Two year olds of 2011

STEVE TAPLIN

Raceform

Front cover: Paul Hanagan and Wootton Bassett win the Grand Criterium Longchamp

Back cover: Some of the Living Legend Partners and friends at Haydock Park in April to see one of our horses.

For an inexpensive way of enjoying the benefits of being a racehorse owner, e-mail stevetaplin@blueyonder.co.uk

Published in 2011 by Raceform
Compton, Newbury, Berkshire, RG20 6NL

Copyright © Steve Taplin 2011

The right of Steve Taplin to be identified as the author of this work has been asserted by him in accordance with the Copyright, Designs and Patents Act 1988.

All rights reserved. No part of this publication may be reproduced, stored in a retrieval system, or transmitted in any form or by any means, electronic, mechanical, photocopying, recording, or otherwise, without the prior written permission of the publishers.

A catalogue record for this book is available from the British Library.

ISBN 978-1-906820-78-7

Designed by Fiona Pike

Printed in Great Britain by CPI Antony Rowe.

Contents

Foreword by Richard Fahey	4
Introduction	5
Fifty to Follow	8
Ten to Follow in Ireland	11
Star Two-Year-Olds	12
The Bloodstock Experts Mark Your Card	13
Trainers' Bargain Buys	23
Two-Year-Olds of 2011	25
Sires Reference	341
Sires Index	356
Racing Trends	360
Horse Index	366
Dams Index	375

Foreword

Training two-year-olds has become a huge part of the job here at Musley Bank Stables over the past couple of seasons. It's very pleasing to pick them out at the yearling sales, win plenty of nice races with them and find yourself in the fortunate position of nurturing the talents of a high-class youngster like Wootton Bassett. Over the past three years our number of wins in two-year-old races has risen from 25 to 34 and to last year's very satisfying total of 75. One thing's for sure; we'll be doing our utmost to increase our season's tally once again.

If you thumb through these pages you'll notice how much of the guesswork in picking winners has been cut out, because Steve's aim is to turn the spotlight on those horses expected to win. Looking back to last season I'm pleased to see that my comments in the book helped readers to spot plenty of future winners. Nice horses like Chiswick Bay, Honeymead, Jamesway, Premier Clarets and Sir Reginald were among 20 individual winners. A very good result – but let's see if we can improve on that this season.

After a long, cold Winter the thoughts of every Flat racing fan turns to the Spring classic trials, the better weather and a new season of two-year-old racing. Not necessarily in that order! I'm sure you'll find that *Two-Year-Olds* is a great way to guide you through the season. Where else will you get perceptive comments from 80 trainers, along with a detailed pedigree profile for each two-year-old?

There are racing books on every aspect of our great sport, but if it's two-year-olds you're interested in, then without a doubt this is the book for you.

RICHARD FAHEY

Introduction

Welcome to the 27th edition of *Two-Year-Olds*, a unique reference book for anyone eager to try their hand at selecting the winners of this season's two-year-old races.

To begin with, I must thank the trainers more than ever for their help this year. In a period stretching for just over three weeks this spring I've managed to interview 80 trainers, which smashes my previous best by some way.

I made tentative enquiries to twelve trainers who are new to the book this year and I'm pleased to say they were all very happy to be interviewed. They are Jane Chapple-Hyam, Denis Coakley, Jessica Harrington, Gary Moore, George Moore, David Nicholls, John Quinn, Linda Stubbs, Roger Varian, Ed Walker, Amy Weaver and John Weymes.

It was sad to see Michael Jarvis stand down from the training ranks this year. He's such a gentleman and a top trainer too of course. It was always a pleasure to visit him at Kremlin House Stables, but in Roger Varian he has an excellent replacement. When talking to Roger I couldn't help noticing that he's very much a chip off the old block.

My research on pedigrees for the book begins in August and finishes at the end of March when the time comes for me to interview trainers. I'm fortunate to get an excellent response from trainers on both sides of the Irish Sea and their comments can be found in italics under the pedigrees of the two-year-olds.

I'm particularly chuffed that Richard Fahey has agreed to write the foreword for me. His record over the past couple of seasons has been phenomenal and Musley Bank Stables is now firmly established as one of the top training yards in the country. Champion jockey Paul Hanagan is based there of course and his part in the Musley Bank success story can hardly be underestimated. I'm certainly looking forward to seeing Paul riding Adlington, one of the horses owned by my Living Legend Racing Partnership this year.

On my trainer visits this year I particularly enjoyed my trips to the gallops at Lambourn. For the first time I watched the impressive Barry Hills string going through their paces on a beautiful spring morning. I must also mention observing the evening stables 'ritual' with Andrew Balding at Park House Stables in Kingsclere. His father Ian was pleased to show me a very special building, now housing all the owners' silks and numerous photographs of past triumphs. It was formerly used as a Catholic chapel for many years and more recently as Mill Reef's hospital ward where his broken leg was repaired so expertly by his surgeon. In common with all the other wonderful buildings at Kingsclere, you can sense the history of the place as you walk around and take in the surroundings.

My visit to Coolmore Stud was a first for me – and what an impressive and beautiful place it is. The stallions were immaculate of course and I was particularly eager to see Sadler's Wells (now retired) and Galileo. I was able mention that my Partnership had a winning daughter of Galileo a few years ago. I know we only leased her, but it still counts!

The 2010 edition of the book included four of the top six rated colts of England and Ireland (Frankel, Wootton Bassett, Casamento and Roderic O'Connor) and the top-rated filly Hooray. The David Simcock trained colt Dream Ahead only missed appearing in the book because he was bought at the Breeze-Up sales just after I'd gone to press. However, the Coventry Stakes winner Strong Suit was most definitely mentioned last year – and mentioned very favourably too by his trainer Richard Hannon.

How did the horses in last year's various "horses to follow" lists fare? Well, in the Fifty To Follow, 44 of the selections ran and they managed to win 45 races between them. The highlights would have to be Liberty Cap (two wins at 20-1), Orientalist (four wins including 10-1 and 12-1), Tullius (two wins including 25-1), Honeymead (two wins including 16-1), Musharakaat (one win at 14-1), Red Presence (one win at 14-1), Sweetie Time (one win at 11-1), Pabusar (one win at 10-1), Byrony (four wins), Face The Problem (three wins) and Temple Meads (three wins).

My "Ten to Follow in Ireland" was led by the good colts Clondinnery and Zoffany, whilst the "Bloodstock Experts" did their bit once again, selecting 32 individual two-year-old winners between them from 70 runners.

Of the 18 "Star Two-Year-Olds", 15 ran and 6 of them made it to winner's enclosure, although I can't claim that any of them really deserved five stars! OK – maybe they were a bit disappointing, so let's hope I improve on that this year.

Please note that this year I haven't given a star rating in the main body of the book for those two-year-olds that don't have a comment from the trainer. I think to give them a rating just based on the pedigree is too speculative.

Finally, what about the "Trainer's Bargain Buys?" The names of 52 two-year-olds were put forward of which 39 actually ran and 18 won – not bad considering they were mostly cheap purchases. I must take my hat off to Eve Johnson-Houghton and Peter Winkworth assistant Anton Pearson for the successes of Orientalist and Tullius at very decent odds (6 wins between them including 25-1, 12-1 and 10-1) and I mustn't forget Sylvester Kirk. He insisted on giving two suggestions and they both won, including Silly Billy who won his race at 11-1.

My Living Legend Racing Partnership managed to get a winner last year and what a great night that was for us. We now have new horses in training and our spirits are high once again – it's certainly a case of "hope springs eternal" in this game!

The following is a rough guide to my description of the ability of family members mentioned in the pedigree assessment of every two-year-old, based upon professional ratings. Please note that these descriptions are standard throughout the book in the vast majority of cases, but there are instances where I rely upon my own judgement of each horse's rating.

Below 60 = moderate
60 – 69 = modest
70 – 79 = fair
80 – 89 = quite useful
90 – 99 = fairly useful
100 – 107 = useful
108 – 112 = very useful
113 – 117 = smart
118 – 122 = very smart
123 – 127 = high-class
128 – 134 = top-class
135 and above = outstanding

The two-year-olds in this book are listed under their trainers and my aim has been to choose those horses most likely to be winners. There are several horses to follow lists, such as the sections 'Fifty To Follow' and 'Star Two-Year-Olds'. These are always useful for those who want to follow a select number of horses. The 'Bloodstock Experts Mark Your Card', is a particularly fruitful section for pinpointing winners and note also that many trainers suggest their 'Bargain Buy'. My only stipulation is that the horse cannot have cost more than 25,000 guineas at the yearling sales. It's always a bit of a problem as to what price I should set. Many trainers won't have a single horse costing that amount, whilst others don't have any below it!

To make it easier to find any specific horse the book is comprehensively indexed. So you'll find an index of the horses, their dams and their sires.

The book is divided into the following sections:

- Fifty To Follow.
- Ten to Follow in Ireland.
- Star Two-Year-Olds. This system gives an instant appraisal of the regard in which a horse is held. Those horses awarded five stars are listed here.
- The Bloodstock Experts Mark Your Card. Bloodstock agents and stud managers suggest potentially smart two-year-olds bought or raised by them.
- Bargain Buys. A list of cheaply bought two-year-olds the trainers feel will turn out to be good deals.
- Two-Year-Olds of 2011. The main section of the book, with each two-year-old listed under the trainer. *Trainers' comments (when given) are in italics after the pedigree assessments.* Readers should bear in mind that all the trainers' comments come from my interviews, which took part in early April.
- Sires Reference, detailing the racing and stud careers of sires with four or more two-year-olds in the book.
- Sires Index.

- Racing Trends. An analysis of some juvenile events that regularly highlight the stars of the future. It includes a list of three-year-olds to follow this season.
- Horse Index.
- Dams Index.

There are inevitably some unnamed horses in the book, but please access my website **www.stevetaplin.co.uk** throughout the season for updates on those horses named after the book was published.

I must say a big "Thank You" to the racing and stud secretaries for their assistance and to the trainers for being so helpful during my interviews with them. In particular, I must also thank my friend Hilda Marshall for assisting me in some of the research, ensuring the book is published on time.

Researched and compiled by
Steve Taplin BA (Hons).

Fifty to Follow

The trainers have spoken highly about this choice selection of two-year-olds.

ALHIRA *"I'd say that at the moment she's the pick of my fillies. She's very natural, very forward and ... a lightish, athletic 2-y-o".* David Simcock.

ALJAMAAHEER (IRE) *"He's a good, strong horse with a good action ... he's very strong looking and has a very natural way of going. I like him".* Roger Varian.

AVON PEARL *"A great big, strong colt ... he appears to be a very nice horse ... I like the way he goes and I'd be hopeful of him".* Henry Candy.

BALTY BOYS (IRE) *"A horse we like a lot and he's one of our picks. He's ready to go now but the longer we wait the better really. He'll get a mile later on I would have thought, but he shows a bit of speed and everyone seems to like him. He's a very attractive horse".* Barry Hills.

BLONDE (IRE) *"One of our nicest fillies, she has a pedigree as long as your arm. She's very tall and very big, so we'll give her a bit of time but we expect quite a lot from her. A lovely mover that has everything going for her".* Richard Hannon.

BURWAAZ *"Very nice ... a strong, powerful colt with a good temperament and if we have a properly precocious 2-y-o, this is the one ... the pedigree is all speed and although it's too early to know yet, if we have a Royal Ascot 2-y-o this could be the one".* Ed Dunlop.

CODE CRACKER *"A July type 2-y-o ... She looks like she'll go on firm ground and that she'll be very willing ... a six/seven furlong 2-y-o".* Sir Mark Prescott.

COMMITMENT *"A lovely horse, he's tall but well put-together. He finds it very easy and he's going to be a seven furlong type in August. Potentially very nice".* Luca Cumani.

CORRECT *"She's in the 'early brigade', she looks like a pocket rocket type ... this is probably our most mature filly. We like her, she's relatively close-coupled, deep-girthed and has a generous backside".* Michael Bell.

CROWNING STAR *"He'll be a pretty decent horse ... he's a fine, big strong colt out of a Group 2 placed filly. He'll win his maiden and hopefully he'll be one we can go to Royal Ascot with. A horse with a lot of ability, he'll keep improving and he's a horse with a big future".* Stan Moore.

DANCE WITH ME (IRE) *"A lovely, big, tall, rangy colt ... he's done a couple of bits of work and looks very nice ... .he gets a double tick from me. A nice horse".* Andrew Balding.

ELECTRIC QATAR *"A very nice horse. He rapidly improved in February and March ... possibly the nicest of my earlier type two-year-olds and he'll be a five/six furlong horse".* Tom Dascombe.

FAIREST (IRE) *"She's going well and I'm pleased with her ... She's a filly I like and she's doing everything the right way so far. If I have a Royal Ascot filly this could be the one".* Jeremy Noseda.

FANOOS *"She's quick, she's working well and will be out fairly soon for the five furlong maidens. A speedy filly".* John Gosden.

FLUCTUATE *"A good, strong, powerful horse that goes well".* John Gosden.

GATEPOST (IRE) *"A lovely horse ... He's good-looking and I like him a lot, I think he's a bloody nice horse and one of the better ones".* Mick Channon.

GREEN LEGACY (USA) *"He's a nice horse, I like him very much ... and he'll be ready to race over six furlongs in May...a nice horse to have around".* Amanda Perrett.

IBTAHAJ "He is doing all that is asked of him with ease ... he's an early foal, well-grown and a nice mover". Godolphin (Saeed bin Suroor).

ICE MISSILE "She's a smashing filly, she has a nice pedigree and quite forward. If I was looking at 2-y-o's that might be Royal Ascot types she'd be on the short list". Sylvester Kirk.

INDIGO IRIS (IRE) "A very nice horse, he works nicely and hopefully he'll be good enough to go to one of the festival meetings". Richard Hannon.

JASIE JAC "He wasn't expensive considering he's quite a nice-looking colt. He pleases us at home ... he could well have a bit more quality than just a five furlong runner. He's quite a nice horse, strong and well-made". Robert Mills.

KNIGHT EXPRESS "A lovely horse, I like him, he's breezed a few times and he'll be a six/seven furlong two-year-old. He's a bonny horse and he'll definitely win". Richard Fahey.

MEHIDI (IRE) "He shouldn't take too long, he probably wants six furlongs but he works really well and we really like him a lot". Brian Meehan.

MENELIK (IRE) "He's done a bit of work ... he'll be out in June and he's a racehorse!" Tom Dascombe.

MIDNIGHT TRYST "A very nice filly, she'll be out later and she's very capable. Very, very attractive, a good mover and a proper filly – just as you would like a filly to be". Ann Duffield.

MORPHIUS "This filly is very nice in every way". Henry Cecil.

MOUNT McLEOD "She's got pace and ... I'd say she's definitely up to winning a maiden at least, early on. A lovely mover, she's quick, small and strong ... I like her a lot and she'd be one of my favourites at the moment". Jamie Osborne.

MUJANNAD (IRE) "This is a horse that I like, he's a definite 2-y-o, he's very solid, has a good mind and he's done quite a lot of work for a seven furlong horse". Marcus Tregoning.

MUKHADRAM "A classy horse, he's big, strong and solid. He'll be a 2-y-o from July/August time and if he wins first time out he'll be heading for some decent races. He's really nice". William Haggas.

MY COLLEEN (USA) "She's a beautiful filly and the best looking of all my 2-y-o's. Very well-made, everything is in the right place ... she has a lovely action". Rae Guest.

NAYARRA "A smashing filly, an absolute diamond. Very, very nice ... I'm very sweet on her at the moment. I think she's very good". Mick Channon.

OBLITEREIGHT (IRE) "He looks a 2-y-o, he has a big, strong shoulder on him and a powerful backside, so he looks like he's going to be a sprinter and he'll be racing in May". William Knight.

PEARL DIVA (IRE) "She's going really nicely and she'll win over five furlongs but be better at six. A filly I like a lot". Peter Chapple-Hyam.

PETALUMA "A gorgeous filly for later on this season. She's big, but she's done everything asked of her and I like her an awful lot". Mick Channon.

POOLE HARBOUR (IRE) "He's a real nice horse and doing everything right. He might start off in a maiden at Newbury in April and he'd one of my picks of all the 2-y-o's" Richard Hannon.

PURPLE 'N GOLD "He's a very nice type and I think an awful lot of him. He's been working very well and would be the most forward of my 2-y-o's ... he shows plenty of speed". George Baker.

PUSSYCAT DREAM "A nicely-made filly, she probably won't be as early as we'd like, but if she runs as well as she looks she'll be OK. A fairly powerful filly ... she's quite flashy-looking". Ed McMahon.

RESPONSIVE "She's always been forward-going and looks like being our first 2-y-o runner. A filly with a good attitude, she'll be a five/six furlong type and I think she's nice". Hughie Morrison.

RIO GRANDE "He's already in fast work and he shows a good level of ability ... A sure-fire winner, so far he's done everything well enough to suggest he could be a Royal Ascot 2-y-o". Jeremy Noseda.

RIOT OF COLOUR "A robust, quite tall filly, but well-grown and quite forward, she should be racing in May or June and she'd be high on the list". Ralph Beckett.

SAJWAH (IRE) "She's a lovely filly. Nice, attractive and bright, she's very forward-going and should be ready by May time. We trained the dam, we liked her and she was a good-looking filly. This one could hopefully be a Royal Ascot job". Barry Hills.

SHOLAAN "This is a 2-y-o, he's strong, very well-made and he goes well – always has done. He's probably the one that I think has a chance to win something nice this year". William Haggas.

SOLAR DEITY (IRE) "A typical Exceed And Excel, he's quite forward and he goes well ... We like him, he's doing really well and he's coming to hand quickly". Marco Botti.

SOVEREIGN DEBT "He's a nice horse that moves well ... probably wants six furlongs but I like him". Michael Bell.

STRINGER BELL "One of our nicest 2-y-o's, he's a liver chestnut and a lovely mover. He was quite exceptional at the sales and he's done everything right since, so we haven't changed our minds. A beautiful colt". Richard Hannon.

SUPERCILIARY "A very good-looking horse and much the nicest out of the mare ... An athletic sort of horse, he'll be a 2-y-o in the second half of the season and he's a really likeable individual, a standout in every way". Ralph Beckett.

SWISS SPIRIT "I've trained a few out of the dam and this is the best specimen of the lot. A big, fine colt ... the mare was fast and she breeds 2-y-o winners, so this colt will be a five/six furlong 2-y-o". David Elsworth.

TOP COP "A big, heavy, rather typical Acclamation. He looks a lovely horse and obviously he's from one of the owner's good families. The mother wasn't short on speed and I bet this colt ends up pretty quick". Andrew Balding.

TOP OFFER "He's a very attractive horse – probably our nicest at this stage. He just looks very nice-natured, strong, well-grown and he moves very well ... if I could only keep one of my 2-y-o's I'd keep him". Roger Charlton.

WARCROWN "A beautiful horse. If I had to pick one at the moment it would be him. Everything about him says quality and ... he certainly stands out ... I like everything about him and I'd say he's got it all – he's a monster!" Richard Fahey.

Ten to Follow in Ireland

AKEED MOFEED "He's a lovely colt, very well-grown and strong. He's done a little bit of fast work and he's a nice, well-balanced horse with a good temperament. Very likeable". John Oxx.

AKEED WAFI (IRE) "He's a lovely looking horse, well balanced and a beautiful mover. Very, very nice, so hopefully he'll be out in mid-summer and he looks promising. He'd like a little distance and might be a seven furlong 2-y-o. A medium-sized, well-balanced colt and very attractive". John Oxx.

FASTIDEOUS "He's a colt I like. He's well-balanced, I hope to run him in May over five/six furlongs and he could well be one to look out for". Dermot Weld.

JEMIMA'S PEARL (USA) "I love this filly, she was a very slow learner but when the penny dropped she became very precocious and she wouldn't be far away from running. I like her and I hope she's black type because I think she could be smart. I have a nice bunch of fillies this year". Ger Lyons.

LANETT LADY (IRE) "A lovely, well-balanced filly that goes well...we like her and she'll be racing at the end of May or in early June. Michael Halford.

NERO EMPEROR (IRE) "He looks to be quite forward and sharp – a real five/six furlong horse ... One of our sharpest, if we do have a Royal Ascot 2-y-o he might be the one". Tommy Stack.

REDOUBTABLE (IRE) "She's lovely and if I was picking one 2-y-o filly this would be the one. She's very nice, not a great big filly but very muscular and in terms of looks the's the nearest to the dam that she's had". Kevin Prendergast.

SLADE POWER (IRE) "We love this horse. He's gorgeous and if he was two-legged he'd be a model. He has a lovely head, he's well-balanced, a great walker and he has loads of quality. He'll be quick enough for six and seven furlongs and although he's a little bit 'on the leg' he might start out in May and he does everything easily". Eddie Lynam.

SPIRIT OF CONCORDE "He's a horse I like a lot and for a horse that's bred to stay he's showing a lot of potential. I would see him running in June or July over seven furlongs. He's a horse that does things nicely and I could run him now because he's that forward. He'll be a very nice horse". Dermot Weld.

TRUE PEARL (USA)
"He'd be the pick of the place at the minute – the number one colt in the yard I would think. He's smart, a seven furlong horse and you won't see him out until late May. They're all being trained with Royal Ascot in mind but it's all subject to them coming right at that time. He's a horse we like a good bit, he's gorgeous, big and he's doing everything we're asking him at the moment". Ger Lyons.

Star Two-year-olds

The stars placed along the side of each two-year-old in the main section of the book give the reader an instant appraisal of the regard in which they are held. The highest rating a horse can attain is five stars.

All the five-star two-year-olds of 2011 are listed below for quick reference

BORN TO SEA (IRE)	John Oxx
CONTINUUM	Henry Cecil
EBBLE	John Gosden
HIT THE JACKPOT (IRE)	Dermot Weld
MIN BANAT ALREEH (IRE)	Roger Varian
MORPHIUS	Henry Cecil
NAYARRA	Mick Channon
PALMETTE	John Gosden
SENTARIL	William Haggas
UTTERANCE	John Gosden
WARCROWN	Richard Fahey
b.br.f. Dixie Union – General Jeanne (Honour And Glory).	Brian Meehan
b.c. Galileo – Kind (Danehill).	Henry Cecil
b.c. Street Cry – Naissance Royale (Giant's Causeway).	Ed Dunlop

The Bloodstock Experts Mark your Card

The honours for top tipster in this section of the book last year goes to Ross Doyle, whose four selections all won. A terrific effort, so let's have more of the same please Ross!

With three winners out of four, the runners-up prize is shared by Angus Gold (his selections included the triple Group placed Elzaam), Bruce Raymond, Gill Richardson and Larry Stratton (Larry had the 20-1 shot Zenella). I must also include David Redvers, whose three winners from five included the 25-1 shot Tullius.

Definitely worth a mention are Robin Sharp (two winners out of three), Tom Goff, Trevor Harris, Chris Richardson (all of them picked two from four), Harry Herbert and Johnny McKeever (both two from five).

In total there were 33 individual winners of 43 races, which easily surpassed the previous year's total of 23 winners of 28 races.

Thank you to all the experts who have had a go at selecting potential winners once again. Remember that most of the two-year-olds selected here can be found in the main section of the book listed under their trainers and highlighted by the symbol ♠

PETER DOYLE
EL DIAMANTE
b.f. *Royal Applause – Lumiere Rouge.*
A lovely filly bought at Deauville from long time successful breeder Haras du Mezeray and trained by Team Hannon.

ENJOYING
b.br.c. *Marju – Jazzy Jan.*
A really nice colt that should do well this year and then become a nice 3-y-o. Trained by Team Hannon.

GREEN LEGACY ★★★★
ch.c. *Discreet Cat – Mira Costa.*
Born to be a 2-y-o and looks the part. Trained by Amanda Perrett.

TRUMPET MAJOR
b.c. *Arakan – Ashford Cross.*
Well grown colt by the sire of "Dick Turpin" and bought at the same sale where we selected "Dick". Trained by Team Hannon.

ROSS DOYLE
INDIGO IRIS
b.c. *Choisir – Sweet Surrender.*
A very mature and imposing horse by Choisir, a very reliable stallion for us over the years. We bought him at the DBS Premier Yearling sale for £65,000 and even though he is a late April foal he was just so mature looking for his age that we had to buy him. He looks like a three year old already and he could be one to run in early May. In training with Team Hannon.

LILBOURNE LAD
b.c. *Acclamation – Sogno Verde.*
I was under bidder on this fellow as a foal for a client so it was nice to be able to buy him as a yearling to race. He is a medium sized, very athletic horse with a great attitude like all the sires progeny and we have been lucky with them over the years. He is the second foal out of the mare and the first foal Bobbyscott was rated 105 plus. We bought him at the DBS Premier Yearling sale for £80,000 and looks like he could be a very early type and he is in training with Team Hannon.

POOLE HARBOUR
b.c. *Elusive City – Free Lance.*
A really nice, compact, sharp looking colt but with a great walk to go with it. He comes from a family that has been good to the Doyle's and Hannon's over the years in Amazing Dream, Billy Allen etc. We bought him at the DBS Yearling sale for £70,000 off the same farm, Redpender Stud that sold Canford Cliffs as a yearling. He looks like he will not take to long to come to hand and is in training with Team Hannon.

UNNAMED
b.f. *Strategic Prince – Murani.*
Very typical of the stallion's progeny, she is very good looking filly, mature and a great mover. She looks very imposing for a filly and seems to have a very good attitude to go with it. We bought her at the Tattersalls Ireland September Yearling sale for €32,000 and it would be nice to think she could go back to win the sales race attached to the sale later in the year. She looks like she will be a middle season type and is in training with Team Hannon.

WILL EDMEADES
RESPONSIVE
b.f. *Dutch Art – Xtrasensory.*
A nice, strong filly bought at DBS for Thurloe Thoroughbreds. We bought the dam, as a yearling, and she was rated 96 as a 2-y-o. Furthermore, her previous three foals have all won at 2, so this filly should be a penalty kick for her trainer Hughie Morrison!

ROCK OF MONET
b.c. *Kyllachy – Level Pegging.*
A very mature, powerful colt, also bought at DBS with the Hannon/Doyle combo as underbidders, which should be a positive. The dam is full-sister to the speedy Flanders and the sire got Tariq from a Sharpen Up line mare. He is owned by Karmaa Racing, who need a change of luck, and trained by David Simcock who feels the colt is pretty forward.

SELF CENTRED
ch.f. *Medicean – Ego.*
This cleverly named filly with a proper 'page' was purchased at Tattersalls for Bunny Roberts. From the marvellous Bloomsbury family of Queen Mary winners Myself and Pushy, her dam achieved a rating of 107 at 2 and she is 3 for 3 with her runners, with her 2-y-o Chef winning on debut the day before the sale. Trained by Barry Hills

SPIRITUAL STAR
b.c. *Soviet Star – Million Spirits*
A really lovely colt with a great presence about him. He is the first foal of a half-sister, by Invincible Spirit, to Gr.1 winner Elusive Wave. Thurloe have sent him to Andrew Balding, who reports him to be rather more precocious than we envisaged when we bought him. He won't be rushed, but he does look exciting. Trained by Andrew Balding.

TOM GOFF
"Hi Steve, may I first congratulate you on your fantastic book which all lovers of 2-y-o racing adore reading, although I am given to asking why you should want my input this time around as I have hardly given you a two-year-old winner since Winker Watson won the Norfolk Stakes which is getting on for five years ago!!! Anyway, some of them won at three (or four!) so we'll give it another whirl".

CHUNKY DIAMOND
b.c. *Diamond Green – Balance The Books*
A really lovely and quite precocious colt who has always displayed a good temperament and attitude to life. A good mover, he was sold by Luke Barry's Manister House Stud to Blandford and Peter Chapple-Hyam at the Doncaster Premier Sale for £42,000. He's got a rather moderate pedigree and falls firmly into that category of a sharp colt at public auction whose pedigree shouldn't be researched in a sales guide as that will only stop you buying a nice horse. Let's hope Peter Chapple-Hyam can work his old magic again. In any event, he's with no better man to get the job done with a sharp two-year-old and Pete loves him at the time of writing.

SOVEREIGN DEBT
br.c. *Dark Angel – Kelsey Rose*
This is a really lovely colt bought at auction in Newmarket at Tattersalls October Part 1 from Yeomanstown Stud. Blandford gave 105,000gns for him on behalf of Mr Lawrie Inman, for whom we purchased Monitor Closely. He is closely related to Puff and Indian Rocket and Michael Bell is very pleased with him so far although obviously it's early days. He's got lots of class and I hope that, if his ability can match his looks, then he may turn out to be above average – he's certainly with a trainer who knows how to get two-year-olds to maximise their potential. Trained by Michael Bell.

FLUCTUATE
ch.c. Exchange Rate – Cut Short.
This is a really strong and very likeable colt indeed. A striking yearling who I'm sure everyone liked at Keeneland September last year, he was bred by Philip Freedman from the family of Daggers Drawn and Brevity. Blandford purchased him from Indian Creek for $160,000 for a client of John Gosden. I don't get the impression from the trainer that he will be enormously early but he is held in good regard by his trainer in what is obviously a decent group of juveniles with John. Fingers crossed, he'll be a successful colt. Trained by John Gosden.

DICK BOS
ch.c. Dutch Art – Cosmic Countess.
Obviously, Peter Chapple-Hyam and I wanted to have a go at a Dutch Art or two last year, even though he was at the time an unproven stallion. We looked at plenty and we felt that this colt from Paul and Sara Thorman's Trickledown Stud was by far the best at Doncaster. He had a distinctive white ring round his near hind cannon bone and was a lovely bright chesnut yearling very like his father with presence and action. We paid a rather exorbitant £48,000 for him but I must say we were really delighted to get him. The Comic Strip Heroes have taken him and I'm delighted about that as they're real sportsmen. He's now a strong colt with more condition on him and Peter thinks he'll be more 6 furlongs than 5 but that would fit with his sire. Let's hope he's lucky for some really stalwart owners. Trained by Peter Chapple-Hyam.

ANGUS GOLD
AFRAAH
b.f. Hard Spun – Sarayir.
This filly is from the first crop of Hard Spun and is a half sister to Ghanaati and Mawatheeq and from the family that has served Sheikh Hamdan so well over the years. Obviously she won't be early and she is still in Dubai as I write, but as an individual she is a very classy filly and I would be hopeful she would be a nice back-end 2-y-o. Trained by Roger Varian.

ALJAMAAHEER
ch.c. Dubawi – Kelly Nicole.
This was a colt we bought as a foal, he's always looked like he should be a 2-y-o, and Roger seems happy with the horse so far. Trained by Roger Varian.

BURWAAZ
b.c. Exceed And Excel – Nidhaal.
This horse is bred to be a 2-y-o, out of a mare who won a Listed race over six furlongs at two, and he is a half brother to a decent filly of last year in Sadafiya. Ed Dunlop says he is showing all the right signs at the moment and that he should certainly be quite early. Trained by Ed Dunlop.

FANOOS
b.f. Dutch Art – Miss Otis.
This was a filly that I fell in love with at the sales and I told Sheikh Hamdan that she would win the Cheveley Park, so she'd better be able to run! She has done very well physically and John Gosden says she has a bit of aggression in her attitude, which I hope is a good thing, and if she is any good she should certainly make a 2-y-o. Trained by John Gosden.

NAWWAAR
ch.c. Distorted Humor – Mostaqeleh.
This is an American homebred out of a decent Rahy mare who looks a proper 2-y-o as an individual. Trained by John Dunlop.

SANAD
b.c. Red Clubs – Knockatotaun.
From the first crop of Red Clubs, this was a nice horse that we bought in Newmarket and Brian Meehan seems to like him so far. Trained by Brian Meehan.

WIDYAAN
b.c. Lawman – Lady Livius
This horse cost 300,000 Gns at Tattersalls Part 1. He has plenty of scope and will take a bit of time but hopefully he'll make a nice horse for the second half of the season. Trained by John Gosden.

CHARLIE GORDON-WATSON

AQUILA
b.f. *Teofilo – Dance Troupe.*
A Teofilo filly, a sire who is my tip along with Dylan Thomas to be the best sires of their generation, her pedigree goes back to Sarah Siddons. She must be showing something as she was one of only three two-year-olds mentioned in Henry Cecil's Racing Post stable tour.

DREAM TUNE
b.c. *Oasis Dream – Play Bouzouki.*
Also with Henry Cecil and in the same ownership as Aquilla, is this big strong powerful Oasis Dream colt, my favourite sire along with Galileo. He was bought at Arqana and would expect to see him from say August onwards.

TIOMAN LEGEND
b.c. *Kyllachy – Elegant Times.*
Runs hopefully at Newbury in April, which is early for Roger Charlton, so hopefully a good sign. A real 2-y-o type from a speedy family out of a Dansili mare.

UNNAMED
b.c. *Dansili – Lady Elgar.*
I have to include this colt, bought at Arqana, maybe more of a 3-y-o but a real quality colt. Trained by Ed Dunlop.

UNNAMED
b.c. *Street Cry – Naissance Royale.*
In the same ownership as the Dansili colt, he's also from Arqana. I saw him a week before the sale and was most keen to buy him and was fortunate to be able to do so thanks to the owner, I hope our faith is justified and should make a very nice 2-y-o. Trained by Ed Dunlop.

UNNAMED
b.c. *Royal Applause – Mazarine Blue.*
Bought from Kirtlington who produce a lot of good winners, he cost a lot less than we expected and is a half brother to Putra Pekan in the same ownership. The mare has bred six 2-y-o winners by Royal Applause who is a very solid reliable sire. Same owner as the 2-y-o Tioman Legend. Trained by Roger Varian.

TREVOR HARRIS

MIDA'S ROSE
b.f. *Royal Applause – Regal Run.*
The dam is by Deputy Minister, is a half sister to two Grade 2 winners in the USA and a half sister to the dam of Palace Episode who won the Racing Post Trophy. She is with Ed Walker who is pleased with her and she should be out mid summer. Trainer: Ed Walker

SWISS SPIRIT
b.c. *Invincible Spirit – Swiss Lake.*
An Invincible Spirit colt out of the speedy Swiss Lake and therefore a half to dual Group 3 and Listed winner Swiss Diva and to Coventry Stakes runner-up Swiss Franc. Like his siblings, he looks precocious and should be out early. Trainer: David Elsworth

UNNAMED
b.c. *Oasis Dream – Hydro Calido.*
A very well bred colt out of a Nureyev mare who won the Prix D'Astarte, was runner-up in the French Guineas and has produced two Stakes winners from her seven winning progeny to date. He looks like he might be out mid summer and could be an exciting prospect. Trainer: Roger Varian.

UNNAMED
b.c. *Manduro – Movie Queen.*
A colt by champion 2-y-o Manduro out of the Danehill mare Movie Queen. He looks a 2-y-o sort but may not be out until mid summer. Trainer: David Elsworth

HARRY HERBERT

APOSTLE
gr.c. *Dark Angel – Rose Dudley.*
John Warren and I were very taken by the Dark Angels at the sales last year and we were delighted to buy this one for 60,000 guineas at Doncaster. He is a very strong, precocious type who should be ready to run in April if everything goes according to plan. The early signs are most encouraging. Trained by Michael Bell.

BOUDOIR
gr.f. *Clodovil – Adultress*.
This filly looks to be very precocious and could easily be one of our first 2-y-o runners. Richard was very positive about her when I spoke to him last week and looking at her physically it is not difficult to see why. She is a very forward going individual who should be ready to roll by the end of April or early May. Trained by Richard Fahey.

COMMITMENT
b.c. *Motivator – Courting*
This is the most beautiful son of Motivator who is also a half brother to Fury. He has found everything incredibly easy so far and, although it is early days I have never heard the trainer so bullish about one of our horses and watching him canter up Warren Hill last week it was easy to see why. This colt just could be very special. Trained by Luca Cumani.

DAMASK
b.f. *Red Clubs – Goldthroat*.
This filly looks fairly precocious and is an absolute beauty to look at. If she continues to progress at her current rate then she could well be ready to run in May and a race such as the Albany at Royal Ascot could be on the agenda. She also has a beautiful pedigree being a half sister to the Group 1 winning daughter of Ofisio, Zafisio. Trained by Richard Hannon

OPINION
b.c. *Oasis Dream – Kiltubber*.
This colt has improved physically out of all recognition in the past few weeks and he really does look to be an exciting prospect in the making. His half brother trained by Mark Johnston recently won a conditions race by five lengths and Opinion himself could make up into a mid summer 2-y-o. Trained by Sir Michael Stoute.

PISTOL
b.c. *High Chaparral – Alinea*
This is a magnificent colt who stands over plenty of ground but despite his size he is finding it all very easy and he gets to the top of Warren Hill without any problem. He is all about next season but it wouldn't surprise me if he were to make an impact towards the back end of this year and it was interesting that Ryan Moore mentioned him in dispatches on the gallops last week! Trained by Sir Michael Stoute.

LUKE LILLINGSTON
TAHLIA REE
b.f. *Acclamation – Dora Carrington*.
We bought this filly by Acclamation out of Dora Carrington who won the Cherry Hinton from Peter Harris' dispersal. She looked the part and Michael has expressed himself pleased with her. Trained by Michael Bell.

UNNAMED
b.f. *Dixie Union – I'm Right*.
We sold two yearlings to the successful Fretwell team who win so many 2-y-o races and they have expressed satisfaction so far. This filly is with Ed McMahon.

UNNAMED
b.f. *Redback – Singitta*.
I bought a couple of yearling fillies for a wonderful man called Paddy Barrett. This filly, now with Ian Wood, was bought to target the Tattersalls sales races (Button Moon who we bought for him the previous year was beaten only a head by Zebedee in the first race in the series). I believe Ian Wood is happy with her

DAVID MCGREAVY
UNNAMED
b.g. *Sir Percy – Carenage*.
He was a really hardy yearling who made very good use of himself. As a January colt I think he will come to hand early and his trainer is very positive about him. Trained by Mick Channon.

PEA SHOOTER
b.c. *Piccolo – Sparkling Eyes*.
A really athletic type who I bought as a foal. He developed into as good a yearling as you could find and has gone to a very good trainer. Trained by Kevin Ryan.

UNNAMED
b.c. *One Cool Cat – Dress Code*.
Another foal purchase who thrived and will maintain his sires winners ratio. He is a half brother to Lucky General and promises much. (Italy)

JOHNNY MCKEEVER
BRILLIANTINE
b.f. *Zamindar – Brilliantly.*
Bought in Deauville October and I love her. Richard Hannon Jr shares my view!

RIGHT TO DREAM
b.c. *Oasis Dream – Granny Kelly.*
One of my new Right Tack syndicate horses who appears to be going the right way and should be ready for the 6 furlong races once they arrive. Trained by Brian Meehan.

MORANT BAY
b.f. *Montjeu – Quad's Melody.*
A filly I bought at Goffs for Noel Martin, owner of Jacqueline Quest. Henry says she could be quite early. Quite a statement for the Cecil/Montjeu combination! Trained by Henry Cecil.

ST BARTHS
b.c. *Cadeaux Genereux – Ile Deserte.*
Another sharp type bought at Doncaster for the same team that had Crown Prosecutor last year. Trained by Brian Meehan.

UNNAMED
ch.c. *Stormy River – Pascarina.*
A really beautiful colt that Tom seemed very pleased with on my first visit to Manor House Stables in March. Tom very kindly allowed me to select 10 yearlings last year and I really hope I did a good job for him.

ROBIN O'RYAN
HOLY ROMAN WARRIOR
br.c. *Holy Roman Emperor – Cedar Sea.*
A big, fine horse, he's very sound, scopey and he'll be a nice 2-y-o in the second half of the season. Trained by Richard Fahey.

LADY'S FIRST
b.f. *Dutch Art – Like A Dame.*
She's a nice filly, she wants a bit of sun on her back but she's a very good-mover. We like the sire, Dutch Art. I would imagine she'd be a six furlong type. Not a robust filly, but she's a real athlete. Trained by Richard Fahey.

PEN BAL CRAG
b.c. *Exceed And Excel – Rosse.*
He does everything right and looks a real 2-y-o over five furlongs. Trained by Richard Fahey.

WARCROWN
b.c. *Azamour – Alikhlas.*
A well-proportioned horse that does everything nicely. A six furlongs type and he's a nice horse and I like him. Trained by Richard Fahey.

YEOMAN OF THE GUARD
b.c. *Librettist – Red Blooded Woman.*
I like him, he's a nice horse and one for the second half of the season over six and seven furlongs. Very sound and a good mover, he does everything nice. Trained by Richard Fahey.

UNNAMED
b.c. *Dark Angel – Guajira.*
He'll be a nice six furlong horse. He's doing everything right and he'll be a nice 2-y-o. Trained by Richard Fahey.

KIRSTEN RAUSING
ALL THAT RULES
b.c. *Galileo – Alba Stella.*
A late foal, this classy colt could still come to hand in the latter part of the 2011 season; he is with a master trainer who knows the sire's stock well. ALL THAT RULES is a third-generation Lanwades-bred and his dam is a twice-winning half-sister to multiple Group One winners Alborada and Albanova, both of whom showed good winning form at 2 years (the former winning the Gr 3 Park Stakes at that age). Another half-sister to ALL THAT RULES' dam, Alakananda, bred Derby second Dragon Dancer. Whatever this good-looking, very athletic colt can do at 2, we hope he will improve further for his 3-y-o season in 2012. Trained by Henry Cecil.

KASHGAR
b.c. *Hernando – Miss Katmandu.*
Owner-breeder Mr J.L.C. Pearce has kept his bloodstock at Lanwades Stud for nearly 30 years and this colt is a third-generation produce of that policy. KASHGAR is bred to be a Classic contender next year (Oaks winner Look

Here is by Hernando out of a Rainbow Quest mare) and his dam is a half-sister to staying Group winners St Expedit and Asian Heights. KASHGAR always caught the eye as a foal and yearling; an athletic, racy type, he has great presence and that indefinable element of class that make us hopeful he can show promise (at the back end of the season) at 2, to go on again next year. Traind by Michael Bell.

MOONSHED
b.c. Arch – Rose of Zollern.
A third-generation Lanwades-bred, this colt was sold under our Staffordstown banner to Sheikh Hamdan at Goffs (€80,000). He was a mature, forward yearling, very good-looking and with a pleasant temperament. His dam was a Stakes winner at 2 who went on to win the German 1,000 Guineas and later become a Stakes winner in the USA, and her (unraced) dam was a half-sister to European Champion 2-Year-Old, Dewhurst winner Kala Dancer. The colt's sire (who had a great year with, amongst others, US Champion Blame in 2010) is infusing some stamina into the pedigree, but it would not surprise me to see MOONSHED doing well at 2 years. Trained by Dermot Weld.

NIMIETY
b.f. Stormy Atlantic – Nadeshzda.
A homebred filly by a very good American sire noted for his speedy produce. This filly's dam (also Lanwades-bred) was useful in Europe (rated 95+) and better still in the USA, where she was only beaten a short head in the Gr 2 Santa Barbara Hcp. Her first foal is a dual winner, her second is the (in March 2011) hitherto unraced Montegonian (M. Treconing) and NIMIETY is her third produce. A well-bred filly with a very strong female pedigree, NIMIETY could be seen out as early as end May or early June. Trained by Mark Johnston.

PEARL FROST
gr.c. Verglas – Eternelle.
Bred, as was his quite useful dam, at Lanwades, and sold as a foal by us from St Simon Stud to Paula Flannery for 28,000 gns. He was resold as a yearling for 50,000 gns. PEARL FROST was a very tough, sturdy sort as a foal and bearing

in mind his highly thought of 3-y-o half sister Encore Une Annee (by Hernando) showed winning form at 2 years (for the same trainer), we would hope that the colt could at least emulate his sister. Trained by Ralph Beckett.

REGAL ENTRANCE
b.c. Royal Applause – Umniya.
Bred at Lanwades by Ptarmigan Bloodstock (just like multiple Group One winner Fame And Glory. This colt was sold by us (from St Simon Stud) as a foal at the 2009 Dec Sales for 47,000 guineas to Hillwood Bloodstock, who resold him nicely to Cheveley Park as a yearling for 100,000 gns. The colt has a sprinty pedigree and conformation and was always quite forward physically and mentally. He should do well at 2 years. Trained by Jeremy Noseda.

YAHROOH
b.f. Medaglia d'Oro – Country Maiden.
Bought at Keeneland for $100,000, she is already showing a lot of quality. She will of course be better over 6f+. Trained by Clive Brittain. n.b. They will all win for sure!

DAVID REDVERS
GURU GIRL
b.f. Ishiguru – Startori.
A very racy homebred filly who looks precocious. Trained by Mrs Karl Burke.

LIGHTENING PEARL
b.f. Marju – Jioconda.
A gorgeous, sharp-looking filly bred by Lady O'Reilly. Sure to be out early. Trained by Ger Lyons.

PROUD PEARL
b.f. Proud Citizen – Pacific Spell.
Full sister to a champion and going nicely. Trained by Brian Meehan.

QATAR'S PEARL
ch.c. Tapit – Arboresque.
The most expensive yearling I have ever bought and the price tag brings some pressure! Trained by Ger Lyons.

SERIOUS SPENDER
b.c. Amadeus Wolf – Meanya).
A proper two-year-old type from Fairyhouse from a very fast family. Trained by Ralph Beckett.

CHRIS RICHARDSON
DARK AMBITION
b.c. Dark Angel – Date Mate.
A half brother to the Group 1 placed Declaration of War and to the Group 2 Princess Margaret Stakes winner and Cherry Hinton runner up Soraaya. Bought for 72,000 Gns at the Tattersalls October Book 2 sale, all being well, he looks a sharp two-year-old type. Trainer William Haggas.

EXTOL
b.c. Exceed and Excel – Dance of Light.
A good looking son of Exceed and Excel out of the listed placed Dance of Light, bred by Reverence's breeders Gary and Lesley Middlebrook. Purchased for 48,000 Gns at the Tattersalls October sale, he looks a lovely balanced colt with a good outlook who, with a bit of luck, could prove a mid season 2-y-o. Trainer John Gosden.

REGAL ENTRANCE
b.c. Royal Applause – Umniya.
A smart looking son of Royal Applause out of the Group 3 placed mare Umniya by Bluebird. Bought for 100,000 Gns at the Tattersalls Book 1 sale, he looks a smart two year-old type – just hope he has an engine. Trainer Jeremy Noseda (who was the underbidder).

DUKE OF FIRENZE
ch.c. Pivotal – Nannina.
The first foal out of Nannina, who was a duel Group 1 winning daughter of Medicean. At two years Nannina won the Meon Valley Stud Fillies' Mile, and at three years won the Group 1 Coronation Stakes at Royal Ascot. A homebred colt who is bred to be followed. Trainer Sir Michael Stoute.

ED SACKVILLE
CATERINA
b.f. Medicean – Senta's Dream.
This attractive filly was bought at Deauville. She was racey looking and had a great step. She has now developed into a very imposing individual and is reportedly pleasing her trainer Trained by Richard Hannon.

RECKONING
b.f. Danehill Dancer – Great Hope.
A beautiful filly whose family goes back to Soldier of Fortune and Intense Focus. I think she will take time and will run towards the backend, but she'll hopefully be worth waiting for. Trained by Jeremy Noseda.

UNNAMED
b.f. Holy Roman Emperor – Gilded Vanity.
I was really thrilled to be able to buy this balanced individual. She was correct and racey looking and is by a good 2-y-o stallion. Trained by Tom Dascombe.

UNNAMED
b.c. Kodiac – Gerobies Girl.
This is a really tough looking colt bought at Fairyhouse, a sale Tom Dascombe and I have been lucky at. His sire Kodiac had over 20 2-y-o winners last year and I hope this chap will add to his 2011 tally. Trained by Tom Dascombe.

PETER STANLEY
STORM LIGHTNING
b.c. Exceed And Excel – All For Laura.
Classy, sharp and a half brother to a brilliant 2-y-o. Trained by Dermot Weld.

PEARL DIVA
b.f. Acclamation – Lassie's Gold
(Seeking The Gold).
Catching pigeons on the gallops. Trained by Peter Chapple-Hyam.

UNNAMED
b.f. Oasis Dream – Rubies From Burma
(Forty Niner).
A sharp sort typical of her very brilliant sire but with scope and class to train on.

MISSISSIPPI
b.c. Exceed And Excel – Ruby Rocket .
Very powerful and strong, a bull of a horse who should be very precocious. Trained by Dermot Weld.

ROBIN SHARP

ORRELL POST
b.f. Kyllachy – Dame Blanche.
A real strong filly who I bought for a top man in David Armstrong. I will be very dissapointed if she is not a 2 year old as I have always liked her. Trained by Richard Fahey.

UNNAMED
f. Shamardal – Misty Waters.
A quality filly with a good pedigree who I know is in the Tatts breeze up. Bred by Houghton Bloodstock, she could be a very good buy for someone. n.b. this filly was bought-in at the breeze up sale for 65,000 guineas.

UNNAMED
c. Tobougg – Billiard.
A smashing colt and I could not understand why he did not make more at the sales, as I always loved him. He will be as hard as iron but is by an underrated stallion and the agents seem to give these kind of horses a wide birth.

UNNAMED
f. Medicean – Palace Affair.
A very powerful filly in mind as well as body. She was always finding trouble when we were preparing her for the sales and had her issues but if ever there was a filly born to run, she is it. Hopefully she'll be a fitting legacy for Miss Swire.

AMANDA SKIFFINGTON

MELTING POT
c. Camacho – Thaw.
I bred this colt and he's a real two-year-old type. He is with a first year trainer, Hugo Palmer, so I very much hope he will be useful for him.

SENTARIL
b.f. Danehill Dancer – Superstar Leo.
A really lovely strong filly with, reportedly, a great mind. With William Haggas, who loved her half-sister, Map of Heaven last year, and likes this one even more.

UNNAMED
b.c. Acclamation – Top Row.
With Richard Hannon, a really attractive colt, who I will be deeply disappointed by if he is not above average.

UNNAMED
b.f. Acclamation – Love Thirty.
For later in the year, I also bought Hugo Palmer this lovely filly; she looks a classy type for later on.

LARRY STRATTON

DON'T TAKE ME ALIVE
br.c. Araafa – Up At Dawn.
Bred by me, he's a half-brother to a Newmarket maiden winning juvenile last year, looks sharp and I am hoping he might be the standout by the sire. Trained by Clive Cox.

GRAY PEARL
b/gr.f. Excellent Art – Divine Grace.
A well-bred filly with a lot of class about her bred by Robert Pocock at Stringston Farm. A foal purchase which could be anything if she runs up to her looks. Trained by Barry Hills.

UNNAMED
b.c. Beat Hollow – Ennobling.
A homebred 2nd foal, he's a half-brother to a filly who won two at two last year. He looks a 2-y-o type and should not be too late appearing. Trained by Nick Littmoden.

ANTHONY STROUD

RIO GRANDE
b.c. Invincible Spirit – Pharma West.
A precocious looking colt who was purchased at the Arqana August Yearling Sale at Deauville and has been showing up very well in his early work. Hopes are high that he will seen at the major meetings this season. Trained by Jeremy Noseda.

SEA ODYSSEY
b.c. Dark Angel – Time To Dream (Gone West).
A smart, early sort who came from Tattersalls Book Two. Looks like a fast two year-old type and has been working well at home. Should be seen out in the first part of the season.. Trained by Barry Hills.

SEASON SPIRIT
ch.c. Shirocco – Shadow Dancing.
A rangy type bred for middle distances, who has been moving well in his paces recently.

Purchased at Tattersalls Book One from his breeder Willie Carson who assures us that he is a black-type performer in the making! He is a half brother to Rasmy, who finished a close third in the G3 Dee Stakes at Chester last year. Trained by James Given.

STENCIVE
b.c. Dansili – Madeira Mist.
A middle-distance bred colt who is a very classy-looking individual from Tattersalls Book One. He is a half brother to last year's G1 Canadian International winner Joshua Tree and since he is owned by Bernard Kantor, Managing Director of Derby sponsor's Investec, it would be wonderful if he could make it to Epsom 2012. Trained by William Haggas.

Trainers' Bargain Buys

How good are the trainers at spotting value for money? The following two-year-olds have been recommended by their handlers as being bargains from the yearling sales. They cost 25,000 guineas or less and, as you can see, some were decidedly at the lower end of the price bracket.

Name	Price	Trainer
Emirates Jack	11,500 gns	George Baker
Goldoni	16,500 gns	Andrew Balding
Ch f Dutch Art – Eloquent Rose	14,500 gns	Ralph Beckett
Operation Tracer	11,500 gns	Michael Bell
Bayleyf	£10 000	John Best
Appealing	€7,500	Marco Botti
Bayton	6,000 gns	Henry Candy
Rooknrasbryripple	7,200 gns	Mick Channon
Seventeen Seventy	3,500 gns	Jane Chapple Hyam
Possibly	6,500 gns	Peter Chapple Hyam
Supreme Quest	£13,000	Roger Charlton
Percy Jackson	6,000 gns	Denis Coakley
Ch f Lucky Story – Soft Touch	12 000 gns	Tom Dascombe
b.c Choisir – Bea's Ruby	15 000 gns	Ann Duffield
Arabian Flight	6,000 gns	Ed Dunlop
Red Mischief	1,500 gns.	Harry Dunlop
Norse Gold	2,400 gns	David Elsworth
Devlin	27 000 gns	Richard Fahey
b.c. Teofilo – Wunders Dream	3,000 gns	James Given
b.f. Jeremy – Misaayef	€2,500	Michael Grassick
b.f. Whipper – Savage	4,000 gns	Rae Guest
Hamble	9,000 gns	William Haggas
Bensoon	15,000 gns	Michael Halford
Redact	85,000 gns	Richard Hannon
Tuibama	7,000 gns	Ben Haslam
Cashmere or Caviar	16,500 gns	Barry Hills
Johnno	18,000 gns	John Hills
Cheviot Quest	11,000 gns	William Jarvis
Bling King	22,000 gns	Eve Johnson Houghton
Mrs Cash	20,000 gns	Sylvester Kirk
Story Writer	10,500 gns	William Knight
Dutch Supreme	15 000 gns	David Larigan
Khyber Pass	10 000 gns	Eddie Lynam
Mount Meru	£7,000	Ger Lyons
Sabusa	3,000 gns	Alan McCabe
Lightning Jet	12 000 gns	Ed McMahon
Maccabees	7,500 gns	Rod Millman
Jasie Jack	16,000 gns	Robert Mills
Isolde's Return	5,500 gns	George Moore
Ginger Monkey	€12,500	Stan Moore
b.f. Dubawi – Enlightened Way	3,000 gns	Patrick Morris
Chil The Kite	13,000 gns	Hughie Morrison
Hollywood All Star	€5,000	Willie Muir
Mount McLeod	€20,000	Jamie Osborne

TRAINER'S BARGAIN BUYS

Bramshill Lass	21,000 gns	Amanda Perrett
ch f Singspiel – Bumble	9,000 gns	John Portman
The Firm	€16,000	Kevin Prendergast
Red Tyke	9,500 gns	John Quinn
Mr Fong	23,000 gns	David Simcock
Latte	16,000 gns	Linda Stubbs
Joe The Coat	11,000 gns	Mark Tompkins
b.f. Intikhab – Ladood	10,000 gns	Marcus Tregoning
Complacent	£6,000	Ed Vaughan
Sparks Might Fly	11,000 gns	Ed Walker
Sweetscot	4,000 gns	Amy Weaver
Celestial Dawn	1,500 gns	John Weymes
b.f. Amadeus Wolf – Am I	€16,500	Peter Winkworth

Two-year-olds of 2011

ERIC ALSTON

1. CHESTER ARISTOCRAT ★★
ch.g. Sakhee – New Light (Generous).
February 16. First foal. 16,000Y. Tattersalls October Book 2. Jeremy Brummitt. The dam, a moderate 9f and 10f placed maiden, is a half-sister to 5 winners including Bygone Days (Group 3 Bentinck Stakes). The second dam, May Light (by Midyan), is a placed half-sister to 10 winners including the Group winners King Luthier and Lighted Glory. (P G Buist). "He was proving quite difficult to handle so we gelded him and since then he's started to grow a bit and he's maturing. I still expect him to be racing in May and despite the stamina in his pedigree I think he'll be alright to start off at six furlongs".

2. KING OF PARADISE (IRE) ★★★
b.c. Hurricane Run – Silly Game (Bigstone).
April 14. Fifth foal. 33,000Y. Tattersalls October Book 2. Jeremy Brummitt. Closely related to the fairly useful 2-y-o 7f winner and 3-y-o 10f listed-placed Better Hand (by Montjeu). The dam, a winner in Italy over 7.5f at 2 yrs and over hurdles, is a half-sister to 5 winners. The second dam, Scarduza (by High Top), won over hurdles in Italy and is a half-sister to 7 winners including the Group 3 winner Midnight Air (dam of the Group 2 Long Island Handicap winner Midnight Line) and to the dams of the Group 1 winners Imperial Beauty and Jan Vermeer. (P G Buist). 'A really nice, good-looking horse, he's not showing any weakness at all at the moment, so I'm expecting him to be out by the end of May. He'll start off at six furlongs but he'll get further in time and he's a very nice colt".

GEORGE BAKER

3. BILLYRAYVALENTINE (CAN) ★★★
b.c. Elusive Quality – Sweet And Careless (Hennessy).
March 23. Fourth foal. Doncaster Premier. £105,000Y. Hugo Merry. Half-brother to the US Grade 1 Alabama Stakes and dual Grade 2 winner Careless Jewel (by Tapit) and to 2 minor winners in Canada and the USA by Crientate. The dam is an unraced half-sister to 4 winners the dual US Grade 1 winner Subordination. The second dam, Not So Careless (by Desert Wine), won at 3 yrs in the USA and is a half-sister to 5 winners including the Grade 1 winners Cacoethes and Fabulous Notion. (Russell, Wheeler, Vail Partnership). "A very nice type, not overly big and he'll be one of our more precocious 2-y-o's. He has a strong American pedigree, so if he does well over here you could see him ending up in the USA at some point. He'll be racing from late May onwards and he's pleasing me very much at the moment. A five/six furlong 2-y-o".

4. DANA'S PRESENT ★★★
ch.c. Osorio – Euro Empire (Bartok).
April 15. Seventh foal. 20,000Y. Tattersalls October Book 2. Blandford Bloodstock. Half-sister to the fair 5f winner Moving Diamonds (by Lomitas and herself dam of the listed winner Dinkum Diamond), to the fair 2-y-o 1m winner Dancing Granny (by Rock Of Gibraltar), the minor US 2-y-o winner Shogun Empire (by Forestry) and 2 winners abroad by Lomitas. The dam, a dual 2-y-o stakes winner in the USA, was placed in two Grade 1 events and is a half-sister to 4 minor winners in the USA. The second dam, Lotta Glory Beau's (by Empire Glory), a stakes winner of 4 races in the USA, is a half-sister to 4 winners. (Michael Wilson & Victor Chandler). "A precocious type that's doing plenty of work on the grass, I would say he'd be running in May and he looks a strong, stocky 2-y-o type for five and six furlongs. Definitely not just a 2-y-o though, he has the scope to go on".

5. EMIRATES JACK ★★★
b.c. Red Clubs – Lady Windley (Baillamont).
April 25. 11,000Y. Tattersalls December. Blandford Bloodstock. Half-brother to the useful 7f (at 2 yrs) and 1m winner Our Teddy (by Grand Lodge), to the fairly useful 7f (at 2 yrs) to 9f winner and listed-placed Talwin (by Alhaarth), to the fairly useful 2-y-o 1m winner Zouave (by Spectrum), the quite useful 10f to 2m winner of 6 races Bergonzi (by Indian Ridge), the fair Irish dual 10f and hurdles winner Lethal Weapon (by Hawk Wing), the modest 9.7f and

10f winner Waseyla (by Sri Pekan) and the minor Italian 2-y-o and 3-y-o winner Reine du Lac (by Dr Devious). The dam, an 11f winner of 3 races in France, is a half-sister to 6 winners and to the placed dam of the Group 1 Tattersalls Gold Cup winner Shiva and the Group 2 Prix Jean du Chaudenay winner Limnos. The second dam, Northern Trick (by Northern Dancer), won the Prix de Diane and the Prix Vermeille. (Mrs V P Baker & Partners). *"A cheap purchase, the sire looks to be stamping his stock with a bit of attitude and this colt certainly has that, but he also has an engine and we'll be pressing on with him".* TRAINERS' BARGAIN BUY

6. MISSUS MILLS (IRE) ★★
ch.f. Notnowcato – Putout (Dowsing).
April 6. Twelfth living foal. 16,000Y. Tattersalls December. Blandford Bloodstock. Half-sister to the 2-y-o Group 3 Premio Primi Passi winner Palanca (by Inchinor), to the fairly useful 2-y-o 6f winner Rajab (by Selkirk), the quite useful 1m and 9f winner Roman Glory (by Soviet Star) and the fair triple 5f winner Bedevilled (by Beveled). The dam, a fair 3-y-o 5f winner, is a half-sister to the Group 2 Sun Chariot Stakes winner Danceabout and to the Group 3 6f Prix de Meautry winner Pole Position. The second dam, Putupon (by Mummy's Pet), a fairly useful 2-y-o 5f winner, is a half-sister to the good horses Jupiter Island (Japan Cup), Pushy (Queen Mary Stakes) and Precocious (Gimcrack Stakes). (Mrs C E S Baker). *"I liked the stallion as a racehorse and this is his first crop of runners. I liked this filly as soon as I saw her, she's quite leggy and not particularly precocious so she's likely to be one to appear from the mid-summer onwards. So far so good, but his sire got better with age and I suspect this filly will be the same".*

7. MOUNT ST MISTRESS ★★★
ch.f. Zamindar – Capannina (Grand Lodge).
January 5. First foal. 25,000Y. Tattersalls October Book 1. Candida Baker. The dam, a fair 2-y-o 7f winner, is a half-sister to 3 winners. The second dam, Mauri Moon (by Green Desert), won 4 races including the listed Oak Tree Stakes and is a half-sister to 5 winners including the Singapore Derby winner Kimbridge Knight. (Miss Emily Asprey & Mrs Susan Roy). *"She looks to have plenty of speed and should be racing by late May. An interesting filly, she has plenty of attitude but it's a willing sort of attitude so I'm not worried because I can channel it in the right direction. A nice stamp of filly, she's well put-together".*

8. PLACE IN MY HEART ★★★
ch.f. Compton Place – Lonely Heart (Midyan).
February 17. 10,000 2-y-o. Ascot January. Not sold. Half-sister to the smart Group 3 7f Tetrarch Stakes winner Leitrim House (by Cadeaux Genereux), to the fairly useful 7f and 1m winner of 5 races Ace Of Hearts (by Magic Ring), the fair 2-y-o 7f winner Missed A Beat (by Mister Baileys) and the fair 7f winner Golden Heart (by Salse). The dam, a useful dual 10f winner, was listed-placed and is a half-sister to 4 winners out of the quite useful 7f to 10f winner Take Heart (by Electric), herself a half-sister to 3 minor winners. (Whitsbury Manor Stud). *"A home-bred and owned by my landlords the Harpers of Whitsbury Manor Stud with whom we have a close relationship. They did plenty of work with her themselves, we've been going steadily with her but we're just stepping up her work now and I'm happy with her. A five/six furlong 2-y-o, she's well put-together, strong-bodied and she definitely has plenty of strength through the neck. A nice horse".*

9. POKER HOSPITAL ★★★
b.f. Rock Of Gibraltar – Empress Anna (Imperial Ballet).
March 12. Third foal. 20,000Y. Tattersalls October Book 2. Blandford Bloodstock. The dam, a minor winner at 3 yrs in the USA, is a half-sister to 5 winners including the Irish listed winner and Group 3 placed Clean Cut. The second dam, Cutlers Corner (by Sharpen Up), a very useful winner of the 5f Rous Stakes, was fourth in the Group 3 King George Stakes and is a half-sister to 6 winners. (Mr J Dwyer & Partners). *"This looks like an 'instant action' 2-y-o because she's pretty much ready to press on with. She's been working well and she'll be racing in late April or early May, she's not over-big but she has a fine action that takes the eye on the gallops. Certainly a horse that we're looking forward to seeing out, she looks the type that should grow again and progress as a 3-y-o next year".*

10. PURPLE 'N GOLD ★★★★
b.c. Strategic Prince – Golden Dew (Montjeu).
March 2. Second living foal. 46,000Y. Tattersalls October Book 2. Blandford Bloodstock. The dam, placed fourth twice over 12f in Ireland, is a half-sister to 5 winners including the Breeders Cup Juvenile (Turf) winner Pounced. The second dam, Golden Cat (by Storm Cat), won over 1m at 3 yrs in Ireland and was listed-placed and is a half-sister to 7 winners including the very useful Irish dual listed winner and subsequent US winner Eurostorm. (M Khan X2). *"He's a very nice type and I think an awful lot of him. He's been working very well and would be the most forward of my 2-y-o's. Because he has such a big stride I initially imagined he'd be a seven furlong 2-y-o, because I didn't think he'd have the speed for anything less, but actually he shows plenty of speed. We'll start him at six furlongs with a view to stepping him up from there".*

11. REFRESHESTHEPARTS (USA) ★★★
ch.f. Proud Citizen – St Francis Wood (Irish River).
March 27. Third foal. Goffs Orby. €35,000Y. Blandford Bloodstock. Half-sister to a minor winner abroad by Giant's Causeway. The dam, a quite useful 1m winner, was listed-placed and is a sister to a stakes winner in the USA and a half-sister to 2 winners. The second dam, Francisco Road (by Strawberry Road), won 3 minor races in the USA and is a half-sister to 5 winners. (Mrs Carvalho-Heineken). *"So named because of her owner! She's doing some nice work on the grass and looks like a seven furlongs or mile 2-y-o. She has a big, round action with a good stride, she's big and strong and although she'll run this year she's likely to improve with age. A horse I like a lot, she should be racing from June onwards".*

12. SWEET OPHELIA ★★★
b.f. Shamardal – Showery (Rainbow Quest).
February 5. Eleventh foal. 24,000Y. Tattersalls December. Blandford Bloodstock. Half-sister to the useful dual 6f (at 2 yrs) and 1m winner Bestam (by Selkirk), to the useful 6f and 1m winner of 7 races Tiger Reigns, the 2011 10f winner Songjiang (both by Tiger Hill), the Hong Kong winner of 6 races Noble Man (by Cadeaux Genereux) and the modest 2-y-o 10f winner Louise Rayner (by Vettori). The dam, a fair 3-y-o 6f winner, is a half-sister to 5 winners including the smart Winter Derby winner Adiemus. The second dam, Anodyne (by Dominion), a useful 6f winner, is a sister to the very useful US Grade 3 winner Domynsky and a half-sister to 8 winners. (George Baker & Partners). *"A really strong type that just continues to progress. I think she'll be racing in May, which is earlier than I first envisaged. She'll start at six furlongs and we'll continue from there, but she's a filly who just thrives on work and her progress over the last few weeks has been eye-catching".*

13. UNNAMED ★★
ch.c. Hurricane Run – Haute Volta (Grape Tree Road).
April 14. Third foal. Goffs Orby. €85,000Y. George Baker. Brother to the quite useful 2-y-o 6f winner Attracted To You and closely related to the Italian dual listed 1m winner (including at 2 yrs) Super Motiva (by Motivator). The dam is an unraced half-sister to 7 winners including the 2-y-o Group 1 National Stakes winner Heart Of Darkness. The second dam, Land Of Ivory (by The Minstrel), a very useful winner over 7f (at 2 yrs) and 1m, was placed in the Prix Cleopatre and Lupe Stakes and is a half-sister to the high-class middle-distance colt Gold and Ivory and to the unraced dams of the Grade 1 winner Anees and the Graded stakes winners and sires Elusive Quality and Rossini. (M Khan X2). *"A gorgeous horse, his sire and his pedigree both suggest he'll be much more of a 3-y-o type and onwards. So we're going steady with him, he's big and fills the eye but he's one for the back-end of the season".*

ANDREW BALDING

14. AMPHORA ★★★★
b.f. Oasis Dream – Carafe (Selkirk).
March 9. Third living foal. £105,000Y. Doncaster Premier. David Redvers. 65,000Y. Tattersalls October Book 2. John Warren. The dam, a quite useful 7f winner, is a half-sister to the fairly useful 1m winner and listed-placed Coyote (herself the dam of two Group 3 stakes winners). The second dam, Caramba (by Belmez), a smart winner of the Group 2 1m Falmouth Stakes and the

Group 2 10f Nassau Stakes, is a half-sister to 7 winners including the Moyglare Stud Stakes and Falmouth Stakes winner Lemon Souffle. (Highclere Thoroughbred Racing, Minoru). *"A very nice filly, she had a bit of a setback with a splint but she's back cantering now. I think she'll be a nice 2-y-o type from June onwards and she's a good-sized filly and a good mover. I must mention that I wasn't that happy with my 2-y-o's last year but I was high on them the year before. I was right both times and I think this crop is the best I've ever had".*

15. AUTUMN FIRE ★★★
b.f. Avonbridge – Brand (Shareef Dancer).
February 21. Half-sister to the very useful Group 3 Badener Meile and listed Doncaster Mile winner of 8 races over 7f and 1m Banknote (by Zafonic), to the useful 6f (at 2 yrs) and 1m winner Royal Warrant (by Royal Applause), the 2-y-o 6f and 7f winner Captain Ginger (by Muhtarram), the 6f to 1m winner Double Brandy (by Elmaamul) and 3 winners over jumps by Broadsword, Elmaamul and Domedriver. The dam is an unraced half-sister to 5 winners out Beacon Hill (by Bustino), herself a half-sister to the dam of Height Of Fashion. (The Queen). *"She should be a mid-summer 2-y-o if not before and she's just started to do really well. A medium-sized filly and a good mover, she hasn't worked yet but she looks relatively precocious".*

16. BACKTRADE (IRE) ★★★★
b.c. Holy Roman Emperor – Braari (Gulch).
March 28. Thirteenth foal. Tattersalls Ireland. €37,000Y. Andrew Balding. Half-brother to the very useful 2-y-o listed 6f winner and Group 3 7f Lanson Champagne Vintage Stakes third Shaard (by Anabaa), to the quite useful 7f and 1m winner Kareeb (by Green Desert), the quite useful 2-y-o 6f winner Marriage Value (by Marju), the Irish 6.5f and 8.5f 2-y-o winner Zaby (by Cadeaux Genereux), the fair 3-y-o 7f winner Mafruz (by Hamas) and a winner in Italy by Danehill Dancer. The dam, a fairly useful 2-y-o 6f winner, is a sister to the US stakes winner Special Alert and a half-sister to 7 winners. The second dam, So Cozy (by Lyphard), was a 2-y-o stakes winner in the USA. (Birkdale Racing). *"A very sharp colt, he'll probably be my first 2-y-o runner. I like him a lot, he goes nicely and I'm hoping to get him out just after the Newmarket Guineas meeting".*

17. BENZANNO (IRE) ★★
b.c. Refuse To Bend – Crossanza (Cape Cross).
March 9. First foal. €14,000Y. Tattersalls Ireland. A Balding. The dam is an unraced half-sister to one winner. The second dam, Alegranza (by Lake Coniston), a winner over 5f at 3 yrs, was listed-placed and is a full or half-sister to 7 winners including the listed winner Army Of Angels and the dam of the Group 1 Cheveley Park Stakes and Canadian Grade 1 6f winner Serious Attitude. (Martin & Valerie Slade and Partner). *"He's a nice colt, we bought him for his 3-y-o career really, but he'll be perfectly alright for a seven furlong maiden or median auction from June onwards. A medium-sized colt with a lot of scope and he's the type that should go on improving".*

18. BONFIRE ★★★
b.c. Manduro – Night Frolic (Night Shift).
February 24. Fourth foal. 90,000Y. Tattersalls October Book 1. John Warren. Half-brother to Joviality (by Cape Cross), unplaced in one start at 2 yrs in 2010, to the fair 2-y-o 5f winner Chicita Banana (by Danehill Dancer) and the fair dual 1m winner Burns Night (by Selkirk). The dam, a modest 1m winner, is a half-sister to 5 winners including the US Grade 3 Cardinal Handicap winner Miss Caerleona (herself dam of the Group winners Karen's Caper and Miss Coronado). The second dam, Miss d'Ouilly (by Bikala), won a listed event over 9f in France and is a half-sister to 6 winners including the Prix Jacques le Marois winner Miss Satamixa and the Group 3 placed Mrs Annie (the dam of four stakes winners). (Highclere Thoroughbred Racing, Pocahontas). *"I was underbidder on him at the sale, so I was fortunate to have him sent to me. He had a trapped testicle which had to be removed and he's done a lot of growing lately, but having said that he's very athletic and really forward going for a middle-distance type. So he should certainly have a couple of runs this year and he looks nice".*

19. BYPASS ★★★
br.f. Passing Glance – Florida Heart (First Trump).
February 27. First living foal. The dam, a fair

2-y-o 1m winner, is a half-sister to 2 winners. The second dam, Miami Dancer (by Seattle Dancer), won at up to 9f in the USA. (Kingsclere Racing Club). *"The first foal of a mare that Dad trained as a 2-y-o, she's been an unlucky producer because she's lost a couple of foals. I don't want to sound biased but I think the sire is very underrated. I like this filly, she's medium-sized and quite classy looking. A good mover for the mid-summer onwards".*

20. CADES REEF (IRE) ★★★
gr.c. Dalakhani – Just Special (Cadeaux Genereux).
March 14. Fifth foal. 60,000Y. Tattersalls October Book 1. Andrew Balding. Half-brother to the French dual 1m winner and listed-placed Best Dating (by King's Best), to the quite useful Irish 7f winner Spesialta (by Indian Ridge) and the fair 1m and hurdles winner Al Qeddaaf (by Alhaarth). The dam, winner of the listed 7f Knockaire Stakes in Ireland and second in the Group 2 Prix d'Astarte is a half-sister to the listed winner Blue Gold. The second dam, Relatively Special (by Alzao), winner of the Group 3 7f Rockfel Stakes at 2 yrs and third in the Irish 1,000 Guineas, is a half-sister to 7 winners including the Dante Stakes winner Alnasr Alwasheek and the Juddmonte International winner One So Wonderful. (Mick & Janice Mariscotti). *"A small, neat, easy-moving colt. He'd be quite forward for a son of Dalakhani, maybe lacking a little in scope, but I'd be disappointed if he didn't have a decent 2-y-o career from when the seven furlong races start".*

21. CAPE CROSSING ★★
br.f. Cape Cross – Dame Hester (Diktat).
March 15. Second foal. 38,000Y. Tattersalls December. Boyce Bloodstock. The dam, a quite useful 1m and 10f winner, was listed-placed and is a half-sister to 5 winners including the Group 2 5f Kings Stand Stakes third My Funny Valentine. The second dam, Aunt Hester (by Caerleon), a modest 2-y-o 5f winner, is closely related to the smart Group 3 9f Prix Daphnis winner L'Irresponsable and a half-sister to 6 winners. (Mildmay Racing/ D★Caslon). *"She's only just come in and she's nice but I wouldn't know an awful lot about her yet".*

22. CHARLES THE GREAT (IRE) ★★★★
b.c. Holy Roman Emperor – Jojeema (Barathea).
March 10. Fourth foal. 30,000Y. Tattersalls October Book 1. G Howson. Half-brother to the fair 1m winner Song To The Moon (by Oratorio) and to the modest 2-y-o 1m winner Hum Cat (by One Cool Cat). The dam is an unraced half-sister to 5 winners including the high-class Group 2 12f Jockey Club Stakes and Group 3 12f Cumberland Lodge Stakes winner Riyadian. The second dam, Knight's Baroness (by Rainbow Quest), a smart filly, won over 7f (at 2 yrs) and the Irish Oaks and was placed in the Oaks, the Lingfield Oaks Trial, the Park Hill Stakes and the May Hill Stakes. (Kennet Valley Thoroughbreds V). *"Very forward, he's a lovely horse and I've never seen one improve as much from the sale to where he's at now. A really nice 2-y-o type, I have reasonably high expectations of him. He was a bit dip-backed and ponified at the sale, but he's really gone the right way and he's a nice horse".*

23. DANCE WITH ME (IRE) ★★★★
b.c. Danehill Dancer – Perpetual Time (Sadler's Wells).
February 22. First foal. 95,000Y. Tattersalls October Book 1. A Balding. The dam is an unraced sister to the Group 2 Prix de Malleret winner Time On. The second dam, Time Away (by Darshaan), won the Group 3 10.4f Musidora Stakes, was third in the Group 1 Prix de Diane and the Group 1 Nassau Stakes and is a half-sister to 6 winners including the 10f winner and Prix de Diane second Time Ahead. (Mr & Mrs R Gorell/Mr & Mrs P Pausewang). *"A lovely, big, tall, rangy colt. He's quite long-backed, as some of the Danehill Dancer's are, he's done a couple of bits of work and looks very nice. He should be ready to go as soon as the six furlong races start and he gets a double tick from me. A nice horse".*

24. DANDY (GER) ★★★★
b.c. Nayef – Diacada (Cadeaux Genereux).
April 11. Fifth foal. Goffs Orby. €65,000Y. Andrew Balding. Half-brother to 3 winners including the German 2-y-o listed 6f winner Diatribe (by Tertullian). The dam, a Group 2 German 1,000 Guineas winner, is a half-sister to 10 winners including the Group 3 winner

Desidera. The second dam, Diasprina (by Aspros), a champion German 2-y-o filly, was a half-sister to 6 winners. (Mr R E Tillett). *"A really nice horse. By Nayef out of a German Guineas winner, he's going to take a bit of time but he's not quite as heavy as some of the Nayef's can be. He's a bit lighter on his feet and a bit more athletic. The mare didn't stay much beyond a mile and this colt will start off at seven furlongs. He should stay a mile and a half next year and I just think he's a thoroughly nice horse".*

25. DISTANT LOVE (IRE) ★★★
b.f. Halling – Conference (Montjeu).
April 3. First foal. 17,000Y. Tattersalls October Book 1. Andrew Balding. The dam is an unraced half-sister to 7 winners including the US stakes winner, Group 3 Chester Vase third and US Grade 3 third Distant Mirage and the listed-placed Roses In The Snow (dam of the US Grade 3 winner Snowdrops). The second dam, Desert Bluebell (by Kalaglow), is a placed half-sister to 10 winners including the Group 3 Solario Stakes winner Shining Waters (herself dam of the Group 1 Grand Criterium winner Tenby). (Mr L L Register). *"A nice filly, my mother bought her and we've always been a fan of Halling. She's having a little break just now but she's nice and neat and she'll be ready to go from July onwards over seven furlongs".*

26. DOLLAR BILL ★★★
ch.c. Medicean – Jardin (Sinndar).
February 9. Second foal. 50,000Y. Tattersalls October Book 1. Andrew Balding. The dam is an unraced half-sister to 7 winners including Sleeping Indian (Group 2 7f Challenge Stakes) and Felicity (Group 3 10f Golden Daffodil Stakes). The second dam, Las Flores (by Sadler's Wells), a useful 10f winner, second in the Lingfield Oaks Trial and third in the Italian Oaks, is a full or half-sister to 5 winners including the Group 2 Royal Whip Stakes winner Bach and the Irish 1,000 Guineas second Dancing Goddess. (Mrs C L Kyle). *"A really nice colt that we bought from Charlie Vigors' stud. I think he was well-bought because if he'd been by a more fashionable sire he would have made double his price tag and yet Medicean can certainly get decent horses. He'll have a couple of runs this year and he'll improve as a 3-y-o, but I'd be very disappointed if he couldn't win this year".*

27. DUTCH MASTER ★★
ch.c. Dutch Art – Duena (Grand Lodge).
April 6. Eighth foal. 5,000Y. Doncaster Premier. Andrew Balding. Half-brother to the fair 2010 2-y-o 1m winner Twice Bitten (by Beat Hollow), to the modest 7f and 11f winner Burnbrake (by Mujahid) and the modest 2-y-o 5f winner Music Teacher (by Piccolo). The dam is an unplaced half-sister to the useful 2-y-o 5f listed and 3-y-o 7f listed winner Presto Vento. The second dam, Placement (by Kris), is an unraced half-sister to 4 winners including the Group 2 Sun Chariot Stakes winner Danceabout and the French dual Group 3 winner Pole Position. (Mr A Brooke-Rankin). *"Probably not your typical Dutch Art because he won't be running until July I wouldn't have thought. He's a big, tall, rangy horse and he's going the right way".*

28. EMPEROR VESPASIAN ★★★
b.c. Royal Applause – Flavian (Catrail).
March 7. Fifth foal. 26,000Y. Tattersalls October Book 2. A Balding. Half-brother to the fairly useful 7f winner and listed-placed Flambeau (by Oasis Dream), to the fair 7f winner Bended Knee (by Refuse To Bend), the moderate 2-y-o 6f and 7f winner Young Flavio (by Mark Of Esteem) and a winner in Scandinavia by Halling. The dam, a fairly useful 6f (at 2 yrs) and 7f winner, is a half-sister to 7 winners including the useful triple 7f winner Mata Cara (herself the dam of a French listed winner). The second dam, Fatah Flare (by Alydar), won over 6f (at 2 yrs) and the Group 3 10.5f Musidora Stakes at 3 yrs and is a half-sister to 8 winners including Sabin, a dual US Grade 1 winner over 9f and 10f. (Mr R Wilmot-Smith). *"I like him a lot and he reminds me very much of a decent Royal Applause horse called Prince Siegfried because he's a similar type in that he's bigger and scopier than most Royal Applause 2-y-o's. He's done very well recently and he'll be a seven furlong 2-y-o from July onwards.*

29. EXPENSE CLAIM (IRE) ★★★
b.c. Intikhab – Indolente (Diesis).
April 28. Third foal. 95,000Y. Tattersalls October Book 2. A Balding. Half-brother to the minor French 3-y-o winner Issacar (by Traditionally). The dam is an unraced half-sister to 2 winners. The second dam, Tycoon's Dolce

(by Rainbows For Life), won the listed Prix de Lieurey and was Group 3 placed three times and is a half-sister to 5 winners (including 3 listed winners in France and Italy). (Another Bottle Racing). *"I loved him as a yearling and since then he's done nothing to suggest anything other than he's a really nice type. A seven furlong 2-y-o for June"*.

30. FLAXEN FLARE (IRE) ★★
ch.c. Windsor Knot – Golden Angel (Slew O'Gold).
February 8. Fifth foal. 20,000Y. Tattersalls October Book 2. G Howson. Half-brother to the modest 10f winner Classical Rhythm (by Traditionally) and to 3 winners abroad by Raise A Grand (2) and Tagula. The dam, a minor French 2-y-o winner, is a half-sister to 5 winners. The second dam, Water Angel (by Halo), is an unraced half-sister to the dual Japanese stakes winner Biwi Shinseiki. (Kennet Valley Thoroughbreds). *"From the first crop of Windsor Knot, he was doing everything right until mid-February when he started a big growth spurt. He now looks quite backward and he needs time, so we'll just have to be patient with him"*.

31. FORTROSE ACADEMY ★★★
b.c. Iceman – Auspicious (Shirley Heights).
April 14. Eighth foal. 16,000Y. Tattersalls October Book 2. A Balding. Half-brother to the fairly useful 2-y-o 7f and 1m winner Doctrine (by Barathea), to the quite useful 2-y-o 1m winner Australian (by Danzero), the quite useful 1m to 10f winner Prince Picasso (by Lomitas), to the fair 2-y-o 1m winner Perfect Vision (by Starcraft) and the fair dual 7f winner Istiqdaam (by Pivotal). The dam, a fairly useful 10.2f winner, is a sister to the smart Group 2 11.9f Great Voltigeur Stakes winner Sacrament and a half-sister to 5 winners and to the unraced dam of the Group 1 winner Chorist. The second dam, Blessed Event (by Kings Lake), winner of the listed 10f Ballymacoll Stud Stakes and placed in the Yorkshire Oaks and the Champion Stakes, is a half-sister to 4 winners. (Mr E Sutherland). *"A neat, 2-y-o type that I hope will be out over six furlongs in mid-May. He's a nice type, a very active walker and a good-bodied horse. Just the sort we can have a bit of fun with this year"*.

32. GOLDONI (IRE) ★★★
ch.c. Dylan Thomas – Lasso (Indian Ridge).
April 27. Second foal. 16,000Y. Tattersalls October Book 1. Andrew Balding. Half-brother to the fairly useful 7f (at 2 yrs) and 1m winner Gunner Lindley (by Medicean). The dam, a modest 7f winner, is a half-sister to 3 winners. The second dam, Rosse (by Kris), a useful dual 7f winner, was listed-placed and is a half-sister to 9 winners including the high-class Group 1 1m Coronation Stakes winner Rebecca Sharp and the smart Group 3 11.5f Lingfield Derby Trial winner Mystic Knight. (Mick & Janice Mariscotti). *"He's done well since the sale and he's a really nice, 3-y-o middle-distance horse in the making. He should have a couple of runs this year – and he'll win I'd like to think"*.
TRAINERS' BARGAIN BUY

33. JUST WHEN ★★
b.c. Dalakhani – Cape Grace (Priolo).
February 23. Closely related to the French 3-y-o 7f winner Alice Town (by Darshaan). The dam, a useful listed 9f winner, is out of the French 3-y-o winner Saffron (by Fabulous Dancer), herself a half-sister to 7 winners. (G Strawbridge). *"Very much a 3-y-o type, he's big and backward but he's very nice, he has a good attitude and is a good mover. I like him and he's a nice horse for next year"*.

34. LAMBEAU FIELD ★★★
b.c. Alhaarth – Weqaar (Red Ransom).
March 19. Fifth foal. 18,000Y. Tattersalls October Book 2. A Balding. The dam, a quite useful 10.2f winner, is a half-sister to 5 winners including Sakhee (Prix de l'Arc de Triomphe and Juddmonte International) and the listed winner Nasheed. The second dam, Thawakib (by Sadler's Wells), won twice over 7f (at 2 yrs) and the Group 2 12f Ribblesdale Stakes. She is a half-sister to 9 winners including the top-class middle-distance colt Celestial Storm (winner of the Group 2 Princess of Wales's Stakes) and to the placed dam of the Group 1 Rothmans International winner River Memories. (A Balding). *"He's a nice type, quite neat and I bought him because he reminded me of Phoenix Reach who is by the same sire. He's grand and he's going to be a nice horse I think"*. The trainer, like me a fan of American Football, tells me he won a tidy sum when the

Green Bay Packers won the Superbowl. Hence this horse has been named after the Packers' stadium in Wisconsin. I was thinking of naming my next Partnerhip horse after the Denver Broncos stadium, but "Mile High" might give people the wrong idea!

35. OMAR KHAYYAM ★★★
b.c. Pivotal – Kithanga (Darshaan).
May 24. Tenth foal. 210,000Y. Tattersalls October Book 1. Norris/Huntingdon. Half-brother to the St Leger and Great Voltigeur Stakes winner Milan, to the fairly useful 12f winners Kahara and Kossack, the fair 11f winner Kibara (all by Sadler's Wells) and the Irish 2-y-o 7f winner and Group 2 Great Voltigeur Stakes third Go For Gold (by Machiavellian). The dam was a smart winner of 3 races including the Group 3 12f St Simon Stakes and the listed 12f Galtres Stakes. The second dam, Kalata (by Assert), ran once unplaced in France and is a half-sister to the dams of the Derby winner Kahyasi, the Yorkshire Oaks winner Key Change, the St Simon Stakes winner Kaliana and the Group 3 10.5f Prix Cleopatre winner Kalajana. (J L C Pearce). *"He was a late foal and he's a bit of a mixture because he's a Pivotal half-brother to a St Leger winner, but he was a neat, really good-looking yearling and my uncle William Huntingdon bought him for John Pearce. We haven't been in a hurry with him but I would hope that he'd be a seven furlong type from August onwards. He's one of the smaller Pivotals, a neat horse and a good mover but he hasn't been asked any questions yet".*

36. PRICE LIST ★★★★
b.f. Red Ransom – Film Script (Unfuwain).
Half-sister to the very useful listed 7f (at 2 yrs) and listed 14f winner Free Agent, to the fair 12f winner Criterion (both by Dr Fong) and the quite useful 12f winner Rainbow's Edge (by Rainbow Quest). The dam, a useful 10f and 12f listed winner, is a half-sister to 4 winners including the fairly useful 6f and 7f winner National Park. The second dam, Success Story (by Sharrood), a modest 10f winner, is a half-sister to the Group 2 13.5f Prix de Pomone winner Interlude. (The Queen). *"Certainly worth putting in the book, she's very nice and looks pretty classy. The last Red Ransom filly I had was our Oaks winner Casual Look, so I hope that's a good omen!"*

37. PROFIT AGAIN (IRE) ★★★
b.c. Tagula – Baileys First (Alzao).
April 20. Eleventh living foal. Doncaster Premier. £23,000Y. Andrew Balding. Half-brother to the quite useful Irish 7f and 1m winner Young Jemmy (by Tagula), to the 2-y-o 7f seller winner Uredale (by Bahhare) and two minor winners in Europe by Spectrum by Salse. The dam is a placed half-sister to 7 winners including the Group 1 Gran Criterium winner Candy Glen and the Group 3 Derrinstown Stud Derby Trial winner Ashley Park. The second dam, Maiden Concert (by Condorcet), ran once unplaced and is a half-sister to 2 winners. (Another Bottle Racing). *"A typical Tagula, he looks just like his Dad and I would hope he'd be an early-season 2-y-o but we had a minor setback with him. We'll see how we go with him but hopefully he'll be out before June".*

38. RENEGOTIATE ★★
ch.c. Trade Fair – L'Extra Honor (Hero's Honor).
March 22. Twelfth foal. 45,000Y. Tattersalls December. Peter Doyle. Half-brother to 6 winners including to the Group 1 1m Sun Chariot Stakes winner Majestic Roi, the very useful 7f (at 2 yrs) and 1m winner and Group 2 Prix Guillaume d'Ornano third Black Spirit (by Black Minnaloushe), the US Grade 3 placed Heza Gone West (by Gone West), the useful 2-y-o 7f winner and listed placed Hiddnah (by Affirmed) and the fair 8.6f winner Ransom Strip (by Red Ransom). The dam won a listed race in France over 10f and is a half-sister to 11 winners including the Group 2 Gallinule Stakes winner Montelimar. The second dam, L'Extravagante (by Le Fabuleux), won 3 races, was third in the Canadian Oaks and is a half-sister to 13 winners including the Canadian champions L'Enjoleur, La Voyageuse and Medaille d'Or and the Grade 2 winner D'Accord and to the unraced dam of the multiple Group 1 winner Holy Roman Emperor. (Birkdale Racing Syndicate). *"I think the sire is a bit under-rated because he's had his share of winners. This colt is nice but he's gone very backward since the sale, so we've just backed off him and he'll be an autumn 2-y-o probably".*

39. SHOT IN THE DARK (IRE) ★★
ch.g. Dr Fong – Highland Shot (Selkirk).
April 6. Half-brother to Great Shot (by Marju),

unplaced in two starts at 2 yrs in 2010 and to the quite useful 1m winner Highland Knight (by Night Shift). The dam, a fairly useful 7f to 9f winner, is a half-sister to numerous winners including the very smart 2-y-o Group 3 7f Solario Stakes winner and Group 1 Dewhurst Stakes third Opera Cape, the high-class stayer Grey Shot and the smart sprint winner of 4 races Night Shot. The second dam, Optaria (by Song), a quite useful 2-y-o 5f winner, is out of the unplaced Electo (by Julio Mariner). (J C Smith). *"He's already been gelded but he's very typical of the offspring of this mare. They don't look much but they improve with work. So he'll probably end up being alright".*

40. SPIRITUAL STAR (IRE) ★★★★ ♠
b.c. Soviet Star – Million Spirits (Invincible Spirit).
February 9. First foal. 80,000Y. Tattersalls October Book 2. Will Edmeades. The dam, a quite useful Irish 7f (at 2 yrs) and 1m winner, is a half-sister to 4 winners including the Group 1 French 1,000 Guineas and 2-y-o Group 3 7f Prix du Calvados winner Elusive Wave. The second dam, Multicolour Wave (by Rainbow Quest), is a placed half-sister to 4 winners. (Thurloe Thoroughbreds XXIX). *"A really nice horse, he's a fine-looking specimen and has a good way of going. We expect him to be seven furlong type 2-y-o in mid-summer. Will Edmeades bought him for Thurloe Thoroughbreds and I put the screws on James Stafford to ensure he came here!"*

41. STIRRING BALLAD ★★★
ch.f. Compton Place – Balnaha (Lomond)
March 31. Half-sister to the Group 1 1m Coronation Stakes winner Balisada (by Kris) and to the quite useful 12f winner Talk To Mojo (by Deploy). The dam, a modest 3-y-o 1m winner, is a sister to Inchmurrin (a very useful winner of the Child Stakes and herself the dam of the very smart and tough colt Inchinor, closely related to the very useful 1m winner Guest Artiste and a half-sister to the Mill Reef Stakes winner Welney. The second dam, On Show (by Welsh Pageant), won over 10f and was second in the November Handicap. (G Strawbridge). *"A nice filly, she's quite rangy and classy-looking. I'm pleased with her and she's probably a six/seven furlong type for mid-summer".*

42. SWAN SONG ★★
b.f. Green Desert – Lochsong (Song).
March 14. Closely related to the useful listed 5f winner Loch Verdi and half-sister to the smart listed 6f winner of 5 races Lochridge (by Indian Ridge), the quite useful dual 6f winner Rapid Water and the quite useful 5f and 6f winner Lochstar (both by Anabaa). The dam, a champion sprinter and winner of the Prix de l'Abbaye (twice), the Kings Stand Stakes and the Nunthorpe Stakes, is a half-sister to the Nunthorpe Stakes winner Lochangel. The second dam, Peckitts Well (by Lochnager), was a fairly useful winner of five races at 2 and 3 yrs from 5f to 6f. (J C Smith). *"She's well-named because she's the last foal out of Lochsong. She's lovely but rather like a lot of the family she doesn't look particularly precocious. They usually end up being fast though, so hopefully she'll be the same. One for the back-end of the season and especially next year".*

43. SWEET LIBERTA (IRE) ★★★
b.f. Cape Cross – Hendrina (Daylami).
March 9. Second foal. 35,000Y. Tattersalls October Book 1. Andrew Balding. The dam, unplaced in 2 starts, is a half-sister to 4 winners including the Irish Group 3 7.5f Concorde Stakes winner Hamairi and the Irish 5f (at 2 yrs) and 3-y-o listed 6f winner Hanabad. The second dam, Handaza (by Be My Guest), a 1m winner at 3 yrs in Ireland, is a half-sister to 6 winners including the Group 3 winners Hazarin and Hazarista. (Mick & Janice Mariscotti). *"A very nice filly, she's done really well since the sale. The Mariscotti's have been very good owners of mine and this filly was very much Janice Mariscotti's pick. At this moment in time it looks like Janice is a good judge. I'm very happy with her and I would say she wants six/seven furlongs. She's not short of speed".*

44. TOPANGA CANYON ★★★
b.c. Nayef – Classical Dancer (Dr Fong).
April 30. Fourth foal. 70,000Y. Tattersalls October Book 1. Not sold. Half-brother to the quite useful 7f, 1m (both at 2 yrs) and 12f winner Zaaqya (by Nayef). The dam, a fairly useful 8.3f winner, was listed-placed twice and is a half-sister to 5 winners including the Group 1 Premio Roma winner Imperial Dancer. The second dam, Gorgeous Dancer (by Nordico),

an Irish 3-y-o 1m winner and third in the listed Irish Oaks Trial, is a half-sister to 3 winners. (Mick & Janice Mariscotti). *"He was bought very much on the recommendation of Charlie Vigors who consigned him to the sale. He didn't make his reserve so we bought him privately afterwards and I'm glad we did. He's very typically Nayef and yet more forward than a lot of them would be. Seven furlongs in June should be alright for him".*

45. TOP COP ★★★★
b.c. Acclamation – Speed Cop
(Cadeaux Genereux).
January 25. Second foal. Half-brother to the fairly useful 2010 2-y-o 6f winner Desert Law (by Oasis Dream). The dam, a useful 2-y-o listed 5.2f winner and third in the Group 2 Flying Childers Stakes, is a sister to the fairly useful triple 5f winner (including at 2 yrs) and listed-placed Siren's Gift and a half-sister to the fair 6f winner Indiana Blues. The second dam, Blue Siren (by Bluebird), a very useful winner of three races from 5f to 7f, was disqualified from first place in two more, notably the Group 1 5f Nunthorpe Stakes (the winner on merit) and is a half-sister to several winners including the quite useful 9f winner Northern Habit. (J C Smith). *"A big, heavy, rather typical Acclamation. He looks a lovely horse and obviously he's from one of the owner's good families. The mother wasn't short on speed and I bet this colt ends up pretty quick. He's strengthened up a lot recently and he's the sort that should be ready by June".*

46. VISCOUNT VERT (IRE) ★★★
br.c. Kheleyf – Viscoumtess Brave
(Law Society).
April 16. Eighth foal. Tattersalls Ireland. €21,000Y. Andrew Balding. Half-brother to 2 minor winners abroad by Desert King and Namid. The dam, a winner of 4 races at 2 and 4 yrs in Italy, was listed-placed and is a half-sister to 4 winners. The second dam, Vadrouille (by Foolish Pleasure), won twice at 3 yrs. (Martin & Valerie Slade and Partner). *"A neat, strong colt and one to crack on with. We'll wait for the six furlong races but he's a proper 2-y-o type".*

47. UNNAMED ★★
b.f. Rock Of Gibraltar – Cherokee Stream
(Indian Ridge).
April 22. Second foal. Half-sister to the quite useful 2010 2-y-o 5f and 6f winner of 4 races Indian Ballad (by Oratorio). The dam, a fair Irish 7f to 9f placed maiden, is a half-sister to 4 winners. The second dam, Moy Water (by Tirol), an Irish 1m (at 2 yrs) and 9f winner, is a half-sister to 8 winners including the very useful listed sprint winners Bufalino and Maledetto. (Mr N N Botica). *"A nice filly and she's beginning to do well but she's tall and rangy and is going to take time. One run at the back-end probably".*

48. UNNAMED ★★
b.c. Dixie Union – No Frills (Darshaan).
April 1. Sixth foal. 40,000Y. Tattersalls October Book 1. Not sold. Half-brother to the US stakes winner and dual Grade 2 placed Singalong, to the quite useful 9f to 11f winner of 5 races Potentiale (both by Singspiel) and the quite useful 10f winner Ephorus (by Galileo). The dam, a modest 9f placed maiden, is a half-sister to 5 winners including the dams of the North American Graded stakes winners Millennium Dragon and J'Ray. The second dam, Bubbling Danseuse (by Arctic Tern), won once over 10f and was second in the Group 3 1m Prix de Sandringham and is a half-sister to 6 winners. (Dr P J Brown). *"He's a nice horse but he's had a setback and is big and backward. He'll run at the back-end of the season though and I like him".*

49. UNNAMED ★★★
b.c. Montjeu – Pescia (Darshaan).
April 22. Seventh foal. 28,000Y. Tattersalls December. Andrew Balding. Brother to the useful 10f winner and listed-placed Stately Home and closely related to the fairly useful 10f winner Snow Blizzard (by Sadler's Wells). The dam, a winner over 10f and 12f in France, was Group 3 placed and is a half-sister to 4 winners. The second dam, Lambada (by Lyphard), won once at 3 yrs in France and was listed-placed and is a half-sister to 4 winners including the champion 2-y-o Tobougg. (Mr N Botica). *"He's quite a small, neat and racey looking colt – not what you'd expect from the pedigree. If he'd been an inch bigger we couldn't have afforded him, but he just lacks that bit of size. He's a good walker, I liked him a lot as a yearling and there's nothing I don't like now".*

50. UNNAMED ★★★
ch.c. Beat Hollow – Sabah (Nashwan).
March 17. First foal. The dam, a fairly useful 1m winner, was listed-placed and is a half-sister to 9 winners including the listed Doncaster Mile, listed City Of York Handicap and subsequent Canadian Grade 2 winner Vanderlin. The second dam, Massorah (by Habitat), won the Group 3 5f Premio Omenoni and was second in the Group 3 Prix du Gros Chene and is a half-sister to 4 winners. (Sir R J Buckley). "He's nice and the dam was unlucky because although she was listed-placed she had an aversion to the stalls which really ruined her career – she could have been very nice otherwise. This colt is not dissimilar in type to the dam's half-brother Vanderlin in many ways. Being by Beat Hollow I'd like to think he'd stay ten furlongs minimum and he's a nice horse. He's done very well physically over the last month".

51. UNNAMED ★★★
b.c. Piccolo – Silken Dalliance (Rambo Dancer).
February 11. £600. Ascot November. Not sold. Half-brother to the quite useful 6f and 7f winner of 4 races Oceana Blue (by Reel Buddy), to the fair 7f (at 2 yrs) to 1m winner Oceana Gold (by Primo Valentino) and the modest 7f (2-y-o seller) and 12f winner Snake Skin (by Golden Snake). The dam was a fairly useful 6f and 1m winner of 4 races at 3 yrs. The second dam, A Sharp (by Sharpo), was unraced. (CHF Partnership). "We've had quite a few out of the mare and this is a nice type of colt that I've always liked. He'll definitely make a 2-y-o, starting at six furlongs and he'll definitely stay seven".

RALPH BECKETT
52. DESPATCH ★★
b.f. Nayef – Time Saved (Green Desert).
May 22. Seventh foal. 65,000Y. Tattersalls October Book 1. Not sold. Half-sister to the smart 7f (at 2 yrs) and Group 2 12f King Edward VII Stakes winner Plea Bargain (by Machiavellian), to the useful listed 6f winner Jira (by Medicean), the useful 2-y-o 7f winner and Group 3 1m Prix des Chenes second Dubai Time (by Dubai Destination) and the quite useful 6f (at 2 yrs) and 1m winner Emirates Sports (by King's Best). The dam, a fairly useful 10f winner, is a sister to the useful 1m winner Illusion and a half-sister to 5 winners including Zinaad and Time Allowed, both winners of the Group 2 12f Jockey Club Stakes and the dams of the Group winners Anton Chekhov, First Charter, Plea Bargain and Time Away. The second dam, Time Charter (by Saritamer), was an exceptional filly and winner of the Oaks, the King George VI and Queen Elizabeth Diamond Stakes, the Champion Stakes, Coronation Cup, Prix Foy and Sun Chariot Stakes. (Mrs I M Beckett). "A very late foal, so it's hard to know. She moves well but she's got a lot of growing to do and she's unlikely to appear before September, but it's a terrific pedigree".

53. IT'S A PRIVILEGE ★★★
gr.c. Verglas – No Rehearsal (Baillamont).
April 23. Fifteenth foal. 22,000Y. Tattersalls October Book 2. David Redvers. Half-brother to the very useful 7f (at 2 yrs) and listed 12f winner Jelani (by Darshaan), to the French 5f and 6f winner and listed-placed Lever To Heaven (by Bluebird), the fair dual 6f winner Kakapuka (by Shinko Forest), the modest 7f to 9f winner Extemporise (by Indian Ridge) and a winner in Singapore by Fairy King. The dam won two minor races in France and is a half-sister to 10 winners including the quite useful 7.5f to 12f winner Tenorio. The second dam, One Life (by L'Emigrant), was unraced and is closely related to the outstanding filly Miesque (herself dam of the Group 1 winners Kingmambo and East of the Moon). (Mr R J Roberts). "He's out of quite an old mare but he's showing a bit already. We've had a few by Verglas and they were tricky, but he seems quite straightforward, he's getting on with it, he's grown quite a lot and I would think he'll be out in July. He has quite long pasterns and he's by Verglas, so I'd say he'd need a bit of cut in the ground. He should get seven furlongs by the end of the year and he's OK".

54. LEXINGTON PEARL (USA) ★★★
ch.f. Elusive Quality – Lexington Girl (Storm Cat).
April 25. Fourth foal. $100,000Y. Keeneland September. David Redvers. Half-sister to the minor US 3-y-o winner Harbin (by Gone West). The dam, a 2-y-o winner in Japan, is a sister to the US dual Grade 2 winners Magicalmysterycat and Burmilla. The second dam, Nannerl (by

Valid Appeal), won two Grade 2 and two Grade 3 events in the USA and is a half-sister to 8 winners. (Pearl Bloodstock Ltd). *"She looks like she'll make a 2-y-o, she's strong, hardy, tough and looks like she'll take a lot of graft. I should imagine she'll be out around July time over six furlongs and she'll go seven later in the year. She has a good way about her"*.

55. MONOPOLI ★★★
ch.f. Cadeaux Genereux – Jump Ship (Night Shift).
March 11. The dam, a modest 12f winner, is a half-sister to 2 winners. The econd dam, Flagship (by Rainbow Quest), a quite useful 10f winner, is a half-sister to numerous winners including Yawl (Group 3 Rockfel Stakes). (Mark Dixon). *"A nice, good-looking individual, she's strong and although the sire doesn't get them to be early 2-y-o's, she'll have a campaign this year. She has a good way about her, she's medium-sized and I'd be hopeful that we can get her racing this year"*.

56. MOON PEARL (USA) ★★★★
b.c. Johannesburg – Moonavvara (Sadler's Wells).
February 5. Fifth foal. €92,000Y. **Arqana Deauville August. David Redvers.** Half-brother the minor French winner Shaheen Hawk (by Hawk Wing) and to a minor winner in the USA at 2 yrs by Shamardal. The dam is an unraced half-sister to 5 winners including the Group 1 Prix Marcel Boussac and Group 1 Moyglare Stud Stakes winner Rumplestiltskin. The second dam, Monevassia (by Mr Prospector), is a placed sister to the French 2,000 Guineas, St James's Palace Stakes and Prix du Moulin winner Kingmambo and to the Group 3 6f Prix de Ris-Oranges winner Miesque's Son and a half-sister to the French 1,000 Guineas, Prix de Diane and Prix Jacques le Marois winner East of the Moon. (Pearl Bloodstock Ltd). *"A well-grown, forward sort of horse. A lot of the Johannesburg's are quirky but he doesn't appear to be. I think he'll appear sometime in May or June, he shows a bit of toe and he's about to be stepped up in his work"*.

57. NICEOFYOUTOTELLME ★★★
b.c. Hernando – Swain's Gold (Swain).
April 25. Fourth foal. 19,000Y. **Tattersalls October Book 3. David Redvers.** Half-brother to the unplaced 2010 2-y-o Mrs Greeley (by Mr Greeley). The dam won 3 minor races at 3 yrs in the USA and is a half-sister to the US stakes winner Brazilian. The second dam, Golden Pond (by Don't Forget Me), won 7 races including the Grade 2 12f Orchid Handicap, the Grade 3 8.5f Suwannee River Handicap and the listed Prix de la Cochere and is a half-sister to 3 winners and to the placed dam of the Group 2 May Hill Stakes winner Pollenator. (Mr R J Roberts). *"I bought him partly on spec, because we've had a lot of success with the sire and it's fairly easy for me to sell 2-y-o's by him. He was a good-walking yearling and quite light-framed, but he's filled out now and he looks a bit further forward than his pedigree would suggest. So I could see him being out around July or August time, he has a great way about him like a lot by the sire, so I'm looking forward to stepping him up. A likeable colt, we should be able to have a campaign with him this year, starting at seven furlongs. I like him"*.

58. PASHAN GARH ★★★★
b.c. Anabaa – Mimisel (Selkirk).
April 1. First foal. 65,000Y. **Tattersalls October Book 1. Will Edmeades.** The dam, a quite useful 2-y-o 7f winner, was listed-placed and is a half-sister to one winner. The second dam, Milly-M (by Cadeaux Genereux), is an unraced half-sister to 3 winners including the useful 6f winner and listed 6f placed Millybaa. (Thurloe Thoroughbreds XXIX). *"A very good-walking yearling, an easy moving horse who really stood out as an athlete. He's pretty forward and I can see him appearing in May. I like the horse, he looks very straightforward, he has a good way about him and he enjoys his work. He was sold to me by Paul Thorman of Trickledown Stud who kept ear-bashing me about the horse and I'm glad he did"*.

59. PEARL FROST ★★★ ♠
gr.c. Verglas – Eternelle (Green Desert).
March 12. Fifth foal. 50,000Y. **Tattersalls October Book 2. David Redvers.** Half-brother to the fair 2010 2-y-o 1m winner Encore Un Annee, to the moderate 11f winner Eloise and the Spanish 7.5f winner Sassicaia (all by Hernando). The dam, a quite useful 9.4f winner, is a sister to the useful winner of 11

races at up to 7f Everset and a half-sister to 5 winners including the champion German horse and dual Group 1 middle-distance winner Caitano and to the US Grade 3 1m winner Lady Lodger. The second dam, Eversince (by Foolish Pleasure), won over 5.5f and 1m in France and is a half-sister to the Group 3 Premio Ellington winner and Italian Derby second Artic Envoy. (Pearl Bloodstock Ltd). *"This horse came to me because we trained his half-sister, Encore Un Annee, last year. He's a big, strong horse – much stronger than his sister, I like him and he'll be a six/seven furlong 2-y-o".*

60. PENINSULA ★★★
ch.f. Rock Of Gibraltar – Kayah (Kahyasi).
January 30. First foal. The dam, a useful 8.3f (at 2 yrs) and listed 11f winner, is a half-sister to one winner. The second dam, Kristina (by Kris), was a quite useful 2-y-o 8.2f winner. (J★Richmond Watson). *"The first foal out of Kayah who won an Oaks Trial for us. She'll need time but the mare, who was quite a tough filly to train, won her only start at two. One for the second half of the year but I'd be hopeful of getting her on the track and trying to win with her as a 2-y-o".*

61. RHAGORI ★★★
b.f. Exceed And Excel – Cresta Gold (Halling).
January 31. First foal. 28,000Y. Ascot Autumn Sales. Not sold (previously 55,000foal, Tattersalls December, R Frisby). The dam, a useful 11f and 12f winner, was listed-placed and is a half-sister to the Group 3 Lingfield Classic Trial and Group 3 Dee Stakes winner African Dream and the listed-placed Fenella's Link and Lone Wolfe. The second dam, Fleet Hill (by Warrshan), winner of the listed Superlative Stakes and third in the Group 3 Rockfel Stakes, is a half-sister to 6 winners including the useful listed 6f Sandy Lane Stakes winner Lee Artiste. (Landmark Racing Ltd). *"She's a lovely filly, I would think she'll be fairly forward and she has a nice way about her. She's still quite light-framed though and needs to furnish a bit more. She shows enough to tell me that she'll appear over six furlongs, but we'll just have to be a bit patient with her for a while".*

62. RIOT OF COLOUR ★★★★
b.f. Excellent Art – Riotous Applause

(Royal Applause).
January 21. First foal. The dam, a fairly useful dual 6f winner (including at 2 yrs), is a sister to one winner and a half-sister to the high-class 2-y-o Group 1 1m Racing Post Trophy winner Crowded House, the French listed 11f winner and Group 3 placed On Reflection and the useful 12f winner Heron Bay and to the placed dam of the US dual Grade 1 winner Ticker Tape. The second dam, Wiener Wald (Woodman), is an unplaced half-sister to 6 minor winners abroad. (The Eclipse Partnership). *"A family we know well because her dam's sister Forest Crown was stakes-placed for us. This is a very different individual to Forest Crown and a much stronger filly. A robust, quite tall filly, but well-grown and quite forward, she should be racing in May or June and she'd be high on the list".*

63. ROYAL RED ★★★
b.f. Holy Roman Emperor – Vermilliann (Mujadil).
January 20. Second foal. 30,000foal. Tattersalls December. Littleton Stud. The dam, fairly useful dual 5f winner, is a sister to the Group 2 6f Mill Reef Stakes winner and Group 1 placed Galeota and a half-sister to the 11f and listed 13f winner Loulwa (by Montjeu) and the fairly useful 2-y-o 5f Weatherbys Supersprint winner Lady Livius (by Titus Livius), the quite useful 7f winner Adoring (by One Cool Cat) and the fair 7f winner Savannah Poppy (by Statue Of Liberty). The second dam, Refined (by Stateblest), a fairly useful dual 5f winner, is a half-sister to 6 winners including the very smart Group 3 7f Criterion Stakes winner Pipe Major. (J C Smith). *"The dam was very quick – I think she won twice as a 2-y-o before the middle of May. This filly is very forward and well-grown, so as soon as she's ready we'll get on with her, starting at five furlongs. She's not a big filly, but she's big enough".*

64. SERIOUS SPENDER (IRE) ★★★★ ♠
b.c. Amadeus Wolf – Meanya (Revoque).
February 7. Fifth foal. Tattersalls Ireland. €45,000Y. David Redvers. The dam, a listed winner of 4 races at 2 and 3 yrs in Italy, is a half-sister to 2 winners and to the dam of the Group 2 July Stakes winner Classic Blade. The second dam, Brazilia (by Forzando), a modest

6f placed 2-y-o, is a half-sister to 4 winners including the Group 2 5f Kings Stand Stakes winner Dominica. (Mr R J Roberts). *"He'll be racing in April, it's a fast family and he goes well. I should think he'll win a maiden and we'll see how we go from there".*

65. SUPERCILIARY ★★★★
b.c. Dansili – Supereva (Sadler's Wells).
January 28. Third foal. Half-brother to Carousel (by Pivotal), unplaced in two starts at 2 yrs in 2010 and to the fair 1m winner Royal Superlative (by King's Best). The dam, an Italian winner of 5 races, is a half-sister to several winners. The second dam, Final Farewell (by Proud Truth), ran once unplaced and is a half-sister to 3 winners and to the dam of Danehill. (HRH The Prince Of Wales & The Duchess Of Cornwall). *"A very good-looking horse and much the nicest out of the mare. There's a lot more of him than either of his half-sisters because there's a lot of size about him, he has good bone and plenty of scope. An athletic sort of horse, he'll be a 2-y-o in the second half of the season and he's a really likeable individual, a standout in every way. He should turn into a nice horse".*

66. TAKEITFROMALADY (IRE) ★★
b.g. Intikhab – Pinheiros (Rock Of Gibraltar).
April 21. First foal. 12,000Y. Tattersalls October Book 2. David Redvers. The dam is an unplaced half-sister to 4 winners including the Group 3 Gallinule Stakes winner Mon Michel. The second dam, Miniver (by Mujtahid), ran once unplaced and is a half-sister to 6 winners including the Champion Stakes winner Legal Case and the dam of the Oaks winner Love Divine. (Mr R J Roberts). *"A hardy little beggar, he'll probably start over six furlongs and he knows plenty about the game already. He should be a good, fun horse for his owner and probably a nursery type 2-y-o".*

67. TANGO SKY (IRE) ★★★
b.c. Namid – Sky Galaxy (Sky Classic).
February 28. Fourth foal. Doncaster Premier. £22,000Y. David Redvers. The dam, a quite useful 2-y-o 6f winner, is a half-sister to 5 winners including the useful 2-y-o 5f winner and Group 3 5f Queen Mary Stakes third Moonshine Girl. The second dam, Fly To The Moon (by Blushing Groom), a fairly useful 3-y-o 1m winner here and subsequently a winner in the USA at 4 yrs, is a sister to the Group 1 Heinz "57" Phoenix Stakes winner Digamist and a half-sister to 5 winners. (A.W.A. Partnership). *"He ran very well on his debut when the ground was probably on the quick side for him, being by Namid. He's a nice horse and he should certainly be up to winning a maiden and we'll go on from there. I like the horse but he'll need some give in the ground or maybe polytrack and he's a five/six furlong 2-y-o".*

68. UNNAMED ★★★
ch.f. Shamardal – Clare Hills (Orpen).
January 30. Second foal. Half-sister to the quite useful 2010 2-y-o 6f winner My Delirium (by Haafhd). The dam won the 2-y-o listed 5f Hilary Needler Trophy and is a half-sister to 2 winners. The second dam, Morale (by Bluebird), is an unraced sister to the Scandinavian listed winner Bluebeard and a half-sister to 3 winners including the useful 1m and 10f winner Sheba Spring. (P K Gardner T/A Springcombe Park Stud). *"She's been quite backward and not that healthy, so I haven't done much with her, but as an individual she's nice. She has a lot more about her and is better looking than her half-sister My Delirium who won at the back-end last year at Newmarket".*

69. UNNAMED ★★★★
b.f. War Front – Ava's Crown (Don't Say Halo).
February 19. Second foal. $20,000Y. Fasig-Tipton November. The dam is an unraced half-sister to 5 winners including the Grade 3 stakes-placed Apremont. The second dam, Choose A Crown (by Ogygian), is an unraced half-sister to 5 winners. *"The sire seems to be carrying all before him in the States. This filly is already showing a bit, she wasn't expensive and she has a very good way about her. She's forward-going and she won't be long in coming to hand either. We like her and she should definitely be on the list".*

70. UNNAMED ★★★
ch.f. Dutch Art – Eloquent Rose (Elnadim).
April 5. First foal. £2,000Y. Ascot November. Not sold (previously 14,000Y Tattersalls December). The dam, a quite useful 2-y-o dual 5f winner, is a half-sister to 3 winners.

The second dam, Quintellina (by Robellino), was a quite useful 2-y-o 7f winner. (Favourites Racing). "A tall, scopey sort of filly but she's already showing more than her physique would suggest. I can see her appearing sometime in May or June. At first I thought she was a bit of a lump in that didn't appear to be getting anywhere, but we got stuck into her and she suddenly blossomed. We like her". TRAINERS' BARGAIN BUY

71. UNNAMED ★★★
gr.f. Footstepsinthesand – Felicita (Catrail).
May 7. Ninth foal. 62,000Y. Tattersalls October Book 1. David Redvers. Half-sister to the promising 2010 2-y-o 5f winner Retainer (by Acclamation), to the fairly useful 2-y-o 5f winner and Group 3 5f Queen Mary Stakes fourth Bunditten (by Soviet Star), the French 6f winner Facilita (by Fasliyev) and the modest 5f and hurdles winner Midnite Blews (by Trans Island). The dam won 3 races in France at 2 yrs including two 5f listed events and is a half-sister to 5 winners. The second dam, Abercwrle (by Absalom), ran unplaced twice at 2 yrs and is a half-sister to 4 winners. (N★T Wrigley). "A late foal from a speed pedigree, she'll have a break shortly just to get some spring grass into her. She's an athletic sort of filly so we should be able to get her on the track in the second half of the year, but she has a bit of growing to do first, just to level off".

72. UNNAMED ★★★
b.f. Montjeu – First Bloom (Fusaichi Pegasus).
February 12. First foal. 92,000Y. Tattersalls October Book 1. Not sold. The dam, a modest 7f placed 2-y-o, is a half-sister to 8 winners including the very smart colt Diffident, winner of the Group 3 6f Diadem Stakes, the Group 3 6f Prix de Ris-Orangis and the listed 7f European Free Handicap and to the dams of 4 stakes winners. The second dam, Shy Princess (by Irish River), a smart French 2-y-o 7f winner and second in the Group 1 Prix Morny, won over 6f as a 3-y-o and is a half-sister to 5 winners including the Breeders Cup Mile winner and Eclipse Stakes second Opening Verse and the US Grade 3 winner So She Sleeps. (Lady N F Cobham). "Her temperament is better than that of most Montjeu fillies. She's made a bit like her pedigree in that she's quite a long, tall, lean sort of filly. She's a good-mover but I think she'll want some give in the ground and plenty of time. She'll be running this year though, I like her and out of the handful of Montjeu fillies we've had she's the nicest. I'd be keen to keep her on the right side because she shows promise".

73. UNNAMED ★★★★
gr.c. Oratorio – Rosamixa (Linamix).
March 21. First foal. €120,000Y. Arqana Deauville August. David Redvers. The dam, a winner at 2 yrs in France and fourth in the Group 3 Prix du Calvados, is a sister to the Group 3 Prix de Fontainebleau winner Rajsaman and the French listed winner Rosara (herself dam of the Group 1 Prix Marcel Boussac winner Rosanara). The second dam, Rose Quartz (by Lammtarra), won once over 13f at 3 yrs in Ireland. (Pearl Bloodstock Ltd). "He was a bit of an ugly duckling when he came in but he's really blossomed over the last few months. He'll need some time, but he's really knuckled down lately and got on with the job, so I could see him making a 2-y-o by the second half of the year. I like the horse, he's turning into a man now and he's a good sort of individual".

MICHAEL BELL
74. ADVERSE (IRE) ★★
b.f. Refuse To Bend – Shadow Roll (Mark Of Esteem).
February 10. Fifth foal. Half-sister to the quite useful 2-y-o 6f winner Undertone (by Noverre). The dam, a fair 2-y-o 7f listed-placed maiden, is a half-sister to one winner and to the listed-placed Shadowless. The second dam, Warning Shadows (by Cadeaux Genereux), won the Group 2 10f Sun Chariot Stakes and was second in the Irish 1,000 Guineas. "She gets up Warren Hill quite nicely and I see her as a filly for the second half of the season. She's well-made but her front legs are immature at this stage".

75. APOSTLE (IRE) ★★★★ ♠
gr.c. Dark Angel – Rosy Dudley (Grand Lodge).
March 25. Fourth foal. Doncaster Premier. £60,000Y. John Warren. Half-brother to the quite useful 2-y-o 5f and 7f winner Grand Honour (by Verglas). The dam, a fair Irish 8.5f winner at 3 yrs, is a half-sister to 6 winners

including the Group 2 Criterium des Ans winner Deadly Dudley and the listed winner Miss Nosey Parker. The second dam, Renzola (by Dragonara Palace), is an unraced half-sister to the dam of the Group/Grade 1 winner Millkom. (Highclere Thoroughbreds). *"I would imagine this colt will have already started his career by the time you go to print. He was bought to be a sharp 2-y-o and that's what he is - an honest, genuine 2-y-o type. He'll do what his pedigree suggests which is stick to five and six furlong races. He's certainly one of the 2-y-o's we've got who is a possible for Royal Ascot and although it's early days yet the work riders are very positive about him".*

76. BACKCOURT (USA) ★★★

ch.f. Street Cry – Badminton (Zieten).
February 11. Half-sister to the quite useful 7f winner Burghley (by Shamardal). The dam, a very useful 2-y-o 6f winner and third in the Group 1 Cheveley Park Stakes, is a half-sister to numerous winners including the useful 2-y-o 7f winner and Group 3 7f Vintage Stakes third Fox, the useful 6f and 7f winner and Group 3 Nell Gwyn Stakes second Cala and the useful 7f winner Rafferty. The second dam, Badawi (by Diesis), was a useful 1m and 9f winner of 4 races. (Marwan Al Maktoum). *"She's a well-made, strong filly that should be racing in mid-summer. Deep-girthed and a good mover, she's likely to want seven furlongs".*

77. BRIDGEHAMPTON ★★

b.c. Lando – Gaze (Galileo).
February 25. First foal. 92,000Y. Tattersalls October Book 1. Kern/Lillingston. The dam, placed over 10f and 12f here, won twice in Germany and is a half-sister to 7 winners including the Irish Derby, Coronation Cup and Tattersalls Gold Cup winner Fame And Glory. The second dam, Gryada (by Shirley Heights), a fairly useful 2-y-o 7f and 8.3f winner, was third in the Group 3 1m Premio Dormello and is a full or half-sister to 4 winners. *"A nice colt, he's good-bodied and very attractive. He has a nice pedigree but he's being trained towards being the high-class middle-distance prospect that his pedigree suggests, so I don't know much about him apart from the fact that he's done well since we bought him, he has a good temperament and he moves well".*

78. BRYANT PARK (USA) ★★★

ch.c. Street Cry – Cala (Desert Prince).
February 25. Third foal. Half-brother to the fair 7f winner Top Draw (by Elusive Quality). The dam, a useful 6f and 7f winner and second in the Group 3 Nell Gwyn Stakes, is a half-sister to 6 winners including the very useful 2-y-o 6f winner and Group 1 Cheveley Park Stakes third Badminton, the useful 2-y-o 7f winner and Group 3 7f Vintage Stakes third Fox and the useful 7f winner Rafferty. The second dam, Badawi (by Diesis), was a useful 1m and 9f winner of 4 races. (Marwan Al Maktoum). *"He's a similar make to Backcourt in a way, in that he's in a similar mould, although she's a filly of course. He's a strong, good-boned, good moving horse and I view him as a 2-y-o type. He hasn't been asked to do more than one canter at this stage however".*

79. CORRECT ★★★★

b.f. Oasis Dream – Dusty Answer (Zafonic).
April 16. Sixth foal. Half-sister to the quite useful 2010 2-y-o 7f and 1m winner Flag Officer (by Dubai Destination), to the French 11f winner and Group 2 Italian Oaks second Counterclaim (by Pivotal) and the quite useful 7f and 1m winner Hamloola (by Red Ransom). The dam, a quite useful 2-y-o 7f winner, was listed placed over 1m and is a half-sister to 4 winners including the listed 1m and subsequent US Grade 2 winner Spotlight. The second dam, Dust Dancer (by Suave Dancer), won 4 races including the Group 3 10f Prix de la Nonette and is a half-sister to 6 winners including the Group 3 7.3f Fred Darling Stakes winner Bulaxie (herself dam of the Group 2 winner Claxon). *"She's in the 'early brigade', she looks like a pocket rocket type and I view her as being a 2-y-o we'll see out in early May. The sire is phenomenal and this is probably our most mature filly. We like her, she's relatively close-coupled, deep-girthed and has a generous backside".*

80. EIGHT LETTERS (USA) ★★

br.f. Mr Greeley – Thara (Hennessy).
February 19. Fourth foal. 42,000Y. Tattersalls October Book 1. C de Moubray. Half-sister to the minor US 4-y-o winner Tawaared (by Unbridled's Song). The dam is an unraced half-sister to the Group 3 Irish 1,000 Guineas Trial and Group 3 C L Weld Park Stakes winner and

triple Group 1 placed Arch Swing. The second dam, Gold Pattern (by Slew O'Gold), a minor US winner of 4 races, is a half-sister to 2 stakes winners in the USA. *"I haven't seen him yet because he's not come in, but apparently he's quite nice"*.

81. FORTIETH AND FIFTH (IRE) ★★★
b.c. Lemon Drop Kid – Maugusta
(Saint Ballado).
April 13. Second foal. 42,000Y. Tattersalls October Book 1. Not sold. The dam is an unraced half-sister to 4 winners including the Japanese stakes winner Forty Oner. The second dam, Heraklia (by Irish River), is an unraced half-sister to 6 winners. *"A horse that's kept on growing, but that's no bad thing because he's not bred to be particularly precocious. He moves well and I like him but he's definitely a second half of the season horse. He's not completely backward though and he's coming"*.

82. HOLY EMPRESS (IRE) ★★★
b.f. Holy Roman Emperor – Kahira
(King's Best).
April 18. Third foal. 25,000Y. Tattersalls October Book 1. Kern/Lillingston. Half-sister to the quite useful 2010 Irish 6f and 7f placed 2-y-o Vastitas (by Green Desert). The dam, a fair 2-y-o 7f placed maiden, is a half-sister to the Group 1 6f Haydock Park Sprint Cup winner Tamarisk. The second dam, Sine Labe (by Vaguely Noble), is an unplaced half-sister to the Group 1 Prix Saint-Alary winner Treble. *"She's not over-big, like a lot of the sire's progeny, and she's just a fun 2-y-o type. We don't have any aspirations for particularly lofty heights but she squirts along really well. A five/six furlong 2-y-o"*.

83. INTENT (IRE) ★★★
b.f. Jeremy – Cant Hurry Love (Desert Prince).
February 17. First foal. Goffs Orby. €65,000Y. John Warren. The dam is an unraced half-sister to 2 winners including the Irish listed winner and Group 2 placed Mister Tee. The second dam, Clipper (by Salse), a useful 1m winner (at 2 yrs) was listed placed over 10f, is a half-sister to 3 winners. (Royal Ascot Racing Club). *"She's done very well physically since she was purchased and she covers the ground nicely. A filly with a bit of a temperament, but that's no bad thing and she'll be a July 2-y-o type. She's not too backward and it'll be interesting to see how she goes when we crank her up a bit"*.

84. KASHGAR ★★★ ♠
b.c. Hernando – Miss Katmandu
(Rainbow Quest).
April 5. The dam, unplaced in one start, is a half-sister to the very smart 7f (at 2 yrs), Group 3 12f September Stakes and Group 3 13.4f Ormonde Stakes winner Asian Heights (by Hernando) and to the smart 10f winner St Expedit. The second dam, Miss Rinjani (by Shirley Heights), a fair 2-y-o 7f winner, was placed over 12f at 3 yrs and is a half-sister to several winners. (Mr J L C Pearce). *"He's done particularly well over the winter and I think he's one of the nicest colts the owner has had with us. He's just thrived and continues to do so. We won't be rushing him because of his pedigree, but he'll be an interesting prospect from the late summer onwards and for next year"*.

85. LE CAGNARD ★★★
b.c. Danehill Dancer – Miss Provence
(Hernando).
February 5. First foal. The dam, a quite useful 9f winner, is a sister to 2 winners including the 7f (at 2 yrs) and listed 10f winner Miss Corniche and a half-sister to 5 winners. The second dam, Miss Beaulieu (by Northfields), was a useful 6f and 10f winner. (Mr J L C Pierce). *"A deep-girthed colt and more mature-looking than a lot of the owner's stock. He could be alright, but I haven't really done a lot with most of my two-year-olds because they aren't bred to be performing over five and six furlongs. I like what I see"*.

86. LOOKS LIKE RAIN ★★★
ch.f. Medicean – Hippogator (Dixieland Band).
May 1. Third foal. 38,000Y. Tattersalls October Book 1. Not sold. The dam, a listed winner of 5 races in the USA, is a half-sister to one winner. The second dam, Gastronomical (by Sunshine Forever), a US Grade 3 winner and Grade 1 placed, is a half-sister to 8 winners including the Italian listed winner and Group 3 Jockey Club Cup third Spanish John. *"We have her full sister and this one is far more precocious. I think she'll be a mid-summer 2-y-o and although she hasn't been out of a swinging canter yet she does it easily"*.

87. MEXICAN WAVE ★★★
b.c. Rock Of Gibraltar – La Belga (Roy).
January 23. Fifth foal. Doncaster Premier. £32,000Y. BBA (Ire)/private sale Kern/Lillingston. Half-brother to 2 minor winners abroad by Giant's Causeway and Singspiel. The dam, a Grade 1 winner in Argentina and Grade 1 placed 3 times, is a half-sister to 2 winners. The second dam, La Baraca (by Mariache), a Grade 1 winner in Argentina, is a half-sister to 6 winners including the Argentine Grade 1 winner Leyden. *"He's done well since we bought him and I think he'll be seen to good effect relatively early in the summer. He was well-bought I think, he has a good temperament and has been easy to train".*

88. OPERATION TRACER ★★★
ch.c. Rock Of Gibraltar – Quite Elusive (Elusive Quality).
February 15. Third foal. 11,000Y. Tattersalls October Book 2. John Warren. The dam is an unraced half-sister to 7 winners including the French listed winner Quittance. The second dam, Quarrel Over Halo (by Halo), a minor US winner of 2 races, is a half-sister to 9 winners including the US Grade 2 winner Suivi. (Highclere Thoroughbreds). *"He'll be a second half of the season horse and we'll be looking for a seven furlong maiden auction for horses that weren't too expensive. He'd be bang in the mix".* TRAINERS' BARGAIN BUY

89. ROSE MADDER ★★★
b.f. Singspiel – Crimson Year (Dubai Millennium).
February 2. First foal. The dam ran twice unplaced at 4 yrs and is a half-sister to 9 winners including the high-class Irish 1,000 Guineas, Coronation Stakes and Nassau Stakes winner Crimplene, the smart Group 3 12.3f Chester Vase winner Dutch Gold and the useful 10f winner Group 2 12f Lancashire Oaks second Loyal Spirit. The second dam, Crimson Conquest (by Diesis), a quite useful 2-y-o 6f winner, is a half-sister to the US stakes winner at around 1m Sword Blade. *"I haven't done a lot with her but she's doing well physically and she moves well. I would hope she'd be a 2-y-o in the second half of the season".*

90. SIGN MANUAL ★★★
b.c. Motivator – New Assembly (Machiavellian).
March 17. Seventh foal. Half-brother to the 2010 7f placed 2-y-o General Synod (by Invincible Spirit), to the useful dual 6f winner (including at 2 yrs) Instalment (by Cape Cross), the quite useful 10f winner Regent's Park (by Green Desert), the quite useful 7f winner Victoria Reel (by Danehill Dancer) and the fair 1m winner Small Fortune (by Anabaa). The dam, a useful 9f and 10f winner, is a sister to the 7f (at 2 yrs) and Group 1 9f Dubai Duty Free Stakes winner Right Approach and a half-sister to 6 winners. The second dam, Abbey Strand (by Shadeed), a fair Irish 10f winner, is a half-sister to numerous winners including the 2-y-o Group 3 winners Grand Chelem and Splendid Moment. (The Queen). *"A quality, staying type, he's cantering and he moves well. He's only just arrived but I know they liked him at the stud. He seems to have a good attitude, he moves well and looks a nice horse".*

91. SOVEREIGN DEBT ★★★★ ♠
br.c. Dark Angel – Kelsey Rose (Most Welcome).
April 22. Sixth foal. 105,000Y. Tattersalls October Book 1. Blandford Bloodstock. Half-brother to the quite useful 2010 2-y-o dual 7f winner Marked Card (by Kheleyf), to the 6f (at 2 yrs) and Group 3 Fred Darling Stakes winner Puff (by Camacho) and the fair 2-y-o 6f winner Golden Rosie (by Exceed And Excel). The dam, a fairly useful 2-y-o 5f winner of 3 races, was listed-placed three times and is a half-sister to 3 winners. The second dam, Duxyana (by Cyrano de Bergerac), is an unraced half-sister to 8 winners including the dam of the Group 2 Mill Reef Stakes winner Indian Rocket. *"He's a nice horse that moves well, he's been in work and probably wants six furlongs but I like him".*

92. TAHLIA REE (IRE) ★★★★ ♠
b.f. Acclamation – Dora Carrington (Sri Pekan).
April 2. Sixth foal. 52,000Y. Tattersalls December. Kern/Lillingston. Closely related to the quite useful 6f (at 2 yrs) and 7f winner Lytton (by Royal Applause) and half-sister to the fairly useful 1m and 10f winner Julienas (by Cape Cross). The dam won the Group 2 6f Cherry Hinton Stakes, was third in the Group 1 6f Phoenix Stakes and is a half-sister to the

Group 1 Middle Park Stakes winner Primo Valentino. The second dam, Dorothea Brooke (by Dancing Brave), won over 9f and is a half-sister to 6 winners. "She goes well, she's a nice, precocious filly and has done a couple of bits of work so she'll be racing in April. She's exactly as she should be, a nice filly with a good temperament and I like her. The sire gets good 2-y-o types, the dam won a Group 2 at that age, she has a good head on her and looks to have some sort of engine, so she'll be one to follow".

93. UNNAMED ★★
gr.f. Dalakhani – Bianca Nera (Salse).
April 16. Tenth foal. 135,000Y. Tattersalls October Book 1. Not sold. Half-sister to the fair 2010 2-y-o 6f winner Biaraafa (by Araafa), to the Irish 2-y-o 7f winner and listed placed Pietra Dura (by Cadeaux Genereux and herself dam of the US Grade 3 winner Turning Top), the fair 12f winner Ever Rigg (by Dubai Destination) and the fair 5f to 7f winner of 5 races Glencairn Star (by Selkirk). The dam, a smart 2-y-o winner of the Group 1 7f Moyglare Stud Stakes and the Group 2 6f Lowther Stakes, is half-sister to 4 winners including the very useful Group 1 Moyglare Stud Stakes second Hotelgenie Dot Com (herself dam of the dual Group 1 winner Simply Perfect). The second dam, Birch Creek (by Carwhite), was placed five times including when third in the Group 3 1m Premio Royal Mares and is a half-sister to 7 winners. "She's not arrived here yet but she's done very well over the winter. Being by Dalakhani you wouldn't expect her to be doing much until late summer at the earliest, but she's a lovely, scopey filly".

94. UNNAMED ★★
b.f. Cape Cross – Charita (Lycius).
April 10. Eighth foal. 50,000Y. Tattersalls October Book 1. Brian Grassick Bloodstock. Half-sister to the smart Irish Group 3 7f and 1m winner Cheyenne Star (by Mujahid), to the fair 2-y-o 5f winner Silent Secret (by Dubai Destination), the fair 10f winner Vivachi (by Red Ransom) and the modest 11f to 2m and hurdles winner Herne Bay (by Hernando). The dam, a listed 1m winner in Ireland, is a half-sister to 4 winners including the Italian Group 2 winner Stanott. The second dam, Seme de Lys (by Slew O'Gold). is a placed half-sister to 4 winners. "She's only just arrived but she seems to go well. I loved her as a yearling and we're literally just getting to know her again now. She conducts herself well and gets up the gallop nicely, but it's too early to assess her ability".

95. UNNAMED ★★
b.c. Lawman – Crystal (Danehill).
March 9. Third foal. 50,000Y. Tattersalls October Book 2. Kern/Lillingston. Half-brother to the fair 11f winner of 5 races Stanley Rigby (by Dr Fong). The dam, a fairly useful 10f winner, is a half-sister to 3 winners including very useful 2-y-o 6f winner and Group 1 Racing Post Trophy third Feared In Flight. The second dam, Solar Crystal (Alzao), won the Group 3 1m May Hill Stakes, was third in the Group 1 1m Prix Marcel Boussac and s a half-sister to 6 winners including the Group 1 Fillies' mile winner Crystal Music, the Group 3 12f Lancashire Oaks winner State Crystal and the Irish Derby third Tchaikovsky. "He fell away after the Sales but he's now beginning to blossom and hopefully he'll turn into a nice horse. We'll know more about him in two months time, but he won't make a 2-y-o until after Royal Ascot".

96. UNNAMED ★★★
b.c. Exceed And Excel – Dubai Surprise (King's Best).
April 5. Third foal. 50,000Y. Tattersalls October Book 1. David Simcock. Half-brother to the fairly useful 2010 2-y-o 7f and 1m winner Star Surprise (by Dubawi) and to the quite useful 2-y-o 6f winner Sand Skier (by Shamardal). The dam, a winner of 4 races here and in Italy including the Group 1 Premio Lydia Tesio and the Group 3 Prestige Stakes, was second in the Group 1 Criterium de Saint-Cloud and is a half-sister to 3 winners. The second dam, Toujours Irish (by Irish River), is an unraced half-sister to 7 winners including the French multiple Group winner Athyka. "A lovely, big, easy-moving colt that'll take a bit of time but he's a particularly good mover. He has a great big stride on him and I see him as a miler".

97. UNNAMED ★★★
b.c. Teofilo – Extreme Beauty (Rahy).
February 19. Third foal. 110,000Y. Tattersalls

October Book 1. Blandford Bloodstock. Half-brother to Little Black Book (by Shamardal), unplaced in one start at 2 yrs in 2010 and to the quite useful 2-y-o 6f winner Extreme Warrior (by Dubawi). The dam, a quite useful 6f (at 2 yrs) and 7f winner, was third in the Group 2 6f Cherry Hinton Stakes is a half-sister to 5 winners including the US Grade 1 Pacific Classic winner Go Between. The second dam, Mediation (by Caerleon), won the listed Irish 1,000 Guineas Trial and was Group 3 placed here and in the USA. *"A well-made horse and a good mover, he has a good temperament and has done everything right, but he's not a whiz-bang and we'll wait until the second half of the season and then we'll see how we go"*.

98. UNNAMED ★★★★
b.c. Intikhab – Jazan (Danehill).
April 1. Fifth foal. Doncaster Premier. £28,000Y. Kern/Lillingston. Half-brother to the modest 2011 3-y-o dual 9f winner Lexi's Boy (by Verglas) and to a minor winner abroad by Best Of The Bests. The dam, a fair 8.5f winner (awarded race), is a half-sister to 5 winners. The second dam, Babita (by Habitat), a very useful 2-y-o 5f winner, was third in the Group 3 6f Cherry Hinton Stakes and is a half-sister to 4 winners. *"A particularly nice horse, he's a very good mover although his temperament has a little bit of a kink. I like him a lot and he's a classy, striking horse to look at. I'm a big fan of the sire – I think he's massively underrated"*.

99. UNNAMED ★★
ch.c. Nayef – Megdale (Waajib).
March 24. Tenth living foal. 95,000Y. Tattersalls October Book 1. Blandford Bloodstock. Half-brother to the smart 7f (at 2 yrs) and triple listed middle-distance winner Frank Sonata (by Opening Verse), to the useful 2-y-o listed 7f Sweet Solera Stakes winner Peaceful Paradise (by Turtle Island), the fairly useful dual 7f winner Coup d'Etat (by Diktat), the quite useful 2-y-o 7f and 1m winner Kinetic Quest (by Haafhd), the fair 2-y-o 6f winner Castellano (by Mujahid), the French 3-y-o winner Lunch Time (by Zamindar) and the German 10f and 11f winner Meg (by Be My Chief). The dam, a fair middle-distance placed maiden, is a sister to the useful 7f to 9f winner Wijara and a half-sister to 10 winners including Alhijaz, a winner of four Group 1 events in Italy. The second dam, Nawara (by Welsh Pageant), was a fair 10.2f winner. *"He's had little setbacks but he's a good mover and has done very well physically. One that's been bought with a middle-distance campaign in mind, so quite what he'll do this year I'm not sure but he's a nice, big, easy-moving type"*.

100. UNNAMED ★★★★
b.f. Galileo – Red Evie (Intikhab).
January 24. First foal. The dam won 9 races including the Group 1 1m Matron Stakes and the Group 1 1m Lockinge Stakes. The second dam, Malafemmena (by Nordico), winner of a listed event in Italy and third in the Group 3 Prix du Calvados, is a half-sister to 7 winners including the smart Group 3 5f Prix du Bois and Group 3 6f Prix de Ris-Orangis winner Export Price. *"The pick of them on pedigree, she moves very well, looks classy and basically we're lucky to have her. The dam didn't actually do anything herself as a 2-y-o but she hurt herself and only ran once at the back-end. I'm under no pressure to press any buttons yet so we'll just see how we go, but she looks like a nice filly, she appears to go well, gets up Warren Hill nicely and all her riders like her"*.

JOHN BEST
101. BAYLEYF (IRE) ★★★
b.c. Kheleyf – Hi Katriona (Second Empire).
January 20. Third foal. £10,000Y. Doncaster Premier. John Best. Half-brother to the fair 2010 2-y-o triple 6f winner Shostakovic (by Fasliyev). The dam, a modest 6f placed Irish 2-y-o, is a half-sister to 11 winners including the Group 2 Premio Melton winner Fred Bongusto. The second dam, Hi Bettina (by Henbit), a fairly useful Irish sprint winner, was second in the Group 3 Debutante Stakes in Ireland and is a half-sister to 5 winners including the Group 3 Norfolk Stakes winner Marouble and the Irish Oaks and Irish 1,000 Guineas second Kitza. (Steve Gabriel & Graham Jones). *"He's probably going to be our first runner and he's a typical Kheleyf in that he's a little bit 'buzzy' and we need to keep his temperament under control, but he shows plenty of speed"*. TRAINERS' BARGAIN BUY

102. GUNG HO JACK ★★★
b.c. Moss Vale – Bijan (Mukaddamah).
February 26. Fourth foal. Doncaster Premier. £28,000Y. John Best. Half-brother to the modest 6f (at 2 yrs) and 5f winner Ramblin Bob (by Piccolo). The dam, a modest 5f (at 2 yrs) and 6f winner, is a half-sister to 6 winners including the Group 3 Ballyogan Stakes winner Yomalo. The second dam, Alkariyh (by Alydar), a fairly useful 2-y-o 6f winner, is a half-sister to 5 winners. (Mr J Fletcher). *"I bought a few Moss Vale yearlings because I thought they were strong and stocky and were going to make 2-y-o's. This colt had a slight setback about a month ago but he's back on track now. He's reasonably early, quite sharp and mentally very good, so I think he'll be out by the end of May, probably over six furlongs".*

103. UNNAMED ★★★
ch.c. Compton Place – Beacon Silver (Belmez).
February 7. £11,000Y. Doncaster Premier. John Best. Half-brother to the quite useful 7f, 1m (both at 2 yrs) and 9f winner Gramm (by Fraam). The dam was placed on the flat and won over hurdles and is a half-sister to 6 winners. The second dam, Nettle (by Kris), a 2-y-o listed winner, is a half-sister to 5 winners. (Kingsgate Racing Syndicate). *"He's big, strong, very mature and doing everything right. I think he'll be a nice horse and I'd like to think he'll run well enough to warrant a place at Royal Ascot. He should be out early enough for us to gauge if he's good enough".*

104. UNNAMED ★★★
b.c. Moss Vale – Celtic Guest (Be My Guest).
April 1. Eighth foal. £5,000Y. Doncaster Premier. John Best. Half-brother to the fair 7f and 1m winner Whispering Spirit (by Catcher In The Rye) and 2 minor winners in Italy and Sweden by Orpen. The dam is a unraced half-sister to 4 winners. The second dam, Gossip (by Sharp Edge), is an unplaced half-sister to 5 winners. (Lingfield Park Owners Club). *"Just like my other Moss Vale's he looks like an obvious 2-y-o, he's doing everything well and I would think he'd be one of the early ones. He's strong, stocky and looks a sprinter type. He's quite broad as well".*

105. UNNAMED ★★★
br.c. Kodiac – Dazzling View (Distant View).
March 11. First foal. Doncaster St Leger Festival. £19,000Y. John Best. The dam is an unraced half-sister to one winner. The second dam, Silver Yen (by Silver Hawk), won twice at 4 yrs in the USA and is a half-sister to the Group 3 Rose Of Lancaster Stakes winner Notable Guest. (H J Jarvis). *"He's very strong and stocky – an absolute 2-y-o type. He looks quite quick and we've just started working him. He's pretty sharp, physically quite mature and I'd be disappointed if he didn't turn out to be quite useful. He'll start at five furlongs to see how we go, probably sometime in May and hopefully he'll be a Royal Ascot horse but it's too soon to judge".*

106. UNNAMED ★★★
b.c. Amadeus Wolf – Kobalt Sea (Akarad).
April 4. Sixth foal. Doncaster Premier. £27,000Y. John Best. Half-brother to the quite useful 1m to 10f winner Punta Galera (by Zafonic), to the French 11f winner Emirati (by Dubai Destination) and the fair Irish 2-y-o 1m winner Kimberley Bay (by Trade Fair). The dam won 3 races in France including over 10.5f, was listed-placed and is a half-sister to 3 winners. The second dam, Karaferya (by Green Dancer), won a 10f listed event in Ireland and is a half-sister to 2 winners and to the placed dam of the dual Group 1 winner Kalanisi. (Kingsgate Racing Syndicate). *"A decent sized colt, he's a little bit backward physically but he's a great character with impeccable manners and I'd be disappointed if he didn't turn out to be really useful. He won't be running before June and physically he'll turn into a really nice horse in time".*

107. UNNAMED ★★★
b.c. Redback – Lady Lucia (Royal Applause).
February 14. Third foal. 17,000Y. Tattersalls October Book 2. J Best. Half-brother to the useful listed 5f winner and listed-placed Mullionmileanhour (by Mull Of Kintyre) and to the modest 2-y-o 5f winner Lady Lube Rye (by Catcher In The Rye). The dam, a moderate maiden, was placed fourth twice over 5f and 7f at 2 yrs and is a half-sister to 3 winners. The second dam, Inventive (by Sheikh Albadou), a quite useful 2-y-o dual 5f winner, is a half-sister

108. UNNAMED ★★★
br.c. Red Clubs – Marasem
(Cadeaux Genereux).
February 10. Fifth foal. Doncaster Premier. £20,000Y. John Best. Half-brother to the 2010 7f placed 2-y-o Spring Bouquet (by King's Best), to the quite useful 7f winner Faleh (by Silver Hawk) and the fair 2-y-o 9f winner Maraca (by Danehill Dancer). The dam, a quite useful 3-y-o 7f winner, is a half-sister to 5 winners including the very useful Group 2 7f Rockfel Stakes winner Sayedah (by Darshaan). The second dam, Balaabel (by Sadler's Wells), a quite useful 1m winner, is a half-sister to 5 winners including the US Grade 2 7f winner Kayrawan and the dam of the Group winners Haatef and Walayef. (H J Jarvis). *"I love him and I thought that Red Clubs was one of the standout first season sires. I was very glad to get this colt, he's strong, stocky and he looks like an out-and-out 2-y-o. He's quite big, so he won't be out that early. Some of the 2-y-o's tend to really grab you and he's one of them. I really like him".*

109. UNNAMED ★★★
b.c. Moss Vale – Vade Retro (Desert Sun).
January 24. Third foal. £13,000Y. Doncaster Premier. John Best. Half-brother to the fairly useful 2010 2-y-o 7f and 1m winner Our Joe Mac (by Celtic Swing) and to the fair 6f winner Zegna (by Clodovil). The dam, a quite useful Irish 2-y-o 7f winner, is a half-sister to 7 winners. The second dam, Mevlana (by Red Sunset), a French 11f and 12f winner, is a sister to the Group 3 10f Royal Whip Stakes winner Dancing Sunset and a half-sister to 4 winners. *"He was very difficult to break and afterwards he needed some time off at stud for some time to make sure he was perfectly OK. When he came back he wasn't quite as forward as some of the others but he's settled down and is working nicely now. He's strengthening up and should be out before June, he moves really well and he has a great attitude".*

110. UNNAMED ★★★
b.c. Amadeus Wolf – Vital Laser
(Seeking The Gold).
April 16. Seventh foal. Doncaster Premier. £22,000Y. John Best. Half-brother to the quite useful Irish 2-y-o 6f winner Belclare (by Verglas) and to 2 winners in the USA and Japan by Stravinsky and Louis Quatorze. The dam is an unraced half-sister to 7 winners including the listed winner Dr Massini. The second dam, Argon Laser (by Kris), a winner at 3 yrs and placed in the Group 2 Premio Chiusura and the Group 3 Child Stakes, is a half-sister to 11 winners including the Group winners Lighted Glory and King Luthier. (Mr S Malcolm, Mr M Winwright & Mr P Tindall). *"He's a bit smaller than my other Amadeus Wolf and more of a 2-y-o type. He moves well and mentally he 's very forward, so all being well he'll be one of our earlier ones, probably over five furlongs".*

111. UNNAMED ★★★
b.c. Iffraaj – Wychwood Wanderer (Barathea).
March 9. First foal. Doncaster Premier. £43,000Y. John Best. The dam, a quite useful triple 6f winner, is a half-sister to the useful 2-y-o triple 6f winner and Group 3 Sirenia Stakes second Diosypros Blue. The second dam, Calamander (by Alzao), a minor Irish 1m winner, is a half-sister to 4 winners including the listed winning 2-y-o Duty Paid and the useful 1m winner and Group 1 Coronation Stakes fourth Lady Miletrian. (Splinter Group). *"One of the nicest we've got, the sire was all the rage at the sales and we just had to be patient and wait to get the right one. I think we got lucky with him because he's doing everything fine, but won't be out early".*

JIM BOLGER
112. AMHRASACH (IRE)
b.f. Teofilo – Irish Question (Giant's Causeway).
March 7. Third foal. Half-sister to the quite useful Irish 2-y-o 5f winner Eireannach (by Rock Of Gibraltar). The dam, a fair Irish 1m winner, is a half-sister to 2 winners. The second dam, Key To Coolcullen (Royal Academy), is an unraced half-sister to numerous winners including the Group 1 6f Phoenix Stakes winner Eva Luna and the Group 3 1m Futurity Stakes winner Cois Na Tine. (Mrs J S Bolger).

113. ANISHA (IRE)
b.f. *Clodovil – Kimola (King's Theatre).*
**April 4. Fourth foal. Goffs Orby. €42,000Y.
Jim Bolger.** Half-sister to the useful Irish 2010 2-y-o 6f winner Whipless (by Whipper) and to the fairly useful Irish 2-y-o dual 6f winner Tomas An Tsioada (by Bachelor Duke). The dam won 9 races in Scandinavia including 2 listed events and is a half-sister to 4 winners. The second dam, La Mortola (by Bold Lad), is an unraced half-sister to 5 winners including the Irish 1,000 Guineas winner Katies. (Mrs J S Bolger).

114. HEAVY WEIGHT (IRE)
b.c. *Teofilo – Sister Angelina (Saint Ballado).*
March 21. Third foal. Half-brother to the very smart 2010 2-y-o Group 1 Phoenix Stakes second and Group 2 Futurity Stakes second Glor Na Mara (by Leroidesanimaux). The dam is an unraced half-sister to one winner. The second dam, Angelina Capote (by Capote), a listed winner of 4 races in the USA, is a half-sister to 7 winners including Do It With Style (Grade 1 Ashland Stakes). (Mrs J S Bolger).

115. JANEY MUDDLES (IRE)
b.f. *Lawman – Slip Dance (Celtic Swing).*
April 25. Second foal. €200,000Y. Arqana Deauville August. BBA (Ire). The dam, a dual sprint listed winner, was second in the Group 3 7f Sweet Solera Stakes and is a half-sister to 5 winners including the listed 6f (at 2 yrs) and listed 7f winner and Group 3 placed Misu Bond. The second dam, Hawala (by Warning), a useful 8.3f winner, is a half-sister to the French Group 3 winner Afaf. (Mrs June Judd)

116. JUST FACTS (IRE)
b.f. *Invincible Spirit – Russian Revolution (Dubai Millennium).*
January 10. Third foal. The dam, a quite useful 2-y-o 1m winner, is a half-sister to 2 winners including the useful 10f winner Russian Society. The second dam, Russian Snows (by Sadler's Wells), a smart winner of the Group 2 12.5f Prix de Royallieu and second in the Irish Oaks, is a sister to the high-class dual Group 2 winner Modhish and a half-sister to the Group 3 10.5f Prix de Royaumont winner Truly Special. (Sheikh Mohammed).

117. MISTEIREACH
b.f. *Cherokee Run – Wild Heaven (Darshaan).*
March 22. The dam, an Irish 2-y-o listed 9f winner, is closely related to the fairly useful 13.4f to 2m winner High Intrigue and a half-sister to the 1m (at 2 yrs) and Group 1 12f Irish Oaks winner Margarula. The second dam, Mild Intrigue (by Sir Ivor), a fairly useful 10f winner, is a half-sister to the useful listed 10f winner Grimesgill, the US stakes winner Determined Bidder and the dam of the South African Grade 1 winner Milleverof. The second dam, Mild Deception (by Buckpasser), won 3 races in the USA at up to 1m, is a half-sister to Arkadina (placed in 3 Irish classics and a high-class broodmare), to the Queen's Vase and Jockey Club Cup winner Blood Royal, the Group 1 Joe McGrath Memorial Stakes winner Gregorian and the Grade 3 Test Stakes winner Ivory Wand (dam of the Group 1 winner Gold And Ivory). (Mrs J S Bolger).

118. RIGOLETTA (IRE)
b.c. *Teofilo – Zavaleta (Kahyasi).*
April 14. Closely related to the fair 12f winner Alessandro (by Galileo) and half-brother to the Group 3 12f Noblesse Stakes winner Danelissima, to the Irish 2-y-o 7f winner and listed placed Daneleta (both by Danehill), the fairly useful Irish 2-y-o 1m winner and listed placed Simonetta (by Lil's Boy), the Irish 3-y-o 6.5f winner and listed-placed Benicio (by Spectrum) and a winner in Japan by Caerleon. The dam a useful dual listed 7f winner, is a half-sister to numerous winners including the 2-y-o Group 1 1m Gran Criterium winner Sholokov and the 2-y-o listed 7f winner Affianced (herself dam of the Irish Derby winner Soldier Of Fortune). The second dam, La Meilleure (by Lord Gayle), a listed winner in Ireland, was Group 3 placed. (Mrs J S Bolger).

119. SOMETHING GRACEFUL
ch.f. *Galileo – Que Puntual (Contested Bid).*
January 26. Second foal. 150,000Y. Tattersalls October Book 1. BBA (Ire). The dam won 5 races from 2 to 5 yrs in Argentina, Canada and the USA including the Canadian Grade 2 Nassau Stakes and is a half-sister to 5 winners including the Argentine Grade 1 placed Delivery Man. The second dam, Repartija (by Tempranero), a Grade 1 and Grade 2 winner in

South America, is a half-sister to the Argentine Grade 1 winner Comisariato. (Mrs June Judd)

120. TEOFOLINA (IRE)
b.f. Teofilo – Moon Unit (Intikhab).
March 4. Third foal. Closely related to Storminateacup (by Galileo), unplaced in two starts at 2 yrs in 2010. The dam, a smart Group 3 6f Greenlands Stakes winner of 6 races, is a half-sister to 4 winners. The second dam, Chapka (by Green Desert), is a placed half-sister to 7 winners including the top-class middle-distance colt Old Vic. (Mrs J Bolger)

121. THOMAS DYLAN (IRE)
b.c. Dylan Thomas – Virginia Rose (Galileo).
February 25. Second foal. €140,000foal. Goffs. J S Bolger. Half-brother to the 2010 French 2-y-o 1m winner and listed placed Rosehill Dew (by Danehill Dancer). The dam, a modest 12f and 14f winner, is a half-sister to 5 winners including the Group 2 10f Prix Guillaume d'Ornano winner Highdown and the Group 2 12f King Edward VII Stakes second Elshadi. The second dam, Rispoto (by Mtoto), a modest 12f winner, is a half-sister to 7 winners including the Group 3 10f Royal Whip Stakes winner Jahafil and the French listed 12f winner Mondschein. (Mrs June Judd)

122. WHILE YOU WAIT (IRE)
b.c. Whipper – Azra (Danehill).
April 4. Brother to the Irish 2-y-o 6f and 1m winner and Group 2 7f Rockfel Stakes second Atasari and half-brother to the Irish 2-y-o 7.5f winner Basra, to the fair 2-y-o 5f winner Russian General (both by Soviet Star), the fair Irish 7f and 10f winner Asafa (by King's Best) and the Irish 3-y-o dual 1m winner Spectacular (by Spectrum). The dam, a useful Irish dual 6f listed winner (at 2 yrs), was third in both the Group 1 Moyglare Stud Stakes and the Group 1 National Stakes and is a half-sister to 3 minor winners. The second dam, Easy To Please (by What A Guest), a useful Irish 2-y-o 1m winner, trained on to win the Queen Alexandra Stakes and is a half-sister to 4 winners including the Group 3 Concorde Stakes winner Pernilla. (Mrs June Judd).

123. WHIP RULE (IRE)
b.c. Whipper – Danemarque (Danehill).
March 23. Brother to the 2010 Irish 2-y-o 1m winner, on his only start, Roches Cross and to the fair Irish 3-y-o 6f winner Whip Hand. The dam ran unplaced in Australia and is a half-sister to 7 winners including the listed winners Lady Shipley and Ellie Ardensky and to the unraced dam of the Group 3 Solario Stakes and US Grade 3 winner Brave Act. The second dam, Circus Ring (by High Top), a joint-champion 2-y-o filly and winner of 3 races at 2 yrs including the Group 2 Lowther Stakes, was a half-sister to 7 winners. (Mrs June Judd). After suffering interference this colt was awarded the first race of the season, at the Curragh in March.

124. ZIP TOP (IRE)
b.c. Smart Strike – Zofzig (Danzig).
March 4. The dam, a minor US 2-y-o winner, is a half-sister to the US Grade 1 Acorn Stakes winner Zaftig. The second dam, Zoftig (by Cozzene), won the Grade 1 Selene Stakes. (Sheikh Mohammed).

MARCO BOTTI
125. APPEALING (IRE) ★★★
b.f. Bertolini – Radiant Energy (Spectrum).
April 17. Fifth foal. €7,500Y. Tattersalls Ireland. Brian Grassick Bloodstock. Half-sister to the 2010 2-y-o Group 3 5f Cornwallis Stakes and listed 5f winner Electric Waves (by Exceed And Excel) and to the fair 2-y-o 7f winner Tut (by Intikhab). The dam, a 1m winner at 3 yrs, is a half-sister to 5 winners. The second dam, Blaine (by Lyphard's Wish), is a placed half-sister to 7 winners including the dam of the dual Group 1 winner Croco Rouge. *"She looks a very sharp 2-y-o and she comes from a nice family especially as the half-sister won a Group 3 last year. She's a strong filly with a good action, she's straightforward and we like her"*. TRAINERS' BARGAIN BUY

126. BEOGRAD SNIPER ★★
b.c. Cape Cross – Messelina (Noverre).
February 28. First foal. 43,000Y. Tattersalls October Book 1. Marco Botti. The dam is an unraced half-sister to 4 winners including the very useful Group 3 6.3f Anglesey Stakes winner Pan Jammer. The second dam, Ingerence (by Akarad), was placed three times in France and

is a half-sister to 6 winners including the Group 3 10.5f Prix Penelope winner La Monalisa. (Op-Center). *"Quite a big horse, he's backward at the moment. He's going to need time, I'd say probably September time over seven furlongs or a mile, but he's a nice horse".*

127. CONFIRMED ★★★
b.c. Authorized – Vas Y Carla (Gone West)
January 30. Fourth foal. 115,000Y. Tattersalls October Book 1. Blandford Bloodstock. Half-brother to the quite useful 7f (at 2 yrs) and 6f winner Alice Alleyne (by Oasis Dream). The dam, a quite useful 7f placed 2-y-o, is a half-sister to 4 winners including the Group 2 Great Voltigeur Stakes third Avalon The second dam, Lady Carla (by Caerleon), a high-class winner over 1m (at 2 yrs) and the Group 1 12f Oaks, is a half-sister to a minor winner. *"He's a scopey horse with a very good action. Being by Authorized, who is a son of Montjeu, I was a bit concerned what sort of attitude he might have because Montjeu's can be hot, but I have to say that his temperament has been fine. We like him a lot, but again it will be late summer over seven furlongs or more before we see him out".*

128. GREY MIRAGE ★★★
b.c. Oasis Dream – Grey Way (Cozzene).
March 24. €62,000Y. SGA (Italy). Not sold. Brother to the quite useful dual 1m winner Tiger Dream and half-brother to the dual Italian Group 1 10f winner Distant Way (by Distant View), the Italian winner and Group 3 14f placed Cima De Pluie (by Singspiel) and the Italian winner and listed 10f placed Secret De Vie (by Fantastic Light). The dam won the Group 2 Premio Lydia Tesio and is a half-sister to 6 winners. The second dam, Northern Naiad (by Nureyev), is a placed half-sister to 7 winners. *"Not the most correct horse, but he's straightforward and he's done really well since he arrived from the sales and he's filled out a lot. He's quite tall and he'll need seven furlongs at least this year, starting in late summer".*

129. LELAPS (USA) ★★★
ch.c. Mr Greeley – Rebecca Parisi
(Persian Heights).
May 4. Half-brother to Becrux (by Glen Jordan), winner of the Grade 1 Woodbine Mile and to 2 minor Italian winners by Docksider and Tibullo. The dam won at 3 yrs in Italy and is a half-sister to 4 other minor winners. The second dam, Busca (by Mr Prospector), is a placed half-sister to 6 winners including the Lancashire Oaks winner and good broodmare Andaleeb. *"I like him a lot. I haven't had much experience of the sire Mr Greeley but this colt is very straightforward and strong. We haven't done a lot with him but he's a good mover. One for seven furlongs to start with, he's a big horse so we're just letting him tick over for now. He was a late foal but he certainly doesn't look it because you'd think he was a 3-y-o already!"*

130. PATTO D'ACCIAIO ★★★
b.c. War Chant – Princess Skippie (Skip Away).
January 21. Second foal. 20,000Y. Tattersalls October Book 2. Not sold. Brother to the 2010 Italian 2-y-o 1m winner Parnassus. The dam is an unplaced half-sister to 3 winners including the Group 1 Italian Derby winner Hailsham and to the unplaced dam of the Group 1 Prix d'Ispahan winner Prince Kirk. The second dam, Halo's Princess (by Halo), won the Grade 1 Princess Elizabeth Stakes in Canada and is a half-sister to 6 winners and to the unraced dam of the Australian Grade 1 winners Curata Storm and Voile d'Or. *"A medium-sized colt, he's a full-brother to an Italian winner over a mile. Mentally he's quite forward but perhaps he'll need six or seven furlongs, so he's not a sharp 2-y-o. We like him and he seems to have a good attitude".*

131. RIGHT REGAL (IRE) ★★★
b.c. King's Best – Royal Esteem
(Mark Of Esteem).
February 28. First foal. 30,000Y. Tattersalls October Book 2. McKeever Bloodstock. The dam won 2 minor races at 3 yrs in the USA and is a half-sister to one winner. The second dam, Inchacooley (by Rhoman Rule), won the listed 1m Brownstown Stakes and a listed event in the USA and is a half-sister to one winner. *"He's good-bodied, medium-sized and I don't think it'll take too long to get him ready to run. Having said that, we'll probably wait for the seven furlong races with him, we like him and he's a good mover".*

132. SECRETS AWAY (IRE) ★★★
ch.f. Refuse To Bend – Lady Zonda
(Lion Cavern).
April 11. Sixth foal. 100,000Y. Tattersalls October Book 1. Dukes Stud. Half-sister to the 2-y-o Group 1 Fillies' Mile and Group 2 12f Ribblesdale Stakes winner Hibaayeb (by Singspiel) and to the Irish 2-y-o 6f winner and listed 6f second (from 2 starts) May Meeting (by Diktat). The dam, a quite useful 7f and 1m winner, is a half-sister to 8 winners. The second dam, Zonda (by Fabulous Dancer), a useful 5f to 8.5f winner and listed-placed here, subsequently won twice in the USA. *"A half-sister to Hibaayeb, she's very elegant and a very smart-looking filly. Quite tall, being by Refuse To Bend she's straightforward and easy to train. We like her a lot".*

133. SILENT PLACE ★★
b.f. Compton Place – Silent Miracle
(Night Shift).
March 15. Seventh foal. 12,000Y. Tattersalls October Book 3. Not sold. Half-sister to the fair 2010 2-y-o 5f winner Silent Wonder (by Diktat), to the fair 7f and 10f winner Annishirani (by Shaamit) and a winner in Russia by Abou Zouz. The am, a fair 6f winner, is a half-sister to 2 minor winners. The second dam, Curie Point (by Sharpen Up), is an unraced half-sister to 9 winners including the US Grade 3 stakes winner Mazilier. (K A Dasmal). *"She only arrived a few weeks ago and she's just been cantering, but so far she's done well and she's a good mover. She looks to me to be an early type, although I've not done enough with her to say for sure".*

134. SOLAR DEITY (IRE) ★★★★
b.c. Exceed And Excel – Dawn Raid
(Docksider).
March 27. Third foal. 35,000Y. Tattersalls October Book 1. Dwayne Woods. Half-brother to the quite useful Irish 7f winner Dance Hall Girl (by Dansili). The dam, a quite useful Irish 3-y-o 7f winner, is a half-sister to 7 winners including the French and Irish 2,000 Guineas and Richmond Stakes winner Bachir, to the smart 7f (at 2 yrs) to 10f and hurdles winner Albuhera and the useful 2-y-o listed 7f winner Elliots World. The second dam, Morning Welcome (by Be My Guest), placed once over 12f at 3 yrs in Ireland, is a half-sister to 9 winners including the Irish listed Debutante Stakes and subsequent US Grade 3 winner Down Again. *"A typical Exceed And Excel, he's quite forward and he goes well, so he'll be able to start at six furlongs. We like him, he's doing really well and he's coming to hand quickly, so I would say he'll be racing by the end of May".*

135. SOTTENMENT (FR) ★★★
ch.c. Manduro – Mantesera (In The Wings).
March 8. Fourth foal. 50,000Y. Tattersalls October Book 1. Half-brother to the very useful listed 7f (at 2 yrs) and listed 10f winner Nideeb (by Exceed And Excel). The dam is an unraced sister to the very smart Group 3 Nell Gwyn Stakes winner and Group 1 Yorkshire Oaks and Group 1 Prix Vermeille placed Cloud Castle and a half-sister to 5 winners including the high-class middle-distance horses and multiple Group 1 winners Warrsan and Luso and the Group 2 winner Needle Gun. The second dam, Lucayan Princess (by High Line), a very useful winner of the listed 6f Sweet Solera Stakes at 2 yrs, was third in the 12.3f Cheshire Oaks and is a half-sister to 7 winners. (Scuderia Rencati Srl). *"Not the biggest horse, he comes from a good family but being by Manduro you would think he'd need a trip. He's a good-moving colt but we're just taking our time with him".*

JIM BOYLE

136. CONFUCIOUS ELITE ★★★
b.c. Bertolini – Cavernista (Lion Cavern).
February 23. Sixth foal. 28,000foal. Tattersalls December. Peter Doyle. Half-brother to the fairly useful 1m to 12f winner of 4 races Celtic Spirit (by Pivotal), to the fairly useful 2-y-o 6f winner She's A Character (by Invincible Spirit), the fair 6f winner Capetown Girl (by Danzero) and the Italian 9f to 11f winner Keycavern (by Key Of Luck). The dam is a placed half-sister to 11 winners including the Group 1 Prix du Cadran winner Give Notice and the 1m listed winner Sovinista. The second dam, Princess Genista (by Ile de Bourbon), a very useful 1m and 8.5f winner, was third in the Musidora Stakes and is a half-sister to 11 winners. (Albert Kwok). *"A big, strong, imposing type, we were quite well-forward with him but he's quite heavy topped and he's had a touch of sore shins, so we've eased off him. He should be out once the six furlong races are here, he's*

quite sharp and has a bit of speed. His owner will be hoping to get him to win or be rated high enough to go to Hong Kong. Most years we're successful in doing that and this colt looks like being no exception. He certainly seems to have ability".

137. DIVINE PAMINA (IRE) ★★★★
br.f. Dark Angel – Greek Symphony (Mozart).
February 25. Second foal. 62,000Y. Tattersalls October Book 1. Peter Doyle. Half-sister to the quite useful 2010 2-y-o 1m winner Music In The Rain (by Invincible Spirit). The dam was placed once over 7f in Ireland and is a half-sister to 3 winners including the Irish dual Group 3 winner Marionnaud. The second dam, Raghida (by Nordico), a fairly useful Irish 2-y-o dual 5f winner, was second in the Group 3 5f Curragh Stakes and the Group 3 Molecomb Stakes and is a full or half-sister to 8 winners including the Group 1 Gran Criterium winner Sholokhov and the dam of the Irish Derby winner Soldier Of Fortune. (Prosser Family Partnership). *"A lovely filly, she was a gorgeous yearling but grew earlier in the year and went a bit weak when I got her doing full canters. We eased off her for a few weeks but she's cantering again now and she'll thrive now that she's getting some sun on her back. She gives a good feel, she covers the ground and looks a smart individual. She's bred to be fairly sharp and I can see her being out when the six furlong maidens start".*

138. FOOLSCAP (IRE) ★★★
ch.c. Choisir – Notepad (King's Best).
April 14. First foal. €15,000Y. Goffs Open. Peter Doyle. The dam is an unplaced half-sister to 8 winners including the useful 2-y-o Group 3 7f C L Weld Park Stakes winner Rag Top and the dam of the listed winner Elnamri. The second dam, Petite Epaulette (by Night Shift), a fair 5f winner at 2 yrs, is a half-sister to 3 winners including the Group 1 1m Gran Criterium second Line Dancer. *"A very sharp sort, he's not very big but as tough as old boots and a very quick learner. He came in later than some of these but leapfrogged them to the front of the queue in terms of precocity We'll have some fun with him early doors in these five furlong races".*

139. ILLUSTRIOUS LAD (IRE) ★★★
ch.c. Bertolini – Squeak (Selkirk).
February 4. Sixth living foal. Doncaster Premier. £30,000Y. Peter Doyle. The dam, winner of the Group 3 Lancashire Oaks and subsequently the Grade 1 Matriarch Stakes and Grade 1 Matriarch Stakes in the USA, is a half-sister to 7 winners. The second dam, Santa Linda (by Sir Ivor), is an unraced half-sister to 5 winners including the Group 1 Premio Roma winner Noble Saint. (Inside Track Racing Club). *"A nice type, he'll cope with five furlongs but I can see him doing better over six. He's sharp enough to start in April because he's come to hand quickly. A real bull of a horse from a good family, he's pretty much bombproof and should give his owners some fun this year".*

140. PALOMA'S PRINCE (IRE) ★★★★
ch.c. Nayef – Ma Paloma (Highest Honor).
April 14. Eighth foal. 50,000Y. Tattersalls October Book 2. Peter Doyle. Half-brother to the Group 2 10.5f Prix Noailles winner of 5 races Ruwi (by Unfuwain), to the quite useful French 12.5f winner Bloke (by Vettori) and 2 minor winners in France and Spain by Vettori and Key Of Luck. The dam won twice, over 8.5f and 10.5f, in France and is a half-sister to 6 winners. The second dam, Palombella (by Groom Dancer), won 3 races at 3 yrs in France and is a half-sister to 11 winners including the Group 3 winner and high-class broodmare Kanmary. (Serendipity Syndicate 2006). *"He won't be the sharpest, but I should think he'll be a mid-season 2-y-o starting at six furlongs and he'll relish seven later on. He's a nice stamp of a horse, he has a lovely stride on him and he really covers the ground. A very straightforward colt, I really like him and he'd be one of my nicest 2-y-o's.*

141. UNNAMED ★★★
b.c. Choisir – Krasivaya (Soviet Star).
February 6. First foal. 11,500Y. Tattersalls October Book 3. Not sold. The dam ran once unplaced and is a half-sister to 3 winners including the Group 2 Challenge Stakes winner Stimulation (by Choisir). The second dam, Damiana (by Thatching), was placed 5 times in France at 2 and 3 yrs and is a sister to the listed Prix Coronation winner and US Grade 2 placed Dirca and a half-sister to 4 winners. *"A three-*

parts brother to Stimulation who is now a stallion. We tried to buy that horse as a yearling but couldn't get near him. This colt reminds me very much of him. He's a really nice, good-sized, good-walking individual. Thankfully he's very laid-back, because I had the dam and she was a bit of a crank. My 2-y-o's are coming to hand quicker this year than they have done in the past and this colt is a good example of that. He'll start in a six furlong maiden and I think he could be quite useful".

142. UNNAMED ★★★
ch.c. Choisir – Sweet Pickle (Piccolo).
February 16. First foal. The dam, a fair 6f (including at 2 yrs) and 7f winner of 12 races, is a half-sister to several winners. The second dam, Sweet Wilhelmina (by Indian Ridge), was a fair 7f (including at 2 yrs) and 1m winner of 8 races. (M Khan x2). *"A nice type, we trained the dam and this is her first foal. He's a bit finer than she was but he's started to come to himself recently and he's starting to please me now. I think we'll be seeing him in a six furlong maiden in May or June. It's a fairly speedy pedigree and he's coming to hand quite quickly now"*.

CLIVE BRITTAIN

143. ECHO OF DUBAI (IRE)
b.f. Echo Of Light – Papabile (Chief's Crown).
March 11. Fifth foal. 30,000Y. Tattersalls October Book 1. Rabbah Bloodstock. Half-sister to the fair 10f winner Papality (by Giant's Causeway). The dam, a useful winner of 3 races over 1m including two listed events, is a sister to the champion 2-y-o Grand Lodge and a half-sister to 5 winners including the dual listed winner La Persiana. The second dam, La Papagena (by Habitat), is an unraced half-sister to 7 winners including the very useful 3-y-o 7f and 1m winner Pamina, the very useful 11f and 12.5f winner Lost Chord. (Mr A Al Mansoori).

144. RED AGGRESSOR (IRE)
b.c. Red Clubs – Snap Crackle Pop (Statoblest).
April 16. Tenth foal. 20,000Y. Tattersalls October Book 2. C Brittain. Half-brother to the useful 2-y-o 6f and listed 7f Washington Singer Stakes winner Sharp Nephew (by Dr Fong), to the fairly useful 5f (including at 2 yrs) and 6f winner Handsome Cross (by Cape Cross), the fair 1m winner Cereal Killer (by Xaar), the fair 2-y-o 6f winner Snip Snap (by Revoque) and the modest 6f winner Miss Frangipane (by Acclamation). The dam, a quite useful 2-y-o 5f listed winner, is a half-sister to 4 minor winners. The second dam, Spinelle (by Great Nephew), a quite useful 11f winner, was second in the Group 3 Oaks Trial and is a half-sister to 5 winners. (C E Brittain).

145. SINGSPIEL SPIRIT
ch.c. Singspiel – Aberavon (Cadeaux Genereux).
January 31. First foal. 26,000Y. Tattersalls October Book 2. C Brittain. The dam is an unplaced sister to the very smart 6f (at 2 yrs) and 7f winner and Group 3 7f Hungerford Stakes second Tarjman and a half-sister to the smart 2-y-o 6f and 3-y-o listed 6f winner Nota Bene and the US stakes winner Porthcawl. The second dam, Dodo (by Alzao), a fairly useful 3-y-o 6f winner, is a half-sister to 7 winners. (Mr A Al Mansoori).

146. UNNAMED
b.f. Shamardal – Blue Parade (Singspiel).
March 31. Second foal. 30,000Y. Tattersalls October Book 1. Blandford Bloodstock. Half-sister to the 2010 French 2-y-o winner Cormeilles (by Dubawi). The dam is an unraced half-sister to 9 winners including the French Group 2 12f winners America and Majorien and the listed 6f Hopeful Stakes winner Rose Indien. The second dam, Green Rosy (by Green Dancer), a French 10f winner and listed-placed, is a sister to the French listed winner Big Sink Hope and a half-sister to 10 winners including the good broodmare Rensaler (dam of the US Grade 1 winner Jovial). (S Ali).

147. UNNAMED
b.f. Authorized – Bunting (Shaadi).
March 17. Tenth foal. 30,000Y. Tattersalls October Book 1. Ed Vaughan. Half-sister to the smart 6f (at 2 yrs) and triple listed 10f winner and Group 2 Royal Lodge Stakes third Parasol (by Halling), to the smart 1m (at 2 yrs) and listed 10f winner and multiple Group 1 placed Mot Juste, the modest 10f winner Northern Acres (both by Mtoto), the fairly useful 6f (at 2 yrs) and 7.5f winner Sudra (by Indian Ridge), the fair 12f winner Longspur (by Singspiel) and the modest 12f winner War

Pennant (by Selkirk). The dam, a useful 1m (at 2 yrs) and 10f winner, was second in the Lingfield Oaks Trial and third in the Group 1 Italian Oaks and is a half-sister to 3 winners. The second dam, Warm Welcome (by General Assembly), a fairly useful 10f winner, was listed-placed and is a half-sister to the Dante Stakes winner Hot Touch. (M Al Nabouda).

148. UNNAMED
b.f. *Dubawi – Fawaayid (Vaguely Noble).*
January 30. Fifteenth foal. $200,000Y. Saratoga August. Blandford Bloodstock. Half-sister to the useful 2-y-o 6f winner Desert Realm (by Desert Prince), to the listed 1m Prix de Bagatelle winner Green Lady, the quite useful 2-y-o 6f winner Shamo (both by Green Desert) and the fairly useful 12f winner Entisar (by Nashwan) and to the placed dam of the Group 2 Hungerford Stakes winner Balthaazar's Gift. The dam, a fairly useful winner of 3 races at 2 yrs from 7f to 10f in Ireland including the Silver Flash Stakes, is a half-sister to 5 winners. The second dam, Clara Bow (by Coastal), was a minor US winner of 3 races and a half-sister to 4 winners. (Mr M Al Shafar).

149. UNNAMED
b.f. *Authorized – Jakarta (Machiavellian).*
March 2. Fifth foal. Half-sister to the fairly useful 2-y-o 7f winner and Group 2 Rockfel Stakes third Puggy (by Mark Of Esteem) and the fairly useful 1m (at 2 yrs) to 11f winner of 6 races Bencoolen (by Daylami). The dam, a fair 3-y-o 7f winner, is a half-sister to 7 winners including the Group 3 10f and 11f winner Blue Monday and the useful 1m to 10f winner Lundy's Lane. The second dam, Lunda (by Soviet Star) is an unplaced half-sister to 6 winners including the high-class middle-distance horses Luso (winner of the Aral-Pokal, the Italian Derby and the Hong Kong International Vase) and Warrsan (Coronation Cup and Grosser Preis von Baden). (S Manana).

150. UNNAMED
b.f. *Cadeaux Genereux – Jules (Danehill).*
April 17. Sixth foal. 25,000Y. Tattersalls October Book 2. Rabbah Bloodstock. Half-sister to the fair 2010 2-y-o 7f winner Romantic Wish (by Hawk Wing), to the useful 6f and 7f winner of 6 races from 2 to 4 yrs Golden Desert (by Desert Prince), the moderate 1m winner The Blue Dog (by High Chaparral) and a winner in Hungary by Fasliyev. The dam, a fair 3-y-o 7f winner, is a half-sister to 10 winners including the dam of the Australian Group 1 winner Prowl. The second dam, Before Dawn (by Raise A Cup), a champion US 2-y-o filly, won two Grade 1 events and is a half-sister to 6 winners. (S Manana).

151. UNNAMED
b.c. *Green Desert – My Amalie (by Galileo).*
April 17. Second foal. The dam, a fairly useful 7f winner, is a half-sister to one winner. The second dam, Princess Amalie (by Rahy). is an unplaced half-sister to 10 winners (including 5 stakes winners) notably the Group 1 1m William Hill Futurity Stakes winner Al Hareb. (S Manana).

152. UNNAMED
b.f. *Acclamation – Needles And Pins (Fasliyev).*
January 25. Third foal. 70,000Y. Tattersalls October Book 2. Rabbah Bloodstock. Half-sister to the fairly useful UAE 7f winner and listed-placed I Am The Best (by King's Best) and to the fair 7f winner Seamster (by Pivotal). The dam, a useful 2-y-o listed 5.2f winner and second in the Group 3 5.5f Prix d'Arenburg, is a half-sister to one winner. The second dam, Fairy Contessa (by Fairy King), is a 6f placed half-sister to 5 winners including River Falls (Group 2, 6f Gimcrack Stakes). (S Manana).

153. UNNAMED
b.f. *Shamardal – Neshla (Singspiel).*
March 31. First foal. 32,000Y. Tattersalls October Book 1. Yeomanstown Stud. The dam, a poor 11f placed maiden, is a half-sister to 9 winners including the Group 3 7.3f Fred Darling Stakes winner and Group 2 10f Nassau Stakes third Sueboog (herself dam of the Group 1 winner Best Of The Bests) and the listed 6f winner Marika. The dam, Nordica (by Northfields), a useful 6f and 1m winner, is a half-sister to 2 winners. (S Manana).

154. UNNAMED
b.c. *Dubawi – Treble Seven (Fusaichi Pegasus).*
January 18. Third foal. 48,000Y. Tattersalls October Book 1. Not sold. Half-brother to the unplaced 2010 2-y-o Jibouti (by Exceed And

Excel) and to the modest 11f winner Stadium Of Light (by Fantastic Light). The dam, placed once over 1m, is a half-sister to 4 winners including the very smart filly Lovers Knot, winner of the Group 2 1m Falmouth Stakes and the US Grade 3 De La Rose Handicap and to the very useful 1m (at 2 yrs) and 9f winner and listed-placed Foodbroker Founder. The second dam, Nemea (by The Minstrel), a fairly useful 10f winner, stayed 2m and is a half-sister to 9 winners. (S Manana).

155. UNNAMED
b.c. Teofilo – Triton Dance (Hector Protector).
February 1. Second living foal. 100,000Y. Tattersalls October Book 1. Kern/Lillingston. Half-sister to the useful Irish dual 7f winner and Group 3 Tetrarch Stakes third Count John (by Intikhab). The dam, an Irish 2-y-o 5f winner, is a half-sister to 4 winners including the 2-y-o Group 2 6f Cherry Hinton Stakes winner Jewel In The Sand and the German 3-y-o listed 6f winner Davignon. The second dam, Dancing Drop (by Green Desert), a useful dual 2-y-o 6f winner, was listed-placed 5 times and is a half-sister to 9 winners including the 2-y-o 5f winner Wisam, the 5f (at 2 yrs) and 7f winner Moon King and the 2-y-o 6f winner Mithl Al Hawa – all useful. (S Manana).

156. UNNAMED
b.f. Authorized – Wimple (Kingmambo).
March 9. Fifth foal. Half-sister to the fairly useful 2-y-o 6f winner and listed-placed Sharnberry (by Shamardal), to the quite useful 2-y-o 6f winner Master Rooney (by Cape Cross) and a winner in Russia by Daylami. The dam, a useful 5f and 6f winner at 2 yrs, was listed-placed and is a half-sister to 2 winners. The second dam, Tunicle (by Dixieland Band), won 4 minor races in the USA and is a half-sister to 5 winners. (S Manana).

157. UNNAMED
b.f. Shamardal – Zamhrear (Singspiel).
February 3. First foal. 35,000Y. Tattersalls October Book 1. Troy Steve. The dam, a modest 7f and 1m winner, is a half-sister to 7 winners including the Group 3 10f and 11f winner Blue Monday. The second dam, Lunda (by Soviet Star), is an unplaced half-sister to 6 winners including the high-class middle-distance horses Luso (winner of the Aral-Pokal, the Italian Derby and the Hong Kong International Vase) and Warrsan (Coronation Cup and Grosser Preis von Baden). (S Manana).

DAVID BROWN
158. FLYING PICKETS (IRE) ★★
b.c. Piccolo – Burn (Selkirk).
January 25. Fourth foal. £3,000. Doncaster Premier. Not sold. Half-brother to the Italian 2-y-o winner Exotic Girl (by Antonius Pius). The dam was placed at 3 yrs and is a half-sister to 6 minor winners. The second dam, River Cara (by Irish River), a French listed 2-y-o 1m winner, is a half-sister to 3 winners. *"He's showing us plenty of speed and he'll be an early 2-y-o over five furlongs. I'm very happy with my new location is at Averham Park near Newark, where Eoghan O'Neill used to train. The facilities are fantastic".*

159. GRIPPER ★★★
ch.c. Avonbridge – Easy Mover (Bluebird).
February 10. Third foal. £10,000Y. Doncaster Premier. Not sold. Half-brother to the fair 2009 2-y-o 5f winner Dispol Keasha (by Kheleyf). The dam, a fair 2-y-o 7f winner, is a half-sister to one winner. The second dam, Top Brex (by Top Ville), won once at 3 yrs in France and is a half-sister to 6 winners including the Italian Group 3 winner Charlo Mio. *"This colt is very strong and has lots of speed, so he'll make a 2-y-o over five furlongs, maybe six later on. He really does look like a bull and people can't believe he's a 2-y-o".*

160. WHISKY BRAVO ★★★
b.c. Byron – Dress Design (Brief Truce).
May 17. Half-brother to the modest 7f winner Whisky Jack (by Bahamian Bounty), to the Italian winner of 4 races Green Target (by Catrail) and the moderate 12f winner Dandarrell (by Makbul). The dam, a minor Irish 2-y-o 5f winner, is a half-sister to 4 winners. The second dam, Lady President (by Dominion), won 2 minor races in Ireland at 3 and 4 yrs and is a half-sister to 6 winners including the Group 3 winner and Group 1 placed Citidancer. *"A smart colt, he's very strong and a five/six furlong 2-y-o type. He should be quite early".*

161. UNNAMED ★★★
ch.f. Captain Rio – Alvarinho Lady (Royal Applause).
Half-sister to the modest 5f (at 2 yrs) and 6f winner Monte Mayor One (by Lujain). The dam, a fair 2-y-o 5f winner, is a sister to the useful 2-y-o winner All Nines and a half-sister to several winners. The second dam, Jugendliebe (by Persian Bold), was a German 10f winner. "She's pure speed. A really, tough, strong filly and she'll be running soon. I expect her to be a nice 2-y-o and I'm still looking for an owner if anyone is interested".

162. UNNAMED ★★★
b.c. Iceman – Colonel's Daughter (Colonel Collins).
May 5. Fifth foal. Half-brother to the useful 6f winner of 4 races (including at 2 yrs) Colonel Mak (by Makbul) and to the modest 2-y-o dual 5f winner Dotty's Daughter (by Forzando). The dam was placed 3 times over 5f at 2 yrs and is a half-sister to several winners. The second dam, Clashfern (by Smackover), was unraced. "This is lovely colt for the middle of the season. He looks like being a bit special, he's a big, strong horse and I have him the Weatherbys Insurance race at Doncaster later in the year".

163. UNNAMED ★★
ch.c. Auction House – Nan Jan (Komaite).
March 14. First foal. The dam, a fair 6f to 1m winner of 7 races, is a half-sister to several winners including the quite useful 6f and 7f winner of 6 races Buxton (by Auction House). The second dam, Dam Certain (by Damister), a moderate 7f to 1m winner, is a half-sister to several winners. "The dam was tough and won plenty of races and this colt looks nice. He'll be running in the middle of the season because he needs to fill out a bit yet".

164. UNNAMED ★★
b.f. Echo Of Light – Sydney Star (Machiavellian).
May 2. Fourth foal. The dam, a quite useful 7f winner, is a half-sister to one winner out of the fairly useful 10.2f winner Sena Desert (by Green Desert), herself a half-sister to the smart Group 3 7f Solario Stakes (at 2 yrs) and Group 2 10f Prix Guillaume d'Ornano winner Best Of The Bests. "She's blind in one eye but she's a lovely filly and certainly worth putting in the book. She'll be one for the back-end of the season, over seven furlongs and she has a touch of class about her".

JULIE CAMACHO

165. ISTAN STAR (USA) ★★
b.c. Istan – Migygian (Ogygian).
February 15. Eighth foal. Half-brother to 4 minor winners including the US winner of 4 races at 2 and 3 yrs Slewgiana (by Slew City Slew). The dam is an unraced half-sister to 7 winners. The second dam, Milingo (by Cougar II), won the Grade 1 Arlington-Washington Lassie Stakes and was Grade 2 placed three times. (Axom XXVIII). This colt is the first crop of the sire Istan, a US Grade 3 winner and a son of Gone West. "A big, strapping colt, we'll probably geld him soon but he's a nice sort. He's not looking like a sharp 2-y-o at the moment, so you're looking at the mid-summer before he comes out. He's just doing swinging canters upsides and I should think we'll wait for seven furlongs with him".

166. NEW ROMANTIC ★★★
b.f. Singspiel – Kalinova (Red Ransom).
February 10. First foal. The dam is an unraced half-sister to the Group 1 Fillies Mile, Falmouth Stakes, Sussex Stakes and Matron Stakes winner Soviet Song and to the useful 5f (at 2 yrs) and triple 6f winner Baralinka. The second dam, Kalinka (by Soviet Star), a quite useful 2-y-o 7f winner, is a half-sister to 2 winners. (Elite Racing Club). "We've done nothing with her yet and she's just cantering away at the moment. James Fanshawe trained the dam and he thought quite a lot of her but she got injured and that's why she never raced. This filly is really strong and she's a nice individual. In training, her mother looked quite sharp so this filly might be a bit earlier than you'd expect from a Singspiel. It depends how she goes because we've been able to take our time with her. Hopefully she'll be racing by mid-summer".

167. UNNAMED ★★
ch.f. Halling – Dixie Favor (Dixieland Band).
May 14. Half-sister to the Italian listed winner and Group 2 Italian 1,000 Guineas third Kiralik, to the fair middle-distance winner of 5 races Favorisio, the hurdles winner Currahee (all by

Efisio), the 2-y-o Group 3 6f Princess Margaret Stakes and subsequent US 3-y-o Grade 2 8.5f winner and Grade 1 9f third River Belle (by Lahib), the useful 3-y-o 7.5f and 1m winner Rio Riva (by Pivotal) and the poor 5f all-weather winner Stately Favour (by Statoblest). The dam was a quite useful Irish 6f (at 2 yrs) to 1m winner. The second dam, Fenne Favor (by Forli), is an unraced half-sister to 4 winners. (Mrs S Camacho). *"We're still in the process of breaking her and she'll be turned out for some spring grass because we knew from her breeding she wasn't going to be sharp. She's the last foal out of the dam and we hope to breed from her because she's a nice sort. One for the back-end of the season".*

HENRY CANDY
168. AILANTHUS ★★★
b.f. Trade Fair – The Abbess
(Bishop Of Cashel).
February 8. First foal. The dam, a quite useful 2-y-o 6f winner from only starts, is a sister to one winner and a half-sister to two more. The second dam, Nisha (by Nishapour), was a lightly-raced maiden. (Girsonfield Ltd). *"She's not very big but she's a great little mover and has a good attitude. A small, lean and active filly, she was an early foal so I would say she should be racing in June over six furlongs. She looks OK and I trained the dam to win first time out as a 2-y-o".*

169. AVON PEARL ★★★★
ch.c. Avonbridge – Warden Rose
(Compton Place).
March 26. Second foal. Doncaster Premier. £52,000Y. David Redvers. The dam is an unplaced half-sister to the Hong Kong listed winner Warden Complex. The second dam, Miss Rimex (by Ezzoud), a quite useful 6f (at 2 yrs) and 1m winner, is a half-sister to 6 winners including the dams of the stakes winners Triple Aspect, Stylish Lass, Guys And Dolls and Pawnbroker. (Pearl Bloodstock Ltd). *"A great big, strong colt, I would think he'd be ready to start working soon and I'd expect him to be running in June. To look at, he appears to be a very nice horse, so if his ability matches his looks he'll be OK. I like the way he goes and I'd be hopeful of him. He was a very nice looking yearling and I tried to buy him, but I don't deal in those sort of figures! So it's nice to have been given him to train".*

170. BYTON ★★★★
b.f. Byron – Arculinge (Paris House).
February 11. Second foal. 6,000Y. Tattersalls October Book 3. Henry Candy. Half-sister to the fair 2010 2-y-o dual 5f winner Normandy Maid (by American Post). The dam, a moderate 6f and 7f placed maiden, is a half-sister to 4 winners including the smart listed 5f winner Corrybrough and to the unplaced dam of the dual Group 3 winning sprinter Amour Propre. The second dam, Calamanco (by Clantime), a fair 5f winner at 3 and 4 yrs, is a sister to the sprint winner Cape Merino (herself dam of the Group 1 Golden Jubilee Stakes winner Cape Of Good Hope) and a half-sister to 3 winners. (Major M G Wyatt). *"You can from the pedigree why I bought her – Amour Propre and Corrybrough were both trained here. She was very small and insignificant at the sales and I didn't pay a lot of money for her, but she's done fantastically well. She's a big, strong filly now and a fantastic mover. I'd say she looks a real sprinter and from July onwards it'll be interesting to see her out".*
TRAINERS' BARGAIN BUY

171. CHORAL BEE ★★★
b.f. Oratorio – Chief Bee (Chief's Crown).
April 2. Ninth living foal. 7,000Y. Tattersalls October Book 2.★Candy. Half-sister to the smart 12f King George V Handicap winner and Melbourne Cup third Beekeeper, to the quite useful 10f winner Argonaut, the fair 11f and hurdles winner Mt Desert (all by Rainbow Quest), the quite useful 2-y-o 7f winner Golden Grace (by Green Desert), the modest French 12f winner Dream Bee (by Oasis Dream) and a winner in Scandinavia by Machiavellian. The dam, a fairly useful winner of 3 races at 4 yrs from 9f to 14.6f, is a sister to the Group 1 Racing Post Trophy winner and useful sire Be My Chief and a half-sister to 5 winners. The second dam, Lady Be Mine (by Sir Ivor), a minor 3-y-o 1m winner, is a half-sister to 6 winners including Mixed Applause (dam of the Group 1 winners Shavian and Paean). (Henry Candy). *"I like her a lot, she's a big strong girl and a fantastic mover, but at the moment I can't get her to stop coughing. I think she'll be nice and I'm in no hurry with her. I don't think there was*

a bid for her at the sale but I loved her then and I still do. I would imagine seven furlongs in August would be her starting point, she's a long-striding beast".

172. GIFTED DANCER ★★
b.f. Cadeaux Genereux – Puteri Sas (Fasliyev).
April 16. Second foal. 5,000Y. Tattersalls October Book 2.★Candy. The dam, a modest 7f placed 2-y-o, is a half-sister to 3 winners including the useful 1m (at 2 yrs) and 9f winner and Group 3 Dee Stakes second Putra Sas. The second dam, Puteri Wentworth (by Sadler's Wells), a quite useful 12f to 2m 4f winner, is a half-sister to 4 winners including the very smart dual listed 5f winner Watching. (Henry Candy). "She looks OK and I would imagine she'll be starting work soon. She's very strong and 'up together', so she's quite forward and although the family doesn't suggest she should be any good she was cheap and I like the sire. I wouldn't be surprised if she was a five/six furlong 2-y-o".

173. MERV ★★★
b.c. Royal Applause – Shauna's Honey (Danehill).
March 17. Eighth foal. 18,000Y. Tattersalls October Book 3. Not sold. Half-brother to the modest 11f to 2m winner of 11 races Ise'Af (by Darshaan) and to a winner in Hong Kong by Indian Ridge. The dam, a quite useful 7f winner at Leopardstown, is a half-sister to 5 winners including the smart Ahohoney, a winner over 6f and 1m here at 2 yrs and the Group 3 10.5f Prix Fille de l'Aire. The second dam, Honey Buzzard (by Sea Hawk II), is a placed half-sister to 5 winners. (Mrs A D Bourne & P Milmo QC). "Not very big, but he's strong and he goes well. He could easily be on the track in the second half of June because he's quite forward. Tough and cheeky, I like him a lot and I like the way he goes. He looks a typical Royal Applause to me and he's a tough little nut".

174. MRS HUFFEY ★★★★
b.f. Acclamation – Passing Hour (Red Ransom).
January 22. First foal. 32,000Y. Tattersalls October Book 1.★Candy. The dam, a winner, is a sister to the Group 3 5f Queen Mary Stakes winner Shining Hour and to the Group 1 Prix Marcel Boussac second Titian Time and is a half-sister to 4 winners. The second dam, Timely (by Kings Lake), a useful 1m winner, was third in the Group 1 Moyglare Stud Stakes and is a half-sister to 3 winners including the dam of the Italian Group 1 winner Le Vie Dei Colori. (Mr J Byrne). "She very big, but she was an early foal so she'll probably get away with it as far as being a 2-y-o is concerned. I can't do very much with her at present because of her size but she's very attractive and she looks quite exciting. One for the second half of the year".

175. RUGGED CROSS ★★★
b.c. Cape Cross – Lunda (Soviet Star).
March 14. Twelfth foal. 55,000Y. Tattersalls October Book 2.★Candy. Half-brother to the very useful 1m to 10f winner and Italian Derby third Lundy's Lane, to the very smart 1m (at 2 yrs) and dual Group 3 middle-distance winner Blue Monday (both by Darshaan), the useful 10f winner and Group 3 placed Bazergan, the fair 7f winner Jakarta (both by Machiavellian), the quite useful 11f winner Multiplication (by Marju), the fair 1m and 10f winner Dancing Tsar (by Salse), the fair 12f winner Najam and the modest 7f and 1m winner Zamhrear (both by Singspiel). The dam is an unplaced half-sister to 6 winners including the high-class middle-distance horses Luso (winner of the Aral-Pokal, the Italian Derby and the Hong Kong International Vase) and Warrsan (Coronation Cup and Grosser Preis von Baden). The second dam, Lucayan Princess (by High Line), won the listed 6f Sweet Solera Stakes at 2 yrs, was third in the 12.3f Cheshire Oaks and is a half-sister to 7 winners. (T Barr). "A colt from one of my favourite families. He's well 'up together' or in other words he's not gangly at all, he's just a nice size, he's burly, carries himself well and he goes nicely. I could be tempted to do a bit with him now because of all that, but his pedigree tells me I must leave him alone until the middle of the summer. He could well be a nice 2-y-o in the autumn".

176. SNOOKY ★★★
b.c. Exceed And Excel – Quintrell (Royal Applause).
February 17. Second foal. 26,000Y. Tattersalls October Book 2. Jill Lamb Bloodstock. The dam, a fair dual 7f winner at 3 yrs, is a half-sister to 7 minor winners. The second dam, Peryllis (by

Warning), a modest 6f (at 2 yrs) to 10.2f placed maiden, is a half-sister to 6 winners including the French listed 11.5f winner Honest Word and the very useful sprinter Cragside. (Mrs J M MacPherson). *"A very big, leggy horse at the moment, he's a lovely mover and I definitely wouldn't want to do anything with him yet. So you're probably talking about July time before he sees a racecourse. He's a nice, big, scopey horse that goes nicely".*

177. UNNAMED ★★★
b.g. Zafeen – Lady Natilda (First Trump).
March 26. Fifth foal. Doncaster St Leger Festival. £18,000Y. Henry Candy. Half-brother to the fairly useful 2010 2-y-o 5f winner Primo Lady and to the quite useful 2-y-o dual 5f winner Lucky Mellor (both by Lucky Story). The dam, a modest 2-y-o 5f winner, is a half-sister to 3 winners. The second dam, Ramajana (by Shadeed), won 2 races at 2 and 4 yrs in Germany and is a half-sister to 6 winners. (Mr Darren May). *"He got very big, heavy and strong, so we gelded him to try and get a bit of weight off him. He looks very nice and he should certainly be a 2-y-o. His knees were x-rayed in February and they were very immature, so we'll leave him alone for a bit. I expect he'll be racing from June onwards and he'll be a sprinting 2-y-o".*

HENRY CECIL
"I like my two-year-olds. I feel there could be a lot of potential and on the whole this crop could be as good or better than those from last year. As a group they will need time and none are in serious work yet, but they have been doing plenty of steady cantering and it will be exciting when they tell me they are ready to move on a little. I'm hopeful that the second half of the season will prove exciting with some of them".

178. ALL THAT RULES ★★ ♠
b.c. Galileo – Alba Stella (Nashwan).
April 30. Fourth foal. Goffs Orby. €90,000Y. Not sold. Half-brother to the quite useful 10f to 12f winner of 6 races at 3 and 4 yrs Aleatricis (by Kingmambo) and to the fair dual 11f winner Alicante (by Pivotal). The dam, a fairly useful dual 12f winner, is a half-sister to 7 winners including the high-class dual Champion Stakes winner Alborada, the triple German Group 1 winner Albanova and the dam of the Epsom Derby second Dragon Dancer. The second dam, Alouette (by Darshaan), a useful 1m (at 2 yrs) and listed 12f winner, is a sister to the listed winner and Irish Oaks third Arrikala and a half-sister to the Nassau Stakes and Sun Chariot Stakes winner Last Second (dam of the French 2,000 Guineas winner Aussie Rules), the Doncaster Cup winner Alleluia (dam of the Group 1 winner Allegretto) and the placed dam of the Group 1 winners Quarter Moon and Yesterday. (W A Tinkler). *"A nice colt with plenty of scope and he's a good mover. His pedigree is that of a middle-distance 3-y-o prospect, so he'll obviously need time".*

179. AMARAJA (GER) ★★
b.f. Galileo – Apsara (Darshaan).
March 15. Closely related to the smart 1m (at 2 yrs) and Group 3 10f Mooresbridge Stakes winner Curtain Call (by Sadler's Wells). The dam is an unplaced half-sister to numerous winners including the Group 1 10.5f Prix Lupin and US Grade 2 1m winner Johann Quatz and the Group 1 Prix du Jockey Club and Group 1 Prix Lupin winner Hernando. The second dam, Whakilyric (by Miswaki), winner the Group 3 7f Prix du Calvados and third in the Prix de la Salamandre and the Prix de la Foret, is a half-sister to 6 winners. (Niarchos Family). *"A nice filly with plenty of size and scope. Time needed".*

180. AQUILLA (IRE) ★★★★ ♠
b.f. Teofilo – Dance Troupe (Rainbow Quest).
April 10. Third foal. 260,000Y. Tattersalls October Book 1. Charlie Gordon-Watson. Half-sister to the quite useful Irish dual 1m (at 2 yrs) and Group 3 10f Ballysax Stakes winner Puncher Clynch (by Azamour). The dam is a placed half-sister to 6 winners including the French listed winner and multiple Group-placed Self Defense. The second dam, Dansara (by Dancing Brave), is an unraced half-sister to 10 winners including the Irish Oaks winner Princess Pati and the Great Voltigeur Stakes winner Seymour Hicks. (Al Asayl). *"This filly is a very good mover. She's big, attractive and very likeable".*

181. CAPE PRIDE ★★★
b.c. Cape Cross – Princess Ellen (Tirol).
April 21. Sixth foal. 48,000Y. Tattersalls October Book 1. Not sold. Half-brother to the useful listed 1m winner Prince Of Dance (by Danehill Dancer), to the French and Belgian winner and 2-y-o listed 5f placed Candelabro (by Elusive Quality), the quite useful 9f to 14f and hurdles winner La Estrella (by Theatrical) and the fair 1m winner Stravella (by Stravinsky). The dam, a smart listed 7f Sweet Solera Stakes winner at 2 yrs, was second in the 1,000 Guineas and the Coronation Stakes and third in the Nassau Stakes (all Group 1 events) She is a half-sister to one winner out of the unraced Celt Song (by Unfuwain), herself a half-sister to 4 minor winners. (Mrs Yvonne Perry). *"A big, good-looking colt, but still backward at present".*

182. CASTILO DEL DIABLO (IRE) ★★
b.br.c. Teofilo – Hundred Year Flood (Giant's Causeway).
February 8. Second foal. Goffs Orby. €300,000Y. Sir Robert Ogden. Half-brother to the moderate 2010 1m placed 2-y-o Bathwick Scanno (by Aptitude). The dam, a minor 2-y-o winner in the USA, is a half-sister to 3 winners including the US Grade 3 winner and Grade 1 placed My Sweet Hope. The second dam, High Heeled Hope (by Salt Lake), won two stakes events at 2 yrs in the USA, was Grade 1 placed twice and is a half-sister to 6 winners. (Sir Robert Ogden). *"He's backward and has done a great deal of growing".*

183. CHECKPOINT ★★★★
ch.c. Zamindar – Kalima (Kahyasi).
February 18. Half-brother to the useful 9f and 10f winner Jet Away (by Cape Cross). The dam is an unraced sister to the very useful 10f (at 2 yrs) and listed 13.8f winner Arrive and to the 2-y-o 5f winner and outstanding broodmare Hasili (dam of the top-class performers Banks Hill, Heat Haze, Intercontinental, Cacique, Champs Elysees and Dansili) and a half-sister to several winners. The second dam, Kerali (by High Line), a quite useful 3-y-o 7f winner, is a half-sister to numerous winners including the Group 3 6f July Stakes winner Bold Fact, the Group 1 Nunthorpe Stakes winner So Factual and the very useful Irish 7f to 1m winner Field Dancer. (Khalid Abdulla). *"A very nice colt and a good mover, he's quite flashy with white legs. I think he's really nice".*

184. CONTINUUM ★★★★★
b.c. Dansili – Clepsydra (Sadler's Wells).
April 22. Eighth foal. Brother to the very smart Group 1 10f Criterium de Saint-Cloud (at 2 yrs) and Group 3 10.3f Musidora Stakes winner Passage Of Time, to the 6f (at 2 yrs) and Group 2 12f King Edward VI Stakes winner Father Time and half-brother to the smart triple listed 1m and 10f winner Timepiece (by Zamindar), the fairly useful 10f winner Sandglass (by Zafonic) and the quite useful 1m and 10f winner Timetable (by Observatory). The dam, a quite useful 12f winner, is a half-sister to several winners including the useful listed 10.5f winner Double Crossed. The second dam, Quandary (by Blushing Groom), a useful winner of 4 races from 9f to 10f including the listed James Seymour Stakes at Newmarket, is a half-sister to the Group 1 Prix du Moulin winner All At Sea. (Khalid Abdulla). *"A big colt, he's a good mover and I like him very much at this stage".*

185. CORSETRY (USA) ★★★
b.f. Distorted Humor – Lingerie (Shirley Heights).
May 4. Half-sister to the Group 1 Oaks winner and Group 1 Irish Oaks second Light Shift (by Kingmambo), to the high-class Group 2 10.5f Tattersalls Gold Cup and Group 3 10f Brigadier Gerard Stakes winner Shiva, the high-class Group 2 12f Prix Jean de Chaudenay and Group 3 12f Prix Foy winner Limnos (both by Hector Protector), the useful 7f and listed 1m winner Burning Sunset (by Caerleon), the fairly useful 1m winner and US Grade 2 9f third Hyades (by Aldebaran) and the fairly useful 10f winner Mahasi (by Woodman). The dam, placed 7 times in France, is a half-sister to 4 winners including the French listed placed Evocatrice. The second dam, Northern Trick (by Northern Dancer), won the Prix de Diane and the Prix Vermeille, was second in the Prix de l'Arc de Triomphe and is a half-sister to the US Grade 1 Jockey Club Gold Cup winner On The Sly. (Niarchos Family). *"This is a nice filly, she's active and from a lovely family that includes a filly I trained to win the Oaks, Light Shift".*

186. DEFY THE ODDS ★★★
b.f. Galileo – Fully Invested (Irish River).
April 27. Half-sister to the French 12f and 15f winner and listed-placed Fully Funded (by Aptitude), to the French 2-y-o 1m winner and listed-placed Gainful, the quite useful 2-y-o 7f winner Safe Investment (both by Gone West) and the fair 10f winner Necessity (by Empire Maker). The dam, a useful 2-y-o 7f winner, is a half-sister to the French 7f (at 2 yrs) and listed 1m winner Multiplex, to the very useful 10f winner Valentine Band, the very useful 10f and Irish Group 3 14f winner Memorise and the useful 7.5f winner and listed 1m placed Sparkling Water. The second dam, Shirley Valentine (by Shirley Heights), a useful 11.8f winner, was fourth in the Park Hill Stakes and the Lancashire Oaks and is a sister to the high class Irish Derby second Deploy and a half-sister to the Derby and Irish Derby winner Commander in Chief, the champion 2-y-o and miler Warning and the Grade 1 10f Flower Bowl Invitational Handicap winner Yashmak. (Khalid Abdulla). *"She'll make up into a nice filly in time".*

187. DR YES (FR) ★★★★
b.c. Dansili – Light Shift (Kingmambo).
February 4. First foal. The dam won the Group 1 12f Oaks and is a half-sister to the Group 2 10.5f Tattersalls Gold Cup and Group 3 10f Brigadier Gerard Stakes winner Shiva and the high-class Group 2 12f Prix Jean de Chaudenay and Group 3 12f Prix Foy winner Limnos. The second dam, Lingerie (by Shirley Heights), placed 7 times in France, is a half-sister to 4 winners including the French listed placed Evocatrice. (Niarchos Family). *"For a first foal he's looks a good type, he makes good use of himself and we like him".*

188. EPOQUE (USA) ★★★
b.f. Empire Maker – Dock Leaf (Woodman).
February 10. Fourth foal. Half-sister to the fairly useful 5f (at 2 yrs) and 6f winner Sea Of Leaves (by Stormy Atlantic), to the fairly useful 10f and 12f winner Distinctive Image (by Mineshaft) and the quite useful 9f winner Point Out (by Point Given). The dam, unplaced in one start, is a half-sister to the Grade 1 9f Hollywood Oaks winner Sleep Easy and to the dual US Grade 1 winner Aptitude. The second dam, Dokki (by Northern Dancer), is an unraced half-sister to the champion US colt Slew O'Gold and the Belmont Stakes winner Coastal. (Khalid Abdulla). *"A good-looking filly that moves well".*

189. FRAGONARD ★★★★
ch.f. Teofilo – Delicieuse Lady (Trempolino).
April 4. Ninth foal. €400,000Y. Arqana Deauville August. Sir Robert Ogden. Half-sister to the Group 1 French Derby winner Blue Canari (by Acatenango), to the smart listed 1m winner Blue Ksar (by Anabaa), the French winner and Group 3 placed Crabapple (by Unfuwain) and the French 2-y-o winner Ballerina Blue (by High Chaparral). The dam won 4 minor races abroad and is a half-sister to 4 winners including the US stakes winner and smart broodmare Quest For Ladies. The second dam, Savoureuse Lady (by Caerleon), winner of the Group 3 10.5f Prix Fille de l'Air and placed in four other Group events, is a full or half-sister to 14 winners including the top-class colt Mtoto and to the dam of the Group 1 winner Mutamam. (Sir Robert Ogden). *"A tall, rangy filly, she makes great use of herself. Nice".*

190. HOLOGRAM ★★★
ch.c. Teofilo – Love Divine (Diesis).
February 25. Closely related to the Group 1 St Leger, Group 2 Jockey Club Cup and Group 3 Gordon Stakes winner Sixties Icon (by Galileo) and half-brother to the useful 10f winner Native Ruler (by Cape Cross) and the fair 9.5f winner Kissing (by Grand Lodge). The dam, winner of the Group 1 12f Oaks and the listed Lupe Stakes, is a half-sister to 4 winners including the listed 12f winner Floreeda. The second dam, La Sky (by Law Society), a useful 10f winner and second in the Lancashire Oaks, is closely related to the Champion Stakes winner Legal Case and a half-sister to 4 winners. (Lordship Stud). *"He's a backward colt but he's nice. Big and scopey".*

191. INTERLOCKING (USA) ★★★
b.f. Awesome Again – Engaging (Private Account).
April 16. Ninth foal. 110,000Y. Tattersalls October Book 1. Course Invest Corp. Half-sister to 5 winners including the US Grade 2 winner Final Pursuit (by Carson City), to the US winner and Grade 3 placed Stage Trick (by

Distorted Humor), the listed-placed winner Space Cruise(by Cape Canaveral) and the minor US winner of 13 races House Of Usher (by Chester House). The dam is an unraced half-sister to 8 winners including the US triple Grade 1 winner Flanders (herself dam of the multiple Grade 1 winner Surfside). The second dam, Starlet Storm (by Storm Bird), won 2 minor races in the USA and is a sister to the Cherry Hinton Stakes winner Storm Star. (Niarchos Family). *"A good-looking American-bred filly, she's likeable".*

192. INTIMACY (IRE) ★★★
ch.f. *Teofilo – Skiphall (Halling).*
March 12. Fifth foal. 65,000Y. Tattersalls December. Brian Grassick. Half-sister to the Grade 1 10f E P Taylor Stakes and Group 2 10f Prix Jean Romanet winner Folk Opera (by Singspiel) and to the quite useful 12f and hurdles winner Art Trend (by Hawk Wing). The dam, placed 5 times at 3 yrs in France, stayed 10.5f and is a half-sister to 7 winners including the 2-y-o listed winner Innocent Air and the French and US listed winner and US Grade 1 placed Skipping. The second dam, Minskip (by The Minstrel), won once at 2 yrs and is a sister to the US Grade 2 winner Savinio and a half-sister to the Italian dual Group 1 winner St Hilarion and the Group 3 winner Ballet De France (dam of the dual Group 1 winner Muhtarram) (Mrs Y M G Jacques). *"She needs to strengthen but she's a nice filly and she moves well".*

193. ISATIS ★★★
ch.f. *Zamindar – Isis (Royal Academy).*
March 9. Second foal. 17,000Y. Tattersalls October Book 1. Not sold. The dam, placed once over 6f from 2 starts at 2 yrs, is a half-sister to 3 winners including the Group 2 6f Gimcrack Stakes winner Sir Gerry. The second dam, Incredulous (by Indian Ridge), a useful 3-y-o 1m winner, is a half-sister to 6 winners. (Dr C M★Wills). *"This is an active filly and she has plenty of character".*

194. JORUM ★★★
b.f. *Dansili – Grail (Quest For Fame).*
January 15. Seventh foal. 70,000foal. Tattersalls December. Airlie Stud. Closely related to the quite useful 4-y-o 7f winner Aliceinwonderland (by Danehill) and half-sister to the fairly useful 2-y-o 6f winner Divine Right (by Observatory) and the fair 6f winner Opus Dei (by Oasis Dream). The dam won once over 12f in France and is a half-sister to 5 winners including the Group 3 Coventry Stakes winner and subsequent US Grade 2 winner Three Valleys. The second dam, Skiable (by Niniski), won four times at up to 9f in France and the USA and is a half-sister to the outstanding broodmare Hasili (dam of the Group/Grade 1 winners Banks Hill, Intercontinental and Heat Haze and the Group 2 winners Cacique and Dansili). (Airlie Stud). *"A nice filly but she won't be an early 2-y-o, she needs a little time".*

195. KING OF DUDES ★★★
b.c. *Dansili – Leto (Diesis).*
February 26. Second foal. 120,000foal. Tattersalls December. Dwayne Woods. The dam is an unplaced half-sister to the Group 1 12f Oaks winner Light Shift, to the Group 2 10.5f Tattersalls Gold Cup and Group 3 10f Brigadier Gerard Stakes winner Shiva, to the high-class Group 2 12f Prix Jean de Chaudenay and Group 3 12f Prix Foy winner Limnos and the useful 7f and listed 1m winner Burning Sunset. The second dam, Lingerie (by Shirley Heights), placed 7 times in France, is a half-sister to 4 winners including the French listed placed Evocatrice. (W A Tinkler). *"A Dansili colt with plenty of scope, he's nice".*

196. MALEKOV (IRE) ★★★
b.c. *Dansili – Young And Daring (Woodman).*
April 11. Half-brother to the useful 2-y-o 6f winner and listed 10f and 12f placed Daring Ransom (by Red Ransom). The dam, a stakes winner in the USA, is a half-sister to 8 winners including two other US stakes winners. (Al Asayl). *"He's grown quite a bit, I like him and he moves well".*

197. MORANT BAY (IRE) ★★★ ♠
b.f. *Montjeu – Quad's Melody (Spinning World).*
April 4. Fourth foal. Goffs Orby. €50,000Y. McKeever Bloodstock. Half-sister to a winner in Hong Kong by Malibu Moon. The dam won the Group 3 Prix d'Aumale at 2 yrs and is a half-sister to 3 winners including Bonapartiste (Grade 2 Del Mar Handicap). The second dam, Fab's Melody (by Devil's Bag), is a placed half-

sister to 2 winners. (N Martin). *"An active filly that uses herself well"*.

198. ~~MORPHIUS~~ POPULAR ★★★★★
b.f. Oasis Dream – Midsummer (Kingmambo).
March 18. Second foal. Sister to the high-class Group 1 Breeders Cup Filly & Mare Turf, Prix Vermeille, Yorkshire Oaks and Nassau Stakes (twice) winner Midday. The dam, a quite useful 11f winner and listed-placed over 12f, is a half-sister to numerous winners including the Oaks and Fillies Mile winner Reams of Verse, the Eclipse Stakes and Phoenix Champion Stakes winner Elmaamul. The second dam, Modena (by Roberto), is an unraced half-sister to the smart 2-y-o 7f winner and Queen Elizabeth II Stakes third Zaizafon – herself the dam of Zafonic. (Khalid Abdulla). *"This filly is very nice in every way. She has quite immature joints at present so we'll take our time with her, but they are improving and she should be worth waiting for"*.

199. MURMUR (IRE) ★★★
b.f. Marju – Siphon Melody (Siphon).
March 22. Second foal. 26,000Y. Tattersalls October Book 2. Anthony Stroud. The dam, a minor winner of 4 races at 3 and 4 yrs in the USA, is a half-sister to 10 winners including the US Grade 2 winner Talloires. The second dam, Logiciel (by Known Fact), a listed-placed winner of 4 races at 3 yrs in France, is a half-sister to 7 winners including the listed winner Frenetique (the dam of 3 stakes winners including the Grade 1 Gran Criterium winner Will Dancer). (R C Tooth). *"An active filly, she should make a 2-y-o"*.

200. NATURAL BLOOM (IRE) ★★★
b.f. Galileo – Dedicated Lady (Pennine Walk).
April 18. Thirteenth living foal. 350,000Y. Tattersalls October Book 1. Sir Robert Ogden. Closely related to the Irish 8.5f (at 2 yrs) and listed 10f winner and Prix de l'Arc de Triomphe fourth Acropolis and to the fair Irish 12f winner De Laurentiis (both by Sadler's Wells) and half-sister to the smart Group 2 12f Ribblesdale Stakes and Group 2 12.5f Prix de la Royallieu winner Fairy Queen (by Fairy King), the smart Group 2 1m Falmouth Stakes winner Tashawak and the fair 6f (at 2 yrs) and 1m winner of 8 races Speedfit Free (both by Night Shift). The dam, a useful Irish 2-y-o 5f and 6f winner, was listed-placed and is a half-sister to 5 winners including the German listed winner and Group 3 third Silk Petal (herself dam of the listed winner Star Tulip). The second dam, Salabella (by Sallust), is a placed half-sister to 7 winners including the Irish St Leger and the Grosser Preis von Baden winner M-Lolshan. (Sir Robert Ogden). *"A nice filly but most of the family have needed time and she'll be the same"*.

201. POLY POMONA ★★★
b.f. Green Desert – Maganda (Sadler's Wells).
January 20. Fourth foal. 450,000Y. Tattersalls October Book 1. Dwayne Woods. Closely related to the useful Irish 2-y-o 6f winner and Group 3 Anglesey Stakes third Rudolf Valentino (by Oasis Dream) and to the quite useful 1m and 10f winner Akhmatova (by Cape Cross). The dam, a quite useful 10f winner, is a sister to the listed winners In The Limelight and On The Nile and a half-sister to 3 winners including the German and Italian Group 1 winner Kutub. The second dam, Minnie Habit (by Habitat), an Irish 4-y-o 9f winner, is closely related to the dual Group 3 sprint winner Bermuda Classic (herself dam of the Coronation Stakes winner Shake The Yoke) and a half-sister to 6 winners. (W A Tinkler). *"A deep filly, but she's only just come in so she's just cantering at this stage"*.

202. PORTRAITOFMYLOVE (IRE) ★★★
b.f. Azamour – Flashing Green (Green Desert).
March 6. Seventh foal. 240,000Y. Tattersalls October Book 2. Dwayne Woods. Half-sister to 3 winners including the German listed winner and Group 3 placed Flashing Colour (by Pivotal). The dam, a German 3-y-o winner, is a half-sister to 6 winners including the 2-y-o 5f and 7f Italian listed winner and Group 2 1m Falmouth Stakes second Croeso Cariad, the Irish listed 12f winner and Coronation Stakes and Irish Oaks third Mona Lisa and the Irish 2-y-o listed 7f Debutante Stakes winner Photogenic. The second dam, Colorsnap (by Shirley Heights), is an unraced half-sister to Colorspin (winner of the Irish Oaks and dam of the Group 1 winners Opera House, Kayf Tara and Zee Zee Top), Bella Colora (winner of the Prix de l'Opera and dam of the very smart colt Stagecraft) and the Irish Champion Stakes winner Cezanne. (W A Tinkler). *"Another filly that's only just arrived, she's nice"*.

203. REGENCY (GER) ★★★
ch.c. Galileo – Reem Dubai (Nashwan).
May 12. Tenth foal. Half-brother to the US Grade 1 Beverly D Stakes winner Royal Highness (by Monsun), to the German Group 3 winner Royal Dubai (by Dashing Blade) and the moderate Irish 9f winner Ardwelshin (by Ajdayt). The dam was placed once over 12f and is a half-sister to 2 winners including the dam of the Group 1 Dubai World Cup winner Electrocutionist and to the placed dam of the Group 1 German Derby winner Robertico. The second dam, Gesedeh (by Ela-Mana-Mou), a smart middle-distance filly and winner of the Group 3 10.5f Prix de Flore and the Pretty Polly Stakes, was second in the Group 2 Sun Chariot Stakes and is a half-sister to the top-class middle-distance stayer Arcross. (Gestut Enzean). *"A well-balanced colt and a good mover, he isn't over-big but he needs to strengthen. His late foaling date suggests he'll take time".*

204. SONGBIRD (IRE) ★★★★
ch.f. Danehill Dancer – Mine Excavation (Galileo).
March 6. Second foal. 330,000Y. Tattersalls October Book 1. Sir Robert Ogden. The dam is an unraced three-parts sister to the Group 1 10.5f Prix Lupin and US Grade 2 1m winner Johann Quatz and to the French 10.5f to 13.5f listed winner Walter Willy and a half-sister to 8 winners including the Group 1 Prix du Jockey Club and Group 1 Prix Lupin winner Hernando. The second dam, Whakilyric (by Miswaki), winner the Group 3 7f Prix du Calvados and third in the Prix de la Salamandre and the Prix de la Foret, is a half-sister to 6 winners. (Sir Robert Ogden). *"A nice filly and a good mover, she'll make a 2-y-o later on".*

205. SPIRITOFTOMINTOUL ★★★
b.br.c. Authorized – Diamond Line (Linamix).
April 19. Fourth foal. 30,000Y. Tattersalls October Book 2. Half-brother to the modest 14f and hurdles winner Diamond Frontier (by Sadler's Wells). The dam ran once unplaced and is a sister to the Group 3 Prix de Royaumont winner Diasilixa and the Group 2 10.5f Prix Greffulhe winner Diamond Mix and a half-sister to 7 winners including the Group 3 10.5f Prix Penelope winner Diamond Dance and the Group 2 placed Diamonaka (the dam of 3 French Group winners). The second dam, Diamond Seal (by Persian Bold), won 3 races including the listed 10f Woodpark Stud Stakes and is a half-sister to 2 winners. (Angus Dundee Distillers plc). *"A tall colt that needs time, he's a good mover".*

206. STATEOS (IRE) ★★
b.c. Acclamation – Mary Arnold (Hernando).
January 28. First foal. €48,000Y. Goffs February. BBA (Ire). The dam ran once unplaced and is a half-sister to numerous winners including the Group 1 Criterium de Saint-Cloud winner Linda's Lad. The second dam, Colza (by Alleged), a quite useful 2-y-o 1m winner, is a half-sister to 10 winners including the Group 3 6f July Stakes winner Wharf and the top-class broodmare Docklands (dam of the Arc winner Rail Link). (Niarchos Family). *"He's a bit of a character but he's beginning to settle down now in his work. Difficult to assess at this stage".*

207. SYMFONY (IRE) ★★★
b.f. Monsun – Musicanna (Cape Cross).
February 5. Second foal. 45,000Y. Tattersalls October Book 1. Charlie Gordon-Watson. The dam, a smart listed 1m winner of 4 races, was third in the Group 1 Falmouth Stakes and the Group 1 Sun Chariot Stakes and is a half-sister to 7 winners. The second dam, Upend (by Main Reef), a smart winner of 3 races from 10f to 12f including the Group 3 St Simon Stakes and the listed Galtres Stakes, was second in the Group 3 Princess Royal Stakes and is a half-sister to 6 winners including the dam of the high-class stayer and champion hurdler Royal Gait. (Al Asayl). *"A good mover, she's a small filly but she has grown a bit".*

208. SYMPOSIA ★★★
ch.f. Galileo – Emplane (Irish River).
March 24. Closely related to the minor French 11f winner Coach Lane (by Barathea) and half-sister to smart 1m (at 2 yrs) and Group 3 10.4f Musidora Stakes winner Aviate, to the very useful 2-y-o dual 7f winner Wingwalker, the 2-y-o Group 3 7f Prix la Rochette winner and Group 1 placed Early March (all by Dansili), the fairly useful French 10f winner Itinerary (by Dr Fong) and the quite useful 7f winner Painted

Sky (by Rainbow Quest). The dam, a useful 3-y-o 1m winner, is a sister to the useful 2-y-o 1m winner Boatman and a half-sister to the quite useful 2-y-o 7f winner Palisade. The second dam, Peplum (by Nijinsky), a useful winner of the listed 11.3f Cheshire Oaks, is a half-sister to the top class filly Al Bahathri, winner of the 1,000 Guineas and the Coronation Stakes. (Khalid Abdulla). *"A nice filly, she's active and should make a 2-y-o later on"*.

209. THOMAS CHIPPENDALE (IRE) ★★★
b.c. *Dansili – All My Loving (Sadler's Wells)*.
February 22. First foal. 375,000Y. Tattersalls October Book 1. Sir Robert Ogden. The dam, a smart 10f winner and third in the Oaks and Irish Oaks, is a sister to the Irish 1,000 Guineas winner Yesterday and to the Group 1 7f Moyglare Stud Stakes winner and Irish 1,000 Guineas, Oaks and Irish Oaks placed Quarter Moon. The second dam, Jude (by Darshaan), a moderate 10f placed maiden, is a sister to the very useful Irish listed 14f winner and Irish Oaks third Arrikala and to the useful Irish 12f listed winner Alouette (herself dam of the Champion Stakes winner Alborada and the German triple Group 1 winner Albanova) and a half-sister to the very smart Group 2 10f Nassau Stakes and Sun Chariot Stakes winner Last Second (dam of the Irish 2,000 Guineas winner Aussie Rules). (Sir Robert Ogden). *"A big, good-moving colt that needs time"*.

210. TICKLED PINK (IRE) ★★★
b.f. *Invincible Spirit – Cassandra Go (Indian Ridge)*.
May 5. Closely related to the fairly useful dual 5f winner Neverletme Go and the fair 5f winner Mannikko (both by Green Desert) and half-sister to Irish 1,000 Guineas, Nassau Stakes and Sun Chariot Stakes winner Halfway To Heaven (by Pivotal) and the Group 3 6f Summer Stakes winner Theann (by Rock Of Gibraltar). The dam, a very smart winner of the Group 2 5f Kings Stand Stakes, is a full or half-sister to 7 winners including the smart Group 3 6f Coventry Stakes winner and Irish 2,000 Guineas second Verglas. The second dam, Rahaam (by Secreto), a fairly useful 3-y-o 7f winner, is a half-sister to 8 winners including the French 2,000 Guineas third Glory Forever. (Trevor Stewart). *"This is an active filly that should make a 2-y-o"*.

211. TIGER CLIFF (IRE) ★★★
b.c. *Tiger Hill – Verbania (In The Wings)*.
March 26. Fifth foal. 27,000Y. Tattersalls October Book 1. Highflyer Bloodstock/ Stefford Bloodstock. Half-brother to the quite useful 2010 2-y-o 7f winner Kalahaag (by Iffraaj), to the fair 12f winner Summerlea (by Alhaarth) and a 2-y-o winner abroad by Bertolini. The dam, an Irish 10f winner, is a half-sister to the useful 2-y-o 5.5f winner Pescara and to the useful French listed 10.8f winner Mistra (herself dam of the Group 1 Prix Saint-Alary winner Marotta). The second dam, Mackla (by Caerleon), won the Group 3 1m Prix d'Aumale and is a half-sister to 6 winners. (W★Ponsonby). *"A nice colt, he's grown and now has plenty of scope. Likeable"*.

212. TOUCH GOLD (IRE) ★★★★
b.c. *Oasis Dream – Seek Easy (Seeking The Gold)*.
February 4. Fifth foal. Half-brother to the very useful 1m winner (at 2 yrs) and dual Group 3 placed Dancing David (by Danehill Dancer), to the quite useful 12f winner Ordination (by Fantastic Light) and a 3-y-o winner in Japan by Boundary. The dam is an unraced half-sister to 3 winners including the US Grade 2 winner Conserve. The second dam, Slew And Easy (by Slew O'Gold), won once at 4 yrs in the USA and is a half-sister to 13 winners including the champion Canadian horses La Voyageuse, L'Enjoleur and Medaille d'Or. (Al Asayl). *"A nice colt with plenty of size and scope"*.

213. VARIETY SHOW (IRE) ★★★
b.f. *Royal Applause – Sensasse (Imperial Ballet)*.
February 7. First foal. Goffs Orby. €45,000Y. Kern/Lillingston. The dam, a quite useful 2-y-o 6f winner, is a half-sister to 2 winners including the Group 3 6f Ballyogan Stakes winner of 6 races and dual Group 1 placed Lesson In Humility. The second dam, Vanity (by Thatching), is a placed half-sister to 4 winners including the listed winner and smart broodmare Ffestiniog. (De La Warr Racing). *"This is a nice filly, she does nothing wrong and it's a speedy pedigree"*.

214. VASTLY (USA) ★★★
b.c. *Mizzen Mast – Valentine Band (Dixieland Band)*.

May 16. Brother to the French 1m, 10f (both at 2 yrs) and listed 9f winner Putney Bridge and half-brother to the Irish 1m (at 2 yrs) and Group 3 10f winner Await The Dawn (by Giant's Causeway) and the fairly useful 11f to 13f winner of 4 races Spruce (by Maria's Mon). The dam, the very useful 10f winner, is a half-sister to the French 7f (at 2 yrs) and listed 1m winner Multiplex, to the very useful 10f and Irish Group 3 14f winner Memorise, the useful 7.5f winner and listed 1m placed Sparkling Water and the useful 2-y-o 7f winner Fully Invested. The second dam, Shirley Valentine (by Shirley Heights), a useful 12f winner, was fourth in the Park Hill Stakes and the Lancashire Oaks and is a sister to the high class Irish Derby second Deploy and a half-sister to the Derby and Irish Derby winner Commander in Chief, the champion 2-y-o and miler Warning and the Grade 1 10f Flower Bowl Invitational Handicap winner Yashmak. (Khalid Abdulla). *"He's grown a lot so he'll need time, but he's a nice colt and a good mover".*

215. ZEYRAN (IRE) ★★★
ch.f. Galileo – Chervil (Dansili).
February 22. Second foal. 80,000Y. **Tattersalls October Book 2. Henry Cecil.** Sister to Thymesthree, unplaced in one start at 2 yrs in 2010. The dam, a quite useful 6f winner, is closely related to the US Grade 1 0f Yellow Ribbon Stakes winner Light Jig and a half-sister to 9 winners including the very useful French 2-y-o listed 1m winner Battle Dore. The second dam, Nashmeel (by Blushing Groom), won the Group 2 1m Prix d'Astarte, was second in the Prix Jacques le Marois, the Yellow Ribbon Invitational and the Matriarch Stakes and is a half-sister to 9 winners. (V I Araci). *"This filly has grown during the winter, she's nice and a good mover".*

216. UNNAMED ★★★★ Elbe
b.f. Dansili – Imroz (Nureyev).
January 30. Half-sister to the fairly useful listed 10f winner Posteritas (by Lear Fan), to the useful 2-y-o dual 7f winner Apex Star (by Diesis) and the fair 10f winner Mainland (by Empire Maker). The dam, a useful 6f (at 2 yrs) and 7f winner, was listed-placed and is a half-sister to 5 winners including the useful 3-y-o listed 1m winner Insinuate. The second dam, All At Sea (by Riverman), a high-class winner of 5 races from 1m to 10.4f including the Group 1 Prix du Moulin, is a half-sister to the Free Handicap winner Over the Ocean, the listed 10f winner Quandary and the US stakes winner Full Virtue. (Khalid Abdulla). *"A very nice filly and I feel she'll make a 2-y-o".*

217. UNNAMED ★★★
b.c. Dansili – Indication (by Sadler's Wells).
March 19. Second foal. The dam, a fair 9.5f winner, is a half-sister to 3 winners including the Group 3 7f Supreme Stakes winner Stronghold. The second dam, Insinuate (by Mr Prospector), a useful listed 1m winner, is a half-sister to numerous winners including the useful 6f and 7f winner and listed-placed Imroz. (Khalid Abdulla). *"A lovely colt, he has scope but is obviously not an early 2-y-o".*

218. UNNAMED ★★★★★
b.c. Galileo – Kind (Danehill).
February 25. Third foal. Brother to the champion 2010 2-y-o, Group 1 7f Dewhurst Stakes and Group 2 1m Royal Lodge Stakes winner Frankel and closely related to the very useful Group 3 11.5f Derby Trial winner Bullet Train (by Sadler's Wells). The dam, a dual listed winner over 5f and 6f, was Group 3 placed and is a half-sister to the Arlington Million and Tattersalls Rogers Gold Cup winner Powerscourt and to the smart 14f winner of 3 races Brimming. The second dam, Rainbow Lake (by Rainbow Quest), a smart winner of 3 races including the Group 3 12f Lancashire Oaks and the listed 10f Ballymacoll Stud Stakes, is a half-sister to several winners including the useful middle-distance winner Vertex. (Khalid Abdulla). *"This colt is stronger looking than his full-brother Frankel was at this stage. He's not a big colt, but he's nice".*

219. UNNAMED ★★★★
b.c. Dansili – Native Justice (Alleged).
May 5. Half-brother to a winner over jumps by Sadler's Wells. The dam, a French listed 10f winner, was third in the Group 2 13.5f Prix de Pomone and is a half-sister to the very smart St Hilarion and to the dam of the Irish Champion Stakes winner Muhtarram. The second dam, Fabulous Native (by Le Fabuleux), is out of a close relative of Exclusive Native. *"A very nice colt, he has plenty of size and scope".*

220. UNNAMED ★★★
b.c. Empire Maker – Reams Of Verse (Nureyev).
May 20. Brother to the US Grade 3 placed Eagle Poise and half-brother to the smart listed 10f winner of 4 races Many Volumes (by Chester House), to the useful 2-y-o 7f winner and Group 3 7f Prestige Stakes second Ithaca (by Distant View), the fairly useful 2-y-o 6f winner Western Verse (by Gone West) and the fair 1m to 10f winner General Knowledge (by Diesis). The dam, a very smart winner of the Oaks, the Fillies Mile, the Musidora Stakes and the May Hill Stakes, is a half-sister to numerous winners including the high-class Group 1 10f Coral Eclipse Stakes and Group 1 10f Phoenix Champion Stakes winner Elmaamul. The second dam, Modena (by Roberto), is an unraced half-sister to the smart 2-y-o 7f winner and Queen Elizabeth II Stakes third Zaizafon – herself the dam of Zafonic. (Khalid Abdulla). *"A nice colt with a good temperament, he has to strengthen and thicken out a great deal. He was a late foal and he's tall, quite narrow and leggy at the moment. Could be nice one day"*.

221. UNNAMED ★★★
b.c. Dalakhani – Top Crystal (Sadler's Wells).
May 5. Half-brother to the smart Group 3 7f Minstrel Stakes winner of 5 races Three Rocks (by Rock Of Gibraltar). The dam ran once unplaced and is a full or half-sister to 6 winners. The second dam, State Crystal (by High Estate), winner of the Group 3 12f Lancashire Oaks and placed in the Yorkshire Oaks and the Prix Vermeille, is a half-sister to 6 winners including the Group 1 Fillies' Mile winner Crystal Music. (M D Poland). *"A lovely colt, but he's backward at the moment and hopefully we'll see him out later in the year"*.

MICK CHANNON

222. ALTONA (IRE) ★★★★
b.f. Redback – Flawless (Warning).
February 4. Seventh foal. 27,000Y. Tattersalls October Book 2. Gill Richardson. Half-sister to the useful 2-y-o 7f and 1m winner Duke Of Tuscany (by Medicean) and to the moderate 10f winner Jelly Mo (by Royal Applause). The dam, a very useful 2-y-o 7f winner, was third in the Group 2 1m Falmouth Stakes and second in the Group 3 1m May Hill Stakes and is a half-sister to 5 winners. The second dam, Made Of Pearl (by Nureyev), a useful French 7f listed winner, was Group 3 placed and is a half-sister to 5 winners. (Mr D Bastian). *"A lovely filly, she needs some sun because she's backward but she shows enough speed and she'll be better off in May than she is now. She's got speed, it's whether the engine's there"*.

223. ARNOLD LANE ★★★
b.c. Footstepsinthesand – Capriole (Noverre).
March 18. Second foal. Goffs Orby. €60,000Y. Gill Richardson. The dam is an unraced half-sister to 8 winners including the dam of the Group 1 winner Hibaayib. The second dam, Zonda (by Fabulous Dancer), a useful listed-placed 5f to 8.5f winner here, subsequently won twice in the USA. (John Webster). *"A nice horse that goes well. Six furlongs in mid-season will suit him and he's a smashing horse – I'm very happy with him, he's a nice colt"*.

224. CAITLIN ★★★
b.f. Dylan Thomas – Kassiopeia (Galileo).
January 30. Second foal. Half-sister to the fair 2010 2-y-o 7f winner Arabian Star (by Green Desert). The dam, a quite useful 12f winner, was fourth in a listed event and is a half-sister to several winners including the French listed-placed Craft Fair. The second dam, Brush Strokes (by Cadeaux Genereux), is an unraced half-sister to several winners including the Group 1 Racing Post Trophy second Mudeer. (George & Jackie Smith). *"One for seven furlongs later on in the year, but she's grand and she goes well, so she'll be alright"*.

225. CALENDAR KING ★★★
b.c. Three Valleys – Fanny's Fancy (Groom Dancer).
February 4. Third foal. £16,000Y. Doncaster Premier. Gill Richardson. Half-brother to the fair 2010 2-y-o 6f winner Jolah (by Oasis Dream). The dam, a fairly useful dual 6f winner, was listed placed. The second dam, Fanny's Choice (by Fairy King), a fairly useful 2-y-o 6f winner, is a half-sister to 3 winners. *"A nice horse that has bags of speed, he's one that we'll get going during April and I like him. From the first crop of Three Valleys, he's one of those who I think is certainly alright, but it's what he does when we start putting a gun to his head"*.

226. CAPTAIN CARDINGTON ★★★
b.c. Strategic Prince – Alkaffeyah
(Sadler's Wells).
April 29. Twelfth foal. 72,000Y. Tattersalls October Book 2. Gill Richardson. Half-brother to the smart 2-y-o 7f winner and Group 2 1m Royal Lodge Stakes second Tholjanan, to the hurdles winner Hashid (both by Darshaan), the listed March Stakes winner and Group 2 Jockey Club Stakes third Ta-Lim (by Ela-Mana-Mou), the 10f and 12f winner Mudaa-Eb and the quite useful 2-y-o 6f winner Kharir (both by Machiavellian). The dam is an unraced sister to the listed 12f Galtres Stakes winner and Group 1 12f Prix Vermeille third Larrocha and a half-sister to the outstanding middle-distance stayer Ardross and the Pretty Polly Stakes winner Gesedeh. The second dam, Le Melody (by Levmoss), won both her starts, over 7f and 10f, and is a half-sister to the Irish 1,000 Guineas winner Arctique Royale (herself dam of the Group winners Modhish and Russian Snows). (John Webster). *"A nice horse, he won't be real early but he'll be ready when the six furlong races come along and he's making up into a nice horse".*

227. DOCTOR BANNER ★★★
b.c. Compton Place – Icing (Polar Falcon).
March 13. Third foal. Doncaster Premier. £21,000Y. Gill Richardson. Half-brother to a 2-y-o winner in Russia by Lando. The dam, a fair 2-y-o 7f winner, is a half-sister to 4 winners including the useful Italian 2-y-o 7f winner and subsequent US stakes winner La Martina. The second dam, Dance Steppe (by Rambo Dancer), showed no form but is a half-sister to 8 winners including the smart 12f winner Carlingford Rose. (Insignia Racing, Ensign). *"A smashing little horse, he's growing all the time and he's doing everything alright. I think he'll probably be better over six/seven furlongs but he certainly goes well enough to say he's capable of winning something".*

228. ESSELL ★★★
ch.f. Singspiel – Londonnetdotcom
(Night Shift).
March 13. Fourth foal. 50,000Y. Tattersalls October Book 1. G Howson. Half-brother to the fair 7f winner Loveinanelevator (by Dr Fong). The dam, a useful 7f (at 2 yrs) and listed 1m winner, was second in the Group 3 Prix du Calvados and is a half-sister to one winner. The second dam, Hopeful Sign (by Warning), ran once unplaced and is a half-sister to 8 winners including the Group 3 winners Ecologist, Green Reef and Infrasonic and the dam of the St Leger winner Toulon. (Derek & Jean Clee). *"Yes, she's nice, she's grown and she's a big filly now. I trained the dam and this filly has the size and scope to be a racehorse, probably starting off at seven furlongs".*

229. FACTORY TIME ★★★
b.c. Baltic King – Mark One (Mark Of Esteem).
January 30. Fourth foal. 20,000Y. Tattersalls October Book 2. Gill Richardson. Half-brother to the fair 6f (at 2 yrs) to 2m and hurdles winner Ambrose Princess (by Chevalier). The dam, a quite useful 10f and 12f winner, is a half-sister to 2 winners. The second dam, One Wild Oat (by Shareef Dancer), won once at 3 yrs in France and is a half-sister to 12 winners including Arctic Owl (Group 1 Irish St Leger) and Marooned (Group 1 Sydney Cup) and the very smart broodmare Much Too Risky (the dam of four stakes winners). (Jaber Abdullah). *"A lovely horse, he has bags of speed and does everything nicely. He's big and strong and he'll be running at the end of April or early May and we'll see how good his is. He'll be better at six furlongs but he'll be fine at five as well".*

230. FILLIONAIRE ★★★
b.f. Kyllachy – Autumn Pearl (Orpen).
April 21. Third foal. 55,000Y. Tattersalls October Book 2. R Frisby. Half-sister to the useful 2010 2-y-o 6f winner and listed-placed Pabusar (by Oasis Dream) and to the modest dual 6f winner Thaliwarru (by Barathea). The dam, a winner of 3 races over 5f and 6f at 2 and 3 yrs, was second in the Group 2 Temple Stakes and is a half-sister to 2 winners abroad. The second dam, Cyclone Flyer (by College Chapel), won once at 3 yrs and is a half-sister to 8 winners including the Group 2 King's Stand Stakes winner Bolshoi. (Mrs Ann Black). *"A lovely filly, she was a slow starter but she needed a bit of time and she's going the right way now. She's nice and I like her, but we won't see her until the middle of the season I wouldn't have thought".*

231. FLASHY STAR ★★★
ch.f. Mr Greeley – Galileo's Star (Galileo).
February 16. First foal. 36,000Y. Tattersalls October Book 1. Gill Richardson. The dam, a useful 2-y-o 7f winner and 7f listed placed, was fourth in a Grade 1 event in the USA and is a half-sister to the Irish 7f (at 2 yrs) and listed 1m winner Anzari. The second dam, Anazara (by Trempolino), a 1m winner at 3 yrs in Ireland, is a half-sister to 8 winners including the high-class Prix Ganay and Prix d'Harcourt winner Astarabad and the useful Irish winner at up to 10f Asmara (herself dam of the triple Group 1 winner Azamour). (Jaber Abdullah). *"Out of a Galileo mare, she's one for the middle of the season. I like her a lot, she's a big filly and she just needs a bit of time".*

232. GATEPOST (IRE) ★★★★
b.c. Footstepsinthesand – Mandama (Warning).
April 1. Sixth foal. €20,000Y. Tattersalls Ireland. Emerald Bloodstock. Half-brother to the unraced 2010 2-y-o Rio Maid (by Captain Rio). The dam, an Irish 2-y-o 7f winner, was listed-placed and is a half-sister to 6 winners including the Group 1 5f Prix de l'Abbaye winner and smart sire Namid and the very useful Group 3 6f and 7.5f winner Noelani. The second dam, Dawnsio (by Tate Gallery), a useful winner of the listed Topaz Sprint Stakes in Ireland, is a half-sister to 3 winners. *"A lovely horse, but again he's one of those that will win but you ask yourself - how good is he going to be? I think he could be a very nice horse. He's good-looking and I like him a lot, I think he's a bloody nice horse and one of the better ones".*

233. GOLD SHOW ★★★
gr.f. Sir Percy – Pearl Bright (Kaldoun).
May 5. Sixth foal. 30,000Y. Tattersalls October Book 2. Gill Richardson. Half-sister to the useful 6f (at 2 yrs) and 7f winner and Group 2 6f Mill Reef Stakes third Berbice (by Acclamation), to the quite useful 10f and 12f winner Bebopalula (by Galileo) and a winner in Greece by Namid. The dam, a quite useful 2-y-o 7f winner, is a half-sister to 4 winners. The second dam, Coastal Jewel (by Kris), is an unraced half-sister to 5 winners. (Jaber Abdullah). *"A lovely filly, she was a fairly late foal but she's showed me that she's OK and I like her an awful lot. We're just going quietly with her really because she's another one for the mid-summer".*

234. GOOD OF LUCK ★★
b.c. Authorized – Oops Pettie (Machiavellian).
May 5. Tenth foal. 38,000Y. Tattersalls October Book 2. Gill Richardson. Half-brother to the useful 14f listed winner Orpington (by Hernando), to the fair 1m winner Oopsie Daisy (by Singspiel) and the modest 11f and 12f winner of 6 races Stuttgart (by Groom Dancer) and the moderate 12f to 2m winner Whoopsie (by Unfuwain). The dam, a fairly useful winner of 3 races over an extended 10f, is a half-sister to 5 winners including the listed Virginia Stakes winner Moselle. The second dam, Miquette (by Fabulous Dancer), won over 12f and 13.5f in France including a listed event and is a half-sister to 6 winners including the Group 3 Prix de Pomone winner Moquerie (herself the dam of 4 listed winners) and the listed winner Rivermaid (dam of the Group 3 winners Movieland and Only Star). (Jaber Abdullah). *"A smashing big horse, but he's not a slob and he'll be one for seven furlongs and a mile. More of a 3-y-o type really".*

235. GRAND GOLD ★★★
b.c. Librettist – Night Symphonie (Cloudings).
April 19. Fifth foal. 8,500Y. Doncaster St Leger Festival. Gill Richardson. Half-brother to the fair 1m, 10f and hurdles winner Buddy Holly (by Reel Buddy) and to a winner in Italy by Diktat. The dam won at 3 yrs in Germany and is a half-sister to 12 winners including the Group 2 winner Network. The second dam, Note (by Reliancve II), won in Germany and is a half-sister to 11 winners. (Jaber Abdullah). *"He was cheap and he'll need a bit of time but he's a nice colt. We like him".*

236. LADY VICTORY ★★★
b.f. Kheleyf – Victoria Lodge (Grand Lodge).
March 19. Third foal. Doncaster Premier. £37,000Y. Gill Richardson. Half-sister to the fairly useful 2010 2-y-o 5f and 6f winner Chiswick Bey (by Elusive City). The dam is an unraced half-sister to one winner. The second dam, Lake Victoria (by Lake Coniston), was listed-placed in Ireland and is a half-sister to 5 winners including the US Grade 1 winner

Delighter and the Oaks third Oakmead. (Jaber Abdullah). *"A nice filly, she's done everything right and although I think she's more of a mid-season type she's good-looking and she has a bit of size and scope, so we're just waiting for her really".*

237. LAUGH OUT LOUD ★★
gr.f. Clodovil – Funny Girl (Darshaan).
April 20. Seventh foal. 30,000Y. Tattersalls October Book 2. Hugo Merry. Half-sister to the useful 6f (at 2 yrs), 10f and listed 12f winner Suzi's Decision (by Act One), to the fairly useful 10f and 12f winner of 4 races Pippa Greene (by Galileo), the fair 5 winner of 3 races Brynfa Boy (by Namid) and the modest 6f winner Nadinska (by Doyen). The dam was placed from 7f to 9f and is a daughter of the minor German winner Just For Fun (by Lead On Time), herself a sister to the listed Prix Herbager winner Judge Decision. (K Al Mudhaf, M Al Qatami & A Black). *"She only comes in this week but I have seen her and she's lovely. She should make a 2-y-o but I can't tell you anything more yet".*

238. LIGHT ZABEEL ★★★★
b.f. Invasor – Ashraakat (Danzig).
February 28. Ninth foal. €100,000Y. Goffs Orby. Gill Richardson. Half-sister to the quite useful 6f to 10f winner of 8 races El Dececy (by Seeking The Gold), to the quite useful 7f winner Ahdaaf (by Bahri) and the quite useful 7f (at 2 yrs) to 12f winner Hezaam (Red Ransom). The dam, a very useful 6f and 7f listed winner, is a sister to the July Cup winner Elnadim, closely related to the Irish 1,000 Guineas winner Mehthaaf and a half-sister to the Group 3 Nell Gwyn Stakes winner Khulood. The second dam, Elle Seule (by Exclusive Native), a very smart winner of the Group 3 1m Prix d'Astarte, is a half-sister to the Group/Grade 1 winners Fort Wood, Hamas and Timber Country and to the dam of Dubai Millennium. (Jaber Abdullah). *"She's a big filly, she's grown and done everything right. We paid a lot of money for her, she has a great pedigree and she'll be a nice filly later on. A lovely filly, I like her a lot but we haven't done much with her yet. She's got the size, the scope and the pedigree to be a good horse".*

239. LILYGLOVES ★★
ch.f. Imperial Dancer – Queen Of Narnia (Hunting Lion).
April 10. Second foal. Sister to the moderate 2010 5f placed 2-y-o Calormen. The dam, a fair 2-y-o 5f winner, is a sister to one winner and a half-sister to 3 winners including the useful 2-y-o 5f winner and Group 3 9f Prix de Conde second Dayglow Dancer. The second dam, Fading (by Pharly), is an unraced half-sister to 5 winners here and abroad including the US stakes-placed Petite Sonnerie. (Norman Court Stud). *"She's already started her career. I'm not worried that she didn't win because I was just getting the show on the road. There'll be a little race in her somewhere".*

240. MAJESTIC ROSE ★★★★
br.f. Imperial Dancer – Solmorin (Fraam).
February 8. Fourth foal. Half-sister to the fairly useful dual 5f winner (including at 2 yrs) Lucky Leigh, to the modest 2-y-o 6f winner Saxonette (both by Piccolo) and the modest dual 1m winner (including at 2 yrs) Alfredtheordinary (by Hunting Lion). The dam is an unplaced half-sister to 2 winners. (Jaber Abdullah). *"It's early days and because she's by Imperial Dancer I keep pinching myself, but I think she's pretty good. I bred her, she's very fast and she'll start at five furlongs but it wouldn't matter what trip she ran over. She's got a bit of size and scope and I just need her to fill out a bit. I'm very pleased with her".*

241. MAJESTIC SOUTH ★★★
ch.f. Bertolini – Tidal Chorus (Singspiel).
February 7. Second foal. £10,000Y. Doncaster Festival. Gill Richardson. Half-sister to the useful 2010 2-y-o Group 3 6f Firth Of Clyde Stakes winner Majestic Dubawi (by Dubawi). The dam ran twice unplaced and is a half-sister to 6 winners including the French listed winner South Rock. The second dam, South Shore (by Caerleon), a useful winner of 4 races at up to 12f, is a half-sister 4 winners including to the Lockinge Stakes winner Soviet Line. (Jaber Abdullah). *"We won't see her until the middle of the season but she's a smashing filly".*

242. MAJESTIC ZAFEEN ★★★
b.f. Zafeen – Arasong (Aragon).
February 15. Ninth foal. 15,000Y. Tattersalls

October Book 3. Gill Richardson. Half-sister to the quite useful triple 5f (at 2 yrs) and 6f winner Gone Hunting, to the fair dual 5f winner Ronnie Howe (both by Hunting Lion), the modest dual 7f winner (including at 2 yrs) Annie's Song (by Farfelu) and the modest 1m and 9f winner La Viola (by Fraam). The dam, a fair dual 5f winner (including at 2 yrs), is a half-sister to 8 minor winners. The second dam, Songstead (by Song), a fairly useful 6f winner of 4 races at 2 and 3 yrs, is a half-sister to 3 winners. (Jaber Abdullah). *"A smashing, big filly, she's a real 'Zafeen' in that she'll need a bit of time, but from the middle of the season I think she could be a very nice horse".*

243. MUSICALLY ★★★
b.f. Singspiel – Pelagia (Lycius).
January 27. Fourth foal. Half-sister to the useful 6f (at 2 yrs) and 1m winner and Group 2 6f Richmond Stakes second Upper Hand (by Mark Of Esteem) subsequently a winner over 1m in Hong Kong as Royal Prince and to the fair 7f (at 2 yrs) and 1m winner Dutiful (by Dubawi). The dam is a 7f fourth-placed half-sister to 4 winners including the Group 1 1m Prix Marcel Boussac and Group 2 1m Prix d'Astarte winner Lady Of Chad and the dual Group 3 Sagaro Stakes winner Alcazar. The second dam, Sahara Breeze (by Ela-Mana-Mou), a quite useful 7f and 1m placed maiden, is a half-sister to 5 winners including the Group 1 Fillies Mile winner Ivanka. (James Reppard). *"This filly has thrived since she came in and she keeps surprising me. I've trained two or three from this family, they've all been alright and I think she will be. She was very small and she's just thrived with work, so I'm very happy with her. I would have thought we'd start her at six furlongs but we'll see. I don't think she'll be out until the end of May or June time, but she's lovely".*

244. NASTROVIA (IRE) ★★★
b.f. Soviet Star – Smile Awhile (Woodman).
March 10. Tenth foal. Goffs Orby. €35,000Y. Emerald. Half-sister to the useful 2-y-o dual 5f winner and listed 7f Debutante Stakes second Caldy Dancer, to the Italian winner Star's Smile (both by Soviet Star), the fair 6f winner Just One Smile (by Desert Prince) and a winner in Japan by Lure. The dam ran once unplaced and is a sister to 3 winners including the useful performer at up to 1m Gypsy Passion. The second dam, Rua d'Oro (by El Gran Senor), won the listed Derrinstown Stud 1,000 Guineas Trial, was third in the Group 3 Matron Stakes and is a sister to the dual Irish listed winner Portico. (Box 41). *"A lovely filly, she's had a few niggling problems and she's a little bit backward, so she'll need time. I like her but you won't see her until June time".*

245. NASEEM ALYASMEEN ★★★
gr.f. Clodovil – Phillippa (Galileo).
March 31. First foal. Doncaster Premier. £44,000Y. Gill Richardson. The dam is an unraced half-sister to 4 winners including the listed Zetland Stakes winner Amir Zaman. The second dam, Kardashina (by Darshaan), won 3 races in France from 11f to 12.5f and is a half-sister to 5 winners including the listed winners Kart Star and Karmifira. (Jaber Abdullah). *"This is a very nice filly, she'll be one for later on this season, probably over seven furlongs".*

246. NAYARRA ★★★★★
b.f. Cape Cross – Massarra (Danehill).
February 12. Fourth foal. Half-sister to the fair Irish 1m winner Middle Persia (by Dalakhani) and to the fair 10f winner Tebee (by Selkirk). The dam, a useful listed 6f winner and second in the Group 2 Prix Robert Papin at 2 yrs, is a sister to one winner, closely related to the Group 1 6f Haydock Park Sprint Cup winner Invincible Spirit and a half-sister to 7 winners including the Group 3 winners Acts Of Grace and Sadian. The second dam, Rafha (by Kris), a very smart winner over 6f (at 2 yrs) and the Group 1 10.5f Prix de Diane, the Group 3 Lingfield Oaks Trial and the Group 3 May Hill Stakes, is a half-sister to 9 winners. (Prince Faisal). *"A smashing filly, an absolute diamond. Very, very nice, she's done everything I could ask of her and I'm very sweet on her at the moment. I think she's very good and we'll see her out in May".*

247. NOOR ZABEEL ★★★
b.c. Elusive Quality – Brave The Storm (Storm Cat).
May 6. Eighth foal. 50,000Y. Tattersalls October Book 1. Gill Richardson. Half-brother to the US stakes-placed winner Film Editor (by Bertrando) and to 2 minor winners

in the USA by Vindication and Cee's Tizzy. The dam was placed once at 4 yrs in the USA and is a half-sister to 11 winners including the US stakes winners Bravo Bull and Russian Tango (herself dam of the US Grade 2 winner and sire Eurosilver) and the dam of the US Grade 2 winner Muntej. The second dam, Brave Raj (by Rajab), a champion US 2-y-o filly, won the Grade 1 Breeders Cup Juvenile Fillies and is a half-sister to 2 winners. (Jaber Abdullah). "A nice horse, he'll be running in May and he shows all the right signs. Not the biggest, but he's quite sharp, he knows his job and he should be alright".

248. PETALUMA ★★★★
b.f. Teofilo – Poppo's Song (Polish Navy).
March 3. Second foal. 70,000foal. Tattersalls December. Gill Richardson. The dam, a Canadian listed stakes winner of 2 races at 3 and 4 yrs, is a half-sister to 2 winners. The second dam, Bridled Song (by Seattle Slew), is a placed half-sister to 4 winners. (Jon & Julia Aisbitt). "A gorgeous filly for later on this season. She's big, but she's done everything asked of her and I like her an awful lot".

249. PITT RIVERS ★★★
br.c. Vital Equine – Silca Boo (Efisio).
February 20. Fifth foal. Doncaster Premier. £42,000Y. Gill Richardson. Half-brother to the modest 2-y-o 6f winner Agent Boo (by Monsieur Bond). The dam, a useful 2-y-o 5f and 6f winner and listed-placed twice, is a half-sister to the very useful dual 6f winner and Group 2 6f Gimcrack Stakes second Zilch. The second dam, Bunty Boo (by Noalto), a very useful filly, won 8 races here and in Sweden including the Group 3 Arthur Guinness Flying Five and a listed 5f event at Sandown Park and is a half-sister to 4 winners. (Jon & Julia Aisbitt). "A nice colt, he's showing the right signs now after a little setback. He should be out in April if everything goes right and he shows a bit of speed".

250. PRINCESS BANU ★★★★
b.f. Oasis Dream – Paradise Isle (Bahamian Bounty).
March 14. First foal. Doncaster Premier. £33,000Y. G Howson. The dam, a useful 5f and 6f winner of 4 races (including at 2 yrs), is a full or half-sister to 9 winners. The second dam, Merry Rous (by Rousillon), a moderate 2-y-o 6f winner, is a half-sister to 5 winners including the dual Group 3 winning sprinter Tina's Pet. (Mrs Theresa Burns). "She runs in early April and she's an absolute flyer. We'll see, but she's so small that I worry about her. She's got the pedigree though and she's very sharp. She's shocked us by the speed she's showed".

251. REPRESENT (IRE) ★★★★
b.f. Exceed And Excel – Craigmill (Slip Anchor).
April 9. Thirteenth foal. 36,000Y. Tattersalls October Book 2. Gill Richardson. Half-sister to the smart 1m winner and listed-placed Castleton, the fairly useful dual 10f winner Craigstown (both by Cape Cross), the German listed winner and Group 3 placed Fleurie Domaine (by Unfuwain), the fairly useful 12f and 2m winner Astyanax (by Hector Protector), the quite useful 2-y-o 1m winner Stirling Castle (by Dubai Destination), the quite useful 10.5f winner Heather Mix (by Linamix), the quite useful 9.5f winner Oscillator (by Pivotal) and the German 2-y-o winner Global Champion (by Elnadim). The dam, a fair 2-y-o 7f winner, is a half-sister to 6 winners including the Group 3 Park Hill Stakes winner Coigach and the Park Hill Stakes second and smart broodmare Applecross. The second dam, Rynechra (by Blakeney), was a useful 12f winner and a half-sister to 6 winners. (Insignia Racing, Ensign). "She could be anything, she shows all the right signs and she's got to go and do it sometime in April or May, then we'll see if she's good enough to send her somewhere nice. I'm not worried about her winning, it's how good she'll be".

252. ROOKNRASBRYRIPPLE ★★★
b.f. Piccolo – Here To Me (Muhtarram).
March 19. Third foal. 7,200Y. Doncaster St Leger Festival. Gill Richardson. Half-sister to the modest 2010 7f placed 2-y-o Dells Breezer (by Kheleyf) and to the quite useful 2-y-o 6f winner Accede (by Acclamation). The dam, a fair 3-y-o 6f winner, is a half-sister to 2 winners out of the unraced Away To Me (by Exit To Nowhere), herself a half-sister to 5 winners. (Nigel Bunter). "She's got the speed to do five furlongs but she'll certainly do six. I do like her and they didn't pay much for her either".
TRAINERS' BARGAIN BUY

253. SAMITAR ★★★★
b.f. Rock Of Gibraltar – Aileen's Gift (Rainbow Quest).
February 1. Sixth foal. 39,000Y. Tattersalls October Book 1. Gill Richardson. Half-sister to the 2-y-o Group 3 Albany Stakes winner Nijoom Dubai (by Noverre), to the fair 7f winner of 6 races La Gifted (by Fraam) and a winner in Greece by Xaar. The dam is an unraced half-sister to 3 winners including the fairly useful listed-placed Roker Park and the dam of the Group 2 Gimcrack Stakes winner Shameel. The second dam, Joyful (by Green Desert), a fair 7f winner at 3 yrs, is a half-sister to 7 winners including the Group 1 1m Coronation Stakes winner Golden Opinion. (John Webster). *"A smashing filly, I loved her when we bought her and she just needs a bit of time. She's grown and she has scope but she shows enough speed now to show that she's going to be a very nice horse. She needs some sun and hopefully she might bloom around Ascot time"*.

254. SAVANNA DAYS ★★★★
ch.f. Danehill Dancer – Dominante (Monsun).
February 19. First foal. 150,000foal. Tattersalls December. Gill Richardson. The dam, a German listed 10f winner and second in the Group 1 German Oaks, is a half-sister to the German listed winner Deauville. The second dam, Dea (by Shareef Dancer), won once at 2 yrs in Germany and is a sister to the German listed winner and smart broodmare Dapprima. (Jon & Julia Aisbitt). *"She's a smashing, big filly with plenty of scope. I haven't done an awful lot with her but she's one for later in the year and I do like her. She could be anything and shows enough already to tell me that she's OK"*.

255. SELINDA ★★★
b.f. Piccolo – Evanesce (Lujain).
March 29. Third foal. Half-sister to the fair dual 7f winner (including at 2 yrs) Alfraamsay (by Fraam). The dam, a fair 2-y-o 6f winner, is a half-sister to one winner. The second dam, Search Party (Rainbow Quest), a fair 8.3f and 10f placed maiden, is a half-sister to the 6f (at 2 yrs) and subsequent Grade 1 10f Santa Barbara Handicap winner Bequest and to the useful 2-y-o 7f winner Fitzcarraldo. (Dave & Gill Hedley). *"She looks sharp and she'll be a 2-y-o for sure. I'm not saying she'll be a superstar but you never know, because she's got enough size and she's shown enough to win"*.

256. SHAMROCKED (IRE) ★★★★
b.c. Rock Of Gibraltar – Hallowed Park (Barathea).
March 29. First foal. Goffs Orby. €72,000Y. Gill Richardson. The dam is an unraced half-sister to 3 winners including the Derby second Walk In The Park. The second dam, Classic Park (by Robellino), won 3 races including the Irish 1,000 Guineas and is a half-sister to 10 winners including the US Grade 2 winner Rumpipumpy. (Box 41). *"A lovely horse, he is. One for later in the year, he looks to have a good attitude and he's a great mover. I think he'll be a very nice horse"*.

257. SHOW FLOWER ★★★★
b.f. Shamardal – Baldemosa (Lead On Time).
April 10. Tenth foal. 54,000Y. Tattersalls October Book 2. Gill Richardson. Half-sister to the very useful 7f winner of 4 races here and in the UAE Sirocco Breeze (by Green Desert), to the 5f and 6f winner of 15 races (including when useful at 2 yrs) Caustic Wit (by Cadeaux Genereux), the modest 8.5f winner Seldemosa (by Selkirk) and a winner in Greece by Diktat. The dam won over 1m in France at 3 yrs and is a half-sister to 4 winners including the Group 1 5.5f Prix Robert Papin winner Balbonella (herself dam of the top-class sprinter Anabaa and the French 1,000 Guineas winner Always Loyal) and the French listed 12f winner Bamwhite. The second dam, Bamieres (by Riverman), was placed fourth twice in France. (Jaber Abdullah). *"A smashing filly, she goes nicely and she'll be running in May, then we'll see how good she is and if she's the type for Royal Ascot. She had a little setback that held us up but she's fine again now and she goes well.*

258. SIGNIFER (IRE) ★★★
br.c. Titus Livius – Extravagance (King's Best).
March 16. First foal. 15,000Y. Tattersalls October Book 3. Gill Richardson. The dam, a fair 6f (at 2 yrs) and 7f placed maiden, is a half-sister to 2 winners. The second dam, Meritxell (by Thatching), won once at 3 yrs in France and is a half-sister to 10 winners including the Group 2 winner Almushtarak. (Insignia,

259. SPLIT SECOND ★★
b.f. Moss Vale – Twenty Questions (Kyllachy).
April 9. First foal. Doncaster St Leger Festival. £16,000Y. Gill Richardson. The dam, an Irish 2-y-o 5f winner, is a half-sister to 4 winners. The second dam, Quiz Show (by Primo Dominie), a quite useful 7f winner, is a half-sister to 4 winners including the high-class sprinter Mind Games, winner of the Group 2 Temple Stakes (twice), the Norfolk Stakes and the Palace House Stakes. (Jaber Abdullah). *"A sweet little filly, she shows a bit of speed and although I don't think she's great she's speedily bred".*

260. TIDAL WAY ★★★
gr.c. Red Clubs – Taatof (Lahib).
April 19. Fifth foal. 18,000Y. Tattersalls October Book 3. Gill Richardson. Half-brother to the fairly useful 12f and 2m winner Silver Suitor (by Swain) and a hurdles winner by High Chaparral. The dam is an unraced half-sister to one winner. The second dam, Labibeh (by Lyphard), won the Group 3 12f Princess Royal Stakes and is a half-sister to 4 winners. (Jaber Abdullah). *"Yes, he's nice and he'll win. A big, grey horse that goes very well and he'll probably be better at six or seven but he certainly shows enough to go with the big boys".*

261. TIDENTIME ★★★
b.br.c. Speightstown – Casting Call (Dynaformer).
February 6. Fifth foal. 75,000Y. Tattersalls October Book 1. Gill Richardson. Half-brother to 2 minor winners in the USA by Siberian Summer and Bertrando. The dam, a minor US 3-y-o winner, is a half-sister to 7 winners, 3 of them stakes-placed. The second dam, Firesweeper (by Drum Fire), a stakes winner of 13 races in the USA, is a half-sister to 7 winners. (Jon & Julia Aisbitt). *"A nice horse, he hasn't grown much but he goes well. A six/seven furlong type and I think he's one to bring out around early June".*

262. TRIGGERLO ★★
ch.c. Piccolo – Elegant Hawk (Generous).
March 17. First foal. 9,000Y. Tattersalls December. Gill Richardson. The dam was a quite useful 9f and 12f winner at 3 yrs. The second dam, Mexican Hawk (by Silver Hawk), a fairly useful 10f winner, is a half-sister to 8 winners. (Lord Ilsley Racing (Medcroft Syndicate)). *"He goes well, he's by Piccolo out of a Generous mare, so we don't know what we've got really but he ran well over five first time out. Top of the ground will be good for him and he hasn't been a problem since day one".*

263. VEXILLUM (IRE) ★★★
br.c. Mujadil – Common Cause (Polish Patriot).
April 30. Eighth foal. 42,000Y. Tattersalls October Book 2. Gill Richardson. Brother to the Irish listed 9f winner of 9 races Wovoka and to the modest 7f winner Banjo Bandit and half-brother to the fair 1m and hurdles winner Letham Island and the moderate 10f and 11f winner Litenup (both by Trans Island). The dam, a quite useful 11.5f and 11.8f winner, is a half-sister to 3 winners. The second dam, Alongside, (by Slip Anchor), an Irish 4-y-o 9f winner, is a half-sister to 3 winners including the Group 2 Prix Eugene Adam winner Kirkwall. (Insignia Racing, Roundel). *"A smashing colt, he shows plenty of speed and he'll certainly be alright. I don't know where to put him in the pecking order but he's a real nice horse. He'll certainly win, he's certainly a 2-y-o and I think he'll get even better in time".*

264. UNNAMED ★★★
b.c. Imperial Dancer – Aunt Ruby (Rubiano).
April 1. Half-brother to the useful 6f (at 2 yrs) and 7f winner of 5 races South Cape (by Cape Cross), to the fairly useful triple 7f winner (including at 2 yrs) and subsequent Hong Kong Group 3 placed 1m winner Relative Order (by Diktat), the fair 7f winner Red Yarn (by Lucky Story), the moderate 5f and 6f winner Eye For The Girls and the poor 1m winner Rubilini (both by Bertolini). The dam, a 7f seller winner at 3 yrs, is out of the US winner Redress (by Storm Cat), herself a half-sister to the Gimcrack Stakes winner Spencent. (Heart Of The South). *"He'll definitely make a 2-y-o, probably over six furlongs a bit later on and he's a very nice colt.*

265. UNNAMED ★★★
b.f. Holy Roman Emperor – Ayla (Daylami).
February 22. First foal. The dam, a fairly

useful 12f winner and fourth in two listed events, is a half-sister to several winners including the Group 1 Irish St Leger and Group 1 Prix du Cadran winner Alandi and Irish 1m (at 2 yrs) and listed 12f winner Aliyfa. The second dam, Aliya (by Darshaan), a dual 12f winner in Ireland, is a sister to the high-class Group 3 12f Lingfield Oaks Trial winner and disqualified Epsom Oaks winner Aliysa and a half-sister to several winners including the useful 2-y-o 7f winner and Group 2 Park Hill Stakes third Altiyna. (Barry Walters Catering). *"A smashing filly, real nice but she was late in, so I've only just got her going and I don't think we'll see her until July. A very nice filly though".*

266. UNNAMED ★★★
b.f. Clodovil – Brigadiers Bird (Mujadil).
February 23. Eleventh foal. Half-sister to the 2-y-o Group 3 Futurity Stakes winner and Group 2 Falmouth Stakes third Lady Lahar (herself dam of the listed winner Classic Legend), the fairly useful 5f winner of 6 races, including at 2 yrs, Captain Carey, the moderate 12f winner Lord Lahar (all by Fraam) and the quite useful 1m 2-y-o winner Sri Pekan Two (by Montjeu). The dam is an unraced half-sister to 3 winners. The second dam, Brigadiers Nurse (by Brigadier Gerard), is an unraced half-sister to 4 minor winners. (Barry Walters Catering). *"She was late coming in and so she's behind the others. I'm very hopeful though and I'd say six furlongs will probably suit her. We trained her half-sister Lady Lahar and this is a smashing filly".*

267. UNNAMED ★★★ ♠
b.g. Sir Percy – Carenage (Alzao).
January 20. Fifth foal. 10,500Y. Tattersalls October Book 3. David McGreavy. Half-brother to the fair 9f winner Caribana (by Hernando). The dam, a quite useful 12f winner, is a half-sister to 4 winners. The second dam, Key Change (by Darshaan), won the Yorkshire Oaks and is a half-sister to 7 winners. (David McGreavy). *"Yes, he goes alright. He'll definitely win, he'll probably be better over six/seven furlongs but he shows a bit of speed. I like the Sir Percy 2-y-o's".*

268. UNNAMED ★★★
b.f. Holy Roman Emperor – Mandavilla (Sadler's Wells).
March 24. Second foal. Goffs Orby. €32,000Y. Gill Richardson. Closely related to the fairly useful Irish 11f winner Seven Summit (by Danehill Dancer). The dam is an unraced full or half-sister to 6 winners including the useful 12f winner and listed-placed Mazaya (herself dam of the dual listed winner and Group 2 placed Munsef). The second dam, Sharaniya (by Alleged), won the Group 2 12f Grand Prix d'Evry, the Group 3 12f Prix Minerve and the Group 3 12.5f Prix de Royallieu and is a half-sister to the Prix Vermeille winner Sharaya and the US Grade 3 winner Shannkara. (John Guest Racing). *"A lovely filly for the mid-season onwards. She has plenty of size and is more like the damsire Sadler's Wells than Holy Roman Emperor in that respect".*

269. UNNAMED ★★
b.br.c. Rakti – Queen Of Fibres (Scenic).
April 20. Sixth foal. 21,000Y. Tattersalls October Book 2. Gill Richardson. Half-brother to the fairly useful 5f to 7f winner of 8 races (including at 2 yrs) Rocket Rob (by Danetime) and to the moderate 7f to 9f winner Hi Spec (by Spectrum). The dam, a moderate 9f and 11f winner at 5 yrs in Ireland, is a half-sister to 3 winners. The second dam, Lightning Bug (by Prince Bee), won 5 races from 12f to 2m and over hurdles and is a half-sister to 8 winners. (Mick Channon). *"He's a smashing big horse. The Raktis I've had have all been nice horses. He'll be the same, but I don't think we'll see him until the end of the year".*

270. UNNAMED ★★★
br.c. Aussie Rules – Scylla Cadeaux (Cadeaux Genereux).
January 14. First foal. 45,000Y. Tattersalls October Book 2. Gill Richardson. The dam, a modest 1m placed maiden, is a half-sister to 3 winners. The second dam, She's Classy (by Boundary), a winner of 2 races at 2 yrs in the USA including a stakes event, was Grade 1 placed twice and is a half-sister to 4 winners in the USA and Japan. (John Guest Racing). *"This a nice, big horse. He's had a few setbacks and little niggles that have just held us up. But I like him, he's a strong horse and he looks to have bit of speed, so we'll just have to wait for him really".*

271. UNNAMED ★★★
ch.c. Bahamian Bounty – Social Storm (Future Storm).
February 16. Sixth foal. 16,000Y. Tattersalls Book 2. Gill Richardson. Half-brother to the quite useful 7f (including at 2 yrs) and 1m winner Stevie Thunder (by Storming Home) and to the modest 5f and 6f winner Kyllachy Storm (by Kyllachy). The dam won 4 races at 2 to 4 yrs in the USA and was listed-placed 3 times. She is a half-sister to 5 winners including the US stakes winner and Grade 3 placed Silver Bandana. The second dam, Datum Line (by High Line), is an unraced sister to the Group 2 winners Ancholia and Quay Line. "He's nice, we'll see how we go with him and he's going the right way".

JANE CHAPPLE-HYAM

272. BULL BAY ★★★
b.c. Bahamian Bounty – Buffy Boo (Agnes World).
January 31. First foal. 16,000Y. Tattersalls October Book 2. Not sold. The dam, unplaced in one start, is a half-sister to the useful 2-y-o 5f and 6f winner and dual listed-placed Silca Boo and to the very useful dual 6f winner and Group 2 6f Gimcrack Stakes second Zilch. The second dam, Bunty Boo (by Noalto), a very useful filly, won 8 races here and in Sweden including the Group 3 Arthur Guinness Flying Five and a listed 5f event at Sandown Park and is a half-sister to 4 winners. (Julie Martin). "He's a lovely, easy-moving colt and I like him a lot. He came to me a bit later than normal because he was broken-in late, but he's got into the routine alright and he's catching up quick. He has a lovely, long stride on him and he's a big, strong individual".

273. COACH MONTANA (IRE) ★★★★
b.c. Proud Citizen – Market Day (Tobougg).
March 14. First foal. 32,000Y. Tattersalls October Book 2. Gordon Li. The dam, a fairly useful dual 6f winner here at 2 yrs, subsequently won a stakes event in the USA and is a half-sister to 2 winners. The second dam, Makhsusah (by Darshaan), is an unraced half-sister to 6 winners. (Mr Gordon Li). "A very nice horse. He's a quick learner and he should start his career at Newbury in mid-April. Although he'll start off at five furlongs he'll be campaigned towards to the six furlong races and I like him a lot. He's so forward it's almost like he's been reincarnated and has done it all before".

274. COCKNEY ROCKER ★★★
br.c. Cockney Rebel – Fur Will Fly (Petong).
April 24. Ninth living foal. Half-brother to the 2-y-o Group 2 5f Flying Childers Rubies (both by Inchinor) and the fair 2-y-o 6f winner Lille Ida (by Hawk Wing). The dam was placed once over 6f at 3 yrs and is a half-sister to 4 winners. The second dam, Bumpkin (by Free State), was a useful sprint winner of 4 races and a half-sister to 7 winners including the prolific 7f to 9f winner On Edge. (Mrs Mette Campbell-Andenaes). "The Cockney Rebel's all came with a bit of a reputation because he was a bit fiery himself but this horse hasn't put a foot wrong. I suppose I'm waiting for the six furlong races with him, he's already done some work on the bridle and I'm happy with him. He's more forward than his foaling date would suggest and as far as his size goes I'd say he's medium to small but he has a lot of heart. I'm planning to run him in late April/early May".

275. FROSTY SECRET ★★
b.f. Echo Of Light – Raze (Halling).
February 23. Third foal. 10,000Y. Tattersalls October Book 2. Jane Chapple-Hyam. The dam, a fair 10f winner, is a half-sister to 5 winners including the Group 3 Queen's Vase second Singleton. The second dam, Rive (by Riverman), won once at 2 yrs in France and is a half-sister to 10 winners. (Mr S Brewster). "I like her a lot but she wants time. A lovely mover, she's still growing so we've had to back-off her a bit. I'd say she's one for the middle of the season, her pedigree tells you she needs time but she's a lovely, scopey filly".

276. JUDGE JEREMY ★★
b.c. Jeremy – Champoluc (Indian Ridge).
May 7. Third foal. 9,000Y. Tattersalls December. Jane Chapple-Hyam. The dam, a quite useful Irish 6f and 7f placed (including at 2 yrs) maiden, is a half-sister to the useful Italian 2-y-o listed 6f winner and Group 3 6f Prix de Seine-et-Oise third Jezebel. The second dam, Just Ice (by Polar Falcon), a fairly useful winner of 3 races over 5f and 6f here and in France including a listed event at Bordeaux, is

a half-sister to 11 winners including the listed winners Always On A Sunday and Palmetto Express. (Gordon Li). *"A bonny little colt, he's on the small side and a bit weak so he's just got to thicken and strengthen. We're taking each fortnight as they come with him and he'll be racing in the second half of the season. A 'cheap and cheerful' 2-y-o, hopefully he'll progress into a horse that the owner can take to Hong Kong at the end of the year".*

277. RED BAY ★★★
b.c. Haafhd – Red Zinnia (Pivotal).
April 15. Second foal. 13,000Y. Tattersalls October Book 3. Not sold. The dam is a half-sister to 3 winners including the useful 7f (at 2 yrs) and 12f winner and Group 3 7f Prestige Stakes third Red Peony. The second dam, Red Azalea (by Shirley Heights), a fairly useful 7f (at 2 yrs) and 10f winner, is a half-sister to 4 winners including the Group 3 Prestige Stakes winner and French 1,000 Guineas third Red Camellia (herself dam of the Fillies Mile winner Red Bloom). (Julie Martin). *"I like him a lot and he'll make a 2-y-o by mid-season, so don't leave him out of the book".*

278. SEVENTEEN SEVENTY ★★
b.c. Byron – Rolexa (Pursuit Of Love).
February 5. First foal. 3,500Y. Tattersalls October Book 3. Jane Chapple-Hyam. The dam, a fair dual 1m placed 3-y-o, is a half-sister to 9 winners including the smart Green Card, a winner from 1m to 10.3f and Group 3 placed three times. The second dam, Dunkellin (by Irish River), a minor 3-y-o winner in the USA, is a half-sister to the Group 1 Criterium des Pouliches winner Oak Hill. (Mrs J F Chapple-Hyam). *"He was a bargain buy because he had no VAT on him! I was just about to leave the sales ring when I saw this easy-moving Byron colt and I bought him for myself. I like him and I've named him after the year Captain Cook landed in Queensland. He'll be a fun horse, he's strong and compact and will be doing his first pieces of work in early April. The sire is a lovely-looking stallion and this colt has a huge backside on him".* TRAINERS' BARGAIN BUY

PETER CHAPPLE-HYAM

279. AL KAHN ★★★★
b.c. Elnadim – Popolo (Fasliyev).
February 5. First foal. The dam, a modest maiden, was placed six times over 5f and 6f and is a half-sister to the very smart Group 3 6f Phoenix Sprint Stakes winner Al Qasi (by Elnadim). The second dam, Delisha (by Salse), won once at 3 yrs in Germany and is a half-sister to 5 winners including the Group 1 Hong Kong Mile winner Ecclesiastical. (Z A Galadari). *"He does everything really well, he's a big horse and I like him a lot. He moves so well, he'll be a six/seven furlong 2-y-o from June onwards and he's a really nice horse. I have a soft spot for him because I trained his three-parts brother Al Qasi".*

280. CHUNKY DIAMOND ★★★★ ♠
b.c. Diamond Green – Balance The Books (Elmaamul).
February 26. Ninth foal. Doncaster Premier. £42,000Y. Blandford Bloodstock. Half-brother to the modest 2-y-o 5f winner Maid Ofiron (by Iron Mask), to the modest 10f and hurdles winner Thecaulofesker (by Imperial Ballet) and the modest 1m to 10f winner Blanco (by First Trump). The dam, a fair 2-y-o 5f winner, is a half-sister to 6 winners. The second dam, Psylla (by Beldale Flutter), a useful 9f and 10f winner, is a half-sister to the Group 2 winners Perpendicular and Prismatic. (Rebel Racing). *"They named him after the way he looked when he first came into the yard! He's changed a lot because he's a strong, muscular colt now. He goes well and he'll probably go to Newbury in mid-April. He'd be my sharpest at the moment, but I think he's got the scope to go on. Whether he'd be a Royal Ascot 2-y-o only time will tell, but I don't think he'll be far away from it".*

281. DICK BOS ★★★ ♠
ch.c. Dutch Art – Cosmic Countess (Lahib).
March 24. Seventh foal. Doncaster Premier. £20,000Y. Blandford Bloodstock. Half-brother to the modest 7f and 1m winner Miss Madame (by Cape Cross) and to a winner in Greece by Bahhare. The dam, a fair 2-y-o 6f winner, is a half-sister to 5 winners. The second dam, Windmill Princess (by Gorytus), a poor 1m and 11f placed maiden, is a half-sister to 4 winners and to the unraced dam of the

September Stakes winner Spartan Shareef. (The Comic Strip Heroes). *"A big colt and he'll be better over six furlongs than five, but I still see him running at the end of May. We'll see then how good he is but he'd be my favourite of the sharper ones".*

282. EVERLONG ★★★★
b.f. Authorized – Crooked Wood (Woodman).
May 9. Third foal. Half-sister to the fair 2-y-o 5f winner Sakile (by Johannesburg). The dam, an Irish 2-y-o 7f and 1m winner and subsequently a minor 4-y-o winner in the USA, is a half-sister to 7 winners. The second dam, Crockadore (by Nijinsky), won 7 races in Ireland and the USA including the Grade 2 12f Orchid Handicap and the Grade 3 11f Sheepshead Bay Handicap (both on turf). She is closely related to the Group 3 Flying Five winner Flowing and a half-sister to 9 winners. (C G P Wyatt). *"A home-bred filly and owned by one of my best friends, I've trained a few cut of the family and this is a lovely filly. I don't see her being out until August time over seven furlongs and she'll want further next year. She has a bit of a temperament, but she's angry rather than bad – which is good! Rather like the sire in fact. She goes very well at the moment and I like her very much".*

283. FLAMING FERRARI (IRE) ★★
b.f. Authorized – Spirit of Pearl
(Invincible Spirit).
March 16. First foal. 3,000Y. Tattersalls October Book 2. Not sold. The dam, a fairly useful Irish 2-y-o 5f and 7f winner, was listed-placed and is a half-sister to several winners. The second dam, Aguilas Perla (by Indian Ridge), is an unraced sister to the Irish listed 7f winner Cool Clarity and a half-sister to the listed winners Artistic Blue and Queen Of Palms. (Mr M J McStay). *"Bred and owned by another good friend of mine, she'll be sharper than my other Authorized, although I don't think she'll be as good. I've started asking her a few questions to see what we've got, she seems to go up the gallop well and she'll be alright".*

284. MY BODY IS A CAGE (IRE) ★★★
ch.f. Strategic Prince – Moonlight Wish
(Peintre Celebre).
April 25. Fourth foal. Goffs Orby. €18,000Y. **Global Equine Group.** Half-sister to the fairly useful 5f (at 2 yrs) and 6f winner Kerry's Requiem (by King's Best). The dam is an unraced half-sister to 6 winners including Group 1 Dewhurst Stakes second Fencing Master. The second dam, Moonlight Dance (by Alysheba), winner of the Group 1 10f Prix Saint-Alary, is a half-sister to the Dante Stakes winner Claude Monet and the smart winners Magdalena and Marignan. *"She hasn't been here that long but she's a fantastic mover. I see her more as a seven furlong filly than six but she does everything just right and she'll be alright".*

285. MY PROPELLER (IRE) ★★★
b.f. Holy Roman Emperor – Incise (Dr Fong).
March 17. Third foal. 45,000Y. Tattersalls October Book 1. Global Equine Group. The dam, a quite useful 2-y-o 5f winner, was listed placed and is a half-sister to 5 winners including the Group 2 5f Duke Of York Stakes winner Twilight Blues. The second dam, Pretty Sharp (by Interrex), a modest 7f placed 2-y-o, is a half-sister to 6 winners. *"She's done a bit of work already but we're waiting a bit now. She'll be out in early May, she goes really well and although I'm not sure how good she is yet I'm happy with everything she's done so far".*

286. PALUS SAN MARCO (IRE) ★★
b.c. Holy Roman Emperor – Kylemore
(Sadler's Wells).
April 14. Eighth foal. Closely related to the fairly useful 2-y-o 7f winner and listed UAE 1,000 Guineas third Purple Sage (by Danehill Dancer) and half-brother to the very useful listed 1m winner Annabelle's Charm (by Indian Ridge) and the fair dual 10f winner Dhan Dhana (by Dubawi). The dam ran twice unplaced and is a sister to the Group 1 Criterium de Saint-Cloud and Grade 1 Canadian International Stakes winner Ballingarry and to the Group 1 1m Racing Post Trophy winner Aristotle and a half-sister to the Group 1 St James's Palace Stakes and Prix Jean Prat winner Starborough. The second dam, Flamenco Wave (by Desert Wine), won the Group 1 6f Moyglare Stud Stakes and is a half-sister to 3 winners. (Eledy Srl). *"He should be sharpish, but the ones I have this year by the sire are a bit bigger than the average. So he'll take a bit of time, he's a bit of a playboy and I can see him being out around*

August-time over six furlongs. Hasn't shown a great deal as yet".

287. PEARL DIVA (IRE) ★★★★ ♠
b.f. Acclamation – Lassie's Gold
(Seeking The Gold).
February 18. Eighth foal. Doncaster Premier. £22,000Y. Blandford Bloodstock. Half-sister to the fair Irish 3-y-o 1m winner Who Could Tell (by Thunder Gulch) and the minor US winner of 9 races Sway Of Passion (by Sea Salute). The dam is an unraced half-sister to 6 winners including the multiple US Grade 1 winner Lemon Drop Kid, the US Grade 2 winner Brulay and the Group 3 Coventry Stakes winner Statue Of Liberty. The second dam, Charming Lassie (by Seattle Slew), won once at 3 yrs in the USA and is a half-sister to 11 winners including the Group 1 Haydock Park Sprint Cup winner Wolfhound and the dam of the top-class US Grade 1 winners A P Indy and Summer Squall. (Mr J C Davies). "She'll be running in May, she's going really nicely and she'll win over five furlongs but be better at six. A filly I like a lot".

288. POSSIBLY ★★★
b.f. Exceed And Excel – One Of The Family
(Alzao).
April 14. 6,500Y. Tattersalls October Book 2. S Ballinger. Half-sister to the fairly useful 14f to 18f winner Som Tala (by Fantastic Light) and to the quite useful 1m to 14f winner of 7 races Pass The Port (by Docksider). The dam, a fair 1m placed 4-y-o, is a sister to the Rockfel Stakes winner Relatively Special and a half-sister to 7 winners including the Juddmonte International Stakes winner One So Wonderful and the Group 2 Dante Stakes winner Alnasr Alwasheek. The second dam, Someone Special (by Habitat), won over 7f, was third in the Coronation Stakes and is a half-sister to the Queen Elizabeth II Stakes winner Milligram. (Miss S J Ballinger). "She'll make a 2-y-o in May, needs to come in her coat at the moment but she does everything well and I'm very happy with her. She'll definitely be better at six furlongs than five". TRAINERS' BARGAIN BUY

289. RIGHT EXPECTATION (IRE) ★★★★
b.c. Holy Roman Emperor – Palacoona
(Last Tycoon).
April 30. Ninth foal. Goffs Orby. €32,000Y.
McKeever Bloodstock. Half-brother to the very useful 1m and subsequent US Grade 3 9f winner Diamond Tycoon (by Johannesburg), to the useful listed 11f winner Cassique Lady (by Langfuhr), the fair 7f winner Sheila Toss and the modest 10f winner Chanrossa (both by Galileo). The dam, a French listed 1m winner, was Group 3 placed and subsequently won in the USA and is a half-sister to 7 winners. The second dam, Palavera (by Bikala), a listed-placed winner in France, is a half-sister to 5 winners including the French Derby winner Polytain. "He's a nice, big colt, he goes really well and he'll be better over seven furlongs this year than shorter but he does everything real nice. In fact I think he's my nicest colt".

290. SAMMINDER ★★★
b.c. Red Ransom – Gimasha
(by Cadeaux Genereux).
January 25. Second foal. The dam, a useful 5f and 6f winner of 5 races, is a half-sister to 5 winners including the very useful triple 1m and hurdles winner Atlantic Rhapsody and the useful French winner of 3 races and Group 3 Prix Thomas Bryon third Gaitero. The second dam, First Waltz (by Green Dancer), winner of the Group 1 6f Prix Morny and second in the Cheveley Park Stakes, is a half-sister to the dam of the Prix Lupin second Angel Falls. (Z A Galadari). "He goes really nicely, I couldn't be happier with him. I like him a lot and his dam was a fast filly. He was an early foal, he's a definite 2-y-o type and he'll be out in May or June as long as everything goes right".

291. SCARABOCIO ★★★
b.c. Shamardal – My Sara
February 10. First foal. 40,000foal. Tattersalls December. (Eledy Srl). The dam, a modest 3-y-o 1m winner, is a half-sister to 6 winners. The second dam, Ancestry (by Persepolis), is an unraced half-sister to a winner in Italy. "He goes really well and I see him as a seven furlong horse, maybe six, around June time. He's more than useful and he goes along nice".

292. TARKOOR ★★
b.c. Cape Cross – Bakhoor (by Royal Applause)
April 13. Second foal. The dam, a fair dual 6f and 7f winner, is a half-sister to numerous winners including the UAE 6f winner Desert

Whisper (by Green Desert) and the very useful triple 1m and hurdles winner Atlantic Rhapsody. The second dam, First Waltz (by Green Dancer), a winner of the Group 1 6f Prix Morny and second in the Cheveley Park Stakes, is a half-sister to the dam of the Prix Lupin second Angel Falls. (Z A Galadari). *"Came in a bit late and he's quite immature so I've given him a break because he needed a bit of time. He'll be a six furlong horse around July time. He's got a bit of character and he'll be alright but I haven't done enough with him comment on his ability yet".*

293. TELWAAR ★★★
ch.c. Haafhd – Waafiah (Anabaa).
February 21. Closely related to the fairly useful triple 1m winner Jaser and to the modest 6f and subsequent UAE 7f winner Ragad (both by Alhaarth). The dam, second over 7f at 3 yrs on her only start, is a half-sister to several winners including the very useful 1m and hurdles winner Atlantic Rhapsody. The second dam, First Waltz (by Green Dancer), winner of the Group 1 6f Prix Morny and second in the Cheveley Park Stakes, is a half-sister to the dam of the Prix Lupin second Angel Falls. (Z A Galadari). *"Quite a small horse but he's grown a lot. I see him as a June type 2-y-o, he does everything right and has a good temperament for a son of Haafhd. The sire is struggling a little bit, but I think this colt will win races".*

294. VENEGAZZU (IRE) ★★★
br.c. Dubawi – Vintage Tipple (Entrepreneur).
April 3. Fifth foal. 35,000foal. Tattersalls December. Not sold. Half-brother to the quite useful Irish dual 7f winner Cape Vintage (by Cape Cross) and to the quite useful 11f winner King's Vintage (by King's Best). The dam, a 7f, 1m (at 2 yrs) and Group 1 Irish Oaks winner, is a half-sister to 4 winners including the useful 2-y-o 7f and 1m winner and Group 1 1m Gran Criterium third Spettro. The second dam, Overruled (by Last Tycoon), a quite useful 1m (at 2 yrs) and 10.2f winner, is a half-sister to 6 winners including the Grade 2 American Derby winner Overbury. (Eledy Srl). *"He goes really well but he's big and is more of an August type 2-y-o. He does everything perfectly at the moment and those who know the dam tell me it's the best looking one she's bred".*

295. UNNAMED ★★★
b.f. Notnowcato – Disco Lights (Spectrum).
March 30. Second foal. €180,000Y. Arqana Deauville August. Paul Hancock B/S. Half-sister to the quite useful 2010 2-y-o 6f winner Tipsy Girl (by Haafhd). The dam, a fair 1m and 9f placed 2-y-o, is a half-sister to the Ebor Handicap winner Tuning and the useful Group 3 7f Rockfel Stakes second Clog Dance. The second dam, Discomatic (by Roberto), a French 9f winner, is a half-sister to the Phoenix Stakes winner Digamist. *"She wants a bit of time but she's coming along really nicely and I couldn't really be happier with her. A seven furlong filly around July time, all being well and I'm very pleased with her".*

296. UNNAMED ★★★
b.f. Holy Roman Emperor – Forever Times (So Factual).
April 14. Third foal. 10,000Y. Tattersalls October Book 2. Not sold. Half-sister to the fairly useful 2010 2-y-o listed 6f placed Question Times (by Shamardal). The dam, a fairly useful 5f (at 2 yrs) to 7f winner, is half-sister to numerous winners including the Group 3 7f Hungerford Stakes and Group 3 6f Bentinck Stakes winner Welsh Emperor and the very useful listed 5f winner Majestic Times. The second dam, Simply Times (by Dodge), ran twice unplaced at 2 yrs and is a half-sister to 5 winners including the US 2-y-o stakes winner Bucky's Baby. (Mr A Belshaw). *"She's going along really nicely, she wasn't an early foal but we'll be asking her a few questions shortly. From what I've seen so far she looks pretty good, I like her and she goes well. Six furlongs will suit her and she should go on any ground. Surprisingly she was bought back at the Sales. She's a better model than her half-sister who'd just been listed-placed".*

297. UNNAMED ★★★
b.c. Excellent Art – Sandtime (Green Desert).
January 26. First foal. Doncaster Premier. £28,000Y. Blandford Bloodstock. The dam, a listed-placed 1m winner in Ireland, is a full or half-sister to 4 winners. The second dam, Key Change (by Darshaan), won the Group 1 Yorkshire Oaks and is a half-sister to 7 winners. *"He'd be better at six furlongs than five, but he does everything right and has a good attitude.*

I like him a lot and I can see him out around June time".

ROGER CHARLTON

298. ALI HOPE (IRE) ★★★
ch.c. Three Valleys – Alexander Duchess (Desert Prince).
May 4. Fourth foal. 24,000Y. Tattersalls October Book 2. Kern/Lillingston. Half-brother to the quite useful triple 5f winner Scarlet Rocks (by Chineur). The dam, a useful dual 7f winner, is a sister to the listed 14f March Stakes winner Jadalee and a half-sister to 4 winners including the dual Group 3 Noblesse Stakes winner Grace O'Malley. The second dam, Lionne (by Darshaan), is an unraced half-sister to 5 winners including the Derby and Dewhurst Stakes winner Sir Percy. (De La Warr Racing). *"I had an order to buy a horse that looked like Three Valleys for less than 25,000 and I got this colt with 1,000 to spare. He's actually quite an interesting pedigree in that the dam was rated 103 and won twice as a 2-y-o and last year's 2-y-o Scarlet Rocks won three times. Having said that, the Derby winner Sir Percy is in there as well. All in all he's got a nice pedigree for his purchase price. A good mover, he was a May foal so he's likely to be a June/July type horse over six/seven furlongs".*

299. BISHOP ROKO ★★★
b.c. Rock Of Gibraltar – Kirk (Selkirk).
February 28. Sixth foal. 58,000Y. Tattersalls October Book 1. Amanda Skiffington. Half-brother to the fairly useful dual 10f winner (including at 2 yrs) and Group 2 Lancashire Oaks third Natalie Jane (by Giant's Causeway), to the fair 1m winner Battlemaiden (by Shamardal) and a winner in Greece by Fasliyev. The dam, a fair 1m winner, is closely related to the smart Group 2 placed Carmelite House and a half-sister to 6 other winners. The second dam, Sancta (by So Blessed), was a useful winner of 3 races at 3 yrs and is a half-sister to the dam of Kris and Diesis. (M Pescod). *"A fine, big, strong colt, he's a good-moving horse but definitely one for the autumn over staying trips and in theory he'll be a better three-year-old".*

300. CAPTAIN CAT (IRE) ★★★
b.c. Dylan Thomas – Mother Of Pearl (Sadler's Wells).
May 1. Eighth foal. 125,000foal. Tattersalls December. Seasons Holidays. Closely related to the French listed 10f winner Danehill's Pearl (by Danehill Dancer) and half-brother to the useful 1m and 10f winner Pearly King, the moderate 1m winner Pearl Island (both by Kingmambo) and a 3-y-o winner in Japan by Fusaichi Pegasus. The dam won both her starts at 2 yrs including the Group 3 1m Prix Saint-Roman and was placed in the Group 3 Prix de la Nonette and the Group 3 Musidora Stakes. She is a closely related to the high-class colt Turtle Island, winner of the Group 1 6f Heinz "57" Phoenix Stakes, the Irish 2,000 Guineas and the Group 2 6f Gimcrack Stakes. The second dam, Sisania (by High Top), won two races in Italy at around 10f and is a half-sister to 3 winners. (Seasons Holidays). *"At 16 hands he's a big horse and he's out of a Sadler's Wells mare, so hopefully he'll run a few times in the autumn but he's much more of a 3-y-o type. An attractive horse, I'm pleased with him and his half-brothers Danehill's Pearl and Pearly King were rated 103 and 105 respectively. A nice, long-term prospect".*

301. CLOWANCE ESTATE (IRE) ★★★
b.c. Teofilo – Whirly Bird (Nashwan).
May 8. Third foal. 115,000Y. Tattersalls December. Roger Charlton. Half-brother to the quite useful dual 7f winner Whirly Dancer (by Danehill Dancer). The dam, a useful 9.5f to 11f winner of 5 races, is a half-sister to 4 winners including the very useful 12f listed Galtres Stakes winner Inchiri and the very useful 2-y-o 8.3f winner and Oaks fourth Inchberry. The second dam, Inchyre (by Shirley Heights), a useful 1m winner and listed-placed over 12f, is a half-sister to 7 winners including the very smart and tough triple Group 3 7f winner Inchinor and the listed winner Ingozi (dam of the Canadian Grade 2 winner Miss Keller). (Seasons Holiday). *"I saw quite a lot of Teofilo yearlings at the sales and I thought they all looked nice, attractive horses and I was pleased to buy this horse. He's from the family of Inchinor, but his dam stayed 12 furlongs and I would imagine this colt will be a ten to twelve furlong type next year. He was a May foal but I would hope that from July onwards we'll see him out. He's a nice horse and I like him".*

302. DAFFYD ★★★
b.c. Green Desert – Ffestiniog (Efisio).
March 6. Closely related to the quite useful 5f and 6f winner Oceans Apart (by Desert Prince) and half-brother to the Group 3 1m Solonaway Stakes winner Border Patrol (by Selkirk), to the smart sprint winner of 11 races (including the Group 3 Prix de Meautry) Eisteddfod (by Cadeaux Genereux), the useful 2-y-o 5f to 7f winner Brecon Beacon (by Spectrum), the useful dual 7f (at 2 yrs) and UAE Group 3 1m winner Boston Lodge (by Grand Lodge), the fairly useful 2-y-o 6f winner Harlech Castle (by Royal Applause) and the quite useful 2-y-o dual 7f winner Tredegar (by Inchinor). The dam, a fairly useful 2-y-o listed 7.3f and 3-y-o 1m winner, is a half-sister to several winners. The second dam, Penny Fan (by Nomination), was placed once over 5f at 3 yrs, is closely related to the listed 5f Scarborough Stakes winner Rivers Rhapsody and a half-sister to the Group 3 5f Prix d'Arenburg winner Regal Scintilla. (Elite Racing Club). *"A half-brother to lots of good horses, he's a very strong, neat horse. A very powerfully made 2-y-o type, I hope he can do as well as the rest of the family. He's had a touch of sore shins so we're going slightly easy with him at the moment, but he'll be racing from June onwards over six furlongs".*

303. DAWN GLORY ★★
b.f. Oasis Dream – Fairy Godmother (Fairy King).
May 13. Half-sister to the smart triple 10f winner and Group 3 placed Kingdom Of Fife (by Kingmambo) and to the useful dual 1m winner (including at 2 yrs) and Group 3 1m Autumn Stakes third Four Winds (by Red Ransom). The dam, a listed 10f winner, is a half-sister to several winners including the Group 2 12f Jockey Club Stakes winner Blueprint. The second dam, Highbrow (by Shirley Heights), a very useful 2-y-o 1m winner, was second in the Group 2 12f Ribblesdale Stakes, is closely related to the good middle-distance colt Milford and a half-sister to the Princess of Wales's Stakes winner Height of Fashion - herself the dam of Nashwan, Nayef and Unfuwain. (The Queen). *"A late foal so she'll need time but she has a nice pedigree and she's attractive. Although some Oasis Dreams can be small and strong and definitely 2-y-o's, most of this mare's progeny need time and I imagine this filly will be the same".*

304. DOGSTAR (IRE) ★★★★
b.f. Nayef – Dolma (Marchand de Sable).
March 5. Third foal. The dam won 6 races over 6f and 7f (including at 2 yrs), notably 3 listed events at 3 yrs. The second dam, Young Manila (by Manila), was listed placed over 10f and is a half-sister to Fabulous Hostess, a winner of three Group 3 events from 11f to 13f. (Lady Rothschild). *"A nice filly, I've had a two out of the mare before but this is by far the nicest. A very good mover out of a tough mare who ran 20 times and won 6 races, she looks like a six/seven furlong filly for the mid-summer onwards and I like what I see".*

305. ESTRELA ★★★
b.f. Authorized – Wannabe Grand (Danehill).
May 6. Eighth foal. 57,000foal. Tattersalls December. Seasons Holidays. Half-sister to the useful 7f to 10f winner King Of Argos (by Sadler's Wells), to the useful 7f (at 2 yrs) to 9f winner of 4 races Wannabe King (by King's Best), the fairly useful triple 7f winner (including at 2 yrs) and subsequent Hong Kong winner Walkonthewildside (by Giant's Causeway), the fairly useful 2-y-o 5f winner Bachelor Of Arts (by Stravinsky), the fair 12f winner Wannabe Free (by Red Ransom) and a winner in Japan by Selkirk. The dam won the Group 1 6f Cheveley Park Stakes and the Group 3 6f Cherry Hinton Stakes and is a half-sister to 4 winners including the useful 2-y-o dual 1m winner and Group 3 second Wannabe Posh. The second dam, Wannabe (by Shirley Heights), a quite useful 1m and 10f winner, is a half-sister to 3 winners including the Group 1 Cheveley Park Stakes second Tanami. (Seasons Holidays). *"A late foal, she's a rangy, good-moving filly. It's difficult to know how far she'll stay because Wannabe Grand won the Cheveley Park and we don't know what to expect from the sire as this is his first season. She'll be one for the second half of the season and probably over seven furlongs or a mile, but you wouldn't know. She's done well because a lot of the mare's progeny have been small, whereas this is a big filly".*

306. EXCAVATOR ★★★
b.c. *Bahamian Bounty – Digger Girl (Black Minnaloushe).*
February 1. Third foal. Doncaster Premier. £25,000Y. Amanda Skiffington. Half-brother to the unplaced 2010 2-y-o Spade (by Halling). The dam ran once unplaced and is a half-sister to 5 winners including the listed 14f winner and Group 3 second Art Eyes. The second dam, Careyes (by Sadler's Wells), is an unraced half-sister to 2 minor winners. (Beckhampton 1). *"He'll hopefully start his career in April and he's quite an attractive horse that moves well. He looks quite speedy and is a six furlong horse to run quite soon".*

307. FAST FOX (IRE) ★★★★
b.c. *Dynaformer – Molasses (Machiavellian).*
April 29. Seventh foal. 170,000Y. Tattersalls October Book 1. Blandford Bloodstock. Half-brother to the Group 3 12f Prix d'Hedouville winner and Group 1 Grand Prix de Paris third Magadan (by High Chaparral), to the modest 7f winner Rock Of Tarik (by Rock Of Gibraltar) and to Musique Magique (by Mozart), a quite useful Irish 2-y-o 7f winner on her only start. The dam is an unraced half-sister to 7 winners including the Oaks winner Light Shift, the champion older mare and Group 1 10.5f Tattersalls Gold Cup winner Shiva and the Group 2 12f Prix Jean de Chaudenay winner Limnos. The second dam, Lingerie (by Shirley Heights), was placed 6 times in France and is a half-sister to 7 winners. (B E Nielsen). *"A colt with a nice pedigree, he was bought-back by his owner at the sales and he's big and strong but not that backward. A July type 2-y-o over seven furlongs and I like him".*

308. GULF PORT ★★
b.f. *Three Valleys – Biloxi (Caerleon).*
April 14. Fifth foal. Half-sister to the quite useful Irish 7f winner (on her only start) Parlour (by Dansili) and to a hurdles winner by Sadler's Wells. The dam is an unraced sister to the useful 10f winner Yaralino and a half-sister to the 1m (at 2 yrs) and Group 1 10f Grand Prix de Paris winner Beat Hollow. The second dam, Wemyss Bight (by Dancing Brave), won 5 races including the Group 1 12f Irish Oaks, the Group 2 12f Prix de Malleret, the Group 3 10.5f Prix Cleopatre and the Group 3 10.5f Prix Penelope. (Khalid Abdulla). *"She'll need time and is one for the end of the season because she's still weak and hasn't been here that long. She might come to hand but she's not in the drive position yet".*

309. HABITA ★★★
b.f. *Montjeu – Minnie Habit (Habitat).*
February 9. Fifteenth foal. 160,000Y. Tattersalls October Book 1. Amanda Skiffington. Closely related to the Irish 2-y-o listed 9f winner On The Nile, the Irish 1m winner In The Limelight, the fair 10f winner Maganda (all by Sadler's Wells) and the Singapore Gold Cup and Gran Premio del Jockey Club winner Kutub (by In The Wings) and half-sister to the 2-y-o 6f winner Child Prodigy (by Ballad Rock) and the Irish 14f winner Blue Bit (by Bluebird) - both quite useful. The dam, an Irish 4-y-o 9f winner, is closely related to the 5f Curragh Stakes and 6f Railway Stakes winner Bermuda Classic (herself dam of the Coronation Stakes winner Shake The Yoke and the Phoenix Sprint Stakes winner Tropical) and a half-sister to 6 winners. The second dam, Minnie Tudor (by Tudor Melody), won over 6f (at 2 yrs) and 1m in Ireland. (Mr John Deer). *"An attractive filly, she's not that backward and she should be running over seven furlongs or a mile from the middle of the summer onwards. She's a sweet filly but it's been a long time since any of the family won a Group race. She's out of an old mare, but doesn't look it and I'd say that she's a nice-looking filly with a good temperament".*

310. HINT OF PROMISE ★★★
b.f. *Beat Hollow – Marching West (Gone West).*
April 29. Closely related to the fairly useful 7f (including at 2 yrs) and 1m winner Marching Time (by Sadler's Wells). The dam, a 2-y-o 6f winner in France, was fourth in the Group 1 5.5f Prix Robert Papin and is a sister to the champion 2-y-o and 3-y-o and sire Zafonic and to the smart Group 3 6f Prix de Cabourg winner and sire Zamindar. The second dam, Zaizafon (by The Minstrel), won twice over 7f at 2 yrs, was placed in the Group 1 1m Queen Elizabeth II Stakes at 3 yrs and is a half-sister to the unraced Modena, herself dam of the Eclipse Stakes and Phoenix Champion Stakes winner Elmaamul. (Khalid Abdulla). *"A fairly late foal, she's a big, strong filly and I quite like her. The sire seems to be doing well and*

the dam is out of a full sister to Zafonic and Zamindar. A good-bodied filly, she's not one to rev up yet. One for the second half of the season and she's OK".

311. INCHINA ★★★
b.f. Montjeu – Incheni (Nashwan).
April 11. Third foal. 360,000Y. Tattersalls October Book 1. Not sold. The dam, a useful 7f (at 2 yrs) and listed 10f winner, is a sister to the very useful 2-y-o 7f winner Inchlonaig and a half-sister to 6 winners including the triple Group 3 7f winner and sire Incinor. The second dam, Inchmurrin (by Lomond), a very useful winner of three races at 2 yrs over 5f and three races at 3 yrs including the Child Stakes, was second in the Group 1 1m Coronation Stakes and is a half-sister to 7 winners including the Mill Reef Stakes winner Welney. (A E Oppenheimer). "She's a very powerful, strong filly, well-made and with good quarters. I imagine she'll be suited by seven furlongs to a mile in the second half of the year. She's bred in a very similar way to the dam of Clowance House, as they're from the same family and both by Montjeu out of Nashwan mares. The Montjeu fillies haven't been so popular or successful as the colts but they can be temperamental and also some of them can be small and a bit 'hot'. This filly is far from being small and she has a good temperament, I'm pleased to report".

312. LA BOCCA (USA) ★★
b.f. Latent Heat – Danzante (Danzig).
April 8. Twelfth foal. Half-sister to the US Grade 1 9.5f Eddie Read Handicap winner Monzante, to the fair 2010 2-y-o 1m winner Marzante (both by Maria's Mon), the useful French 2-y-o 7f winner Alpha Plus (by Mr Prospector), the fairly useful 2-y-o triple 5f winner and listed-placed Tentative (by Distant View), the 10f winner Roman Villa (by Chester House), the 7f winner Dance West (by Gone West) and the 2-y-o 5f winner Forante (by Forty Niner) – all quite useful. The dam, a sprint winner in France and in the USA, is a half-sister to the Breeders Cup Classic winner Skywalker and to the French Group 3 7f winner Nidd. The second dam, Bold Captive (by Boldnesian) was a sprinter. (Khalid Abdulla). "She's probably the last foal out of Danzante and I've trained quite a lot of them. The sire won the Grade 1 Malibu Stakes over seven furlongs. This filly is small and a bit weak, but because of her size she'll have to be a 2-y-o. She had a bit of a setback and I don't know a lot about her yet. We'll press on with her when we can".

313. LOVAGE ★★★
b.f. Exceed And Excel – Name Of Love (Petardia).
April 12. Closely related to the fair 7f winner Love Match (by Danehill Dancer) and half-sister to the US Grade 3 8.5f placed Perilous Pursuit (by Lemon Drop Kid) and the fair 9.5f winner Almavara (by Fusaichi Pegasus). The dam, a very useful 2-y-o Group 3 7f Rockfel Stakes and listed 7f Oh So Sharp Stakes winner, is a half-sister to 3 winners including the useful 7f winner (at 2 yrs) and 9f listed placed Annapurna. The second dam, National Ballet (by Shareef Dancer), is an unraced half-sister to 7 winners including the listed winners Broken Wave, Guarde Royale, Clifton Chapel and Saxon Maid. (Lady Rothschild). "The mare was a good 2-y-o and she's had winners but they've been a bit disappointing. I would say that having trained most of them that this is the most attractive out of the mare. She's a good prospect, the sire is a good influence for speed and I'm happy with her. A nice filly, she's not small but she looks the type to make a 2-y-o over six furlongs because she looks mature and I'll certainly press on with her".

314. MINCE ★★★
ch.f. Medicean – Strut (Danehill Dancer).
January 27. Second foal. The dam, a 2-y-o listed 5.2f winner, was Group 3 placed twice and is a half-sister to the quite useful 2-y-o 5f winner Brag (by Mujadil). The second dam, Boast (by Most Welcome), a useful 5f and 6f winner, is a half-sister to 6 winners including the fairly useful 2-y-o 5f and 4-y-o 1m winner Great Bear. (Lady Rothschild). "The dam was a huge, strong, speedy filly by Danehill Dancer and this filly looks a bit like her because she's got very big quarters on her and is a powerful filly. She has a bit of growing to do and she had a small setback a month ago so I don't know as much about her as the others. She does look like a 2-y-o prospect though".

315. NIMBLE THIMBLE ★★★
ch.f. Mizzen Mast – Skiable (Niniski).
April 3. Half-sister to the 2-y-o Group 3 6f Coventry Stakes and disqualified Group 1 6f Middle Park Stakes winner Three Valleys (by Diesis), to the quite useful triple 10f winner Ski Jump (by El Prado), the quite useful 2-y-o 6f winner Morzine (by Miswaki), the fair 1m winner Lahberhorn (by Affirmed), the modest 12f winner Back Pass and to the French 12f winner Grail (both by Quest For Fame). The dam won four times at up to 9f in France and the USA and is out of a half-sister to the smart sprinter So Factual. (Khalid Abdulla). *"Quite a strong, deep filly, she's not as eye-catching a mover as her half-brother Three Valleys but she's a stronger filly than her half-sister Morzine who I also trained. She's in the second wave of horses to run so I'll be pressing her soon. It's a mixed pedigree because the dam is by Niniski and you wouldn't know how strong the stamina influence will be, but we'll see and I quite like her".*

316. PICK THREE ★★
ch.c. Three Valleys – Magic Number (Dansili).
March 16. First foal. The dam, a minor French 12.5f winner, is a half-sister to the French 2-y-o 7f and 1m winner and Group 1 Prix Marcel Bousac second Conference Call. The second dam, Phone West (by Gone West), was placed over 1m at 3 yrs in France. (Khalid Abdulla). *"A big, rather backward and very relaxed horse – unlike his father who wasn't particularly relaxed. Again, the Danehill influence is there and it's a typical Juddmonte family. In reality, this horse is probably more about stamina than speed. He doesn't show me any speed at the moment and he seems quite sleepy – hopefully he'll wake up shortly! Sometimes they can".*

317. PRICELESS JEWEL ★★★
b.f. Selkirk – My Branch (Distant Relative).
May 22. Half-sister to the Group 1 6f Haydock Sprint Cup winner Tante Rose (by Barathea), to the useful 2-y-o listed 7f winner Bay Tree (by Daylami), the useful 1m winner and listed-placed Melodramatic (by Sadler's Wells), the quite useful 2-y-o 5.7f winner Rosie's Posy (by Suave Dancer) and the quite useful 3-y-o 7f winner Future Flight (by Polar Falcon). The dam, a very useful winner of the listed 6f Firth Of Clyde Stakes (at 2 yrs) and the listed 7f Sceptre Stakes, was fourth in the 1,000 Guineas and third in the Irish 1,000 Guineas. The second dam, Pay The Bank (by High Top), a quite useful 2-y-o 1m winner, stayed 10f. (B E Nielsen). *"Her half-sister Tante Rose unfortunately died having a Pivotal foal, so there's a lot hanging on this filly. She's attractive but she's also a late foal by Selkirk who you wouldn't associate with siring precocious types. So it's hard to read, but if you didn't know all that you'd think she could be running by July because she doesn't look backward. So she ought to make a 2-y-o by mid-summer".*

318. REX IMPERATOR ★★★
b.c. Royal Applause – Elidore (Danetime).
March 27. First foal. 75,000Y. Tattersalls October Book 2. Amanda Skiffington. The dam, a fairly useful 6f and 7f winner at 2 yrs, also won twice over 1m at 4 yrs and is a half-sister to 4 winners including the listed 6f winner Bright Edge. The second dam, Beveled Edge (by Beveled), won once at 4 yrs and is a half-sister to 2 winners. (M Pescod). *"He has a lot of speed in his pedigree and he's a powerful horse who didn't do quite as well as some of the others in the early spring but he's catching up now. He could be running in May or June, he shows good promise and is a typical Royal Applause 2-y-o".*

319. ROSSLYN CASTLE ★★★
ch.c. Selkirk – Margarula (Doyoun).
March 9. Fourth foal. Brother to the quite useful 11f winner Marywell and half-brother to the fair 12f winner Set The Scene (by Sadler's Wells). The dam, a 1m (at 2 yrs) and Group 1 12f Irish Oaks winner, is a half-sister to the Irish 2-y-o listed 9f winner Wild Heaven. The second dam, Mild Intrigue (by Sir Ivor), a fairly useful 10f winner, is a half-sister to the useful listed 10f winner Grimesgill, the US stakes winner Determined Bidder and the dam of the South African Grade 1 winner Milleverof. (Lady Rothschild). *"A more typical Selkirk than the 2-y-o Priceless Jewel, he's one for the autumn and next year. His dam won the Irish Oaks but she hasn't produced much as yet. This is her first colt though, I like him and he seems to go well. Some Selkirk 2-y-o's can be quite narrow and weak-looking, but he's a well-made colt".*

320. SUPREME QUEST ★★★
ch.f. Exceed And Excel – Spanish Quest (Rainbow Quest).
March 2. Fifth foal. Doncaster Premier. £18,000Y. Roger Charlton. Half-sister to the fair 2-y-o 7f winner Hey Up Dad (by Fantastic Light). The dam is an unraced half-sister to 2 winners including the listed winner Spanish Don. The second dam, Spanish Wells (by Sadler's Wells), won at 3 yrs in France and is a full or half-sister to 6 winners including the Irish Oaks winner Wemyss Bight (dam of the Group 1 winner Beat Hollow) and the dams of the Group 1 winners Oasis Dream, Zenda and Reefscape. (Messrs Inglett, Allen, Carter & Kennedy). *"I particularly liked her at the sale, she's sharp, has a nice temperament and is a very good mover. A typical Exceed And Excel, she'll want fast ground and she should be running in late April or early May. It's a very good pedigree and although the mare has been disappointing this filly could be OK, she goes well and for what she cost I'm happy".* TRAINERS' BARGAIN BUY

321. THAT'S DANGEROUS ★★★
ch.c. Three Valleys – St Edith (Desert King).
April 9. Sixth foal. 9,000Y. Doncaster Premier. Amanda Skiffington. The dam is an unplaced half-sister to several winners. The second dam, Carnelly (by Priolo), was an Irish 9f winner was listed-placed and is a sister to the winner and Group 3 placed Wenda. (Mr D Carter & Mr P Inglett). *"I was looking at yearlings by Three Valleys for obvious reasons and I thought this colt looked like him, he walked well and looked quite attractive. He's actually got quite a bit of stamina in his pedigree, but he's a tough little horse and was ready to run early. Not a flying machine but he's OK".* This colt finished second on his debut in early April.

322. TIOMAN LEGEND ★★★ ♠
b.c. Kyllachy – Elegant Times (Dansili).
February 12. Second foal. 82,000Y. Tattersalls October Book 2. Charlie Gordon-Watson. The dam, a modest 6f winner, is a half-sister to 6 winners including the Group 2 7f Hungerford Stakes and Group 3 6f Bentinck Stakes winner Welsh Emperor, the very useful listed 5f winner Majestic Times and the useful 6f and 7f winner and Group 3 6f third Brave Prospector. The second dam, Simply Times (by Dodge), ran twice unplaced at 2 yrs and is a half-sister to 5 winners including the US 2-y-o stakes winner Bucky's Baby. (HRH Sultan Ahmad Shah). *"He's powerful, strong, has a good temperament and he could run in the next few weeks. He'll start at five furlongs and I don't think he'll be inconvenienced by soft ground, being by Kyllachy. He's OK I think – so far so good".*

323. TOP OFFER ★★★★
b.c. Dansili – Zante (Zafonic).
March 29. Half-brother to the modest 10f winner Kefalonia (by Mizzen Mast). The dam, a very useful 1m and listed 10f winner, is a half-sister to the 11f winner and dual US Grade 1 second Requete. The second dam, Danthonia (by Northern Dancer), a quite useful 2-y-o 5f winner, is closely related to the Group 3 1m Prix Quincey winner Masterclass and a half-sister to the Group 3 10.5f Prix Corrida winner Diese. (Khalid Abdulla). *"The mare has been a bit disappointing but this is her first colt. It's a very good family and he's a very attractive horse – probably our nicest at this stage. He just looks very nice-natured, strong, well-grown and he moves very well. He's sixteen hands, he's a nice horse and if I could only keep one of my 2-y-o's I'd keep him".*

324. WATERCLOCK (IRE) ★★
ch.c. Notnowcato – Waterfall One (Nashwan).
February 2. Fourth foal. Half-brother to the unplaced 2010 2-y-o Waterborne (by Diktat) and to the fair 2-y-o 7f winner Water Biscuit (by Bertolini). The dam is an unplaced half-sister to 3 winners. The second dam, Spout (by Salse), was a very smart winner of the Group 3 12f John Porter Stakes and the Group 3 Lancashire Oaks and is a half-sister to numerous winners including the French listed winner Mon Domino. (Lady Rothschild). *"He's from the first crop of Notnowcato and he's a good-looking, good-moving horse but I think he's going to need time. We should see him out the second half of the season, but he'll want middle distances next year. So he wouldn't be in the top flight, but he's an attractive looking horse".*

325. ZAMARELLE ★★★
b.f. Zamindar – Kardelle (Kalaglow).
February 24. Eighth living foal. 20,000Y.

Tattersalls October Book 2. Not sold. Half-sister to the 6f (at 2 yrs) to 1m and subsequent US winner and Group 1 National Stakes second King's County (by Fairy King), to the quite useful 1m, 8.5f and subsequent UAE winner Airbuss (by Mozart), the modest 6f winner Deuxieme (by Second Empire), a winner in Italy by Grand Lodge and a multiple winner in Hong Kong by Salse. The dam, a quite-useful middle-distance placed maiden, is a half-sister to 6 winners including the John Porter Stakes and Lancashire Oaks winner Spout and the French listed winner Mon Domino. The second dam, Arderelle (by Pharly), a quite useful 3-y-o 10f winner, is a half-sister to 8 winners including the Group 2 Prix Greffulhe winner Arokar. (Beckhampton Stables Ltd). *"I bred this filly, she went to the sales where I bought my partner out and I'm glad I did. She's very strong – I think the sire has put some strength into a rather backward family. She's a very good mover, shows a little bit of temperament at times but for a filly that's got a lot of stamina in the pedigree and for a filly that's over sixteen hands, I'm cautiously optimistic that we'll have some fun with her this year".*

326. UNNAMED ★★
b.c. Dansili – Bionic (Zafonic).
January 25. Half-brother to the Group 3 9f Earl Of Sefton Stakes winner Phoenix Tower (by Chester House), to the quite useful 2-y-o 7f winner Winter Bloom (by Aptitude) and the quite useful 2-y-o 5f winner Krynica (by Danzig). The dam, a very useful 2-y-o 7f winner, is a half-sister to the multiple Group 3 middle-distance winner and French Derby fourth Day Flight. The second dam, Bonash (by Rainbow Quest), a very useful filly, won 4 races in France from 1m to 12f including the Prix d'Aumale, the Prix Vanteaux and the Prix de Malleret and is a full or half-sister to 4 winners. (Khalid Abdulla). *"An enormous horse – he's 16.2 hands and strong with it. The dam looked like being very good for Henry Cecil, but unfortunately broke a pelvis. She's produced some good horses though and as regards this colt if you were Nicky Henderson or Paul Nicholls you'd be looking forward to running him in a bumper! A sweet-natured, kind horse but it's much too early to judge him. You couldn't be pressing him yet and patience is the order of the day with him".*

327. UNNAMED ★★★
b.c. Jeremy – Graceful Air (Danzero).
March 22. Fourth foal. 31,000Y. Tattersalls October Book 2. Not sold. Half-brother to the useful 2010 2-y-o 5f and 6f winner Forjatt (by Iffraaj) and to the quite useful 6f winner of 4 races (including at 2 yrs) Amenable (by Bertolini). The dam, a fair 8.3f and 10f winner, is a half-sister to 3 winners including the very useful 2-y-o 5f winner and Group 2 6f Mill Reef Stakes second Mystical Land. The second dam, Samsung Spirit (by Statoblest), a fair dual 6f winner (including at 2 yrs), is a half-sister to 7 winners and to the placed dam of the Group 2 6f Mill Reef Stakes winner Indian Rocket. (R A Pegum). *"A big, strong horse, he has a bit of a knee action so he might prefer some cut in the ground. He has a nice temperament and there's a bit of speed in the pedigree. He's quite big, so he won't be early but he's OK and his pedigree is quite interesting because he has Danehill on both sides. I'm happy with him".*

328. UNNAMED ★★
b.c. Mizzen Mast – Red Dot (Diesis).
January 23. Third foal. The dam is an unraced half-sister to 4 winners including the Grade 1 9f Kentucky Oaks and the Grade 1 10f Alabama Stakes winner Flute. The second dam, Rougeur (by Blushing Groom), a winner over 10f in France and 12f in the USA, was Grade 2 placed and is a half-sister to the Park Hill Stakes winner and good broodmare Eva Luna. (Khalid Abdulla). *"I like him and he seems to go quite nicely. This is the family of Workforce, whose dam is out of Eva Luna. I would guess that this colt should stay well. He doesn't look the type I should be revving up any time soon, but he's slowing filling out and maturing and he goes OK without being a champion".*

DENIS COAKLEY
329. ENTHRALL (IRE) ★★★
b.f. Holy Roman Emperor – Intriguing (Fasliyev).
April 19. Third foal. £8,000Y. Doncaster Premier. Denis Coakley. Half-sister to Lady Intrigue (by Hurricane Run), unplaced on her only start at 2 yrs in 2010. The dam, a quite useful 2-y-o 6f winner, is a half-sister to 7 winners including the Group 3 6f Greenlands

Stakes winner Nautical Pet. The second dam, Sea Mistress (by Habitat), is an unraced half-sister to 2 minor winners. (Miss Y M G Jacques). *"She was a fairly late foal so she'll take a bit of time and won't make a 2-y-o until July onwards over six furlongs. A medium-sized, lovely-looking filly".*

330. FLY IN STYLE ★★★
b.c. Sir Percy – Fly In Style (Hernando).
March 19. Sixth foal. 6,000Y. Tattersalls October Book 3. Denis Coakley. Half-brother to the fair 2010 dual 6f placed 2-y-o Kraleeji (by Kyllachy), to the modest 9f and 10f winner Sternian (by Where Or When) and the moderate 2-y-o 6f seller and subsequent Spanish winner Distant Flash (by Mujahid). The dam is an unraced half-sister to 2 minor winners abroad. The second dam, Fly Don't Run (by Lear Fan), is a placed sister to the Group 2 Premio Ellington winner Run Don't Fly and a half-sister to 5 winners. (Count Calypso Racing). *"For just six grand I think this colt was a bargain. He's a compact 2-y-o type that should be out as soon as the six furlong races start".* TRAINERS' BARGAIN BUY

331. ROYAL DUTCH ★★★
ch.c. Nayef – Shersha (Priolo).
April 8. Third foal. 26,000Y. Tattersalls October Book 2. Norris/Huntingdon. Half-brother to the fair 2010 dual 7f placed 2-y-o Ransom Request (by Red Ransom). The dam, a useful Irish 6f (listed) and dual 1m winner at 3 and 6 yrs, is a half-sister to 2 winners. The second dam, Sheriya (by Green Dancer), was an unraced half-sister to 2 winners. (C T Van Hoorn). *"A nice colt but he's quite big and will take a bit of time. I would imagine he'll be out in August-time over seven furlongs. A big horse and a great mover".*

332. GABRIEL'S LAD (IRE) ★★★
b.c. Dark Angel – Catherine Wheel (Primo Dominie).
March 4. Fourth foal. 17,000Y. Tattersalls October 2. Denis Coakley. Half-brother to the 2010 2-y-o winner Eshoog (by Kyllachy). The dam, a fairly useful 3-y-o 5f and 6f winner, is a half-sister to 4 winners including the very useful 6f (at 2 yrs) and 7f listed winner Levera

The second dam, Prancing (by Prince Sabo), a useful listed-placed 2-y-o 5f winner, stayed 1m and is a full or half-sister to 4 winners including the Group 1 6f Middle Park Stakes winner First Trump. *"He's grown quite a bit and he's a slightly leggy colt. so I wouldn't imagine he'd be out before July. A nice horse, on breeding he should be suited by sprint distances".*

PAUL COLE

333. ALMOST GEMINI (IRE)
gr.c. Dylan Thomas – Streetcar (In The Wings).
May 7. Ninth foal. Goffs Orby. €70,000Y. Hugo Merry. Closely related to the US Grade 1 winner and Irish 1,000 Guineas third Luas Line (by Danehill) and to the fair Irish 9.5f winner Street Style (by Rock Of Gibraltar) and half-brother to the quite useful 2010 2-y-o 7f winner Marden, the fairly useful dual 1m winner Lost In The Moment and the Japanese winner of 4 races Rendir (all by Danehill Dancer). The dam was placed fourth once over 8.5f at 2 yrs and is a half-sister to 9 winners including the Group 3 May Hill Stakes winner Intimate Guest and the dam of the US Grade 1 winner Prince Arch. The second dam, As You Desire Me (by Kalamoun), won 2 listed events in France over 7.5f and 1m and is a half-sister to 7 winners including the Group 2 King Edward VII Stakes winner Classic Example. (Mrs F H Hay).

334. CARDINAL WALTER (IRE)
br.c. Cape Cross – Sheer Spirit (Caerleon).
February 15. Seventh foal. Goffs Orby. €160,000Y. Alex Cole. Half-brother to the fairly useful Irish 2010 7f winner Manieree (by Medicean), to the useful 6f (at 2 yrs) and 7f winner River Bravo (by Indian Ridge), the fairly useful 10f winner and listed-placed Bold Choice (by Dubai Destination), the fairly useful 2-y-o 6f to 1m winner and listed-placed Solid Rock (by Rock Of Gibraltar) and the fair 12f to 14f winner Sovereign Spirit (by Desert Prince). The dam won over 12f at 3 yrs and is a half-sister to 9 winners including the Derby winner Oath and the triple Group 1 winner Pelder. The second dam, Sheer Audacity (by Troy), was placed twice in Italy and is closely related to the Ribblesdale Stakes winner and good broodmare Miss Petard. (Mrs F H Hay).

335. COMMISSAR
b.c. Soviet Star – Sari (Faustus).
March 9. Seventh foal. 32,000Y. Tattersalls October Book 2. P Cole. Brother to the quite useful dual 7f winner Pravda Street and half-brother to the 2010 2-y-o listed 7f winner Lily Again (by American Post), the fairly useful 2-y-o 6f and 1m winner Genari (by Generous) and the fairly useful dual 5f (at 2 yrs) and dual 6f winner Saristar (by Starborough). The dam, a quite useful 7f winner of 2 races (including at 2 yrs), is a half-sister to one winner. The second dam, Fire Lily (by Unfuwain), is a placed half-sister to one winner.

336. DANSABLE (IRE)
b.f. Dansili – Sheepscot (Easy Goer).
February 27. Eighth foal. Goffs Orby. €180,000Y. Hugo Merry. Half-sister to 4 winners including the French 2,000 Guineas winner Astronomer Royal (by Danzig), the US Grade 2 Pan American Handicap winner Navesink River (by Unbridled) and a minor winner in the USA by Fusaichi Pegasus. The dam, a minor stakes winner of 5 races in the USA, is a half-sister to 8 winners including the dual US Grade 1 winner Vicar. The second dam, Escrow Agent (by El Gran Senor), a winner at 2 yrs in Ireland and stakes-placed in the USA, is a half-sister to 7 winners. (RCUK).

337. MACDONALD MOR (IRE)
b.c. Dansili – Imperial Beauty (Imperial Ballet).
March 29. Fifth foal. 110,000Y. Tattersalls October Book 1. Blandford Bloodstock. The dam, winner of the Group 1 5f Prix de l'Abbaye and second in the Group 1 6f Cheveley Park Stakes, is a full or half-sister to 5 winners. The second dam, Multimara (by Arctic Tern), was placed at 2 yrs in the USA and is a half-sister to 8 winners including the Group 3 May Hill Stakes winner Midnight Air (herself dam of the Group 3 Prestige Stakes, Group 3 May Hill Stakes and US Grade 1 winner Midnight Line) and the dam of the 2-y-o Group 1 Criterium International winner Jan Vermeer. (Mrs F H Hay).

338. PERFECT DAY
b.f. Holy Roman Emperor – Yesterday (Sadler's Wells).
May 11. Second foal. 225,000Y. Tattersalls October Book 1. Not sold. The dam won the Irish 1,000 Guineas, was placed in the Prix de l'Opera, Prix Vermeille and Breeders Cup Filly and Mare Turf (all Grade 1 events) and is a sister to the Group 1 7f Moyglare Stud Stakes winner Quarter Moon. The second dam, Jude (by Darshaan), a moderate 10f placed maiden, is a sister to the very useful Irish listed 14f winner and Irish Oaks third Arrikala and to the useful Irish 12f listed winner Alouette (herself dam of the Champion Stakes winner Alborada and the dual Group 1 winner Albanova) and a half-sister to the very smart Group 2 10f Nassau Stakes and Sun Chariot Stakes winner Last Second (dam of the French 2,000 Guineas winner Aussie Rules). (RCUK).

339. PINK DAMSEL (IRE)
b.f. Galileo – Riskaverse (Dynaformer).
March 27. Second foal. 600,000Y. Tattersalls October Book 1. Hugo Merry. Closely related to the quite useful 2010 2-y-o 1m winner Sadler's Risk (by Sadler's Wells). The dam won 9 races from 2 to 6 yrs in the USA including the Grade 1 Flower Bowl Invitational (twice) and the Grade 1 Queen Elizabeth II Challenge Cup Stakes and is a half-sister to 2 winners including the US Grade 3 winner Cozzy Corner. The second dam, The Bink (by Seeking The Gold), won the Grade 3 Interborough Breeders Cup Handicap in the USA and is a half-sister to 4 winners. (Mrs F H Hay).

340. RAINBOW CHORUS
b.c. Royal Applause – Seren Devious (Dr Devious).
April 27. Fourth foal. 50,000Y. Tattersalls October Book 1. Not sold. Half-brother to the Group 3 Prix Thomas Bryon winner and dual Group 3 placed Circumvent (by Tobougg) and to the fairly useful 2-y-o 7f and 1m winner Seradim (by Elnadim). The dam is an unraced half-sister to 6 winners including the smart Group 3 11.5f Lingfield Derby Trial winner Saddler's Quest and the useful French listed 12.5f winner Seren Hill. The second dam, Seren Quest (by Rainbow Quest), was a fairly useful 10f winner. (The Fairy Story Partnership).

341. ROYAL BLUSH
b.f. Royal Applause – Applaud (Rahy).
March 23. Half-sister to the fairly useful listed 1m Masaka Stakes winner Jazz Jam (by Pivotal),

to the quite useful 2-y-o 5f winner Reebel (by Danehill), the fair 2010 2-y-o 5f and 6f winner One Cool Bex (by One Cool Cat), the fair 2-y-o 6f winner Velvet Band (by Verglas), the minor US winner of 8 races Pagliacci (by Gone West) and the minor French 3-y-o winner Framboise (by Diesis). The dam, a smart 2-y-o winner of the Group 2 6f Cherry Hinton Stakes, is a sister to the useful 2-y-o 7f winner Houston Time and a half-sister to 4 winners including the listed winner Sauterne. The second dam, Band (by Northern Dancer), is a placed half-sister to 5 winners including the US Grade 3 9f New Orleans Handicap winner Festive. (Derford Stud Ltd).

342. SILVERHEELS (IRE)
gr.c. Verglas – Vasilia (Dansili).
January 20. First foal. 30,000Y. Tattersalls October Book 2. Paul Cole. The dam is an unraced half-sister to 6 winners including the Group 1 6f Cheveley Park Stakes and dual Group 2 winner Airwave. The second dam, Kangra Valley (by Indian Ridge), a moderate 2-y-o 5f winner, is a half-sister to 7 minor winners. This colt was a winner on his debut at Kempton.

343. STORMBOUND (IRE)
b.c. Galileo – A Footstep Away (Giant's Causeway).
January 29. First foal. 52,000Y. Tattersalls December. Margaret O'Toole. The dam is an unraced half-sister to the US dual Grade 1 winner Lu Ravi and to the dam of the US dual Grade 1 winner and champion 2-y-o filly Halfbridled. The second dam, At The Half (by Seeking The Gold), won 5 races including the Grade 3 Golden Rod Stakes in the USA and is a half-sister to 7 winners including the US Grade 1 winner Spruce Needles. (P F Cole Ltd).

LUCA CUMANI
344. ASHYANE (IRE) ★★★
b.f. Dubawi – Tarabaya (Warning).
March 24. Sixth foal. 100,000Y. Tattersalls October Book 2. L Cumani. Half-sister to the fair 2010 2-y-o 7f winner Askaud (by Iffraaj), to the fair Irish triple 12f winner Taralga (by Sinndar), the French 2-y-o 1m winner Taralan (by Kahyasi) and the French 13f winner Taraba (by Inchinor). The dam, a fairly useful 9f winner, is a half-sister to 6 winners including the useful listed 12f Galtres Stakes winner and Group 3 Noblesse Stakes third Tarakala. The second dam, Tarakana (by Shahrastani), won over 9f in Ireland at 3 yrs, was placed in four listed events from 7f to 12f and is a half-sister to 6 winners. (Sheikh Mohammed Obaid Al Maktoum). *"So far, so good. She seems likeable but she's not particularly early. Seven furlongs or a mile in the second half of the season will be right for her and she's a good-looking filly".*

345. AVALANCHE ★★★
b.c. Three Valleys – Silent Waters (Polish Precedent).
February 15. Fifth foal. 40,000Y. Tattersalls October Book 2. Charlie Gordon-Watson. Half-brother to the fair 12f winner Silver Waters (by Fantastic Light) and to a hurdles winner by Dubai Destination. The dam, placed fourth once over 11f, is a half-sister to 8 winners including the 10f, 12f and subsequent UAE Group 3 12f winner Gower Song. The second dam, Gleaming Water (by Kalaglow), a quite useful 2-y-o 6f winner, is a sister to the Group 3 Solario Stakes winner Shining Water (herself dam of the Group 1 Grand Criterium winner Tenby) and a half-sister to 8 winners. (P Silver). *"A very good-looking horse, he should be one of my earlier ones and I'd expect him to have the speed for six furlongs in June/July. There's plenty of stamina in the pedigree but he's got a bit of speed from Three Valleys I think".*

346. CITY OF CANTON ★★
b.c. Monsun – Snow Crystal (Kingmambo).
April 13. Second foal. 80,000Y. Tattersalls December. Rachel Boffey. The dam, a quite useful 2-y-o 7f winner, is a half-sister to 6 winners including the Group 1 Fillies' mile winner Crystal Music, the Group 3 1m May Hill Stakes winner Group 1 1m Prix Marcel Boussac third Solar Crystal and the Group 3 winners Dubai Success and State Crystal. The second dam, Crystal Spray (by Beldale Flutter), a minor Irish 4-y-o 14f winner, is a half-sister to 8 winners including the Group 2 winner Crystal Hearted. (Mr S A Stuckey). *"Typical of the sire in that he'll need time, he's quite light and immature looking. He needs time to strengthen so he might not run until the autumn at the earliest".*

347. COMMITMENT ★★★★ ♠
b.c. Motivator – Courting (Pursuit Of Love).
April 17. Seventh foal. 85,000Y. Tattersalls October Book 1. John Warren. Half-brother to the very promising 2010 2-y-o dual 7f winner Fury (by Invincible Spirit), to the fairly useful 7f to 10f winner of 6 races Secret Liaison (by Medicean), the fairly useful 7f and 10f winner Tryst (by Highest Honor), the quite useful 9f to 12f winner Speed Dating (by Pivotal) and the modest 6f winner Vibe (by Danzero). The dam, a fairly useful winner of four 2-y-o 7f events and two listed races over 1m and 10f at 3 yrs, is a half-sister to 7 winners including the Group 3 Horris Hill Stakes winner Cupid's Glory. The second dam, Doctor's Glory (by Elmaamul), a fairly useful 5.2f (at 2 yrs) and 6f winner, is a half-sister to 6 winners including the useful On Call, a winner of 7 races at up to 2m (herself dam of the US Grade 2 winner One Off). (Highclere Racing – Diamond Jubilee). *"A lovely horse, he's tall but well put-together. He finds it very easy and he's going to be a seven furlong type in August. Potentially very nice".*

348. DULKASHE (IRE) ★★★
b.r.f. Pivotal – Saik (Riverman).
April 19. Eighth foal. Goffs Orby. €120,000Y. Luca Cumani. Half-sister to the quite useful 3-y-o 7f winner Wistman (by Woodman), to the fair 7f (including at 2 yrs) to 10f winner Hallingdal, the fair 9f and hurdles winner Halling Gal (both by Halling) and 2 winners in Japan by Jade Robbery. The dam is an unraced half-sister to 5 winners including the smart Group 3 10f Brigadier Gerard Stakes and Group 3 10f Scottish Classic winner Husyan and the dam of the triple Group 2 winner Mubtaker. The second dam, Close Comfort (by Far North), is an unraced half-sister to the champion French 2-y-o filly Ancient Regime (herself dam of 3 good winners in Crack Regiment, Rami and La Grande Epoque) and to the Group 2 Prix Maurice de Gheest winner Cricket Ball. (Sheikh Mohammed Obaid Al Maktoum). *"She's very nice – a very good-looking filly, a bit leggy and tall and might not be at her best this year but she'll be good in time".*

349. EMIRATES QUEEN ★★★
b.f. Street Cry – Zomaradah (Deploy).
February 17. Half-sister to the high-class National Stakes (at 2 yrs), Irish 2,000 Guineas and Prix Jacques le Marois winner and sire Dubawi (by Dubai Millennium), to the listed 10f winner Princess Nada (by Barathea) and the quite useful 8.5f winner Suba (by Seeking The Gold). The dam, a winner of 6 races including the Group 1 Italian Oaks, the Group 2 Royal Whip Stakes and the Group 2 Premio Lydia Tesio, is a half-sister to several winners. The second dam, Jawaher (by Dancing Brave), was placed over 1m and 9f and is a half-sister to the Derby winner High Rise. (Sheikh Mohammed Obaid Al Maktoum). *"She's a sister to Dubawi and she's a good-looking filly. Unfortunately she has a bit of a temperament and is not the most co-operative, so whether she'll consent to being a racehorse we'll have to see. It's a shame because it's a great pedigree, she's really good-looking and she goes well".*

350. FURZANAH ★★★
b.f. Dubawi – Latent Lover (In The Wings).
February 24. Second foal. 120,000Y. Tattersalls October Book 1. L Cumani. Half-sister to the unplaced 2010 2-y-o Hal Of A Lover (by Halling). The dam is an unraced half-sister to 4 winners including the listed King Charles II Stakes and subsequent US Grade 3 winner and Grade 2 placed Millennium Dragon. The second dam, Feather Bride (by Groom Dancer), won once at 3 yrs in France and is a half-sister to 5 winners. (Sheikh Mohammed Obaid Al Maktoum). *"She's a nice filly, good-looking and could be a bit earlier than the previous Dubawi we spoke about. She's more mature and stronger, so she should make a 2-y-o half way through the season".*

351. GALLETTO ★★
b.c. Azamour – Galleta (Hernando).
April 30. Third living foal. 50,000Y. Tattersalls October Book 2. Charlie Gordon-Watson. The dam is an unraced half-sister to 8 winners including the useful triple 7f winner Mata Cara (herself the dam of a French listed winner). The second dam, Fatah Flare (by Alydar), won over 6f (at 2 yrs) and the Group 3 10.5f Musidora Stakes at 3 yrs and is a half-sister to 8 winners including Sabin, a dual US Grade 1 winner over 9f and 10f. (L Marinopoulos & Partners). *"A good-looking horse, he has a staying pedigree but he could*

be alright in the autumn, otherwise he'll be better next year".

352. INFINITE HOPE (USA) ★★★
b.br.f. Dynaformer – Shared Dreams (Seeking The Gold).
February 16. First foal. The dam, a fairly useful 10f winner, was listed placed and subsequently fourth in a Grade 3 stakes in the USA. The second dam, Coretta (by Caerleon), won the Grade 2 Long Island Handicap and the Grade 2 La Prevoyante Handicap and is a half-sister to the very useful 10f winner and listed-placed Trumpet Sound, the very useful 10.5f winner and listed placed Rosa Parks and the 2-y-o 9f listed winner Mikado. (Miss S J E Leigh). "A nice, good-looking filly from a good family. A first foal and slightly on the small side, she's nice and from a family I know very well. Dynaformers normally want a bit of a trip and this branch of the family stays as well, so she'll be one to start off at seven furlongs to a mile later on this season".

353. KALILY ★★★
b.c. Dubawi – Mail Express (Cape Cross).
March 20. Second foal. The dam, a fair 6f winner at 3 yrs, is a half-sister to 5 winners including the Group 1 1m Premio Vittorio di Capua, Group 2 Challenge Stakes and Group 2 Italian 2,000 Guineas winner Le V e dei Colori. The second dam, Mystic Tempo (by El Gran Senor), won over 6f at 2 yrs and two 6f sellers at 3 yrs and is a half-sister to 3 winners including the useful dual 3-y-o 1m winner and Group 1 Moyglare Stud Stakes third Timely. (Sheikh Mohammed Obaid Al Maktoum). "A good-looking horse, he's quite big and he doesn't strike me as an early type. He should start coming to himself from the middle of the season onwards".

354. KEEP IT DARK ★★
b.c. Invincible Spirit – Tarneem (Zilzal).
February 28. Tenth foal. 80,000Y. Tattersalls October Book 1. Charlie Gordon-Watson. Half-brother to the smart 7f (at 2 yrs) and Group 3 9f Darley Stakes winner and Group 1 Coronation Cup third Enforcer, to the quite useful 2-y-o dual 5f winner Lord Of The Inn, the modest 1m winner Uncle Brit (all by Efisio), the fair 5.7f winner Innstyle (by Daggers

Drawn) and the Italian winner of 9 races at up to 13.5f Kris's Bank (by Inchinor). The dam, a quite useful 3-y-o 1m winner, is a half-sister to 4 minor winners abroad. The second dam, Willowy Mood (by Will Win), won 14 races including two Grade 3 events in the USA and is a half-sister to 9 winners. (A Marinopoulos). "He had a slight setback earlier on, so he might not make it back as a 2-y-o. We'll just have to see how he goes".

355. KIWAYU ★★
b.c. Medicean – Kibara (Sadler's Wells).
April 13. Third foal. The dam, a fair 11f winner, is a sister to 4 winners including the St Leger and Great Voltigeur Stakes winner Milan and half-sister to the Irish 2-y-o 7f winner and Group 2 Great Voltigeur Stakes third Go For Gold. The second dam, Kithanga (by Darshaan), was a smart winner of 3 races including the Group 3 12f St Simon Stakes and the listed 12f Galtres Stakes. (Fittocks Stud Ltd). "A good-looking horse from a great family, he's a little bit backward in his development. Again, it's a staying family but he's a horse that has got possibilities".

356. MANKINI ★★
b.c. Dansili – Fashion Statement (Rainbow Quest).
March 15. First foal. 100,000Y. Tattersalls October Book 2. Charlie Gordon-Watson. The dam, a 1m (at 2 yrs) and Group 2 Italian Oaks winner, is a half-sister to one winner. The second dam, Shabby Chic (by Red Ransom), winner of the listed 10f Prix de Liancourt and third in both the Grade 1 Yellow Ribbon Stakes and the Group 3 Prix Chloe, is a sister to the Oaks winner Casual Look and a half-sister to 7 winners. (L Marinopoulos & Partners). "He's a small horse and after buying him we turned him out for a while to give him a chance to grow. He's doing that and he's a likeable individual but his pedigree suggests he'll want a trip next year, so hopefully he'll be capable of doing something at the back-end of his 2-y-o career".

357. MEZZOTINT (IRE) ★★★
b.c. Diamond Green – Aquatint (Dansili).
February 6. Third foal. Doncaster Premier. £31,000Y. G Howson. Half-brother to the

2010 2-y-o Missile Attack (by Majestic Missile) and to the useful 6f (at 2 yrs) and 7f winner and listed placed Kaptain Kirkup (by Captain Rio). The dam is an unraced half-sister to 5 winners including the listed 12f winner and Group 2 12f Ribblesdale Stakes third Marani. The second dam, Aquamarine (by Shardari), won the listed Cheshire Oaks and is a half-sister to the St Leger winner Toulon. (L Marinopoulos & Partners). *"A good-looking yearling, he was relatively inexpensive and he should be good enough to win as a 2-y-o".*

358. OUT DO ★★★
ch.c. Exceed And Excel – Ludynosa (Cadeaux Genereux).
May 16. Fifth foal. 55,000Y. Tattersalls October Book 1. Charlie Gordon-Watson. Half-brother to Psitta (by Grand Lodge), a winner of 6 races in Italy and listed placed, to the fair 6f winner Siren Party (by Pivotal) and a winner in Greece by Baratea. The dam, a fairly useful 6f and 7f winner, is a half-sister to 8 winners including the Group 2 1m Prix d'Astarte winner Daneskaya and the French dual Group 3 middle-distance winner Silverskaya. The second dam, Boubskaia (by Niniski), a listed-placed winner in France, is a half-sister to 7 winners including the Group 1 1m Gran Criterium winner Will Dancer and the Group 2 6f Premio Umbria winner Dancing Eagle. (L Marinopoulos & Partners). *"He doesn't look like an Exceed And Excel because he's big and scopey and seems to want a bit of time. He's also a late foal so we'll have to see, but the family is quite good and they have horses that are fairly fast, so let's hope he'll come together one of these days".*

359. PARAMYTHI (IRE) ★★★★
ch.c. Peintre Celebre – The Spirit Of Pace (In The Wings).
April 6. Fourth foal. Goffs Orby. €55,000Y. Charlie Gordon-Watson. Half-brother to the fairly useful 12f winner of 4 races Spirit Is Needed (by No Excuse Needed) and to a winner in Greece by Celtic Swing. The dam is an unraced half-sister to 3 winners including the German Group 1 and French Group 2 winner of 16 races Yavana's Pace and the listed winner Littlepacepaddocks. The second dam, Lady In Pace (by Burslem), a dual 5f winner in Ireland, is a half-sister to 2 winners. (A Marinopoulos). *"A good-looking horse that moves very well, despite his middle-distance pedigree he should win as a 2-y-o if nothing goes wrong. He's an athletic horse and not at all backward-looking. For the pedigree he's a precocious looking horse".*

360. PETROL ★★★
ch.c. Danehill Dancer – Pongee (Baratea).
March 21. Third foal. Half-brother to the quite useful 2010 2-y-o 1m winner Poplin (by Medicean) and to the fair 10f winner Paisley (by Pivotal). The dam, a very useful Group 2 12f Lancashire Oaks winner, is closely related to the smart listed 12f and listed 14f winner Lion Sands and to the very useful 10f (at 2 yrs) and 11f winner and listed-placed Pukka and a half-sister to 2 winners. The second dam, Puce (by Darshaan), a very useful listed 12f winner, is a half-sister to 7 winners. (Fittocks Stud). *"Another family that I know well and it's a staying family that come to themselves at three. So anything they do at two is a bonus. This colt is likeable and good-looking, so if he copies his sister and wins over a mile this year that would be good".*

361. QANAN ★★★★
b.c. Green Desert – Strings (Unfuwain).
March 30. Fourth foal. 145,000Y. Tattersalls October Book 2. Rachel Boffey. Half-brother to the fairly useful 2010 2-y-o 1m winner State Opera (by Shamardal), to the quite useful dual 7f (at 2 yrs) and 10f winner Bahamian Flight (by Bahamian Bounty) and a winner abroad by Exceed And Excel. The dam is an unraced half-sister to 6 winners including the French 2,000 Guineas winner Victory Note. The second dam, Three Piece (by Jaazeiro), an Irish placed 2-y-o, is a half-sister to 8 winners including Orchestration (Group 2 Coronation Stakes) and Welsh Term (Group 2 Prix d'Harcourt). (Mr S A Stuckey). *"A nice, good-looking horse that moves well and he should be a 2-y-o even though he's quite big. One for August or September time, I like him and he should hopefully do some good at two".*

362. QUALITY PEARL (USA) ★★★
b.f. Elusive Quality – Marianka (Ascot Knight).
February 14. Eighth foal. $150,000Y.

Keeneland September. David Redvers. Half-sister to the Canadian Grade 3 winners Matt's Broken Vow (by Broken Vow) and High Button Shoes (by Carson City), to the Canadian stakes winner Victory Thrill (by Victory Gallop) and 2 minor winners by Broken Vow and Mr Greeley. The dam, a stakes winner of 3 races at 3 yrs in Canada, is a half-sister to the Canadian stakes winner Super You. The second dam, Unforgetable You (by Vice Regent), was a stakes winner of 3 races at 3 yrs. (Pearl Bloodstock Ltd). *"A good-looking filly, she's tall and quite leggy. One for the second part of the season I'd say, around August or September, probably over seven furlongs or a mile to begin with".*

363. ROCKALONG (IRE) ★★★
b.br.c. Rock Of Gibraltar – High Spot (Shirley Heights).
April 23. Sixth foal. 170,000Y. Tattersalls October Book 2. Charlie Gordon-Watson. Half-brother to the very useful 2-y-o 6f and subsequent US Grade 2 Providencia Stakes winner and Group 2 7f Rockfel Stakes second Missit (by Orpen) and to the quite useful Irish 2-y-o 7f winner Night Sphere (by Night Shift). The dam was placed over middle-distances and is a half-sister to 3 winners including the listed-placed Allergy. The second dam, Rash Gift (by Cadeaux Genereux), is a placed half-sister to 7 winners. (Mr Nagy El Azar). *"A very good-looking horse, he goes well and I'm pleased with him, but he's out of a staying mare and I don't know the family very well. I think the jury is still out on Rock Of Gibraltar, nobody has a real handle on them at the moment".*

364. SCRUPUL ★★★★
b.c. Dylan Thomas – Pearl Quest (Rainbow Quest).
May 1. First foal. 38,000Y. Tattersalls December. Ama al Shorafa. The dam was placed 6 times at 3 yrs in France and is a half-sister to one winner. The second dam, Oyster Catcher (by Bluebird), an Irish listed 5.6f winner and Group 3 placed, is a half-sister to 4 winners including the Group 1 7f Moyglare Stud Stakes winner Sequoyah (dam of the multiple Group 1 winning miler Henrythenavigator) and the 2-y-o Group 1 Fillies' Mile winner Listen. (Salice). *"A nice colt, I like him and he shouldn't be too backward despite being out of a Rainbow

Quest mare. All being well he should run two or three times this year from August onwards, starting off at seven furlongs".*

365. SEA FEVER ★★★
b.c. Footstepsinthesand – Love And Laughter (Theatrical).
March 1. Second foal. 115,000Y. Tattersalls October Book 1. De La Warr Racing. Half-brother to the very smart 1m (at 2 yrs) and triple 10f winner and subsequent US Grade 1 second Wigmore Hall (by High Chaparral). The dam, a fair 2-y-o 7f winner, is a half-sister to 3 winners including the French listed winner Kissing The Camera. The second dam, Hoh Dear (by Sri Pekan), won 4 races here and in North America including the 6f Empress Stakes (at 2 yrs) and the Grade 3 Natalma Stakes and was second in the Group 2 Cherry Hinton Stakes. (Delaware Racing). *"He's a nice, neat, well-proportioned 2-y-o that should be alright as a 2-y-o come July or August. He should be OK and I'd say he'll want seven furlongs".*

366. SEEMA (USA) ★★★★
b.c. Dubawi – The Sound Of Music (Galileo).
April 15. First foal. The dam is an unraced to 6 winners including the St Leger and Coronation Cup winner Scorpion, the US Grade 2 and Grade 3 winner Memories and the listed winners Garuda and Danish Rhapsody and the dam of the Australian Group 1 winner Zipping. The second dam, Ardmelody (by Law Society), is an unraced half-sister to 8 winners. (Sheikh Mohammed Obaid Al Maktoum). *"He's nice, he's a good-looking horse and he should be up to winning this year".*

367. SPUNKY ★★★
b.c. Invincible Spirit – Passe Passe (Lear Fan).
April 9. Ninth foal. 26,000Y. Tattersalls October Book 1. Charlie Gordon-Watson. Half-brother to La Troupe (by King's Best), placed fourth over 7f on her only start at 2 yrs in 2007, to the fairly useful 7f (at 2 yrs) and 10f winner Cabinet (by Grand Lodge), the fairly useful 10.2f and 12f winner and Australian Grade 2 placed Magic Instinct (by Entrepreneur), the quite useful 2-y-o 5f winner Ryedale Ovation (by Royal Applause) and the fair 7f winner Great Art (by One Cool Cat). The dam, a fair 7f to 12f placed maiden, is a half-sister to the Irish listed winner and French

Group 2 placed Windermere. The second dam, Madame L'Enjoleur (by L'Enjoleur), a 2-y-o stakes winner in the USA, was placed in two Grade 1 events over 8.5f and is a half-sister to the Grade 1 9f Hollywood Derby winner Labeeb and the Grade 2 winners Fanmore and Alrassam. (L Marinopoulos & Partners). *"He should make a 2-y-o. He's neat, quite strong and well put-together. He'll be working earlier than most of the others and he should run in May or June".*

368. STRADA FACENDO (USA) ★★★★
ch.c. Street Cry – What A Treasure
(Cadeaux Genereux).
April 10. First foal. $190,000Y. Keeneland September. John Ferguson. The dam, a fair dual 7f winner, is a half-sister to 4 winners including the German Group 3 6.5f winner Toylsome. The second dam, Treasure Trove (by The Minstrel), is a placed half-sister to the US Graded stakes winners Dance Parade and Ocean Queen. (P Agostini). *"I like him, he's got a bit of speed and I trained the dam. He's likeable and he should be a July type 2-y-o".*

369. SUBTRACTION (IRE) ★★
b.c. Pivotal – Attraction (Efisio).
April 15. Third foal. 200,000Y. Tattersalls October Book 1. Luca Cumani. Half-brother to the quite useful 2010 2-y-o 1m winner Devastation (by Montjeu) and to the fair 2-y-o winner Elation (by Cape Cross). The dam, a high-class 1,000 Guineas, Irish 1,000 Guineas, Coronation Stakes, Matron Stakes and Sun Chariot Stakes winner, is a half-sister to 2 winners. The second dam, Flirtation (by Pursuit Of Love), ran unplaced once over 7f at 3 yrs and is a half-sister to 4 winners including the French listed 12f winner and Group 2 placed Carmita. (Mrs M Marinopoulos, Duke Of Roxburghe & Mrs Sara Cumani). *"A huge horse, probably the biggest 2-y-o we have, so I doubt him doing anything this year. He's lovely to look at but he's weak and I look forward to having him at three and four".*

370. SYNCOPATE ★★★
b.c. Oratorio – Millistar (Galileo).
February 15. First foal. 42,000Y. Tattersalls October Book 1. Charlie Gordon-Watson. The dam, a fair dual 10f winner, is a half-sister to 4 winners and to the unplaced dam of the Group 2 Sun Chariot Stakes winner Kissogram. The second dam, Milligram (by (by Mill Reef), won the Group 1 1m Queen Elizabeth II Stakes, the Group 2 1m Coronation Stakes and the Group 2 Waterford Crystal Mile and is a half-sister to the Coronation Stakes placed Someone Special - herself dam of the Group winners One So Wonderful, Alnasr Alwasheek and Relatively Special. (L Marinopoulos & Partners). *"He should make a 2-y-o, he's neat and well put-together and not backward. Her should be racing in late May or June, possibly over six or seven furlongs".*

371. TWELVE STRINGS (IRE) ★★★
b.c. Iffraaj – Favoritely (Favorite Trick).
February 17. First foal. 110,000Y. Tattersalls October Book 2. Rachel Boffey. The dam, placed four times at 4 yrs in the USA, is a half-sister to 9 winners including the US stakes winner and Grade 2 placed Happy Gini (herself the dam of 3 Group winners). The second dam, Keep Her Happy (by Sham), won twice at 3 yrs in the USA and is a half-sister to 12 winners including the US Grade 3 winner Private Thoughts. (Mr S A Stuckey). *"A good-looking horse, his temperament isn't great and he may have to be gelded, but he should be a six furlong 2-y-o in May or June".*

TOM DASCOMBE

372. BAROLO TOP (IRE) ★★★
b.c. Amadeus Wolf – Princess Mood
(Muhtarram).
April 13. Seventh foal. 50,000Y. Tattersalls October Book 1. McKeever Bloodstock. Half-brother to the very useful 6f and 7f listed winner and subsequent UAE Group 1 placed Kingsgate Prince (by Desert Sun), to the useful 2-y-o listed 7f winner of 3 races Captain Ramius (by Kheleyf), the fairly useful 6f and 7f winner Avenuesnalleyways (by Bertolini) and the fair 8.5f winner Smugglers Bay (by Celtic Swing). The dam, placed over 1m in Germany, is a half-sister to 5 winners in Germany and Italy. The second dam, Princess Nana (by Bellypha), won the Group 2 German 1,000 Guineas and is a half-sister to 6 winners. (Jones, Seed, Woodgate). *"A very nice type of horse and since we bought him his half-brother Kingsgate Prince (renamed Sunny King) was third in*

a Group 1 in Meydan on Dubai World Cup night. He's been sold to some very enthusiastic owners and he'll probably go to Chester for the May meeting. That'll be just to get him going and then he'll want six furlongs. He's improved an awful lot, he's strong and quite forward. We bought him from Book 1 of Tattersalls Sales so he could be entered in the sprint sales race in the autumn".

373. BROCKWELL ★★
b.c. Singspiel – Noble Plum (King's Best).
February 22. First foal. 70,000Y. Tattersalls October Book 2. D Elsworth. The dam, a quite useful dual 12f winner, is a half-sister to one winner. The second dam, Perfect Plum (by Darshaan), won the Group 2 1m Prix Saint-Roman and the Group 3 1m Prix des Reservoirs (both at 2 yrs) and is a half-sister to 3 winners. (South Wind Racing 3). "He's only just come in and he's a big horse by Singspiel so we haven't done much with him yet. So as far as his ability is concerned I couldn't say just yet and he'll be one for the back-end of the season. He's entered for the 2012 Derby, so we'll see if that's a sensible entry or not!"

374. CONQUERATA ★★
gr.f. Motivator – Park Acclaim (Clodovil).
January 10. First foal. The dam is an unraced half-sister to the Group 3 7f Jersey Stakes winner Rainfall. The second dam, Molomo (Barathea), an Irish 12f winner and second in both the Group 2 10f Pretty Polly Stakes and the Group 2 10f Royal Whip Stakes, is a sister to the Irish 1m and 9f winner and listed-placed Pepperwood and a half-sister to 2 winners. (Manor House Stables LLP). "For a January foal she doesn't have a lot of substance to her. Small and light, she'll take a bit of time and is one for the second half of the season".

375. ELECTRIC QATAR ★★★★
b.c. Pastoral Pursuits – Valandraud (College Chapel).
March 30. Fifth foal. Doncaster Premier. £46,000Y. Kern/Lillington. Half-brother to the quite useful 2-y-o 5f and subsequent Hong Kong winner Final Answer (by Kyllachy) and to Rio Ther (by Bertolini), a winner of 8 races in Italy from 2 to 5 yrs. The dam is an unraced half-sister to 2 winners. The second dam, Guana Bay (by Cadeaux Genereux), is an unraced sister to one winner and a half-sister to 5 winners including the Group 2 winners Prince Sabo and Millyant. (Manor House Stables LLP). "A very nice horse. He rapidly improved in February and March and he has a couple of race entries already, so he might have run before your book comes out. Possibly the nicest of my earlier type two-year-olds and he'll be a five/six furlong horse. Certainly a first half of the season 2-y-o".

376. EQUALIZER ★★★
b.c. Authorized – Octaluna (Octagonal).
February 15. Third foal. €90,000Y. Arqana Deauville August. Kern/Lillington. The dam, placed once at 2 yrs, is a half-sister to the Group 2 King Edward VII Stakes and Group 2 Princess Of Wales's Stakes winner Papal Bull. The second dam, Mialuna (by Zafonic), is an unplaced half-sister to the 5 winners including the Italian multiple Group 3 winner St Paul House. (Manor House Stables LLP). "He's a French-bred colt and a latter part of the season type. He's just doing canters at the moment, he only came in the yard in March and he'll be aimed at a novice event around July time with a view to finding out how good he is before going to France. If he's good enough he'll follow the route followed by our colt Hung Parliament last year. So he'll be contesting the seven furlong and mile races over there".

377. GOAL HANGER ★★★
b.f. Exceed And Excel – Mrs Gray (Red Sunset).
January 17. Fourteenth foal. Doncaster Premier. £18,000Y. Kern/Lillington. Half-sister to the very useful 6f and 7f (at 2 yrs) and subsequent US stakes winner Steelaninch, to the quite useful 2-y-o 1m winner Snowey Mountain (both by Inchinor), the quite useful 2-y-o 5f winner Exgray (by Exceed And Excel), the quite useful 7f (at 2 yrs) to 10f winner Anuvasteel (by Vettori), the fair 4-y-o 6f winner Lucayan Beach (by Cyrano de Bergerac), the fair 9f winner Scrupulous (by Dansili), the fair 7f (at 2 yrs) and 10f winner Flying Applause (by Royal Applause), a winner of 8 races in Sweden by Rambo Dancer and a bumpers winner by Rock Hopper. The dam, a modest 2-y-o 5f winner, is a full or half-sister to 11 winners here and abroad including the German 2-y-o Group

2 6f winner Amigo Sucio and the dam of the Group 2 Prix Robert Papin winner Rolly Polly. The second dam, Haunting (by Lord Gayle), is a placed half-sister to 7 minor winners. (Owen Promotions Ltd). *"She looked very sharp and was going to be an early 2-y-o, but she went completely off her grub and we had to give her a bit of time off. But we got her going again, she's got speed and she's tall and leggy. I think she's got ability and she'll have the pace for five furlongs from late May onwards".*

378. GONDOLIER (FR) ★★★
b.c. Anabaa – Grenade (Bering).
March 6. Third foal. €60,000Y. Arqana Deauville October. Kern/Lillingston. Brother to the French 1m (at 2 yrs) and listed 7f winner Gotlandia. The dam, a minor winner at 3 yrs in France, is a half-sister to 8 winners including the Group 1 Fillies' Mile winner Gloriosa. The second dam, Golden Sea (by Saint Cyrien), won 4 minor races at 2 and 4 yrs in France and is a half-sister to 8 winners including Glity (Group 2 Prix Guillaume d'Ornano). (Auld Hayes and Murphy). *"Another of our French-bred horses (we bought a few because the premiums are fantastic), he's the most stunning looking horse. He'll go for a novice race or something similar, as an introduction before sending him to Deauville in August. He'll have three runs maximum this year and he'll make a lovely 3-y-o. Having said that, if any of these French-breds show that they've got a lot of ability I'd rather win something like the Superlative Stakes than cross the channel".*

379. LEXI'S PRINCE (IRE) ★★★
gr.c. Clodovil – Bent Al Fala (Green Desert).
January 26. Ninth foal. Goffs Orby. €58,000Y. McKeever Bloodstock. Closely related to the quite useful dual 5f winner Indigo Nights (by Danehill Dancer) and half-brother to 6 winners including the Group 3 La Coupe de Maisons-Laffitte winner Pallodio (by Medicis), the fair Irish 6f winner Iron Major (by Titus Livius) and the modest 7f and 1m winner Nok Twice (by Second Empire). The dam, a modest 2-y-o 5f winner, is a half-sister to 8 winners including the fair listed winner Bashful. The second dam, Clunk Click (by Star Appeal), is a placed half-sister to 10 winners including the triple Group 2 winner Sure Blade. (Dr M Koukash). *"We're delighted to be training for Dr Marwan Koukash. This horse was bought for Chester, he'll be running at Chester and will be running at every available race at Chester from now until October! He's a nice horse but he shows that he probably wants six furlongs and probably a bit of cut in the ground".*

380. LORD ALI McJONES ★★★
b.c. Elusive City – Combloux (Southern Halo).
April 9. Fourth foal. €40,000Y. Arqana Deauville August. McKeever Bloodstock. Brother to the French 6f to 1m winner of 4 races, listed second and Group 3 fourth Bolt City and half-brother to a minor French winner by Enrique. The dam was laced once at 2 yrs in France and is a half-sister to 6 winners including the listed winner and Group 2 Criterium de Maisons-Laffitte second Black Escort and the French Group 3 placed Contexte. The second dam, Company (by Nureyev), won once as a 2-y-o at Longchamp, was third in the listed Prix Zeddaan and fourth in the Group 3 5f Prix d'Arenburg. She is a sister to the very useful sprinter King's Signet, is closely related to the good sprinter Sicyos and a half-sister to the 2-y-o Group 3 6.5f Prix Eclipse winner Radjhasi. (Manor House Stables LLP). *"A very racey type of 2-y-o, the owners are very keen to run at Chester's May meeting and he might go for a maiden before that so we can decide which of the Chester races to go for. He's not over-big, she's sharp and has bags of speed, so I'll be disappointed if he doesn't win races in April or May. He's also eligible for the French bred premiums".*

381. MARFORD MISSILE (IRE) ★★★★
b.c. Majestic Missile – Khawafi (Kris).
January 28. Seventh foal. Tattersalls Ireland. €14,000Y. Kern/Lillingston. Half-brother to the fair 7f and 1m winner of 10 races Kipchak (by Soviet Star) and to the modest 10f winner Paymaster General (by Desert Style). The dam won once over 10f and is a half-sister to 4 winners including the dual listed winner Tolpuddle. The second dam, Tabdea (by Topsider), won the listed Firth Of Clyde Stakes and listed Sceptre Stakes and is a half-sister to 8 winners including the French 1,000 Guineas winner Ta Rib. (The MHS 4x10 Partnership). *"It was nice to see him win first time out but the time of the race was slow.*

He'll go to Newcastle again in April for a novice race and if he's successful there he'll go for the Lily Agnes Stakes at Chester. He's a bull of a horse and was fifty kilos bigger than any other horse in the race and he won despite the fact he went there mainly for an educational run. Very straightforward and professional".

382. MENELIK (IRE) ★★★★
b.c. Oasis Dream – Chica Roca (Woodman).
March 31. Fourth foal. Goffs Orby. €50,000Y. Kern/Lillingston. Half-brother to the 2010 Irish 2-y-o 7f winner Qubuh (by Invincible Spirit) and to the fair Irish 6f (at 2 yrs) and 7f winner Chibcha (by High Chaparral). The dam, placed twice at 2 yrs in France, is a half-sister to the Group 2 Criterium de Maisons-Laffitte winner Zinziberine. The second dam, Amenixa (by Linamix), a 4-y-o 10f winner, is a sister to the dual Group 1 Prix Royal-Oak winner Amilynx and the listed winner Amie De Mix and a half-sister to the Group 2 Criterium de Maisons-Laffitte winner Amiwain. (L A Bellman). "He's done a bit of work but it transpired that physically it was a bit too soon and he wasn't quite up to it. He's had a couple of easy weeks since then, he'll be out in June – and he's a racehorse! Six furlongs should suit him to begin with, he's looking stronger now. One to note".

383. MISTY CONQUEST (IRE) ★★★
b.f. Mujadil – Polish Belle (Polish Precedent).
March 20. Seventh foal. Doncaster Premier. £5,000Y. Kern/Lillingston. Half-sister to the fair 2011 1m and 9f 3-y-o winner Tijori (by Kyllachy), to the quite useful 2-y-o 6f winner Jairzihno (by Royal Applause) and a winner in Italy by Red Ransom. The dam is an unraced half-sister to 5 winners including the very smart sprinter Danehurst, winner of the Cornwallis Stakes (at 2 yrs), the Curragh Flying Five, the Prix de Seine-et-Oise and the Premio Umbria (all Group 3 events) and the smart Group 3 10.5f Prix Penelope winner Humouresque. The second dam, Miswaki Belle (by Miswaki), second over 7f on her only start, is a half-sister to 8 winners including the smart Group 3 6f Cherry Hinton Stakes winner and 1,000 Guineas third Dazzle. (Deva Racing Mujadil Partnership). "We got lucky with this filly because a couple of weeks after the sales her half-brother Jairzihno was second in a Grade 2 in America. She's a precocious type and she'll be racing in late April or early May. Sharp and racey, she'll have the speed for five furlongs but she'll probably get seven in the end".

384. MUSICAL VALLEY ★★★
ch.c. Three Valleys – Musical Horizon (Distant View).
April 23. Second foal. €2,000Y. Tattersalls Ireland. Kern/Lillingston. The dam is an unplaced sister to the champion 2-y-o Distant Music (winner of the Group 1 7f Dewhurst Stakes, the Group 2 7f Champagne Stakes and the Group 2 9f Goffs International Stakes) and a half-sister to 3 winners including the useful 10f winner and Group 3 Lancashire Oaks third New Orchid (herself dam of the Group 1 6f Haydock Sprint Cup winner African Rose). The second dam, Musicanti (by Nijinsky), a French 14.5f winner, is a half-sister to the top-class American middle-distance colt Vanlandingham, winner of the Washington D.C. International, the Jockey Club Gold Cup and the Suburban Handicap. (The MHS 4x10 Partnership). "He was going very nicely but he hasn't really developed behind as well as he could have and I think that's because he has a high testicle, so we're going to get him gelded. He should still be out in May and he's done enough to suggest he'll win a race. He was very cheap, despite being out of a full sister to a champion 2-y-o, so that's very strange. I'm looking forward to running him".

385. PALMETTO (FR) ★★★★
b.c. Anabaa – Porretta (Indian Ridge).
April 14. Fifth foal. €55,000Y. Arqana Deauville August. Kern/Lillingston. Half-brother to 2 minor French winners by Numerous. The dam, a minor French 3-y-o winner, is a half-sister to 4 winners including the Group 3 placed Pescia. The second dam, Lambada (by Lyphard), a French listed-placed winner, is a half-sister to the dual Group 1 winning 2-y-o and sire Tobougg. (The MHS 8x8 Partnership). "He looked great at the sales but when we brought him home he fell apart. He must be 16.2 hands now, we sent him to Bearstone Stud and they've done a lovely job with him because he's strong and he looks fantastic. He'll be another one I'll run in July all being well and then take to Deauville. A gorgeous horse".

386. PYMAN'S THEORY (IRE) ★★★
ch.f. Exceed And Excel – Gazebo (Cadeaux Genereux).
March 29. Third foal. Doncaster Premier. £42,000Y. Kern/Lillingston. Half-sister to the Irish 2-y-o listed 6f Flame Of Tara Stakes winner Forthefirsttime (by Dr Fong) and to the quite useful 1m to 10f winner Oat Cuisine (by Mujahid). The dam, a modest 6f placed 2-y-o, is a half-sister to the US sprint winner of 13 races and listed-placed Hardball, to the listed-placed winner Injaaz and to the winner Corndavon (herself dam of the July Stakes winner Nevisian Lad). The second dam, Ferber's Follies (by Saratoga Six), a winning 2-y-o sprinter, was third in the Grade 2 6f Adirondack Stakes and is a half-sister to 11 winners including the US 2-y-o Grade 2 6f winner Blue Jean Baby. (Owen Promotions Ltd). *"A very sharp, five furlong 2-y-o, she's had sore shins but she'll be racing in late April or early May because although we went easy on her for a bit, she's ready to go".*

387. SPRING DAISY (IRE) ★★★
b.f. Bertolini – Charlotti Carlotti (Celtic Swing).
January 23. First foal. Doncaster St Leger Festival. £10,500Y. Kern/Lillingston. The dam, a fair 2-y-o 5f winner, is a half-sister to 4 winners. The second dam, Kunucu (by Bluebird), a fairly useful sprint winner of 4 races and listed placed, is a full or half-sister to 7 winners. (The MHS 4x10 Partnership). *"A very sharp, speedy 2-y-o. She'll be racing in April and she's very straightforward. Not a star but she's a nice type and there's a race in her".*

388. VIOLA D'AMOUR (IRE) ★★★
b.f. Teofilo – Dame's Violet (Groom Dancer).
March 14. Sixth foal. Tattersalls Ireland. €44,000Y. Kern/Lillingston. Closely related to the fairly useful 2-y-o 7f winner Marina Of Venice (by Galileo) and half-sister to the useful 1m and listed 10f winner Dawnus, the fair 2-y-o 7f winner Maximus Aurelius and the fair 5f winner Maigue Violet (all by Night Shift). The dam, a 1m winner of 2 races at 3 yrs in France, is a half-sister to 6 winners including the high-class Group 2 and Group 3 middle-distance winner Wagon Master. The second dam, Sunny Flower (by Dom Racine), placed twice in France, was a half-sister to 5 winners including the top-class broodmare Sunny Valley (the dam of Sun Princess and Saddlers Hall). (L A Bellman). *"A beautiful Teofilo, she's a nice, sharp filly with a bit of quality and a nice pedigree. She's had a couple of tiny problems and we've looked after her rather than push on, she's not over-big but she looks quick".*

389. WINTER HILL ★★★
b.f. Three Valleys – White Turf (Tiger Hill).
April 22. Second foal. £5,000Y. Doncaster Festival. Kern/Lillingston. Half-sister to the unplaced 2010 2-y-o These Dreams (by Sleeping Indian). The dam, a minor French 1m winner at 3 yrs, is a half-sister to the winner and German listed-placed Wonderful Day. The second dam, Wonderful Dreams (by Dashing Blade), a listed winner at 3 yrs in Germany, is a sister to the stakes winner and German Group 2 placed Winning Dash. (The MHS 4x10 Partnership). *"A German pedigree with a bit of stamina, she's tall and leggy so she won't be rushed. I'd like to think that we'd get a run into her in June sometime. A nice type, but she won't be early".*

390. UNNAMED ★★★★
b.c. Vital Equine – Alexander Ballet (Mind Games).
May 19. Fifth foal. 50,000Y. Tattersalls October Book 2. McKeever Bloodstock. Half-brother to the Group 1 Gran Criterium winner and Group 1 St James Palace Stakes third Hearts Of Fire (by Firebreak). The dam, an Irish 3-y-o 5f winner, is a half-sister to 4 winners. The second dam, Dayville (by Dayjur), a quite useful triple 6f winner, is a half-sister to 4 winners including the Grade 1 Yellow Ribbon Handicap winner Spanish Fern. (Manor House Stables LLP). *"A very nice horse, he was a late foal but his half-brother Hearts Of Fire was a May foal and he won the Brocklesby and then a Group 1 as a 2-y-o. We've forgotten about the Brocklesby – we just want to win the Group 1! He's a nice type, he should have plenty of speed when we actually ask him for it and he looks like a 2-y-o but he won't run until June".*

391. UNNAMED ★★★
b.f. Diamond Green – Amorous Pursuits (Pursuit Of Love).
February 5. Fourth foal. Doncaster Premier. £20,000Y. McKeever Bloodstock. Half-

sister to the fair Irish 2-y-o 6f winner Lovers Quest (by Pyrus) and to the modest 1m seller winner Rakhine. The dam ran once unplaced and is a half-sister to 6 winners including the very smart 2-y-o Group 3 Horris Hill Stakes winner Peak To Creek and the dual listed winner Ripples Maid. The second dam, Rivers Rhapsody (by Dominion), a useful winner of the listed 5f Scarborough Stakes and third in the Group 2 5f Temple Stakes, is a half-sister to the Group 3 5f Prix d'Arenberg winner Regal Scintilla. (The MHS 8x8 Partnership). "A funny little thing, because the sire's first 2-y-o's last year did better towards the end of the season when they got seven furlongs and soft ground, whereas she looks like she wants five furlongs and that she's an out-and-out sprinter. She's sharp and 'buzzy' so we'll fiddle away with her for a bit and probably go for a six furlong fillies' maiden in May".

392. UNNAMED ★★★
b.f. Whipper – Bahamamia (Vettori).
January 30. Third foal. Doncaster Premier. £32,000Y. Kern/Lillingston. Half-sister to the useful 2-y-o 6f winner Marine Boy and to fairly useful 2-y-o 6f winner and listed placed Jeanie Johnston (both by One Cool Cat). The dam won over 1m at 2 yrs in France and is a half-sister to 4 winners including the German Group 2 winner Accento. The second dam, Daeside Ladybird (by Tolomeo), won over 6f (at 2 yrs) and 5f and is a half-sister to one winner. (Manor House Stables LLP). "A half-sister to a nice horse we have called Marine Boy and to a black-type filly, this is a very nice filly. She's tall, scopey and rangy. She'll probably start off in May over six furlongs and she'll improve for the run because we're not getting stuck into her as if she were a five furlong out-and-out sprinter. She's big, so we'll start her off on a galloping track somewhere".

393. UNNAMED ★★★
b.c. Oasis Dream – Barathiki (Barathea).
February 10. Fifth foal. 38,000Y. Tattersalls October Book 1. Kern/Lillingston. Brother to the fair 7f winner Whitechapel and half-brother to the quite useful 2-y-o 6f winner and listed 6f Bosra Sham Stakes third Albertine Rose (by Namid) and a winner abroad by Docksider. The dam, a quite useful 2-y-o dual 6f winner, is a half-sister to 3 winners including the useful Peacock Alley, a winner of 3 races at around 7f and listed-placed. The second dam, Tagiki (by Doyoun), won once over 7f at 2 yrs in Italy and is a half-sister to 8 winners including the listed Ulster Harp Derby winner Tijara. (Manor House Stables LLP). "A very tall, narrow horse, we've given him plenty of time and he's filled out a bit. He was bought with the Tattersalls Sales sprint race in the autumn. So he'll have a run for experience and if he shows us enough he'll go for that. Probably more of a 3-y-o type".

394. UNNAMED ★★★★
b.c. Kyllachy – Czarna Roza (Polish Precedent).
April 18. Third foal. 52,000Y. Tattersalls October Book 1. Kern/Lillingston. Brother to the very smart listed 1m winner of 7 races and Group 3 Diomed Stakes third Mabait and half-brother to the fair 1m winner Gypsy Carnival (by Trade Fair). The dam is an unraced half-sister to 9 winners including the dam of the Group 2 Queen Mary Stakes winner Elletelle. The second dam, Nemesia (by Mill Reef), a very useful 10.2f and 4-y-o 13.4f listed winner, is a full or half-sister to 8 winners including the smart Tattersalls Rogers Gold Cup winner Elegant Air. (A G Bloom). "A nice type and a strong colt, but I sometimes feel that Kyllachy's aren't as sprinterish as they appear to be. So I think he'll probably want six furlongs and for that reason alone he probably won't be out before mid-May at the earliest. We like to think that he might have a bit of quality".

395. UNNAMED ★★★★
b.c. Amadeus Wolf – Darby Shaw (Kris).
April 5. Third foal. €30,000Y. Arqana Deauville August. Kern/Lillingston. The dam won 5 minor races in Italy and is a half-sister to 11 winners including the US stakes winner and Grade 2 second Skytrial and the dams of the US Graded stakes winners Gleam Of Hope and Trickey Trevor. The second dam, Try Sympathy (by Habitat), is a placed half-sister to 3 winners including the Group 2 Gallinule Stakes winner Welsh Fantasy. (The MHS 8x8 Partnership). "A big, strong horse, he's a French-bred 2-y-o and he's lovely. He'll have a run here, perhaps in June, and then he'll be aimed at the French premiums and probably spend a few weeks in Deauville in August. I'll be amazed if he doesn't

do quite well and pay his way. At the sales I was trying to buy a horse for less than 30,000 and although he didn't actually look that great at the time he's now developed into one of our nicer types".

396. UNNAMED ★★
b.c. Piccolo – Fizzy Treat (Efisio).
April 4. Sixth foal. Doncaster Premier. £25,000Y. Kern/Lillingston. Half-brother to the modest 9f to 12f winner Formidable Guest (by Dilshaan) and to a winner in Greece by Kyllachy. The dam, a fair 5f and 6f winner at 4 yrs, is a sister to the useful 2-y-o 5f and 6f winner and Group 3 placed Hoh Chi Min and a half-sister to 7 winners including the listed 7f winner Cragganmore and the dam of the Group 3 Molecomb Stakes winner Inya Lake. The second dam, Special Guest (by Be My Guest), a modest 2-y-o 7f winner, is a half-sister to 3 minor winners. (The MHS 8x8 Partnership). "A very big and heavy colt, he's grown an awful lot throughout the winter. He's not going to be early because he's done so well physically and we're very happy with that. You would think that in the middle of the season a five furlong maiden would be well within his remit".

397. UNNAMED ★★★ ♣
b.c. Kodiac – Gerobies Girl (Deposit Ticket).
April 21. Fifth living foal. Tattersalls Ireland. €27,000Y. Kern/Lillingston. Half-brother to the moderate dual 1m winner Ufallya (by Statue Of Liberty). The quite useful 1m winner in Ireland, is a half-sister to 8 winners. The second dam, Galway (by Irish River), won twice at 2 and 5 yrs in France and the USA including a listed stakes, is a half-sister to 6 winners including the Group winners Gracias and Gramy. (Manor House Stables LLP). "He was galloping at the end of March and we thought he'd be an early type but he's just gone a little bit backward. He's a big horse, so there's no problem and we like him. Five or six furlongs in May should be fine for him and he's a nice horse".

398. UNNAMED ★★★★ ♣
b.f. Holy Roman Emperor – Gilded Vanity (Indian Ridge).
April 13. Fifth foal. Goffs Orby. €65,000Y. Kern/Lillingston. Half-sister to the Irish 2-y-o Group 3 6f placed maiden A Mind Of Her Own (by Danehill Dancer) and to the fair 2-y-o 6f winner Desert Icon (by Desert Style). The dam, a minor Irish 5f winner, is a sister to 2 winners including the smart 1m winner and Irish 2,000 Guineas second Fa-Eq and a half-sister to 4 winners including the smart listed 7.3f and 1m winner Corinium and the useful dual 5f winner (including at 2 yrs) Ellway Star. The second dam, Searching Star (by Rainbow Quest), a modest 6f (at 2 yrs) to 11.3f placed maiden, is a half-sister to 8 winners including the smart listed Blue Riband Trial winner Beldale Star. (Manor House Stables LLP). "She's beautiful, looks like a colt and is very strong. We've given her time because she was growing and it looks like it's been worthwhile. She has a semi-decent pedigree and she's a really good-looking type. Six furlongs in May will be her starting point and hopefully she'll be a proper horse".

399. UNNAMED ★★★★
ch.c. Bahamian Bounty – Intellibet One (Compton Place).
January 30. Fourth foal. Doncaster Premier. £50,000Y. McKeever Bloodstock. Half-brother to the fair 5f and 6f winner of 4 races Taurus Twins (by Deportivo). The dam, a fair 5f (including at 2 yrs) and 6f winner of 3 races, is a half-sister to 8 winners. The second dam, Safe House (by Lyphard), a winner at 3 yrs, is a half-sister to 4 other minor winners. (Manor House Stables LLP). "He looked for all the world like he'd be racing in the first week of the season, in the Brocklesby Stakes. He's a real good-looking, strong, January foal and very racey. But actually he's gone a bit weak, so we've gone easy on him. He's not been sold yet so we don't have to push on with him and I think he's one that's a bit better than an ordinary maiden winner".

400. UNNAMED ★★★★
ch.f. Dubawi – Lady Causeway (Giant's Causeway).
February 16. First foal. Goffs Orby. €45,000Y. Kern/Lillingston. The dam, a modest 12f winner in Ireland, is a half-sister to one winner. The second dam, Lady Upstage (by Alzao), a smart Group 2 10f Pretty Polly Stakes winner and Group 1 second, is a half-sister to the useful 6f (at 2 yrs) winner and 1m listed second Lycility. (Dr M Koukash). "A beautiful filly and

I have Andrew Tinkler to thank for her really because he let me have her by stopping bidding for her at the sale. She's very strong, a little bit backward and wants six or seven furlongs. For a horse that's bred for a trip she's got speed. I think there's a fillies' maiden at Chester at the end of June and I'd like to start her there".

401. UNNAMED ★★★
b.c. Holy Roman Emperor – Mackenzie's Friend (Selkirk).
May 8. Fifth foal. Goffs Orby. €55,000Y. McKeever Bloodstock. Half-brother to the fair 12f and hurdles winner Know The Law (by Danehill Dancer) and to the fair 13f winner Anfield Road (by Dr Fong). The dam is an unraced half-sister to 5 winners including the Group 2 winners Allied Powers and Dane Friendly. The second dam, Always Friendly (by High Line), a very useful winner of 3 races including the Group 3 12f Princess Royal Stakes, was second in the Group 1 Prix Royal-Oak and is a half-sister to 5 winners. (Manor House Stables LLP). "A May foal and we're in no rush with him, but he's done quite well. He's had one or two half-speeds and he should be out by the end of May, then we'll see what happens".

402. UNNAMED ★★★★
ch.c. Footstepsinthesand – Melisendra (Highest Honor).
March 24. Eighth foal. €42,000Y. Arqana Deauville August. Kern/Lillingston. Half-brother to the useful 2-y-o 7f and 1m winner Roskilde (by Danehill), to the fairly useful 10.3f winner Murray (by Darshaan), the quite useful 1m and 10f winner Mafeking, the fair 10f and 12f winner Haljaferia (both by Halling) and the modest 9f to 14f winner Three Thieves (by Jade Robbery). The dam, a listed-placed winner of 3 races in France, is a full or half-sister to 8 winners including the Group 3 10.5f Prix Fille de l'Air second On Credit (herself dam of the Group 2 Great Voltigeur Stakes winner Stowaway). The second dam, Noble Tiara (by Vaguely Noble), won twice in France and was fourth in two Group 3 events. (Manor House Stables LLP). "He was a little bit disappointing after we got him home from the sales. He just looked a bit small and plain, but in fairness to him he had a little issue with a testicle and he must have grown four inches in 3 weeks Now

he looks different class, we're pushing on with him and being French-bred he'll probably run a couple of times here and a couple of times in France. He's a 2-y-o type, so we won't be saving him for next year. I should think he'll start over six furlongs and get seven. He looks a proper 2-y-o".

403. UNNAMED ★★★★ ♠
ch.c. Stormy River – Pascarina (Exit To Nowhere).
March 5. Sixth foal. 60,000Y. Tattersalls October Book 2. McKeever Bloodstock. Half-brother to the quite useful 2-y-o 5f winner Carson's Spirit (by Carson City), to the minor French dual 3-y-o winner Hope Of The Irish (by Strong Hope) and 2 winners in Sweden by Distant View and Horse Chestnut. The second dam, Hersande (by Pink), won 2 minor races at 2 and 3 yrs in France and is a half-sister to 9 winners including Fabulous Hostess (Group 2 Prix de Royallieu). (Manor House Stables LLP). "I said at our Open Day a few months ago that he was my favourite and I see no reason to change my mind. He's very big, very strong and a French-bred that's also qualified for the yearling bonus races. In an ideal world he'll win a six furlong maiden in July and go to Deauville in August. A really nice type of horse".

404. UNNAMED ★★★
b.c. Oratorio – Penelewey (Groom Dancer).
March 22. Fourth foal. Tattersalls Ireland. €35,000Y. Kern/Lillingston. Half-brother to the useful 1m (at 2 yrs) and 10f winner Jedediah (by Hernando). The dam, a useful 6f and 7f winner of 3 races, is a half-sister to 7 winners here and abroad. The second dam, Peryllys (by Warning), is a placed half-sister to 6 winners. (The MHS 8x8 Partnership). "This colt was bought specifically for the Tattersalls Ireland Sales race over seven furlongs and (probably) soft ground. So that's what he'll be aimed at after a run or two beforehand. He's in a Partnership of 8 horses we've put together that includes some early types and some later ones".

405. UNNAMED ★★★
ch.f. Nayef – Princess Luna (Grand Lodge).
February 26. Third foal. 100,000Y. Tattersalls October Book 2. Blandford Bloodstock. Half-sister to the fairly useful 1m and 10f

winner Space War (by Elusive City). The dam, a minor German 3-y-o winner, is a half-sister to 5 winners and to the placed dam of the listed winners Captain Ramius and Kingsgate Prince. The second dam, Princess Nana (by Bellypha), won the Group 2 German 1,000 Guineas and is a half-sister to 6 winners. (A W Black). "She's going to take time, she's steady cantering and she'll be a second half of the season 2-y-o. She was pretty small and she's growing a bit, but she's improving all the time and we're happy with her".

406. UNNAMED ★★★
ch.f. Lucky Story – Soft Touch (Petorius).
March 22. Fifth living foal. £12,000Y. Doncaster St Leger Festival. Kern/Lillingston. Half-sister to the quite useful 2010 2-y-o 6f winner Gentle Lord, to the fair 6f (including at 2 yrs) and 5f winner of 5 races Gentle Guru (both by Ishiguru) and the minor Italian winner of 3 races Beecroft (by Fraam). The dam, a fair 1m and hurdles winner, is a full or half-sister to 9 winners including the dual French listed winner and Group 3 Horris Hill Stakes second Hollow Hand. The second dam, Fingers (by Lord Gayle), won over 12f in Ireland, is a full or half-sister to 6 winners. (The MHS 8x8 Partnership). "We had the half-brother Gentle Lord last year and this filly will be racing very soon. She's one of those that has enough speed for five furlongs even though it's not really her trip and I think she'll want seven. We'll run her in a maiden over five and I think she can win that. But there's not a lot of her so we'll then give her a bit of time and hope she improves enough physically to get further". TRAINERS' BARGAIN BUY

407. UNNAMED ★★★
b.f. Aussie Rules – Sticky Green (Lion Cavern).
April 21. Fifth foal. Tattersalls Ireland. €17,000Y. Kern/Lillingston. Half-sister to the useful Irish 2-y-o 6f and subsequent Hong Kong winner Emerald Hill (by Piccolo), to the fairy useful 1m (at 2 yrs) to 14f winner Lethal Glaze (by Verglas) and a winner of 3 races in Italy by Clodovil. The dam, a fair 12f winner, is a half-sister to 2 winners including the useful sprint winner of 8 races Piccled. The second dam, Creme de Menthe (by Green Desert), is an unraced half-sister to 7 winners including the top class filly In the Groove, winner of the Champion Stakes, Juddmonte International Stakes, Irish 1,000 Guineas and the Coronation Cup. (The MHS 8x8 Partnership). "She's had one or two niggling issues but nothing serious, so she'll start off over six furlongs in May. She's a little bit of a nervy type, but she's got size and she's got a bit about her, so you'd be disappointed if she didn't win a maiden".

408. UNNAMED ★★
b.c. Haafhd – Treble Heights (Unfuwain).
February 25. Fourth foal. Half-brother to the 2010 2-y-o 7f winner, on only start, Brown Panther (by Shirocco) and to two hurdles winners by Pivotal. The dam, a listed 12f winner, was Group 2 placed over 14f in France and is a half-sister to numerous winners including the very useful winner of 5 races and Group 1 Ascot Gold Cup third Warm Feeling and the useful 7.6f (at 2 yrs) and 10f winner Rainbow Heights. The second dam, Height Of Passion (by Shirley Heights), is an unplaced half-sister to 8 winners. (Owen Promotions Ltd). "One of Michael's home-breds, you'd think he'd want a trip so we're giving him time and he's not even here at the moment. I can't tell you anything about his ability but his half-brother last year didn't come in until June and he won as a 2-y-o over seven furlongs. You would hope that this colt would follow a similar path".

409. UNNAMED ★★★★
b.f. Invincible Spirit – Winding (Irish River).
March 17. Fourth foal. Doncaster Premier. £60,000Y. McKeever Bloodstock. The dam is an unplaced half-sister to 4 winners including the Group 3 placed Silver Desert. The second dam, Silver Fling (by The Minstrel), won the Group 1 Prix de l'Abbaye and the Group 3 King George Stakes and was placed in the William Hill Sprint Championship at York and the Vernons Sprint Cup (twice). She is a sister to the high-class filly Silverdip, winner of the Salisbury 1,000 Guineas Trial, the Strensall Stakes and the Montrose Handicap and a half-sister to 2 other stakes winners. (Manor House Stables LLP). "A very racey type, she's got a really nice pedigree and she's a small, sharp filly. I've probably given her too much time but I do like her and she'll be out within the next month over five furlongs. She has a good attitude, she's as hard as nails and I'm looking forward to running her".

ANN DUFFIELD

410. BEECHEY'S BEAUTY ★★★
b.c. Camacho – Mix It Up (Linamix).
April 29. Third foal. £8,000Y. Doncaster St Leger Festival. Ann Duffield. The dam ran twice unplaced and is a half-sister to 6 winners including the useful 7f and 1m winner Bishr and the dam of the Group 3 Hackwood Stakes winner High Standing. The second dam, Hawayah (by Shareef Dancer), a modest 2-y-o 7f winner, is a half-sister to 7 winners including the stakes winner and smart broodmare Promptly. (Middleham Park Racing XXXVI). *"A tough, hardy, honest sort. He's very nice and five or six furlongs should suit him from mid-May onwards".*

411. CHEVANAH (IRE) ★★★
b.f. Chevalier – Omanah (Kayrawan).
March 27. Fourth foal. £6,000Y. Doncaster St Leger Festival. Not sold. Sister to the fairly useful Irish dual 1m winner Chevie and half-sister to the fair Irish 1m and 9f winner Cul A Dun (by Soviet Star) and the modest dual 5f winner Rann Na Cille (by Agnes World). The dam was placed in the USA and is a half-sister to 5 winners including the lkisted Masaka Stakes winner Nasij. The second dam, Hacuiyah (by Genrous), won at 3 yrs and is a half-sister to 2 winners. *"She's going very nicely and she should make a genuine 2-y-o. Capable of winning".*

412. GOODFELLOWS QUEST (IRE) ★★★★
ch.c. Intikhab – Poppys Footprint (Titus Livius).
March 20. Third foal. Goffs Orby. €40,000Y. Ann Duffield. Half-brother to the unplaced 2010 Irish 2-y-o Lake Wanaka (by Fasliyev). The dam, a fair dual 6f (at 2 yrs) and 1m winner, is a half-sister to 4 winners. The second dam, Mica Male (by Law Society), won twice in Italy and is a half-sister to 7 winners. (Mr J Gatesby). *"A nice colt, a little bit lazy, very athletic, very strong and he should be running in May. He's capable, he's got the pace to win at five or six furlongs because he'll be out early, but I think later on we'll see a better horse when he runs over further".*

413. IBERIAN ROCK ★★★
b.f. Rock Of Gibraltar – Karsiyaka (Kahyasi).
March 7. Eighth foal. Goffs Orby. €16,000Y. Ann Duffield. Half-sister to the quite useful 2-y-o 6f winner Isabella Grey (by Choisir), to the useful dual 7f winner (including at 2 yrs) Contractor (by Spectrum), the quite useful 10f winner Planetarium (by Fantastic Light), the fair 1m winner Pearl's Girl (by King's Best) and the modest dual 11f winner Altos Reales (by Mark Of Esteem). The dam is an unraced half-sister to 4 winners including the dam of the May Hill Stakes winner Karasta. The second dam, Karlafsha (by Top Ville), won twice in France including the listed 1m Prix des Lilas and is a half-sister to the 5 winners. (Middleham Park Racing). *"A quality filly, a good mover and very athletic. A very pretty filly with a strong neck, she wouldn't want to be running too soon because although she's got a bit of pace she's still growing".*

414. MARIA ANNA (IRE) ★★★
b.f. Amadeus Wolf – Corryvreckan (Night Shift).
February 14. Fourth foal. Goffs Orby. €8,000Y. Ann Duffield. Half-sister to the modest 2010 5f placed 2-y-o Mollyow (by Iceman), the quite useful 2-y-o 5f winner Leftontheshelf (by Namid) and the modest Irish 2-y-o 7f winner Dearg (by Intikhab). The dam, a fair Irish 7f and 1m placed maiden, is a half-sister to 9 winners including the very useful listed sprint winners Bufalino and Maledetto. The second dam, Croglin Water (by Monsanto), is an unplaced half-sister to the smart sprinter Governor General. (Mrs★Baines & Mrs J Anderton). *"Sharp and early, capable of winning something, she's very strong and looks like a colt".*

415. MARIA MEDECIS (IRE) ★★★
b.f. Medicis – Aweigh (Polar Falcon).
February 21. Second foal. £9,000Y. Doncaster St Leger Festival. Not sold. The dam ran once unplaced and is a half-sister to 5 winners including the dual Group 1 Lockinge Stakes winner Soviet Star. The second dam, Shore Line (by High Line), a very useful 7f winner, was fourth in the Oaks and is a sister to the Group 2 winners Ancholia and Quay Line (grandam of the Oaks winner Pure Grain). (Girls On Top partnership). *"She goes well, she's very attractive, tough and hardy. A good-looking filly with scope but she'll run early. A nice sort".*

416. MIDNIGHT TRYST ★★★★
ch.f. Cockney Rebel – Shaken And Stirred (Cadeaux Genereux).
April 8. Fourth foal. Doncaster Premier. £14,000Y. Ann Duffield. Half-sister to the fairly useful 5f and 6f winner and Group 3 Firth Of Clyde Stakes second Midnight Martini (by Night Shift). The dam is an unraced half-sister to 3 winners including the Group 3 Musidora Stakes third Sues Surprise. The second dam, My Micheline (by Lion Cavern), is an unraced half-sister to 4 winners including the listed winner Well Beyond (herself dam of the US Grade 3 winner Out Of Reach). (Middleham Park Racing XXXVII). *"A very nice filly, she'll be out later and she's very capable. Very, very attractive, a good mover and a proper filly – just as you would like a filly to be. Quite scopey, she's the type to keep improving".*

417. ONENITEINHEAVEN (IRE) ★★
ch.f. Choisir – Westlife (Mind Games).
March 24. Sixth foal. £5,000Y. Doncaster Premier. Not sold. Half-sister to the fair triple 5f winner Ryan Style (by Desert Style), to the 2-y-o 6f seller winner Pearo (by Captain Rio) and the moderate 5f winner Orpenlina (by Orpen). The dam is an unplaced half-sister to the listed Roses Stakes winner Pepperoni. The second dam, Enchantica (by Timeless Times), is a placed half-sister to 7 winners. (Mr J Kent & Mr B Woods). *"A nice filly, she's genuine, game, honest and capable. Quite tall and scopey, she just needs to fill out a bit more".*

418. VULCAN MISSION (IRE) ★★★
b.c. Excellent Art – Puck's Castle (Shirley Heights).
March 11. Tenth foal. Goffs Orby. €75,000Y. Ann Duffield. Half-brother to the useful listed 5f winner and Group 2 5f Flying Childers Stakes second Emerald Peace (by Green Desert and herself dam of the 2-y-o listed winner Vital Statistics), to the fairly useful 7f and 1m winner Day Of The Eagle (by Danehill Dancer), the Irish 2-y-o 1m winner and listed placed Cobra and the Irish 12f winner Down Mexico Way (both by Sadler's Wells). The dam, a fairly useful 2-y-o 1m winner and third in the listed 10f Zetland Stakes, is a half-sister to 6 winners including the champion 2-y-o filly and Cheveley Park Stakes winner Embassy and to the Group 2 Pretty Polly Stakes winner Tarfshi. The second dam, Pass The Peace (by Alzao), won 5 races including the Cheveley Park Stakes, was second in the French 1,000 Guineas and is a half-sister to 3 winners. (Mr J Gatesby). *"He's growing, rather lazy and a strong, stocky, backward sort. He won't be early, but obviously the hope is that he'll be very good because we paid a lot of money for him. The talk about Excellent Art is that his first 2-y-o's are very good and of all the horses here, he has the best pedigree but he'll want seven furlongs to start with".*

419. UNNAMED ★★★
b.c. Choisir – Bea's Ruby (Fairy King).
March 25. Fifth foal. Doncaster Premier. £15,000Y. Ann Duffield. Half-brother to the modest Irish 1m winner of 8 races Kilmannin (by College Chapel) and to the moderate 10f winner Miss Monica (by Grand Lodge). The dam, a quite useful 7f and 1m winner, is a half-sister to 4 winners including the US dual listed stakes winner Crystal Mine. The second dam, Beautiful Secret (by Secreto), is an unraced sister to a winner and a half-sister to 4 winners including the stakes winner and Grade 1 placed Lord Lister. (Mrs A Duffield). *"Very nice, he's going really well. Quite tall, very big and scopey, he's one for the future but saying that he'll probably be running any time from mid-May onwards. He's got ability".* TRAINERS' BARGAIN BUY

420. UNNAMED ★★★
b.c. Key Of Luck – Bermuxa (Linamix).
February 2. Second foal. €7,000Y. Goffs Orby. Not sold. The dam was placed in France at 3 yrs and is a half-sister to 7 winners including the Group winners Bernimixa and Miraculous. The second dam, Bernique (by Affirmed), a winner of 5 races in the USA and Grade 3 placed, is a half-sister to 10 winners. *"He goes well, a bit tall and a bit 'bolshie' but he's a lovely mover that wants a bit of time and we think he's got a bit of an engine".*

421. UNNAMED ★★★
b.c. Diamond Green – Pivotal Role (Pivotal).
March 27. Third foal. £11,500Y. Doncaster Premier. Not sold. The dam is an unplaced half-sister to 2 winners including the dual Hong Kong Stakes winner Algol. The second

dam, Heckle (by In The Wings), won at 3 yrs in Germany and is a half-sister to 3 winners. "Wants a bit more time but he's very genuine and very straightforward. Good-looking, he reminds me of a good 2-y-o we had last year called Alaskan Spirit – I hope he can go as well as he did".

422. UNNAMED ★★★
b.c. Indesatchel – Statuette (Statoblest).
March 23. £7,500Y. Doncaster November. Not sold. Half-brother to the modest 5f winner of 5 races Nomoreblondes (by Ishiguru). The dam won at 2 yrs and is a half-sister to 3 winners. The second dam, La Pirouette (by Kennedy Road), won twice and is a half-sister to 6 minor winners. "He goes well, he's sharp, early and very capable of winning. Very much a 2-y-o, we like him, he has a good way of going. We're still looking for an owner if anyone is interested".

ED DUNLOP
423. AEGAEUS ★★
b.c. Monsun – Ouija Board (Cape Cross).
February 14. Second foal. Half-brother to the unraced 2010 2-y-o Voodoo Prince (by Kingmambo). The dam was a top-class winner of 10 races from 7f (at 2 yrs) to 12f including seven Group/Grade 1 races and is a half-sister to 6 winners. The second dam, Selection Board (by Welsh Pageant), was placed over 7f at 2 yrs and is a sister to the top-class Queen Elizabeth II Stakes and Budweiser Arlington Million winner Teleprompter. (The Earl of Derby). "A backward colt, he's having a break now and will be a back-end type 2-y-o. He's a very good-looking horse, taller and slightly narrower than his 3-y-o half-brother but he's obviously going to need time. Ouija Board has a beautiful Galileo yearling filly, she's about to have a Galileo colt and then she'll visit Dubawi".

424. ALMUNDER ★★★
b.c. Intikhab – Adraaj (Sahm).
April 17. Second foal. The dam, a quite useful 10f winner, is a half-sister to 4 winners including the useful 6f (at 2 yrs) and listed 1m winner and dual Group 3 third Nasij. The second dam, Hachiyah (by Generous), a fairly useful 10f winner, is closely related to the Italian Derby third Mutawwaj and a half-sister to the Peruvian champion Faaz. (Hamdan Al Maktoum). "He's a good looking horse that came in a bit late after having had a slight setback as a yearling. He's just coming to us now, he's a very good-looking horse and quite strong. Probably one for the latter part of the season and he looks nice so far".

425. ARABIAN FLIGHT ★★★
b.f. Exceed And Excel – Emirates First (In The Wings).
February 20. Second foal. 6,000Y. Tattersalls October Book 2. Ed Dunlop Racing. The dam, a modest 9f winner, is a half-sister to 4 winners including the smart 1m (at 2 yrs) and German dual Group 1 12f winner Mamool. The second dam, Genovefa (by Woodman), a useful winner of the Group 3 10.5f Prix de Royaumont, is closely related to the Group 3 10f Prix de la Nonette winner Grafin and a half-sister to the US Grade 3 8.5f winner Miss Turkana. (Serendipity Partnership). "A racey filly, she wasn't expensive but she goes OK and I think she's quite nice. A six furlong type 2-y-o, don't leave her out". TRAINERS' BARGAIN BUY

426. ART SHOW ★★★
b.f. Dutch Art – Regina (Green Desert).
February 13. Second foal. 34,000Y. Tattersalls October Book 2. Rabbah Bloodstock. Half-sister to the fair 2-y-o dual 5f winner Six Wives (by Kingsalsa). The dam, a fairly useful 2-y-o dual 5f winner, is a half-sister to 3 winners including the fairly useful dual 1m winner Dubois. The second dam, Dazzle (by Gone West), a smart winner of the Group 3 6f Cherry Hinton Stakes and placed in both the Cheveley Park Stakes and the 1,000 Guineas, is a half-sister to the listed winners Fantasize and Hypnotize, and to the placed dam of the Group 2 winner Danehurst. (M Jaber). "I quite like her, she looks neat and racey and could do with warmer weather but she goes OK and shows some speed. A five/six furlong 2-y-o, she's strongish, has a slight knee action and moves quite well. Looks OK".

427. BURWAAZ ★★★★ ♠
b.c. Exceed And Excel – Nidhaal (Observatory).
February 20. Second foal. Half-brother to the quite useful 2010 2-y-o 5f and 6f winner Sadafiya (by Oasis Dream). The dam, a very

useful 2-y-o listed 6f winner and second in the Group 3 6f Princess Margaret Stakes, is a half-sister to 2 winners. The second dam, Jeed (by Mujtahid), a quite useful 2-y-o 6f winner, is a half-sister to 2 winners. (Hamdan Al Maktoum). "Very nice. I trained his half-sister last year who was very small and had knee issues, but they're like chalk and cheese. This is a strong, powerful colt with a good temperament and if we have a properly precocious 2-y-o, this is the one. He's very nice, the pedigree is all speed and although it's too early to know yet, if we have a Royal Ascot 2-y-o this could be the one".

428. CORN RIGS ★★★
b.f. Exceed And Excel – Corndavon (Sheikh Albadou).
April 8. Half-sister to the smart 2-y-o Group 2 6f July Stakes winner Nevisian Lad (by Royal Applause), to the fairly useful 5f (at 2 yrs) and 6f winner and listed-placed Woodnook and the quite useful dual 7f winner Windermere Island (both by Cadeaux Genereux). The dam, a fairly useful 6f winner of 3 races, is a sister to the listed-placed winner Injaaz and a half-sister to the US sprint winner of 13 races and listed-placed Hardball. The second dam, Ferber's Follies (by Saratoga Six), a winning 2-y-o sprinter, was third in the Grade 2 6f Adirondack Stakes and is a half-sister to 11 winners including the US 2-y-o Grade 2 6f winner Blue Jean Baby. (Julia Scott). *"She's only recently come to us so that will hold her up a bit, but the family is very fast and she should be earlyish. She's small, very athletic and looks to have a good temperament, so I'm happy so far".*

429. DIAMOND FINESSE (IRE) ★★★
b.f. Red Clubs – Birthday Present (Cadeaux Genereux).
April 5. Fifth foal. Goffs Orby. €45,000Y. Peter Doyle. Half-sister to the quite useful 2010 2-y-o 7f winner Red Presence (by Redback), to the 2-y-o 6f winner and Group 3 6f third May Day Queen (by Danetime) and the 2-y-o 7f and 1m winner Call It On (by Raise A Grand) – all quite useful. The dam is an unraced half-sister to 3 winners including the Group 1 Moyglare Stud Stakes third Supposition. The second dam, Topicality (by Topsider), won once at 3 yrs and is a sister to the Cherry Hinton and Fred Darling Stakes winner Top Socialite and a half-sister to the US Grade 1 winners Expelled and Exbourne. (Thurloe Thoroughbreds XXIX). *"I like her, she's racey and early. She just needs to strengthen up and warmer weather will help that. A tough filly that looks to go quite well, she'll be OK".*

430. ESHAAB (USA) ★★
b.br.c. Dynaformer – Jaish (Seeking The Gold).
February 15. Second foal. The dam, a useful 2-y-o 6f winner, was listed-placed over 1m and 10f and is a half-sister to 2 winners. The second dam, Khazayin (by Bahri), was placed over 10f and is a sister to the high-class Prix de l'Arc de Triomphe and Juddmonte International winner Sakhee and closely related to the useful 7f (at 2 yrs) and 10f winner Nasheed. (Hamdan Al Maktoum). *"Still in Dubai at the moment (early April)".*

431. HATTAAK ★★★★
b.c. Royal Applause – Blue Echo (Kyllachy).
February 8. First foal. 240,000Y. Tattersalls October Book 1. Shadwell Estate Co. The dam won 3 races including two listed events over 6f is a half-sister to 6 winners including the smart dual 2-y-o 6f winner and subsequent US Grade 2 9f stakes winner Sapphire Ring and the smart dual listed winner Putra Pekan. The second dam, Mazarine Blue (by Bellypha), a modest sprint winner at 3 yrs, is a half-sister to 7 winners including the Group 2 6f Richmond Stakes winner Rich Charlie. (Hamdan Al Maktoum). *"He cost a lot of money and he's obviously well-bred. There's plenty of speed in the pedigree and he's a very good-looking horse but he isn't going to be that precocious. I think he's a July type of horse and he has a very good temperament for a Royal Applause. A very strong and powerful individual".*

432. HOMERIC ★★
b.c. Montjeu – Al Saqiya (Woodman).
March 2. Seventh foal. Goffs Orby. €100,000Y. John Warren. Half-brother to the quite useful Irish 6f winner Rock Of Veio, to the Japanese winner Rock Balloon (by Rock Of Gibraltar) and the French 10f winner Cashel Blue (by Aljabr). The dam was placed at 2 yrs and is a half-sister to 5 winners including the Grade 2 Sorrento Stakes winner Buffythecenterfold. The second dam, Augusta Springs (by Nijinsky), a

US stakes-placed winner, is a half-sister to 4 winners including the Grade 1 Starlet Stakes winner Cuddles. (Highclere Thoroughbred Racing – Jackson). *"Stating the obvious, he's not going to be precocious. He's a nice, big horse, but one for the back-end and for next year".*

433. MAQARAAT ★★★
b.c. Acclamation – Raghida (Nordico).
March 31. Tenth foal. 100,000Y. Tattersalls October Book 1. Ed Dunlop. Half-brother to the smart Irish 5f (at 2 yrs) and dual Group 3 (7.5f and 1m) winner Marionnaud (by Spectrum), to the useful Irish dual 6f winner (including at 2 yrs) and Group 3 placed Rock Moss, the fair 5f and 7f winner Bravely (both by Rock Of Gibraltar) and the fair 12f winner Sky Mystic (by Galileo). The dam, a fairly useful Irish 2-y-o dual 5f winner, was second in the Group 3 5f Curragh Stakes and the Group 3 Molecomb Stakes and is a sister to the useful 6f to 7f winner and Group 3 placed Nordic Fox and a half-sister to 7 winners including the Group 1 Gran Criterium winner Sholokhov and the listed winner Affianced (dam of the Group 1 Irish Derby winner Soldier Of Fortune). The second dam, La Meilleure (by Lord Gayle), a quite useful listed 1m winner in Ireland at 3 yrs, is a half-sister to 6 winners. (Mrs V I Araci). *"He was popular at the sales, he's good-looking and strong. Not as precocious as I first envisaged but he moves well and will be a mid-season 2-y-o. A nice colt".*

434. MIKDAAR (IRE) ★★
b.c. Elnadim – Jeed (Mujtahid).
February 27. Half-brother to the very useful 2-y-o listed 6f winner and Group 3 6f Princess Margaret Stakes second Nidhaal (by Observatory), to the fairly useful 12f winner of 5 races on the Flat and dual hurdles winner Maslak (by In The Wings) and the fair 9f winner Riqaab (by Peintre Celebre). The dam, a quite useful 2-y-o 6f winner, is a half-sister to 2 winners. The second dam, Secretary Bird (by Kris), is an unraced half-sister to the classic winners Assert (French and Irish Derby) Bikala (French Derby) and Eurobird (Irish St Leger). (Hamdan Al Maktoum). *"Still in Dubai at the moment (early April)".*

435. RUNNING THE SHOW ★★★
b.c. Sir Percy – Ann Veronica (Sadler's Wells).
February 13. Eighth foal. 25,000Y. Tattersalls October Book 2. Charlie Gordon-Watson. Half-brother to the modest 2-y-o 10f winner Marjeune (by Marju), to the minor French and Swiss winner of 2 races Adina (by Persian Bold) and a winner in Greece by Sakhee. The dam is an unraced half-sister to 2 winners in Japan and one in the USA. The second dam, Verily (by Known Fact), is a placed half-sister to 6 winners including the Group 3 winner Dancing Bloom, the Group 1 placed River Dancer (the dam of Spectrum) and the dam of the St Leger winner Millenary. (A & A). *"I know the sire won over six furlongs as a 2-y-o, but this colt is out of a Sadler's Wells mare, so you can't expect precocity. He's a good-looking horse, strong, powerful and with a good temperament. He moves well and goes OK, but I think he's probably a seven furlong horse for later in the season. The sire seems to be stamping them well, but it'll be interesting to see if they have any speed".*

436. STILL I'M A STAR (IRE) ★★★
b.f. Lawman – Aminata (Glenstal).
April 8. Fifteenth foal. 32,000Y. Tattersalls October Book 1. Charlie Gordon-Watson. Half-sister to the very useful Group 3 1m Desmond Stakes winner Swift Gulliver (by Gulch), to the useful 2-y-o 6f and subsequent dual US stakes winner Abderian, the modest 1m winner Prince Minata (both by Machiavellian), the fairly useful 1m and 10f winner Requested Pleasure (by Rainbow Quest), the Irish 2-y-o 6f winner and listed-placed Minatonic (by Zafonic), the Irish 2-y-o 1m winner Musadaf (by Pennekamp), the quite useful staying winner Turquoise Sea (by Shirley Heights), the modest 6f winner Mint Whip (by Whipper), the Irish 3-y-o 6f winner Amandian (by Indian Ridge) and a winner in Japan by King's Best. The dam, a useful winner of the Group 3 5f Curragh Stakes and the listed 6f Smurfit Italia Stakes, is a half-sister to 3 winners. The second dam, Belle Epoque (by Habitat), was a placed sister to the Group 1 Prix de l'Abbaye winner Double Form and a half-sister to the Lupe Stakes winner Scimitarra. (A & A). *"I like her and I'm getting good vibes about the first-season sire Lawman. She's not going to be precocious,*

but she has a big, honest head with big floppy ears and she moves OK. One for seven furlongs later in the season and I like what I see".

437. ZIMIRA (IRE) ★★★
b.f. Invincible Spirit – Zibilene (Rainbow Quest).
March 5. Seventh foal. 350,000Y. Tattersalls October Book 1. Not sold. Half-sister to the fairly useful 2010 2-y-o 7f winner Oracle (by Danehill Dancer), to the French 6f (at 2 yrs) and 7.5f winner and Group 2 1m third Mathematician (by Machiavellian) and the quite useful 10f winner Aryaamm (by Galileo and herself the dam of the 2-y-o Group 2 7f Champagne Stakes winner Saamidd). The dam, a useful 12f winner and listed-placed over 10f, is a half-sister to 7 winners including the Breeders Cup Mile, Irish 2,000 Guineas and Queen Anne Stakes winner Barathea and the Fillies Mile and Irish 1,000 Guineas winner Gossamer. The second dam, Brocade (by Habitat), won 5 races including the Group 1 7f Prix de la Foret and is a half-sister to 7 winners. (Mr N Bizakov). *"A well-bred filly that cost a lot of money, she's good-looking but being out of a Rainbow Quest mare she'll need a bit of time".*

438. UNNAMED ★★★
b.br.c. Dark Angel – Absolute Pleasure (Polar Falcon).
April 17. Third foal. 62,000Y. Tattersalls October Book 2. Rabbah Bloodstock. Half-sister to the moderate 2010 6f placed 2-y-o Box Of Frogs (by One Cool Cat) and to the modest dual 9f winner True Pleasure (by Choisir). The dam is an unplaced half-sister to 8 winners including the smart listed 6f Abernant Stakes winner and good broodmare Splice. The second dam, Soluce (by Junius), won the Group 3 Irish 1,000 Guineas Trial and is a half-sister to 3 winners. (Saeed Manana). *"Out of a Polar Falcon mare, he's strong – as I believe most of the Dark Angel's are. A good-looking horse that was popular at the sale, I think he'll need a minimum of six furlongs but he's a horse that keeps improving. He looks tough, he's sound, has no issues and has a slight knee action so wouldn't want firm ground".*

439. UNNAMED ★★★
b.f. Dubawi – Arsad (Cape Cross).
March 10. First foal. 65,000Y. Tattersalls October Book 1. Portanova Bloodstock. The dam, a modest 11f and 14f winner, is a half-sister to 2 winners including the useful Irish 2-y-o listed 5f winner Flash McGahon. The second dam, Astuti (by Waajib), a quite useful 2-y-o 6f winner, is a half-sister to 6 winners including the Group 2 Kings Stand Stakes and Group 3 5f King George V Stakes winner The Tatling and the fairly useful 5.2f listed and 6f Tattersalls Breeders Stakes winner Amazing Dream. (S Ali). *"A strong, powerful filly that moves well. Probably one for six furlongs and she'll be ok".*

440. UNNAMED ★★★★
b.br.c. Arch – Insan Mala (Bahhare).
March 24. Second foal. 35,000Y. Tattersalls December. Charlie Gordon-Watson. The dam, a the US listed stakes winner of 3 races, was fourth in a Grade 1 event and is a half-sister to 3 minor winners. The second dam, Madame Claude (by Paris House), a fair 2-y-o 6f winner, is a half-sister to 4 winners. (A & A). *"I really like this colt. He's strong, not too big and moves very well. He caught the others up fast having come into the yard late, he's very well-balanced and he's one for six furlongs plus. So far so good".*

441. UNNAMED ★★★★♠
b.c. Dansili – Lady Elgar (Sadler's Wells).
February 20. Eighth foal. €400,000Y. Arqana Deauville August. Charlie Gordon-Watson. Half-brother to the US dual Grade 1 12f Sword Dancer Handicap and Turf Classic Invitational winner Grand Couturier (by Grand Lodge), to the smart 10f winner of 4 races Alainmaar (by Johar), the very useful 7f and listed 10f winner Yaqeen (by Green Desert) and the quite useful 10f winner Sir Edward Elgar (by King's Best). The dam, unplaced in one start in France, is a sister to the Sha Tin Trophy winner and Irish Derby third Desert Fox and a half-sister to the US Grade 3 winners Poolesta and Home Of The Free. The second dam, Radiant (by Foolish Pleasure), won at 3 yrs and is a half-sister to the multiple German Group 1 and Group 2 Royal Lodge Stakes winner Gold And Ivory. (Mr V I Araci). *"He cost a lot of money and he's very well-bred, but he's bred to win the Derby, so*

he's beautiful but he'll take time. A big, scopey individual, he's a very good mover and goes well already, but everything about him says next year".

442. UNNAMED ★★★★★ ♠♠
b.c. Street Cry – Naissance Royale
(Giant's Causeway).
January 25. First foal. €320,000Y. Arqana Deauville August. Charlie Gordon-Watson. The dam won 6 races at 2 to 5 yrs in France, the USA and Canada including the Nassau Stakes, Lake Placid Stakes and the Las Palmas Handicap (all Grade 2 events) and is a half-sister to the winner and Group 3 Musidora Stakes second Spinning World. The second dam, Net Worth (by Forty Niner), won 2 races over 8.5f and 9f in the USA at 3 yrs and is a half-sister to 6 other minor winners. (Mrs V I Araci). "A very good looking horse, I envisage him to be a seven furlong 2-y-o, he has a very good temperament for a Street Cry and he's a beautiful individual. One for the second half of the season and he should be one to follow".

443. UNNAMED ★★★
b.f. Oasis Dream – River Belle (Lahib).
April 13. Third foal. 230,000Y. Tattersalls October Book 1. Ed Dunlop. Half-sister to the useful 7f (at 2 yrs) and listed 1m UAE 1,000 Guineas winner Siyaadah (by Shamardal) and to the quite useful 2010 2-y-o 7f and 1m winner Bridal Belle (by Dansili). The dam, winner of the Group 3 6f Princess Margaret Stakes and subsequently the US Grade 2 8.5f Mrs Fevere Stakes, was Grade 1 placed and is a half-sister to 5 winners including the Italian listed winner and Group 2 Italian 1,000 Guineas third Kiralik and the useful 7.5f and 1m winner of 5 races Rio Riva. The second dam, Dixie Favor (by Dixieland Band), was a quite useful Irish 6f (at 2 yrs) to 1m winner of 3 races. (St Albans Bloodstock LLP). "A neatish filly when she came in, but she's gone a bit lanky and leggy on me. That's a good thing because she's grown up into quite a nice filly and she just needs to thicken out now. She has a good temperament and is one for the middle of the season".

444 UNNAMED ★★★★
b.c. Cape Cross – Starlit Sky (Galileo).
March 1. Second foal. 235,000Y. Tattersalls

October 1. Ed Dunlop. Closely related to the fair 2010 6f placed 2-y-o Green Warrior (by Green Desert). The dam is an unraced half-sister to 8 winners including the Group 2 13.5f Prix de Pomone winner Interlude and the dam of the stakes winners Barney McGrew, National Park and Film Script. The second dam, Starlet (by Teenoso), won 7 races from 7f (at 2 yrs) to 12f including a Group 2 event in Germany and is a half-sister to 8 winners including the US Grade 1 Arlington Handicap winner Unknown Quantity. (Mrs V I Araci). "He's a nice horse and an expensive purchase with a goodish pedigree. A very good-moving horse, he's a little bit weak but he's strengthening up well and I envisage him to be a seven furlong 2-y-o. Goes nicely".

445. UNNAMED ★★★
b.f. Shamardal – Sunsetter (Diesis).
March 10. Fourth foal. Goffs Orby. €40,000Y. Charlie Gordon-Watson. Half-sister to the quite useful 1m winner Sundowner (by Galileo) and to the modest 10f winner Regal Sunset (by Desert Prince). The dam is a placed half-sister to 5 winners. The second dam, Hushi (by Riverman), a US stakes winner of 9 races and Grade 3 placed, is a half-sister to 6 winners. (S Ali). "A racey filly, she's quite 'buzzy' and will probably be earlyish. Strong, powerful and neat, she'll be OK".

446. UNNAMED ★★
b.br.f. Henny Hughes – Zanoubia
(Our Emblem).
February 14. Half-sister to the fair 2-y-o 6f winner Hunt The Bottle (by Bertolini). The dam won at 2 yrs in France and was listed-placed and is a half-sister to 4 winners including a US stakes winner. The second dam, Broadcast (by Broad Brush), a minor US 3-y-o winner, is a sister to the Grade 1 Breeders Cup Classic winner Concern and to the US Grade 3 winner Tennis Lady. (N Mourad). "A backward filly and typical of the family in that regard, I know there's speed on the stallion's side but I don't see her making a 2-y-until much later in the season".

HARRY DUNLOP

447. POLYDAMOS ★★★
b.c. Nayef – Spotlight (Dr Fong).
February 13. Third foal. 20,000Y. Tattersalls

October Book 1. Bluehills Racing. Half-brother to the fair 9f placed 2-y-o Coachlight (by Cape Cross). The dam, a listed 1m and subsequent US Grade 2 Lake Placid Handicap winner, is a full or half-sister to 4 winners including the listed-placed Dusty Answer. The second dam, Dust Dancer (by Suave Dancer), won 4 races including the Group 3 10f Prix de la Nonette and is a half-sister to 6 winners including the Group 3 7.3f Fred Darling Stakes winner Bulaxie (herself dam of the Group 2 winner Claxon). (Bluehills Racing Ltd). *"A lovely mover by Nayef, he's quite a big horse and I think he'll take a bit of time because he's quite backward and he'll start off later in the season over seven furlongs. He's good-bodied, scopey and a little bit cheeky but nothing to worry about at this stage".*

448. RAFAELLA ★★★
b.f. Holy Roman Emperor – Cliché (Diktat).
February 17. First foal. 8,000Y. Tattersalls October Book 2.★Dunlop. The dam, a useful 8.3f winner, was listed placed over 10f and is a half-sister to one winner. The second dam, Sweet Kristeen (by Candy Stripes), a fair 7f winner at 3 yrs, is a half-sister to 3 winners. (Rupert Hambro, David & Jennifer Sieff). *"She's a nice filly and obviously the dam was useful. We didn't pay a great deal for her and yet she's a good, strong-bodied filly. She goes nicely, her size suggests 'two-year-old' and I would certainly hope to be starting her at six furlongs before progressing to seven".*

449. RED MISCHIEF ★★
b.f. Red Clubs – Mujadilly (Mujadil).
March 27. Fifth living foal. 1,500Y. Tattersalls October Book 3. Harry Dunlop Racing. Half-sister to the quite useful 5f winner of 11 races (including twice at 2 yrs) and listed-placed Guto (by Foxhound) and to the modest 2-y-o 5f and 6f winner Genethni (by Primo Valentino). The dam is a placed half-sister to 4 winners including the listed winner Sabre Rattler. The second dam, Casbah Girl (by Native Bazaar), won 3 races at 3 yrs and is a half-sister to 2 winners. (Harry Dunlop Racing Partnership). *"She was very cheap, but the mare has bred a listed-placed winner and the sire is very good. This filly looks strong behind the saddle and she's a 2-y-o type that will improve as the year goes on. We'll start her at six furlongs".* TRAINERS' BARGAIN BUY

450. SUBTLE EMBRACE ★★★
b.f. Acclamation – Subtle Affair (Barathea).
February 23. Third foal. Doncaster Premier. £15,000Y. Kern/Lillingston. Half-sister to the unplaced 2010 2-y-o Dustland Fairytale (by Noverre). The dam, a quite useful dual 11f winner, is a half-sister to 9 winners including the useful 12.3f and 14f winner and Group 2 Henry II Stakes second Lochbuie, the Irish 7f (at 2 yrs) and 9f winner and Group 2 placed Prize Time and the useful 12f and 14f winner Direct Bearing. The second dam, Uncertain Affair (by Darshaan), a quite useful Irish 14f winner, is a half-sister to 3 winners. *"She's working now and she's another that should start her at six furlongs in May. She goes OK, taking a bit of time just to completely mature, but very much going the right way".*

451. SURREY SPIRIT ★★★★
b.f. Invincible Spirit – Anse Victorin (Mt Livermore).
March 25. First foal. 47,000Y. Tattersalls December. Mark Vickers. The dam is an unraced half-sister to 10 winners including the French Oaks, French 1,000 Guineas, Prix Marcel Boussac, Prix d'Astarte and Prix Morny winner (all Group 1's) Divine Proportions and the Prix Jacques Le Marois, Prix Maurice de Gheest and Prix Morny winner (all Group1's) Whipper. The second dam, Myth To Reality (by Sadler's Wells), a triple listed winner of 4 races at 3 yrs in France, was second in the Group 3 Prix de Minerve and is a half-sister to 6 winners. (Mark Vickers). *"Not very big but obviously she's beautifully bred, she has a lot of speed and I've entered in the Supersprint and races like that. I do like her, she's quick and considering her pedigree if she was a bit taller she would have cost an awful lot of money".*

452. VILLA ROYALE ★★★
b.f. Val Royal – Villa Carlotta (Rainbow Quest).
May 10. Half-sister to the useful 1m (at 2 yrs) and listed 10f winner Ceilidh House, to the fairly useful 10f winner Shela House (both by Selkirk), the quite useful 10f winner Villa Sonata (by Mozart) and the quite useful 9f and hurdles winner Bothy (by Pivotal). The dam, a

smart 12f listed winner of four races, is a half-sister to the fairly useful 10f winner Seeyaaj. The second dam, Subya (by Night Shift), was a very useful winner of 5 races from 5f (at 2 yrs) to 10f including the Lupe Stakes, the Masaka Stakes and the Milcars Star Stakes (all listed events). (J★Richmond-Watson). *"She's having a spring break at present but I like her a lot. She'll take time and is very much a 3-y-o in the making, but I wouldn't be surprised if we did some damage later in the season. She's a smashing mover, tall and quite leggy and will only improve. Sadly the mare has died which is a real shame".*

JOHN DUNLOP

453. AAZIF ★★★
ch.c. Nayef – Ayun (Swain).
March 2. Fourth foal. Half-brother to the very useful Group 2 2m and Group 3 2m winner of 8 races Akmal (by Selkirk) and to the fair 14f winner Albeed (by Tiger Hill). The dam, a useful 1m and 10f winner, is a half-sister to 3 winners including the smart 7f (at 2 yrs) and Group 3 1m Desmond Stakes winner Haami. The second dam, Oumaldaaya (by Swain), a very useful filly, won over 7f at 2yrs and the Group 2 10f Premio Lydia Tesio and listed 10f Lupe Stakes at 3 yrs. She is a half-sister to 6 winners including the Derby winner Erhaab. (Hamdan Al Maktoum). *"A good-moving colt and a powerful sort".*

454. AFNOON (USA) ★★★
b.c. Street Cry – Tashawak (Night Shift).
March 3. Half-brother to the unplaced 2010 2-y-o Misk Khitaam (by Distorted Humor) and to the quite useful 7f and 1m winner Nadawat (by Kingmambo). The dam, a smart 6f (at 2 yrs) and Group 2 1m Falmouth Stakes winner, is a sister to the fair 6f (at 2 yrs) and 1m winner of 8 races Speedfit Free and a half-sister to the Irish 8.5f (at 2 yrs) and 10f winner and Group 1 1m Criterium International third Acropolis and the smart Group 2 12f Ribblesdale Stakes and Group 2 12.5f Prix de la Royallieu winner Fairy Queen. The second dam, Dedicated Lady (by Pennine Walk), a useful Irish 2-y-o 5f and 6f winner, is a half-sister to 5 winners including the German listed winner and Group 3 10.5f Prix de Flore third Silk Petal (herself dam of the listed Sandy Lane Stakes winner Star Tulip). (Hamdan Al Maktoum). *"A stocky, powerful filly".*

455. ALRAASED (USA) ★★★★
b.c. Exchange Rate – Alabaq (Riverman).
February 27. Closely related to the fairly useful 7f winner Aamaaq (by Danehill) and half-brother to the fair dual 10f winner Asaateel (by Unfuwain). The dam, a smart winner of the Group 3 1m Premio Bagutta and listed 10f Pretty Polly Stakes, is a half-sister to the Group 3 Rockfel Stakes winner Bint Salsabil and to the very useful 2-y-o 6f and 7f winner Sahm. The second dam, Salsabil (by Sadler's Wells), won the Prix Marcel Boussac, the 1,000 Guineas, the Irish Derby, the Epsom Oaks and the Prix Vermeille - all Group 1 events. She is a half-sister to the high-class colt Marju, winner of the St James's Palace Stakes. (Hamdan Al Maktoum). *"She's a likeable filly, tall and strong with a touch of class".*

456. BALADY ★★
b.f. Zamindar – Faydah (Bahri).
March 28. Sixth foal. The dam, unplaced in 2 starts, is closely related to the top-class Group 1 1m Queen Elizabeth II Stakes and Group 2 1m Queen Anne Stakes winner Lahib and to the useful 10f winner Eshtiaal and a half-sister to the smart 2-y-o 6f winner and Group 3 1m Craven Stakes third Nwaamis, the useful 7f (at 2 yrs) and listed 1m winner Hawriyah and the very useful US miler Maceo. The second dam, Lady Cutlass (by Cutlass), won three races from 5f to 7f in the USA and was stakes placed. (Hamdan Al Maktoum). *"A nice filly, but she's rather backward at the moment and needs some time".*

457. BETTER BE MINE (IRE) ★★★
br.f. Big Bad Bob – Cara Fantasy (Sadler's Wells).
April 1. Fourth foal. Half-sister to the very smart Group 3 7f Acomb Stakes and Group 3 1m Craven Stakes winner and Group 1 Racing Post Trophy second Elusive Pimpernel (by Elusive Quality) and to the smart 1m (at 2 yrs), Group 3 10f Strensall Stakes and listed 9f winner Palavicini (by Giant's Causeway). The dam, a quite useful dual 12f winner, is closely related to the Group 2 winner Lucky Guest and a half-sister to numerous winners. (Windflower Overseas Holdings Inc). *"A lovely filly and she isn't terribly backward so she should make a 2-y-o a bit later on".*

458. CAPHENE ★★★
b.f. Sakhee – Claxon (Caerleon).
April 19. Eighth foal. 100,000Y. Tattersalls October Book 1. Not sold. Half-sister to the fairly useful 2-y-o triple 7f winner and listed-placed Clarietta (by Shamardal), to the useful 7f (at 2 yrs) and listed Lingfield Oaks Trial and subsequent US Grade 3 winner and Group 1 Nassau Stakes second Cassydora (by Darshaan), the listed 10f winner Classic Remark (by Dr Fong) and the quite useful 10f winner Circle Of Love (by Sakhee). The dam, a very useful 1m (at 2 yrs) and Group 2 10f Premio Lydia Tesio winner, is a half-sister to 3 winners including the Group 2 placed Bulwark. The second dam, Bulaxie (Bustino), a very useful winner of the Group 3 7.3f Fred Darling Stakes, was second in the Group 2 Premio Lydia Tesio and is a half-sister to 6 winners including the Group 3 10f Prix de la Nonette winner and smart broodmare Dust Dancer. (Bluehills Racing Ltd). *"This is a tall, leggy, unfurnished filly that needs a bit of time".*

459. ESTABSAAL (IRE) ★★★★
b.c. Dansili – Bunood (Sadler's Wells).
January 19. Second foal. Half-brother to the fair 2010 6f and 7f placed 2-y-o Bakoura (by Green Desert). The dam, a fairly useful 2-y-o 1m winner, was third in the Group 3 12f Princess Royal Stakes, is a half-sister to 4 winners. The second dam, Azdihaar (by Mr Prospector), a quite useful dual 7f at 3 yrs is a half-sister to the high-class and genuine filly Shadayid, winner of the 1,000 Guineas and the Prix Marcel Boussac and to the very useful listed 7f winner and Jersey Stakes third Dumaani. (Hamdan Al Maktoum). *"This is a nice colt and he has a touch of quality about him".*

460. FAREEDHA ★★★★
b.f. Green Desert – Shahaamah (Red Ransom).
March 1. Fifth foal. Closely related to the quite useful 7f winner Mutafajer (by Oasis Dream) and half-sister to the fairly useful 2-y-o 7f winner Zakhaaref (by Daylami) and the fair 2-y-o 5f winner Azwa (by Haafhd). The dam is an unraced half-sister to 4 winners including the very useful 2-y-o 6f winner and Group 2 6f Lowther Stakes second Khulan and the useful 7f (at 2 yrs) and 1m winner Thajja. The second dam, Jawlaat (by Dayjur), a fairly useful dual 6f winner, is closely related to the July Cup winner Elnadim and a half-sister to the Irish 1,000 Guineas winner Mehthaaf. (Hamdan Al Maktoum). *"A sharp filly, she's bred for speed and she'll make a 2-y-o".*

461. MANBAA (USA) ★★★
b.f. Jazil – Itnab (Green Desert).
March 9. Fifth foal. Half-sister to the fair 2010 2-y-o 1m winner Istishaara (by Kingmambo) and to the useful 7f (at 2 yrs), 10f and subsequent UAE 6f winner and Group 3 6f second Alazeyab (by El Prado). The dam won the Group 3 12f Princess Royal Stakes and is a sister to the very useful 6f winner of 4 races Haafiz and the useful 7f and 1m winner and Irish 1,000 Guineas third Umniyatee and a half-sister to numerous winners including the Group 1 Epsom Oaks winner Eswarah. The second dam, Midway Lady (by Alleged), won the Prix Marcel Boussac, the 1,000 Guineas and the Oaks and is a half-sister to 5 winners including the very useful 11.8f listed winner Capias. (Hamdan Al Maktoum). *"This is a nice, well-balanced filly and a good mover".*

462. NAWWAAR (USA) ★★★★ ♣
ch.c. Distorted Humor – Mostaqeleh (Rahy).
April 4. Second foal. The dam, a very useful 2-y-o 6f and 7f winner, was second in the Group 2 1m Prix de Sandringham and is a half-sister to the very smart listed 7f (at 2 yrs) and listed 10f winner Muqbil. The second dam, Istiqlal (by Diesis), is an unraced half-sister to the Group 1 1m St James's Palace Stakes and Group 1 1m Queen Elizabeth II Stakes winner Bahri and to the high-class 2-y-o Group 2 7f Laurent Perrier Champagne Stakes winner Bahhare. (Hamdan Al Maktoum). *"This colt is precocious and will be racing much sooner than most of my 2-y-o's".*

463. ZAAHYA (IRE) ★★★
b.f. Shamardal – Najah (Nashwan).
March 28. Half-sister to the fair 2010 2-y-o 1m winner Tameen (by Shirocco) and to the fair 4-y-o dual 1m winner Waabel (by Green Desert). The dam, a smart Group 2 10f Premio Lydia Tesio winner, is a sister to 3 winners and a half-sister to the useful 10f winner and listed-placed Tanaghum. The second dam, Mehthaaf (by Nureyev), won the Irish 1,000 Guineas, the Tripleprint Celebration Mile and the Nell Gwyn

Stakes and is closely related to the Diadem Stakes winner Elnadim and to the French 2-y-o 7.5f winner Only Seule (herself dam of the Group 1 7f Prix de la Foret and Group 1 6.5f Prix Maurice de Gheest winner Occupandiste). (Hamdan Al Maktoum). *"This filly is a typical Shamardal in that she has lots of strength but needs time".*

464. UNNAMED ★★★
b.f. *Elusive Quality – Elrehaan (Sadler's Wells).*
March 1. Fifth foal. Half-sister to the fairly useful 1m (including at 2 yrs) and 7f winner Tarteel (by Bahri). The dam, a fairly useful 2-y-o 7f winner, was third in the listed Cheshire Oaks and is a half-sister to 3 winners including the useful 2-y-o 7f winner Wahsheeq. The second dam, Moss (by Woodman), ran once unplaced in the USA and is a half-sister to the William Hill Sprint Championship and Prix de l'Abbaye winner Committed (herself dam of the US Grade 1 winner Pharma). (Hamdan Al Maktoum). *"A big, strong, powerful type".*

TIM EASTERBY

465. HADRIAN'S RULE (IRE)
b.c. *Holy Roman Emperor – Farbenspiel (Desert Prince).*
April 5. Second foal. 32,000Y. Tattersalls October Book 2. Tim Easterby. The dam won once at 3 yrs in Germany and is a half-sister to 5 winners including the US Grade 3 Miesque Stakes winner Louvain. The second dam, Flanders (by Common Grounds), a very useful sprint winner of 6 races including the listed Scarborough Stakes, was second in the Group 2 Kings Stand Stakes and is a half-sister to 7 winners. (Mrs J E Pallister).

466. PREMIER CHOICE
b.c. *Exceed And Excel – Simply Times (Codge).*
March 21. Eighth foal. 60,000Y. Tattersalls October Book 1. R O'Ryan. Sister to the Group 2 7f Hungerford Stakes and Group 3 6f Bentinck Stakes winner Welsh Emperor (by Emperor Jones), to the very useful listed 5f winner of 4 races Majestic Times (by Bluebird), the useful 6f and 7f winner and Group 3 third Brave Prospector, the fair 6f winner Timeless Dream (both by Oasis Dream), the fairly useful 5f (at 2 yrs) to 7f winner Forever Times (by So Factual), the quite useful 5f and 6f winner Distant Times (by Orpen) and the modest 6f winner Elegant Times (by Dansili). The dam ran twice unplaced at 2 yrs and is a half-sister to 5 winners including the US 2-y-o stakes winner Bucky's Baby. The second dam, Nesian's Burn (by Big Burn), was a stakes-placed winner at up to 1m in the USA and is a half-sister to 9 winners. (Sir Alex Ferguson & Jack Hanson).

467. REGAL ACCLAIM (IRE)
b.c. *Acclamation – Certain Charm (Thunder Gulch).*
May 2. Seventh foal. Doncaster Premier. £30,000Y. Highflyer Bloodstock. Closely related to the fair 12f winner Onatha (by Dansili) and half-sister to the unplaced 2010 2-y-o Lady Charm (by Oratorio), to the useful 7f winner Sanserif (by Fasliyev) and the Irish 2-y-o 6f winner Nerys (by Namid). The dam was placed over 1m and 10f and is a half-sister to 2 minor winners. The second dam, Style n'Elegance (by Alysheba), is a placed half-sister to 11 winners including the Irish 1,000 Guineas winner Trusted Partner (herself dam of the US Grade 1 winner Dress To Thrill) and to the Group 3 winner and good broodmare Easy To Copy. (Mr & Mrs J D Cotton).

468. ZAFFY (IRE)
b.f. *Iffraaj – Silkie Smooth (Barathea).*
February 4. First foal. Doncaster Premier. £28,000Y. Tim Easterby. The dam, a fair 6f and 7f placed 2-y-o, is out of the placed Whassup (by Midyan), herself a half-sister to 5 winners including the US stakes winner and Grade 2 placed Colchis Island. (Mrs J P Connew).

DAVID ELSWORTH

469. ELUSIVE FLAME ★★★
b.f. *Elusive City – Dimelight (Fantastic Light).*
March 5. Second foal. Half-sister to the fair 2011 3-y-o 7f winner Odin (by Norse Dancer). The dam, a fair 9f and 10f placed maiden, is a half-sister to numerous winners including the smart Group 3 Prix La Rochette winner Guys And Dolls, the smart 1m (including at 2 yrs) to 11f listed winner Pawn Broker and the useful dual 7f 2-y-o winner and Group 3 placed Blushing Bride. The second dam, Dime Bag (by High Line), a quite useful winner of 4 races at up to 2m, is a half-sister to 7 minor winners. (J C Smith). *"She's a smart little filly. I think she'll*

be a 2-y-o type – she certainly looks it. One of our earlier runners".

470. ENGROSSING ★★★★
b.c. Tiger Hill – Pan Galactic (Lear Fan).
March 5. Ninth living foal. 20,000Y. Tattersalls October Book 1. D Elsworth. Half-brother to the fair 2-y-o 6f winner Pan American (by American Post), to the 9f and multiple jumps winner Megaton (by Nashwan) and 3 winners in France by Polish Precedent, Zafonic and Bering. The dam, a French listed-placed 1m winner, is a sister to the French and US winner of 10 races and stakes-placed Jirhan and a half-sister to 5 winners. The second dam, Scierpan (by Sharpen Up), was placed over 5f and 6f at 2 yrs and is a half-sister to 7 winners including the Group/Grade 3 middle-distance winners Tralos and Polemic. (Mr B M C Wong). *"This is one to watch out for. I know he's by Tiger Hill and he'll take time but he's a lovely 2-y-o. One for July onwards – I do like him and he has a lot of quality".*

471. FIRESTARTER ★★★★
b.c. Cockney Rebel – Good Girl (College Chapel).
May 4. Fourth foal. 80,000Y. Tattersalls October Book 2. P Cunningham. Half-brother to the quite useful 2010 2-y-o 6f winner Cruiser (by Oasis Dream), to the fairly useful 6f (at 2 yrs) to 1m winner of 4 races Good Again (by Dubai Destination) and the quite useful 7f winner Ink Spot (by Diktat). The dam, a useful winner of the 2-y-o listed 5f Hilary Needler Trophy and third in the Group 1 6f Cheveley Park Stakes, is a half-sister to 6 winners. The second dam, Indian Honey (by Indian King), is an unraced half-sister to 7 winners. (D Hanafin & P Cunningham). *"He'll be one to watch out for. I think the sire is very underrated and this colt is lovely. Tall and leggy, he wouldn't want to see a racecourse until July time, but he goes well and he's quite precocious. He'll improve as the season goes on and I do like him. One of his owners, Mr Cunningham, owns Cockney Rebel".*

472. GOLDEN SONG ★★★
ch.f. Singspiel – Premier Prize (Selkirk).
January 31. Fourth foal. Half-sister to the fair 7f and 1m winner Hidden Fire (by Alhaarth). The dam, a useful 7f (at 2 yrs) and listed 10f winner, was third in the Group 2 Sandown Mile and is a half-sister to 4 winners including the Group 2 15f Prix Kergorlay winner Gold Medallist. The second dam, Spot Prize (by Seattle Dancer), a useful filly, won over 5f at 2 yrs and was fourth in the Oaks. (J C Smith). *"A good-looking filly. I'd like to see her on the racecourse from July onwards and then go on to make a nice 3-y-o. A fine, big filly".*

473. MONYMUSK ★★★
b.c. Norse Dancer – Bee One (Catrail).
April 26. Half-brother to the fair 5f to 1m winner of 6 races Highland Harvest (by Averti), to the fair dual 7f winner (including at 2 yrs) Highland Quaich (by Compton Place) and the modest 1m (at 2 yrs) and 11f winner Highland River (by Indian Creek). The dam was placed over 5f and 6f and is a half-sister to several winners. The second dam, Ruwy (by Soviet Star) won over 1m. (J Wotherspoon). *"He looks like making a 2-y-o because he's quite precocious, but I haven't done much with him yet".*

474. NIFTY SHIFTIN ★★
b.c. Norse Dancer – Reciprocal (Night Shift).
April 15. Half-brother to the modest 2-y-o 7f winner Highland Bridge (by Avonbridge). The dam, a fairly useful 3-y-o dual 9f winner, is a half-sister to several winners. The second dam, African Light (by Kalaglow), was placed once over 9f and is out of the Park Hill Stakes winner African Dancer (by Nijinsky). (J Wotherspoon). *"A different model to the previous 2-y-o on the list, Monymusk, who is by the same sire and I think this will be more of a 3-y-o type. Seven furlongs or a mile at the back-end will be his starting point".*

475. NORSE GOLD ★★★
ch.c. Norse Dancer – Rainbow End (Botanic).
April 18. Third foal. 2,400Y. Tattersalls October 3. Not sold. Half-brother to the fair 2011 3-y-o 5f winner Morermaloke (by Bahamian Bounty) and to a minor winner abroad by Dr Fong. The dam, a fairly useful 10f winner, is a half-sister to 2 winners. The second dam, High Finish (by High Line), is an unplaced full or half-sister to 11 winners including Munwar (Group 3 Lingfield Derby Trial). *"The sire's stats show that he's only had*

8 runners and 4 have won. This colt might be more precocious than you'd expect because he does look that way and the sire won first time out as a 2-y-o, so I might start getting on with him soon". TRAINERS' BARGAIN BUY

476. PERCYTHEPINTO (IRE) ★★★
b.c. Tiger Hill – Tullawadgeen (Sinndar).
April 20. Third foal. 7,000Y. Tattersalls October Book 3. David Elsworth. Half-brother to the quite useful 2010 2-y-o 9f winner Weapon Of Choice (by Iffraaj) and to the modest triple 7f winner Eager To Bow (by Acclamation). The dam is an unplaced half-sister to 3 winners including the French 1,000 Guineas winner Tie Black. The second dam, Tender Is Thenight (by Barathea), won once at 3 yrs in France and is a half-sister to 10 winners including the Breeders Cup Mile and William Hill Sprint Championship winner Last Tycoon and the dam of the French 1,000 Guineas winner Valentine Waltz. "I gave him the name because he's got so much white all over him. His pedigree says he can't make a 2-y-o, but if you look at him as an individual he's as sharp as a needle. He might surprise a few people".

477. PLUM BAY ★★★
ch.f. Nayef – Pelican Key (Mujadil).
March 10. First foal. 20,000Y. Tattersalls October Book 2. Not sold. The dam, a quite useful 2-y-o 5f winner, is a half-sister to one winner. The second dam, Guana Bay (by Cadeaux Genereux), is an unraced sister to one winner and a half-sister to 5 winners including the Group 2 winners Prince Sabo and Millyant, and the listed winner Bold Jessie (dam of the Group 2 Gimcrack Stakes winner Abou Zouz). (Khalifa Dasmal). "A nice little filly, she looks precocious and could well make a 2-y-o by mid-summer. Very nice".

478. POETIC POWER (IRE) ★★★★
b.c. Dylan Thomas – Chalice Wells (Sadler's Wells).
March 18. Fourth foal. 70,000foal. Tattersalls December. Littleton Stud. Half-brother to the fair 10f and hurdles winner Jolly Roger (by Oratorio). The dam is an unraced sister to the Group 1 Coronation Cup and triple Group 1 Ascot Gold Cup winner Yeats and a half-sister to the Group 2 Royal Whip Stakes winner Solskjaer and the Japanese stakes winner and Grade 1 fourth Tsukuba Symphony. The second dam, Lyndonville (by Top Ville), a minor Irish 3-y-o 14f winner, is a half-sister to 4 winners including the Group 1 Fillies Mile winner Ivanka. (J C Smith). "He's a very nice colt and his dam is a sister to Yeats. If you weren't aware of his pedigree and you watched him cantering you'd think he was early, but then a lot of potentially good horses do that. Hes an exciting horse to have around".

479. SALFORD DANCER (IRE) ★★★
ch.f. Sir Percy – Millay (Polish Precedent).
January 29. Fourth foal. Goffs Orby. €40,000Y. David Elsworth. Half-sister to the moderate 2m winner M'Lady Rousseur (by Selkirk) and to a winner in Switzerland by Red Ransom. The dam, a minor winner at 3 yrs in France, is a half-sister to 6 winners including the listed winner Millstreet. The second dam, Mill Path (by Mill Reef), ran once unplaced and is a half-sister to 4 winners including the Irish Oaks winner Give Thanks. (A J Thompson & Matthew Green). "Her half-sister carried an injury all her life and still managed to win at Kempton over 2 miles. I liked her – she had a great temperament but was a bit difficult to train. This is a much better model and I'd be optimistic that she'd make a 2-y-o in mid-season".

480. SALFORD DREAM ★★★
ch.c. Halling – Spitting Image (Spectrum).
February 20. Third foal. 38,000Y. Tattersalls October Book 2. D Elsworth. Half-brother to the unplaced 2010 2-y-o Time For Applause (by Royal Applause) and to a winner abroad by Observatory. The dam, a modest 2m winner of 6 races, is a half-sister to 4 winners. The second dam, Decrescendo (by Polish Precedent), is an unraced half-sister to 4 winners including Calando (Group 3 May Hill Stakes). (A J Thompson). "A very nice colt, he's bred to get a trip but he does show a lot of class. A very good-moving colt, he has bags of scope. Rather an attractive sort and in my dreams I think about the Racing Post Trophy this year and the Derby next year. If that doesn't materialise we'll look for something a bit smaller! I'd be wrong to push him this early, so we'll just have to take our time with him"

481. SWISS SPIRIT ★★★★ ♠
b.c. *Invincible Spirit – Swiss Lake (Indian Ridge).*
February 25. Fifth foal. Closely related to the quite useful 7f (at 2 yrs) and 6f winner Swiss Cross (by Cape Cross) and half-brother to the smart Group 3 6f Prix de Meautry and Group 3 5f Prix de Petit Couvert winner Swiss Diva (by Pivotal) and the smart 2-y-o 5f winner and triple Group 2 placed Swiss Franc (by Mr Greeley). The dam, a dual listed 5f winner (including at 2 yrs), is a half-sister to the useful 2-y-o dual 5f winner and listed placed Dubai Princess. The second dam, Blue Iris (by Petong), a useful winner of 5 races over 5f and 6f including the Weatherbys Super Sprint and the Redcar Two-Year-Old Trophy, is a half-sister to 9 winners. (Lordship Stud). *"I've trained a few out of the dam and this is the best specimen of the lot. A big, fine colt, he's over 16 hands now but he's a beautiful colt and I'd be disappointed if he doesn't do well. Despite his size he's quite precocious and I like him. The mare was fast and she breeds 2-y-o winners, so this colt will be a five/six furlong 2-y-o".*

JAMES EUSTACE

482. BALCARY BAY ★★★
ch.g. *Zamindar – Chantress (Peintre Celebre).*
February 25. Second foal. 26,000Y. Tattersalls October Book 2. James Eustace. The dam, a fairly useful 9.3f and 10.3f winner, was listed-placed and is a half-sister to 3 winners including the Group 3 6f Coventry Stakes winner Red Sea and the useful 7f (at 2 yrs) and Italian Group 3 12f winner Sailing. The second dam, Up Anchor (by Slip Anchor), won four races including the Group 3 12f St Simon Stakes, was third in the Italian Oaks and is a half-sister to 5 winners including the triple US Grade 3 winner at around 8.5f Just Class. (The MacDougall Two). *"He's a flashy chestnut and he's that way in temperament as well, hence he's been gelded. Having said that he enjoys his work, so I've no worries on that score. He does look athletic and he's forward enough to be a mid-season 2-y-o. I do like him and I don't think he was expensive given his pedigree".*

483. CARIBBEAN ACE (IRE) ★★★
b.f. *Red Clubs – Caribbean Escape (Pivotal).*
March 9. Sixth foal. €24,000foal. Goffs. Littleton Stud. Half-sister to the fairly useful 2-y-o listed 5f winner Knavesmire (by One Cool Cat), to the quite useful triple 6f winner Honey Monster (by Choisir) and the quite useful dual 6f winner (including at 2 yrs) Sleeping Storm (by Danehill Dancer). The dam is an unraced half-sister to 8 winners including the smart listed 6f Abernant Stakes winner and good broodmare Splice. The second dam, Soluce (by Junius), won the Group 3 Irish 1,000 Guineas Trial and is a half-sister to 3 winners. (J C Smith). *"Quite a nice little filly, she's attractive and looks like she'll be a 2-y-o. Her knees are slightly open so she won't be very early – probably a mid-summer type. She's already going nicely and she's already shown a bit of speed. Five/six furlongs should suit".*

484. DENTON DANCER ★★★
b.br.c. *Halling – Rapid Revalation (Bianconi).*
March 4. Second living foal. 20,000Y. Tattersalls October Book 2. J Eustace. The dam won 5 minor races in the USA at 3 and 4 yrs and is a half-sister to 6 winners. The second dam, Rapid Raja (by Darby Creek Road), a stakes-placed winner of 3 races in the USA, is a half-sister to 4 winners including the US Grade 2 winner Native Raja. (Mr A E B Wiegman). *"I like him and he's probably the most forward of them all. He's done some work already, seems to have a good attitude and he's got some speed from the dam's side. I suspect he takes after her because he's not a great big Halling, rather he's quite a neat, compact horse. He's working nicely and he does look like he'll be a 2-y-o, quite possibly over as short as five furlongs. The breeder did tell me that the dam won over sprint distances in America".*

485. IRON BUTTERFLY ★★★
b.f. *Shirocco – Coh Sho No (Old Vic).*
February 26. Half-sister to the fair dual 12f winner Iron Condor (by Tobougg) and to the fair 14f to 2m and hurdles winner At The Money (by Robellino). The dam was a modest 15.4f and hurdles winner. The second dam, Castle Peak (by Darshaan), a fairly useful 12f winner, is a half-sister to the Prix du Cadran winner Sought Out and to the listed winners Queen Helen and Greektown (herself dam of the Geoffrey Freer Stakes winner Multicolored) and the dam of the Great Voltigeur Stakes

winner Bonny Scot. (H D Ness). *"A very nice filly, the whole family have done me well and this would seem to be the one with the most quality. Potentially a genuinely nice middle-distance filly for next year, but she's physically mature already so she'll certainly run this year and I'd like to think that she's classy enough to do something as well. One for the late summer onwards, she rather belies her pedigree in physical terms already. She wants to do it and she's quite capable but I'm having to deliberately hold her back".*

RICHARD FAHEY

486. ALEJANDRO ★★
b.c. Dark Angel – Carallia (Common Grounds).
April 20. Fourth foal. 25,000Y. Tattersalls October Book 2. R O'Ryan. Half-brother to the 2010 French 2-y-o 1m winner Maitres Des Airs (by Hawk Wing) and to the fairly useful Irish 2-y-o 7f winner Carazam (by Azamour). The dam won over 6f at 2 yrs in Ireland and was listed-placed and is a half-sister to 4 winners including the Group 1 Prix de la Foret winner Caradak. The second dam, Caraiyma (by Shahrastani), won over 9f in Ireland and is a sister to the Irish dual Group 3 winner Cajarian. (Frank Lenny). *"He's a bit on the small side but he wants to run, he's sharp and he'll be an early runner for the yard. He's what I call a 'north of England' sort of 2-y-o and he'll be a 5/6 furlong type".*

487. ARTISTS CORNER ★★
ch.f. Dutch Art – Justbetweenfriends (Diesis).
March 22. Sixth foal. 10,000Y. Tattersalls October Book 2. R O'Ryan. Half-sister to the quite useful Irish 2-y-o 1m winner Fikrah (by Medicean), to the modest 2m winner Deuce (by Where Or When) and the modest 11f winner Dosti (by Zamindar). The dam was placed over 12f and is a half-sister to 7 winners including the smart Group 3 7f Hungerford Stakes winner With Reason and the useful Group 3 1m Curragh Futurity Stakes and 7f Sweet Solera Stakes winner Jural. The second dam, Just Cause (by Law Society), is an unraced half-sister to 5 winners. (The Derwent Arms). *"She's not very big, but she tries and the lads in the pub own her. She shows a bit of speed and she's one for five and six furlongs".*

488. ART OF STONE ★★★
b.br.c. Dutch Art – Starstone (Diktat).
May 8. Third foal. 32,000Y. Tattersalls December. R O'Ryan. Half-brother to the 2010 Irish 2-y-o 7f winner (on her only start) Handassa (by Dubawi) and to the fair 2-y-o 6f winner Emirates Hills. The dam is an unraced half-sister to the Group 1 July Cup winner Pastoral Pursuits and the Group 1 Haydock Park Sprint Cup winner Goodricke. The second dam, Star (by Most Welcome), a quite useful 5f winner, is a half-sister to 7 winners including the useful 2-y-o listed 5f winner Four-Legged-Friend and the US Grade 3 7f winner Superstrike. (John Rhodes & P Timmins). *"Quite a nice horse, I haven't done any fast work with him at all but he's done real well since the Sales. A good mover, he gets on with his job and we're still learning about him".*

489. BACCARAT ★★★
ch.c. Dutch Art – Zut Alors (Pivotal).
February 8. First foal. €420,000Y. Arqana Deauville August. Sir Robert Ogden. The dam won once at 2 yrs in France and was third in the Group 3 Prix Miesque and is a half-sister to 4 winners. The second dam, Zeiting (by Zieten), won 4 listed events in France and is a half-sister to the Group 3 Prix du Bois winner Dolled Up. (Sir Robert Ogden). *"Quite a nice colt but he'll take a bit of time and he's one for the back-end of the season. A horse we like a lot, he's quite a big, scopey horse and we won't be in any hurry with him".*

490. BORDER REVIA ★★★
b.c. Celtic Swing – Maraami (Selkirk).
March 24. Fifth foal. Tattersalls Ireland. €32,000Y. Robin O'Ryan. Half-brother to the modest 2010 6f and 7f placed 2-y-o High On The Hog (by Clodovil) and to the quite useful 2-y-o 1m winner Calaloo (by Dansili). The dam, placed 5 times from 6f (at 2 yrs) to 2m, is a half-sister to 4 winners including the Group 3 Meld Stakes winner Latino Magic. The second dam, Tansy (by Shareef Dancer), won once at 2 yrs and is a half-sister to 7 winners including the Lockinge Stakes winner Most Welcome. (Jed Gaffney). *"He's done very well since the sales, we're pleased with him but he'll be a seven furlong two-year-old and we'll just take our time with him. I like him and we'll try and get him ready for the Sales race".*

491. BOUDOIR ★★★ ♠
b.f. Clodovil – Adultress (Ela-Mana-Mou).
February 13. Ninth foal. Goffs Orby. €32,000Y. John Warren. Half-sister to the very useful 2-y-o 10f listed winner Forest Magic (by Charnwood Forest) and the French 2-y-o 1m winner Please Be Good (by Prince Of Birds). The dam is an unraced half-sister to 6 winners including the Group 3 9f Prix Chloe winner Adaiyka (herself dam of the dual Group 3 winner Adilabad). The second dam, Adarika (by Kings Lake), is an unraced half-sister to 6 winners. (Highclere Thoroughbreds). *"Quite a nice filly, a five/six furlong type and very forward going. She's still learning but she's got plenty of toe and will be an early runner".*

492. CHAPTER SEVEN ★★★
ch.c. Excellent Art – My First Romance (Danehill).
March 31. Twelfth foal. 20,000Y. Tattersalls December. Not sold. Half-brother to the Group 3 5f Queen Mary Stakes winners Romantic Myth (by Mind Games) and Romantic Liason (by Primo Dominie), the useful 2-y-o 5f winner Power Packed (by Puissance), the fairly useful 2-y-o 6f winner Alkhafif (by Royal Applause), the fairly useful dual 5f winner Zargus (by Zamindar), the quite useful 2-y-o 7f winner Wedaad (by Fantastic Light), the fair 7f winner Romantic Destiny (by Dubai Destination), the fair 2-y-o 5.5f winner Chance For Romance (by Entrepreneur) and the UAE 7f winner Maath Gool (by Dubawi). The dam ran twice unplaced and is a half-sister to 6 minor winners here and abroad. The second dam, Front Line Romance (by Caerleon), won once and was Group 3 placed over 1m at 2 yrs in Ireland and is a full or half-sister to 10 winners including the multiple Italian Group 3 winner Knight Line Dancer. (Terry Holdcroft). *"He's only just come to us, so we haven't had him long but he looks a nice horse and I like the Excellent Art's because they seem to have good attitudes. He hasn't done anything quick but I do like him. He canters up really well".*

493. CLARETINTHEBLOOD ★★
b.c. Elusive City – River Abouali (Bluebird).
May 21. Eighth foal. Goffs Orby. €40,000Y. Robin O'Ryan. Half-brother to the fair 2-y-o 5f winner Maugwenna (by Danehill and herself dam of the Group 2 placed 2-y-o Bould Mover), to the fair 6f, 7f (both at 2 yrs) and 1m winner Vito Volterra (by Antonius Pius), the modest 6f winner Trouble Maker (by Green Desert) and 2 minor winners abroad by Bertolini and Diktat. The dam is an unraced half-sister to the Irish listed winner Queen Titi (herself dam of the Group 1 Dewhurst Stakes winner Beethoven) and to the very useful 1m winner and subsequent US stakes-placed winner The Editor. The second dam, Litani River (by Irish River), was listed-placed in France and is a sister to the French 5.5f and 7f winner Or Vision (herself dam of the Group/Grade 1 winners Dolphin Street, Insight and Saffron Walden) and a half-sister to 7 winners including the dam of the Group 1 winners Sequoyah and Listen. (The Matthewman). *"He'll take time because he was a very late foal. He's just doing routine canters and he looks immature, but the sire's alright".*

494. COSMIC HALO ★★★
ch.f. Halling – Cosmic Case (Casteddu).
February 12. Half-sister to the fair 2010 2-y-o 7f winner Cosmic Moon (by Doyen) and to the fairly useful 12f and 13f winner Cosmic Sun (by Helissio). The dam was a modest winner of 10 races on the Flat from 1m to 14f and 8 races over hurdles. The second dam, La Fontainova (by Lafontaine), was an unraced half-sister to 8 winners. *"She's probably the nicest one out of the mare and despite being by Halling out of a jumping mare she could well make a 2-y-o, which is a bit of a shock! One for the back-end of the season but worth putting in the book".*

495. DEVLIN ★★★
b.c. Auction House – Dancing Loma (Danehill Dancer).
February 22. First foal. £9,500Y. Doncaster Premier. Robin O'Ryan. The dam is an unraced half-sister to 7 minor winners. The second dam, Jabali (by Shirley Heights), is an unplaced half-sister to 4 winners including the French Group 2 winner Dadarissime and the French Group 3 winner Floripedes (the dam of Montjeu). (Jed Gaffney). *"He's a good hardy horse and he was well-bought, cheap in fact. He'll definitely win".*
TRAINERS' BARGAIN BUY

496. DIVINE SUCCESS ★★★
b.c. Amadeus Wolf – Divine Pursuit (Kris).
April 29. Ninth foal. 27,000Y. Tattersalls October Book 2. R O'Ryan. Half-brother to the useful 5f to 7f winner and listed-placed Quest For Success (by Noverre), to the fair 4-y-o 10f winner Blazing The Trail (by Indian Ridge) and a minor winner in the USA by Marju. The dam, a fair 7f to 8.5f placed maiden, is a sister to the smart Group 2 Prix du Gros Chene and Group 2 Prix du Ris-Orangis winner Divine Danse and a half-sister to 5 winners including the Group 2 Prix Maurice de Gheest winner Pursuit Of Love. The second dam, Dance Quest (by Green Dancer), a smart winner of 3 sprint races, is a half-sister to 6 winners including the Prix de la Salamandre winner Noblequest. (Steve Clayton). *"He's grown a lot since we bought him and he's done real well since the Sales. A very good mover, he's a horse that I like but I haven't done much with him yet because he was a fairly late foal, so I'm not in any hurry with him".*

497. DOUBLE CEE ★★★
ch.c. Haafhd – Razzle (Green Desert).
April 6. Fourth foal. 40,000Y. Tattersalls October Book 2. R O'Ryan. Brother to the fairly useful dual 7f winner Infiraad and half-brother to the 2010 7f fourth-placed 2-y-o King Of The Ring (by Indesatchel). The dam, a modest 10f placed 3-y-o, is a sister to the very smart triple Group 3 6f and 7f winner and sire Desert Style and a half-sister to 2 winners. The second dam, Organza (by High Top), a useful 3-y-o 10f winner, is a full or half-sister to 7 winners including the Group 1 Prix de la Foret winner Brocade (herself dam of the Group 1 winners Barathea and Gossamer). (John Coleman). *"Quite a nice horse, he'll want six/seven furlongs, he's breezed a few times and he shows a good attitude. We're not in any hurry with him but he gets on with his job".*

498. EASTERN DESTINY ★★★★
gr.f. Dubai Destination – Night Haven (Night Shift).
February 6. Seventh foal. Half-sister to the useful 2-y-o 7f and listed 10f winner Rosa Grace (by Lomitas), to the fairly useful 5f and 6f winner and listed-placed Secret Night (by Dansili) and the moderate 5f winner of 4 races Duke Of Rainford (by Bahamian Bounty). The dam, a fairly useful 5f (at 2 yrs) and 6f winner and 6f listed-placed, is a sister to 3 winners including the French 2-y-o listed 5f and subsequent UAE winner Shoalhaven. The second dam, Noble Haven (by Indian King), won once at 2 yrs and is a half-sister to 6 winners. (Mr Farr Snr). *"A lovely filly and a six/seven furlong two-year-old, she's a model – a sweet filly. I like her and she's a good sort".*

499. EBONY CLARETS ★★★
b.f. Kyllachy – Pachanga (Inchinor).
March 10. Third foal. 14,000Y. Tattersalls October Book 2. R O'Ryan. Half-sister to the modest 10f and 11f winner Broughtons Swinger (by Celtic Swing). The dam, placed once at 3 yrs in France, is a half-sister to 3 winners. The second dam, Gai Bulga (by Kris), a very useful triple 10f winner, is a full or half-sister to 8 winners including the 2-y-o Group 3 7f Prestige Stakes winner Glatisant (dam of the 2,000 Guineas winner Footstepsinthesand) and to the placed dam of the very smart 2-y-o Superstar Leo. (The Matthewman). *"Quite a sharp filly and she'll run early. She shows a bit of ability and I'm sure she'll win. Five or six furlongs will be her trip".*

500. EDGE LANE ★★
b.f. Dutch Art – Cape Trafalgar (Cape Cross).
April 12. Fourth foal. 3,000Y. Tattersalls October Book 3. Not sold. Half-sister to the quite useful 9f winner Gritstone (by Dansili). The dam, a fair 5f and 6f 2-y-o winner of 4 races, was subsequently stakes-placed in the USA and is a half-sister to 3 winners. The second dam, West Escape (by Gone West), a fairly useful 1m winner at 3 yrs, is a half-sister to 6 winners. (D W Armstrong). *"I'd like to kick on early with her but she's had sore shins. Not very big, but she looks genuine and she tries".*

501. GABRIAL (IRE) ★★★★ ♠
b.c. Dark Angel – Guajira (Mtoto).
April 2. Second foal. Doncaster Premier. £28,000Y. Bobby O'Ryan. The dam, a minor French 11f winner, is a half-sister to 9 winners including Jaunatxo and Iron Deputy (both US Grade 2 winners). The second dam, Femme de Fer (by Iron Duke), won twice in France and is a half-sister to 3 winners. (Dr M Koukash). *"I like him and funnily enough although the dam was*

a middle-distance winner by Mtoto this colt has speed. He's certainly not slow and he's a big, scopey horse that you'd like".

502. GIORGIO'S DRAGON ★★★★
b.c. Le Vie Dei Colori – Broadways Millie
(Imperial Ballet).
March 7. First foal. Doncaster Premier. £120,000Y. Sir Robert Ogden. The dam is an unraced half-sister to 5 winners including the dual Group 3 winner Eastern Purple. The second dam, Broadway Rosie (by Absalom), a useful Irish listed winner of 4 races from 5f to 7f, is a half-sister to 5 winners including the Irish listed winner Mora. (Sir Robert Ogden). *"A nice horse for six/seven furlongs, I like him. He's breezed a few times, he'll be out in May if not earlier and he'll definitely win".*

503. GOING GREY ★★
b.c. Diamond Green – Incendio
(Siberian Express).
March 7. Ninth foal. €38,000foal. Goffs. Norman Steel. Half-brother to 5 winners including the Group 2 6f Diadem Stakes and Group 3 5f Norfolk Stakes winner Baron's Pit (by Night Shift), the Irish 6f (at 2 yrs) and 7f winner Set Fire (by Bertolini), the fair 5f (at 2 yrs) and 6f winner Candela Bay (by Captain Rio) and the modest 1m winner Burton Ash (by Diktat). The dam, an Italian winner of 9 races from 2 to 4 yrs, is a half-sister to 5 winners including the Italian listed winner of 10 races Infiel. The second dam, Indocina (by Indian King), a listed-placed winner of 4 races in Italy, is a half-sister to 7 winners. (Norman Steel). *"A huge horse, he'd be 16.2 so I haven't done a lot of work with him, he's just been cantering every day so I don't know enough to comment at the moment".*

504. GONE BY SUNRISE ★★★
b.c. Three Valleys – Quadrophenia
(College Chapel).
February 11. First foal. 15,000Y. Doncaster Premier. Not sold. The dam, a modest 2-y-o 5f winner, is a half-sister to 3 winners. The second dam, Truly Madly Deeply (by Most Welcome), is an unplaced half-sister to 10 winners including the very smart Group 2 5f Flying Childers Stakes and Weatherbys Super Sprint winner Superstar Leo. *"Quite sharp, he'll be an early season two-year-old and he shows a bit of speed. Whether he'll train on to the back-end I don't know but he'll run early".*

505. HILLCROFT ★★★
br.f. Kyllachy – Skyelady (Dansili).
March 7. First foal. 30,000Y. Tattersalls October Book 3. Bobby O'Ryan. The dam, a quite useful 5f (at 2 yrs) and dual 7f winner, was second in the listed 6f Empress Stakes and is a half-sister to 2 winners. The second dam, Song Of Skye (by Warning), a quite useful 5f (at 2 yrs) and 7f winner, is a half-sister to 7 winners. (D W Armstrong). *"A good, hardy filly that'll run early. We'll be kicking on with her".*

506. HOLY ROMAN WARRIOR ★★★★ ♠
br.c. Holy Roman Emperor – Cedar Sea
(Persian Bold).
February 25. Fifth foal. Doncaster Premier. £70,000Y. Mrs Jeanette Penman. Half-brother to Geblah (by Green Desert), placed fourth on her only start at 2 yrs in 2010 and to the smart 1m (at 2 yrs) and Group 3 13f winner Corsica (by Cape Cross). The dam, a French 1m winner and second in the listed Prix Yacowlef, is a half-sister to 3 winners including the Group 3 6f Coventry Stakes winner CD Europe. The second dam, Woodland Orchid (by Woodman, is an unplaced half-sister to the Group 3 Derrinstown Stud Derby Trial winner Truth Or Dare, the UAE Group3 winner D'Anjou and the listed winner Sandstone. *"A big, scopey horse, he'll want six/seven furlongs and we like him but he wouldn't want the ground too quick because he hits the ground hard. Quite a nice horse – a good sort".*

507. KNIGHT EXPRESS ★★★★
b.c. Bahamian Bounty – Broughtons Revival
(Pivotal).
February 15. First foal. Doncaster Premier. £80,000Y. Gill Richardson. The dam, a quite useful 11f to 14f winner, is a half-sister to 2 winners. The second dam, Ella Lamees (by Statoblest), a modest 6f winner, is a half-sister to 7 winners. (Norman Steel). *"A lovely horse, I like him, he's breezed a few times and he'll be a six/seven furlong two-year-old. He's a bonny horse and he'll definitely win".*

508. LADY AUTHOR ★★
b.f. Authorized – Kelucia (Grand Lodge).
March 6. Second foal. 40,000Y. Tattersalls October Book 1. Not sold. Half-sister to Monel (by Cadeaux Genereux), unplaced in 3 starts at 2 yrs in 2010. The dam, a useful 2-y-o dual 1m winner and third in the Group 2 7f Rockfel Stakes, is a half-sister to 3 winners. The second dam, Karachi (by Zino), won 5 races in Spain at 2 yrs and is a half-sister to 7 other minor winners. (Frank Brady). *"She's not very big and she could do with growing. Her pedigree suggests she'll stay and yet she canters up there like she wants to run, but I'm not in any hurry with her".*

509. LADY'S FIRST ★★★★ ♣
b.f. Dutch Art – Like A Dame (Danehill).
March 26. Second foal. Goffs Orby. €100,000Y. N Steel. The dam, a minor 3-y-o winner in France, is a half-sister to 5 other minor winners. The second dam, Anysheba (by Alysheba), a minor French 3-y-o winner, is a half-sister to 8 winners including the Group 3 winner Sadler's Wells. (Norman Steel). *"A filly I really like. She's a great-moving filly and I like her a lot, but my fillies are further behind than normal so I haven't done much with them yet. One to watch out for I'd say".*

510. LET YOUR LOVE FLOW ★★
b.f. Iffraaj – Miss Odlum (Mtoto).
March 3. Fifth foal. €19,000Y. Tattersalls Ireland. Glen Devlin. Half-sister to the fair 7f (including at 2 yrs) and 6f winner Suhayl Star (by Trans Island). The dam, a fair 10f winner in Ireland, is a half-sister to one winner. The second dam, Trexenta (by Green Desert), is a placed half-sister to 5 winners including the French Group 3 winner Caprarola and the French 1,000 Guineas second Cortona. (Glen Devlin). *"Quite a scopey filly, she'll take a bit of time".*

511. LEXINGTON SPIRIT (IRE) ★★★
b.f. Iffraaj – Festivite (Fasliyev).
February 3. Third foal. Doncaster Premier. £26,000Y. Robin O'Ryan. The dam, the minor French 3-y-o winner, is a half-sister to 4 winners including the useful 2-y-o 1m and smart hurdles winner Fire And Rain. The second dam, Quatre Saisons (by Homme de Loi), is an unraced half-sister to 3 winners and to the dam of the Group 1 National Stakes winner Beckett. *"I haven't done a lot with her but I like her. She could just do with growing a bit, but she's fine and gets on with her job".*

512. LILY'S ANGEL ★★
b.f. Dark Angel – Noyelles (Docksider).
March 29. First foal. Doncaster Premier. £8,000Y. Richard Fahey. The dam is an unraced half-sister to 8 winners including the Group 3 Prix de Flore winner In Clover and the French listed winner Bayourida. The second dam, Bellarida (by Bellypha), won the Group 3 Prix de Royaumont and is a half-sister to 2 winners. *"She didn't cost a lot and she'll run early. A sharp filly, she tries and she'll do a job".*

513. LISIERE ★★
b.f. Excellent Art – Sahara Sky (Danehill).
January 24. First foal. 65,000Y. Tattersalls October Book 2. BBA (Ire). The dam is an unraced half-sister to 9 winners including the Group 1 6f July Cup and Group 2 6f Moet and Chandon Rennen winner Owington. The second dam, Old Domesday Book (by High Top), a fairly useful 10.4f winner, was listed-placed over 10f. (David Blunt). *"I haven't done a lot with her and although she's a good sort of filly she'll take a bit of time".*

514. LITTLE MR SUNSHINE ★★
b.c. Azamour – Tagula Sunrise (Tagula).
March 31. First foal. The dam, fairly useful 6f (including at 2 yrs) and 7f winner, was listed-placed and is a sister to one winner and a half-sister to 2 winners. The second dam, Lady From Limerick (by Rainbows For Life), a modest 2-y-o sprint-placed maiden, is a half-sister to several winners. (Mel Roberts). *"The first foal out of a mare I trained, he's not very big but he'll be a 'north of England' sort of horse. The dam was quite quick and this colt seems to have taken after her more than the sire, so he'll run as a 2-y-o over six/seven furlongs".*

515. MFIFTYTHREE FORD (IRE) ★★★
b.f. Royal Applause – Maid For Romance (Pursuit Of Love).
February 16. Sixth foal. Goffs Orby. €20,000Y. Robin O'Ryan. The dam was placed over 10f

on her only outing and is a half-sister to 8 winners including the Group 2 10f Sun Chariot Stakes winner Lady In Waiting, the Group 3 15f Prix du Lutece winner Savannah Bay and the dam of the Group 3 Prix Eclipse winner Tremar. The second dam, High Savannah (by Rousillon), a fair middle-distance placed maiden, is a half-sister to 6 winners including the useful sprinters Maid For The Hills and Maid For Walking (herself dam of the US Grade 1 winner Stroll). (M53 Motors). *"A big, strong filly, she looks like a colt and she's quite forward. She'll be suited by five/six furlongs, we're still learning about her but she goes OK"*.

516. MISS WORK OF ART ★★★
ch.f. Dutch Art – Lacework (Pivotal).
March 13. First foal. Doncaster Premier. £29,000Y. Robin O'Ryan. The dam, a fairly useful 7f (at 2 yrs) to 10f winner, is a sister to the multiple Scandinavian listed winner Entangle and a half-sister to 2 winners. The second dam, Entwine (by Primo Dominie), a quite useful 2-y-o dual 5f winner, is a half-sister to 5 winners including the Group 2 Lowther Stakes winner Soar and the very smart 6f and 7f winner Feet So Fast. (Mel Roberts & Richard Fahey). *"A very sharp filly with loads of speed. She'll have had her first race well before your book is out and although she still hasn't come in her coat she's still one of the quickest we have at the moment. She'll stay further than five furlongs but she's got loads of boot"*.

517. MOONVILLE ★★★★
gr.c. Clodovil – Moone Cross (Cape Cross).
February 6. First foal. Doncaster Premier. £22,000Y. Emerald Bloodstock/private sale Robin O'Ryan. The dam, a fairly useful dual 6f winner at 3 yrs in Ireland, was listed-placed and is a half-sister to 3 winners. The second dam, Cannikin (by Lahib), a quite useful 2-y-o 6f winner, is a half-sister to 7 winners. (Mike Wynne). *"Quite a good sort and a hardy horse, I like him, he shows speed and he'll definitely win early. Five or six furlongs will do but he's a horse that could get better. He shows a bit"*.

518. NAYEF FLYER ★★
ch.c. Nayef – Abunai (Pivotal).
February 4. First foal. 30,000Y. Tattersalls October Book 1. Highflyer Bloodstock. The dam, a quite useful 2-y-o 5f and 6f winner, is a half-sister to 8 winners including the very useful listed placed Tissifer, the useful Tattersalls Houghton Sales Stakes winner and German Group 1 fourth Sir George Turner, the Group 2 May Hill Stakes second Kotsi and the Canadian Grade 2 second Miss Keller. The second dam, Ingozi (by Warning), a fairly useful winner over 7f and 1m at 3 yrs including a listed event at Sandown Park, is a half-sister to 7 winners including the very smart and tough triple Group 3 7f winner Inchinor. (John Cotton). *"He hasn't grown much since we bought him, so we're just giving him time and we haven't done a lot with him. He's just cantering away and we're not in any hurry"*.

519. NEMUSHKA ★★★
ch.f. Sakhee – Dame de Noche (Lion Cavern).
January 21. First foal. The dam, a useful 5f to 1m winner of 4 races, is a sister to the Japanese 7f stakes winner Dublin Lion. The second dam, Goodnight Kiss (by Night Shift), was placed 7 times including a second in the Irish 1,000 Guineas and is a half-sister to 3 winners. (G Guck Group). *"She's quite a nice filly but she'll take time. I wouldn't leave her out because she has a bit of speed but I won't rush her"*.

520. NORTHERN JEWEL ★★★
b.f. Nayef – Tekindia (Indian Ridge).
April 3. Sixth foal. Goffs Orby. €90,000Y. Norman Steel. Half-brother to the useful Irish dual 1m winner and dual Group 3 placed Wade Giles (by Azamour) and to the fair 12f winner Reciprocation (by Singspiel). The dam won once over 7f at 3 yrs in France and is a half-sister to 6 winners including the US stakes winner and Grade 2 third The Key Rainbow. The second dam, Te Kani (by Northern Dancer), won once in France and is a half-sister to 7 winners including the US triple Grade 1 winner Ogygian. (Norman Steel). *"A lovely filly but she'll take time. A good mover"*.

521. ONE KOOL DUDE ★★★
ch.c. Iceman – Hiraeth (Petong).
April 14. Sixth foal. 9,000Y. Doncaster Premier. Aiden O'Ryan. Half-brother to the modest 2010 6f placed 2-y-o New Springs (by Acclamation) and to the fair dual 5f winner (including at 2 yrs) Cocabana (by Captain Rio).

The dam, a fair 6f winner, is a half-sister to 6 winners including the dual Group 3 5f winner Ringmoor Down. The second dam, Floppie (by Law Society), a minor 3-y-o winner in France, is a sister to a listed-placed winner there and a half-sister to 4 winners including the French listed winner Love Shack. (Let's Go Racing 1). "A typical 'north of England' horse, he ran OK on his debut and I'm sure he'll win. He probably lacks a gear but he'll get six furlongs definitely. A good, hardy little horse and they'll have some fun with him". This colt was only beaten by a short head on his debut at Dundalk in late March.

522. ORRELL POST ★★★★ ♣
b.f. Kyllachy – Dame Blanche (Be My Guest).
April 13. Fifth foal. 40,000Y. Tattersalls October Book 2. R O'Ryan. Half-sister to the quite useful French 10f winner and Group 3 Prix Cleopatre third Excellent Girl (by Exceed And Excel) and to a winner abroad by Xaar. The dam, a modest 1m placed 3-y-o, is a half-sister to 4 winners including the US Grade 1 winner and Irish 1,000 Guineas third Luas Line. The second dam, Streetcar (by In The Wings), is a placed half-sister to 9 winners. (D W Armstrong). "A nice filly, she could be early but she's had a touch of sore shins and a dirty nose so she's a little bit behind. Could be the owner's nicest 2-y-o, she's worked alright, shows a bit and has speed".

523. OUR BOY JACK ★★★
b.c. Camacho – Jina (Petardia).
February 25. Seventh foal. 35,000Y. Tattersalls October Book 2. R O'Ryan. Half-brother to the fair 2-y-o 7f winner Heather Heath (by Tendulkar) and to the Italian winner of 11 races from 2 to 6 yrs Mr Mamo (by Indian Rocket). The dam, a poor maiden, was placed fourth twice over 1m and is a half-sister to 4 winners. The second dam, Crimson Crest (by Pampapaul), a modest Irish sprint maiden, is a half-sister to 3 winners including the Group 3 Curragh Stakes winner Crimson Heather. (Middleham Park Racing). "Quite a nice horse, I like him, he works well and he's a hardy racehorse. He probably wants six furlongs but he will win".

524. PEN BAL CRAG ★★★ ♣
b.c. Exceed And Excel – Rosse (Kris).
April 19. Seventh foal. 16,000Y. Tattersalls October Book 2. George R Hunnam. Half-brother to the fairly useful 6f (at 2 yrs) and 10f winner Upton Grey (by Dalakhani), to the fairly useful 1m winner and listed-placed Fidelia (by Singspiel), the fair 9f winner La Tizona (by Alhaarth) and the modest 7f winner Lasso (by Indian Ridge). The dam, a useful dual 7f winner, is a half-sister to 9 winners including the high-class Group 1 1m Coronation Stakes winner Rebecca Sharp and the smart Group 3 11.5f Lingfield Derby Trial winner Mystic Knight. The second dam, Nuryana (Nureyev), was a useful winner of the listed 1m Grand Metropolitan Stakes and is a half-sister to 5 winners. (Mr Hunnam). "Quite sharp, he's got a lot of boot and he would have been early but he got sore shins. I hope we don't miss the boat with him because he's a typical early two-year-old and he should be running early".

525. PERSONAL TOUCH ★★★
ch.c. Pivotal – Validate (Alhaarth).
April 11. Second foal. 65,000Y. Tattersalls October Book 2. R O'Ryan. Closely related to the quite useful 2010 2-y-o 5f winner Little Lion Man (by Kyllachy). The dam is an unraced half-sister to 3 winners including the fairly useful dual 6f winner (including at 2 yrs) and listed-placed Enact. The second dam, Constitute (by Gone West), a quite useful 1m winner, is a half-sister to 5 winners including the dual listed winner and Group 3 10f Select Stakes second Battle Chant. (Mr N Wrigley & Mr K Hart). "A nice horse and I like him but Pivotal's just take a bit of time. We're not in any great hurry with him but he's breezed a few times and he'll definitely win. A six/seven furlong type".

526. PETERS PURSUIT ★★
ch.c. Bertolini – Xarzee (Xaar).
February 17. First foal. 22,000Y. Tattersalls December. McKeever Bloodstock, (previously 37,000Y, Tattersalls October Book 2, Global Equine). The dam is an unplaced half-sister to 6 winners including Paco Boy (Lockinge Stakes, Queen Anne Stakes and Prix de la Foret). The second dam, Tappen Zee (by Sandhurst Prince),

a dual 7f winner at 3 yrs in Ireland, is a half-sister to 7 winners including the dual listed winner and Irish 2,000 Guineas third Cape Town. (Peter Foden). *"A big, raw sort of horse, he's huge. Quite lazy at home, it's hard to get to grips with him so I'm not sure where we're up to with him"*.

527. RIVINGTON ★★★
b.c. Oasis Dream – Kiralik (Efisio).
March 31. Fourth foal. 45,000Y. Tattersalls December. Not sold. Half-brother to the fair 2010 dual 7f placed 2-y-o Adlington (by Dansili). The dam, an Italian listed winner and third in the Group 2 Italian 1,000 Guineas, is a full or half-sister to 5 winners including the 2-y-o Group 3 6f Princess Margaret Stakes and subsequent US 3-y-o Grade 2 8.5f winner and Grade 1 9f third River Belle. The second dam, Dixie Favor (by Dixieland Band), was a quite useful Irish 6f (at 2 yrs) to 1m winner. (D W Armstrong). *"He's been a little bit disappointing for an Oasis Dream but it's still early doors. He's not very big, but he's a good sort of colt and he'll take a bit of time I'd say. Six furlongs in mid-season will do for starters probably"*.

528. SHEVINGTON ★★★
b.c. Choisir – Miss Dixie (Bertolini).
January 27. Second foal. Doncaster Premier. £20,000Y. Robin O'Ryan. The dam, placed over 5f and 6f at 2 yrs, is a half-sister to 6 winners including the 2-y-o Group 3 6f Princess Margaret Stakes and subsequent US 3-y-o Grade 2 8.5f winner and Grade 1 9f third River Belle and the Italian listed winner and Group 2 Italian 1,000 Guineas third Kiralik. The second dam, Dixie Favor (by Dixieland Band), was a quite useful Irish 6f (at 2 yrs) to 1m winner. (D W Armstrong). *"We won't mess about with him, he'll run early, I'd say six furlongs will suit him even more than five and he's a good, hardy horse"*.

529. SUGARPINE ★★★
b.f. Oratorio – Maria Luisa (King's Best).
February 9. Second foal. Goffs Orby. €34,000Y. Norman Steel. The dam, a fair Irish dual 1m winner, is a half-sister to 5 winners. The second dam, Miss Amy R (by Deputy Minister), won 2 races at 2 and 3 yrs in the USA and is a half-sister to 8 winners including Glory Forever (Group 3 Prix Thomas Bryon) and the dam of the Group winners Verglas and Cassandra Go. (Norman Steel). *"I haven't done a lot with her yet but she's a good mover, she has a bit of a temperament but she's fine. Probably a mid-season type 2-y-o"*.

530. SUMMER LANE ★★
b.f. Chevalier – Greta d'Argent (Great Commotion).
March 11. Third foal. Doncaster Premier. £10,000Y. Robin O'Ryan. Half-sister to the fairly useful 2-y-o dual 5f winners Coolminx and Baycat (both by One Cool Cat). The dam, a fairly useful 1m (at 2 yrs) to 12f winner of 4 races, is a half-sister to 5 winners including the listed winner and Group 2 placed Winged d'Argent. The second dam, Petite-D-Argent (by Noalto), won over 6f (at 2 yrs) and 7f and is a half-sister to one winner. (Norman Steel). *"She seems a good-moving filly, but although I can't knock her I don't know much about her yet. She hasn't got a sprinting mentality so we'll have to wait and see with her"*.

531. VALLEY OF HOPE ★★★
gr.g. Three Valleys – Zaragossa (Paris House).
March 31. Fifth living foal. £8,500Y. Doncaster Festival. Robin O'Ryan. Half-brother to the fair 6f (including at 2 yrs) and 5f winner The Name Is Frank (by Lujain). The dam, a fair 2-y-o 5f winner, is a sister to one 5f winner and a half-sister to 3 other sprint winners. The second dam, Antonia's Folly (by Music Boy), a modest 2-y-o 5f winner, stayed 6f and is a half-sister to 2 minor winners. (Middleham Park Racing & Richard Fahey). *"He was an absolute sod, so we had to geld him! He'll run early though and I think he'll do a job because he seems genuine enough now and if he keeps his temperament right he'll be OK"*.

532. VENTURA SPIRIT ★★★★
b.c. Royal Applause – Jalissa (Mister Baileys).
March 10. Third foal. 70,000Y. Tattersalls October Book 2. R O'Ryan. Half-brother to the fair 2010 2-y-o 6f winner Bahamian Sunset (by Bahamian Bounty) and to the fairly useful 6f (including at 2 yrs) and 7f winner Folly Bridge (by Avonbridge). The dam, a quite useful 6f winner, is a half-sister to 3 winners including the smart 7f (at 2 yrs) to 10f winner of 7 races Vintage

Premium. The second dam, Julia Domne (by Dominion), placed fourth over 5f and 1m is a sister to two listed winners and a half-sister to the Hungerford Stakes winner Norwich. Keith Denham). "*He's a nice, good-moving horse and I like him a lot, but you're looking at the middle to back- end of the season for him. He'll want six/seven furlongs and maybe a bit further, he'll take time but he's nice*".

533. WARCROWN ★★★★★ ♣
b.c. Azamour – Alikhlas (Lahib).
January 31. Eighth foal. €42,000foal. Goffs. Norman Steel. Half-brother to the fairly useful triple 7f winner (including at 2 yrs) Sik Fan (by Unfuwain), to the fairly useful Irish Blasket Spirit (by King's Best), the quite useful 7f winner Anne Tudor (by Anabaa) and the fair 6f winner Imperial Rule (by Second Empire). The dam was a fair 3-y-o 1m winner and is a half-sister to 3 winners including the listed winner and Group 2 Lancashire Oaks second Sahool and the dam of the dual Group 2 Hardwicke Stakes winner Maraahel. The second dam, Mathaayl (by Shadeed), a quite useful 6f and 10f winner, is a half-sister to 3 winners including the Group 3 Princess Margaret Stakes winner Muhbubh. (Norman Steel). "*A beautiful horse. If I had to pick one at the moment it would be him. Everything about him says quality and although I haven't done a lot with him yet I'd say he's a racehorse. He certainly stands out and although you might think on pedigree he'd want seven furlongs, he's definitely not slow either. Possibly Royal Ascot bound, I like everything about him and I'd say he's got it all – he's a monster!*"

534. WORTHINGTON ★★
b.f. Kodiac – Idle Fancy (Mujtahid).
March 20. Eighth foal. Doncaster Premier. £45,000Y. Highfield Farm. Closely related to the fairly useful 8.3f (at 2 yrs) to 12f winner Come On Jonny (by Desert King) and half-sister to the fairly useful 2-y-o dual 5f winner and listed placed Crafty Fancy (by Intikhab), to the fairly useful 5f (at 2 yrs) to 7f winner of 14 races Idle Power (by Common Grounds) and the fair 1m winner Bint Alhaarth (by Alhaarth). The dam, a fair Irish 3-y-o 1m winner, is a half-sister to 7 winners including the French listed 1m winner Danish Field and the useful French 2-y-o winner Femme Grise and the dam of the Lancashire Oaks winner Ela Athena. The second dam, Pizziri (by Artaius), won over 6f and 1m in Italy and is a half-sister to 7 winners. (D W Armstrong). "*She seems a nice filly but I haven't done enough with her yet to really comment. Like a lot of my fillies she's just a bit behind at the moment, but she will be a two-year-old*".

535. YEOMANOFTHEGUARD ★★★★ ♣
b.c. Librettist – Red Blooded Woman (Red Ransom).
April 3. First foal. The dam, a fair 7.6f winner, is a half-sister to the Irish 2-y-o 7f winner and Group 1 Criterium de Saint-Cloud second Drumbeat. The second dam, Maskaya (by Machiavellian), an Irish 2-y-o 5f winner, is a half-sister to 4 winners including the dual Irish listed 7f winner and Group 2 placed Modeeroch and the Irish 2-y-o 6f winner and Group 1 6f Cheveley Park Stakes third Danaskaya. (Mr Farr Jnr). "*A fine horse, he's quite a handful so he's being gelded at the moment, but God, he's some mover! A big, strong horse, we'll kick on with him because he's worth persevering with. A really good-moving horse*"

536. UNNAMED ★★★
b.f. Teofilo – Bedara (Barathea).
February 18. Seventh foal. 36,000Y. Tattersalls October Book 1. Bobby O'Ryan. Half-sister to the useful 1m and 10f winner of 4 races and listed-placed Mutajarred (by Alhaarth), to the fairly useful 7f (at 2 yrs) and 1m and subsequent US stakes-placed winner Arm Candy (by Nashwan) and the quite useful 2-y-o 1m winner Mozafin (by Zafonic), subsequently a winner in Austria at 3 yrs. The dam, a quite useful 10.5f winner, was listed-placed and is a half-sister to 2 minor winners abroad. The second dam, Cutting Reef (by Kris), a staying winner of 2 races in France including a listed event at Maisons-Laffitte, is a half-sister to 7 winners. (Dr M Koukash). "*A good-moving filly, we were keen on Teofilo at the Sales but we couldn't afford them. She'll take time and she'll want a trip, so I'd say seven furlongs or a mile from the middle to the back end of the season for her. She gets on with her job, she's a good mover and I like her*".

537. UNNAMED ★★★★
b.c. Rock Of Gibraltar – Dakota Sioux
(College Chapel).
**March 26. Fourth foal. Goffs Orby. €68,000Y.
Robin O'Ryan.** Half-brother to the 2-y-o listed 6f winner Max One Two Three and to the modest 7f winner of 9 races Straight Face (both by Princely Heir). The dam, a fairly useful 7f and 1m winner of 8 races from 3 to 5 yrs, is a half-sister to 3 winners including a listed winner in Italy. The second dam, Batilde (by Victory Piper), is a placed half-sister to 7 minor winners. (Paul Towell). *"A big, scopey horse, he's a good mover and I like him. He'll take time, I used to train the dam and he's probably the nicest horse she's bred. I like him a lot".*

538. UNNAMED ★★★★
b.c. Cockney Rebel – Gibraltar Bay
(Cape Cross).
February 9. Second foal. Doncaster St Leger Festival. £20,000Y. Bobby O'Ryan. Half-brother to the fair 2010 2-y-o 7f winner Kalkan Bay (by Pastoral Pursuits). The dam, a quite useful 9f and 12f winner of 3 races, is a half-sister to 4 winners. The second dam, Secrets Of Honour (by Belmez), is an unraced half-sister to 6 winners including the Group 1 July Cup winner Mr Brooks and to the placed dam of the Group 1 Middle Park Stakes winner First Trump. (Dr M Koukash). *"The most handsome horse you've ever seen. He'll take a bit of time because he's big and scopey and I imagine he'll want seven furlongs. The best looking horse in the yard".*

539. UNNAMED ★★★★
b.f. Dubawi – Magical Cliché (Affirmed).
March 9. Eighth foal. 70,000Y. Tattersalls October Book 1. Form Bloodstock. Half-sister to the Irish 3-y-o 6f winner Clever Myth (by Green Desert) and to the Irish 9f to 12f winner Legend Has It (by Sadler's Wells). The dam was placed 4 times at up to 1m and is a sister to several good winners including the Group 2 Premio Legnano winner Easy To Copy and the Irish 1,000 Guineas winner Trusted Partner (dam of the high-class filly Dress To Thrill). The second dam, Talking Picture (by Speak John), a champion American 2-y-o filly, won at up to 7f. (Sheikh Mohammed bin Khalifa Al Maktoum). *"A nice, big, scopey filly. I like her a lot and she'll make a 2-y-o from the mid-season onwards".*

540. UNNAMED ★★★★
b.c. Dubawi – Ribot's Guest (Be My Guest).
March 21. Eighth foal. 360,000Y. Tattersalls October Book 1. Form Bloodstock. Half-brother to the Group 1 Prix de l'Opera and Group 2 1m May Hill Stakes winner Kinnaird (by Dr Devious) and to the quite useful 12f winner Tourism by Dubai Destination). The dam ran unplaced in Italy and is a half-sister to 6 winners including the Italian listed winner Raysiza and the dam of the Hong Kong Derby winner Salford Mill. The second dam, Raysiya (by Cure The Blues), a fairly useful Irish 10f and 12f winner, is a half-sister to 5 winners including the Group 3 10f Royal Whip Stakes winner Rayseka. (Sheikh Mohammed bin Khalifa Al Maktoum). *"Quite a nice horse, he seemed to be stood still after the Sales but he's just starting to pick up now and he'll be racing from mid-summer onwards. A good-moving horse with a good attitude – everything's right. A nice horse".*

541. UNNAMED ★★★
gr.c. Clodovil – Tahtheeb (Muhtarram).
February 2. First foal. Goffs Orby. €60,000Y. Aidan O'Ryan. The dam, a listed-placed 9f winner here at 2 yrs and subsequently a winner in the USA, is a half-sister to 3 winners. The second dam, Mihnah (by Lahib), a quite useful 6f (at 2 yrs) and 1m winner, is a half-sister to 9 winners including the smart Group 2 14.6f Park Hill Stakes winner Ranin. (Mike Browne). *"A six/seven furlong type 2-y-o, he's a good sort and just gets on with his job, so there are no issues about him. He should win".*

JAMES GIVEN
542. BUSTER BROWN (IRE) ★★★
ch.c. Singspiel – Gold Dodger (Slew O'Gold).
March 5. Seventh foal. 20,000Y. Tattersalls October Book 2. Anthony Stroud. Half-brother to the Group 3 C L Weld Park Stakes winner Chintz (by Danehill Dancer), to the French dual 13f winner Fruela (by Fasliyev), the minor French 3-y-o winner Artful (by Green Desert) and a winner in Daylami. The dam, a listed 10f winner of 2 races in France, is a half-sister to 9 winners including the French Group 2 winner Prospect Wells and the dual Group

3 winner Prospect Park. The second dam, Brooklyn's Dance (by Shirley Heights), won the Group 3 Prix Cleopatre and is a half-sister to 8 winners. (Mrs L P Fish). "Although he has a look of being slightly backward because he's a bit unfurnished, we've given him a bit of a spin and he's more forward than his physique suggests, which is very exciting because when he matures we could have quite a nice horse. He'll be a mid-season 2-y-o at best, but the jockeys have already had a bit of a squeeze on him and he responded nicely, so he's one we're very much looking forward to running".

543. FINBAR ★★★
b.c. Nayef – Baralinka (Barathea).
March 17. Half-brother to the fairly useful 2010 2-y-o listed 5f winner of 3 races Mara inka and to the fair 1m winner State Fair (both by Marju). The dam, a useful 5f (at 2 yrs) and triple 6f winner, is a half-sister to the Group 1 Fillies Mile, Falmouth Stakes, Sussex Stakes and Matron Stakes winner Soviet Song (by Marju). The second dam, Kalinka (by Soviet Star), a quite useful 2-y-o 7f winner, is a half-sister to 2 winners. (Elite Racing Club). "He's going through a huge growth spurt, but before that he was showing us quite a bit and he was the most forward 2-y-o we had. So it certainly looks like he'll make a 2-y-o and I don't think it'll be too long either".

544. HARBOUR SANDS ★★★
b.c. Bahamian Bounty – Sahara Silk (Desert Style).
January 25. Second foal. 16,000Y. Tattersalls October Book 2. Not sold. Brother to the modest 2010 dual 5f placed 2-y-o Silk Bounty. The dam, a fair winner of 10 races over 5f and 6f, is a half-sister to one winner. The second dam, Buddy And Soda (by Imperial Frontier), is a half-sister to 9 winners. (Danethorpe Racing Partnership). "We had his full-brother last year and he was small, but this is a bigger version. He's very muscular and very well-developed. I'd say he'll be a mid-season 2-y-o".

545. KUNG HEI FAT CHOY (USA) ★★★
b.c. Elusive Quality – Lady Succeed (Brian's Time).
March 14. First foal. $120,000Y. Keeneland September. Not sold. The dam, a winner in Japan at 3 and 5 yrs, is a half-sister to 4 winners including the French listed 7f winner Esperero. The second dam, Hydro Calido (by Nureyev), a very useful filly and winner of the Group 2 1m Prix d'Astarte, was second in the French 1,000 Guineas and is a half-sister to the champion European 2-y-o and 2,000 Guineas second Machiavellian, to the smart Group 1 Prix Morny and Group 1 Prix de la Salamandre winner and 1,000 Guineas third Coup de Genie and the very smart Group 1 Prix Jacques le Marois winner Exit to Nowhere. (Danethorpe Racing Partnership). "A good-looking horse, he's more of a 3-y-o both to look at and in the way he's training. That's not to say he's weak or backward, because he's not. He's big and strong. So although he's one for the late summer onwards, he's one to keep an eye on".

546. MALINDI ★★
b.f. Compton Place – Mana Pools (Brief Truce).
March 30. Sister to the fairly useful 2-y-o 7f and 1m winner of 4 races Cesc. The dam, a fair 1m to 10f of 3 races, is a half-sister to 5 winners. The second dam, Pipers Pool (by Mtoto), is a placed half-sister to 8 winners. (H J P Farr). "She's been growing recently and has developed a backside that you can expect for a Compton Place! It'll be a while before we start doing anything more with her but she looks like she'll be a six furlong horse".

547. NIGHT FLASH (GER) ★★★
b.c. Oratorio – Night Woman (Monsun).
February 7. Fifth foal. 30,000Y. Tattersalls October Book 2. Anthony Stroud. Half-brother to the Group 1 German Oaks winner Night Magic (by Sholokov), to the German listed-placed winner Night Prince (by Dashing Blade) and 2 minor winners in Germany by Sholokov and Lord Of England. The dam, a listed-placed winner of 4 races in Germany, is a half-sister to one winner. The second dam, Noveka (by Kalaglow), won 3 races at 2 and 3 yrs in Germany. (Danethorpe Racing Partnership). "A nice horse, he was bought with his eligibility for the Chesham Stakes at Royal Ascot in mind because Oratorio's have won that race once and been third once. At the time we bought him he looked like he'd be a 2-y-o type and he's developed that way as well. At the moment he's done nothing to suggest he

couldn't have a run beforehand to see if he's good enough for Ascot".

548. NO DOMINION (IRE) ★★★★
b.c. Dylan Thomas – Boast (Most Welcome).
April 4. Fifth foal. 125,000Y. Tattersalls October Book 1. Not sold. Closely related to the useful 2-y-o listed 5.2f winner and dual Group 3 placed Strut (by Danehill Dancer) and half-brother to the quite useful 2-y-o dual 5f winner and subsequent US Grade 3 placed Vaunt (by Averti) and the quite useful 2-y-o 5f and subsequent US winner Brag (by Mujadil). The dam, a useful 5f and 6f winner, is a half-sister to 6 winners including the fairly useful 2-y-o 5f and 4-y-o 1m winner Great Bear. The second dam, Bay Bay (by Bay Express), a useful 7.6f winner, was listed-placed twice and is a half-sister to 7 winners. (Mr J A Barson). "A very nice horse. We're lucky this year in that we have a bunch of what you would expect to be 3-y-o types and yet they're doing well already. He's had a couple of spins, he knows what he's doing and although I wouldn't say it's all there now, it is coming and it's coming in advance of what you'd expect given his sire. I'm excited about him and he's a good looking horse that looks like he could start off at six furlongs".

549. SALLY PEPPER (USA) ★★★
b.br.f. Rock Hard Ten – La Sila (Danzig).
April 27. Seventh foal. $80,000Y. Keeneland September. Anthony Stroud. Half-sister to the minor US stakes-placed winner Short Circuit (by Lemon Drop Kid). The dam was unplaced in one start and is a half-sister to 3 winners. The second dam, La Spia (by Capote), winner of the Grade 2 Del Mar Debutante Stakes, was Grade 1 placed and is a half-sister to 3 winners. (Danethorpe Racing Partnership). "A very nice filly. She's big, scopey, level-headed and takes everything in her stride. We had a filly by the same sire here last season called Fenella Fudge and she came very close to winning some decent maidens. This filly is more forward than she was at this stage. She's an exciting horse to look forward to and I'd say she's likely to want seven furlongs and a galloping track because she has a huge stride on her".

550. SEASON SPIRIT ★★★★ ♠
ch.c. Shirocco – Shadow Dancing (Unfuwain).
February 5. Fourth foal. 45,000Y. Tattersalls October Book 1. Anthony Stroud. Half-brother to the useful 2-y-o 1m winner and Group 3 10.3f Dee Stakes third Rasmy (by Red Ransom), to the fair 2-y-o 1m winner Hazy Dancer (by Oasis Dream). The dam, winner of the listed Cheshire Oaks, was third in the Oaks and second in the Group 2 Ribblesdale Stakes and in the Group 2 Prix de Pomone and is a half-sister to 6 winners. The second dam, Salchow (by Niniski), won the listed Cheshire Oaks, was second in the Park Hill Stakes and is a half-sister to 7 winners. (Mr D J Fish). "This colt is the apple of my eye – I think he's something special. He's a very big horse but he doesn't carry himself like one, he carries himself like a well-balanced horse and if I told you he was a 4-y-o you wouldn't argue. He's a very good-looking horse, a good size and he carries himself with strength and purpose. He has a good attitude, he shows good paces already and I just think we could have dropped lucky with this one. He's very nice".

551. UNNAMED ★★★
b.c. Teofilo – Wunders Dream (Averti).
March 21. Fourth foal. 3,000Y. Tattersalls October 2. Not sold. Half-sister to the modest 5f placed 2-y-o Paradise Dream (by Kyllachy). The dam, a winner of 4 races at 2 yrs including the Group 2 5f Flying Childers Stakes and the Group 3 5f Molecomb Stakes, is a half-sister to 4 winners including the Irish Group 3 winner Grecian Dancer. The second dam, Pizzicato (by Statoblest), a modest 5f and 5.3f winner at 3 yrs, is a half-sister to 5 winners including the high-class Hong Kong horses Mensa and Firebolt. (Bolton Grange). "When you think about it this colt is by a champion 2-y-o and out of the fastest filly of her generation. He's developed very nicely and isn't a squat, sprinter type on looks, so I suspect he'll be a six/seven furlong type 2-y-o. The sire has had a winner already and although this colt hasn't got the perfect conformation one of my work riders has already said he wouldn't swap him for anything". TRAINERS' BARGAIN BUY

552. UNNAMED ★★
b.f. Three Valleys – Oomph (Shareef Dancer).
February 7. 3,000Y. Tattersalls October Book 3. Not sold. Half-sister to the fairly

Star truly Bolts in

STARSPANGLEDBANNER was described as the "**Usain Bolt of horse racing**" after producing a world-class performance to win the Group 1 Golden Jubilee Stakes at Royal Ascot yesterday.

Ray Thomas, Daily Telegraph, 21st June 2010

Top sprinters from the Danzig sire line that became top stallions include:

Horse	Timeform Rated
Oasis Dream	129
Green Desert	127
Danehill	126
Danetime	121
Invincible Spirit	121

STARSPANGLEDBANNER is rated 128 by Timeform.

hampion sprinter in rope & Australia.

- n Golden Jubilee Stakes-**Gr.1**, 6f.
- n July Cup-**Gr.1**, 6f.
- n Caulfield Guineas-**Gr.1**, 8f.
- n Oakleigh Plate-**Gr.1**, 5½f.
- n Nunthorpe Stakes-**Gr.1**, 5f.

tarspangledbanner

COOLMORE

Contact: **Coolmore Stud**, Fethard, Co. Tipperary, Ireland. Tel: 353-52-6131298. Fax: 353-52-6131382. **Christy Grassick, David O'Loughlin, Eddie Fitzpatrick, Tim Corballis, Maurice Moloney, Gerry Aherne** or **Mathieu Alex. Tom Gaffney, David Magnier, Joe Hernon** or **Cathal Murphy.** 3-25-31966/31689. **Kevin Buckley** (UK Rep.) 44-7827-795156. E-mail: sales@coolmore.ie Web site: www.coolmore.com All stallions nominated to EBF.

Tally-Ho Stud
SIRES FOR 2011

ZEBEDEE
INVINCIBLE SPIRIT - COZY MARIE - COZZENE
THE SPEEDIEST 2-Y-O OF HIS YEAR
GROUP WINNER OF 6 RACES FROM 7 STARTS AT 2
WON Gr2 FLYING CHILDERS S (5f), Gr3 MOLECOMB S (5f)
"He's got explosive speed, an absolute star" RICHARD HANNON
FAMILY OF MISS ALLEGED (CHAMPION IN EUROPE & USA)

NEW FOR 2011

BUSHRANGER
DANETIME - DANZ DANZ - EFISIO
CHAMPION 2-Y-O IN ENGLAND & FRANCE
WON Gr1 PRIX MORNY, Gr1 MIDDLE PARK S - both in record time
RATED 121 ON INTERNATIONAL CLASSIFICATION AT 2
COVERED THE DAMS OF 28 GROUP/LISTED WINNERS,
HALF SISTERS TO 130 GROUP/LISTED WINNERS,
25 GROUP/LISTED WINNERS/PLACED,
DAUGHTERS OF 33 GROUP/LISTED WINNERS in his 1st season

KODIAC
DANEHILL - RAFHA - KRIS
Gr1 PLACED WINNER OF 4 SPRINT RACES IN ENGLAND & DUBAI
1/2 BROTHER TO TOP SIRE INVINCIBLE SPIRIT (By GREEN DESERT)
DAM RAFHA - Gr1 & CLASSIC WINNER. FAMILY OF PITCAIRN
1st CROP SIRE IN 2010 OF 17 INDIVIDUAL 2-Y-O WINNERS
incl 3 STAKES WINNERS
BATHWICK BEAR, ILENY PRINCESS, SWEET CECILY

BALTIC KING
DANETIME - LINDFIELD BELLE - FAIRY KING
RECORD BREAKING SPRINTER - RATED 120 BY TIMEFORM ANNUAL
STAKES WINNER OF 8 RACES AT 5-6f AND €400,000
DEFEATED 114 GROUP/LISTED WINNERS
FULL BROTHER TO DOMINGUES (Gr3 winning 2-Y-O)
FIRST CROP OF 2-Y-O's RUN IN 2011

TALLY-HO STUD BREEDERS AND VENDORS OF **GR1 WINNE**
DREAM AHEAD, BUSHRANGER, KINGSGATE NATIVE, MYBOYCHARLIE, LAHAL

TALLY-HO STUD, MULLINGAR, CO. WESTMEATH, IRELAND
Tel 04493-48450. Fax 04493-42807. E-Mail info@tallyhostud.com
Contact Tony O'Callaghan (Mob 086-2424416) or Roger O'Callaghan (Mob 087-9690629)
www.tallyhostud.com

8-Horse 2yo Partnership
shares available with
TOM DASCOMBE
at Manor House Stables

Anabaa ex Poretta bc €58,300
Piccolo ex Fizzy Treat bc £26,500
Oratorio ex Penelewey bc €37,100
Moss Vale ex Cape Sydney bc €27,560
Amadeus Wolf ex Darby Shaw bc €31,800
Diamond Green ex Amorous Pursuits bf £15,900
Lucky Story ex Soft Touch chf £12,720
Aussie Rules ex Sticky Green bf €18,020

1/8th share £50,000 all-inclusive until 31 October 2011

For more information call 01948 820485 or visit

www.manorhousestables.com

"Of the eight horses, two will qualify for the **75% French Bred Owners' Premium**s having been bought at Arqana, three were bought at Doncaster, two at Tattersalls Ireland and one at **Goffs**. We carefully selected the eight horses so that the partners will have an interest throughout the season. Some, like the Doncaster purchases, are **proper early two year olds**, some will be more for the mid season and a couple will be more **scopey types** that the partners could even retain as three year olds. The gender mix is five colts and three fillies, so there really is **something for everyone** in this partnership."

Tom Dascombe

useful 7f (at 2 yrs) to 10f winner of 5 races The Which Doctor (by Medicean) and to the quite useful 12f winner Very Agreeable (by Pursuit Of Love). The dam, a quite useful 7f winner, is a half-sister to the UAE listed 1m winner Swiss Law. The second dam, Seductress (by Known Fact), a useful 2-y-o listed 5f winner, is a half-sister to 11 winners including the middle-distance Group winners Little Rock, Short Skirt and Whitewater Affair. (C G Rowles Nicholson). *"She's just started to show us a bit now, she's a nice size for a 2-y-o and she's developing and getting stronger all the time. It's still too early to press any buttons with her but the signs are encouraging. One for the mid-season onwards".*

GODOLPHIN (SAEED BIN SUROOR)

Diana Cooper has kindly helped me out with these comments on Saeed's lovely two-year-olds.

553. A'JUBA ★★★★
b.c. Kingmambo – Arlette (King Of Kings).
March 15. Brother to the 2-y-o Group 3 6f Prix de Cabourg and subsequent UAE Group 3 9f winner, Group 1 6f Prix Morny third and German Group 1 third Alexandros and half-brother to the 2010 2-y-o 1m winner Margravine (by King's Best). The dam is closely related to the Breeders Cup Turf, Coronation Cup and Grand Prix de Saint-Cloud winner In The Wings, to the smart Group 2 10.5f Prix Greffuhle winner Hunting Hawk and the very useful 10f and 11.5f winner Hawker's News. The second dam, High Hawk (by Shirley Heights), won 6 races from 10f to 14.5f including the Group 1 Premio Roma, the Group 2 Ribblesdale Stakes and the Group 2 Park Hill Stakes and is a half-sister to the useful miler Heron's Hollow and to the dam of Infamy (Rothman's International, Sun Chariot Stakes, etc). *"A well-balanced type, he is mature mentally and seems straightforward like his brother Alexandros. He's a nice type who could start over six furlongs, but at the moment more likely seven during the summer".*

554. ALMAAS (USA) ★★★
ch.c. Hard Spun – Summer Dream Girl (Unbridled).
March 15. Fourth foal. $160,000Y. Keeneland September. John Ferguson. Half-brother to 2 winners including the minor US winner Family Pride (by Arch). The dam is an unraced half-sister to 4 winners including the Prix de l'Abbaye and July Cup winner Agnes World and the champion Japanese sprinter/miler Hishi Akebono. The second dam, Mysteries (by Seattle Slew), was third in the Group 3 Musidora Stakes. *"A good-sized colt with lots of quality and a good action. He won't be early and will need seven furlongs, but he's a nice type for later this year".*

555. AL SAHAM ★★★
b.c. Authorized – Local Spirit (Lion Cavern).
February 19. Second foal. The dam, a useful 10f winner, was second in the Group 2 12f Lancashire Oaks and is a sister to the high-class Irish 1,000 Guineas, Coronation Stakes and Nassau Stakes winner Crimplene and a half-sister to 7 winners including the smart Group 3 12.3f Chester Vase winner Dutch Gold. The second dam, Crimson Conquest (by Diesis), a quite useful 2-y-o 6f winner, is a half-sister to the US stakes winner at around 1m Sword Blade. *"We're looking forward to seeing Authorized's progeny and this is a good example of a good-looking, classy colt who certainly looks an interesting prospect at this early stage. He's another seven furlong type for the second half of the season".*

556. FA'IZ (IRE) ★★★
b.c. Dansili – Carisolo (Dubai Millennium).
March 15. Second foal. Half-brother to Midnight Moon (by Singspiel), unplaced in one start at 2 yrs in 2010. The dam, placed once over 10f, is a half-sister to numerous winners including the Group 1 Irish Oaks winner Moonstone, the Breeders Cup second L'Ancresse and the Group 1 10f Prix Saint-Alary winner Cerulean Sky (herself dam of the Group 2 Doncaster Cup winner Honolulu). The second dam, Solo de Lune (by Law Society), a French 11f winner, is a half-sister to 6 winners including the Grade 2 E P Taylor Stakes winner Truly A Dream and the French Group 2 winner Wareed. *"Going through the motions at the moment, with a view to later in the season. He's done nothing wrong at this stage and we are looking forward to seeing him develop".*

557. FAMOUS POET (IRE) ★★★
b.c. Exceed and Excel – Asfurah (Dayjur).
April 15. Half-brother to the quite useful 9f winner Asfurah's Dream (by Nayef), to the quite useful 10.2f winner Ijtihad (by Darshaan), to the fair UAE 1m winner Africanus (by Dubai Millennium) and a minor 1m winner abroad by Machiavellian. The dam, a very useful winner of the Group 3 6f Cherry Hinton Stakes and the listed 5f Windsor Castle Stakes, is closely related to the fairly useful 5.3f (at 2 yrs) and 6f winner Alumisiyah and a half-sister to the US dual Grade 3 winner Istintaj. The second dam, Mathkurh (by Riverman), a useful 5f (at 2 yrs) and 6f winner, is a half-sister to the Group 3 6f Princess Margaret Stakes winner Muhbubh. *"This colt is strong, energetic and is bred to show plenty of speed. He has a good temperament, is generally pleasing and at this stage could make his racecourse debut in June over six furlongs".*

558. HANDSOME MAN (IRE) ★★★
ch.c. Nayef – Danceabout (Shareef Dancer).
February 28. Fifth foal. 140,000Y. Tattersalls October Book 1. John Ferguson. Half-brother to the French listed 9f winner and Group 3 placed Rainbow Dancing (by Rainbow Quest) and to the fairly useful 2-y-o 6f winner Zaffaan (by Efisio). The dam won the Group 2 Sun Chariot Stakes and the listed 7f Oak Tree Stakes and is a half-sister to 3 winners including the Group 3 6f Prix de Meautry winner Pole Position. The second dam, Putupon (by Mummy's Pet), a fairly useful 2-y-o 5f winner, is a full or half-sister to 10 winners including the good horses Jupiter Island (Japan Cup), Pushy (Queen Mary Stakes) and Precocious (Gimcrack Stakes). *"This colt is still a little on the weak side, so will not be rushed, but he has a lovely action, is very laid back and is one to look forward to later in the season".*

559. IBTAHAJ ★★★★
b.c. Invincible Spirit – Maroussies Wings (In The Wings).
January 20. First foal. 200,000Y. Tattersalls October Book 1. John Ferguson. The dam, a very useful French Group 3 13f Prix Minerve winner, was third in the Group 2 Ribblesdale Stakes and is a half-sister to 3 winners including the listed Sceptre Stakes winner Mamounia. The second dam, Maroussie (by Saumarez), won 3 races including the Group 3 10f Prix Fille de l'Air and is a half-sister to 7 winners. *"He is doing all that is asked of him with ease, there's not a lot of precocity on his dam's side, but he's an early foal, well-grown and a nice mover who should be able to start mid-summer".*

560. IHSAS (USA) ★★★
ch.f. Rahy – Express Way (Ahmad).
Sister to the Group 1 Prix Jean Luc Lagardere, Group 1 Premio Vittorio de Capua and Group 1 Premio Roma winner Rio De La Plata and closely related to the Argentine Grade 1 winner El Expressivo (by Candy Stripes). The dam was placed in Argentina and is a half-sister to 2 minor winners. The second dam, Escaline (by Hawk), was unraced. *"Rio de la Plata's full sister, she has just gone through a growth spurt, but is beginning to shape up nicely. She moves well and could be a mid-summer debutant over six furlongs, before stepping up in distance, like her brother".*

561. LAST FIGHTER (USA) ★★★
b.c. Cape Cross – Launch Time (Relaunch).
April 14. Eleventh foal. 90,000foal. Tattersalls December. John Ferguson. Brother to the smart 2-y-o Group 2 7f Superlative Stakes and Group 2 Bosphorus Cup winner Halicarnassus and half-brother to the fair 8.3f winner Follow My Lead (by Night Shift), the US stakes-placed winner My Lucky Strike (by Smart Strike) and 2 minor winners in the USA by Hennessy and Two Punch. The dam is a US placed half-sister to 4 winners including the US Grade 2 winner Palace March and the US Grade 1 second Executive Pride. The second dam, Pride's Palace (by Majestic Palace), won once at 2 yrs and is a half-sister to 5 winners including the US Grade 1 winner Winds Of Thought. *"He is going through a growth spurt at the moment, but there is plenty to like about this colt, especially if he proves to be as tough as Halicarnussus. Eager to please and could be earlier than initially thought".*

562. MAHKAMA (USA) ★★★
b.f. Bernardini – Rahy Rose (Rahy).
March 16. Seventh foal. $270,000Y. Keeneland September. John Ferguson. Half-sister to 3 winners including the US Grade 3

Tempted Stakes winner Summer Raven (by Summer Squall and herself dam of the US Grade 3 winner Winslow Homer). The dam won 2 minor races at 4 yrs in the USA and is a half-sister to 5 winners including the dual Grade 1 winner Wild Rush. The second dam, Rose Park (by Plugged Nickel), a US stakes winner and fourth in the Grade 1 CCA Oaks, is a half-sister to 7 winners. *"This a lively filly who shouldn't take much getting ready. She lacks a little scope and although there is plenty of stamina in her distaff side, she is mature and appears to be one to go forward with quite early".*

563. MIZBAH ★★★★
b.c. *Dubai Destination – Candice (Caerleon).*
March 25. Half-brother to the quite useful 2-y-o 6f winner Red And White (by Red Ransom) and to the French 12f winner Sweet Shop (by Grand Lodge). The dam, a useful 2-y-o 1m winner and third in the Group 3 1m May Hill Stakes, is a half-sister to 2 winners. The second dam, Criquette (by Shirley Heights), a useful 2-y-o and winner of the 7.3f Radley Stakes, is a half-sister to the top-class miler Markofdistinction. *"This colt has strengthened well in the last month and looks like he could come to hand quite quickly. Six furlongs will be his trip at this stage and he could debut next month".*

564. NAJM KABIR ★★★★
b.c. *Teofilo – See You Later (Emarati).*
February 13. Sixth living foal. 220,000Y. Tattersalls October Book 1. John Ferguson. Half-brother to the very useful 5f (including at 2 yrs) and listed 6f winner of 6 races Aahayson (by Noverre), to the fairly useful 6f and 7f winner of 8 races Thebes (by Cadeaux Genereux), the fairly useful 5f and 6f winner of 4 races (including at 2 yrs) Take Ten (by Bahamian Bounty) and the quite useful 2-y-o 5f winner Annatalia (by Pivotal). The dam, a fairly useful dual 5f winner (including at 2 yrs), was listed-placed 3 times and is a half-sister to 6 winners including the very smart 2-y-o Group 3 Horris Hill Stakes winner Peak To Creek and the dual listed winner Ripples Maid. The second dam, Rivers Rhapsody (by Dominion), a useful winner of the listed 5f Scarborough Stakes and third in the Group 2 5f Temple Stakes, is a half-sister to the Group 3 5f Prix d'Arenberg winner Regal Scintilla. *"Hopefully* this colt will be a good advertisement for his sire. He is well-grown, has a very professional attitude, moves well and it would be nice to see him out in July".

565. RAHEEBA ★★★★
b.f. *Invincible Spirit – Wild Gardenia (Alhaarth).*
January 26. First foal. 90,000Y. Tattersalls October Book 1. John Ferguson. The dam, placed fourth once over 12f, is a half-sister to 3 winners including Thakafaat (Group 2 Ribblesdale Stakes). The second dam, Frappe (by Inchinor), a fairly useful 2-y-o 6f winner, is a half-sister to the 2,000 Guineas winner Footstepsinthesand. *"This is certainly a mature-looking filly, with a very laid-back attitude, and indeed sometimes too much so. She gives the impression that she should be out in June or July and have the speed for six furlongs".*

566. ROYAL EMPIRE (IRE) ★★★★
b.c. *Teofilo – Zeiting (Zieten).*
April 14. Eighth foal. €200,000Y. Arqana Deauville August. John Ferguson. Half-brother to 5 winners including the useful 2-y-o 7f winner and triple Group 3 placed Bikini Babe (by Montjeu), to the French 2-y-o 6f winner and Group 3 7f Prix Miesque third Zut Alors (by Pivotal), the useful 2-y-o 6f winner Mutawajid (by Zafonic) and the quite useful 1m winner Mohathab (by Cadeaux Genereux). The dam won 6 races from 6f to 1m including the listed Prix Zeddaan and 3 minor US stakes events and is a half-sister to 5 winners including the Group 3 Prix du Bois winner Dolled Up out of the Irish 13f winner Belle de Cadix (by Law Society), herself a half-sister to 5 winners. *"Another Teofilo that is very athletic and pleasing at this stage. There is plenty of precocity in his family and it will be very interesting to see what he shows us mid-summer".*

567. SHAJJA ★★★
b.c. *Pivotal – Poised (Rahy).*
May 17. Sixth foal. Brother to the very useful 2-y-o 6f and 7f winner Gothenburg and to the fair 12f winner Ipswich Lad (both by Halling). The dam, second over 9f at Chantilly at 3 yrs, is a sister to the Group 1 Sussex Stakes winner Noverre and closely related to the outstanding 2-y-o Arazi, winner of the Breeders Cup

Juvenile, the Prix Robert Papin, the Prix Morny, the Prix de la Salamandre and the Ciga Grand Criterium (all Group 1 events between 5f and 8.5f). The second dam, Danseur Fabuleux (by Northern Dancer), was placed in the Group 3 12f Prix de Minerve and is closely related to the US Grade 1 winner Joyeux Danseur and the very useful 12f winner Fabulous Dancer. *"A nice, forward-going type from the family of Arazi, he is a May foal, like his dam's brother Noverre. He finds life pleasantly easy at the moment and should have the speed to debut over six furlongs in May".*

568. SHIHAB ★★★★
b.f. Dubawi – Baya (Nureyev).
March 26. Half-sister to the Group 3 1m Prix d'Aumale winner Birthsite (by Machiavellian), to the fairly useful 10f winner and listed placed Bayberry (by Bering), the quite useful 7f winner Kafhanee (by Seeking The Gold) and the French 2-y-o 1m winner Quelea (by Gone West). The dam was a very useful Group 3 1m Prix de la Grotte winner and was second in the Group 1 10.5f Prix de Diane. The second dam, Barger (by Riverman), won the Group 3 9.5f Prix Vanteaux, was third in the Group 1 10f Prix Saint Alary and is a sister to that wonderful mare Triptych, winner of the Champion Stakes, Irish 2,000 Guineas, etc. *"An exciting colt on pedigree, he is also pleasing in his work. There will be no rush with him, but he is nice and strong with a wonderfully laid-back attitude at the moment. It is easy to imagine him waking up and making his debut over seven furlongs in July".*

569. SPECIAL BOY (IRE) ★★★
b.c. Invincible Spirit – Ezilla (Darshaan).
May 13. Ninth foal. Goffs Orby. €110,000Y. John Ferguson. Closely related to the fairly useful Irish 10f winner Ezalli (by Cape Cross) and half-brother to the smart 1m, listed 10f and listed 12f winner Ezima and to the fairly useful Irish 12f winner Gentle On My Mind (both by Sadler's Wells). The dam is an unraced sister to the top-class broodmare Ebaziya, a triple listed winner from winner from 7f (at 2 yrs) to 12f in Ireland (herself dam of the Group 1 winners Edabiya, Ebadiyla and Enzeli) and a half-sister to 7 winners. The second dam, Ezana (by Ela-Mana-Mou), a winner in France at 3 yrs over 11.5f, is a half-sister to 5 winners including the Group 3 10.5f Prix de Flore and Group 3 10.5f Prix Penelope winner Demia. *"Despite his age, this little colt is a smart, forward type. He is strong, physically mature and should be one of our first two-year-old runners, although he will prefer six furlongs to five. He has an excellent attitude".*

570. TADMIR (USA) ★★★
b.br.c. Bernardini – Owsley (Harlan).
April 7. Fourth foal. $200,000Y. Saratoga August. John Ferguson. Brother to the 2011 3-y-o US Grade 1 9f Wood Memorial Stakes second Arthur's Tale and half-brother to 2 winners in the USA by Pulpit and War Chant. The dam won 8 races in the USA including the Grade 2 Galaxy Stakes and the Grade 2 New York Handicap and is a half-sister to 4 winners. The second dam, Insipid (by Sham), is a placed sister to the stakes-placed winner Petite Diable (herself dam of the Grade 1 Metropolitan Handicap winner Dixie Brass). *"His full-brother, Arthur's Tale, has entered the Kentucky Derby picture recently when finishing second in the Wood Memorial, but he didn't break his maiden until the fourth time of asking in December last year. This colt won't be early either and still has a lot of daylight under him, but he is very light on his feet and one to look forward to seeing mature in due course".*

571. TAJAMAL (IRE) ★★★
b.c. Dubai Destination – Aryaamm (Galileo).
March 2. Second foal. Half-brother to the 2010 2-y-o Group 2 7f Champagne Stakes winner Saamidd (by Street Cry). The dam, a quite useful 10f winner, is a half-sister to the French 6f (at 2 yrs) and 7.5f winner and Group 2 1m third Mathematician. The second dam, Zibilene (by Rainbow Quest), a useful 12f winner and listed-placed over 10f, is a half-sister to 7 winners including the Breeders Cup Mile, Irish 2,000 Guineas and Queen Anne Stakes winner Barathea and the Fillies Mile and Irish 1,000 Guineas winner Gossamer. *"Obviously it would be great to see the same kind of ability as his half-brother showed when winning the Champagne Stakes but it is still very much early days for this colt, as indeed it was for Saamidd at this stage last year. He is a good-looking individual though, who will just need a little time".*

GODOLPHIN (SAEED BIN SUROOR) – JOHN GOSDEN

572. TAJRIBA (IRE) ★★★
b.f. Teofilo – Caumshinaun (Indian Ridge).
March 7. Seventh foal. 200,000Y. Tattersalls October Book 1. John Ferguson. Closely related to the Group 1 Irish 1,000 Guineas winner Nightime (by Galileo) and half-sister to the Irish 2-y-o 1m winner and listed-placed Mermaid Island (by Mujadil) and the fairly useful dual 7f winner Gunga Din (by Green Desert). The dam won 5 races from 6f to 1m in Ireland at 3 and 4 yrs including a listed event and was Group 3 placed. She is a half-sister to one winner out of the Irish 2-y-o 6f winner Ridge Pool (by Bluebird). *"This is a professional filly who has the makings of a nice type in time. She has a lot of energy though and can get a little tense. She won't be rushed but should be out mid-summer and have the speed for six furlongs".*

573. TAMARRUD (IRE) ★★★
b.c. Authorized – Miss Hepburn (Gone West).
February 20. Second foal. 50,000Y. Tattersalls October Book 1. R. Frisby. The dam is an unplaced daughter of the Group 3 Prestige Stakes winner and subsequent US Grade 2 third Circle Of Gold (by Royal Academy), herself a sister to the listed winner Crystal Crossing (dam of the St Leger winner Rule Of Law) and a half-sister to 4 winners. *"This is a colt with a nice way about him. He is an easy mover, has a good temperament and although we won't see him at the races until the second half of the season, September was early enough for his sire to debut".*

574. TASRIH (USA) ★★★
b.c. Hard Spun – Rare Gift (Unbridled's Song).
April 5. Third foal. $180,000Y. Fasig-Tipton Kentucky July. John Ferguson. The dam won 3 races in the USA at 2 and 3 yrs including the Grade 3 Ladies Handicap and is a half-sister to 2 winners. The second dam, Rare Blend (by Bates Motel), won 10 races including the Grade 2 Molly Pitcher Handicap and three Grade 3 events. *"A fine, athletic individual with plenty to like about him. He is going well and could be out the second half of the season, over seven furlongs".*

575. USTURA (USA) ★★★
b.c. Nayef – Calando (Storm Cat).
April 7. Seventh foal. Half-brother to the useful 2-y-o listed 7f Chesham Stakes winner Champlain (by Seeking The Gold) and to the modest 5f to 1m winner of 10 races Sovereignty (by King's Best). The dam won the Group 3 1m May Hill Stakes, was second in the Group 1 Fillies Mile and third in the French 1,00 Guineas and is a half-sister to 2 winners. The second dam, Diminuendo (by Diesis), won the Hoover Fillies Mile, Cherry Hinton Stakes (both at 2 yrs), Epsom Oaks, Irish Oaks (in a dead-heat), Yorkshire Oaks and Musidora Stakes. *"Another Nayef with a similar profile to Handsome Man. He appears to have plenty of quality but is one for the back end of the season".*

JOHN GOSDEN

576. AIM HIGHER ★★★★
ch.c. Exceed And Excel – Enemy Action (Forty Niner).
January 24. Sixth foal. 60,000Y. Tattersalls October Book 2. Hugo Merry. Half-brother to the 1,000 Guineas third Super Sleuth (by Selkirk), to the quite useful 2-y-o 6f winner Duelling (by Diesis) and a winner abroad by Shamardal. The dam, a very useful 2-y-o dual 6f winner and subsequently stakes-placed in the USA, is a half-sister to 4 winners including the smart Daggers Drawn, winner of the Group 2 6f Richmond Stakes and the Group 2 7f Laurent Perrier Rose Champagne Stakes. The second dam, Sun And Shade (by Ajdal), a useful 2-y-o 6f winner, is a half-sister to the very smart Group 2 Park Hill Stakes and Group 2 Prix de Royallieu winner Madame Dubois (herself dam the Irish 2,000 Guineas winner Indian Haven and the Group 1 Gran Criterium winner Count Dubois). *"He's done a bit of work, he goes well and he's a promising colt".*

577. ALAREEF ★★★
gr.c. Oasis Dream – Karliyna (Rainbow Quest).
March 7. Second foal. 180,000Y. Tattersalls October Book 1. Shadwell Estate Co. Half-brother to the fair 9f winner Qamar (by Pivotal). The dam, a fairly useful 10f winner, was listed-placed and is a half-sister to 7 winners including the 2-y-o Group 3 1m May Hill Stakes winner and Group 1 Prix Marcel Boussac second Karasta and the Group 2 2m 2f Doncaster Cup

dead-heat winner Kasthari and the Group 3 Gladness Stakes winner Kargari. The second dam, Karliyka (by Last Tycoon), a French winner of 4 races, was listed placed over 1m and 10f and is a half-sister to 4 winners. *"A neat colt, a good mover and well-balanced, he'll start off at six furlongs but I bet he goes up to a mile"*.

578. APOTHECARY ★★★
b.f. Manduro – Sister Maria (Kingmambo).
February 9. First foal. 60,000Y. Tattersalls October Book 1. John Ferguson. The dam, a fair dual 10f winner, is a half-sister to Mischief Making, a winner of 4 races from 9f to 13f winner of 4 races including a listed event and second in the Group 3 Sagaro Stakes. The second dam, Fraulein (by Acatenango), won over 7f and 1m at 2 yrs, the Grade 1 10f E P Taylor Stakes and a listed 1m event at Ascot and is a half-sister to 4 winners. *"A good mover, she's a light framed, sound type of filly but she's going to take a little time to come to herself"*.

579. ASTRONOMY DOMINE ★★★
b.f. Galileo – Platonic (Zafonic).
February 26. Fifth living foal. €280,000Y. Arqana Deauville August. Badgers Bloodstock. Half-sister to the French listed 11f winner Prudenzia (by Dansili) and to the fairly useful 12f winner of 9 races Hatton Flight (by Kahyasi). The dam, a minor winner at 4 yrs in France, is a half-sister to 5 winners including the Group 2 12f Lancashire Oaks winner Pongee and the dual listed winner Lion Sands. The second dam, Puce (by Darshaan), a very useful listed 12f winner, was Group 3 placed and is a half-sister to 7 winners including the dam of the triple Group 1 winner Alexandrova and the Cheveley Park Stakes winner Magical Romance. *"A nice mover and a quality filly, she's a nice type for seven furlongs to a mile in the second half of the season"*.

580. BINABEE ★★★
b.f. Galileo – Quenched (Dansili).
March 10. Second foal. Closely related to the quite useful 2010 2-y-o 1m winner Rain Mac (by Beat Hollow). The dam, a useful listed 12f winner, is a sister to the French dual 13f winner Lifting Cloud and a half-sister to the very useful 7f (at 2 yrs) and 10f winner and Group 2 Dante Stakes second Raincoat (by Barathea). The second dam, Love The Rain (by Rainbow Quest), a winner over 11f in France, is a sister to the very useful Prix d'Aumale, Prix Vanteaux and Prix de Malleret winner Bonash and a half-sister to 3 winners. (Khalid Abdulla). *"A nice filly and like her mother she has a lot of character. She's a lovely mover and is a nice type for August or September time"*.

581. CHALET GIRL ★★★
b.f. Oasis Dream – Sauterne (Rainbow Quest).
March 10. Sixth foal. 85,000Y. Tattersalls October Book 2. Blandford Bloodstock. Half-sister to the unplaced 2010 2-y-o Daa'iman (by Dansili), to the useful 10f and 12f winner Senate (by Pivotal) and the fair 2-y-o 7f winner Determined Stand (by Elusive Quality). The dam, a listed winner of 3 races from 7f to 10f, is a half-sister to 6 winners including the smart 2-y-o Group 2 6f Cherry Hinton Stakes winner Applaud. The second dam, Band (by Northern Dancer), is a placed half-sister to 5 winners including the US Grade 3 9f New Orleans Handicap winner Festive. *"She's goes alright, she's a nice type and is improving. One for the middle of the season onwards"*.

582. DANEKING ★★
b.c. Dylan Thomas – Sadie Thompson (King's Best).
March 6. Second foal. 35,000Y. Tattersalls October Book 2. Blandford Bloodstock. Half-brother to a winner in Italy by Halling. The dam, a fair 2-y-o 7f winner, is a half-sister to one winner. The second dam, Femme Fatale (by Fairy King), a useful dual 6f winner of 2 races (including a listed event at 2 yrs), was second in the Group 2 Sun Chariot Stakes and is a half-sister to 3 winners including the smart dual listed 10f winner Foodbroker Fancy. *"A nice middle-distance colt in the making"*.

583. EASTERN SUN (IRE) ★★★★
b.c. Kodiac – Always Friendly (High Line).
March 21. Eighth living foal. 78,000Y. Tattersalls October Book 2. Blandford Bloodstock. Closely related to the Group 2 Premio Ribot winner and Group 1 placed Dane Friendly (by Danehill) and half-brother to the Group 2 Grand Prix de Chantilly winner Allied Powers (by Invincible Spirit), the useful triple 10f winner Arabie, the fairly useful 12f

winner of four races Warsaw Pact, the Irish 13f and hurdles winner Impartial (all Polish Precedent). The dam won 3 races including the Group 3 12f Princess Royal Stakes, was second in the Prix Royal-Oak and is a half-sister to 5 winners. The second dam, Wise Speculation (by Mr Prospector), is an unplaced half-sister to 6 winners. *"A nice colt, he goes well, has a good action and looks like being out when the six furlong maidens come".*

584. EBBLE ★★★★★
b.f. *Oasis Dream – Sulk (Selkirk).*
April 13. Half-sister to the smart UAE listed 7f winner and Group 2 placed Ibn Battuta (by Seeking The Gold) and a minor winner abroad by Kingmambo. The dam, a smart winner of the Group 1 1m Prix Marcel Boussac and the Group 1 10f Nassau Stakes, is a half-sister to 4 winners including the Group 1 Hong Kong Cup and Group 2 Beresford Stakes winner Eagle Mountain and the smart 1m listed winner Wallace. The second dam, Masskana (by Darshaan), a minor 9f and 10f winner in France, is a half-sister to 3 winners including the US Grade 3 Arcadia Handicap winner Madjaristan and the Group 2 Gallinule Stakes winner Massyar. *"She's a neat, racey filly and she goes nicely. A six furlong 2-y-o".*

585. ELECTRICIAN ★★★
b.c. *Echo Of Light – Primrose Lane (Sunday Silence).*
April 25. The dam was placed over 10f and is a sister to the smart Group 3 8.5f Princess Elizabeth Stakes and US Grade 3 9f winner Sundrop. The second dam, Oenothera (by Night Shift), an Irish 10f and 11f and German listed winner, is closely related to the high-class Grade 1 Breeders Cup Turf and Grade 1 Oak Tree Invitational winner Northern Spur and a half-sister to the high-class Doncaster Cup, Jockey Club Gold Cup and Tote Ebor Handicap winner Kneller and the smart Jockey Club Gold Cup and Doncaster Cup winner Great Marquis. *"He did a swinging canter upsides this morning and he's a likeable colt. I think he's going to need seven furlongs".*

586. EX ORIENTE ★★★
b.c. *Azamour – Little Whisper (Be My Guest).*
April 2. Fourth foal. 55,000Y. Tattersalls October Book 1. Blandford Bloodstock. Half-brother to the fair 2010 1m placed 2-y-o If You Whisper (by Iffraaj). The dam, an Irish 2-y-o 6f and 7f winner and listed-placed, is a half-sister to 3 winners including the dual Group 3 winner Confuchias. The second dam, Schust Madame (by Second Set), won over 11f in Ireland and is a half-sister to 4 winners including the dual US Grade 2 winner Sweet Ludy and the Italian Group 3 winner Late Parade. *"A nice, big, powerful colt, he goes very well and he'll be out when the seven furlong maidens start".*

587. EXTOL ★★★ ♣
b.c. *Exceed And Excel – Dance Of Light (Sadler's Wells).*
February 22. First foal. 48,000Y. Tattersalls October Book 2. Cheveley Park Stud. The dam, a fairly useful 10f winner, was listed-placed and is a half-sister to 3 winners. The second dam, Flamelight (by Seattle Slew), was unplaced in one start in Ireland and is a half-sister to 8 winners including the smart 1m Magnolia Stakes and 10.4f Glasgow Stakes winner Dr Massini and the smart 2-y-o 1m winner and Group 3 Dante Stakes second Weigh Anchor. *"He goes OK and he's a mid-season 2-y-o".*

588. FALLEN FOR YOU ★★★★
b.f. *Dansili – Fallen Star (Brief Truce).*
April 7. Closely related to the quite useful 12f winner Star Of Gibraltar (by Rock Of Gibraltar) and half-sister to the smart 7f (at 2 yrs) and listed 1m winner Fallen Idol (by Pivotal) and the useful 2-y-o 1m winner and Group 2 12f Lancashire Oaks second Fallen In Love (by Galileo). The dam, a listed 7f winner and Group 3 placed twice, is a half-sister to 6 winners including the Group 1 7f Lockinge Stakes winner Fly To The Stars. The second dam, Rise And Fall (by Mill Reef), is an unplaced full or half-sister to 7 winners including the listed winners Special Leave, Spring To Action and Laughter. (Normandie Stud). *"A nice filly, she goes well, has a good action and is one for seven furlong maidens on the July course. A nice type".*

589. FANOOS ★★★★ ♣
b.f. *Dutch Art – Miss Otis (Danetime).*
April 8. Second foal. 120,000Y. Tattersalls

October Book 2. Shadwell Estate Co. The dam, a fair 2-y-o 5f winner, is a half-sister to 2 winners including the sprint winner and Group 3 Palace House Stakes second Hoh Hoh Hoh. The second dam, Nesting (by Thatching), is an unplaced full or half-sister to 3 winners and to the dams of the Group 2 winners Tariq and Wi Dud. (Hamdan Al-Maktoum). *"She's quick, she's working well and will be out fairly soon for the five furlong maidens. A speedy filly".*

590. FENCING ★★★
ch.c. Street Cry – Latice (Inchinor).
March 2. The dam won the Group 1 Prix de Diane and is a half-sister to the Group 1 French Derby and Group 1 Prix Jean Prat winner Lawman and the Group 3 Prix du Palais-Royal winner and Group 1 second Satri. The second dam, Laramie (by Gulch), placed fourth once over 7f at 3 yrs in Ireland, is a half-sister to 2 minor winners. *"A nice sort of colt that moves well, he'll come out around September time and he's very likeable".*

591. FLUCTUATE ★★★★ ♣
ch.c. Exchange Rate – Cut Short (Diesis).
April 11. Fourth foal. $160,000Y. Keeneland September. Blandford Bloodstock. Half-brother to the useful 2010 2-y-o listed 6f winner Brevity (by Street Cry) and to the fair 5f winner Special Quality (by Elusive Quality). The dam, a quite useful 1m winner, is a sister to the smart Daggers Drawn (winner of the Group 2 6f Richmond Stakes and the Group 2 7f Laurent Perrier Rose Champagne Stakes) and a half-sister to the very useful 2-y-o dual 6f winner Enemy Action. The second dam, Sun And Shade (by Ajdal), a useful 2-y-o 6f winner, is a half-sister to the very smart Group 2 Park Hill Stakes and Group 2 Prix de Royallieu winner Madame Dubois (herself dam of the Irish 2,000 Guineas winner Indian Haven and the Group 1 Gran Criterium winner Count Dubois). *"A good, strong, powerful horse that goes well".*

592. GALLIPOT ★★★
b.f. Galileo – Spinning Queen (Spinning World).
January 27. Second foal. The dam, winner of the Group 1 1m Sun Chariot Stakes and the Group 3 7f Brownstown Stakes and third in the Group 2 Cherry Hinton Stakes, is a half-sister to 4 winners including the useful 10f and 12f winner and 2-y-o 7f listed-placed Shannon Springs. The second dam, Our Queen Of Kings (by Arazi), is an unraced half-sister to 7 winners including the Grade 1 9f Hollywood Derby winner Labeeb, the Grade 2 Arlington Handicap winner Fanmore and the Group 2 9f Budweiser International Stakes winner Alrassaam. *"A nice filly, she's a good mover and will start over seven furlongs in mid-season".*

593. GATHERING ★★★
b.f. Street Cry – Seebe (Danzig).
March 13. Half-sister to the promising 2010 2-y-o 1m winner (on his only start) Seelo (by Dynaformer). The dam, winner of the 2-y-o Group 3 6f Princess Margaret Stakes and second in the French 1,000 Guineas, is a sister to the smart dual listed winner Rimrod and a half-sister to Selkirk. The second dam, Annie Edge (by Nebbiolo), a smart 7f and 1m winner, subsequently won in the USA. (Mr G Strawbridge). *"She goes alright. A nice sort of filly and a good mover, she'll start in the middle of the season".*

594. GINGERNUT ★★★
ch.c. Galileo – Foodbroker Fancy (Halling).
February 16. Half-brother to the smart 7f (at 2 yrs), listed 10f and subsequent US Grade 3 12f winner Dalvina (by Grand Lodge) and to the very useful 7f (at 2 yrs) and listed 10f winner Soft Centre (by Zafonic). The dam, a smart 6f (at 2 yrs) and dual listed 10f winner, is a half-sister to the useful listed 2-y-o 6f winner Femme Fatale. The second dam, Red Rita (by Kefaah), a fairly useful 4-y-o 6f winner, was second in the Group 3 6f Cherry Hinton Stakes and the Group 3 6f Princess Margaret Stakes at 2 yrs and is a half-sister to 3 minor winners. (Normandie Stud). *"A nice colt, he's well-balanced and moves well".*

595. GREAT HEAVENS ★★★
b.f. Galileo – Magnificent Style (Silver Hawk).
April 28. Sister to the promising 2010 dual 1m placed Nathaniel, closely related to the Group 1 Fillies' Mile winner Playful Act, to the Group 3 11.5f Lingfield Derby Trial winner Percussionist and the 10f winner and Group 3 10f Prix de Psyche second Changing Skies (all by Sadler's Wells) and half-sister to the Group 2 1m Sun

Chariot Stakes and Group 2 14.6f Park Hill Stakes winner Echoes In Eternity (by Spinning World), the US stakes winner and Grade 3 placed Stylelistick (by Storm Cat), the 1m (at 2 yrs) and listed 9f winner and Group 2 placed Petara Bay (by Peintre Celebre) and the quite useful 9f winner Distinctive Look (by Daneh ll). The dam won the Group 3 10.5f Musidora Stakes and is a half-sister to the Grade 1 10f Charles H Strub Stakes winner Siberian Summer. The second dam, Mia Karina (by Icecapade), a minor 3-y-o winner in France, is a half-sister to the dam of the US Grade 1 Pegasus Handicap winner Silver Ending. *"A nice type of filly with a good action and a good stride, she's like a lot of my 2-y-o's in that she'll start from July onwards. A nice filly".*

596. GREGORIAN ★★★★
b.c. Clodovil – Three Days In May
(Cadeaux Genereux).
April 16. Third living foal. 85,000Y. Tattersalls October Book 1. Blandford Bloodstock. Brother to the fairly useful 2-y-o 6f winner Kalam Daleel. The dam, a fair 3-y-o 6f winner, is a half-sister to 7 winners including the very useful 6f winner and Cheveley Park Stakes, Queen Mary Stakes and Cherry Hinton Stakes placed Crazee Mental – herself dam of the triple Group 2 winner Premio Loco. The second dam, Corn Futures (by Nomination), a fair 2-y-o 6f winner, is a half-sister to 7 winners. *"He goes fine, he did a half-speed upsides today and he's a likeable colt, probably one to start off at six furlongs".*

597. HEPWORTH ★★★
b f. Singspiel – Annalina (Cozzene).
February 22. Third foal. Half-sister to the quite useful 12f winner Sagamore (by Azamour) and to the Japanese Grade 3 placed Kyoei Basara (by Aussie Rules). The dam is an unraced half-sister to 4 winners including the US Grade 2 Long Island Handicap winner Olava. The second dam, Solaia (by Miswaki), won the listed Cheshire Oaks and was second in the Group 3 Lancashire Oaks and is a half-sister to 3 winners. *"A typical Singspiel in that she'll take some time, but she's got some quality and she moves well".*

598. HILL STREET ★★★
ch.c. Street Cry – Utrecht (Rock Of Gibraltar).
January 24. First foal. The dam won two races including the Group 3 9f Prix Chloe and is a half-sister to 2 winners. The second dam, Maria Isabella (by Kris), a fairly useful 8.2f winner, was listed placed over 8.5f and 10f and is a half-sister to the classic winners Bosra Sham, Hector Protector and Shanghai. *"A very likeable colt and a nice mover. He's a bit backward and has gone a little long at this stage, but he'll come along".*

599. INFINITUM ★★★
gr.f. Dalakhani – Time Honoured
(Sadler's Wells).
March 11. Fourth living foal. 135,000Y. Tattersalls October Book 1. Cheveley Park Stud. Closely related to the fair 10f to 12f winner Bona Fortuna (by Mark Of Esteem). The dam, a quite useful 2-y-o 1m winner, is a sister to the very useful Group 3 12f Princess Royal Stakes winner Time Allowed and a half-sister to Group 3 12f Jockey Club Stakes winner Zinaad and the dams of the Group winners Anton Chekhov, First Charter, Plea Bargain and Time Away. The second dam, Time Charter (by Saritamer), was an exceptionally talented filly and winner of the Oaks, the King George VI and Queen Elizabeth Diamond Stakes, the Champion Stakes, the Coronation Cup, the Prix Foy and the Sun Chariot Stakes. *"A nice type of filly, very much one for the mile maidens towards the back-end but she's got quality and moves well".*

600. MAIN FOCUS ★★★★
b.c. Mizzen Mast – Tsar's Pride (Sadler's Wells).
March 3. Brother to the quite useful Irish 7f winner Signal Fire and half-brother to the smart Italian Group 3 10f and 12f winner Exhibit One (by Silver Hawk) and to a minor 1m winner abroad by Distant View. The dam won over 12f in France and was listed-placed over 10f. The second dam, Bold Empress (by Diesis), a 2-y-o 6f winner, is a half-sister to the champion 2-y-o and 3-y-o Zafonic and to the smart Zamindar. (Khalid Abdulla). *"He goes well, he shows speed and he'll be out in a six furlong maiden, hopefully in mid-May".*

601. MARIA LETIZIA ★★★
b.f. Galileo – Napoleon's Sister (Alzao).
March 18. Half-sister to the useful 9f winner and Group 2 Lancashire Oaks third Queen Of Naples (by Singspiel), to the 2-y-o 6f winner Halle Bop (by Dubai Millennium), the 2-y-o 1m winners Louis Napoleon (by Indian Ridge) and Elise (by Fantastic Light) – all quite useful – and the fair 9f winner Maria Nunziata. The dam, a useful 10f listed winner, is a half-sister to 7 winners including the top-class colts Oath (winner of the Derby) and Pelder (winner of the Group 1 1m Gran Criterium, the Group 1 1m Premio Parioli and the Group 1 10.5f Prix Ganay). The second dam, Sheer Audacity (by Troy), placed twice in Italy, is closely related to the Ribblesdale Stakes winner and good broodmare Miss Petard. *"A nice filly, she moves well and will be aimed at maidens over seven furlongs or a mile".*

602. MICHELANGELO ★★★
b.c. Galileo – Intrigued (Darshaan).
February 23. Second foal. 550,000Y. Tattersalls October Book 1. Charlie Gordon-Watson. Brother to No Heretic, placed over 7f on his only start at 2 yrs in 2010. The dam, a very useful 2-y-o 8.5f winner, was listed-placed and fourth in the Group 1 Prix Marcel Boussac and is a sister to the 7.5f (at 2 yrs) and listed 10f winner and US Grade 2 second Approach (dam of the Group 2 Irish Derby Trial winner Midas Touch) and a half-sister to the French 2,000 Guineas and US Grade 1 winner Aussie Rules. The second dam, Last Second (by Alzao), winner of the 10f Nassau Stakes and the 10f Sun Chariot Stakes, is a half-sister to 7 winners including the Moyglare Stud Stakes third Alouette (herself dam of the Group 1 winners Albanova and Alborada), the Group 2 Doncaster Cup winner Alleluia (dam of the Group 1 Prix Royal-Oak winner Allegretto) and to the placed dam of the Group 1 winners Yesterday and Quarter Moon. *"He cost a lot of money, he's a strong, good-going colt and he'll start off in a seven furlong maiden".*

603. MONEY NEVER SLEEPS ★★★
b.c. Kyllachy – Shine Like A Star (Fantastic Light).
February 17. First foal. The dam is an unplaced half-sister to the smart 7f (at 2 yrs) and listed 1m winner Fallen Idol and to the useful 2-y-o 1m winner and Group 2 12f Lancashire Oaks second Fallen In Love. The second dam, Fallen Star (by Brief Truce), a listed 7f winner and Group 3 placed twice, is a half-sister to 6 winners including the Group 1 7f Lockinge Stakes winner Fly To The Stars. (Normandie Stud). *"A decent type of colt that could be out in a six furlong maiden in June".*

604. MOROCCO ★★★
b.c. Rock Of Gibraltar – Shanghai Lily (King's Best).
March 13. Third foal. 58,000Y. Tattersalls October Book 1. Kern/Lillingston. Half-brother to the fairly useful 2010 2-y-o 6f and 1m winner Cafe Elektric (by Pivotal). The dam, a very useful 6f and 7f 2-y-o winner, is a half-sister to the very useful dual 1m winner (including at 2 yrs) and listed-placed General Eliott and the useful 7f (at 2 yrs) and 1m winner Eden Rock. The second dam, Marlene-D (Selkirk), a minor Irish 3-y-o 9f winner, is a half-sister to 7 winners including the useful Queen's Vase winner Arden and the French listed winner Kerulen and to the placed dam of the US Grade 1 winner Kiri's Clown. *"A nice type of colt with a nice easy action, but Rock Of Gibraltar's aren't precocious".*

605. OPERA CLOAK ★★★
b.f. Cape Cross – Opera Comique (Singspiel).
March 19. Third foal. Half-sister to the Grade 1 10f Arlington Million, Group 2 10f Prix Eugene Adam and Group 3 10f Huxley Stakes winner Debussy (by Diesis) and to the quite useful Irish 1m winner Lightening Stricks (by King's Best). The dam, a 2-y-o Irish 9f winner and third in the Group 3 7f C L Weld Park Stakes, is a half-sister to numerous winners including the top-class King George VI and Queen Elizabeth Diamond Stakes, Great Voltigeur Stakes and Chester Vase winner Belmez. The second dam, Grace Note (by Top Ville), a fairly useful 10f Chepstow winner and second in the Group 3 12f Lingfield Oaks Trial, is a half-sister to the dams of the high-class 10.5f Prix de Diane winner Lypharita and the very useful winners Arousal and In Focus. *"She's grown and is now 'up behind' but she's a quality filly and a good mover".*

606. PALMETTE ★★★★
b.f. Oasis Dream – Arabesque (Zafonic).
April 24. Eighth foal. Sister to the Group 2 6f Gimcrack Stakes winner Showcasing and to the fairly useful triple 6f winner (including at 2 yrs) and listed-placed Bouvardia and half-sister to the very smart listed 6f winner Camacho (by Danehill). The dam, a useful listed 6f winner, is a sister to 2 winners including the useful 5f and 6f winner Threat and a half-sister to 5 winners including the Group 2 1m Prix de Sandringham winner Modern Look. The second dam, Prophecy (by Warning), was a very useful winner of the Group 1 6f Cheveley Park Stakes and was second in the Group 3 7f Nell Gwyn Stakes. (Khalid Abdulla). *"A strong filly, she's a lot like her brother Showcasing and is a speedy type that should be out around June time".*

607. PATEGONIA ★★★
b.c. Oasis Dream – Cozy Maria (Cozzene).
February 27. Fifth foal. 320,000Y. Tattersalls October Book 1. Not sold. Half-brother to the 2010 2-y-o Group 2 5f Flying Childers Stakes and Group 3 5f Molecomb Stakes winner Zebedee (by Invincible Spirit). The dam, a useful 10f winner, was listed-placed twice and is a half-sister to 6 winners in the USA. The second dam, Mariamme (by Verbatim), won twice at 3 yrs in the USA and is a half-sister to 7 winners including the Grade 1 Breeders Cup Turf winner Miss Alleged. *"He's alright, he's a nice sort and coming along fine. He probably won't be quite as early as his half-brother but he's doing everything right at this stage".*

608. PROOFREADER ★★★★
b.c. Authorized – Blixen (Gone West).
January 27. Fourth foal. Half-brother to the quite useful 1m and 9f winner Storybook (by Halling) and to the French 1m winner African Story (by Pivotal). The dam, a listed-placed Irish 2-y-o 6f winner, is a half-sister to 2 winners. The second dam, Danish (by Danehill), was a Grade 1 winner in Australia and the USA and is a half-sister to 9 winners including the multiple Grade 1 placed Hawkeye and the good chaser Sybillin. *"A grand sort of horse, he did a little half-speed today and I liked him. He's a nice sort and a seven furlong maiden will beckon when they come".*

609. RED HAND (USA) ★★★
b.br.f. Mr Greeley – Helena Molony (Sadler's Wells).
January 30. Second foal. 425,000Y. Tattersalls October Book 1. MHGoodbody. The dam, a fairly useful Irish 10f winner, was listed-placed and is a sister to the Derby, Irish Derby and Breeders Cup Turf winner High Chaparral and to the Group 2 Dante Stakes winner Black Bear Island and a half-sister to 4 winners. The second dam, Kasora (by Darshaan), is an unraced full or half-sister to 8 winners. *"A nice type of filly that goes well. She has a good action and is all about the second half of the season".*

610. SEE EMILY PLAY ★★★
b.f. Galileo – Tree Tops (Grand Lodge).
March 8. Fourth foal. Sister to the French 1m (at 2 yrs) and 15f winner and listed-placed Martial Law. The dam, a fair 1m to 10f placed maiden, is a half-sister to the US Grade 1 winner Tuscan Evening. The second dam, The Faraway Tree (by Suave Dancer), a very useful 6f and 14f winner, was second in the Group 3 Park Hill Stakes and is a half-sister to 12 winners including the Prix d'Ispahan winner Sasuru, the Challenge Stakes and Jersey Stakes winner Sally Rous and the dam of the French 1,000 Guineas winner Rose Gypsy. *"She should be racing in July over seven furlongs. She's a neat filly with a quick action".*

611. THE NILE ★★★★
ch.c. Three Valleys – Delta (Zafonic).
March 23. Fourth foal. Half-brother to the fairly useful 2010 2-y-o 7f winner and listed-placed Flood Plain (by Orpen), to the fairly useful 2-y-o 7f winner Hunting Tartan (by Oasis Dream) and the quite useful 2-y-o 1m winner Sampi (by Beat Hollow). The dam was a French 3-y-o dual 1m winner. The second dam, Fleet River (by Riverman), a fairly useful 2-y-o 7f winner, is a half-sister to the very smart Eltish, winner of the 7f Lanson Champagne Stakes and the 1m Royal Lodge Stakes and runner-up in the Grade 1 8.5f Breeders Cup Juvenile, to the useful 8.3f winner Yamuna, the useful 5f and 6f winner Forest Gazelle and the French listed 10f winner Souplesse. (Khalid Abdulla). *"An attractive colt, he's good-looking and a nice mover".*

612. THOUGHT WORTHY ★★★★
b.c. Dynaformer – Vignette (Diesis).
March 22. Brother to the Group 1 St Leger and dual Group 2 12f winner Lucarno and half-brother to the promising 2010 2-y-o 7f winner Morning Charm (by North Light). The dam, a US stakes winner, is a half-sister to numerous winners. The second dam, Be Exclusive (by Be My Guest), won 5 races in France and the USA including the Group 3 Prix Chloe and is a half-sister to 2 winners. (Mr G Strawbridge). *"A nice colt, he's well-balanced, good-looking and has a good shape. He's grand".*

613. TIGHTLACED (USA) ★★★
b.f. Tiznow – Polaire (by Polish Patriot).
April 28. Half-sister to Polygon (by Dynaformer), placed third over 1m on his only start at 2 yrs in 2010 and to the fairly useful 2-y-o 7f winner Cold Quest (by Seeking The Gold). The dam, winner of the Group 2 10f Pretty Polly Stakes and third in both the Group 1 Phoenix Stakes and the Grade 1 Beverly Hills Handicap, is a half-sister to numerous winners. The second dam, Headrest (by Habitat), is an unplaced sister to the Group 3 Princess Royal Stakes winner One Way Street (herself dam of the Group winners Grape Tree Road, Red Route and Windsor Castle) and to the dam of the May Hill Stakes and Hungerford Stakes winner Ever Genial. *"A filly with a good action and a good attitude, she's a nice type and one for the mid-season onwards".*

614. TOP BILLING ★★★★
br.c. Monsun – La Gandilie (Highest Honor).
February 14. Fifth living foal. €320,000Y. Arqana Deauville August. Juddmonte Farms. Half-brother to the useful 2-y-o 6f listed winner Fashion Rocks (by Rock Of Gibraltar), to the quite useful 9f to 12f winner Aktia (by Danehill Dancer) and the quite useful 10f winner Art Broker (by Pivotal). The dam, a dual 2-y-o winner in France including a listed event, was third in the Group 3 Prix Chloe and is a half-sister to 4 winners including the Italian listed winner Totostar and also to the placed dams of the French Group 3 winners Linda Regina and Star Of Akkar. The second dam, Prospector's Star (by Mr Prospector), a minor winner at 3 yrs in Ireland, is out of the Grade 1 Oak Leaf Stakes winner Astrious. *"A big, fine horse, he goes quite well, he's very likeable and he'll be one for the seven furlong maidens".*

615. TROVE (IRE) ★★★
b.c. Rock Of Gibraltar – Cache Creek (Marju).
April 14. Third foal. Goffs Orby. €100,000Y. Cheveley Park Stud. Half-brother to the fair Irish 2-y-o 6f winner Ballycahill (by Barathea). The dam, a listed 9.5f winner of 6 races in Ireland, was Group 3 placed twice. The second dam, Tongue River (by Riverman), is an unraced half-sister to 7 winners including the Group 3 winners Lady Roberta and Tursanah. *"A nice sort of horse but very much one for the mid-season, he's fine at this stage".*

616. TURN OF THE SUN ★★★
ch.c. Galileo – Something Mon (Maria's Mon).
February 10. Sixth foal. 90,000Y. Tattersalls October Book 2. Blandford Bloodstock. Half-brother to the useful 2-y-o 5f and Group 3 7f Oh So Sharp Stakes winner Raymi Coya (by Van Nistelrooy), the US 2-y-o and 4-y-o winner and stakes-placed Olympia Fields (by Alydeed), the minor Canadian winner Rag And Bone (by Street Cry) and the minor US 2-y-o and 4-y-o winner Cape Cod Gal (by Cape Town). The dam is an unraced half-sister to 5 winners including the champion German 2-y-o and Group 2 winner Somethingdifferent. The second dam, Try Something New (by Hail The Pirates), won the Grade 1 Spinster Stakes in the USA and is a half-sister to 5 winners. *"An attractive colt and a good mover, but very much one for the September mile maidens".*

617. UMAYYAD (IRE) ★★★
b.c. Montjeu – Janoubi (Dansili).
February 23. First foal. 150,000Y. Tattersalls October Book 1. Blandford Bloodstock. The dam is an unraced half-sister to 6 winners including the Group 2 Prix Eugene Adam and Group 3 Prix La Force winner Radevore. The second dam, Bloudan (by Damascus), is an unraced half-sister to the Irish 1,000 Guineas and Coronation Stakes winner Al Bahathri (dam of the 2,000 Guineas and Champion Stakes winner Haafhd), the US Grade 2 winner Geraldine's Store and the listed Cheshire Oaks winner Peplum. *"A nice type of horse, he's another I'll be aiming at the mile maidens".*

618. UTTERANCE ★★★★★
b.c. Dansili – Valentine Waltz (Be My Guest).
February 18. Half-brother to the useful 1m (at 2 yrs) and listed 11f winner Dyna Waltz (by Dynaformer). The dam won 3 races including the French 1,000 Guineas and the Group 3 Nell Gwyn Stakes and was third in the 1,000 Guineas and the Coronation Stakes. The second dam, Save Me The Waltz (by Kings Lake), won once in France over 6.5f at 2 yrs and is a half-sister to 10 winners including the Breeders Cup Mile, Kings Stand Stakes and William Hill Sprint Championship winner Last Tycoon, the Group 2 Premio Melton winner Astronef and the Group 3 Prix du Bois winner The Perfect Life. *"He goes well, he did a half-speed this morning and is a talented sort of colt. He'll be out when the seven furlong maidens start towards the end of June and he's a nice type".*

619. VERY FRENCH ★★★
b.c. Iffraaj – Very Nice (Daylami).
April 28. Third foal. 57,000Y. Tattersalls October Book 2. John Ferguson. Half-brother to the fair 2-y-o 7f winner Dream Number (by Fath) and to the fairly useful triple 7f winner Seek N' Destroy (by Exceed And Excel). The dam is an unraced half-sister to 2 winners including the Group 3 Prix de Cabourg second Atlantic High. The second dam, All Time Great (by Night Shift), a fairly useful 2-y-o 6f winner and fourth in the 7.3f Fred Darling Stakes, is closely related to the Dante Stakes and Craven Stakes winner Alnasr Alwasheek and a half-sister to 6 winners including the Juddmonte International Stakes winner One So Wonderful and the Rockfel Stakes winner Relatively Special. *"He did a little half-speed this morning and went OK. He looks like a ready made 2-y-o".*

620. VINNIE JONES ★★★★
ch.c. Piccolo – Fen Guest (Woodborough).
March 15. First foal. The dam, a moderate 6f winner, is a half-sister to numerous winners including the useful 7f (at 2 yrs) and listed 11f winner Ronaldsay and the quite useful 5.7f (at 2 yrs) to 10f winner Crackle (herself dam of the US Grade 3 winner Pickle). The second dam, Crackling (by Electric), a modest 9f and 12f winner, is a half-sister to 4 winners including the Group 1 7f Moyglare Stud Stakes winner Bianca Nera and the Moyglare Stud Stakes and Fillies Mile placed Hotelgenie Dot Com. *"He goes fine and might start off in April. Hopefully the jockey will get him to the start because he's quite good at doing U-turns. But he's a tough little beggar and he'll win some races".*

621. WIDYAAN (IRE) ★★★ ♠
b.c. Lawman – Lady Livius (Titus Livius).
February 14. First foal. 300,000Y. Tattersalls October Book 1. Shadwell Estate Co. The dam, a fairly useful 2-y-o 5f Weatherbys Superprint winner of 3 races, is a half-sister to 5 winners including the Group 2 6f Mill Reef Stakes winner and Group 1 placed Galeota and the listed 13f winner Loulwa. The second dam, Refined (by Statoblest), a fairly useful dual 5f winner, is a half-sister to 6 winners including the very smart Group 3 7f Criterion Stakes winner Pipe Major. *"He's grown a lot and I feel you won't see him until the seven furlong maidens in August".*

622. WINDSOR COUNTY ★★★
br.f. Elusive Quality – Ascutney (Lord At War).
February 11. Sister to the Grade 1 10f Breeders Cup Classic and Group 1 1m Queen Elizabeth II Stakes winner Raven's Pass and half-sister to the US stakes winner and Grade 2 placed Gigawatt (by Wild Again) and to the minor US 4-y-o winner New Age (by Touch Gold). The dam won the US Grade 3 Miesque Stakes and is a sister to the US stakes winner Words Of War (herself dam of the Grade 1 Del Mar Oaks winner No Matter What and the US Grade 2 winner E Dubai) and a half-sister to 8 winners. The second dam, Right Word (by Verbatim), is a placed sister to the stakes winner Spruce Song. *"A sister to Raven's Pass, she's a nice type of filly but won't be quite as precocious as her brother".*

623. UNNAMED ★★★
b.c. Rock Of Gibraltar – Evita (Selkirk).
March 21. First foal. 60,000Y. Tattersalls October Book 1. Not sold. The dam, a modest 9f and 12f placed maiden, is a half-sister to 9 winners including the triple Group 1 winner Da Re Mi, the Hong Kong Group 1 winner Diaghilev, the Group 2 12.5f Prix Maurice de Nieuil winner Darazari and the Derby third

Rewilding. The second dam, Darara (by Top Ville), won the Group 1 12f Prix Vermeille and is a half-sister to 11 winners including the Prix du Jockey Club winner and high-class sire Darshaan. *"He's alright, he's a big, powerful colt that's done very well. Expect to see him about September time".*

624. UNNAMED ★★★★
b.c. Galileo – Insinuate (Mr Prospector).
March 26. Closely related to the listed 10f winner Take The Hint (by Montjeu), to the quite useful 8.7f winner Imply (by Beat Hollow) and the fair 9.5f winner Indication (by Sadler's Wells) and half-brother to the Group 3 7f Supreme Stakes winner Stronghold (by Danehill). The dam, a useful listed 1m winner, is a half-sister to numerous winners including the useful 6f and 7f winner and listed-placed Imroz. The second dam, All At Sea (by Riverman), was a high-class winner of 5 races from 1m to 10.4f including the Group 1 Prix du Moulin and was second in the Oaks, the Juddmonte International and the Nassau Stakes. (Khalid Abdulla). *"A nice type of colt, he's a good mover, good-looking and he's from a nice family. I like him and he'll debut at seven furlongs".*

625. UNNAMED ★★★
gr.f. Dansili – Light Of Morn (Daylami).
March 17. Third foal. Half-sister to Splendid Light (by Selkirk), placed fourth over 1m on his only start at 2 yrs in 2010. The dam, a useful 11.5f winner, is a half-sister to the smart 12f and listed 14f winner Moments Of Joy. The second dam, My Emma (by Marju), a smart winner of the Group 1 12f Prix Vermeille, is a half-sister to 5 winners including the Group 1 St Leger and Group 1 Ascot Gold Cup winner Classic Cliché. *"She's obviously a staying filly, but she's a nice type and I like her".*

626. UNNAMED ★★
b.f. Shamardal – Mango Mischief (Desert King).
February 3. First foal. 78,000Y. Tattersalls October Book 2. John Ferguson. The dam, a Group 3 10f Daffodil Stakes winner of 5 races, is a half-sister to 4 winners including the useful 2-y-o 6f and 7f and subsequent US Grade 3 winner Eurolink Raindance and the smart 7f (at 2 yrs) and 10f winner Bonecrusher. The second dam, Eurolink Mischief (by Be My Chief), a quite useful 3-y-o 12f winner, is a half-sister to 3 winners including the useful middle-distance colt and listed winner Duke Of Eurolink. *"She goes fine – a regular type of filly".*

627. UNNAMED ★★★
b.c. Invincible Spirit – Dubai Sunrise (Seeking The Gold).
April 27. The dam is an unraced sister to Dubai Millennium, winner of the Dubai World Cup, the Prix Jacques le Marois, the Prince Of Wales's Stakes and the Queen Elizabeth II Stakes (all Group 1 events) and a half-sister to the Group 2 10.5f Prix Greffulhe second Denver County. The second dam, Colorado Dancer (by Shareef Dancer), a very smart winner of the Group 2 13.5f Prix de Pomone and the Group 3 12f Prix de Minerve and Group 1 placed, is closely related to the Grade 1 Gamely Handicap winner Northern Aspen, to the Group 1 July Cup winner Hamas and the Group 1 Grand Prix de Paris winner Fort Wood and a half-sister to the Prix d'Astarte winner Elle Seule (herself dam of the Irish 1,000 Guineas winner Mehthaaf) and the champion US 2-y-o colt Timber Country. *"A small colt, but he goes OK".*

628. UNNAMED ★★★
b.f. Shamardal – Woodbeck (Terimon).
March 31. Ninth foal. Doncaster Premier. £62,000Y. Blandford Bloodstock. Half-sister to the very smart 7f (at 2 yrs), Group 2 Yorkshire Cup and Group 3 11.8f Lingfield Derby Trial winner Franklins Gardens (by Halling), to the very smart Group 3 7f and Group 3 1m winner Polar Ben (by Polar Falcon), the fairly useful 10f winner and listed placed Wood Chorus (by Singspiel) and the modest 7f winner Wood Fairy (by Haafhd). The dam, a fairly useful 3-y-o dual 7f winner, is a half-sister to 8 winners including the fairly useful 2-y-o winners Optimistic and Carburton. The second dam, Arminda (by Blakeney), is an unraced half-sister to the Group 1 Prix de Diane winner Madam Gay. *"She goes fine and she's a nice, strong filly for mid-season".*

MICHAEL GRASSICK
629. LOTUS ROOTS ★★★
b.f. Whipper – Star Of Akkar (Distant Relative).
February 7. Half-sister to the French 10f

winner Parcimonie (by Whipper). The dam, a winner over 1m (at 2 yrs) and three Group 3 events in France over 9f and 10f, was second in the Group 1 Prix de Diane and is a half-sister to 3 minor winners. The second dam, Donna Star (by Stately Don), was placed three times at 2 yrs and is a half-sister to 9 winners. (Marquesa de Moratella). *"She's cantering away and she's not over-big but we're happy with her. One for the second half of the season, she's nice and progressing well at the moment".*

630. UNNAMED ★★
b.f. Dylan Thomas – Bounce (Trempolino).
March 1. Third foal. 28,000Y. Tattersalls October Book 1. Not sold. Half-sister to the French 2011 dual 3-y-o winner Berniere (by Montjeu). The dam won 2 minor races at 3 yrs in France and is a half-sister to the French listed winner and Group 1 Criterium de Saint-Cloud second Simplex. The second dam, Russyskia (by Green Dancer), won once at 3 yrs in France and is a half-sister to 6 winners including the very smart Group 1 15.5f Prix Royal-Oak and Group 2 15f Prix Kergorlay winner Top Sunrise and the useful stayer Old Rouvel. (Mrs M J Grassick). *"A nice, big, scopey filly. You'd be looking at seven furlongs in August/September with her. We like her and she's a good actioned filly with a good attitude".*

631. UNNAMED ★★★
b.f. Dylan Thomas – Jinskys Gift (Cadeaux Genereux).
April 6. Third foal. Goffs Orby. €26,000Y. Dermot Farrington. The dam is an unraced half-sister to 8 winners including the triple listed 7f winner Modeeroch, the 2-y-o 8 5f winner and Group 1 1m Gran Criterium third Chinese Whisper and the useful Irish 2-y-o 6f winner and Group 1 6f Cheveley Park Stakes third Danaskaya. The second dam, Majinskaya (by Marignan), winner of the listed 12f Prix des Tuileries, is a half-sister to 6 winners including the dam of the Group 1 5f Prix de l'Abbaye winner Kistena. (Fenpark Syndicate). *"A similar type, though not as big as our other Dylan Thomas filly, so she should be a bit earlier. She's only cantering at the moment, we're pleased with her and she'll want seven furlongs from around July/August time".*

632. UNNAMED ★★★★
b.f. Jeremy – Misaayef (Swain).
March 15. Fourth foal. €2,600Y. Goffs Open. M C Grassick. Half-sister to the useful 2010 2-y-o dual 5f winner and listed-placed Cape To Rio (by Captain Ric) and to the quite useful 6f and 7f winner Solar Spirit (by Invincible Spirit). The dam, a quite useful 10.5f winner, is a half-sister to 3 winners including the dam of the US Grade 1 winner Alwajeeha. The second dam, Zakiyya (by Dayjur), a minor US 3-y-o winner, is a half-sister to 11 winners including the dam of the US Grade 1 winner Scorpion. *"We like her and we couldn't believe we bought her as cheaply as we did. A strong, athletic type of filly, we'll be looking at running her in May or June over five or six furlongs. People didn't seem to want these Jeremy's at the Sales but the tide has turned and seemingly a good number of the breeders are going back to him".* TRAINERS' BARGAIN BUY

633. UNNAMED ★★★
ch.f. Indian Haven – Gentle Wind (Gentleman).
April 26. Fourth foal. €1,500Y. Goffs Open. M C Grassick. Closely related to the very useful UAE 5f and 6f winner Happy Dubai (by Indian Ridge). The dam, a minor US 4-y-o winner, is a half-sister to 10 winners including the US Grade 2 winner and Grade 1 placed Talloires. The second dam, Logiciel (by Known Fact), a listed-placed winner of 4 races at 3 yrs in France, is a half-sister to 7 winners including three French listed winners. *"It's amazing we got her so cheaply because there's nothing wrong with her. A nice filly, she's progressing well and hopefully she'll be out in May or June over five or six furlongs. A strong filly with a nice temperament, we're happy with her".*

RAE GUEST
634. ALICE ROSE (IRE) ★★
ch.f. Manduro – Bold Assumption (Observatory).
March 9. Third foal. 11,000Y. Tattersalls October Book 2. Rae Guest. The dam is an unraced half-sister to 4 winners and to the unraced dam of the German Group 2 winner Daring Love. The second dam, Bold Empress (by Diesis), a fairly useful 2-y-o 6f winner, is a half-sister to the champion 2-y-o and 3-y-o and sire Zafonic, and to the smart Group 3

6f Prix de Cabourg winner and sire Zamindar. (Mrs J E Lury & Mr O T Lury). *"She's a very nice, correct filly and we thought she'd take a long time being by Manduro, but she hasn't grown a lot so we're thinking she'll be running later on this year. A neat filly, well-made and everything's in the right place. This year I think we have a nice bunch of horses and we've also got more than we usually have. As a bunch they're probably the best set of 2-y-o's I've ever had".*

635. BE MY ROCK ★★★
b.f. *Rock Of Gibraltar – Supa Sal (King's Best).*
March 28. First foal. 10,000Y. Tattersalls December. Rae Guest. The dam, a fair dual 7f winner (including at 2 yrs), is a half-sister to 5 winners including the useful dual 1m winner and Group 3 third Supaseus. The second dam, Supamova (by Seattle Slew), a quite useful 8.5f winner at 3 yrs, is a sister to the very smart Group 1 7f Prix de la Foret winner Septieme Ciel and a half-sister to 7 winners including the Group 1 1m Prix Marcel Boussac winner Macoumba. (D J Willis). *"She had an injury so couldn't go to Book 1 of Tattersalls Sales. I think we got her at a very reasonable price because she's grown into a beautiful filly and we're very pleased with her. We won't be rushing her but she shows a lot of natural speed and has a lovely temperament. Hopefully she'll be out in late summer over six furlongs".*

636. GUILETTA (IRE) ★★
gr.f. *Dalakhani – Guilia (Galileo).*
February 3. First foal. The dam, a useful 2-y-o 7f winner, was listed-placed over 10f and 13f and is a half-sister to 2 winners. The second dam, Lesgor (by Irish River), won over 10f in France, was third in the Group 3 10f Prix de Psyche and is a half-sister to 3 winners. (The Hornets). *"A very nice filly but she's going to be a late developing type. She should run at the back-end of the season but we're very pleased with her. She's light-framed just like her mother and looks like a staying type".*

637. HEADLINE NEWS (IRE) ★★★★
ch.f. *Peintre Celebre – Donnelly's Hollow (Docksider).*
February 2. Second foal. 12,000Y. Tattersalls October Book 1. Rae Guest. Half-sister to the 2010 1m placed 2-y-o Elfine (by Invincible Spirit). The dam, a modest 1m placed Irish maiden, is a half-sister to 5 winners including the Group 1 12f Italian Derby winner and King George VI and Queen Elizabeth Stakes second White Muzzle and the Group 2 German St Leger winner Fair Question and the listed 10f winner Elfaslah (dam of the Dubai World Cup winner Almutawakel). The second dam, Fair of the Furze (by Ela-Mana-Mou), won the Group 2 10f Tattersalls Rogers Gold Cup and is a half-sister to the listed winners Majestic Role, Norman Style and Proconsular. (Chestnuts). *"Although she's a 3-y-o type she's a very nice filly and it's a better family than it looks on the Sales page. She'll start off in late summer and is one of the nicest we have. She's not a great big backward Peintre Celebre, she goes along nicely and is an athletic type".*

638. MACCHIARA ★★★
ch.f. *Medicean – Castaway Queen (Selkirk).*
January 19. Third living foal. 32,000Y. Tattersalls October Book 1. Rae Guest. Sister to the modest 9f (including at 2 yrs) and 1m winner of 5 races Tuscan King and half-sister to a winner in Greece by Singspiel. The dam was placed 13 times from 6f (at 2 yrs) to 10f and is a half-sister to 8 winners including the useful 6f to 9.4f winner and subsequent US Grade 3 All American Handicap winner Mister Fire Eyes and the Hong Kong stakes winner Bumper Storm. The second dam, Surfing (by Grundy), a fair 7f placed maiden, is a sister to the Group 3 Prix d'Arenburg winner Glancing and a half-sister to the Group 1 Middle Park Stakes winner Bassenthwaite. (David Fish). *"A very nice filly, not too big but well-made, she should be running in August if the plan comes together".*

639. MY COLLEEN (USA) ★★★★
ch.f. *Discreet Cat – Navasha (Woodman).*
April 29. Fifth foal. 55,000Y. Tattersalls October Book 2. Not sold. Half-sister to the US stakes-placed winner Silver Navasha (by Silver Hawk) and to the fairly useful 5f (including at 2 yrs) and 6f winner of 8 races Piscean (by Stravinsky). The dam is an unraced half-sister to 2 minor winners. The second dam, Wendy Vaala (by Dayjur), is an unraced half-sister to the Group 1 winners Alydaress,

Desirable (dam of the dual Group 1 winner Shadayid) and Park Appeal (dam of the high-class sire Cape Cross). (E P Duggan). *"She's a beautiful filly and the best looking of all my 2-y-o's. She's by a first season sire so we don't know what sort of trip she'll want, but I think a mile would be the furthest she'd go. She's done everything right so far and she's a speedier type than most of the others, but she still won't be rushed. Very well-made, she has nice colouring and everything is in the right place. When you see her walk and trot she has a lovely action".*

640. POISSON D'OR ★★
b.f. Cape Cross – Lille Hammer (Sadler's Wells).
February 18. Twelfth foal. 20,000Y. Tattersalls October Book 1. Rae Guest. Half-sister to 7 winners including the French listed 12f winner Olimpic Girl (by Darshaan) and the French listed-placed (by Tiger Hill) and L'Olympique (by Machiavellian). The dam won the listed 12f Harvest Stakes, was third in the Group 2 Prix de Royallieu and second in the Group 2 Park Hill Stakes and is a half-sister to 8 winners including the German Group 2 winner Soto-Grande. The second dam, Smeralda (by Nebos), won 3 races in Germany and is a half-sister to the Group 2 German Oaks winner Slenderella and to the unraced dam of the German Group 1 winner Solon. (The Family Fish). *"A bit small when we bought her but she's grown and done well. Cape Cross wasn't the flavour of the month at the Sales and yet he's knocking out winners left, right and centre. She was cheap, she's from a middle-distance family and we'll take our time with her. She's not a great big filly, just a perfect size, so she'll probably start off in late summer all being well".*

641. SHAMAKAT ★★★
ch.f. Shamardal – Katina (Danzig).
February 26. Sixth foal. 18,000Y. Tattersalls October Book 2. Rae Guest. Half-sister to the quite useful 2010 Irish 7f and 1m placed 2-y-o Hold The Aces and to the Japanese 2-y-o winner Zetto Spiel (both by Singspiel). The dam, a modest 3-y-o 6f winner, is a half-sister to 2 winners. The second dam, Alisidora (by Nashwan), a useful Irish 12f winner and listed-placed, is a full or half-sister to 5 winners. (Chestnuts). *"A filly we hope will make a* 2-y-o, she's well put-together and looks speedy. Doing everything right at the moment and she has a happy outlook on life. A 2-y-o for the mid-summer onwards".

642. SPINNACLE ★★
ch.f. Pivotal – Anthos (Big Shuffle).
March 25. Fourth foal. 20,000Y. Tattersalls October Book 2. Rae Guest. Half-sister to the modest 2010 6f and 7f placed 2-y-o Hortensis (by Iceman). The dam, a quite useful 2-y-o 6f winner, is a half-sister to 3 winners. The second dam, Anemone (by Motley), won 5 races in Germany from 2-5 yrs. *"A typical Pivotal, she looks nice and goes well. She's grown a lot so she won't be early but she was cheap for a Pivotal and she's grown into a nice horse since the Sales. We thought she'd be earlyish but because of her growth spurt we're just taking our time with her for now".*

643. UNNAMED ★★★★
b.f. Kyllachy – Black Belt Shopper (Desert Prince).
March 18. 3,000Y. Tattersalls October Book 2. Not sold. Half-sister to the quite useful 2010 2-y-o 7f winner Cheque Book (by Araafa) and to the modest dual 6f winner Exit Strategy (by Cadeaux Genereux). The dam, a quite useful 2-y-o 6f winner, was listed-placed and is a half-sister to the quite useful 2-y-o 1m winner Lucayan Beauty. The second dam, Koumiss (by Unfuwain), a French maiden, stayed 10f and is a half-sister to 8 winners including the useful 7f (at 2 yrs) and 11.5f winner Mystery Play, the Queen's Vase winner Arden, the French listed winner Kerulen and the dam of the US Grade 1 winner Kiri's Clown. (The Hightailers). *"She's nice and looks like making a 2-y-o. Very athletic, with a lot of Go about her, I'm pleased with her. She came in late but she's done well and picked up. A very nice filly, she's a good shape and a good size".*

644. UNNAMED ★★★
b.f. Holy Roman Emperor – Dreams Come True (Zafonic).
February 10. Second foal. 8,000Y. Tattersalls December. Rae Guest. Half-sister to My Ruby (by Oasis Dream), unplaced in one start at 2 yrs in 2010. The dam won 4 races from 2 to 5 yrs in France and the USA including a stakes event

and was Grade 3 placed and is a half-sister to 2 winners. The second dam, Moonlight Dreams (by Caerleon), won 3 minor races at 3 and 4 yrs in France and is a half-sister to 10 winners including the listed winner Party Doll (herself dam of the dual Group 2 winner and sire Titus Livius). (D J Willis). *"Like most by this sire she's small and hopefully she'll be one of our 2-y-o types. She goes very well, she's perfectly formed, moves nicely and has a good attitude. There's plenty of Go about her and when she gets her act together she'll be one of our first to run".*

645. UNNAMED ★★★★
ch.f. Exceed And Excel – Millyant (Primo Dominie).
March 12. Half-sister to the useful 6f winner and listed 6f placed Millybaa (by Anabaa), to the fairly useful 2-y-o 5f winner Juantorena (by Miswaki), the quite useful 5f winner of 4 races Millinsky (by Stravinsky) and the quite useful 6f winner Mirza (by Oasis Dream). The dam, winner of the Group 2 5f Prix du Gros-Chene, is a half-sister to the Group 2 5f Flying Childers winner and very useful sire Prince Sabo and to the Irish listed winner Bold Jessie (herself dam of the Gimcrack Stakes winner Abou Zouz). The second dam, Jubilee Song (by Song), won once at 3 yrs and is a sister to the dual winner and Nell Gwyn Stakes second Shark Song and to the winner of 10 races and listed-placed Band On The Run. (Mr C Mills). *"We trained the dam and this is her last foal. I think it's the nicest one she's had and she's had some decent ones. She came in late but I'm very pleased with her, she's settled into the job well and is a little professional. We have high hopes for her, she'll be a five furlong filly and if she gets six I'd be pleased".*

646. UNNAMED ★★★★
b.f. Oasis Dream – Mina (Selkirk).
February 15. Second foal. 40,000Y. Tattersalls October Book 1. Not sold. The dam, a modest 6f winner at 4 yrs, is a half-sister to 5 winners including the Group 3 5f Ballyogan Stakes winner Miss Anabaa. The second dam, Midnight Shift (by Night Shift), a fair dual 6f winner at 3 yrs, is a half-sister to 8 winners including the high-class Group 1 6f July Cup winner Owington. (Mr C Mills). *"The dam's half-sister Miss Anabaa won a Group 3 for us and this is a nice Oasis Dream filly. Mina was a nice filly but she was placed a lot more than she won. The Oasis Dream – Selkirk cross is very good and this is a very nice filly for the late summer. Some Oasis Dreams can be small but she's not, she's just about the perfect size and she has a lot of Go about her so I think she'll be alright".*

647. UNNAMED ★★★
b.f. Green Desert – Miss Anabaa (Anabaa).
March 19. Fifth foal. 28,000foal. Tattersalls December. Catridge Farm. The dam, a winner of 3 races including the Group 3 5f Ballyogan Stakes, is a half-sister to 5 winners including Out After Dark, a smart 5f and 6f winner of 6 races, including the Portland Handicap. The second dam, Midnight Shift (by Night Shift), a fair dual 6f winner at 3 yrs, is a half-sister to 8 winners including the high-class Group 1 6f July Cup winner Owington. (Mr C Mills). *"Green Desert's can be small but she's not. A nice filly, not quite as good at the moment as the 2-y-o's out of Millyant and Mina we discussed, but you never know she may end up better next year. She's coming along nicely and she's the nicest one out of the dam that we've had".*

648. UNNAMED ★★★
b.f. Whipper – Savage (Polish Patriot).
March 13. 4,000Y. Tattersalls December. Rae Guest. Half-sister to the smart triple 7f winner (at 2 yrs) and Irish 1,000 Guineas third Soul City (by Elusive City), to the French listed 1m winner Sentinelese (by Cape Cross), the quite useful 2-y-o 5f winner Chinese Temple (by Namid), the fair 11f and 12f winner Fascinating (by Desert King), the fair Irish 9f winner Yes Missus (by Alamshar) and the modest 7f and 1m winner Grande Terre (by Grand Lodge). The dam won 2 races at 2 and 3 yrs in Germany, was Group 2 placed over 6f at 2 yrs and is a half-sister to 2 other winners abroad. The second dam, Special Meeting (by Persian Bold), is an unraced half-sister to 4 minor winners. *"A very nice filly, she was bought for 26,000 as a foal and we got her for just 4. So she's looking like a bargain. A nice, big filly, she shows speed, has a good attitude and I think she'll be one of our 2-y-o types this year".* TRAINERS' BARGAIN BUY

WILLIAM HAGGAS

649. AFAAL (USA) ★★★
b.c. Hard Spun – Alattrah (Shadeed).
April 10. Half-brother to the fair 2-y-o 7f winner Bahraj (by Key Of Luck) and to a number of disappointing horses. The dam is an unraced sister to the high-class and genuine filly Shadayid, winner of the 1,000 Guineas and the Prix Marcel Boussac and placed in the Coronation Stakes, the Sussex Stakes and the Queen Elizabeth II Stakes and a half-sister to numerous winners including the smart 6f and 7f winner Fath and the very useful 1994 3-y-o listed 7f winner and Jersey Stakes third Dumaani. The second dam, Desirable (by Lord Gayle), won the Group 1 6f Cheveley Park Stakes and the 6f Princess Margaret Stakes, was third in the 1,000 Guineas and is a half-sister to the Irish Oaks winner Alydaress, the Cheveley Park winner Park Appeal and the very useful middle-distance colt Nashamaa. (Hamdan Al Maktoum). *"Only just arrived here from Dubai, so I don't know anything about him. They liked him over there though".*

650. AL JABREIAH ★★★
b.f. Bertolini – Nihal (Singspiel).
April 17. Second foal. The dam, a quite useful dual 7f (at 2 yrs) and 12f winner, is a half-sister to numerous winners including the Irish 9f to 14f winner and listed-placed Catherina and the fairly useful 7f (at 2 yrs) to 10f winner Secretary General. The second dam, Katie McLain (by Java Gold), an Irish 3-y-o 7f and 10f winner, is a half-sister to 7 winners including the Group 3 Desmond Stakes and Group 3 7f C L Weld Park Stakes winner Asema. (Mohammed Jaber). *"She goes alright, she's got a bit of pedigree and the sire should speed her up a bit. A very nice mover, she has a long stride and although I wouldn't know how good she is yet she has a nice temperament and a nice action. She doesn't look like a sharp 2-y-o but she doesn't look slow either".*

651. ANISEED (IRE) ★★★
gr.f. Dalakhani – Anna Karenina (Atticus).
March 16. Fifth foal. 60,000Y. Tattersalls October Book 1. Norris/Huntingdon. Half-brother to the 2010 1m fourth placed 2-y-o Muqtarrib (by Medicean), to the useful Irish 7f (at 2 yrs) and listed 7.5f winner Anna's Rock (by Rock Of Gibraltar) and the useful 1m winner and listed-placed Sugar Mint (by High Chaparral). The dam is an unraced half-sister to the Group 3 Prix de Psyche winner and French 1,000 Guineas and French Oaks placed Agathe (herself dam of the Grade/Group 1 winners Artiste Royale and Aquarelliste), to the Breeders Cup Classic winner Arcangues and the dams of the Group/Grade 1 winners Cape Verdi and Angara. The second dam, Albertine (by Irish River), a smart winner of two races at up to 10f, was placed in the Group 2 Prix de l'Opera and is a half-sister to 8 winners including the high-class middle-distance stayer Ashmore and the smart middle-distance filly Acoma. (M J & L A Taylor). *"She's obviously not going to be that early, being by Dalakhani, but she's fine, a good mover, knows what to do and she's done well. I don't know yet how far she'll go but I think she'll be a 2-y-o in the second half of the season over seven furlongs. She's not very big but she's done well since the Sales and she's fine".*

652. ASHBINA ★★★
b.f. Royal Applause – Crystal Power (Pleasant Colony).
January 31. Fourth foal. 72,000Y. Tattersalls October Book 2. Shadwell Estate Co. Half-sister to the useful 2-y-o 7f winner and Group 3 Sweet Solera second Misdaqeya (by Red Ransom) and to a winner in Belgium by Averti. The dam won once at 3 yrs in the USA and is a half-sister to 5 winners including the US Grade 1 Flower Bowl Invitational Handicap winner Chelsey Flower (herself dam of the French Group 3 winner Kentucky Dynamite). The second dam, Chelsey Dancer (by Affirmed), is an unplaced half-sister to 10 winners. (Sheikh Ahmed Al Maktoum). *"She's a scopey filly, but I'm not sure if that's how a Royal Applause should be. She moves well, she's quite lazy and the jury's out at the moment".*

653. ASHKAN ★★★
b.c. Nayef – South Club Hill (Danehill).
February 19. Third foal. 30,000Y. Tattersalls October Book 2. Rabbah Bloodstock. The dam is an unraced half-sister to 6 minor winners. The second dam, Chantereine (by Trempolino), a minor winner at 3 yrs in France, is a half-sister to 3 winners including

the Cheveley Park Stakes second Line Of Thunder (herself dam of the Kentucky Derby and Belmont Stakes winner Thunder Gulch). (Mohammed Jaber). *"This is quite a good cross, Nayef on Danehill, he's nice and although the dam was tiny it seems that sending her to Nayef has worked because this horse is quite strong and a good mover".*

654. CAPE FERRAT (IRE) ★★★
b.f. Nayef – Anyaas (Green Desert).
January 29. Fourth foal. Sister to the fair 2010 dual 7f placed 2-y-o Above All and half-sister to the fair 2-y-o 7f winner Pearl Dealer (by Marju) and the moderate Irish 7f winner Non Tiscordadime (by Haafhd). The dam was a 1m winner at 3 yrs in the UAE. The second dam, Anwaar (by Machiavellian), was an Irish 2-y-o 1m winner. (Hadi Al Tajir). *"She hasn't arrived here yet but they like her. Her year-older sister is enormous but she's a lot smaller and neater. Hopefully she'll be a seven furlong 2-y-o in the second half of the season".*

655. CELLIST ★★★★
b.c. Halling – Ae Kae Ae (King Of Kings).
March 30. Third foal. 42,000Y. Tattersalls October Book 2. John Warren. Half-brother to the modest 2010 6f placed 2-y-o Barkston Ash (by Kyllachy). The dam is an unraced half-sister to 7 winners including the Group 3 placed Charlock. The second dam, Charmante (by Alydar), won over 7f at 2 yrs in Ireland and a minor 1m stakes event in the USA and is a half-sister to the top-class miler Zilzal. (Royal Ascot Racing Club). *"A nice-moving colt for July onwards, he should be a nice 2-y-o, he's a good mover and he'll get better next year. I like him".*

656. CLASSIC FALCON ★★★
ch.f. Dubawi – Livius Lady (Titus Livius).
April 30. Fifth foal. 180,000Y. Tattersalls October Book 2. Shadwell Estate Co. Half-sister to the smart 2010 2-y-o Group 3 6f Round Tower Stakes winner Dingle View and to the quite useful 5f and 6f winner of 8 races (including at 2 yrs) and listed-placed Vhujon (both by Mujadil). The dam is an unraced half-sister to 2 minor winners. The second dam, Gitchee Gumee Rose (by Paris House), ran twice unplaced and is a half-sister to 5 winners.

(Sheikh Hamdan bin Maktoum). *"A well-bred filly, she cost very little as a foal but then 180,000 as a yearling. She'll take a bit of time as I think most Dubawi's do and she's almost a May foal, but she'll be a second half of the season 2-y-o. A filly with a nice temperament and a nice attitude, so I think she'll be fine".*

657. COUNTESS FERRAMA ★★
b.f. Authorized – Madame Dubois (Legend Of France).
March 18. Fourteenth foal. 90,000Y. Tattersalls October Book 1. W Haggas. Half-sister to the Irish 2,000 Guineas winner Indian Haven (by Indian Ridge), to the smart Group 1 Gran Criterium winner Count Dubois (by Zafonic), the useful dual 12f winner Massif Centrale (by Selkirk), the useful dual 12f winner Place de l'Opera (by Sadler's Wells and herself the dam of 3 stakes winners), the fairly useful 10f winner Paragon Of Virtue (by Cadeaux Genereux), the fairly useful 12f winner Galette (by Caerleon), the quite useful 12f winner Richelieu (by Kris) and the fair 17f winner Saggiatore (by Galileo). The dam, a very smart filly, won 5 races from 9f to 14.6f including the Group 2 Park Hill Stakes and the Group 2 Prix de Royallieu and is a half-sister to 4 winners including the dam of the very smart 2-y-o Daggers Drawn. The second dam, Shadywood (by Habitat), a useful 10f winner, was second in the Lancashire Oaks and is a half-sister to 8 winners. (Mr B Kantor & Mr M Jooste). *"She's done very well, but she'll be a one mile plus 2-y-o. I don't think she's that strong but she'll change. I think she was well-bought at 90 grand because she'll be worth that as a broodmare even if she never runs".*

658. DARK AMBITION (IRE) ★★★ ♠
b.c. Dark Angel – Date Mate (Thorn Dance).
March 3. Seventh foal. 72,000Y. Tattersalls October Book 2. Cheveley Park Stud. Half-brother to the 2010 2-y-o Group 3 6f Princess Margaret Stakes winner Soraaya (by Elnadim), to the listed 2-y-o Woodcote Stakes winner and Group 1 Prix Jean-Luc Lagardere second Declaration Of War (by Okawango), the quite useful 6f to 10f winner of 4 races Freak Occurrence (by Stravinsky) and a winner over hurdles by Idris. The dam, placed in the USA, is a half-sister to 4 winners including the dams

of the Italian Group 1 winner Le Vie Dei Colori and the Queen Mary Stakes winner Shining Hour. The second dam, Doubling Time (by Timeless Moment), a smart winner at 3 yrs in France and second in the Group 3 10.5f Prix de Flore, is a full or half-sister to 8 winners including the Prix Ganay and Prix d'Ispahan winner Baillamont. (Cheveley Park Stud). *"He'll be one of our earlier runners. Quite a well-made 2-y-o, he goes nicely and moves well. I hope he'll run at the Guineas meeting, he's a strong colt and although I don't know how much class he's got, he's ready to go".*

659. DARLING GRACE ★★★
b.c. Nayef – Lady Grace (Orpen).
April 7. First foal. The dam, a useful winner of 5 races over 6f and 7f at 2 and 3 yrs including a 3-y-o listed event, was Group 3 placed twice and is a sister to the useful Group 3 7f Prestige Stakes winner Gracefully and to the useful 2-y-o 6f winner and Group 3 Sirenia Stakes third Visionist and half-sister to the useful 2-y-o 6f winner Speedball. The second dam, Lady Taufan (by Taufan), was placed 5 times in Ireland and stayed 9f and is a sister to the listed National Stakes winner and Lowther Stakes third Princess Taufan. *"She's the first foal out of a mare we used to train who was very tough, very genuine and a stakes winner. This filly is a bit small and may need a bit of time but she's an athletic filly who will do well if she is anywhere near as good as her mother".*

660. DISTRICT ATTORNEY ★★★★
b.c. Lawman – Mood Indigo (Indian Ridge).
January 30. Sixth foal. 135,000Y. Tattersalls October Book 1. Anthony Stroud. Half-brother to the Group 3 7f Silver Flash Stakes winner Luminous Eyes (by Invincible Spirit) and to the Irish 1m winner Michikabu (by Grand Lodge). The dam, an Irish 3-y-o 7f winner, is a half-sister to 2 winners including the minor US stakes winner Got A Crush (herself dam of the US Grade 3 winner Palmilla). The second dam, Glowing Ardour (by Dancing Brave), won the Group 3 1m Silken Glider Stakes in Ireland and is a half-sister to 7 winners including the top-class Breeders Cup Turf, Japan Cup, Champion Stakes and Eclipse Stakes winner Pilsudski and the Japanese £2.5 million earner Fine Earner. (Mr B Kantor & Mr M Jooste). *"Quite*

an early foal but he's a huge horse with longish pasterns. He's got such a swagger and has great presence. He really looks a good horse, he has a great walk to him and he's a good mover. One for the second half of the season".

661. DREAM ATTRACTION ★★★★
ch.f. Bahamian Bounty – Vax Star (Petong).
March 18. Ninth foal. 30,000Y. Tattersalls October Book 2. W Haggas. Half-sister to the fairly useful 2-y-o dual 6f winner Negligee (by Night Shift), to the quite useful dual 6f (at 2 yrs) and 5f winner Yurituni (by Bahamian Bounty), the quite useful 3-y-o 7f winner Vandal (by Entrepreneur), the fair 2-y-o 5f winner River Crossing (by Zafonic), the 2-y-o 5f seller winner Trick Or Two (by Desert Style) and the French 2-y-o 6f winner Silver Shadow (by Fasliyev). The dam, a fairly useful 2-y-o 5f listed winner, is a half-sister to 4 winners. The second dam, the fairly useful listed sprint winner Vax Lady (by Millfontaine), is a half-sister to 2 winners. (Options O Syndicate). *"Yes, she's alright – I bought her to try and win the Supersprint, she's bred to be fast and although she's not that precocious she'll come and she'll be alright. I like her".*

662. ENTIFAADHA ★★★★
b.c. Dansili – Model Queen (Kingmambo).
March 25. Seventh foal. 360,000Y. Tattersalls October Book 1. Shadwell Estate Co. Half-brother to the Group 1 6f Haydock Sprint Cup and Group 3 Hackwood Stakes winner Regal Parade (by Pivotal), to the useful 1m (at 2 yrs) and 10f winner and Group 3 Derby Trial third Hot Prospect (by Motivator), the useful French 11f and 12f winner and Group 2 Prix Noailles fourth Mount Helicon (by Montjeu) and the minor French 10f winner Sister Sylvia (by Fantastic Light). The dam, a fair 3-y-o 7f winner, is a half-sister to 5 winners including the French listed 1m winner Arabride. The second dam, Model Bride (by Blushing Groom), is an unraced half-sister to 6 winners including the smart Queen Elizabeth II Stakes third Zaizafon (herself the dam of Zafonic and Zamindar) and to the unraced Modena (the dam of Elmaamul and Reams Of Verse). (Hamdan Al Maktoum). *"He looks very much a 2-y-o type, I don't think he's bred to be one but he's a tough colt, he's strong, he looks like he*

wants to go and I think he'll be a 2-y-o so we'll be training him that way".

663. FARAWAY ★★★
b.c. Royal Applause – Somersault (Pivotal).
February 28. Second foal. 18,000Y. Tattersalls October 2. Rabbah Bloodstock. The dam, a fair 1m winner, is a half-sister to 6 winners. The second dam, Rash (by Pursuit Of Love), is an unraced half-sister to 6 winners including the useful 2-y-o dual 6f winner Maid For The Hills and the useful 2-y-o 5f and 6f winner Maid For Walking (herself dam of the US Grade 1 winner Stroll). (Mohammed Jaber). *"Likely to be one of our first runners, he's quite a small, strong, well-made horse. He'll be running in late April/early May, he'll want quick ground and five furlongs. I think he'll be alright and we like him as a sharp 2-y-o".*

664. FAST OR FREE ★★★
ch.c. Notnowcato – Ewenny (Warrshan).
February 26. Eighth foal. 26,000Y. Tattersalls October Book 2. W Haggas. Half-brother to the fairly useful 6f and 7f winner Johnny The Fish (by Most Welcome), to the fair 6f winner of 4 races (including at 2 yrs) Bazguy (by Josr Algarhoud), the moderate 7.5f seller winner Hymns And Arias (by Mtoto) and a hurdles winner by Reset. The dam, a fair 2-y-o 5f winner, is a half-sister to 5 winners. The second dam, Laleston (by Junius), won two races at 2 and 3 yrs. (Ian & Christine Beard). *"Quite a strong, well-made colt, he's a good mover and although the sire was best as a 4-y-o I think this colt might well make a 2-y-o".*

665. HAMBLE ★★★
b.c. Librettist – Time For Tea (Imperial Frontier).
April 18. 9,000Y. Tattersalls October Book 2. MHBastard. Half-brother to the quite useful 7f and 1m winner Frazzled (by Greensmaith), to the fair 7f to 10f winner of 7 races Trifti (by Vettori), the quite useful 7f winner Sugar Land (by Dansili), the modest 6f and 7f winner Moon Bird (by Primo Dominie) and a winner in France by Zamindar. The dam is a placed half-sister to 2 minor winners. The second dam, a listed-placed winner of 3 races, is a half-sister to Kalaglow and the Ribblesdale Stakes winner Armarama. (Mrs C Cyzer). *"A big horse with a dipped back, he has plenty of strength and he should make a 2-y-o".* TRAINERS' BARGAIN BUY

666. HUMMINGBIRD ★★★
b.f. Nayef – Artistic Blue (Diesis).
February 28. Sixth foal. Half-sister to the useful 7f to 10f winner of 3 races Indigo Way (by Encosta De Lago), to the fairly useful 12f winner Wandle (by Galileo) and a 3-y-o winner in Japan by Machiavellian. The dam won the listed 7f Tyros Stakes, was second in the Group 3 7f Boland Stakes and is a half-sister to 6 winners including the Irish listed winners Queen Of Palms and Cool Clarity. The second dam, Tapolite (by Tap On Wood), won the listed 7f Tyros Stakes, is a sister to the 2-y-o Group 3 1m Killavullen Stakes winner Sedulous and a half-sister to 3 winners. *"She's done very well since she came in and is a strong, attractive filly, even though she's a little bit small. Her half brother stayed well and I expect this filly to get a mile this year and she could prove useful".*

667. JAFOOL ★★
b.f. Cape Cross – Ghazal (Gone West).
February 20. Fifth foal. Closely related to the quite useful 5f to 1m winner Muftarres (by Green Desert) and half-sister to the quite useful triple 1m winner at 3 to 5 yrs Hassaad (by Danehill). The dam, a useful dual 6f winner (including at 2 yrs), is a sister to the US dual Grade 3 winner and good sire Elusive Quality and closely related to 4 winners including the 2-y-o Group 2 5.5f Prix Robert Papin winner Rossini. The second dam, Touch Of Greatness (by Hero's Honor), is an unraced half-sister to the German Group 1 and Royal Lodge Stakes winner Gold And Ivory and to the dam of the Group 1 National Stakes winner Heart Of Darkness. (Hamdan Al Maktoum). *"She's been in Dubai, I've had a few of the family but I don't know anything about her".*

668. KAHRUMAN ★★★
b.c. Mr Greeley – Jaleela (Kingmambo).
February 1. First foal. The dam, a quite useful 1m winner, is closely related to the very useful 7f (at 2 yrs) and subsequent UAE Group 2 1m winner Derbaas. The second dam, Sultana (by Storm Cat), is an unraced sister to the

high-class Group 1 7f Prix de la Salamandre and Group 1 1m Sussex Stakes winner Al abr. (Hamdan Al Maktoum). *"I trained the dam to win a maiden at Newmarket. This colt is still in Dubai, but they do like him".*

669. KHAZEENA ★★★
b.f. Oasis Dream – Shamaiel (Lycius).
March 11. Fifth foal. 170,000Y. Tattersalls October Book 1. Shadwell Estate Co. Half-sister to the useful 9f and 10f winner Shamali (by Selkirk), to the quite useful dual 1m winner Dear Maurice (by Indian Ridge) and the fair 12f winner Parhelion (by Fantastic Light). The dam, a useful listed 14f March Stakes winner, is a half-sister to the high-class dual Group 2 7f winner Naayir and to the very smart UAE Group 3 12f winner and Group 1 Coronation Cup second Highest. The second dam, Pearl Kite (by Silver Hawk), a useful 2-y-o 1m winner and third in the Group 2 12f Ribblesdale Stakes, is a half-sister to 3 winners. (Hamdan Al Maktoum). *"We have her half-sister Shamali. I loved this filly as a yearling but she went off a bit when she got here. She's just coming back nicely now and she'll be a 2-y-o alright".*

670. MAMA QUILLA (USA) ★★★★
ch.f. Smart Strike – Myth To Reality (Sadler's Wells).
March 13. Fourteenth foal. Half-sister to the French Oaks, French 1,000 Guineas, Prix Marcel Boussac and Prix Morny winner Divine Proportions, to the French 10f and 11f winner and listed-placed Indigo Myth (both by Kingmambo), the Prix Jacques Le Marois winner and sire Whipper (by Miesque's Son), the French listed winner Assos (by Alleged) and the useful 7f winner and Group 3 placed Mythical Kid (by Lemon Drop Kid). The dam, a listed winner of four races at 3 yrs in France, was second in the Group 3 Prix de Minerve and is a half-sister to 6 winners. The second dam, Millieme (by Mill Reef), a useful French Group 3 1m placed maiden, is a sister to Shirley Heights and to the dam of the Ribblesdale Stakes winner and high-class broodmare Gull Nook. (Mr & Mrs G Middlebrook). *"She's beautifully-bred and the apple of her breeder's eye, so I'm privileged to train her. It's a lovely pedigree, she'll need a bit of time but she has a nice frame, a nice physique and looks to*

have a good temperament. She's one for the late summer onwards and she'll be better next year. Not wholly backwards, but she'll be better as a 3-y-o".

671. MUJANNADA ★★
b.f. Jazil – Wasnah (Nijinsky).
April 29. Eleventh foal. Closely related to the fair 1m winner Amwaal (by Seeking The Gold) and half-sister to the top-class colt Bahri, a winner over 6f (at 2 yrs) and the Group 1 1m St James's Palace Stakes and Group 1 1m Queen Elizabeth II Stakes, to the fair 12f winner Winsa (both by Riverman), the very smart Bahhare (by Dayjur), winner of the Group 2 7f Laurent Perrier Champagne Stakes and third in the Champion Stakes and the fair 1m winner Ashwaaq (by Gone West). The dam, a fairly useful maiden, was placed five times from 7f (at 2 yrs) to 10.5f. She is closely related to the Group 3 Tetrarch Stakes winners Dance Bid and Northern Plain and a half-sister to the US Grade 2 winner Winglet. The second dam, Highest Trump (by Bold Bidder), won the Group 2 5f Queen Mary Stakes at Royal Ascot. (Hamdan Al Maktoum). *"Still in Dubai".*

672. MUKHADRAM ★★★★
b.c. Shamardal – Magic Tree (Timber Country).
February 8. Second foal. €190,000foal. Goffs. Shadwell Estate Co. The dam ran once unplaced and is a half-sister to the Group 1 winner Gran Criterium winner Kirklees and the Group 1 St Leger and Group 2 Italian Derby winner Mastery. The second dam, Moyesii (by Diesis), won once and is a half-sister to the Group 3 Prix de Fontainebleau winner Bowman. (Hamdan Al Maktoum). *"A classy horse, he's big, strong and solid. He'll be a 2-y-o from July/August time and if he wins first time out he'll be heading for some decent races. He's really nice".*

673. NINE REALMS ★★★
b.c. Green Desert – Bourbonella (Rainbow Quest).
April 24. Sixth foal. 100,000Y. Tattersalls December. Not sold. Closely related to the high-class Group 1 1m Prix du Moulin, Group 2 Summer Mile and Group 3 7f Jersey Stakes winner Aqlaam (by Oasis Dream) and half-brother to the fair 12f to 15f winner Curacao

(by Sakhee). The dam is an unraced half-sister to 9 winners including the high-class and multiple winning stayer Persian Punch and the Group 3 7f Solario Stakes winner Island Magic. The second dam, Rum Cay (by Our Native), a fair 14.6f winner, is a half-sister to 3 winners including the listed winner of 10 races Gymcrak Premiere. (Mr David Hearson). *"A very neat horse, he's very active and he's out at the moment recovering from a problem he had last year. So I'm not really qualified to comment any further, except to say that I like the way he goes".*

674. NOBLE THOUGHT ★★
b.c. Rock Of Gibraltar – Apache Dream (Indian Ridge).
February 7. First foal. 125,000Y. Tattersalls October Book 2. Jill Lamb. The dam, a fair 2-y-o 6f winner, is a half-sister to 4 winners including the smart 7f and 1m winner and Group 3 Desmond Stakes third Middlemarch and the useful 2-y-o 6f and 7f winner and Group 2 6f Cherry Hinton Stakes second Lady High Havens. The second dam, Blanche Dubois (by Nashwan), is an unraced half-sister to 8 winners including the Irish 2,000 Guineas winner Indian Haven, the Group 1 Gran Criterium winner Count Dubois and the listed-placed Place de l'Opera (the dam of 3 stakes winners including the Group 2 Scottish Derby winner Imperial Stride). *"One for the second half again, but he's a strong horse. I don't have many precocious types this year. This colt is one of those that'll do nothing for a few months and then all of a sudden the penny will drop around June/July time. He's a nice mover and I think the sire is underrated. I think this colt will be better next year".*

675. OCEAN MYTH ★★★
b.f. Acclamation – Mystery Ocean (Dr Fong).
January 24. First foal. 85,000Y. Tattersalls October Book 1. Cheveley Park Stud. The dam, a quite useful 2-y-o 5f winner, was third in the listed Masaka Stakes and is a half-sister to 4 winners including the useful Group 3 7f Dubai Duty Free (Fred Darling Stakes) and 2-y-o 7f listed winner and Irish 1,000 Guineas second Penkenna Princess. The second dam, Tiriana (by Common Grounds), is a placed half-sister to 6 winners including the 2-y-o listed 5.2f winner Head Over Heels. (Cheveley Park Stud). *"She's quite sharp and she's a January foal. The dam was quite a good 2-y-o and this filly is quite light-framed, she likes her work and I think she'll be one of those tough ones that runs quite a bit. She'll be fine".*

676. PEARL NATION ★★★
b.c. Speightstown – Happy Nation (Lear Fan).
March 4. Sixth foal. $150,000Y. Keeneland September. David Redvers. Half-brother to 3 winners including the US stakes winner Happy Humor (by Distorted Humor) and a minor winner in the USA by Silver Deputy. The dam was unplaced in one start and is a half-sister to the US stakes winner and Grade 2 placed Happily Unbridled. The second dam, Spire (by Topsider), a US stakes winner and Grade 3 placed, is a half-sister to 5 winners. (Pearl Bloodstock Ltd). *"A nice, solid horse that goes well, he should make a 2-y-o and be even better next year".*

677. PEARL WAR ★★★★
b.f. War Front – B. W. Chargit (Meadowlake).
April 23. Tenth foal. $100,000Y. Keeneland September. David Redvers. Half-sister to 4 minor winners including the US stakes winner B. W. Beetle. The dam, a minor US 2-y-o winner, is a half-sister to 2 winners. The second dam, Recharged (by Key To The Mint), a US stakes winner of 3 races, is a half-sister to 9 winners including the US Grade 2 winner Stalwart Charger. *"She's done very well this Spring and is a rangy filly with a good action. I think she'll be a July 2-y-o and I hope she'll develop into something smart".*

678. PICKLED PELICAN ★★★
b.c. Dylan Thomas – Starship (Galileo).
March 13. Second foal. Closely related to the fairly useful 2010 Irish 2-y-o 7f and 1m winner Alexander Pope (by Danehill Dancer). The dam, a fair 7f (at 2 yrs) to 8.3f winner, is a half-sister to numerous winners including the very smart Group 2 5f Flying Childers Stakes and Weatherbys Super Sprint winner Superstar Leo. The second dam, Council Rock (by General Assembly), a fair 9f and 10f placed 3-y-o, is a half-sister to 6 winners including the Group 3 Prestige Stakes winner Glatisant and the listed Virginia Stakes winner

Gai Bulga. (Des Scott & L Piggott). *"Very small, he's as big as the dam's half-sister Superstar Leo was. He looks like he'll be a 2-y-o and he's quite a good mover, but I can't believe that a 2-y-o by Dylan Thomas out of a Galileo mare could make a 2-y-o type. We're going to carry on training him and we'll see what happens".*

679. POLAR VENTURE ★★★
b.c. Invincible Spirit – Sharplaw Venture (Polar Falcon).
March 3. Third foal. 60,000Y. Tattersalls October Book 1. Cheveley Park Stud. Half-brother to the very useful listed 6f and listed 7f winner Dever Dream (by Medicean). The dam, a useful 2-y-o 5f and 6.5f winner, was listed placed over 1m and is a half-sister to 8 winners including the Group 2 Mill Reef Stakes and Group 2 Godolphin Mile winner Firebreak. The second dam, Breakaway (by Song), a useful 5f winner, was listed-placed and is a half-sister to 5 winners. (Cheveley Park Stud). *"He's a half-brother to Dever Dream who was good last year as a 3-y-o. He's very similar, he'll need a bit of time and has a lot of Polar Falcon in him. I like him but he's definitely one for the second half of the season. A powerful horse, he was quite well-bought".*

680. SAITAIA ★★★★
b.f. Shamardal – Neila (Diktat).
April 3. First foal. 50,000Y. Tattersalls October Book 2. Shadwell Estate Co. The dam won twice at 2 yrs in Germany and is a half-sister to 4 winners. The second dam, Nigella (by Limbo), a German listed-placed winner of 3 races, is a half-sister to 7 winners. (Sheikh Ahmed Al Maktoum). *"A very nice filly with lots of quality. She's a good mover with a good attitude. I like her and she'll probably start off at six furlongs".*

681. SENTARIL ★★★★★ ♣
b.f. Danehill Dancer – Superstar Leo (College Chapel).
February 14. Half-sister to the very smart Group 3 5f Molecomb Stakes and Group 3 5f King George Stakes winner Enticing (by Pivotal) and to the quite useful dual 5f winner (including at 2 yrs) Speed Song (by Fasliyev). The dam, a very smart 2-y-o, won 5 races including the Group 2 5f Flying Childers Stakes and the Weatherbys Super Sprint and is a full or half-sister to numerous winners. The second dam, Council Rock (by General Assembly), a fair 9f and 10f placed 3-y-o, is a half-sister to 6 winners including the Group 3 Prestige Stakes winner Glatisant and the listed Virginia Stakes winner Gai Bulga. (Lael Stable). *"She's lovely, has a bit of a temperament but she's strong and well-made. I think she'll be a 2-y-o alright. She might want slower ground and she's certainly alright".*

682. SEVENTH SIGN ★★★
b.c. Pivotal – Rahayeb (Arazi).
March 17. Seventh foal. 250,000Y. Tattersalls October Book 1. Dwayne Woods. Half-brother to the French listed 9f and subsequent US Grade 1 10f and Grade 1 11f winner Lahudood (by Singspiel), to the French listed 10f winner Kareemah (by Peintre Celebre) and the fair 1m and hurdles winner Wujood (by Alzao). The dam, a fair 12.3f winner, is a full or half-sister to 4 winners. The second dam, Bashayer (by Mr Prospector), a useful dual 1m winner, is closely related to Nayef and a half-sister to the top-class colt Nashwan and the dual Group 2 winner Unfuwain. (Andrew Tinkler). *"A nice, big horse that's been too backward to come into training as yet, but he's a lovely mover with a good attitude and a good mind and he should be one for later on in the season".*

683. SHATTER (IRE) ★★★★
b.f. Mr Greeley – Watership Crystal (Sadler's Wells).
February 25. Third foal. Goffs Orby. €100,000Y. Cheveley Park Stud. Half-sister to the 2010 Irish 2-y-o 7f winner, from 2 starts, Cocozza and to the minor French 3-y-o 10f winner Black Crystal (both by Elusive Quality). The dam is an unplaced sister to the Group 3 John Porter Stakes winner Dubai Success and to the Irish Derby third Tchaikovsky and a half-sister to the Group 1 Fillies' Mile winner Crystal Music, the Group 3 1m May Hill Stakes winner Solar Crystal and the Group 3 Lancashire Oaks winner State Crystal. The second dam, Crystal Spray (by Beldale Flutter), a minor Irish 4-y-o 14f winner, is a half-sister to 8 winners including the Group 2 winner Crystal Hearted. (Cheveley Park Stud). *"She's nice, her pedigree*

suggests she won't be that early but she's strong, very well-made and she's always gone well since day one. A mid-season type 2-y-o".

684. SHOLAAN ★★★★
b.c. Invincible Spirit – Jazz Up (Cadeaux Genereux).
March 1. Sixth foal. 75,000Y. Tattersalls October Book 1. Shadwell Estate Co. Half-brother to the smart 2-y-o Group 3 7f C L Weld Park Stakes and Group 3 7f Athasi Stakes winner Jazz Princess (by Bahhare) and the fair 8.5f winner Rudry Dragon (by Princely Heir). The dam is an unraced half-sister to 6 winners including the dual Italian listed winner Mister Cavern. The second dam, Slow Jazz (by Chief's Crown), a French 6f, 6.7f and listed 1m winner, is a three-parts sister to the smart Group 1 6f Middle Park Stakes winner Zieten and the Group 1 6f Cheveley Park Stakes winner Blue Duster and a half-sister to 8 winners. (Sheikh Ahmed Al Maktoum). *"This is a 2-y-o, he's strong, very well-made and he goes well – always has done. He's probably the one that I think has a chance to win something nice this year".*

685. SIR PALOMIDES ★★★★
b.br.c. Mr Greeley – Glatisant (Rainbow Quest).
March 19. Tenth foal. 70,000Y. Tattersalls October Book 1. Not sold. Half-brother to the 2,000 Guineas winner Footstepsinthesand (by Giant's Causeway), to the fairly useful 2-y-o 6f winner Frappe (by Inchinor and herself dam of the Ribblesdale Stakes winner Thakafaat) and the Irish 12f to 2m and bumper winner Theme Song (by Singspiel). The dam, a very useful winner of the Group 3 7f Prestige Stakes at 2 yrs, is a half-sister to 8 winners including the listed winner and Group 1 placed Rockerlong and the very useful triple 10f winner Gai Bulga and to the placed dam of the very smart 2-y-o Superstar Leo. The second dam, Dancing Rocks (by Green Dancer), won over 5f and 6f at 2 yrs and the Group 2 10f Nassau Stakes at 3 yrs and is a half-sister to 4 winners. (Mr A Oppenheimer). *"A lovely horse with a nice temperament and a good, fluent mover. He's a half brother to a classic winner, he has a pedigree to be a good horse and he certainly looks the part".*

686. STENCIVE ★★★ ♠
b.c. Dansili – Madeira Mist (Grand Lodge).
March 18. Fourth foal. 260,000Y. Tattersalls October Book 1. Anthony Stroud. Half-brother to the Group 2 1m Royal Lodge Stakes (at 2 yrs) and Grade 1 Canadian International winner Joshua Tree (by Montjeu). The dam won 8 races in the USA and Canada including the Grade 3 Dance Smartly Handicap and is a half-sister to 6 winners including the Irish listed winner Misty Heights. The second dam, Mountains Of Mist (by Shirley Heights), a quite useful 10f winner, is a half-sister to 7 winners including the Group 2 Lowther Stakes winner Enthused. (Mr B Kantor & Mr M Jooste). *"A real classy horse, but he's one for the Dante and the Derby next year. He'll run in a maiden in September or October and I doubt him running in a decent race this year, but he's got some class, definitely".*

687. TA AJAAB ★★★
b.c. Pastoral Pursuits – First Eclipse (Fayruz).
March 24. Second foal. 55,000Y. Tattersalls October Book 2. Shadwell Estate Co. The dam, a modest 2-y-o 5f winner, is a half-sister to 3 winners. The second dam, Naked Poser (by Night Shift), a quite useful 2-y-o 6f winner, is a half-sister to 4 winners including the useful sprinter Damalis. (Sheikh Ahmed Al Maktoum). *"A strong, well-made horse, he's had a setback unfortunately but he's definitely a 2-y-o. He's in light work now and he'll be out in June over five furlongs. Quite a fluent mover, I should think he'd be OK on fastish ground".*

688. TAWAASUL ★★★★
b.f. Haafhd – Muwakleh (Machiavellian).
March 4. Half-sister to the quite useful 7f (at 2 yrs) and 1m winner Manaal (by Bahri). The dam, winner of the UAE 1,000 Guineas and second in the Newmarket 1,000 Guineas, is a sister to the high-class Dubai World Cup and Prix Jean Prat winner Almutawakel and to the useful 10f winner Elmustanser and a half-sister to the smart 10f winner Inaaq. The second dam, Elfaslah (by Green Desert), a useful winner of three races from 10f to 10.4f at 3 yrs including a listed event at the Curragh, is a half-sister to the Group 1 12f Italian Derby winner and 'King George' second White Muzzle. (Hamdan Al Maktoum). *"This is a lovely, rangy filly and she*

has the pedigree to be useful. Her mother was second in the 1,000 Guineas and despite being quite old now, this filly looks like a 2-y-o out of a young mare and she has great presence. I have high hopes for her".

689. TEACHER ★★
ch.c. Danehill Dancer – Lac Dessert (Lac Ouimet).
April 28. Seventh foal. Goffs Orby. €100,000Y. John Warren. Half-brother to the fair 1m and 12f winner Exclusive Air (by Affirmed). The dam, a dual 2-y-o 7f winner and subsequently a US stakes winner, is a half-sister to one winner. The second dam, Tiramisu (by Roberto), won at 3 yrs in France and is a half-sister to 7 winners including the dam of the Group 1 winners Pas de Reponse and Green Tune. (Highclere Thoroughbred Racing). "A big, scopey, backward horse but he's a good mover and has a good temperament. A 3-y-o in the making".

690. VALIANT ★★★
ch.c. Galileo – Whazzis (Desert Prince).
March 9. First foal. 90,000Y. Tattersalls October Book 1. John Warren. The dam won 3 races here and in Italy including the Group 3 1m Premio Sergio Cumani and is a half-sister to 4 winners including the listed Chesham Stakes winner Whazzat. The second dam, Wosaita (by Generous), a fair 12.3f placed maiden, is a half-sister to 10 winners including the very smart Group 1 10.5f Prix de Diane winner Rafha (herself the dam of 4 stakes winners including the Haydock Sprint Cup winner Invincible Spirit) and the Group 3 12f Blandford Stakes winner Chiang Mai. (Highclere Thoroughbred Racing). "He's lovely, he was relatively inexpensive and we trained the dam. He's quite long and quite backward, definitely a 3-y-o type, but he's a nice horse. He'll want seven furlongs or a mile as a 2-y-o and he should get further next year".

691. VITAL GOLD ★★★
b.c. Vital Equine – Golden Nun (Bishop Of Cashel).
May 14. Third foal. 27,000Y. Tattersalls October Book 2. W Haggas. Half-sister to the unplaced 2010 2-y-o Say A Prayer (by Indesatchel) and to the quite useful 6f (at 2 yrs) and dual 5f winner Confessional (by Dubawi). The dam, a very useful Group 3 6f Ballyogan Stakes winner, is a half-sister to 7 winners including the fairly useful 2-y-o 5f winner and Group 3 third Amber Valley. The second dam, Amber Mill (by Doulab), a useful winner over 5f (twice) and 6f, is a half-sister to 4 winners. (Ian & Christine Beard). "Out of a tough mare that ran lots of times, he's a late foal by a first crop sire, so although I don't know how precocious he'll be, I should be fast. Possibly a five furlongs type".

692. VIVID BLUE ★★★
ch.f. Haafhd – Vivianna (Indian Ridge).
March 28. Fifth foal. Half-sister to the 6f, 7f and subsequent US Grade 2 1m and Grade 3 1m winner Diamond Diva (by Dansili), to the quite useful 10f winner Kaylianni (by Kahyasi) and the quite useful 1m winner Lazy Days (by Bahamian Bounty). The dam won at 3 yrs in France and is a half-sister to one winner. The second dam, Kundalini (by El Gran Senor), a champion 3-y-o filly in South Africa, won 6 races including the Grade 1 Bloodline Classic, is a sister to the minor US stakes winner Pixie Spirit and a half-sister to the French Group 3 winner Lime Garders. (Mrs F Woodd & Mrs J Scott). "Quite a nice, backward filly, she'll take a bit of time to pull together but she'll be a 2-y-o a bit later on. She'll be fine".

693. VOW ★★★★
b.f. Motivator – Frog (Akarad).
April 19. Ninth foal. 60,000Y. Tattersalls October Book 2. John Warren. Half-sister to the unraced 2010 2-y-o Beaten Up (by Beat Hollow), to the listed 12f and listed 14f winner Harris Tweed (by Hernando), the fair 2m winner of 3 races Froglet (by Shaamit), the fair 7f (at 2 yrs) to 12f winner Val de Lobo (by Loup Sauvage) and the modest 2-y-o 7f winner Sel (by Selkirk). The dam, a fair 10f and 12f winner of 5 races, is a half-sister to 6 winners. The second dam, Best Girl Friend (by Sharrood), is an unraced half-sister to 4 winners including the French dual Group 3 winner Comrade In Arms. (Highclere Thoroughbred Racing). "A nice mover, I hope she'll be a bit more precocious than her half-brothers Beaten Up and Harris Tweed. She'll be better next year, but I still think she'll be a mile 2-y-o and I expect we'll be looking at something nice this autumn with her".

694. WELL PAINTED ★★★
ch.c. Excellent Art – Aoife (Thatching).
February 12. Eighth foal. Goffs Orby. €42,000Y. Not sold. Half-brother to the smart Group 3 5f winner Resplendent Glory (by Namid), to the quite useful 6f (including at 2 yrs) and 5f winner Esuvia (by Whipper), the quite useful 2-y-o 5f and 6f winner of 5 races Matuza (by Cadeaux Genereux) and minor winners abroad by Night Shift, Were Or When and Entrepreneur. The dam, a quite useful dual 6f winner, is a half-sister to 5 winners including the Group 2 5f Kings Stand Stakes third My Funny Valentine. The second dam, Aunt Hester (by Caerleon), a modest 2-y-o 5f winner, is closely related to the smart Group 3 9f Prix Daphnis winner L'Irresponsable and a half-sister to 6 winners. (Options O Syndicate). *"I bought him privately at Goffs and he's an interesting horse. He's a half-brother to Resplendent Glory and yet he's quite a long, backward-looking thing but I think there's a 2-y-o engine there. I think he'll pull together and I've got three Excellent Art's – they're all backward-looking and yet they're all out of speedy dams. So maybe Pivotal, the sire of Excellent Art, is influential there and they'll be better 3-y-o's. He looks a real genuine, very solid, good-tempered horse".*

695. WINDY LANE ★★★
b.f. Dubai Destination – Wendylina (In The Wings).
February 24. Sixth foal. 41,000Y. Tattersalls October Book 1. Anthony Stroud. Half-sister to the very smart 2-y-o Group 3 Solario Stakes and 3-y-o Group 2 10f Prix Guillaume d'Ornano winner Sri Putra (by Oasis Dream) and to the fairly useful 11f and hurdles winner Duty (by Rainbow Quest). The dam is an unraced half-sister to 9 winners including the Group 1 10.5f Prix de Diane winner Caerlina. The second dam, Dinalina (by Top Ville), a French 2-y-o 10f winner, is a half-sister to 8 winners including the Doncaster Cup winner Karadar and the dams of the Group 1 winners Kartajana and Khariyda. (Mr B Kantor & Mr M Jooste). *"She's quite well-made and strong. One for the second half of the season".*

696. UNNAMED ★★★★
ch.c. Galileo – Bordighera (Alysheba).
April 30. Half-brother to the Phoenix Stakes, National Stakes, 2,000 Guineas and Queen Elizabeth II Stakes winner George Washington (by Danehill), to the Irish Champion Stakes, Prince Of Wales's Stakes and Singapore Airlines International Cup winner Grandera, the UAE 1m and 10f winner Ampelio, the modest 13f, 2m and hurdles winner Wyeth (all by Grand Lodge), the fair 2m winner Old Hundred (by Tiger Hill) and the French 10f winner Fifty Five (by Lake Coniston). The dam won once over 13f in France, was second in the listed 12f Prix des Tuileries and is a half-sister to 7 winners. The second dam, Blue Tip (by Tip Moss), won 4 races including the Group 3 10.5f Prix Penelope, was Group 2 placed and is a half-sister to 7 winners. (Lael Stable). *"He was two boards slapped together when he came but he's done terrifically well. What a pedigree he's got and it's an honour to have him. God knows what he'll be like but he's done really well, he's matured a lot but he'll be one for the back-end and hopefully a Derby horse. He has a good brain and he moves fine".*

697. UNNAMED ★★★★
b.c. Oasis Dream – Loulwa (Montjeu).
January 29. First foal. The dam, a fairly useful 11f and listed 13f winner, is a half-sister to 5 winners including the Group 2 6f Mill Reef Stakes winner and Group 1 placed Galeota and the fairly useful 2-y-o 5f Weatherbys Supersprint winner Lady Livius. The second dam, Refined (by Statoblest), a fairly useful dual 5f winner, is a half-sister to 6 winners including the very smart Group 3 7f Criterion Stakes winner Pipe Major. (Saleh Al Homaizi & Imad Al Sagar). *"A nice colt with a bit of strength about him, he should be running in mid-summer and has the scope to go and be a decent horse as a three year old too but he should do well this year".*

MICHAEL HALFORD
698. AUTONOMOUS ★★★
b.c. Jeremy – Princess Caraboo (Alzao).
April 4. Fourth living foal. 45,000Y. Tattersalls October Book 2. Michael Halford. Half-brother to the winner Josiah Bartlett (by Invincible Spirit). The dam is an unraced half-

sister to 9 winners including the Group 1 Fillies Mile winner Fairy Heights and the very useful Group 3 12f St Simon Stakes winner Persian Brave and the Irish Group 3 winner Puerto Rico. The second dam, Commanche Belle (by Shirley Heights), was placed four times from 10f to 2m and is a half-sister to 11 winners including the Yorkshire Cup winner Band and the Ormonde Stakes winner Zimbalon. (Mr P Redmond). *"A nice, well-balanced colt that looks like making his debut in May. He's been working nicely, he's shown promise and I'll possibly start him at six furlongs but he'll get seven this year".*

699. BENSOON (IRE) ★★★
b.c. Refuse To Bend – Monsoon Wedding (Monsun).
February 11. First foal. 15,000Y. Tattersalls October Book 2. Emerald Bloodstock. The dam, a modest 9f winner, is a half-sister to 5 winners including the dual Group 3 winner Poet and the dam of the Group 3 winner and Irish 2,000 Guineas second France. The second dam, Hyabella (by Shirley Heights), won three races over 1m at 3 yrs including the listed Atalanta Stakes and the listed Ben Marshall Stakes and is a half-sister to 6 winners including the high-class Prince of Wales's Stakes winner Stagecraft. (Mr G McDonald). *"A nice horse that's pleasing us in his work, he'll make a 2-y-o in the second half of the year. A good, well-balanced horse that'll want seven furlongs or a mile, we like him and he could be well-bought".*
TRAINERS' BARGAIN BUY

700. BLUE CORNER (IRE) ★★★★
b.c. Teofilo – Indian Belle (Indian Ridge).
April 11. Fifth foal. 135,000foal. Tattersalls December. John Ferguson. Half-sister to the fairly useful Irish 5f winner Sioduil (by Oasis Dream), a fairly useful Irish 10f winner, is a half-sister to 3 winners. The second dam, Abyat (by Shadeed), is an unraced half-sister to 9 winners including the Group 1 Middle Park Stakes winner Hayil. (Sheikh Mohammed). *"A very big horse, he's only been doing strong canters but he has a lovely temperament and great balance. We like him but it'll be the second half of the year before we see him".*

701. DILIZAN (IRE) ★★★
b.c. Dubai Destination – Dibiya (Caerleon).
February 13. Half-brother to the fairly useful Irish 7f winning 2-y-o's Dirar (by King's Best) and Dilinata (by Spinning World) and to the Irish 12f winner Dibella (by Observatory). The dam, a fairly useful 12f and 14f winner, was listed-placed. The second dam, Dabtiya (by Shirley Heights), won the listed Ballyroan Stakes. (H H Aga Khan). *"A nice, straightforward, tough colt, he'll probably start off at seven furlongs in mid-season and he'll get a mile no problem".*

702. FREE SPIN (IRE) ★★★
ch.c. Iffraaj – Romea (Muhtarram).
March 20. Third foal. Goffs Orby. €85,000Y. John Ferguson. The dam won 2 races at 3 and 4 yrs in Italy and is a half-sister to 5 winners including the US Grade 3 winner Where We Left Off. The second dam, Rekindled Affair (by Rainbow Quest), is an unraced half-sister to 4 winners and to the unraced smart broodmare Summer Trysting (the dam of two Group winners). (Sheikh Mohammed). *"A sharp colt, he's showing a nice bit of pace and he should be able to start at six furlongs in mid to late May. A well-balanced horse with a good attitude, he's a nice, straightforward colt".*

703. LANETT LADY (IRE) ★★★★
br.f. Teuflesburg – Smoken Rosa (Smoke Glacken).
February 23. First foal. 30,000Y. Tattersalls October Book 2. Emerald Bloodstock. The dam, placed 3 times in the USA, is a half-sister to 4 winners including Snowdrops (three Grade wins). The second dam, Roses In The Snow (by Be My Guest), a useful 1m winner and listed-placed here, subsequently won in the USA and is a half-sister to 6 winners. (Mr N Hartery). *"A lovely, well-balanced filly that goes well. She'll start at six furlongs and will probably get seven. We like this filly, she goes well and she'll be racing at the end of May or in early June. The sire is an American horse by Johannesburg".*

704. MULTITASKING ★★★
b.c. Multiplex – Ryan's Quest (Mukaddamah).
March 8. Second foal. Doncaster Premier. £20,000Y. Frank Berry. Half-brother to the moderate 2010 5f placed 2-y-o Glenns Princess (by Needwood Blade). The dam, a

modest 5f placed maiden, is a half-sister to 6 winners including the Group 3 winner and Group 1 placed Dhanyata. The second dam, Preponderance (by Cyrano de Bergerac), a quite useful 2-y-o dual 5f winner, is a half-sister to 6 winners. *"A nice, sharp colt, he's a five/six furlong horse that probably wants good ground. I could see him being out anytime from the end of May and he's a sharp colt that's showing a nice bit of pace",*

705. SINETTA (IRE) ★★★
b.f. Red Ransom – Siniyya (Grand Lodge).
April 8. Second foal. The dam, placed from 12f to 2m in Ireland, is a sister to the top-class middle-distance colt Sinndar (by Grand Lodge), winner of the Derby, the Irish Derby and the Prix de l'Arc de Triomphe and a half-sister to the fairly useful 1m winner (at 2 yrs) and listed-placed Simawa. The second dam, Sinntara (by Lashkari), won 4 races in Ireland at up to 2m. (H H Aga Khan). *"She's one for the second half of the year over seven furlongs or a mile. She's grown quite a bit so she's only been doing half-speeds but she's a well-balanced filly. We like her and she goes well".*

706. ZAMBELOT (IRE) ★★
ch.c. Street Cry – Camlet (Green Desert).
March 26. Brother to Abergeldie, placed third over 7f from two starts at 2 yrs in 2010 and half-brother to the quite useful 2-y-o 6f winner Cheviot (by Rahy). The dam, a fairly useful dual 6f winner (including at 2 yrs), is a half-sister to the Group 1 Fillies Mile and Irish 1,000 Guineas winner Gossamer, to the high-class Breeders Cup Mile, Irish 2,000 Guineas and Queen Anne Stakes winner Barathea and the smart colt Zabar, a winner of three Group 3 1m events. The second dam, Brocade (by Habitat), was a high-class filly at up to 1m, winning five races including the Group 1 7f Prix de la Foret and the Group 3 7f Bisquit Cognac Challenge Stakes. She is a sister to the very useful 2-y-o Cause Celebre and a half-sister to 5 winners. (Sheikh Mohammed). *"He's a very big colt so we haven't done a lot with him at the moment but he has a lovely pedigree and he's a smashing horse to go with it. He's well-balanced and has a good attitude, but his size means he'll be one for the back-end of the season".*

707. ZALANGA (IRE) ★★
b.f. Azamour – Zanara (Kahyasi).
April 24. Half-sister to the quite useful Irish 9f, 13f and hurdles winner Zanderi (by Kalanisi), to the quite useful Irish 12f winner Zamiyla (by Daylami) and the fair Irish 12f winner Zanoubiya (by Dalakhani). The dam, an Irish 12f winner, is a half-sister to 5 winners including the 1m winner and dual Group 3 placed Zarad. The second dam, Zarannda (by Last Tycoon), won two listed events in France over 7f and 1m at 3 yrs. (H H Aga Khan). *"She's a fine, big filly, well-balanced and with a good temperament, but she won't be ready until the back-end of the season over seven furlongs and she'll get a mile no problem. We like her and for what she's doing she's doing it very well".*

708. UNNAMED ★★★
ch.f. Medicean – Arameen (Halling).
January 26. Half-sister to the fair Irish 12f winner Aracena (by Grand Lodge). The dam, an Irish 2-y-o dual 7f winner, is a half-sister to numerous winners including the Irish Champion Stakes and St James's Palace Stakes winner Azamour. The dam, a useful winner in Ireland at up to 10f, is a half-sister to the high-class Prix Ganay and Prix d'Harcourt winner Astarabad. The second dam, Anaza (by Darshaan), only ran at 2 yrs when she was a useful 1m winner in France. (H H Aga Khan). *"A lovely filly for the second half of the year and the way she's bred she'll want seven furlongs minimum, but she's nice and strong – stronger even than some of the more forward types. Any time from June onwards she'll be ready to go".*

709. UNNAMED ★★★
b.c. Clodovil – Delphie Queen (Desert Sun).
April 5. Third foal. 5,000Y. Tattersalls October Book 3. Emerald Bloodstock. The dam, a fairly useful 6f (at 2 yrs) and 7f winner of 3 races, is a half-sister to 4 minor winners. The second dam, Serious Delight (by Lomond), is an unraced half-sister to 8 winners. (Mr N Hartery). *"He's showing us a nice bit of pace at the moment, he's a well-balanced horse and he'll start off at six furlongs from the end of May onwards. He's been working nicely and working well enough for me to think he's good enough to win this year".*

710. UNNAMED ★★★★
b.f. Invincible Spirit – Interpose (Indian Ridge).
April 7. Seventh living foal. Goffs Orby. €100,000Y. Michael Halford. Half-sister to the fairly useful 6f (at 2 yrs) and subsequent US winner and Grade 3 placed Rinterval, to the fair 7f, 10f and hurdles winner Go Figure (both by Desert Prince), the fair 10f winner Interdiamonds (by Montjeu) and a minor winner in France by Sinndar. The dam is an unraced half-sister to 7 winners including the French Group 3 winner Short Pause, the French 1m listed winner Cheyenne Dream and the dams of the Group 1 winners Continent and Zambezi Sun. The second dam, Interval (by Habitat), a high-class sprinting winner of four races from 5f to 1m including the Group 2 Prix Maurice de Gheest, is a half-sister to 5 winners. (Gigginstown House Stud). *"She's a filly that we like, she shows plenty of pace and she'll be racing by the end of May over five or six furlongs. We like her".*

711. UNNAMED ★★★
ch.f. Hurricane Run – Miss Intimate (War Chant).
January 28. Second foal. 25,000Y. Tattersalls October Book 1. Margaret O'Toole. Half-sister to the unplaced 2010 Irish 2-y-o Inexcused (by Medicean). The dam is an unraced half-sister to the Irish 2,000 Guineas winner Bachelor Duke and the German listed 12f winner Translucid. The second dam, Gossamer (by Seattle Slew), a winner of 2 races in the USA at up to 9f, is a half-sister to 5 winners including the German Group 3 winner Miss Tobacco. (Gigginstown House Stud) *"A nice, big filly, she's well-grown and has a good attitude. She's going to want seven furlongs or a mile and she'll make a back-end 2-y-o. A well-balanced filly with a good action".*

RICHARD HANNON

712. AIRBORNE AGAIN (IRE) ★★★
gr.c. Acclamation – Bunditten (Soviet Star).
January 20. Third foal. 40,000Y. Tattersalls October Book 2. Peter Doyle. The dam, a fairly useful 2-y-o 5f winner, was listed-placed and fourth in the Group 3 5f Queen Mary Stakes and a half-sister to 3 winners. The second dam, Felicita (by Catrail), won 3 races in France at 2 yrs including two 5f listed events, was Group 3 placed and is a half-sister to 5 winners. (Kennet Valley Thoroughbreds II). *"A nice, good-looking horse, he'll be fairly early even though he's still growing a bit and I expect him to be racing in May."*

713. ALUPKA (IRE) ★★★
b.f. Acclamation – Array Of Stars (Barathea).
March 4. First foal. Doncaster Premier. £30,000Y. Peter Doyle. The dam, a modest Irish 4-y-o 9f winner, is a half-sister to 2 winners including the Group 2 Beresford Stakes second Going Public. The second dam, Gifts Galore (by Darshaan), is a placed half-sister to 7 winners. (The Socrates Partnership). *"She was a bit too keen to get on with things at first and wanted to do everything quickly. We've now got her settled down and she's a very nice, big, good-looking filly that goes well but hasn't worked yet".*

714. AMIS REUNIS ★★★
b.f. Bahamian Bounty – Spring Clean (Danehill).
February 2. Fourth foal. Doncaster Premier. £30,000Y. Peter Doyle. Half-sister to the 2011 3-y-o 6f winner Hocver (by Sleeping Indian) and to the quite useful 6f winner Duster (by Pastoral Pursuits). The dam, a quite useful 2-y-o 6f winner, is a half-sister to 2 winners in France. The second dam, Spring Haven (by Lear Fan), is a placed half-sister to 6 winners including the German Group 3 winner Tahreeb. (Mrs Julie Wood). *"Very stocky, she's getting better all the time and she'll probably want six furlongs a bit later one but she's certainly a 2-y-o and she's nice".*

715. AVAILABLE (IRE) ★★★
b.f. Moss Vale – Divert (Averti).
January 26. First foal. €20,000foal. Goffs. Maestro Bloodstock. The dam, a quite useful Irish 5f winner at 3 yrs, is a half-sister to 6 winners including the Irish 7f (at 2 yrs) to 10f and subsequent Hong Kong stakes winner Solid Approach and the useful Irish 7f winner and listed-placed Dangle. The second dam, Dawn Chorus (by Mukaddamah), is an unraced half-sister to 6 winners including Barrier Reef, a winner of 8 races and second in the Group 3 Beresford Stakes. (Mrs Julie Wood). *"She's quite long and light but we like*

the Moss Vales, we've got three of them and they all go quite well".

716. BALM ★★★
b.f. Oasis Dream – Alovera (King's Best).
March 17. First foal. The dam, a fairly useful 2-y-o 6f winner, is a sister to the smart 6f (at 2 yrs) and listed 8.3f winner Army Of Angels and a half-sister to numerous winners including the useful 2-y-o 6f winner and Group 2 Lowther Stakes second Seraphina. The second dam, Angelic Sounds (by The Noble Player), a minor 2-y-o 5f winner, is a half-sister to 7 winners including the Group 1 Prix de la Foret winner Mount Abu. (Rockcliffe Stud). *"Very small but very pretty, she's quite tidy although she came in a bit late really. She ought to have a bit of speed".*

717. BEACH CANDY (IRE) ★★★
ch.f. Footstepsinthesand – Endure (Green Desert).
January 21. Second foal. Goffs Orby. €30,000Y. Peter Doyle. Sister to the quite useful 2-y-o 6f winner Atacama Crossing. The dam ran twice unplaced and is a half-sister to 6 winners including the Canadian Grade 3 winner Alexis and the Irish listed winner Freshwater Pearl. The second dam, Sister Golden Hair (by Glint Of Gold), a listed-placed winner at 2 yrs in Germany, is a half-sister to 2 winners. (S Mahal, R Morecombe & Anderson). *"She's a little bit backward but she'll make a 2-y-o alright and she's quite a nice filly".*

718. BELLA VENTO ★★★
ch.f. Shirocco – Annabelle Ja (Singspiel).
February 17. Second foal. 30,000Y. Tattersalls October Book 1. Not sold. Half-sister to the 2010 2-y-o Group 2 July Stakes and Group 2 Richmond Stakes winner Libranno (by Librettist). The dam, a quite useful 2-y-o 7f winner, is a half-sister to 11 winners in Europe (mainly Germany). The second dam, Alamea (by Ela-Mana-Mou), won 2 minor races at 2 and 3 yrs in Germany and is a half-sister to 8 winners. (McDowell Racing Ltd). *"A very nice filly, a 2-y-o type despite being by Shirocco and she'll be OK".*

719. BIG TIME CHARLIE (IRE) ★★
b.c. Elusive City – Brennie (Grand Lodge).
April 15. Third foal. Goffs Orby. €35,000Y. Peter Doyle. The dam was placed 8 times from 11f to 2m and is a half-sister to 6 winners. The second dam, Brentsville (by Arctic Tern), won once over 6f at 2 yrs and was Group 3 placed and is a half-sister to 7 winners. (Mr D L Dixon). *"We sold him quickly after the sales but so far we haven't done a lot with him. He's a horse for later, we haven't been anywhere near him yet".*

720. BLACK MASCARA (IRE) ★★★
br.f. Authorized – Pina Colada (Sabrehill).
April 18. Fifth foal. Doncaster Premier. £80,000Y. Peter Doyle. Half-sister to the quite useful 2010 Irish 2-y-o 5f winner, on his only start, Mr Mojito and to the quite useful dual 1m winner Colonel Carter (both by Danehill Dancer). The dam, a winner of 3 races here and in the USA including a minor stakes, was Grade 2 placed and is a half-sister 5 winners and to the unraced dam of Canford Cliffs. The second dam, Drei (by Lyphard), is a placed full or half-sister to 3 winners. (Mrs Julie Wood). *"One for the six and seven furlong races, she's by a Derby winner and came in late so she has time on her side but she's very nice and cost a fair bit of money".*

721. BLONDE (IRE) ★★★★
ch.f. Pivotal – Sister Golden Hair (Glint Of Gold).
March 8. Thirteenth foal. 60,000Y. Tattersalls October Book 1. Peter Doyle. Half-sister to the US Grade 3 Dance Smartly Handicap and French 1m listed winner Alexis, to the 2-y-o listed 6f winner Freshwater Pearl, the Irish 2-y-o listed 1m winner Miss Helga (all by Alzao), the Irish 7.5f and hurdles winner Straycat Strut (by Fasliyev), the modest 1m winner Golden Rock (by Rock Of Gibraltar), the modest 8.5f winner Nuit d'Or (by Night Shift) and the moderate 4-y-o 1m winner Et Dona Ferentes (by Green Desert). The dam, a 2-y-o winner and listed-placed in Germany, is a half-sister to 2 winners. The second dam, Rain Again (by Relko), won at 3 yrs in Germany and is a half-sister to 7 winners. (Mrs Julie Wood). *"One of our nicest fillies, she has a pedigree as long as your arm. She's very tall and very big, so we'll give her a bit of time but we expect quite a lot from her. A lovely mover that has everything going for her".*

722. BRILLIANTINE (FR) ★★★ ♠
b.f. Zamindar – Brilliantly (Priolo).
April 14. Fifth live foal. €62,000Y. Arqana Deauville October. McKeever Bloodstock. Half-sister to two minor winners in France by Marchand De Sable and Key Of Luck. The dam is a placed sister to the Group 2 Prix Saint-Alary winner Brilliance. The second dam, Briesta (by Cresta Rider), is an unplaced half-sister to the German and Italian Group 3 winner Dictator's Song. *"A lovely, leggy filly with natural speed and a lot of scope".*

723. BRONTERRE ★★★
b.c. Oasis Dream – Wondrous Story (Royal Academy).
February 18. Third foal. 110,000Y. Tattersalls October Book 1. Peter Doyle. The dam, a quite useful 2-y-o 7f winner, is closely related to a winner in the USA by Caerleon and a half-sister to 5 winners including the very useful 6f Cherry Hinton Stakes, 7f Rockfel Stakes and 7.3f Fred Darling Stakes winner Musicale and the very useful 2-y-o 1m winner and Group 2 12f King Edward VII Stakes third Theatre Script. The second dam, Gossiping (by Chati), a minor winner over 6f in the USA at 3 yrs, is a half-sister to 5 winners including the high-class sprinter and smart broodmare Committed (herself dam of the US Grade 1 winner Pharma). (M Pescod). *"We don't get too many Oasis Dream's because they're expensive now. This colt will take a bit of time but he's a grand horse".*

724. CATERINA ★★★★ ♠
b.f. Medicean – Senta's Dream (Danehill).
February 1. First foal. €110,000Y. Arqana Deauville August. Kern/Lillingston. The dam is an unraced half-sister to one minor winner. The second dam, Starine (by Mendocino), won the Grade 1 Breeders Cup Filly and Mare Turf and the Grade 1 Matriarch Stakes and is a half-sister to 3 winners. (De La Warr Racing). Richard Jnr tells me *"This is a really nice filly. There's one share left in her and I recommend that if anyone is looking for a share in a filly you won't do any better. She's a very nice, thick-set filly by a good stallion and she's got a real future".*

725. CHANDLERY (IRE) ★★
b.c. Choisir – Masai Queen (Mujadil).
March 10. Second foal. Doncaster Premier. £88,000Y. Peter Doyle. The dam is an unraced sister to the useful Irish 5f (at 2 yrs) and 1m winner and listed-placed Mombassa and a half-sister to the very useful 2-y-o listed 1m winner and Group 3 1m Prix Thomas Bryon third Gwaihir. The second dam, Twilight Tango (by Groom Dancer), is an unraced sister to the very useful 7f and 1m (at 2 yrs) and Group 3 12.3f Dalham Chester Vase winner Twist and Turn and a half-sister to the Group 3 Gallinule Stakes winner Meath. (Mrs Julie Wood). *"A lovely, big horse and a six/seven furlong type, but he's backward and we won't see him until the back-end of the season I'd say".*

726. CITY DAZZLER ★★★
b.f. Elusive City – Shady Nook (Key Of Luck).
March 23. Second foal. Tattersalls Ireland. €34,000Y. Peter Doyle. The dam is an unplaced half-sister to the dual Group 3 winner Wake Up Maggie. The second dam, Kalagold (by Magical Strike), won at 2 yrs and is a half-sister to 7 winners. (Ms E C Chivers). *"A really likeable filly with a very sweet nature, she looks like she'll try hard and is a real 'trainer's filly'. She kept going lame for a bit but she was just growing and she's over all that now".*

727. CLARE ISLAND BOY (IRE) ★★★★
ch.c. Strategic Prince – Tea Chest (In The Wings).
January 25. First foal. Doncaster Premier. £62,000Y. Peter Doyle. The dam is an unraced half-sister to one minor winner in the USA. The second dam, Tea Service (by Roi Danzig), a winner of 3 races in Ireland and the USA and listed-placed, is a half-sister to 9 winners including the US Grade 1 winner Danish and the Group 3 winners Ace and Hawkeye. (Middleham Park Racing XIV). *"A smashing horse, he's very, very strong and carries a bit of weight. He has a bit of an attitude in that he thinks he's pretty good, but time will tell. A nice horse for when the six furlong races start".*

728. CLASSY STRIKE (IRE) ★★
b.c. Oratorio – Goldster (Intikhab).
April 29. Fourth foal. Doncaster Premier. £32,000Y. Peter Doyle. The dam is an

unraced half-sister to 4 minor winners here and abroad. The second dam, Almela (by Akarad), placed in France and is a half-sister to 9 winners including the Group 3 winners Altayan and Altashar. (Mr M S Al Shahi). *"A mid-season type, he's doing everything right but he's on the back burner at the moment. A nice-looking colt though"*.

729. COPLOW ★★★
ch.f. Manduro – Anna Oleanda (Old Vic).
March 2. Fifth living foal. 78,000Y. Tattersalls October Book 1. Peter Doyle. Closely related to the French dual 10.5f winner and Group 3 Prix de Royaumont third Anna Mona (by Monsun) and half-sister to the Group 3 Prix d'Astarte winner Middle Club (by Fantastic Light) and the German winner and listed-placed Anna Royal (by Royal Dragon). The dam won twice at 3 yrs in Germany and is a sister to the German Group 3 winner Anno Luce and a half-sister to the dams of the Group winners Annus Mirabilis, Anna of Saxony, Annaba and Pozarica. The second dam, Anna Paola (by Prince Ippi), won the Group 2 German Oaks and is a half-sister to 7 winners. (R J McCreery). *"This a beautiful, big filly but she's backward at the moment. One to start over seven furlongs from August onwards"*.

730. COUPE DE VILLE (IRE) ★★★
b.c. Clodovil – Fantastic Account (Fantastic Light).
April 21. Third foal. 82,000Y. Tattersalls October Book 1. Peter Doyle. Half-brother to the fairly useful 2010 Irish 2-y-o 7f winner and listed placed Tell The Wind (by Mujadil) and to the US stakes winner and Grade 3 placed Fantastico Roberto (by Refuse To Bend). The dam is an unraced half-sister to 3 minor winners. The second dam, Fabulous Account (by Private Account), is a placed half-sister to 9 winners including the US Grade 1 winner Joyeux Danseur and the Group 3 placed Danseur Fabuleux (dam of the outstanding 2-y-o Arazi and the Sussex Stakes winner Noverre). (Coupe de Ville Partnership). *"He's working well, he carries his head a little bit high but we've noticed that with a few of the Clodovil's we've had. He'll probably be better off waiting for the six furlong races, but he'll be pretty straight when he does run and he's a nice colt"*.

731. CRESTA STAR ★★★
b.f. Teofilo – Fleet Hill (Warrshan).
March 1. Seventh foal. 20,000Y. Tattersalls October Book 2. Not sold. Half-sister to the Group 3 Lingfield Classic Trial and Group 3 Dee Stakes winner African Dream (by Mark Of Esteem), to the useful 11f and 12f winner and listed-placed Cresta Gold (by Halling), the Irish 9f winner and listed-placed Fenella's Link (by Linamix), the fairly useful 6f and 7f winner and listed-placed Lone Wolfe (by Foxhound) and a winner in the USA by Miner's Mark. The dam, winner of the listed Superlative Stakes and third in the Group 3 Rockfel Stakes, is a half-sister to 6 winners including the useful listed 6f Sandy Lane Stakes winner Lee Artiste. The second dam, Mirkan Honey (by Ballymore), a quite useful Irish 4-y-o 16f winner, is a half-sister to 12 winners. (P T Tellwright). *"A lovely filly, she's going the right way but she's nowhere near ready in her coat yet so I don't know when we'll be starting her. One for six or seven furlongs this year"*.

732. CRISTAL GEM ★★★★
ch.f. Cadeaux Genereux – Desert Cristal (Desert King).
March 7. Second foal. 22,000Y. Tattersalls October Book 2. Peter Doyle. Half-sister to the fair 2010 5f and 6f placed 2-y-o Cristaliyev (by Fasliyev). The dam, a fairly useful 7f to 10f winner, is a half-sister to the Group 2 7f Challenge Stakes winner Stimulation. The second dam, Damiana (by Thatching), was placed 5 times in France at 2 and 3 yrs and is a half-sister to 5 winners including the listed Prix Coronation winner and US Grade 2 placed Dirca. (R A Gander). *"A nice filly, she's small and petite. Quite quick, she's a Supersprint type and is working well at the moment, so she won't be long in running"*.

733. DAMASK (IRE) ★★★★ ♠
b.f. Red Clubs – Goldthroat (Zafonic).
April 3. Sixth foal. Goffs Orby. €110,000Y. John Warren. Half-sister to Sandtail (by Verglas), unplaced in 2 starts at 2 yrs in 2010, to the 2-y-o Group 1 Criterium International and dual Group 3 winner Zafisio (by Efisio),

the fairly useful 1m and 9f winner of 4 races Harald Bluetooth (by Danetime) and the quite useful 9.5f (at 2 yrs) and 10f winner New Beginning (by Keltos). The dam, a fair 7f winner at 2 yrs, is a half-sister to 2 winners. The second dam, Winger (by In The Wings), a fair Irish 9f winner, is a half-sister to 6 winners. (Highclere Thoroughbred Racing – Rockingham). *"A beautiful filly and a half-sister to a Group 1 winner, she has a bit of grey in her tail. I wouldn't think we'd see her until after Royal Ascot and over six or seven furlongs".*

734. DEMOCRETES ★★★★
ch.c. Cadeaux Genereux – Petite Epaulette (Night Shift).
April 25. Fourteenth foal. 60,000Y. Tattersalls October Book 2. Dan O'Donnell. Half-brother to the useful 2-y-o Group 3 7f C L Weld Park Stakes winner Rag Top, to the fair 2-y-o 7f winner Seamstress (herself dam of the 2-y-o listed winner Elhamri), the quite useful 2-y-o 5f winner Dress Code (all by Barathea), the fairly useful 2-y-o dual 5f winner Lady Sarka (by Lake Coniston), the fairly useful 7.6f and subsequent US 1m winner Red Top (by Fasliyev), the quite useful 2-y-o 5f winner Shalford's Honour (by Shalford), the fair 2-y-o 6f winner Petite Spectre (by Spectrum) and the modest 7f winner One Giant Leap (by Pivotal). The dam, a fair 5f winner at 2 yrs, is a sister to the 2-y-o listed second The Jotter and a half-sister to the Group 1 1m Gran Criterium second Line Dancer. The second dam, Note Book (by Mummy's Pet), a fairly useful 5f winner, is a sister to the Norfolk Stakes winner Colmore Row and a half-sister to 8 winners including the Horris Hill Stakes winner Long Row. (John Reddington). *"He was tailor made for our place, we loved him at the sales and because we've had most of the family there was never any doubt he'd end up here".* Jockey Richard Hughes told me *"This is a lovely horse, he'll be ready to run in late April/early May, he goes well and looks a real 2-y-o. He was bought to run at Windsor and I'm sure he'll end up there".*

735. DYNAMIC DUO (IRE) ★★★
ch.c. Iffraaj – Collada (Desert Prince).
March 5. Fourth foal. €27,000foal. Goffs. Catridge Farm Stud. Brother to the fair

useful 2010 2-y-o 7f and 1m winner Cai Shen and half-brother to a winner in Greece by Celtic Swing. The dam is an unplaced half-sister to 3 winners including the very smart 2-y-o Group 3 7f Horris Hill Stakes winner and French 2,000 Guineas second Clearing and to the useful dual 7f winner (including at 2 yrs) Blazing Thunder. The second dam, Bright Spells (by Alleged), a French 12f winner, is a half-sister to the Group 2 German winner Non Partisan, the Grade 3 Canadian stakes winner Jalaajel and the useful dual 2-y-o 7f winner and Group 3 Prix d'Aumale third Suntrap (herself dam of the Grade/Group 1 winners Raintrap and Sunshack). (Mrs Julie Wood). *"He's just like his full brother Cai Shen, a very big colt that'll want seven furlongs from August onwards. Hopefully he'll do exactly as it says on the tin"!*

736. EIGHTFOLD ★★★
b.c. Cadeaux Genereux – Nirvana (Marju).
April 1. Half-brother to the fair 2010 2-y-o 7f winner Isolate (by Verglas) and to the fair dual 1m and hurdles winner Ultimate (by Anabaa). The dam, a quite useful 11.7f winner, is a half-sister to 5 winners including the very smart Group 2 12f King Edward VII Stakes winner Kingfisher Mill and the Group 3 12f St Simon Stakes and Group 3 10f Prix Gontaut-Biron winner Wellbeing. The second dam, Charming Life (by Sir Tristram), won over 7f in Australia and is a sister to the Australian Grade 1 1m winner Zabeel and a half-sister to the Australian Grade 1 winner Baryshnikov. (Lady G De Walden). *"A very nice colt, we like him a lot. He wouldn't be a five furlong horse though because there's plenty of stamina in the family".*

737. EL DIAMANTE (FR) ★★★★ ♠
b.f. Royal Applause – Lumiere Rouge (Indian Ridge).
April 19. Fourth living foal. €200,000Y. Arqana Deauville August. Sir Robert Ogden. Half-sister to the German listed winner Lumiere Noire (by Dashing Blade) and the French listed-placed winner Lumiere Astrale (by Trempolino). The dam is a placed half-sister to 5 winners including the Group 2 Criterium de Maisons-Laffitte winner Signe Divin. The second dam, Lumen Dei (by Raise A Native), a

French listed placed maiden, is a half-sister to 6 winners. (Sir Robert Ogden). *"You must put her down on your list, she's a nice filly that's showing plenty. Not quite there in her coat yet, but when she blooms she'll be a standout"*. Richard Hughes also commented *"She's real nice, doing everything right and hasn't put a foot wrong. A lovely filly that moves well, she probably wants six furlongs"*.

738. ELUSIVE LIGHT (FR) ★★★★
b.f. *Elusive City – Bonne Mere (Stepneyev)*.
March 5. Third foal. €190,000Y. Arqana Deauville August. Sir Robert Ogden. Sister to the very useful 5f and 6f winner of 4 races and listed-placed Mister Hughie. The dam, a listed-placed winner of 5 races, is a half-sister to 2 minor winners in France. The second dam, Gardine (by Fast Topaze), a listed-placed winner of 5 races, is a half-sister to 3 winners. (Sir Robert Ogden). *"A very nice filly that we like a lot, she's started working and she'll begin over six furlongs. She was expensive but looks worth her money at the moment"*.

739. ENDOWING (IRE) ★★★★
b.c. *Danehill Dancer – Brazilian Samba (Sadler's Wells)*.
April 5. Third foal. 62,000Y. Tattersalls October Book 1. Peter Doyle. The dam is an unraced half-sister to 5 winners including the 2-y-o Group 3 6f Swordlestown Stud Sprint Stakes winner Brazilian Bride and the 2-y-o 7.5f winner and Group 3 7f second Brazilian Star. The second dam, Braziliz (by Kingmambo), placed fourth once over 5f at 2 yrs, is a half-sister to 8 winners including Or Vision (dam of the Group 1 winners Saffron Walden, Insight and Dolphin Street). (Mr B C M Wong). *"A nice horse, we thought we got him pretty cheap at the Sales. We'll give him his time and physically there's nothing wrong with him"*.

740. ENJOYING ★★★ ♠
b.br.c. *Marju – Jazzy Jan (Royal Academy)*.
February 21. First foal. Goffs Orby. €88,000Y. Peter Doyle. The dam is an unplaced daughter of the 2-y-o listed 1m winner and Group 3 Prix Saint-Roman second La Vita E Bella (by Definite Article), herself a half-sister to the 2-y-o dual listed 5f winner and Group 2 Criterium de Maisons-Laffitte third Bella Tusa.

741. ESENTEPE (IRE) ★★★
b.f. *Oratorio – Mythie (Octagonal)*.
April 13. Fourth living foal. 22,000Y. Tattersalls October Book 2. Peter Doyle. Half-sister to the fair 2010 dual 7f placed 2-y-o Yojimbo (by Aussie Rules) and to the fairly useful 2-y-o 6f winner Versaki (by Verglas). The dam, a minor French 3-y-o 1m winner, is a half-sister to 4 winners including the French listed winner Mytographie. The second dam, Mythologie (by Bering), won two races at 2 and 3 yrs in France and is a half-sister to 7 winners including Malaspina (Group 3 Prix Perth). (Middleham Park Racing XXI). *"A sweet filly, she's got a bit of speed and she wasn't expensive. Could be one for the Supersprint"*.

742. ESSEXVALE (IRE) ★★★★
b.f. *Moss Vale – Danccalli (Traditionally)*.
February 12. First foal. Tattersalls Ireland. €20,000Y. Peter Doyle. The dam is an unplaced half-sister to 4 winners including Whitbarrow (Group 3 Molecomb Stakes). The second dam, Danccini (by Dancing Dissident), won at 2 yrs and is a half-sister to 4 winners. (Morecombe, Elsom, Jopson, Burnham & Notley). *"Quite a sharp filly. I was a bit surprised when we worked her because although she does look a bit backward she does go well. Hopefully she'll be lucky for her owners and I think she'll win quite early"*.

743. EUREKA (IRE) ★★★
b.c. *Kheleyf – Fancy Theory (Quest For Fame)*.
April 18. Fifth foal. Doncaster St Leger Festival. £20,000Y. Peter Doyle. Half-brother to the modest 12f and jumps winner Mad Professor (by Mull Of Kintyre). The dam is an unraced half-sister to 3 winners. The second dam, Latest Creation (by Affirmed), an Irish 10f and 12f winner, is a half-sister to 5 winners. (Noodles Racing). *"A really nice horse, I won't rush him because he's big, but I can see him being out by the end of May over six furlongs"*.

744. EURYSTHEUS (IRE) ★★★★
b.c. *Acclamation – Dust Flicker (Suave Dancer)*.
March 18. Fourth foal. Doncaster Premier. £80,000Y. Peter Doyle. Brother to the 2-y-o listed 5f winner and Group 3 6f Princess Margaret Stakes third Sweepstake and half-brother to the unplaced 2010 2-y-o Sabys

Gem (by Diamond Green) and the modest 2-y-o 6f winner Luxuria (by Kheleyf). The dam, placed fourth once over 10f, is a half-sister to 6 winners including the Group 3 winners Dust Dancer (dam of the US Grade 2 winner Spotlight) and Bulaxie (herself dam of the Group 2 winner Claxon). The second dam, Galaxie Dust (by Blushing Groom), a quite useful 2-y-o 6f winner, is a half-sister to 2 minor winners. (Sir Alex Ferguson, S Hassiakos & P Nicholls). *"He goes well. He's a really nice, classy-looking 2-y-o type and yet I think he'll want seven furlongs in the end".*

745. FAIRY MOSS (IRE) ★★★
b.f. Amadeus Wolf – Frond (Alzao).
March 28. Tenth foal. Goffs Orby. €40,000Y. Peter Doyle. Half-sister to the smart triple listed winner (from 7f to 10f) Nashmiah (by Elusive City), to the useful 2-y-o 7f and listed 1m winner Streets Ahead (by Beat Hollow), the fairly useful 2-y-o 6f winner and listed-placed Ridder (by Dr Fong), the fair dual 10f winner Addikt (by Diktat), the German 10f winner Portcullis (by Pivotal) and the Scandinavian 1m and 10f winner Azolla (by Cadeaux Genereux). The dam, a quite useful 2-y-o 7f winner, is a half-sister to 8 winners. The second dam, Fern (by Shirley Heights), a useful 12f winner and third in the listed 10f Lupe Stakes, is a half-sister to 6 winners including the Group 1 Fillies Mile winner and Oaks second Shamshir. (Peter Fagan). *"She's very small but she's sharp and she's got an awesome pedigree. We'll start getting into her now and if she shows anything at all I would think she'll be very good".*

746. FORCE THREE (FR) ★★
b.f. Shirocco – Drei (Lyphard).
February 6. Tenth foal. €45,000Y. Arqana Deauville August. Peter Doyle. Half-sister to the 5.3f (at 2 yrs) and US winner and Grade 2 placed Pina Colada (by Sabrehill), to the fairly useful 2-y-o 6f winner and listed fourth Baltic Dip (by Benny The Dip), the quite useful 10f winner Triple Sharp (by Selkirk), the quite useful triple 9.4f winner Trois (by Efisio), a winner in Holland by Darshaan and the unraced dam of the Irish 1,000 Guineas and St James's Palace winner Canford Cliffs. The dam, placed fourth over 1m at 3 yrs on her only outing, is a half-sister to the useful 1m winner Triode. The second dam, Triple Tipple (by Raise A Cup), won 10 races here and in the USA including the Grade 2 Wilshire Handicap, the Grade 3 Palomar Handicap and the listed Strensall Stakes and is a half-sister to 6 winners. (Pall Mall Partners). *"A very backward filly, it's a family of winners but she will take a bit of time".*

747. FORGIVE ★★★
b.f. Pivotal – Amira (Efisio).
March 7. Third foal. 110,000Y. Tattersalls October Book 1. John Warren. Closely related to the quite useful 2010 2-y-o 5f and 6f winner Loki's Revenge (by Kyllachy). The dam, a modest 5f winner, is a half-sister to 5 winners including the Group 2 6f Diadem Stakes winner of 6 races and good sire Acclamation and the fairly useful 6f and 7f winner Waypoint (herself dam of the Group 2 Prix Robert Papin winner Never A Doubt). The second dam, Princess Athena (Ahonoora), a very smart winner of the Group 3 5f Queen Mary Stakes and placed in numerous Group events over sprint distances, is a half-sister to 4 winners. (Highclere Thoroughbred Racing – Spearmint). *"A nice, black filly she's lovely and she'll go six furlongs alright, probably seven".*

748. FORT BASTION (IRE) ★★★
b.c. Lawman – French Fern (Royal Applause).
March 24. Second foal. €420,000Y. Arqana Deauville August. Robert Ogden. The dam, placed at 2 yrs in Ireland and a minor US winner, is a half-sister to 3 winners including the Group 3 Criterium de Maisons-Laffitte winner Captain Marvelous. The second dam, Shesasmartlady (by Dolphin Lady), is an unplaced half-sister to 7 winners including the Irish listed winners Dashing Colours and Dash Of Red. (Sir Robert Ogden). *"He's working now and he's a nice horse, as his price tag suggests he should be, but he wants seven furlongs. He goes well".*

749. FREDDY Q (IRE) ★★★★
ch.c. Iffraaj – Barnabas (Slip Anchor).
February 2. Ninth foal. 45,000Y. Tattersalls October Book 2. Peter Doyle. Half-brother to Carimo (by Fasliyev), a winner of 7 races in France including over a mile at 2 yrs, to the quite useful 2-y-o 7f and subsequent

US stakes-placed winner Mighty Empire (by Second Empire) and a minor winner in the USA by Statue Of Liberty. The dam is an unraced half-sister to 7 winners including three Japanese stakes winners. The second dam, Bubble Prospector (by Miswaki), won at 3 yrs and is a half-sister to 5 winners including the Group 1 Criterium de Saint Cloud winner Intimiste. (N Hunt). *"A nice horse, he has a little bit of a knee action but he's learning all the time. He might be one for the six furlong races and he's working well".*

750. FREE VERSE ★★★★
b.f. Danehill Dancer – Fictitious (Machiavellian).
March 8. Sister to the useful 6f, 7f (both at 2 yrs) and 1m winner and listed-placed Quadrille and half-sister to the quite useful dual 1m winner Hunting Tower (by Sadler's Wells) and the fair triple 6f winner Cardinal (by Pivotal). The dam, a useful 10f listed winner, is a sister to the smart Group 2 12f Ribblesdale Stakes and Group 2 13.3f Geoffrey Freer Stakes winner Phantom Gold (herself dam of the Oaks second Flight Of Fancy). The second dam, Trying For Gold (by Northern Baby), was a useful 12f and 12.5f winner at 3 yrs. (The Queen). *"She goes very well and as soon as she comes in her coat we'll be travelling with her. I was thinking of Newbury in mid-April, but there isn't a race restricted to fillies' only. As soon as I can find a suitable race I'll run her".*

751. GLEE ★★★★
b.f. Bahamian Bounty – Syrian Queen (Slip Anchor).
March 3. Ninth foal. 42,000Y. Tattersalls October Book 1. Peter Doyle. Half-sister to the fairly useful triple 6f winner (including at 2 yrs) Dark Mischief (by Namid), to the modest 9f winner Sham Sharif (by Be My Chief) and two minor French winners by Oscar and Croco Rouge. The dam, a quite useful 10f winner, is a half-sister to 8 winners including the Cherry Hinton Stakes winner and 1,000 Guineas second Kerrera and the Coventry, July, Gimcrack, Greenham and Criterion Stakes winner Rock City. The second dam, Rimosa's Pet (by Petingo), won the Group 3 8.5f Princess Elizabeth Stakes (at 2 yrs) and the Group 3 10.5f Musidora Stakes and is a half-sister to 5 winners. (Mrs Julie Wood). *"A nice filly, we thought was going to be very early but she isn't. She's worked since and done very well. An early type".*

752. GOLD SCEPTRE (FR) ★★★★
b.c. Gold Away – Cap Serena (Highest Honor).
March 24. Second foal. €620,000Y. Arqana Deauville August. Will Edmeades. The dam is an unraced half-sister to the US dual listed winner Cap Beino and to the placed dam of the Group 2 and Group 3 winner Major Cadeaux. The second dam, Capades (by Overskate), won six graded stakes events in the USA including the Grade 1 Selima Stakes and is a half-sister to 3 winners including the dam of the French Group 2 winner Vangelis. (Mr John Manley & Mr N A Woodcock). *"A smashing horse by the family of Major Cadeaux and owned by the same man, hopefully lightning can strike twice. He's a lovely colt and a 2-y-o type".*

753. GRAPHIC (IRE) ★★★★
ch.c. Excellent Art – Follow My Lead (Night Shift).
March 12. Third foal. 48,000Y. Tattersalls October Book 1. John Warren. Half-brother to the fair 2010 Irish 7f fourth placed 2-y-o Crystal Morning (by Cape Cross) and to the modest 7f winner Amity (by Nayef). The dam, a fair 8.3f winner, is a half-sister to 5 winners including the Group 2 Superlative Stakes and Group 2 Bosphorus Cup winner Halicarnassus. The second dam, Launch Time (by Relaunch), is a US placed half-sister to 4 winners including the US Grade 2 winner Palace March and Grade 1 placed Executive Pride. (The Royal Ascot Racing Club). *"A lovely horse but he won't be about until the seven furlong races start. He had a slight setback early on but he's fine now. You may see him out around Royal Ascot time and he might even run there. A lovely, strapping chestnut colt".* Jockey Richard Hughes added more compliments about him. *"A lovely colt – he has to be decent".*

754. GUAVA ★★★★
b.f. Kyllachy – Spunger (Fraam).
January 22. First foal. Doncaster Premier. £30,000Y. Peter Doyle. The dam, a modest 1m and 10f winner, is a half-sister to 2 winners including useful 2-y-o 7f winner and

Group 3 7f Acomb Stakes second Gweebarra. The second dam, Complimentary Pass (by Danehill), a quite useful 1m placed maiden, is a half-sister to 5 minor winners. (Middleham Park Racing XXI). *"An early sort, she was going to be our first runner but she just got a little problem and we gave her a couple of weeks off. She'll be running soon in the auction races".*

755. HARBOUR WATCH (IRE) ★★★
b.c. Acclamation – Gorband (Woodman).
March 28. Fourth foal. 58,000Y. Tattersalls December. Peter Doyle. Half-brother to a winner in South Africa by Rock Of Gibraltar. The dam was placed in the UAE and is a three-parts sister to the very useful 14f winner Sharaf Kabeer and a half-sister to 6 winners including the very smart Group 2 1m Prix du Rond-Point and Group 2 Prix Guillaume d'Ornano winner Kabool. The second dam, Sheroog (by Shareef Dancer), a fair 3-y-o 1m winner, is a sister to the very smart Prix ce Pomone winner Colorado Dancer (the dam of Dubai Millennium), closely related to the Group/Grade 1 winners Hamas, Northern Aspen and Fort Wood and a half-sister to the Grade 1 winner Timber Country and the dams of the Group 1 winners Medaaly, Methaaf and Elnadim. (Mr H R Heffer). *"A nice horse, we don't know why but the weight fell off him after the sale. He's getting it all together again now, he's working quite well and he'll want six furlongs."*

756. HEFNER (IRE) ★★
b.c. Tagula – Classic Style (Desert Style).
April 6. Second foal. €12,000foal. Goffs. Catridge Farm Stud. The dam, a moderate 1m placed 3-y-o, is a half-sister to 6 winners including the useful 5f and 6f winner of 9 races and listed-placed Seven No Trumps and the fairly useful 6f to 10f winner of 19 races and Group 3 Norfolk Stakes second Waterside. The second dam, Classic Ring (by Auction Ring), a 2-y-o 7f seller winner, is a half-sister to 6 winners. (Mrs Julie Wood). *"A great big, backward horse and we won't see him until the seven furlong races start".*

757. IMPEL (IRE) ★★★★
b.c. Excellent Art – Tencarola (Night Shift).
April 3. Sixth foal. 50,000Y. Tattersalls October Book 2. Peter Doyle. Half-brother to the minor US winner of 5 races at 4 to 6 yrs O'Gulch (by Gulch). The dam, a listed-placed winner at 3 yrs in France, is a half-sister to 5 winners. The second dam, Vanya (by Busted), won the listed Prix d'Automne and is a full or half-sister to 7 winners including the French Group 3 winner Muroto and the smart broodmare Zivania (dam of 5 stakes winners). (Mrs Y M G Jacques). *"A very nice horse, he's very tall and we'll wait until the six furlong races. Typical of the Excellent Art's, he's showing plenty and he looks a 2-y-o. Really nice".*

758. IMPERIAL ORDER (IRE) ★★★
b.c. Excellent Art – Sao Gabriel (Persian Bold).
February 20. Sixth foal. Doncaster Premier. £75,000Y. Sir Robert Ogden. Half-brother to the quite useful Irish 3-y-o 7f winner Spring Snowdrop (by Danehill Dancer). The dam is an unraced half-sister to 6 winners including the Champion Stakes winner Legal Case and the dam of the Oaks winner Love Divine. The second dam, Maryinsky (by Northern Dancer), won twice in the USA and is a half-sister to 4 stakes winners. (Sir Robert Ogden). *"A nice horse and very classy looking but we've been nowhere near him yet. Hopefully he'll turn out to be a good one. We'll more than likely wait for seven furlongs with him".*

759. INDIGO IRIS (IRE) ★★★★ ♠
b.c. Choisir – Sweet Surrender (Pennekamp).
April 24. Sixth foal. Doncaster Premier. £65,000Y. Peter Doyle. Half-brother to the fair 2010 2-y-o 6f to 1m winner of 3 races Daas Rite (by Byron), to the fair Irish 10f and 12f winner Shanghai Star (by Soviet Star) and a winner in Spain by Intikhab. The dam, a fair Irish dual 9f winner, is a half-sister to 5 winners including the very smart 6f and 7f (at 2 yrs) and Group 2 10f Prix Guillaume d'Ornano winner Highdown and the useful 2-y-o 1m and 8.5f winner and Group 2 12f King Edward VII Stakes second Elshadi. The second dam, Rispoto (by Mtoto), a modest 12f winner, is a half-sister to 7 winners including the Group 3 10f Royal Whip Stakes winner Jahafil and the French listed 12f winner Mondschein. (Mr M S Al Shahi). *"A very nice horse, he works nicely and hopefully he'll be good enough to go to*

one of the festival meetings". Richard Hughes also pointed out to me that this colt is one to follow.

760. INTUITION ★★
b.c. Multiplex – Shallow Ground (Common Grounds).
April 4. Sixth foal. Doncaster Premier. £70,000Y. Sir Robert Ogden. Half-brother to the unraced dam of the Group 3 Horris Hill Stakes winner Carnaby Street. The dam won over 6f in Ireland, was listed-placed and is a half-sister to 5 winners including the US Grade 2 winner Shanawi. The second dam, Shabarana (by Nishapour), won two minor races in France and is a half-sister to 3 winners. (Sir Robert Ogden). *"A great big horse, he had trouble with his shins early on but we like him and he'll be given time".*

761. JACOB CATS ★★★
b.c. Dutch Art – Ballet (Sharrood).
April 2. Thirteenth foal. 38,000Y. Tattersalls October Book 1. Peter Doyle. Half-brother to the moderate 2010 1m placed 2-y-o Dr Darcey (by Dr Fong), to the smart 1m winner and Group 3 1m Joel Stakes third Fair Trade (by Trade Fair), the smart 1m (at 2 yrs) and listed 10f winner Island Sound (by Turtle Island), the useful 10f and 11.6f winner Serge Lifar (by Shirley Heights), the fairly useful Irish 10f winner Ballyhaunis (by Daylami), the quite useful 10f winner Quintoto (by Mtoto), the German 7f winner Batanga (by Primo Dominie) and the modest 14.8f winner Charlie's Gold (by Shalford). The dam, a moderate 5f and 6f placed maiden, is a half-sister to 10 winners including the May Hill Stakes winner Satinette. The second dam, Silk Stocking (by Pardao), won 3 races including the listed 9f Strensall Stakes and is a half-sister to 5 winners including the smart sprinter Shiny Tenth. (Michael Pescod & Justin Dowley). *"He's shown us a bit and he'll probably be running in May. He has a bit of attitude but he's shown us enough".*

762. JUVENAL (IRE) ★★★
b.c. Holy Roman Emperor – Final Opinion (King's Theatre).
February 4. Third foal. Goffs Orby. €60,000Y. Peter Doyle. Half-brother to the 2010 French 1m winner Footsteppy (by Footstepsinthesand) and to the fair Irish 10f and 12f winner Fammi Sognare (by Bertolini). The dam, an Irish dual 13f winner, is a half-sister to 5 winners including the Group 3 6f Greenlands Stakes winner Final Exam and the 2-y-o Group 2 6f Lowther Stakes third Spirit Of Chester. The second dam, It Takes Two (by Alzao), is an unplaced half-sister to 2 minor winners. (Noodles Racing). *"One of the nicest looking two-year-olds we've got, but although he looks ready to run we're not fooled by that, because he wants another few weeks yet. A very attractive horse".*

763. KARUGA ★★★★
ch.f. Kyllachy – Bolshaya (Cadeaux Genereux).
February 14. Eighth foal. Doncaster Premier. £26,000Y. Peter Doyle. Half-sister to the fair 2010 2-y-o 5f winner Inagh River (by Fasliyev) and to the Irish 2-y-o 7f and subsequent Hong Kong winner Carnegie Hall (by Danehill). The dam, a fair triple 6f winner, is a half-sister to 8 winners including the very smart King's Stand Stakes and Temple Stakes winner Bolshoi and the useful sprinters Mariinsky, Great Chaddington and Tod. The second dam, Mainly Dry (by The Brianstan), is an unraced half-sister to 4 winners. (Fairway Racing). *"Out of a very fast family, we like her big time and she'll be running in April. She's very sharp and is another one for the Supersprint".*

764. MR KNIGHTLEY (IRE) ★★★
ch.c. Strategic Prince – Emma's Surprise (Tobougg).
February 22. First foal. Doncaster Premier. £20,000Y. Peter Doyle. The dam, a fair 2-y-o 6f winner, is a half-sister to 7 winners including the Group 2 6f Mill Reef Stakes winner and July Cup third Indian Rocket and the useful 2-y-o listed 6f Woodcote Stakes winner The Bonus King. The second dam, Selvi (by Mummy's Pet), was a placed full or half-sister to 8 winners. (P A Deal). *"He's a nice horse, he goes well and could be anything. One for May or June".*

765. KYLIN ★★
ch.f. Kyllachy – Descriptive (Desert King).
March 28. Third foal. 40,000Y. Tattersalls October Book 3. Peter Doyle. Half-sister to a 2-y-o winner in Norway by Xaar. The dam, a quite useful 2-y-o 6f winner, is a half-sister

to 5 winners. The second dam, Ridiya (by Last Tycoon), an Irish 1m and 9f winner, was listed placed over 6f and is a half-sister to 6 winners. (R C Tooth). *"A lovely big, backward filly, we've only been cantering her so far so she'll take a bit of time"*.

766. LILBOURNE LAD (IRE) ★★★★ ♠
*b.c. Acclamation – Sogno Verde
(Green Desert).*
March 7. Second foal. Doncaster Premier. £80,000Y. Peter Doyle. Half-brother to the very useful Irish 2-y-o 7f winner and 3-y-o Group 3 10f Gallinule Stakes second Bobbyscot (by Alhaarth). The dam, a fair Irish 9f winner, is closely related to the 7f (at 3 yrs) and 4-y-o listed 12f winner Chartres and a half-sister to 5 winners including the listed 10f and listed 14f winner Pugin. The second dam, Gothic Dream (by Nashwan), a winner over 7f in Ireland at 2 yrs and third in the Irish Oaks, is a half-sister to 3 winners. (Mr A T J Russell). *"He goes very well and we might run him at Newbury in April. He was a little bit narrow when we bought him but he's put on weight and done well"*.

767. LORD OFTHE SHADOWS (IRE) ★★★★
ch.c. Kyllachy – Golden Shadow (Selkirk).
March 10. Third foal. 70,000Y. Tattersalls October Book 2. Peter Doyle. Half-brother to the unplaced 2010 2-y-o Tigerino (by Tiger Hill). The dam, a fair 2-y-o dual 1m placed maiden, is a half-sister to 3 winners including the Group 1 1m Coronation Stakes winner Balisada. The second dam, Balnaha (by Lomond), a modest 3-y-o 1m winner, is a sister to Inchmurrin (a very useful winner of the Child Stakes and herself dam of the very smart and tough colt Inchinor) and a half-sister to 6 winners including the Mill Reef Stakes winner Welney. (Richard Hitchcock & Alan King). *"He'll have won before your book comes out, even though he probably wants six furlongs. He's had one run already and he did alright after they'd gone too quick early on"*.

768. MADGENTA (IRE) ★★
br.f. Manduro – Ruby Affair (Night Shift).
March 16. Ninth foal. 50,000Y. Tattersalls October Book 1. Arlington Bloodstock. Half-sister to the useful 2-y-o 6f and UAE listed 5f winner Hammadi (by Red Ransom), to the very useful 6f (including at 2 yrs) and 6.5f winner Khabfair (by Intikhab), the quite useful 2-y-o 6f winner Frances Cadell (by Cadeaux Genereux) and the quite useful dual winner (including at 2 yrs) Red Kyte (by Hawk Wing). The dam, a modest 7f placed 3-y-o, is a half-sister to 5 winners including the 2,000 Guineas winner Island Sands. The second dam, Tiavanita (by J O Tobin), is an unplaced half-sister to 8 winners including the Group 2 Great Voltigeur Stakes winner Corrupt. (Woodcote Stud). *"A nice filly, but she's small and we'll just have to see how soon we can run her. Being by Manduro you wouldn't expect her to be a sharp -y-o, but she is small"*.

769. MAGIC CITY (IRE) ★★★★
*b.c. Elusive City – Annmarie's Magic
(Flying Spur).*
February 17. Third foal. Doncaster Premier. £42,000Y. Peter Doyle. The dam, placed twice at 4 yrs, is a half-sister to 4 winners and to the unraced dam of the Group 3 winner and Group 1 Cheveley Park Stakes second Aspen Darlin. The second dam, Magic Garter (by Precocious), is an unraced half-sister to 7 winners and to the unraced dam of Grand Lodge. (D W Barker). *"A nice horse, he's a 2-y-o type and we liked him at the sales. One to follow and he'll be racing in April"*.

770. MAGLEV ★★
b.f. Rail Link – Tenable (Polish Precedent).
April 26. Half-sister to the fair 9f winner Tagansky (by Barathea), to the fair 1m and 9f winner Milla's Rocket (by Galileo) and the fair 2-y-o 1m winner Armour (by Azamour). The dam is an unraced half-sister to Day Flight, a winner of 6 races at up to 13.5f including three Group 3 12f events. The second dam, Bonash (by Rainbow Quest), was a very useful winner of 4 races in France from 1m to 12f including the Prix d'Aumale, the Prix Vanteaux and the Prix de Malleret. (Mrs Julie Wood). *"A great big filly by the Arc winner Rail Link. She's lovely, but backward so we'll be leaving her until later on and giving her all the time she needs"*.

771. MAKE UP ★★★
b.f. Kyllachy – Christmas Tart (Danetime).
April 4. Tenth foal. Doncaster Premier. £30,000Y. Peter Doyle. The dam, a fair 2-y-o

5f winner, is a half-sister to 9 winners including the smart Group 3 6f Prix de Meautry winner Andreyev. The second dam, Missish (by Mummy's Pet), is an unraced full or half-sister to 4 minor winners here and abroad including the dam of the Group 3 winners Asian Heights and St Expedit. (Mrs Julie Wood). *"Over the last two weeks she's started to turn the corner, she's doing well and taking the eye all of a sudden. I'd expect her out sometime in May or early June".*

772. MANMANMANMAN (IRE) ★★★★
b.f. *Royal Applause – Alsharq (Machiavellian).*
April 7. Third foal. Doncaster Premier. £34,000Y. Peter Doyle. Half-sister to the fair dual 5f winner, including at 2 yrs, Commanche Raider (by Tale Of The Cat). The dam, a modest 7f winner, is a sister to one winner and a half-sister to 4 winners including the very useful Group 2 7f Rockfel Stakes winner Sayedah. The second dam, Balaabel (by Sadler's Wells), a quite useful 1m winner, is a half-sister to 5 winners including the US Grade 2 7f winner Kayrawan and the good broodmare Sayedat Alhadh (dam of the Group winners Haatef and Walayef). *"Goes very well, we'll be running her in late April or early May and physically she's a 2-y-o type".*

773. MARCUS AUGUSTUS (IRE) ★★★★
b.c. *Holy Roman Emperor – Lulua (Bahri).*
March 4. Second foal. Doncaster Premier. £32,000Y. Dwayne Woods. Half-brother to the fair Irish 7f winner Samba School (by Sahm). The dam, a minor winner of 2 races at 3 yrs in the USA, is a half-sister to 7 winners. The second dam, Sajjaya (by Blushing Groom), a useful 2-y-o 7f and 3-y-o 1m winner, was second in the Group 3 Matron Stakes and is a half-sister to 8 winners including the top-class Group 1 1m Queen Elizabeth II Stakes winner Lahib. (Mr W A Tinkler). *"A very nice horse, he's a little bit 'buzzy' at the moment and needs to settle a bit, but he goes very well".*

774. MAYO LAD (IRE) ★★★★
b.c. *Holy Roman Emperor – Mrs Marsh (Marju).*
February 22. Third foal. 100,000Y. Tattersalls October Book 1. Peter Doyle. Half-brother to the Irish 2,000 Guineas, Sussex Stakes and St James's Palace Stakes winner Canford Cliffs (by Tagula) and to a winner in Sweden by Barathea. The dam is an unraced half-sister to 6 winners including the US Grade 2 and Grade 3 winner Pina Colada. The second dam, Drei (by Lyphard), placed fourth over 1m at 3 yrs on her only outing, is a half-sister to 3 winners. (Middleham Park Racing XXI). *"Canford Cliffs' brother, he's a nice big horse that needs a bit of time. We've gone very easy with him and we'll treat him like a good one until he proves otherwise".*

775. MISS ASTRAGAL (IRE) ★★★
b.f. *Oratorio – Mansiya (Vettori).*
February 7. Second foal. Goffs Orby. €35,000Y. Peter Doyle. Half-sister to the fair 2010 7f and 1m placed 2-y-o Cadore (by Hurricane Run). The dam, a modest 7f (at 2 yrs) to 9f placed maiden, is a half-sister to 6 winners including the useful listed 11.4f Cheshire Oaks winner Abury and to the dam of the South African dual Group 1 winner Bad Girl Runs. The second dam, Bay Shade (by Sharpen Up), a fairly useful 2-y-o 7f and Italian 1m listed winner, is a half-sister to 12 winners including the Group/Grade 3 winners Daarik and Bex (herself the dam of 4 stakes winners). (Richard Hitchcock & Alan King). *"A sharp filly, she's not very big but she'll make a racehorse. I wouldn't know what trip exactly, but I would imagine five or six furlongs. We like her".*

776. MORE THAN WORDS (IRE) ★★★
b.f. *Lawman – Gilded (Redback).*
March 11. First foal. Goffs Orby. €145,000Y. Peter Doyle. The dam, a winner of 5 races including the Group 2 5f Queen Mary Stakes, is a half-sister to one winner. The second dam, Tumbleweed Pearl (by Aragon), a fairly useful 5.7f (at 2 yrs) and 6f winner, is a half-sister to 6 winners including the Group 3 Horris Hill Stakes, Ballycorus Stakes and Prix de la Porte Maillot winner Tumbledown Ridge. (Mrs Julie Wood). *"The first foal out of our Queen Mary winner Gilded, she goes very well and will probably go to one of the bigger, nicer meetings".*

777. MR KNIGHTLEY (IRE) ★★★
ch.c. *Strategic Prince – Emma's Surprise (Tobougg).*

February 22. First foal. Doncaster Premier. £20,000Y. Peter Doyle. The dam, a fair 2-y-o 6f winner, is a half-sister to 7 winners including the Group 2 6f Mill Reef Stakes winner and July Cup third Indian Rocket and the useful 2-y-o listed 6f Woodcote Stakes winner The Bonus King. The second dam, Selvi (by Mummy's Pet), was a placed full or half-sister to 8 winners. (P A Deal). *"He's a nice horse, he goes well and could be anything. One for May or June".*

778. MR MAJEIKA (IRE) ★★★★
b.c. Oasis Dream – Before The Storm (Sadler's Wells).
March 5. Second foal. Goffs Orby. €55,000Y. Peter Doyle. The dam is a placed half-sister to 4 winners including the very useful listed 7f (at 2 yrs) and listed 11.4f Cheshire Oaks winner Valentine Girl. The second dam, Set Fair (by Alleged), a French 10f winner, is a sister to the smart Group 2 winning stayer Non Partisan and a half-sister to the Grade 3 Canadian stakes winner Jalaajel and the useful dual 2-y-o 7f winner and Group 3 Prix d'Aumale third Suntrap (herself dam of the Group/ Grade 1 winners Raintrap and Sunshack). (Mr D C McKay). *"He's working very nicely. He'll probably start off at Doncaster in April and he's capable of winning one of the bonus races".*

779. MRS MOP (IRE) ★★
b.f. Amadeus Wolf – Look Who's Dancing (Observatory).
March 2. Second foal. Doncaster Premier. £15,000Y. Barry Bull. The dam is an unplaced half-sister to 5 winners including the listed 1m and subsequent US Grade 2 winner Spotlight. The second dam, Dust Dancer (by Suave Dancer), won 4 races including the Group 3 10f Prix de la Nonette and is a half-sister to 6 winners including the Group 3 7.3f Fred Darling Stakes winner Bulaxie (herself dam of the Group 2 winner Claxon). (Barry Bull & K Ivory). *"She finished third first time out, she's a plater but she's alright and can win a few sellers. If they don't buy her she'll win nurseries".*

780. MY QUEENIE ★★★★
b.f. Nayef – Margay (Marju).
March 11. Sixth foal. 26,000Y. Tattersalls October Book 2. Peter Doyle. Half-sister to the fair 2010 7f placed 2-y-o Cross Culture (by Cape Cross) and to minor winners in France (by Pulpit) and the USA (by Hennessy). The dam, an Irish 2-y-o 7f winner, was second in the Group 2 German 1,000 Guineas and is a half-sister to 5 winners. The second dam, Almarai (by Vaguely Noble), is a placed half-sister to 5 winners including the US Grade 1 winner Buckhar. (N A Woodcock). *"The first Nayef we've had, she's a smashing filly and not over-big either. Nice".*

781. NANT SAESON (IRE) ★★★
b.c. Elusive City – Lady Power (Almutawakel).
February 28. First foal. €12,000foal. Goffs. Catridge Farm Stud. The dam, a fair Irish 4-y-o dual 6f winner, is a half-sister to 3 minor winners. The second dam, Daily Double (Unfuwain), is an unraced half-sister to 4 minor winners in France and Germany. (Mrs Julie Wood). *"We'll probably leave him until the six/seven furlong races, so he's not one of the early 2-y-o's but he's a nice colt and we'll make something of him".*

782. NORTH STAR BOY (IRE) ★★★★
b.c. Acclamation – Isla Azul (Machiavellian).
March 7. Fourth foal. 57,000Y. Tattersalls October Book 2. Peter Doyle. Half-brother to the moderate 1m winner Blue Savannah (by Anabaa) and to a winner in Bahrain by Pivotal. The dam, placed fourth once over 7f at 3 yrs, is a sister to the high-class Group 1 1m Coronation Stakes winner Rebecca Sharp and a half-sister to 9 winners including the smart Group 3 11.5f Lingfield Derby Trial winner Mystic Knight and the useful listed 11.4f Cheshire Oaks winner Hidden Hope. The second dam, Nuryana (by Nureyev), was a useful winner of the listed 1m Grand Metropolitan Stakes and is a half-sister to 5 winners. (Mr R W Tyrrell). *"A nice, big strong colt, he just wants a bit more time but he goes very well and he's a nice horse".*

783. NOT BAD FOR A BOY (IRE) ★★★
b.c. Elusive City – Reign Of Fire (Perugino).
March 30. Third foal. Doncaster Premier. £26,000Y. Peter Doyle. Half-brother to the unplaced 2010 2-y-o Miss Cosette (by Diamond Green) and to the multiple Italian winner Very Glamour (by Pyrus). The dam was placed at 2 yrs and is a half-sister to 4 winners

including the US Grade 3 winner Media Mogul. The second dam, White Heat (by Last Tycoon), was placed at 2 yrs and is a half-sister to 5 winners including the dual listed winner Watching. (Middleham Park Racing XXI). *"He goes well, he's very nice and does everything right. Not the biggest horse, but he'll make a 2-y-o and he's a good-looker".*

784. PEARL CHARM (USA) ★★★★
ch.c. *Distorted Humor – Charmed Gift (A P Indy).*
March 15. Fifth foal. $155,000Y. Keeneland September. David Redvers. Brother to the US Grade 3 winner Endorsement and half-brother to a winner in Mexico by Fusaichi Pegasus. The dam won 4 races in the USA, was Grade 3 placed twice and is a half-sister to 2 winners. The second dam, Potridee (by Potrillazo), a champion 2-y-o and Group 1 winner in Argentina, is a sister to 3 other Group 1 winners there. (Pearl Bloodstock Ltd). *"Goes well. We've put him back a bit because he looks like he's ready but he's not. He wants seven furlongs, he's a horse that we like and hopefully he'll turn into a good one".*

785. PHILIPSTOWN ★★★
ch.c. *Notnowcato – Tahara (Caerleon).*
April 29. Tenth foal. 35,000Y. Tattersalls October Book 1. Not sold. Half-brother to the Group 1 5f Prix de l'Abbaye and Group 3 Ballyogan Stakes winner Gilt Edge Girl (by Monsieur Bond), to the Group 2 5f Flying Childers Stakes winner Godfrey Street (by Compton Place), the quite useful 7f winner Always Ready (by Best Of The Bests), the modest 7f winner Tamora (by Dr Fong) and a winner abroad by Zamindar. The dam is an unplaced half-sister to 2 winners and to the unraced dam of the Group 1 Prix Morny winner Arcano. The second dam, Tarwiya (by Dominion), won the Group 3 C L Weld Park Stakes, was third in the Group 1 Irish 1,000 Guineas and is a half-sister to the Norfolk Stakes winner Blue Dakota. (Mr W P Drew & Mr J N Reus). *"A very thick-set horse but quite athletic, he goes alright and he's bred to a fast horse".*

786. POETIC LORD ★★★★
b.c. *Byron – Jumairah Sun (Scenic).*
April 5. Eleventh foal. 38,000Y. Tattersalls October Book 2. Peter Doyle. Half-brother to the Group 3 7f Gladness Stakes winner Millennium Force (by Bin Ajwaad), to the useful dual 1m winner Chrysander (by Cadeaux Genereux), the fairly useful dual 6f winner (including at 2 yrs) Sunoverregun (by Noverre), the quite useful 6f winner of 5 races Najeebon, the quite useful 2-y-o 6f winner Joonayh (by Warning) and the minor French dual 1m winner Kitaj (by Sakhee). The dam, a fairly useful 10f winner, was listed placed over 12f and is a half-sister to 3 winners. The second dam, Sun On The Spey (by Glint Of Gold), was unplaced twice over 12f and is closely related to the useful listed winners River Spey and Spinning. (Mrs John Lee). *"He's a lovely horse and one of the nicest movers we've got. A lovely colt, he was relatively cheap and it's a pleasure to watch him come by every day".*

787. POOLE HARBOUR (IRE) ★★★★ ♠
b.c. *Elusive City – Free Lance (Grand Lodge).*
March 18. Second foal. Doncaster Premier. £70,000Y. Peter Doyle. Brother to the 2010 Irish 2-y-o 5f winner (from two starts) Machaputo. The dam is an unplaced half-sister to 3 winners including the Irish listed winner Flash McGahon. The second dam, Astuti (by Waajib), a quite useful 2-y-o 6f winner, is a half-sister to 6 winners including the Group 2 Kings Stand Stakes and Group 3 5f King George V Stakes winner The Tatling and the fairly useful 5.2f listed and 6f Tattersalls Breeders Stakes winner Amazing Dream. (The Heffer Syndicate). Stable jockey Richard Hughes told me *"He's a real nice horse and doing everything right. He might start off in a maiden at Newbury in April and he'd one of my picks of all the 2-y-o's. He was in the same box at the sale that Canford Cliffs had been in as a yearling – so I hope that turns out to be lucky"!*

788. REDACT (IRE) ★★★★
b.c. *Strategic Prince – Rainbow Java (Fairy King).*
April 26. Seventh foal. Goffs Orby. €25,000Y. Peter Doyle. Half-brother to the quite useful Irish 5f listed-placed New Spirit (by Invincible Spirit), to the fair 2-y-o 7f winner Abandagold

(by Orpen) and the Italian 2-y-o winner Meciapino (by Glen Jordan). The dam, a 5f winner at 3 yrs in Italy, is a half-sister to 5 winners including the Group 1 Ascot Gold Cup winner Mr Dinos. The second dam, Spear Dance (by Gay Fandango), won twice at 3 yrs and is a sister to the Group 3 winner Rasa Penang and a half-sister to 7 winners including the Group 3 winner Darcy's Thatcher. (Kennet Valley Thoroughbreds III). *"He's working really well, he's pleasing us all the time and he ought to be a nice early-season 2-y-o. He came up the gallop the other day like he was on fire! He'll win races"*. TRAINERS' BARGAIN BUY

789. REIGNS OF GOLD (IRE) ★★★★
b.c. Dylan Thomas – Lolita's Gold
(Royal Academy).
March 21. Fifth foal. Doncaster Premier. £85,000Y. Peter Doyle. Half-brother to the fair 2010 2-y-o 7f winner Sextons House (by King's Best) and to the modest 2-y-o 7f winner Sienna Lake (by Fasliyev). The dam, placed at 2 and 3 yrs over 9f and 10f, is a half-sister to 3 winners including the Group 3 Jersey Stakes winner Membership. The second dam, Shamisen (by Diesis), a fairly useful 2-y-o 7f winner and second in the Group 2 6f Lowther Stakes, is a sister to the Group 3 8.5f Diomed Stakes winner Enharmonic and a half-sister to 9 winners including the dual listed winner Soprano. (Mr M S Al Shahi). *"A beautiful horse, but I wouldn't be worried if he didn't run this year because he's an extremely nice horse. One with a future"*.

790. ROCK BAND ★★
b.c. Rock Of Gibraltar – Decision Maid (Diesis).
February 27. Sixth foal. 24,000foal. Tattersalls December. Catridge Farm Stud. Half-brother to the useful 2-y-o 7f winner and dual listed placed Latin Lad (by Hernando) and to the quite useful 1m to 10f winner of 4 races Shake On It (by Lomitas). The dam a quite useful 2-y-o 7f winner, is a half-sister to 5 winners including the listed 7f winner Miss Ivanhoe. The second dam, Robellino Miss (by Robellino), won 7 races at up to 9f in the USA, was stakes-placed and is a half-sister to the listed winners Grangeville and Palana. (Mrs Julie Wood). *"A big, backward horse and one for later in the year"*.

791. ROEDEAN (IRE) ★★
b.f. Oratorio – Exotic Mix (Linamix).
April 1. Second foal. 50,000Y. Tattersalls October Book 1. Peter Doyle. Half-sister to Glass Mountain (by Verglas), unplaced in one start at 2 yrs in 2010. The dam, placed once at 3 yrs in France, is a sister to a listed-placed winner and a half-sister to the Group winners Spinola and Shot To Fame. The second dam, Exocet (by Deposit Ticket), won once at 3 yrs in the USA and is a half-sister to 5 winners. (Mrs Julie Wood). *"She goes well and she has a good pedigree but we haven't done anything with her yet"*.

792. SEEMPLES (IRE) ★★★
b.f. Exceed And Excel – Secret History (Bahri).
March 20. Third foal. 50,000Y. Tattersalls October Book 1. Not sold. The dam won 4 races including the Group 3 Musidora Stakes and is a half-sister to 5 winners including the very smart 2-y-o 6f winner and Group 3 7f Prix du Calvados second Laureldean Gale and the US stakes winner Costume Designer. The second dam, Ravnina (by Nureyev), is an unraced half-sister to 2 stakes-placed winners. (Mrs Julie Wood). *"Coming along nicely, we'll probably hang on a bit with her but she's a nice filly and we like her"*.

793. SIR LEXINGTON (IRE) ★★★★
b.c. Desert Style – Shulammite Woman
(Desert Sun).
March 15. Second foal. Goffs Orby. €95,000Y. Peter Doyle. The dam is an unraced half-sister to 7 winners. The second dam, Bold Meadows (by Persian Bold), won twice in Ireland at 2 and 3 yrs, was second in the Group 2 Blandford Stakes and is a half-sister to 8 winners including the dam of the triple Group 1 winner Kiljaro. (Middleham Park Racing XXI). *"A great, big horse by the same sire as Paco Boy, we've been very lucky with Desert Style. He'll want seven furlongs but he's a very nice horse and we like him a lot"*.

794. SIZE (IRE) ★★★
b.c. Oratorio – Primissima (Second Set).
February 10. First foal. Doncaster Premier. £110,000Y. Sir Robert Ogden. The dam won at 3 yrs in Germany and is a half-sister to 5 winners there. The second dam, Princess

Taufan (by Taufan), won the listed National Stakes and was third in the Group 2 Lowther Stakes and is a half-sister to the dam of the stakes winners Gracefully and Lady Grace. (Sir Robert Ogden). *"He's had a few minor problems and just seems to find trouble, but he is a nice horse. He was very small when he came in, but he's grown and he goes quite well".*

795. SPUTNIK SWEETHEART ★★★★
b.f. Oasis Dream – Sachet (Royal Academy).
March 22. Fourth living foal. €50,000Y. Arqana Deauville August. Peter Doyle. Half-sister to the quite useful 2010 2-y-o 1m winner Chain Lightning (by Hurricane Run). The dam ran once unplaced and is a sister to the US listed winner and the Group 1 6f Cheveley Park Stakes third Royal Shyness and a half-sister to 8 winners. The second dam, Miss Demure (by Shy Groom), won the Group 2 6f Lowther Stakes. (Mr M Pescod). *"A half-sister to a colt we like a lot in Chain Lightning, she's very nice, she's working very well and she'll be running in late April or early May. She could well win first time out".* Jockey Jimmy Fortune was riding out when I was at the yard and he suggests this filly as one to follow.

796. STRINGER BELL ★★★★
ch.c. Cockney Rebel – Heckle (In The Wings).
April 14. Eighth foal. Goffs Orby. €110,000Y. Ross Doyle. Half-brother to the 2010 6f placed 2-y-o Muffraaj (by Iffraaj), to the fairly useful 2-y-o triple 6f and subsequent Hong Kong Chairman's Sprint Prize winner Algol (by Kyllachy) and the moderate 4-y-o 6f winner Pintano (by Dr Fong). The dam was placed fourth once over 6f at 2 yrs and is a half-sister to 4 winners including the Irish listed sprint winner Mitsubishi Vision. The second dam, Valiant Cry (by Town Crier), won over 9f at 4 yrs in France and is a half-sister to 2 winners. (Mr M Pescod). *"One of our nicest 2-y-o's, he's a liver chestnut and a lovely mover. He was quite exceptional at the sales and he's done everything right since, so we haven't changed our minds. A beautiful colt".*

797. SWING IT ★★
b.c. Bahamian Bounty – Haiyfoona (Zafonic).
February 24. Fifth foal. 30,000Y. Tattersalls October Book 2. Peter Doyle. Half-brother to a winner in the Czech Republic by Lomitas. The dam ran once unplaced and is a half-sister to 5 winners including the smart Group 1 1m Gran Criterium and US Grade 3 8.5f winner Hello. The second dam, Itqan (by Sadler's Wells), a fairly useful winner of 3 races from 12f to 14.8f and is a half-sister to 3 winners and to the dams of the Group 2 winners Atlantis Prince and Dano-Mast. (The Calvera Partnership No.2). *"He was the biggest yearling we bought last year. We like him a fair bit physically, but he carries a lot of weight and you won't see him until August or September".*

798. TEA CUP ★★★★
b.f. Danehill Dancer – Quiet Storm (Desert Prince).
February 11. Fourth foal. Goffs Orby. €65,000Y. Peter Doyle. Half-sister to the unplaced 2010 2-y-o Romano (by Haafhd) and to the useful Irish 2-y-o 7f winner and listed placed Forest Storm (by Galileo). The dam, a fairly useful 7f and 10f winner, was listed-placed twice and is a half-sister to 4 winners. The second dam, Hertford Castle (by Reference Point), is an unplaced half-sister to 6 winners here and abroad. (P A Byrne). *"A good filly, she'll probably have run and won before your book comes out. She goes well, looks like a very nice filly and might well be the one to aim at the Albany Stakes or the Queen Mary, something like that".* Jockey Jimmy Fortune chose this filly as one of his 'picks' among the 2-y-o's".

799. TELL DAD ★★★
b.c. Intikhab – Don't Tell Mum (Dansili).
February 7. Third foal. 72,000Y. Tattersalls October Book 1. Dwayne Woods. Brother to the 2010 French 2-y-o dual 6f winner and Group 3 6f Prix de Cabourg third Khawatim. The dam, a useful 5f (at 2 yrs) and 6f winner and second in the Supersprint, is a half-sister to 2 winners including the listed National Stakes winner and Group 3 third Icesolator. The second dam, Zinnia (by Zilzal), ran once unplaced and is a half-sister to 4 winners including the dam of the Group 3 Cornwallis Stakes winner Mubhij.

800. THE NEW BLACK (IRE) ★★★
b.f. Oratorio – Zarawa (Kahyasi).
March 15. Seventh living foal. 10,000Y. Tattersalls October Book 2. Not sold. Half-brother to the quite useful 10f winner Plymouth Rock (by Sadler's Wells), to the fair 12f winner Dawaarr (by Indian Ridge) and the smart hurdles winner Big Eared Fran (by Danehill). The dam ran once unplaced in France and is a half-sister to 3 winners including the French listed winner Zarannda and the dam of the Group 3 Prix de Sandringham winner Zarkyta. The second dam, Zarna (by Shernazar), won once at 3 yrs and is a half-sister to 4 winners including the dam of the French Oaks and Prix Saint-Alary winner Zainta. (Mrs Julie Wood). "She's carrying a lot of weight but she won't be like that all her life. She had an infection but she's OK now, we like her, she's speedy and she wasn't expensive. So if she's any good she'll make it to the Supersprint or something similar".

801. TONES (IRE) ★★★
b.br.c. Strategic Prince – Social Honour (Entrepreneur).
February 12. First foal. Doncaster Premier. £25,000Y. Kern/Lillingston. The dam won 4 races at 3 and 4 yrs in Italy and is a half-sister to 4 other minor winners. The second dam, Social Upheaval (by Twilight Agenda), a listed-placed winner of 8 races in Italy, is a half-sister to 8 winners. (Ivan Murphy). "He's a horse we like a fair bit, and he's a nice, big black horse. He's started work and we'll find a nice six furlong race for him from late May onwards. He didn't cost a lot but he'll give the owners a lot of fun in the auction races".

802. THRONE ★★★
b.f. Royal Applause – Pretty Poppy (Song).
February 19. Sixteenth foal. Doncaster St Leger Festival. £65,000Y. Peter Doyle. Half-sister to the quite useful 2010 2-y-o 5f winner Dubai Celebration (by Dubai Destination) to the top-class Group 1 5f Nunthorpe Stakes winner and sire Kyllachy, the modest triple 6f winner Tadlil (both by Pivotal), the very useful triple 5f winner Borders (by Selkirk), the useful 5f winner of 4 races Speed On, the quite useful 2-y-o 5f winner Loving And Giving (both by Sharpo), the fairly useful dual 5f winner Follow Flanders, the quite useful 2-y-o 5f and 6f winner High Curragh (both by Pursuit Of Love), the quite useful 7f winner Ela Paparouna (by Vettori) and the fair dual 5f winners (including at 2 yrs) Pretty Miss (by Averti) and Poppy's Song (by Owington). The dam, a modest 2-y-o 5f winner, stayed 7.6f and is a half-sister to 4 winners including the Criterium de Maisons-Laffitte winner Corviglia. The second dam, Moonlight Serenade (by Crooner), is a placed sister to the winner and Group 3 5f Duke Of York Stakes third Blackbird. (Mrs Julie Wood).

803. TRAVELLER'S TALES ★★
b.f. Cape Cross – Lost In Wonder (Galileo).
January 30. First foal. The dam, a fairly useful 2-y-o 7.5f winner, is closely related to the 7f (at 2 yrs) and listed 12f winner Juliette and a half-sister to the useful Irish 6f (at 2 yrs) and 1m winner and subsequent US Grade 2 placed Plato. The second dam, Arutua (by Riverman), is an unraced half-sister to the Group 2 Prix Greffulhe Stakes winner Along All. (The Queen). "Quite backward, she's moving well but we haven't done much with her yet".

804. TRUMPET MAJOR (IRE) ★★★ ♠
b.c. Arakan – Ashford Cross (Cape Cross).
March 5. Second foal. €20,000Y. Tattersalls Ireland. Peter Doyle. The dam is an unraced half-sister to 7 winners. The second dam, Risen Raven (by Risen Star), a dual Group 2 winner in Germany, is a half-sister to 3 winners. (J D Manley). "We bought this colt basically because one of our good horses last year, Dick Turpin, is by the same sire. He didn't cost a lot of money but he's pleased us and will probably want six or seven furlongs. He's going well".

805. VALLEY OF DESTINY ★★★★
ch.c. Three Valleys – Nouvelle Lune (Fantastic Light).
April 24. Second foal. 50,000Y. Tattersalls October Book 2. Peter Doyle. The dam is an unraced half-sister to 6 winners including the Group 3 Prix de Flore winner Audacieuse and the Irish listed 14f winner Lord Jim. The second dam, Sarah Georgina (by Persian Bold), a quite useful 2-y-o 6f winner, is a half-sister to 11 winners including the French 1,000 Guineas winner Danseuse du Soir (herself dam of the Group 1 Gran Criterium winner Scintillo). (Mr

W P Drew). *"A nice horse, he's had sore shins so we've backed off him a bit, but he's not unlike the stallion".*

806. VARNISH ★★
ch.f. Choisir – Bronze Star (Mark Of Esteem).
February 24. First foal. 40,000Y. Tattersalls October Book 2. John Warren. The dam, a modest dual 10f winner, is a half-sister to 3 winners including the Group 2 12f Ribblesdale Stakes second Eldalil. The second dam, White House (by Pursuit Of Love), a quite useful 10f winner, is a half-sister to 11 winners including the middle-distance Group winners Little Rock, Whitewater Affair and Short Skirt. (Highclere Thoroughbred Racing – Eleanor). *"A long-legged, scopey filly, we've sent her home for a break because she's going to need a bit of time. One for the late summer onwards".*

807. VIEWPOINT (IRE) ★★★
b.c. Exceed And Excel – Lady's View (Distant View).
February 21. Fourth foal. 35,000Y. Tattersalls October Book 1. Peter Doyle. Half-brother to Making Eyes (by Dansili), unplaced in two starts at 2 yrs in 2010. The dam, an Irish 2-y-o 7f winner, is a half-sister to 2 winners including the US stakes winner Krasnaya. The second dam, Karasavina (by Sadler's Wells), is an unraced sister to the very useful 10f winner and St Leger fourth In Camera, to the very useful 11.5f winner and Yorkshire Oaks second Bineyah and the useful Group 2 1m Royal Lodge Stakes winner Desert Secret and a half-sister to 6 other winners. (The Heffer Syndicate). *"This is a nice horse, we quite like him and we thought we got him cheap at the sale. He carries his head a bit high but other than that you couldn't fault him. He's done nothing wrong and has worked as well as anything".*

808. WHIMSICAL (IRE) ★★★★
b.f. Strategic Prince – Sweet Namibia (Namid).
January 30. First foal. Goffs Orby. €76,000Y. Peter Doyle. The dam, a modest 5f winner, is a half-sister to 7 winners including the useful 2-y-o 7f and listed 7.5f winner Bakewell Tart and the useful listed 7f winner Macaroon. The second dam, Almond Flower (by Alzao), won over 5f in Ireland at 2 yrs and was second in the listed Oral B Marble Hill Stakes. (Miss Y M G Jacques). *"A filly we like, she had a lung infection early on so she's a little bit behind the others. But she's one of the nicest fillies we bought at the sales and she was showing up very well. We love the Strategic Prince 2-y-o's we have and this filly looks like being nice".*

809. WREATHS OF EMPIRE (IRE) ★★
b.c. Dalakhani – Eyrecourt (Efisio).
February 3. Third foal. 50,000Y. Tattersalls October Book 1. Peter Doyle. The dam ran twice unplaced and is a sister to the Group 1 Prix Vermeille and Group 2 Prix de Malleret winner Piffle and a half-sister to 3 winners including the US Grade 1 Hollywood Turf Handicap and Group 3 Beresford Stakes winner Frenchpark. The second dam, Piffle (by Shirley Heights), a quite useful 12f winner, is a sister to the useful stayer El Conquistador and a half-sister to 5 winners. (Mrs Julie Wood). *"A nice horse, but he's going to want seven furlongs or a mile later on and he was bought with his 3-y-o career in mind".*

810. UNNAMED ★★★★
b.f. Teofilo – Aguilas Perla (Indian Ridge).
May 11. Fifth foal. 46,000Y. Tattersalls October Book 2. Rabbah Bloodstock. Half-sister to the fairly useful Irish 2-y-o 5f and 7f winner and listed-placed Spirit Of Pearl (by Invincible Spirit), to the fair 6f (at 2 yrs) to 1m winner of 6 races Annes Rocket (by Fasliyev), the fair dual 10f winner Saint Thomas (by Alhaarth) and the modest Irish dual 6f winner Hazelwood Ridge (by Mozart). The dam is an unraced sister to the Irish listed 7f winner Cool Clarity and a half-sister to 6 winners including the listed winners Artistic Blue and Queen Of Palms. The second dam, Tapolite (by Tap On Wood), won the listed 7f Tyros Stakes, is a sister to the 2-y-o Group 3 1m Killavullen Stakes winner Sedulous and a half-sister to 3 winners. (Mr H R Bin Ghadayer). *"She goes very well and we want to run her soon. She was a May foal but don't worry about that - she's not backward or anything like that. A nice filly".*

811. UNNAMED ★★★★
ch.f. Danehill Dancer – In Safe Hands (Intikhab).
March 1. First foal. Goffs Orby. €110,000Y. Peter Doyle. The dam, a fairly useful 1m

winner, was listed-placed twice and is a half-sister to 5 winners including the Group 2 5f Flying Childers Stakes winner and French 2,000 Guineas fourth Cayman Kai and the useful 2-y-o 6f and subsequent Hong Kong winner Tajasur. The second dam, Safiya (by Riverman), is an unraced sister to the German Group 2 winner and Group 1 Premio Parioli third Sulaafah and a half-sister to 3 winners. (Mrs S Magnier). *"A small filly but she's quite pleasing. She seems to be very tough and you'll see her in mid-summer. A nice filly, we like her".*

812. UNNAMED ★★★★
b.c. War Chant – Miss Kilroy (A P Indy).
April 18. Seventh foal. Goffs Orby. €100,000Y. Peter Doyle. Half-brother to the Irish 10f winner and Group 1 Irish Oaks second Miss Jean Brodie (by Maria's Mon), to the US listed stakes winner and Grade 3 second Abby's Angel and the minor US winner Sunburst (both by Touch Gold). The dam is an unraced half-sister to 5 winners including the US Grade 2 winner Miss Coronado and the Group 3 Nell Gwyn Stakes and US dual Grade 3 winner Karen's Caper. The second dam, Miss Caerleona (Caerleon), a useful French 10f performer and subsequently winner of the Grade 3 Cardinal Handicap in the USA, is a half-sister to 5 winners. (Mr M S Al Shahi). *"After we'd worked him he really started to do well, as if it had turned him on. He's one to look out for".* Richard Hughes commented *"This is a proper horse. He did one piece of work and caught the eye when we weren't expecting it".*

813. UNNAMED ★★★★ ♠
b.f. Strategic Prince – Murani (Marju).
April 22. Second foal. Tattersalls Ireland. €32,000Y. Peter Doyle. The dam is an unplaced half-sister to 4 winners including the very useful 7f (at 2 yrs) to 12f winner and listed-placed Falak. The second dam, Tafrah (by Sadler's Wells), a fair 10f winner, is a sister to the Group 1 2m 4f Prix du Cadran winner Chief Contender and closely related to the Group 1 6f Phoenix Stakes winner Aviance (herself dam of the Coronation Stakes winner Chimes of Freedom and the Hollywood Derby and Turf Classic winner Denon). (Tom Grossman). Richard Jnr told me *"I met the owner at the Breeders Cup. I told him that if he gave me a lift home in his private jet I'd buy him an aeroplane – so hopefully by buying him this filly I have done! She's in the Tattersalls Fairyhouse Sales race and she's a lovely, long-striding filly. She'll probably want seven furlongs".*

814. UNNAMED ★★ ♠
b.c. Acclamation – Top Row (Observatory).
February 12. Second foal. Doncaster Premier. £23,000Y. Amanda Skiffington. The dam is an unplaced half-sister to 8 winners including the useful 2-y-o Group 3 7f C L Weld Park Stakes winner Rag Top and the dam of the 2-y-o Goffs Million winner Lucky General. The second dam, Petite Epaulette (by Night Shift), a fair 5f winner at 2 yrs, is a full or half-sister to 3 winners including the Group 1 1m Gran Criterium second Line Dancer. (Coriolan Links Partnership III). *"Hasn't arrived here yet".*

815. UNNAMED ★★★
b.f. Red Ransom – Whoopsie (Unfuwain).
March 16. First foal. 25,000Y. Tattersalls October Book 2. Peter Doyle. The dam, a moderate 12f to 2m winner, is a half-sister to 4 winners including the listed winner and Group 3 placed Orpington. The second dam, Oops Pettie (by Machiavellian), a fairly useful winner of 3 races over an extended 10f, is a half-sister to 5 winners including the listed 10.4f Middleton Stakes and listed 10.2f Virginia Stakes winner Moselle. (Mr D J Cox & Partners). *"Quite nice, she didn't make a lot at the Sales but she's very pretty and she goes very well".*

816. UNNAMED ★★★
b.c. Avonbridge – Zephrina (Zafonic).
February 13. Second foal. Doncaster Premier. £40,000Y. Peter Doyle. Half-brother to the modest 2010 6f and 7f placed 2-y-o Piccoluck (by Piccolo). The dam is an unplaced half-sister to one winner abroad. The second dam, Fairlee Mixa (by Linamix), won twice at 2 and 4 yrs in France and the USA and is a half-sister to 4 winners including the Group 1 Prix Ganay winner Fair Mix. (Mr D L Dixon). *"He carries his head a little bit awkwardly and we had a bit of trouble breaking him in, but he's OK. He's caught up with the others and I'd say he'll be racing in May because he seems to be catching on now quite quickly".*

JESSICA HARRINGTON

817. ABSOLUTE CRACKERS (IRE) ★★★
ch.f. Giant's Causeway – El Laoob
(Red Ransom).
May 3. First foal. Tattersalls Ireland. €52,000Y. BBA (Ire). Half-sister to the useful 7f (at 2 yrs) and dual listed winner over 10f and 12f Pachattack (by Pulpit) and to the US listed stakes winner La Mina (by Mineshaft). The dam, a fairly useful 10f winner and listed 12f placed, is a half-sister to 6 winners including the useful 2-y-o 6f and subsequent UAE and US winner Mutamayyaz. The second dam, Ajfan (by Woodman), a very useful winner of 3 races from 7f (at 2 yrs) to 1m and third in the 1,000 Guineas, is a half-sister to 7 winners including the St Leger second Minds Music and the French Group 3 winner Turning Wheel. (John Harrington). *"She's lovely, not over-big and a May foal, but she's showing all the right signs. She might not appear before July".*

818. GUSH (USA) ★★★
b.f. Empire Maker – Enthused
(Seeking The Gold).
February 8. Sixth foal. $170,000Y. Keeneland September. Not sold. Half-sister to the useful 1m winner and subsequent US Grade 3 turf 8.5f second Ea (by Dynaformer), to the very useful 2-y-o Group 3 6f Round Tower Stakes winner and Group 2 6f Criterium de Maisons-Laffitte second Norman Invasion (by War Chant) and the quite useful 2-y-o dual 6f winner Erytheis (by Theatrical). The dam won the Group 2 6f Lowther Stakes and the Group 3 6f Princess Margaret Stakes and is a half-sister to the listed 12f Prix Vulcain winner From Beyond. The second dam, Magic Of Life (by Seattle Slew), won the Group 1 1m Coronation Stakes and the Group 2 Mill Reef Stakes and is a half-sister to 4 winners. (Course Investment Co). *"A very nice, very straightforward filly and she's done everything right so far. A good moving filly, she's quite strong, not over-big but not too small either and she has a very good temperament. She'll start over six or seven furlongs in early summer".*

819. MAID TO MASTER (IRE) ★★★
ch.f. Danehill Dancer – Starlight Dreams
(Black Tie Affair).
February 28. Eighth foal. Sister to the multiple Group 1 winner (Phoenix Stakes, National Stakes, Irish 1,000 Guineas and St James's Palace Stakes) Mastercraftsman, and to the Irish 2-y-o 7f winner and Group 1 7f Moyglare Stud Stakes second Famous, closely related to the US Grade 3 winner Genuine Devotion (by Rock Of Gibraltar) and the fairly useful 2010 2-y-o 6f winner Queen Of Spain (by Holy Roman Emperor) and half-sister to the 2-y-o 6f seller winner Nordhock (by Luhuk). The dam won twice at 3 yrs in the USA and is a half-sister to 5 winners including the listed Zetland Stakes winner Matahif and the dams of the Group 1 Premio Roma winner Pressing and the Group 3 Princess Royal Stakes winner Mazuna. The second dam, Reves Celeste (by Lyphard), a quite useful 1m winner, is a three-parts sister to the Ribblesdale Stakes winner Thawakib (dam of the 'Arc' winner Sakhee) and a half-sister to the Group 2 Princess Of Wales's Stakes winner Celestial Storm. (Gavin Murphy, SF Bloodstock LLC). *"A full-sister to Mastercraftsman, she's a big filly and she's doing a lot of growing at the moment, but she's strong. She might not appear before August over seven furlongs because she needs a bit more time".*

820. PRINCESS SINEAD (IRE) ★★★
b.br.f. Jeremy – Princess Atoosa (Gone West).
March 5. Fifth foal. Half-sister to 3 winners including the fair 1m winner Elmfield Giant (by Giant's Causeway) and a minor Canadian winner by A P Indy. The dam is an unraced half-sister to 2 winners in Japan. The second dam, Kooyonga (by Persian Bold), won the Coronation Stakes, Eclipse Stakes and Irish 1,000 Guineas and is a half-sister to the listed winner Hatton Gardens, herself dam of the champion South African filly Kundalini. (Mrs Elizabeth Moran). *"She's a big filly and when she came in I thought she'd be backward but in fact she isn't, she has a very good temperament and she's doing everything right. A good mover, she's a big, strong filly and I expect she'll start off over six or seven furlongs".*

821. REMEMBER ALEXANDER ★★★★
b.f. Teofilo – Nausicaa (Diesis).
April 8. Sixth foal. 120,000Y. Tattersalls October Book 1. Tally-Ho Stud. Half-sister to the 2010 2-y-o Group 2 Cherry Hinton Stakes

and Group 3 6f Princess Margaret Stakes winner Memory, to the quite useful 6f (at 2 yrs) and 7f winner Kafuu (both by Danehill Dancer), the quite useful Irish 9f winner Hedaaya (by Indian Ridge) and the quite useful 6f (at 2 yrs) and 1m winner Naughty Frida (by Royal Applause). The dam won 3 races at 2 and 3 yrs in France and the USA over 7f and 1m, was third in the Grade 3 Miesque Stakes and is a half-sister to 3 winners. The second dam, Blushing All Over (by Blushing Groom), won 6 races in France and the USA including a listed event and is a half-sister to 8 winners including the good broodmare Come On Rosi. *"She's very forward and a half-sister to Memory. A lovely big filly, she's a very good mover and I like her a lot. She's seems to be quite precocious so I'm hopeful that she'll make a nice 2-y-o".*

822. UNNAMED ★★★
b.f. Montjeu – Helsinki (Machiavellian).
April 16. Half-sister to the Dewhurst Stakes, French 2,000 Guineas, French Derby and St James's Palace Stakes winner Shamardal, the fairly useful 10f and 12f winner Yougonnabelucky (by Giant's Causeway) and the modest 7f winner Lushs Lad (by Wolfhound). The dam, listed placed over 10f at 3 yrs in France, is a sister to the Dubai World Cup and US Grade 1 winner Street Cry and a half-sister to 7 winners including the useful 8.3f to 11.6f winner Grecian Slipper (herself the dam of the Group 3 winners Magna Graecia and Graikos). The second dam, Helen Street (by Troy), won 3 races including the Irish Oaks. *"A tall filly, she's a half-sister to Shamardal. She has a lovely temperament for a Montjeu and she's a good mover that looks very racey. I would think seven furlongs would be her starting point".*

BEN HASLAM
823. DREAM LIONESS ★★
b.f. Acclamation – Dream Vision (Distant View).
February 21. Second foal. £5,500Y. Doncaster Premier. Ben Haslam. Half-sister to the modest 2010 dual 6f placed 2-y-o Night Vision (by Oratorio). The dam is an unraced half-sister to the French listed winner and Group 1 Criterium de Saint-Cloud third Putney Bridge (by Mizzen Mast). The second dam, Valentine Band (by Dixieland Band), a listed-placed 3-y-o winner, is a half-sister to the Group 3 winners Memorise and Multiplex. (Blue Lion Racing IX). *"A little bit smaller and racier than my other Acclamation filly, she'll run in May and if she does anything it'll be this year rather than the next".*

824. KING LAERTIS (IRE) ★★★
br.c. Baltic King – Vltava (Sri Pekan).
March 20. Sixth foal. 9,000Y. Tattersalls October Book 2. Ben Haslam. Half-brother to the modest 1m to 12f winner of 8 races Hucking Heat (by Desert Sun) and to the minor Italian 3-y-o winner of 4 races Nonna Giuseppina (by Mull Of Kintyre). The dam, a 7f placed 2-y-o, is a half-sister to 7 winners. The second dam, Tatra (by Niniski), won once at 4 yrs and is a half-sister to 3 winners including the dam of the Irish 2,000 Guineas winner Turtle Island. *"A strong 2-y-o type, he'll probably run over five but I'd be disappointed if he didn't win over six furlongs this year".*

825. OH SO BLUE (IRE) ★★
b.c. Majestic Missile – Oh So Rosie (Danehill Dancer).
April 2. The dam, a quite useful 2-y-o 6f and 7f winner of 3 races, is a sister to one winner and a half-sister to the fairly useful winners Sonning Rose, New Jersey and Vienna's Boy (all three listed-placed). The second dam, Shinkoh Rose (by Warning), placed over 9f at 3 yrs in Ireland, is a half-sister to one winner. (Miss Karen Theobald). *"He came in quite late, he's on the small side and bit immature still, so I haven't done a lot with him, but he's a little 2-y-o type".*

826. TUIBAMA (IRE) ★★★★
ch.c. Bertolini – Supportive (Nashamaa).
May 7. 7,000Y. Tattersalls December. Ben Haslam. Half-brother to the Irish 2-y-o 5f winner and Group 1 Phoenix Stakes fourth Galloway Boy, to the useful 5f and 6f winner and Group 3 Cornwallis Stakes third Grand Lad (both by Mujtahid), the fairly useful 6f winner Loyal Royal (by King Charlemagne), the quite useful 5f and 6f winners Wunderbra (by Second Empire) and La Stellina (by Marju) and a winner in Germany by Last Tycoon. The dam won four races over 5f at 2 and 3 yrs in Ireland and is a half-sister to 3 winners. The

second dam, Amiga Mia (by Be Friendly), won at 3 yrs and is a half-sister to 6 winners. (Mr M J James). *"I like this colt and although he's a May foal he's very strong and a real sprinter type. He should be racing in April and I'd be very surprised if he didn't win as a 2-y-o. I'll start him over five furlongs but he'll definitely go six as well. The way he's going now and the fact that he's a May foal and a half-brother to listed winners, if everything went correct there's a slight chance he might be a bit better than a maiden winner".* TRAINERS' BARGAIN BUY

827. UNNAMED ★★★
ch.f. Motivator – Chetwynd (Exit To Nowhere).
April 29. Fifth foal. 9,000Y. Tattersalls October Book 2. B Haslam. Half-sister to the Italian Group 3 10f winner Wickwing (by In The Wings), to the fair 2-y-o dual 5f winner Metroland (by Royal Applause) and a winner in Japan by Singspiel. The dam is an unraced half-sister to 4 winners including the listed and subsequent US stakes winner Secret Garden. The second dam, Chalamont (by Kris), a quite useful 2-y-o dual 6f winner, is a half-sister to 5 winners including the dual Ascot Gold Cup winner Gildoran. (Mr M J James). *"I like her, she's big but I can see her racing at the end of June in six/seven furlong races. She's definitely nice and although her pedigree suggests she'll be better next year, she'll make a 2-y-o alright. She's showing plenty and if her ability matches her size it wouldn't be a surprise if she turns out to be quite nice".*

828. UNNAMED ★★★
b.f. Acclamation – Discover Roma (Rock Of Gibraltar).
March 12. First foal. 7,000Y. Tattersalls October Book 2. B Haslam. The dam won 3 races at 2 and 3 yrs in Italy, was listed-placed over 9f and is a half-sister to 3 winners. The second dam, Soltura (by Sadler's Wells), is an unraced half-sister to 9 winners including the US Grade 2 winner Sword Dance. (Middleham Park Racing). *"She was on the weak side during the winter but she's just coming to hand now. She hasn't done a great deal, just working upsides, but I do quite like her. I think the penny will drop during the summer, maybe from the end of May onwards. She's got size and scope and she'll be OK".*

829. UNNAMED ★★★
b.c. Dark Angel – Red Slipper (Alzao).
April 24. Fourth foal. €3,000Y. Goffs Orby. Not sold. Half-brother to the Italian 3-y-o winner Bellicoso (by Bachelor Duke). The dam was placed at 3 yrs in France and is a half-sister to 4 winners including the smart dual listed 10f winner Foodbroker Fancy (herself the dam of two stakes winners) and the listed winner Femme Fatale. The second dam, Red Rita (by Kefaah), a fairly useful 4-y-o 6f winner, was second in the Group 3 6f Cherry Hinton Stakes and the Group 3 6f Princess Margaret Stakes at 2 yrs and is a half-sister to 3 minor winners. (Mrs Sheila Mason & Mr Robert Stipetic). *"He'll be one to keep an eye on in the second half of the season. He was small but he's grown a lot and I don't mind him at all, he'll be OK. He moves nicely and he'll probably want a bit of cut in the ground the way he moves".*

BARRY HILLS

I had a pleasant morning discussing the two-year-olds at Faringdon Place with Assistant Trainer Charlie Hills in early April.

830. ALFURSAAN ★★★
b.c. Dansili – Almurooj (Zafonic).
April 28. Tenth foal. Half-brother to the useful listed 6f winner Judhoor (by Alhaarth), to the fairly useful 7f and 1m winner Muzher (by Indian Ridge), the quite useful 2-y-o 6f winner Al Sifaat (by Unfuwain) and a hurdles winner by Nayef. The dam, a moderate 5f and 6f placed maiden, is a half-sister to 7 winners including the smart 6f (at 2 yrs), Group 2 7f Challenge Stakes and Group 3 7f Greenham Stakes winner Munir and the very useful Irish 1m listed stakes winner and Group 1 Coronation Stakes second Hasbah. The second dam, Al Bahathri (by Blushing Groom), was a high-class winner of 6 races from 6f to 1m, notably the Irish 1,000 Guineas and the Coronation Stakes. (Hamdan Al Maktoum). *"Everyone who rides him seems to like him, but he's been growing and is likely to be a June/July 2-y-o. He has a nice action and a nice way about him".*

331. AMBER SILK (IRE) ★★★★
b.br.f. Lawman – Faraday Light
(Rainbow Quest).
**April 2. Second foal. Goffs Orby. €52,000Y.
BBA (Ire).** The dam ran twice unplaced and is a half-sister to the Group 3 St Simon Stakes winner and dual Group 1 placed High Heeled. The second dam, Uncharted Haven (by Turtle Island), won two US Grade 2 events and is a half-sister to 4 winners. *"She looks lovely, she has a good temperament and she'll make a 2-y-o without a doubt. Built very strongly, she has a nice action and seems to enjoy everything she does. A bonny filly"*.

832. ANGELS WILL FALL (IRE) ★★★★
b.f. Acclamation – Coconut Squeak
(Bahamian Bounty).
February 15. Second foal. 90,000Y. Tattersalls October Book 1. BBA (Ire). The dam, a useful 6f winner of 3 races including a listed event, is a half-sister to 3 winners. The second dam, Creeking (by Persian Bold), a modest maiden, was placed 7 times at up to 10f and is a half-sister to 5 winners including the useful Heinz 57 Phoenix Stakes and July Stakes placed Fast Eddy and the 6f (at 2 yrs) to 10.2f winner and dual Group 2 placed Stone Mill. *"Everyone seems to like her a lot but she's backward in her coat so we're just giving her a bit more time. She looks like she has a lot of natural speed but she just needs a bit of sunshine. There's plenty of length to her and when she fills out her frame she'll be a very nice looking animal. Although she seems to have plenty of speed I would have thought she'd get seven furlongs later on"*.

833. BALTY BOYS (IRE) ★★★★
b.c. Cape Cross – Chatham Islands
(Elusive Quality).
February 14. First foal. 100,000Y. Tattersalls October Book 1. BBA (Ire). The dam, a fair 2-y-o 6f winner, is a half-sister to 4 winners including the useful 2-y-o listed 6f winner and Group 2 6f Cherry Hinton Stakes second Pearl Grey. The second dam, Zelanda (by Night Shift), a very useful winner of 4 races over 5f and 6f including a listed event, is a half-sister to the Group 3 1m Prix des Reservoirs winner Emily Bronte. *"He's another horse we like a lot and he's one of Dad's picks. He's ready to go now but the longer we wait the better really. He'll get a mile later on I would have thought, but he shows a bit of speed and everyone seems to like him. He's a very attractive horse"*.

834. BASSETERRE (IRE) ★★
b.c. Cape Cross – Higher Love (Sadler's Wells).
April 15. Third foal. 55,000Y. Tattersalls October Book 2. Anthony Stroud. Half-brother to the winner Frances Stuart (by King's Best). The dam, a fairly useful 9.7f winner, was second in the listed Cheshire Oaks and is a half-sister to 2 winners. The second dam, Dollar Bird (by Kris), a useful 2-y-o 8.2f winner and second in the listed 11.5f Oaks Trial, is a half-sister to 7 winners including the Group 2 12f King Edward VII Stakes winner Amfortas and the Group 3 10.5f Prix de Royaumont winner Legend Maker (dam of the 1,000 Guineas winner Virginia Waters). *"He's been growing an awful lot and so he's changed since we bought him as a yearling. He's obviously going to take a bit of time, but he's a well-made horse that could be anything. Certainly more of a 3-y-o than a 2-y-o type"*.

835. BRIMSTONE HILL (IRE) ★★★
b.c. Royal Applause – Right As Rain
(Rainbow Quest).
April 16. First foal. 46,000Y. Tattersalls October Book 2. Anthony Stroud. The dam is an unraced sister to the winner and Group 3 Chester Vase third Risk Taker and a half-sister to the French listed winner Chasing Stars. The second dam, Post Modern (by Nureyev), is an unraced sister to the Fillies' mile and Oaks winner Reams Of Verse and a half-sister to 7 stakes winners including the Eclipse Stakes and Irish Champion Stakes winner Elmaamul and the dam of the multiple Group 1 winner Midday. *"We did a little bit of work early on with him but he just looks like he wants a bit of time. He seems fairly natural, has a good temperament and a nice action, so he shouldn't have any problem winning races"*.

836. CARABINIERI ★★★
ch.c. Notnowcato – Bidding Time
(Rock Of Gibraltar).
January 28. First foal. Doncaster Premier. £40,000Y. BBA (Ire). The dam ran twice unplaced and is a half-sister to 2 winners

including the listed placed Pietra Dura (herself the dam of a stakes winner in the USA). The second dam, Bianca Nera (by Salse), won the Group 1 Moyglare Stud Stakes and the Group 2 Lowther Stakes and is a half-sister to 4 winners including the dam of the Group 1 Fillies' Mile and Falmouth Stakes winner Simply Perfect. *"He's had sore shins and a splint so he's missed some time, but he has strong quarters and a strong back-end so he'll definitely make a 2-y-o, starting off at six furlongs".*

837. CASHMERE OR CAVIAR ★★★
b.f. Tagula – Sandystones (Selkirk).
February 17. £16,500Y. Doncaster Premier. BBA (Ire). Half-sister to the quite useful 2-y-o 5f winner Sighting (by Eagle Eyed), to the modest 5f winner Tatweer (by Among Men) and the hurdles winner Shingle Street (by Bahhare). The dam, a modest 9f placed maiden, is a half-sister to 3 winners including the Group 3 placed Sonic Boy. The second dam, Sharanella (by Shareef Dancer), is an unraced half-sister to 6 winners including the Prix Jean Prat second Satin Wood. *"She's a filly that's started to thrive and she's growing into a very nice, straightforward 2-y-o. Certainly one for the first part of the season and she goes well".* TRAINERS' BARGAIN BUY

838. COCKNEY DANCER ★★★★
ch.f. Cockney Rebel – Roo (Rudimentary).
March 23. Sixth living foal. Doncaster Premier. £75,000Y. Blandford Bloodstock. Half-sister to the very smart 6f (at 2 yrs) and 7f winner and Group 2 Prix Morny second Gallagher (by Bahamian Bounty), to the useful 7f (including at 2 yrs) and 1m winner Quick Wit (by Oasis Dream), the useful 5f (at 2 yrs) and 7f winner and listed-placed Roodeye (by Inchinor), the quite useful 7f (at 2 yrs) and 10f winner Roodolph (by Primo Valentino) and the fair 6f winner of 6 races Averoo (by Averti). The dam, a quite useful 2-y-o 5f and 6f winner, is a half-sister to 4 winners including the Group 2 6f Gimcrack Stakes winner Bannister (by Inchinor). The second dam, Shall We Run (by Hotfoot), placed once over 5f at 2 yrs, is a full or half-sister to 8 winners including the Group 1 6f Cheveley Park Stakes winner Dead Certain. *"She looks a bit of a standout really. She's done a bit of work this morning up the grass and she went very well. A very imposing filly to look at, she has a bit of size and scope, plus a good temperament. Given her pedigree you'd expect some speed as well and hopefully she'll start at Newmarket's Craven meeting".*

839. CRYPTIC CHOICE (IRE) ★★★★
b.c. Johannesburg – Royal Fupeg (Fusaichi Pegasus).
April 7. First foal. Doncaster Premier. £45,000Y. BBA (Ire). The dam won 3 minor races at 3 yrs in the USA and is a half-sister to 5 winners including the Group 3 Tetrarch Stakes second Emerald Cat. The second dam, Heeremandi (by Royal Academy), winner of the listed Silver Flash Stakes and third in the Group 1 Prix Morny, is a half-sister to 4 stakes winners (including the dam of the Group 1 Prix Saint-Alary winner Nadia) and to the dam of the multiple US Grade 1 winner Flawlessly. *"He looked to be a very forward going horse and he's been working but he's shown us that he needs a bit more time. A very athletic horse, he certainly seems to be one to look out for because he seems to have plenty of natural ability".*

840. DARK DON (IRE) ★★★
b.c. Dark Angel – Bint Al Hammour (Grand Lodge).
March 25. Third foal. Goffs Orby. €65,000Y. BBA (Ira). The dam is an unplaced half-sister to 11 winners including the Group 3 Meld Stakes winner Muakaad. The second dam, Forest Lair (by Habitat), won once at 2 yrs and is a half-sister to 4 winners including the triple Group 3 winner Pampabird. *"A horse we always liked as a yearling, but he's grown an awful lot and you wouldn't recognise him now. He has a very good temperament and he'll be out by mid-season if not before. I expect he'll have plenty of speed, so we'll start him at six furlongs I should think".*

841. ELLAAL ★★★★
b.c. Oasis Dream – Capistrano Day (Diesis).
April 17. Sixth foal. 220,000Y. Tattersalls October Book 1. Shadwell Estate Co. Brother to the fairly useful 2-y-o 6f winner and Group 3 Nell Gwyn Stakes second Dream Day, closely related to the fair 7f and 1m winner of 4 races Green Agenda (by Anabaa) and a

winner in Greece (by Green Desert) and half-brother to the useful 6f (at 2 yrs) to 1m winner and Group 3 Supreme Stakes third Sabbeeh (by Red Ransom). The dam, a smart listed 7f winner, was fourth in the 1,000 Guineas and is a full or half-sister to 5 winners. The second dam, Alcando (by Alzao), a smart 5f (at 2 yrs) to 10f winner here, subsequently won the Grade 1 9f Beverly Hills Handicap in the USA and is a half-sister to 5 winners. (Hamdan Al Maktoum). "A nice, athletic horse with a good action, we'll wait until the six furlong races and he'll get seven alright. A good-bodied colt, he's well-bred and he'll hopefully be a nice 2-y-o".

842. ENSEJAAM (IRE) ★★★
b.br.f. Dynaformer – Catch The Ring (Seeking The Gold).
April 23. Sixth foal. $400,000Y. Keeneland September. Shadwell Estate Co. Sister to a minor winner in Canada and half-sister to the Canadian champion 2-y-o filly Catch The Thrill and the minor Canadian winner Catch The Luck (both by A P Indy). The dam, a champion Canadian 3-y-o filly, won 7 races including the Grade 3 Maple Leaf Stakes and is a sister to two other Canadian stakes winners. The second dam, Radiant Ring (by Halo), won 11 races including the Grade 2 Matchmaker Stakes in the USA. (Hamdan Al Maktoum). "She's only just come in because she's been in Dubai. A little bit 'on the leg' at the moment, I suspect she's one for later in the year, but she seems to have a good temperament".

843. FORGOTTEN HERO (IRE) ★★★★
b.br.c. High Chaparral – Sundown (Polish Precedent).
April 4. Fifth foal. Goffs Orby. €110,000Y. BBA (Ire). Half-brother to the fairly useful Irish 5f and 6f winner of 5 races Copper Dock (by Docksider). The dam is a 6f placed half-sister to 5 winners. The second dam, Ruby Setting (by Gorytus), a fairly useful 10f winner at 3 yrs, is a half-sister to 6 winners including the high-class 2-y-o Prince Of Dance, winner of the Dewhurst Stakes (in a dead-heat) and the Group 2 Scottish Derby winner Princely Venture and to the unraced dam of the Japanese Derby winner Fusaichi Concorde. "A lovely looking animal, he's done very well over the last couple of weeks and we like the stallion very much. We obviously won't be running him until the seven furlong races come out, but he has a good temperament and should be one to watch out for".

844. GLASGOW BOY (IRE) ★★★
gr.c. Iffraaj – Alphilde (Ezzoud).
March 11. Sixth foal. Doncaster Premier. £22,000Y. BBA (Ire). Half-brother to a winner in Sweden by Namid. The dam, a quite useful 2-y-o 6f winner, is a half-sister to 3 winners including the South African listed winner L'Passionata and to the Italian listed winner Firebelly. The second dam, Desert Delight (by Green Desert), is an unraced half-sister to 9 winners including the Group 3 May Hill Stakes winner Intimate Guest. "He looks like an early sort but he's had a couple of setbacks which have put him behind. Once he gets over his problems I should think he'll come to hand fairly quickly and he'll definitely make a 2-y-o. A very forward going horse, I should think six furlongs will be his trip".

845. GLEN MOSS (IRE) ★★★
b.c. Moss Vale – Sail With The Wind (Saddlers' Hall).
May 8. Fourth foal. Doncaster Premier. £62,000Y. Half-brother to the fair 2010 2-y-o dual 7f winner Fifth Dimension (by Acclamation) and to Expensive Detour (by Namid), a quite useful 6f winner here and subsequently a winner in France and Greece. The dam, a 10f to 12f winner of 5 races, is a sister to one winner and a half-sister to 5 winners including the useful 2-y-o 10f and Group 3 10f Sandown Classic Trial winner Shield. The second dam, Shesadelight (by Shirley Heights), was placed at up to 2m and is a sister to the Grade 1 Rothmans International winner Infamy (herself the dam of three Group winners). "One of the more expensive Moss Vale's at the sales, he's quite a good-looking colt but he was quite a late foal so he's just going to take a bit of time. We'll take our time with him, but he'll make a 2-y-o in the second half of the year".

846. GRAY PEARL ★★★ ♠
gr.f. Excellent Art – Divine Grace (Definite Article).
March 17. Sixth foal. 95,000Y. Tattersalls

October Book 1. Anthony Stroud. Half-sister to the German Group 2 6f Goldene Peitsche winner of 5 races Electric Beat (by Shinko Forest), to the fairly useful 2-y-o 7f winner and listed placed Blakey's Boy (by Hawk Wing) and the modest 5.2f winner Divalini (by Bertolini). The dam ran unplaced twice and is a half-sister to 2 winners. The second dam, Grey Patience (by Common Grounds), is an unraced half-sister to 8 winners including the listed winners Cape Town and Regiment. *"She's a big filly and has some immature joints so she'll just need a bit more time. I would have thought she'd start at six furlongs but she'll get further. As a yearling she was a beauty and she'll be a nice looking filly one day".*

847. HEYAARAAT (IRE) ★★★
b.f. Lawman – Lanzana (Kalanisi).
January 29. First foal. 48,000foal. Tattersalls December. Shadwell Estate Co. The dam is an unraced half-sister to 8 winners, notably the top-class broodmare Ebaziya, a triple listed winner from 7f (at 2 yrs) to 12f in Ireland and dam of the Group 1 winners Edabiya, Ebadiyla and Enzeli. The second dam, Ezana (by Ela-Mana-Mou), a winner in France at 3 yrs over 11.5f, is a half-sister to 5 winners including the Group 3 10.5f Prix de Flore and Group 3 10.5f Prix Penelope winner Demia. (Hamdan Al Maktoum). *"We've started doing a bit of steady work with her, so we should see her out in May and she seems to have a lot of natural speed. We have two Lawman 2-y-o's and we like them both. She looks like she'll be quite nice and we'll start her off at six furlongs, although she'll get seven later on".*

848. HEY FIDDLE FIDDLE (IRE) ★★★★
b.f. One Cool Cat – Crystal Valkyrie (Danehill).
May 4. Sixth foal. Goffs Orby. €110,000Y. BBA (Ire). Half-sister to the Group 3 Classic Trial winner Above Average (by High Chaparral), to the 2-y-o Group 3 7f Prestige Stakes winner Sent From Heaven (by Footstepsinthesand) and the modest 2-y-o 6f winner Spinning Crystal (by Spinning World). The dam, a fair 10f winner, is a half-sister to 3 minor winners. The second dam, Crystal Cross (by Roberto), a quite useful winner of 4 races at up to 14f, is a half-sister to the Group 1 Haydock Park Sprint Cup winner Iktamal, the French Group 2 winner First Magnitude and the US Grade 2 winner Rockamundo. *"She seems very straightforward, she has a bit of spirit about her which you need in all good fillies really and obviously she's well-bred being a half-sister to Above Average and Sent From Heaven. She looks like she's got a bit more speed than those two and she'll make a 2-y-o. She's not the biggest filly, but they don't have to be".*

849. I'M HARRY ★★★
b.c. Haafhd – First Approval (Royal Applause).
February 11. Second foal. The dam, a fair 6f winner, is a half-sister to 6 winners including the high-class 7f to 11f winner Hawksley Hill (by Rahy), winner of the Arcadia Handicap, El Rincon Handicap and San Francisco Mile (all US Grade 2 events) and the dam of the Group 1 Prix de l'Abbaye winner Benbaun. The second dam, Gaijin (by Caerleon), a useful 2-y-o 6f winner, is a full or half-sister to 5 winners including Thousla Rock (Group 3 Premio Umbria). (Whickfield Stud). *"He's a bit backward in his coat at the moment but he's improving, he has a nice action and seems a very straightforward horse. He should be running around July time and he'll be suited by six/seven furlongs".*

850. INUNDATE (USA) ★★★
b.c. Pleasant Tap – Tinge (Kingmambo).
January 25. Third foal. The dam is an unraced half-sister to the triple US Grade 1 winner Empire Maker and the US Grade 1 winners Honest Lady (herself dam of the US Grade 1 winner First Defence), Chester House and Chiselling. The second dam, Toussaud (by El Gran Senor), a 6f and 7f winner here, subsequently won a Grade 1 in North America. (Khalid Abdulla). *"A lovely looking horse for the back-end of the year and as a 3-y-o. He has a nice temperament and we all seem to like him".*

851. LAUREL LAD (IRE) ★★★
b.c. Oratorio – Laurel Delight (Presidium).
May 24. Tenth foal. 65,000Y. Tattersalls October Book 1. BBA (Ire). Half-brother to the Group 1 Irish Derby and Group 2 Dante Stakes winner Cape Blanco (by Galileo), to the US Grade 2 Argent Dixie Stakes and Grade 2 Kelso Breeders Cup Handicap winner and Grade 1

second Mr O'Brien (by Mukaddamah), the fair 2-y-o 5f winner Laurel Pleasure (by Selkirk) and a winner in Italy by Emperor Jones. The dam, a useful winner of 4 races over 5f, is a half-sister to 5 winners including the high-class sprinter Paris House. The second dam, Foudroyer (by Artaius), ran unplaced twice and is a half-sister to 2 minor winners. *"He was a late foal so we're just taking our time with him. He has a good action and seems fairly athletic but he's one for the second half of the season".*

852. LAWN JAMIL (USA) ★★★
b.c. Jazil – Khazayin (Bahri).
May 15. Fifth foal. Closely related to the useful 2-y-o 6f winner Jaish (by Seeking The Gold) and half-brother to the quite useful 12f and 2m winner Dalhaan (by Fusaichi Pegasus) and the fair 11f winner Jawaaneb (by Kingmambo). The dam was placed over 10f and is a sister to the high-class Prix de l'Arc de Triomphe and Juddmonte International winner Sakhee and closely related to the useful 7f (at 2 yrs) and 10f winner Nasheed. The second dam, Thawakib (by Sadler's Wells), a useful dual 7f (at 2 yrs) and Group 2 12f Ribblesdale Stakes winner, is a half-sister to numerous winners including the top-class middle-distance colt Celestial Storm (winner of the Group 2 Princess of Wales's Stakes). (Hamdan Al Maktoum). *"He's just arrived from Dubai so we don't know much about him. But he seems a very good-looking horse. We need to take our time with the Dubai horses, let them get over their trip and take it from there".*

853. LETSGOROUNDAGAIN (IRE) ★★★
b.c. Redback – Starring (Ashkalani).
April 10. Fifth foal. Doncaster Premier. £32,000Y. BBA (Ire). Half-brother to the quite useful 7f to 9f winner of 11 races Spinning (by Pivotal), to the quite useful 7f to 12f winner Goodwood Starlight (by Mtoto) and the fair 2-y-o 5f winner Daisy Moses (by Mull Of Kintyre). The dam, placed once at 3 yrs in France, is a half-sister to 4 winners the very smart dual listed 5f winner Watching. The second dam, Sweeping (by Indian King), a useful 2-y-o 6f winner, is a half-sister to 10 winners. *"He's working but he's had a touch of sore shins so he probably wouldn't want the ground too fast. He'll be racing sometime in April and he's an attractive looking horse and a good, willing partner. Although he'll start at five furlongs I should think he'll be better over six".*

854. LITMUS (USA) ★★★
ch.f. Latent Heat – Fairy Glade (Gone West).
March 7. Fourth foal. Half-sister to the fair 2-y-o 7f winner Fairy Promises (by Broken Vow). The dam is an unraced half-sister to several winners including the very smart Skimming, a winner of 5 races from 1m to 10f here and in the USA including the Grade 1 Pacific Classic. The second dam, Skimble (by Lyphard), a fairly useful 6f (at 2 yrs) and 10.4f winner here, subsequently won 7 stakes events in the USA. She is a sister to the dam of the 1,000 Guineas winner Wince and closely related to the Grade 1 Washington Lassie Stakes winner Contredance, the listed Roses Stakes winner Old Alliance and to the dam of the Lanson Champagne Stakes winner Eltish. (Khalid Abdulla). *"She should make a 2-y-o, she looks very 'set', has a good temperament and is a straightforward filly. She'll be running when the six furlong races start".*

855. LLANARMON LAD (IRE) ★★★
b.c. Red Clubs – Blue Crystal (Lure).
March 9. Seventh foal. Goffs Orby. €25,000Y. BBA (Ire). Half-brother to the quite useful 2010 2-y-o 1m winner Aciano (by Kheleyf), to the Italian 2-y-o winner and listed placed Golden Liberty (by Statue Of Liberty) and a minor winner in Italy by Grand Lodge. The dam, a fair 10.5f winner in Ireland, is a half-sister to 3 minor winners including the dam of the Group 3 winners Above Average and Sent From Heaven. The second dam, Crystal Cross (by Roberto), a quite useful winner of 4 races at up to 14f, is a half-sister to 7 winners including the Group 1 Haydock Park Sprint Cup winner Iktamal, the French Group 2 winner First Magnitude, the Grade 2 Arkansas Derby winner Rockamundo and the dam of the Group 2 Gimcrack Stakes winner Conquest. *"A bonny horse, he's done well physically and he has a good temperament like a lot by Red Clubs, he's certainly a stallion we like a lot. He'll be a mid-season 2-y-o, he's a good model with good limbs and he's an attractive looking horse".*

856. MARGATE ★★
b.f. Mizzen Mast – Cinnamon Bay (Zamindar).
February 16. First foal. The dam, a French listed 1m winner, is a half-sister to the Group 2 14f Prix Maurice de Nieuil and Group 3 12f Prix d'Hedouville winner Bellamy Cay. The second dam, Trellis Bay (Sadler's Wells), a useful 12f winner, is a sister to the 12f winners Coraline, Spanish Wells and New Abbey and a half-sister to the very smart Group 1 Irish Oaks and Group 2 Prix de Malleret winner Wemyss Bight. (Khalid Abdulla). *"A big filly that's going to need a bit of time and I would think she'll be one for the back-end of the year. She has a good temperament and hasn't done anything wrong, but she's 'on the leg' at the moment".*

857. MASHAER (USA) ★★
b.br.f. Street Cry – Judhoor (by Alhaarth).
April 4. Fourth foal. The dam, a useful listed 6f winner, is a half-sister to 2 winners including the fairly useful 7f and 1m winner Muzher. The second dam, Almurooj (by Zafonic), a moderate 5f and 6f placed maiden, is a half-sister to 7 winners including the smart 6f (at 2 yrs), Group 2 7f Challenge Stakes and Group 3 7f Greenham Stakes winner Munir and the very useful Irish 1m listed stakes winner and Group 1 Coronation Stakes second Hasbah. (Hamdan Al Maktoum). *"Not arrived here yet".*

858. MEZMAAR ★★★★
b.c. Teofilo – Bay Tree (Daylami).
April 29. Third foal. 120,000Y. Tattersalls October Book 1. Shadwell Estate Co. Half-brother to the modest 2010 7f placed 2-y-o The Bells O Peover (by Dynaformer). The dam, useful 2-y-o listed 7f winner, was third in the Group 3 Musidora Stakes and is a half-sister to 4 winners including the Group 1 6f Haydock Sprint Cup winner Tante Rose. The second dam, My Branch (by Distant Relative), a very useful winner of the listed 6f Firth Of Clyde Stakes (at 2 yrs) and the listed 7f Sceptre Stakes, was second in the Group 1 Cheveley Park Stakes and third in the Irish 1,000 Guineas and is a half-sister to 5 winners. (Hamdan Al Maktoum). *"A very good-actioned horse, he's very attractive, we always liked him as a yearling and luckily we ended up with him. He was a little bit of a boy early on, but now he's done a bit of work he's fine. He should hopefully* make a nice 2-y-o and certainly train on as a 3-y-o as well. One to look out for".

859. MODEL PUPIL ★★★
b.c. Sinndar – Modesta (Sadler's Wells).
March 12. Third foal. Half-brother to Monopolize (by Oasis Dream), unplaced in one start at 2 yrs in 2010 and to the fairly useful 7f (at 2 yrs) and 1m winner Intense (by Dansili). The dam, a useful 11.5f and listed 14f winner, is closely related to the Oaks, Fillies Mile, Musidora Stakes and May Hill Stakes winner Reams of Verse and to the smart 2-y-o 1m winner and Group-placed High Walden and a half-sister to the high-class Group 1 10f Coral Eclipse Stakes and Group 1 10f Phoenix Champion Stakes winner Elmaamul. The second dam, Modena (by Roberto), is an unraced half-sister to the smart 2-y-o 7f winner and Queen Elizabeth II Stakes third Zaizafon – herself the dam of Zafonic. (Khalid Abdulla). *"A very attractive looking, strong colt. His pedigree tells us we need to take our time with him a bit and start him off at seven furlongs in the second half of the season. He has a nice temperament and a very forward way about him, so he should be OK all being well".*

860. PIECE OF CAKE ★★
b.f. Exceed And Excel – Sundae Girl (Green Dancer).
February 25. Ninth foal. 65,000Y. Tattersalls October Book 1. BBA (Ire). Half-sister to the useful 2-y-o 6f winner and Group 2 May Hill Stakes second High Heel Sneakers (by Dansili), to the French 6f winner and listed-placed Easy Sundae (by Diableneyev), the modest 13f winner Arctic Cove (by Vettori) and a minor French winner by Dr Fong. The dam, a fair 2-y-o 6f winner, is a half-sister to 6 winners including the Peruvian champion Faaz. The second dam, Charmie Carmie (by Lyphard), was placed 9 times in the USA and is a half-sister to 8 winners including the triple Grade 1 winner Chris Evert (the grandam of Chief's Crown) and the dams of the Kentucky Derby winner Winning Colors and the US Grade 1 winners Confessional and Missed The Storm. *"She got a little injury so she's having that attended to at the moment. She looked to be a very nice filly but she might not been seen this year unfortunately".*

861. PRIVATE MEANS ★★★★
b.f. Dansili – Market Forces (Lomitas).
February 18. The dam, a fairly useful 12f and 14f winner, was listed-placed and is a half-sister to several winners including the useful 2-y-o listed 7f winner Protectress. The second dam, Quota (by Rainbow Quest), a useful 10f winner, is a sister to 4 winners including the top-class Group 1 1m Racing Post Trophy winner and St Leger second Armiger and the useful 2-y-o 1m and 8.5f winner and Group 1 Racing Post Trophy fourth Besiege. (Khalid Abdulla). *"She's very backward in her coat so we're hoping for a bit of sun to help her, but she looks to be very athletic and she'll certainly make a 2-y-o. Not the biggest filly in the world, she's one for June/July time over six furlongs and we all like her at the moment".*

862. QANNAAS (USA) ★★★
b.br.c. Hard Spun – Windsong (Unbridled).
April 30. Fifth foal. $250,000Y. Keene and September. Shadwell Estate Co. Half-brother to a minor winner in the USA by Forestry The dam won 4 races in the USA and was placed in five Graded stakes events including the Grade 2 Orchid Handicap and is a half-sister to 5 winners. The second dam, Falconese (by Imperial Falcon), was a stakes winner of 6 races in the USA. (Hamdan Al Maktoum). *"Just arrived from Dubai, he's just doing steady canters but he does look to be more of a 2-y-o type than some of them".*

863. RED ART (IRE) ★★★★
b.c. Excellent Art – All Began (Fasliyev).
February 1. First foal. Doncaster Premier. £50,000Y. BBA (Ire). The dam ran twice unplaced and is a half-sister to 8 winners including the Group 3 winner Nautilus Pet. The second dam, Sea Mistress (by Habitat), is an unraced half-sister to 2 winners. *"He certainly seems to be a 2-y-o type but we haven't pressed any buttons with him yet. He's just a bit backward in his coat so we'll give him a chance and start him off at six furlongs. He looks very uncomplicated and he might turn out to be a Royal Ascot horse. He's quite 'set' and gives the impression that he might have a bit of quality".*

864. RED DANZIG (IRE) ★★★
b.c. Desert Style – Hemaca (Distinctly North).
April 4. Sixth foal. 80,000Y. Tattersalls October Book 2. BBA (Ire). Brother to the dual 6f (including at 2 yrs) and Group 3 7f Oh So Sharp Stakes winner Souter's Sister and half-brother to the fairly useful 5f (at 2 yrs) to 7f winner of 3 races Premier Fantasy (by Pivotal), the fair 2-y-o 5.5f winner Ficoma (by Piccolo) and a winner abroad by Diktat. The dam is an unraced daughter of the 2-y-o 5f and 6f winner Herora (by Heraldiste), herself a half-sister to 6 winners including the Group 2 Mill Reef Stakes winner Kahir Almaydan. *"He seems very laid back at the moment and doesn't know whether it's Christmas or Easter. Once the penny drops I think he'll make up into a very nice horse, he's very strong and well-made. Built like a sprinter with strong shoulders and a big back-end".*

865. RED SENOR (IRE) ★★★★
b.c. Red Clubs – Belsay (Belmez).
March 4. Tenth foal. Goffs Orby. €130,000Y. BBA (Ire). Half-brother to the 6f, 7f (at 2 yrs) and Group 3 Craven Stakes winner and Group 2 second Killybegs (by Orpen), to the fairly useful Irish 1m (at 2 yrs) and 7.5f winner Pyrenees, a minor winner in Switzerland (both by Rock Of Gibraltar), the fairly useful Irish 2-y-o 6f winner Lady's Mantle (by Sri Pekan), the quite useful Irish 7f winner Dreamalittledream (by Danehill Dancer), the fair 6f (at 2 yrs) and 1m winner Tsaroxy, the minor German 3-y-o winner Beaumont (both by Xaar) and a winner in Hong Kong by Cape Cross. The dam ran unplaced twice and is a half-sister to 4 winners including the Group 3 7f Nell Gwyn Stakes winner and 1,000 Guineas third Crystal Gazing. The second dam, Crystal Bright (by Bold Lad, Ire), won once in the USA and is a half-sister to 4 minor winners. *"He was one of my picks as a yearling. Physically he's done very well since the sale because he's now a strong 2-y-o that should have plenty of speed. He has a lovely action and hopefully he'll turn into a Royal Ascot horse. He won't just be a 2-y-o either, because he has plenty of scope as well".*

866. RED TRUMP (IRE) ★★★
b.c. Red Clubs – Wolf Cleugh (Last Tycoon).
April 22. €82,000foal. Goffs. BBA (Ire). Half-brother to the Group 2 5f Prix du Gros-Chene and dual Group 3 5f winner Moss Vale (by Shinko Forest), to the fairly useful 6f winner and Group 3 6f third Alexander Youth, the modest 2-y-o 6f winner Spennymore (both by Exceed And Excel), the fairly useful dual 6f winner Jarrow (by Shamardal), the fairly useful dual 1m winner Natural Force (by King's Best), the quite useful 2-y-o dual 6f winner Cape Vale (by Cape Cross) and the quite useful 10f winner of 3 races Street Life (by Dolphin Street). The dam is an unplaced half-sister to 8 winners including the Irish listed 6f winner King's College. The second dam, Santa Roseanna (by Caracol), won the listed 9f The Minstrel Stakes, was second in the Group 2 6f Moyglare Stud Stakes and is a half-sister to 9 winners. *"He's slightly weak at the moment so we're giving him a bit of time and letting him enjoy the sunshine. He could be anything but we don't know just yet".*

867. REVEAL THE STAR (USA) ★★★
b.f. Aptitude – Rouwaki (Miswaki).
February 21. Fifth foal. Sister to the smart 7f (at 2 yrs) and listed 1m winner Critical Moment and half-sister to the smart 2010 2-y-o 6f and Group 3 7f Somerville Tattersall Stakes winner Rerouted (by Stormy Atlantic), the quite useful 1m winner Rattan (by Royal Anthem) and the fair dual 1m winner Cornish Castle (by Mizzen Mast). The dam is an unplaced half-sister to the Grade 1 Kentucky Oaks winner Flute. The second dam, Rougeur (by Blushing Groom), won over 10f and 12f in the USA. (Khalid Abdulla). *"A very forward-going filly, she just lacks a bit of scope at the moment so we'll give her a bit of time and get some sun on her back. She's very natural, very racey and knows what she's here for. I should think we'll run her over six/seven furlongs from mid-season".*

868. REVELETTE (USA) ★★★
b.f. Mizzen Mast – Skimble (Lyphard).
May 7. Half-sister to the very smart Skimming (by Nureyev), a winner of 5 races from 1m to 10f here and in the USA including the Grade 1 Pacific Classic, to the quite useful 2-y-o 7f winner Search Mission (by Red Ransom) and the quite useful 10f winner Cloud Hopping (by Mr Prospector). The dam, a fairly useful 6f (at 2 yrs) and 10.4f winner here, subsequently won 7 stakes events in the USA. She is a sister to the fair 10f winner Flit (dam of the One Thousand Guineas winner Wince) and is closely related to the Grade 1 Washington Lassie Stakes winner Contredance, the listed Roses Stakes winner Old Alliance and to the dam of the Lanson Champagne Stakes winner Eltish. The second dam, Nimble Folly (by Cyane), is an unraced sister to the very useful 2-y-o Group 3 winner and Group 1 third Misgivings. (Khalid Abdulla). *"A good-looking filly, we haven't done anything with her yet but physically she's started to do very well and she's not going to be backward, so she'll make a 2-y-o".*

869. SAFARJAL (IRE) ★★
b.f. Marju – Wijdan (Riverman).
May 16. Sister to the Group 2 1m Premio Ribot winner Oriental Fashion and to the quite useful dual 10f winner Tanfidh and half-sister to the very useful listed 7f and subsequent US Grade 2 10f winner Makderah (by Danehill), the useful 1m and 10f winner Ezdiyaad (by Galileo), the useful 10f winner and listed-placed Fatanah (by Green Desert) and the fair 10f winner Mohafazaat (by Sadler's Wells). The dam, a useful 1m and 10.4f winner, is a sister to the 7f (at 2 yrs) and 1m listed winner Sarayir and a half-sister to the brilliant 2,000 Guineas, Derby, Eclipse and King George winner Nashwan and to the high-class middle distance colt Unfuwain. The second dam, Height of Fashion (by Bustino), a high-class winner of 5 races from 7f to 12f including the Group 2 Princess of Wales's Stakes, is a half-sister to the good middle-distance colt Milford. (Hamdan Al Maktoum). *"Not arrived here yet".*

870. SAJWAH (IRE) ★★★★
b.f. Exceed And Excel – Tahrir (Linamix).
February 14. Third foal. Half-sister to the quite useful 2-y-o 7f winner Tamaathul (by Tiger Hill). The dam, a useful dual 7f winner, is a sister to the listed 7f Prix Djebel winner and dual Group 3 placed Mister Charm and to the French listed 7f winner Green Channel and a half-sister to the Group 3 Prix de Guiche winner Mister Sacha. The second dam, Miss

Sacha (by Last Tycoon), won the listed Topaz Sprint Stakes in Ireland at 3 yrs and is a half-sister to 6 winners including the Italian listed 7.5f winner Pinta. (Hamdan Al Maktoum). *"She's a lovely filly. Nice, attractive and bright, she's very forward-going and should be ready by May time. We trained the dam, we liked her and she was a good-looking filly. This one could hopefully be a Royal Ascot job".*

871. SEA ODYSSEY (IRE) ★★★★ ♠
b.c. Dark Angel – Time To Dream (Gone West).
March 19. Second foal. 65,000Y. Tattersalls October Book 2. Anthony Stroud. The dam is an unraced half-sister to 3 winners and to the placed dam of the dual Group 2 winner Pipedreamer. Half-sister to the useful 12f and 13f winner Elusive Dream (by Rainbow Quest) and to the modest 10f winner Dance A Daydream (by Daylami). The second dam, Dance A Dream (by Sadler's Wells), a smart winner of the Cheshire Oaks and second in the Epsom Oaks, is a sister to the 2,000 Guineas winner Entrepreneur and to the very useful middle-distance listed winner Sadler's Image and a half-sister to numerous winners including the Coronation Stakes winner Exclusive. *"He ran at Windsor at the start of the season and just showed too much speed, getting tired in the end. We're hoping to run him at Chester in May and he's one to keep an eye on. He's got plenty of speed, his sire had the right attitude for the job and he got better with racing and I'm sure this colt will do the same".*

872. SELF CENTRED ★★★ ♠
ch.f. Medicean – Ego (Green Desert).
March 13. Fourth living foal. 32,000Y. Tattersalls October Book 2. Will Edmeades. Half-sister to the fair 2010 2-y-o 7f winner Chef, to the fair 3-y-o 7f winner I'm Sensational (both by Selkirk) and the fair dual 7f winner (including at 2 yrs) Cut And Thrust (by Haafhd). The dam, a very useful 2-y-o dual 6f winner, was listed-placed twice and is a half-sister to 2 winners including the useful 2-y-o 6f winner and Group 2 7f Champagne Stakes third Ghayth. The second dam, Myself (by Nashwan), a smart winner of the Group 3 7f Nell Gwyn Stakes, is a half-sister to 12 winners including the Group 3 Princess Margaret Stakes winner Bluebook. (Mrs E Roberts).

"She seems very straightforward and she'll make a 2-y-o but we'll wait until June time I would think and take it from there. She has a good action and although she isn't the biggest there's plenty of her".

873. SEQUOIA ★★★
b.c. Sharmardal – Atnab (Riverman).
March 10. Tenth foal. 55,000Y. Tattersalls October Book 1. Highflyer Bloodstock. Half-brother to the useful French 9.5f (at 2 yrs) to 15f winner and listed-placed Grey Mystique (by Linamix), to the quite useful 2-y-o 8.3f and subsequent US winner Millestan (by Invincible Spirit) and 2 winners in Greece by Fasliyev and Refuse To Bend. The dam, a modest 12f winner, is a half-sister to 6 winners including the useful 2-y-o 6f and 7f winner Muhab. The second dam, Magic Slipper (by Habitat), a useful 10f and 11.5f winner, is a half-sister to the 1,000 Guineas winner Fairy Footsteps and to the St Leger winner Light Cavalry. *"He unfortunately threw a splint so it set him back a bit, but he's a strong looking colt and he was always going to make a 2-y-o. Once we get him back and going I would have thought he'd be a mid-season type. He should get a mile eventually but he has a bit of speed so we'll set him off at six or seven furlongs".*

874. SHAME ON YOU (IRE) ★★★★
ch.f. Shamardal – Woodlass (Woodman).
April 6. Fourth foal. 75,000Y. Tattersalls October Book 1. BBA (Ire). Half-sister to Makheelah (by Dansili), placed fourth once over 7f from 2 starts at 2 yrs in 2010, to the French 2-y-o 7f and subsequent US listed stakes winner and Grade 3 placed Duke Of Homberg (by Dynaformer) and the modest 7f winner Always Dazzling (by Cadeaux Genereux). The dam won 3 races in France and the USA, was stakes-placed and is a half-sister to 8 winners including the 2-y-o listed Prix Herod winner Vitaba. The second dam, Vitola (by Sallust), won 3 races in France and was Grade 2 placed in the USA and is a half-sister to 5 winners. *"She's going to make a 2-y-o when the six furlong races start. A strong looking filly, she's a proper 2-y-o type with a good temperament and she's a willing partner. We haven't done any fast work with her yet, but I don't think it'll take too long and she'll be ready to go".*

875. SHAWKA ★★★
b.f. Oasis Dream – Wissal (Woodman).
April 22. Closely related to the very useful 2-y-o listed 7f Star Stakes winner and Group 3 7f Prestige Stakes second Mudaaraah (by Cape Cross) and to the useful listed 6f winner Ethaara (by Green Desert) and half-sister to the useful 2-y-o listed 7f winner Sudoor (by Fantastic Light). The dam is an unraced sister to the high-class 2-y-o Group 2 7f Laurent Perrier Champagne Stakes Bahhare and a half-sister to the Group 1 1m St James's Palace Stakes and Group 1 1m Queen Elizabeth II Stakes winner Bahri. The second dam, Wasnah (by Nijinsky), a fairly useful maiden, was placed at up to 10.5f and is a half-sister to the Group/Graded stakes winners Dance Bid, Northern Plain and Winglet. (Hamdan Al Maktoum). *"She looks to be quite sharp although she's a bit backward in her coat so we'll give her a bit more time. She'll be a 2-y-o if anything and she's done very well recently. A 2-y-o type for six furlongs".*

876. WEST LEAKE DIMAN (IRE) ★★★
b.c. Namid – Roselyn (Efisio).
March 22. Sixth foal. £20,000Y. Doncaster Premier. BBA (Ire). Brother to the fair 2010 2-y-o 6f winner Squires Gate and half-brother to the fair 1m to 10f winner of 5 races Kimono My House (by Dr Fong) and to a minor Italian 4-y-o winner by Mark Of Esteem. The dam, a modest maiden, was placed fourth 3 times at 2 yrs over 6f and 7f. She is a half-sister to 3 winners including Riberac, a winner of 3 listed events and third in the Group 2 Sun Chariot Stakes. The second dam, Ciboure (by Norwick), a fair 6f (at 2 yrs) and 1m winner of 3 races, is a half-sister to 4 winners. *"A full-brother to Squires Gate who started off in the Brocklesby last year. He's slightly different in that he's a little bit more 'on the leg', but the riders seem to like him. He's very straightforward, with a good temperament and once he fills his frame he'll make up into a nice colt".*

877. WEST LEAKE HARE (IRE) ★★★
b.c. Choisir – March Hare (Groom Dancer).
April 21. Ninth foal. 25,000Y. Tattersalls October Book 2. BBA (Ire). Closely related to the minor Italian 3-y-o winner Krone (by Danehill Dancer) and half-brother to the quite useful triple 10f winner (including at 2 yrs) Toy Show (by Danehill), the quite useful 11.6f winner Kappelmeister (by Mozart) and the quite useful 12f winner Boxhall (by Grand Lodge). The dam, a modest middle-distance placed maiden, is a half-sister to 7 winners including the smart 1m and 10f listed winner Inglenook. The second dam, Spring (by Sadler's Wells), a very useful winner of 3 races from 12f to 14f including a Group 3 event in Italy, was placed in several other Group races and is a half-sister to 7 winners including Pentire, winner of the King George VI and Queen Elizabeth Diamond Stakes. *"A fine, big horse, there's plenty of him and he won't be too backward either. He should have plenty of speed because he's built like a sprinter, so hopefully he'll be out around May time".*

878. WILLIES WONDER (IRE) ★★★
b.c. Moss Vale – Red Letter (Sri Pekan).
January 31. Fifth foal. 26,000Y. Doncaster Premier. BBA (Ire). Half-brother to the fair 7f and 1m winner Hessian (by Barathea) and to the fair 1m winner Reverend Green (by Tagula). The dam, a quite useful 2-y-o 6f winner, is a half-sister to 3 winners. The second dam, Never Explain (by Fairy King), a quite useful 10f winner, is a half-sister to 8 winners including the Irish 1,000 Guineas winner Matiya. *"He's a strong looking colt that's going to make a 2-y-o. He has a good action and although he's a bit heavy through his shoulders that shouldn't be a problem. He seems to have a good temperament, so there's hope for him and we should be starting him off at six furlongs".*

879. ZENAAD (USA) ★★
b.br.c. Henny Hughes – Lady Cruella (Capote).
May 1. Sixth foal. $240,000Y. Keeneland September. Shadwell Estate Co. Half-brother to 3 winners including the triple US Grade 2 winner Leah's Secret (by Tiger Hill) and the Canadian Grade 3 winner Bear Tough Guy (by Roar Of The Tiger). The dam, a minor winner of 4 races at 3 and 5 yrs, is out of the minor US 4-y-o winner Mary's Spirit (by Mr Prospector), herself a full or half-sister to 11 winners including the US Grade 1 winner of 25 races Lady's Secret. (Hamdan Al Maktoum). *"He's a fine, big horse but he was quite a late foal and I*

should think he's one for seven furlongs around September time".

880. UNNAMED ★★
ch.f. Pivotal – Australian Dreams (Magic Ring).
April 6. Fifth foal. 60,000Y. Tattersalls October Book 2. Brian Grassick Bloodstock. Half-sister to the quite useful 12f winner Wadnaan (by Shamardal). The dam, a listed winner of 7 races at 3 and 4 yrs in Germany, is a half-sister to 6 winners including the smart Group 3 5f Palace House Stakes and subsequent US Grade 3 9f winner Needwood Blade and the US Grade 3 winner Islay Mist. The second dam, Finlaggan (by Be My Chief), a quite useful 11f to 2m winner, is a half-sister to 7 winners. "She's only just come in having been in a pre-training yard. She looks like she's going to need a bit of time and we're still learning about her at the moment. I would have thought she's be out in the second half of the season over seven furlongs".

881. UNNAMED ★★★★
b.f. Holy Roman Emperor – Briery (Salse).
March 12. Fifth foal. Half-sister to the quite useful 6f and 7f winner of 6 races Great Charm (by Orpen), to the quite useful 7f to 15f winner of 5 races Fregate Island, the fair 10f, 11f and hurdles winner Pearl (both by Daylami) and the Swiss 2-y-o winner Story Of Dubai (by Dubai Destination). The dam, a modest 3-y-o 7f winner, is out of the unraced Wedgewood (by Woodman), herself a half-sister to 10 minor winners. (Mr & Mrs G Middlebrook). "Although she's only been here about six weeks she's a filly that's not going to need too much work to get her onto the racecourse. She looks very natural and she knows what she's here for. Very tough, she's certainly going to be fairly sharp and we like her".

882. UNNAMED ★★★
b.c. Speightstown – High Walden (El Gran Senor).
April 19. Half-brother to the quite useful dual 7f winner Portodora (by Kingmambo) and to the fair 1m winner Heather Moor (by Diesis). The dam, a smart 2-y-o 1m winner, was Group-placed and is closely related to the Oaks, Fillies Mile, Musidora Stakes and May Hill Stakes winner Reams of Verse and a half-sister to the Group 1 10f Coral Eclipse Stakes and Group 1 10f Phoenix Champion Stakes winner Elmaamul (by Diesis). The second dam, Modena (by Roberto), is an unraced half-sister to the smart 2-y-o 7f winner and Queen Elizabeth II Stakes third Zaizafon – herself the dam of Zafonic. (Khalid Abdulla). "He's a lovely-actioned horse, very well-made horse and very athletic, but we won't be running him until the second half of the year over seven furlongs. Everyone seems to like him".

883. UNNAMED ★★
b.c. Oratorio – Louve Sereine (Sadler's Wells).
April 15. Sixth foal. 25,000Y. Tattersalls October Book 2. BBA (Ire). Half-brother to the moderate 1m winner Louve Heureuse (by Peintre Celebre) and to a minor French winner by Red Ransom. The dam, a fair Irish 12f winner, is a half-sister to 4 winners. The second dam, Louve Romaine (by Alydar), a smart French 10f winner and placed in the Group 1 Prix de Diane and the Group 1 Prix Saint-Alary, is a half-sister to the 5 stakes winners including Louveterie (herself dam of the Group 1 Grand Criterium winner Loup Solitaire). "We've just been taking our time with him because he's just a bit timid and he needs to build his confidence, but he's turning into a lovely-looking horse and he'll certainly make up into a nice 3-y-o I would have thought".

884. UNNAMED ★★★★
b.c. Acclamation – Milly-M (Cadeaux Genereux).
April 20. Seventh foal. 62,000Y. Tattersalls October Book 2. BBA (Ire). Half-brother to the quite useful 7f winner and listed-placed Mimisel (by Selkirk) and to the fair 6f winner Conrad (by Royal Applause). The dam is an unraced half-sister to 3 winners including the useful 6f winner and listed 6f placed Millybaa. The second dam, Millyant (by Primo Dominie), winner of the Group 2 5f Prix du Gros-Chene, is a half-sister to 5 winners including the Group 2 5f Flying Childers winner and very useful sire Prince Sabo and to the Irish listed winner Bold Jessie (herself dam of the Gimcrack Stakes winner Abou Zouz). "A fine, big horse, we like him an awful lot and we're just giving him a bit of time off at the moment because he's so big. He has a very good temperament and a good

action, he covers the ground and we'll start him off at six or seven furlongs in June/July time. A colt with a lot of natural ability".

885. UNNAMED ★★★
b.f. *Holy Roman Emperor – On The Nile (Sadler's Wells).*
February 21. Sixth foal. Goffs Orby. €40,000Y. BBA (Ire). Closely related to the fairly useful 1m and 10f winner Tommy Toogood (by Danehill). The dam, an Irish 2-y-o listed 9f winner, is a sister to the Irish listed 1m winner In The Limelight, closely related to the Singapore Gold Cup and Gran Premio del Jockey Club winner Kutub and a half-sister to 3 winners. The second dam, Minnie Habit (by Habitat), an Irish 4-y-o 9f winner, is closely related to the dual sprint Group 3 winner Bermuda Classic (herself dam of the Coronation Stakes winner Shake The Yoke) and a half-sister to 6 winners. *"A strong looking filly, we still haven't sold her but she seems to have a nice attitude and a good action. Very straightforward, she'll be a seven furlong type in mid-season".*

886. UNNAMED ★★★
b.f. *Excellent Art – Reprise (Darshaan).*
February 14. Fourth foal. 100,000Y. Tattersalls October Book 1. BBA (Ire). Half-sister to the useful 10f winner and Group 3 12f second Leo Gali and to the minor French 12f winner Orient Meissa (both by Galileo). The dam, placed fourth once over 10f, is a half-sister to 3 winners. The second dam, Rapid Repeat (by Exactly Sharp), a quite useful 2-y-o 7f winner, is a half-sister to 5 winners including the Irish Group 3 winner Artema. *"She's a lovely filly and we like her an awful lot. We always liked her as a yearling, she has a bit of class and a nice action. One for the second half of the year over seven furlongs and we're still looking for an owner for her".*

887. UNNAMED ★★★
b.f. *Rail Link – Well Warned (Warning).*
March 7. Half-sister to the very useful listed 5f winner and Group 3 placed Prohibit (by Oasis Dream), to the French listed 6f winner and Group 3 placed Emergency (by Dr Fong) and the French 7f (at 2 yrs) and listed 6.5f winner Prior Warning (by Barathea). The dam, a useful 2-y-o 6f winner, was third in the Group 3 6f Cherry Hinton Stakes and is a sister to the very useful listed 1m winner Out Of Reach and a half-sister to 4 winners. The second dam, Well Beyond (by Don't Forget Me), was a useful filly and winner of the listed 1m October Stakes. (Khalid Abdulla). *"She's got some stride on her. A lovely looking, big, imposing filly. She's had a small setback, but once we get her back she'll be lovely".*

JOHN HILLS

888. B FIFTY TWO (IRE) ★★★★
br.c. *Dark Angel – Petite Maxine (Sharpo).*
February 1. Twelfth foal. 43,000Y. Tattersalls October Book 2. Amanda Skiffington. Half-brother to the fairly useful 2-y-o 7f winner of 3 races Under My Thumb, the fair 1m to 10f winner of 4 races Luck Will Come (both by Desert Style), the fairly useful 5f and 6f winner of 8 races from 2 to 4 yrs Pipadash, a winner in Sweden (both by Pips Pride), the quite useful 2-y-o 6f winner Moonlight Affair (by Distant Music), the fair 12f winner of 3 races Pont Neuf (by Revoque) and a hurdles winner by Definite Article. The dam, a modest 6f and 7f placed maiden, is a full or half-sister to 11 winners. The second dam, Penny Blessing (by So Blessed), won twice at 2 yrs, was fourth in the Cheveley Park Stakes and is a half-sister to 8 winners. (G Woodward). *"He's nice, he's working now but I think he'll go better over six furlongs rather than five. A horse with a bit of natural ability and he's a really likeable colt with a very laid-back attitude. I was a bit concerned by the way he sticks his head out a bit, but apparently Dark Angel did the same sort of thing. In his work so far he just does whatever the lead horse sets him to do, so he could be a nice horse. Definitely one to give four stars to at the moment".*

889. BOHEMIAN RHAPSODY (IRE) ★★★
b.c. *Galileo – Quiet Mouse (Quiet American).*
April 30. Sixth foal. 50,000Y. Tattersalls December. Bobby O'Ryan. Brother to the unplaced 2010 2-y-o First Sea Lord and half-brother to the Group 3 7f 2-y-o C L Weld Park Stakes and 3-y-o 6f listed winner and Group 1 7f Moyglare Stud Stakes second Ugo Fire (by Bluebird) and to the quite useful Irish 2-y-o 7f winner Houston Dynimo (by Rock Of

Gibraltar). The dam is an unraced half-sister to 6 winners including the fairly useful 2-y-o 6f and 7f winner and smart broodmare Witch Of Fife. The second dam, Fife (by Lomond), a fairly useful 1m winner, is a half-sister to 5 winners including Piffle (dam of the Group 1 winners Frenchpark and Pearly Shells). (4x4 Partnership). *"He's a smaller, more 'together' horse than my other Galileo colt. He's got some speed, he's a very racey looking colt and we'll be getting on with him shortly because he'll make a 2-y-o. He has a nice way about him and he doesn't over-do himself. He looks like one of those Galileo's that has natural speed as opposed to being a middle-distance 3-y-o type".*

890. BOOMERANG BOB (IRE) ★★★
b.c. Aussie Rules – Cozzene's Pride (Cozzene). **April 9. Sixth foal. Goffs Orby. €30,000Y. John Hills.** Half-brother to 4 winners including the French 7f winner and listed-placed Tsar Xsar (by Xsar) and a minor winner abroad by Northern Hill. The dam is an unraced half-sister to 6 winners. The second dam, Goodnight Moon (by Ela-Mana-Mou), a winner at 2 yrs and third in the Group 3 Killavullen Stakes, is a half-sister to 6 winners. (R J Tufft). *"He's been coming along very nicely and he should be racing in late April. He's been thriving, he's got a lovely way about him and he really 'lays down' when you ask him to pick up a bit. So I think he's quite promising, he's a medium-sized colt with very powerful hind-quarters and he has a lovely, relaxed attitude".*

891. GOLD COIN ★★★
b.f. Rail Link - Rosa De Mi Corazon (Cozzene). **February 6. First foal. €9,000Y. Goffs Orby. Not sold.** The dam, a fair 6f and 7f winner, is a half-sister to the fairly useful 2-y-o dual 7f winner and subsequent German dual listed placed Flor Y Nata. The second dam, Rose Of Zollern (by Seattle Dancer), won 9 races including the German 1,000 Guineas and a stakes event in the USA and is a half-sister to 3 winners. (Peter Stopp, Paul Gold, Luke Tofts). *"Quite a big, scopey filly, she's lovely and yet she wasn't at all expensive. She probably didn't fit the bill at that sale because they were all looking for 2-y-o types there. This filly is by an Arc winner and from a decent family and she's definitely got some natural speed. In my eye she could be anything, I don't expect her to be early but a lot of her riders think she could be – which is slightly surprising. She'll be a 2-y-o from the mid-season onwards, probably over seven furlongs and she's a nice filly".*

892. GRANDE ILLUSION ★★
br.c. Singspiel – Larousse (Unfuwain). **February 19. 16,000Y. Tattersalls October Book 2. Not sold.** Half-brother to a hurdles winner by King's Best. The dam, a moderate dual 12f winner, is a half-sister to the Irish listed winner Cruzspiel (by Singspiel). The second dam, Allespagne (by Trempolino), a French listed winner of 5 races, is a half-sister to 6 winners. *"Very much a horse for the end of the year and as a 3-y-o, but he's probably as good a mover as I've got. He was inexpensive but he just has something about him and we've had a fair bit of luck with Singspiel's. So I just think he's a horse I'll really like one day and he'll probably come out in a seven furlong maiden in the autumn".*

893. INFINITE JEST ★★★
ch.c. Danehill Dancer – Noelani (Indian Ridge). **April 1. Second foal.** Half-brother to the quite useful 2010 2-y-o dual 5f winner Natalisa (by Green Desert). The dam, a Group 3 6f and Group 3 7f in Ireland, is a sister to the Group 1 5f Prix de l'Abbaye winner and smart sire Namid and to the very useful Group 3 6f and 7.5f winner Noelani and a half-sister to the useful Irish 2-y-o 7f winner and dual Group placed Natalis. The second dam, Dawnsio (by Tate Gallery), a useful winner of the listed Topaz Sprint Stakes in Ireland, is a half-sister to 3 winners including the Cherry Hinton Stakes third Miss Bluebird. (D J Abbott & Partners). *"His half-sister has done well but he's a big baby and he's one that's definitely a second half of the year 2-y-o. Without being unkind to him he's one of those Danehill Dancer horses you'd describe as a bit coarse looking. So although I haven't done an awful lot with him he's got size and stature and he moves well".*

894. JOHNNO ★★★★
br.c. Excellent Art – Vert Val (Septieme Ciel). **March 16. 18,000Y. Tattersalls October 1. Not sold.** Half-brother to the 2-y-o Group 3 5f Norfolk Stakes winner Russian Valour (by

Fasliyev), to the modest 5f to 7f winner of 3 races Come Away With Me (by Machiavellian), the moderate 6f winner Valverde (by Sinndar) and 3 winners in France by Bering, In The Wings and Peintre Celebre. The dam won 5 races in France including the listed 7f Prix du Pin and is a half-sister to 4 minor winners. The second dam, Valthea (by Antheus), won once in France and is a half-sister to 12 winners including the French 2,000 Guineas winner and good sire Green Dancer and the US Grade 2 winner Val Danseur and to the unplaced dam of the Dewhurst Stakes winner Alhaarth. (G Woodward). *"I have three Excellent Art 2-y-o's and I like them all. This is a great big horse, rather imposing and absolutely able to do anything I want him to do at this stage, despite his size. I'm slightly frightened of pushing him too quickly, but for me I say he'll make a 2-y-o. He's got size and scope and it looks like he has a bit of ability, so he's one of the most promising 2-y-o's I've got"*. TRAINERS' BARGAIN BUY

895. LIMONCELLO ★★★
b.br.f. Lemon Drop Kid – Tinaca (Manila).
March 18. $100,000foal. Keeneland. Blandford Stud. Half-sister to 7 winners including the US triple Grade 2 winner Quest Star (by Broad Brush), the fair 10f winner Lucky Rainbow (by Rainbow Quest), the minor US 3-y-o winner Zurs Victory (by Storm Cat) and the modest 12f to 14f winner Distant Cousin (by Distant Relative). The dam is an unplaced half-sister to 5 winners including the dual Grade 2 winner Mariah's Storm (the dam of Giant's Causeway) and the Group 2 Prix d'Harcourt winner Panoramic. The second dam, Immense (by Roberto), won 5 races in the USA including a Grade 3 stakes. (4x4 Partnership). *"A beautiful filly, she's one of the nicest we've got, she's a half-sister to a lot of winners and the sire is successful. She's going to need a bit of time to fill her frame, but she looks as though she might have that bit extra. She does everything easily, she has natural speed and she's a really good-looking filly. I love her"*.

896. PAPAL POWER (IRE) ★★★
b.c. Holy Roman Emperor – Summerhill Parkes (Zafonic).
May 2. Fourth foal. Half-brother to the 2010 7f placed 2-y-o, on her only start, Lucky Meadows (by Noverre), to the fair 8.5f and subsequent minor Italian winner Seleet (by Sakhee) and a winner over hurdles by Haafhd. The dam, a useful 3-y-o listed 6f winner, is a half-sister to 7 winners including the useful 2-y-o 5f and 6f winner Ace Of Parkes, the useful dual 5f winner and Moyglare, Lowther and Queen Mary Stakes placed My Melody Parkes and the useful winner of 13 races over 5f Lucky Parkes. The second dam, Summerhill Spruce (by Windjammer), a fair 3-y-o 6f seller winner, is a half-sister to 6 winners including the German Group 2 winner Jimmy Barnie. (Corinthian Partnership). *"He's a workmanlike colt with a bit of a scrappy action and he looks like he's going to be quick. The sire gets them quick and his dam was pretty fast too. I'd say he's a not a beauty but he looks like being a fast performer"*.

897. VIRGINIA GALLICA (IRE) ★★
b.f. Galileo – Papering (Shaadi).
April 28. Ninth foal. 60,000Y. Tattersalls December. Peter Doyle. Half-sister to the Irish 3-y-o listed 1m winner and Group 2 Matron Stakes third Dossier (by Octagonal) and a winner over hurdles by Singspiel. The dam, winner of the Group 2 10f Premio Lydia Tesio, was second in the Yorkshire Oaks, the Prix Vermeille and the Nassau Stakes and is a half-sister to 2 winners. The second dam, Wrapping (by Kris), was placed in the Italian Oaks, the Meld Stakes and the Lancashire Oaks and is a sister to the Group 2 Royal Lodge Stakes winner Reach. (Corinthian Partnership). *"The dam was a really useful filly and it's a lovely family. This filly is a lovely, elegant, unfurnished type and she looks exactly like you'd expect a potential 3-y-o middle distance Group race filly to look at this stage. She's weak and we're only ticking her over, but she's lovely"*.

898. WESTWARD HOPE (USA) ★★★
b.c. Mr Greeley – Morning Cry (Danzig).
January 17. First foal. 50,000Y. Tattersalls October Book 1. Amanda Skiffington. The dam is an unraced half-sister to 10 winners including the Oaks and Irish Derby winner Balanchine, the Group 2 10f Sun Chariot Stakes winner Red Slippers (herself dam of the Prix de Diane winner West Wind) and the Derby third Romanov and to the unraced

smart broodmare Alleged Devotion (the dam of four stakes winners). The second dam, Morning Devotion (by Affirmed), was a useful 2-y-o 6f winner and was third in the Hoover Fillies Mile. (Mr P A Abberley). *"A nice horse, he's done a bit of work and he's a big, strapping colt out of a half-sister to Balanchine. I haven't had many Mr Greeley's but he's got a real, powerful look to him. He's got a great action, he'll make a 2-y-o from May onwards over six furlongs and he'll develop into a miler later on. A very nice horse".*

899. XINBAMA (IRE) ★★★
b.c. Baltic King – Persian Empress (Persian Bold).
February 26. £10,000Y. Doncaster Premier. Amanda Skiffington. Half-brother to the useful 7f to 10.3f winner Scotty's Future, to the Italian 2-y-o winner Persian Net (both by Namaqualand), the fair 6f (at 2 yrs) to 11f winner Rhodamine (by Mukaddamah), the modest 6f to 1m winner of 7 races Wrighty Almighty (by Danehill Dancer), the modest 12f winner Gearbox (by Tillerman) and a winner in Italy by Imp Society. The dam, a modest placed 2-y-o, is a sister to the listed Irish Cambridgeshire winner Persian Royale and a half-sister to 7 winners. The second dam, Route Royale (by Roi Soleil), is an unraced half-sister to 7 winners. *"He's an interesting horse, a half-brother to the Victoria Cup winner Scottish Future and the sire was a similar type, winner of the Wokingham. So he's from a workmanlike family but Baltic King was a tough horse. This colt has a fantastic attitude and he looks like he might be fast enough to start at five furlongs. He's a very happy horse and he'll be racing shortly, he didn't cost much money and he'll start in auction races and go from there. I think he's a cracking little horse".*

900. UNNAMED ★★★
b.f. Dylan Thomas – Clinet (Docksider).
April 12. First foal. 30,000Y. Tattersalls October Book 2. Not sold. The dam won 5 races at 2 to 4 yrs and from 7f to 9f, including a listed event in the UAE, was Grade 2 placed in the USA and is a half-sister to 3 winners. The second dam, Oiche Mhaith (by Night Shift), won once at 3 yrs and is a half-sister to 7 winners. (Wood Hall Stud Ltd). *"She's a lovely filly out of a mare that I trained and she was pretty good. So she's a bit close to my heart and I see her coming to hand in mid-season. She's a medium-sized filly with a bit of quality about her and I like her. She's certainly smaller than her mother but she was like a battleship, so that's not really saying much!"*

901. UNNAMED ★★★
b.c. Diamond Green – Molaaf (Shareef Dancer).
February 2. Fourth foal. €12,500Y. Tattersalls Ireland. Amanda Skiffington. Half-brother to a winner in Russia by Monashee Mountain. The dam is a placed half-sister to 7 winners including Cool Jazz (dual Group 3 winning sprinter). The second dam, Amber Fizz (by Effervescing), ran once unplaced and is a half-sister to 9 winners. *"He's a nice colt, the sire did well with his first crop last year and the dam's a half-sister to a fast horse in Cool Jazz. This fellow looks tough, workmanlike and solid. He had a few spots, which put him out of action for a few weeks, otherwise he'd have been up there doing faster work. He's started that now though, so he's going to be a 2-y-o and I like him. I'm still looking for an owner".*

902. UNNAMED ★★★
b.f. Exceed And Excel – Porthcawl (Singspiel).
February 18. Second foal. 10,000Y. Tattersalls October Book 2. Rod Millman. The dam, a fairly useful triple1m winner here, subsequently won a stakes event in the USA and is a half-sister to the very smart 6f (at 2 yrs) and 7f winner and Group 3 7f Hungerford Stakes second Tarjman and the smart 2-y-o 6f and 3-y-o listed 6f winner Nota Bene. The second dam, Dodo (by Alzao), a fairly useful 3-y-o 6f winner, is a half-sister to 7 winners. (Usk Valley Stud). *"She's very nice, she carries herself very well, her dam was a stakes winner in the USA and she seems to have natural speed. She just needs to furnish up a bit, but she's going to make a 2-y-o for sure and she needs a bit of sun. She was 'bought in' at the yearling sales for just 10,000 guineas which was just ridiculous really, because she was a little bit 'on the leg' which may have put a few people off, but that's all. I can see that she just needs a bit more time yet so maybe the Singspiel influence is telling there".*

WILLIAM JARVIS

903. ASHDOWN LAD ★★★
ch.c. Sir Percy – Antibes (Grand Lodge).
March 25. Second foal. 12,000Y. Tattersalls October Book 2. W Jarvis. The dam, placed over 7f (at 2 yrs) and 1m, is a half-sister to 6 winners including the 1m (at 2 yrs) and Group 3 10.5f winner Prix de Flore winner Australie and the smart 7f and 1m winner and Group 3 placed Forgotten Voice. The second dam, Asnieres (by Spend A Buck), a minor winner in France at 4 yrs, is a half-sister to 9 winners including the Breeders Cup Classic and 9.3f Prix d'Ispahan winner Arcangues, the Prix de Psyche winner and French 1,000 Guineas second Agathe (dam of the triple Group 1 winner Alexandrie) and the dam of the 1,000 Guineas winner Cape Verdi and to the placed dam of the US Grade 1 winner Angara. (The FOPs). *"He's quite a sharp little horse, I have two by Sir Percy and I think they'll both be OK. It shouldn't be long before he's running, although I think he'll be better over six furlongs than five. He's certainly got a chance".*

904. BERLUSCA (IRE) ★★★
b.c. Holy Roman Emperor – Shemanikha (Sendawar).
February 8. First foal. 22,000Y. Tattersalls October Book 2. Bobby O'Ryan. The dam is an unraced half-sister to 5 winners including the French Group 3 10f and Group 3 15f winner Shemima and the French listed winners Shemala and Shemaya. The second dam, Shemaka (by Nishapour), a smart filly and winner of the Group 1 10.5f Prix de Diane, the Group 3 10f Prix de la Nonette and the Group 3 9f Prix de Conde, is a half-sister to 5 winners. *"We quite like this colt and he seems to be going the right way. We had a bit of luck with a 2-y-o by this sire last year and this colt seems a similar type. Quite a forward-going horse, he shouldn't take too long so he'll be a five/six furlong 2-y-o and he's absolutely straightforward".*

905. CAPPIELOW PARK ★★★★
b.c. Exceed And Excel – Barakat (Bustino).
March 16. Fourteenth foal. 25,000Y. Tattersalls October Book 2. Not sold. Half-brother to the 10.3f and US stakes winner and Grade 2 placed Mabadi (by Sahm), to the useful 10f winner and listed-placed Ta Awun (by Housebuster), the fairly useful 10f winner Mudalal (by Dixieland Band), the fairly useful middle-distance and jumps winner Mumaris (by Capote), the quite useful 11.7f winner Mabrooka (by Bahri), the quite useful dual 12f winner Killcara Boy (by Tobougg), the fair 8.5f winner Tadawul (by Diesis) and the fair 7f winner Fakih (by Zilzal). The dam, a fairly useful 14.6f winner, is a half-sister to 6 winners including the Group 1 winners Ibn Bey and Roseate Tern. The second dam, the useful 7.5f and 1m winner Rosia Bay (by High Top), is a half-sister to 5 winners including the Queen Elizabeth II Stakes and Arlington Million winner Teleprompter and to the laced dam of the top-class filly Ouija Board. (Dr J Walker). *"I like this horse, he's out of an old mare but he has a lot of Bustino about him. A very strong colt, he'll be a mid-summer 2-y-o, he has the scope to go on at three and at the moment he looks very promising. We like him a lot – he's very attractive".*

906. CHEVIOT QUEST (IRE) ★★★
ch.c. Sir Percy – Cushat Law (Montjeu).
February 27. First foal. 11,000Y. Tattersalls October Book 3. Not sold. The dam, a modest 12f winner, is a half-sister to one winner. The second dam, Blush With Love (by Mt Livermore), ran twice unplaced in the USA and is a half-sister to numerous winners including Tuesday's Special (Group 3 Prix Exbury). (Mr Anthony Reed). *"He's a very well-balanced horse, the cross looks like a good mating and he's a nice, attractive colt. We think he could be OK, he has a bit of size and scope and there's a bit of quality about him. He was in Book 3 at Tattersalls and I think he slipped through the net".* TRAINERS' BARGAIN BUY

907. LOTHIAN SKY (IRE) ★★★
b.c. Authorized – Golly Gosh (Danehill).
April 9. Third foal. 48,000Y. Tattersalls October Book 2. Ric Wylie. Half-brother to the fair 1m winner Miss Fritton (by Refuse To Bend). The dam won 3 races over 12f and was listed-placed in Ireland and is a half-sister to the Irish listed-placed Misty Peak. The second dam, Miss Declared (by Alleged), is an unraced half-sister to 9 winners in the USA. (Dr J Walker). *"He's an Authorized colt that we*

think a fair bit of. A late-summer type 2-y-o, he's a good mover and straightforward. I'd say he's a good advertisement for his sire, I like him and he'll be a strong horse from mid-summer onwards, probably over seven furlongs".

908. NIP AND TUCK ★★
b.c. Green Desert – Coveted (Sinndar).
April 5. Third foal. 14,000Y. Tattersalls October Book 2. BBA (Ire). The dam is an unraced half-sister to 6 winners including the Group 1 1m St James's Palace Stakes and Group 2 6f Mill Reef Stakes winner Excellent Art. The second dam, Obsessive (by Seeking The Gold), a useful 2-y-o 6f winner and third in the Group 3 10.4f Musidora Stakes, is a half-sister to 7 winners. (Mrs Melba Bryce). *"There's not much of him, but we like him and he's quite a nice individual. It's important for the owner-breeder that he wins a race".*

909. SILKE TOP ★★★
b.f. Librettist – Zaza Top (Lomitas).
February 6. Half-sister to the dual 7f (at 2 yrs) and German Group 2 11f winner and Group 1 German Derby second Zazou (by Shamardal) and to the French 12f and 2m 2f winner Zoe Dream (by Galileo). The dam was second in the Group 3 1m Premio Dormello at 2 yrs and is a half-sister to several winners. The second dam, Zorina (by Shirley Heights), won over 1m at 2 yrs in Ireland and is a half-sister to several winners. (Mr K J Hickman). *"Definitely a 2-y-o type, she's quite nippy and she goes well, so don't miss her out of the book. One to look out for".*

910. SCRIPTURIST ★★★
b.c. Oratorio – Lambroza (Grand Lodge).
March 19. Second foal. The dam is an unplaced half-sister to the US Grade 3 9f winner Good Mood. The second dam, Pillars Of Society (by Caerleon), a fairly useful Irish 10f winner, is a half-sister to 5 winners. (Lady Howard De Walden). *"A nice, big, fine horse. When he really thrives and furnishes I can see him being a very attractive horse in mid-summer. He has a good action and I think he has every chance".*

911. UNNAMED ★★
b.c. Dutch Art – Masandra (Desert Prince).
March 21. Second foal. 9,000Y. Tattersalls October Book 2. W Jarvis. The dam is an unplaced half-sister to 2 winners including the 1m Irish Cambridgeshire winner and subsequent Grade 1 Hong Kong Derby fourth Beverly Green (named Masani in Ireland). The second dam, Masawa (by Alzao), an Irish 3-y-o 1m winner, is a half-sister to the very useful Group 2 10f Gallinule Stakes winner Massyar, to the French 1m to 10f and subsequent Grade 3 1m Arcadia Stakes winner Madjaristan and the high-class broodmare Masskana (dam of the Group 1 winners Eagle Mountain and Sulk). (Rupert Villers & Partners). *"He had a setback from which he's now recovered but he won't be the early type I was looking forward to. He's on the back burner now, but I like him and it's a shame that we'll have to wait until late summer for him now".*

EVE JOHNSON HOUGHTON

912. BLING KING ★★★★
b.c. Haafhd – Bling Bling (Indian Ridge).
March 10. Third foal. 24,000Y. Tattersalls October Book 2. Eve Johnson Houghton. Half-brother to the quite useful 2010 2-y-o 7f winner Male Model (by Iffraaj). The dam, a fair fourth over 1m and 10f, is a sister to the very smart dual listed 5f winner Watching and a half-sister to 4 winners. The second dam, Sweeping (by Indian King), a useful 2-y-o 6f winner, was listed placed and is a half-sister to 10 winners. (Peter Deal & Charlie Brown). *"A cracking horse, I'm a big Haafhd fan even if no one else is! He looks the part, he goes the part and he is the part. He'll be out in May and I just think he's a real nice horse. He'll start at six furlongs and he'll get better as he goes further. He's strong and compact – a dark version of my nice horse from last year Orientalist. He's a real professional and I like him a lot".* TRAINERS' BARGAIN BUY

913. BLUEBELLS ARE BLUE (IRE) ★★★
b.g. Three Valleys – Blue Bamboo (Green Desert).
January 22. First foal. Doncaster Premier. £22,000Y. Eve Johnson Houghton. The dam, a modest 7f winner, is a half-sister to one winner. The second dam, Silver Bandana (by Silver Buck), a US stakes winner of 6 races at 3 to 5 yrs and Grade 3 placed twice, is a half-sister to 5 winners. (S Dartnell). *"He looks sharp*

and early. I was asked to buy a 2-y-o type and that's what it says on the tin really. I had to geld him because he was quite cheeky, but I expect him to be racing from late April onwards. He'll get six furlongs later on but I doubt him getting any further and although he's not very big there's plenty of him".

914. LUNAR DEITY ★★★
b.c. Medicean – Luminda (Danehill).
March 17. Fifth foal. 20,000Y. Tattersalls October Book 2. Eve Johnson Houghton. Half-brother to the quite useful 2010 2-y-o 6f winner Rhythm Of Light (by Beat Hollow), to the French 1m listed-placed Lazy Afternoon (by Hawk Wing) and the quite useful triple 7f winner She's In The Money (by High Chaparral). The dam won 2 races in France (including at 2 yrs) and is a half-sister to 3 winners including the US Grade 2 winner Little Treasure. The second dam, Luminosity (by Sillery), won once at 2 yrs in France and is a half-sister to 4 minor winners. (Eden Racing III). "He's not going to be early but he's a beautiful mover, a professional horse and I really like him. He's a good-looking, good-moving horse. He's bred to be a seven furlong or mile 2-y-o, so I'll be patient with him. I'm really pleased my 2-y-o's this year – particularly the colts".

915. ORDERS FROM ROME (IRE) ★★★★
b.c. Holy Roman Emperor – Fatat Alarab (Capote).
May 1. Third foal. 30,000Y. Tattersalls October Book 1. Eve Johnson Houghton. Half-brother to Gentle Audrey (by Elusive Quality), a winner of 2 races in the USA at 2 and 3 yrs and Grade 1 fourth. The dam won once at 3 yrs in the USA and is a half-sister to the dam of the US Grade 3 winner Mrs Kipling. The second dam, Quinpool (by Alydar), a winner of 3 races in the USA and third in the Grade 1 third Kentucky Oaks, is a half-sister to 7 winners. (G C Stevens). "He's lovely – a really good stamp of a horse. The sire isn't that popular because his stock have the reputation of being quirky. This colt is a little bit that way but there's no badness in him and he'd be the best ride up the gallop of any of my 2-y-o's. He behaves immaculately and he works really well, so I expect him to be a nice 2-y-o. I don't want to rush him because he was quite a late foal but I'd like him to be out in May or June. He'll definitely get six furlongs".

916. RASPBERRY FIZZ ★★★
b.f. Red Ransom – Dubai Spirit (Mt Livermore).
April 2. Fifth foal. €10,000Y. Tattersalls Ireland. Eve Johnson-Houghton. Half-sister to the Italian winner of 4 races from 2 to 4 yrs Singdubai (by Singspiel) and to the quite useful 1m winner Canary Islands (by El Prado). The dam, a minor 3-y-o winner in France, is a half-sister to the Japanese stakes winner Vril. The second dam, Phantom Creek (by Mr Prospector), a 6f winner at 3 yrs in the UAE, is a half-sister to 7 winners including Arazi and Noverre. "She's lovely and I'm still looking for an owner for her. If you look at her pedigree you'll see Arazi and Noverre – so there's a lot of speed there. She's quite speedy and tough too and she'll be racing in a couple of weeks. She'll go as fast as the one next door to her – and that doesn't matter if the one next door is slow or fast! A real tough little filly, there's nothing flash about her and I really like her".

917. RUN OF THE DAY ★★
b.f. Three Valleys – Shall We Run (Hotfoot).
April 15. Half-sister to the Group 2 6f Gimcrack Stakes winner Bannister, to the fair 10f winner Ghantoot (both by Inchinor), the quite useful 2-y-o 5f and 6f winner Roo (by Rudimentary), the fair 7f winner Peace Lily (by Dansili), the fair triple 12f winner Strathcal (by Beat Hollow) and the modest 9.4f winner Absolute Majority (by Absalom). The dam, placed once over 5f at 2 yrs, is a full or half-sister to 8 winners including the Group 1 6f Cheveley Park Stakes winner Dead Certain. The second dam, Sirnelta (by Sir Tor), won from 1m to 10f in France. (Mrs F M Johnson Houghton). "She's a bit more backward than I'd hoped. I thought she was going to be sharp and early but she's gone pretty weak on me, so there's every chance that I'll throw her in a field for three weeks when we get some sunshine. When she does come right I'd expect her to be a sprinter, both on pedigree and the way she looks".

918. ZINGANA ★★
b.f. Zamindar – Change Partners (Hernando).
April 7. Fourth foal. 14,000Y. Tattersalls October Book 2. Eve Johnson Houghton.

Half-sister to the fair 2010 dual 1m placed 2-y-o Lady Bridget (by Hawk Wing). The dam, a fair 12f winner, is a half-sister to 8 winners including the useful 2-y-o 6f winner and Group 3 7f Rockfel Stakes third Total Love and the useful middle-distance winner Shonara's Way. The second dam, Favorable Exchange (by Exceller), won 3 races in France from 10f to 12f and is a half-sister to 6 winners including the Group 1 Grosser Preis von Baden winner Valour. "She's a really nice filly but she'll take a bit of time. Quite classy, she'll definitely run as a 2-y-o but not until July or August. She looks like a nice, staying filly so there's no point pushing her".

919. UNNAMED ★★★
b.c. Halling – Red Shareef (Marju).
April 2. Seventh foal. 27,000Y. Tattersalls October Book 2. Eve Johnson Houghton. Half-brother to the smart 6f and 1m winner of 10 races here, in the UAE and USA and listed placed Caesar Beware (by Daggers Drawn), to the fair 5f and 6f winner Radio City, the modest dual 7f winner Orangeleg (both by Intikhab), the modest dual 6f winner (including at 2 yrs) Gainshare and the minor French 1m winner Zylig (both by Lend A Hand). The dam won 3 races at 2 and 3 yrs in Italy and is a half-sister to 5 winners. The second dam, Dash Of Red (by Red Sunset), won the listed Silver Flash Stakes in Ireland at 2 yrs and is a half-sister to 7 winners. (Anthony Pye Jeary & Mel Smith). "He's going to take a bit of time. He's really nice and will be out in the second half of the year. I'd like to think he could win as a 2-y-o but he's definitely a 3-y-o in waiting".

MARK JOHNSTON
920. AIRD SNOUT (USA)
b.br.c. Giant's Causeway – Gold Pattern (Slew O'Gold).
February 18. Ninth foal. $100,000Y. Keeneland September. Mark Johnston. Half-brother to the Group 3 Irish 1,000 Guineas Trial and Group 3 C L Weld Park Stakes winner and triple Group 1 placed Arch Swing (by Arch) and to a 2-y-o winner in Japan by Swain. The dam, a minor US winner of 4 races, is a half-sister to 2 stakes winners in the USA. The second dam, Pattern Step (by Nureyev), won the Grade 1 Hollywood Oaks and is a half-sister to the Grade 2 winner Motley. (A G D Hogarth)

921. ALIANTE
ch.f. Sir Percy – Alexandrine (Nashwan).
April 24. Seventh foal. 50,000Y. Tattersalls October Book 1. Not sold. Half-sister to the promising 2010 2-y-o 1m winner Rasheed (by Oasis Dream), to the fairly useful 12f to 14f winner of 6 races and listed-placed Alambic (by Cozzene), the quite useful 1m (at 2 yrs) and 10f winner Algarade (by Green Desert), the quite useful 11f and 12f winner and listed-placed Allannah Abu (by Dubawi), the quite useful 1m, 10f (both at 2 yrs) and 11f winner Alcalde (by Hernando) and the modest 11f and 12f winner Astrodome (by Domedriver). The dam, a fair 10f to 13f winner of 4 races, is a half-sister to 7 winners including the Nassau Stakes and Sun Chariot Stakes winner Last Second (dam of the French 2,000 Guineas winner Aussie Rules), the Doncaster Cup winner Alleluia (dam of the Prix Royal-Oak winner Allegretto) and the Moyglare Stud Stakes third Alouette (herself dam of the dual Champion Stakes winner Alborada and the triple German Group 1 winner Albanova) and to the placed dam of the Group 1 winners Yesterday and Quarter Moon. The second dam, Alruccaba (by Crystal Palace), a quite useful 2-y-o 6f winner, is out of a half-sister to the dams of Aliysa and Nishapour. (Miss K Rausing).

922. BOUNTY SEEKER (USA)
b.c. A P Indy – Plenty Of Light (Colony Light).
March 1. Sixth foal. $285,000Y. Keeneland September. Mark Johnston. Half-brother to 3 winners including one in Japan by Gone West. The dam won 5 races including the Grade 1 Spinster Stakes and is a half-sister to one stakes winner. The second dam, Iceycindy (by Northrop), a US stakes winner of 7 races at 2 and 4 yrs, is a half-sister to 7 winners. (A D Spence)

923. CRAVAT
b.c. Dubai Destination – Crinolette (Sadler's Wells).
March 20. Ninth foal. Half-brother to the useful 2-y-o 6f winner and Group 2 6f Richmond Stakes third Cedarberg (by Cape Cross) and to

the fair 2011 3-y-o 7f winner Materialism (by Librettist). The dam, unplaced over 8.2f on her only start at 2 yrs, is a half-sister to the very smart Group 3 7f Tetrarch Stakes and Group 3 7f Ballycorus Stakes winner Desert Style. The second dam, Organza (by High Top), a useful 3-y-o 10f winner, is a half-sister to the Group 1 Prix de la Foret winner Brocade – herself the dam of Barathea and Gossamer. (Sheikh Hamdan Bin Mohammed Al Maktoum).

924. DRUMMOYNE (USA)
ch.c. Street Cry – Strike Hard (Green Desert).
February 3. Half-brother to the useful 2-y-o 7f winner and Group 3 6f Sirenia Stakes third Red Alert Day (by Diktat) and to the Japanese winner at 2 and 3 yrs Chorus Master (by Singspiel). The dam won 3 races at 2 and 3 yrs including the Group 3 6f Greenlands Stakes and is a half-sister to 4 winners. The second dam, Chinese Justice (by Diesis), an Irish listed 6f winner, is a half-sister to 4 winners including the dam of the Australian Grade 1 winner Isolda. (Sheikh Hamdan Bin Mohammed Al Maktoum).

925. ERAADA
ch.f. Medicean – Elfaslah (Green Desert).
February 4. Half-sister to 12 winners including the high-class Dubai World Cup and Prix Jean Prat winner Almutawakel, to the UAE 1,000 Guineas winner and Newmarket 1,000 Guineas second Muwakleh, the useful 10f winner Elmustanser (all by Machiavellian), the smart 10f winner Inaaq (by Lammtarra), the fairly useful 7f (at 2 yrs) and 10f Dubai winner Mawjud (by Mujtahid), the useful 1m to 11f winner Alhabeeb and the quite useful 7f and 1m winner Multakka (both by Alhaarth). The dam, a useful winner of three races from 10f to 10.4f at 3 yrs including a listed event at the Curragh, is a half-sister to the Group 1 12f Italian Derby winner and 'King George' second White Muzzle. The second dam, Fair of the Furze (by Ela-Mana-Mou), won the Group 2 10f Tattersalls Rogers Gold Cup and is a half-sister to the listed winners Majestic Role, Norman Style and Proconsular. (Hamdan Al Maktoum).

926. FALCONINTHEDESERT (IRE)
b.c. Clodovil – Mise (Indian Ridge).
January 16. Fourth foal. Goffs Orby. €80,000Y. Mark Johnston. Brother to the Group 1 1m Falmouth Stakes and Group 2 6f Lowther Stakes winner Nahoodh and half-brother to the quite useful 7f (at 2 yrs) and 1m winner Silver Games (by Verglas). The dam is an unraced half-sister to 6 winners including the French Group 3 winner Not Just Swing and the French listed winner Minoa. The second dam, Misbegotten (by Baillamont), a French listed 1m Prix Finlande winner, was second in the Group 2 Prix de l'Opera and is a half-sister to 4 winners. (J Abdullah).

927. FULBRIGHT
b.c. Exceed And Excel – Lindfield Belle (Fairy King).
March 1. Thirteenth foal. 52,000foal. Tattersalls December. R O'Gorman. Closely related to the 2-y-o Group 3 7f Prix Eclipse winner Domingues and to the smart listed 5f winner and Group 2 Diadem Stakes second Baltic King (both by Danetime) and half-brother to the fairly useful 7f (at 2 yrs) and 1m winner Huygens (by Zieten), the fair 9f winner Superior Star (by Superior Premium), the fair 2-y-o 6f winner Red Amazon (by Magic Ring), the Italian 7f (at 2 yrs) and 7.5f winner Whetly (by Dilum), the modest 5f winner of 3 races at 5 yrs Distant King (by Distant Relative) and a winner in Scandinavia by Kirkwall. The dam, a fair 2-y-o 5f winner, is a half-sister to 3 minor winners here and abroad. The second dam, Tecmessa (by Home Guard), is an unraced sister to the Group 3 5f Prix du Petit Couvert winner Manjam. (Sheikh Hamdan Bin Mohammed Al Maktoum)

928. GHOST TRAIN (IRE)
b.c. Holy Roman Emperor – Adrastea (Monsun).
February 24. Second foal. €85,000Y. Arqana Deauville August. Mark Johnston. The dam won 5 minor races in France and Germany and is a half-sister to 8 winners including the Group 2 German 2,000 Guineas winner Aviso and the dam of the Group 1 German Oaks winner Amarette. The second dam, Akasma

(by Windwurf), won 3 minor races in Germany and is a half-sister to 5 winners including the German Group 2 winner Ajano. (A D Spence).

929. HAMIS AL BIN (IRE)
b.c. Acclamation – Paimpolaise (Priolo).
May 6. Sixth foal. Goffs Orby. €52,000Y.
M Johnston. Half-brother to the Group 2 7f Hungerford Stakes and Group 3 7f Solario Stakes winner Shakespearean (by Shamardal). The dam, placed twice at 3 yrs in France, is a half-sister to 7 winners including the Group 3 Prix de Saint-Georges winner Pont-Aven (herself dam of the Group 2 winners Josr Algarhoud and Sainte Marine). The second dam, Basilea (by Frere Basile), is a placed half-sister to 7 winners including the Group winners Bold Apparel and Conte Grimalci. (J Abdullah).

930. HAJRAS (IRE)
b.c. Dubai Destination – Nufoos (Zafonic).
May 11. Third foal. Half-brother to the 2-y-o Group 1 6f Middle Park Stakes and Group 2 6f Mill Reef Stakes winner Awzaan (by Alhaarth) and to the fair 2010 2-y-o 7f winner Tasfeya (by Haafhd). The dam, a useful 5f, 6f (both at 2 yrs) and listed 7f winner, is a half-sister to the 5 winners including the fairly useful 2-y-o sprint winner of 3 races Valiant Romeo. The second dam, Desert Lynx (by Green Desert), a fair dual 6f winner, is a half-sister to the very smart dual listed 5f winner Watching. (Hamdan Al Maktoum).

931. IDLER (IRE)
b.c. Exceed And Excel – Dilly Dally (Rubiton).
March 5. Half-brother to the 2010 French 7f placed 2-y-o Procrastination (by Pivotal). The dam, an Australian dual Group 2 6f winner of 6 races, was Group 1 placed twice and is a half-sister to the Australian Group 1 placed Li Lo Lil out of Faricca (by Millionaire). (Sheikh Hamdan Bin Mohammed Al Maktoum).

932. JOHN LIGHTBODY
b.c. Teofilo – Patacake Patacake (Bahri).
February 27. Sixth foal. 55,000Y. Tattersalls October Book 1. Blandford Bloodstock. Closely related to the Irish 2-y-o 7.5f winner and Group 2 Dante Stakes second Fremantle (by Galileo) and half-brother to the smart triple listed 10f winner Mashaahed (by In The Wings). The dam, a modest 6f and 1m placed 2-y-o, is a half-sister to 9 winners including the Group 2 Champagne Stakes winner Bog Trotter and the US stakes winner and 2,000 Guineas second Poteen. The second dam, Chaleur (by Rouge Sang), a stakes winner in Canada and Grade 3 placed, is a half-sister to 4 winners. (Netherfield House Stud).

933. LEQQAA (USA)
b.c. Street Cry – Guerre Et Paix (Soviet Star).
May 9. Seventh foal. $310,000Y. Keeneland September. Shadwell Estate Co. Half-brother to the very useful listed 10f winner and multiple Group 3 placed Zaham, to the quite useful Irish 10f and hurdles winner Alqaab (both by Silver Hawk), the quite useful 2-y-o 1m winner Haashed (by Mr Greeley) and a winner in the USA by Quiet American. The dam, a 1m winner in France at 2 yrs and listed placed, subsequently won once in the USA and is a half-sister to 6 winners. The second dam, Fire and Shade (by Shadeed), a fairly useful 2-y-o 6f winner, is a half-sister to 7 winners. (Hamdan Al Maktoum).

934. LOST HIGHWAY (IRE)
b.f. Danehill Dancer – En Garde (Irish River).
March 14. Ninth foal. 48,000Y. Tattersalls October Book 1. Mark Johnston. Sister to the Group 3 12f Gordon Stakes winner Rebel Soldier and half-sister to the fairly useful 7f (at 2 yrs), 1m and jumps winner Rifleman (by Starborough), the quite useful 10f winner Fabia and the minor French 3-y-o winner Marie de Bansha (both by Sadler's Wells). The dam, a quite useful 2-y-o 5.7f winner, is a half-sister to 7 winners including the top-class Group 1 1m Queen Elizabeth II Stakes and Group 1 9.3f Prix d'Ispahan winner Observatory and the Group 2 Prix de Malleret winner High Praise. The second dam, Stellaria (by Roberto), won from 5f to 8.5f including the listed 6f Rose Bowl Stakes and is a half-sister to 8 winners. (S J Macdonald).

935. MABROOR (USA)
b.c. Hard Spun – Mayfield (Exploit).
April 7. Fourth foal. $300,000Y. Keeneland September. Shadwell Estate Co. Half-brother to 2 minor winners in he USA by Golden

Missile and Saint Liam. The dam won 2 minor races at 3 yrs in the USA and is a half-sister to 11 winners including 4 stakes winners, notably the Grade 2 winner and Grade 1 placed Penny's Reshoot. The second dam, Ahpo Hel (by Mr Leader), won twice at 3 yrs and is a half-sister to 3 stakes winners including the Grade 2 winner Pok Ta Hok.

936. MASTER OF AGES (IRE)
b.c. Exceed And Excel – Historian (Pennekamp).
March 16. Half-brother to the French 10f and 11f winner and listed placed Antiquities (by Kaldounevees), to the quite useful 2-y-o 9f winner Book Of Facts (by Machiavellian) and the French 10f and hurdles winner Patterning (by Pivotal). The dam, a French listed 10.5f winner, is a sister to one winner and a half-sister to numerous winners including the Dubai World Cup winner Street Cry. The second dam, Helen Street (by Troy), won 3 races including the Irish Oaks. (Sheikh Hamdan Bin Mohammed Al Maktoum).

937. NICE ROSE
ch.f. Teofilo – Souvenance (Hernando).
January 21. First foal. Goffs Orby. €50,000Y. Mark Johnston. The dam, a fairly useful 2-y-o 7.2f winner, subsequently won a listed event in Germany, was third in the Group 1 Italian Oaks and is a sister to the 2-y-o Group 3 1m Prix des Reservoirs winner Songerie and a half-sister to 4 winners including the useful listed winners Soft Morning and Sourire. The second dam, Summer Night (by Nashwan), a fairly useful 3-y-o 6f winner, is a half-sister to 7 winners including the Group 3 Prix d'Arenburg winner Starlit Sands. (J Abdullah).

938. NIMIETY ♠
b.f. Stormy Atlantic – Nadeszhda (Nashwan).
March 17. The dam, a quite useful triple 12f winner, is a half-sister to the useful 2-y-o 6f winner and 7f Group 3 placed Nataliya. The second dam, Ninotchka (by Nijinsky), a listed winner in Italy and third in the Group 3 12f Lancashire Oaks and the Group 3 12f Princess Royal Stakes, is a half-sister to 5 winners. (Miss K Rausing).

939. OASIS LOVE
b.c. Oasis Dream – Lunathea (Barathea).
March 21. First foal. 72,000Y. Tattersalls October Book 2. M Johnston. The dam won 3 races over 11f in France and is a half-sister to 6 winners including the Group 3 Prix de Psyche winner Luna Kya. The second dam, Luna Caerla (by Caerleon), won once at 4 yrs in France and is a half-sister to 7 winners including the Group 1 10f Prix Saint-Alary winner Luna Wells, the French 2,000 Guineas winner Linamix, the Group 2 Grand Prix d'Evry winner Long Mick. (Crone Stud Farms Ltd).

940. PARTY LINE
b.f. Montjeu – Party (Cadeaux Genereux).
February 6. First foal. 42,000Y. Tattersalls October Book 1. Mark Johnston. The dam won the 2-y-o listed 7f Radley Stakes and is a half-sister to 2 winners. The second dam, Forty Belles (by Forty Niner), was placed 6 times in France and is a half-sister to 7 winners including the French Group 3 winner In Clover. (S R Counsell).

941. QUIET APPEAL (IRE)
b.f. Cape Cross – Rise And Fall (Quiet American).
March 21. Fifth foal. Goffs Orby. €35,000Y. Mark Johnston. Half-sister to the fairly useful 2-y-o 6f winner and listed-placed Prime Delivery (by More Then Ready) and to the minor US winner Elite Wildcat (by Forest Wildcat). The dam won once at 3 yrs in the USA and is a half-sister to 3 winners including the listed winner and multiple Group 3 placed Zaham. The second dam, Guerre Et Paix (by Soviet Star), a winner at 2 yrs in France, was listed-placed and is a half-sister to 6 winners.

942. RAFEEJ
b.c. Iffraaj – Muffled (Mizaaya).
April 18. Sixth foal. 80,000Y. Tattersalls October Book 2. Shadwell Estate Co. Half-brother to the fairly useful 2010 2-y-o 5f winner and listed-placed Excello (by Exceed And Excel), to the French 2-y-o 7f winner Hushed (by Cape Cross), the modest dual 10f winner Benbrook (by Royal Applause) and the modest 2-y-o 6f winner Chandrayaan (by

Bertolini). The dam, a modest 3-y-o 7f winner, is a half-sister to 3 other minor winners. The second dam, Sound It (by Believe It), is a placed half-sister to 7 winners including the Cheveley Park Stakes winner Pas de Reponse and the French 2,000 Guineas winner Green Tune. (Hamdan Al Maktoum).

943. TOPCOAT (IRE)
b c. *Exceed And Excel – Janaat (Kris).*
March 1. Half-brother to the very smart Group 1 1m Gran Criterium winner and 2,000 Guineas second Lend A Hand (by Great Commotion), to the fairly useful 1m and 10f winner Emirates Champion (by Haafhd), the quite useful 2-y-o 5f winner Grand Fleet (by Green Desert), the quite useful 10f and 12f winner Soldiers Quest (by Rainbow Quest) and the quite useful 10f to 14f winner Double Deputy (by Sadler's Wells), is a sister to the French 3-y-o listed 10.5f winner Trefoil and a half-sister to numerous winners including the smart middle-distance winners Maysoon, Richard of York, Three Tails (dam of the high-class middle-distance colt Tamure) and Third Watch. The second dam, Triple First (by High Top), won seven races including the Group 2 10f Nassau Stakes and the Group 2 10f Sun Chariot Stakes. (Sheikh Hamdan Bin Mohammed Al Maktoum).

944. VOCATIONAL (USA)
b.f. *Exceed And Excel – Carry On Katie (Fasliyev).*
February 22. Fourth foal. Half-sister to Circus Act (by Cape Cross), unplaced in one start at 2 yrs in 2010. The dam won 3 races at 2 yrs including the Group 1 6f Cheveley Park Stakes and the Group 2 6f Lowther Stakes and is a half-sister to 2 winners. The second dam, Dinka Raja (by Woodman), a minor French 3-y-o 1m winner, is a half-sister to 3 winners. (Sheikh Hamdan Bin Mohammed Al Maktoum).

945. VOCIFEROUS (USA)
b.br.f. *Street Cry – Sander Camillo (Dixie Union).*
March 17. First foal. The dam, winner of the Group 2 Cherry Hinton Stakes and the Group 3 Albany Stakes at 2 yrs, is a half-sister to 3 winners. The second dam, Staraway (by Star de Naskra), won 20 races in the USA including three listed stakes and is a half-sister to 5 winners. (Sheikh Hamdan Bin Mohammed Al Maktoum).

946. UNNAMED
b.f. *Dylan Thomas – Marlene-D (Selkirk).*
April 4. Seventh foal. Goffs Orby. €30,000Y. Mark Johnston. Closely related to the very useful dual 1m winner (including at 2 yrs) and listed-placed General Eliott (by Rock Of Gibraltar) and to the useful 7f (at 2 yrs) and 1m winner Eden Rock (by Danehill) and half-sister to the very useful 6f and 7f 2-y-o winner Shanghai Lily (by King's Best). The dam, a minor Irish 3-y-o 9f winner, is a half-sister to 7 winners including the useful Queen's Vase winner Arden and the French listed winner Kerulen and to the placed dam of the US Grade 1 winner Kiri's Clown. The second dam, Kereolle (by Riverman), is a placed half-sister to 5 winners including the dam of the Group 1 winners Lydian and Ballinderry. (Dr M B Q S Koukash).

SYLVESTER KIRK
947. ACCUSTOMED HH
ch.f. *Motivator – Duty Paid (Barathea).*
March 12. Fifth foal. Half-sister to the modest 7f and 1m winner Duty Doctor (by Dr Fong). The dam, a useful 2-y-o listed 6f winner, is a sister to the useful 1m winner and listed-placed Lady Miletrian and a half-sister to 3 winners. The second dam, Local Custom (by Be My Native), was placed at up to 7f at 2 yrs and is a sister to the listed winner Tribal Rite and a half-sister to the Middle Park Stakes winner Balla Cove. (J C Smith). *"A nice, big, tall, leggy filly. She'll probably take a bit of time and I trained the only winner out of the mare. Seven furlongs or a mile will suit her later on this year".*

948. BERWIN (IRE) ★★★
b.f. *Lawman – Topiary (Selkirk).*
March 25. Fourth foal. €34,000foal. Goffs. Half-sister to the fair 2010 2-y-o 7f winner Bassett Road (by Byron) and to the fairly useful triple 6f winner (including at 2 yrs) Gramercy (by Whipper). The dam, a minor winner in France at 3 yrs, is a half-sister to 4 winners including the Group 3 Prix d'Aumale winner Top Toss. The second dam, Tossup (by

Gone West), won the listed Irish 1,000 Guineas Trial and is a full or half-sister to 5 winners. (Mr & Mrs R G Kelvin Hughes). *"A beautiful mover, she's big and growing all the time. A filly with a good attitude, I like her and it was good to see her 2-y-o half-brother win last year after we bought her. She's precocious mentally but she's getting bigger so I'd like to look after her for a bit, but there's speed in there, so maybe she's one for six furlongs. I like her".*

949. DICKENS RULES ★★★
gr.c. Aussie Rules – Lisfannon (Bahamian Bounty).
March 20. Second foal. Half-brother to the quite useful 2010 2-y-o 5f winner Dress Up (by Noverre). The dam is a placed half-sister to 3 winners including the listed 5f winner of 5 races Dazed And Amazed. The second dam, Amazed (by Clantime), a modest 5f placed 3-y-o, is a sister to the Group 3 Prix du Petit Couvert winner Bishops Court and a half-sister to 5 winners including the listed winning sprinter Astonished. *"Not quite as precocious as his half-brother Dress Up was last year, he's a lot lighter, leaner and has more scope. I love him to death, he's had sore shins so I'm going easy with him now but that will allow him to come on physically. He's just a nice horse with a good attitude. Six furlongs will suit him".*

950. DON'T TEMPT ME ★★★
b.f. Moss Vale – Banutan (Charnwood Forest).
March 23. Fourth foal. Tattersalls Ireland. €24,000Y. Sylvester Kirk. Half-sister to the fair 2010 2-y-o winner Temptingfaith (by Acclamation) and to the fair Irish 10f winner Walter De La Mare (by Barathea). The dam is a placed half-sister to 2 winners. The second dam, Banariya (by Lear Fan), a minor 3-y-o winner, is a half-sister to 5 winners including the US Grade 3 winner Blue Stellar. (Mr T Cummins). *"I loved her at the sales and I paid a bit more for her than usual. She seems precocious enough and the penny has just dropped but the owner's in no panic to get her out early. She just goes along on the bridle nicely but I still think she'll be reasonably early – probably a six/seven furlong 2-y-o".*

951. ELMORA ★★★
ch.f. Elnadim – Ringarooma (Erhaab).
January 30. Second foal. 22,000Y. Tattersalls October Book 2. S Kirk. The dam, a moderate 4-y-o 10f winner, is a half-sister to 2 winners and to the dams of the Group 2 winners Wi Dud and Tariq. The second dam, Tatouma (by The Minstrel), a quite useful 2-y-o 5f and 6f winner, is a half-sister to 4 winners. (Messrs Nicholson, Doran & Wilson). *"A beautiful moving filly with a great attitude and the sire is one of my favourites. I'll give her a bit more time, I loved her at the sales and had to have her. She's strong, forward-looking and one for six or seven furlongs".*

952. ICE MISSILE ★★★★
br.f. One Cool Cat – Exorcet (Selkirk).
February 18. Half-sister to the fair 2010 2-y-o 6f winner Guided Missile, to the very useful 6f winner of 4 races and Group 2 6f Diadem Stakes second Dark Missile, the fair dual 6f winner Night Rocket (all by Night Shift) and the fairly useful dual 1m winner Breakheart (by Sakhee). The dam, a fair 3-y-o 6f winner, is a half-sister to 2 winners including the useful UAE 7f and 1m winner Rock Music. The second dam, Stack Rock (by Ballad Rock), was a very useful winner of 9 races from 5f to 1m including the listed Hopeful Stakes and was second in the Group 1 Prix de l'Abbaye. (J C Smith). *"She's a smashing filly, she has a nice pedigree and quite forward. I did think she'd be early and then she started to grow a bit, but she'll be early enough. If I was looking at 2-y-o's that might be Royal Ascot types she'd be on the short list. When she started off I was rubbing my hands and thinking we'd got a nice one. We'll kick on with her soon, then we'll see".*

953. L'ARLESIENNE ★★★
ch.f. Dutch Art – Angry Bark (Woodman).
February 20. Fourth foal. 26,000Y. Tattersalls October Book 2. Peter Doyle. Half-sister to the fair 2010 2-y-o 9f winner Mattoral (by High Chaparral) and the fair 3-y-o 9f winner Plutocraft (by Starcraft). The dam was placed over 9f and is a half-sister to 4 winners including the French listed winner and US Grade 2 placed Cyrillic. The second dam, Polemic

(by Roberto), a winner over 6.5f at 2 yrs and second in the Prix Saint-Alary, subsequently won a Grade 3 event and was Grade 1 placed in the USA and is a sister to the Group 3 winner Tralos. (Wood Street Syndicate III). *"She's grown quite a bit since we bought her and yet prior to that I did think she'd be early. She had a minor problem and because she's so big I put her on the back burner, but everything's settled down now and we can carry on. A beautiful filly with a nice pedigree and physically she's fine, so she should be running from the middle of the season onwards"*.

954. LONE FOOT LADDIE (IRE) ★★★
b.g. Red Clubs – Alexander Phantom (Soviet Star).
April 3. Third foal. 15,000Y. Tattersalls October Book 2. S Kirk. Half-brother to the fairly useful 2010 2-y-o dual 6f winner Alaskan Spirit (by Kodiac) and to the quite useful 7f winner Ghost (by Invincible Spirit). The dam is an unraced half-sister to 4 minor winners. The second dam, Phantom Waters (by Pharly), won twice at 3 yrs and is a full or half-sister to 9 winners including the Group 3 Solario Stakes winner Shining Water (herself dam of the Grand Criterium and Dante Stakes winner Tenby). (Dr J Wilson). *"A weirdo, but a smashing horse. He has a good 2-y-o pedigree, he'll lead the string as if he was an older horse and loves to be in front and he'll gallop all the time. A tall, leggy horse and physically he needs time. If I get him onto the track from mid-season onwards he could be anything"*.

955. LUCIFERS SHADOW (IRE) ★★★
br.c. Dark Angel – Marianne's Dancer (Bold Fact).
April 28. Second foal. 14,500Y. Tattersalls December. S Kirk. The dam is an unplaced half-sister to 3 winners including the Group 3 placed Lock And Key and the 2-y-o listed 6f and subsequent minor US stakes winner Akanti. The second dam, Lock's Heath (by Topsider), won over 6f and 7.8f in Ireland at 3 yrs and is a half-sister to 4 winners. (Dr J Wilson). *"A nice horse, he's grown a bit so he's not going to be out that early, but he has a good attitude and he'll be racing in May or June. I do like him"*.

956. MRS CASH (IRE) ★★★
b.f. Holy Roman Emperor – Ring Of Fire (Nureyev).
February 13. Eighth foal. 20,000Y. Tattersalls October Book 2. S Kirk. Half-brother to 4 winners including two in Japan by Seeking The Gold and Danehill Dancer. The dam is an unraced sister to the multiple Grade 1 winner Spinning World and a half-sister to 2 winners. The second dam, Imperfect Circle (by Riverman), winner of the 2-y-o listed 6f Firth of Clyde Stakes and second in the Cheveley Park Stakes, is a half-sister to the Group/Grade 1 winners Denon and Chimes of Freedom (herself the dam of 2 Grade 1 winners) and the dam of the German Group 1 winner Saddex. (Mr D O'Loughlin & Mr P Shanahan). *"A smashing, sharp little filly, she has a good attitude and being small she's typical of the sire. An early type with a nice pedigree and she might even be better than she looks"*.
TRAINERS' BARGAIN BUY

957. OPERA BUFF ★★★
b.c. Oratorio – Opera Glass (Barathea).
April 4. Third foal. Half-brother to the quite useful 10f and 11f winner Opera Gal (by Galileo). The dam, a quite useful 8.5f winner, is a sister to the very smart 2-y-o Group 3 7f Solario Stakes winner and Group 1 Dewhurst Stakes third Opera Cape and a half-sister to the high-class stayer Grey Shot and the smart sprint winner of 4 races Night Shot. The second dam, Optaria (by Song), was a quite useful 2-y-o 5f winner. (J C Smith). *"Andrew Balding has the half-sister Opera Gal and he thinks a lot of her. This is a smashing horse with a good attitude, a beautiful head and a nice shoulder. He could be anything and I'm thinking he'll make a 2-y-o in the second half of the season. The pedigree is a mixture of speed and pedigree so it's a bit hard to judge at the moment but he's a nice horse and I like him a lot. One of those with plenty of scope and he'll make a real nice 3-y-o next year"*.

958. NUDE (IRE) ★★
b.f. Redback – Flower Bowl (Anabaa).
February 10. 5,000Y. Tattersalls October Book 3. Sylvester Kirk. Half-sister to the minor French winner (at 2 and 3 yrs) Roadster (by Hawk Wing). The dam, a minor French

winner at 3 yrs, is a half-sister to 4 winners including the French 2,000 Guineas and French Derby winner Lope De Vega and the French Group 3 winner Bal De La Rose. The second dam, Lady Vettori (by Vettori), won the Group 3 Prix du Calvados and is a half-sister to 5 winners. *"A nice little filly, she's owned by a small partnership of my wife Fanny, her sister Lizzie and Tony McCoy's wife. This filly had a sore mouth, otherwise she'd have been ready to run, but she's precocious and she'll be out early enough".*

959. RAFFINN ★★★
b.c. Sakhee – Blue Mistral (Spinning World).
February 9. First foal. 9,500Y. Tattersalls October Book 3. F Kirk. The dam, a modest 1m and 10f winner, is a half-sister to 3 winners including the useful 6f winner of 6 races (including at 2 yrs) and listed-placed Johannes. The second dam, Blue Sirocco (by Bluebird), ran once unplaced and is a half-sister to 8 winners including the listed 7f winner and Group 1 7f Moyglare Stud Stakes second Tamnia, the Group 2 13.3f Geoffrey Freer Stakes winner Azzilfi and the Group 3 15f Coppa d'Oro di Milano winner Khamaseen. (Mr N Simpson). *"He's looking more like a 2-y-o type than any of the others at the moment, which is a bit of a conundrum because he's by Sakhee. He travels along well and I'll wait for as long as possible but if he keeps doing well I'll start him at six furlongs. He looks all 2-y-o, he's forward and he's clean limbed and working well".*

960. ROCK ON CANDY ★★★
b.f. Excellent Art – Rock Candy
(Rock Of Gibraltar).
January 10. First foal. Doncaster St Leger Festival. £20,000Y. Tom Hayes. The dam is an unraced half-sister to 2 winners. The second dam, Strawberry Roan (by Sadler's Wells), a winner of the listed 1,000 Guineas Trial and second in the Irish 1,000 Guineas, is a sister to the Irish 1,000 Guineas and Oaks winner Imagine and a half-sister to 7 winners including the Derby, Irish Derby and King George winner Generous. (Mr T Hayes). *"A big, home-bred filly, she has a good attitude and she's tall and leggy. Precocious enough mentally, she's just a bit 'buzzy' and as far as her physique is concerned I think she'll take time, so I haven't done enough with her yet".*

961. ROMAN MYST (IRE) ★★★
b.c. Holy Roman Emperor – Mystiara (Orpen).
April 2. Fourth foal. 15,000Y. Tattersalls October Book 3. S Kirk. Closely related to Kendwa (by Danehill Dancer), a winner of 4 races abroad. The dam is an unraced half-sister to 10 winners including the Group 3 placed On Credit (dam of the Group 2 Great Voltigeur Stakes winner Stowaway). The second dam, Noble Tiara (by Vaguely Noble), won twice in France and was fourth in the Group 3 Prix de Flore and the Group 3 Prix de Royallieu. (Sapphire Racing Partnership). *"A precocious, sharp looking colt, we'll start him off at five furlongs but he'll probably get better over six. Not typical of the sire on looks because he's tall and leggy, he's not missed a day since I've had him".*

962. TUNDRIDGE ★★★
b.c. Authorized – Salanka (Persian Heights).
February 24. Twelfth foal. 60,000Y. Tattersalls October Book 1. Not sold, 30,000Y. Tattersalls December. Not sold. Half-brother to the useful 6f, 6.5f (both at 2 yrs) and listed 1m winner Salamanca (by Pivotal), to the fairly useful 2-y-o 7f winner and listed-placed Penmayne, the fairly useful 1m and 8.5f winner Salinor (both by Inchinor), the quite useful 7f (at 2 yrs) to 12.3f winner Kaiapoi (by Elmaamul), the fair 9f winner King Kenny (by Lomitas), the poor Irish 7f and 1m winner Set Barabbas Free (by Bishop Of Cashel) and a winner over hurdles by Halling. The dam, a fair 3-y-o 10f winner, is a half-sister to one winner abroad. The second dam, Haskeir (by Final Straw), is an unraced half-sister to 7 winners and to the dams of the Group winners Reprimand, Wiorno, Ozone Friendly, Ardkinglass and Soft Currency. (Mr T Hayes). *"I have a soft spot for him because he's from a family I know well. He's a smashing horse, the sire puts me off a bit because otherwise he's a strong, forward-going horse so it's a conundrum as to whether we should let him rattle on or give him more time".*

963. UNNAMED ★★★
ch.c. Redback – Counting Blessings (Compton Place).
April 19. Third foal. 4,500Y. Tattersalls October Book 3. F Kirk. The dam, a moderate 1m placed maiden, is out of the 3-y-o winner Banco Suivi (by Nashwan), herself a half-sister to 5 winners including the dual listed winner and Group 1 placed My Branch (dam of the Group 1 Sprint Cup winner Tante Rose). "He doesn't have much of a pedigree but he's a smashing horse. A straightforward colt, he just has a touch of sore shins so I've eased off him, but as soon as they've settled down he'll be running. There's a one-third share left in him, so if anyone's interested he'd be a smashing horse to have considering the keep fees will be low".

964. UNNAMED ★★★
b.f. Rock Of Gibraltar – Starry Messenger (Galileo).
April 20. First foal. €70,000Y. Goffs Orby. Not sold. The dam, a fair 12f winner, is a half-sister to the US dual Grade 2 1m winner Tuscan Evening. The second dam, The Faraway Tree (by Suave Dancer), a very useful 6f and 14f winner, was second in the Group 2 Park Hill Stakes and is a half-sister to 12 winners including the high-class 9.3f Prix d'Ispahan winner Sasuru, the high-class Challenge Stakes and Jersey Stakes winner Sally Rous and the dam of the French 1,000 Guineas winner Rose Gypsy. "A nice filly, she's a bit small and wasn't sold at the sales so I was fortunate to get her. She's changed shape physically and grown taller and she has a nice pedigree. A good mover, she's one for later on over seven furlongs".

965. UNNAMED ★★
br.f. Dark Angel – Tanda Tula (Alhaarth).
April 12. Third foal. 6,000Y. Tattersalls December. Fanny Kirk. The dam is an unplaced half-sister to 7 winners including the German Group 2 winner Stormont. The second dam, Legal Steps (by Law Society), won once at 3 yrs and is a half-sister to 5 winners including the South African Group 1 winner Super Sheila. "A big, leggy filly and a good mover with a good attitude. She's going along nicely, she's a little bit backward, but she'll make a 2-y-o later on".

WILLIAM KNIGHT

966. DANCE COMPANY ★★★
b.f. Aussie Rules – Corps de Ballet (Fasliyev).
March 16. Fourth foal. 16,000Y. Tattersalls October Book 3. Not sold. Half-brother to the promising 2010 2-y-o 6f winner (on his only start) Georges Lane (by Diamond Green), to the quite useful dual 6f winner (including at 2 yrs) Dark Lane (by Namid) and the fair 7f winner Compton Park (by Compton Place). The dam, a fairly useful 5f (at 2 yrs) and 6f winner, is a half-sister to 7 winners including the prolific Hong Kong winner of 8 races and over half a million pounds Quick Action and the listed winners Doowaley and Misraah. The second dam, Dwell (by Habitat), a fairly useful 3-y-o 1m winner, was listed-placed and is a half-sister to the dams of the South African Grade 2 winner Gleaming Sky and the smart winner of the Cambridgeshire Cap Juluca. (Mrs P G M Jamison). "She's a really nice filly, a lovely mover and I reckon that looking at her she'll be out around July or August time over seven furlongs. She has plenty of size about her, she has a good temperament and I like her, she seems nice".

967. FLY HAAF (IRE) ★★★
b.c. Haafhd – Rose Indien (Crystal Glitters).
May 5. Twelfth foal. 17,000Y. Tattersalls October Book 2. Blandford Bloodstock. Half-brother to 7 winners including the useful 2-y-o dual 7f winner Sahara Kingdom (by Cozzene), the US stakes winner Salty Sea (by Siberian Express) and the US stakes-placed War Tempo (by Quiet American) and Darkwood (by Fit To Fight). The dam, winner of the listed 6f Hopeful Stakes, is a half-sister to 8 winners including the French Group 2 12f winners America and Majorien. The second dam, Green Rosy (by Green Desert), a French 10f winner and listed-placed, is a sister to the French listed winner Big Sink Hope and a half-sister to 9 winners including the good broodmare Rensaler (dam of the US Grade 1 winner Jovial). (Pheasant Rew Partnership). "I like him, he'll take a bit of time because he's shot up behind but he has a nice way of going, he's a nice mover and I'd say we'd be looking for seven furlongs around August for him".

968. FRAMED ★★★★
ch.f. Elnadim – Photo Flash (Bahamian Bounty).
January 19. Sixth foal. 27,000Y. Tattersalls October Book 2. Not sold. Half-sister to the fairly useful 2-y-o 5f winner and listed placed Deal Breaker (by Night Shift) and to the Group 2 6f Richmond Stakes winner Prolific (by Compton Place). The dam, a fair 1m winner, is a half-sister to 8 winners including the smart 2-y-o Group 2 1m Royal Lodge Stakes winner Atlantis Prince. The second dam, Zoom Lens (by Caerleon), placed once over 7f at 2 yrs, is a half-sister to 4 winners. (Mrs P G M Jamison). *"A nice, scopey filly, a lovely mover and with a bit of class about her. She doesn't look like she's going to be a sprinter and I think we'll be starting her off at seven furlongs".*

969. HOONOSE ★★★★
ch.c. Cadeaux Genereux – Roodeye (Inchinor).
March 15. Second foal. 48,000Y. Tattersalls October Book 1. Portanova Bloodstock. Half-brother to the fairly useful 2-y-o 5f winner Roodle (by Xaar). The dam, a useful 5f (at 2 yrs) and 7f winner, was listed-placed and is a half-brother to 5 winners including the Group 1 Prix Morny second Gallagher. The second dam, Roo (by Rudimentary), a quite useful 2-y-o 5f and 6f winner, is a half-sister to 5 winners including the Group 2 6f Gimcrack Stakes winner Bannister. (Four Men and a Dream Partnership). *"He's just starting to really come to himself now and he should have a lot of speed, looking at his pedigree. I never rush the two-year-olds but this is a nice, solid, medium-sized colt and a well-made horse with a good backside on him. He should start off at six furlongs and I like him. Being by Cadeaux he's just taking that little extra time to come to hand but he's one I certainly wouldn't leave out".*

970. JAMBOBO ★★
b.c. Acclamation – Hovering (In The Wings).
March 6. First foal. Goffs Orby. €50,000Y. Portanova Bloodstock. The dam, a fairly useful Irish 1m and hurdles winner, was listed placed and is a half-sister to 2 winners. The second dam, Orlena (by Gone West), a minor 2-y-o 7f winner in France, is a half-sister to 6 winners including the listed winner and 1,000 Guineas third Vista Bella. (Mr J B Henderson). *"I think he takes more after the damsire In The Wings than Acclamation because he's quite a scopey horse and a bit gormless at the moment, so it looks like he'll want a trip. He's a well-made colt and I would say about August time he'll be out over seven furlongs".*

971. NASSAU STORM ★★★
b.c. Bahamian Bounty – Got To Go (Shareef Dancer).
February 19. Sixth foal. 50,000Y. Tattersalls October Book 2. Portanova Bloodstock. Closely related to the fairly useful triple 7f winner (including at 2 yrs) Swift Gift and half-brother to the quite useful 7f and 1m winner Piano Player (by Mozart), to the fair 12f winner Morning Farewell (by Daylami) and a winner in Spain by Sakhee. The dam, a useful 2-y-o 6f winner, was listed placed and is a half-sister to 3 winners. The second dam, Ghost Tree (by Shareef Dancer), a quite useful 7f winner, is a sister to a Japanese stakes winner and a half-sister to 4 winners. (The Oil Men Partnership). *"A nice, strong, powerful little colt, he should be starting off at six furlongs around May/June time. He looks like he's got ability".*

972. OBLITEREIGHT (IRE) ★★★★
ch.c. Bertolini – Doctrine (Barathea).
March 8. Fourth foal. Doncaster Premier. £30,000Y. Portanova Bloodstock. Half-brother to the fairly useful dual 6f winner (including at 2 yrs) Sunraider (by Namid) and to the fairly useful Irish dual 7f winner Always Be True (by Danehill Dancer). The dam, a fairly useful 2-y-o 7f and 1m winner, is a half-sister 4 winners. The second dam, Auspicious (by Shirley Heights), a fairly useful 10.2f winner, is a sister to the smart Group 2 11.9f Great Voltigeur Stakes winner Sacrament and a half-sister to 5 winners and to the unraced dam of the Group 1 winner Chorist. (The Oil Men Partnership). *"He looks a 2-y-o, he has a big, strong shoulder on him and a powerful backside, so he looks like he's going to be a sprinter and he'll be racing in May".*

973. RING FOR BAILEYS ★★★
ch.f. Kyllachy – Ring Of Love (Magic Ring).
April 12. Eighth foal. 23,000Y. Tattersalls October Book 3. William Knight. Half-sister

to the fair 2010 6f fourth placed 2-y-o Proper Charlie (by Cadeaux Genereux) and to the very useful 6f (at 2 yrs) and 1m dual listed winner and dual Group 2 placed Bahia Breeze (by Mister Baileys). The dam, a fair 5f winner of 4 races (including at 2 yrs), is a half-sister to 7 winners. The second dam, Fine Honey (by Drone), a fairly useful 2-y-o 5f winner, is a half-sister to 7 winners. (G R Bailey Ltd). "She's small, compact and a 2-y-o type on looks, but she's met with a small setback which means she'll not be out until the second half of the season. A powerful looking filly with a big back-end on her and she's quite typical of the sire and will be suited by six furlongs".

974. ROMAN AROUND ★★
b.f. Antonius Pius – Koniya (Doyoun).
April 14. Seventh foal. 20,000Y. Tattersalls October Book 2. T G Roddick. Half-sister to the fairly useful 9f and 10f winner and Group 3 9f Dahlia Stakes second Casilda (by Cape Cross), to the fairly useful dual 10f winner King Of Dreams (by Sadler's Wells) and the minor French 14f winner Kekova (by Montjeu). The dam, a minor winner over 15f at 3 yrs in France, is a half-sister to 7 winners including the listed 7f Irish 1,000 Guineas Trial winners Khanata and Kotama, and to the unraced dam of the dual Derby winner High Chaparral. The second dam, Kozana (by Kris), won 4 races at 3 yrs over 1m (3 times) and 10f including the Group 2 Prix de Malleret and the Group 3 Prix de Sandringham and was third in the Prix de l'Arc de Triomphe. (Mr T G Roddick). "She had a little setback early on, she's quite small but compact and without the injury she'd have been an early type. She's cantering again now but it's early days and I haven't been able to do enough with her to really work her out".

975. STORY WRITER ★★★
b.c. Sakhee – Celestial Princess (Observatory).
March 11. Third foal. 10,500Y. Tattersalls October Book 3. Portanova Bloodstock. Half-sister to the quite useful 2010 2-y-o 7f winner Bloodsweatandtears (by Barathea). The dam, a quite useful 2-y-o 7f winner, is a half-sister to 9 winners including the useful 2-y-o listed 6f and 7f winner Bibury Flyer. The second dam, Affair Of State (by Tate Gallery), a very useful Irish 2-y-o 6f winner, is a half-sister to 7 minor winners. "He's a lovely, big, scopey horse, probably a mile or ten furlongs horse next year but I'm sure he'll be running over seven furlongs this year. He's similar to the 3-y-o half-brother we have called Bloodsweatandtears. I've always liked this colt and he has a bit of class about him". TRAINERS' BARGAIN BUY

976. TENDERLY PLACE ★★★
ch.f. Compton Place – Tender (Zieten).
March 9. Half-sister to the fair 3-y-o 7f winner Mackten (by Makbul). The dam, a modest triple 5f winner (including at 2 yrs), is a half-sister to several winners. The second dam, Jayess Elle (by Sabrehill), is an unplaced half-sister to the very useful listed 7f winner Supercal. (Mrs F Ashfield). "I like this filly, I've trained the brothers and sisters and they've all had weakness in their knees but she's quite racey. A bit small, she's one we should be getting on with, so she's probably one of the early 2-y-o's over five/six furlongs".

977. VIOLA DA GAMBA (IRE) ★★★★
b.f. Alhaarth – Addaya (Persian Bold).
May 20. Tenth foal. 30,000Y. Tattersalls October Book 1. Blandford Bloodstock. Sister to the quite useful 1m winner Udabaa and half-sister to the Group 2 Celebration Mile and listed 7f winner Priors Lodge (by Grand Lodge), the useful 7f to 8.5f winner and listed-placed Penny Cross, the fair 10f winner Kentmere (both by Efisio), the fair 9f to 14f winner Alonso de Guzman, the fair 12f and 2m winner Night Cruise (both by Docksider) and the modest 7f winner Mystical Star (by Nicolotte). The dam ran once unplaced and is a half-sister to 8 winners abroad. The second dam, Night Of Stars (by Sadler's Wells), won a listed event in Germany over 1m and is a half-sister to 3 winners including the Beeswing Stakes, Hungerford Stakes and Kiveton Park Stakes winner Hadeer. (Mrs S M Mitchell). "A lovely filly and a lovely mover, she's just starting to go a bit weak on me but not too badly and don't forget she is a late May foal. But she does have a bit of class about her. She's a bit edgy but if we can keep the lid on her she could turn out to be a really nice filly for the future. Seven furlongs in August will suit her I would have thought".

978. ZAMURAI ★★
ch.g. Zamindar – Indian Mystery (Indian Ridge).
February 17. Third foal. 40,000Y. Tattersalls October Book 2. Portanova Bloodstock. Half-brother to the listed Doncaster Mile winner and Group 1 Racing Post Trophy third Medicine Path (by Danehill Dancer). The dam, a modest Irish 3-y-o 5f winner, is a half-sister to 2 winners. The second dam, Mystic Reason (by Lyphard), won once at 3 yrs and was listed-placed in France and is a half-sister to 9 winners. (Mr B & Mrs D Willis, Mr & Mrs M Tracey). *"He was quite weak but has now started to fill out and he has plenty of size about him. He was always bought to be a back-end 2-y-o but I like him and given the time I think he'll make up into a nice horse".*

979. ZUZU ANGEL (IRE) ★★★
gr.f. Clodovil – Zither (Zafonic).
February 12. Fifth foal. Goffs Orby. €26,000Y. Portanova Bloodstock. Half-brother to Lady Gabrielle (by Dansili), placed fourth once over 1m at 2 yrs in 2010, to the French 2-y-o winner Istimlaak (by Marju) and the fair 8.5f winner Themwerethedays (by Olden Times). The dam, a fairly useful 6f (at 2 yrs) and 7f winner, is a half-sister to 3 winners including the useful 2-y-o listed 6f winner Dowager and the useful 1m (at 2 yrs) and 10f winner Dower House. The second dam, Rose Noble (by Vaguely Noble), a modest 3-y-o 11.5f winner, is a half-sister to 7 winners including the champion two-year-old and high-class sire Grand Lodge, winner of the Dewhurst Stakes and the St James's Palace Stakes. (Mrs N J Welby). *"She's nice, quite precocious and not over-big. A nice mover, she seems to have a good temperament and is one for six or seven furlongs I would have thought".*

980. UNNAMED ★★
ch.f. Teofilo – Dust Dancer (Suave Dancer).
February 11. Half-sister to the listed 1m and subsequent US Grade 2 winner Spotlight, to the quite useful 2-y-o 7f winner Dusty Moon (both by Dr Fong), the fairly useful dual 7f winner Tyranny (by Machiavellian) and the quite useful 2-y-o 7f winner and listed 1m placed Dusty Answer (by Zafonic). The dam won 4 races including the Group 3 10f Prix de la Nonette and is a half-sister to 6 winners including the Group 3 7.3f Fred Darling Stakes winner Bulaxie (herself dam of the Group 2 winner Claxon). The second dam, Galaxie Dust (by Blushing Groom), a quite useful 2-y-o 6f winner, is a half-sister to 2 minor winners. (Bluehills Racing Ltd). *"A backward filly, she didn't come in until quite late but she's a nice mover, a nice size and I would have thought she'd be a back-end 2-y-o. I think most Teofilo's are like that from what I can gather and I don't dislike her at all".*

981. UNNAMED ★★
b.f. Intikhab – Jacaranda Ridge (Indian Ridge).
February 9. First foal. Tattersalls October Book 2. Not sold. The dam, a quite useful 7f winner, is a half-sister to the very smart Group 1 12f Gran Premio del Jockey Club and listed 10f winner Rainbow Peak and the smart 7f (at 2 yrs) and 1m listed winner Celtic Heroine. The second dam, Celtic Fling (by Lion Cavern), a fair 3-y-o 8.3f winner, is a half-sister to the outstanding champion 2-y-o Celtic Swing, winner of the French Derby and the Racing Post Trophy. (Mrs M Bryce). *"I like her, she's a big scopey filly so she won't be early, but she has a good temperament and she's a lovely mover, so I'd say she'll start off around August time over seven furlongs".*

DAVID LANIGAN

982. DUTCH SUPREME ★★★
ch.c. Dutch Art – Barnacla (Bluebird).
April 6. Eighth foal. 15,000Y. Tattersalls October Book 2. Charlie Gordon-Watson. Half-brother to the fair 2-y-o 6f winner Suesam (by Piccolo), to the modest 3-y-o 6f winner Milldown Story (by Lucky Story) and the modest 1m winner Princess Zada (by Best Of The Bests). The dam, a fairly useful 6f winner, is a half-sister to 4 winners including the fairly useful 12f winner Palua. The second dam, Reticent Bride (by Shy Groom), a fair 6f winner in Ireland, is a sister to the Group 2 Lowther Stakes winner Miss Demure. (Mr Trevor Benton). *"He's a big, strong horse, we'll just feel our way with him. There's a lot of speed in the family, he needs a little bit of time to strengthen up but he's got loads of scope and he wasn't expensive. Hopefully he'll be a nice six furlong horse in the mid-summer".*
TRAINERS' BARGAIN BUY

983. IRONICALLY ★★
b.c. Refuse To Bend – Dutch Auction
(Mr Greeley).
April 7. First foal. The dam is an unraced daughter of the minor French winner of 4 races Best Buy (by Danehill), herself a half-sister to 5 winners including the dams of the Group winners Prolix, Bad Bertrich Again, Danefair, Vortex and Prove. (David, Bob & Jane Lanigan & Mrs John Magnier). *"A nice, attractive filly with a lovely stride and hopefully she'll be useful later on this summer. She's strengthened up an awful lot in the last two months and she'll continue doing that. She might not be a really nice filly but she could be useful and she's not useless!"*

984. LEAN ON PETE (IRE) ★★★
b.c. Oasis Dream – Superfonic (Zafonic).
March 22. Fifth foal. 125,000Y. Tattersalls October Book 1. Charlie Gordon-Watson. Half-brother to the minor French 2-y-o winner Paradisiac (by Hernando). The dam, a minor French 3-y-o winner, is a half-sister to 9 winners including the outstanding multiple Group 1 winner Goldikova and the French Group 3 winners Gold Sound and Gold Round. The second dam, Born Gold (by Blushing Groom), won over 8.3f and is a sister to the Group 1 1m Prix Marcel Boussac and Group 1 1m Coronation Stakes winner Gold Splash. (Mr Charles Wentworth). *"He's a nice horse for later on in the summer. He has quite a rounded action but I think that's just because he's growing and his knees are quite open. He should be a nice horse in time and six furlongs should suit him".*

985. MAIN LINE ★★★★
b.c. Rail Link – Cooden Beach
(Peintre Celebre).
January 29. Half-brother to the 2-y-o Group 2 6f Gimcrack Stakes winner and Group 1 7f National Stakes second Shaweel (by Dansili). The dam, a moderate 1m winner, is a half-sister to 2 winners including the listed-placed Roker Park. The second dam, Joyful (by Green Desert), a fair 7f all-weather winner at 3 yrs, is a half-sister to 5 winners including the top-class filly Golden Opinion, winner of the Group 1 1m Coronation Stakes and placed in the French One Thousand Guineas and the July Cup. (Bill McAlpine). *"A lovely horse, it took a bit of time to get him to settle but he's switched off now and he's a very attractive colt. We'll get him out in July or August time and he's a nice sort".*

986. MAIN SEQUENCE (USA) ★★
ch.c. Aldebaran – Ikat (Pivotal).
February 13. First foal. The dam, a French 2-y-o 7f winner, was second in the Group 3 1m Prix d'Aumale and is a half-sister to 2 winners. The second dam, Burning Sunset (by Caerleon), a useful 7f and listed 1m winner, is a half-sister to the Group 1 Oaks winner Light Shift, to the Group 2 10.5f Tattersalls Gold Cup and Group 3 10f Brigadier Gerard Stakes winner Shiva and the Group 2 12f Prix Jean de Chaudenay and Group 3 12f Prix Foy winner Limnos. (Niarchos Family). *"More of a 3-y-o type but he's a very nice horse and he might be the nicest I've had from the Niarchos family. He's very straightforward and growing all the time and although he's a very raw looking horse now he'll be very good-looking in time. Anything he does this year will be a bonus though and he'll not be out before September".*

987. MELODRAMA (IRE) ★★★★
b.f. Oratorio – Lila (Zafonic).
March 11. Fourth foal. 40,000Y. Tattersalls October Book 1. Not sold. The dam, a 3-y-o 1m winner, is a sister to the 2-y-o 1m winner and Group 2 King Edward VII Stakes second Zafonium and a half-sister to 7 winners including the very useful winner of 7 races (including the Group 3 10f Gran Premio Citta di Napoli) Revere. The second dam, Bint Pasha (by Affirmed), won the Group 1 12f Yorkshire Oaks, the Group 1 12f Prix Vermeille and the Group 2 10f Pretty Polly Stakes. (Mr Bob Lanigan & Partners). *"A good, big, strong filly who'll get nicer during the year and she could be OK as a 2-y-o. The sire can get a 2-y-o, he's a bit unfashionable at the moment but his statistics aren't bad at all. She's just a very strong, good-looking filly and seven furlongs should be OK for her".*

988. PROTANTO ★★★
b.c. Lawman – Incoming Call (Red Ransom).
February 10. First foal. 120,000Y. Tattersalls

October Book 2. Charlie Gordon-Watson. The dam, placed third over 7f at 3 yrs on her only start, is a half-sister to 4 winners including the French Group 3 10.5f winner Dance Dress (herself dam of the US Grade 2 winner Costume). The second dam, Private Line (by Private Account), a useful 7f (at 2 yrs) and listed 1m winner, is a half-sister to 8 winners including the French 2-y-o listed 1m Prix de Lieurey winner and Group 1 placed Most Precious (the dam of 4 stakes winners including the French 1,000 Guineas winner Matiara). (Mr B Nielsen). *"He's only just arrived, he's a very good-looking horse and we'll take our time with him. We bought him with the idea that he'd make a mid-summer 2-y-o and he's an attractive colt that goes well but we haven't done anything with him at this stage, so we'll just take our time and see how we go on".*

989. SHESTHEMAN ★★★
b.f. Manduro – Clear Vision (Observatory).
February 22. Second foal. 60,000Y. Tattersalls October Book 1. Not sold. The dam, a moderate 12f and 13f placed maiden, is a half-sister to 4 winners including the useful 2-y-o 7f winner, Group 1 Nassau Stakes second and subsequent US Grade 3 winner Cassydora. The second dam, Claxon (by Caerleon), a very useful 1m (at 2 yrs) and Group 2 10f Premio Lydia Tesio winner, is a half-sister to 3 winners. (Fergus Anstock & Partners). *"In my head I had the idea that she'd take time, being by Manduro, but she's a very scopey filly and not overly big – just a good size. She's a strong filly that goes quite nicely and hopefully in the middle of the summer we'll be able to start her off at six furlongs and maybe win a maiden over seven".*

990. UNNAMED ★★★★
b.f. Shamardal – Cheerleader (Singspiel).
April 16. Third foal. 28,000Y. Tattersalls October Book 2. D Lanigan. Half-sister to the quite useful triple 12f winner Leader Of The Land (by Halling). The dam, quite useful 10f winner, is a half-sister to 8 winners including the smart US Grade 2 1m Colonel F W Koester Handicap and German Group 3 1m winner Ventiquattrofogli and the German 6f to 11f listed winner Irish Fighter. The second dam, India Atlanta (by Ahonoora), is an unraced half-sister to 7 winners including the German Group 3 1m winner Sinyar. (Mr Saeed Altayer). *"Like a lot of the sire's offspring she's not the most attractive looking filly, but very workmanlike and she does everything nicely. Very straightforward, she has a nice action and we like to think that from August onwards she'll be alright".*

991. UNNAMED ★★★
b.c. Teofilo – Deveron (Cozzene).
April 3. Second foal. 50,000Y. Tattersalls October Book 1. Anthony Stroud. Half-brother to the quite useful 2010 2-y-o 7f winner Dffar (by Shamardal). The dam, a very useful 2-y-o 7f winner, was third in the Group 1 1m Prix Marcel Boussac and is a sister to the Canadian stakes winner and Grade 2 placed Windward Islands and a half-sister to 5 winners including the minor US stakes winner Hunter Cruise. The second dam, Cruisie (by Assert), won 3 minor races at 3 yrs in the USA and is a half-sister to 4 stakes winners including the dam of the US Grade 1 winner Capote Belle. (Mr Saif Ali). *"A very good-looking horse, he's big, strong, scopey and has a lovely action. The longer we give him the better, but there's a lot to like about him and he's got a lot going for him. We'll nurse him through the early part of the summer and see how we go, but the 2-y-o half-brother last year was sharp. He's a big, strong horse now and he looks like he'll be a better 3-y-o, but there's a lot to like about him as a potential 2-y-o as well".*

992. UNNAMED ★★★★
b.c. Cape Cross – Eve (Rainbow Quest).
March 11. Sixth living foal. 38,000Y. Tattersalls October Book 1. Rabbah Bloodstock. Half-brother to the useful 7f, 11f and 12f winner Charm School (by Dubai Destination) to the fairly useful 1m winner and listed-placed Admission (by Azamour) and the fairly useful 1m and subsequent UAE 10f winner Dubai Twilight (by Alhaarth). The dam, a quite useful winner of 3 races over 1m, is a half-sister to 7 winners including the listed winners Birdie and Fickle and the French middle-distance winner of 10 races (including 4 listed events) Faru. The second dam, Fade (by Persepolis), is an unraced half-sister to Tom Seymour, a winner of five Group 3 events in Italy. (Mr Saif Ali). *"A

nice horse, he's very straightforward he's going through a little growth spurt at the moment but he's precocious and a good-looker. He has a very good mind, he's a promising looking horse and one for the middle of the season onwards. He'll handle quick ground like all those Cape Cross horses and he's a horse that you'd like to step up during April to see if he could handle six furlongs, although I just have it in my mind that being by Cape Cross he'll want further".

993. UNNAMED ★★★★
b.c. Oasis Dream – Prospectress (Mining).
March 3. Sixth foal. 50,000Y. Tattersalls October Book 1. Rabbah Bloodstock. Half-brother to the fair 2-y-o 5f winner Bellini Rose (by Bertolini) and to a jumps winner by Giant's Causeway. The dam, a US Grade 2 La Prevoyante Handicap winner, is a half-sister to 5 winners including the dam of the Group 3 Princess Royal Stakes winner Trick Or Treat. The second dam, Seductive Smile (by Silver Hawk), is an unraced half-sister to 6 winners including the Group 1 Premio Roma winner Nizon, the US Grade 3 winner Don Roberto and the South African Grade 3 winner Lord Ba merino. (Mr Saif Ali) "A very good-looking horse, he's big and strong but he'll need a bit of time and hopefully we'll be able to get him out in the middle of the summer. He's done everything right and he's a horse that I like. If he turns out to be really nice we'll start him off in a Newmarket maiden over six furlongs and then win his maiden over seven. There's a lot of speed in the family".

994. UNNAMED ★★★
b.f. Dubai Destination – Purple Tiger (Rainbow Quest).
March 15. Fourth foal. 30,000Y. Tattersalls October Book 2. David Lanigan. Half-sister to the smart 2-y-o 6f winner and Group 2 6f Gimcrack Stakes second Taajub (by Exceed And Excel) and to the quite useful 5f and 6f winner Polish Pride (Polish Precedent). The dam is an unraced half-sister to 5 winners including the German Group 2 winner and Italian Group 1 second Notability and the Group 3 Prix La Force winner Simon De Montfort. The second dam, Noble Rose (by Caerleon), won the Group 3 Park Hill Stakes and the listed Galtres Stakes and is a half-sister to 4 winners including Simeon (Group 3 Sandown Classic Trial). (Mr Saif Ali). "A nice, compact, good-actioned filly. She missed a bit of time because she had a spot on her back but she's going again now. She's quite straightforward and should make a 2-y-o over six furlongs".

995. UNNAMED ★★★
b.f. Teofilo – Saabiq (Grand Slam).
February 14. Second foal. 80,000Y. Tattersalls October Book 1. Huntingdon/ Norris. The dam, a fairly useful 2-y-o 6f winner, was listed-placed over 6f and 7f and is a half-sister to one winner in the USA. The second dam, Lucky Lineage (by Storm Cat), a minor winner at 3 and 5 yrs in the USA, is a half-sister to 2 other minor winners. (Mr Saif Ali). "The two Teofilos I have are very similar to each other. This filly is big and strong and she'll get better as the year goes on".

996. UNNAMED ★★★★
b.c. Dubawi – Star Express (Sadler's Wells).
March 10. Fifth foal. 85,000Y. Tattersalls October Book 2. David Lanigan. Half-brother to the 2010 7f placed 2-y-o Desert Shine (by Green Desert), to the modest 5f winner Star Twilight and the moderate 6f winner Haedi (both by King's Best). The dam, a minor 12f winner in France, is a sister to the Group 3 7f Greenham Stakes winner and Irish 2,000 Guineas fourth Yalaietanee and a half-sister to 5 winners including the Group 3 5f Molecomb Stakes winner Sahara Star (herself dam of the Group 2 5f Flying Childers Stakes winner Land Of Dreams). The second dam, Vaigly Star (by Star Appeal), a smart sprint winner of 3 races, was second in the Group 1 July Cup and a half-sister to 6 winners including the high-class sprinter Vaigly Great. (Dr Ali Rhida). "He's a horse I like and he'll be a 2-y-o alright. He missed a bit of time with a niggling problem but he's back trotting now and when we get him back cantering we'll kick on with him. I like him and he's an out-and-out 2-y-o. A nice colt by the right stallion".

997. UNNAMED ★★★
ch.c. Kheleyf – Tarbela (Grand Lodge).
February 10. Fourth foal. 75,000foal. Tattersalls December. A O Nerses. Half-brother to the smart 2-y-o listed 7f and

listed 1m winner Big Audio (by Oratorio) and to the modest 6f winner Spiritual Healing (by Invincible Spirit). The dam, a moderate 7f placed 2-y-o in Ireland, is a half-sister to 2 winners. The second dam, Tarwiya (by Dominion), won the Group 3 7f C L Weld Park Stakes, was third in the Irish 1,000 Guineas and is a half-sister to 5 winners including the Group 3 Norfolk Stakes winner Blue Dakota. (Saleh Al Homaizi & Imad Al Sagar). *"A small, compact 2-y-o type. He looks well, he's got a good stride and we want to get going with him in May if we can, maybe starting him at five furlongs, but more likely six".*

998. UNNAMED ★★★
ch.f. *Galileo – Tilbury (Peintre Celebre).*
April 8. Second foal. 48,000Y. Tattersalls October Book 1. Not sold. The dam, placed fourth over 7f from two runs, is a half-sister to 11 winners including the Group 3 6f July Stakes and listed 3-y-o 9f winner Wharf, the top-class broodmare Docklands (the dam of 3 Group winners including the Arc winner Rail Link) and the dam of the Group 1 winner Linda's Lad. The second dam, Dockage (by Riverman), a winner over 1m at 2 yrs and a 9f listed event at 3 yrs in France, is a half-sister to 3 winners. (Miss Jane Lanigan, Mr Bob Lanigan & Partners). *"When she came in she was very weak and backward, but she's done very well. Strengthening all the time, she has a good attitude and a nice action. She'll strengthen further as the summer goes on and we'll probably start her off at seven furlongs or a mile from August onwards".*

999. UNNAMED ★★★
b.br.c. *Rock Of Gibraltar – Tis Me (Notebook).*
April 3. Half-brother to the fair 12f winner Woodford Belle (by Arch) and to a winner in Canada by Peace Rules. The dam won over 1m in the USA including at 2 yrs and is a half-sister to the dam of the Dubai World Cup winner Well Armed. (Catesby Clay). *"A very attractive colt whose paces are much better when he's cantering. Strong and attractive, hopefully he'll be a June/July sort of horse".*

EDDIE LYNAM

1000. ARMED GUARD (IRE) ★★★
b.c. *Medicean – Fairest Of All (Sadler's Wells).*
March 11. First foal. Goffs Orby. €36,000Y. Eddie Lynam. The dam is an unraced half-sister to 5 winners including the US and Canadian Grade 1 winner Relaxed Gesture and the US Grade 2 winner Evolving Tactics. The second dam, Token Gesture (by Alzao), won the Group 3 C L Weld Park Stakes and is a half-sister to 6 winners including the US Grade 2 winner Wait Till Monday. (Aileen Lynam). *"A lovely horse by Medicean, he's going to be a second half of the season 2-y-o and he'll be a decent 3-y-o but he's a particularly nice colt. He has the same cross as Bankable (by Medicean out of a Sadler's Wells mare). A well-made colt, he's a good walker and a good mover".*

1001. ATTICUS FINCH (IRE) ★★★
b.c. *Kodiac – Hayley's Affair (Night Shift).*
April 8. Sixth foal. Tattersalls Ireland. €20,000Y. Eddie Lynam. Closely related to the Italian winner of 5 races from 2 to 5 yrs Golden Nautical (by Danetime). The dam is an unplaced half-sister to 8 winners including the Group 3 Greenlands Stakes winner Nautical Pet. The second dam, Sea Mistress (by Habitat), is an unraced half-sister to 2 winners. (Edward Lynam). *"He shows a nice bit of speed, he's just getting over a little throat infection but he'll be out in June and he's a sprinting 2-y-o".*

1002. BELOVED LEADER ★★
b.c. *Medicean – Esclarmonde (In The Wings).*
March 29. First foal. 4,000Y. Tattersalls December. Edward Lynam. The dam, a fair 12f placed maiden, is a sister to the Group 3 10f Prix Corrida and Group 3 10.5f Prix de Flore winner Trumbaka and a half-sister to the listed winners Arctic Hunt and Spirit Of Dubai. The second dam, Questina (by Rainbow Quest), won twice at 3 yrs in France and is a half-sister to 6 winners. (Aileen Lynam). *"He could turn out well-bought because he's a nice horse. He'll want a bit of a trip, so you won't see him out until later in the year".*

1003. DIMITAR ★★★
b.c. *Mizzen Mast – Peace And Love (Fantastic Light).*
February 25. First foal. 18,000Y. Tattersalls

December. **Eddie Lynam.** The dam, a quite useful 2-y-o 7f winner, is a half-sister to 2 winners. The second dam, Muschana (by Deploy), a quite useful dual 10f winner, is a half-sister to 4 winners including Jeune, winner of the Group 2 12f Hardwicke Stakes here and the Melbourne Cup in Australia and the very useful Group 2 12f King Edward VII Stakes winner Beneficial. (Edward Lynam). *"A speedy horse, he's a little bit immature at present but we like him a lot. The dam was second in her maiden as a 2-y-o to Flashy Wings, she was quick and she's a half-sister to a nice horse we had called Senior that we sold to Hong Kong. I like this colt and he shows speed".*

1004. FRENCH EMPEROR (IRE) ★★★
b.c. Holy Roman Emperor – Se La Vie (Highest Honor).
February 7. Second foal. €14,000Y. Tattersalls Ireland. Eddie Lynam. The dam won 2 minor races at 2 and 3 yrs in France and is a half-sister to 4 winners including the Canadian stakes winner and Grade 2 placed Daylight Come. The second dam, Lady Winner (by Fabulous Dancer), won the Group 2 Prix d'Astarte and the Grade 3 Chrysanthemum Handicap and is a half-sister to 4 winners. (T Dalzell). *"He's had a run already when he shaped with promise. He'll be out again in May, stepping up to six furlongs and he shouldn't have a problem winning his maiden. He'll get a mile later and he's a nice horse with a nice page. He lacks a bit of scope, but he's a stocky horse".*

1005. HUGENOT (IRE) ★★★
ch.c. Choisir – All Elegance (Key Of Luck).
January 31. First foal. The dam ran twice unplaced and is a half-sister to 7 winners including the smart Irish 5f and listed 6f winner Rolo Tomasi, the useful 5f and 10f winner Eastern Breeze, the useful German 6.5f winner and German Group 2 1,000 Guineas second Elegant Ridge and the Irish 2-y-o 1m winner and listed 6f placed Summer Sunset. The second dam, Elegant Bloom (by Be My Guest), a quite useful Irish 2-y-o 6f winner, stayed 7f and is a full or half-sister to 12 winners including two stakes winners. (Oxford Racing Partnership). *"He shows a bit of speed, he'll start his career in April over five furlongs and then he'll probably step up to six. He's out of a half-sister to a nice horse I trained called Rolo Tomasi".*

1006. KHYBER PASS ★★★★
b.c. Three Valleys – My Golly (Mozart).
March 5. Third foal. 10,000Y. Tattersalls October Book 3. BBA (Ire). Half-brother to the promising 2010 2-y-o 6f winner (on her only start) Hallelujah (by Avonbridge) and to the fair triple 5f winner (including at 2 yrs) Tom Folan (by Namid). The dam is an unraced half-sister to 3 minor winners. The second dam, Bedazzling (by Darshaan), a dual 7f winner and fourth in the Group 2 1m Falmouth Stakes, is a sister to the listed 10f winner and Group 2 12f Great Voltigeur Stakes fourth Bustan and a half-sister to 3 winners. (Aileen Lynam). *"One of my better 2-y-o's I'd say, I like him an awful lot. He's a little bit immature mentally but he has loads of natural speed".* TRAINERS' BARGAIN BUY

1007. MERKEL (IRE) ★★★★
b.f. Manduro – Queen Of Palms (Desert Prince).
April 20. Fourth foal. 34,000Y. Tattersalls December. Eddie Lynam. Half-sister to the quite useful Irish 7f winner Palm Ridge (by Indian Ridge). The dam, an Irish listed 7.5f winner, is a half-sister to the Irish listed winners Artistic Blue and Cool Clarity. The second dam, Tapolite (by Tap On Wood), winner of the listed 7f Tyros Stakes, is a sister to the 2-y-o Group 3 1m Killavullen Stakes winner Sedulous and a half-sister to 3 winners. (Edward Lynam). *"Possibly my nicest filly, she's a little bit weak of her joints at the moment but she has a lot of class and she shows a good attitude. I love her, but being by Manduro I have to let her develop a bit more. She has gears and I'd expect her out over six furlongs but she'll get further later on".*

1008. REGAL POWER ★★★
b.c. Royal Applause – Be My Charm (Polish Precedent).
April 3. Second foal. 8,000Y. Tattersalls December. Edward Lynam. The dam, a fair maiden, was placed 5 times over 5f and 6f including at 2 yrs and is a half-sister to the Group 1 5f Nunthorpe Stakes winner Sole Power and to the fairly useful 5f (including

at 2 yrs) to 7f winner of 15 races and Group 3 Cornwallis Stakes second Cornus. The second dam, Demerger (by Distant View), is an unraced half-sister to 4 winners. (Mrs S Power). *"A colt that shows me plenty of speed, he's a little bit immature at the moment and he has to strengthen up behind a bit".*

1009. ROMAN GENERAL (IRE) ★★
b.c. Holy Roman Emperor – Tawoos (Rainbow Quest).
February 18. Third foal. Tattersalls Ireland. €21,000Y. Eddie Lynam. Half-brother to a winner in Norway by Tiger Hill. The dam, a Swedish listed winner, is a half-sister to 6 winners. The second dam, Queen Of Dance (by Sadler's Wells), a 2-y-o winner in France, is a half-sister to 4 winners. (Edward Lynam). *"He's out of a Rainbow Quest mare that won a stakes race over a bit of a trip, so he'll probably start off at seven furlongs or a mile, but he goes OK. He's much bigger and has more scope than my other Holy Roman Emperor 2-y-o".*

1010. SLADE POWER (IRE) ★★★★
b.c. Dutch Art – Girl Power (Key Of Luck).
April 2. First foal. £5,000Y. Doncaster Premier. Eddie Lynam. The dam, a quite useful 5f winner, is a sister to the fairly useful Irish 2-y-o 6f winner and listed-placed Key Rose and a half-sister to the useful Irish 6f and 7f winner of 6 races Empirical Power. The second dam, Rumuz (by Marju), was placed 4 times at up to 10f and is a half-sister to 7 winners. (Mrs S Power). *"We love this horse. He's gorgeous and if he was two-legged he'd be a model. He has a lovely head, he's well-balanced, a great walker and he has loads of quality. He'll be quick enough for six and seven furlongs and although he's a little bit 'on the leg' he might start out in May and he does everything easily".*

1011. STAGECOACH ★★★
ch.c. Medicean – La Spezia (Danehill Dancer).
March 28. First foal. 34,000Y. Tattersalls October Book 1. Eddie Lynam. The dam, a fair 9f winner and third in the listed 10f Pretty Polly Stakes, is a half-sister to 5 winners including the listed winner Brindisi. The second dam, Genoa (by Zafonic), a fairly useful 11.5f winner, was listed placed over 10f and is a half-sister to 3 winners. (Lady O'Reilly). *"He's grown well since we bought him at the sales and he should make a nice seven furlong 2-y-o. A nice moving colt, he'll be running around June time".*

1012. UNNAMED ★★
br.f. Lawman – Theben (Monsun).
April 19. Third foal. 8,000Y. Tattersalls October Book 1. Not sold. The dam won once at 3 yrs in Germany and is a half-sister to one winner. The second dam, Toja (by Windwurf), won two races at 3 and 4 yrs in Germany and is a half-sister to 7 winners. (Edward Lynam). *"I love this filly, we've given her a break so she can benefit from the spring grass. She's a good mover, has a beautiful head and she's lovely but we think she'll be a middle-distance filly. We'll take our time with her".*

GER LYONS

1013. BURNIE BRAES (IRE) ★★★
b.c. Moss Vale – Etica (Barathea).
March 8. Fourth foal. Doncaster Premier. £26,000Y. BBA (Ire). Half-brother to two 2-y-o winners in Italy by Acclamation. The dam won two races at 2 yrs in Italy and is a half-sister to 4 winners. The second dam, Minodora (by Marju), was listed-placed in Italy and a half-sister to 5 winners. (Mr S Jones). *"A lovely horse, he's big and heavy but he holds his condition well. Big and powerful, he has an engine and I like him. I'd like to think he's a bit better than a maiden winner, he's forward and we'll see him out in May or June".*

1014. CHOICE PEARL ★★
b.br.f. Any Given Saturday – Horns Gray (Pass The Tab).
May 20. Ninth foal. $150,000Y. Keeneland September. David Redvers. Closely related to 2 winners by Distorted Humor, including the US Grade 1 Spinaway Stakes winner Awesome Humor and half-sister to 5 winners including the US stakes-placed Dignified Donovan (by Regal Classic). The dam, a stakes winner of 12 races, is a half-sister to 3 winners. The second dam, Cox's Angel (by Cox's Ridge), is an unraced half-sister to the US Grade 1 winner All Fired Up. (Pearl Bloodstock Ltd). *"A nice filly, she's done a lot of growing and is very high behind the saddle. She has a great*

temperament and is doing everything I ask of her but I'm in no rush because she's a late foal and she'll be the last filly I run".

1015. DARK PASSION (IRE) ★★★
b.c. Dark Angel – Prince's Passion (Brief Truce).
April 18. Fifth foal. £10,000Y. Doncaster Premier. BBA (Ire). Half-brother to the fair 2-y-o 1m and hurdles winner Whipperway (by Whipper) and a winner over jumps by Captain Rio. The dam, a fair 2-y-o 6f winner, is a half-sister to 4 minor winners. The second dam, Green Bonnet (by Green Desert), is a placed sister to the listed winner Mauri Moon and a half-sister to the Singapore Derby winner Kimbridge Knight. (Mr S Jones). "A big, strapping horse and a seven furlong auction maiden winner hopefully. A good, honest horse, I see the first-season sire is having winners and this guy should be another".

1016. DISAGREE ★★★
b.c. Ishiguru – Clancassie (Clantime).
February 27. Sixth foal. Doncaster Premier. £26,000Y. BBA (Ire). Half-brother to the very useful Mecca's Mate (by Paris House), a winner of two listed events over 5f and third in the Group 2 Temple Stakes, and to a winner in Sweden by Presidium. The dam is an unplaced half-sister to 4 winners. The second dam, Casbar Lady (by Native Bazaar), won 4 races at 2 and 4 yrs and is a half-sister to one winner abroad. (Mr S Jones). "A nice horse, he'll definitely win his maiden and hopefully he'll be a bit better than that. He's a slow learner but the penny is dropping and he's improving week by week. I could see him being out sooner rather than later but not over five furlongs, he's more of a six/seven furlong type. I have two Ishiguru 2-y-o's and they're both definite maiden winners, but whether they're up to winning any black type is another matter".

1017. GIN RUMMY ★★★★
b.c. Red Clubs – Litewska (Mujadil).
February 24. Third foal. 20,000Y. Tattersalls October Book 2. Ger Lyons. Half-brother to the modest 5f winner Mistress Cooper (by Kyllachy). The dam, a quite useful 5f (including at 2 yrs) and 6f winner, is a half-sister to 3 winners. The second dam, Old Tradition (by Royal Academy), is a placed half-sister to 4 minor winners. (Mr S Jones). "He's likely to run in mid-April and he's a horse we like. He'd be in the same category of another of our 2-y-o's, Shukhov. A very honest colt with a great temperament, I'd be disappointed if he wasn't a stakes horse. A good, big, strong horse, I can see him improving as the season goes on".

1018. GREEK CANYON (IRE) ★★★
br.c. Moss Vale – Lazaretta (Dalakhani).
March 28. First foal. 15,000Y. Tattersalls October Book 2. Ger Lyons. The dam is an unraced half-sister to one winner in Germany. The second dam, Siringas (by Barathea), won the Grade 2 Nassau Stakes in Canada and is a half-sister to 4 winners. (Mr S Jones). "A small colt, he'll have raced before your book comes out and he's a real "die for you" Moss Vale – a real honest horse. I would say he's an auction maiden winner in the making and let's see how he improves when we get him to the track".

1019. HURRICANE HUGO (IRE) ★★
b.c. Hurricane Run – All Time Great (Night Shift).
March 16. Seventh foal. 28,000Y. Tattersalls October Book 2. Ger Lyons. Half-brother to the French 2-y-o 7f winner and Group 3 Prix de Cabourg second Atlantic High (by Nashwan) and to the quite useful 9f, 12f and hurdles winner High Day (by Monsun). The dam, a fairly useful 2-y-o 6f winner and fourth in the 7.3f Fred Darling Stakes, is closely related to the Dante Stakes and Craven Stakes winner Alnasr Alwasheek and a half-sister to the Juddmonte International Stakes winner One So Wonderful and the Rockfel Stakes winner Relatively Special. The second dam, Someone Special (by Habitat), won over 7f, was third in the Coronation Stakes and is a half-sister to the Queen Elizabeth II Stakes winner Milligram. (Mr S Jones). "A very backward horse, you won't see him out until the middle to back-end of the season. A typical Hurricane Run, he'll just take time. He was very feminine but then did a lot of growing over the winter and I'm happy with him now, but you definitely won't see him for a while yet".

1020. JAMMING ★★
b.c. Jeremy – Perfect Sound (Halling).
April 29. Second foal. €7,000Y. Goffs Orby.

Ger Lyons. The dam, a minor French 3-y-o winner, is a half-sister to 5 winners including the French listed 12f Prix de la Porte de Madrid and Group 2 placed Sibling Rival and the dam of the listed winner Imperial Guest. The second dam, Perfect Sister (by Perrault), a minor French winner, is a half-sister to the US Grade 1 winner Frankly Perfect and the French listed winner and US Grade 1 placed Franc Argument. (Mrs L Lyons). *"Very backward. My wife chose, picked, owned and named him – he's her baby. No matter how long it takes for my other backward 2-y-o's to race, you won't see him out before them".*

1021. JEMIMA'S PEARL (USA) ★★★★
b.f. Distorted Humor – Jemima (Owington).
April 15. Sixth foal. $100,000Y. Keeneland September. David Redvers. Half-sister to the US stakes winner of 5 races English Colony (by Rock Of Gibraltar) and to the US winner and Grade 3 placed Pinckney Hill (by A P Indy). The dam, a winner of 5 races here and in the USA including the Group 2 Lowther Stakes, is a half-sister to 3 winners. The second dam, Poyle Fizz (by Damister), is an unraced full or half-sister to 3 winners. (Pearl Bloodstock Ltd). *"I love this filly, she was a very slow learner but when the penny dropped she became very precocious and she wouldn't be far away from running. I like her and I hope she's black type because I think she could be smart. I have a nice bunch of fillies this year".*

1022. KASHMIR PEAK (IRE) ★★
b.c. Tiger Hill – Elhareer (Selkirk).
January 16. Second foal. 11,000Y. Tattersalls October Book 2. Ger Lyons. Half-brother to the moderate 2010 5f placed 2-y-o Bobby Smith (by Elnadim). The dam, a modest 2-y-o 5f winner, is a half-sister to the fairly useful 5f and 6f winner of 11 races Figaro Flyer (by Mozart). The second dam, Ellway Star (by Night Shift), a useful dual 5f winner (including at 2 yrs), was listed-placed and is a half-sister to 6 winners including the smart 1m winner and Irish 2,000 Guineas second Fa-Eq and the smart listed 7.3f and 1m winner Corinium. (Mr S Jones). *"He's in the same bracket as my Hurricane Run and Authorized 2-y-o's in that he's backward. He looked very precocious until he started to grow and I'm just giving him time. But he has a bit of an engine and I could see him winning a maiden. He'll want a minimum of six/seven furlongs and the precocity he was showing earlier must come from his dam".*

1023. KING'S WARRANT (IRE) ★★★★
b.c. King's Best – Ask Annie (Danehill).
March 1. First foal. The dam is an unraced half-sister to the high-class Group 1 12f Grand Prix de Saint-Cloud and Group 1 12f Preis von Europa winner Youmzain, to the Group 1 1m Lockinge Stakes and triple Group 3 winner Creachadoir and the Irish Group 3 9.5f winner Shreyas. The second dam, Sadima (by Sadler's Wells), a fairly useful Irish 10f winner, is a half-sister to 2 winners in Chile. (Mr F Dunne). *"He's a three-parts brother to Creachadoir who was also by King's Best. This is a smart horse and he'll not be far behind the best in the yard. We like him, he's very straightforward, he's maturing into a lovely physical specimen and the longer we give him the better he'll get. We'll be in no rush to run him but we think he has an engine and I think we'll see him out at the Curragh Guineas meeting".*

1024. LADY ROCHFORD (IRE) ★★★
b.f. Invincible Spirit – Sheezalady (Zafonic).
March 20. Sixth foal. 110,000foal. Tattersalls December. John Ferguson. Half-sister to the Group 3 6f Acomb Stakes winner and Group 1 7f Dewhurst Stakes third Fast Company (by Danehill Dancer). The dam is an unraced half-sister to 5 winners including Hawajiss, winner of the Group 2 10f Nassau Stakes, the Group 3 1m May Hill Stakes and the Group 3 10.4f Musidora Stakes. The second dam, Canadian Mill (by Mill Reef), was a smart 2-y-o 6f winner and second in the Group 1 6f Cheveley Park Stakes, is a half-sister to 4 winners including the Royal Lodge Stakes second Khozaam. (Sheikh Mohammed). *"A smart Invincible Spirit filly, she's typical of the sire in that your biggest job is to make sure she keeps going forward as opposed to kicking the head off you! She has ability and should be racing in May. We like her a lot and I hope she's better than a maiden winner, I've won with every Invincible Spirit I've had and she'd be typical".*

1025. LIGHTENING PEARL (IRE) ★★★★ ♣
b.f. Marju – Jioconda (Rossini).
February 15. Second foal. Goffs Orby. €125,000Y. David Redvers. Sister to the 2010 2-y-o Group 3 Tyros Stakes third Jo ie Jioconde. The dam won the listed Silken Glider Stakes and was third in the Group 3 Killavullan Stakes. The second dam, La Joconde (by Vettori), is an unraced half-sister to 4 winners. (Pearl Bloodstock Ltd). *"A very nice filly, she's small and very precocious and I'd be disappointed if she's not black type. Definitely a five/six furlongs filly because she's has speed and hopefully she'll get a stride further. She has 2-y-o written all over her".*

1026. MOUNT MERU
b.c. Red Clubs – Shangazi (Miswaki).
March 24. First living foal. Doncaster Premier. Not sold/private sale BBS (Ire). The dam, placed fourth once over 7f at 3 yrs, is a half-sister to 3 minor winners in North America. The second dam, Gran Ole Flag (by El Gran Senor), is an unplaced half-sister to 7 winners. (Mr S Jones). *"An auction maiden horse, he's small but he'd be the one I'd pick out for value for money, he's not as smart as the better Red Clubs colt I have, Gin Rummy, but he'll still be alright".* TRAINERS' BARGAIN BUY

1027. MUCKLE BAHOOCHIE (IRE) ★★★★
b.f Moss Vale – Multiple (Mull Of Kintyre).
February 15. First foal. Tattersalls Ireland. €27,000Y. David Redvers. The dam, a fair dual 5f at 2 yrs, subsequently won 3 races at 3 yrs in the USA and is a half-sister to 3 winners including the German Group 3 winner Shinko's Best. The second dam, Sail Away (by Platini), won at 2 yrs in Germany and is a half-sister to 10 winners including 2 German listed winners. (Mr D Redvers). *"David Redvers and I have had some luck with fillies, this one is very precocious, she'll start off in mid-April and we like her a lot. I reckon the first-season sire Moss Vale will do well this summer. Our biggest job with this filly will be to try and get her to stay a trip because she's speedy but I'll be disappointed if she doesn't stay seven furlongs later on".*

1028. MUNRO BAGGER ★★
b.c. Whipper – Prashock (Traditionally).
February 11. First foal. Goffs Orby. €27,000Y. Ger Lyons. The dam is an unraced half-sister to 2 winners including the Irish listed winner Shizao. The second dam, Shigeru Summit (by Be My Chief), won 2 races at 2 yrs including the Group 3 Prix du Calvados and is a half-sister to 8 winners. (Mr S Jones). *"A big, strong, strapping colt. One for the middle of the season and for six and seven furlongs. I would hope he'd win an auction maiden".*

1029. PC HENRY ★★★
b.c. Ishiguru – Elhida (Mujtahid).
January 30. Seventh living foal. Doncaster Premier. £40,000Y. Hugo Merry. Half-brother to the quite useful triple 5f winner (including at 2 yrs) Hadaf (by Fasliyev), to the fair 6f winner Katheer (by Anabaa) and the modest 5f winner of 7 races Lithaam (by Elnadim). The dam, a useful 2-y-o 6f winner, is a sister to the useful 2-y-o 6f winner and Group 3 July Stakes second Juwwi and a half-sister to 2 winners. The second dam, Nouvelle Star (by Luskin Star), won from 5f to 8.2f in Australia including a Grade 2 event and was the champion older filly at 4 yrs. (Mr R Pegum). *"I named him after my German shepherd who was a police dog! He's a lovely-looking colt, with quality written all over him. He'd be in the same bracket as my other Ishiguru 2-y-o except that I couldn't see him running over shorter than seven furlongs. I like him, he'd have to improve to get black type but I would hope he'd win a maiden".*

1030. PITLOCHRY (IRE) ★★★
b.c. Chineur – Knapton Hill (Zamindar).
March 7. First foal. €21,000Y. Tattersalls Ireland. E Daly BS/Action Horse. The dam, a quite useful 7f winner at 3 yrs, is a half-sister to one winner in Germany. The second dam, Torgau (by Zieten), a Group 2 6f Cherry Hinton Stakes winner, was second in the Group 1 7f Moyglare Stud Stakes and is a half-sister to 9 winners. (Mr S Jones). *"He's a nice colt, but he's at an immature stage right now. Once he's out of that he'll be ready to roll, he's done plenty of work and is very similar to a Chineur we had last year. He'll be placed in his maidens, hopefully win one and then we'll see how we go. A good-looking horse, I'd like to see him on the track sooner rather than later".*

1031. QATAR'S PEARL (USA) ★★★★ ♠
ch.c. Tapit – Arboresque (Cure The Blues).
April 21. Seventh foal. $420,000Y. Keeneland September. David Redvers. Half-brother to 5 winners including the US stakes winner of 10 races Meadow Blue (by Meadow Monster) and the US 2-y-o stakes-placed winner Brickyard Fast (by Sharp Humor). The dam was placed once at 2 yrs in the USA. The second dam, General Tree (by General Assembly), is an unraced half-sister to the US dual Grade 3 winner Paying Dues. (Pearl Bloodstock Ltd). "A fast ground horse for seven furlongs and we'll probably start him off at Dundalk in late May, so he's forward enough. A gorgeous-looking horse, he's medium-sized, a good walker and a quick learner. He does his job well but I'd expect him to want a minimum of seven furlongs. He definitely doesn't want soft ground and I like what he's doing without getting too excited".

1032. SHUKHOV (IRE) ★★★★
b.c. Ivan Denisovich – Just One Smile (Desert Prince).
January 29. Fourth foal. €25,000Y. Tattersalls Ireland. Edward Daly BS/Action Horse. Brother to the minor Italian 2-y-o winner Via Di Fuga and half-brother to the fair 6f winner Agent Stone (by Night Shift) and the minor Italian 2-y-o winner Chikorita (by Verglas). The dam, a fair 6f winner, is a half-sister to 3 winners including the useful 2-y-o dual 5f winner and Group 3 7f Debutante Stakes second Caldy Dancer. The second dam, Smile Awhile (by Woodman), ran once unplaced and is a full or half-sister to 3 winners. (Mr S Jones). "He missed the break and ran very green on his debut, but he's a big, strong, powerful horse with a bit of a knee action. I'd like to see him over seven furlongs with a bit of ease in the ground. In my opinion he's definitely a stakes horse and he'll only get better as the year goes on".

1033. THE KERNIGAL (IRE) ★★★
b.c. Red Clubs – Ellens Princess (Desert Prince).
March 30. Second foal. 35,000Y. Tattersalls October Book 2. Ger Lyons. Half-brother to the unplaced 2010 2-y-o One Fat Cat (by One Cool Cat). The dam, a modest 7f winner, is a half-sister to 8 winners including the Irish 2-y-o 6f winner and Group 1 6f Phoenix Stakes second Miss Beabea and the very useful multiple sprint winner Ellen's Lad. The second dam, Lady Ellen (by Horage), won 3 races in Ireland from 7f to 1m and is a half-sister to 3 winners including Indian Ridge. (Mr S Jones). "I have three by Red Clubs and they're nice – he's my tip to become leading sire. This colt wouldn't be as forward as the other two and I see him as being one for auction maidens from mid-May onwards".

1034. TRUE PEARL (USA) ★★★★
b.c. Yes It's True – Sirocco Dream (Gone West).
March 7. First foal. Goffs Orby. €55,000Y. David Redvers. The dam is an unplaced daughter of the US Grade 3 winner and Irish 1,00 Guineas third Storm Dream (by Catrail), herself a half-sister to 7 winners. (Pearl Bloodstock Ltd). "He'd be the pick of the place at the minute – the number one colt in the yard I would think. He's smart, a seven furlong horse and you won't see him out until late May. They're all being trained with Royal Ascot in mind but it's all subject to them coming right at that time. He's a horse we like a good bit, he's gorgeous, big and he's doing everything we're asking him at the moment".

1035. ZERMATT (IRE) ★★★
ch.c. Strategic Prince – Await (Peintre Celebre).
March 18. Second foal. Doncaster Premier. £30,000Y. BBA (Ire). Half-brother to the 2011 3-y-o US Grade 2 9f and Grade 3 7f winner Cambina (by Hawk Wing). The dam is an unraced half-sister to 6 winners including the Irish 2-y-o 1m and subsequent US stakes winner Lightning Hit and the French 1m and 11f winner and Group 3 9f Prix Daphnis third Blasket Island. The second dam, Starring Role (by Glenstal), is an unraced half-sister to 5 winners including the Group 3 5f King George Stakes winner Title Roll and the Irish listed sprint winner Northern Express. The second dam, Tough Lady (by Bay Express), was a fairly useful 2-y-o 6f winner and a half-sister to 5 winners. (Mr S Jones). "He has 'time' written all over him, but his half-sister has recently won a Grade 2 and a Grade 3 in the USA. This colt has impressed me all winter but he's now on a huge growth spurt and we have him on the back burner for now. He's a big horse now so we'll give him a chance. When we were

breaking them all he was the one that stood out".

1036. UNNAMED ★★★
b.f. Exceed And Excel – Rawabi (Sadler's Wells).
March 25. Fifth foal. Half-sister to the French 10f and 11f winner and listed-placed Honour System (by King's Best). The dam is an unraced sister to the Group 1 Dewhurst Stakes winner In Command and a half-sister to the champion European 2-y-o and Group 1 Keeneland Nunthorpe Stakes winner Lyric Fantasy and the Group 1 Middle Park Stakes and Group 1 Haydock Sprint Cup winner and sire Royal Applause. The second dam, Flying Melody (by Auction Ring), a sprint winner of 2 races in France, is a half-sister to the listed winners Pearl Star, Portese and Seadiver. (Sheikh Mohammed). *"A lovely filly, she's small but starting to grow and show a bit of speed. Not as precocious you'd expect from her sire but she's getting there and she'll be ready to run at the end of May. She's doing everything I'm asking her, she's honest and has a lovely temperament, but how good she is time will tell".*

GEORGE MARGARSON

1037. ARTFUL LADY (IRE) ★★★
b.br.f. Excellent Art – Fear And Greed (Brief Truce).
March 25. Fifth living foal. 32,000Y. Tattersalls October Book 2. G Margarson. Half-sister to the fair 2-y-o 6f winner Falcolnry (by Hawk Wing) and to the minor Irish 5f winner Live In Fear (by Fasliyev). The dam, an Irish 2-y-o 6f winner and second in the Group 1 7f Moyglare Stud Stakes, is a half-sister to the 2-y-o 6.5f Goffs Challenge winner Serious Play. The second dam, Zing Ping (by Thatching), a quite useful 2-y-o 7f placed maiden, is a half-sister to 4 winners here and abroad. (Mrs E L Hook). *"I think my 2-y-o's this year are proper horses, with substance. This is a very nice filly, I loved her at the Sales and I still do. A proper little 2-y-o, but she's gone through a growing spurt so although I was trying to get her ready for April because she's worked well with older horses she's a bit immature still, so I'll wait for a bit and train her for six furlongs".*

1038. FACTOR THREE ★★
ch.c. Three Valleys – Desert Daisy (Desert Prince).
February 23. Third foal. 7,000Y. Tattersalls Book 3. Not sold. Half-brother to the 2-y-o winner Michaelmas Daisy (by Camacho). The dam was placed twice at 2 yrs and was a moderate 4-y-o 7f winner and is a half-sister to one winner. The second dam, Pomponette (by Rahy), is an unraced half-sister to 4 winners. (Matt Sharkey). *"Worth putting in the book, he'll be my first 2-y-o runner, he's got scope and I see him needing six furlongs and being a nursery type. Maybe not one of my nicer ones but there's a lot to like about him and he might get seven furlongs".*

1039. UNNAMED ★★★★
b.c. Cockney Rebel – Marisa (Desert Sun).
April 6. Fourth foal. 54,000Y. Tattersalls October Book 2. G Margarson. Half-brother to the fairly useful 2-y-o 5f and listed 6f winner Smokey Storm (by One Cool Cat) and to the fairly useful 2-y-o 5f winner and listed-placed Di Stefano (by Bahamian Bounty). The dam is an unraced half-sister to 6 minor winners here and abroad. The second dam, Mithl Al Hawa (by Salse), a useful 2-y-o 6f winner, was listed placed is a half-sister to 9 winners. (John Guest Racing). *"He's the apple of my eye at the moment. I'm in love with him and I think he's a gorgeous horse. He'll probably just be a 2-y-o because the family are that way, but having said that the sire did train on of course. He's a bit sparky, temperament-wise, just like his Dad and he's one of the nicer Cockney Rebels from the Sales. I can't get him off the bit with anything, he's a proper horse".*

1040. UNNAMED ★★★
b.c. Exceed And Excel – Polar Jem (Polar Falcon).
March 30. Third foal. 48,000Y. Tattersalls December. Not sold. The dam, a very useful 9f to 12f winner of 8 races (including 3 listed events), is a half-sister to 2 winners. The second dam, Top Jem (by Damister), a fair 9f and 10f winner of 5 races, is a half-sister to 5 winners including Aldora (a winner of 4 listed events at around 1m) and the smart 10f performer Polar Red (by Polar Falcon). (Norcroft Park Stud). *"I have a lot of time for him although I'm a bit*

worried about the covering because the dam was a ten furlong filly and yet everyone tells me Exceed And Excel doesn't get horses that go beyond seven. Having said that I noticed he had a twelve furlongs winner the other day! This colt looks the type that should run well over six furlongs but on pedigree he should need seven and I'll train him with that in mind. He's got his mother's temperament in that he'd do anything for you, he's not over tall and he looks a racey 2-y-o type but with scope. He's a sound horse with a good head on him".

1041. UNNAMED ★★★
b.c. Indian Haven – Princess Speedfit (Desert Prince).
March 21. Fifth foal. 48,000Y. Tattersalls October Book 2. G Margarson. Half-brother to the useful 6f winner of 4 races (including a 2-y-o listed event) Imperial Guest (by Imperial Dancer) and to the quite useful 6f (at 2 yrs) and 7f winner Excellent Guest (by Exceed And Excel). The dam, a fair 8.3f winner at 3 yrs, is a half-sister to the French listed 12f winner and dual Group 2 placed Sibling Rival. The second dam, Perfect Sister (by Perrault), a minor French winner, is a sister to the US Grade 1 winner Frankly Perfect and a half-sister to the French listed winner and US Grade 1 placed Franc Argument. (John Guest Racing). *"From a good family that I know really well, this fellow is a gorgeous horse and I went well over budget for him. He's typical of the family, although the sire worries me a bit, but he's has a lot of Imperial Guest about him. I worked him in February but I stopped him because he started to grow and get a bit edgy. He's just doing steady canters now and I'll wake him up in the middle of April with a view to running him over six and seven furlongs. He's worked really nicely with older horses and I'm very happy with him".*

1042. UNNAMED ★★
b.c. Shamardal – Tarandot (Singspiel).
March 9. Second foal. 75,000Y. Tattersalls December. Not sold. Half-brother to the 2010 6f placed 2-y-o Calaf (by Dubai Destination). The dam, a listed 14f winner, is a half-sister to 4 winners including the smart Group 2 12f Prix Hocquart winner Rifapour. The second dam, Rifada (by Ela-Mana-Mou), a useful winner of 2 races over 12f, is a half-sister to 5 winners including the Group 3 Royal Whip Stakes winner Rayseka. (Norcroft Park Stud). *"He's giving me crossed messages because he's big but he's not tall and he could be a 2-y-o but his half-sister last year wasn't. I've done little bits with him but I need to be careful with him because he's more of a 3-y-o type really. A heavy topped horse, but I've lightened him up a bit. I'll just take my time with him, but he wants to go and he's a nice horse".*

ALAN McCABE
1043. DAWN LIGHTNING ★★★
b.f. Dark Angel – River Crossing (Zafonic).
April 11. Second foal. 2,500Y. Tattersalls December. A McCabe. Half-sister to the unplaced 2010 2-y-o Billyruben (by Bertolini). The dam, a fair 2-y-o 5f winner, is a half-sister to numerous 2-y-o winners including the fairly useful 2-y-o dual 6f winner Negligee. The second dam, Vax Star (by Petong), a fairly useful 2-y-o 5f listed winner, is a half-sister to 4 winners. *"A very nice filly that's going well, she'll be racing in early April and she's a strong filly, so she looks the type to get six furlongs. The reports of the sire are very good and this filly goes well".*

1044. LIEBESZIEL ★★★
b.c. Pursuit Of Love – Pretty Miss (Averti).
March 23. First foal. 3,000Y. Doncaster St Leger Festival. A McCabe. The dam, a fair dual 5f winner (including at 2 yrs), is a half-sister to numerous winners including the top-class Group 1 5f Nunthorpe Stakes winner and sire Kyllachy, the very useful triple 5f winner Borders, the useful 5f winner of 4 races Speed On and the fairly useful dual 5f winner Follow Flanders. The second dam, Pretty Poppy (by Song), a modest 2-y-o 5f winner, stayed 7.6f and is a half-sister to 4 winners including the Criterium de Maisons-Laffitte winner Corviglia. (Mrs D E Sharp). *"I like him a lot, he's a speedy, compact individual. He's got a bit of an attitude but hopefully it'll be of the right sort. He'll be early, he's very speedy and hopefully he'll go six as well".*

1045. OUTLAW TORN (IRE) ★★★
ch.c. Iffraaj – Touch And Love (Green Desert).
April 2. Sixteenth foal. Doncaster Premier. £57,000Y. Tom Malone/Alan McCabe. Half-

brother to 5 winners including the French 2-y-o listed 7f winner Bashful (by Brief Truce) and the fair 7f winner Forest Of Love (by Brief Truce). The dam, a 2-y-o winner in France, was second in the Group 2 Prix du Gros-Chene and is a half-sister to 8 winners out of the unraced Clunk Click (by Star Appeal), herself a half-sister to 10 winners including the Group winners Sure Blade, Only A Pound and Sure Sharp. (C V Wentworth). *"A very nice individual, he should be racing soon and although I think he probably warrants six furlongs he should be sharp enough for five. He hasn't grown as much as I expected but he's what I'd call a handy horse".*

1046. REVE DU JOUR (IRE) ★★★
b.f. Iffraaj – Melaaya (Aljabr).
February 14. Second foal. Doncaster Premier. £55,000Y. Tom Malone/Alan McCabe. The dam, a quite useful 2-y-o 6f winner, is a half-sister to 2 winners. The second dam, Saint Emilia (by Saint Ballado), a Group 3 winner of 13 races in Peru, is a sister to the Peruvian Group 2 winner Domingo. (Mrs Z Wentworth). *"A very nice filly, just on the back burner at the minute because she's growing but she's going through the motions well. I think I'll probably start her off at six furlongs, she's a nice filly that moves very well and covers a lot of ground."*

1047. SABUSA ★★★
b.c. Kheleyf – Black Tribal (Mukaddamah).
March 21. March 21. Sixth foal. 3,000Y. Tattersalls October Book 2. Not sold. Half-brother to the quite useful 5f (at 2 yrs), 6f and subsequent UAE winner Satwa Street (by Elusive City) and to 2 winners in Italy by Captain Rio (at 2 yrs) and Dr Devious. The dam won once at 2 yrs in Italy and is a half-sister to 6 winners including the Italian 1m listed winner Silent Tribute. The second dam, Tribal Rite (by Be My Native), a fairly useful Irish 2-y-o listed 6f and 3-y-o 10f winner, is a half-sister to the Middle Park Stakes winner Balla Cove, the US stakes winner Burning Issue and the Irish listed winner Blasted Heath. (K Dasmal). *"He goes well, he's working above average and he's got '2-y-o type' written all over him".* TRAINERS' BARGAIN BUY

1048. TURN THE PAGE ★★★
b.c. Lucky Story – Maid For Running (Namaqualand).
April 8. Fourth foal. Doncaster Premier. £50,000Y. Tom Malone/Alan McCabe. Half-brother to the moderate 2010 5f placed 2-y-o Bigalo's Vera B, to the fair 2-y-o 5f winner Sheka (both by Ishiguru) and a winner in Hong Kong by Fraam. The dam, a quite useful 2-y-o 5f winner, is a half-sister to the useful winners Polar Kingdom and Goodwood Prince. The second dam, Scarlet Lake (by Reprimand), is an unplaced half-sister to 6 winners and to the dams of the US Grade 1 winner Stroll and the Group 2 Sun Chariot Stakes winner Lady In Waiting. (C V Wentworth). *"A nice, big colt that's similar to our Iffraaj filly in that he's on the back burner at the moment but he's going through his paces well. A big, strong colt, he'd probably want a stiff five furlongs or six. He has a bit of a knee action so I don't think he'd want quick ground".*

ED McMAHON
1049. ARCHERS PRIZE (IRE) ★★★
b.c. Dark Angel – Silver Arrow (Shadeed).
April 28. Seventh foal. 20,000Y. Tattersalls October Book 2. J Fretwell. Closely related to the modest dual 6f winner (including a seller at 2 yrs in 2010) Slatey Hen (by Acclamation) and half-brother to the very useful Group 3 6f Norfolk Stakes winner of 6 races Masta Plasta (by Mujadil) and the fairly useful 2-y-o 5f winner Kheleyf's Silver (by Kheleyf). The dam was placed once at 2 yrs and is a half-sister to 3 winners including the listed-placed Ras Shaikh. The second dam, Aneesati (by Kris), a quite useful 1m winner, is a half-sister to 10 winners including the Prix de la Salamandre second Bin Nashwan and the US Grade 2 winner Magellan and the Supreme Stakes second Alanees. (J C Fretwell). *"He's a late foal and not over-big so I haven't got him going yet, but he moves quite nicely and we'll just have to wait and see".*

1050. ARTISTIC JEWEL (IRE) ★★★
ch.f. Excellent Art – Danish Gem (Danehill).
April 15. Sixth foal. €30,000Y. Goffs Orby. Not sold. Half-sister to the fairly useful 5f and 6f (at 2 yrs) and listed 1m winner Ponty Rossa (by Distant Music), to the fair dual 6f winner

Jimmy The Poacher (by Verglas), the modest dual 9f winner Midnight Strider (by Golan) and a winner in Greece by Marju. The dam, a 1m winner at 3 yrs in France, is a half-sister to 6 winners. The second dam, Gemaasheh (by Habitat), is an unraced half-sister to 5 winners. (R L Bedding). *"She's fairly well-forward and I think she'll be quite early. One to start off at five furlongs, she's a good-actioned filly, fairly professional, quite well-made and athletic. I think she'll know her job first time".*

1051. FAST ON (IRE) ★★
gr.c. Verglas – Dream State (Machiavellian).
April 1. Second foal. Doncaster Premier. £11,000Y. John Fretwell. Half-brother to Minimoi (by Byron), last of 16 on her only start at 2 yrs in 2010. The dam is an unraced half-sister to 5 winners. The second dam, Reveuse de Jour (by Sadler's Wells), a fair 7f placed 3-y-o, is a half-sister to 8 winners including the Group 2 6f Lowther Stakes winner Enthused. (J C Fretwell). *"He's a fairly straightforward little horse, what you see is what you get with him. He's going the right way and because his action is a little bit rounded as long as there's a drop of rain we'll have him out in May".*

1052. FLUGELHORN (IRE) ★★★
b.c. Elusive City – Prepare For War (Marju).
April 10. Fourth foal. Doncaster Premier. £42,000Y. John Fretwell. Half-brother to the fair 6f winner Johannesgray (by Verglas). The dam ran once unplaced and is a half-sister to 4 winners. The second dam, Fadaki Hawaki (by Vice Regent), is a placed half-sister to 5 winners including the Group winners and sires Fruits Of Love and Mujadil. (J C Fretwell). *"He's a big-topped colt, the last one to come to me from the breaking yard and so he's a bit immature mentally. He could turn out to be anything really, he's only cantering at the moment, but he's a well-made colt and a good walker".*

1053. IMPASSIVE ★★★
ch.f. Choisir – Frigid (Indian Ridge).
April 1. First foal. £9,000Y. Doncaster Premier. John Fretwell. The dam ran once unplaced and is a half-sister to the very useful 12f and listed 14f winner Savarain. The second dam, Frangy (by Sadler's Wells), a fair dual 12f winner, is a full or half-sister to 8 winners including the German 1m to 9.5f winner of 7 races and listed-placed Flying Heights. (J C Fretwell). *"I wouldn't say she was over-big but she's going the right way and she should be out in late May or early June".*

1054. KODIAC ISLAND ★★★
b.f. Kodiac – Inveraray (Selkirk).
March 10. Second foal. Doncaster Premier. £25,000Y. John Guest. The dam is an unplaced half-sister to 4 winners including the Group 2 12f Hardwicke Stakes and Group 2 12f Blandford Stakes winner Predappio and the dam of the Group 3 winner Bonus. The second dam, Khalafiya (by Darshaan), won the Group 3 12f Meld Stakes and is a half-sister to 4 winners. (Mr D Botterill & Mr J Guest). *"A nice, deep-bodied filly, she probably has a bit of a temperament and she won't be running until mid-season. She's going the right way and as long as her attitude stays the same she'll be alright".*

1055. LIGHTNING JET ★★★
ch.f. Dutch Art – Glint (Pivotal).
February 3. First foal. 12,000Y. Tattersalls October Book 2. Ed McMahon. The dam is an unraced half-sister to 3 minor winners. The second dam, Flame Valley (by Gulch), a smart listed 10f winner, was placed in the Group 2 10f Sun Chariot Stakes and in the Grade 1 10f E P Taylor Stakes and is a half-sister to 3 winners including the US Grade 2 winner Beyrouth. (Petros Partnership). *"She was a fairly cheap purchase and partly because of that I've entered her for the Supersprint. She has a bit of growing to do but she's a good walker and a decent size, so hopefully she'll turn out to be a nice filly".* TRAINERS' BARGAIN BUY

1056. LOOK HERE'S LADY ★★★
b.f. Kyllachy – Look Here's Carol (Safawan).
March 14. Third foal. Half-sister to the modest 2010 2-y-o 1m winner Imperial Look (by Royal Applause) and to the fair 2-y-o 5f winner Look Whos Next (by Compton Place). The dam, a fairly useful 6f and 7f winner of 3 races, was listed-placed and is a half-sister to several winners including the smart listed 6f winner Now Look Here. The second dam, Where's Carol (by Anfield), was a fair 2-y-o 6f

winner of 4 races. (S L Edwards). "I know this family well and they're all on the small side. She's a bit temperamental, like some fillies can be but fairly well forward. She'll want a bit of ease in the ground and I expect her to be out in the next few weeks. It's a fairly genuine family and she'll be the same".

1057. PIVOTAL BAY ★★★
b.c. Pivotal – Jewel In The Sand (Bluebird).
March 19. Second foal. 50,000Y. Tattersalls October Book 2. Ed McMahon. The dam, a winner of 4 races including the Group 2 6f Cherry Hinton Stakes and the Albany Stakes, is a half-sister to 4 winners including the German 3-y-o listed 6f winner Davignon. The second dam, Dancing Drop (by Green Desert), a useful dual 2-y-o 6f winner, was listed-placed and is a half-sister to 9 winners. (Mr J Coleman). "He's not over-big but his conformation is correct and he's fairly professional. He'll want decent ground and hopefully he'll be racing in May".

1058. POINT MADE (IRE) ★★★★
b.c. Aussie Rules – Princess Clara (Dr Fong).
April 10. Second foal. Doncaster Premier. £20,000Y. John Fretwell. The dam is an unraced half-sister to 2 winners. The second dam, Delirious Moment (by Kris), a listed-placed winner of 3 races in France, is a half-sister to 4 winners including the dam of the dual Group 3 winner Buccellati. (J C Fretwell). "He's a nice, big horse, still green mentally but he looks nice. You could take him to Ascot, Goodwood or York and he wouldn't look out of place in the paddock. If he keeps sound and keeps going the right way he could be anything".

1059. PUSSYCAT DREAM ★★★★
b.f. Oasis Dream – The Cat's Whiskers (Tale Of The Cat).
March 11. Second living foal. 65,000Y. Tattersalls October Book 2. J Fretwell. Half-sister to the fairly useful 2-y-o dual 6f winner Walk On Water (by Exceed And Excel). The dam, a winner over 7f and 1m in New Zealand, is a half-sister to 2 winners including the Australian Group 3 winner and Group 2 placed Tully Dane. The second dam, Good Faith (by Straight Strike), a Group 1 and Group 3 winner in New Zealand, is a half-sister to 6 winners. (J

C Fretwell). "A nicely-made filly, she probably won't be as early as we'd like, but if she runs as well as she looks she'll be OK. A fairly powerful filly, John doesn't usually pay so much at the sales so he went a bit over the top for her, but she's quite flashy-looking and I just hope she does well for him".

1060. SAMBA NIGHT (IRE) ★★★
b.c. Dark Angel – Brazilia (Forzando).
March 18. Ninth foal. 30,000Y. Tattersalls October Book 2. J Fretwell. Half-brother to the Italian listed winner Meanya (by Revoque), to the fairly useful winner of 8 races at around 7f Santisima Trinidad (by Definite Article), the fair triple 5f winner Lost In Paris (by Elusive City) and the unplaced dam of the Group 2 July Stakes winner Classic Blade. The dam, a modest 6f placed 2-y-c, is a half-sister to 4 winners including the Group 2 5f Kings Stand Stakes winner Dominica. The second dam, Dominio (by Dominion), a useful winner of the listed 5f St Hugh's Stakes and second in the Group 2 Temple Stakes, is a half-sister to 6 winners including the Group 1 Nunthorpe Stakes winner Ya Malak. (J C Fretwell). "A nice sort and quite strong, he's just coming to himself now. He's not as early as his pedigree suggests because he's been growing a fair bit, but I should think he'll be out by late May and then we'll see how good he is".

1061. SMALL STEPS (IRE) ★★★
b.f. Acclamation – Last Tango (Lion Cavern).
March 23. Fourth foal. 29,000Y. Tattersalls October Book 2. J Fretwell. Half-sister to I Want To Tango (by Northern Afleet), a minor winner of 5 races at 3 and 4 yrs in the USA. The dam, a fairly useful Irish 2-y-o 7f winner, subsequently won 6 races in the USA and is a half-sister to 4 winners including the Irish listed winner Apparatchik. The second dam, Last Exit (by Dominion), a listed-placed 2-y-o winner, is a half-sister to one winner. (J C Fretwell). "She's a nice big filly, a deep-bodied sort and as long as she keeps going the right way she should be a nice 2-y-o".

1062. VERBEECK ★★★
b.c. Dutch Art – Tesary (Danehill).
February 23. Third foal. Doncaster Premier. £34,000Y. J Fretwell. Half-brother to the

unraced 2010 2-y-o Merton Lady (by Beat Hollow). The dam, a useful 5f (at 2 yrs) to 7f winner, is a half-sister to the fairly useful 7f and 1m winner Baldour. The second dam, Baldemara (by Sanglamore), is an unraced half-sister to 5 winners including the Group 1 5.5f Prix Robert Papin winner Balbonella (herself dam of the top-class sprinter Anabaa, the French 1,000 Guineas winner Always Loyal and the useful sire Key Of Luck). (J C Fretwell). *"He's a nice looking sort and he'll probably get him out in May. I just have a concern about his demeanour, because he could be one of those horses that might throw the towel in if he has too hard a race. But he might change once he finds it's not too hard. He's going the right way".*

1063. VESPASIA ★★★★
b.f. Medicean – Agrippina (Timeless Times).
March 11. Fifth foal. Sister to the dual listed 6f winner and Group 3 third Cartimandua and half-sister to the useful 5f winner of 5 races (including at 2 yrs) Terentia (by Diktat) and the fair 2-y-o 9f winner Sejanus (by Dubai Destination). The dam, a useful 2-y-o listed 7f winner, is a half-sister to one winner. The second dam, Boadicea's Chariot (by Commanche Run), an Irish 12f and hurdles winner, is a half-sister to 6 winners. (Mrs F S Williams): *"A full sister to Cartimandua who was a stakes winner for us, I'd say she's lighter framed but it's early on in her career and she's a big-topped filly. I expect she'll be out in mid-summer over six furlongs".*

1064. UNNAMED ★★★ ♠
b.f. Dixie Union – I'm Right (Rahy).
April 5. Second foal. 20,000Y. Tattersalls October Book 2. J Fretwell. The dam, a fair 7f winner, is a half-sister to 5 winners. The second dam, Sheer Reason (by Danzig), won the listed Criterium d'Evry and was Group 2 placed and is a half-sister to 6 winners. (J C Fretwell). *"She's been going well and she'll be sharp, but when we'll get her out is another thing. A 2-y-o type, she's fairly compact".*

1065. UNNAMED ★★★
ch.f. Vital Equine – Its Another Gift (Primo Dominie).
April 8. Eighth foal. 11,000Y. Tattersalls October Book 2. J Fretwell Racing. Half-brother to the 2-y-o listed-placed 5f winner Gifted Gamble (by Mind Games), to the 2-y-o 6f winner and Group 3 Princess Margaret Stakes second Reel Gift (by Reel Buddy) and the 2-y-o listed-placed 5f winner Scented Present (by Foxhound) – all fairly useful. The dam, a modest sprint placed maiden, is a half-sister to 5 winners. The second dam, Margaret's Gift (by Beveled), won 4 races from 2 to 4 yrs, was listed placed and is a half-sister to 4 winners including the French 1,000 Guineas second Peony. (Premspace Ltd). *"Not over-big and a little bit narrow, but she's very game and she should have run already but she got a touch of a sore shin. As soon as she's alright we'll get her out over five furlongs because she's quite sharp. The people who own her also had the sire, Vital Equine".*

BRIAN MEEHAN

1066. ACROSS ARABIA (IRE) ★★★
b.f. Invincible Spirit – Nofa's Magic (Rainbow Quest).
March 28. Third foal. The dam, placed over 10f and 12f, is a half-sister to 5 winners including the Group 1 9f Prix Jean Prat winner Olden Times. The second dam, Garah (by Ajdal), a very useful winner of 4 races over 6f, was second in the Group 3 5f Duke Of York Stakes and is a half-sister to 6 winners. (J Abdullah). *"A nice filly, she's quite sharp and she should be racing over six furlongs sometime around late May, but I don't know how good she is yet".*

1067. ALFAATEH (USA) ★★★
b.br.c. Stevie Wonderboy – Winner Takes All (Hennessy).
April 24. Second foal. Doncaster Premier. £20,000Y. McKeever Bloodstock. The dam won 2 races at 3 yrs in the USA and is a half-sister to 2 winners including the US Grade 3 winner Around The Cape. The second dam, Song Of Africa (by Alzao), a US listed winner and Grade 3 placed, is a half-sister to 7 winners including the US Grade 3 winner and Grade 1 placed Intensive Command. (Mr A Alkhallaf). *"A lovely horse, he looks nice, he wants six furlongs to start with and he's been working very well. I hope to have him out sometime in early May".*

1068. ANGELIC NOTE (IRE) ★★★
b.f. Excellent Art – Evangeline (Sadler's Wells).
**February 14. Fifth foal. 130,000foa.
Tattersalls Foals. Adrian Maxwell.** Half-sister to the 2-y-o Group 2 6f Lowther Stakes winner Infamous Angel (by Exceed And Excel). The dam is an unraced half-sister to 4 winners including the listed winner Sgt Pepper. The second dam, Amandine (by Darshaan), won once at 3 yrs in France and is a half-sister to 3 winners. (B V Sangster). *"A big filly that wants plenty of time, I would think she'd be ready in July and she moves very well".*

1069. ARABIAN FALCON ★★★
ch.c. Dutch Art – Castilian Queen (Diesis).
**April 26. Eleventh foal. Goffs Orby. €36,000Y.
Gill Richardson.** Half-brother to the high-class Group 1 5f Prix de l'Abbaye winner Carmine Lake (by Royal Academy), the useful 2-y-o 5f and 6f winner Major Eazy (by Fasliyev), the fairly useful 3-y-o 7f winner and listed-placed Three Secrets (by Danehill), the fairly useful Irish 2-y-o 6f and subsequent Hong Kong winner Progreso (by Danehill Dancer) and the fair 2-y-o 7f winner Star Of Grosvenor (by Last Tycoon). The dam, a fair 2-y-o 6f winner, is a half-sister to 4 winners including the useful 6f and 7f winner and Diomed Stakes third Regal Sabre. The second dam, Royal Heroine (by Lypheor), won 10 races including the 6f Princess Margaret Stakes (at 2 yrs) and the 9f Hollywood Derby, the 9f Matriarch Stakes and the Breeders Cup Mile (all Grade 1 events). (J Abdullah). *"He starts his career at Newbury in mid-April and although he'll probably need the run he looks sharp and he looks nice and I think he'll get six furlongs".*

1070. ART LAW (IRE) ★★★
b.g. Kheleyf – Snippets (Be My Guest).
April 6. Fourth foal. 42,000Y. Tattersalls October Book 2. McKeever Bloodstock. Half-brother to the quite useful 2010 2-y-o dual 6f winner Hortensia (by Holy Roman Emperor) and to a hurdles winner by Oasis Dream. The dam was an Irish 7f, 1m (both at 2 yrs) and listed 12f winner and is a half-sister to 2 winners. The second dam, Sniffle (by Shernazar), is an unpaced half-sister to 4 winners including the Grade 1 12f Hollywood Turf Cup and Group 3 1m Beresford Stakes winner Frenchpark and the Group 1 Prix Vermeille winner Pearly Shells. (R C Tooth) *"He's having a couple of weeks off after a gelding operation, but he goes well".*

1071. BAYAN (IRE) ★★★★
b.c. Danehill Dancer – Kindling (Dr Fong).
**February 11. Second foal. 210,000Y.
Tattersalls October Book 1. Angie Sykes.**
The dam, a useful 9f, 12f and listed 2m winner, is a half-sister to 8 winners including the French listed 9f winner Thattinger. The second dam, Isle Of Flame (by Shirley Heights), was unraced. (I Parvizi). *"A big horse, he's going to need time. I'd say August would be his starting point but he goes really well and I'm very happy with him. He should be one to look out for".*

1072. BULLDOG BEASLEY (USA) ★★★
b.c. Van Nistelrooy – Dixie Eyes Blazing (Gone West).
February 10. Eleventh foal. Doncaster Premier. £45,000Y. McKeever Bloodstock.
Half-brother to the quite useful 2-y-o 7f winners Greyt Big Stuff (by Aljabr) and Damietta (by More Than Ready), to the fair 1m winner Johnny Reb (by Danehill), the Italian winner of 7 races Dixie General (by Kris) and a 2-y-o 6f winner in Japan by Barathea. The dam ran twice and was placed once over 7f on the . She is a half-sister to 4 winners including the useful 5f (at 2 yrs) and 1m winner Well Beyond (herself dam of the US Grade 3 winner Out Of Reach and the Cherry Hinton Stakes third Well Warned). The second dam, Mariakova (by The Minstrel), placed over 6f at 2 yrs and 1m at 3 yrs, is a sister to the smart filly Zaizafon (the dam of Zafonic) and a half-sister to the unraced Modena (the dam of Elmaamul and Reams of Verse). *"He's done very well lately and has grown a lot. He has a wonderful attitude, he'll be racing in June and he looks very progressive".*

1073. BURANO (IRE) ★★★
ch.c. Dalakhani – Kalimanta (Lake Coniston).
February 23. Sixth foal. Goffs Orby. €82,000Y. McKeever Bloodstock. Half-brother to Sinnfonia (by Sinndar), unplaced in one start at 2 yrs in 2010, to the useful 7f (at 2 yrs) and 1m winner and Group 3 Brownstown Stakes third Kalidaha (by Cadeaux Genereux)

and the quite useful Irish 11f and 12f winner Kallithea (by Dr Fong). The dam ran twice unplaced and is a half-sister to 5 winners including the top-class Champion Stakes and Breeders Cup Turf winner Kalanisi and the high-class 1m listed winner and Group 1 St James's Palace Stakes second Kalaman. The second dam, Kalamba (by Green Dancer), was placed over 9f and 10f and is a full or half-sister to 3 winners. (Mr J Harvey). *"He's got a touch of sore shins at the moment so I've had to back off him. He goes really well, he's a nice horse and I like him a lot. Considering his pedigree he's actually very sharp".*

1074. CLEAN BOWLED (IRE) ★★★★
b.c. Footstepsinthesand – Miznapp (Pennekamp).
May 6. Sixth foal. 31,000Y. Tattersalls October Book 2. McKeever Bloodstock. Half-brother to the minor US winner of 2 races at 3 and 4 yrs Violet Sky (by Montjeu) and to the moderate dual 5f winner (including at 2 yrs) Boga (by Invincible Spirit). The dam is an unraced half-sister to 3 winners including the Group 3 Ballycorus Stakes winner Al Tadh. The second dam, Tithcar (by Cadeaux Genereux), is a placed half-sister to 6 winners including the dual Group 2 winner Zindabad. *"I have two colts by Footstepsinthesand and I like them both very much. He's quite a sharp colt, he'll want six furlongs and he should be racing by the end of May".*

1075. DIAMONDHEAD (IRE) ★★★
b.c. Kyllachy – Hammrah (Danehill).
January 30. First foal. Goffs Orby. €50,000Y. Sir Robert Ogden. The dam is an unraced half-sister to 3 winners. The second dam, Wardat Allayl (by Mtoto), a fairly useful 2-y-o 7f winner, is a half-sister to 7 winners including the high-class 2-y-o Group 2 6f Lowther Stakes winner Bint Allayl, the Group 3 7f Jersey Stakes winner and smart sire Kheleyf and the Group 3 Prix Quincey winner Laa Reyb. (Sir Robert Ogden). *"He's had a touch of sore shins but he's a very nice colt and he goes very well. A strong colt, six furlongs should be fine for him in late May".*

1076. EBEN ZAABEEL (IRE) ★★★
b.c. Invincible Spirit – Easy Lover (Pivotal).
January 28. First foal. Tattersalls October Book 1. Shadwell Estate Co. The dam won 2 races at 2 yrs including the listed Radley Stakes and is a half-sister to one winner. The second dam, Easy To Love (by Diesis), a quite useful 4-y-o 11.5f winner, is a sister to the Oaks winner Love Divine (herself dam of the St Leger winner Sixties Icon) and a half-sister to 3 winners including the listed 12f winner Floreeda. (Hamdan Al Maktoum). *"He's had a bit of a setback so he'll need a month or two off, but he's a very nice colt".*

1077. FINLEY CONNOLLY (IRE) ★★★★
b.c. Cockney Rebel – Impetious (Inchinor).
March 27. First foal. Goffs Orby. €30,000Y. Hugo Merry. The dam, a useful German listed 1m winner, was third in the Group 3 C L Weld Park Stakes and is a out of the modest 11f winner Kauri (by Woodman), herself a half-sister to 3 minor winners in the USA. (Mrs Mette Campbell-Andenaes). *"A lovely horse, I really like him, since he came in he's done nothing but get stronger, he has a great temperament and he should be ready in a month or so. A good-looking horse".*

1078. FREE HOUSE ★★★
ch.c. Sir Percy – Coming Home (Vettori).
April 3. Fourth foal. 80,000Y. Tattersalls October Book 2. McKeever Bloodstock. Half-brother to the very useful 2010 2-y-o 7f and 1m winner Mantoba (by Noverre) and to the fair 2-y-o 6f winner Via Mia (by Namid). The dam, a minor French middle-distance winner, is a half-sister to 3 winners. The second dam, Bonne Etoile (by Diesis), a fairly useful winner of 3 races at 3 yrs including a listed event over 10f, is a half-sister to 5 winners. *"A very nice horse, he goes very well. He's had a touch of sore shins so he won't be ready until mid-summer anyway and he'll want six or seven furlongs, but I like him a lot".*

1079. GOOD CLODORA (IRE) ★★★
b.f. Red Clubs – Geht Schnell (Fairy King).
April 15. Thirteenth foal. Goffs Orby. €48,000Y. Gill Richardson. Half-sister to the Irish 2-y-o 6f listed winner Alexander Alliance (by Danetime), to the listed 5f and 6f winner

and Group 3 placed Ruby Rocket (by Indian Rocket), the German listed winner and Group 3 6.5f Prix Eclipse second Inzar's Best (by Inzar), the quite useful 2-y-o dual 7f winner Cool Panic (by Brave Act), the quite useful 12f and hurdles winner Spiderback (by Redback), the minor Irish 12f winner Voodoo Lily (by Petardia) and 3 minor winners abroad by Runnett and Petardia (2). The dam is a placed half-sister to one winner abroad. The second dam, Anita's Princess (by Miami Springs), is an unraced half-sister to 7 winners including the very smart sprinter Anita's Prince. (J Abdullah). *"She shouldn't take too long because she's very sharp and she's been working well. Five or six furlongs will be her trip".*

1080. GREAT NAMOOS ★★★
b.c. Dansili – Flashy Wings (Zafonic).
February 12. First foal. The dam, a winner of 4 races including the Group 2 6f Lowther Stakes and Group 2 5f Queen Mary Stakes, was Group 1 placed three times and is a half-sister to 5 winners. The second dam, Lovealoch (by Lomond), a very useful 7f (at 2 yrs) and 9f winner here and placed in the Group 2 Falmouth Stakes and the Group 2 Premio Lydia Tesio, subsequently won once in the USA and is a half-sister to 7 winners. (J Abdullah). *"A lovely horse but he wants plenty of time and he's very typical of the stallion".*

1081. JUNIOR DIARY (USA) ★★★
ch.f. Mr Greeley – Cross Channel (Giant's Causeway).
January 27. First foal. The dam, a fairly useful 2-y-o 7f winner, was fourth in a listed event and is a half-sister to the US Grade 2 Tom Fool Handicap winner Exchange Rate and to the Group 3 10.5f Rose Of Lancaster Stakes winner Sabre d'Argent. The second dam, Sterling Pound (by Seeking The Gold), won five races including the Grade 3 Honey Bee Handicap. (Mrs L J Freedman). *"A tall filly, I think she wants plenty of time but I like her a lot. She's very classy".*

1082. KELNER'S CROSS ★★★
b.c. Cape Cross – Gretna (Groom Dancer).
February 18. Third foal. 75,000Y. Tattersalls October Book 2. McKeever Bloodstock. Closely related to the fair 1m and 9f winner of 3 races Wedding Dream (by Oasis Dream) and half-brother to the 2010 French 1m placed 2-y-o Kingston Tiger (by Tiger Hill). The dam, a fair 9.7f winner, is a half-sister to 5 winners including the Group 2 Princess Of Wales's Stakes winner Sans Frontieres and the very useful triple listed 1m winner (including at 2 yrs) and Group 2 Falmouth Stakes third Kootenay. The second dam, Llia (by Shirley Heights), a fairly useful 2-y-o 7f winner, was third in the listed 10f Pretty Polly Stakes and is a half-sister to 5 winners including the Italian Group 3 winner Guest Connections and the useful 2m listed winner Lady Of The Lake. (R P Foden). *"He's got a great attitude, he's very laid-back and he's going to want plenty of time but he goes very well".*

1083. LOVED BY ALL (IRE) ★★★
b.f. Elusive City – Bianca Cappello (Glenstal).
April 9. Eighth foal. 24,000Y. Tattersalls October Book 2. McKeever Bloodstock. Half-sister to the useful 2-y-o Group 3 6.5f Prix Eclipse winner Potaro (by Catrail) and to the fair 7f winner Gemini Future (by Flying Spur). The dam is an unplaced half-sister to 4 winners including Idris (a winner of four Group 3 events in Ireland at up to 12f) and the US Grade 3 placed Sweet Mazarine. The second dam, Idara (by Top Ville), was a very useful winner over 11f and 12f and was third in the Group 2 Prix de Pomone. (J Abdullah). *"I trained her half-brother Potaro a few years ago and she's a similar type to him. She's had a break but she's on her way back now and I really like her".*

1084. MAROOSH ★★★
br.c. Kyllachy – Madamoiselle Jones (Emperor Jones).
March 19. Third foal. 25,000Y. Tattersalls October Book 2. McKeever Bloodstock. Half-brother to the 2010 5f and 6f placed 2-y-o Abidhabidubai (by Dubai Destination). The dam, a fair winner of 3 races at around 1m, is a half-sister to 4 winners including the useful Group 3 7f Dubai Duty Free (Fred Darling Stakes) and 2-y-o 7f listed winner and Irish 1,000 Guineas second Penkenna Princess. The second dam, Tiriana (by Common Grounds), is a placed half-sister to 4 winners including the 2-y-o listed 5.2f winner Head Over Heels.

"A very typical Kyllachy, he's a nice horse, straightforward, his temperament is very good and he moves well. He's going to want a little bit more time and he'll probably get seven furlongs".

1085. MEHIDI (IRE) ★★★★
b.c. Holy Roman Emperor – College Fund Girl (Kahyasi).
April 19. Fourth foal. 50,000Y. Tattersalls October Book 1. Angie Sykes. Half-brother to the quite useful 1m and hurdles winner Final Approach (by Pivotal). The dam, a fair 12f winner, is a half-sister to the dual Group 2 7f winner Nayyir, to the UAE Group 3 12f winner and Group 1 placed Highest and the listed 14f winner Shamaiel. The second dam, Pearl Kite (by Silver Kite), a useful 2-y-o 1m winner and third in the Group 2 12f Ribblesdale Stakes, is a half-sister to 3 winners including the Group 2 Goodwood Cup third Jaseur. (I Parvizi). *"He shouldn't take too long, he probably wants six furlongs but he works really well and we really like him a lot".*

1086. MENTION (IRE) ★★★
b.f. Acclamation – Somaggia (Desert King).
February 4. Second foal. 20,000Y. Tattersalls October Book 2. McKeever Bloodstock. The dam is an unplaced half-sister to 8 winners including the listed winner and Group 1 Prix de la Salamandre third Speedfit Too. The second dam, Safka (by Irish River), a useful 2-y-o 5f winner, was third in the Group 3 5f Cornwallis Stakes and is a half-sister to 9 winners including the Group 2 7f Lockinge Stakes winner Safawan. (R C Tooth). *"A nice, sharp filly. We eased back on her recently but she's come through nicely from that break. I can see her starting off in mid-May over six furlongs".*

1087. MOST IMPROVED (IRE) ★★★
b.c. Lawman – Tonnara (Linamix).
May 3. Second foal. €65,000Y. Arqana Deauville August. Angie Sykes. The dam, unplaced in two starts, is a half-sister to 5 winners including the Group 3 Prix de Flore winner Albisola. The second dam, Mahalia (by Danehill), won the listed Prix Imprudence and is a half-sister to 7 winners including the French Group 3 winner Muroto and the good broodmare Zivania (the dam of 5 stakes winners). (I Parvizi). *"A colt that came from Deauville in August so he's had plenty of time, he's a nice size, scopey and just needs a bit more time. Probably one for seven furlongs".*

1088. ORWELLIAN ★★★
b.g. Bahamian Bounty – Trinny (Rainbow Quest).
March 8. Third foal. Doncaster Premier. £22,000Y. McKeever Bloodstock. Half-brother to the unraced 2010 2-y-o Apassionforfashion (by Best Hollow). The dam is an unraced half-sister to one winner in France. The second dam, Mall Queen (by Sheikh Albadou), won the listed Prix Yacowlef and is a half-sister to 8 winners including two listed winners. *"He's just been gelded so he's having a little break. He's quite leggy and wants a bit of time but he has a nice attitude and I'm very pleased with him. A typical Bahamian Bounty in that what you see is what you get, and you always get your money's worth".*

1089. PROUD PEARL (USA) ★★★★ ♠
b.f. Proud Citizen – Pacific Spell (Langfuhr).
May 17. Sixth foal. $250,000Y. Keeneland September. David Redvers. Sister to the US Grade 1 Kentucky Oaks and Grade 1 Alabama Stakes winner Proud Spell. The dam, a minor winner at 3 and 4 yrs in the USA, is a half-sister to 4 winners including the US stakes winner Call Her Magic. The second dam, Malibu Magic (by Encino), won 2 minor races at 5 yrs and is a half-sister to 7 winners including the Grade 1 Santa Anita Oaks winner Imaginary Lady. (B V Sangster). *"She looks really nice, she goes very well and she's very uncomplicated. Looks a smart filly".*

1090. RAWAAFED (IRE) ★★★
b.br.c. Invasor – Holly's Kid (Pulpit).
February 15. Second foal. $300,000Y. Keeneland September. Shadwell Estate Co. The dam won 2 minor races in the USA at 2 and 3 yrs and is a sister to the US Grade 1 Del Mar Oaks winner Rutherienne. The second dam, Ruthian (by Rahy), a listed winner of 4 races in the USA, is a half-sister to 2 minor winners. (Hamdan Al Maktoum). *"He's only just come in, he's a well-grown colt that wants a lot of time and I don't know an awful lot about him*

yet. Looking at him I'd say he could be a very nice horse".

1091. RIGHT DIVINE (IRE) ★★
gr.c. Verglas – Yellow Trumpet (Petong).
February 15. Sixth foal. 56,000Y. Tattersalls October Book 2. McKeever Bloodstock. Brother to the fair 10f winner Silverglas and half-brother to the useful dual 5f (including at 2 yrs) and subsequent Hong Kong winner and listed-placed City Of Tribes (by Invincible Spirit), the quite useful 2-y-o 5f winner Canary Island (by Groom Dancer) and the quite useful 2-y-o 1m winner Golden Aria (by Rakti). The dam, a fair 2-y-o 5f winner, is a sister to 3 winners including the listed 5.2f St Hugh's Stakes winner Petula and a half-sister to 3 winners including the very useful Group 3 Ballycorus Stakes winner Naahy. The second dam, Daffodil Fields (by Try My Best), placed 6 times in Ireland, is a half-sister to 3 winners. (Right Tack Partnership). "A nice horse, he threw a splint which took him out of action for a while, so he won't be ready until late May".

1092. RIGHT TO DREAM (IRE) ★★★ ♠
b.c. Oasis Dream – Granny Kelly (Irish River).
February 20. Eighth foal. 60,000Y. Tattersalls October Book 1. McKeever Bloodstock. Brother to the minor French 3-y-o winner Aisy and half-brother to the quite useful 2-y-o 6f and Italian 7.5f listed winner Six Hitter (by Boundary), to the quite useful dual 7f winner (including at 2 yrs) of 4 races Hustle (by Choisir) and the minor French 10f and 11f winner of 3 races Heavenly Light (by Montjeu). The dam, placed once over 7f at 2 yrs in Ireland, is a half-sister to 4 minor winners. The second dam, Deviltante (by Devil's Bag), a minor US 3-y-o winner, is a half-sister to 5 winners including the US stakes winner and Grade 2 placed Arrowtown. (Right Tack Partnership). "He should be racing in May, he has a lovely action and shows speed".

1093. RUBY GLASS (IRE) ★★★
b.c. Red Clubs – Gold Bar (Barathea).
March 21. Fifth foal. The dam, a 10f placed maiden, is closely related to the high-class Group 1 7f Dewhurst Stakes dead-heater Prince of Dance and to the Group 2 Scottish Derby winner Princely Venture. The second dam, Sun Princess (by English Prince), a top-class winner of the Oaks, the St Leger and the Yorkshire Oaks, is a half-sister to the high-class middle-distance colt Saddlers Hall. (Ballymacoll Stud Farm). "A nice horse, he's done particularly well recently and he's goes well. One for June onwards, he comes from a particularly nice family".

1094. SAFARI STORM (USA) ★★★
b.c. Dubawi – Londolozi (Forest Wildcat).
February 23. First foal. 36,000Y. Tattersalls October Book 2. McKeever Bloodstock. The dam, a modest 7f placed 2-y-o, is a half-sister to 3 winners including the listed winner subsequent US Grade 2 placed True Cause. The second dam, Dearly (by Rahy), won the Group 3 Blandford Stakes and is a half-sister to 4 winners including Balletto (Grade 1 Frizette Stakes in the USA). (N Attenborough, Mrs L Mann, Mrs L Way). "He's had a run and his jockey was pleased with him. He said he should win next time. He'll get six furlongs but he'll be able to win over five before that".

1095. SANAD (IRE) ★★★ ♠
b.c. Red Clubs – Knockatotaun (Spectrum).
March 16. Fourth foal. 62,000Y. Tattersalls October Book 2. Shadwell Estate Co. Half-brother to the fairly useful 2010 Irish 2-y-o triple 6f winner Knock Stars (by Soviet Star), to the fair Irish dual 1m winner Rassi Maguire (by Intikhab) and the moderate 6f winner Donard Lodge (by Elnadim). The dam, a moderate 12f and 13f winner, is a half-sister to 3 winners including the Irish dual listed 11f winner and multiple Group 3 placed Indiana Gal. The second dam, Genial Jenny (by Danehill), won 4 minor races over 9f in Ireland and is a half-sister to 7 other minor winners. (Hamdan Al Maktoum). "He wants six furlongs but he's very sharp in his mind. He goes well and it won't take long to get him ready".

1096. SANDBETWEENOURTOES (IRE) ★★★★
b.c. Footstepsinthesand – Callanish (Inchinor).
April 7. Third foal. 32,000Y. Tattersalls October Book 2. McKeever Bloodstock. The dam ran twice unplaced and is a half-sister to the 9.5f (at 2 yrs) and Grade 2 La Prevoyante Handicap winner and Group 1 10f Prix Saint-

Alary third Arvada and to the Group 3 7f Craven Stakes winner Adagio. The second dam, Lalindi (by Cadeaux Genereux), a fair middle-distance winner of 7 races, is a half-sister to 5 winners including the useful 2-y-o winner Sumoto (herself dam of the Group 1 winners Summoner and Compton Admiral). *"I like him a lot and apart from being a slightly different colour you'd say my two Footstepsinthesand 2-y-o's were like two peas out of a pod. Nice, precocious horses, they both want six furlongs and they won't take long"*.

1097. SHARK IN THE SEA ★★★
b.c. Sakhee – Wassendale (Erhaab).
April 5. First foal. 25,000Y. Tattersalls October Book 2. McKeever Bloodstock. The dam was placed over 10f and is a half-sister to 7 winners including the smart 7f (at 2 yrs) and triple listed middle-distance winner Frank Sonata and the useful 2-y-o listed 7f Sweet Solera Stakes winner Peaceful Paradise. The second dam, Megdale (by Waajib), a fair middle-distance placed maiden, is a sister to the useful 7f to 9f winner Wijara and a half-sister to 10 winners including Alhijaz, a winner of four Group 1 events in Italy. (J Abdullah). *"A big, strong colt with a great attitude. He's going to want seven furlongs and a bit of time but he goes well"*.

1098. SHE'S FLAWLESS (USA) ★★★
b.f. Smart Strike – Diva (A P Indy).
April 2. Second foal. $140,000Y. Keeneland September. Not sold. The dam, a minor US 3-y-o winner, is a sister to the US stakes winner Full Mandate and a half-sister to the US dual Grade 3 winner and Grade 1 placed Newfoundland. The second dam, Clear Mandate (by Deputy Minister), won 10 races in the USA including three Grade 1 stakes and is a half-sister to the US Grade 2 winner Dream Scheme. (I Parvizi). *"I'd say she was well-bought, she goes well and isn't going to take long. I think she'll be better over seven furlongs but she'll win over six first"*.

1099. SIR BEDIVERE (IRE) ★★★
b.c. Dansili – Miss Ivanhoe (Selkirk).
March 16. 82,000Y. Tattersalls October Book 1. Brian Meehan. The dam, a listed 7f winner, is a half-sister to 6 winners. The second dam, Robellino Miss (by Robellino), won 7 races at up to 9f in the USA, was stakes-placed and is a half-sister to the listed winners Grangeville and Palana. *"A strong, well-built colt, he goes well and even at this stage he does everything easily but we'll give him plenty of time"*.

1100. STATEMENTOFINTENT (IRE) ★★★
b.c. Tagula – Key Girl (Key Of Luck).
February 27. First foal. Doncaster Premier. £85,000Y. McKeever Bloodstock. The dam is an unplaced half-sister to 8 winners including the smart Irish 5f and listed 6f winner Rolo Tomasi and the Group 2 German 1,000 Guineas second Elegant Ridge. The second dam, Elegant Bloom (by Be My Guest), a quite useful Irish 2-y-o 6f winner, stayed 7f and is a full or half-sister to 12 winners. *"A nice horse, he wants time, he has a good attitude and he goes well like all the Tagula's. I like him a lot but he needs time"*.

1101. ST BARTHS ★★★ ♠
b.c. Cadeaux Genereux – Ile Deserte (Green Desert).
January 3. First foal. Doncaster Premier. £40,000Y. McKeever Bloodstock. The dam is an unraced half-sister to one winner. The second dam, Audacieuse (by Rainbow Quest), winner of the Group 3 Prix de Flore, is a half-sister to 3 winners including the Irish listed 14f winner Lord Jim. *"He looks like a horse that would need a bit further but the way he worked the other day I may run him quite soon. A typical Cadeaux, he has a great attitude and I like him a lot"*.

1102. STRICTLY PRIVATE ★★★
ch.c. Rahy – Al Theraab (Roberto).
March 11. Thirteenth foal. 40,000Y. Tattersalls October Book 1. Not sold. Brother to the quite useful 1m and 9f winner Caldercruix and half-brother to the Group 2 Beresford Stakes winner Albert Hall, to the listed French Prix Yacowlef winner Barsine, the useful French 6f and 7f winner Algallarens (all by Danehill), the useful 7f (at 2 yrs) to 8.5f winner of 8 races Flighty Fellow (by Flying Spur), the quite useful 7f winner Sabhaan (by Green Desert) and the French 1m winner Ebdaa (by Nashwan). The dam, a quite useful 1m winner, is a half-sister to 5 winners including the US stakes winner

Meadowlamb. The second dam, Golden Lamb (by Graustark), won at 3 yrs and is a sister to several good US horses including the Grade 3 winner Java Moon and the dam of the champion US turf horse Sunshine Forever. (B E Nielsen). *"He wants plenty of time, he's quite well-grown and forward but still a bit weak. A nice horse".*

1103. THE BLUE BANANA (IRE) ★★★
b.c. Red Clubs – Rinneen (Bien Bien).
March 25. Third foal. Doncaster Premier. £20,000Y. McKeever Bloodstock. The dam, a modest 6f (at 2 yrs) and 12f placed maiden, is a half-sister to 5 winners including the dual listed 6f winner (including at 2 yrs) Lady Links (herself dam of the dual listed winner Selinka). The second dam, Sparky's Song (by Electric), a moderate 10.2f and 12f winner, is a half-sister to the very smart Group 1 6.5f winner Bold Edge and to the listed winner and Group 3 5f Temple Stakes second Brave Edge. (Lanesborough). *"He goes really well and looks sharp but he's not quite ready yet. He should be out by the end of May and I like him".*

1104. VOODOO RHYTHM (USA) ★★★
b.g. Proud Citizen – Enchanted Kiss (Afternoon Deelites).
April 28. Fourth foal. 30,000Y. Tattersalls October Book 2. McKeever Bloodstock. The dam is an unraced half-sister to the US stakes winner Homemaker. The second dam, Open House (by Deputy Minister), is an unraced half-sister to 6 minor winners in the USA. (Decadent Racing). *"A good-looking horse, he's been gelded but he goes really well and he's going to want seven furlongs probably. He was a cheap horse".*

1105. UNNAMED ★★★★
b.br.f. Dixie Union – General Jeanne (Honour And Glory).
April 8. Sixth foal. $390,000Y. Keeneland September. Hugo Merry. Sister to the US dual Grade 2 winner and Grade 1 placed Justwhistledixie and half-sister to the US Grade 2 winner Chace City (by Carson City) and a minor winner in the USA by Victory Gallop. The dam, a minor US 3-y-o winner of 2 races, is a half-sister to 11 winners including the US Grade 2 winner Penny's Reshoot. The second dam, Ahpo Hel (by Mr Leader), won 2 minor races at 3 yrs in the USA and is a sister to the Grade 2 winner Pok Ta Pok. (Mr A Rosen). *"Very classy to look at, she moves very well but she wants a bit of time so she'll be out June or July. I like her a lot".*

1106. UNNAMED ★★★
ch.g. Hawk Wing – Give A Whistle (Mujadil).
February 6. Sixth foal. Doncaster Premier. £35,000Y. Agent Allison. Half-brother to the Irish 2-y-o listed 5f and subsequent US Grade 3 6f winner Pasar Silbano (by Elnadim), to the quite useful UAE 3-y-o 6f winner Call For Liberty and the fair Irish 2-y-o 6f winner Laldie (both by Statue Of Liberty). The dam, a dual 5f winner at 3 and 4 yrs, is a half-sister to one winner. The second dam, Repique (by Sharpen Up), is a winning half-sister to the Group winners Indian Lodge, Sarhoob and Sifting Gold. *"He goes very well, has a great attitude and a nice temperament, likely to be out by late May".*

1107. UNNAMED ★★★
gr.g. Verglas – La Caprice (Housebuster).
April 12. Seventh foal. Doncaster Premier. £20,000Y. Agent Allison. Half-brother to the unplaced 2010 2-y-o Deveze, to the fair 5f and 6f winner of 8 races La Capriosa (both by Kyllachy), the quite useful 2-y-o 5f winner and listed-placed Empire's Ghodha (by Mujadil) and the fair 5f and 6f winner of 4 races Milton Of Campsie (by Medicean). The dam, a quite useful 5f winner at 2 and 3 yrs, is a half-sister to 8 winners including the Group 2 6f Richmond Stakes winner Muqtarib and the listed winners Ra'A and Janib. The second dam, Shicklah (by The Minstrel), a useful 2-y-o 5f and 6f winner here, subsequently won a Group 2 event in Germany and is a half-sister to 3 winners. (Lanesborough). *"A sharp, good sort and a typical Verglas. He has a nice attitude and he'll be racing in May".*

1108. UNNAMED ★★★
b.f. Rail Link – Monkshill (Fraam).
February 6. First foal. 36,000Y. Tattersalls October Book 2. Hugo Merry. The dam ran twice unplaced and is a half-sister to 8 winners including the useful triple 7f winner Mata Cara (herself the dam of a French listed winner). The

second dam, Fatah Flare (by Alydar), won over 6f (at 2 yrs) and the Group 3 10.5f Musidora Stakes at 3 yrs and is a half-sister to 8 winners including Sabin, a dual US Grade 1 winner over 9f and 10f. (Ladyswood Stud). *"She hasn't been in long, but she goes well, she's very forward in herself, very relaxed and a nice filly"*.

1109. UNNAMED ★★★
b.f. *Bernardini – Promenade Girl (Carson City)*.
March 23. First foal. The dam won the US Grade 2 8.5f Molly Pitcher Handicap, was Grade 1 placed twice and is a half-sister to 6 winners. The second dam, Promenade Colony (by Pleasant Colony), a minor US 3-y-o winner, is a sister to the US Grade 2 winner Dance Colony and a half-sister to the US Grade 1 winners Another Review and No Review. (B V Sangster). *"She's very typical of the horses I've seen by the stallion, she's a nice, good-looking filly and I'm pleased with her"*.

1110. UNNAMED ★★★
gr.c. *Verglas – Roystonea (Polish Precedent)*.
March 30. Fourth foal. Goffs Orby. €90,000Y. BBA (Ire). Half-brother to the quite useful Irish 2-y-o 7f winner Take A Chance (by Hawk Wing) and a minor winner abroad by Xaar. The dam, a winner of 2 races over 7f and 1m at 3 and 4 yrs in France, was listed-placed and is a half-sister to the French listed winners Bermuda Grass and Bermuda Rye. The second dam, Alleluia Tree (by Royal Academy), a French 2-y-o winner, is a half-sister to 7 winners including the Irish listed 9f winner Rimpa and to the unraced Ardmelody (dam of the Coronation Cup, St Leger and Grand Prix de Paris winner Scorpion, the US Grade 2 winner Memories and the smart listed winners Danish Rhapsody and Garuda). (Mrs S Tucker, & Ed McCormack). *"A very typical Verglas, he's a nice horse and although he needs a little bit of time six furlongs will be fine for him and he won't be long"*.

1111. UNNAMED ★★★
ch.f. *Distorted Humor – Wile Cat (Storm Cat)*.
January 21. First foal. $375,000Y. Keeneland September. Oliver St Lawrence. The dam is an unraced sister to the Grade 2 La Canada Stakes winner Cat Fighter and a half-sister to the Group 3 winner and sire Ishiguru.

The second dam, Strategic Maneuver (by Cryptoclearance), winner of the Grade 1 6f Spinaway Stakes, the Grade 1 7f Matron Stakes and two Grade 2 events at 2 yrs in the USA, is a half-sister to 9 winners including the US stakes winners Ashford Castle and Missionary. (Mr F Nass). *"A sharp filly, she goes well and has a great attitude. She'll be racing from mid-May onwards and she's nice"*.

1112. UNNAMED ★★★
b.f. *Van Nistelrooy – Yousefia (Danzig)*.
April 27. Eleventh foal. Goffs Orby. €78,000Y. McKeever Bloodstock. Half-sister to the very useful Group 3 6f Princess Margaret Stakes (at 2 yrs) and 1m winner Mythical Girl, to the minor US winner of 4 races Occidental Tourist (both by Gone West), to the quite useful 7f winner Bullsefia (by Holy Bull) and 4 winners abroad by Private Account, Silver Hawk, Seeking The Gold and Johannesburg. The dam, a useful 2-y-o 6f winner here, subsequently won a 5.5f stakes event in the USA at 4 yrs and is a sister to the high-class July Cup winner and sire Green Desert and to the useful 2-y-o 6f winners Kissogram Girl and Blue Ocean. The second dam, Foreign Courier (by Sir Ivor), is an unraced half-sister to 15 winners, notably the Grade 1 winners Althea (dam of the champion Japanese 2-y-o filly Yamanin Paradise), Ali Oop and Ketoh, and the Grade 2 winners Aishah (dam of the US Grade 1 winner Aldiza), Aquilegia and Twining. *"She's typical of the sire, she has the right attitude and she goes well. I can see her being ready by the end of May and she's a nice filly"*.

ROD MILLMAN
1113. BLACKDOWN FAIR ★★★
b.f. *Trade Fair – Shielaligh (Aragon)*.
March 21. Second foal. £2,200Y. Not sold. Ascot November. Half-sister to the modest 6f winner Blackdown Boy (by Sampower Star). The dam, a fair 2-y-o 6f winner, is a sister to 2 winners including the quite useful 5f (at 2 yrs) and 6f winner of 4 races Seamus Shindig and a half-sister to one winner. The second dam, Sheesha (by Shadeed), was unplaced in one start and is a half-sister to 8 winners including the smart 12f King George V Handicap winner and St Leger fourth Samraan and the useful 6f (at 2 yrs) and 7f winner Star Talent. (Mr R

Brooke). "We had her half-brother last year and we managed to win with him but unfortunately he fractured a joint. This is quite a nice filly, she's a lot more forward than he was and a nicer type. She'll be racing over sprints from May onwards. The family is quite reasonable, a bit wayward but talented".

1114. DOVILS DATE ★★
gr.c. Clodovil – Lucky Date (Halling).
April 17. Third foal. 8,000Y. Tattersalls October Book 2. Rod Millman. Closely related to the fair 9f winner Highkingofireland (by Danehill Dancer) and half-brother to the French 1m (at 2 yrs) to 10f winner Rava (by Nayef). The dam, a fairly useful 2-y-o 7f winner, was second in the listed 1m Masaka Stakes and is a half-sister to 3 winners. The second dam, Hesperia (by Slip Anchor), a winner over 11f and 12f including a listed event in Italy, is a half-sister to the French listed winners Wavey and Rebuff. (Always Hopeful Partnership). "He's coming along nicely and he'll be running in April. At the moment I'd say that he'll benefit from having a couple of runs but he'll improve when he can race over six and seven furlongs. He's not over-big but well put-together and quite a relaxed character".

1115. GARRARUFA ★★★
ch.c. Chineur – Face The Storm (Barathea).
April 29. Sixth foal. 13,000Y. Tattersalls October Book 2. Rod Millman. Brother to the useful 2-y-o 5f and 6f winner and Group 2 7f Superlative Stakes second Roi de Vitesse and half-brother to the quite useful 2010 2-y-o 6f winner Kojak (by Kodiac) and the quite useful 6f (at 2 yrs) and 9f winner Cavort (by Vettori). The dam, a fair 2-y-o 1m winner, is a half-sister to 3 winners including the listed winner Santa Isobel. The second dam, Atlantic Record (by Slip Anchor), is an unraced half-sister to 4 winners. "We had his good full-brother Roi de Vitesse and although he's not as forward as him, he's a similar type. Although he's lazy like his brother was, he is at least showing us a bit, which his brother never did at home. If he's to be as good as him he has a lot to live up to, but so far he doesn't seem too bad at all".

1116. ISHI ★★★
b.f. Ishiguru – Chorus (Bandmaster).
March 27. £3,000Y. Not sold. Ascot November. Half-sister to Madame Kintyre (by Trade Fair), unplaced in one start at 2 yrs in 2010 and to the fair 5f winner Mrs Boss (by Makbul). The dam was a fair 5f to 7f winner of 5 races. The second dam, Name That Tune (by Fayruz), was unplaced. (Kintyre Racing). "Quite a nice filly, she's probably the best 2-y-o type to come out of the mare so far. She's also more straightforward than her half-sister Mrs Boss. Quite an imposing filly, she's entered in the Supersprint and because she went through the sales ring at Ascot she'll be heading for that Sales race as well, although it should be more competitive this year because there were some nice types at that sale this time".

1117. IVOR'S PRINCESS ★★★
b.f. Atraf – Rosina May (Danehill Dancer).
February 5. Fifth foal. Half-sister to the quite useful 2010 2-y-o 5f and 6f winner Rosina Grey (by Proclamation). The dam won all three of her starts, over 5f at 2 yrs. The second dam, Gay Paris (by Paris House), was an unraced half-sister to 3 winners. "She's a stronger type and better put-together than her half-sister Rosina Grey, who we had last year, but she's been coughing and we've missed a lot of work with her. By the time May comes along she'll be fine, she'll be a sprinter. Her sister was quite hard to train and this one isn't the quietest either".

1118. MACCABEES ★★★★
b.g. Motivator – Takarna (Mark Of Esteem).
February 17. Sixth foal. 7,000Y. Tattersalls October Book 2. Rod Millman. Brother to the quite useful 2-y-o 1m winner Jibrrya (by Motivator). The dam is a placed half-sister to 6 winners including the Group 2 Royal Whip Stakes winner Takali and the Group 3 12f Meld Stakes winner Takarian, subsequently winner of the Bay Meadows Derby in the USA. The second dam, Takarouna (by Green Dancer), a very useful winner of the Group 2 12f Pretty Polly Stakes at the Curragh, is a sister to the smart Group 2 Dante Stakes winner Torjoun. (Mr C Roper). "This is a nice horse. He'll probably have one run over six furlongs and then we'll move him up in trip. We've gelded

him and he's much easier to handle now. Quite a light-framed horse, he's quick to learn and going off his work you'd think he'd been doing it for six months. He's a tough horse and if there was a seven furlong race in April he could run in it. He wouldn't have a turn of foot, but he'll go on to be a nice dual-purpose horse one day". TRAINERS' BARGAIN BUY

1119. MELONERAS ★★★
b.f. Kyllachy – Overcome (Belmez).
March 8. Seventh foal. £9,000Y. Doncaster Premier. Not sold. Half-sister to the quite useful 2-y-o 5f winner Royal Desert (by Pastoral Pursuits), to the fair 6f (at 2 yrs) and 12f winner River Ardeche, the modest 2-y-o 6f winner Bridget's Team (both by Elnadim) and the fair 1m winner of 3 races Brace Of Doves (by Bahamian Bounty). The dam won once over 10f in Germany and is a half-sister to 8 winners. The second dam, Olivana (by Sparkler), is an unraced half-sister to the German Derby winners Orofino and Ordos. (The Not Too Far Boys). "She's showing good early form and hopefully she'll show some speed but get further than five furlongs because she's out of a staying dam. Worth putting in the book".

1120. MISTER MUSICMASTER ★★
b.c. Amadeus Wolf – Misty Eyed (Paris House).
May 2. Fourth foal. £5,000Y. Doncaster Premier. Jan Fuller. The dam, a smart 2-y-o winner of 4 races including the Group 3 5f Molecomb Stakes, was Group 2 placed twice and is a half-sister to several winners. The second dam, Bold As Love (by Lomond), is an unraced half-sister to 3 winners abroad. (Mrs J Fuller). "A little bit on the small side, he's a May foal and was very small at the Sales but he's done quite well since and he's caught the others up. He won't run until May and he'll be a sprinter. The dam was smart but she's been a disappointing broodmare. Having said that, this is the first of her foals that actually looks like a racehorse".

1121. NIGHT ANGEL (IRE) ★★★★
gr.f. Dark Angel – Dangle (Desert Style).
April 14. Fourth foal. Doncaster Premier. £10,000Y. Not sold, private sale Rod Millman. Half-sister to the moderate 5f (at 2 yrs) and 6f winner Watch Chain (by Traditionally). The dam, a useful Irish 7f winner, was listed-placed and is a half-sister to 6 winners including the Irish 7f (at 2 yrs) to 10f and subsequent Hong Kong stakes winner Solid Approach. The second dam, Dawn Chorus (by (Mukaddamah), is an unraced half-sister to 6 winners including Barrier Reef, a winner of 8 races and second in the Group 3 Beresford Stakes. (The Links Partnership). "She's very small but very well put-together and she'll be running in the early 2-y-o races trying to win one of the bonus races. She'll be one to aim at the Supersprint because she'll get in off a low weight. She might not be a top horse but she's pretty sharp and she might pick up a bit of early season black type".

1122. UNNAMED ★★
b.f. Trade Fair – Che Chic (Daggers Drawn).
March 16. Third foal. £400. Not sold. Ascot November. The dam won 3 races at 3 yrs in Italy and is a half-sister to 4 winners including the listed winner and Group 3 placed Royale Figurine. The second dam, Cree's Figurine (by Creetown), won once at 2 yrs and is a half-sister to 2 winners. (Rod Millman Racing Club). "Despite the price tag she's quite a nice filly actually. She's been coughing so she's missed some work otherwise she would have been early. Cheap and cheerful, it's almost impossible for a breeder to sell average fillies and I got her for the minimum bid. She'll be OK, a bit on the small side but big enough to win races and be competitive in small fillies' races later on. We put her in my Racing Club, which has 4 horses and costs just £150 per share – it's just an attempt to stir some interest and we've had 2 winners this year already".

1123. UNNAMED ★★★
b.f. Royal Applause – Fuschia (Averti).
January 19. First foal. Doncaster Premier. £17,000Y. Rod Millman. The dam, a fair 3-y-o 7f winner, is a half-sister to one winner. The second dam, Big Pink (by Bigstone), is an unraced half-sister to 8 winners including the French triple Group 3 winner Pink. (Mr D J Deer). "She's only just arrived after being prepared by the owner's stud but she's an attractive filly and I think she'll be quite nice. An average-sized filly, she's only cantering at the moment but she does everything right".

ROBERT MILLS

It was a pleasure to once again speak to Assistant Trainer Richard Ryan about the Loretta Lodge two-year-olds.

1124. DESERT SPREE ★★★
ch.f. Byron – Babaraja (Dancing Spree).
February 22. Fourth foal. Half-sister to the modest 2010 dual 5f placed 2-y-o Zarazar (by Statue Of Liberty). The dam is an unraced half-sister to numerous minor winners. The second dam, Ceramic (by Raja Baba), ran once unplaced and is a half-sister to 8 winners. *"A very nice filly and a sharp, 2-y-o type that will probably be one of our earlier runners".*

1125. EWELL PLACE ★★★
br.g. Namid – Miss Gibraltar (Rock Of Gibraltar).
February 4. First foal. Doncaster Premier. £22,000Y. Robert Mills. The dam ran once unplaced and is a half-sister to 2 winners. The second dam, Photogenic (by Midyan), a fairly useful 6f and listed 7f winner at 2 yrs, is a half-sister to numerous winners including the listed winner and Group 1 placed Mona Lisa and the very useful 2-y-o 5f and 7f Italian listed winner and Group 2 1m Falmouth Stakes second Croeso Cariad. (Exors of the late T G Mills). *"He's a strong, very well-made colt that should be early. A tough horse, he'll probably be seen to better advantage over six furlongs than five".*

1126. HIGH ENDEAVOUR ★★★★
b.f. High Chaparral – Green Tambourine (Green Desert).
January 28. Seventh foal. Goffs Orby. €72,000Y. R Mills. Half-sister to the quite useful 2-y-o 7f and subsequent US stakes winner Maid For Music (by Dubai Destination). The dam, a quite useful 2-y-o 6f winner, is a half-sister to 6 winners including the useful 2-y-o 7f winner Artistic Lad and the useful 7f (at 2 yrs) and 10f winner Maid To Perfection. The second dam, Maid For The Hills (by Indian Ridge), was a useful 2-y-o and won twice over 6f including the listed Empress Stakes. She is a half-sister to 5 winners including the dams of the US Grade 1 winner Stroll and the Group winners Lady In Waiting and Savannah Bay. (Exors of the late T G Mills). *"She's got a lot of quality, we like her a lot and although she hasn't been asked any questions she's done everything with very little effort. She's a tall, strong filly with scope and will probably be seen at her best up to a mile this year towards the autumn".*

1127. JASIE JAC ★★★★
b.c. Namid – Dynah Mo Hum (Key Of Luck).
March 11. First foal. 16,000Y. Tattersalls October Book 2. R Mills. The dam, a fair 7f winner, is a half-sister to 4 winners including the very useful dual listed 5f winner Dairine's Delight (by Fairy King). The second dam, Silius (by Junius), won the 1m Irish Cambridgeshire and is a half-sister to 7 winners including the dam of the 2-y-o Group 1 1m Racing Post Trophy winner Seattle Rhyme. (Portish Holdings Ltd). *"He wasn't expensive considering he's quite a nice-looking colt. He pleases us at home and has done some upsides work and although no buttons have been pressed he threatens to be out before mid-season. He may not be an out-and-out five furlong horse and he may need six furlongs but he could well have a bit more quality than just a five furlong runner. He's quite a nice horse, strong and well-made and probably the type to train on at three. A lot of horse for the money".* TRAINER'S BARGAIN BUY

1128. LA PASSIONATA ★★★
ch.f. Proclamation – Miss Madame (Cape Cross).
February 28. Second foal. The dam, a modest 7f and 1m winner, is a half-sister to a winner in Greece. The second dam, Cosmic Countess (by Lahib), a fair 2-y-o 6f winner, is a half-sister to 5 winners. *"An autumn type two-year-old but she's lovely and has a lot of quality".*

1129. MACY ANNE ★★★
b.f. King's Best – Gilah (Saddlers Hall).
January 30. Sixth foal. 20,000Y. Tattersalls October Book 2. R Mills. Sister to the fairly useful 2-y-o dual 1m winner Night Of Joy (by King's Best) and half-sister to the quite useful 10f to 2m and hurdles winner Ainama (by Desert Prince) and the quite useful 2-y-o 8.3f winner Congressional (by Grand Lodge). The dam is an unraced half-sister to 7 winners including the very useful 10.2f winner Cocotte

(the dam of 6 stakes winners including the top-class colt Pilsudski). The second dam, Gay Milly (by Mill Reef), a fair 3-y-o 1m winner, is out of the Irish 1,000 Guineas winner Gaily. (Portish Holdings Ltd). *"A neat, sharp little filly, she's well-made and I think she'll want six/seven furlongs whereas her full sister wanted a bit further. She'll be in action this year".*

1130. ROCK CANYON ★★★
b.c. Rock Of Gibraltar – Tuesday Morning (Sadler's Wells).
March 4. Fourteenth living foal. 30,000Y. Tattersalls October Book 2. R Mills. Brother to the fair Irish 14f winner Rocky Wednesday, closely related to the Irish dual 7f (at 2 yrs) and Group 3 1m Park Express Stakes winner Danehill Music (by Danehill Dancer) and the fair 2-y-o 6f winner Danetime Music (by Danetime) and half-brother to the minor 8.5f winner Ruby Estate (by High Estate), the 10f seller winner Purple Dawn (by Tirol), the Italian 3-y-o winner Su Colle (by College Chapel) and a winner in Turkey by Eagle Eyed. The dam is an unraced half-sister to one winner in Germany. The second dam, Mourwara (by Wolver Hollow), is a placed half-sister to 5 winners including the French 1,000 Guineas winner Masarika (herself dam of the Group winners Massyar and Madjaristan). *"He's very pleasing and has answered every question asked of him so far. I imagine he'll probably be seen over six furlongs plus, and he looks a neat, well-made 2-y-o type. He takes much more after his Dad than his full-brother who won over 14 furlongs!"*

1131. UNNAMED ★★★
ch.c. Excellent Art – Gentle Night (Zafonic).
January 26. Fifth foal. 200,000Y. Tattersalls October Book 2. J Humphreys. Half-brother to the quite useful 2-y-o 7f winner Oratory, to the quite useful Irish 7f winner Rockymountainhigh (both by Danehill Dancer) and the 4-y-o UAE triple 7f winner Knight Of Dance (by Singspiel). The dam ran once unplaced and is a half-sister to 6 winners including the Group 2 Flying Childers Stakes winner Land Of Dreams (herself dam the dual Group 1 winning 2-y-o Dream Ahead). The second dam, Sahara Star (by Green Desert), won the Group 3 Molecomb Stakes and is a half-sister to 6 winners including the Group 3 Greenham Stakes winner Yalaietanee. *"An expensive purchase but there's a lot happening in the pedigree particularly through Dream Ahead who was a big, brute of a 2-y-o last year by Diktat. This colt was a similar stamp to Dream Ahead at the Sales, although a chestnut by Excellent Art. He'll probably be a seven furlong type two-year-old because although he's a January foal he's a very big individual and won't be rushed".*

GARY MOORE

1132. ART NEWS (IRE) ★★
b.c. Dansili – Lucky (Sadler's Wells).
April 16. Fourth foal. 48,000Y. Tattersalls October Book 2. G L Moore. The dam, winner of the Group 3 Athasi Stakes, is a sister to the Leopardstown 1,000 Guineas Trial winner and Irish 1,000 Guineas second Amethyst and to the 2,000 Guineas and Group 1 National Stakes winner King Of Kings and a half-sister to the Group 2 5.5f Prix Robert Papin winner General Monash. The second dam, Zummerudd (by Habitat), is an unplaced sister to the Irish Group 3 and US Grade 3 winner Ancestral. (R Green). *"A nice horse, he's an athletic type but backward and I haven't done a great deal with him yet. It looks like he's going to need plenty of time but he's very nice. He has loads of size and scope about him and if I did any more than I am doing with him at the moment I'd be doing too much, he's just doing nice canters".*

1133. ROYAL ACADEMICIAN ★★★★
b.c. Mr Greeley – Alta Moda (Sadler's Wells).
January 24. First foal. 55,000Y. Tattersalls October Book 1. G L Moore Racing. The dam is an unraced half-sister to the listed Prix Petite Etoile winner Alvarita. The second dam, Alborada (by Alzao), winner of the Champion Stakes (twice), the Group 2 Nassau Stakes and the Group 2 Pretty Polly Stakes, is a sister to the triple German Group 1 winner Albanova and a half-sister to 6 winners including the fairly useful dual middle-distance winner Alakananda (herself dam of the Derby second Dragon Dancer). (R Green). *"He's quite a big, strong colt and a bit further forward than my Dansili colt. He's forward-going, we like him a lot, he goes well and he won't just be a two-year-old. He's very willing, a really nice horse*

1134. VENETIAN VIEW (IRE) ★★★★
b.c. Amadeus Wolf – Twilight Tango (Groom Dancer).
March 21. Seventh living foal. Goffs Orby. €60,000Y. G L Moore. Half-brother to the very useful 2-y-o listed 1m winner and Group 3 1m Prix Thomas Bryon third Gwaihir (by Cape Cross) and to the useful Irish 5f (at 2 yrs) and 1m winner and listed-placed Mombassa (by Mujadil). The dam is an unraced sister to the very useful 7f and 1m (at 2 yrs) and Group 3 12 3f Dalham Chester Vase winner Twist and Turn and a half-sister to the Group 3 Gallinule Stakes winner Meath. The second dam, Twyla (by Habitat), a useful dual 6f winner, is a sister to the smart 2-y-o sprinter Defecting Dancer. (R Green). "A lovely horse and we like him a lot. He's big and strong and looks like a 3-y-o already. He's got a great attitude, he's very laid-back and I couldn't speak more highly of him. He hasn't done a lot yet but everything he has done has been good. On pedigree you'd expect him to be fairly sharp but he's such a big, strong horse I'm a bit wary of starting him off too soon".

1135. JUPITER STORM ★★★
ch.c. Galileo – Exciting Times (Jeune Homme).
February 9. Sixth foal. 55,000Y. Tattersalls December. G L Moore. Half-brother to the US Grade 1 Beverly D Stakes, Group 2 Prix de Sandringham and dual US Grade 2 winner Gorella (by Grape Tree Road), to the US stakes and French listed winner Porto Santo and dual US Grade 2 second (by Kingsalsa), the fair 1m winner Squall (by Dubawi) and the French listed-placed winner Thanks Again (by Anabaa Blue). The dam is a placed half-sister to 7 winners. The second dam, Eloura (by Top Ville), won twice in France and is a half-sister to 4 other minor winners. (Heart of the South Racing). "A lovely horse, I couldn't believe we got him for that amount and I keep waiting for something to turn up, but so far so good. He's quite backward and fairly big but he goes along nicely and you couldn't wish to see a nicer horse. He's very well-mannered, I like him and he's one for late August onwards".

1136. WHINGING WILLIE (IRE) ★★★★
b.c. Cape Cross – Pacific Grove (Persian Bold).
February 3. Tenth foal. 44,000Y. Tattersalls October Book 2. G L Moore. Brother to the German 2-y-o Group 2 6f winner Mokabra and half-brother to the fairly useful Irish 6f winner and listed-placed John Doran's Melody (by Bluebird), the fairly useful 2-y-o 6f winner Caroline Island (by Catrail), the quite useful 2-y-o 6f winner Major Speculation (by Spectrum). The dam, a fairly useful winner of 3 races from 7f to 1m, is a half-sister to 5 winners including the listed Oak Tree Stakes winner Mauri Moon. The second dam, Dazzling Heights (by Shirley Heights), a useful winner of 4 races from 7f (at 2 yrs) to 11f including a listed event at Toulouse, is a full or half-sister to 6 winners. (P B Moorehead). "He's the only one of my two-year-olds that isn't very big! He looks a fairly early type, he goes along nicely and has a fantastic attitude. Watching him work you wouldn't think he'd want soft ground and I like him a lot. I'd say he'd be the first of ours to run, I love the sire and although this is a small colt he has a big heart".

GEORGE MOORE

1137. ALMOND BRANCHES ★★★
ch.f. Dutch Art – Queens Jubilee (Cayman Kai).
February 2. Fourth foal. £14,000Y. Doncaster Premier. Not sold. Half-sister to the fair 7f and 1m winner Fibs And Flannel (by Tobougg). The dam, a modest 2-y-o 6f winner, is a half-sister to 6 winners including Dubai Dynamo and Sadeek (both listed winners) and the useful 2-y-o 5f winner Pachara. The second dam, Miss Mercy (by Law Society), a modest 2-y-o 6f winner, is a half-sister to 3 minor winners. (J A & M A Knox). "She only came in late but she'd already been broken-in and was cantering, so they'd done a brilliant job with her and I expect her to be racing in April. Not a big filly, but she looks quick and the family have had 2-y-o and 3-y-o winners, so that won't bother her and she'll be quick enough. A proper little 2-y-o".

1138. ISOLDE'S RETURN ★★★
b.f. Avonbridge – Up And About (Barathea).
April 18. Ninth foal. 5,500Y. Tattersalls October 2. George Moore. Half-sister to the fairly useful 2-y-o 6f and 10f winner Take It To The Max (by Bahamian Bounty), to the

fairly useful 2-y-o 8.3f and UAE 3-y-o winner Tamarillo (by Daylami and herself dam of the Group 3 Oak Tree Stakes winner Summer Fete), the fairly useful 6f (at 2 yrs) and 7f winner and listed-placed Wake Up Call (by Noverre), the modest 2-y-o 9f winner Tiger Spice (by Royal Applause) and the moderate 12f and hurdles winner Park's Prodigy (by Desert Prince). The dam, a fair all-weather 14.8f winner, is a half-sister to 7 winners including the listed winner and Group 1 placed Musicanna. The second dam, Upend (by Main Reef), a smart winner of 3 races from 10f to 12f including the Group 3 St Simon Stakes and the listed Galtres Stakes, is a half-sister to 6 winners including the dam of the high-class stayer and champion hurdler Royal Gait. (Mrs M E Ingham). "She's done nothing but grow since I bought her and she's a bonny filly now. I'm very happy with her and she's doing little bits of work now. She does look like a 2-y-o but because of her growth spurt we've had to wait a bit with her but she does everything right, we do like her and fingers crossed she'll do her job. She looks like she'll be fairly quick, so five/six furlongs will do for her". TRAINERS' BARGAIN BUY

1139. UNNAMED ★★★
ch.f. Notnowcato – Exclusive Approval (With Approval).
March 23. Sixth foal. 23,000Y. Tattersalls October Book 2. George Moore. Half-sister to the modest 2009 7f placed 2-y-o Turf Trivia (by Alhaarth), to the very useful 6f and 10.5f winner and listed-placed In The Light (by Inchinor), the quite useful 1m, 10f and hurdles winner Thumbs Up (by Intikhab), the French 1m to 10f winner of 5 races By Appointment (by Mojave Moon) and a hurdles winner by Alhaarth. The dam, a minor US 3-y-o winner, is a sister to the stakes winner Be Elusive and a half-sister to 8 winners including the US stakes winner Vignette (dam of the St Leger winner Lucarno). The second dam, Be Exclusive (by Be My Guest), won 5 races in France and the USA including the Group 3 Prix Chloe and is a half-sister to 2 winners. (D Parker). "She's a bit backward at the moment but she's a lovely filly of a good size and with plenty of scope. We've not pressed any buttons yet but she's been doing a few bits of upsides work and we're just letting her enjoy what she's doing. She's a really scopey filly, so seven furlongs in mid-season should be about right for her. We're hopeful of having a bit of luck with her".

1140. UNNAMED ★★
b.f. Acclamation – Hufflepuff (Desert King).
April 19. Third foal. £5,000Y. Doncaster Premier. Not sold. Half-sister to the modest 2010 5f and 6f placed 2-y-o Indian Shuffle (by Sleeping Indian). The dam, a quite useful 6f (at 2 yrs) and 5f winner, is a half-sister to 4 winners. The second dam, Circle Of Chalk (by Kris), a fair 3-y-o 10.7f winner in the French provinces, is a sister to the useful French listed 12f winner From Beyond and a half-sister to 6 winners including the Group 2 Lowther Stakes winner Enthused. (A Crute & Partners). "We broke her in and got her going but she wants a bit of time because she was a bit weak, so we've sent her home for a holiday. We'll take another look at her around May time but she looks the type to be quick enough for five and six furlongs".

1141. UNNAMED ★★★
b.f. Sakhee – Tipsy Me (Selkirk).
March 1. Second foal. 40,000Y. Tattersalls October Book 2. George Moore. The dam, a modest 1m placed maiden, is a half-sister to 4 winners including the Group 2 12f King Edward VII Stakes winner Plea Bargain and the useful listed 6f winner Jira. The second dam, Time Saved (by Green Desert), a fairly useful 10f winner, is a sister to the useful 1m winner and listed-placed Illusion and a half-sister to 5 winners including Zinaad and Time Allowed, both winners of the Group 2 12f Jockey Club Stakes and the dams of the Group winners Anton Chekhov, First Charter, Plea Bargain and Time Away. (S P Graham). "She's a cracker – I like her a lot. Her physique is brilliant and I couldn't fault her in any way. All she needs is time – how much time, God knows! She'll want seven furlongs to a mile this year I would think, but I'm very happy with her".

STAN MOORE
1142. CROWNING STAR ★★★★
b.c. Royal Applause – Dossier (Octagonal).
January 25. 16,000Y. Tattersalls October Book 2. Margaret O'Toole. Half-brother to a winner of 7 races at 4 and 5 yrs in Greece by Daylami and to the Italian 3-y-o dual winner

Cima Galaxy (by Singspiel). The dam, an Irish 3-y-o listed 1m winner, was third in the Group 2 Matron Stakes and in the Group 3 Blandford Stakes and is a half-sister to a hurdles winner. The second dam, Papering (by Shaadi), winner of the Group 2 10f Premio Lydia Tesio, was second in the Yorkshire Oaks, the Prix Vermeille and the Nassau Stakes and is a half-sister to 2 winners. "He'll be a pretty decent horse, he was third in the Brocklesbury and he's a fine, big strong horse out of a Group 2 placed filly. He'll win his maiden and hopefully he'll be one we can go to Royal Ascot with. A horse with a lot of ability, he'll keep improving and hopefully he'll go to Redcar for the Racecall Trophy at the end of the year. A horse with a big future".

1143. EVERVESCENT (IRE) ★★
*b.g. Elnadim – Purepleasureseeker
(Grand Lodge)*
February 22. Fourth foal. €3,500Y. Tattersalls Ireland. Stan Moore. Half-brother to the modest 2010 2-y-o 7f seller winner Kissing Clara (by Elusive City). The dam is an unplaced half-sister to the useful 2-y-o Group 3 6.5f Prix Eclipse winner Potaro. The second dam, Bianca Cappello (by Glenstal), is an unplaced half-sister to Idris, a winner of four Group 3 events in Ireland at up to 12f and to the winner and US Grade 3 placed Sweet Mazarine. (Ever Equine) "I would have run him in the Brocklesbury but he got a bit of ringworm. He goes really well and he wasn't expensive so he'll be quite a nice horse for the money he cost. He's very good-looking and I trained his half-sister who ran about 15 times and won or got placed nearly every time. I think he'll be the same – a very genuine horse for six/seven furlongs and I think he'll win races this year alright".

1144. GINGER MONKEY (IRE) ★★★★
*ch.c. Cockney Rebel – Miss Interpret
(Danehill Dancer)*
February 3. Second foal. Tattersalls Ireland. €12,500Y. Stan Moore. The dam is an unplaced half-sister to 6 winners including the German listed winner Symboli Kildare. The second dam, Quiche (by Formidable), a fair dual 6f winner, is a half-sister to 3 winners. (Phil Cunningham & Mr J S Moore). "A very strong horse, he goes real well and I've had to lay off him a bit through immaturity, but I think at the end of the season he'll be one of the best 2-y-o's I'll have. He seems to have a lot of class and I think the sire could be one of the dark horses among the first season stallions for this year. He could be a five/six furlong 2-y-o in mid-season but he'll be going for proper races because he's got gears". TRAINERS' BARGAIN BUY

1145. IDYLLIC STAR ★★★
ch.f. Choisir – Idolize (Polish Precedent).
Half-sister to the quite useful 1m and hurdles winners Sacrilege (by Sakhee) and Golden Feather (by Dr Fong). The dam, a fairly useful 1m and 10.2f winner, is a sister to the high-class Group 2 12f Jockey Club Stakes and Group 3 12f Cumberland Lodge Stakes winner Riyadian and a half-sister to the useful 1m (at 2 yrs) and 12f winner Wales. The second dam, Knight's Baroness (by Rainbow Quest), a smart filly, won over 7f (at 2 yrs) and the Irish Oaks and was placed in the Oaks, the Lingfield Oaks Trial, the Park Hill Stakes and the May Hill Stakes. (Mr Ray Styles & J S Moore). "A big filly, she'll be a seven furlong type and she'll hopefully have three or four runs later on. She goes real nice, has a lovely pedigree and I'll probably enter her in the Fillies' Mile, just in case she proves up to it. I think she's a quality filly".

1146. IMELDA MAYHEM ★★★
*ch.f. Byron – Halland Park Girl
(Primo Dominie).*
April 16. Seventh foal. £10,000Y. Doncaster Premier. Margaret O'Toole. Half-sister to the quite useful 5.2f and 6f winner Lindbergh, to the modest 7f 2-y-o winner Hallandale (both by Bold Edge), the quite useful 2-y-o 5f winner Top Town Girl (by Efisio) and the modest dual 7f winner Party In The Park (by Royal Applause). The dam won 5 races at 2 yrs including the listed Doncaster Stakes and is a half-sister to 2 minor winners. The second dam, Katsina (by Cox's Ridge), a useful 2-y-o 7f winner, was placed in two listed events and is a half-sister to 9 winners including the listed 10f Virginia Stakes winner Rambushka. "She well-bred, she's quick and definitely a five furlong type. The Hilary Needler Trophy at Beverley might be one race for her and she's a possible for Royal Ascot. A speedy filly, she'll win her races".

1147. ISLAND MELODY (IRE) ★★★
b.c. Oratorio – Pout (Namid).
February 8. Second foal. 2,000Y. Ascot Sales. Faye Bramley (previously 24,000Y Tattersalls October Book 1, not sold). The dam won 3 races including the Group 2 1m Ridgewood Pearl Stakes and is a half-sister to two listed winners in India. The second dam, Symphony (by Cyrano de Bergerac), is an unraced half-sister to 5 winners including the dual listed winner Dairine's Delight. *"He was pretty sharp early on but he's grown a bit. Out of a Group 2 winner, he'll be a six/seven furlongs 2-y-o and he'll be one of our nicer 2-y-o's I think. We'll kick start his career in May and hopefully he'll end up in black-type races".*

1148. LYRICAL GANGSTER (IRE) ★★★
ch.c. Redback – Feet Of Flame (Theatrical).
February 14. Sixth foal. Doncaster Premier. £15,000Y. Jim McCartan/private sale to Stan Moore. Brother to the fairly useful 2-y-o 8.7f winner Fullback and half-brother to the fair 7f to 10f winner and listed-placed Kinky Afro (by Modigliani) and the fair 2-y-o 7f winner Orpen Fire (by Orpen). The dam is a placed half-sister to one winner in the USA. The second dam, Red Hot Dancer (by Seattle Dancer), is a US placed half-sister to 5 winners including the minor US stakes winner at around 1m Madame Secretary (herself dam of the French 1,000 Guineas winner Ta Rib) and the Stewards Cup winner Green Ruby. (Phil Cunningham & Mr J S Moore). *"A lovely-moving horse, he's one for August onwards over seven furlongs. He goes nicely and hopefully he'll win a maiden later on before progressing to be a better 3-y-o".*

1149. PURPLE AFFAIR (IRE) ★★★
gr.c. Clodovil – Akariyda (Salse).
April 18. Sixth foal. £17,000 2-y-o. Goffs Kempton Breeze Up. Not sold. Half-brother to the quite useful 5f winner of 4 races Captain Coke (by Fath). The dam is an unraced half-sister to 7 winners including the Group 2 Henry II Stakes winner Akbar and the useful Irish 2-y-o 1m and 4-y-o 1m listed winner Akhiyar. The second dam, Akishka (by Nishapour), is an unraced daughter of the Prix de l'Arc de Triomphe winner Akiyda (by Labus), herself a half-sister to the French Derby winner Acamas and the Grand Prix de Saint-Cloud winner Akarad. *"He has a lovely pedigree and although we've only just got him from the breeze up sales he seems to be really nice. I expected him to be a back-end type 2-y-o but even though we've only been on the gallops with him a few times we can see now that he'll be running in May. Six furlongs will probably be his trip and he seems to be quality. When I first saw him on the gallops I had a big smile and because he's for sale if anyone wants to be his owner they'll have to be quick!"*

1150. TITUS STAR ★★★
ch.g. Titus Livius – The Oldladysays No (Perugino).
April 10. €4,000Y. Tattersalls Ireland. M Wanless. Half-brother to the modest 2-y-o 6f winner Merseyside Star (by Kheleyf) and to a winner in Italy by Daggers Drawn. The dam, placed 6 times at 2 and 4 yrs, is a half-sister to 7 minor winners. The second dam, Calash (by Indian King), is an unplaced half-sister to 9 winners. *"He could be a dark horse because he was cheap and he'll be aimed at the seven furlong Sales race in Ireland. He'll kick start over six furlongs in May or June, he'll be a tough horse and he could be a surprise package. Maybe the type to win a nursery before going to the Sales race".*

PATRICK MORRIS

1151. PROFESSOR TIM (IRE) ★★
gr.g. Verglas – Cool Chron (Polar Falcon).
The dam, a poor 3-y-o 1m winner, is a half-sister to numerous other minor winners. The second dam, Lough Graney (by Sallust), an Irish 12f winner, is a sister to the 2,000 Guineas winner Tap On Wood and the Irish listed winner Americus and a half-sister to 3 winners. *"If there's some cut in the ground he'll be our first 2-y-o runner of the year. Worth putting in the book".*

1152. ROUGHLYN ★★★★
ch.c. Haafhd – Dime Bag (High Line).
April 1. Half-brother to the smart Group 3 Prix La Rochette winner Guys And Dolls (by Efisio), to the smart 1m (including at 2 yrs) to 11f listed winner Pawn Broker (by Selkirk), the useful dual 7f 2-y-o winner and Group 3 placed Blushing Bride (by Distant Relative), the fairly useful Irish 7f winner Blushing Melody

(by Never So Bold) and the quite useful 8.3f winner Nouveau Riche (by Entrepreneur). The dam, a quite useful winner of 4 races at up to 2m (including on the), is a half-sister to 7 minor winners. The second dam, Blue Guitar (by Cure The Blues), a fairly useful winner of 2 races over 1m and 8.3f, is a half-sister to the listed winners Polished Silver and Melody. (Chester Racing Club Ltd). *"We haven't done a lot with him yet but whatever he's done he's answered our questions. I'd say that of all our two-year-olds he's the one with the most potential. It's a cracking pedigree and I expect him to start off at six furlongs in early summer before he moves up in trip. A medium-sized colt, he's not over-robust and I wouldn't run him on quick ground".*

1153. UNNAMED ★★
b f. Dubawi – Enlightened Way (Indian Ridge).
April 9. Second foal. 3,000 2-y-o. Ascot January. Pat Morris. The dam is an unraced half-sister to the US Grade 1 8.5f Citation Handicap and dual Grade 2 winner Ashkal Way. The second dam, Golden Way (by Cadeaux Genereux), a quite useful 10f and 11f winner, is a half-sister to numerous winners. (Chester Racing Club Ltd). *"She's small and 'chancey' and that's why she cost so little at the sales. But she's probably the only Dubawi that's qualified for the minimum amount in a median auction. Being out of a half-sister to a Grade 1 winner, if we can win a race with her she'll be worth a lot more than her Sales price"* TRAINER'S BARGAIN BUY

1154. UNNAMED ★★
b.c. Kheleyf – Royal Lady (Royal Academy).
March 26. Sixth foal. Doncaster St Leger Festival. £28,000Y. Bobby O'Ryan. Half-brother to the moderate 2010 dual 5f placed 2-y-o Look 'N' Listen (by Fasliyev) and to a minor winner in France by Verglas. The dam is an unplaced half-sister to 6 winners including the dual listed winner and US Grade 1 placed Bouccaneer. The second dam, Shahoune (by Blushing Groom), is a placed half-sister to the US dual Grade 3 winner Amal Hayati. (Odysian Ltd/TA Cruise Nightspot). *"I thought he'd come quicker but he's grown so we're just going to have to wait with him. He's a gorgeous, big, black horse and he should come around June time over six or seven furlongs. A nice horse and like most of my two-year-olds he's not an early, five furlongs type - they seem to have a bit more scope than the ones we had last year".*

1155. UNNAMED ★★★
b.c. Diamond Green – Sirindiya (Night Shift).
March 31. First foal. Doncaster Premier. £20,000Y. Bobby O'Ryan. The dam, a fair Irish 7f placed 2-y-o, is a half-sister to the smart hurdler Simarian. The second dam, Sinnariya (by Persian Bold), is a placed half-sister to 6 winners including the Derby, Irish Derby and Arc winner Sinndar. (Mr A McNamara). *"I thought on his pedigree he'd need more time but he's the most sensible, laid-back, perfect-sized horse you'd ever come across. A nice colt for the mid-summer onwards".*

HUGHIE MORRISON

1156. BELLA OPHELIA (IRE) ★★★
b.f. Baltic King – Banco Solo (Distant Relative).
March 28. £9,000Y. Doncaster Premier. Hughie Morrison. Closely related to the Italian listed winner of 20 races Golden Danetime and to the fair 1m (including at 2 yrs) to 10f winner of 6 races Bridge Of Fermoy (both by Danetime) and half-sister to the useful 8.2f to 10f winner Internationalguest (by Petardia), the fairly useful 8.3f winner Bold Act (by Brave Act) and the quite useful 12f to 2m winner The Last Don (by Redback). The dam is an unraced sister to the dual listed winner and Irish 1,000 Guineas third My Branch (herself dam of the Group 1 Haydock Park Sprint Cup winner Tante Rose) and a half-sister to 5 winners. The second dam, Pay The Bank (by High Top), a quite useful 2-y-o 1m winner, stayed 10f and is a half-sister to 4 winners. (Mrs Belinda Scott & Partners). *"She's quite sharp but still very much 'up behind' and we'll get on with her when she levels out, but she looks the part. A late summer 2-y-o over five furlongs, maximum six. She has a very nice temperament, is very forward-going and looks quite like the sire really".*

1157. BURNHAM ★★★
b.c. Nayef – Salim Toto (Mtoto).
May 10. Fifth foal. 30,000Y. Tattersalls October Book 1. Not sold. Half-brother to the quite useful 12f winner Touchdown (by

Singspiel). The dam won 4 races from 10f to 12f including a listed event and is a half-sister to 8 winners. The second dam, Villasanta (by Corvaro), is a placed half-sister to 8 winners including 4 stakes winners and the very smart broodmare Zivania. (The Hill Stud). *"He's quite 'together' physically but given the pedigree we'll sit on him until later in the summer, but he's forward-going, he has a nice action and a good attitude, so I think he'll be alright later in the day".*

1158. CALEDONIAN LAD ★★★★
ch.g. *Pastoral Pursuits – Jasmick (Definite Article).*
February 14. 3,200Y. Ascot Sales. Not sold. Brother to the quite useful 2010 2-y-o 7f winner Sagramor and half-brother to the modest 12f and 13f winner Jasmeno (by Catcher In The Rye). The dam, a quite useful 10f and 14f winner, is a half-sister to 2 winners. The second dam, Glass Minnow (by Alzao), was placed three times from 5f to 9f. (The Caledonian Racing Society). *"A full-brother to a very nice colt we won with last year called Sagramor. He's quite straightforward – probably more so since we gelded him. Hopefully he'll be out in the middle of the summer and I should think we'll start him over six furlongs. He's very nice and easy to have around".*

1159. CHIL THE KITE ★★★★
b.c. *Notnowcato – Copy-Cat (Lion Cavern).*
April 11. Sixth living foal. 18,000Y. Tattersalls October Book 2. H Morrison. Half-brother to the fairly useful dual 6f winner (including at 2 yrs) Pastoral Player (by Pastoral Pursuits), to the 2-y-o 7f and subsequent Hong Kong winner Copywriter (by Efisio), the 2-y-o 6f winner Chataway (by Mujahid) – all fairly useful, the quite useful dual 7f winner (including at 2 yrs), Laudatory (by Royal Applause) and the quite useful 2-y-o 5f winner Gilt Linked (by Compton Place). The dam is an unplaced half-sister to 7 winners including the very useful Group 3 5f King George Stakes winner Averti. The second dam, Imperial Jade (by Lochnager), a useful sprint winner of 4 races and second in the Group 2 Lowther Stakes, is a sister to the Greenlands Stakes, Palace House Stakes and Temple Stakes winner Reesh and a half-sister to 3 winners. (Hazel Lawrence & Graham Doyle). *"I think he was well-bought. He's an easy-going half-brother to a 3-y-o we have called Pastoral Player. Being by Notnowcato I'll give this colt a chance and wait for the late summer or early autumn, but he's a nice sort and I couldn't be happier with him. The dam has bred a lot of 2-y-o winners, but mostly later in the season".* TRAINERS' BARGAIN BUY

1160. FLEXIBLE FLYER ★★★
b.c. *Exceed And Excel – Windermere Island (Cadeaux Genereux).*
April 14. Second foal. 16,000Y. Tattersalls October Book 2. Hugh Morrison. Half-brother to the modest 6f winner Yes We Can (by Alhaarth). The dam, a quite useful dual 7f winner, is a half-sister to 3 winners including the 2-y-o Group 2 6f July Stakes winner Nevisian Lad. The second dam, Corndavon (by Sheikh Albadou), a fairly useful 6f winner of 3 races, is a sister to 2 winners. (Mr A J Struthers, Mr J Dean, Mrs J Scott). *"A tall, leggy horse, he's more backward than the pedigree would suggest, but he's a lovely mover and forward-going, so I'd like to give him at least a couple of runs before the end of the season".*

1161. GLAZE ★★
ch.f. *Kyllachy – Raindrop (Primo Dominie).*
April 10. Sixth foal. 30,000Y. Tattersalls October Book 2. G Howson. Half-sister to the useful 1m listed winner of 6 races Kasumi (by Inchinor), to the fair 5f winner of 4 races (including at 2 yrs) Enodoc (by Efisio) and the modest 6f and 7f winner of 3 races Glencal (by Compton Place). The dam, placed fourth once over 7f, is a half-sister to 4 winners. The second dam, Thundercloud (by Electric), is a placed half-sister to 9 winners including the St Leger winner Julio Mariner, the Oaks winner Scintillate and the Irish Oaks winner Juliette Marny. (Lady Margadale, Viscountess Trenchard, Mrs A Usher). *"A nice filly, she's grown a lot in the last month or two but she should be out later in the season. She's easy-going, I know the family well and I won't push her if she doesn't want me to. Probably a six/seven furlong type".*

1162. ISOBELLA ★★★
b.f. *Royal Applause – Gwyneth (Zafonic).*
April 15. Third foal. 11,000Y. Tattersalls

October Book 2. Hugh Morrison. The dam is an unplaced half-sister to 6 winners including the Italian Group 3 winner Guest Connections and the smart broodmare Llia. The second dam, Llyn Gwynant (by Persian Bold), won the Group 3 1m Desmond Stakes and the Group 3 1m Matron Stakes and is a half-sister to 2 winners. (The End-R-Ways Partnership). "She's starting to come to hand now after being backward. She still has a fair bit of growing to do but hopefully she'll make a 2-y-o by the late summer, possibly over six furlongs. A nice type, she has plenty of personality and she's a typical Royal Applause".

1163. PORT CHARLOTTE ★★★
b.f. Oasis Dream – Maria Theresa (Primo Dominie).
March 17. Half-sister to the very useful Group 3 6f winner of 5 races (including at 2 yrs) Intrepid Jack (by Compton Place), to the fairly useful 7f and 1m winner Fervent Prince (by Averti) and the quite useful 1m and 10f winner Pagan Crest (by Indian Ridge). The dam is an unraced half-sister to the Group 2 Sandown Masai Mile and Group 2 Premio Emilio Turat winner Nicobar. The second dam, Duchess Of Alba (by Belmez), a fair 13.8f winner, is a half-sister to 7 winners including 4 listed winners. (The Caledonian Racing Society). "A very attractive filly, she's quite weak in herself but she's a talented type. An easy-moving filly, she just looks a natural athlete. I know the family well and she reminds me of her great aunt Jolly Bay who won the Pretty Polly Stakes. So she's too nice to push on with too soon".

1164. RESPONSIVE ★★★★ ♠
b.f. Dutch Art – Xtrasensory (Royal Applause).
January 31. Fourth foal. Doncaster Premier. £50,000Y. Will Edmeades. Half-sister to the quite useful 2-y-o 5f and 6f winner Tishtar (by Kyllachy), to the fair 7f (at 2 yrs) and 1m winner Redsensor (by Redback) and the fair 6f winner Fenella Rose (by Compton Place). The dam, a fairly useful 2-y-o 6f winner, is a half-sister to 7 winners. The second dam, Song Of Hope (by Chief Singer), a useful 2-y-o 5f winner and second in the listed Firth of Clyde Stakes, is a half-sister to 10 minor winners. (Thurloe Thoroughbreds XXIX). "She's always been forward-going and looks like being our first 2-y-o runner. A filly with a good attitude, she'll be a five/six furlong type and I think she's nice".

1165. SEA FRET ★★★
b.f. Nayef – Shifting Mist (Night Shift).
February 8. Eleventh foal. 20,000Y. Tattersalls October Book 2. Not sold. Half-sister to the 2-y-o Group 3 6f Premio Primi Passi winner Shifting Place, to the quite useful 5f and 6f winner Misty Glade (both by Compton Place), the fairly useful 1m and 8.5f winner Cal Mac (by Botanic), the fair 6f winner of 4 races Our Sheila (by Bahamian Bounty) and a winner in Poland by Bin Ajwaad. The dam, a modest 10f to 14f winner of 5 races, is a half-sister to 7 winners including the smart broodmare Finlaggan (the dam of 3 stakes winners). The second dam, Misty Halo (by High Top), a fairly useful winner of 22 races here and in the Isle Of Man and from 1m to 2m 2f, is a half-sister to 4 winners. (Mrs C R Philipson). "A nice filly that moves well, she's big and strong and she could be alright later in the year. She's still growing but she's a nice type and we hope she'll make a 2-y-o later on".

1166. SUPAHEART ★★★
b.f. Lion Heart – Supamova (Seattle Slew).
May 14. Eleventh living foal. 31,000Y. Tattersalls October Book 1. Not sold. Half-sister to the useful dual 1m winner and Group 3 third Supaseus (by Spinning World), to the fair dual 7f winner (including at 2 yrs) Supa Sal (by King's Best), the fair 8.7f winner Supaverdi (by Green Desert), the modest 10f and 12f winner Swellmova (by Sadler's Wells) and a winner in Japan by Danehill. The dam, a quite useful 8.5f winner at 3 yrs, is a sister to the very smart Group 1 7f Prix de la Foret winner Septieme Ciel and a half-sister to 7 winners including the Group 1 1m Prix Marcel Boussac winner Macoumba. The second dam, Maximova (by Green Dancer), won the Group 1 7f Prix de la Salamandre (in a dead-heat) and was placed in the French and Irish 1,000 Guineas. She is a half-sister to 5 winners including the Group winners Navratilovna and Vilikaia. (Ben and Martyn Arbib). "She's naturally talented and like all the family she's a bit tall but she seems to have much better conformation than the last three out of the mare. The lads think I should

push on with her, but it's because she's a natural athlete and really she isn't ready yet. She's a nice person, a mid-May foal and I'll wait until the early autumn with her. I think she'll be alright".

1167. UNNAMED ★★★
ch.f. Dylan Thomas – Maskaya (Machiavellian).
April 27. Fifth foal. 45,000Y. Tattersalls October Book 2. Not sold. Half-sister to the Irish 2-y-o 7f winner and Group 1 Criterium de Saint-Cloud second Drumbeat (by Montjeu), to the fair 7.6f winner Red Blooded Woman (by Red Ransom) and a winner in Japan by Giant's Causeway. The dam, an Irish 2-y-o 5f winner, is a half-sister to 4 winners including the dual Irish listed 7f winner and Group 2 placed Modeeroch and the Irish 2-y-o 6f winner and Group 1 6f Cheveley Park Stakes third Danaskaya. The second dam, Majinskaya (by Marignan), winner of the listed 12f Prix des Tuileries, is a half-sister to 6 winners including the French 2-y-o 7f winner Mabrova (herself dam of the Group 1 5f Prix de l'Abbaye winner Kistena). (P A Byrne). "Small and quite sharp, she had a bit of a setback early on but she's just starting to do some fast work now so she might still be running in May. She's sharp in many ways, because she hospitalised her rider on one occasion and herself on another!"

1168. UNNAMED ★★★
ch.f. Teofilo – Suntory (Royal Applause).
May 5. Fifth foal. Half-sister to the fair 1m winner Sunceleb (by Peintre Celebre). The dam, an Irish 6f and 7f winner, is a half-sister to 7 winners including the Group 2 Derrinstown Stud Derby Trial winner Fracas. The second dam, Klarifi (by Habitat), a fairly useful winner of the 7f Ballycorus Stakes at 3 yrs, is a half-sister to the smart Irish miler Captivator and the very useful 12f winners Eileen Jenny, Kasmayo and Bahamian – the latter also dam of the Irish Oaks winner Wemyss Bight. "She looks as if she'll make a 2-y-o around May or June time. I trained Sunceleb out of the dam and she was tiny. This filly is slightly bigger, she's grown enough and she wants to get on with it. I'm still looking for an owner if anyone is interested".

WILLIE MUIR

1169. ALICE'S DANCER (IRE) ★★★★
br.f. Clodovil – Islandagore (Indian Ridge).
March 24. Seventh foal. 28,000Y. Tattersalls October Book 2. Willie Muir. Sister to the quite useful 2010 2-y-o 6f winner (on his only start) Iron Range and to the quite useful Irish 2-y-o 7f winner Tintean and half-sister to the fairly useful 7f (at 2 yrs) to 10f winner of 5 races Island Sunset (both by Trans Island), the fair 7f (at 2 yrs) and 1m winner Right Ted and the fair 2-y-o 6f winner Toby's Dream (both by Mujadil). The dam, a 3-y-o 7f winner in Ireland, was second in a listed event over 9f on her only other start and is a half-sister to the 2-y-o listed 6f winner Lady Of Kildare. The second dam, Dancing Sunset (by Red Sunset), a smart winner of the Group 3 10f Royal Whip Stakes, is a full or half-sister to 5 winners including the US stakes winner Truly. (Perspicacious Punters Racing Club). "I know a bit about the family because I trained Island Sunset who won four races for me despite having little problems with her fetlock joints. This filly is very clean, her full-brother Iron Range won on his debut at the back-end of last season and this filly looks sharper. She looks like a 2-y-o, she's going well and she shows she's got ability. I wouldn't want to rush her, but she's really nice".

1170. ARMIGER ★★★
b.c. Araafa – Welsh Valley (Irish River).
March 21. Fifth foal. Half-brother to the fairly useful 2-y-o 7f winner Brecon (by Unfuwain) and the fair 4-y-o 9.5f and 10f winner Man Of Gwent (by In The Wings). The dam, a modest 6f placed maiden, is a half-sister to 8 winners including the Group 2 6f Gimcrack Stakes winner Chilly Billy and the US Grade 3 placed Mister Approval. The second dam, Sweet Snow (by Lyphard), won over an extended 10f in France and is a half-sister to 9 winners including the US stakes winners Windansea and Sing And Swing. (Muir Racing Partnership – London). "I like him a lot. Being by Araafa you possibly wouldn't think he'd be my sharpest - but he is. He was always a bit too keen and nervy after we broke him, but he's now a strong, sharp 2-y-o. He shows he has enough ability to win and I don't think it'll be long before he's out".

1171. BREAKING THE BANK ★★★
ch.c. Medicean – Russian Dance (Nureyev)
February 12. Fourth foal. 50,000Y. Tattersalls October Book 2. Willie Muir. Half-brother to the fairly useful 7f to 9f winner Dance East (by Shamardal). The dam, a fairly useful 2-y-o 6f winner, is a half-sister to 9 winners including the Group 1 Racing Post Trophy winner Saratoga Springs. The second dam, Population (by General Assembly), is a placed half-sister to the Group/Grade 1 winners Play It Safe and Providential. (Mr R Devlin). "A lovely-moving son of Medicean and a good-looking individual. He shows enough and he's strong enough for me to say that he'll be able to win races at two, but he will go on at three. I really like him".

1172. CHARITABLE ACT (FR) ★★★
b.c. Cadeaux Genereux – Acatama (Efisio).
February 24. First foal. 40,000Y. Tattersalls October Book 1. Willie Muir. The dam is an unraced half-sister to 4 winners including the US Grade 1 John C Mabee Handicap and Grade 1 Del Mar Oaks winner Amorama. The second dam, Tanzania (by Alzao), was a minor Irish 12f and 13f winner. (Muir Racing Partnership – Chester). "This colt is phenomenal to look at. He's a big horse and sometimes those types can lose their strength, but if he doesn't he'll be an exciting type of horse. I love the Cadeaux's and I've done well with them. I have to take my time with him but I'll be hoping to have him out in mid-summer".

1173. EMPRESSIVE ★★
b.f. Holy Roman Emperor – Dodo (Alzao).
January 14. Eighth foal. 5,000Y. Tattersalls October Book 2. Not sold. Half-sister to the very smart 6f (at 2 yrs) and 7f winner and Group 3 7f Hungerford Stakes second Tarjman (by Cadeaux Genereux), to the smart 2-y-o 6f and 3-y-o listed 6f winner Nota Bene (by Zafonic) and the fairly useful 1m winner of 3 races Porthcawl (by Singspiel). The dam, a fairly useful 3-y-o 6f winner, is a half-sister to 7 winners including the very useful 2-y-o 5f and 6f winner and Cornwallis Stakes second Deadly Nightshade. The second dam, Dead Certain (by Absalom), a very smart winner of the Group 1 6f Cheveley Park Stakes and the Group 2 6.5f Prix Maurice de Gheest, is a half-sister to 7 winners.

(Muir Racing Partnership – York). "Typical of the sire in that she's not very big, she was cheap because she was small as a yearling. She's sharp, I really like her and I just want to wait until she comes in her coat. She'll be one of the early ones to run and she has a great pedigree".

1174. HOLLYWOOD ALL STAR ★★★
b.c. Kheleyf – Camassina (Taufan).
April 28. Ninth foal. €6,000Y. Tattersalls Ireland. Not sold. Half-brother to the fairly useful Irish 7f (at 2 yrs) and 1m winner of 4 races Bricks And Porter (by College Chapel), to the fair 7f, 10f and hurdles winner Paintball (by Le Vie Dei Colori), the fair 2-y-o 5f winner Mujassina, the fair 2-y-o 6f winner On Offer (by Clodovil) and the moderate Irish 7f winner Idle Journey (both by Mujadil). The dam was placed once over 7f at 3 yrs and is a half-sister to 2 winners. The second dam, Kaskazi (by Dancing Brave), won twice at 3 yrs and is a half-sister to 7 winners. (Mr M Lavelle). "I had his half-brother, Paintball. I loved this colt at the Sales so as he didn't make his reserve I bought him straight afterwards. Paintball took a bit of time because he had immature joints, but this colt will be early. He just loves life, he enjoys whatever you do with him. The sire gets a lot of winners, I like the colt a lot and he will be a 2-y-o". TRAINERS' BARGAIN BUY

1175. INNISCASTLE BOY ★★★
b.c. Sir Percy – Galapagar (Miswaki).
March 20. Fourth foal. 46,000Y. Tattersalls October Book 2. Not sold. Half-brother to the moderate 2010 dual 1m placed 2-y-o Highcliffe (by Bertolini) and to the fair 6f winner Magic Jack (by Trade Fair). The dam, a French 1m and 9f winner, is a half-sister to 4 other minor winners in the USA. The second dam, Runaway Fair Lady (by Runaway Groom), was a stakes winner of 5 races in the USA. (Mr M Lavelle). "A good, strong-bodied colt, he looks sharp and I haven't got after him seriously yet but I will do soon. He's quite laid-back, he has a good temperament and I like him a lot".

1176. LAST SHADOW ★★
b.c. Notnowcato – Fairy Queen (Fairy King).
March 18. Seventh living foal. 25,000Y. Tattersalls October Book 2. Willie Muir. Half-brother to the fair 12f, 2m and hurdles

winner Fin Vin De Leu (by Dr Fong) and to the minor US 4-y-o winner of 2 races Oberon's Girl (by Coronado's Quest). The dam won 5 races including the Group 2 12f Ribblesdale Stakes and the Group 2 12.5f Prix de la Royallieu and is a half-sister to 4 winners including the smart Group 2 1m Falmouth Stakes winner Tashawak and the listed 10f winner and Prix de l'Arc de Triomphe fourth Acropolis. The second dam, Dedicated Lady (by Pennine Walk), a useful Irish 2-y-o 5f and 6f winner, is a half-sister to 5 winners. (Mr M J Caddy). *"I had my doubts about the sire when he first went to stud but I have to say I love this horse. He's big and scopey and he won't be a 2-y-o, that's for sure. But you just look at him and he reminds you of some of those other horses that Newsells Park have bred – like Soapy Danger. He's a big, scopey horse like him. You can put him in the string and he doesn't look out of place and of course you wouldn't over do him, but he's one of those horses that jumps out at you all the time. He'd be on my list of high hopes".*

1177. LONDON WELSH ★★★★
b.f. *Cape Cross – Croeso Cariad*
(Most Welcome).
January 22. Fifth foal. Half-sister to the fairly useful dual 1m winner (including at 2 yrs) Saboteur (by Shamardal) and to the moderate 10f winner Monmouthshire (by Singspiel). The dam, a very useful 2-y-o 5f and 7f Italian listed winner, was second in the Group 2 1m Falmouth Stakes and is a half-sister to 5 winners including the Irish listed winner and multiple Group 1 placed Mona Lisa. The second dam, Colorsnap (by Shirley Heights), is an unraced half-sister to 9 winners including the Irish Oaks winner Colorspin (dam of the Group 1 winners Opera House, Zee Zee Top and Kayf Tara), the Prix de l'Opera winner Bella Colora (dam of the very smart colt Stagecraft) and the Irish Champion Stakes winner Cezanne. (M Graham & Mr K Mercer). *"One of the best-bred fillies we've got. She came in later than the others because we thought she'd need time but she caught the others up in two weeks. You can see she wants time to develop but she's naturally talented. She's just a really nice type of filly and I'd like to hope she could win a maiden later on before going for the Fillies' Mile – that the sort of time scale you'd be looking at. Potentially very nice".*

1178. MOMENT IN THE SUN ★★★
b.f. *Dubai Destination – Special Moment*
(Sadler's Wells).
February 16. Second foal. 4,000Y. Tattersalls October Book 2. Not sold. Half-sister to the fair 2010 2-y-o 7f winner Midas Moment (by Danehill Dancer). The dam is a placed sister to 2 winners including the Irish listed 1m winner and Irish 1,000 Guineas third Starbourne and a half-sister to 3 winners. The second dam, Upper Circle (by Shirley Heights), ran twice unplaced and is a sister to the dam of the Oaks winner Lady Carla. (Foursome Thoroughbreds). *"I won with her sister as a 2-y-o and this filly isn't as big and she's much sharper. She's shows me she's got ability and I like her a lot".*

1179. MOODY DANCER ★★
b.f. *Cape Cross – Bluebelle Dancer*
(Danehill Dancer).
February 10. First foal. 25,000Y. Tattersalls October Book 1. Willie Muir. The dam, a modest 6f (at 2 yrs) and 7f winner, is a half-sister to 8 winners including the useful Irish 2-y-o 6f winner and Group 1 Phoenix Stakes third Catch A Glimpse (herself the dam of a US Grade 3 winner). The second dam, Spring To Light (by Blushing Groom), a winner over 6f and 7f and second in the Group 3 C L Weld Park Stakes, is a half-sister to 7 winners. (Mr S Jones). *"We trained her dam who was a bit of a tramp because she had the ability to run in decent company but she let herself down by refusing to co-operate half the time. This is her first foal, she's a really good-looking, good-bodied filly and she's another one for the middle-to-back-end. So I won't be in any rush with her, but she moves well and does everything right".*

1180. PICURA ★★★
ch.f. *King's Best – Picolette (Piccolo).*
April 21. Half-sister to the fairly useful 6f (at 2 yrs) to 9f winner Pintura (by Efisio), to the quite useful 2-y-o 6f and 7f winner Pomme Frites (by Bertolini) and the 12f seller winner Ruby Delta (by Delta Dancer). The dam was placed once at 2 yrs and is a half-sister to one winner. The second dam, Poyle Jezebelle (by Sharpo), won once at 4 yrs and is a full or half-sister to 7 winners. (Dulverton Equine). *"This filly has got a lovely temperament – unlike a lot by the*

sire. She's sharp and we'll be kicking on with her, she does everything asked, she's neat, she's put condition on and I like her. She just could be what you're looking for and she'll definitely win this year. She'll start off at six furlongs".

1181. PRINCESS KAIULANI (IRE) ★★★
b.f. Royal Applause – Scottish Exile (Ashkalcni).
March 24. Third foal. 17,000Y. Tattersalls October Book 2. Willie Muir. Half-sister to the smart 5f and 6f 2-y-o winner and multiple Group 3 second Bonnie Charlie (by Intikhab). The dam, a fair triple 5f winner, is a sister to the fairly useful 6f winner of 11 races and listed-placed Million Percent and a half-sister to 4 winners. The second dam, Royal Jade (by Last Tycoon), a fairly useful 7f winner, is a half-sister to 6 winners including the Group 3 5f King George Stakes winner Averti. (Mr David Knox and Partners). *"She's sharp and shows she's got ability. Looking at her you might think she's ready, but I just think she's starting to mature and I feel I have to back off a fraction. I like her and she's got a great way about her. I think she'll be a 2-y-o and I've entered her for the Supersprint, so I do think she's alright".*

1182. ROCCOTAKI (IRE) ★★
b.c. Shirocco – Otaki (King's Best).
March 30. First foal. 12,500Y. Tattersalls October Book 2. Willie Muir. The dam, a moderate 4-y-o 2m winner, is a half-sister to 5 winners including the US Grade 2 winner One Off and the Swedish listed winner Oblique. The second dam, On Call (by Alleged), a useful listed winner of 7 races at up to 2m, was Group 3 placed and is a half-sister to 6 winners including the fairly useful Doctor's Glory (herself the dam of 3 stakes winners). (The Breakfast Club). *"Being by Shirocco you'd think he'd need all day but he's probably showing me more now than any 2-y-o I've got. He's a nice 2-y-o size and I'm resisting working him because on his pedigree he should get a trip and yet he looks sharp – and that doesn't seem right. A beautiful looking horse, he moves well".*

1183. STEPPER POINT ★★★
b.c. Kyllachy – Sacre Coeur (Compton Place).
February 25. First foal. 45,000Y. Tattersalls October Book 2. Willie Muir. The dam, a fair 2-y-o 6f winner, is a half-sister to 5 winners including the useful dual 10f winner and listed-placed Lonely Heart (herself dam of the Group 3 Tetrarch Stakes winner Leitrim House) and the useful 6f and 7f winner of 4 races Indian Trail. The second dam, Take Heart (by Electric), a quite useful 7f to 10f winner of 4 races, is a half-sister to 3 winners. (Mr C L A Edginton). *"He goes well and looks like being one of the early 2-y-o's. He's showing speed, he's laid-back, big-bodied and I could run him in April. I've never had so many 2-y-o's that are actually 2-y-o types. This is one of them, I like him and he has a fantastic temperament. He'll start at five furlongs".*

1184. WELSH ROYALE ★★★
b.c. Royal Applause – Brecon (Unfuwain).
March 25. Third foal. Half-brother to the modest 2011 1m placed 3-y-o Mountain Myst (by Val Royal). The dam, a fairly useful 2-y-o 7f winner and fourth in two listed events, is a half-sister to one winner. The second dam, Welsh Valley (by Irish River), a modest 6f placed maiden, is a half-sister to 8 winners including the Group 2 6f Gimcrack Stakes winner Chilly Billy. (Muir Racing Partnership – London). *"I like him, he was a bit light-framed but he's really putting on condition right now. We'll see him out around June or July and he looks like a fast ground horse".*

1185. UNNAMED ★★
br.c. Kheleyf – Adeptation (Exceller).
April 30. Ninth foal. 10,000Y. Doncaster Premier. Not sold. Half-brother to the quite useful 8.5f all-weather (at 2 yrs) and 9f winner Retirement (by Zilzal), to the fair 1m winner Turnstone (by Pivotal) and 2 winners in Greece by Elnadim and Rakti. The dam, a French 10f and 12f winner, is out of the US Grade 1 and dual Grade 3 winner Adept (by Grey Dawn II). *"He looks quite sharp, he's strong-bodied, doing plenty of work and I'm pressing on with him. A really nice individual and he's still for sale. But when he's ready to run I'll just name him and away we'll go".*

1186. UNNAMED ★★★
b.c. Sleeping Indian – Tintern (Diktat).
March 3. First foal. 14,000Y. Tattersalls October Book 3. Not sold. The dam is an unraced half-sister to 4 winners including the

dual 10f and subsequent US stakes winner and Grade 2 placed Solva. The second dam, Annapurna (by Brief Truce), a useful 2-y-o 7f winner, was listed placed over 9f and is a half-sister to 4 winners including the 2-y-o Group 3 7f Rockfel Stakes and listed 7f winner Name Of Love. (Muir Racing Partnership – Bath). *"I like him a lot and I had a Sleeping Indian last year that was a bit more backward than this colt. He's laid-back and he has a great temperament so you can graft him and he takes the work. I think when the penny drops he'll be a nice 2-y-o and they'll have a lot of fun with him".*

DAVID NICHOLLS

1187. IMPERIAL LEGEND (IRE) ★★★
b.c. *Mujadil – Titian Saga (Titus Livius).*
February 28. First foal. Doncaster Premier. £23,000Y. Tall Trees Racing. The dam, a fair 2-y-o 6f winner, is a half-sister to 7 winners. The second dam, Nordic Living (by Nordico), is an unplaced half-sister to one winner. (Pinnacle Racing). *"He goes really nicely, he's a well-balanced individual and he's forward going. A five/six furlong 2-y-o".*

1188. J J LEARY (IRE) ★★★
b.g. *Amadeus Wolf – Nautical Design (Seeking The Gold).*
April 16. First foal. Doncaster Premier. £25,000Y. Bobby O'Ryan. The dam won over 9f in Ireland at 4 yrs. The second dam, Well Designed (by Sadler's Wells), a minor winner at 4 yrs in the USA, is a sister to the Irish Oaks winner Dance Design and a half-sister to 4 winners including the Grade 3 winner Hibernian Rhapsody. (Dr M B Q S Koukash). *"He starts his career in mid-April and he'll be our first 2-y-o runner of the season. He's a strong, compact colt but he still looks a bit green and nervy, so he'll come on a lot for his first run".*

1189. LEXI'S DARLING (IRE) ★★★
b.f. *Windsor Knot – Sunrise (Sri Pekan).*
February 27. Seventh foal. Tattersalls Ireland. €25,000Y. Bobby O'Ryan. Half-sister to the useful 2-y-o 5f winner of 3 races and listed-placed Vale Of Belvoir (by Mull Of Kintyre) and to the modest 7f (at 2 yrs) to 2m and hurdles winner Mystified (by Raise A Grand). The dam, a modest 5f placed 2-y-o, is a half-sister to 5 winners including the Group 3 Phoenix Sprint Stakes winner March Star. The second dam, Grade A Star (by Alzao), an Irish 2-y-o 1m winner, is a half-sister to 2 winners. (Dr M B Q S Koukash). *"She was almost ready to run but she met with a little setback. She's got plenty of speed but we need a drop of rain before I can run her".*

1190. PRINCE GABRIAL (IRE) ★★★★
b.g. *Moss Vale – Baileys Cream (Mister Baileys).*
February 9. Sixth foal. Doncaster Premier. £52,000Y. Bobby O'Ryan. Half-brother to the 2-y-o listed 6f winner and Group 3 second Baileys Cacao (by Invincible Spirit), to the minor Italian winner of 5 races Rich Of Promises (by Imperial Ballet) and a winner in Switzerland by Camacho. The dam, a fair 2-y-o 7f winner, is a full or half-sister to 5 winners including the listed Chesham Stakes winner Fair Cop. The second dam, Exclusive Life (by Exclusive Native), won once in the USA and is a half-sister to 8 winners including the US Grade 2 winner Special Warmth. (Dr M B Q S Koukash). *"A big colt, I had been hoping to run him early but he had problems with his shins. He goes very well and he'll be a five furlong 2-y-o. The horses have done plenty of work but we desperately need some rain. We haven't seen a drop for weeks".*

1191. RALPHY BOY (IRE) ★★★★
b.c. *Acclamation – Silcasue (Selkirk).*
January 16. First foal. The dam is an unraced half-sister to one winner. The second dam, Golden Silca (by Inchinor), a smart Group 2 6f Mill Reef Stakes and German Group 2 winner, was second in the Group 1 Coronation Stakes and the Group 1 Irish 1,000 Guineas and is a half-sister to 6 winners including the smart 2-y-o Group 1 6f Prix Morny winner Silca's Sister and the very useful multiple 5f and 6f winner Green Manalishi. (Frank Lowe). *"A very nice horse, he's a great walker and there's a lot of Go about him".*

1192. UNNAMED ★★
b.g. *One Cool Cat – Monsusu (Montjeu).*
March 7. Second foal. £15,000Y. Doncaster Premier. Bobby O'Ryan (private sale after being unsold at £10,000). Half-brother to the fair 2010 2-y-o dual 5f winner Tro Nesa (by Chineur). The dam, a fair Irish 7f winner, is

a half-sister to several winners including the fairly useful 9f and 10f winner. The second dam, Susun Kelapa (St Jovite), won twice over 7.8f (at 2 yrs) and 9f and is a half-sister to the US stakes winner Lac Dessert. (Dr M B Q S Koukash). "The One Cool Cat's are funny individuals sometimes, you can think they'll be early but they end up taking more time, although they go well enough. This colt will come into his own over six furlongs in the middle of the season".

1193. UNNAMED ★★
b.g. Bachelor Duke – Petite Arvine (Gulch).
February 21. First foal. Tattersalls Ireland. €20,000Y. David Nichols. The dam is an unplaced half-sister to one minor winner in the USA. The second dam, Grapevine (by Sadler's Wells), second in the listed Cheshire Oaks and later a listed-placed winner of 2 races in the USA, is a half-sister to 6 winners including the multiple Group 3 winner Musicale. (Mr M Browne). "He was going really well but he's had a setback. He won't be that long but he was almost ready to go. I'd describe him as a compact, bonny horse with a lovely head on him".

JEREMY NOSEDA
1194. ACTOR (IRE) ★★
b.c. Montjeu – Original (Caerleon).
April 28. Seventh foal. 100,000Y. Tattersalls October Book 1. John Warren. Closely related to the useful 10f winner and listed 12f placed Aunt Julia (by In The Wings) and half-brother to the French 10f and 12f winner and listed-placed Ucandri (by Refuse To Bend) and the modest 9f winner Rainbow Zest (by Rainbow Quest). The dam is an unraced three-parts sister to the listed winner Xtra and a half-sister to 3 winners. The second dam, Oriental Mystique (by Kris), a fairly useful 3-y-o 7f and 1m winner, is a sister to the Group 2 Park Hill Stakes second Guilty Secret and a half-sister to 6 other winners. "A good-moving horse, I'm very pleased with what I see at the moment but realistically we're looking at him being an autumn 2-y-o and he'll be a better horse next year. I like him though, he's an athletic horse with plenty of scope".

1195. AMERICAN BLING (USA) ★★★
b.c. Johannesburg – American Jewel (Quiet American).

April 15. Fifth foal. $100,000Y. Keeneland September. Jane Allison. Brother to the Irish 2-y-o 7f and subsequent US winner Sawtooth Mountain and half-brother to the US stakes winner Awsugahnow (by Forestry). The dam, placed at 2 yrs in the USA, is a half-sister to the US stakes winner and Grade 3 placed U R Unforgetable and the US stakes winner Turko's Turn (dam of the champion colt and multiple Grade 1 winner Point Given). The second dam, Turbo Launch (by Relaunch), a US stakes winner of 4 races, is a half-sister to the US Grade 2 winner Dignitas. (Mrs Susan Roy). "He's been in fast work in America and I was there to see him in February working over two furlongs. We decided that he was a strong set horse who we really need to kick on with. He'll be arriving here any day now and he should be on the track in May. My initial thoughts are that he'll win as a 2-y-o".

1196. BIBA DIVA (IRE) ★★★
b.f. Danehill Dancer – Mowaadah (Alzao).
April 11. Fourth foal. €80,000Y. Arqana Deauville August. Jane Allison. Half-sister to the 2010 French fourth placed 2-y-o Villerville (by Gulch) and to the fair 1m winner Balloura (by Swain). The dam won 3 races over 1m including a listed event and is a half-sister to 5 winners including the Eclipse Stakes and Irish Champion Stakes winner Oratorio and the English and US winner and US Grade 1 second Fahim. The second dam, Mahrah (by Vaguely Noble), a fairly useful 3-y-o 1m winner, is a half-sister to 6 winners including the very useful Group 2 12f Blandford Stakes winner Andros Bay. "A neat filly, I did a bit of work with her because her size implied to me that she might be early, but I decided to be more patient and she's going to be more of a mid-summer 2-y-o. She's improving and going forward however".

1197. DELFT ★★
b.f. Dutch Art – Plucky (Kyllachy).
March 8. First foal. The dam, a quite useful 7f winner, is a half-sister to the 2-y-o Group 2 5f Flying Childers Stakes and Group 3 5f Molecomb Stakes winner Wunders Dream and to the very useful Irish Group 3 Ridgewood Pearl Stakes winner Grecian Dancer. The second dam, Pizzicato (by Statoblest), a

modest 5f and 5.3f winner at 3 yrs, is a half-sister to 5 winners including the high-class Hong Kong horses Mensa and Firebolt. *"At the moment she's having a little break, but from what I've seen of her early on I'm happy. A good-moving filly with a straightforward attitude, she's one for the second half of the season over six/seven furlongs".*

1198. FAIREST (IRE) ★★★★
ch.f. Elusive Quality – Joan Joan Joan (Touch Gold).
March 20. Third foal. 72,000Y. Tattersalls October Book 2. John Warren. Half-sister to a minor 3-y-o winner in the USA by Repent. The dam, a minor US 3-y-o winner, is a half-sister to 9 winners including the Group 3 Acomb Stakes winner Big Timer. The second dam, Moonflute (by The Minstrel), a listed-placed 2-y-o winner, is a half-sister to 4 winners. *"She's going well and I'm pleased with her. Physically she looks at this point as if she's quite 'together' and she'll be a six/seven furlong type 2-y-o. We'll see how she progresses and hopefully she'll be racing by the second half of May. She's a filly I like and she's doing everything the right way so far. If I have a Royal Ascot filly this could be the one".*

1199. FALCON IN FLIGHT ★★
b.f. Shamardal – Marine City (Carnegie).
April 7. Fourth foal. 100,000Y. Tattersalls October Book 1. Rabbah Bloodstock. Half-sister to the modest 2m winner Dubai Diva (by Dubai Destination) and to the moderate 14f winner Light The City (by Fantastic Light). The dam, a fair 12f winner, is a half-sister to 4 winners including the Group 1 12f Prix de l'Arc de Triomphe and dual German Group 1 winner Marienbard. The second dam, Marienbad (by Darshaan), a French 1m winner at both 2 and 3 yrs, is a half-sister to 6 winners. *"She's just a bit weak and unfurnished at present. I think she'll definitely make a 2-y-o, but in the second half of the season. A good mover, but it would be unfair to comment any more than that at the moment".*

1200. FURBELOW ★★
b.f. Pivotal – Red Tiara (Mr Prospector).
March 13. Seventh foal. Sister to the US 5f (minor stakes) to 8.5f winner Red Diadem, closely related to the useful 2-y-o 6f winner and Group 1 6f Cheveley Park Stakes fourth Adorn (by Kyllachy) and half-sister to the modest 8.3f winner Argent (by Barathea). The dam, a moderate 7.6f fourth-placed maiden, is closely related to the Japanese sprint stakes winner Meiner Love and a half-sister to 2 winners. The second dam, Heart Of Joy (by Lypheor), won 10 races including the Grade 2 Palomar Handicap and the Group 3 Nell Gwyn Stakes, is a half-sister to 8 winners. (Cheveley Park Stud). *"A backward filly, she's been a little bit immature of her knees and is having a break currently. A good mover, but I haven't done enough with her to say any more than that".*

1201. GOLD EDITION ★★★★
ch.c. Mr Greeley – Triple Edition (Lear Fan).
March 24. Second foal. Half-brother to the fair 11f winner Ana Emarati (by Forestry). The dam, placed at 2 yrs in France, is a sister to the winner and listed-placed Starfan and a half-sister to the Group 1 Prix de la Foret winner Etoile Montante. The second dam, Willstar (by Nureyev), a minor French 3-y-o winner, is a sister to the listed winner Viviana (herself dam of the Grade 1 winners Sightseek and Tates Creek) and a half-sister to US Grade 2 winner Revasser. *"A colt that's done really well, he's a good physical specimen and a good mover. I like him and he's done everything he's been asked very comfortably. If he keeps moving forward throughout April he'll be doing fast work at the end of the month. Even if that proves too soon I still view him as definitely a 2-y-o type by mid-season. I like him, he's a nice, straightforward, strong individual and he should do a decent job at two".*

1202. GRANDEUR (IRE) ★★★
gr.c. Verglas – Misskinta (Desert Sun).
April 9. Second foal. Goffs Orby. €85,000Y. Brian Grassick Bloodstock. Half-brother to the 2010 Irish 1m placed Sixty Eight Guns (by Noverre). The dam, a minor Irish 12f winner at 4 yrs, is a half-sister to 4 winners including the Group 3 2m 2f Doncaster Cup winner Far Cry and the dam of the US Grade 3 winner Dress Rehearsal. The second dam, Darabaka (by Doyoun), is an unraced half-sister to 6 winners including the Group 3 Prix Minerve winner Daralinsha (herself the dam of numerous

winners) and the listed winner Darata (dam of the French Oaks winner Daryaba). "A solid horse, a July type 2-y-o, he has a good temperament and is doing everything in the right way. My experience of Verglas is that they tend to come to hand a bit later than you'd think, but this one looks to me like a horse that will have a 2-y-o campaign".

1203. HARVARD N YALE (USA) ★★★
ch.c. Smart Strike – Compete (El Prado).
January 30. Fourth foal. Half-brother to the Grade 3 All Along Stakes winner and dual Grade 3 placed Lady Digby (by Grand Slam). The dam, a minor winner in the USA, is a half-sister to 3 other minor winners. The second dam, Pete's Heiress (by Peteski), is an unraced half-sister to 7 winners including the US Grade 2 winner Private Treasure. (Earle Mack). "He's about to arrive here soon, but I've seen him a couple of times in America and talked to the people there. He's a great-moving colt, everything's in the right place, he's got a lot of quality and he'll be a 2-y-o in the last third of the season. He's a horse with a great action and I'm looking forward to training him".

1204. HERBACEOUS ★★
b.f. Medicean – Red Blossom (Green Desert).
January 27. First foal. The dam, a fair 9f winner, is a half-sister to the smart Group 1 Fillies' Mile and Group 2 10f Blandford Stakes winner Red Bloom and to the smart 10f, 12f and listed 13f winner Red Gala. The second dam, Red Camellia (by Polar Falcon), winner of the Group 3 7f Prestige Stakes and third in the French 1,000 Guineas, is a half-sister to the German middle-distance winner Red Bouquet. (Cheveley Park Stud). "A solid filly that's cantering away, I haven't done much more than that with her as yet but I'm pleased with how she goes. She really needs some warmer weather to start thriving. There's speed in the pedigree and she should make a 2-y-o type".

1205. ICE (IRE) ★★★
b.c. Elusive City – Ice Box (Pivotal).
February 10. First foal. Doncaster Premier. £120,000Y. Sir Robert Ogden. The dam, a modest 1m winner at 3 yrs, is out of the French placed Thaisy (by Tabasco Cat), herself a half-sister to 5 winners including the triple Group 2 winner Fruits Of Love and the Group 3 Cornwallis Stakes winner Mujadil. "He's ready to go into some fast work now and he's definitely a six furlongs 2-y-o type. A strong, well put-together sort, he's good-looking and a solid, racey horse".

1206. INTEGRITY (IRE) ★★★
b.c. Dark Angel – Law Review (Case Law).
March 7. Eighth foal. Goffs Orby. €65,000Y. John Warren. Half-brother to the useful 6f (at 2 yrs) and 9f winner Layazaal (by Mujadil), to the fairly useful 5f (at 2 yrs) and 6f winner Falasteen, the quite useful 2-y-o 5f and 6f winner Latin Review and the quite useful 6f to 1m winner of 7 races Opus Maximus (all by Titus Livius). The dam was placed once over 1m and is a half-sister to 9 winners including the Group 1 July Cup winner and sire Lake Coniston. The second dam, Persian Polly (by Persian Bold), a useful Irish 2-y-o 7f winner, was third in the Group 3 Park Stakes and is a half-sister to 2 winners. "A horse I was really pleased with but unfortunately he had a setback which means he's not going to return to full training until May. But I was pleased with what I saw before, he's a good-moving horse and he does have size and scope. A nice 2-y-o for the second half of the season".

1207. JOY FOR LIFE ★★★
b.f. Pivotal – Gallivant (Danehill).
February 27. Fifth foal. Sister to the quite useful dual 6f winner Pumpkin and half-sister to the fair 6f winner Junket (by Medicean). The dam, a quite useful 2-y-o 6f winner, is a closely related to the smart 2-y-o Group 2 6f Mill Reef Stakes winner Byron and a half-sister to 3 winners including the useful 1m and 10.3f winner Gallant Hero. The second dam, Gay Gallanta (by Woodman), a very smart winner of the Group 1 6f Cheveley Park Stakes and the Group 3 5f Queen Mary Stakes, was second in the 1m Falmouth Stakes and is a half-sister to 10 winners including the Group 2 10f Gallinule Stakes winner Sportsworld. (Cheveley Park Stud). "Quite a big, coarse filly at the moment but she has lots of size and scope. She moves well and although we'll have to be patient with her she's a filly that I like and she could develop into a nice type for later on this year".

1208. JUBILANCE (IRE) ★★★
b.c. Oratorio – Literacy (Diesis).
April 30. Third foal. 32,000Y. Tattersalls October Book 1. Kern/Lillingston. The dam, a modest 10f and 11f winner here, subsequently won in the USA and was second in the Grade 2 Long Island Handicap and is a half-sister to 2 winners. The second dam, Tuviah (by Eastern Echo), is a placed half-sister to 5 winners including the Group 3 Park Stakes winner of 7 races Duck Row. *"He showing a bit of ability and I have done a bit of work with him. I was pleased but he's just started growing again, so I've just eased off him. He'll definitely run at two, but whereas I was hoping it was going to be April, it's now looking more like June or July. But he's a good, solid individual and he has a good attitude".*

1209. KOGERSHIN (USA) ★★★
ch.f. Giant's Causeway – Kokadrie (Coronado's Quest).
April 12. Fifth foal. $450,000Y. Keeneland September. Charlie Gordon-Watson. Half-sister to 2 winners including the US triple Grade 1 winner and champion sprinter Kodiac Kowboy (by Posse). The dam is an unraced half-sister to the US Grade 1 Nassau County Handicap winner West By West. The second dam, West Turn (by Cox's Ridge), is a placed sister to the US Grade 1 winner Little Missouri. *"A good mover and a nice type, she's just having a break for a few weeks now so she'll take a bit of time, but I like her and physically she's done really well since she's been with us. I was lucky enough to see her half-brother Kodiac Kowboy when he was a 2-y-o at Vinery Stud in America. This filly is a very different type, she's got size and scope, so she's more of a seven furlong/mile filly".*

1210. MONNOYER ★★★★
b.c. Dutch Art – Ellebanna (Tina's Pet).
April 15. Thirteenth foal. 50,000Y. Tattersalls October Book 2. Jane Allison. Half-brother to the smart 1m Royal Hunt Cup winner Mine (by Primo Dominie), to the useful 3-y-o 7f winner King Midas (by Bluebird), the fairly useful 7f winner of 5 races Gift Of Gold (by Statoblest), the quite useful dual 1m winner Christmas Carnival, the fair 1m winner (on his only start) City Bonus (both by Cadeaux Genereux), the modest 7f winner Ours (by Mark Of Esteem) and a winner in Belgium by Distant Relative. The dam, a fair winner of 3 races over 5f, is a half-sister to 8 winners including the high-class sprinter Bolshoi, winner of the Group 2 Kings Stand Stakes and the Group 2 Temple Stakes. The second dam, Mainly Dry (by The Brianstan), is an unraced half-sister to 4 winners. *"This horse is working and I'm pleased with what he's showing me at the moment. A sharp, racey type, he'll be running in the second half of April. I like him, he looks really well in himself at present and he appears to have all the attributes that you'd want in a really early season 2-y-o".*

1211. NET WHIZZ (USA) ★★★
b.br.c. Mr Greeley – Reboot ((Rubiano).
February 5. Eighth foal. $240,000Y. Keeneland September. Jane Allison. Brother to the very smart 2-y-o 6f winner, Group 1 Middle Park Stakes second and Group 2 Mill Reef Stakes third Rebuttal and half-brother to the US stakes winner Summer Cruise (by Vicar) and minor US winners Bluegrass Cat, Carson City and Strong Hope. The dam, a minor winner of 4 races in the USA at 3 and 4 yrs, is a half-sister to 2 other minor winners. The second dam, Launch Light Tek (by Relaunch), a stakes winner in the USA and second in a Grade 3 event, is a sister to another minor US stakes winner. (Mrs Susan Roy & Tom Ludt). *"I've seen him twice and since the sales he's grown and has a lot more size and scope. They've been very pleased with how he's gone in America through the winter and spring, they really like him and I really liked what I saw when I was there. He's a 2-y-o to run in July over six/seven furlongs and he's a horse that I like. He arrives here in early April".*

1212. NIGER (IRE) ★★★
ch.c. Pivotal – Tithcar (Cadeaux Genereux).
March 11. Tenth foal. Goffs Orby. €95,000Y. Sir Robert Ogden. Half-brother to the very useful Irish Group 3 7f Ballycorus Stakes winner An Tadh, to the fairly useful 3-y-o 1m winner Chetak (both by Halling) and the fair 10f and 12f winner of 8 races Timocracy (by Cape Cross). The dam, a modest maiden, was placed 6 times from 5f to 7f at 3 yrs. She is a half-sister to 5 winners including the smart 1m

(at 2 yrs) and listed 10f winner Zindabad. The second dam, Miznah (by Sadler's Wells), winner of a 6f listed event at 2 yrs at the Curragh, is a full or half-sister to 9 winners including the useful listed 6f Silver Flash Stakes winner and Group 1 6f Prix Morny third Heeremandi, the Irish Group 3 winners Lake Como and Single Combat and the dam of the multiple US Grade 1 winner Flawlessly. *"A nice, straightforward colt, he moves well and I'm pleased with him but although he will make a 2-y-o we're talking about the second half of the season, once he's strengthened up and furnished"*.

1213. NOCTURN ★★★★
b.c. Oasis Dream – Pizzicato (Statoblest).
April 18. Eighth foal. 130,000Y. Tattersalls October Book 1. John Warren. Closely related to the quite useful Irish 5f and 1m winner Astonish (by Cape Cross) and half-brother to the moderate 2010 5f and 6f placed 2-y-o Pizzarra (by Shamardal), the 2-y-o Group 2 5f Flying Childers Stakes and Group 3 5f Molecomb Stakes winner Wunders Dream (by Averti), to the very useful Irish Group 3 Ridgewood Pearl Stakes winner Grecian Dancer (by Dansili), the fairly useful 6f (at 2 yrs) and 7f winner Go Between (by Daggers Drawn), the quite useful 7f winner Plucky (by Kyllachy) and a winner in Greece by Royal Applause. The dam, a modest 5f and 5.3f winner at 3 yrs, is a half-sister to 5 winners including the high-class Hong Kong horses Mensa and Firebolt. The second dam, Musianica (by Music Boy), was a fairly useful 2-y-o dual 6f winner. (Miss Y M G Jacques). *"This horse has done really well, I like him and he's got the make and shape of a fast horse. Not a real precocious type for April, but he's a fast, 2-y-o type for July onwards. Everything is in place but he just needs time to furnish and pull himself together. He looks to me all the world like a sprinter, he's a good mover and does everything the right way even now"*.

1214. PEARL CITY (IRE) ★★
b.f. Zamindar – Miss Hawai (Peintre Celebre).
January 27. Fifth foal. €140,000Y. Arqana Deauville August. Cheveley Park Stud. Half-sister to the 2010 2-y-o Evening Dress (by Medicean), to the Irish listed 9f winner and Group 1 Pretty Polly Stakes second Beach Bunny (by High Chaparral) and the quite useful 6f winner Robinson Cruso (by Footstepsinthesand). The dam is an unraced half-sister to 4 winners including the French dual listed winner Mer de Corail. The second dam, Miss Tahiti (by Tirol), won the Group 1 Prix Marcel Boussac and is a half-sister to 3 winners. *"An athletic filly that moves well, but she's a 2-y-o for the last third of the season. I haven't done enough with her to make a proper assessment but she's a good-moving filly with plenty of scope"*.

1215. REGAL ENTRANCE ★★★★ ♠
b.c. Royal Applause – Umniya (Bluebird).
February 17. Third foal. 100,000Y. Tattersalls October Book 1. Cheveley Park Stud. The dam, a quite useful 2-y-o 6f winner, was fourth in the Group 1 Moyglare Stud Stakes and third in the Group 3 Premio Dormello and is a half-sister to 5 winners including the dual listed 6f winner Lady Links (herself dam of the dual listed winner Selinka). The second dam, Sparky's Song (by Electric), a moderate 10.2f and 12f winner, is a half-sister to 3 winners including the very smart Group 1 6.5f winner Bold Edge and the listed winner and Group 2 5f Temple Stakes second Brave Edge. *"He's in fast work and he's a strong, robust individual and a sharp, early type. He could be running before the end of April and I'm just getting a feel for him now. I think he's definitely got the ability to win a couple of races as a 2-y-o. A solid individual, we'll start him off at five furlongs but he'll get six no problem"*.

1216. REGAL REALM ★★
b.f. Medicean – Regal Riband (Fantastic Light).
February 20. Second foal. The dam, a fair 6f (including at 2 yrs) and 5f winner of 7 races is a half-sister to 2 winners by Medicean including the fairly useful 2-y-o 6f winner Regal Royale. The second dam, Regal Rose (by Danehill), won both her starts including the Group 1 6f Cheveley Park Stakes and is a sister to the Japanese 10f stakes winner Generalist and a half-sister to 7 winners including the very useful listed-placed Regal Flush. *"A good mover, she's a filly with a bit of quality but she needs another month and some warm weather before we decide how to go forward. She's doing plenty of cantering and I like the way she

goes. She'll definitely run this year but I haven't done enough with her yet".

1217. RIO GRANDE ★★★★ ♠
b.c. *Invincible Spirit – Pharma West* (Gone West).
April 19. Third living foal. €180,000Y. Arqana Deauville August. Sir Robert Ogden. The dam won 2 minor races in France at 3 and 4 yrs and is a half-sister to one winner. The second dam, Pharma (by Theatrical), won the Grade 1 Santa Ana Handicap and the Grade 3 Wilshire Handicap and is a half-sister to the multiple US Grade 2 winner Hap. "He's already in fast work and he shows a good level of ability. He should be running in the second half of April and he's definitely a five/six furlong type. A sure-fire winner, so far he's done everything well enough to suggest he could be a Royal Ascot 2-y-o".

1218. ROMAN SOLDIER (IRE) ★★★
b.c. *Holy Roman Emperor – Fermion* (Sadler's Wells).
January 22. First foal. Goffs Orby. €80,000Y. Jane Allison. The dam, a listed 12f winner, is a sister to the listed winners Rave Review and Sail and a half-sister to the Group 3 winner Hearthstead Maison. The second dam, Pieds De Plume (by Seattle Slew), placed second once over 1m at 3 yrs in France, is closely related to the French listed and US stakes winner Slew The Slewor and a half-sister to the Group 1 Prix Lupin winner and sire Groom Dancer, the French Group 3 winner Tagel and the dam of the French Group 1 winner Plumania. "A neat horse, but he has a bit of scope to him as well. A good, solid individual, he's working and doing it well. He just needs to strengthen up a touch, but he shows a bit of ability, has a good attitude and he's a good mover. In late April/early May he'll be on the go and five or six furlongs shouldn't be a problem".

1219. ROXELANA (IRE) ★★
b.f. *Oasis Dream – Macadamia* (Classic Cliché).
January 21 Fourth foal. 100,000Y. Tattersalls October Book 1. Badgers Bloodstock. Sister to the fairly useful 2-y-o 7f winner Kona Coast. The dam, a smart winner of 5 races including the Group 2 1m Falmouth Stakes, is a half-sister to 7 winners including the very useful winner and listed-placed Azarole and the useful 2-y-o 5f and 6f winner Pistachio – subsequently a Group 3 winner in Scandinavia. The second dam, Cashew (by Sharrood), a quite useful 1m winner, is a half-sister to 6 winners here and abroad. "She hasn't arrived here yet because she's been quite backward. They've assured me that she will make a 2-y-o type, but she's just taking plenty of time".

1220. STAR BONITA (IRE) ★★
b.f. *Invincible Spirit – Honour Bright* (Danehill).
March 10. Second foal. 115,000Y. Tattersalls October Book 1. Willie Browne. The dam is an unraced half-sister to 4 winners including the listed 10f Ballyroan Stakes winner and Group 3 placed Dabtiya and the 10f winner and listed-placed Dabaya. The second dam, Dabiliya (by Vayrann), is an unraced half-sister to 12 winners including the top-class French Derby winner and sire Darshaan, the top-class Prix Vermeille winner Darara (dam of the Group 1 winners Diaghilev, Dar Re Mi and Darazari) and the Prix de Royallieu winner Dalara (dam of the Coronation Cup winner Daliapour). "I was really pleased with her and then she started growing in February and went through a weak stage. She's coming back to me now and she's a filly that I like because she has great strength and scope, but I haven't done anything fast with her at this stage to allow me to be more precise about her ability".

1221. STARFLY (IRE) ★★★
b.f. *Invincible Spirit – Mythologie* (Bering).
March 3. Ninth living foal. 56,000Y. Tattersalls October Book 2. John Warren. Half-sister to the French listed 2-y-o 6f winner Mytographie (by Anabaa) and to 4 minor winners in France by Octagonal (2), Anabaa and Sillery. The second dam, Mythologie (by Bering), won two races at 2 and 3 yrs in France and is a half-sister to 7 winners including Malaspina (Group 3 Prix Perth). (Highclere Thoroughbreds). "She was ready to go into fast work but her front ankles showed me that she needed a bit more time, so I eased back on her. She'll be back in full work in mid-April, she should be an early type and looks all over a five/six furlong filly".

NEW FOR 2011

MAWATHEEQ

DANZIG - SARAYIR by Mr PROSPECTOR

Out of a red-hot maternal family, brother to 2009 Guineas winner GHANAATI, from the direct family of NASHWAN, UNFUWAIN and NAYEF.

BRILLIANTLY BRED GROUP WINNING SON OF DANZIG

SHADWELL
STANDING FOR SUCCESS

Contact Richard Lancaster, Johnny Peter-Hoblyn or Audrey Leyval
+44 (0)1842 755913 I nominations@shadwellstud.co.uk I www.shadwellstud.co.uk

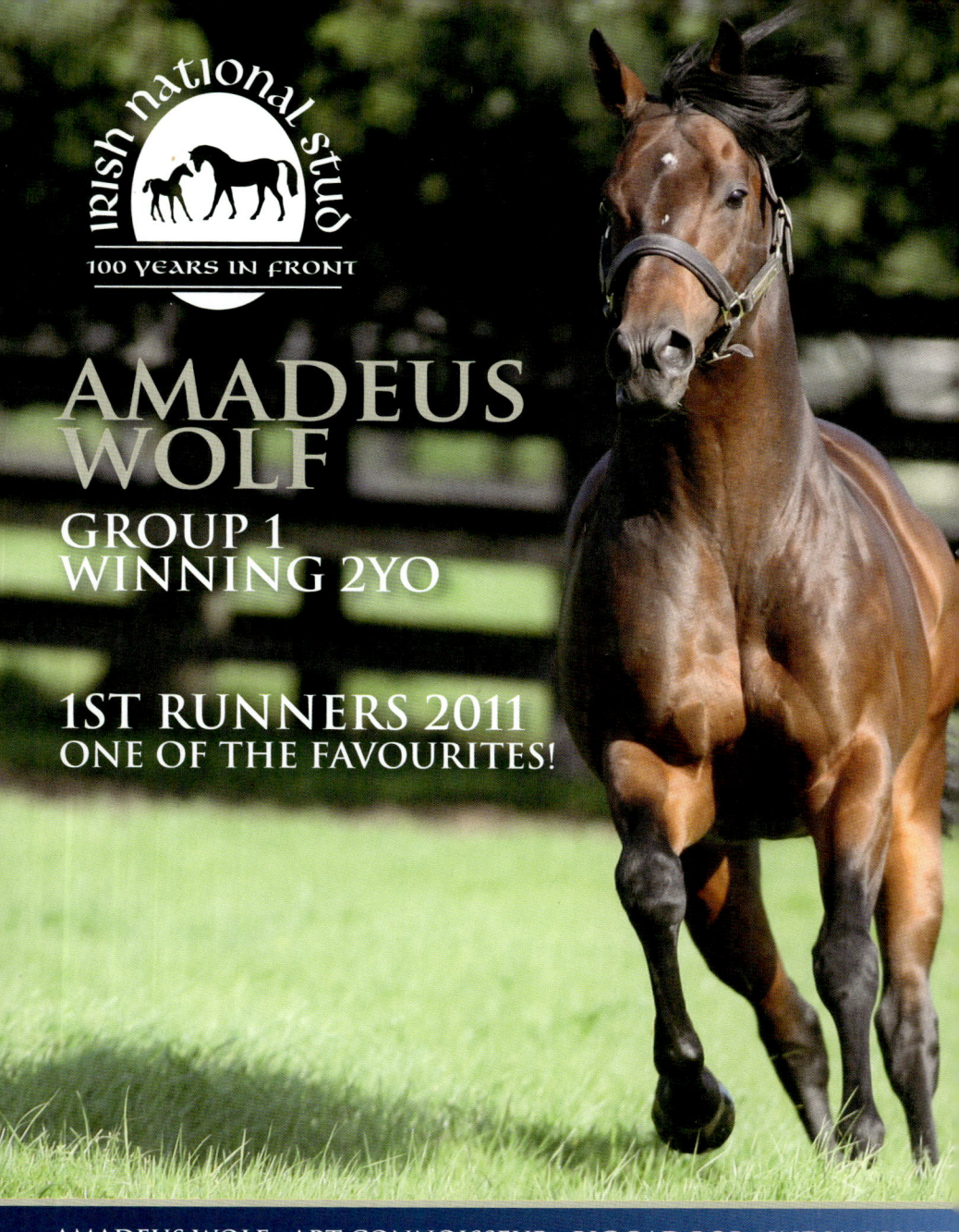

JEREMY

DANEHILL DANCER
Gr.1 winning 2yo

GLINT IN HER EYE
By Arazi (Rated 135 at 2 years)

WIND IN HER HAIR
By Alzao (Champion First Season Sire)

DAM OF DEEP IMPACT
(Champion First Season Sire in Japan 2010)

FAMILY OF NAYEF

AMADEUS WOLF   ART CONNOISSEUR   BIG BAD BOB   INDIAN HAVEN
INVINCIBLE SPIRIT   JEREMY   LORD SHANAKILL   VERGLAS

Contact: **JOHN OSBORNE** tel: +353 (0)45 521251
email: stud@irish-national-stud.ie   www.irish-national-stud.ie

The Perfect Arrangement...

Your mare and a Cheveley Park Stud stallion

Dutch Art
- Dual **Gr.1** winning unbeaten 2yo by **MEDICEAN**
- First crop yearlings fetched **€180,000, 120,000gns**, etc.

First runners in 2011

■ **FEE: £5,000**

Kyllachy
- Sire of **105 individual winners** in 2010
- 2010 successes included **Gr.1** Nunthorpe Stakes winner **SOLE POWER**

■ **FEE: £8,000**

Medicean
- Dual **Gr.1** winning miler by **MACHIAVELLIAN**
- Sire of **6 Gr.1 winners** from his first 5 crops

■ **FEE: £12,000**

Pivotal
- Sire of **19 individual Stakes winners** in 2010
- Sire of **18 individual Gr.1 winners** (2 in 2010)

■ **FEE: £55,000**

Virtual
- **Gr.1** winning miler by **PIVOTAL**
- Dam from the **Gr.1** family of **SARISKA** and **ECHELON**

First crop foals in 2011

■ **FEE: £4,000**

All fees 1st October terms LF Free Return.

Duchess Drive, Newmarket, Suffolk CB8 9DD
Telephone: **(01638) 730316** Fax: **(01638) 730868**
enquiries@cheveleypark.co.uk www.cheveleypark.co.uk

JEREMY NOSEDA

1222. TALWAR (IRE) ★★★
b.c. Acclamation – Moore's Melody (Marju).
February 23. First foal. 140,000Y. Tattersalls October Book 1. Willie Browne. The dam won twice over 1m at 3 and 4 yrs in France and is a sister to the Irish listed winner Bruges and a half-sister to 2 winners. *"He's done a little bit of work and he's a good, straightforward type that's strengthening all the time. A nice 'together' horse that should be on the track at the back end of April/early May and he looks like a real hardy 2-y-o type. We haven't done anything serious with him but he looks like he'll have the speed for five furlongs".*

1223. VALBCHEK (IRE) ★★★
b.c. Acclamation – Spectacular Show (Spectrum).
March 12. Second foal. 110,000Y. Tattersalls October Book 1. J McCalmont. Half-brother to Aussie Dollar (by Dansili), unplaced in one start at 2 yrs in 2010. The dam, a quite useful 2-y-o 5f winner, is a half-sister to the Group 3 7f Sweet Solera Stakes winner and Group 1 Fillies' Mile third English Ballet. The second dam, Stage Presence (by Selkirk), a 7f and 1m 3-y-o winner, is a half-sister to 6 winners including the 6f (at 2 yrs) and Group 3 7f Ballycorus Stakes winner Rum Charger (herself dam of the dual US Grade 1 winner Winchester). *"A good, scopey horse, he's more of a 2-y-o for the second half of the season. A bit immature in his development, but he's a good mover and has a good attitude. He's a colt that I like and he's a nice type of horse with plenty of size and substance".*

1224. UNNAMED ★★★
b.c. Azamour – Amoureux (Deputy Minister).
March 22. Second foal. Goffs Orby. €90,000Y. Citywest Inc. The dam is a placed half-sister to the Group 1 Criterium de Saint-Cloud winner Passion For Gold. The second dam, dam. Cest L'Amour (by Thunder Gulch), won the Grade 2 Nassau County Handicap in the USA and was Grade 1 placed and is a half-sister to 4 winners. *"A 3-y-o type, when we got him at the sales he was a neat, quality horse but he's grown a lot. Having said that he's grown into a fine, strong horse and he's a good mover. I like him a lot but he's a horse for a run or two in the autumn".*

1225. UNNAMED ★★★★
b.f. Red Clubs – Esterlina (Highest Honor).
February 22. Fifth foal. 54,000foal. Tattersalls October 1. Emerald Bloodstock. Half-sister to the smart 7f (at 2 yrs) and listed 1m Heron Stakes winner and Group 1 1m Criterium International third Redolent (by Redback), to the fair 6f winner Hightime Heroine (by Danetime) and the minor French 2-y-o winner Zomorroda (by Chineur). The dam won over 1m at 3 yrs in Ireland and is a half-sister to 3 minor winners in France. The second dam, Shaquick (by Shadeed), won in France and is a half-sister to 8 winners including the dual Group 3 winner Leap Lively (dam of the Irish 1,000 Guineas winner Forest Flower). *"A filly I like, she's very athletic and she could be a Royal Ascot filly. I haven't done anything serious with her yet but I like the way she goes about things. She has scope to go beyond that too, I really like her and she'll do a job as a 2-y-o, so she's one to look out for".*

1226. UNAMED ★★
b.f. Teofilo – Kootenay (Selkirk).
March 25. Half-sister to the quite useful 1m winner Kelowna (by Pivotal). The dam, a useful 2-y-o Italian listed 1m winner, is a half-sister to 3 winners including the fairly useful 2-y-o dual 7f winner Jay Gee's Choice. The second dam, Llia (by Shirley Heights), a fairly useful 2-y-o 7f winner, was third in the listed 10f Pretty Polly Stakes and is a half-sister to 3 winners including the useful 2m listed winner Lady Of The Lake. *"She's cantering along and is a neat filly that's improving all the time. She needs some warm weather now to help her come to hand, she does her canters well but I haven't done any more than that. A solid filly that maybe could do with growing a touch more".*

1227. UNNAMED ★★★
b.c. Iffraaj – Limit (Barathea).
March 29. Third foal. 62,000Y. Tattersalls October Book 2. Kern/Lillingston. Half-brother to the fairly useful triple 6f winner Kellys Eye (by Noverre). The dam, a modest 2-y-o 7f winner, is a half-sister to 2 winners. The second dam, Orlena (by Gone West), a minor 2-y-o 7f winner in France, is a half-sister to 6 winners including the listed winner and 1,000 Guineas third Vista Bella. *"Very much a*

colt for the last third of the season, he's big and scopey and he moves well. He's done everything in absolutely the right manner but he's quite an unfurnished fellow at the moment. I'm happy with him though and his sire looks like a proper stallion in the making".

1228. UNNAMED ★★★
ch.f. *Giant's Causeway – Lizzy Cool (Saint Ballado)*.
February 5. Fifth foal. $190,000Y. Keeneland September. Demi O'Byrne. Half-sister to the 2010 listed 7f placed 2-y-o Caspar's Touch (by Touch Gold) and to the US stakes winner Cool Bullet (by Red Bullet). The dam, a stakes winner in the USA at 3 yrs, is a half-sister to 8 winners. The second dam, Well Supported (by Key To The Mint), is an unplaced daughter of the US dual Grade 1 winner Windy's Daughter. (Messrs Tabor, Magnier & Smith). *"She's one for the last third of the season and she's done everything right since she's been with us but we just require a bit of patience with her".*

1229. UNNAMED ★★★
b.c. *Danehill Dancer – May Kiersey (Sadler's Wells)*.
January 20. Second foal. Goffs Orby. €75,000Y. Jane Allison. Brother to the fair 2010 Irish 7f and 1m placed 2-y-o Nucals Star. The dam is an unraced sister to the Group 3 Prix Penelope and Group 3 Prix des Reservoirs winner and Group 1 French and Irish Oaks placed Gagnoa. The second dam, Gwynn (by Darshaan), is an unraced half-sister to 2 minor winners. *"A 2-y-o for the second half of the year. He's just going through a growing stage and has gone a bit weak on me, but up to that point I'd been pleased with all he'd done. A seven furlong or mile type 2-y-o".*

1230. UNNAMED ★★
b.f. *Cape Cross – Miss Lacey (Diktat)*.
February 17. Second foal. 70,000foal. Tattersalls December. Knockenduff Stud. The dam is an unraced half-sister to 5 winners including the Group 2 Superlative Stakes and Group 3 Rose Of Lancaster Stakes winner Halicarnassus. The second dam, Launch Time (by Relaunch), is a US placed half-sister to 4 winners including the US Grade 2 winner Palace March and the Group/Grade 1 placed Executive Pride. (S E Construction). *"She's only been with me for a few days but I know they were happy with her at Ballylinch Stud in Ireland. I'm happy with her too, she moves well and has length and scope. I see her as a late season 2-y-o, but I haven't had her long enough to properly assess her really".*

1231. UNNAMED ★★★
b.c. *Kyllachy – Murrieta (Docksider)*.
February 16. Second foal. 90,000Y. Tattersalls October Book 1. Kern/Lillingston. Half-brother to the quite useful 2010 2-y-o 1m winner Maywood (by Cape Cross). The dam, a moderate 12f placed maiden, is a half-sister to 2 winners including the 2-y-o 6f and 7f winner and Group 1 1m Racing Post Trophy second Charlie Farnsbarns (by Cape Cross). The second dam, Lafleur (by Grand Lodge), is an unplaced half-sister to 9 winners including the smart 7f (at 2 yrs) and 11.5f winner and Epsom Oaks third Crown Of Light and the very useful 2-y-o listed 1m Stardom Stakes winner and Group 1 Grand Criterium third Alboostan. *"A good mover, he's a colt I like and he'll make a 2-y-o from July onwards. He needs to furnish and go in the right direction, but there's something about the way he's gone through the early part of his preparation that suggests to me he has ability. For an unfurnished horse he's done everything in a good manner to this point".*

1232. UNNAMED ★★★
ch.c. *Johannesburg – Mythical Echo (Stravinsky)*.
March 12. First foal. 100,000Y. Tattersalls October Book 2. Kern/Lillingston. The dam, a quite useful 2-y-o 6f winner, is a half-sister to 7 winners including the US Grade 2 winner Chinese Dragon. The second dam, Fabulous Fairy (by Alydar), a fair 3-y-o 10f winner, is a half-sister to 5 winners and to the dam of the top-class miler Desert Prince. *"A big, scopey horse, very much a colt for just a run or two at the back-end of the season. I like the way he handles himself and the way he moves, but he needs time. A horse with a good attitude and a great frame, he'll be a good, strong type if we're patient with him".*

1233. UNNAMED ★★★
b.f. *Galileo – Simply Perfect (Danehill)*.

January 7. First foal. The dam won the Group 1 Fillies' Mile and the Group 1 Falmouth Stakes. The second dam, Hotelgenie Dot Com (by Selkirk), a 7f winner at 2 yrs, was second in the Group 1 7f Moyglare Stud Stakes and third in the Group 1 Fillies' Mile and is a half-sister to 4 winners including the Moyglare Stud Stakes and the Group 2 6f Lowther Stakes winner Bianca Nera. *"She's cantering away and has done things in the right manner so far. I just need her to furnish a bit and get a bit more muscle tone and definition. One week I feel she's going in the right direction and is almost ready to kick on with, but the next week I change my mind. She's a good, solid type and the same sort of size as her mum but very different to look at. I don't think she'll be quite as precocious, but she should make a 2-y-o from July onwards. Simply Perfect was a great servant to me at two and three. She was a real tough 2-y-o and I hope that at some stage we're going to find a streak that runs through this filly similar to her mum".*

1234. UNNAMED ★★★
b.f. Haafhd – Valjarv (Bluebird).
March 3. Third foal. Tattersalls December. Redwall Bloodstock. Half-sister to the modest 2010 1m placed 2-y-o Destiny Of Dreams (by Dubai Destination) and to the modest 5f winner Val C (by Dubawi). The dam, a fairly useful 2-y-o 6f winner, was listed-placed and is a half-sister to 5 winners including the listed-placed Qadar and Ikan. The second dam, Iktidar (by Green Desert), a quite useful Irish 1m placed maiden, is a half-sister to 6 winners. *"We've done one little piece of work with her but then decided she's not a five furlong 2-y-o and we've eased off her. She's quite a nice, solid, hard-knocking filly with a great attitude'.*

1235. UNNAMED ★★★
b.c. Oasis Dream – Varenka (Fasliyev).
May 8. Third foal. 100,000Y. Tattersalls October Book 1. Kern/Lillingston. Half-brother to the useful dual 7f winner (including at 2 yrs) Meezaan (by Medicean). The dam, a fairly useful 2-y-o 7.5f winner, was listed-placed in Italy and a half-sister to one winner. The second dam, Castara Beach (by Danehill), placed fourth once over 7f at 2 yrs, is a sister to the useful Group 3 7f Criterion Stakes winner Hill Hopper (herself dam of the dual Group 1 winner Nannina) and a half-sister to 5 winners including the Australian Grade 1 winner Water Boatman. *"He was a late foal and is very much a 2-y-o for the last third of the season and then moving on at three. A good mover, he has a good attitude and he's a neat, 'together' horse that I'm happy with'.*

1236. UNNAMED ★★
ch.f. Giant's Causeway – Walker's Gal (Woodman).
May 25. Fourth foal. $250,000Y. Keeneland September. Demi O'Byrne. Sister to the minor US 3-y-o winner The Flats. The dam was placed at 4 yrs in the USA and is a sister to the 1,000 Guineas, Champion Stakes and Fillies' Mile winner Bosra Sham and to the French 2,000 Guineas winner Hector Protector and a half-sister to the French 2,000 Guineas winner Shanghai. The second dam, Korveya (by Riverman), won the Group 3 9f Prix Chloe and is a sister to the German Group 2 winner Keos and a half-sister to the high-class 6f to 7f filly Proskona. *"She was a late foal and she's ready for a little break now. A good, scopey type that moves well, at this moment in time she's done everything right and given time she could be a nice filly. One for the late summer/ early autumn".*

AIDAN O'BRIEN

1237. AHIMSA (IRE)
b.f. Holy Roman Emperor – Blue Cloud (Nashwan).
March 30. Eighth foal. Goffs Orby. €18,000Y. Bobby O'Ryan. Half-sister to the useful 2010 2-y-o 7f winner and 3-y-o listed-placed Blue Angel (by Oratorio), to the Group 3 7f Irish 1,000 Guineas Trial winner Enouraging (by Encosts De Lago), the French 1m and 9f winner Bank Guard (by Peintre Celebre), the French 9f winner Bomber Pilot (by Numerous) and another minor French winner by Polish Precedent. The dam, winner of the listed 7f Prix Imprudence at 3 yrs, is a half-sister to the top-class miler Bigstone and the French listed winner Bague Bleue. The second dam, Batave (by Posse), a 3-y-o 6f winner here, subsequently won in France and was placed in both the Group 3 5f Prix de Meautry and the Group 3 5f Prix de Saint-Georges.

1238. AMONG EQUALS
b.c. Oasis Dream – First (Highest Honor).
February 17. Fifth foal. 320,000Y. Tattersalls October Book 1. Demi O'Byrne. Brother to the smart listed 1m and listed 10f winner and dual Group 3 third Perfect Stride and half-brother to the French 2-y-o listed 6f winner Law Lord (by Diktat) and the French 10f winner Next (by In The Wings). The dam, a listed 1m winner at 3 yrs in France, is a half-sister to 12 winners including the smart Group 3 winners Bluebook and Myself. The second dam, Pushy (by Sharpen Up), a very useful 2-y-o winner of 4 races including the Group 2 Queen Mary Stakes, is a half-sister to 10 winners including the high-class 2-y-o Precocious and the Group 1 Japan Cup winner Jupiter Island.

1239. ATHENS (IRE)
b.c. Dylan Thomas – Rafina (Mr Prospector).
April 2. Closely related to the 2-y-o Group 2 1m Royal Lodge Stakes and Group 3 10.3f Dee Stakes winner Admiralofthefleet (by Danehill) and half-sister to the Irish 2-y-o 7f winner and Group 3 Acomb Stakes third Lucifer Sam (by Storm Cat), the useful 2-y-o 8.5f winner Canberra and the minor French 14f winner Gallo's Wells (both by Sadler's Wells). The dam was placed three times in France and is a sister to the champion European 2-y-o Machiavellian and to the smart Group 1 Prix Morny and Group 1 Prix de la Salamandre winner Coup de Genie, closely related to the Group 2 1m Prix d'Astarte winner Hydro Calido and a half-sister to the Group 1 Prix Jacques le Marois winner Exit to Nowhere. The second dam, Coup de Folie (by Halo), won four races from 6f to 10f including the Group 3 1m Prix d'Aumale and was stakes placed in the USA.

1240. BORIS GRIGORIEV (IRE)
b.br.c. Excellent Art – Strategy (Machiavellian).
February 21. Third foal. 130,000Y. Tattersalls October Book 1. Demi O'Byrne. Half-brother to a minor winner in the USA by Danehill Dancer. The dam, a quite useful 10f and 11f winner, is a half-sister to 2 winners. The second dam, Island Story (by Shirley Heights), a quite useful 10f winner, is a half-sister to 6 winners. *Second on his debut over five furlongs in mid-April.*

1241. ERNEST HEMINGWAY (IRE)
b.c. Galileo – Cassydora (Darshaan).
April 10. Second foal. The dam, a useful 7f (at 2 yrs), listed Lingfield Oaks Trial and subsequent US Grade 3 winner, was second in the Group 1 Nassau Stakes and is a half-sister to 3 winners including the listed 10f winner Classic Remark. The second dam, Claxon (by Caerleon), a very useful 1m (at 2 yrs) and Group 2 10f Premio Lydia Tesio winner, is a half-sister to 3 winners including the Group 2 placed Bulwark.

1242. HOMECOMING QUEEN (IRE)
b.f. Holy Roman Emperor – Lagrion (Diesis).
April 23. Closely related to the top-class middle-distance winner of 6 Group 1 events (including the Prix de l'Arc de Triomphe) Dylan Thomas (by Danehill) and to the Group 1 12f Oaks second Remember When (by Danehill Dancer) and half-sister to the champion 2-y-o filly and Group 1 6f Cheveley Park Stakes winner Queen's Logic (by Grand Lodge), the useful maiden and Group 2 Blandford Stakes second Love To Dance (by Sadler's Wells), the quite useful 3-y-o 1m winner Chatifa (by Titus Livius), the poor 10f winner Tulsa (by Priolo) and a winner of 10 races in Italy by Lahib. The dam was placed 5 times in Ireland and stayed 12f and is a sister to the Group 1 Middle Park Stakes second Pure Genius. The second dam, Wrap It Up (by Mount Hagen), is a placed half-sister to 6 winners including the Oaks Trial winner Gift Wrapped.

1243. ISHVANA (IRE)
b.f. Holy Roman Emperor – Song Of The Sea (Bering).
March 17. Fourth foal. Goffs Orby. €50,000Y. Not sold. The dam, placed fourth once over 12f, is a half-sister to 5 winners. The second dam, Calypso Run (by Lycius), ran once unplaced and is a half-sister to 9 winners including the good broodmare Grecian Sea and the Group 3 winner Sailor's Mate. *This filly won over five furlongs on her debut in April.*

1244. KNOW (IRE)
b.f. Excellent Art – For Evva Silca (Piccolo).
March 13. Fifth foal. 150,000Y. Tattersalls October Book 1. Demi O'Byrne. Half-sister to the very useful Irish listed 5f (at 2 yrs), 6f and UAE 7f winner Warsaw (by Danehill Dancer).

The dam, placed once at 2 yrs, is a half-sister to 7 winners including the 2-y-o Group 1 6f Prix Morny winner Silca's Sister, the Group 2 6f Mill Reef Stakes and German Group 2 winner and Group 1 placed Golden Silca and the very useful 5f winner and listed 6f winner of 12 races (including at 2 yrs) Green Manalishi. The second dam, Silca-Cisa (by Hallgate), a fairly useful dual 5f winner, was listed placed over 5f at 4 yrs and is a half-sister to the Group 3 placed sprinter Azizzi.

1245. PLUTORIUS (IRE)
b.c. Holy Roman Emperor – Almaaseh (Dancing Brave).
March 22. Twelfth living foal. Goffs Orby. €67,000Y. Demi O'Byrne. Half-brother to the very useful Group 3 5f Curragh Stakes and Group 3 5f Molecomb Stakes winner Almaty (by Dancing Dissident), to the useful 10f winner and listed-placed Salee (by Caerleon), the fairly useful 7f (at 2 yrs) to 10f winner of 9 races Impeller (by Polish Precedent), the fair 1m winner Miss Brown To You (by Fasliyev), the fair 6f winner Sarah Stokes (by Brief Truce) and the modest Irish 7f and hurdles winner Collingwood (by Machiavellian). The dam, placed once over 6f at 3 yrs, is a half-sister to 8 winners including the 2,000 Guineas and Champion Stakes winner Haafhd and the Group 2 Challenge Stakes winner Munir and to the unraced dam of the Group 1 Dubai Duty Free Stakes winner Gladiatorus. The second dam, Al Bahathri (by Blushing Groom), won the Irish 1,000 Guineas and is a half-sister to the US Grade 2 winner Geraldine's Store and to the dam of the US Grade 1 winner Spanish Fern.

1246. POWER
b.c. Oasis Dream – Frappe (Inchinor).
March 6. Ninth foal. 50,000Y. Tattersalls October Book 1. Not sold. Half-brother to the 7f (at 2 yrs) and Group 2 12f Ribblesdale Stakes winner Thakafaat (by Unfuwain), to the fairly useful 10f winner Quantum (by Alhaarth) and the quite useful 2-y-o 7f winner Applauded (by Royal Applause). The dam, a fairly useful 2-y-o 6f winner, is a half-sister to 2 winners including the 2,000 Guineas winner Footstepsinthesand. The second dam, Glatisant (by Rainbow Quest), winner of the Group 3 7f Prestige Stakes, is a half-sister to 8 winners and to the placed dam of the very smart 2-y-o Superstar Leo.

1246. RAPHAEL SANTI (IRE)
b.c. Excellent Art – Jamrah (Danehill).
March 1. Second foal. Tattersalls Ireland. €70,000Y. Eddie Fitzpatrick. Half-brother to For That Reason (by Medicean), last of 12 on his only start at 2 yrs in 2010. The unraced dam is closely related to the Group 3 Anglesey Stakes winner Walk On Bye. The second dam, Pipalong (by Pips Pride), won 10 races including the Group 1 6f Haydock Park Sprint Cup, the Group 3 Duke Of York Stakes and the Group 3 Palace House Stakes and is a half-sister to 9 winners including the fairly useful 2-y-o 6f listed winner Out Of Africa. *Fourth over five furlongs on his debut and then ran second over six, both in April.*

1247. SOON (IRE)
b.f. Galileo – Classic Park (Robellino).
April 19. Ninth foal. 75,000Y. Tattersalls October Book 1. Demi O'Byrne. Closely related to the French 2-y-o 1m winner, Group 1 1m Criterium International third and Epsom Derby second Walk In The Park and to the quite useful dual 2m winner Regal Park (both by Montjeu) and half-sister to the smart 1m winner Secret World (by Spinning World) and the quite useful Irish 6f and 7f winner Mufradat (by Desert Prince). The dam won 3 races including the Irish 1,000 Guineas and is a half-sister to 10 winners including the US Grade 2 winner Rumpipumpy. The second dam, Wanton (by Kris), a useful 2-y-o 5f winner and third in the Group 2 Flying Childers Stakes, is a half-sister to 8 winners including the listed 5f St Hugh's Stakes winner and Group 2 5f Prix du Gros-Chene second Easy Option (herself dam of the dual Group 1 winner Court Masterpiece).

1248. SECRETARY OF STATE (IRE)
b.c. Danehill Dancer – Akuna Bay (Mr Prospector).
April 25. Brother to the useful 2-y-o 5f and 6f winner and Group 3 Solario Stakes third Gaspar Van Wittel, closely related to the useful 10f and 12f winner and Group 3 Cumberland Lodge Stakes second Sugar Ray (by Danehill)

and half-brother to the fair Scandinavian listed 12f winner Demeanour (by Giant's Causeway) and a minor winner abroad by King Of Kings. The dam, a 2-y-o 7f winner, is a half-sister to 3 winners including the Ribblesdale Stakes second Gothic Dream. The second dam, Dark Lomond (by Lomond), won the Irish St Leger and is a half-sister to 5 winners including the Irish Group winners South Atlantic and Forlene.

1249. STORMBOUND (IRE)
b.c. *Galileo – A Footstep Away (Giant's Causeway).*
January 29. First foal. 52,000Y. Tattersalls December. Margaret O'Toole. The dam is an unraced half-sister to the US dual Grade 1 winner Lu Ravi and to the dam of the US dual Grade 1 winner and champion 2-y-o filly Halfbridled. The second dam, At The Half (by Seeking The Gold), won 5 races including the Grade 3 Golden Rod Stakes in the USA and is a half-sister to 7 winners including the US Grade 1 winner Spruce Needles.

1250. UNNAMED
b.f. *Kingmambo – Alexandrova (Sadler's Wells).*
January 12. First foal. The dam, winner of the Oaks, the Irish Oaks and the Yorkshire Oaks, is a sister to the smart listed 2-y-o 1m winner and Group 2 1m Beresford Stakes third Masterofthehorse and closely related to the 2-y-o Group 1 6f Cheveley Park Stakes winner Magical Romance and the smart Group 2 second Washington Irving. The second dam, Shouk (by Shirley Heights), a quite useful 10.5f winner, is closely related to the listed winner and Group 3 Park Hill Stakes third Puce and a half-sister to 6 winners.

1251. UNNAMED
b.f. *Galileo – Ask For The Moon (Dr Fong).*
January 16. Third foal. 400,000foal. Tattersalls December. Demi O'Byrne. The dam won 5 races including the Group 1 10f Prix Saint-Alary and is a half-sister to one winner. The second dam, Lune Rouge (by Unfuwain), won once and was listed-placed in France and is a half-sister to 7 winners including the dam of the French Group 3 winner Celimene.

1252. UNNAMED
ch.c. *Pivotal – Cape Merino (Clantime).*
March 21. Sixth living foal. 230,000Y. Tattersalls October Book 1. Demi O'Byrne. Half-brother to the Group 1 Golden Jubilee Stakes and Australian Group 1 winner Cape Of Good Hope, to the fair 6f winner Cape Cobra (both by Inchinor), the useful 2-y-o 6f winner and Group 1 Coronation Stakes fourth Cape Columbine (by Diktat) and the quite useful triple 6f winner Cape St Vincent (by Paris House). The dam, a useful winner of 4 races over 5f and 6f, is a sister to the fair dual 5f winner Calamanco (herself dam of the listed winner Corrybrough) and a half-sister to 3 winners. The second dam, Laena (by Roman Warrior), was placed once at 2 yrs and is a half-sister to one winner.

1253. UNNAMED
b.c. *Galileo – Dietrich (Storm Cat).*
April 13. Brother to the useful 2-y-o 7f winner Eskimo and half-brother to the Irish 2-y-o 7f winner and Group 3 6f second Marquesa, to the fairly useful Irish 7f winner Greatwallofchina (both by Kingmambo), the Irish 5f (at 2 yrs) and Group 3 6f winner Beauty Bright and the fair 7f winner Port Of Spain (both by Danehill). The dam won the Group 3 5f King George Stakes and Group 3 5f Ballyogan Stakes. The second dam, Piquetnol (by Private Account), a French 3-y-o winner and second in the Group

1254. UNNAMED
b.c. *Galileo – Four Roses (Darshaan).*
May 3. Sixth foal. 340,000Y. Tattersalls October Book 1. Demi O'Byrne. Half-sister to the Group 2 10f Blandford Stakes winner Four Sins (by Sinndar) and to a 4-y-o winner in Germany by Seattle Dancer. The dam is an unraced half-sister to 9 winners including the Group 3 7f Rockfel Stakes winner Germane and the very useful German 10f winner Fabriano. The second dam, Fraulein Tobin (by J O Tobin), a fair 1m winner, is a half-sister to 6 winners including the very smart 10f performer Running Stag.

1255. UNNAMED
b.f. *Galileo – Gwynn (Darshaan).*
March 24. Fifth foal. 900,000Y. Tattersalls October Book 1. John Magnier. Closely

related to the 2010 French 2-y-o 9f winner Pour Moi (by Montjeu), to the Group 3 1m Prix des Reservoirs and Group 3 10.5f Prix Penelope winner and Group 1 placed Gagnoa and the fairly useful French 2-y-o 1m winner Rendezvous (both by Sadler's Wells). The dam is an unplaced half-sister to 2 minor winners. The second dam, Victoress (by Conquistador Cielo), won over 11f in France and is a half-sister to 7 winners including the dual Group 1 winner Awaasif (herself dam of the Oaks winner Snow Bride and thus the grandam of Lammtarra) and the 1,000 Guineas second Konafa (the grandam of Hector Protector, Shanghai and Bosra Sham).

1256. UNNAMED
b.f. Galileo – Jude (Darshaan).
May 13. Eleventh foal. Closely related to the Irish 1,000 Guineas winner Yesterday, to the Group 1 7f Moyglare Stud Stakes winner and Irish 1,000 Guineas, Oaks and Irish Oaks placed Quarter Moon, the Group 2 placed winners All My Loving and Hold Me Love Me, the listed-placed winner Magicalmysterytour and the fair 2-y-o 1m winner Man Of God (all by Sadler's Wells). The dam, a moderate 10f placed maiden, is a sister to the very useful Irish listed 14f winner and Irish Oaks third Arrikala and to the useful Irish 12f listed winner Alouette (herself dam of the Group 1 winners Albanova and Alborada) and a half-sister to the very smart Group 2 10f Nassau Stakes and Sun Chariot Stakes winner Last Second (dam of the dual Group 1 winner Aussie Rules) and the Group 2 Doncaster Cup winner Alleluia (dam of the Group 1 winner Allegretto). The second dam, Alruccaba (by Crystal Palace), a quite useful 2-y-o 6f winner, is a half-sister to 3 winners.

1257. UNNAMED
b.c. Galileo – Kasora (Darshaan).
February 3. Closely related to six winners by Sadler's Wells including the Racing Post Trophy (at 2 yrs), Epsom Derby, Irish Derby and dual Breeders Cup Turf winner High Chaparral, the Group 2 10.4f Dante Stakes winner Black Bear Island and the useful Irish 10f winner and listed-placed Helena Molony and half-brother to the Irish 2-y-o 7f winner and listed-placed Treasure The Lady (by Indian Ridge)

and the Irish 8.5f and 9f winner Oriental Ben (by Ridgewood Ben). The dam is an unraced full or half-sister to 6 winners including the Irish 1,000 Guineas Trial winners Kotama and Khanata and the Group 1 National Stakes, Group 1 Premio Parioli and Grade 1 Oak Tree Turf Championship placed Khoraz. The second dam, Kozana (by Kris), won the Group 2 10f Prix de Malleret and the Group 3 1m Prix de Sandringham, was third in the Prix de l'Arc de Triomphe and is a half-sister to the Prix du Cadran winner Karkour and to the dam of the Cumberland Lodge Stakes winner Kazaroun.

1258. UNNAMED
b.c. Galileo – La Chunga (More Than Ready).
January 31. First foal. The dam won the Group 3 6f Albany Stakes (at 2 yrs) and the Group 3 6f Summer Stakes. The second dam, Gypsy Monarch (by Wavering Monarch), a minor winner in the USA, is a half-sister to the US Grade 3 6f winner Mint.

1259. UNNAMED
b.c. Galileo – Lady Lohar (Fraam).
February 13. Sixth foal. 270,000Y. Tattersalls October Book 1. Demi O'Byrne. Brother to the fairly useful listed 1m (at 2 yrs) and 10f winner Classic Legend, closely related to the useful 10f winner and listed-placed Popmurphy (by Montjeu) and half-brother to the fairly useful 7f (at 2 yrs) and 1m winner of 5 races Kilburn (by Grand Lodge) and the quite useful 7f (at 2 yrs) and 1m winner Syrian (by Hawk Wing). The dam, a useful 2-y-o Group 3 7f Futurity Stakes and 3-y-o 8.3f winner, was third in the Group 2 Cherry Hinton Stakes and the Group 2 Falmouth Stakes and is a half-sister to 3 winners. The second dam, Brigadier's Bird (by Mujadil), is an unraced half-sister to 3 winners.

1260. UNNAMED
ch.c. Proud Citizen – Legend Maker (Sadler's Wells).
April 30. Half-brother to the 7f (at 2 yrs) and 1,000 Guineas winner Virginia Waters (by Kingmambo), to the Irish 2-y-o 1m winner and Group 1 1m Criterium International second Chevalier, the Group 3 Gallinule Stakes winner Alexander Of Hales (both by Danehill) and the 2-y-o 7f winner and Group 3 placed Chief Lone Eagle (by Giant's Causeway). The dam won the

Group 3 10.5f Prix de Royaumont, was third in the Group 2 13.5 Prix de Pomone and is a half-sister to the Group 2 12f King Edward VII Stakes winner Amfortas. The second dam, High Spirited (by Shirley Heights), a quite useful winner over 14f and 2m, is a sister to the Premio Roma, Ribblesdale Stakes and Park Hill Stakes winner High Hawk (herself dam of the Breeders Cup Turf winner In the Wings) and a half-sister to the dams of the Derby winner High Rise and the Rothmans International winner Infamy.

1261. UNNAMED
b.c. Kingmambo – Liscanna (Sadler's Wells).
January 20. First foal. The dam, an Irish 2-y-o Group 3 6f Ballyogan Stakes winner, is a half-sister to the Irish 7.5f (at 2 yrs) and Group 3 10f Kilternan Stakes winner and dual Group 2 placed The Bogberry. The second dam, Lahinch (by Danehill Dancer), a useful listed 5f (at 2 yrs) and listed 6f winner, is a half-sister to 7 winners including the smart 2-y-o 5f and subsequent US stakes winner Perugino Bay.

1262. UNNAMED
b.c. Dylan Thomas – Monevassia (Mr Prospector).
March 17. Closely related to the 2-y-o Group 1 Moyglare Stud Stakes and Group 1 Prix Marcel Boussac winner Rumplestiltskin, to the quite useful 1m winner Denbera Dancer (both by Danehill) and the 2010 Irish 2-y-o 5f winner Catherineofaragon (by Holy Roman Emperor) and half-brother to the fairly useful Irish 2-y-o 6f winner Great Rumpuscat (by Storm Cat) and a hurdles winner by Sadler's Wells. The dam is a placed sister to the French 2,000 Guineas, the St James's Palace Stakes and Prix du Moulin winner Kingmambo and to the smart Group 3 6f Prix de Ris-Oranges winner Miesque's Son, closely related to the listed winner Moon Is Up and a half-sister to the high-class French 1,000 Guineas, Prix de Diane and Prix Jacques le Marois winner East of the Moon. The second dam, Miesque (by Nureyev), was a great filly and the winner of 10 Group or Grade 1 events including the Breeders Cup Mile (twice), the Prix Jacques le Marois (twice), the 1,000 Guineas, the French 1,000 Guineas and the Prix du Moulin.

1263. UNNAMED
b.f. Galileo – Necklace (Darshaan).
April 18. Fourth foal. The dam won the 2-y-o Group 1 7f Moyglare Stud Stakes and was Grade 1 placed in the USA. The second dam, Spinning The Yarn (by Barathea), ran once unplaced and is closely related to the top-class King George VI and Queen Elizabeth Diamond Stakes winner Opera House and the Ascot Gold Cup and Irish St Leger winner Kayf Tara and a half-sister to the Group 1 Prix de l'Opera winner Zee Zee Top.

1264. UNNAMED
b.c. Galileo – Nell Gwyn (Danehill).
January 30. First foal. The dam, a useful 2-y-o 1m winner, was second in the Group 3 Irish 1,000 Guineas Trial and is a sister to the top-class miler Rock Of Gibraltar (winner of the Dewhurst Stakes, Grand Criterium, 2,000 Guineas, Irish 2,000 Guineas, Prix du Moulin, Sussex Stakes and St James's Palace Stakes) and to the very useful Irish 2-y-o 6f winner Great Pyramid and a half-sister to 5 winners. The second dam, Offshore Boom (by Be My Guest), an Irish 2-y-o 6f winner, is a half-sister to 5 winners including the Irish listed winner Outside Pressure and the Group 1 Gran Criterium third Winning Venture.

1265. UNNAMED
b.c. Dansili – Race For The Stars (Fusaichi Pegasus).
March 17. Second foal. The dam, winner of the listed 7f Oh So Sharp Stakes (at 2 yrs) and the Group 3 9.5f Denny Cordell Fillies' Stakes, is a sister to the Irish 10f winner and Group 2 placed Zulu Chief, closely related to the National Stakes, Eclipse Stakes and Lockinge Stakes winner Hawk Wing and the minor Canadian stakes winner Alexandrina and a half-sister to numerous winners including the US dual Grade 3 placed Dr Sardonica. The second dam, La Lorgnette (by Val De L'Orne), was a champion 3-y-o filly in Canada.

1266. UNNAMED
eib.f. Kingmambo – Sequoyah (Sadler's Wells).
January 1. Sister to the 2,000 Guineas, Irish 2,000 Guineas, St James's Palace Stakes and Sussex Stakes winner Henrythenavigator and to the Group 3 Irish 1,000 Guineas Trial winner

Queen Cleopatra and half-sister to the fairly useful Irish 2-y-o 7.5f winner Abide With Me (by Danehill). The dam, winner of the Group 1 7f Moyglare Stud Stakes, is a sister to the 2-y-o Group 1 Fillies' Mile winner Listen and a half-sister to the Irish listed 5.6f winner and Group 3 7f placed Oyster Catcher. The second dam, Brigid (by Irish River), a minor French 3-y-o 1m winner, is a sister to the French listed 7f winner Or Vision (herself dam of the Group/Grade 1 winners Dolphin Street, Insight and Saffron Walden) and a half-sister to 6 winners.

1267. UNNAMED
b.f. *Montjeu – Shadow Song (Pennekamp).*
April 23. Third foal. 400,000Y. Tattersalls October Book 1. Charlie Gordon-Watson. Sister to the 2-y-o Group 1 1m Criterium International winner and Irish Derby third Jan Vermeer and closely related to the 2010 2-y-o Group 3 7f Silver Flash Stakes winner and Group 1 Fillies' Mile second Together (by Galileo). The dam won once at 3 yrs in France and is a half-sister to 7 winners including the Group 3 May Hill Stakes winner Midnight Air (herself dam of the Group 3 and subsequent US Grade 2 winner Midnight Line) and to the placed dam of the Group 1 Prix de l'Abbaye winner Imperial Beauty. The second dam, Evening Air (by J O Tobin), is an unraced half-sister to 5 winners including the Irish Derby Trial second Ancient Times.

1268. UNNAMED
b.c. *Dylan Thomas – Sheer Bliss (Sadler's Wells).*
February 20. Fifth foal. 300,000Y. Tattersalls October Book 1. Demi O'Byrne. Half-brother to the fairly useful 2010 Irish 2-y-o 7f winner When Not Iff (by Iffraaj). The dam, a fair 2-y-o 1m winner, is a half-sister to 9 winners including the Derby winner Oath and the triple Group 1 winner Pelder. The second dam, Sheer Audacity (by Troy), was placed twice in Italy and is closely related to the Ribblesdale Stakes winner and good broodmare Miss Petard.

1269. UNNAMED
b.c. *Galileo – Silverskaya (Silver Hawk).*
April 13. Third foal. Brother to the very smart 2010 Irish 2-y-o 7f winner and Group 1 1m Racing Post Trophy second Seville. The dam, a French

dual Group 3 middle-distance winner, is a half-sister to numerous winners including the Group 2 1m Prix d'Astarte winner Daneskaya. The second dam, Boubskaia (by Niniski), a listed-placed winner in France, is a half-sister to 7 winners including the Group 1 1m Gran Criterium winner Will Dancer and the Group 2 6f Premio Umbria winner Dancing Eagle.

1270. UNNAMED
b.c. *Galileo – Tarascon (Tirol).*
April 12. Seventh foal. Goffs Orby. €260,000Y. Demi O'Byrne. Closely related to the quite useful Irish 10f winner Estephe (by Sadler's Wells) and to the Irish dual 9f Beucaire (by Entrepreneur) and half-brother to the useful 2010 2-y-o listed 6f winner High Award (by Holy Roman Emperor), the French dual 7f winner (including at 2 yrs) and listed-placed Mayano Sophia (by Rock Of Gibraltar) and the Irish 12f winner Perfecto (by Peintre Celebre). The dam, winner of the 7f Moyglare Stud Stakes and the Irish 1,000 Guineas, is a half-sister to the Group 2 Prix Guillaume d'Ornano winner Mister Monet and to the very useful 5f winner and Moyglare Stud Stakes and Cheveley Park Stakes placed Mala Mala. The second dam, Breyani (by Commanche Run), a useful winner at up to 2m, is a half-sister to 4 winners.

1271. UNNAMED
b.c. *Montjeu – Tarfah (Kingmambo).*
March 5. Second foal. 525,000Y. Tattersalls October Book 1. Demi O'Byrne. Closely related to Ideal (by Galileo), unplaced in two starts at 2 yrs in 2010. The dam was a useful winner of 5 races over 1m and 9f including the Group 3 Dahlia Stakes and the listed Rosemary Stakes and is a half-sister to one winner. The second dam, Fickle (by Danehill), a fairly useful 1m and listed 10f winner, is a half-sister to 7 winners including the useful 11.5f listed winner Birdie and the French middle-distance winner of four listed events Faru.

1272. UNNAMED
b.c. *Giant's Causeway – Vallee Des Reves (Kingmambo).*
April 10. Brother to the Group 1 1m Coronation Stakes and Group 2 7f Rockfel Stakes winner Maid's Causeway and half-brother to the Irish

7f winner and Group 3 9f placed Uimhir A Haon (by Montjeu), the quite useful 10f, 14f and hurdles winner Corum (by Galileo) and the fair 7f and 1m winner Manhattan Dream (by Statue Of Liberty). The dam is an unraced half-sister to the Group 2 Prix du Muguet winner Vetheuil, the Group 3 Prix de l'Opera winner Verveine (herself dam of the Grade 1 winners Vallee Enchantee and Volga) and the dam of the Group 1 Grand Prix de Paris winner Vespone. The second dam, Venise (by Nureyev), is an unraced three-parts sister to the Mill Reef Stakes and Richmond Stakes winner Vacarme and a half-sister to the Prix Jacques le Marois winner Vin de France.

1273. UNNAMED
b.c. Galileo – Winds Of Time (Danehill).
March 10. Second foal. 380,000Y. Tattersalls October Book 1. Demi O'Byrne. Half-brother to the very useful 2010 2-y-o 6f winner and Group 2 Richmond Stakes second The Paddyman (by Giant's Causeway). The dam, a fairly useful 2-y-o 6f winner, subsequently won in the USA and Canada and is a half-sister to 2 winners. The second dam, Windmill (by Ezzoud), a fair 13.8f winner, is a half-sister to 8 winners including the very smart Group 2 12f Ribblesdale Stakes winner Gull Nook (herself dam of the top-class colt Pentire), the equally smart Group 2 12f Princess Royal Stakes winner Banket and the useful Group 3 Ormonde Stakes winner Mr Pintips.

JAMIE OSBORNE

1274. APPLAUDERE ★★★
b.f. Royal Applause – Let Alone (Warning).
February 7. Seventh foal. Doncaster Premier. £22,000Y. Jamie Osborne. Half-sister to the US winner of 5 races and Italian listed-placed Mac Rhapsody (by Night Shift), to the quite useful triple 6f winner (including at 2 yrs) Rash Judgement (by Mark Of Esteem), the modest 1m and 10f winner Tabulate (by Dansili), a winner in Sweden by Exceed And Excel and the useful hurdles winner Shalone (by Tobougg). The dam, a fair 1m winner, is a half-sister to 5 minor winners. The second dam, Mettlesome (by Lomond), a French 1m (at 2 yrs) and 9f winner, is a half-sister to 5 winners including the Group 3 Rose Of Lancaster Stakes and subsequent Grade 1 Santa Anita Handicap winner Urgent Request. (Mr Simon Griffiths). *"She's a nice filly but not as forward as I thought she'd be. Originally I expected her to be a pre-Ascot filly but maybe she's more likely to be a mid-summer type. She's grown a bit, but she moves well and five/six furlongs will be her sort of trip".*

1275. BYRON BLUE (IRE) ★★★★
br.c. Dylan Thomas – High Society (Key Of Luck).
February 11. Fourth foal. 43,000Y. Tattersalls October Book 1. Not sold. Closely related to Irish listed 6f winner and Group 1 Golden Jubilee Stakes second Society Rock (by Rock Of Gibraltar) and half-brother to the minor German 2-y-o 6f winner Johannesburg Cat (by Johannesburg). The dam, an Irish 2-y-o listed 6f and subsequent US stakes winner, was Grade 2 placed and is a half-sister to 4 winners. The second dam, Ela's Gold (by Ela-Mana-Mou), a moderate 6f placed maiden, is a full or half-sister to 6 winners. (Mr & Mrs I H Bendelow). *"I love this horse, he was a sharper looking Dylan Thomas as a yearling than a lot of them seemed to be at the sales. Obviously there's a bit of speed in the pedigree, he goes along nicely and he's very mature, so there's a chance he'll start at six furlongs, but if so you'd have to think he'd improve for going further later on. There's a lot of quality there and, very tentatively, I'm hoping he'll have the ability to be a Chesham Stakes horse".*

1276. CUTIE PIE (IRE) ★★
b.f. Iffraaj – Easter Parade (Entrepreneur).
January 31. Fourth foal. Doncaster Premier. £18,000Y. Jamie Osborne. Half-sister to the modest dual 10f winner Sharakti (by Rakti) and to the modest Irish 7f winner All In Clover (by Bahri). The dam, a fair 12f and 14f winner, is a half-sister to 7 winners including Interlude (Group 2 Prix de Pomone). The second dam, Starlet (by Teenoso), won 7 races from 7f (at 2 yrs) to 12f including a Group 2 event in Germany and is a half-sister to 8 winners including the US Grade 1 Arlington Handicap winner Unknown Quantity. (Miss J Kask). *"She's grown a lot, she's very nice but not that forward. I see her as a second half of the season filly and I wouldn't have a view on ability yet because she wouldn't have done a lot".*

1277. EESTI POISS (IRE) ★★
b.c. Oratorio – Pivotalia (Pivotal).
February 20. First foal. Doncaster Premier. £20,000Y. Jamie Osborne. The dam, a modest 9.5f winner, is a half-sister to 3 winners. The second dam, Viscaria (by Barathea), an Irish 1m (at 2 yrs) and 10f winner, is closely related to the UAE Group 3 winner Stagelight and a half-sister to 7 winners including the 1,000 Guineas third Hathrah, the smart Group 2 12f Premio Ellington winner Ivan Luis and the French/German listed winners Amathia and Zero Problemo. The second dam, Zivania (by Shernazar), a useful Irish winner of 4 races from 1m to 9.5f, is a half-sister to 4 stakes winners. (Miss J Kask). *"He's done well, he's changed a fair bit over the winter and spring and I wouldn't have too much of a view as to ability, but he looks very nice and he moves well".*

1278. FISTFUL OF DOLLARS (IRE) ★★
b.g. Holy Roman Emperor – Taking Liberties (Royal Academy).
March 31. Ninth foal. 42,000Y. Tattersalls October Book 1. Jamie Osborne. Closely related to the listed 1m winner of 7 races here and in Hong Kong Troubadour, to the fair 2-y-o 6f winner Danapali (both by Danehill) and the fair 10f and 12f winner Mons Calpe (by Rock Of Gibraltar) and half-brother to the fair 1m to 10f winner Eccollo, the French 2-y-o winner and 5f listed-placed Agapimou (both by Spectrum), the quite useful 5-y-o dual 1m winner Saponi and the minor French dual winner Tosca's Impulse (both by Indian Ridge). The dam ran once unplaced and is a sister to the Irish 2-y-o Group 3 1m Futurity Stakes winner Equal Rights and a half-sister to 6 winners including the Australian Grade 3 winner Freedom Fields. The second dam, Lady Liberty (by Noble Bijou), won the Grade 1 12f South Australian Oaks and is a half-sister to 4 winners. (Mr D L Dixon). *"We gelded him because he was a little bit over-inclined not to concentrate on his work! He goes OK but he's quite big and he'll be a 2-y-o from mid-summer onwards".*

1279. GREATEST DANCER (IRE) ★★★★
b.f. Iffraaj – Seasonal Style (Generous).
March 9. Seventh foal. Tattersalls Ireland. €33,000Y. Jamie Osborne. Half-sister to the 2010 Spanish 2-y-o winner Sergei, to the fair Irish 2-y-o 7f and subsequent German winner Hard Warrior (both by Gulch), the fairly useful Irish and US 6f to 1m winner Perfect Casting (by Diesis), to the fairly useful Irish triple 12f winner Rich Sense (by Mt Livermore), the quite useful 10f winner Tropical Chic (by Thunder Gulch). The dam, a fairly useful Irish 9f and 10f winner, is a half-sister to 3 winners. The second dam, Just Society (by Devil's Bag), won over 5f and 6f at 3 yrs in Ireland and is a half-sister to 3 winners including the Group 1 7f National Stakes fourth Smooth Performance. (Mr D L Dixon). *"She nice, she goes well and she'll be early. I'd say she's just a notch behind the Holy Roman Emperor filly at the moment but I can see her progressing. I like her a lot and she's definitely up to winning a maiden early on. She's not enormous, she's just got stronger rather than grow and she's a real 2-y-o type".*

1280. HEARTS AND MINDS ★★★
b.g. Clodovil – Heart's Desire (Royal Applause).
March 16. Fourth foal. 32,000Y. Tattersalls October Book 2. Jamie Osborne. Half-brother to the Irish 2-y-o listed 6f winner Heart Of Fire (by Mujadil) and to the fairly useful Irish 1m (at 2 yrs) and 14f winner Knight Eagle (by Night Shift). The dam, a fair 7f and 1m placed maiden, is a half-sister to 5 winners including the French listed winner and Group 3 placed Bashful. The second dam, Touch And Love (by Green Desert), a 2-y-o winner in France, was second in the Group 2 Prix du Gros-Chene and is a half-sister to 8 winners. (Mr G Gill). *"A beautiful mover, he goes well and he'll be racing in May or June. A nice horse, he'll be OK".*

1281. MOUNT McLEOD ★★★★
b.f. Holy Roman Emperor – Northern Gulch (Gulch).
April 14. Seventh foal. €20,000Y. Goffs Orby. (Private Sale). Half-sister to the 2-y-o Group 2 6f Richmond Stakes winner Hamoody (by Johannesburg) and to the US winner and Grade 3 placed Arcodoro (by Medaille d'Or). The dam, placed three times in the USA, is a half-sister to 9 winners including the US dual Grade 3 winner Stylish Star. The second dam, Northern Style (by Ack Ack), a US stakes winner and Grade 3 placed, is a full or half-sister to 4

winners. (Ken Rhatigan & Partners). *"She's got pace and she could be our first runner. I'd say she's definitely up to winning a maiden at least, early on. A lovely mover, she's quick, small and strong and a look at her pedigree suggests you wouldn't be surprised if she turned out to be a nice horse. I like her a lot and she'd be one of my favourites at the moment".* TRAINERS' BARGAIN BUY

1282. PRIDE AND JOY (IRE) ★★★★
b.c. Dark Angel – Fey Rouge (Fayruz).
March 24. Eighth foal. Doncaster Premier. £20,000Y. Jamie Osborne. Half-brother to the Irish 7f and 1m winners and Group placed Crystal View (by Imperial Ballet) and Miss Trish (by Danetime), the Irish 5f winner Bye Bye Ben (by Beckett) and the minor Italian winner of 8 races Schumichel (by Imperial Ballet). The dam is an unplaced full or half-sister to 9 winners. The second dam, Isa (by Dance In Time), is an unraced half-sister to 4 winners. (Miss J Kask). *"In full training, he's working away and he goes well. I thought I'd be starting him off at five furlongs, but I think I'm going to wait until he can start over six. A quality colt that moves well, hopefully he'll be one of the better early colts".*

1283. RUSSIAN BULLET ★★★
b.g. Royal Applause – Gandini (Night Shift).
February 8. Fifth foal. Doncaster Premier. £10,000Y. Jamie Osborne. Half-brother to the Italian winner of 5 races and listed-placed Powerful Speed (by Compton Place) and to 2 minor winners in Italy and Spain by Diktat and Tagula. The dam, a minor winner at 3 yrs in Italy, is a full or half-sister to 8 winners. The second dam, Actress (by Arctic Tern), is a placed half-sister to 2 winners. (Miss J Kask). *"He's a bit of a playboy and we may have to geld him, but he goes OK, he'll be racing in the first half of the season and although I don't think he'll be quite as good as the owner's 2-y-o Pride And Joy, I certainly think he'll be up to winning a maiden".*

1285. UNNAMED ★★
b.br.f. Clodovil – Clochette (Namaqualand).
April 2. Fourth living foal. 6,000Y. Tattersalls October Book 3. Jamie Osborne. Half-sister to the fair 2-y-o 5f winner Calypso Girl (by Verglas) and to the moderate 6f winner Time Share (by Danetime). The dam was placed twice over 6f at 3 yrs in Ireland and is a half-sister to 5 winners including the Group 1 Cheveley Park Stakes and Group 1 Moyglare Stud Stakes winner Capricciosa. The second dam, Clanjingle (by Tumble Wind), is a placed half-sister to 4 winners. *"A sharp little filly, she's grown a bit but stayed strong and she'll be racing in the first half of the season. She goes along alright and she'll be OK. I'll start her off at five furlongs".*

1286. UNNAMED ★★
b.f. Holy Roman Emperor – Moonshadow (Diesis).
February 28. Second foal. 15,000Y. Tattersalls October Book 2. Jamie Osborne. The dam is a 12f placed sister to the Group 1 12f Oaks winner Love Divine (herself dam of the Group 1 St Leger winner Sixties Icon) and a half-sister to 4 winners including the useful listed 12f winner Floreeda. The second dam, La Sky (by Law Society), a useful 10f winner and second in the Lancashire Oaks, is closely related to the Champion Stakes winner Legal Case. (Hearn, Pennick, Durkan & Co). *"She's a little bit behind where I'd like her to be, due to a couple of niggling problems she had during the winter, but she's going along alright. I can see her starting off at seven furlongs".*

1287. UNNAMED ★★
b.g. Marju – Royals Special (Caerleon).
April 29. Sixth foal. 7,000Y. Tattersalls December. Jamie Osborne. Half-brother to the very useful 9f to 2m winner of 4 races and listed-placed Yes Mr President (by Montjeu). The dam is an unplaced half-sister to 5 winners including Ezzoud, winner of the Eclipse Stakes and the Juddmonte International Stakes (twice) and Distant Relative, winner of the Sussex Stakes and the Prix du Moulin. The second dam, Royal Sister II (by Claude), a winner over 10f at 4 yrs in Ireland, also won 7 races in Italy from 3 to 5 yrs and is a half-sister to 4 winners. (Hearn, Pennick, Durkan & Co). *"Leave him in the book because he might have a future, but we had to geld him and I haven't been able to assess him properly yet".*

1288. UNNAMED ★★★
b.c. Amadeus Wolf – Slieve (Selkirk).
February 2. Second foal. Goffs Orby. €58,000Y. Jamie Osborne. Half-brother to the fair 2010 2-y-o 1m winner Census (by Cacique). The dam is an unraced sister to the Group 1 Gran Premio di Milano winner Leadership and a half-sister to 3 minor winners abroad. The second dam, Louella (by El Gran Senor), is a placed half-sister to 7 minor winners in Europe and the USA. (J Duddy). *"A beautiful horse and a beautiful mover, he's grown a lot and so he'll take a little bit of time. One for the second half of the season but you'd love watching him going up the gallop pointing his toe, he's lovely".*

1289. UNNAMED ★★★
b.c. Royal Applause – Three Gifts (Cadeaux Genereux).
April 22. Fourth foal. 30,000Y. Tattersalls October Book 1. Jamie Osborne. Half-brother to Sunny Peace (by Vision Of Night), a minor winner of 5 races at 4 and 5 yrs in the USA. The dam is an unraced half-sister to 5 winners. The second dam, Thracian (by Green Desert), a fairly useful 2-y-o 6f and 7f winner, is a half-sister to 12 winners including the Group 2 12f Ribblesdale Stakes winner Third Watch, the Group 3 Prix Foy winner Richard of York, the Group 2 Premio Dormello winner Three Tails (herself dam of the high-class colts Tamure, Three Cheers and Sea Wave), the Group 3 Fred Darling Stakes winner Maysoon and the dams of the Group winners Lend A Hand and Talented. *"A beautiful mover and a very good-looking horse, but he's done a fair bit of growing and I'll just have to keep the hand brake on him for a bit. I'm hoping he'll be a second half of the season 2-y-o and he has a lot of quality".*

1290. UNNAMED ★★
ch.f. Sharp Humor – Tip The Scale (Valiant Nature).
April 19. Third foal. Goffs Orby. €15,000Y. Jamie Osborne. Half-sister to the French listed-placed winner Wildcat Wizard (by Forest Wildcat) and to a minor US winner by Hussonet. The dam, a minor stakes winner of 9 races at 4 and 5 yrs in the USA, is a half-sister to 9 winners including the US Grade 2

winner Eleusis. The second dam, Balancing Act (by Spectacular Bid), a minor winner of 2 races at 3 yrs, is a half-sister to 9 winners including the champion Canadian 3-y-o colt and dual Grade 1 winner Peaks And Valleys. *"She's having a couple of months off due to a setback, but she will be a 2-y-o in the second half of the season. It's a shame really because she was quite forward looking, but she looks like she'll be alright once we get this problem sorted".*

1291. UNNAMED ★★★
b.c. Ishiguru – To The Woods (Woodborough).
March 28. Fifth foal. Doncaster St Leger Festival. £15,000Y. Jamie Osborne. Brother to a minor winner at 2 and 3 yrs in Hungary and half-brother to the modest 10f winner Wood Fair (by Trade Fair). The dam, a fairly useful 5f and 7f winner (including at 2 yrs), is a half-sister to 7 winners including the 2-y-o 6f winner and Group 2 6f Lowther Stakes fourth Valjarv. The second dam, Iktidar (by Green Desert), a quite useful Irish 1m placed maiden, is a half-sister to 6 winners. (Hearn, Pennick, Durkan & Co). *"He goes very well and I was hoping to have him more forward, but he's just gone on a growing spurt so I need to leave him alone for a bit. But he'd done a few bits of work and he does go very well. Hopefully he'll be out pre-Ascot and he's certainly shown me enough to suggest he'll win his maiden".*

1292. UNNAMED ★★
b.f. Oasis Dream – Venturi (Danehill Dancer).
March 12. Fourth foal. 12,000Y. Tattersalls October Book 2. Jamie Osborne. Half-sister to the quite useful 1m winner Call To Reason (by Pivotal) and to the quite useful Irish 1m and 11f winner Cilium (by War Chant). The dam, winner of the Group 3 7f C L Weld Park Stakes, was subsequently second in two US Grade 3 events and is a sister to the French listed winner and Group 1 Criterium de Saint-Cloud third Feels All Right. The second dam, Zagreb Flyer (by Old Vic), is an unraced half-sister to 8 winners including the listed winner and Group 1 Italian Oaks second Flying Girl. (Hearn, Pennick, Durkan & Co). *"Obviously her price tag shows she has a lot more pedigree than physique, so she's 'chancey' but she seems to get across the ground OK. The chances are she's not a bad buy for what she cost and*

despite her physique she's holding up alright at the moment, doing half and three-quarter speeds and doing them nicely".

JOHN OXX

1293. AFRAZ (IRE) ★★★★
b.c. Red Ransom – Adelfia (Sinndar).
February 8. Second foal. Half-brother to the fairly useful 2010 2-y-o 1m winner Adilapour (by Azamour). The dam, a quite useful 12f winner, is a half-sister to several winners including the smart dual Group 3 winner Adilabad. The second dam, Adaiyka (by Doyoun), was a smart winner of the Group 3 9f Prix Chloe. *"A lovely horse, he'll be a nice 2-y-o and you should put him in the book".*

1294. AKEED MOFEED ★★★★
b.c. Dubawi – Wonder Why (Tiger Hill).
February 14. First foal. The dam is an unraced half-sister to 5 winners including the German listed winners Whispered Secret and Wells Present. The second dam, Wells Whisper (by Sadler's Wells), was placed over 1m and 10f and is a sister to the very useful Group 1 10.5f Prix Lupin and US Grade 2 1m winner Johann Quatz and to the smart French 10.5f to 13.5f listed winner Walter Willy and a half-sister to the top-class middle-distance colt Hernando. *"He's a lovely colt, very well-grown and strong. He's done a little bit of fast work and he's a nice, well-balanced horse with a good temperament. Very likeable".*

1295. AKEED WAFI (IRE) ★★★★
b.c. Street Cry – Shy Lady (Kaldoun).
April 18. Eighth foal. Closely related to the very useful listed 7f winner Atlantic Sport (by Machiavellian) and half-brother to the quite useful 2010 2-y-o 1m winner (from two starts) Happy Today (by Gone West), to the high-class Group 1 1m St James's Palace Stakes and Group 2 6f Mill Reef Stakes winner Zafeen (by Zafonic), the useful 2-y-o Group 3 7f Prix du Calvados winner Ya Hajar (by Lycius), the fair dual 7f winner Fantastic Dubai (by Fantastic Light) and the Irish 1m winner (on his only start) Youm Mutamiez (by Seeking The Gold). The dam, winner of a listed event over 6f in Germany, was fourth in the Group 2 6f Moet and Chandon Rennen and is a half-sister to 4 winners. The second dam, the minor French 3-y-o winner Shy Danceuse (by Groom Dancer), is a half-sister to the dual Group 3 winner Diffident. (Jaber Abdullah). *"He's a lovely looking horse, well balanced and a beautiful mover. Very, very nice, so hopefully he'll be out in mid-summer and he looks promising. He'd like a little distance and might be a seven furlong 2-y-o. A medium-sized, well-balanced colt and very attractive".*

1296. ALIZARI (IRE) ★★★
b.c. Oratorio – Alaya (Ela-Mana-Mou).
April 3. Half-brother to the dual 7f (at 2 yrs) and Group 3 10f Mooresbridge Stakes winner Alayan (by Sri Pekan), to the very useful listed 12f winner and Grade 2 winning hurdler Alaivan (by Kalanisi) and the useful 2-y-o 1m winner and Group 2 10f Royal Whip Stakes second Alarazi (by Spectrum). The dam won over 12f in Ireland and is a half-sister to the Irish Derby and King George winner Alamshar. The second dam, Alaiyda (by Shahrastani), a minor Irish 3-y-o 10f winner, is a half-sister to the smart Group 3 1m Craven Stakes winner and Group 2 10.4f Dante Stakes second Desert Story (by Green Desert). (H H Aga Khan). *"A good-looking, correct sort of colt, he'll probably need a bit of time. The dam has bred some useful horses but they all take a bit of time – Alayan probably did better at two than most of the others. This colt is nice looking and he's done well over the winter. We like him but it'll be the second half of the year before he's out.*

1297. BADGED ★★★
b.c. High Chaparral – Meshhed (Gulch).
February 16. Ninth foal. 60,000Y. Tattersalls October Book 2. De Burgh Equine. Half-brother to the useful 2-y-o 1m winner Montaff (by Montjeu), to the quite useful 2-y-o 5f and 6f winner Tangled Up In Blue (by Marju) - subsequently a winner of 5 races the USA and to a winner in Greece by In The Wings. The dam, a useful triple 7f winner (including at 2 yrs) and listed placed, is closely related to the useful 7f and 1m winner Jarah and a half-sister to 3 winners. The second dam, Umniyatee (by Green Desert), a useful 3-y-o winner of 2 races over 7f and 1m, was third in the Irish 1,000 Guineas and is a half-sister to the Oaks winner Eswarah. (Mr L J Williams). *"He's a good-looking horse, very athletic and a nice medium-sized,*

correct colt. He has a very fluent stride on him and he's a very good mover. Quite a nice horse, he'll be a second half of the season 2-y-o".

1298. BORN TO SEA (IRE) ★★★★★
b.c. Invincible Spirit – Urban Sea (Miswaki).
March 2. Closely related to the outstanding colt Sea The Stars (by Cape Cross), a winner of seven Group 1's including the Derby and the Prix de l'Arc de Triomphe and half-brother to the Derby, Irish Derby and King George VI and Queen Elizabeth Diamond Stakes winner Galileo, the Group 1 12f Gran Premio del Jockey Club and Group 1 10.5f Tattersalls Gold Cup winner Black Sam Bellamy, the Group 3 10.5f Middleton Stakes winner All Too Beautiful (all by Sadler's Wells), the US dual Grade 2 8.5f winner My Typhoon (by Giant's Causeway), the smart listed 10f Pretty Polly Stakes winner and Oaks third Melikah (by Lammtarra) and the smart 1m (at 2 yrs) and Group 2 10f Gallinule Stakes winner Urban Ocean (by Bering). The dam, a top-class winner of 8 races from 1m (at 2 yrs) to 12f including the Group 1 Prix de l'Arc de Triomphe and the Group 2 Prix d'Harcourt, is closely related to the 2,000 Guineas winner King's Best and a half-sister to numerous winners. The second dam, Allegretta (by Lombard), a useful 2-y-o 1m and 9f winner and second in the Lingfield Oaks Trial, is a sister to the German St Leger winner Anno. (Mr C Tsui). *"He's a nice colt, a good-looker and very handsome and correct. Probably a bit more precocious than his half-brother Sea The Stars, but that's the influence of Invincible Spirit because he's a good 2-y-o sire. Hopefully he'll be out in mid-summer and it's so far so good with him, he hasn't done any serious work so although he's nice at this stage he's just another well-bred horse. He'll be a 2-y-o though, because he's really precocious looking and he could well start at six furlongs".*

1299. CALL TO BATTLE (IRE) ★★★
b.c. King's Best – Dance The Classics (Sadler's Wells).
February 23. First foal. The dam, a fairly useful Irish 12f winner, is a sister to the smart 10f and listed 13f winner Roses For The Lady. The second dam, Head In The Clouds (by Rainbow Quest), a smart Group 3 12f Princess Royal Stakes winner, is a sister to the high-class St Leger, Chester Vase and Jockey Club Stakes winner Millenary and a half-sister to the very smart 1m (at 2 yrs) and 10f winner and Derby third Let The Lion Roar. (Mr N Jones). *"A nice colt, he's not been in long because he was broken and got-going elsewhere, but he's a nice-looking horse, very correct and a good mover. A nice horse for the second half of the season".*

1300. CHOLESKY (IRE) ★★★★
b.c. Galileo – Funsie (Saumarez).
February 7. Fifth foal. Closely related to the Epsom Derby, Juddmonte International Stakes and Racing Post Trophy winner Authorized and to the quite useful Irish 2-y-o 1m winner Sirgarfieldsobers (both by Montjeu) and half-brother to the fairly useful 10f and 12f winner Empowered (by Fasliyev). The dam is an unraced half-sister to 8 winners including the Group 3 10.5f Prix Cleopatre winner Brooklyn's Dance (herself the dam of 5 stakes winners) and the dam of the Group 1 winners Okawango and Quijano. The second dam, Valle Dansante (by Lyphard), won once in France and is a full or half-sister to 12 winners including the French 2,000 Guineas winner and sire Green Dancer. (Mr P Makin). *"A good-looking horse, very beautifully balanced and a lovely mover. He's medium sized, very attractive and obviously he has a great pedigree and he's a good prospect. It'll be the autumn before he runs but he's very nice".*

1301. CRISTAL GROOVE (IRE) ★★★
b.f. Marju – Mango Groove (Unfuwain).
January 18. Third foal. Goffs Orby. €40,000Y. J McDonald. Sister to Emmeline Pankhurst, unplaced in 2 starts at 2 yrs in 2010. The dam is an unplaced half-sister to 4 winners including very useful 2-y-o 6f winner and Group 1 Racing Post Trophy third Feared In Flight. The second dam, Solar Crystal (Alzao), won the Group 3 1m May Hill Stakes, was third in the Group 1 1m Prix Marcel Boussac and is a half-sister to 6 winners including the Group 1 Fillies' Mile winner Crystal Spirit, the Group 3 winners State Crystal and Dubai Success, and the Irish Derby third Tchaikovsky. (Mr J McDonald). *"She's a nice filly, well grown and a good mover. A straightforward type, she's a*

biggish filly so she won't be early. One for the mid-summer".

1302. ENGLISH NIGHT (IRE) ★★★
b.c. Dalakhani – Sassenach (Night Shift).
April 17. Eighth foal. Half-brother to the Irish listed 7f winner Fairy Of The Night, to the minor Irish 10f winner Night Fairy (both by Danehill), the US Grade 3 and Irish listed winner Dress Rehearsal (by Galileo) and the useful dual 1m winner Gold Sovereign (by King's Best). The dam, a winner over 13f at 4 yrs in Ireland, is a half-sister to 4 winners including the Group 3 2m 2f Doncaster Cup winner Far Cry. The second dam, Darabaka (by Doyoun), is an unraced half-sister to 5 stakes winners including the Group 3 Prix Minerve winner Daralinsha. (Mr C Tsui). *"An extremely good-looking colt, he'll take some time and I don't expect to be running him until the autumn, but he's particularly attractive and a good mover with a nice temperament".*

1303. KASTOVIA (USA) ★★★
ch.f. Giant's Causeway – Kastoria (Selkirk).
March 5. Second foal. The dam, winner of the Group 1 14f Irish St Leger, is a half-sister to several winners. The second dam, Kassana (by Shernazar), winner of the Group 3 12.5f Prix Minerve, is a half-sister to the Group 2 15f Prix Kergorlay winner Kassani. (H H Aga Khan). *"She's very nice, she had a little setback before Christmas but I think she could make her mark as a 2-y-o in the second half of the season. Hopefully the sire will have injected a bit of speed and precocity into a stamina-laden mare".*

1304. KEY TO DANCE (IRE) ★★★
b.f. Dansili – Key Change (Darshaan).
March 20. Half-sister to the fairly useful Irish 2m and very smart hurdles winner Pittoni (by Peintre Celebre), to the quite useful Irish 1m winner and listed-placed Sandtime, the Irish 10f winner and listed-placed Calorando (both by Green Desert) and the quite useful 12f winners Interchange (by Montjeu) and Carenage (by Alzao). The dam, a winner of 4 races including the Group 1 12f Yorkshire Oaks, is a full or half-sister to numerous minor winners. The second dam, Kashka (by The Minstrel), a winner over 12f at 3 yrs in France, is a half-sister to the Italian Group 3 winner Karkisiya and to the dams of the Derby winner Kahyasi and the Group 3 winners Kaliana and Kalajana and Kithanga. (Lady Clague). *"She's a nice filly, correct and a very good mover, by a good sire and out of a good racemare. The Dansili's are not always precocious and the dam's side certainly isn't. One for the later months of the year".*

1305. LA BARACCA (IRE) ★★★
b.f. Hurricane Run – Hoity Toity (Darshaan).
February 2. Fourth foal. 100,000Y. Tattersalls October Book 2. Oaklawn Stud. Half-sister to the Group 1 1m Coronation Stakes and Group 1 1m Matron Stakes winner Lillie Langtry (by Danehill Dancer). The dam is an unraced half-sister to 4 winners. The second dam, Hiwaayati (by Shadeed), is an unraced half-sister to 6 winners including Great Commotion (winner of the Group 3 6f Cork and Orrery Stakes and the Group 3 7f Beeswing Stakes and second in both the July Cup and the Irish 2,000 Guineas) and Lead on Time (winner of the Group 2 7f Criterium de Maisons-Laffitte and the Group 2 6.5f Prix Maurice de Gheest). (Mrs C McStay). *"She's a nice filly, she'll take a bit of time and probably won't appear until much later on, but she's nice. Not too big, she's a bit light-framed but correct, a good mover and she behaves herself. I can't say much more at this stage".*

1306. LONAN (IRE) ★★★
b.c. Dubawi – Chartres (Danehill).
April 19. Fourth foal. Half-brother to the quite useful 11f and 12f winner Colourways (by Singspiel). The dam, a 7f (at 3 yrs) and 4-y-o listed 12f winner, is a half-sister to 4 winners including the listed 10f and listed 14f winner Pugin. The second dam, Gothic Dream (by Nashwan), won over 7f in Ireland at 2 yrs and was third in the Irish Oaks. (Lady Clague & Mr J D Clague). *"He's a very big, strong horse and he'll take a bit of time. It's difficult to know what he'll do this year but he's by a good stallion so hopefully we'll get him out later in the season. He's quite nice".*

1307. RAYADOUR (IRE) ★★★★
b.c. Azamour – Rayyana (Rainbow Quest).
February 25. Half-brother to the 2-y-o Group 3 7f Killavullan Stakes and 3-y-o listed 6f

winner Rayeni (by Indian Ridge) and to the fair Irish 12f winner Rayena (by Sinndar). The dam, an Irish 10f winner, is a half-sister to several winners out of the Group 3 Royal Whip Stakes winner Rayseka (by Dancing Brave). (H H Aga Khan). *"This is a particularly nice colt, he's big, strong and a great mover with a good temperament. You wouldn't see much nicer than him"*.

1308. ROYAL SEA (IRE) ★★★
b.c. Refuse To Bend – Janayen (by Zafonic)
April 28. Third foal. Half-brother to the modest 2010 2-y-o 5f winner Secret Gold (by Exceed And Excel) and to the quite useful 2-y-o 5f winner Nadeen (by Bahamian Bounty). The dam, a fairly useful dual 1m winner, is a half-sister to the useful 2-y-o 7f winner Manntab. The second dam, Saafeya (by Sadler's Wells), a very useful listed 10f winner of 6 races, is a half-sister to one winner. (Jaber Abdullah). *"He's improved a lot since he came in. He's grown and developed a lot but he's nearly a May foal, so he's probably going to grow even more and take a bit of time, but he's a nice colt"*.

1309. RUBINA (IRE) ★★★★
b.f. Invincible Spirit – Riyafa (Kahyasi).
April 11. Closely related to the quite useful 9f winner Riynaaz (by Cape Cross) and half-sister to the listed 10f Pretty Polly Stakes winner Riyalma (by Selkirk) and to the minor French 12.5f winner Risayla (by Polish Precedent). The dam was a smart 12f listed winner at Ascot. The second dam, Riyama (by Doyoun), won over 10f in Ireland and is a half-sister to numerous winners including the useful triple 12f winner Ridaiyma. (H H Aga Khan). *"She's a nice filly and of course being by Invincible Spirit she might do something at two. She's a very good mover, very athletic and attractive with a good temperament. She's a nice prospect and I like her although she hasn't done any fast work yet, but that won't be too far away"*.

1310. SHALAMAN (IRE) ★★★
b.c. Oratorio – Shalama (Kahyasi).
April 13. Half-brother to the 10f and 12f winner and Irish Derby third Shalapour (by Dalakhani), to the quite useful 10f and 12f winner Shibina (by Kahyasi) and the quite useful 2-y-o 1m winner Shalaya (by Marju). The dam, a fairly useful 9f and 10f placed maiden, is a half-sister to the Derby and Irish Derby winner Shahrastani. The second dam, Shademah (by Thatch), won 3 races from 7f to 8.2f and is a half-sister to the Grand Prix de Saint-Cloud winner Shakapour, the US Grade 1 Bowling Green Handicap winner Sharannpour and the dam of the Prix de Diane winner Shemaka. (H H Aga Khan). *"A very good-looking horse and half-brother to a good horse in Shalapour. He'll take a bit of time because it's not a precocious family, but he's a very attractive colt that we'll see in the autumn"*.

1311. SHAMOODA (IRE) ★★★
b.f. Azamour – Shemaka (Nishapour).
March 19. Half-sister to the French Group 3 10f and Group 3 15f winner Shemima (by Dalakhani), to the French listed 10f winner Shemala (by Danehill), the French listed 9f winner Shemaya (by Darshaan), the French 9f winner and listed-placed Shediyama (by Red Ransom) and the minor 11f, 12f (in France) and hurdles winner Shemdani (by Unfuwain). The dam was a smart filly and winner of the Group 1 10.5f Prix de Diane, the Group 3 10f Prix de la Nonette and the Group 3 9f Prix de Conde and is a half-sister to the French winner and Group 3 placed Sheshara. The second dam, Shashna (by Blakeney), was unplaced in both her races (over 10f) and is a half-sister to the Grade 1 11f Bowling Green Handicap winner Sharannpour, the Group 1 12f Grand Prix de Saint-Cloud winner Shakapour and to the dam of the dual Derby winner Shahrastani. (H H Aga Khan). *"A nice, big, strong filly and she should come to hand reasonably early I would think. She has a great action and a beautiful stride to her and is enthusiastic about her work. So she's a nice filly and we like her. She has a big, long stride so she's probably one for seven furlongs"*.

1312. SHARENI (IRE) ★★★
b.c. Azamour – Sharesha (Ashkalani).
April 20. Fifth foal. Half-brother to the useful Irish Group 3 8.5f winner Shareen (by Bahri) and to the useful 6f (at 2 yrs) and 7f winner and listed-placed Sharleez (by Marju). The dam, a fairly useful Irish 10f winner, is a half-sister to 4 winners out of the 1m placed Sharemata

(by Doyoun). (H H Aga Khan). *"A nice colt, a very good-mover and I'd say he'll need time and a distance but the dam has bred a couple of useful ones already. So I'd be hopeful that he'll make a 2-y-o later on, starting at seven furlongs and then moving on from there".*

1313. SHELFORD (IRE) ★★★
b.c. Galileo – Lyrical (Shirley Heights).
April 9. Fifth foal. Closely related to the fairly useful 11f to 15f winner and listed-placed Wells Lyrical (by Sadler's Wells) and half-sister to a minor winner in Italy by Grand Lodge. The dam, a modest 12f placed maiden, is a half-sister to 5 winners including the Oaks winner Love Divine (herself dam of the St Leger winner Sixties Icon). The second dam, La Sky (by Law Society), a useful 10f winner and second in the Group 3 Lancashire Oaks, is closely related to the Champion Stakes winner Legal Case. (Mr L J Williams). *"A nice colt, a very fluent mover and he's done well over the winter. We didn't get him until a little bit late but he's caught up with the others fairly well. A nice horse, he'd like good ground and being a Galileo out of a Shirley Heights mare he'd want distance".*

1314. URBAN BALL (IRE) ★★★
b.f. Galileo – Ball Chairman (Secretariat).
May 13. Closely related to the US Grade 1 Shadwell Mile and dual Grade 2 winner Perfect Soul (by Sadler's Wells) and half-sister to the US stakes-placed winner Dimontina (by Dixieland Band). The dam is a placed half-sister to several winners. The second dam, A Status Symbol (by Exclusive Native), was a stakes winner of 7 races. (Mr C Fipke). *"She's a nice filly, she had a setback after she was broken but she's going on again after a couple of months rest. She's a particularly good-looking filly, very nice with a good temperament and she's a good mover. A late season 2-y-o".*

1315. UNNAMED ★★★
b.f. Halling – Behra (Grand Lodge).
February 3. Half-sister to the fair 2-y-o 7f winner and high-class hurdler Barizan (by Kalanisi). The dam, a quite useful 10f winner, is a half-sister to numerous winners including the Group 2 15f Prix Hubert de Chaudenay winner Behkara, the Irish listed 11f winner Behkiyra and the very useful Group 3 15.5f Prix Berteux winner Bayrika. The second dam, Behera (by Mill Reef), won the Group 1 10f Prix Saint-Alary and the Group 3 10.5f Prix Penelope and was second in the Prix de l'Arc de Triomphe. *"A nice-looking filly, she's big and rangy and is a second half of the year type. She's quite nice and although she's by Halling she'll probably make a 2-y-o".*

1316. UNNAMED ★★★
ch.c. Lemon Drop Kid – Ebaza (Sinndar).
March 24. Half-brother to the promising Irish 2011 7f winner Emiyna (by Maria's Mon) and to the quite useful 11f and 2m winner Emrani (by Rahy). The dam is an unplaced half-sister to the Group 1 winners Ebadiyla, Edabiya and Enzeli. The second dam, Ebaziya (by Darshaan), won from 7f (at 2 yrs) to 12f including three listed races and was third in the Group 2 12f Blandford Stakes. (H H Aga Khan). *"A nice colt out of a young mare, he's very good-looking, very correct and medium-sized, and a very fluent mover".*

1317. UNNAMED ★★★
b.c. Nayef – Handaza (Be My Guest).
February 3. Half-brother to the Irish Group 3 7.5f Concorde Stakes winner Hamairi (by Spectrum), to the Irish 5f (at 2 yrs) and 3-y-o listed 6f winner Hanabad (by Cadeaux Genereux), the quite useful Irish 12f winner Hadarama (by Sinndar), the fair 1m winner Hanakiyya (by Danehill Dancer) and the modest Irish 10f winner Hannda (by Dr Devious). The dam, a 1m winner at 3 yrs in Ireland, is out of Hazaradjat (by Darshaan), herself a half-sister to the Middle Park Stakes winner Hittite Glory. (H H Aga Khan). *"He's a good-looking horse, big, rangy, and lengthy. A very nice horse with a grand temperament, he has a big frame and he'll take a bit of time to develop, but I do like him and I'd say he has an engine so hopefully he'll make the track in the second half of the season".*

1318. UNNAMED ★★★
b.f. Include – Sindirana (Kalanisi).
April 10. The dam won over 7f (at 2 yrs) and the listed 11f Lingfield Oaks Trial and is a half-sister to 2 winners. The second dam, Sindiya (by Pharly), won over 13f and is a half-sister to Sinndar. *"She's a real nice filly, the dam won the*

Oaks Trial and the stallion won plenty of good races in America. This filly is quite racey and will hopefully be out in mid-season".

1319. UNNAMED ★★★
ch.c. Giant's Causeway – Timarwa (Dayjami).
April 29. First foal. The dam, an Irish Group 3 9.5f winner, is a half-sister to 4 winners. The second dam, Timarida (Kalaglow), a high-class 10f filly, won the Group 1 Irish Champion Stakes, the Group 1 Dallmayr-Preis and the Grade 1 Beverly D Stakes and is a half-sister to numerous winners and to the dam of the listed winners Miss Sacha and Pinta. (H H Aga Khan). *"He's a nice colt that will take a bit of time to build up and develop, but he's a good mover, medium-sized with a good action and he'll be alright".*

1320. UNNAMED ★★★
ch.c. Dalakhani – Zalaiyma (Rainbow Quest).
February 1. Half-brother to the 2010 7f placed 2-y-o Zabarajad (by Invincible Spirit). The dam won twice in France over 1m and was listed-placed. The second dam, Zalaiyka (by Royal Academy), won the French 1,000 Guineas. *"He's particularly nice, a good-looking colt and a half-brother to a useful horse I have called Zabarajad. Hopefully he'll be out in mid-summer, he's strong, a fluent mover and a powerful galloper".*

AMANDA PERRETT
1321. ALTARIA ★★★
b.f. Rail Link – Costa Rica (Sadler's Wells).
May 12. Fourth foal. Half-sister to the fairly useful 7f (at 2 yrs) to 12f winner Casual (by Nayef). The dam is an unraced half-sister to 10 winners including the Group 3 winners Vortex, Danefair and Prove. The second dam, Roupala (by Vaguely Noble), a fair 3-y-o 1m winner, is a half-sister to 4 winners including the useful 6f and 7f winner Ajuga (dam of the German Group 2 winner Bad Bertrich Again and the Group 3 Scottish Classic winner Prolix) and to the unraced dam of the US Grade 2 winner Daros. (Khalid Abdulla). *"She's a lovely filly, a very scopey individual and one for seven furlongs later in the year".*

1322. ARCH VILLAIN (IRE) ★★★
b.c. Arch – Barzah (Darshaan).
May 6. Sixth foal. 60,000Y. Tattersalls October Book 1. Peter Doyle. Half-brother to Thubiaan (by Dynaformer), unplaced on his only start at 2 yrs in 2010. The dam, a 2-y-o 6f winner, was listed placed over 11f and is a half-sister to a winner in Japan. The second dam, Lepikha (by El Gran Senor), won once at 3 yrs and is a half-sister to 5 winners including the dual Group 3 winner and Derby second Glacial Storm. (Mr & Mrs F Cotton, Mr & Mrs P Conway). *"Similar to the Rail Link filly Altaria, he's quite a scopey individual and likely to want seven furlongs later in the year".*

1323. ATTAIN ★★★★
b.c. Dansili – Achieve (Rainbow Quest).
April 12. Fifth foal. Brother to the fair 6f winner High Achieved. The dam is an unraced sister to the Derby and Hollywood Turf Handicap winner Quest For Fame and to the Group 3 Queens Vase second Silver Rainbow and a half-sister to the Grade 2 Long Island Handicap winner and Prix Vermeille second Yenda. The second dam, Aryenne (by Green Dancer), was a high-class winner of the French 1,000 Guineas and the Criterium des Pouliches and is a half-sister to 3 winners. (Khalid Abdulla). *"A really nice colt with a good attitude and a good action. One to make a 2-y-o by mid-season".*

1324. AUTARCH (USA) ★★★★
ch.c. Gone West – Vargas Girl (Deputy Minister).
March 30. Second foal. 140,000Y. Tattersalls October Book 1. Peter Doyle. The dam is an unplaced half-sister to 6 winners including the US Grade 1 Futurity Stakes winner Bevo and the US Grade 3 winner Moonlight Sonata. The second dam, Wheatly Way (by Wheatly Hall), a 2-y-o listed winner in the USA, is a half-sister to 7 winners. (John Connolly & Odile Griffiths). *"A grand stamp of a horse, one for a little later in the year over seven furlongs but he has a good straight action. A good-bodied individual, he may come to hand for a run in late May and then we'll see how we go, but I would guess he's more of a long term prospect".*

1325. BLACK MINSTREL (IRE) ★★
b.c. Dylan Thomas – Overlook (Generous).
March 28. Second foal. €100,000Y. Arqana Deauville August. Amanda Perrett. The dam is a placed half-sister to 9 winners including the very smart Group 2 1m Oettingen-Rennen and Group 3 8.5f Diomed Stakes winner Passing Glance, the smart Group 3 7f Prix de Palais-Royal and European Free Handicap winner Hidden Meadow, the smart listed 11f winner Scorned and the useful 6f (at 2 yrs) and listed 1m winner Kingsclere. The second dam, Spurned (by Robellino), a fairly useful 2-y-o 7f winner, later stayed 10f. (A D Spence). *"The dam won over two miles but under the second dam there's some mile speed. He's a little bit immature still but he's done some quite nice work".*

1326. BLANK CZECH (IRE) ★★★★
b.c. Clodovil – Shambodia (Petardia).
March 6. Fifth foal. 45,000Y. Tattersalls October Book 1. Peter Doyle. Half-brother to the fairly useful triple 7f winner (including at 2 yrs) Bettalatethannever (by Titus Livius) and to the fair 6f (at 2 yrs) and 1m winner Master Of Dance (by Noverre). The dam is an unraced half-sister to 5 winners. The second dam, Lucky Fountain (by Lafontaine), is an unraced sister to the Group 2 Geoffrey Freer Stakes winner Shambo and a half-sister to 4 winners. (G D P Materna). *"He's working nicely, he'll be a six furlong 2-y-o in May and he's a nice, rangy individual and forward-going".*

1327. BLUE SURF ★★★
ch.c. Excellent Art – Wavy Up (Brustolon).
March 3. Eighth foal. 28,000Y. Tattersalls December. Peter Doyle. Half-sister to the useful 7f winner Cousteau (by Spinning World), to the useful 11f to 14f winner and listed-placed Ti Adora (by Montjeu) and the fair 10f, 12f and hurdles winner Beaubrav (by Falbrav). The dam won once at 3 yrs in France and is a half-sister to 5 winners including Wavy Run, a winner of 13 races in Spain, France and the USA including the US Grade 2 San Francisco Mile Handicap. The second dam, Wavy Reef (by Kris), ran once unplaced and is a half-sister to 8 winners including the Group 2 Sun Chariot Stakes winner Talented. (The Green Dot Partnership). *"Quite sharp, he's straightforward in everything he's done. He's shown a bit of speed but he's nearly sixteen hands so he isn't going to be really early. He should hopefully be running at the end of May or early June over six furlongs".*

1328. BRAMSHILL LASS ★★★
ch.f. Notnowcato – Disco Ball (Fantastic Light).
April 5. Second foal. 21,000Y. Tattersalls December. Amanda Perrett. The dam, a fair 6f and 7f placed maiden, is a half-sister to the French listed 9f winner and Group 3 placed Rainbow Dancing (by Rainbow Quest). The second dam, Danceabout (Shareef Dancer), won the Group 2 Sun Chariot Stakes and the listed 7f Oak Tree Stakes and is a half-sister to 3 winners including the Group 3 6f Prix de Meautry winner Pole Position. (Mrs K J L Hancock). *"Quite a rangy filly, she's done some nice, swinging canter work, but being out a Fantastic Light mare I don't think we'll see her much before the seven furlong races".*
TRAINERS' BARGAIN BUY

1329. BRIEF CHAT (USA) ★★★
b.br.f. Pleasant Tap – Sambac (Mr Prospector).
February 11. Half-sister to the French 2-y-o 6f winner Spinning Globe (by Spinning World) and to the French 7f winner Full Measure (by Southern Halo). The dam, a useful 2-y-o triple 6f winner, is a closely related to the French 2-y-o 6f winner and Group 1 7f Prix de la Salamandre third Wooden Doll and the very useful 6f (at 2 yrs) and listed 7f winner Welcome Friend and a half-sister to the smart Group 3 1m Prix de Fontainebleu winner Rainbow Corner and the useful 2-y-o 7f listed winner Baltic State. The second dam, Kingscote (by Kings Lake), won 3 races from 5f to 6f including the Lowther Stakes and is a full or half-sister to 8 winners. (Khalid Abdulla). *"The sire was a decent horse in America and the dam was a useful 2-y-o. This filly goes nicely, but she's only cantering at present".*

1330. GREEN LEGACY (USA) ★★★★ ♠
ch.c. Discreet Cat – Mira Costa (Thunder Gulch).
February 19. First foal. 52,000Y. Tattersalls October Book 1. Peter Doyle. The dam is an unplaced half-sister to 3 winners including the US Grade 1 Secretariat Stakes and Grade

1 Arlington Million winner Kicken Kris and the US stakes winner and Grade 2 placed Kris' Sis. The second dam, Kicken Grass (by Jade Hunter), a US listed-placed winner, is a half-sister to 11 winners including the US Grade 1 Hollywood Derby winner Live The Dream and the US Grade 3 winner Warcraft. (The Green Dot Partnership). *"He's a nice horse, I like him very much. He's by a first season sire and the dam is also an unknown at the moment, but he's a nice individual and he'll be ready to race over six furlongs in May. He's 15.3 hands and a nice horse to have around".*

1331. HIDDEN JUSTICE (IRE) ★★★
b.c. Lawman – Uncharted Haven (Turtle Island).
February 3. Fifth foal. €100,000Y. Arqana Deauville August. Peter Doyle. Half-sister to the Group 3 St Simon Stakes winner and Oaks third High Heeled. The dam, a French 2-y-o 1m and subsequent US Grade 2 San Clemente Handicap and Grade 2 San Gorgonio Handicap winner, is a half-sister to 4 winners including the useful 2-y-o 7f winner Torinmoor. The second dam, Tochar Ban (by Assert), a quite useful 10f winner, is a half-sister to 6 winners. (G D P Materna). *"I like the dam and the second dam because they seem to be very tough running and producing families. This colt will run at Goodwood over six furlongs in early May. He'll want further but he's been quite a mature horse to train".*

1332. HYACINTH ★★★
ch.f. Haafhd – Agnus (In The Wings).
January 31. Half-sister to the listed 1m winner and Group 2 1m Sun Chariot Stakes second Dolores (by Danehill) and to the fairly useful 10f winner Rachel (by Spectrum). The dam, a winner twice in Belgium, is a half-sister to 4 other winners abroad including Wavy Run, a winner of 13 races in Spain, France and the USA including the US Grade 2 San Francisco Mile Handicap. The second dam, Wavy Reef (by Kris), ran once unplaced and is a half-sister to 7 winners including Talented, winner of the Group 2 Sun Chariot Stakes. (Normandie Stud). *"A lovely filly for a little bit later in the year, we trained her half-sister Dolores so we know the family. She's a nice filly but even though she was a January foal she'll need time to mature and she looks a nice filly for seven furlongs later in the year".*

1333. KNOYDART ★★★
b.br.c. Forest Wildcat – Chasenthebluesaway (Real Quiet).
January 25. First foal. $50,000Y. Keeneland September. James Delahooke. The dam won 3 minor races in the USA at 3 and 4 yrs and is a half-sister to 3 winners including the stakes winner and Grade 2 placed Gibson County. The second dam, Miss Gibson County (by Winrightt), a US stakes winner of 11 races, is a sister to 2 stakes winners. (Guy Harwood). *"He's a big horse at 16 hands, but he's bred to be quite quick and he's got a sprinting action on him. He's starting to come to hand now."*

1334. LANCASTER GATE ★★★
b.c. Zamindar – Bayswater (Caerleon).
March 14. Closely related to the fairly useful 7f winner Portland and to the quite useful 1m winner Art Work (both by Zafonic) and half-brother to the fairly useful 10f winner Montbretia (by Montjeu) and the fair 12f winner Park View (by With Approval). The dam, a fair 12.3f winner, is a sister to the high-class Group 1 1m Ciga Grand Criterium and Group 2 10.4f Dante Stakes winner Tenby, to the very useful 1m (at 2 yrs) and 10f winner Bright Water and the useful 2-y-o 7f and 1m winner River Usk. The second dam, Shining Water (by Kalaglow), was a very useful winner of the Group 3 7f Solario Stakes and was placed in the Group 2 Park Hill Stakes. (Khalid Abdulla). *"He's a nice, big, strapping horse and I like him. The dam won over twelve furlongs and she's a sister to Tenby, so he's going to be all for next year really. He's got the right attitude and he'll be racing later in the year over seven furlongs and a mile".*

1335. OPUS (IRE) ★★★
b.c. Danehill Dancer – Mixed Blessing (Lujain).
March 15. Second foal. 95,000Y. Tattersalls October Book 1. Peter Doyle. The dam, a 2-y-o Group 3 6f Princess Margaret Stakes winner, is a half-sister to 3 minor winners. The second dam, Marjorie's Memory (by Fairy King), a fair 5f winner at 2 and 3 yrs, is a half-sister to 4 winners. (John Connolly & Odile Griffiths). *"He's quite precocious I would say.*

A nice, strong sort for six furlongs at the end of May".

1336. PLUS FOURS (USA) ★★★
gr.c. Mizzen Mast – Quick To Please (Danzig).
April 29. Sixth foal. The dam, a useful 2-y-o 1m winner, was listed-placed over 1m and is a sister to the top-class sprinter and sire Danehill, the US Grade 2 9f winner Eagle Eyed and the very smart Group 3 Criterion Stakes winner Shibboleth. The second dam, Razyana (by His Majesty), was placed over 7f at 2 yrs and 10f at 3 yrs. (Khalid Abdulla). *"He's quite a late foal, a neat horse and it's a nice pedigree. I like the Mizzen Mast's, so this colt should be alright, especially as they say he's the best of the mare's foals so far".*

1337. ROCK SONG ★★★
b.c. Rock Of Gibraltar – Jackie's Opera (Indian Ridge).
February 20. Fifth foal. 35,000Y. Tattersalls October Book 2. J Delahooke. Half-brother to the fairly useful Irish 2-y-o 7f winner and listed-placed Glisten (by Oasis Dream) and to the fair 7f to 9f winner Final Tune (by Grand Lodge). The dam is an unraced half-sister to 5 winners including the dual French listed winner Arabian King. The second dam, Escaline (by Arctic Tern), won the Group 1 Prix de Diane and is a half-sister to 4 winners. (Harwoods Racing Club Ltd). *"I like the sire, we've got quite a nice older filly by him. This is a nice horse, he's quite big at 16.1, pretty strong and with a good attitude. He might have a run over six furlongs around May/June time, but I should think he'll be stepped up in trip fairly soon after".*

1338. SIR GLANTON (IRE) ★★★
ch.c. Choisir – Ctesiphon (Arch).
March 23. Third foal. Doncaster Premier. £26,000Y. Peter Doyle. Half-brother to the fair 6f winner Kielder (by Shinko Forest). The dam, a moderate 9f placed maiden, is a half-sister to 5 winners including the Grade 2 E P Taylor Stakes winner Wandering Star. The second dam, Beautiful Bedouin (by His Majesty), is an unraced half-sister to 6 winners including the Group 3 Craven Stakes winner and Irish Derby second Silver Hawk. (Slade, Clouting, Ross, Wells). *"He's bred to be fairly sharp and he's a bonny colt we'll be kicking on with. We should see some 2-y-o action with him".*

1339. TREASURED DREAM ★★★
b.f. Oasis Dream – Maid To Treasure (Rainbow Quest).
April 22. Fourth foal. Half-sister to the very useful 12f, 14f and listed 2m winner King Of Wands (by Galileo) and to the modest 9f winner Queen Of Wands (by Sakhee). The dam, a fair 7f (at 2 yrs) and 10f placed maiden, is a half-sister to numerous winners including the useful 7f (at 2 yrs) and 10f winner Maid To Perfection and the useful 2-y-o 7f winner Artistic Lad. The second dam, Maid For The Hills (by Indian Ridge), was a useful 2-y-o and won twice over 6f including the listed Empress Stakes and is a half-sister to 5 winners including the Group 3 6f Princess Margaret Stakes second Maid For Walking. (Normandie Stud). *"She's a half-sister to the listed two miles winner King Of Wands, but I don't think she'll be going that far! She's an attractive, strong, compact filly, a late foal with a bit of growing to do. She should be able to start off at six furlongs in the middle of the season".*

1340. TRUE PRINCE (USA) ★★★
ch.c. Yes It's True – Whenthedoveflies (Dove Hunt).
February 22. First foal. $100,000Y. Keeneland September. James Delahooke. The dam, a stakes winner of 14 races in the USA, is a half-sister to 2 minor winners. The second dam, Notesn'discretion (by Notebook), is an unraced half-sister to 7 winners. (Harwoods Racing Club Ltd). *"The dam was obviously tough, she won 14 races over sprint distances and this colt is going nicely. A nicely topped horse, 15.3 hands, so he'll make a 2-y-o".*

1341. WELSH NAYBER ★★★
ch.c. Nayef – Aberdovey (Mister Baileys).
March 3. Third foal. 24,000Y. Tattersalls October Book 2. J Delahooke. The dam, a fair 6f (at 2 yrs) and 1m winner, is a half-sister to 2 winners including the dual 10f and subsequent US stakes winner and Grade 2 placed Solva. The second dam, Annapurna (by Brief Truce), a useful 2-y-o 7f winner, was listed placed over 9f and is a half-sister

to 4 winners including the 2-y-o Group 3 7f Rockfel Stakes and listed 7f winner Name Of Love. (Coombelands Racing Syndicate). *"He's quite an athletic individual, not very big and hopefully he'll give my Coombelands Racing Syndicate a bit of 2-y-o action over seven furlongs from the middle of the season".*

1342. UNNAMED ★★★
b.f. Aptitude – Diese (Diesis).
March 15. Half-sister to the useful French 6f (at 2 yrs) and 1m winner Speak In Passing (by Danzig), to the useful 7f (at 2 yrs) and 10f winner Senure, the useful winner at up to 15f in France Terrazzo (both by Nureyev), the fairly useful 9f winner Power Series (by Mizzen Mast), the quite useful 10f winner Serious Impact (by Empire Maker), the quite useful 4-y-o 8.2f winner Dexterity (by Kingmambo) and the fair 10f winner Five Fields (by Chester House). The dam, winner of the Group 3 10.5f Prix Corrida and a listed event over 10f in France, is a half-sister to numerous good winners including the champion European 2-y-o Xaar, winner of the Group 1 Dewhurst Stakes and the Group 1 Prix de la Salamandre and the Group 3 1m Prix Quincey winner Masterclass. The second dam, Monroe (by Sir Ivor), a useful Irish 5f and 6f winner, is a sister to the good 2-y-o Gielgud and to the very smart Malinowski and a half-sister to the dual Grade 1 winner Blush With Pride and to Sex Appeal - the dam of El Gran Senor and Try My Best. (Khalid Abdulla). *"She's a nice, neat filly, with a lovely pedigree. I haven't done much with her yet but she should make a 2-y-o at some point".*

1343. UNNAMED ★★★
gr.c. Mizzen Mast – Single Market (Dynaformer).
February 4. The dam over 1m in the USA and is a half-sister to the Group 1 Grand Prix de Saint-Cloud second Perfect Sunday (by Quest For Fame) and the smart US 10f winner Barter Town. The second dam, Sunday Bazaar (by Nureyev), won over 12f in France and is a half-sister to numerous winners including the US Grade 1 winners Bates Motel and Hatim and the Horris Hill Stakes winner Super Asset. (Khalid Abdulla). *"He's a big, strong individual and ready to be trained. Seven furlongs should suit him this year".*

1344. UNNAMED ★★★
br.c. Dansili – Tuning (Rainbow Quest).
March 23. Half-brother to the smart 10.5f winner and Group 2 10.4f Dante Stakes second Tuning Fork (by Alzao), to the quite useful French 2-y-o 1m winner Prototype (by Beat Hollow) and the modest 10f and 12f winner Mixing (by Linamix). The dam, a smart winner of the 14f Ebor Handicap, is a sister to the fairly useful French 12f winner Raincloud and a half-sister to the useful Group 3 7f Rockfel Stakes second Clog Dance. The second dam, Discomatic (by Roberto), a French 9f winner, is a half-sister to the Phoenix Stakes winner Digamist. (Khalid Abdulla). *"A neat colt and he's been doing some quite nice work. Although the dam won the Ebor, this horse should be racing by early summer".*

JON PORTMAN

1345. COURTLAND AVENUE ★★
b.g. Kodiac – Chingford (Redback).
May 2. First foal. £400. Ascot Sales. The dam, a modest 5f placed 2-y-o, is a half-sister to a fair 2-y-o winner. The second dam, Beverley Macca (by Piccolo), a fair 5f winner of 4 races including at 2 yrs, is a half-sister to 5 winners including the 2-y-o Group 1 Cheveley Park Stakes and dual Group 2 winner Airwave. (Prof. C D Green). *"He was going to be early but he got sore shins, but he's quite nice. A neat, average-sized colt, I was disappointed with the shins because he hadn't done a lot. He looks like a 2-y-o and he'll be alright".*

1346. ISOLA BELLA ★★★
ch.f. Sleeping Indian – Tetravella (Groom Dancer).
April 6. Eighth foal. £10,000Y. Doncaster Premier. J Portman. Half-sister to the fairly useful 10f to 12f winner Island Odyssey (by Dansili), to the fair 7f (at 2 yrs) and 12f winner Mizooka (by Tobougg), the fair 12f and hurdles winner Ellerslie Tom (by Octagonal), the minor Italian 2-y-o winner King Beat (by Beat Hollow) and the minor French winner of 3 races at 4 yrs Berissimo (by Bering). The dam, a French 12f and 15f winner, is a half-sister to 5 winners. The second dam, Vanya (by Busted), won the listed Prix d'Automne and is a full or half-sister to 7 winners including the French Group 3 winner Muroto. *"A big filly and she's*

still growing, but I like her. A mid-summer type 2-y-o, possibly over six furlongs to begin with but more likely seven, she has a bit of scope for later on. She's not ready to do any fast work yet, so apart from the fact she goes nicely when cantering that's all I can say really. Big and strong, she moves well and I like her".

1347. LADRAM BAY (IRE) ★★
b.f. Oratorio – Ringmoor Down (Pivotal).
April 25. Third foal. 10,000Y. Tattersalls October Book 2. Not sold. Half-sister to the modest 9f winner Cuckoo Rock (by Refuse To Bend). The dam won 6 races from 2 to 5 yrs including the Group 3 5f King George Stakes and the Group 3 Flying Five and is a half-sister to 6 winners. The second dam, Floppie (by Law Society), a minor 3-y-o winner in France, is a sister to a listed-placed winner there and a half-sister to 4 winners including the French listed winner Love Shack. (Prof. C D Green). "She's very small but she shows a bit of speed. The family tend to need a bit of time though and she's had a slight problem that's given her a month off. She's as tough as nails".

1348. PURPLE ANGEL ★★
b.f. Dark Angel – Cocabana (Captain Rio).
March 3. First foal. The dam was a fair dual 5f winner (including at 2 yrs). The second dam, Hiraeth (Petong), a fair 6f winner, is a half-sister to numerous winners including the dual Group 3 5f winner Ringmoor Down. (R C Dollar). "She's was late being broken-in, so she's behind the other 2-y-o's mentally and has a bit to learn, but she shouldn't take long to get ready. She's quite small and I trained the dam who was the same. She's got a bit of speed, she's OK and I think she'll pull herself together, so she might well be out in April".

1349. SILENT LAUGHTER ★★★
b.f. Shamardal – Tease (Green Desert).
February 9. Fourth foal. 50,000Y. Tattersalls October Book 2. Emma O'Gorman. Half-sister to the fairly useful 2-y-o 7f winner and listed-placed Jazz Police (by Beat Hollow). The dam, a fair 3-y-o 7f winner, is a half-sister to the Irish listed winner Galistic. The second dam, Mockery (by Nashwan), won 2 minor races in France over 10.5f and 15f and is a half-sister to 3 other minor winners. (Mr D O Joly). "She's very nice, not very big and she's had some growing pains in her knees but I like her. She looks sharp and she's an early foal but in terms of maturity I don't think she's as sharp as she looks. When she's ready she'll be quite nice".

1350. WHITE FLIGHT ★★
gr.f. Doyen – Reason To Dance (Damister).
March 17. Half-sister to the triple South African Group 1 winner (from 1m to 11f) Dancer's Daughter (by Act One), to the very useful 2-y-o Group 3 7f Somerville Tattersall Stakes winner Diktatorial (by Diktat), the quite useful 9f winner Stands To Reason (by Hernando), the fair 9f winner Lanterns Of Gold (by Fantastic Light) and the 10f seller winners Princess Magdalena (by Pennekamp) and Twist (by Suave Dancer). The dam, a useful 2-y-o 5f and 5.8f winner, was third in the Group 2 1m Falmouth Stakes and is a half-sister to 4 minor winners. The second dam, La Nureyeva (by Nureyev), is a placed half-sister to 7 winners including the South African Grade 1 winner Icona. (The Hon. D Joly). "She hasn't come in yet and she's still being broken. Leggy and a bit weak at the moment, she needs time but she has very good reports. Her breeder thinks she's the best thing she's bred and as she bred the half-sister Dancer's Daughter, I hope she's right, but I imagine she'll need a bit of time".

1351. UNNAMED ★★★
gr.f. Aussie Rules – Akoya (Anabaa).
April 9. First foal. £7,000Y. Doncaster Premier. Jon Portman. The dam was placed over 1m at 3 yrs in France and is a half-sister to 2 winners including Roman Saddle (Group 3 Prix Berteux). The second dam, Galitzine (by Riverman), a 3-y-o winner in France, is a half-sister to 6 winners including the French Group 3 winners Gay Minstrel and Greenway. "She's nice, quite forward and although I wouldn't be sure what her trip is yet she looks sharp enough to be a 2-y-o. She's cantering nicely at the moment and I'll probably wait for six furlongs with her".

1352. UNNAMED ★★
b.c. Aussie Rules – Aptina (Aptitude).
Second foal. Half-brother to the modest 2010 6f placed 2-y-o and dual 5f 3-y-o winner

Finn's Rainbow (by Iffraaj). The dam is an unraced half-sister to 4 winners including the Scandinavian Group 3 and listed Strensall Stakes winner Binary File. The second dam, Binary (by Rainbow Quest), a smart French listed 10f winner, is a full or half-sister to 10 winners including the listed winners Bequeath and Bal Harbour. (Compton Racing Club). *"A bit weak and leggy, he's a beautiful mover and he goes alright but he won't be rushed. He's one of those horses about which there's more than meets the eye and I wouldn't be surprised if he turned out alright one day but he's not an obvious, early 2-y-o".*

1353. UNNAMED ★★★★
ch.f. Singspiel – Bumble (Rainbow Quest)
April 1. Sixth foal. 9,000Y. Tattersalls October Book 2. S A Clifford. Half-sister to the useful 5f winner of 4 races and 2-y-o Group 2 6f July Stakes second Northern Empire (by Namid), to the quite useful Minus Fifteen (by Trans Island) and the fair 1m winner Scutch Mill (by Alhaarth). The dam is an unraced half-sister to 6 winners including the Group 1 Racing Post Trophy winner Be My Chief. The second dam, Lady Be Mine (by Sir Ivor), a minor 3-y-o 1m winner, is a half-sister to 6 winners including Mixed Applause (dam of both the high-class miler Shavian and the Ascot Gold Cup winner Paean). (W Clifford). *"She's very nice Quite narrow, very light-framed, a little bit hot-headed and she does everything easily I like her a lot and if she wasn't by Singspiel I almost be ready to run her – that's how easy she's doing everything. In that regard she belies her pedigree. She moves like a dressage horse, her limbs are very tidy and they don't react to work, but I'll have to sit on her and wait for the six furlong races".* TRAINERS' BARGAIN BUY

1354. UNNAMED ★★
b.f. Notnowcato – Kozmina (Sadler's Wells).
March 28. Sixth foal. 12,000Y. Tattersalls October Book 2. J Portman. Half-sister to a minor winner in France by Mark Of Esteem. The dam is an unraced half-sister to 8 winners including the listed 7f Irish 1,000 Guineas Trial winners Khanata and Kotama, and to the unraced dam of the dual Derby winner High Chaparral. The second dam, Kozana (by Kris), won 4 races at 3 yrs over 1m (3 times) and 10f including the Group 2 Prix de Malleret and the Group 3 Prix de Sandringham and was third in the Prix de l'Arc de Triomphe. (P Deal & Partners). *"She's in a pre-training yard and she's nice, if a bit weak in the hocks and a bit temperamental. A late season 2-y-o, but she's quite nice".*

1355. UNNAMED ★★
b.f. Whipper – Pink Sovietstaia (Soviet Star).
April 23. 3,000Y. Tattersalls December. Sophie Portman. Half-sister to the fairly useful 2-y-o 6f winner and listed-placed Russian Rosie (by Traditionally), to the fair dual 6f winner (including at 2 yrs) Observatory Star (by Observatory), the quite useful 6f (at 2 yrs) and 1m winner King's Icon (by King's Best) and the quite useful 2-y-o 6f and 7f winner Russian Ruby (by Vettori). The dam, awarded a 9f event at 4 yrs in France, is a half-sister to 9 winners including the listed winner Pinaflore (herself dam of the Group/Graded stakes winners Pinakaral, Pinfloron and Pinmix). The second dam, Pink Satin (by Right Royal V), won once at 2 yrs and is a half-sister to the French Group 1 winners Amber Rama and Blue Tom. *"She's a mid-summer type 2-y-o and she's quite nice. Still growing a bit, but she looks a 2-y-o sort and she's worth putting in the book".*

KEVIN PRENDERGAST

1356. AARAAS ★★★
b.f. Haafhd – Adaala (Sahm).
April 29. Third foal. Closely related to the useful Irish 2-y-o 6f winner and Group 3 7f Silver Flash Stakes third Alshahbaa (by Alhaarth) and half-sister to the quite useful 2010 Irish 7f and 1m placed 2-y-o Asheerah (by Shamardal). The dam, an Irish 7f (at 2 yrs) and listed 9f winner, is a half-sister to the Irish listed 9f winner Adaala. The second dam, Alshoowg (by Riverman), is an unraced half-sister to 4 winners. (Hamdan Al Maktoum). *"A nice filly, she'll take a bit of time but I'd hope to see her out in June and she'll be alright, I like her. A six/seven furlong 2-y-o, she's not a big filly but she's well-made".*

1357. AEGEAN SKY (IRE) ★★★
b.f. Galileo – Alambic (Cozzene).
February 4. First foal. 130,000Y. Tattersalls October Book 1. BBA (Ire). The dam, a fairly

useful 12f to 14f winner of 6 races, was listed-placed and is a half-sister to 4 winners. The second dam, Alexandrine (by Nashwan), a fair 10f to 13f winner of 4 races, is a half-sister to 7 winners including the Nassau Stakes and Sun Chariot Stakes winner Last Second (dam of the French 2,000 Guineas winner Aussie Rules), the Doncaster Cup winner Alleluia (dam of the Prix Royal-Oak winner Allegretto) and the Moyglare Stud Stakes third Alouette (herself dam of the dual Champion Stakes winner Alborada and the triple German Group 1 winner Albanova) and to the placed dam of the Group 1 winners Yesterday and Quarter Moon. (Lady O'Reilly). *"A nice filly, she's big and tall and a good mover. One for August or September over seven furlongs or more".*

1358. ALNAAHEE (IRE) ★★★★
ch.c. Teofilo – Redstone Dancer (Namid).
March 26. Second foal. Goffs Orby. €85,000Y. Shadwell Estate Co. The dam, a very useful Group 3 7f Brownstown Stakes and Group 3 7f Minstrel Stakes winner, is a half-sister to 2 winners including the useful dual 6f (at 2 yrs) and 7f winner Red Liason. The second dam, Red Affair (by Generous), an Irish listed 10f winner, is a half-sister to 6 winners including the smart 7.6f to 10f winner Brilliant Red. (Hamdan Al Maktoum). *"A nice horse that'll start in May. Not a big fellow but a nice, active sort and a good mover. He'll want dry ground and I'm very fond of him".*

1359. AZAMATA (IRE) ★★
b.c. Azamour – Brave Madam (Invincible Spirit).
January 26. Second foal. Tattersalls Ireland. €40,000Y. Frank Barry. The dam is an unraced half-sister to 4 winners including the US listed stakes winner Insan Mala. The second dam, Madame Claude (by Paris House), a fair 2-y-o 6f winner, is a half-sister to 4 winners including the Irish dual listed winner Nashcash. (Mr McAuley). *"A back-end type 2-y-o but we like him, he's a fine, big, tall horse and a good mover".*

1360. BAHAMA SPIRIT (IRE) ★★★
b.f. Invincible Spirit – Braziliz (Kingmambo).
April 13. Sister to the quite useful 2-y-o 5f and 7f winner Brazilian Spirit and half-sister to the very useful 2-y-o 7.5f winner and Group 3 7f second Brazilian Star, the quite useful 7f winner Brazilian Beauty (both by Galileo), the 2-y-o Group 3 6f Swordlestown Stud Sprint Stakes winner Brazilian Bride (by Pivotal) and the fair 6f winner Brazilian Sun (by Barathea). The dam is an unplaced half-sister to the 2-y-o winner Or Vision (dam of the Irish 2,000 Guineas winner Saffron Walden, the Grade 1 E P Taylor Stakes winner Insight and the Group 1 7f Prix de la Foret winner Dolphin Street). The second dam, Luv Luvin' (by Raise a Native), won 2 races in the USA. (Lady O'Reilly). *"She looks a 2-y-o and she should be ready in late May. It's a proper 2-y-o family and she looks just the same, they aren't very big but they're usually 2-y-o types. A fairly forward filly, I'd say she'd want dry ground".*

1361. BEAT THE STARS (IRE) ★★★★
gr.f. Verglas – Dazzling Dancer (Nashwan).
March 21. Fourth foal. Sister to the Irish listed-placed 2-y-o 7f winner and subsequent US 1m winner and Grade 3 placed Driving Snow and half-sister to the fairly useful 2009 Irish 2-y-o 7f winner Dazzling Day (by Hernando). The dam, a quite useful Irish 12f winner, is a half-sister to one winner. The second dam, Danse Classique (by Night Shift), a listed-placed winner in Ireland, is a half-sister to the triple Group 1 winner Petrushka. (Lady O'Reilly). *"A full-sister to a horse I had that was the only horse to beat Sea The Stars – hence the name! We like her quite a lot, she'll be racing in May and she looks like a filly that will improve as she goes on. She would have sold well because she's a very good-looker, tall and a very good mover".*

1362. BIG BLUE SPIRIT ★★★
b.c. Invincible Spirit – Blue Sail (Kingmambo).
April 12. Second foal. 85,000Y. Tattersalls October Book 1. Ben McElroy. Half-brother to the 2010 French 1m placed 2-y-o Blue Hollow (by Beat Hollow). The dam was placed once at 2 yrs in France and is a sister to the French 1,000 Guineas winner and Coronation Stakes third Bluemamba. The second dam, Black Penny (by Private Account), is a placed half-sister to 7 winners including the Group 1 Prix Morny winner Orpen and the US Grade 3 winner Jules. (Mr & Mrs Hamilton). *"He's a*

little bit more backward than he should be, but he's nice but he'll make a 2-y-o in August over seven furlongs".

1363. BULBUL (IRE) ★★★
b.f. Shamardal – Oriental Fashion (Marju).
March 24. Half-sister to the very useful 2-y-o 6f and 7f winner Oriental Warrior, to the useful dual 1m winner (including at 2 yrs) and Group 3 Irish 2,000 Guineas third Famous Warrior (by Alhaarth), the useful 7f and UAE 1m winner Green Coast, the fairly useful 7f and 1m winner Desert Chief (both by Green Desert) and the Irish 2-y-o 7f winner Oriental Melody (by Sakhee). The dam won 3 races including the Group 2 1m Premio Ribot and is a half-sister to 3 winners including the US Grade 2 winner Makderah. The second dam, Wijdan (by Riverman), a useful 1m and 10.4f winner, is a sister to the 7f (at 2 yrs) and listed 1m winner Sarayir and a half-sister to Nashwan, Nayef and Unfuwain. (Hadi Al Tajir). *"We haven't had here here long but she looks a 2-y-o. I had her half-brother Oriental Warrior but this is a completely different type. She's very muscular and looks a nice, quality filly".*

1364. CATAMOUNT ★★★
b.f. Notnowcato – Feathers Flying (Royal Applause).
January 28. Fifth foal. Goffs Orby. €24,000Y. A O'Ryan. Half-sister to the modest 11f to 2m winner Featherlight (by Fantastic Light). The dam, a fairly useful 2-y-o 7f winner, was listed placed and is a full or half-sister to 5 winners including the 1m (listed) and 9f winner of 4 races at 4 yrs Wagtail. The second dam, Dancing Feather (by Suave Dancer), a fair 4-y-o 1m winner, stayed 12f and is a half-sister to 8 winners including the Group 3 Prix Cleopatre winner Spring Oak and the 10f Lupe Stakes winner Fragrant Hill (herself dam of the French Group 1 winners Fragrant Mix and Alpine Rose). (Lady O'Reilly). *"I thought she'd be a bit more forward but she's grown a lot and I'd say it'll be June before we see her out. She looks a 2-y-o, but she's biggish and very well-developed so I think she'll improve as the season goes on. We don't know about the sire yet but he was a very good racehorse and very durable".*

1365. DANTE INFERNO (IRE) ★★★★
b.c. Galileo – Ugo Fire (Bluebird).
April 28. Second foal. 100,000Y. Tattersalls December. Aidan O'Ryan. Closely related to the promising 2010 dual 7f placed 2-y-o Puttore (by High Chaparral). The dam, a 2-y-o Group 3 7f C L Weld Park Stakes and 3-y-o 6f listed winner, was second in the Group 1 7f Moyglare Stud Stakes second and is a half-sister to one winner. The second dam, Quiet Mouse (by Quiet American), is an unraced half-sister to 6 winners including the fairly useful 2-y-o 6f and 7f winner and smart broodmare Witch Of Fife (the dam of 3 stakes winners). (Norman Ormiston). *"He's a very nice horse and we're very happy with him. He was a late foal but he's maturing nicely and we won't see him out until August. He's only cantering now but he's a very good mover with a lovely temperament and we're very fond of him".*

1366. DARK RANGER (IRE) ★★★★
b.f. Amadeus Wolf – Danzelline (Danzero).
February 6. Third foal. Half-brother to Head Space (by Invincible Spirit), a 5f winner on his only start at 2 yrs in Ireland in 2010 and to the fair Irish 2-y-o 6f winner Diva Dolce (by Domedriver). The dam, a fair Irish 1m and 10f winner, is a half-sister to 4 winners including the high-class Group 1 10.5f Tattersalls Gold Cup and Group 2 10f Pretty Polly Stakes winner Rebelline, the Group 2 Blandford Stakes and Group 3 Gallinule Stakes winner Quws and the useful 2-y-o 6f and 7f winner and listed-placed Moonlight Man. The second dam, Fleeting Rainbow (by Rainbow Quest), a modest 10f placed 3-y-o, is a half-sister to 3 winners. (Lady O'Reilly). *"A nice filly, we're very fond of her. She was ready to run early but she scoped bad, she'll be racing sometime in May. A quality filly, not over-tall but strong and very muscular".*

1367. EKBAAL ★★
b.c. Red Ransom – Tamazug (Machiavellian).
February 22. Second foal. The dam, a useful Irish 7f and 1m winner, was third in the Group 3 Derrinstown Stud 1,000 Guineas Trial and is a sister to the quite useful Irish 7f to 10f winner Mutadarek. The second dam, Nasheed (by Riverman), a useful 7f (at 2 yrs) and 10f winner,

is a half-sister to the high-class Prix de l'Arc de Triomphe and Juddmonte International winner Sakhee. (Hamdan Al Maktoum). *"He's a backward horse and we won't see him until the back-end of the season and I think he'll get a little further than his dam did"*.

1368. FREEDOM REIGNS (IRE) ★★★
b.f. Jeremy – For Freedom (King Of Kings).
February 25. Fourth foal. Goffs Orby. €28,000Y. Ben McElroy. Half-sister to Dust Cloud (by Verglas), unplaced in two starts at 2 yrs in 2010 and to the fair 10f winner Belletlou (by Peintre Celebre). The dam, placed once over 7f at 2 yrs, is a half-sister to 3 winners including the Grade 1 Breeders Cup Mile and Grade 1 Santa Anita Derby winner Castledale. The second dam, Louju (by Silver Hawk), is an unraced half-sister to 10 winners. (Liberty Partnership). *"A very nice filly, she had a small setback which has put us back a bit, but she'll be fine and we like her a lot. A nice, big filly, she'll get seven furlongs and a mile later on "*.

1369. JIMTOWN ★★★
b.c. Avonbridge – Gorgeous Dancer (Nordico).
April 4. Tenth foal. Doncaster Premier. £40,000Y. Ben McElroy. Half-brother to the Group 1 Premio Roma winner of 11 races Imperial Dancer (by Primo Dominie), to the useful 8.3f winner and listed-placed Classical Dancer (by Dr Fong), the useful 10.4f listed winner Lafite (by Robellino), the fairly useful 6f (at 2 yrs) to 1m winner Perfect Storm (by Vettori), the moderate 11f winner Shraayef (by Nayef) and a winner abroad by Nordico. The dam, an Irish 3-y-o 1m winner and third in the listed Irish Oaks Trial, is a half-sister to 3 winners including the Group 3 placed Campalto. The second dam, Simply Gorgeous (by Hello Gorgeous), is an unraced half-sister to 4 winners including the Irish Oaks winner Give Thanks (herself grandam of the 1,000 Guineas winner Harayir). (Mr & Mrs Hamilton). *"A nice horse, he'll be ready to run in May and he's a half-brother to 6 winners including a stakes winner. I bought him at Doncaster and he's a lovely colt"*.

1370. LA COLLINA (IRE) ★★★
ch.f. Strategic Prince – Starfish (Galileo).
April 24. Second foal. Doncaster Premier. £42,000Y. K Prendergast. Half-sister to the quite useful 2010 2-y-o 7f winner Next Edition (by Antonius Pius). The dam is an unraced half-sister to 2 winners including the Group 3 placed Icon Dream. The second dam, Silver Skates (by Slip Anchor), is a placed half-sister to 8 winners including the Group 2 Derrinstown Derby Trial winner Fracas. (M Vasicheck). *"A very nice filly, she'll be racing in May over six furlongs. She's grand and we like her a lot"*.

1371. LEATHERWOOD (IRE) ★★★
ch.c. Peintre Celebre – Seraphine (Dashing Blade).
February 15. Second foal. Goffs Orby. €88,000Y. Frank Barry. The dam, a winner of 4 races in Germany and Italy including a listed event, was Group 3 placed and is a half-sister to 6 winners including the dam of the dual Group 1 winner Indian Ink. The second dam, Sovereign Touch (by Pennine Walk), is an unraced half-sister to 7 winners including the Group 2 winners Royal Touch and Foresee. (Mr & Mrs Hamilton). *"A nice horse, he's just starting work and we like him a lot. He'll want good ground and seven furlongs to a mile"*.

1372. MADEIRA PACK (IRE) ★★
ch.c. Haafhd – Birdsong (Dolphin Street).
March 23. Sixth foal. 34,000Y. Tattersalls October Book 2. F Barry. Half-brother to the fairly useful 2-y-o dual 5f winner Mubaashir, to the fair 10f winner Mecox Bay (both by Noverre) and the minor French 1m winner of 4 races Filimeala (by Pennekamp). The dam, a fair dual 6f winner at 3 yrs, is a half-sister to 7 winners including the 2-y-o listed 6f Sweet Solera Stakes winner Lucayan Princess (herself the dam of four Group winners including the Group 1 winners Luso and Warrsan). The second dam, Gay France (by Sir Gaylord), a fairly useful 2-y-o 6f winner, is a half-sister to 10 winners including the dam of the Group 1 winner and sire Common Grounds. (Comerford Brothers). *"A very nice horse, we like him a lot but he had a little setback and although he's improving now I'd say it'll be the back-end before he's ready"*.

1373. MUNTHER (IRE) ★★
b.c. Lawman – Requested Pleasure
(Rainbow Quest).
February 6. Second foal. Goffs Orby. €120,000Y. Shadwell Estate Co. Half-brother to the modest 2011 3-y-o 1m winner Govenor General (by Araafa). The dam, a fairly useful 1m and 10f winner in Ireland, is a half-sister to 8 winners including the very useful Group 3 1m Desmond Stakes winner Swift Gulliver and the useful 2-y-o 6f and subsequent dual US stakes winner Abderian. The second dam, Aminata (by Glenstal), a useful winner of the Group 3 5f Curragh Stakes, is a half-sister to 3 winners. (Hamdan Al Maktoum). *"A big, backward horse, he goes well and we like him but he needs time, probably an August type 2-y-o".*

1374. MURAAFIQAH ★★★
b.f. Haafhd – Ulfah (Danzig).
February 28. Fourth foal. Half-sister to the fairly useful 2010 Irish 6f and 7f placed 2-y-o Tashqeel (by Medicean). The dam, an Irish dual listed 6f winner, is a sister to the Group 2 6f Diadem Stakes winner Haatef, to the listed winner and Group 1 Moyglare Stud Stakes second Shimah and the listed 6f (at 2 yrs) and Group 3 7f Athasi Stakes winner Waneyef. The second dam, Sayedat Alhadh (by Mr Prospector), a US 7f winner, is a sister to the US Grade 2 7f winner Kayrawan and a half-sister to the useful winners Amaniy, Elsaamri and Mathkurh. (Hamdan Al Maktoum). *"She goes well, will take a bit of time, she's not a big filly and six or seven furlongs will be her trip. We've been lucky with the family, they aren't usually big, robust types though and she'd be like that".*

1375. PINKISTHECOLOUR (IRE) ★★★
b.f. Red Clubs – Delicia (Rainbow Quest).
April 11. Second foal. Goffs Orby. €38,000Y. Frank Barry. Half-sister to the 2010 French 2-y-o winner Grey Delice (by Verglas). The dam is a placed half-sister to 2 winners including the dam of the US listed winner and Grade 3 placed Driving Snow. The second dam, Danse Classique (by Night Shift), an Irish listed-placed 7f winner, is a half-sister to 5 winners including the high-class Irish Oaks, Yorkshire Oaks and Prix de l'Opera winner Petrushka. (Mr K Prendergast). *"She started off at the Curragh, she ran well and I'll now aim her for Navan over five furlongs. She'd prefer six a bit later on. Not a great big filly, but very correct and muscular and she's done well since her run".*

1376. QASSER (IRE) ★★★
b.c. Intikhab – Surrender To Me
(Royal Anthem).
February 19. Second foal. Goffs Orby. €85,000Y. Shadwell Estate Co. The dam is an unraced half-sister to 4 winners including the Italian listed winner Six Hitter. The second dam, Granny Kelly (by Irish River), was placed once over 7f at 2 yrs in Ireland and is a half-sister to 4 minor winners. (Hamdan Al Maktoum). *"He's a big, strong, robust horse. There's a seven furlong race at Gowran Park at the end of April and we might run him there. He's very nice but he's a bit cheeky and I want to run him early just to concentrate his mind on his job".*

1377. RAYON ROUGE (IRE) ★★
b.f. Manduro – Regalline (Green Desert).
February 21. First foal. The dam, a fair Irish 1m winner, is closely related to the Group 3 Irish 2,000 Guineas Trial winner Recharge. The second dam, Rebelline (by Robellino), won 6 races from 7f to 10.5f including the Group 1 10.5f Tattersalls Gold Cup and the Group 2 10f Pretty Polly Stakes and is a half-sister to 4 winners including the Group 2 Blandford Stakes winner Quws. (Lady O'Reilly). *"A nice filly but she's backward. I've trained a lot of the family and they take time".*

1378. REDOUBTABLE (IRE) ★★★★
b.f. Invincible Spirit – Rebelline (Robellino).
March 29. Fifth foal. Closely related to the smart Group 3 Irish 2,000 Guineas Trial and listed 1m winner and Group 1 10.5f Tattersalls Rogers Cup second Recharge (by Cape Cross) and to the fair Irish 1m winner Regalline (by Green Desert). The dam won 6 races from 7f to 10.5f including the Group 1 10.5f Tattersalls Gold Cup and the Group 2 10f Pretty Polly Stakes and is a half-sister to 4 winners including the Group 2 Blandford Stakes winner Quws. The second dam, Fleeting Rainbow (by Rainbow Quest), a modest 10f placed 3-y-o, is a half-sister to 3 winners. (Lady O'Reilly).

"She's lovely and if I was picking one 2-y-o filly this would be the one. She's very nice, not a great big filly but very muscular and in terms of looks the's the nearest to the dam that she's had".

1379. RIGHT REASON ★★
ch.f. Manduro – Right Key (Key Of Luck).
March 20. Third foal. Half-sister to the 2010 Irish 2-y-o 1m winner and listed 1m placed Rising Wind (by Shirocco) and to the fair Irish 2-y-o 1m winner Rightside (by High Chaparral). The dam, a very useful Irish 7f (at 2 yrs) and Group 3 10f and 12f winner, is a sister to several winners including the Irish dual 7f (at 2 yrs) and listed 1m winner and dual Group 2 placed Wrong Key. The second dam, Sarifa (by Kahyasi), is an unraced half-sister to the Group 3 Prix du Palais Royale winner Saratan. (Lady O'Reilly). *"I like her a lot but she wouldn't be a very robust filly so we'll look after her. She has a great way about her and a good way of going".*

1380. THE FIRM (IRE) ★★★
b.c. Acclamation – Aspen Falls (Elnadim).
March 10. Second foal. €16,000Y. Tattersalls Ireland. Frank Barry. Half-brother to the 2010 French 2-y-o 1m winner Filozef (by Footstepsinthesand). The dam, a fair 2-y-o 7f winner, is a half-sister to the useful 6f to 8.2f and subsequent US stakes winner Wixoe Express. The second dam, Esquiline (by Gone West), is an unplaced half-sister to 5 minor winners in France. *"He would have ran early on but he got a setback. He's back now and I'd say he'll be a winner".* TRAINERS' BARGAIN BUY

1381. WOT A SHOT (IRE) ★★
b.c. Refuse To Bend – Ashdali (Grand Lodge).
February 18. Second foal. €16,000Y. Tattersalls Ireland. Frank Barry. The dam is an unraced half-sister to 9 winners including the listed winner Sinntara. The second dam, Sidama (by Top Ville), won 4 races in France at 3 yrs and is a half-sister to 5 winners including the dual Group 2 winner Sadjiyd. (On Target Syndicate). *"A good-looking horse, he's a good walker and mover. He'll want seven furlongs or more".*

SIR MARK PRESCOTT
1382. ABSTAIN ★★★
ch.f. Araafa – Anna Amalia (In The Wings).
April 19. Fourth foal. Half-sister to the 7f (at 2 yrs), Grade 1 10f Flower Bowl International and Group 3 9.5f winner Ave (by Danehill Dancer) and to the useful 2-y-o 7f winner and Group 3 7f Solario Stakes third Dubai Phantom (by Dubawi). The dam won once at 3 yrs in France and is a half-sister to 5 winners including the smart French 2-y-o Group 3 1m Prix d'Aumale winner and smart broodmare Anna Palariva. The second dam, Anna Of Saxony (by Ela-Mana-Mou), a very useful winner of the Group 2 14.6f Park Hill Stakes, is a half-sister to 10 winners including the Group 2 winners Annaba and Pozarica. (Mrs Perle O'Rourke). *"A well-bred filly, she's been away for a break, she's sharp-actioned and not very big, so she might be quicker than her pedigree would indicate, but she won't appear until later in the year".*

1383. ALBAMARA ★★★
b.br.f. Galileo – Albanova (Alzao).
January 28. Third foal. Half-sister to the fair 10f winner Albertus Pictor (by Selkirk). The dam, a triple Group 1 12f winner in Germany, is a sister to the dual Group 1 10f Champion Stakes winner Alborada. The second dam, Alouette (by Darshaan), a 1m (at 2 yrs) and listed 12f winner, is a half-sister to the Nassau Stakes and Sun Chariot Stakes winner Last Second (dam of the Group 1 winner Aussie Rules) and the dams of the Group 1 winners Yesterday and Quarter Moon and the Group 2 winner Allegretto. (Miss K Rausing). *"Very nice, she's a lovely big filly but don't forget the sire is usually an influence for stamina and the dam was at her best when she was five! So she'll be an autumn filly".*

1384. ALBASPINA (IRE) ★★★
b.c. Selkirk – Alabastrine (Green Desert).
March 21. Fourth foal. Half-brother to the useful Irish 7.5f (at 2 yrs) and 9f winner Hail Caesar (by Montjeu). The dam, placed over 7f at 2 yrs, is a half-sister to 8 winners including the Nassau Stakes and Sun Chariot Stakes winner Last Second (dam of the French 2,000 Guineas winner Aussie Rules), the Doncaster Cup winner Alleluia (dam of the Prix Royal-Oak

winner Allegretto), the Moyglare Stud Stakes third Alouette (dam of the dual Champion Stakes winner Alborada and the triple German Group 1 winner Albanova) and to the placed dam of the Group 1 winners Yesterday and Quarter Moon. The second dam, Alruccaba (by Crystal Palace), a quite useful 2-y-o 6f winner, is out of a half-sister to the dams of Aliysa and Nishapour. (Miss K Rausing). *"A tall, leggy filly, she looks like she'll prefer firm ground and I'd expect her out around August time".*

1385. ARTISTIC THREAD (IRE) ★★★
b.c. Barathea – Jellett (Green Desert).
March 30. Third foal. Goffs Orby. €38,000Y. Sir M Prescott. Half-sister to the fairly useful Irish dual 7f winner Smart Striking (by Smart Strike). The dam is an unraced sister to the Irish 2,000 Guineas, Prix du Moulin and Queen Elizabeth II Stakes winner Desert Prince and a half-sister to 6 winners including the 2-y-o Group 3 6.5f Anglesey Stakes winner Ontario. The second dam, Flying Fairy (by Bustino), placed twice at up to 12f, is a half-sister to 6 winners including the Group 3 Prix Penelope third Fleet Fairy. (W E Sturt – Osborne House III). *"A July type 2-y-o, he's big, strong and straightforward".*

1386. AWESOME PEARL (USA) ★★★
b.br.c. Awesome Again – Gottcha Last (Pleasant Tap).
February 13. Third foal. $210,000Y. Keeneland September. David Redvers. Half-brother to the US dual Grade 3 winner and Grade 1 placed Gottcha Gold (by Coronado's Gold). The dam, a stakes winner of 5 races in the USA, is a half-sister to 9 winners including the US Grade 3 winner Stem The Tide. The second dam, Temper The Wind (by Elocutionist), won 3 races at 3 yrs in the USA. (Pearl Bloodstock Ltd). *"A big, scopey horse for around mid-September and he'll be better when he's a 3-y-o but he's a grand, big horse".*

1387. BETWEEN US ★★★
b.f. Galileo – Confidante (Dayjur).
February 5. Ninth foal. Half-sister to the Group 3 7f (at 2 yrs) and Group 1 10.5f Prix de Diane winner Confidential Lady (by Singspiel), to the fairly useful 7f winner Crown Counsel and the fair 5f and 7f winner Registrar (both by Machiavellian), the quite useful 1m winner Censored (by Pivotal) and the moderate 1m and 10f winner Confide In Me (by Medicean). The dam, a fairly useful 3-y-o dual 7f winner, is a half-sister to 6 winners including the 2-y-o 6f winner Wind Cheetah, the Group 3 7f Solario Stakes winner White Crown and the 11.8f winner Zuboon – all useful. The second dam, Won't She Tell (by Banner Sport), a minor stakes winner of 9 races in the USA at up to 9f, is a half-sister to the American Triple Crown winner Affirmed. (Cheveley Park Stud). *"A tall, staying filly, she looks to have plenty of quality. We liked her and then we turned her out for a break and she'll be racing in the autumn. I know the family backwards and whatever she does this year she'll be much better as a 3-y-o".*

1388. CODE CRACKER ★★★★
b.f. Medicean – Confidential Lady (Singspiel).
January 26. The dam, winner of the Group 3 7f Prix du Calvados (at 2 yrs) and the Group 1 10.5f Prix de Diane, is a half-sister to 4 winners. The second dam, Confidante (by Dayjur), a fairly useful 3-y-o dual 7f winner, is a half-sister to 6 winners including the 2-y-o 6f winner Wind Cheetah, the Group 3 7f Solario Stakes winner White Crown and the 11.8f winner Zuboon – all useful. (Cheveley Park Stud). *"A July type 2-y-o, she was a very small foal and has done well considering that. She looks like she'll go on firm ground and that she'll be very willing but without her mother's size and scope. I would think that she'll be a six/seven furlong 2-y-o".*

1389. FRESA ★★★
b.f. Selkirk – Flor Y Nata (Fusaichi Pegasus).
February 6. First foal. The dam, a fairly useful 2-y-o dual 7f winner, was listed placed twice in Germany. The second dam, Rose Of Zollern (Seattle Dancer), won 9 races including the German 1,000 Guineas and a stakes event in the USA and is a half-sister to 3 winners. (Miss K Rausing). *"This is a big filly with a high action, which is part of the family. But it's a powerful action. I should think she'll want a mile this year".*

1390. GASSIN GOLF ★★★
b.c. Montjeu – Miss Riviera Golf (Hernando).
March 7. Half-brother to the fairly useful 2-y-

o 1m winner Mont Agel (by Danehill Dancer), to the listed 7f winner Hotel Du Cap, the fairly useful 10f and 12f winner The Carlton Cannes (both by Grand Lodge) and the fair 7f and 1m winner Gassin (by Selkirk). The dam won a listed event over 1m in France at 3 yrs and is a half-sister to several winners including the useful 2-y-o 6f winner and listed-placed Miss Riviera. The second dam, Miss Beaulieu (by Northfields), was a useful 6f and 10f winner. (Mr J L Pearce). *"He could be a nice horse, he has a proper pedigree but he's a staying horse and will probably need some cut in the ground. An autumn 2-y-o"*.

1391. GENIALITY ★★
b.g. Dansili – Hotelgenie Dot Com (Selkirk).
February 26. Seventh foal. 82,000Y. Tattersalls October Book 1. Sir Mark Prescott. Closely related to the Group 1 Fillies' Mile and Group 1 Falmouth Stakes winner Simply Perfect (by Danehill). The dam, a 7f winner at 2 yrs, was second in the Group 1 7f Moyglare Stud Stakes and third in the Group 1 Fillies' Mile and is a half-sister to 4 winners including the Moyglare Stakes and the Group 2 6f Lowther Stakes winner Bianca Nera. The second dam, Birch Creek (by Carwhite), was placed five times including when third in the Group 3 1m Premio Royal Mares and is a half-sister to 7 winners including the useful Group 3 winning sprinter Great Deeds. (W E Sturt – Osborne House IV). *"He's been gelded and comes back in during May. I hadn't done a lot with him beforehand, he's an expensive horse and a nice one, but I didn't do enough to be able to gauge his ability"*.

1392. GOOSEBERRY FOOL ★★
br.f. Danehill Dancer – Last Second (Alzao).
April 14. Tenth living foal. Closely related to the French 2,000 Guineas and US Grade 1 winner Aussie Rules (by Danehill) and half-sister to the useful 7.5f (at 2 yrs) and listed 10f winner and US Grade 2 second Approach, the very useful 2-y-o 8.5f winner and Group 1 Prix Marcel Boussac fourth Intrigued (both by Darshaan), the fairly useful 9f winner Fork Lightning (by Storm Bird), the quite useful 10f winner Bold Glance and the minor US 2-y-o winner Pampered King (both by Kingmambo). The dam, winner of the Group 2 10f Nassau Stakes and the Group 2 10f Sun Chariot Stakes, is a half-sister to 7 winners including the Moyglare Stud Stakes third Alouette (herself dam of the Group 1 winners Albanova and Alborada) and the Group 2 Doncaster Cup winner Alleluia (dam of the Group 1 winner Allegretto) and to the placed dam of the Group 1 winners Yesterday and Quarter Moon. The second dam, Alruccaba (by Crystal Palace), a quite useful 2-y-o 6f winner, is out of a half-sister to the dams of Aliysa and Nishapour. (Denford Stud). *"A very small filly and she has a paralysed tail – I've never trained a horse with one before and I don't know anyone else who has. She can't move it at all and the hair hasn't grown in it. She must have had done it when she was a foal but nobody knows how. She's small and correct, she has a lovely pedigree but the only one out of the mare previously that didn't win was very small. I don't think she'll be ready until July or August"*.

1393. ITALIAN RIVIERA ★★★
b.br.c. Galileo – Miss Corniche (Hernando).
March 4. Fifth foal. Half-brother to the very useful 1m winner and listed-placed Moyenne Corniche (by Selkirk) and to the quite useful 2-y-o 6f winner Miss Eze (by Danehill Dancer). The dam, a 7f (at 2 yrs) and listed 10f winner, is a sister to 2 winners and a half-sister to numerous winners including the listed 1m winner Miss Riviera Golf. The second dam, Miss Beaulieu (by Northfields), was a useful 6f and 10f winner. (Mr J L Pearce). *"He'll need time and he's closely related on the dam's side to another 2-y-o of mine called Gassin Golf. He's an elegant, staying 2-y-o and you'd think he'd run in July or August"*.

1394. KINETICA ★★★★
b.f. Stormy Atlantic – Kiswahili (Selkirk).
March 13. Second foal. Half-sister to the unplaced 2010 2-y-o Four Nations (by Langfuhr). The dam won 4 races including a listed 14f event in Germany and is a half-sister to 3 winners. The second dam, Kiliniski (by Niniski), a very smart winner of the Group 3 12f Lingfield Oaks Trial, was second in the Yorkshire Oaks and fourth in the Epsom Oaks and is a half-sister to 5 winners including the dam of the US Grade 2 winner Bienamado. (Miss K Rausing). *"The dam stayed very well, this

is a big, strong, attractive filly and she canters strongly. I think she'll run in July or August".

1395. LUCKY MONEY ★★★
ch.c. Selkirk – Autumn Wealth
(Cadeaux Genereux).
February 8. Third foal. 45,000Y. Tattersalls October Book 1. Highflyer Bloodstock. Half-brother to Blazing Field (by Halling), unplaced in one start at 2 yrs in 2010 and to the fairly useful 6f (a 2 yrs) and 7f winner Colepeper (by Cape Cross). The dam, a useful listed 12f winner of 3 races, is a half-sister to 3 winners including the useful 2-y-o 7f winner and Group 2 7f Futurity Stakes third Wilful. The second dam, Prickwillow (by Nureyev), a fair 3-y-o 10.2f winner, is a half-sister to 4 winners. (J M Brown). "A good-natured, solid and very relaxed horse. The mare stayed well and I suppose he'll be a seven furlong or mile 2-y-o from July or August".

1396. MUTUAL REGARD (IRE) ★★★
b.c. Hernando – Hidden Charm
(by Big Shuffle)
March 20. Second foal. Half-brother to the useful 2010 Irish 2-y-o 7f winner and dual listed-placed Triple Eight (by Royal Applause). The dam, a quite useful 5f and 6f winner, is a half-sister to one winner. The second dam, Polite Reply (by Be My Guest), a quite useful Irish 7f and 1m winner, is a half-sister to 2 winners. (Moyglare Stud Farm). "He's not very big but he'll need time. I broke him in and turned him away, he'll come back in May".

1397. NEIGE D'ANTAN ★★★
gr.f. Aussie Rules – Ninotchka (Nijinsky).
March 8. Half-sister to the useful 2-y-o 6f winner and 7f Group 3 placed Nataliya (by Green Desert), to the quite useful triple 12f winner Nadeszhda (by Nashwan) and the quite useful 12f winner Nezhenka (by With Approval). The dam, a listed winner in Italy and third in the Group 3 12f Lancashire Oaks and the Group 3 12f Princess Royal Stakes, is a half-sister to 5 winners. The second dam, Puget Sound (by High Top), was a fairly useful 7f and 1m winner and a half-sister to the Group 3 Oaks Trial Stakes winner Kiliniski.

(Miss K Rausing). "She's growing, so I shouldn't think she'd be ready until July or August over seven furlongs or a mile".

1398. PEARL SPIRIT (IRE) ★★★
b.f. Invincible Spirit – Millennium Tale
(Distant Relative).
February 12. Eighth foal. 185,000Y. Tattersalls October Book 1. David Redvers. Sister to the Group 1 6f July Cup and dual Group 2 winner Fleeting Spirit and half-sister to the fair 2010 2-y-o 6f winner Half Truth (by Verglas) and the fairly useful Irish 6f to 1m winner and listed-placed Alone He Stands (by Flying Spur). The dam is an unraced half-sister to 5 winners. The second dam, The Bean Sidhe (by Corvaro), won the Group 3 Irish 1,000 Guineas Trial and is a half-sister to 4 winners. (Pearl Bloodstock Ltd). "Expensive, very good-looking, she's grown a lot and I wouldn't be surprised if she alright, but it won't be until the autumn. Fleeting Spirit never even ran at two".

1399. PONCHO ★★
b.f. Cape Cross – Pixie Ring (Pivotal).
February 16. First foal. The dam, a fair 2-y-o dual 6f winner, is a half-sister to 3 winners. The second dam, Ard Na Sighe (by Kenmare), is an unraced half-sister to 9 winners including the champion sprinter Marwell (herself dam of the high-class Coronation Stakes and Sussex Stakes winner Marling and of the good 5f to 1m colt Caerwent) and the Group 2 Mill Reef Stakes winner Lord Seymour. (Nicholas Jones). "A nice, big filly but she's growing and won't be seen out until the autumn".

1400. POSITION ★★★
b.c. Medicean – Poise (Rainbow Quest).
March 18. Third foal. The dam, a fairly useful 10f winner, is a half-sister to 2 minor winners. The second dam, Crepe Ginger (by Sadler's Wells) was placed fourth once over 12f in Ireland and is a half-sister to 5 winners including the French listed winner Daltawa (herself dam of the top-class horses Daylami and Dalakhani). (Cheveley Park Stud). "A seven furlong/mile 2-y-o in September I would think. He's a very pleasant horse and he looks a firm ground type".

1401. QUITE A THING ★★★★
ch.f. Dutch Art – Amazed (Clantime).
March 25. Seventh foal. 25,000Y. Tattersalls October Book 2. Sir M Prescott. Half-sister to the quite useful 2010 2-y-o 6f winner Mayhab (by Cadeaux Genereux), to the useful 2-y-o listed 6f and 3-y-o listed 5f winner Dazed And Amazed (by Averti) and the quite useful dual 5f winner (including at 2 yrs) Nawaaff (by Compton Place). The dam, a modest 5f placed 3-y-o, is a sister to the Group 3 Prix du Petit Couvert winner Bishops Court and a half-sister to 5 winners including the listed winning sprinter Astonished. The second dam, Indigo (by Primo Dominie), a quite useful 2-y-o 5f winner, is a half-sister to 5 winners. (Lady Fairhaven & The Hon. C & H Broughton). *"She'll be the first one of ours to work. It's a speedy family and she's round and cheerful and she'll be running in June hopefully".*

1402. REPEATER ★★★
b.c. Montjeu – Time Over (Mark Of Esteem).
February 12. First foal. 115,000Y. Tattersalls October Book 1. Cheveley Park Stud. The dam, a fair 1m winner, is closely related to the Group 3 10.4f Musidora Stakes winner and Group 1 Prix de Diane third Time Away and a half-sister to 5 winners including the 10f winner and Group 1 French Oaks second Time Ahead. The second dam, Not Before Time (by Polish Precedent), is an unraced half-sister to the Group 3 12f Jockey Club Stakes winner Zinaad and to the Group 3 12f Princess Royal Stakes winner Time Allowed. (Cheveley Park Stud). *"A seven furlong horse in June or July, he's not over-big but he's athletic and unlike a lot of Montjeu's it looks like firm ground will be fine".*

1403. SEVEN VEILS (IRE) ★★★
b.f. Danehill Dancer – Ahdaab (Rahy).
February 23. Sixth foal. 330,000Y. Tattersalls October Book 1. Kern/Lillingston. Sister to the Canadian Grade 2 Nassau Stakes winner Callwood Dancer, to the Group 2 Italian Oaks winner Contredanse and the fairly useful Irish 2-y-o 7f winner and Group 1 Juddmonte International third Set Sail and closely related to the fair 2-y-o 5f and subsequent US winner and Grade 3 placed Walklikeanegyptian (by Danehill). The dam, placed once over 10f, is a half-sister to 8 winners including the Group 1 1m Queen Elizabeth II Stakes winner Maroof and to the placed dam of the Irish Derby winner Desert King. The second dam, Dish Dash (by Bustino), won the Group 2 12f Ribblesdale Stakes and is a half-sister to 6 winners. (Mrs Olivia Hoare). *"A very nice, big, scopey, lengthy filly. She's growing a lot and needs plenty of time".*

1404. SOLAR VIEW (IRE) ★★★
ch.c. Galileo – Ellen (Machiavellian).
April 24. Fourth foal. 50,000Y. Tattersalls October Book 1. Sir Mark Prescott. Half-brother to the fair 2010 5f and 7f placed 2-y-o Mujrayaat (by Invincible Spirit) and to the French 4.5f and 5.5f 2-y-o winner and Group 3 Prix du Bois third Faslen (by Fasliyev). The dam is an unraced half-sister to 2 winners including the Group 3 Winter Derby winner Gentleman's Deal. The second dam, Sleepytime (by Royal Academy), won the 1,000 Guineas and is a sister to the Group 1 winner Ali Royal and a half-sister to the Group 1 winner Taipan. (Neil Greig – Osborne House). *"He'll be running in mid to late summer and he's essentially a staying horse and a 3-y-o. He'll probably need a bit of cut in the ground".*

1405. THE BARONET ★★★
b.c. Sir Percy – Windmill (Ezzoud).
February 14. Sixth living foal. Tattersalls October Book 2. Sir M Prescott. Closely related to a winner abroad by Mark Of Esteem and half-brother to the quite useful 2-y-o 6f winner and subsequent US and Canadian winner Winds Of Time (by Danehill) and to the fair 9f winner Inis Boffin (by Danehill Dancer). The dam, a fair 13.8f winner, is a half-sister to 8 winners including the very smart Group 2 12f Ribblesdale Stakes winner Gull Nook (herself dam of the top-class colt Pentire), the equally smart Group 3 12f Princess Royal Stakes winner Banket and the useful Group 3 Ormonde Stakes winner Mr Pintips. The second dam, Bempton (by Blakeney), was placed three times at up to 11f and is a half-sister to 7 winners including the Shirley Heights. (Charles C Walker – Osborne House). *"It was rather impudent of them to name the horse after me! I think he'll be a 2-y-o and the sire was a leading 2-y-o, which people*

often forget. Obviously being out of an Ezzoud mare he'll stay, so he won't run until the seven furlong/mile races, but he'll be ready to run before some of the more backward types. A medium-sized colt with an almost white tail, which is most unusual".

1406. TRANSFIX ★★★
b.f. Pivotal – Hypnotize (Machiavellian).
March 25. Seventh foal. Sister to the quite useful 2-y-o 6f winner Hip and half-sister to the very smart 2010 2-y-o Group 1 6f Cheveley Park Stakes and Group 2 6f Lowther Stakes winner Hooray (by Invincible Spirit), the useful 2-y-o listed 8.3f winner of 7 races Hypnotic (by Lomitas), the fairly useful 2-y-o 1m winner Notorize (by Hernando) and the quite useful dual 7f winner Macedon (by Dansili). The dam, a useful 2-y-o dual 7f winner, is closely related to 2 winners including the Group 3 6f Cherry Hinton Stakes winner Dazzle and a half-sister to 5 winners including the useful 7f (at 2 yrs) and 1m listed winner Fantasize and to the placed dam of the Group 2 winning sprinter Danehurst. The second dam, Belle et De uree (by The Minstrel), won over 1m (at 2 yrs) and 10f in France and is a half-sister to the very useful 6f and 1m winner and Cheveley Park Stakes second Dancing Tribute (herself dam of the Group/Grade 2 winners Souvenir Copy and Dance Sequence). (Cheveley Park Stud). *"Very different to her half-sister Hooray and doesn't look as zippy at this stage"*.

1407. YOURS EVER ★★
b.f. Dansili – Love Everlasting (Pursuit Of Love).
March 18. Fifth foal. 180,000Y. Tattersalls October Book 1. Cheveley Park Stud. Half-sister to the fairly useful 12f winner Acquainted (by Shamardal). The dam, a very useful 2-y-o 7.5f and 3-y-o listed 12f winner, is a half-sister to 6 winners including the smart Group 3 10f Scottish Classic winner Baron Ferdinand. The second dam, In Perpetuity (by Great Nephew), a fairly useful 10f winner, is a half-sister to the Derby winner Shirley Heights and to Bempton (dam of the Group 2 winner Gull Nook and the Group 3 winners Mr Pintips and Banket). (Cheveley Park Stud). *"Very expensive and bought by Cheveley Park for the paddocks eventually. She's a very big, good-looking filly who, from what we've seen, is very much a 3-y-o type and she'd need to be very good to win this year. But she'll be a grand looking filly in time"*.

1408. UNNAMED ★★
b.f. Acclamation – Ziria (Danehill Dancer).
January 3. Fourth foal. 26,000Y. Tattersalls October Book 2. Axom. Half-sister to the fairly useful 2010 2-y-o 7f winner and listed 7f placed Zacynthus (by Iffraaj) and to the fair French 1m winner Ixalos (by Hawk Wing). The dam, winner of the Group 3 5f Prix du Bois and the Group 3 5f Prix du Petit-Couvert, is a half-sister to 5 winners including the useful dual 7f winner Tashkil. The second dam, Surprise Visitor (by Be My Guest) was placed once in France and is a half-sister to 9 winners including the dual German listed winner Mirage (herself dam of the Group 2 winner Swallow Flight) and the champion Scandinavian older horse Red Hero. (AXOM XXXI). *"She's very big and we turned her away in January. She'll come back in May but she needed time because she was so big"*. Sir Mark is such a stickler for demanding that his owners name their 2-y-o's before the New Year, it's surprising he's allowed Axom to get away with leaving this filly without a name for so long. Let's hope he isn't losing it!

NOEL QUINLAN

1409. AMOURE MEDICI ★★★
b.c. Medicean – Lifetime Romance (Mozart).
March 23. Second foal. 39,000Y. Tattersalls October Book 2. Charlie Gordon-Watson. The dam, a quite useful Irish 2-y-o 7f winner, is a half-sister to 3 winners. The second dam, Josh's Pearl (by Sadler's Wells), a minor Irish 13f winner, is a half-sister to 2 winners. *"A lovely, big, scopey horse and a late summer type that does everything well. One for the second half of the season"*.

1410. DARK AGES ★★★
bl.f. Dark Angel – Prosaic Star (Common Grounds).
May 6. Eleventh foal. 36,000Y. Tattersalls October Book 2. BBA (Ire). Half-sister to the Irish 2-y-o dual 5f winner and listed-placed Blue Crush (by Entrepreneur), to the fairly useful 2-y-o triple 5f winner Barringer (by Nicollote), the quite useful 2-y-o 5f winner Lupine (by Lake Coniston), the quite useful

2-y-o 6f winner Folsomprisonblues (by Mull Of Kintyre), the modest 2-y-o 6f winner Kapelad Junior (by Clodovil), the Irish 10f and hurdles winner Puck Out (by Topanoora) and the moderate 2m and hurdles winner Sea Cliff (by Golan). The dam, a quite useful Irish 2-y-o 1m winner, is a half-sister to 4 winners. The second dam, Starduster (by Lucifer), won the listed Irish November Handicap and is a half-sister to 4 winners. (Newtown Anner Stud). *"Bred by the ex- jockey Willie Robinson in Ireland, she'll start off in April at Newmarket, she's a nice filly and a typical Acclamation (the sire of Dark Angel) in terms of her good temperament. Very relaxed, she's more like a colt in that she does what she has to do without any bother".*

1411. HARMONIE ★★★
b.f. Teofilo – Harmonist (Hennessy).
March 17. Fourth foal. 55,000Y. Tattersalls October Book 2. BBA (Ire). The dam won twice at 3 yrs in the USA and is a half-sister to 4 winners including the US Grade 2 placed Country Store. The second dam, Geraldine's Store (by Exclusive Native), won 13 races including the Grade 2 Diana Handicap and is a half-sister to the Irish 1,000 Guineas and Coronation Stakes winner Al Bahathri (herself dam of the 2,000 Guineas and Champion Stakes winner Haafhd). (Newtown Anner Stud). *"There are no buttons pressed with her yet, but I'd say she's potentially very nice and we hear nice words about the first season sire Teofilo. A proper nice filly but we'll wait with her until June I should think".*

1412. LEMON ROCK ★★★★
b.f. Green Desert – Lady Links (Bahamian Bounty).
January 19. Sixth foal. 32,000Y. Tattersalls October Book 1. BBA (Ire). Closely related to the quite useful 2-y-o 7f winner Swanky Lady (by Cape Cross) and to a minor winner abroad by Oasis Dream and half-sister to the useful listed 6f (at 2 yrs) and listed 7f winner Selinka (by Selkirk). The dam, a dual listed 6f winner (including at 2 yrs), is a half-sister to 5 winners including the quite useful 2-y-o 6f winner and Group 3 placed Umniya. The second dam, Sparky's Song (by Electric), a moderate 10.2f and 12f winner, is a half-sister to 3 winners including the Group 1 6.5f winner Bold Edge.

"I would imagine she'd be the best 2-y-o in the yard and we're hoping her debut will be in a fillies' maiden at Newmarket in May. If she's not ready we'll give her a bit more time. She would have made more at the sale because she's a fine filly but she's a little bit offset in front which allowed us in to get her. A real good type with size, scope and strength. I think potentially she's very good".

1413. UNNAMED ★★
b.f. Rock Of Gibraltar – Dixie Belle (Diktat).
April 30. Second foal. 18,000Y. Tattersalls October Book 2. Not sold. Half-sister to the quite useful 2010 2-y-o 6f winner Blanche Dubawi (by Dubawi). The dam, a Group 3 5f and listed 6f winner, is a half-sister to one winner. The second dam, Inspiring (by Anabaa), is an unraced half-sister to 5 winners. *"An ugly duckling to begin with but now that the spring is here she's changing every day. That's how the family seem to be, she was tall, lean and angular but she's getting better every day now".*

1414. UNNAMED ★★
b.f. Le Vie Dei Colori – Heres The Plan (Revoque).
March 31. Third foal. 13,000Y. Tattersalls October Book 3. Not sold. Sister to the fairly useful 2010 2-y-o triple 5f winner Belle Bayardo and to the modest 10f, 12f and hurdles winner Plan A. The dam, a 2-y-o winner, is a half-sister to 5 winners. The second dam, Fanciful (by Mujtahid), ran once unplaced and is a half-sister to 5 winners. *"The dam's first two foals were by the same sire and they've both won. She's a nice filly but a little bit weak at the moment so we'll have to wait and see how she progresses".*

1415. UNNAMED ★★★★
b.c. Dutch Art – Tidal (Bin Ajwaad).
March 21. Fourth foal. €10,500Y. Goffs Orby. Not sold. Half-brother to the quite useful 1m and 10f winner Faldal (by Falbrav). The dam, a quite useful 10f and 12f winner of 4 races, was third in the Group 3 Golden Daffodil Stakes and is a half-sister to 4 winners. The dam, a modest 9f to 17f winner of 3 races, is out of the unplaced Saucy Bird (by Henbit), herself a sister to 2 minor winners. *"An exciting colt,*

he's good-looking and although we haven't pressed any buttons yet his work has been extraordinary. He's as laid-back as could be, he doesn't sweat, he doesn't pull and you wouldn't know he was in the yard because he's no trouble at all. He goes up the gallop so easily it's unbelievable".

JOHN QUINN
1416. DORA'S SISTER ★★★
b.f. Dark Angel – Teodora (Fairy King).
April 25. Eighth foal. Doncaster Premier. £19,000Y. John Quinn. Half-sister to the fair 2010 5f placed 2-y-o Lady Kildare (by Bachelor Duke), to the fairly useful 5f winner of 4 races (including 3 times at 2 yrs) Duchess Dora, the quite useful 2-y-o 7f winner Fadhb Ar Bith (both by Tagula), the fair 2-y-o 7f winner Feeling Wonderful and the useful 2-y-o dual 7f winner Prince Of Love (both by Fruits Of Love). The dam, a fairly useful 2-y-o 6f winner, was fourth in the Group 3 6f Princess Margaret Stakes and is a half-sister to 6 winners. The second dam, Pinta (by Ahonoora), won over 5f in Ireland and a listed event in Italy over 7.5f and is a half-sister to 6 winners. (The Clay Family). "I have the half-sister Duchess Dora and she's grand. This is quite a nice sort of filly that she should make a 2-y-o from late April onwards. She's quite a tall filly, but so is Duchess Dora, and in Dark Angel she's by a sire that should get plenty of 2-y-o winners".

1417. RED TYKE (IRE) ★★★
b.c. Red Clubs – Teutonic (Revoque).
February 5. First foal. £9,500Y. Doncaster Premier. John Quinn. The dam, a poor 11f placed maiden on the flat, won over hurdles and is a half-sister to 5 winners including the useful 5f and 6f winner of 6 races Seven No Trumps and the quite useful 6f winner and Group 3 Norfolk Stakes second Waterside. The second dam, Classic Ring (by Auction Ring), a 2-y-o 7f seller winner, is a half-sister to 7 winners. (Mr T Woods). "He's a grand type of horse that should start off in April over five furlongs. There's plenty of speed in the family and he's a neat horse that might like a bit of cut in the ground, if you consider one or two others in the family. You wouldn't want to run him on firm ground". TRAINER'S BARGAIN BUY

1418. VALLEY ACE ★★★
b.c. Three Valleys – First Ace (First Trump).
March 5. 19,000Y. Tattersalls October Book 2. John Quinn. Half-brother to Mrs G (by Ad Valorem), unplaced in 2 starts at 2 yrs in 2010. The dam is an unraced sister to the 2-y-o Group 2 5f Flying Childers Stakes winner Mrs P, a three-parts sister to the very useful sprinter and Portland Handicap winner Sarcita (herself the dam of two listed winners) and a half-sister to 7 winners. The second dam, Zinzi (by Song), won over 5f at 4 yrs in Ireland and is a half-sister to 4 winners including the Irish listed winner Checker Express. (Roberts, Green, Savidge, Whittal, Williams). "He's a nice sort of colt that moves well. We haven't really pressed any buttons yet but we like the look of him. He looks like a 2-y-o and you'd be hoping he'd have the speed to start off at five furlongs from May onwards. He'll want decent ground and he's a nice, neat colt, not over-big but big enough and well put-together".

KEVIN RYAN
1419. ARDMAY (IRE)
b.c. Strategic Prince – Right After Moyne (Imperial Ballet).
April 26. Third foal. Tattersalls Ireland. €28,000Y. Stephen Hillen. Half-brother to the useful 2010 2-y-o 5f winner and Group 3 Molecomb Stakes third Choose Wisely (by Choisir) and the 6f (at 2 yrs) and 10f winner Tamanaco (by Catcher In The Rye). The dam is an unraced half-sister to 3 winners. The second dam, Trojan River (by Riverman), won twice over 10f and 14f and is a half-sister to 6 winners including Air Marshall (Group 2 Great Voltigeur) and Break Bread (Group 3 Prix la Force).

1420. BOGART
ch.c. Bahamian Bounty – Lauren Louise (Tagula).
March 1. Second foal. Doncaster Premier. £32,000Y. Stephen Hillen. The dam, a moderate 6f winner at 4 yrs, is a half-sister to 3 winners including the French listed-placed Golden Accolade. The second dam, Movie Star (by Barathea), ran once unplaced and is a full or half-sister to 3 winners including the French listed winner Kilometre Neuf. (Mrs A Bailey).

1421. CHURCH MUSIC
b.c. Amadeus Wolf – Cappella
(College Chapel).
April 7. Eighth foal. Doncaster Premier. £42,000Y. Kern/Lillingston (private sale, Stephen Hillen). Half-sister to the fair 2010 2-y-o 6f winner Rafella (by Iffraaj), to the useful 2-y-o 6f and 7f winner Dickensian (by Xaar), to the quite useful 1m to 10f and jumps winner of 5 races Red Birr (by Bahhare), the moderate triple 6f winner (including a 2-y-o seller) Azuree (by Almutawakel) and a winner in Cyprus by Noverre. The dam, a fair dual 5f winner at 2 yrs, is a full or half-sister to 5 winners including the fairly useful 5f (at 2 yrs) and 7f winner and Group 2 placed Queenfisher. The second dam, Mavahra (by Mummy's Pet), a fairly useful 5f and 6f winner, is a half-sister to 5 winners including the dam of the Group 2 Coventry Stakes winner Hellvelyn. (J C Fretwell).

1422. DISCRESSION
b.c. Indesatchel – Night Gypsy (Mind Games).
April 3. Seventh foal. 30,000Y. Tattersalls October Book 2. Stephen Hillen. Half-brother to the useful 2-y-o 6f and listed 7f winner Electric Feel (by Firebreak), to the fairly useful 2-y-o 6f winner and listed placed Aunt Nicola (by Reel Buddy) and the quite useful 5f winner of 6 races from 3 to 5 yrs Safari Mischief (by Primo Valentino). The dam, a fair 2-y-o 5f winner, is a sister to the listed 2-y-o winner On The Brink and a half-sister to 4 winners including the listed winner and Group 2 placed Eastern Romance and the useful 2-y-o triple 6f winner Blue Tomato. The second dam, Ocean Grove (by Fairy King), a quite useful 2-y-o 6f winner, is a half-sister to 5 winners here and abroad. (Kenneth MacPherson & Mr and Mrs T Holdcroft).

1423. FORGET ME NOT LANE (IRE)
b.c. Holy Roman Emperor – Mrs Arkada (Akarad).
April 9. Seventh foal. 45,000Y. Tattersalls October Book 1. Stephen Hillen. Half-brother to the French listed 1m winner Marque Royale (by Royal Academy and herself the dam of two listed winners in France), to the French 11f winner and dual Group 3 placed Mister Kick (by Linamix) and 2 minor winners in France by Peintre Celebre and Linamix. The dam, a French listed 1m winner, was third in the Group 1 Prix Saint-Alary and is a half-sister to the French Group 3 winners Mister Sicy, Mister Riv and Manninamix. The second dam, Mrs Annie (by Bolkonski), a French 2-y-o winner and third in the Group 3 Prix d'Arenburg, is a half-sister to 6 winners including Satamixa (Group 1 Prix Jacques le Marois).

1424. HAMZA (IRE)
b.c. Amadeus Wolf – Lady Shanghai (Alhaarth).
April 21. Second foal. Doncaster Premier. £25,000Y. Stephen Hillen. The dam, a quite useful Irish 5f to 1m placed 2-y-o, is a half-sister to 4 winners including the Group 3 Palace House Stakes winner and Group 1 placed Dandy Man. The second dam, Lady Alexander (by Night Shift), won the Group 3 6.3f Anglesey Stakes and Group 3 5f Molecomb Stakes and is a half-sister to 2 winners. (Mr Mubarak Al Naimi).

1425. INDEPUB
b.c. Indesatchel – Champenoise (Forzando).
April 4. Tenth foal. Doncaster Premier. £30,000Y. Stephen Hillen. Half-brother to the fairly useful 2-y-o dual 5f winner Dreams Desire, to the fair 5f and 6f winner Brut (both by Mind Games), the fair 2-y-o 5f and 6f winner Bebe de Cham (by Tragic Role), the modest 6f to 1m winner Drink To Me Only (by Pursuit Of Love) and a winner in Jersey by Tragic Role. The dam, a 1m seller winner at 4 yrs, is a half-sister to 3 winners. The second dam, Migoletty (by Oats), won at 3 yrs and is a half-sister to 5 winners. (D W Barker).

1426. KODIAC KING (IRE)
b.c. Kodiac – Prodigal Daughter (Alhaarth).
April 12. Third foal. Doncaster Premier. £24,000Y. Stephen Hillen. Half-brother to the very useful 2-y-o Group 3 7f Horris Hill Stakes winner Carnaby Street (by Le Vie Dei Colori). The dam is an unraced daughter of the Irish 6f winner and listed-placed Shallow Ground (by Common Grounds), herself a half-sister to 5 winners including the US Grade 2 winner Shanawi. (Mr N I O'Callaghan).

1427. MARCHING ON (IRE)
b.c. Rock Of Gibraltar – Miss Delila (Malibu Moon).
January 30. First foal. 31,000Y. Tattersalls October Book 2. Not sold. The dam is an unplaced half-sister to 3 winners including Sander Camillo (Group 2 Cherry Hinton Stakes and Group 3 Albany Stakes). The second dam, Staraway (by Star de Naskra), won 20 races in the USA including three listed stakes and is a half-sister to 5 winners. (Highbank Stud).

1428. MY PEARL (IRE)
b.c. Sleeping Indian – My-Lorraine (Mac's Imp).
February 11. Tenth foal. Doncaster Premier. £32,000Y. David Redvers. Half-brother to the useful 1m and 8.5f winner Bolodenka (by Soviet Star), the fairly useful 5f of 3 races (including at 2 yrs) listed-placed Izmail (by Bluebird), the fair 2-y-o 7f winner Ajara (by Elusive City), the modest 6f winner Cross Of Lorraine (by Pivotal) and a winner in Japan by Captain Rio. The dam, a minor Irish 3-y-o 5f and 6.5f winner, is a half-sister to 6 winners including the Group 3 5f Ballyogan Stakes winner and Group 1 Haydock Park Sprint Cup third Catch The Blues. The second dam, Dear Lorraine (by Nonoalco), won over 10f in France and is a half-sister to 4 winners. (Fearl Bloodstock Ltd).

1429. PEA SHOOTER ♠
b.c. Piccolo – Sparkling Eyes (Lujain).
February 25. First foal. Doncaster Premier. £30,000Y. Stephen Hillen. The dam, a fairly useful dual 5f winner (including at 2 yrs), was fourth in the Group 2 5f Queen Mary Stakes, is a half-sister to 3 winners here and abroad. The second dam, Lady Georgia (by Alzao), a useful 3-y-o 7.8f winner, was fourth in the Group 3 7f Prestige Stakes at 2 yrs. (Mrs M Forsyth).

DAVID SIMCOCK

1430. AL MAMZAR (IRE) ★★★
b.c. Teofilo – Avila (Ajdal).
May 17. Fourteenth foal. 32,000Y. Tattersalls October Book 2. David Simcock. Half-brother to the very smart Group 1 1m Racing Post Trophy and Group 2 10.4f Dante Stakes winner Dilshaan, to the fair staying winner of 6 races Aveiro (both by Darshaan), the smart 7f (at 2 yrs) and listed 10f winner and Group 1 1m Prix Marcel Boussac second Darrfonah, the quite useful 12f winner Calakanga (by Dalakhani), the modest 1m winner Al Joza (by Dubawi), the modest 10.5f winner Mama-San (by Doyoun) and two minor winners abroad by Royal Applause and Shirley Heights. The dam, a fair 7f placed maiden, is a half-sister to the smart middle-distance colts Alleging, Monastery and Nomrood. The second dam, Sweet Habit (by Habitat), is an unraced half-sister to 5 winners including the Group 2 Pretty Polly Stakes winner Fleur Royale. "A nice, good-actioned horse, he's quite mature and he's one you'll see over seven furlongs in mid-summer. He's very likeable, he was picked up for a song and there's nothing wrong with him".

1431. ALHIRA ★★★★
b.f. Royal Applause – Taghreed (Zamindar).
January 19. First foal. The dam, a modest 6f and 7f placed maiden from 3 starts, is a half-sister to 2 winners including the fairly useful triple 1m winner Jaser. The second dam, Waafiah (by Anabaa), second over 7f at 3 yrs on her only start, is a half-sister to several winners including the very useful 1m and hurdles winner Atlantic Rhapsody. "I'd say that at the moment she's the pick of my fillies. She's very natural, very forward and she should be out over six furlongs in May. She's a lightish, athletic 2-y-o".

1432. ANDALIEB ★★★★
b.c. Zamindar – Sakhya (Barathea).
February 22. Third foal. Half-brother to the fair 7f winner Falakee (by Sakhee). The dam, unplaced in one start, is a half-sister to 4 winners including the useful 2-y-o 6f winner Mr Sandancer and the useful 2-y-o 7f winner Fantasy Island. The second dam, Um Lardaff (by Mill Reef), a winner over 11f and 12f at 3 yrs in France, is a sister to the Derby winner and high-class sire Shirley Heights and a half-sister to the good mare Bempton – dam of the Group 3 winners Mr Pintips and Banket and of the Group 2 winner Gull Nook (herself dam of the smart filly Spring). (Z A Galadari). "A very straightforward, mature and attractive horse, he'll be a seven furlong or mile 2-y-o. A very likeable colt".

1433. CAPE SAVANNAH ★★★
b.c. Cape Cross – Lady High Havens (Bluebird).
April 10. Fifth foal. 34,000Y. Tattersalls October Book 2. Blandford Bloodstock. Half-brother to the 2010 dual 6f placed 2-y-o Formal Demand (by Invincible Spirit) and to the moderate 1m winner Nurai (by Danehill Dancer). The dam, a useful 2-y-o 6f and 7f winner and second in the Group 2 6f Cherry Hinton Stakes, is a half-sister to 4 winners including the smart dual 1m winner and Group 3 Desmond Stakes third Middlemarch. The second dam, Blanche Dubois (by Nashwan), is an unraced half-sister to 8 winners including the Irish 2,000 Guineas winner Indian Haven and the Group 1 Gran Criterium winner Count Dubois. *"A very likeable, attractive horse, but he will need a little bit of time and I'd hope he'd be running over seven furlongs and a mile a little later on".*

1434. COFFEE KING (IRE) ★★
b.c. King's Best – Passarelle (In The Wings).
January 29. First foal. Goffs Orby. €20,000Y. Blandford Bloodstock. The dam, a fair 12f winner, is a half-sister to 2 winners including the very useful listed 8.5f winner of 3 races Fort Dignity. The second dam, Kitza (by Danehill), won 3 races including the listed Irish 1,000 Guineas Trial and was second in the Irish Oaks and the Irish 1,000 Guineas. She is a half-sister to 5 winners including the fairly useful Irish sprinter Hi Bettina (dam of the Group 2 winner Fred Bongusto) and the Group 3 Norfolk Stakes winner Marouble. *"A cheap purchase from Goffs, he was broken and has done everything asked but he's on a break at the moment just so he can mature and develop – no more than that. A horse that you'll see later on this season".*

1435. GHOST PROTOCOL (IRE) ★★★★
b.c. Cockney Rebel – Stroke Of Six (Woodborough).
March 25. Fourth living foal. 33,000Y. Tattersalls October Book 1. Blandford Bloodstock. Half-brother to the fairly useful 2-y-o 6f and 7f winner Sohcahtoa (by Val Royal), to the quite useful 2-y-o dual 6f winner Marcus Cicero (by Le Vie Dei Colori) and the fair 7f (at 2 yrs) and jumps winner Miss Phoebe (by Catcher In The Rye). The dam, a quite useful 6f (at 2 yrs) and 1m winner, is a full or half-sister to 6 winners including the Group 2 10f Prix Eugene Adam winner Revelation. The second dam, Angelus Chimes (by Northfields), a quite useful Irish 4-y-o 12f winner, is a half-sister to 4 winners. *"A very natural, very forward horse, he goes well, has a little bit of an attitude but generally I'm very happy with him. He shows plenty of speed, he'll be a six/seven furlong 2-y-o and he'll be one of the earlier types. He might just lack a little bit of substance but he's likeable to watch".*

1436. GREY FALCON (FR) ★★
gr.c. Clodovil – Sugar (Nashwan).
January 27. Ninth living foal. €30,000Y. Arqana Deauville August. Gill Richardson. Half-brother to the French 12-time winner Multiverse (by Hernando), to the French winner of 6 races Pur Sucre (by Zamindar) and a minor winner in France by Observatory. The dam won once in France at 3 yrs and is a half-sister to 9 winners including the French Group 3 winner and US Grade 1 placed Angel In My Heart (herself dam of the Derby winner Kris Kin), the Group 1 Prix de la Salamandre winner and useful sire Common Grounds and the listed winner Lightning Fire (dam of the US Grade 2 winner Beyrouth). The second dam, Sweetly (by Lyphard), won 3 races in the USA and is a full or half-sister to 10 winners. *"He'll need plenty of time, he's really workmanlike and a big, raw horse. A staying horse for the future".*

1437. GUCCI D'ORO ★★★
b.br.c. Medaglia D'Oro – Ninette (Alleged).
May 7. Eighth foal. $85,000Y. Keeneland September. Rabbah Bloodstock. Half-brother to 4 winners including the fairly useful 2-y-o 7f winner Quartet (by Quest For Fame), the French 6f and 1m winner of 9 races Summer Shrill (by Summer Squall) and the modest 8.5f winner Ninth House (by Chester House). The dam, a useful 10f winner and listed-placed here, subsequently won over 9f in the USA and is a half-sister to the top-class miler Observatory, winner of the Queen Elizabeth II Stakes. The second dam, Stellaria (by Roberto), won from 5f to 8.5f including the listed 6f Rose Bowl Stakes and is a half-sister to numerous winners including the US Grade

1 placed horses Potentiate and Cogency. 'He's just stepped up a group and he's a workmanlike, attractive colt that I'd like to think will be a high summer horse over seven furlongs. He's done everything asked of him".

1438. HELLO DUBAI ★★
ch.f. Teofilo – Bush Cat (Kingmambo).
April 12. Fifth foal. 30,000Y. Tattersalls October Book 2. Blandford Bloodstock. Half-sister to the quite useful 2010 2-y-o 7f winner Blue Tiger's Eye (by Motivator, to the quite useful 2-y-o 1m winner and subsequent US Grade 3 placed Meer Kat (by Red Ransom) and the moderate dual 1m seller winner Ask Dan (by Refuse To Bend). The dam, a quite useful 2-y-o 7f winner, is a half-sister to 6 winners. The second dam, Arbusha (by Danzig), won a listed 1m stakes in Germany, was third in the Group 3 Royal Whip Stakes and is a sister to the Group 2 6f Goldene Peitsche winner Nicholas and a half-sister to 9 winners including the dam of the dual Group 1 winner Strategic Choice. "She's surprised me, she's grown and done very well since the New Year after showing me very little early on. I see her as a seven furlong filly from mid-summer onwards and I quite like her".

1439. MR FONG ★★★★
ch.c. Dr Fong – Selkirk Sky (Selkirk).
February 24. First foal. 23,000Y. Tattersalls October Book 1. Blandford Bloodstock. The dam, a moderate 7f winner, is a half-sister to the triple listed winner and Group 2 6f Gimcrack Stakes second Andronikos. The second dam, Arctic Air (by Polar Falcon), a quite useful 2-y-o 7f winner, is a sister to the useful listed 7f winner Arctic Char and a half-sister to 6 winners including the Group 2 winners Barrow Creek and Last Resort and the dam of the Group 2 winner Trans Island. "A very likeable horse, probably the best looking individual we bought at the Sales. His brain is very good for a Dr Fong and he looks like a bigger version of a nice horse we had called Metropolitan Man. A horse that doesn't seem to get tired, he'll be a seven furlong 2-y-o and he's a horse that we like". TRAINERS' BARGAIN BUY

1440. ROCK OF MONET ★★★★ ♠
b.c. Kyllachy – Level Pegging (Common Grounds).
March 5. Seventh foal. Doncaster Premier. £85,000Y. Will Edmeades. Half-brother to the fair 5f and 6f winner of 6 races Even Bolder and to the fair 2-y-o 6f winner Bold Tie (both by Bold Edge). The dam, unplaced on her only 2 starts at 2 yrs, is a sister to the listed Scarborough Stakes winner and Group 2 Kings Stand Stakes second Flanders (herself dam of the US Grade 3 winner Louvain) and a half-sister to 6 winners. The second dam, Family At War (by Explodent), won once over 5f at 2 yrs and is a half-sister to 4 winners. "A very forward colt and a good type, he'll be running over six furlongs in May. Very likeable and mature, he probably wouldn't want the ground too quick but won't have a problem winning a maiden in May or June and he's all 2-y-o".

1441. WAVEGUIDE (IRE) ★★
b.f. Dubawi – Million Waves (Mull Of Kintyre).
February 12. Second foal. 78,000foal. Tattersalls December. Dunchurch Lodge Stud. The dam, an Irish 2-y-o 7f winner, was listed-placed and is a half-sister to several winners including the 2-y-o Group 3 7f Prix du Calvados winner Elusive Wave. The second dam, Multicolour Wave (by Rainbow Quest), is a placed half-sister to 4 winners. "From the family of Elusive Wave, she's a big, raw horse that needs plenty of time but she's a likeable, attractive filly".

1442. YAZDI (IRE) ★★
b.c. Galileo – Lucky Spin (Pivotal).
March 6. Second foal. 55,000Y. Tattersalls October Book 1. Angie Sykes. The dam, a winner of 5 races including the Group 3 7f Chartwell Stakes and the Group 3 6f Summer Stakes, is a half-sister to 4 winners. The second dam, Periscope (by Legend Of France), was placed over 6f in Scandinavia and is a half-sister to 4 minor winners. "A narrow, raw horse, he wasn't particularly expensive for a Galileo out of a good racemare. He's a good actioned horse, very light on his feet and very athletic for a horse that we won't see until the autumn".

1443. UNNAMED ★★★
b.f. Exceed And Excel – Areyaam
(Elusive Quality).
February 3. First foal. The dam, a fair maiden, was placed three times over 1m and is a half-sister to 2 winners. The second dam, Yanaseeni (by Trempolino), is an unplaced sister to the German-trained middle-distance dual Group 1 winner Germany (by Trempolino) and to 4 minor winners in the USA. *"A very natural filly, very light on her feet and she'll be one of our early runners – hopefully in May".*

1444. UNNAMED ★★★★
b.f. Invincible Spirit – Baize (Efisio).
April 14. Tenth foal. 95,000Y. Tattersalls October Book 1. Hugo Lascelles. Half-sister to the Grade 1 Del Mar Oaks winner Singhalese, to the 2010 Irish 2-y-o 6f winner Isis Song, the US winner at 2 and 3 yrs Kid Edward (all by Singspiel), the useful 7f and 1m winner of 4 races at 2 and 3 yrs and listed-placed Docofthebay (by Docksider), the fairly useful 6f (at 2 yrs) to 1m winner Masterpoint (by Mark Of Esteem), the quite useful 3-y-o 6f winner Patterdale (by Octagonal), the quite useful 9f to 14f and hurdles winner Baizically (by Galileo) and the Italian winner of 5 races Farhad (by Red Ransom). The dam, a fairly useful 2-y-o 5f winner and third in the Group 3 Molecomb Stakes, subsequently won 3 races at up to 6f in the USA and is a sister to the listed-placed winner Bayleaf. The second dam, Bayonne (by Bay Express), a dual 5f winner at 3 yrs, is a half-sister to 7 winners. *"She's the fastest we've got. Very likeable, she goes well and she'll be seen on the racecourse at the end of April/early May. Very natural, she goes well and looks one to follow".*

1445. UNNAMED ★★★
b.c. War Front – Ball Gown (Silver Hawk).
March 6. $40,000Y. Keeneland September. Blandford Bloodstock. Half-brother to the useful 11f and multiple jumps winner and Group 3 15f Prix du Lutece third Palomar (by Chester House), to the French 2-y-o listed 1m winner Putyball (by Silver Deputy), the fair 9f and 11f winner and listed-placed Hayhaat (by Irish River) and the fair 2-y-o 6f winner Trepa (by Hennessy). The dam is an unraced half-sister to 3 winners including the US stakes winner and Grade 3 placed Dance Account. The second dam, Dancing Rags (by Nijinsky), a minor winner at 3 yrs in the USA, is a sister to the US Grade 2 winner Terpsichorist and a half-sister to the high-class 2-y-o and Group 2 Champagne Stakes winner Gorytus. *"A lovely horse by an exciting American stallion. He's a huge colt but very natural with it and he's a horse I really like. I like everything he does and despite his size he's natural enough to shape, so I would think he'd start off at seven furlongs and make up into a nice mile and a half horse next year".*

1446. UNNAMED ★★★
b.f. Shamardal – Bronwen (King's Best).
April 13. Third foal. 110,000Y. Tattersalls October Book 1. David Simcock. Sister to Heatherbird (by Shamardal), placed fourth over 7f on her only start at 2 yrs in 2010. The dam, a fairly useful 9f to 15f winner, is a half-sister to 5 winners including the Group 1 Fillies' Mile and Group 3 May Hill Stakes winner Teggiano. The second dam, Tegwen (by Nijinsky), a quite useful 10f winner, is a half-sister to 4 winners. *"A very attractive filly, it's a family I know well. They all need time and she'll be no different, but as an individual she's as attractive a filly that you could see. Everything she's done, she's done well, but she won't be rushed in any way. A filly for the autumn".*

1447. UNNAMED ★★★
b.c. Rail Link – For Example (Northern Baby).
February 3. Twelfth foal. Goffs Orby. €35,000Y. Blandford Bloodstock. Half-brother to the smart 1m (at 2 yrs) to 10f winner and Group 3 placed Forbearing (by Bering), the useful Italian listed 12f winner Viz (by Darshaan), the fairly useful 1m and 8.3f winner Dryden House (by Cadeaux Genereux), the quite useful 2-y-o 1m winner Miss Emma May (by Hawk Wing) and a winner over hurdles by Fantastic Light. The dam, an Irish 10f placed maiden, is a half-sister to 5 winners and to the dams of the Group/Grade 1 winners Awe Inspiring, Culture Vulture, Polish Precedent and Zilzal. The second dam, Bold Example (by Bold Lad, USA), a US stakes-placed winner at up to 7f, is a half-sister to the dams of the Sussex Stakes winner Posse and the US Grade 1 winner Wavering Monarch. (Dr Marwan

Koukash). *"Another typical one of our buys, he's a big, raw brute and a really likeable sort. For his breeding he's a very natural horse. I try to buy the owner horses that stay a mile and a half and this colt a classic example. I like him a lot but he's one for much later on".*

1448. UNNAMED ★★★
b.f. Dutch Art – Haretha (Alhaarth).
April 29. Second foal. 50,000Y. Tattersalls October Book 2. Rabbah Bloodstock. The dam is an unraced half-sister to 5 winners including the Group 1 10f Nassau Stakes and Group 10.4f Musidora Stakes winner Zahrat Dubai. The second dam, Walesiana (by Star Appeal), won the German 1,000 Guineas and is a half-sister to 8 winners. *"She's lovely, lacking in pedigree a bit, but she's as nice an individual as we've bought. She's very attractive and very natural. A six/seven furlong 2-y-o".*

1449. UNNAMED ★★★
b.f. Dutch Art – Miss Respect
(Mark Of Esteem).
February 15. First foal. 21,000Y. Tattersalls October Book 1. Rabbah Bloodstock. The dam is an unraced half-sister to 2 winners including the 2-y-o Group 1 Fillies' Mile and Group 2 12f Ribblesdale Stakes winner Hibaayeb. The second dam, Lady Zonda (by Lion Cavern), a quite useful 7f and 1m winner, is a half-sister to 8 winners. *"She's slightly more forward than our other Dutch Art filly. I see her as a six/seven furlong horse in May or June, she's mature and well put-together".*

1450. UNNAMED ★★★
ch.c. Shamardal – Oystermouth (Averti).
February 16. First foal. 55,000Y. Tattersalls October Book 1. Mr A O Nerses. The dam, a modest 5.7f winner, is a half-sister to the Group 1 5f Prix de l'Abbaye winners Avonbridge and Patavellian. The second dam, Alessa (by Caerleon), a quite useful 2-y-o 7f winner, is a sister to the Group 2 14.6f Park Hill Stakes winner Casey and a half-sister to 4 winners. *"A likeable individual, he has a big, ugly head on him but he's surprised me how forward he is considering the dam's two good half-brothers got better with age. I suspect he'll be the same and yet he's one that could go forward very quickly. I'd like to think he's a seven furlong horse for the mid-season, he's a good boned horse and there's a lot of him".*

1451. UNNAMED ★★
b.c. Iffraaj – Pretty Majestic (Invincible Spirit).
March 22. First foal. The dam, a quite useful 2-y-o dual 6f winner, is a sister to the quite useful 7f (at 2 yrs) and 6f Golden Shaheen and a half-sister to several winners. The second dam, Cheeky Weeky (Cadeaux Genereux), was placed five times in France at up to 1m and is a half-sister to 4 winners. *"A bit of a playboy, everything's a game with him at the moment. He's quite a compact, neat horse and I'll find out a bit more about him during April. There's speed in the pedigree and we'll get on with him soon".*

1452. UNNAMED ★★★
b.f. Invincible Spirit – Reform Act
(Lemon Drop Kid).
March 16. First foal. 85,000Y. Tattersalls October Book 1. A O Nerses. The dam, 1m (at 2 yrs), 10f and listed 12f winner in Ireland and third in the Grade 2 Long Island Handicap in the USA, is a half-sister to the US winner and Grade 1 Spinster Stakes second Soul Search. The second dam, Solar Colony (by Pleasant Colony), won twice at 3 yrs and is a sister to the US Grade 1 winner Pleasant Stage and to the US Graded stakes winners Colonial Play (herself dam of the dual Grade 1 winner Marsh Play) and Stage Colony. *"She lacks a bit of size so she ought to make a 2-y-o because she's very much a 2-y-o type. She has that Invincible Spirit spark in her. I wouldn't say she's lightning, she lacks a bit of scope but she's a good actioned filly".*

1453. UNNAMED ★★★
b.c. Bernardini – Royal Tigress (Storm Cat).
January 31. Second foal. $50,000Y. Keeneland September. Blandford Bloodstock. The dam, winner of the listed Irish 1,000 Guineas Trial, is a half-sister to the Group 3 Norfolk Stakes winner Warm Heart and the 2-y-o listed 6f winner Miguel Cervantes. The second dam, Warm Mood (by Alydar), won 4 races at up to 9f in the USA and is a half-sister to a stakes winner in Japan. *"A really strong horse that we bought in America. I like the stallion and he's done well in Britain. This colt is big and*

raw and there's lots of him but he'll step up quite considerably. Not one that's going to be particularly early, but he'll be a seven furlong/mile horse by the summer".

1454. UNNAMED ★★★
gr.c. Verglas – Sahara Lady (Lomitas).
January 19. First foal. 35,000Y. Tattersalls October Book 2. David Simcock. The dam, a minor French 10f (including at 2 yrs) and 12f winner, is a half-sister to the winner and dual Group 2 placed Darley Sun. The second dam, Sagamartha (by Rainbow Quest), a minor French 3-y-o winner, is a half-sister to 4 winners including the Group 2 Lowther Stakes and Group 2 Queen Mary Stakes winner Flashy Wings. *"A likeable horse, he's closely related to Darley Sun and was bought with getting a trip in mind, but surprisingly he shows a little bit of speed. A very natural horse, a lot of Verglas horses need cut in the ground and I imagine he'll be the same. I like everything he's done and he has a good attitude".*

1455. UNNAMED ★★★
b.f. Green Desert – Soviet Terms (Soviet Star).
February 15. Second foal. 27,000Y. Tattersalls October Book 1. David Simcock. Half-sister to the fair dual 6f winner Pirate's Song (by Bahamian Bounty). The dam ran twice unplaced and is a half-sister to 2 winners. The second dam, Sharp Terms (by Kris), is an unraced half-sister to 8 winners including the Group 2 winners First Charter and Anton Chekhov and the Group 1 Italian Derby second Private Terms. *"A six furlong filly, she's showing plenty and she'll be racing in May. My fillies seem to be far more forward than my colts and you shouldn't leave this one out of the book".*

TOMMY STACK

1456. CRAZYLITTLETHING (IRE) ★★
b.f. Oratorio – Feather Bride (Groom Dancer).
April 16. Eleventh living foal. Tattersalls Ireland. €27,000Y. James Stack. Half-sister to the listed 7f King Charles II Stakes and subsequent US Grade 3 winner Millennium Dragon (by Mark Of Esteem), the fair 10.2f winner Bless The Bride (by Darshaan), the minor Italian 3-y-o winner of 3 races Enduring Freedom (by In The Wings) and a winner in Greece by Bluebird. The dam, a minor 10.5f winner at 3 yrs in France, is a half-sister to 5 winners. The second dam, Bubbling Danseuse (by Arctic Tern), won once and was second in the Group 3 1m Prix de Sandringham and is a half-sister to 6 winners. *"She's not over-big and I'd say she'd want fastish ground and six/seven furlongs. She'll be running shortly and she goes OK".*

1457. HESTIAN (IRE) ★★★
b.c. Kodiac – Tides (Bahamian Bounty).
January 26. Third foal. Doncaster Premier. £46,000Y. Cormac McCormack. Half-brother to Foxtrot Golf (by Diamond Green), unplaced in one start at 2 yrs in 2010. The dam is an unplaced half-sister to 5 winners including the listed winner Amazing Bay. The second dam, Petriece (by Mummy's Pet), won at 3 yrs and is a half-sister to 5 winners including the dam of the Group 1 winning sprinters Lochsong and Lochangel. *"A good-moving, good-bodied colt, he should be racing in May. His pedigree suggests he should be speedy and he looks a proper 2-y-o type".*

1458. MAKALALI ★★★
b.c. Kodiac – Hawattef (Mujtahid).
February 26. Seventh foal. Doncaster Premier. £35,000Y. Cormac McCormack. Half-brother to 3 winners in Italy (two of them at 2 yrs) by Danetime, Fath and Chevalier. The dam is an unraced half-sister to 2 minor winners. The second dam, Madary (by Green Desert), won twice at 3 yrs and is a half-sister to 6 winners and to the unraced Dievotchka (the dam of three Group 2 winners). *"A good-moving sort, he looks like he'll want fastish ground and he's more of a seven furlong type, so we'll be ready to run him when those races start".*

1459. MOLDOWNEY ★★★★
ch.c. Dalakhani – Danehill's Dream (Danehill).
March 14. Third foal. 100,000Y. Tattersalls October Book 1. C McCormack. Half-brother to Viking Storm (by Hurricane Run), unplaced in two starts at 2 yrs in 2010. The dam is an unraced sister to the 2-y-o winner and Group 1 Criterium de Saint-Cloud second Summerland and a half-sister to 2 minor winners. The second dam, Summerosa (by Woodman), a fair

3-y-o 8.5f winner, is a half-sister to 4 winners including the Group 1 Racing Post Trophy second Zind and to the unraced dam of the Derby winner Dr Devious. "He looks quite nice, he's a good-moving horse and one we'll probably set off in June over seven furlongs and then a mile. A grand colt with plenty of size and scope, he should progress as time goes on".

1460. NERO EMPEROR (IRE) ★★★★
b.c. Holy Roman Emperor – Blue Iris (Petong).
April 5. Tenth foal. Goffs Orby. €50,000Y. De Burgh Equine. Half-brother to the dual listed 5f winner (including at 2 yrs) Swiss Lake (by Indian Ridge), to the 5f (including at 2 yrs) and 6f winner and listed-placed Dubai Princess (by Dubai Destination) and the fairly useful 6f and 7f winner of 5 races Hajoum (by Exceed And Excel). The dam, a useful winner of 5 races over 5f and 6f including the Weatherbys Super Sprint and the Redcar Two-Year-Old Trophy, is a half-sister to 9 winners including the quite useful triple 6f winner Abbajabba. The second dam, Bo' Babbity (by Strong Gale), a fair 2-y-o 5f winner, is a half-sister to 6 winners including the high-class Group 3 5f King George Stakes winner Anita's Prince. "He looks to be quite forward and sharp – a real five/six furlong horse and he should be out shortly. He'll do most of his running as a 2-y-o because he looks just as his pedigree suggests he should do. One of our sharpest, if we do have a Royal Ascot 2-y-o he might be the one".

1461. PENNISTON LINE (IRE) ★★★
b.c. Holy Roman Emperor – Willowbridge (Entrepreneur).
May 13. Sixth foal. Goffs Orby. €28,000Y. C McCormack. Closely related to the quite useful triple 1m winner Willow Dancer (by Danehill Dancer) and to the fairly useful 2-y-o 6f winner Aerodynamic (by Oratorio). The dam is an unraced half-sister to 6 winners including the Breeders Cup Turf winner Northern Spur and the Doncaster Cup winners Great Marquess and Kneller. The second dam, Fruition (by Rheingold), was second in the 12f Lupe Stakes and is a half-sister to 9 winners including the top-class broodmare Flame of Tara (the dam of Salsabil

and Marju). "A typical 2-y-o and a typical Holy Roman Emperor, I'd say he's going to want six or seven furlongs this year".

1462. STRADATER (IRE) ★★★★
b.c. Catcher In The Rye – Starring Role (Glenstal).
May 5. Twelfth foal. Half-brother to the Irish 2-y-o 1m and subsequent US stakes winner Lightning Hit (by Orpen), to the French 1m and 11f winner and Group 3 9f Prix Daphnis third Blasket Island (by Kenmare), the fairly useful Irish 5f to 7f winner of 6 races Baggio (by Foxhound), the fair dual 9f winner Stagecoach Jade (by Peintre Celebre), the Irish 2-y-o 7f winner Globe Theatre (by Tirol) and the minor French 2-y-o winner Paymaker (by Spectrum). The dam is an unraced half-sister to 5 winners including the Group 3 5f King George Stakes winner Title Roll and the Irish listed sprint winner Northern Express. The second dam, Tough Lady (by Bay Express), was a fairly useful 2-y-o 6f winner and a half-sister to 5 winners. "Quite a big, good-looking horse, he's a good walker and a good mover. One for the middle of the summer onwards, he's from a family we've been lucky with".

1463. VAN ROONEY (IRE) ★★★
ch.c. Van Nistelrooy – Royal Shyness (Royal Academy).
April 11. Sixth foal. 52,000Y. Tattersalls October Book 1. De Burgh Equine. Half-brother to the useful 7f and 1m winner and listed-placed Commander Cave and to the fair 7f to 10f winner Shy Glance (by Red Ransom). The dam, a useful 2-y-o 6f winner, was third in the Group 1 6f Cheveley Park Stakes and subsequently won a listed stakes race in the USA. She is a half-sister to 8 winners including the useful 2-y-o 6f winner Missel. The second dam, Miss Demure (by Shy Groom), won the Group 2 6f Lowther Stakes. "A big, good-looking horse and a good walker, he's starting to thrive and come together now. He should definitely pay his way this year and hopefully he'll be horse that'll be up there around June time".

1464. VEGAS ROCKS (IRE) ★★★
b.c. Elusive City – Chehalis Sunset
(Danehill Dancer).
February 12. First foal. 45,000Y. Tattersalls October Book 2. Not sold. The dam is an unraced half-sister to 5 winners including the US Grade 2 9f Honeymoon Handicap winner and Grade 1 placed Country Garden. The second dam, Totham (by Shernazar), a quite useful 12f winner, is a half-sister to 6 winners. *"A good-bodied colt, he's strong and probably a six/seven furlong 2-y-o. He goes OK, he'll be running in May and he should definitely pay his way as a 2-y-o".*

1465. VERY SOCIAL (IRE) ★★★
ch.f. Danehill Dancer – Pillars Of Society
(Caerleon).
May 11. Sixth foal. €17,000Y. Goffs Orby. C McCormack. Sister to the fair 2010 Irish 7f placed 2-y-o Poltava and to the French 2-y-o and subsequent US Grade 3 9f Regret Stakes winner Good Mood. The dam an Irish 10f winner, was Group 3 placed and is a half-sister to 5 winners. The second dam, Grise Mine (by Crystal Palace), won the Group 1 10f Prix Saint-Alary and the Group 3 Prix Vanteaux and is a half-sister to 3 winners including the triple US Grade 1 winner Kostroma. *"She's not over-big but she's very strong and she'll be running shortly although I think she'll be better over six or seven furlongs as the year goes on. She was a May foal, but she doesn't look it".*

1466. UNNAMED ★★★
b.c. Oratorio – Bluebell Wood (Bluebird).
April 22. Sixth foal. Doncaster Premier. £30,000Y. Cormac McCormack. Closely related to the fair 2-y-o 7f winner Dancing Marabout and to the Group 1 Moyglare Stud Stakes third Beyond Our Reach (both by Danehill Dancer). The dam, a quite useful triple 10f winner, is a half-sister to 5 winners including the useful 2-y-o 5.7f and 6f winner and Group 3 7f Criterion Stakes third Lady Lindsay. The second dam, Jungle Jezebel (by Thatching), a very useful 2-y-o 7f winner, was listed-placed twice. *"He looks like a horse that wants fast ground and he should be racing in May. He'll make a 2-y-o because he's not over-big, he's sharp looking and I'd say he probably needs six or seven furlongs".*

1467. UNNAMED ★★★
b.c. Windsor Knot – Exponent (Exbourne).
March 26. Seventh living foal. Goffs Orby. €32,000Y. C McCormack. Half-brother to the smart Irish dual listed 2-y-o 5f winner and Group 2 Railway Stakes second Drayton (by Danetime), to the quite useful 5f (at 2 yrs) and 6f winner Exponential (by Namid), the fair 2-y-o 5f winner Cian Rooney (by Camacho) and a winner over jumps by Desert King. The dam is an unraced half-sister to 6 minor winners here and abroad. The second dam, Water Angel (by Halo), is an unraced half-sister to 2 winners. *"We had the half-brother Drayton and this is a bigger colt that seems to move well but he won't be as forward. He'll be out by the middle of the season".*

1468. UNNAMED ★★★
b.c. Royal Applause – Fabine
(Danehill Dancer).
February 1. First foal. Doncaster Premier. £36,000Y. John O'Byrne. The dam won at 3 yrs and is a half-sister to 3 winners including the very useful 2-y-o Group 2 5.5f Prix Robert Papin winner Never A Doubt. The second dam, Waypoint (Cadeaux Genereux), a fairly useful 6f and 7f winner, is a half-sister to the Group 2 Diadem Stakes winner and high-class sire Acclamation. *"He looks a typical 2-y-o type and his pedigree suggests he should be quite quick. If all goes according to plan he should be running shortly and he'll be a five/six furlong type".*

1469. UNNAMED ★★★
b.c. Galileo – In My Life (Rainbow Quest).
April 4. Third foal. 150,000Y. Tattersalls October Book 1. Blandford Bloodstock. Closely related to the modest 2010 7f fourth placed 2-y-o Jeu De Vivre (by Montjeu) and half-brother to the very useful 9f winner and listed-placed Fighter Boy (by Rock Of Gibraltar). The dam, placed once at 3 yrs in Japan, is a sister to the 2-y-o Group 1 10f Criterium de Saint-Cloud winner Special Quest and a half-sister to 9 winners including the 2-y-o Group 2 7f Criterium de Maisons-Laffitte winner Moiava. The second dam, Mona Stella (by Nureyev), a smart winner of the Group 2 9.2f Prix de l'Opera, is closely related to the French 1,000 Guineas and Prix Vermeille

winner Dancing Maid. *"A horse that's done well, he's maturing all the time and he wouldn't be your typical Galileo, he's not too backward and with a bit of luck he'll be running in the next few weeks. A good-moving horse that should progress as the year goes on, he should be suited by seven furlongs to start with".*

1470. UNNAMED ★★★
b.f. *Holy Roman Emperor – Non Dimenticar Me (Don't Forget Me).*
May 2. Eleventh foal. 35,000Y. Tattersalls October Book 2. Fozzy Stack. Closely related to the useful 1m (including at 2 yrs) and listed 6f winner and Irish 1,000 Guineas second Dimenticata (by Danetime) and half-sister to the useful listed 6f winner Master Fay, the fair 2-y-o 5f winner Louvolite (both by Fayruz), the useful 7f winner and listed-placed Zarin (by Inzar), the quite useful triple 6f winner Didn't We and the German winner at up to 11f Sambucan Daze (both by Mujadil). The dam, a modest 3-y-o 5f winner, stayed 7f and is a half-sister to 7 winners. The second dam, Amboselli (by Raga Navarro), was a fair 5f placed 2-y-o and a half-sister to 9 winners. *"She's a filly that's really started to thrive in the last few weeks, she might take a bit more time but she seems to be a good mover. One to start in May or June and she seems to have more scope than most of them by the sire".*

1471. UNNAMED ★★★★
b.f. *Royal Applause – Opopmil (Pips Pride).*
February 13. Sixth living foal. Doncaster Premier. £26,000Y. John O'Byrne. Half-sister to the quite useful dual 10f winner Poppy Seed, to the fair triple 5f winner (including at 2 yrs) Don't Tell Sue, the fair dual 6f winner Orange Pip (all by Bold Edge) and the quite useful 3-y-o 6f winner Mission Man (by Revoque). The dam was placed twice at 2 yrs and is a sister to the Group 1 6f Haydock Park Sprint Cup winner Pipalong and a half-sister to 9 winners including the 2-y-o 6f listed winner Out Of Africa. The second dam, Limpopo (by Green Desert), a poor 5f placed 2-y-o, is a half-sister to 8 winners here and abroad. *"A very strong filly, she looks like one that should pay her way as a 2-y-o. A good mover and a good walker, she seems to have all the credentials to make a racehorse. Hopefully one of our nicer 2-y-o's".*

SIR MICHAEL STOUTE

1472. ALBANKA (USA)
ch.f. *Giant's Causeway – Alidiva (Chief Singer).*
April 9. Fourteenth foal. $350,000Y. Keeneland September. Charlie Gordon-Watson. Sister to the quite useful dual 1m and subsequent US Grade 2 winner Oonagh Maccool and half-sister to the high-class Group 1 1m Sussex Stakes winner Ali Royal, the 1,000 Guineas winner Sleepytime (both by Royal Academy), the Group 1 12f Europa Preis and Group 1 10f Premio Roma winner Taipan (by Last Tycoon), the useful 10f winner Curtain Time (by Sadler's Wells), the minor French 4-y-o winner Dear Girl and the minor US winner Anytime (both by Fairy King). The dam, a useful listed winner of 3 races from 6f to 1m, is a half-sister to the dual Group1 winner Croco Rouge. The second dam, Alligatrix (by Alleged), a very useful 2-y-o 7f winner, was third in the Hoover Fillies Mile.

1473. CANTAL
ch.f. *Pivotal – Canda (Storm Cat).*
April 7. Third foal. Half-sister to the 2-y-o Group 3 7f winner Horris Hill Stakes winner and Group 1 St James's Palace Stakes fourth Evasive (by Elusive Quality). The dam is an unraced half-sister to 3 winners including the 2-y-o Group 3 5.5f Prix d'Arenburg winner Moon Driver and the US winner and Grade 2 Californian Stakes second Mojave Moon. The second dam, East Of The Moon (by Private Account), was a high-class winner of the French 1,000 Guineas, the Prix de Diane and the Prix Jacques le Marois and is a half-sister to the top class miler and sire Kingmambo and to the smart Miesque's Son.

1474. DEBATING SOCIETY (IRE)
b.c. *Invincible Spirit – Drama Class (Caerleon).*
April 1. Half-brother to the smart 1m (at 2 yrs) and Group 2 10f Blandford Stakes winner Eleanora Duse (by Azamour), to the listed 10f winner and Group 1 12f Irish Oaks second Scottish Stage (by Selkirk), the fairly useful 10f winner and subsequent Australian Group 3 placed Voice Coach (by Alhaarth) and the quite useful 10f winner Namibian Orator (by Cape Cross). The dam, a useful 10.2f winner, is a half-sister to the Group 2 10.3f winner Stage Gift. The second dam, Stage Struck (by

Sadler's Wells), a quite useful 12f winner, is a sister to the high-class Group 1 7f Dewhurst Stakes winner (in a dead-heat) Prince of Dance and to the useful middle-distance winners Ballet Prince and Golden Ball.

1475. DUKE OF FIRENZE ♠
ch.c. Pivotal – Nannina (Medicean).
February 22. First foal. The dam, winner of the Group 1 Fillies' Mile and the Group 1 1m Coronation Stakes, is a half-sister to numerous winners. The second dam, Hill Hopper (by Danehill), a useful winner of 4 races including the Group 3 7f Criterion Stakes, is a half-sister to 4 winners including the Australian Grade 1 West End Adelaide Cup winner Water Boatman.

1476. ELITE
b.f. Invincible Spirit – Garah (Ajdal).
February 23. Half-sister to the Group 1 9f Prix Jean Prat winner Olden Times (by Darshaan), to the useful 1m (at 2 yrs) and listed 6f winner and Group 1 Cheveley Park Stakes third Festoso (by Diesis), the quite useful 10f and 12f winner And Again (by In The Wings), the modest 12f winner All Good Things (by Marju) and the minor US 6f winner Idma (by Midyan). The dam, was a very useful winner of 4 races over 6f, was second in the Group 3 5f Duke Of York Stakes and is a half-sister to 3 winners. The second dam, Abha (by Thatching), a very smart 5f and 6f winner of 4 races, was fourth in the Group 1 5f Kings Stand Stakes and is a half-sister to the listed Princess Margaret Stakes winner Sarissa.

1477. ELYSIAN
b.f. Galileo – Echelon (Danehill).
February 4. First foal. The dam won the Group 1 1m Matron Stakes, the Group 2 Celebration Mile and four Group 3 events and is a half-sister to the dual Group 2 1m Celebration Mile winner Chic . The second dam, Exclusive (Polar Falcon) winner of the Group 1 1m Coronation Stakes, is a half-sister to the 2,000 Guineas winner and Derby fourth Entrepreneur, the smart Cheshire Oaks winner and Epsom Oaks second Dance a Dream, the very useful middle-distance listed winner Sadler's Image and the useful French 2-y-o listed 7f winner Irish Order.

1478. GLITTERBALL (IRE)
b.f. Smart Strike – Crystal Music (Nureyev).
April 5. Sixth foal. 260,000Y. Tattersalls October Book 1. Cheveley Park Stud. Half-sister to the fairly useful 201 2-y-o dual 7f winner Treasury Devil (by Bernardini) and to the fairly useful 2-y-o 6f winner and listed-placed Crystany (by Green Desert). The dam, a smart winner of the Group 1 Fillies' Mile at 2 yrs, is closely related to the Group 3 12f John Porter Stakes winner Dubai Success and the smart 7f (at 2 yrs) and 10f winner Tchaikovsky and a half-sister to the Group 3 1m May Hill Stakes winner Solar Crystal and the Group 3 12f Lancashire Oaks winner State Crystal. The second dam, Crystal Spray (by Beldale Flutter), a minor Irish 4-y-o 14f winner, is a half-sister to 8 winners including the Group 3 Scottish Classic winner Crystal Hearted.

1479. HONOUR
b.f. Dansili – Virtuous (Exit To Nowhere).
May 2. Half-sister to the Group 1 1m Lockinge Stakes and dual listed winner Virtual, to the quite useful 10f winner Virtuosity (both by Pivotal), the very smart 2-y-o Group 2 6f Coventry Stakes winner and Group 1 6f Middle Park Stakes third Iceman (by Polar Falcon), the quite useful 10f winner Peace (by Sadler's Wells) and the fair 2-y-o 6f winner Liberty (by Singspiel). The dam, a fairly useful 2-y-o 1m winner, was third in the listed 11.5f Oaks Trial and is a sister to one winner. The second dam, Exclusive Virtue (by Shadeed), a fairly useful 2-y-o 7f winner, stayed 12f and is a half-sister to 8 winners including the 2,000 Guineas winner and Derby fourth Entrepreneur and the Coronation Stakes winner Exclusive. (Cheveley Park Stud).

1480. KING'S GUEST (IRE)
b.f. King's Best – Temple Street (Machiavellian).
March 3. Fourth foal. 80,000Y. Tattersalls October Book 1. Rabbah Bloodstock. Half-sister to the 2-y-o Group 2 5f Queen Mary Stakes winner Langs Lash (by Noverre), to the quite useful 1m winner Bougainvilia (by Bahamian Bounty) and a winner in Greece by Danehill Dancer. The dam is an unraced half-sister to 4 winners and to the placed dam of the French 1,000 Guineas winner Elusive Wave. The second dam, Echoes (by Niniski), won the

Group 3 Prix Corrida and is a half-sister to 5 winners.

1481. LADYSHIP
b.f. Oasis Dream – Peeress (Pivotal).
April 23. First foal. The dam, a very smart winner of 7 races including the Group 1 1m Lockinge Stakes and the Group 1 1m Sun Chariot Stakes, is a half-sister to 2 winners. The second dam, Noble One (by Primo Dominie), a useful dual 5f winner, is a full or half-sister to 5 winners.

1482. LASHYN (USA)
ch.f. Mr Greeley – Sleepytime
(Royal Academy).
April 16. Ninth foal. $625,000Y. Keeneland September. Charlie Gordon-Watson. Half-sister to the Group 3 Winter Derby winner of 9 races Gentleman's Deal, to the Irish 2-y-o 7f winner and Group 3 Gallinule Stakes second Spanish Harlem (both by Danehill) and the minor US stakes winner Dame Ellen (by Elusive Quality). The dam, a very smart filly and winner of the 1,000 Guineas and third in the Coronation Stakes and the Fillies' Mile, is a sister to the Group 1 1m Sussex Stakes winner Ali Royal and a half-sister to the dual Group 1 winner Taipan and the US Grade 2 winner Oonagh Maccool. The second dam, Alidiva (by Chief Singer), a useful winner of 3 races from 6f to 1m including a listed event, is a half-sister to 6 winners including the dual French Group 1 winner Croco Rouge.

1483. MARTIN CHUZZLEWIT (IRE)
ch.c. Galileo – Alta Anna (Anabaa).
March 17. First foal. €420,000Y. Arqana Deauville August. Sir Robert Ogden. The dam is an unraced half-sister to the Group 3 Prix Penelope winner Abbatiale (herself dam of the listed winner Bewitched) and to the listed winner Aubergade. The second dam, Anna Edes (by Fabulous Dancer), is a placed half-sister to 7 winners.

1484. MAWASEM
b.c. Street Cry – Saree (Barathea).
February 4. Third foal. 375,000Y. Tattersalls October Book 1. Shadwell Estate Co. Half-brother to the quite useful 2-y-o 7f winner North East Corner (by Giant's Causeway). The dam, a fairly useful 2-y-o 7f winner, subsequently won once at 3 yrs in the USA and was Grade 3 placed in Canada and is a sister to the 2-y-o Group 1 6f Cheveley Park Stakes winner Magical Romance and a half-sister to the high-class 1m (at 2 yrs), Oaks, Irish Oaks And Yorkshire Oaks winner Alexandrova. The second dam, Shouk (by Shirley Heights), a quite useful 10.5f winner, is closely related to the listed winner and Group 3 Park Hill Stakes third Puce (herself dam of the Group 2 Lancashire Oaks winner Pongee) and a half-sister to 9 winners.

1485. MINOAN DANCER (IRE)
b.f. Galileo – Grecian Dancer (Dansili).
March 15. First foal. Goffs Orby. €240,000Y. Cheveley Park Stud. The dam, a very useful Irish Group 3 Ridgewood Pearl Stakes winner, is a half-sister to 5 winners including the 2-y-o Group 2 5f Flying Childers Stakes and Group 3 5f Molecomb Stakes winner Wunders Dream. The second dam, Pizzicato (by Statoblest), a modest 5f and 5.3f winner at 3 yrs, is a half-sister to 5 winners including the high-class Hong Kong horses Mensa and Firebolt.

1486. MODERN TUTOR
b.c. Selkirk – Magical Romance (Barathea).
February 9. Second foal. Half-brother to the 2010 7f placed 2-y-o Dean Swift (by Dansili). The dam, a 2-y-o Group 1 6f Cheveley Park Stakes winner, is a sister to the fairly useful 2-y-o 7f winner and subsequent Canadian Grade 3 placed Saree and closely related to the Oaks, Irish Oaks and Yorkshire Oaks winner Alexandrova and the smart listed 2-y-o 1m winner and Group 2 1m Beresford Stakes third Masterofthehorse. The second dam, Shouk (by Shirley Heights), a quite useful 10.5f winner, is closely related to the listed winner and Group 3 Park Hill Stakes third Puce and a half-sister to 6 winners.

1487. MR MAYNARD
ch.c. Notnowcato – Crystal Cavern
(Be My Guest).
January 21. Half-brother to the useful 2-y-o listed 7f Radley Stakes winner and Group 3 Fred Darling Stakes second Crystal Star, to the fair 2-y-o 1m winner True Dream (both by Mark Of Esteem), the fairly useful 1m and 12f

winner The Fonz (by Oasis Dream), the Irish 4-y-o 7f to 8.5f winner of 4 races Christavelli (by Machiavellian), the fair 12f and hurdles winner E Major (by Singspiel) and the French 10f winner Vracca (by Vettori). The dam, a fairly useful 2-y-o 7f winner here and subsequently a dual winner in Canada, is a half-sister to 6 winners including the French 1,000 Guineas winner Rose Gypsy. The second dam, Krisalya (by Kris), a fairly useful 10.4f winner, is a half-sister to 12 winners including the high-class 9.3f Prix d'Ispahan winner Sasuru and the high-class Challenge Stakes and Jersey Stakes winner Sally Rous.

1488. OPINION ♠
b.c. Oasis Dream – Kiltubber (Sadler's Wells).
March 21. Fifth foal. 210,000Y. Tattersalls October Book 1. John Warren. Half-brother to the 2010 Irish 2-y-o 6f winner Anam Allta (by Invincible Spirit), to the fairly useful 10f winner Fox Hunt (by Dubawi), the fair 12f winner Spinning Well (by Pivotal) and a winner over hurdles by Daylami. The dam, an Italian listed 12f winner, is a half-sister to 3 winners. The second dam, Priory Belle (by Priolo), winner of the 2-y-o Group 1 7f Moyglare Stud Stakes, is a half-sister to 7 winners including the Group 1 Premio Lydia Tesio winner Eva's Request and the Irish Group 3 7f Concorde Stakes winner Wild Bluebell. (Highclere Thoroughbreds).

1489. PISTOL ♠
b.c. High Chaparral – Alinea (Kingmambo).
April 28. Seventh living foal. 110,000Y. Tattersalls October Book 2. John Warren. Half-brother to 2 minor winners in France and Italy by Inchinor and Priolo. The dam is an unraced half-sister to 7 winners including the Group/Grade 2 winners El Angelo, Miswaki Tern and Via Borghese. The second dam, Angela Serra (by Arctic Tern), won the Group 2 12f Premio Legnano. (Highclere Thoroughbreds).

1490. PRIME RUN
b.f. Dansili – Silca-Cisa (Hallgate).
February 28. Tenth foal. 140,000Y. Tattersalls October Book 1. Charlie Gordon-Watson. Half-sister to the smart 2-y-o Group 1 6f Prix Morny winner Silca's Sister, to the smart Group 2 6f Mill Reef Stakes and German Group 2 winner and Group 1 placed Golden Silca (both by Inchinor), the smart 2-y-o 6f winner and dual Group 1 placed Silca Chiave (by Pivotal), the useful sprint winner of 14 races (including at 2 yrs) Green Manalishi (by Green Desert), the quite useful 2-y-o dual 6f winner Silca Legend (by Efisio), the quite useful 6.8f winner King Silca (by Emarati) and the Italian 2-y-o 5f winner Muso Corto (by Reprimand). The dam, a fairly useful dual 5f winner, was listed placed over 5f at 4 yrs and is a half-sister to the Group 3 placed sprint winner Azizzi. The second dam, Princess Silca-Key (by Grundy), was a modest 7f winner and a half-sister to 3 winners.

1491. PROXIMITY
b.f. Nayef – Contiguous (Danzig).
March 5. Sister to the very smart 7f (at 2 yrs) and Group 3 1m winner Confront and half-sister to the fairly useful 2010 2-y-o 7f winner Tuscania and the French 3-y-o listed-placed 10f winner Nearby (both by King's Best). The dam is an unraced three-parts sister to Reams of Verse, winner of the Oaks and the Group 1 Fillies Mile and a half-sister to the Group 1 10f Coral Eclipse Stakes and Group 1 10f Phoenix Champion Stakes winner Elmaamul. The second dam, Modena (by Roberto), is an unraced half-sister to the smart 2-y-o 7f winner and Queen Elizabeth II Stakes third Zaizafon – herself dam of Zafonic. (Khalid Abdulla).

1492. SAMAAH (IRE)
br.f. Cape Cross – Native Force (Indian Ridge).
February 24. Fifth foal. 140,000Y. Tattersalls October Book 1. Shadwell Estate Co. Half-sister to the modest 2010 2-y-o 6f winner Native Picture (by Kodiac), to the Group 1 Golden Jubilee Stakes and Group 1 Nunthorpe Stakes winner Kingsgate Native (by Mujadil), the quite useful 2-y-o 5f winner Vanishing Grey (by Verglas) and the 7f seller winner Assumption (by Beckett). The dam, a quite useful 1m winner, is a half-sister to 2 winners. The second dam, La Pellegrina (by Be My Guest), is a placed half-sister to 5 winners including the 1,000 Guineas winner Las Meninas.

1493. SAMUEL PICKWICK (IRE)
b.c. Holy Roman Emperor – Save The Table (Tale Of The Cat).
March 27. Second foal. Goffs Orby. €220,000Y. Sir Robert Ogden. Brother to the fair 2010 2-y-o 5f and 6f winner Jollywood. The dam was unplaced at 2 yrs in the USA and is a half-sister to 5 winners including the listed Thirsk Classic Trial winner Royal Dignitary. The second dam, Star Actress (by Star de Naskra), is an unplaced half-sister to 5 winners including the US Grade 1 winner Dreamy Mimi.

1494. STAR RATING (IRE)
b.f. Dansili – Islington (Sadler's Wells).
January 8. Third foal. The dam was a high-class winner of 6 races including the Group 1 Yorkshire Oaks (twice), the Grade 1 Filly and Mare Turf and the Group 1 Nassau Stakes. She is a half-sister to the smart stayer Election Day, the smart 10f performer Greek Dance and the useful 7f and 1m winner Desert Beauty. The second dam, Hellenic (by Darshaan), won the Yorkshire Oaks and the Ribblesdale Stakes and is a half-sister to 8 winners.

1495. STEPTURN
b.c. Invincible Spirit – Gay Gallanta (Woodman).
March 28. Ninth foal. Closely related to the smart 2-y-o Group 2 6f Mill Reef Stakes winner Byron, to the fairly useful 7f to 9f winner of 11 races Gallantry, the quite useful 6f winner Light Hearted (all by Green Desert) and the fairly useful 7f and 1m winner Resort (by Oasis Dream) and half-brother to the useful 1m and 10.3f winner Gallant Hero, the fairly useful 9f winner Gallant (both by Rainbow Quest), the useful 10.4f listed-placed maiden Gay Heroine (by Caerleon) and the quite useful 2-y-o 6f winner Gallivant (by Danehill). The dam, a very smart winner of the Group 1 6f Cheveley Park Stakes and the Group 3 5f Queen Mary Stakes, was second in the 1m Falmouth Stakes and is a half-sister to the smart Group 2 10f Gallinule Stakes winner Sportsworld. The second dam, Gallanta (by Nureyev), a useful winner of 3 races from 5.5f to 1m including the Prix de Coburg, was second in the Group 1 Prix Morny and is a half-sister to the top-class French middle-distance colt Gay Mecene and to the dam of Wolfhound. (Cheveley Park Stud).

1496. ULTRASONIC (USA)
b.f Mizzen Mast – Quickfire (Dubai Millennium).
March 7. Second foal. The dam, a useful 2-y-o 7f winner, was second in the Group 3 Musidora Stakes and the Group 3 7f Oak Tree Stakes and is a half-sister to 2 winners. The second dam, Daring Miss (by Sadler's Wells), won 4 races in France including the Group 2 12f Grand Prix de Chantilly and is a half-sister to several winners including the Group 3 12f Prix de Royaumont winner Apogee. (Khalid Abdulla).

1497. UPRISE
b.c. Pivotal – Soar (Danzero).
March 25. Third foal. Brother to the fair 2010 1m fourth placed 2-y-o Levitate and half-brother to the quite useful 2-y-o 6f winner Racy (by Medicean). The dam, winner of the Group 2 6f Lowther Stakes and the Group 3 Princess Margaret Stakes at 2 yrs, is a half-sister to numerous winners including the very smart 6f and 7f winner of 7 races Feet So Fast. The second dam, Splice (by Sharpo), a smart winner of the listed 6f Abernant Stakes, is a full or half-sister to several winners including the fairly useful 1m winner and subsequent Italian winner Alfujairah. (Cheveley Park Stud).

1498. WILD SILK
b.f. Dansili – So Silk (Rainbow Quest).
March 3. First foal. 165,000Y. Tattersalls October Book 1. Cheveley Park Stud. The dam is an unraced half-sister to 2 winners including the 2-y-o Group 1 Racing Post Trophy winner Ibn Khaldun. The second dam, Gossamer (by Sadler's Wells), won the Group 1 Fillies' Mile and the Group 1 Irish 1,000 Guineas and is a sister to the Breeders Cup Mile and Irish 2,000 Guineas winner Barathea and a half-sister to the Group 3 winners Zabar and Free At Last (herself dam of the US multiple Grade 2 winner Coretta).

1499. ZUMBI (IRE)
b.c. Dubawi – Star Studded (Cadeaux Genereux).
February 28. Fourth foal. 140,000foal. Tattersalls December. London Thoroughbred Services. Half-brother to the useful 1m winner and listed-placed Say No Now (by Refuse To

Bend). The dam is an unraced sister to the Group 2 5f Flying Childers Stakes and Group 3 5f King George V Stakes winner Land Of Dreams (herself the dam of a listed winner) and a half-sister to 4 winners. The second dam, Sahara Star (by Green Desert), won the Group 3 5f Molecomb Stakes, was third in the Lowther Stakes and is a half-sister to 6 winners.

1500. UNNAMED
ch.f. Pivotal – Our Queen Of Kings (Arazi).
March 15. Eighth foal. 240,000Y. Tattersalls October Book 1. Mr A O Nerses. Half-sister to the fair 2009 2-y-o 6f winner Our Dream Queen (by Oasis Dream), to the Group 3 Brownstown Stakes winner and Group 2 Cherry Hinton Stakes third Spinning Queen (by Spinning World), the useful 10f and 12f winner and 2-y-o 7f listed-placed Shannon Springs (by Darshaan), the fairly useful dual 7f winner Amber Queen (by Cadeaux Genereux) the quite useful 2-y-o 5f , 7f and 10f winner Changing The Guard (by King's Best) and the Italian winner of 4 races Jekill (by Royal Academy). The dam is an unraced half-sister to 7 winners including the Grade 1 9f Hollywood Derby winner Labeeb, the Grade 2 Arlington Handicap winner Fanmore and the Group 2 9f Budweiser International Stakes winner Alrassam. The second dam, Lady Blackfoot (Prince Tenderfoot), a very useful Irish listed winning sprinter, is a half-sister to 3 winners.

1501. UNNAMED
b.f. King's Best – Sadima (Sadler's Wells).
March 22. Sister to the Group 1 1m Lockinge Stakes and triple Group 3 winner Creachadoir and half-sister to the high-class Group 1 12f Grand Prix de Saint-Cloud and Group 1 12f Preis von Europa winner Youmzain (by Sinndar), to the Irish Group 3 9.5f winner Shreyas and the Irish 2-y-o 1m winner Sagacious (both by Dalakhani). The dam, a fairly useful Irish 10f winner, is a half-sister to 2 winners in Chile. The second dam, Anima (by Ajdal), was placed once at 3 yrs and is a half-sister to 8 winners including the multiple Group 1 winner Pilsudski.

LINDA STUBBS

1502. FOREVERTHEOPTIMIST (IRE) ★★★
gr.g. Verglas – Hankering (Missed Flight).
April 17. Fourth foal. 14,000Y. Tattersalls October Book 2. L Stubbs Racing. The dam is an unraced half-sister to 4 winners including the US Grade 3 winner Media Mogul and the fairly useful 2-y-o dual 6f winner and listed-placed Dhekraa. The second dam, White Heat (by Last Tycoon), was placed at 2 yrs and is a half-sister to 5 winners including the dual listed winner Watching. (G & T Bloodstock). "A very nice type and a big, strong horse with plenty of ability. We'll start him off at five furlongs in April but he'll need six I should think".

1503. LATTE ★★★
b.g. Multiplex – Coffee To Go (Environment Friend).
March 21. Seventh foal. 2,000Y. Tattersalls October Book 3. L Stubbs Racing. Half-brother to the moderate 1m winner Daily Double (by Needwood Blade) and to Mr Tosi (by Wizard King), a winner of 3 races at 2 and 3 yrs in Italy. The dam is an unraced half-sister to 8 winners here and abroad. The second dam, Piney Lake (by Sassafras), is a placed half-sister to 10 winners including the Group 1 placed Beeshi and Chaumiere. (Time Partnership). "Only a cheap horse but he's nice and he shows plenty of ability. A very big, strong horse, he's well-built and a proper 2-y-o. He'll start off in April and I can see him getting further later on. He definitely wants six furlongs but he shows enough speed to win over five". TRAINERS' BARGAIN BUY

1504. TARQUIN (IRE) ★★★★
b.g. Excellent Art – Umlani (Great Commotion).
April 29. Fifth foal. 16,000Y. Tattersalls October Book 2. Not sold. Half-brother to the fairly useful 2-y-o 5f winner and Group 3 5f Molecomb Stakes third Safari Sunset (by Fayruz). The dam is an unraced half-sister to 3 minor winners. The second dam, Travel Magic (by Henbit), a quite useful 7f winner, is a half-sister to 7 winners. (Mr D Arundale). "I suppose he's the most expensive horse we've ever bought and he's developing and getting stronger all the time. He won't run until May, he wants six furlongs and he's very nice".

1505. XYZZY ★★
b.f. Royal Applause – Out Like Magic (Magic Ring).
March 28. Sixth foal. 6,000Y. Tattersalls October Book 3. R W Stubbs. Sister to the quite useful 2-y-o 6f winner Bahamian Magic and half-sister to the fair 2010 2-y-o 5f winner Ice Trooper (by Iceman), the fair 6f and 7f winner Nubar Boy (by Compton Place) and a minor winner in Greece by Vetto-. The dam, a quite useful 2-y-o 5f winner, is a half-sister to 4 winners including the listed Heron Stakes second In Like Flynn. The second dam, Thevetia (by Mummy's Pet), is a placed half-sister to 7 winners. (J P Hames). *"A small filly, she's very sharp and she'll be very early. Five furlongs is her distance and I don't see her staying further".*

TOM TATE

1506. BEYOND CONCEIT (IRE)
b.c. Galileo – Baraka (Danehill).
March 12. Fourth foal. 250,000Y. Tattersalls October Book 1. Alex Cole. The dam, a listed 11f winner, is a sister to the Japanese Grade 1 winner Fine Motion and a half-sister to 6 winners including Pilsudski (winner of the Grade 1 12f Breeders Cup Turf, Grade 1 12f Japan Cup, Group 1 10f Grosser Preis von Baden and Group 1 10f Coral-Eclipse Stakes) and the Irish 2-y-o Group 3 1m winner Glowing Ardour. The second dam, Cocotte (by Troy), a very useful 10.2f winner, was second in the Group 3 Prix de Psyche, fourth in the Group 2 10f Nassau Stakes and is a half-sister to the listed winner Gay Captain. (Mrs F H Hay).

1507. KEEP SWINGING (IRE)
b.c. Oasis Dream – Whisper To Dream (Gone West).
April 24. Fourth foal. Goffs Orby. €250,000Y. Alex Cole. Half-brother to the quite useful 10f winner Royaaty (by Singspiel). The dam won twice at 3 yrs in France and is a half-sister to 4 winners. The second dam, Hatoof (by Irish River), a high-class filly and winner of 7 races notably the 1,000 Guineas, the Champion Stakes and the Beverly D Stakes, is a half-sister to the US Grade 1 winner Irish Prize and the French listed winners Fasateen and Irsijaam. (Mrs F H Hay).

1508. KEY APPOINTMENT
b.c. Pivotal – Appointed One (Danzig).
February 21. Eighth foal. 150,000Y. Tattersalls October Book 1. Alex Cole. Half-brother to the smart 7f and 1m winner (at 2 yrs) and Group 3 10f Select Stakes second Battle Chant (by Coronado's Quest), to the fairly useful 7f winner Matoaka (by A P Indy), the quite useful 1m winner Constitute (by Gone West), the quite useful 2-y-o 1m winner Commissionaire, the fair triple 1m winner Officer (both by Medicean) and the Japanese 2-y-o winner Appointed Day (by Red Ransom). The dam, a minor US stakes winner, is a sister to 3 winners including the Group 2 1m Lockinge Stakes winner Emperor Jones and the listed 6f Sirenia Stakes winner and Group 1 Middle Park Stakes third Majlood and a half-sister to 6 winners including the Group 1 1m William Hill Futurity Stakes winner Bakharoff. The second dam, Qui Royalty (by Native Royalty), a winner of 5 races at up to 1m in the USA, was second in the Grade 3 Boiling Springs Handicap and is a half-sister to 8 winners including the US Grade 3 winner Qui Native. (Mrs F H Hay).

1509. MEAN IT (IRE)
b.c. Danehill Dancer – Lilissa (Doyoun).
January 29. Eleventh foal. Goffs Orby. €200,000Y. Alex Cole. Half-brother to the Irish and US winner of 9 races and Group 1 second Livadiya (by Shernazar), to the French 3-y-o 9f winner and Group 3 placed Liska (by Bigstone), the useful 10f and 12f winner and smart broodmare Lidakiya (by Kahyasi), the fairly useful 10f winner Lishtar (by Mtoto), to the fair 12f winner Cape Express (by Cape Cross), the modest dual 2m winner Leo McGarry (by Fantastic Light) and the modest 10f winner Foxilla (by Foxhound). The dam, a French 9f and 10.5f winner, is a half-sister to 5 winners including the Group 3 12f Prix Minerve winner Linnga. The second dam, Lisana (by Alleged), won twice at 3 yrs in France. (Mrs F H Hay).

1510. NEVER PERFECT (IRE)
b.c. Galileo – Dapprima (Shareef Dancer).
May 13. Eleventh foal. Brother to the very useful Irish 7f (at 2 yrs) and 10f winner and Group 1 Criterium de Saint-Cloud fourth Don Carlos and to the German 2-y-o 7f winner and listed-placed Dubai, closely related to

the German Group 3 9f winner Davidoff (by Montjeu) and half-brother to the German Group 2 9f winner Denaro, the German listed 11f winner and Group 3 placed Duellant (both by Dashing Blade) and three minor winners abroad by Danehill, Fasliyev and Platini. The dam, a listed winner in Germany and second in the Group 2 German 1,000 Guineas, is a half-sister to 8 winners. The second dam, Diaspora (by Sparkler), won twice and was second in the German 1,000 Guineas and is a half-sister to 7 winners. (Mrs F H Hay).

1511. PARC DE LAUNAY
ch.c. Monsieur Bond – Franglais (Lion Cavern).
April 5. Fifth foal. Doncaster Premier. £50,000Y. Tom Tate. Half-brother to the 2-y-o listed 5f Windsor Castle Stakes winner and US Grade 3 placed Flashman's Papers (by Exceed And Excel) and to the quite useful dual 6f winner Temple Of Thebes (by Bahri). The dam won 3 races from 6f to 1m at 3 and 4 yrs in Germany and is a half-sister to 4 winners including the Grade 1 E P Taylor Stakes winner Fraulein. The second dam, Francfurter (by Legend Of France), a quite useful 3-y-o dual 10f winner, was a half-sister to 7 winners. (Mrs F H Hay).

1512. PINK DELIGHT (IRE)
ch.f. Rock Of Gibraltar – Turkana Girl (Hernando).
February 28. Third foal. Doncaster Premier. £46,000Y. Tom Tate. Half-sister to the 2010 2-y-o Group 2 Prix Robert Papin winner Irish Field (by Dubawi). The dam, placed once over 7f, is a half-sister to the Group 2 Royal Lodge Stakes winner Leo and to the dual Italian listed winner Balkenhol. The second dam, Miss Penton (by Primo Dominie), was placed 3 times at up to 7f and is a half-sister to 8 winners including the very useful listed 6f Sirenia Stakes winner Art of War. (Mrs F H Hay).

1513. THANE OF CAWDOR (IRE)
b.c. Danehill Dancer – Holy Nola (Siler Deputy).
May 5. Eighth foal. 280,000Y. Tattersalls October Book 1. Alex Cole. Half-brother to the US Grade 2 and dual Grade 3 winner Preachinatthebar (by Silver Charm), to the French winner and German Group 3 placed Nolas Lolly (by Lomitas) and the French 2-y-o 1m winner and listed placed Royal Revival (by King's Best). The dam, a stakes winner of 5 races in the USA, is a sister to the triple US Grade 3 winner Bare Necessities and a half-sister to 4 winners. The second dam, Shrewd Vixen (by Spectacular Bid), a US listed-placed winner of 6 races, is a half-sister to 3 winners.

MARK TOMPKINS

1514. ASTROGOLD ★★★
ch.f. Motivator – Mega (Petardia).
April 29. 7,000Y. Tattersalls October Book 2. Not sold. Half-sister to the fair 2010 2-y-o 7f winner, on her only start, Mystic Winds (by Shirocco), to the quite useful 7f (at 2 yrs) to 9f winner of 4 races Marvo (by Bahamian Bounty), to the fair 9f (at 2 yrs) and 1m winner of 4 races Astrodonna (by Carnival Dancer) and the fair 1m and 9f winner Mercoliano (by Medicean). The dam is an unplaced half-sister to 7 winners including the listed winners Bolino Star and Don Fayruz. The second dam, Gobolino (by Don), won over 7f in Ireland at 2 yrs and is a half-sister to 4 winners. (Mystic Meg Ltd). *"Everything out of the dam that's run has won. This is a great big, old-fashioned type of filly who I really like. One for the back-end of the season and she's definitely worth putting on your radar".*

1515. CHANKILLO ★★
ch.c. Observatory – Seasonal Blossom (Fairy King).
April 14. Half-brother to the very useful 6f to 12f winner of 4 races (including the listed Galtres Stakes) Brushing (by Medicean), to the fair 10f to 14f winner of 6 races Wee Charlie Castle (by Sinndar) and the fair 1m winner of 4 races Seasonal Cross (by Cape Cross). The dam is an unplaced half-sister to 7 winners including the US Grade 2 winner Wait Till Monday and the Irish Group 3 winner Token Gesture (herself dam of the Grade 1 winner Relaxed Gesture). The second dam, Temporary Lull (by Super Concorde), is an unraced sister to the Group 3 Nell Gwyn Stakes winner Martha Stevens. *"A strong, well-grown colt and showing plenty of ability now despite his size. I'm sure he's going to be a nice horse. The family always churns out good winners".*

1516. CHONBERG ★★★
b.c. Bahamian Bounty – Qilin (Second Set).
March 1. Fifth foal. Half-brother to the fair 1m and 12f winner Drum Dragon (by Beat Hollow). The dam, a fairly useful 6f (including at 2 yrs) and 7f winner, was listed-placed. And is a half-sister to 5 winners The second dam, Usance (by Kronankranich), a German winner and listed-placed, is a half-sister to two German listed winners. (Kenneth MacPherson). *"A well-grown, strong, typical Bahamian Bounty colt. The mother was quick and this is the best one of her foals by far. I really like him, he's got a good temperament and he could be one for the mid-season onwards. A grand horse".*

1517. EANANS BAY ★★
b.c. Tiger Hill – Gold Hush (Seeking The Gold).
February 26. First foal. Tattersalls October Book 2. Not sold. The dam, a quite useful 1m and 10f winner, is a half-sister to several winners including the useful 2-y-o 1m winner and Group 3 1m Autumn Stakes second Menokee. The second dam, Meniatarra (by Zilzal), unplaced in one run at 2 yrs, is a sister to the smart 1m to 10f winner Kammtarra and the useful 10f winner Haltarra and a half-sister to the top-class colt Lammtarra, winner of the Derby, the King George and the Prix de l'Arc de Triomphe. *"A big, strong, lengthy colt. He's going to need a bit of time but he's very attractive and he's from the Lammtarra family. Although the sire is a bit unfashionable, now he's gone back to Germany he'll no doubt get plenty of winners! One for the late summer onwards and he's certainly got a future".*

1518. JENNIFER J ★★
ch.f. Motivator – Trew Class (Inchinor).
March 11. Third foal. Half-brother to the fair 11f and 12f winner Kathleen Frances (by Sakhee). The dam, a fairly useful 10f winner of 4 races, was listed-placed and is a half-sister to 2 winners. The second dam, Inimitacle (by Saveur), a modest 10f winner, is a half-sister to 3 winners. (Russell Trew Ltd). *"Motivator tends to get them big I think and both my fillies by that sire are that way. They won't be early but they'll certainly be having a run or two from August onwards and they could develop into very nice horses".*

1519. JOE THE COAT ★★★
gr.c. Act One – Torcross (Vettori).
April 27. Third living foal. 11,000Y. Tattersalls October Book 3. M H Tompkins. Half-brother to the fair 10f and 12f winner Bagber (by Diktat). The dam, a useful 2-y-o 7f winner, is a half-sister to the very useful 6f (at 2 yrs), Group 3 7.5f Concorde Stakes and dual listed winner Sheppard's Watch. The second dam, Sheppard's Cross (by Soviet Star), a quite useful 7f winner, is a half-sister to 5 winners including the Irish listed sprint winner Clean Cut. (Roalco Ltd). *"He's like a 'spotted wonder' because he's grey and looks a bit like The Tetrarch did! I hope he's as good as him. He's cantering well and he'll make a 2-y-o from mid-season onwards. A very strong, attractive colt he is".* TRAINERS' BARGAIN BUY

1520. LADY BELLATRIX ★★★
b.f. Singspiel – Humility (Polar Falcon).
March 15. Second foal. 35,000Y. Tattersalls October Book 2. M Tompkins. Half-sister to the fair 2010 2-y-o 7f winner Home Office (by Nayef). The dam was a moderate 7f and 1m winner of 2 races at 4 and 5 yrs. The second dam, Rich In Love (by Alzao), a fairly useful 6f (at 2 yrs) and 7f winner, was listed-placed and is a half-sister to 6 winners. (J Benchley). *"A most attractive filly, she'll need a bit of time but she does everything right, has a good temperament and is a good mover. Out of a Polar Falcon mare, which I quite like, there won't be a problem with her. She's very nice".*

1521. LIKE CLOCKWORK ★★
b.c. Rail Link – Tenpence (Bob Back).
April 25. Half-brother to the fair 2010 1m placed 2-y-o Barwick (by Beat Hollow). The dam, unplaced in two starts, is a sister to the 2-y-o 1m winner and Group 3 Prix Saint-Roman second Ten Bob I and a half-sister to one winner. The second dam, Tiempo (by King Of Spain), was unplaced. (Dullingham Park). *"He's the nicest looking of the dam's foals so far. By a first-season sire, Rail Link, that won the Arc, you wouldn't know what he's going to do but I always liked him as a racehorse. This is a lovely looking colt with a fantastic temperament. He's a lovely mover and he could develop into a very nice horse".*

1522. PHANTOM RANCH ★★
b.c. Act One – Highbrook (Alphabatim).
April 6. Eighth foal. 12,000Y. Tattersalls October 2. Not sold. Half-brother to Ruby Brook (by Sakhee), a 1m winner on his only start at 2 yrs in 2010, to the fairly useful 9f winner Ted Spread (by Beat Hollow), the quite useful 6f (at 2 yrs) to 10f and hurdles winner Niagara (by Rainbows For Life) and the fair 2-y-o 6f winner Pink Sapphire (by Bluebird). The dam, a quite useful 10f to 13f and hurdles winner, is a half-sister to 5 minor winners in the USA. The second dam, Tellspot (by Tell), is a placed half-sister to 10 winners. *"I've trained most of them out of the dam and this colt goes as well as any of them at this stage in his life. A very easy-moving horse with a good temperament, he'll certainly want a bit of a trip but there won't be a problem with him. Seven furlongs to a mile will suit him this year".*

1523. RAYVIN BLACK ★★★★
b.c. Halling – Optimistic (Reprimand).
February 26. Half-brother to the quite useful 2-y-o 7f winner Such Optimism, to the moderate dual 10f winner Astrolibra (both by Sakhee), the quite useful 2-y-o 7f winner Astrobella (by Medicean) and the modest 2m 2f and hurdles winner Rajayoga (by Kris). The dam, a fairly useful 2-y-o dual 7f winner, is a half-sister to several winners including the fairly useful 3-y-o dual 7f winner Woodbeck (dam of the Group 2 Yorkshire Cup winner Franklins Gardens) and the fairly useful 7f (at 2 yrs) and 10f winner Carburton. The second dam, Arminda (by Blakeney), is an unraced half-sister to the Group 1 Prix de Diane winner Madam Gay. (Mr R White). *"A very attractive colt and the mare is a sister to the dam of Franklins Gardens, who was by Halling, so the cross works well. He's doing everything he's being asked now and he's a cracking horse. I might start him at six furlongs but he definitely wants seven or a mile and he could be a really nice horse".*

1524. SLEIGH BELLS ★★★
b.f. Three Valleys – Dolls House (Dancing Spree).
March 24. Second foal. The dam is an unplaced half-sister to several winners including the smart listed 6f winner and Group 1 Sprint Cup fourth Steenburg and the useful 1m and 12f winner Thingmebob. The second dam, Kip's Sister (by Cawston's Clown), is an unraced half-sister to several winners from the family of the smart sprinter Grey Desire. (Dullingham Park). *"This filly goes alright and looks like being a real 2-y-o. I think the sire might do well because I think his yearlings looked very attractive. She's sharp, goes well and is very healthy-looking all the time. I won't be messing about with her, she'll be out in May and could well be alright. She'll start her at five but I should think six furlongs will suit her better".*

1525. TOPTEMPO ★★★
ch.f. Halling – Topatoo (Bahamian Bounty).
February 25. First foal. The dam, a Group 3 10.3f Middleton Stakes winner of 4 races, was second in the Group 3 9f Dahlia Stakes and is a half-sister to several winners. The second dam, Topatori (by Topanoora), was a quite useful 7f to 11f winner of 4 races. (Roalco Ltd). *"By a good sire and the dam won the Middleton at York. She does everything right, looks the right shape and size, her temperament is fine and she has everything in her favour. I absolutely love her and she'll be one that won't be hurried because she could be a proper filly. One for the mid-season onwards".*

1526. UNNAMED ★★★
b.f. Piccolo – Sosumi (Be My Chief).
January 22. Fifth foal. 8,000Y. Half-sister to the fair 7f and 1m winner of 4 races Tevez (by Sakhee), to the modest 2-y-o 1m seller winner Benayoun (by Inchinor) and the modest 11f winner Edward Whymper (by Bahamian Bounty). The dam, a useful 2-y-o dual 5f winner, was fourth in the Group 3 Prix du Calvados. The second dam, Princess Deya (by Be My Guest), ran twice unplaced and is a half-sister to the Eclipse Stakes winner Compton Admiral and the Group 1 1m Queen Elizabeth II Stakes winner Summoner. (The Fat Boys). *"She's a strong, attractive filly that looks the part and does everything right. She'd be one of my favourite fillies and there won't be a problem with her. With a bit of luck she'll be out at the end of April or the beginning of May".*

MARCUS TREGONING

1527. ALWAFFAA (USA) ★★★
b.f. Discreet Cat – Elaflaak (Gulch).
March 23. Fifth foal. The dam, a useful listed 5f winner, is a half-sister to the US triple Grade 3 9f winner Indescribable. The second dam, Catnip (by Flying Paster), a US 12f winner, is a half-sister to the Belmont Stakes winner Editor's Note. (Hamdan Al Maktoum). "I trained the dam and she was all speed. She was also quite highly strung but that's often the case with sprinters. She's been a disappointing broodmare really but considering this filly's sire is Discreet Cat she should be a five furlong 2-y-o. I haven't seen her because she hasn't arrived from Dubai yet".

1528. BRONZE ANGEL (IRE) ★★★
b.c. Dark Angel – Rihana (Priolo).
March 3. Third foal. Doncaster Premier. £42,000Y. Peter Doyle. Ha f-brother to the unplaced 2010 2-y-o Zahraan (by Elusive City). The dam, placed fourth once over 9f in Ireland, is a half-sister to 6 minor winners. The second dam, Ridaya (by Last Tycoon), an Irish 1m and 9f winner, was listed placed and is a half-sister to 6 winners. (Lacy Tennant). "I like him, he was bought reasonably well by Peter Doyle I think. He goes alright, he's ready to run and I'll get him out in late April or early May. He's quite scopey, so he's not short coupled or anything and he seems to have a good mind. He has enough speed, I should think he'd be quite happy to start at five furlongs and six would be fine for him. He goes quite nicely and he's very sound".

1529. CAVALEIRO (IRE) ★★★★
ch.c. Sir Percy – Khibraat (Alhaarth).
March 6. First foal. 78,000Y. Tattersalls October Book 2. Oliver St Lawrence. The dam is an unplaced half-sister to 10 winners including the smart Group 2 14.6f Park Hill Stakes winner Ranin. The second dam, Nafhaat (by Roberto), a fairly useful 12f winner, was listed-placed and stayed 15f. (Mr G C B Brook). "When we saw him at the sales I thought that as an individual he was the nicest yearling colt there. I was very keen to buy him, he was well-proportioned like Sir Percy and apart from his colour he's very much like him in many ways. That's to say he's a very relaxed horse in his work, he wouldn't be a flashy worker but I should think he'd have the pace to start over six furlongs in May. I like the way he goes, he's very well-made and I fully expect him to be a winner".

1530. EBTISAMA ★★★
b.f. Kingmambo – Misterah (Alhaarth).
March 19. Half-sister to the useful 2010 2-y-o 6f winner and Group 3 5f Cornwallis Stakes third Darajaat (by Elusive Quality) and to the useful 6f (at 2 yrs) and listed 1m winner and Group 3 7f Oak Tree Stakes third Shabiba. The dam, a very useful listed 6f (at 2 yrs) and Group 3 7f Nell Gwyn Stakes winner, is sister to one winner and a half-sister to 2 winners including the useful 2-y-o 6f winner Muqtarb. The second dam, Jasarah (by Green Desert), was a fair 7f placed maiden. (Hamdan Al Maktoum). "Well, the dam was a good enough 2-y-o and she trained on to win the Nell Gwyn, but she didn't have the best of joints which was a shame because I thought an awful lot of her. I never saw this filly in Dubai, but people who have seen her, and who I could trust, liked her as a type and thought she'd make a 2-y-o. So that's encouraging and she's about to arrive here soon".

1531. EKRAAM ★★★
b.c. Shamardal – Shawahid (A P Indy).
March 26. The dam is an unraced half-sister to 6 winners including the 1,000 Guineas and Coronation Stakes winner Ghanaati and the Group 3 12f Cumberland Lodge Stakes winner Mawatheeq. The second dam, Sarayir (by Mr Prospector), the winner of a 1m listed event, is closely related to the top-class Champion Stakes winner Nayef and a half-sister to numerous winners including the 2,000 Guineas, Eclipse, Derby and King George winner Nashwan and the high-class middle distance colt Unfuwain. (Hamdan Al Maktoum). "Shamardal doesn't get flashy individuals, they're quite plain horses, that's just the way he stamps them. Anyway, he's a good stallion and it's nice to get one. This colt hasn't done a lot yet but he's a reasonable mover and he'll be alright when the mile races come round".

1532. ESTEMAALA (IRE) ★★★
b.f. Cape Cross – Elutrah (Darshaan).
January 31. Sister to the quite useful 2-y-o 1m winner Multames. The dam is an unraced sister to the very useful Group 2 7f Rockfel Stakes winner Sayedah and a half-sister to 4 winners. The second dam, Balaabel (by Sadler's Wells), a quite useful 1m winner, is a half-sister to 3 winners including the US Grade 2 7f winner Kayrawan. (Hamdan Al Maktoum). *"She's rather good-looking and definitely the nicest one out of the mare that I've seen so far. She's scopey and has a lot of quality about her, so you wouldn't mind waiting for her and anything by Cape Cross is good enough for us. She's only cantering at the moment and she's one for later in the year, but hopefully one with a future".*

1533. LULLA ★★★
b.f. Oasis Dream – Dominica (Alhaarth).
March 6. Fifth foal. Sister to the quite useful French 2-y-o 7f winner Jungle Bay and closely related to the modest 5f and 6f winner of 3 races Todber (by Cape Cross). The dam, winner of the Group 2 5f Kings Stand Stakes and the Group 3 Cornwallis Stakes, is a half-sister to 3 winners including the listed-placed sprinter Bowness. The second dam, Dominio (by Dominion), a 2-y-o listed 5f winner, was second in the Group 2 5f Temple Stakes and is a half-sister to 6 winners including the very smart Group 1 5f Nunthorpe Stakes winner Ya Malak. (Mrs R B Kennard). *"I think she's probably the nicest out of the mare so far and that includes the full sister Jungle Bay. I'm very happy with her, she does everything right and is quite straightforward. She's done her work and I expect to see her out in May and she'll win this year. The sire can get horses at all distances, but in her case given the speed on her dam's side you'd think if she was any good she'd be a sprinter".*

1534. MISS BLAKENEY ★★★
b.f. Sir Percy – Misplace (Green Desert).
April 30. Half-sister to the French 1m to 10f winner and Group 3 third Mayweather (by Nayef), to the French 2-y-o 1m winner and Group 3 fourth Mistaken Identity (by Vettori) and the minor French 7f winner Milhaarth (by Alhaarth) and to the unraced dam of the Group 1 1m Falmouth Stakes and Group 2 6f Lowther Stakes winner Nahoodh. The dam ran once unplaced and is a half-sister to 6 winners including the French Group 3 winner Not Just Swing and the French listed winner Minoa. The second dam, Misbegotten (by Baillamont), a French listed 1m Prix Finlande winner, was second in the Group 2 Prix de l'Opera and is a half-sister to 4 winners. (Mr & Mrs A E Pakenham). *"This is rather a nice-looking filly, she did a lot of growing and I had to leave her alone for a while but she's a very good-looking filly and I really do like her as a type. It's hard to fault her as an individual, she's lovely and a good mover but we'll have to wait a bit.*

1535. MUJANNAD (IRE) ★★★★
b.c. Red Ransom – Hureya (Woodman).
February 3. Sixth foal. Brother to the 2-y-o listed 7f Star Stakes and 3-y-o Group 3 7f Fred Darling Stakes winner Muthabara and half-brother to the fairly useful 7f (including at 2 yrs) and 1m winner of 4 races Aqmaar (by Green Desert) and the quite useful 9f winner Estiqraar (by Alhaarth). The dam, a quite useful 3-y-o 1m winner, is a half-sister to the very smart listed 7f (at 2 yrs) and listed 10f winner Muqbil. The second dam, Istiqlal (by Diesis), is an unraced half-sister to the Group 1 1m St James's Palace Stakes and Group 1 1m Queen Elizabeth II Stakes winner Bahri and to the high-class 2-y-o Group 2 7f Laurent Perrier Champagne Stakes winner Bahhare. (Hamdan Al Maktoum). *"This is a horse that I like, he's a definite 2-y-o, he's very solid, has a good mind and he's done quite a lot of work for a seven furlong horse. I think it's lovely when you can get on with a horse, teach them their job when the ground's good and you can get them up the grass. That's the huge advantage of getting them to trainers on time and not sending them late and having them hacking round on polytrack or sand or woodchip – it's not the same. If you've got good grass you make the most of it in the spring. I've done plenty with this colt and he could start off in a race like the Strutt & Parker maiden at Newmarket in July".*

1536. MUTANAWWER ★★★
br.c. Red Ransom – Nasheed (Riverman).
January 16. Seventh foal. Half-brother to the useful Irish 7f and 1m winner Tamazug, to the

quite useful Irish 7f to 12f and hurdles winner Mutadarek (both by Machiavellian) and the modest 11f and 14f winner Al Azy (by Nayef). The dam, a useful 7f (at 2 yrs) and 10f winner, is a half-sister to the high-class Prix de l'Arc de Triomphe and Juddmonte International winner Sakhee. The second dam, Thawakib (by Sadler's Wells), a useful dual 7f (at 2 yrs) and Group 2 12f Ribblesdale Stakes winner, is a half-sister to numerous winners including the top-class middle-distance colt Celestial Storm (winner of the Group 2 Princess of Wales's Stakes). (Hamdan Al Maktoum). "I'm a fan of the sire, having had Ekraar who was away for some time but then came back to us a few years later and won a Group 1. That was quite a moving story for me because I loved him as a 2-y-o and it was great when he returned and did so well for us. Red Ransom can get you a really good horse, this is another one I like and later on he'll be a seven furlong/mile 2-y-o. A nice individual".

1537. SCARLET BELLE ★★★
ch.f. Sir Percy – Nicola Bella (Sadler's Wells).
March 30. Eighth foal. 50,000Y. Tattersalls October Book 1. Marcus Tregoning. Half-sister to the 7f to 9.5f and subsequent US Grade 2 1m winner Beautyandthebeast (by Machiavellian), to the German 2-y-o Group 3 8.5f winner Neatico (by Medicean), the German 11f winner and listed placed Narcisco (by Fantastic Light), a minor German winner by Rainbow Quest and to the unraced dam of the French dual Group 3 winner Calvados Blues. The dam, an Irish 9.6f winner, is a sister to the 10f winner and Group 1 Irish Oaks third Sister Bella and a half-sister to 3 winners. The second dam, Valley Of Hope (by Riverman), is an unraced half-sister to the Mill Reef Stakes and Richmond Stakes winner Vacarme and to the Prix Jacques le Marois winner Vin de France. (The FOPS). "She's not overly-big and hence we'll be getting on with her quite soon, but she's very well-made, has a good, sound constitution and good limbs. Because of her size she'll have to race very soon and in May she'll be battling it out at Goodwood".

1538. SHY ROSA (USA) ★★★
b.f. Dixie Union – Lethal Temper (Seattle Slew).
February 25. Third foal. $130,000Y. Keeneland September. Oliver St Lawrence. Half-sister to the US stakes-placed winner Lethal Quality (by Elusive Quality). The dam, a winner of 3 minor races at 3 and 4 yrs in the USA, is a half-sister to numerous winners including the very smart colt Diffident, winner of the Group 3 6f Diadem Stakes, the Group 3 6f Prix de Ris-Orangis and the listed 7f European Free Handicap. The second dam, Shy Princess (by Irish River), a smart French 2-y-o 7f winner and second in the Group 1 Prix Morny, won over 6f as a 3-y-o and is a half-sister to the Breeders Cup Mile winner and Eclipse Stakes second Opening Verse and the US Grade 3 winner So She Sleeps. (Mr G C B Brook). "I'm very keen on her, it's not a typical 2-y-o family and yet she looks to me like a six furlong type. I think she's speedy, she has a really strong constitution, very good limbs and a very powerful behind – she's built like a sprinter. She'll be at her best as a 3-y-o but if she shows us enough she'll run this summer and win".

1539. SPINNING SILK (IRE) ★★★
ch.f. Redback – Silk Point (Barathea).
April 11. Sixth foal. €14,000Y. Goffs Orby. M Tregoning. Half-sister to the quite useful dual 7f winner (including at 2 yrs) All Of Me (by Xaar), to the modest dual 9f winner (including at 2 yrs) Empress Leizu (by Chineur) and a minor 3-y-o winner in Germany by Noverre. The dam is an unraced half-sister to 4 winners including the dam of the Group 3 Cornwallis Stakes winner Captain Gerrard. The second dam, Scimitarra (by Kris), a very useful 2-y-o 6f and 7.2f and 3-y-o 10f Lupe Stakes winner, is a half-sister to 6 winners including the top class sprinter Double Form. (Park Walk Racing). "She's very nice and I waited for three days at the sales to buy her because she was in the ring on the last day. She's turned out alright, she's quite scopey and taller than I'd hoped because she grew quite a lot. Possibly a bit immature, but from mid-summer onwards hopefully she'll be nice".

1540. THAWABEL (IRE) ★★★
b.f. Nayef – Shohrah (Giant's Causeway).
April 16. Second foal. Half-sister to the quite useful 2-y-o 9f winner Shaayeq (by Dubawi). The dam, a useful 2-y-o 6f winner, is a half-

sister to the useful 7f winner and 1m listed second Ma-Arif. The second dam, Taqreem (by Nashwan), was second four times over middle-distances and is a half-sister to the high class middle distance colt Ibn Bey, winner of 4 Group 1 events including the Irish St Leger and second in the Breeders Cup Classic and to the very smart Group 1 Yorkshire Oaks winner Roseate Tern. (Hamdan Al Maktoum). *"Not the most precocious of types and more of a back-end 2-y-o, although her dam won over six furlongs at Ascot at two. I suppose you'll have to wait for seven furlongs later in the season to see her but she's a nice mover and like all Nayef's she's very sound".*

1541. WAAFID ★★★
b.c. Oasis Dream – Hazimah (Gone West).
January 1. Fifth foal. The dam, a fair 7f and 1m placed maiden, is a half-sister to numerous winners including the high-class 2-y-o Mujahid, winner of the Group 1 7f Dewhurst Stakes and subsequently third in the 2,000 Guineas. The second dam, Elrafa Ah (by Storm Cat), was a useful winner of 3 races over 5f and 6f including the listed Bentinck Stakes. The second dam, Bubbles Darlene (by Fappiano), won twice at up to 1m. (Hamdan Al Maktoum). *"He should be alright because he's a reasonable mover, short coupled and quite nice – or so I'm told, but he's not arrived yet from Dubai".*

1542. WEAAM (IRE) ★★★
b.c. Shamardal – Merayaat (Darshaan).
March 23. Third foal. Half-brother to the fair 2010 2-y-o 1m winner, from 2 starts, Hawaafez (by Nayef). The dam was a quite useful 14f winner. The second dam, Maddelina (by Sadler's Wells), is an unplaced half-sister to 2 winners. (Hamdan Al Maktoum). *"It's a staying family and you're talking about mile races later in the year".*

1543. UNNAMED ★★★★
b.c. Street Sense – Cajun Two Step (Tabasco Cat).
March 11. Sixth foal. $250,000Y. Keeneland September. Oliver St Lawrence. Half-brother to the US Grade 2 California Stakes and Grade 2 San Diego Handicap winner Informed (by Tiznow) and to a minor US winner by Old Trieste. The dam, a minor US winner at 3 yrs, is a half-sister to the US Grade 3 winner Discreet Hero. The second dam, Tapstress (by Desert Wine), a US stakes winner of 3 races, is a half-sister to 6 winners including the US Grade 2 winner Triple Tipple. (F Nass). *"I'm really glad I've got this horse. I was in America and this was one we tried to buy but couldn't afford. Fortunately for me, when the owner found out how much I liked him he told the agent to send him to me – so that was very nice! This horse isn't overly big, he's a six/seven furlong 2-y-o, he's in full work and he's almost ready to go. He could easily win over six and hopefully you'll see plenty of him".*

1544. UNNAMED ★★★
b.f. Intikhab – Ladood (Unfuwain).
April 21. Second foal. 10,000Y. Tattersalls October Book 2. Marcus Tregoning. The dam ran once unplaced and is a half-sister to 2 winners. The second dam, Alshakr (by Bahri), won the Group 2 Falmouth Stakes and is a half-sister to 4 winners including the dam of the 1,000 Guineas winner Harayir. (Mr J A Tabet). *"I was wondering how I could get a Snow Fairy, but obviously lightning doesn't strike twice! I like this filly and there's something nice about her. When people see her they say 'that's a nice filly' because she has presence. She has a good head, a bold eye, she's a good mover and we're looking forward to whatever she can do. It's a half decent family so you can make a case for her".* TRAINERS' BARGAIN BUY

ROGER VARIAN

1545. ABARRAT (IRE) ★★
b.f. Cape Cross – Malyana (Mtoto).
March 1. First foal. The dam, a quite useful 1m (at 2 yrs) to 1m winner, is a sister to the useful 7f, 1m (both at 2 yrs) and Group 2 10f Pretty Polly Stakes winner Tarfshi and half-sister to 4 winners including the champion 2-y-o filly and Group 1 6f Cheveley Park Stakes winner Embassy. The second dam, Pass The Peace (by Alzao), won the Cheveley Park Stakes and was second in the 1,000 Guineas. (Sheikh Ahmed Al Maktoum). *"We trained the mother to win as a 3-y-o and this filly is good-bodied, a bit on the small side but very correct. She canters OK and shows a good attitude but we won't be doing anything early. She'll start off in late summer".*

1546. AFRAAH (USA) ★★★ ♠
b.f. Hard Spun – Sarayir (Mr Prospector).
Closely related to the Group 3 12f Cumberland Lodge Stakes winner and Group 1 Champion Stakes second Mawatheeq and to the quite useful 1m winner Itqaan (both by Danzig) and half-sister to the 1,000 Guineas and Coronation Stakes winner Ghanaati (by Giant's Causeway), the useful 1m (at 2 yrs) and listed 9f winner Rumoush, the fair 12f winner Atayeb (both by Rahy) and the quite useful 10f winner Sundus (by Fairy King). The dam, winner of a 1m listed event, is closely related to the Champion Stakes winner Nayef and a half-sister to Nashwan and Unfuwain The second dam, Height Of Fashion (by Bustino), a high-class winner of 5 races from 7f to 12f including the Group 2 Princess of Wales's Stakes, is a half-sister to the good middle-distance colt Milford. (Hamdan Al Maktoum). "I haven't seen her yet, she's wintered in Dubai, but she has a pedigree to be very excited about. Richards Hills and Angus Gold will have called in to see her two or three times over there and they say she's a nice type, so we're looking forward to getting her here".

1547. ALJAMAAHEER (IRE) ★★★★ ♠
ch.c. Dubawi – Kelly Nicole (Rainbow Quest).
March 13. Third foal. 100,000foal. Tattersalls December. Shadwell Estate Co. Half-brother to the quite useful 2010 2-y-o dual 7f winner Tinkertown (by Verglas). The dam, a fair 1m to 10f winner of 3 races, is a half-sister to 3 winners including the Irish dual 9f and subsequent US stakes winner Cold Cold Woman. The second dam, Banquise (by Last Tycoon), won over 2m in France and is a half-sister to 8 winners including the French dual Group 2 winner Modhish, the French Group 2 12.5f Prix de Royallieu winner Russian Snows and the Group 3 winner and good broodmare Truly Special. (Hamdan Al Maktoum). "He's a good, strong horse with a good action. It might not be unrealistic to think he could be a May/June runner. He hasn't done any fast work yet but he's very strong looking and has a very natural way of going. I like him".

1548. ALZAHRA ★★★
b.f. Exceed And Excel – Aunty Mary (Common Grounds).
February 15. Fifth foal. 115,000Y. Tattersalls October Book 2. Shadwell Estate Co. Half-sister to the 3-y-o 7f winner Ertikaan (by Oasis Dream), to the 7f and 1m winner Pride Of Kings (by King's Best) and the 5f (at 2 yrs), 7f and hurdles winner King's Bastion (by Royal Applause) – all quite useful. The dam, a quite useful 2-y-o 5f winner, is a half-sister to the 1,000 Guineas, Irish 1,000 Guineas, Coronation Stakes, Matron Stakes and Sun Chariot Stakes winner Attraction. The second dam, Flirtation (by Pursuit Of Love), ran unplaced once over 7f at 3 yrs and is a half-sister to 4 winners including the French listed 12f winner and Group 2 placed Carmita. (Sheikh Ahmed Al Maktoum). "This filly is quite forward and she could take training earlier than some of our 2-y-o's. She could be out in May or June, she's strong and a good mover. We wouldn't know too much about her ability yet but I quite like her".

1549. AMBIVALENT (IRE) ★★
b.f. Authorized – Darrery (Darshaan).
February 26. Tenth foal. 24,000Y. Tattersalls October Book 2. James Given. Half-sister to the very useful 1m, 10f (both at 2 yrs) and 14f winner and listed-placed Sunday Symphony (by Sunday Silence), to the useful 2-y-o 7f winner and Group 1 1m Gran Criterium third Al Waffi (by Fairy King), the 2-y-o 1m and subsequent Triumph Hurdle winner Made In Japan (by Barathea), the triple winner in Greece Diary (by Green Desert and herself dam of the Group 1 Prix de l'Abbaye winner Total Gallery) and the quite useful Irish 11f winner Home Secretary (by Machiavellian). The dam, a useful 10f and 12f winner, was listed-placed and is a half-sister to 3 winners out of the Group 3 Waterford Candelabra Stakes winner Flamenco (by Dance Spell). (A Saeed). "She's got a bit of size and scope about her, she moves quite nicely and comes from a good family. Being by Authorized I'm not expecting her to do an awful lot this year, perhaps one or two runs at the back-end. But she has a bit of scope and she moves well".

1550. ATHB (IRE) ★★
b.f. Teofilo – Anbella (Common Grounds).
February 12. Fourth foal. 150,000foal. Tattersalls December. Shadwell Estate Co.

Half-sister to the useful 2010 2-y-o 5f and 7f winner and Group 3 fourth Masaya, to the fair 6f winner Anacreon (both by Dansili) and to the minor French winner Reasons (by Malabar Gold). The dam, a French 2-y-o listed 7f winner, is a half-sister to 8 winners including the Group 1 Criterium de Saint-Cloud winner Spadoun and the dual Group 1 Prix de l'Opera winner Satwa Queen. The second dam, Tolga (by Irish River), is a placed half-sister to 6 winners including the dam of the Group 2 winner and Group 1 placed Signe Divin. (Hamdan Al Maktoum). *"Haven't seen her yet, she's still in Dubai".*

1551. BAHEEJA ★★★
b.f. *Dubawi – Hasty Words (Polish Patriot).*
February 8. Seventh foal. 50,000Y. Tattersalls October Book 2. Shadwell Estate Co. Half-sister to the useful 5f and 6f winner of 6 races (including at 2 yrs) Grigorovitch (by Fasliyev) and to the quite useful 9f winner Ashes Regained (by Galileo). The dam won over 6f (at 2 yrs) and the listed Doncaster Mile at 4 yrs and was third in the Group 2 7f Rockfel Stakes. She is a half-sister to 2 winners including the fairly useful 5f and 6f winner Katya. The second dam, Park Elect (by Ahonoora), won over 7f and 9f in Ireland at 3 yrs and is a half-sister to 3 winners. (Sheikh Ahmed Al Maktoum). *"She's not had a smooth winter but saying that she's doing fine now and she could be a summertime 2-y-o around July or August. I don't know anything about her ability yet, but to look at she's the right type of model. The stallion's done well, so you'd be hopeful without having a proper guide".*

1552. BU NAAJI (IRE) ★★★
b.c. *Kheleyf – Atamana (Lahib).*
February 5. Sixth foal. Half-brother to the modest 2010 2-y-o 1m and 9f winner Skeleton (by Tobougg), to the Group 3 10.5f Rose Of Lancaster Stakes winner of 6 races Mulaqat and the fair 10f winner Emshabb (both by Singspiel). The dam, a quite useful 1m winner, is a half-sister to 6 winners including the Irish 2-y-o 6f winner and Group 3 7f Killavullen Stakes third Dance Clear - subsequently a winner of 4 races and Grade 3 placed in the USA. The second dam, Dance Ahead (by Shareef Dancer), a quite useful 2-y-o 7f winner, is a half-sister to 6 winners. (Sheikh Ahmed Al Maktoum). *"He could be a sharp sort and it might not be unrealistic to suggest he'll be on the racecourse in May or June. He's doing well and although it's a bit early to tell his ability he's a good mover, a strong horse and he could be campaigned throughout he summer. He looks a 2-y-o and six furlongs might be his distance".*

1553. BUZKASHI (IRE) ★★
b.f. *Nayef – Min Alhawa (Riverman).*
February 13. Ninth foal. 175,000Y. Tattersalls October Book 1. Blandford Bloodstock. Half-sister to the smart 10f, 12f and UAE listed winner Mutasallil (by Gone West), to the useful 10f and 12f winner Nuzooa (by A P Indy), the useful 10f and 11f winner and Group 3 Cumberland Lodge Stakes third Ajhar (by Diesis), the fairly useful 10f winner Matraash (by Elusive Quality) and the fairly useful 12.3f winner Tasneef (by Gulch). The dam, a useful 7f (at 2 yrs) to 10f winner, is a sister to the very smart 1,000 Guineas and Celebration Mile winner Harayir and a half-sister to 3 winners. The second dam, Saffaanh (by Shareef Dancer), a quite useful 12.2f winner, is a half-sister to 4 winners including the Group 2 Falmouth Stakes winner Alshakr. (B E Nielsen). *"She's an attractive filly, an easy mover and one for the second half of the season, probably from the end of summer onwards ".*

1554. EKTIHAAM (IRE) ★★★
b.c. *Invincible Spirit – Liscune (King's Best).*
March 26. Second foal. 250,000foal. Tattersalls December. Shadwell Estate Co. The dam, a fair 1m and 12f winner in Ireland, is a half-sister to 4 winners including the Group 3 Prix du Lys winner Lycitus and to the placed dam of the Group 1 Premio Roma winner Sunstrach. The second dam, Royal Lorna (by Val de l'Orne), won the Group 3 Premio Bagutta and is a half-sister to 7 winners including the Group 1 Yorkshire Oaks winner Awaasif (dam of the Oaks winner Snow Bride). (Hamdan Al Maktoum). *"He's an attractive colt who fills the eye. He has plenty of size and presence and is a very natural mover. I'd be hopeful of him being an August or September 2-y-o and I quite like him".*

ROGER VARIAN

1555. ELYASSAAT ★★★
b.c. Nayef – Blue Symphony (Darshaan).
April 7. Fifth foal. 525,000Y. Tattersalls October Book 1. Shadwell Estate Co. Half-brother to the very smart Group 3 7f Prestige Stakes (at 2 yrs) and Group 3 Nell Gwyn Stakes winner and dual Group 1 placed Fantasia (by Sadler's Wells), to the useful 10f w nner and 10f listed-placed Pink Symphony (by Montjeu) and the fair 2-y-o 7f winner Blue Rhapsody (by Cape Cross). The dam, a fair 10f winner, is a half-sister to one winner. The second dam, Blue Duster (by Danzig), w nner of the Group 1 6f Cheveley Park Stakes, the Group 3 6f Princess Margaret Stakes and the Group 3 5f Queen Mary Stakes, is a sister to the smart Group 1 6f Middle Park Stakes and Group 2 7f Challenge Stakes winner Zieten and a half-sister to 9 winners. (Hamdan Al Maktoum). "A nice type of horse with a nice way of going. He's grown and he's a big morse now, so we're looking forward to running h'm a couple of times from late summer onwards. He was expensive but he looks that way – a good-looking horse and a good mover, so you'd be hopeful of him being a nice horse. We're still at the guessing stage but you'd be encouraged by what he's shown so far".

1556. FARRAAJ (IRE) ★★★
b.c. Dubai Destination – Pastorale (Nureyev).
April 23. Brother to the quite useful 2010 2-y-o 1m and 9f winner Makeynn and to the useful 7 winner of 4 races and listed-placed Taqdeyr and half-brother to the high-class triple Group 2 7f winner and sire Iffraaj, the useful 2-y-o Group 3 7f Prix du Calvados winner Kareymah, the fair 7f winner Akrmina (all by Zafonic), the useful dual 1m winner Jathaabeh (by Nashwan), the fairly usefu 1m winner Mofarij (by Bering), the fair 1m and 11.5f winner Krosno (by Kris) and the French 11f winner In Arcadia (by Slip Anchor) The dam, a fairly useful 3-y-o 7f winner, is a half-sister to 7 winners including Cape Cross. The second dam, Park Appeal (by Ahonoora), won four 6f races including the Group 1 Cheveley Park Stakes and the Group 1 Moyglare Stud Stakes and is a sister to the Group 3 9f winner Nashamaa and a half-sister to the Irish Oaks and Ribblesdale Stakes winner Alydaress and the Cheveley Park Stakes winner Desirable – herself dam of the 1,000 Guineas winner Shadayid. (Sheikh Ahmed Al Maktoum). "A half-brother to Iffraaj, so it's a family we know well, he's quite an attractive colt that moves well. The sire doesn't get too many early 2-y-o's but there's a possibility he could be out in July and the dam is a good broodmare".

1557. FIRDAWS (USA) ★★★
b.f. Mr Greeley – Eswarah (Unfuwain).
February 26. Second foal. The dam won 3 races including the Group 1 Epsom Oaks and is a half-sister to 9 winners including the Group 3 12f Princess Royal Stakes winner Itnab, the very useful 6f winner of 4 races Haafiz and the useful 7f and 1m winner and Irish 1,000 Guineas third Umniyatee. The second dam, Midway Lady (by Alleged), won the Prix Marcel Boussac, the 1,000 Guineas and the Oaks and is a half-sister to 5 winners including the very useful 11.8f listed winner Capias. (Hamdan Al Maktoum). "A filly to get excited about on paper, she's very attractive and she moves well. It's too early to say really, but from what I've seen of her so far I like her and it's nice to have a filly from this family in the yard".

1558. GO DUTCH (IRE) ★★
ch.c. Dutch Art – Paix Royale (Royal Academy).
May 3. Ninth foal. 27,000Y. Tattersalls October Book 2. M Jarvis. Half-brother to the French listed 7f winner Peach Pearl (by Invincible Spirit), to the French 7f and subsequent US stakes-placed winner Peacefally (by Grand Lodge), the fair 5f and 6f winner Captain Royale (by Captain Rio), the French 1m and 10f winner Soul Of Love (by Desert Prince) and two minor winners in France (by Trempolino) and Italy (by Alzao). The dam won once at 2 yrs in France and was listed-placed and is a half-sister to 6 winners including the French listed winners Playact and Play Around. The second dam, Play Or Pay (by Play Fellow), a French listed-placed winner, is a half-sister to 9 winners. (K Allen, R Marchant, G Moss & M Jarvis). "He's had a winter hiccup but he's a late foal and he's grown a lot so it might not have done him any harm. We might still be able to get him out in mid-summer. You'd hope he'd be a six furlong type of horse".

1559. HAVIN' A GOOD TIME (IRE) ★★
b.f. Jeremy – Flanders (Common Grounds).
May 7. Eighth foal. 45,000Y. Tattersalls October Book 2. M Jarvis. Half-sister to the US Grade 3 Miesque Stakes winner Louvain (by Sinndar), to the fairly useful Irish 10f Lagoon (by Montjeu), the fair 2-y-o 6f winner My Love Thomas (by Cadeaux Genereux), the quite useful 5f (including at 2 yrs) and 6f winner Desert Poppy (by Oasis Dream), the modest 7f winner Wallonia (by Barathea) and the minor German 3-y-o winner Farbenspiel (by Desert Prince). The dam, a very useful sprint winner of 6 races including the listed Scarborough Stakes, was second in the Group 2 Kings Stand Stakes and is a half-sister to 7 winners. The second dam, Family at War (by Explodent), a fair 2-y-o 5f winner, is a half-sister to 4 minor winners in the USA. (A D Spence). *"She's not over-big but she was a late foal and weak as a yearling, so she's still growing and developing. At the end of things I think she'll be big enough and she has a good action but we've got quite a long way to go yet".*

1560. HENRY ALLINGHAM ★★★
ch.c. Three Valleys – Hoh Dancer (Indian Ridge).
March 10. Eighth foal. 32,000Y. Tattersalls October Book 2. R J Baines. Half-brother to the fairly useful dual 7f winner (including at 2 yrs) Dixey, to the fair 7f to 9f winner of 9 races Dichoh (both by Diktat) and the fairly useful 5f and 6f winner of 3 races (including at 2 yrs) Harry Patch (by Lujain). The dam was placed over 5f and is a half-sister to 3 winners including the listed Doncaster Stakes winner Infanta Real. The second dam, Alteza Real (by Mansingh), won 3 sprint races at 2 and 3 yrs and is a full or half-sister to 10 winners including the US Grade 1 winner and useful sire Forzando. (R J Baines). *"He's a half-brother to Harry Patch, so we know the family quite well. A very attractive horse, he's big but he's one for July/August and he should be strong enough to race perhaps three times and give the owner a bit of fun. He's a likeable character, he's got a bit of size and presence and he moves well".*

1561. KEYAADI ★★★
b.c. Iffraaj – Arabescato (Gone West).
February 3. Fifth foal. Tattersalls October Book 2. 110,000Y. Shadwell Estate Co. Half-brother to the minor French 13f winner Askhada (by Alhaarth). The dam is an unraced half-sister to 2 winners including the French listed winner and Group 3 placed Vernoy. The second dam, Marble Maiden (by Lead On Time), won the Grade 2 All Along Stakes and the Group 3 Prix de Sandringham and is a half-sister to 5 winners. (Sheikh Ahmed Al Maktoum). *"A horse with a bit of size and presence. A nice type, he moves quite nicely and he won't be early but I'd hope he'd be a second half of the season 2-y-o. We liked him at the Sales very much and he's done nothing to discourage us.*

1562. KHAJOOL (IRE) ★★★
ch.f. Haafhd – Khulood (Storm Cat).
January 20. Fifth foal. Half-sister to the quite useful dual 7f winner Imaam (by Pivotal) and to the quite useful 2-y-o 5f winner Kashoof (by Green Desert). The dam, a useful listed 7f (at 2 yrs) and Group 3 7f Nell Gwyn Stakes winner, is a half-sister to numerous winners including the Irish 1,000 Guineas winner Mehthaaf and the July Cup winner Elnadim. The second dam, Elle Seule (by Exclusive Native), a very smart winner of the Group 3 1m Prix d'Astarte, also won over 10.5f and is a half-sister to the Group/Grade 1 winners Fort Wood, Hamas and Timber Country and to the Group winners Northern Aspen, Colorado Dancer and Mazzacano. (Hamdan Al Maktoum). *"Still in Dubai".*

1563. MAZEYDD ★★★
b.c. Motivator – Jathaabeh (Nashwan).
March 26. Seventh foal. Half-brother to the very useful 1m (including at 2 yrs) and 9f winner Yaddree (by Singspiel) and to the quite useful dual 1m winner Sky More (by Xaar). The dam, a useful dual 1m winner, is a half-sister to several winners including the high-class sire Iffraaj and the useful 2-y-o Group 3 7f Prix du Calvados winner Kareymah. The second dam, Pastorale (by Nureyev), a fairly useful 3-y-o 7f winner, is a half-sister to the Group 1 Lockinge Stakes winner and high-class sire Cape Cross out of the dual Group 1 winning 2-y-o Park Appeal. (Sheikh Ahmed Al Maktoum). *"This horse has done well since he came in. He was a shy character but he's got his confidence now*

and he's improved physically as well. There's no reason to think he can't be a runner in the second half of the season".

1564. MIN BANAT ALREEH (IRE) ★★★★★
b.f. Oasis Dream – Tariysha (Daylami).
March 4. Third foal. 700,000Y. Tattersalls October Book 1. Shadwell Estate Co. Sister to the 2-y-o Group 1 6f Prix Morny and Group 2 6f July Stakes winner Arcano (by Oasis Dream) and half-sister to the quite useful 2010 7f and 1m placed 2-y-o El Muqbil (by Medicean). The dam is an unraced half-sister to 2 winners and to the dam of the Group 1 Prix de l'Abbaye winner Gilt Edge Girl and the Group 2 Flying Childers Stakes winner Godfrey Street. The second dam, The second dam, Tarwiya (by Dominion), won the Group 3 7f C L Weld Park Stakes, was third in the Irish 1,000 Guineas and is a half-sister to 5 winners including the Group 3 Norfolk Stakes winner Blue Dakota. (Hamdan Al Maktoum). "This filly cost a pretty penny at the Sales and quite rightly because she's a very attractive filly with a lot of strength and depth to her. We haven't pressed any buttons but she's a nice mover, she's strong and she should be able to start her career this summer, hopefully over six furlongs. She's got good quarters and a good girth, we're looking forward to getting going with her and I do like her".

1565. MOKBIL (IRE) ★★
b.c. Dansili – Chatifa (Titus Livius).
April 9. Fifth foal. Half-brother to a hurdles winner by Key Of Luck. The dam, a quite useful 1m winner, is a half-sister to the champion 2-y-o filly and Group 1 6f Cheveley Park Stakes winner Queen's Logic and to the top-class multiple Group 1 winner Dylan Thomas. The second dam, Lagrion (by Diesis), was placed 5 times in Ireland and stayed 12f and s a full or half-sister to 3 winners. (Hamdan Al Maktoum). "This horse is OK, he's not over-big but he's a good-mover. The type to run two or three times from August onwards".

1566. MORATAB (IRE) ★★★
b.c. Dubai Destination – Bahr (Generous).
February 6. Seventh foal. Half-brother to the very useful dual listed 1m winner Baharah (by Elusive Quality), to the fairly useful 7.5f (at 2 yrs) and UAE 7f winner Naaddey (by Seeking The Gold), the fairly useful 1m to 10f winner Sarrsar (by Shamardal), the fairly useful 2-y-o 1m winner In Dubai (by Giant's Causeway) and the quite useful 2-y-o 7f winner Raaeidd (by King's Best). The dam, winner of the listed 7f Washington Singer Stakes (at 2 yrs), the Group 3 12f Ribblesdale Stakes and the Group 3 10.4f Musidora Stakes, is a half-sister to numerous winners. (Sheikh Ahmed Al Maktoum). *"The family is very familiar to us and the dam has bred some good animals, they're usually very attractive and this is no exception. He's a very good-looking colt, he's grown and gone a bit weak on us so he's one for the late summer onwards. He has a good action and he's good-looking".*

1567. MOSSBRAE ★★
ch.c. Selkirk – Frosty Welcome (With Approval).
February 13. Fifth foal. 65,000Y. Tattersalls October Book 2. John Warren. Half-brother to the fair 12f to 2m winner Casual Garcia (by Hernando), to a winner over hurdles by War Chant and a winner in Slovakia by Sadler's Wells. The dam, a useful 9f and 12f winner, is a half-sister to 6 minor winners. The second dam, Light Ice (by Arctic Tern), won 4 races at up to 10f in the USA and is a half-sister to 12 winners including the US Grade 1 winners Al Mamoon and La Gueriere. (Highclere Thoroughbred Racing – Spearmint). *"A big horse, very good-looking and for a big colt he's quite active and light on his feet which is encouraging. One to race at the back-end really, because his future lies as a 3-y-o, but I'm quite encouraged by the way he moves at this stage".*

1568. MUTAALEQ (IRE) ★★
b.c. Oasis Dream – Siringas (Barathea).
March 28. Fifth foal. 480,000Y. Tattersalls October Book 1. Shadwell Estate Co. Closely related to a minor German 3-y-o winner by Green Desert. The dam won the listed 1m Brownstown Stakes, was Grade 2 placed in Canada and was Grade 3 placed in the USA and is a half-sister to 4 winners including the Irish listed 1m winner Castle Quest. The second dam, In Unison (by Eellypha), won over 1m at 3 yrs and is a half-sister to 4 winners including the Group 1 6f Haydock Park Sprint Cup winner

Cherokee Rose. (Hamdan Al Maktoum). *"This horse isn't with us yet, he had a setback after the Sales but nothing too serious. Obviously he has a price tag on him and he's a good-looking colt, so we're looking forward to getting him here. You'd be quite hopeful he'd be a nice horse because of the way he looked at the Sales and because of the stallion".*

1569. MUTASADDER (USA) ★★
b.br.c. Distorted Humor – Dessert (Storm Cat).
March 26. Half-brother to the quite useful 2-y-o 6f winner Almoutaz (by Kingmambo). The dam won the Grade 1 Del Mar Oaks and is a half-sister to the Grade 1 12f Breeders Cup Turf and Grade 1 Hollywood Derby winner Johar. The second dam, Windsharp (by Lear Fan), won 11 races in France, Canada and the USA including the Grade 1 San Luis Rey Stakes and the Grade 1 Beverly Hills Handicap. (Hamdan Al Maktoum). *"Still in Dubai".*

1570. MUZDAAN (IRE) ★★
ch.f. Exceed And Excel – Belle Genius (Beau Genius).
April 4. Half-sister to the quite useful 2-y-o 6f winner Wisecraic, to the fair 2-y-o 7f winner Zelloof (both by Kheleyf), the quite useful 6f and 7f winner Birjand, the quite useful 2-y-o 6f winner Dellini (both by Green Desert), the quite useful 1m winner Bin Rahy (by Rahy), the fair Irish 1m and 9f winner Fereeji (by Cape Cross) and the minor Irish 12f winner Battish (by Pennekamp). The dam won the Group 1 7f Moyglare Stud Stakes. The second dam, Time And Tide (by Mr Leader), a minor US 4-y-o winner, is a half-sister to the Brigadier Gerard Stakes winner Hibernian Gold. (Sheikh Ahmed Al Maktoum). *"She's a sweet filly and we've had a few out of the mare but although the majority of Exceed And Excels are quite sharp, strong horses, this filly is on the weak side. So while she moves well and has a very sweet temperament, she's going to be a back-end of the season runner I think".*

1571. OOJOOBA ★★
b.f. Monsun – Ameerat (Mark Of Esteem).
March 19. Half-sister to the fairly useful 2-y-o 1m winner Sowaylm (by Tobougg) and to the quite useful 7f winner Own Boss (by Seeking The Gold). The dam won the 1,000 Guineas and is a full or half-sister to 3 winners including the smart UAE 1m winner of 11 races Walmooh. The second dam, Walimu (by Top Ville), a quite useful winner of 3 races from 1m to 12f, is a half-sister to 6 winners. (Sheikh Ahmed Al Maktoum). *"We're lucky to have in the yard the progeny of Michael's two classic winners and this is one of them. We've not had all of Ameerat's stock actually, but in features this filly looks very much like her. So I hope that's a good thing, but being by Monsun she won't be doing too much too early. She moves quite nicely and at this early stage I'd be hopeful that come the autumn she'll be running".*

1572. SHALEEK ★★★
ch.f. Pivotal – Dorrati (Dubai Millennium).
April 12. Third foal. Half-sister to the quite useful 2-y-o 6f winner Dahakaa (by Bertolini). The dam is an unraced half-sister to 4 winners including the 7f (at 2 yrs) and dual listed 1m winner Baharah and the fairly useful 2-y-o winners In Dubai and Naaddey. The second dam, Bahr (Generous), winner of the listed 7f Washington Singer Stakes (at 2 yrs), the Group 3 12f Ribblesdale Stakes and the Group 3 10.4f Musidora Stakes, is a half-sister to numerous winners. (Sheikh Ahmed Al Maktoum). *"It did look like she'd be sharp and that we could have a go at her early, but she's since gone through a growing phase and gone a bit weak with it. So now she'll be a filly for the second half of the summer, she's quite likeable but she needs time to mature and strengthen".*

1573. SIGNOR SASSI ★★★★
b.c. Acclamation – Fairy Contessa (Fairy King).
March 27. Seventh foal. 140,000Y. Tattersalls October Book 2. M Jarvis. Half-brother to the Irish 2010 2-y-o 7f winner Fred Archer (by Iffraaj), to the useful 2-y-o listed 5.2f winner and Group 3 5.5f Prix d'Arenburg second Needles And Pins (by Fasliyev) and the quite useful 2-y-o 6f winner Perfect Choice (by Daylami). The dam is a 6f placed half-sister to 5 winners including the very smart colt River Falls, a winner of three races at 2 and 3 yrs including the Group 2 6f Gimcrack Stakes and third in the Group 1 Middle Park Stakes. The second dam, More Fizz (by Morston), won once over an extended 9f in France at 3 yrs and is a half-sister to 6 winners. (Mr P D Smith).

"He's a very likeable colt and has a good action. There's a bit of strength to him so we'll see how we go but we should be able to get him out in June if all goes well. I like him".

1575. TAZWEED (IRE) ★★★★
b.c. Dubawi – Albahja (Sinndar).
March 13. Third foal. Half-brother to the quite useful 2010 2-y-o 7f winner Jaaryah (by Halling) and to the fair 10f winner Kronful (by Singspiel). The dam, a useful 12f winner, was second in the Group 3 10f Golden Daffodil Stakes and in the listed 12f Galtres Stakes and is a half-sister to the fair 11f to 14f winner of 4 races Efrhina. The second dam, Eshq Albahr (by Riverman), is an unraced half-sister to the useful 1m to 10f winner Dayflower. (Sheikh Ahmed Al Maktoum). *"A very attractive colt, we trained the mare who was quite useful but took time to mature and we also trained both the mare's first foals and they've both won. This colt would have a bit more quality than those two winners at the same stage, so bearing in mind he's by Dubawi who can't do a lot wrong at the moment you'd be hopeful of him making up into a nice horse. I don't think he's going to be early and from mid-*

1574. SPORTING GOLD (IRE) ★★★
b.c. Shirocco – Pink Stone (Bigstone).
March 22. Seventh foal. 130,000Y. Tattersalls October Book 1. M Jarvis. Half-brother to the useful but ill-fated 2-y-o 7f winner Tiger Eye (by Danehill Dancer), to the quite useful 2-y-o 8.3f winner Alright My Son (by Pennekamp), the quite useful 12f winner Battleoftrafalgar (by Galileo) and a minor winner abroad by Agnes World. The dam was placed three times in France and stayed 10f and is a half-sister to 8 winners including the triple Group 3 winner Pink and the French listed winners Ring Pink and Lypink. The second dam, Pink Valley (by Never Bend), won the listed Prix d'Aumale and is a half-sister to 12 winners including the French 2,000 Guineas winner and sire Green Dancer. (A D Spence). *"A lovely, attractive colt, he's a half-brother to a very good filly that we sadly lost called Tiger Eye. He'll get better as we go through the year and he's a real 3-y-o prospect but saying that he has a little bit of quality about him, so I would hope he'd run once or twice this year. A nice type of horse".*

summer onwards we could have a look at him. Probably a seven furlong type 2-y-o to start with, bearing in mind the dam was a twelve furlong winner by Sinndar".

1576. TOP HANA (IRE) ★★
b.f. Pivotal – Tarfshi (Mtoto).
March 21. Half-sister to several disappointing horses by Green Desert and Selkirk. The dam, a winner of 5 races from 7f (at 2 yrs) to 10f including the Group 2 Pretty Polly Stakes, is a full or half-sister to 4 winners including the champion 2-y-o filly and Cheveley Park Stakes winner Embassy. The second dam, Pass The Peace (by Alzao), won the Cheveley Park Stakes, was second in the French 1,000 Guineas and is a half-sister to 3 winners. (Sheikh Ahmed Al Maktoum). *"The dam was a wonderful filly for Michael but as a broodmare she's been disappointing and she needs to come up with a good one. This is an attractive filly with size and scope, so she's perhaps one of the best models we've seen out of the dam, which gives you a bit of hope, but she's a bit backward so she's likely to run just the once at the back-end".*

1577. UNNAMED ★★ ♠
b.c. Oasis Dream – Hydro Calido (Nureyev).
March 13. Half-brother to the French listed 7f winner Esperero (by Forty Niner), to the fair 10f winner Best Intent (by King's Best) and the moderate 9f winner Lady Calido (by El Prado). The dam, a very useful filly and winner of the Group 2 1m Prix d'Astarte, was second in the French 1,000 Guineas and is a half-sister to the champion European 2-y-o and 2,000 Guineas second Machiavellian, to the smart Group 1 Prix Morny and Group 1 Prix de la Salamandre winner and 1,000 Guineas third Coup de Genie and the very smart Group 1 Prix Jacques le Marois winner Exit to Nowhere (by Irish River). The second dam, Coup de Folie (by Halo), won four races from 6f to 10f including the Group 3 1m Prix d'Aumale and was stakes-placed in the USA. The third dam, Raise the Standard (by Hoist the Flag), is an unraced half-sister to Northern Dancer. (Lordship Stud). *"Quite an attractive colt with a great pedigree, but we haven't got too far with him at the moment and I don't see him as an early runner. One for the second half of*

the season over six or seven furlongs, but I'd be guessing as to his ability at the moment".

1578. UNNAMED ★★
b.f. Exceed And Excel – Intrum Morshaan (Darshaan).
April 4. Sixth foal. 30,000Y. Tattersalls October Book 2. Rabbah Bloodstock. Half-sister to the smart listed 10f Doonside Cup winner and Group 1 Criterium International second Prince Siegfried (by Royal Applause), to the useful French listed 13f winner Bigzam (by Zamindar), the fair 9f winner Peking Beauty (by Kendor) and the modest 11f, 14f and hurdles winner Zed Candy (by Medicean). The dam, a fairly useful 2m winner, is a half-sister to 4 winners including the useful Irish 2-y-o listed 6f and subsequent US Grade 3 winner Coney Kitty. The second dam, Auntie Maureen (by Roi Danzig), a fair Irish 9f and 10f winner, is a half-sister to 3 minor winners. (S Ali). "She's a very attractive filly and I think she takes after the dam because she's not particularly precocious, she's tall and leggy at the moment. But she moves well and she's a half-sister to Godolphin's Prince Seigfried who got better with age. Even though she's by Exceed And Excel who gets his 2-y-o's, I see her more as a 3-y-o type".

1579. UNNAMED ★★
b.c. Galileo – Landmark (Arch).
May 11. Third foal. 310,000Y. Tattersalls October Book 1. Charlie Gordon-Watson. Brother to Field Of Miracles, placed fourth once over 7f on her only start at 2 yrs in 2010 and half-brother to the fairly useful 10f winner Sour Mash (by Danehill Dancer). The dam, a minor 2-y-o winner in the USA, is a sister to the Grade 1 E P Taylor Stakes and Grade 1 Del Mar Oaks winner Arravale. The second dam, Kalosca (by Kaldoun), won 3 races in France and the USA, was Grade 2 placed and is a half-sister to the listed winners Mykonos and Crillon. (HRH Sultan Ahmad Shah). "An attractive colt with a very good action. He's a late foal, still growing and developing, so he won't be doing anything until August time. I quite like him as an individual but we don't know if he has ability or not just yet".

1580. UNNAMED ★★★
b.f. Street Cry – Marienbad (Darshaan).
May 17. Tenth foal. 145,000Y. Tattersalls October Book 1. Not sold. Half-sister to the fairly useful 2010 2-y-o 7f and 1m winner Borug (by Kingmambo), to the Group 1 12f Prix de l'Arc de Triomphe and dual German Group 1 winner Marienbard (by Caerleon), the fair 12f and 14f winner Cape Marien (by Cape Cross), the fair 12f winner Marine City (by Carnegie), the modest 12f winner Genscher (by Cadeaux Genereux) and a 3-y-o winner in Japan by Polish Precedent. The dam, a French 1m winner at both 2 and 3 yrs, is a half-sister to 6 winners including the French and Italian listed winner Kentucky Coffee. The second dam, Marie de Fontenoy (by Lightning), won once in France and is a half-sister to 7 winners including the Group 1 Prix Morny winner Sakura Reiko. (S Ali). "From a family we know very well and she might be a bit stronger than some of them – I think perhaps courtesy of Street Cry. I don't see why the filly wouldn't be running around August time because although she was a late foal she's got a bit of strength to her and she's quite solid. She's bred to improve with age and I'm sure she will, but I think we'll get her out a bit earlier than some of the family".

1581. UNNAMED ★★★ ♠
b.c. Royal Applause – Mazarine Blue (Bellypha).
March 30. Eleventh living foal. 40,000Y. Tattersalls October Book 2. Charlie Gordon-Watson. Half-brother to the smart dual 2-y-o 6f winner and subsequent US Grade 2 9f stakes winner Sapphire Ring, to the Swedish winner of 7 races Sufian, the fair 9f and jumps winner Blue Mariner (all by Marju), the smart 7f (at 2 yrs) to 9f winner of 9 races including 2 listed events Putra Pekan (by Grand Lodge), the dual listed 6f winner (including at 2 yrs) Blue Echo (by Kyllachy), the modest 5f and 6f winner Ice Age (by Chilibang) and the modest 2-y-o 5f winner Orange And Blue (by Prince Sabo). The dam, a modest sprint winner at 3 yrs, is a half-sister to 7 winners including the Group 2 6f Richmond Stakes winner Rich Charlie. The second dam, Maiden Pool (by Sharpen Up), a quite useful 5f winner of 3 races, is a half-sister to 3 winners here and abroad. (HRH

Sultan Ahmad Shah). *"We've trained two smart animals out of the mare in Putra Pekan and Blue Echo. This colt is a 2-y-o type, he's got a bit of strength to him and he'll be a summer 2-y-o from June onwards".*

1582. UNNAMED ★★★
b.c. *Street Cry – Mehthaaf (Nureyev).*
March 23. Half-brother to the smart Group 2 10f Premio Lydia Tesio winner Najah, to the fairly useful 12.3f winner Raaqi, the fairly useful 10f winners Eljohar and Zaajel, (all by Nashwan), the useful 7f and 1m winner Tasdeer (by Rahy), the useful 10f winner and listed-placed Tanaghum (by Darshaan) and the quite useful 10f winner Thaahira (by Dynaformer). The dam won the Irish 1,000 Guineas, the Tripleprint Celebration Mile and the Nell Gwyn Stakes and is closely related to the Diadem Stakes winner Elnadim and the French 2-y-o 7.5f winner Only Seule (herself dam of the Group 1 7f Prix de la Foret and Group 1 6.5f Prix Maurice de Gheest winner Occupandiste). The second dam, Elle Seule (by Exclusive Native), won the Group 3 1m Prix d'Astarte and is a half-sister to the Group/Grade 1 winners Fort Wood, Hamas and Timber Country and to the Group winners Northern Aspen, Colorado Dancer (herself the dam of Dubai Millennium) and Mazzacano. (Hamdan Al Maktoum). *"It's a great pedigree but he's still in Dubai and we haven't seen him".*

1583. UNNAMED ★★★★
b.f. *Iffraaj – Spiritual Air (Royal Applause).*
February 2. Third foal. Doncaster Premier. £55,000Y. David Redvers. Half-sister to the fair 2-y-o 7f winner Andean Margin (by Giant's Causeway) and to the moderate 1m winner Emeralds Spirit (by Rock Of Gibraltar). The dam, a fairly useful 2-y-o 6f winner, subsequently won at 4 yrs in the USA and is a half-sister to 3 winners including the very useful 2-y-o 5f winner and Group 2 6f Mill Reef Stakes second Mystical Land. The second dam, Samsung Spirit (by Statoblest), a fair dual 6f winner (including at 2 yrs), is a half-sister to 7 winners and to the placed dam of the Group 2 6f Mill Reef Stakes winner Indian Rocket. (Clipper Group Holdings Ltd). *"A very attractive filly, she has a bit of size about her and a good action, but I don't know about her ability as yet because she had a bit of a cough and we went quiet with her. But I'm looking forward to training her, especially knowing how well the sire did last year. Certainly when you see her stood up in the box you'd like her and there's every chance she'll make a 2-y-o in July".*

1584. UNNAMED ★★★★
b.f. *Iffraaj – Why Now (Dansili).*
March 3. Third foal. 40,000Y. Tattersalls October Book 2. Rabbah Bloodstock. Half-sister to the quite useful 2010 2-y-o 6f winner What About You (by Statue Of Liberty) and to the quite useful dual 5f winner Here Now And Why (by Pastoral Pursuits). The dam, a fair 5f and 6f winner, is a half-sister to 4 winners including the fairly useful 10.8f and jumps winner In Question. The second dam, Questionable (by Rainbow Quest), is an unraced sister to the Group 3 15f Prix Berteux winner Ecologist and a half-sister to 7 winners including the St James's Palace Stakes second Greensmith, the Group 3 winners Infrasonic and Green Reef and the dam of the St Leger winner Toulon. (S Ali). *"A very strong filly, the dam was very precocious and this filly has real strength to her, a deep girth and great quarters. She wants training as a 2-y-o and she could be out in May or June and have a proper summer campaign with her. One to look out for".*

1585. UNNAMED ★★
b.c. *Nayef – Yaqeen (Green Desert).*
February 22. First foal. The dam, a very useful 7f and listed 10f winner, is a half-sister to the US dual Grade 1 12f Sword Dancer Handicap and Turf Classic Invitational winner Grand Couturier and to the smart 10f winner of 4 races Alainmaar. The second dam, Lady Elgar (by Sadler's Wells), unplaced in one start in France, is a sister to the Sha Tin Trophy winner and Irish Derby third Desert Fox and a half-sister to the US Grade 3 winners Poolesta and Home Of The Free. (Hamdan Al Maktoum). *"Still in Dubai and I haven't seen her but we trained the dam and she was quite smart".*

ED VAUGHAN

1586. CLAPPED ★★★
b.c. *Royal Applause – Susun Kelapa (St Jovite).*
April 30. Eighth foal. 21,000Y. Tattersalls October Book 2. Ed Vaughan. Brother to the modest 2010 fourth placed 2-y-o St Oswald and half-brother to the fairly useful 9f and 10f winner Military Power (by Dubai Destination), to the fair Irish 7f winner Monsusu (by Montjeu), the modest 5f winner Royal Composer (by Mozart) and the 1m seller winner Non Ultra (by Peintre Celebre). The dam, a fairly useful 7.8f (at 2 yrs) and 9f winner, is a half-sister to the US stakes winner Lac Dessert. The second dam, Tiramisu (by Roberto), a minor French 3-y-o winner, is a half-sister to 7 winners including the dam of the French 2,000 Guineas winner Green Tune and the Cheveley Park Stakes winner Pas de Reponse. (Hamer & Hawkes). *"A very late foal, he's grown a lot, he has a good action and he'll be one for the second half of the season, from July onwards, over seven furlongs. A nice colt".*

1587. COMPLACENT (IRE) ★★★
b.f. *Kheleyf – Mambodorga (Kingmambo).*
March 4. £6,000Y. Doncaster Premier. Blandford Bloodstock. Half-sister to the quite useful 5f, 6f (including at 2 yrs) and 7f winner Mambo Spirit (by Invincible Spirit). The dam is an unplaced half-sister to 11 winners including the French Group 2 and US Grade 2 winner Spring Star. The second dam, L'Irlandaise (by Irish River), won the listed Prix de Honfleur and is a half-sister to 2 winners. (E F Vaughan). *"She goes well this little filly, I have a sharp bunch this year, they've done plenty of work and they're quite early. This filly goes OK, she looks like she'll need six furlongs and she has a very good constitution".* TRAINERS' BARGAIN BUY

1588. QUIZZED ★★★★
b.f. *Oratorio – Tree Peony (Woodman).*
April 2. Fifth foal. 22,000Y. Tattersalls October Book 2. Blandford Bloodstock. Half-sister to Primevere (by Singspiel), a promising 1m winner on her only start at 2 yrs in 2010, to the moderate 1m seller winner Molly The Witch (by Rock Of Gibraltar) and a winner in Saudi Arabia by Indian Ridge. The dam, a fair 3-y-o 7f winner, is a half-sister to 5 winners including the Group 3 placed Evening World. The second dam, Pivoine (by Nureyev), is an unraced half-sister to 7 winners including the dam of the champion European 3-y-o Peintre Celebre. (The Eloquently Partnership). *"A very nice filly that should be out pretty early and she looks to be quick enough for six furlongs. Very much a 2-y-o type, her half-sister Primevere broke the track record on her only start last year. She was very impressive so we bought this filly the next morning and she's probably the one I like the most at present".*

1589. VERGE ★★★
b.f. *Acclamation – Marliana (Mtoto).*
January 25. Fifth living foal. Doncaster Premier. £23,000Y. Ed Vaughan. Half-sister to the quite useful 2-y-o winner The Dial House (by Tagula), to the dual 2-y-o 7f seller winner Marmite (by Vettori) and the fair 2-y-o dual 6f winner Zambach (by Namid). The dam, a French 2-y-o 6f winner, is a half-sister to 4 winners including the Group 3 Prix de Flore winner Albisola. The second dam, Mahalia (by Danehill), won the listed Prix Imprudence and is a half-sister to 7 winners including the Group 3 winner Muroto and the dam of the Ivan Luis and Stagelight. (Hungerford Park Ltd). *"A half-sister to three 2-y-o winners, physically she looks the nicest of my 2-y-o's. She has a really nice action, so hopefully she'll do as her pedigree suggests and be quick enough for six furlongs. I've done a couple of bits of work with her and I'm just waiting for the six furlong maidens in early May".*

1590. UNNAMED ★★★
b.c. *Bahamian Bounty – Andramad (Fasliyev).*
January 26. First foal. Doncaster Premier. £56,000Y. David Redvers. The dam, a quite useful 2-y-o 6f winner, is a half-sister to 3 winners including the listed winner Desert Fantasy. The second dam, Petite Fantasy (by Mansooj), a very useful Irish sprinter, won the listed Belgrave Stakes, was placed in numerous other Group races in Ireland and is a half-sister to 3 winners. (Pearl Bloodstock Ltd). *"He's a little bit immature of his joints so I'm being careful with him, but otherwise he's a big, strong, mature-looking 2-y-o. He won't be out for a while but I do like him and he's a good actioned horse".*

ED WALKER

1591. DUKE OF DESTINY (IRE) ★★★
b.c. Bachelor Duke – Marghelan (Soviet Star).
May 12. Third foal. Tattersalls Ireland. €11,500Y. Kern/Lillingston. Brother to the unplaced 2010 2-y-o Mama Sox. The dam was placed 4 times at 3 yrs in France and is a half-sister to 8 winners. The second dam, Marcotte (by Nebos), won 5 races in Belgium, was fourth in the Group 2 Grand Criterium d'Ostende and is a full or half-sister to 10 winners including the multiple German Group 1 winner Mondrian. (Dubai Thoroughbred Racing). *"A nice, athletic 2-y-o type that I bought at Fairyhouse. He's built to be a 2-y-o but he was a May foal so he's one for the mid-summer onwards. He goes well at this stage, he's a very likeable chap and although I haven't turned any screws yet he's ticking the right boxes so far. The sire hasn't set the world on fire but this was a cheaply-bought colt and if he'd been by a fashionable sire he'd have cost fifty grand rather than ten because he's a nice individual".*

1592. LIVIA'S DREAM (IRE) ★★★★
b.f. Teofilo – Brindisi (Dr Fong).
April 28. Third foal. 45,000Y. Tattersalls October Book 1. Olivia Hoare. Half-sister to the modest 10f winner Halyard (by Halling). The dam, a listed 1m winner, is a sister to one winner and a half-sister to 5 winners. The second dam, Genoa (by Zafonic), a fairly useful 11.5f winner, was listed placed over 10f and is a half-sister to 3 winners. (Mrs O Hoare). *"A lovely filly out of a listed winning mare, she was quite a late foal but she's not very big so I'm hoping she'll be an earlier 2-y-o than her foaling date might suggest. A very racy, very athletic filly with a great attitude and by an exciting first-season sire. I think she'll certainly make a two-year-old".*

1593. SPARKS MIGHT FLY ★★★★
ch.c. Sakhee – Angel Rays (Unfuwain).
March 7. First reported foal. 11,000Y. Tattersalls October Book 2. Kern/Lillingston. The dam, a modest maiden, was placed fourth over 7f (at 2 yrs) and 6f and is a sister to the useful 10f and 12f listed winner Film Script (herself dam of the listed winner Free Agent) and a half-sister to the Group 3 Chipchase Stakes winner Barney McGrew and the fairly useful 6f and 7f and subsequent US stakes winner National Park. The second dam, Success Story (by Sharrood), a modest 10f winner, is a half-sister to the Group 2 13.5f Prix de Pomone winner Interlude. (The Leg Men). *"I think he was very well-bought. Sakhee is an unfashionable stallion so I don't think this colt was on many people's lists and they missed him. He's one for the late summer and he's a very athletic, very good-looking horse. At the moment he goes very nicely and I'm looking forward to when he fills his frame because he'll be a very good-looking horse. I should think a mile to ten furlongs should suit him as a 3-y-o".* **TRAINERS' BARGAIN BUY**

1594. WILLIE WAG TAIL (USA) ★★★
b.c. Theatrical – Night Risk (Wild Again).
January 21. Tenth foal. 40,000Y. Tattersalls October Book 2. Kern/Lillingston. Half-brother to the fairly useful 6f and 7f winner of 6 races Nightjar (by Smoke Glacken), to the French listed-placed Blow The Lot (by Stravinsky), 3 minor winners in the USA by Polish Numbers, Private Terms and Smoke Glacken and a jumps winner by With Approval. The dam, a minor US 3-y-o winner, is a half-sister to 9 winners including the minor stakes winners Vignette, On A Cloud and Be Elusive. The second dam, Be Exclusive (by Be My Guest), won the Group 3 Prix Chloe. (One Carat Partnership). *"A very big horse, he's a strapping, good-looking colt. A Theatrical with a good temperament (some of them aren't), for a big horse he's light on his feet and he moves well. He's not at all a cumbersome type despite his size and is an athletic colt that covers the ground well. I'll start him off at the back-end of the summer".*

1595. UNNAMED ♣♣
gr.f. Nayef – Miss Satamixa (Linamix).
May 7. Twelfth foal. 8,000Y. Tattersalls October Book 2. Not sold. Half-sister to the fair 2010 5f laced 2-y-o X Rated (by Dubai Destination), to the quite useful 2-y-o dual 7f winner Brambleberry (by Cape Cross), the quite useful Irish 2-y-o 1m winner Byzantine, the minor French middle-distance winner of 3 races Mister Wells (both by Sadler's Wells) and the minor French 3-y-o 7f winner Man O Desert (by Green Desert). The dam, winner of

the Group 1 1m Prix Jacques le Marois, is a half-sister to 6 winners including the dams of the Group/Graded stakes winners Miss Caerleona, Mister Riv, Mister Sicy and Manninamix. The second dam, Miss Satin (by Satingo), won the listed 7f Prix de l'Obelisque and is a half-sister to 6 winners including the Italian Group 2 winner Mister Ski. *"A filly out of a Group 1 winning mare, she's available for lease and is a very likeable sort. A slow-maturing type, she did a lot of growing and changing shape in the early part of the year so I sent her back to the stud for a rest. I expect her to come back into training in April and she should be racing from late-summer onwards".*

CHRIS WALL

1596. CHARITY BOX ★★★★
b.f. Haafhd – Bible Box (Bin Ajwaad).
March 16. Fifth foal. Half-sister to the useful listed 6f winner of 5 races (including at 2 yrs) Bounty Box, to the French 2-y-o 9f listed-placed Bahamian Box (both by Bahamian Bounty) and the fairly useful 2-y-o 6f winner and listed-placed Vive Les Rouges (by Acclamation). The dam, a quite useful 7f to 9f winner of 3 races, is out of the 2-y-o 1m seller winner Addie Pray (by Great Commotion), herself a half-sister to 7 winners. (J E Sims). *"The mare's done well and this looks an athletic filly. The 3-y-o is no good but she's quite big, whereas this filly is more typical of the ones we've had out of the mare in the past. She'll be a 2-y-o in the second half of the season, we haven't done a lot with her but she does everything nicely. Certainly a promising sort and she should have the speed for six furlongs, but I think being by Haafhd she should get seven".*

1597. INTENSE PINK ★★★
b.f. Pivotal – Clincher Club (Polish Patriot).
April 1. Tenth foal. 75,000Y. Tattersalls October Book 1. Chris Wall. Half-sister to the useful 2010 2-y-o 6f winner and Group 2 6f Gimcrack Stakes third Sir Reginald (by Compton Place), to the smart 2-y-o 6f winner and Group 1 1m Racing Post Trophy third Henrik (by Primo Dominie), the quite useful 2-y-o 6f winners Bishop's Lake (by Lake Coniston) and Spritzeria (by Bigstone), the quite useful dual 7f winner Sard (by Bahamian Bounty) and a minor winner abroad by Soviet Star. The dam, a fair 5f (at 2 yrs) and 7.5f winner, is a half-sister to 9 winners. The second dam, Merry Rous (by Rousillon), won once at 2 yrs and is a half-sister to 5 winners including the dual Group 3 winning sprinter Tina's Pet. (Mr D S Lee). *"A nice type of filly from a family we know well, she's just going through a growing phase now so I wouldn't expect her to make a 2-y-o too early. I like her, she seems to have the right attitude and she just has to get her act together through the first part of the summer and then we'll see. A six/seven furlong type 2-y-o, she's strong and physically more forward than most of my others".*

1598. NORFOLK SKY ★★★
ch.f. Haafhd – Cayman Sound (Turtle Island).
March 10. Fifth foal. Half-sister to the fair 1m and 9f winner of 3 races Charlevoix (by King Charlemagne) and to the moderate 1m and 9f winner Key Breeze (by Exceed And Excel). The dam, a minor 12f winner, is a half-sister to 6 winners. The second dam, Kukri (by Kris), is an unraced half-sister to 3 winners. *"A nice type of filly, we trained her half-sister Charlevoix. An athletic type and well put-together, she ought to make a 2-y-o because she's a slightly different model to the others in the family and I think she'll be a bit more precocious".*

1599. PEARL MAGIC ★★★★
ch.f. Speightstown – Nature's Magic (Nijinsky).
April 24. Twelfth foal. $50,000Y. Keeneland September. David Redvers. Half-sister to 9 winners including the very smart 7f (at 2 yrs) and Group 3 1m winner and Group 2 1m Queen Anne Stakes third Tough Speed, the Irish jumps winner Mouftari (both by Miswaki), the minor US stakes winner Asyouwish (by Pioneering) and to 2 minor winners in the USA by Pioneering and Devil's Bag. The dam is a placed half-sister to the US dual Grade 3 9f winner Stalwars and the French listed 7f winner and German Group 2 second Joy Of Glory. The second dam, Joy Returned (by Big Spruce), was a stakes winner of 6 races in the USA. (Pearl Bloodstock). *"A nice, well-grown, strong filly, she looks like being a summer 2-y-o. A nice type and certainly worth putting in the book".*

1600. SILVER LACE (IRE) ★★
gr.f. Clodovil – Rockahoolababy (Kalanisi)
March 23. First foal. 20,000Y. Tattersalls October Book 2. C Wall. The dam is an unraced half-sister to 7 winners including the useful dual Group 3 sprint winner of 10 races Proud Native and the useful Irish listed middle-distance winner Karikata The second dam, Karamana (by Habitat), is an unraced half-sister to 6 winners including 3 listed winners and the minor French winner Kaysama (dam of the stakes winners Air Of Distinction, Kayfa and Rabican). (The Equema Partnership). "Quite a backward filly, she's had a few niggling problems so we've had to take our time with her. But she's a nice enough filly, certainly not one for the first half of the season but she's athletic and we'd be hopeful of her achieving something. If it's not this year, then maybe as a 3-y-o".

1601. WORLD CLASS ★★★★
ch.f. Galileo – Out West (Gone West).
May 6. Closely related to the Derby, Racing Post Trophy and Dante Stakes winner Motivator and to the Group 2 12f Hardwicke Stakes winner Macarthur (both by Mortjeu) and half-sister to the smart listed 10f winner Imperial Star (by Fantastic Light) and a minor 4-y-o winner in the USA (by Polish Precedent). The dam, a useful 7.5f (at 2 yrs) and 1m lsted winner, is a half-sister to 3 winners including the US Grade 3 placed Auggies Here. The second dam, Chellingoua (by Sharpen Up) was placed over 1m and is half-sister to 5 winners including the dual Grade 1 winner Wavering Monarch. (Ms A Fustoq). "A beautifully-bred filly and she's a very nice type too. You always worry about horses with names like hers, but she's certainly bred to be something! I've had two others out of the dam and they weren't much good, but this filly is in a different mould. A scopey filly, temperamentally everything's OK with her, she's a bigger and stronger type than her half-sisters and I like her. Not bred to be an early 2-y-o obviously, but I'd like to get some experience into her at the back-end of the season. She's one of those you dream about, but we don't know how good she is yet".

1602. ZE KING ★★
b.c. Manduro – Top Flight Queen (Mark Of Esteem).
May 4. Seventh foal. 32,000Y. Tattersalls October Book 1. Not sold. Half-brother to the very useful 7f (at 2 yrs) to 10f winner Big Robert (by Medicean), to the quite useful 5f and 6f winner of 5 races Anne Of Kiev (by Oasis Dream), the fair 1m to 10f winner of 5 races King's Masque (by Noverre) and a French hurdles winner by Vettori. The dam, a quite useful 10f winner, is a half-sister to 6 winners including the smart Group 2 11.9f Great Voltigeur Stakes winner Sacrament and to the unraced dam of the Group 1 Pretty Polly Stakes winner Chorist. The second dam, Blessed Event (by Kings Lake), winner of the listed 10f Ballymacoll Stud Stakes, was placed in 5 Group races including the Yorkshire Oaks and the Champion Stakes and is a half-sister to 4 winners. (Ms A Fustoq). "A nice type of horse, but he's destined to be a 3-yo. He has a good attitude and I trained the dam who was quite a nice filly and she was a tough mare with the right attitude. I'd be hopeful for him, but not as a 2-y-o".

AMY WEAVER

1603. POND LIFE (IRE) ★★★
b.c. Teofilo – Water Feature (Dansili).
February 14. Second foal. 18,000Y. Doncaster Premier. BBA Ire. The dam is an unraced half-sister to 13 winners including the high-class Group 1 1m Ciga Grand Criterium and Group 2 10.4f Dante Stakes winner Tenby, the very useful 1m (at 2 yrs) and 10f winner Bright Water and the useful 2-y-o 7f and 1m winner River Usk. The second dam, Shining Water (by Kalaglow) was a very useful winner of the Group 3 7f Solario Stakes and was placed in the Group 2 Park Hill Stakes. (Mrs M Bryce). "He's going quite nicely and although on pedigree you'd think he'd want a bit more time he's actually a compact, sprinting type and we'll hopefully get him on the track in April. He'd quite forward and looks to have a bit of speed".

1604. SWEETSCOT (IRE) ★★★
b.f. Selkirk – So Sweet (Cape Cross).
March 29. First foal. 4,000Y. Tattersalls October Book 3. Amy Weaver. The dam, a

fairly useful 2-y-o dual 7f winner, is a sister to the smart 6f (at 2 yrs), 7f and listed 12f winner and Group 3 placed Crosspeace and a half-sister to 3 winners. The second dam, Announcing Peace (by Danehill), is an unplaced full or half-sister to 5 minor winners. (Mrs M Bryce). *"She was quite small at the Sales but she's grown an awful lot. A filly with a nice pedigree, she's starting to shape up now and is much more Cape Cross looking than Selkirk. She should make a summertime 2-y-o, starting at seven furlongs and she has the action of a good ground horse"*. TRAINERS' BARGAIN BUY

1605. UNNAMED ★★★
br.f. Excellent Art – Siena Gold (Key Of Luck).
March 1. Second foal. 14,000Y. Tattersalls October Book 2. Not sold. The dam, a useful winner of the 2-y-o 5f Weatherbys Supersprint, is a half-sister to 6 winners including the very useful 2-y-o Crazee Mental (a winner over 6f and placed in the Cheveley Park Stakes, the Queen Mary Stakes and the Cherry Hinton Stakes). The second dam, Corn Futures (by Nomination), a fair 2-y-o 6f winner, is a half-sister to 7 winners including the dam of the March Stakes and Glorious Stakes winner Midnight Legend. (C G Rowles Nicholson). *"She's a lovely, big filly. A strong type from a 2-y-o family, I imagine she'll be out in June or July. She'll probably want a bit of ease in the ground because she's quite a heavy-topped horse"*.

1606. UNNAMED ★★
b.c. Hurricane Run – Violette (Observatory).
April 5. Second foal. The dam, a Group 3 6f Firth Of Clyde Stakes winner, was second in the Group 2 Rockfel Stakes and is a half-sister to 4 winners including the useful 2-y-o 5f and 6f winner and Group 3 placed Virginia Hall and the listed 6f (at 2 yrs) and Group 3 7f Nell Gwyn Stakes winner Silca's Gift. The second dam, Odette (by Pursuit Of Love), a fair 3-y-o 5f and 5.7f winner, is a half-sister to 4 winners including the useful 6f (at 2 yrs) and 7f winner and Group 2 5f Flying Childers Stakes fourth Caballero. (C G Rowles-Nicholson). *"A smashing looking horse – he's big, strong and really nice. He's very well-bred and although he's more of a 3-y-o type both on looks and on pedigree he's already showing the right signs.*

He's well able to keep up with the others and so not as backward as you might think. If we look after him he'll have a run or two from August onwards and then be a nice horse next year. A big, long-striding horse, we'll start him off at seven furlongs"*.

DERMOT WELD

1607. ACORN VALLEY (USA) ★★★
ch.c. Kitten's Joy – Mambo With G (Old Trieste).
March 27. Second foal. Goffs Orby. €50,000Y. Bobby O'Ryan. The dam, a stakes-placed winner of 4 races in the USA, is a half-sister to 4 winners including the stakes winner Congo Kaye. The second dam, Palau (by Kingmambo), a minor winner at 2 yrs in the USA, is a half-sister to 6 winners including the US Grade 3 winner High Strike Zone. (Dr R Lambe). *"I think he'll be a nice horse in the second half of the season. I see him going seven furlongs or a mile in July/August. The sire was a Grade 1 winner in America and was beaten a neck for the Breeders Cup Turf. This is his second crop"*.

1608. ANGEL BRIGHT (IRE) ★★★
b.f. Dark Angel – Cover Girl (Common Grounds).
April 24. Sixth foal. Goffs Orby. €115,000Y. Bobby O'Ryan. Closely related to the fair Irish 7f and 1m winner Luxie (by Acclamation) and half-sister to the very useful dual listed 6f winner Mister Manannan and the useful 2-y-o 5f and 5.7f winner, Group 3 Cornwallis Stakes third and subsequent US Grade 3 placed Shermeen (both by Desert Style). The dam, a fair 2-y-o 6f and 7f and subsequent Scandinavian listed winner, is a half-sister to 2 winners. The second dam, Peace Carrier (by Doulab), was placed over 12f in Ireland and is a half-sister to 6 winners including the listed winner Sandhurst Goddess – herself dam of the dual Group 3 winner Lady Alexander. (Mrs C L Weld). *"Owned by my mother, this is a nice filly and a three-parts sister to Luxie who we trained. It's a good family and she'll be a nice six furlong 2-y-o around June/July time"*.

1609. CRIMSON SUNRISE (IRE) ★★★★
b.f. Holy Roman Emperor – Zanida (Mujadil).
March 17. First foal. Goffs Orby. €75,000Y.

Bobby O'Ryan. The dam, a quite useful 2-y-o 5f winner, is a half-sister to 5 winners including the useful sprinter and listed winner of 6 races Double Quick. The second dam, Haraabah (by Topsider), a useful 5f to 7f winner, is a half-sister to 3 winners. (Dr R Lambe). *"A very sharp filly, she'll start off in April and she goes nicely. She'll win as a 2-y-o over five furlongs".*

1610. CUSTOM CUT (IRE) ★★★
b.c. Notnowcato – Polished Gem (Danehill).
February 2. Second foal. Half-brother to Sapphire (by Medicean), unplaced in one start at 2 yrs in 2010. The dam, an Irish 2-y-o 7f winner, is a sister to 2 winners including the Grade 1 9f Matriarch Stakes and Group 2 1m Sun Chariot Stakes winner Dress To Thrill and a half-sister to 6 winners. The second dam, Trusted Partner (by Affirmed), was a very useful winner of the Group 3 7f C.L. Weld Park Stakes (at 2 yrs) and the Irish 1,000 Guineas and is a sister to the useful middle distance performers Easy to Copy and Epicure's Garden and to the useful Irish 7f listed and US Grade 3 winner Low Key Affair. (Moyglare Stud Farm). *"He's interesting, a medium sized colt and he'll be a 2-y-o in mid-summer over six/seven furlongs".*

1611. ENCRYPTED MESSAGE (IRE) ★★★★
b.c. Dansili – Where We Left Off (Dr Devious).
April 26. Half-brother to the 2010 Irish 2-y-o 1m winner Late Day Sun (by Montjeu) and to the quite useful Irish 11f winner Walk Beside Me (by Theatrical). The dam, a US Grade 3 9f winner, is a half-sister to the Australian Group 2 10f winner Rekindled Interest (by Redoute's Choice) and the French listed 11f winner Porticcio. The second dam, Rekindled Affair (by Rainbow Quest), is an unraced half-sister to 4 winners and to the unraced smart broodmare Summer Trysting (the dam of two Group winners). (Moyglare Stud Farms Ltd). *"A very nice colt. He'll be racing July or August and he's a strong, powerful horse".*

1612. FASTIDEOUS ★★★★
b.c. Exceed And Excel – Felicitous (King's Best).
February 10. Half-brother to the Australian dual Group 1 placed Praecido (by One Cool Cat). The dam, the fairly useful 6f and 7f winner, is a half-sister to the useful 2-y-o 7f winner Grosvenor Square. The second dam, Embassy (by Cadeaux Genereux), a champion 2-y-o filly and winner of the Cheveley Park Stakes, is a half-sister to the smart 7f (at 2 yrs) and Group 2 Pretty Polly Stakes winner Tarfshi and the fairly useful 2-y-o 1m winner Puck's Castle. (Sheikh Mohammed). *"He's a colt I like. He's well-balanced, I hope to run him in May over five/six furlongs and he could well be one to look out for".*

1613. FIERY AMBITION ★★★★
b.c. Shamardal – Xaluna Bay (Xaar).
February 6. First foal. 68,000Y. Tattersalls October Book 1. Bobby O'Ryan. The dam, a fair 5f (at 2 yrs) and 6f winner, is a half-sister to 3 winners including the useful Irish 7f winner and dual Group 3 placed Kyniska. The second dam, Lunadine (by Bering), is an unplaced half-sister to 3 winners including the Group 3 winner Prix Corrida winner Luna Mareza. (Dr R Lambe). *"He's going to be a very strong colt, one for the late summer and he's a horse I like".*

1614. HASEEN (IRE) ★★★
b.c. Invincible Spirit – Elshamms (Zafonic).
February 8. Seventh foal. Closely related to the moderate 6f winner Minwir (by Green Desert) and half-brother to the fairly useful Irish 7f and 10f winner Aqraan (by In The Wings), the useful triple 6f (including at 2 yrs) and subsequent UAE listed 5f winner Taqseem (by Fantastic Light) and the fair 1m winner Ishraaqat (by Singspiel). The dam, a fairly useful 2-y-o 7f winner and third in the Group 3 Prestige Stakes, is a half-sister to numerous winners including the very useful 10f winner Shaya. The second dam, Gharam (by Green Dancer), a very useful 2-y-o 6f winner, was third in the French 1,000 Guineas and is a half-sister to the US Grade 1 9f winner Talinum. (Hamdan Al Maktoum). *"He's one for the second part of the season, he'll make a 2-y-o though".*

1615. HIT THE JACKPOT (IRE) ★★★★★
ch.c. Pivotal – Token Gesture (Alzao).
January 22. Tenth foal. Half-brother to the 7f (at 2 yrs in Ireland) and Grade 1 Canadian International winner Relaxed Gesture, to the useful 10f winner and Group 3 10f Gallinule Stakes third Central Station (both by Indian

Ridge), the Irish 1m and subsequent US Grade 2 9.5f American Derby winner Evolving Tactics (by Machiavellian), the fairly useful 7f (at 2 yrs) to 13f winner Braveheart Move (by Cape Cross) and the Irish 1m, 12f and hurdles winner Turn Of Phrase (by Cadeaux Genereux). The dam, a smart winner of the Group 3 7f C L Weld Park Stakes, is a half-sister to the US Grade 2 9f winner Wait Till Monday, to the useful Irish 10f to 12.3f winner Blazing Spectacle and the useful Irish middle-distance stayer and Triumph Hurdle winner Rare Holiday. The second dam, Temporary Lull (by Super Concorde), is an unraced sister to the Nell Gwyn Stakes winner Martha Stevens. (Moyglare Stud Farm). *"A good, strong colt and a mid-summer 2-y-o over seven furlongs. One to note".*

1616. KAASEB (USA) ★★
b.c. Jazil – Thawakib (Sadler's Wells).
May 1. Closely related the fair 4-y-o 7f winner Haasem (by Seeking The Gold) and half-brother to the Prix de l'Arc de Triomphe and Juddmonte International winner Sakhee (by Bahri), to the useful 7f (at 2 yrs) and 10f winner Nasheed (by Riverman), the fairly useful 2-y-o 7f winner Alharir (by Zafonic), the quite useful 10.2f winner Weqaar (by Red Ransom) and the fair 1m winner Yathreb (by Kingmambo). The dam, a useful filly, won twice over 7f (at 2 yrs) and the Group 2 12f Ribblesdale Stakes. She is a half-sister to numerous winners including the top-class middle-distance colt Celestial Storm (winner of the Group 2 Princess of Wales's Stakes) and to the placed dam of the Group 1 Rothmans International winner River Memories. The second dam, Tobira Celeste (by Ribot), won twice at up to 9f in France and was third in the Group 3 12f Prix de Minerve. (Hamdan Al Maktoum). *"Only just arrived from Dubai, but as the sire won the Belmont I should imagine this colt will be more of a 3-y-o".*

1617. MAHAAZEN (IRE) ★★
b.f. Cape Cross – Innclassic (Stravinsky).
March 1. Third foal. Goffs Orby. €125,000Y. Shadwell Estate. Half-sister to the 2010 2-y-o Italian winner Pile Ou Face (by Exceed And Excel). The dam, a modest 6f winner, is a half-sister to 5 winners including the US dual Grade 1 winner Daytona. The second dam, Kyka (by Blushing John), is an unraced half-sister to 5 winners including the French 1,000 Guineas winner Madeleine's Dream and the US Grade 3 9f Bewitch Stakes winner Miss Lenora (herself dam of the triple Grade 3 winner Stylish). (Hamdan Al Maktoum). *"More of a second half of the season 2-y-o".*

1618. MISSISSIPPI ★★★ ♣
b.c. Exceed And Excel – Ruby Rocket (Indian Rocket).
March 14. Third foal. 180,000Y. Tattersalls October Book 1. Sir Robert Ogden. The dam, a listed 5f and 6f winner, was Group 3 placed twice and is a half-sister to 8 winners including the Irish 2-y-o 6f listed winner Alexander Alliance and the German listed winner and Group 3 6.5f Prix Eclipse second Inzar's Best. The second dam, Geht Schnell (by Fairy King), is a placed half-sister to one winner abroad. (Sir Robert Ogden). *"A nice colt, he's strong but he's growing a lot. So I see him as more of a second half of the season 2-y-o".*

1619. MOONSHED (USA) ★★ ♣
b.c. Arch – Rose Of Zollern (Seattle Dancer).
February 2. Fifth foal. Goffs Orby. €80,000Y. Shadwell Estate Co. Half-brother to the fairly useful 2-y-o dual 7f winner and subsequent German dual listed placed Flor Y Nata (by Fusaichi Pegasus), to the fair 6f and 7f winner of 3 races Rosa De Mi Corazon (by Cozzene) and the fair 1m winner Tarooq (by War Chant). The dam won 9 races including the German 1,000 Guineas and a stakes event in the USA, was Group 1 placed and is a half-sister to 3 winners. The second dam, Kalisha (by Rainbow Quest), is an unraced half-sister to the Dewhurst Stakes winner Kala Dancer. (Hamdan Al Maktoum). *"He's only just arrived from Dubai so it's hard to say, but and he's a good-sized colt. I see him as being more of a 3-y-o type".*

1620. MULHEB (USA) ★★★★
b.c. Bernardini – Private Status (Alydar).
February 13. Tenth foal. $800,000Y. Keeneland September. Shadwell Estate Co. Half-brother to the Grade 1 Mother Goose Stakes and Grade 1 Kentucky Oaks winner Secret Status, to the US Grade 3 winner Alumni Hall (both by A P Indy) and the US stakes

winner Private Gift (by Unbridled). The dam, a US stakes winner, was Grade 1 placed and is a half-sister to two Grade 1 winners in Chile The second dam, Miss Eva (by Con Brio II), won twice at 3 yrs in Chile. (Hamdan Al Maktoum). *"A very nice colt, he's just arrived from Dubai and he's a good-sized colt. I would see him as a very nice horse from August onwards".*

1621. NILE VENTURE ★★★
b.c. Oasis Dream – Strike Lightly (Rainbow Quest).
February 5. Fourth foal. Half-brother to the fair 10f winner Significant Move (by Montjeu). The dam is an unraced sister to the very smart middle-distance winner Ulundi and the French winner and Group 1 Prix Saint-Alary second Fleeting Glimpse (herself dam of the Group 3 May Hill Stakes winner Half Glance) and a half-sister to the 1,000 Guineas winner Wince (dam of the Group 1 Yorkshire Oaks winner Quiff). The second dam, Flit (by Lyphard), a fair 3-y-o 10f winner, is a sister to the US Grade 2 winner Skimble (dam of the US Grade 1 winner Skimming) and closely related to the Grade 1 Washington Lassie Stakes winner Contredance and to the dam of the Larson Champagne Stakes winner Eltish. (Khalid Abdulla). *"I should imagine he'll make a 2-y-o by mid-summer, but it's a bit early for me to say where he fits in".*

1622. PALE MIMOSA (IRE) ★★★
b.f. Singspiel – Katch Me Katie (Danehill).
February 21. Fifth foal. Goffs Orby. €80,000Y. Bobby O'Ryan. Sister to the fairly useful 12f and 2m winner and listed-placed Suailce. The dam, a fair 9f winner, is a half-sister to 4 winners including the Grade 2 E P Taylor Stakes winner and Grade 1 Gamely Handicap and Group 2 Sun Chariot Stakes second Kool Kat Katie and to the smart 8.3f (at 2yrs) and Group 3 10.4f Musidora Stakes winner, Epsom Oaks second and Grade 1 Beverley Hills Handicap third Kalypso Katie. The second dam, Miss Toot (by Ardross), a fair 10f and 15f winner on her only starts, is a half-sister to one winner. *"A lovely, big filly. She's one for the autumn but she's a very powerful, big girl".*

1623. PRINCESS HIGHWAY (USA) ★★★★
b.f. Street Cry – Irresistible Jewel (Danehill).
April 4. Half-sister to the smart Irish Group 3 7f Gladness Stakes winner and multiple Group 1 placed Mad About You (by Indian Ridge) and to the fairly useful 14f winner of 4 races Royal Diamond (by King's Best). The dam won the Group 2 12f Ribblesdale Stakes and the Group 3 10f Blandford Stakes and is a half-sister to numerous winners including the listed 12f winner Diamond Trim and the useful Irish 1m winner Legal Jousting. The second dam, In Anticipation (by Sadler's Wells), won over 12f and 14f in Ireland. (Moyglare Stud Farms Ltd). *"She's a quality filly for August or September and one of the nicest 2-y-o's I have".*

1624. QUICK GLIMPSE ★★★
b.f. Galileo – Half Glance (Danehill).
April 25. Fourth foal. Closely related to the quite useful dual 12f winner Brief Look (by Sadler's Wells) and to the fair Irish 11f winner Catchafallingstar (by Montjeu). The dam won 3 races including the 2-y-o Group 3 1m May Hill Stakes and is a half-sister to the Irish Derby, St Leger and Turf Classic placed Tycoon. The second dam, Fleeting Glimpse (by Rainbow Quest), a 10f winner in France, was second in the Group 1 10f Prix Saint-Alary and is a half-sister to the 1,000 Guineas winner Wince (herself dam of the Group 1 Yorkshire Oaks winner Quiff). (Khalid Abdulla). *"A very sweet filly, she'll make a 2-y-o in August or September".*

1625. RADIO CALL ★★★
b.c. Rail Link – Aspiring Diva (Distant View).
March 10. Closely related to the Group 3 7f Concorde Stakes winner Emulous and to the listed 5f winner Daring Diva (by Dansili) and half-sister to the fairly useful 2-y-o 6f winner Striking Spirit (by Oasis Dream). The dam, placed at up to 1m in France, is a half-sister to numerous winners including the useful 10.2f winner Private Song. The second dam, Queen Of Song (by His Majesty), won 14 races in the USA including the Grade 2 8.5f Shuvee Handicap and the Grade 3 8.5f Sixty Sails Handicap (twice), was Grade 1 placed and is a sister to the Grade 1 Jersey Derby winner Cormorant. (Khalid Abdulla). *"He's a nice colt, but one for later in the season".*

1626. RANSOMED ROSE ★★★
b.f. Oasis Dream – Rapid Ransom
(Red Ransom).
January 29. Sister to the fairly useful Irish 7f (at 2 yrs) and 1m winner and Group 3 7f Debutante Stakes third Rare Ransom, closely related to the fairly useful Irish 10f and 11f winner and listed-placed Ransomed Bride (by Cape Cross) and half-sister to the quite useful Irish 12f winner Rafaello Santi (by Medicean). The dam, a quite useful Irish 10f winner, was Grade 3 placed in the USA and is a half-sister to the Irish 2-y-o listed winner and Group 3 Queen Mary Stakes third Warrior Queen (herself dam of the US Grade 2 winner and Grade 1 placed A P Warrior). The second dam, Call Me Fleet (Afleet), is an unraced half-sister to several winners including Soundings dam of the French Group 1 winners Green Tune and Pas de Reponse). (Lady O'Reilly). *"A big filly, she's very nice and one for August or September".*

1627. RIVIERA POET (IRE) ★★★★
b.br.c. Footstepsinthesand – Dance Clear
(Marju).
March 5. Seventh foal. Goffs Orby. €135,000Y. Dermot Weld. Half-brother to the quite useful 2010 2-y-o winner Man Of The Match (by Iffraaj), to the fair 14f and 2m winner Twist Again (by Sakhee), the fair 12f and hurdles winner Rosecliff (by Montjeu) and the modest 8.7f winner Dyanita (by Singspiel). The dam, an Irish 2-y-o 6f winner and third in the Group 3 7f Killavullan Stakes, subsequently won 4 races and was Grade 3 placed twice in the USA. She is a half-sister to 7 winners out of Dance Ahead (by Shareef Dancer), a quite useful 2-y-o 7f winner and herself a half-sister to 6 winners. (Dr R Lambe). *"A quality colt, he goes nicely and I would hope to run him in around June time over seven furlongs".*

1628. SPEAKING OF WHICH (IRE) ★★★
b.c. Invincible Spirit – Suitably Discreet
(Mr Prospector).
April 19. Half-brother to the Irish 2-y-o 7f winner and Group 2 1m Beresford Stakes second Capital Exposure, to the quite useful Irish 9f and 11f winner Designated Decoy (both by Danzig) and a winner over jumps by Giant's Causeway. The dam is an unraced half-sister to the Group 2 1m Goffs International Stakes and US Grade 2 Arcadia Handicap winner Century City. The second dam, Alywow (by Alysheba), a champion filly in Canada, won 7 races including the Grade 3 8.5f Nijana Stakes and was second in the Grade 1 Rothmans International and the Grade 1 Flower Bowl Invitational. (Moyglare Stud Stakes). *"He's a nice colt, he'll be a 2-y-o but in September or October because he's a big horse".*

1629. SPIRIT OF CONCORDE ★★★★
gr.c. Authorized – Lucky Token (Key Of Luck).
April 8. Second foal. 80,000Y. Tattersalls October Book 1. Bobby O'Ryan. The dam, a fair 9f winner, is a half-sister to 8 winners including the 2-y-o Group 3 6f Round Tower Stakes winner Arctic and the very useful 10f (at 2 yrs) and 2m Queens Vase winner Shanty Star. The second dam, Shawanni (by Shareef Dancer), a useful 2-y-o 7f winner, is a half-sister to the UAE Group 3 winner Blatant and the Group 3 Prix Thomas Bryon winner Songlark. (Dr R Lambe). *"He's a horse I like a lot and for a horse that's bred to stay he's showing a lot of potential. I would see him running in June or July over seven furlongs. He's a horse that does things nicely and I could run him now because he's that forward. He'll be a very nice horse".*

1630. STORM LIGHTNING ★★★★ ♠
b.c. Exceed And Excel – All For Laura
(Cadeaux Genereux).
February 14. Second foal. 85,000Y. Tattersalls October Book 1. D K Weld. Half-brother to the Group 2 6f Cherry Hinton Stakes winner and Group 1 Cheveley Park Stakes second Misheer (by Oasis Dream). The dam, a fairly useful 2-y-o 5f winner, was listed-placed and is a full or half-sister to 3 winners. The second dam, Lighthouse (by Warning), a fairly useful 3-y-o 8.3f winner, is a half-sister to 4 winners including the Group 1 Middle Park Stakes winner First Trump. (Dr R Lambe). *"He's a nice, sharp colt and I would hope to see him out in mid-summer over six or seven furlongs".*

1631. SUNDRENCHED COAST (USA) ★★★
ch.c. Van Nistelrooy – Harve De Grace
(Boston Harbor).
April 7. Fourth foal. $120,000Y. Keeneland September. Ben McElroy. Half-brother to 2

winners including the US Grade 2 9 and Grade 3 9f winner Concord Point (by Tapit). The dam, a minor US winner at 3 and 4 yrs, is a half-sister to the US Grade 3 winner Tasha's Miracle. The second dam, Ms. Cuvee Papa (by Relaunch), a minor US winner from 3 to 5 yrs, is a half-sister to one winner. *"A big colt for the second half of the season"*.

1632. SWEET MYSTERY (IRE) ★★★★
b.c. Dark Angel – Hartstown House (Primo Dominie).
January 26. Sixth foal. Goffs Orby. €110,000Y. Bobby O'Ryan. Half-brother to the fairly useful 7f and 1m winner Hacienda (by Kheleyf), to the fairly useful Irish 2-y-o 6f winner Sheltingham (by Intikhab) and the fair dual 7f winner Little Wing (by Hawk Wing). The dam, a fairly useful Irish 2-y-o dual 5f winner, is a half-sister to 6 winners including the smart 1m winner and Irish 2,000 Guineas second Fa-Eq and the smart listed 7.3f and 1m winner Corinium. The second dam, Searching Star (by Rainbow Quest), a modest 6f (at 2 yrs) to 11.3f placed maiden, is a half-sister to 8 winners including the listed winners Beldale Star and Moon Drop. (Dr R Lambe). *"A good, strong colt and I would hope to be running him in May or June over six furlongs"*.

1633. SWERVE ★★★
b.f. Oasis Dream – Avoidance (Cryptoclearance).
February 7. Fourth foal. Sister to the fairly useful 6f and 7f winner Brushed Aside and to the quite useful Irish 2-y-o 7f winner Broad Meaning. The dam, a fairly useful 7f and 1m winner at 2 yrs, is a half-sister to several winners including the useful 1m and 10f winner Averted View. The second dam, Averti (by Known Fact), a fairly useful 7f (at 2 yrs) and 6f winner, is a half-sister to the US Grade 1 winner Defensive Play. (Khalid Abdulla). *"A bit backward at the moment and one for the second half of the year"*.

1634. TENDEM ★★★
b.c. Dansili – Light Ballet (Sadler's Wells).
May 13. Brother to the quite useful 1m (at 2 yrs in France) to 12f winner of 4 races Porgy and half-brother to the French listed 11f winner Penchee (by Grand Lodge) and the quite useful Irish 1m winner Move (by Observatory). The dam, a French 11f winner, was Group 3 placed and is a sister to the Group 2 12.5f Prix de Royallieu winner Dance Routine and the useful French listed 10f winner Concentric and a half-sister to the 2-y-o Group 3 1m Prix Thomas Bryon winner Apsis and the French listed 12f winner Space Quest. The second dam, Apogee (by Shirley Heights), won the Group 3 12f Prix de Royaumont and is a half-sister to the Group 2 12f Grand Prix de Chantilly winner Daring Miss. (Khalid Abdulla). *"He's a nice colt, but you won't see him before September I don't think"*.

1635. TWO PATHS (USA) ★★★
ch.c. Giant's Causeway – Hymn Of Love (Barathea).
February 16. Half-brother to the quite useful Irish 10f winner Stroke Of Love (by Smart Strike). The dam, an Irish listed 1m winner, is a half-sister to several winners including the Irish 6f and subsequent US winner Still As Sweet. The second dam, Perils Of Joy (by Rainbow Quest), a 3-y-o 1m winner in Ireland, is a half-sister to 5 winners including the Italian Group 3 winner Sweetened Offer. (Moyglare Stud Farm). *"A strong colt, I'd like to run him in June or July over seven furlongs"*.

1636. WHITE NILE (IRE) ★★★★
b.c. Galileo – Super Gift (Darshaan).
May 13. Eighth foal. Goffs Orby. €215,000Y. Sir Robert Ogden. Brother to the fairly useful 2-y-o 1m winner and listed-placed Sense Of Purpose, closely related to the fairly useful 1m winner and listed-placed Dance Pass (by Sadler's Wells) and half-sister to the Irish 7f winner Rare Delight (by Indian Ridge), the quite useful Irish 7f and 1m winner Polite Reply (by Be My Guest) and the fair Irish 10f winner All In A Mix (by Definite Article). The dam, a dual 2-y-o 1m winner and second in the Group 3 C L Weld Park Stakes, is a half-sister to 6 winners. The second dam, Speciality Package (by Blushing Groom), is a placed half-sister to 4 winners including the dam of the dual Group 1 winner Grey Swallow. (Sir Robert Ogden). *"Although he's quite backward at the moment I still see him running in September or October because he's an extremely good mover. I think he'll be a very nice horse"*.

1637. WILLOW ISLAND (IRE) ★★★
b.c. Dark Angel – Cidaris (Persian Bold).
May 14. Ninth foal. Goffs Orby. €40,000Y.
Bobby O'Ryan. Half-brother to the useful Italian listed 1m winner Carioca (by Rakti), to the 5f Windsor Castle Stakes winner and Group 2 6f Mill Reef Stakes second Irony, the fair Irish 2-y-o 6.5f winner District Six (both by Mujadil) and the minor Irish 8.5f winner Manavic (by Clodovil). The dam ran once unplaced and is a half-sister to 3 winners including the dam of the South African Grade 1 winner Rabiya. The second dam, Secret Sunday (by Secreto), a minor Irish 12f winner, is a sister to the 2,000 Guineas winner Mystiko and a half-sister to 6 winners. (Dr R Lambe). *"He's not your typical Dark Angel, he's more lengthy and he's going to be out in July or August over seven furlongs".*

1638. YELLOW ROSEBUD (IRE) ★★★★
b.f. Jeremy – Nebraas (Green Desert).
April 25. Fifth foal. Goffs Orby. €75,000Y.
Bobby O'Ryan. Half-sister to the useful 2010 Irish 2-y-o listed 6f winner Seeharn (by Pivotal), to the quite useful 7f (at 2 yrs) and 6f winner of 5 races My Kingdom and the quite useful 7f winner Royalist (both by King's Best). The dam is an unraced three-parts sister to the very useful 6f winner (including at 2 yrs) Mutaakkid and a half-sister to 4 winners including the Group 1 Golden Jubilee Stakes winner Malhub. The second dam, Arjuzah (by Ahonoora), a useful winner of the listed 7f Sceptre Stakes, is a half-sister to the Irish listed winner Ormsby. (Dr R Lambe). *"A very nice filly. I see her as a seven furlong type for July/August. She looks particularly nice".*

1639. ZAIDAAN (IRE) ★★★
b.c. Acclamation – Tasha's Dream (Woodman).
April 10. Fifth foal. Goffs Orby. €140,000Y.
Shadwell Estate Co. Brother to the fair 1m winner Truly Asia and half-brother to the 2010 2-y-o 6f winner and Group 2 1m May Hill Stakes second Al Madina (by Noverre) and the fairly useful Irish 2-y-o 7f winner and subsequent French listed-placed winner Unquenchable Fire (by Invincible Spirit). The dam is a placed sister to the Group 3 Tetrarch Stakes winner Major Force and a half-sister to 7 winners including the Peruvian Grade 2 winner Dancing Action and the Group 3 Curragh Cup winner Quality Team. The second dam, Ready For Action (by Riverman), won at 3 yrs and is a half-sister to 4 winners. (Hamdan Al Maktoum). *"A big horse, he's strong and one for the second half of the season".*

1640. UNNAMED ★★★
b.f. Selkirk – Daring Diva (Dansili).
February 6. First foal. The dam, a French 2-y-o listed 5f winner, is a sister to the smart listed 1m winner Emulous and a half-sister to the fairly useful 2-y-o 6f winner Striking Spirit. The second dam, Aspiring Diva (by Distant View), was placed at up to 1m in France and is a half-sister to numerous winners including the useful 10.2f winner Private Song. (Khalid Abdulla). *"She's forward enough to run as a 2-y-o later in the season, but she's more of a 3-y-o type".*

1641. UNNAMED ★★★
b.c. Amadeus Wolf – Fabuco (Mujadil).
February 28. Fifth foal. 55,000Y. Tattersalls October Book 1. Blandford Bloodstock. Half-brother to the quite useful 2-y-o dual 7f and subsequent South African Group 3 winner Purple Orchid (by Dr Fong) The dam, a modest 2-y-o 5f winner, is a sister to the useful 2-y-o 5f winner and Group 3 placed Connemara and to the fairly useful 2-y-o 5f winner and Cherry Hinton Stakes fourth Presentation and a half-sister to 3 winners. The second dam, Beechwood (by Blushing Groom), won over 10.8f in France and is a half-sister to 5 winners. (Dr R Lambe). *"I'd hope to have him running in mid-summer, but it's too early to comment on his ability".*

1642. UNNAMED ★★★★
b.f. Flower Alley – Search Mission (Red Ransom).
February 23. Fourth foal. The dam, a quite useful 2-y-o 7f winner, is a half-sister to the very smart Skimming, a winner of 5 races from 1m to 10f here and in the USA including the Grade 1 Pacific Classic (twice). The second dam, Skimble (by Lyphard), a fairly useful 6f (at 2 yrs) and 10.4f winner here, subsequently won 7 stakes events in the USA. She is a sister to the fair 10f winner Flit (dam of the One Thousand Guineas winner Wince) and is closely related to the Grade 1 Washington

Lassie Stakes winner Contredance, the listed Roses Stakes winner Old Alliance and to the dam of the Lanson Champagne Stakes winner Eltish. (Khalid Abdulla). "Quite a sharp filly, she'll be racing in May or June over six furlongs. Probably one of the most forward of the ones I have for Prince Khalid".

1643. UNNAMED ★★★
b.f. Dalakhani – Truly Mine
(Rock Of Gibraltar).
February 20. First foal. 72,000Y. Tattersalls October Book 1. Not sold. The dam, a useful listed 11f winner in Ireland and third in the Group 3 1m Park Express Stakes, is a half-sister to one winner. The second dam, Truly Yours (by Barathea), a 2-y-o 1m winner in France, is a half-sister to 4 winners including the French 2,000 Guineas second Catcher In The Rye. (Newtown Anner Stud). "A very sweet filly, one for September or October and she'll make a lovely 3-y-o".

JOHN WEYMES
1644. ARTISTIC DAWN ★★★
b.f. Excellent Art – Midnight Mist
(Green Desert).
March 8. Third foal. 3,000Y. Tattersalls October Book 2. John Weymes. Half-sister to the quite useful 2010 Irish 2-y-o 1m winner Midnight Music (by Dubawi). The dam, a fair Irish 7f and 1m winner, is a half-sister to the Canadian Grade 3 winner Madeira Mist and to the listed 8.5f winner and Group 1 7f Moyglare Stud Stakes fourth Misty Heights (by Fasliyev), the Irish 2-y-o 7f winner Mountain Snow (by Barathea), the quite useful 1m, 10f and hurdles winner Fortune Point (by Cadeaux Genereux) and the Irish dual 12f winner Mist Of Magic (by Caerleon). The second dam, Mountains Of Mist (by Shirley Heights), a quite useful 10f winner, is a half-sister to 7 winners including the Group 2 Lowther Stakes winner Enthused and the listed 12f Prix Vulcain winner From Beyond. (T A Scothern). "She's a well-grown, good-sized filly and a beautiful mover. We haven't done a lot with her yet and I think she'll probably be one to start off over seven furlongs. The sire, Excellent Art, should do very well and I reckon we stole this filly on just one bid. She had a couple of splints but that didn't deter me and since we bought her the half-sister won her maiden in Ireland. If you look at this filly in the paddock there's just a touch of class about her. She'll want decent ground – you wouldn't run her in a bog. Once we'd got all the 2-y-o's broken and we had had them up on the moor doing a figure of eight, they struck me as the best moving bunch we've had for a few years".

1645. CATARACT ★★★
ch.f. Avonbridge – Catspraddle (High Yield).
January 20. First foal. £6,500Y. Doncaster November. John Weymes. The dam, a fair 5f (at 2 yrs) and 6f winner, is a half-sister to one winner in the USA. The second dam, Beaux Dorothy (by Dehere), won twice and is a half-sister to 4 winners. (Mrs R L Heaton). "She's quite a big, heavy filly that's been half-asleep all winter but she's just starting to show a bit of improvement. I expect her to keep on improving throughout the season and I can see it taking 3 or 4 runs before she gets cherry-ripe, so she might be one for a nursery. Looking at her pedigree you'd expect her to be a five or six furlong type, she's a lovely filly and I loved her at the Sales but I got her for well under budget, so I'm quite happy. She's very laid-back but she's started to improve just lately".

1646. CELESTIAL DAWN ★★
b.f. Echo Of Light – Celestial Welcome
(Most Welcome).
March 8. Sixth foal. 1,500Y. Tattersalls October Book 3. A Crombie. Half-sister to the modest 2010 2-y-o 6f winner Shesastar (by Bahamian Bounty), to the quite useful 2-y-o dual 7f winner and listed-placed Startori (by Vettori), the fair 2-y-o 7f winner Celestial Tryst (by Tobougg) and the moderate 10f to 13f winner of 5 races Shekan Star (by Sri Pekan). The dam, a useful 7f to 12f winner of 8 races, is a sister to 2 winners and a half-sister to 3 winners including the smart Group 2 12f King Edward VII Stakes second Snowstorm. The second dam, Choral Sundown (by Night Shift), a quite useful winner of 4 races at up to 12f, is a half-sister to 5 winners. "She looks like a proper 2-y-o. All the half-siblings out of the dam by 2-y-o type stallions seem to have won. A really bonny filly, she's enthusiastic, loves her work and she's pleased us all winter. She's what I'd call a 'proper northern trainer's horse'

in that we can crack on with her and race her plenty of times". TRAINERS' BARGAIN BUY

1647. ENDANGERD SPECIES ★★
ch.c. Lucky Story – Lucky Dip (Tirol).
April 21. Eleventh foal. 17,000Y. Tattersalls October Book 2. T A Scothern. Half-brother to the useful 2-y-o listed 5f and subsequent US stakes winner Fortunately (by Forzando), to the winner Halsion Chancer (by Atraf), the fair 2-y-o 5f winner Wittily (by Whittingham), the modest 6f winner Diamond Surprise (by Mark Of Esteem), the modest 7f winner Kinky (by Kingsinger), the moderate 9f winner Master Of Light (by Bertolini) and the moderate 5f winner Madam Isshe (by Ishiguru). The dam, a modest 3-y-o 5f winner, is a half-sister to 8 winners. The second dam, Miss Loving (by Northfields), a fairly useful 2-y-o 5f and 7f winner, is a half-sister to 6 winners including the useful 5f to 1m winner Cremation and is the dam of the Australian Group 1 winner Sapieha. (T A Scothern). *"He's a well-grown sort with a big, long stride on him and I ride him quite a bit. I would think he'd want seven furlongs to a mile and I haven't rushed him but he's done everything asked of him so far. He was good to break-in, he has a good temperament and he's a gentleman. He's not the sharpest but I think he'll be alright and I'm just kicking on with him now".*

1648. JUST DIXIE ★★
b.f. Avonbridge – Fly South (Polar Falcon).
March 27. Ninth foal. £3,500Y. Doncaster St Leger Festival. John Weymes. Closely related to the quite useful triple 5f winner (including twice at 2 yrs) and listed-placed Just Joey (by Averti) and half-sister to the fair 7f (at 2 yrs) and 1m winner Whitgift Rock (by Piccolo) and a jumps winner by Bishop Of Cashel. The dam is an unraced half-sister to 4 winners. The second dam, Vallauris (by Faustus), won at 3 yrs and was third in the listed Atalanta Stakes and is a half-sister to 4 winners. (High Moor Racing 1 & Mrs R Morley). *"We trained her half-brother Just Joey and she's ready to rock 'n roll, so I think we'll give her an run at Wolverhampton before going for a maiden auction that has a ten grand bonus at Ripon in mid-April. She's a sharp, early type that does everything easily and she should run quite* often but also develop as the season goes along".

1649. SELECTIVE SPIRIT ★★★
ch.f. Exceed And Excel – Our Sheila (Bahamian Bounty).
February 13. Second foal. £10,000Y. Doncaster Premier. John Weymes. Half-sister to the unplaced 2010 2-y-o Place And Chips (by Compton Place). The dam, a fair 6f winner of 4 races at 3 yrs, is a half-sister to 4 winners including the Italian Group 3 winner Shifting Place. The second dam, Shifting Mist (by Night Shift), a modest 10f to 14f winner of 5 races, is a half-sister to 7 winners including the dam of the Group/Grade 3 winner Needwood Blade. (T A Scothern). *"She's doing everything easily, she absolutely floats on the ground – a really good mover. Not as big as some, but she's a good, handy size. At the moment I'm not sure what trip she'll want, but maybe six furlongs. I'm looking after her a bit because the mother was half-crackers! But she's by a good sire so I think she'll be OK and she'll want genuinely good, fast ground".*

1650. UNNAMED ★★
b.f. Cadeaux Genereux – Sister Bluebird (Bluebird).
April 25. Fifth foal. 8,000Y. Tattersalls December. John Weymes. The dam, a 2-y-o listed 7f winner, is a half-sister to 2 winners. The second dam, Pain Perdu (by Waajib), a minor 3-y-o 10f winner in France, is a half-sister to 8 winners including the Group 3 1m Prix la Rochette winner Fine Fellow. (T A Scothern). *"A good-sized filly, she looks like a 3-y-o already. Her conformation is correct and she's a good-mover. The mother was a listed winner and although her previous foals have been useless we liked this filly at the Sales and thought we'd take a chance because she's the first filly out of the mare. Unfortunately Stan Moore must have thought the same because we were the only two bidding and maybe I paid more than I expected, but she's a lovely filly with a really good attitude. I ride her a bit myself and I think she'll probably want seven furlongs, so we'll bring her along accordingly. A nice filly".*

PETER WINKWORTH

1651. FOXTROT INDIA (IRE) ★★
b.c. Tagula – Mayfair (Green Desert).
April 24. €20,000Y. Tattersalls Ireland. Tom Malone. Brother to the quite useful 5f (at 2 yrs) to 1m winner of 5 races Kirsty's Boy and half-brother to a winner in Greece and to a hurdles winner (both by Fleetwood). The dam, a quite useful 2-y-o 6f winner, is a sister to the Group 3 5f Cornwallis Stakes and Group 3 5f Norfolk Stakes winner Magic Ring and a half-sister to 6 winners. The second dam, Emaline (by Empery), won over 7f at 2 yrs in France and is a half-sister to 4 winners. (Foxtrot Racing Partnership V). *"He'll be an early runner. We had his half-brother who was by Needwood Blade and he was useless, but this is a nice-looking horse and I would have thought he'd be able to win a race. He'll start early over five furlongs".*

1652. SHANGHAI BLAZE (IRE) ★★★
b.f. Acclamation – Laheen (Bluebird).
March 13. Second foal. Doncaster Premier. £19,000Y. David Redvers. The dam is an unplaced half-sister to 2 winners. The second dam, Ashirah (by Housebuster), is an unraced half-sister to the US dual Grade 3 winner Mustanfar and the listed winner Tadris. (Mrs Jessica Muddle). *"She'll be running before the other Acclamation we have, she looks a good type and has a lovely attitude".*

1653. SIR FREDLOT (IRE) ★★★★
ch.g. Choisir – Wurfklinge (Acatenango).
February 19. Fourth foal. Goffs Orby. €32,000Y. Davis Redvers. Half-brother to the fair 2-y-o 7f winner Nora Mae (by Peintre Celebre). The dam won over 1m at 2 yrs in Germany and is a sister to 2 winners including the German dual Group 2 winner Wurftaube and a half-sister to 6 winners including the German dual Group 3 winner Wurfscheibe. The second dam, Wurfbahn (by Frontal), won once at 3 yrs in Germany and is a half-sister to one winner. (Mr Rupert Williams). *"He's a beautiful individual and a great big strong horse. He'll be alright, he's definitely a racehorse and I love his relaxed attitude to it all. He's very nice".*

1654. UNNAMED ★★★
b.f. Amadeus Wolf – Am I (Thunder Gulch).
April 28. Second foal. Tattersalls Ireland. €16,500Y. David Redvers. Half-sister to the fairly useful 2010 2-y-o 1m winner Questioning (by Elusive Quality). The dam, a minor 2-y-o winner in the USA, is a half-sister to 6 winners including the US Grade 3 winner Certainly Classic and the French Group 3 winner Mahfooth. The second dam, I Certainly Am, a minor winner in the USA, is a sister to the Group 2 Premio Lydia Tesio winner Medi Flash and a half-sister to the US Grade 1 Flower Bowl Invitational winner Laugh And Be Merry. *"Not over-big, she's a proper racehorse, has a lovely attitude and she'll be very sharp and fast. She hasn't been sold yet, so we're looking for an owner for her".* TRAINERS' BARGAIN BUY

1655. UNNAMED ★★★
b.f. Trans Island – Athlumney Dancer (Shareef Dancer).
April 15. Fifth foal. Goffs Orby. €24,000Y. David Redvers. Sister to the Italian listed 11f winner Apprimus and to the minor Italian winner of 15 races West Nile. The dam is an unraced half-sister to 2 minor winners. The second dam, Shanira (by Shirley Heights), is an unraced half-sister to 5 winners. (NH Bloodstock Ltd). *"Out of all the 2-y-o's she was the last one to be broken, she's lovely and we like her a lot. Quite a big, well-grown filly and we're talking seven furlongs to start with".*

1656. UNNAMED ★★★
b.f. Acclamation – Cutpurse Moll (Green Desert).
May 1. Eleventh foal. Doncaster Premier. £32,000Y. David Redvers. Closely related to the smart listed winning sprinter Colonel Cotton and to the modest 6f to 12f winner Comrade Cotton (both by Royal Applause) and half-sister to the fairly useful 6f winner Cyclone Connie (by Dr Devious), the quite useful 7f (at 2 yrs) and 12f winner Lola Sapola (by Benny The Dip), the modest 2-y-o 7f seller winner Inch Pincher (by Inchinor) and the moderate 8.6f to 11f winner Lake Diva (by Docksider). The dam, a fair 7f winner at 3 yrs, is a half-sister to the dual listed winner Polka Dancer. The second dam, Pretty Pol (by Final Straw), won the Group 3 10f Premio Carlo Porta and is a

half-sister to 5 winners including the smart 1m to 10f colt Wylfa. (NH Bloodstock Ltd). *"I love the sire. I think Acclamation's all look the same and that's always a good starting point for a horse. Stallions should produce individuals that look very much the same. This filly has taken time to come to hand, she looks well and she's as wide as she is deep. I like her a lot and she's just started to do fast work.*

1657. UNNAMED ★★
b.g. Oratorio – Estivau (Lear Fan).
April 24. Fifth foal. 22,000Y. Tattersalls October Book 1. Highflyer Bloodstock. Half-brother to a winner in Switzerland by Alhaarth. The dam, an Irish 3-y-o 10f winner, is a half-sister to 8 winners including the very smart Group 2 1m Berlin Brandenburg Trophy and Hong Kong Group 2 International Mile winner Docksider. The second dam, Pump (by Forli), is an unraced daughter of a half-sister to Thatch. (Mr P L Winkworth). *"Not many people like the sire but he does seem to get a good horse every year. When this fellow arrived he looked like two boards slapped together and he was so colty and badly behaved we cut him straight away. He's pleasing me now, he'll be a later 2-y-o and he's come on no end".*

1658. UNNAMED ★★★
b.g. Tagula – Mooching Along (Mujahid).
February 11. First foal. Tattersalls Ireland. €34,000Y. David Redvers. The dam is an unraced half-sister to one winner. The second dam, Inching (by Inchinor), was placed 9 times over 5f and 6f from 2 to 4 yrs and is a half-sister to 7 winners including the triple Group 3 winning sprinter Majestic Missile. (Mr P L Winkworth). *"A lovely individual, he'll definitely win races and being an early foal it won't be long before he's out".*

Sires Reference

This section deals with sires that have several two-year-old representatives in the book. Please note the index immediately following this reference.

ACCLAMATION 2000 *Royal Applause – Princess Athena (Ahonoora)* Racing record: Won 6 times, including Diadem Stakes. Also placed in King's Stand and Nunthorpe. Stud record: First crop now five-year-olds, he was an instant hit with his first crop in 2007, notably with his Group 1 winner Dark Angel. His subsequent good winners include the Group 1 King's Stand winner Equiano and the King's Sand third Angelzarke. His 2009 two-year-olds won 14 races. Standing at Rathbarry Stud, Ireland. €15,000 in 2011.

ALHAARTH 1993 *Unfuwain – Irish Valley (Irish River)* Racing record: Champion 2-y-o of 1995 when winner of 4 group races, notably Dewhurst Stakes. Showed very smart form up to 10f at 3/4 yrs, winning three Group 2 events. Stud record: First runners in 2001. Sire of Awzaan (2009 2-y-o Group 1 6f Middle Park Stakes), Haafhd (2000 Guineas and Champion Stakes), Bandari and Phoenix Reach (Canadian International, Hong Kong Vase and Dubai Sheema Classic) and the smart performers Bouguereau, Dominica, Hoh Buzzard, Maharib, Mourayan and Mutajarred. Standing at Derrinstown Stud, Ireland. 2011 fee: €5,000.

AMADEUS WOLF 2003 *Mozart – Rachelle (Mark of Esteem)* ran 17, won 4, including Gimcrack St, Middle Park Stakes, Duke of York Stakes. Standing at Irish National Stud, 2011 fee 6,000 €. First runners 2011.

ANABAA 1992 *Danzig – Balbonella (Gay Mecene)* Racing record: Won 8 races including the July Cup and the Prix Maurice de Gheest. Stud record: First runners in 2000. Sire of the top-class filly Goldikova, Anabaa Blue (Prix du Jockey Club), Martillo (multiple German Group 2 winner), Precision (Hong Kong Cup) and the smart performers Amonita, Ana Marie, Celtic Slipper, Blue Ksar, Loup Breton, Marshall, Miss Anabaa, Morana, Passager, Rouvres, Shaard, Tarzan City and Victorieux. Died.

ARAAFA 2003 *Mull of Kintyre – Resurgence (Polar Falcon)* Racing Record: Won 3 races including the G1 St James's Palace Stakes and the Irish 2,000 Guineas. Stud record: First runners 2010. Standing at Plantation Stud, Newmarket. 2011 fee: Price on application

ARAKAN 2000 *Nureyev – Far Across (Common Grounds)* Racing record: Won 6 races including the Group 3 Criterion Stakes, the Supreme Stakes (both 7f), the listed Abernant Stakes and the City Of York Stakes (both 6f). Stud record: His first runners appeared in 2009 and his 8 winners included the Group 2 Richmond Stakes and Tattersalls Ireland Sales Race winner Dick Turpin. Standing at Ballyhane Stud. 2011 fee: €4,000.

ARCH 1995 *Kris S – Aurora (Danzig)* Racing Record: 5 wins including Super Derby and Fayette Stakes. Stud record: Sire of Arravale (Grade 1 Del Mar Oaks), Les Arcs (Golden Jubilee Stakes and July Cup), Pine Island (dual US Grade 1 winner), Overarching (South African Group 1 winner), Prince Arch (US Grade 1 winner) and Montgomery's Arch (Group 2 Richmond Stakes). Standing at Claiborne Farm, Kentucky, 2011 fee $30,000.

AUSSIE RULES 2003 *Danehill – Last Second (Alzao)* Racing Record: Won 4 races including the Shadwell Turf Mile and the French 2,000 Guineas. Stud record: First runners 2010. Winners include Dinkum Diamond, Chinese Wall and Private Jet. Standing at Coolmore Stud, Ireland. 2011 fee: €6,000.

AUTHORISED 2004 *Montjeu – Funsie (Saumarez)* Won 4 races including the Racing Post Trophy, G1 Juddmonte International 10½f; Derby Stakes. Standing at Dalham Hall Stud, fee for 2011 £15,000. First runners 2011.

AVONBRIDGE 2000 *Averti – Alessia (Caerleon)* Racing record: Won the Prix de l'Abbaye and the Palace House Stakes, second in the July

Cup. Stud record: 19 winners among his first runners in 2009 including the smart listed 5f winner Iver Bridge Lad. In 2010 Temple Meads won Mill Reef Stakes and Weatherbys Super Sprint. Standing at Whitsbury Manor Stud. 2011 fee: £3,500.

AZAMOUR 2001 *Night Shift – Azmara (Lear Fan)* Race record: Won St James's Palace Stakes, Irish Champion Stakes, Prince of Wales's Stakes and King George VI and Queen Elizabeth Diamond Stakes. Stud record: Best winners include Native Khan (Craven Stakes, Solario Stakes), Eleonora Duse (Group 2 Blandford Stakes), Azmeel (dual Group 3) and Puncher Clynch (Group 3 Ballysax Atakes). Standing at Gilltown Stud, Ireland. 2011 fee: €15,000.

BAHAMIAN BOUNTY 1994 *Cadeaux Genereux – Clarentia (Ballad Rock)* Racing Record: Winner of 3 races at 2 yrs, notably Prix Morny and Middle Park. Also fourth in July Cup at 3 yrs. Stud record: First runners in 2001. Sire of high-class performer Pastoral Pursuits (July Cup), very smart Goodricke (Sprint Cup) and Mister Napper Tandy (US Grade 2) and smart performers Gallagher, Babodana, Dubaian Gift, Naahy, Paradise Isle and Topatoo. Standing at the National Stud, Newmarket. 2011 fee: £10,000.

BALTIC KING 2000 *Danetime – Lindfield Belle (Fairy King)* Race record: Won 8 races including the Wokingham Hcp. Stud record: Standing at Tally Ho Stud, 2011 fee 3,000€. First runners 2011.

BARATHEA 1990 *Sadler's Wells – Brocade (Habitat)* Racing record: 5 wins, notably Breeders Cup Mile and Irish 2000 Guineas. Stud record: First runners in 1998. Sire of high-class Tobougg (Prix de la Salamandre and Dewhurst) and Tante Rose (Sprint Cup), and numerous smart performers including Alasha, Apsis, Barathea Guest, Barshiba, Cornelius, Enrique, Hazarista, Jumbajukiba, Lost Soldier Three, One Off, Opera Cape, Pongee, Port Vila, Raincoat, Sanaya, Shield, Sina Cova and Stotsfold. Barathea died in 2009.

BEAT HOLLOW 1997 *Sadler's Wells – Wemyss Bight (Dancing Brave)* Racing record: Won 7 races Grand Prix de Paris, Arlington Million, Woodford Reserve Turf Classic. Stud record: To stud 2003. Sire of 5 stakes winners including Proportional (Group 1 Prix Marcel Boussac). Standing at Banstead Manor Stud, Newmarket. 2011 fee £5,000.

BERNARDINI 2003 *A P Indy – Cara Rafaela (Quiet American)* Racing Record: Won 5 Grade 1 events in the USA including the 1mWithers Stakes, the 9.5f Preakness Stakes, the 9f Jim Dandy Stakes, the 10f Jockey Club Gold Cup and the 10f Travers Stakes. Sire of Biondetti, Premio Grand Criterium G1, Theyskens Theory, G3 Prestige Stakes. Standing at Darley Stud, Kentucky. 2011 fee: $70,000.

BERTOLINI 1996 *Danzig – Aquilega (Alydar)* Racing record: Won 2 races, including July Stakes at 2 yrs, and placed in July Cup, Sprint Cup and Nunthorpe Stakes. Stud record: First runners in 2005. Sire of Donna Blini (Cheveley Park), New Zealand Group 1 winner Juice, the smart winners Moorhouse Lad and Prime Defender and the useful performers Blades Girl, Bobs Surprise, Come Out Fighting, Mac Gille Eoin, Medic Power (in Hong Kong), Signor Peltro, Suits Me and Tabaret. Standing at Overbury Stud, Gloucestershire. 2011 fee: £3,000.

BYRON 2001 *Green Desert – Gay Gallanta (Woodman)* Racing Record: Won 3 races including the Group 2 6f Mill Reef Stakes (at 2 yrs) and the Group 2 7f Betfair Cup (Lennox Stakes). Stud record: First runners 2010, sire of 8 individual winners. Standing at Woodlands Stud, Ireland. 2011 fee €2,500.

CADEAUX GENEREUX 1985 *Young Generation – Smarten Up (Sharpen Up)* Racing record: 7 wins notably July Cup and William Hill Sprint Championship. Stud record: Best winners include high-class Bijou d'Inde (Group 1 St James's Palace Stakes), Donativum (Grade 1 Breeders Cup Juvenile) and Touch of The Blues (Atto Mile in Canada) and numerous smart performers including Bahamian Bounty (Group 1 Middle Park Stakes), Desert Deer (Group 2 Sandown Mile), Embassy (Group 1 Cheveley Park Stakes), Hoh Magic (Prix Morny), Land Of Dreams (Group 2 Flying Childers Stakes), Major

Cadeaux (Group 2 Sandown Mile), Stage Gift (Group 2 York Stakes) and Toylsome (Group 1 Prix de la Foret). Died 2010.

CAMACHO 2002 *Danehill – Arabesque (Zafonic)* Racing record: Won a listed race over 6f and was second in the Group 3 7f Jersey Stakes. Stud record: Had his first runners in 2009. Best winners include Puff (Group 3) and the listed winners Star Rover and Arctic Feeling). Standing at Morristown Lattin Stud, Ireland. 2011 fee: €4,000.

CAPE CROSS 1994 *Green Desert – Park Appeal (Ahonoora)* Racing record: Won 4 races, including Lockinge Stakes, Queen Anne Stakes and Celebration Mile. Stud record: First runners in 2003. Sire of the outstanding colt Sea The Stars (2,000 Guineas, Derby, Prix de l'Arc de Triomphe etc,), top-class Ouija Board (7 Group 1 wins including the Oaks & the Breeders' Cup Filly and Mare Turf), Hong Kong Group 1 winner Able One and numerous smart performers including Borthwick Girl, Cape Fear, Castleton, Charlie Farnsbarns, Crossing The Line, Crosspeace, Crystal Capella, Halicarnassus, Hatta Fort, Hazyview, Mad Love, Madrid, Mazuna, Musicanna, Privy Seal, Russian Cross, Cape Dollar and I Love Me Standing at Kildangan Stud, Ireland 2011 Fee 35,000€.

CHOISIR 2000 *Danehill Dancer – Great Selection (Lunchtime)* Racing record: Group 1 winner in both Australia and Britain, including King's Stand Stakes and Golden Jubilee Stakes. Stud record: His winners include the Australian dual Group 1 winner Starspangledbanner, Group 2 Challenge Stakes winner Stimulation, Australian Group 2 winners Dreamscape Gold Water and Hurried Choice, Group 3 Somerville Tattersalls Stakes Sir Parky, Group 3 C L Weld Park Stakes winner Lady Springbank and the listed winners Choose Me, Fat Boy, Luna Nel Pozz, Meydan Princess, Porto Marmay, Prime Champion. Standing at Coolmore Stud, Ireland. 2011 fee: €12,500.

CLODOVIL 2001 *Danehill – Clodora (Linamix)* Racing record: Won 5 races, including Poule d'Essai des Poulains. Stud record: His first crop were two-year-olds in 2007 and from relatively small crops his best winners to date are the Group 1 Falmouth Stakes winner Nahoodh and the very useful Beacon Lodge (Group 3 Horris Hill Stakes) and the Group 3 placed Dovil Boy. Standing at Rathasker Stud, Ireland. 2011 fee: €9,000.

COCKNEY REBEL 2004 *Val Royal – Factice (Known Fact)* Won 3 races including the 2,000 Guineas and Irish 2,000 Guineas. Stands at National Stud Newmarket for £4,500. First runners 2011.

COMPTON PLACE 1994 *Indian Ridge – Nosey (Nebbiolo)* Racing record: Won 3 races, notably July Cup. Stud record: First runners in 2002. Sire of the Group 1 Nunthorpe Stakes winner Borderlescott, the smart Boogie Street and Intrepid Jack, US Grade 2 winner Passified, the Group 2 winners Godfrey Street and Prolific, and numerous useful performers including Compton's Eleven, If Paradise, Judd Street, Hunter Street and Pacific Pride. Standing at Whitsbury Manor Stud, Hampshire. 2011 fee: £6,000.

DALAKHANI 2001 *Darshaan – Daltawa (Miswaki)* Racing record: Won 8 of 9 starts, including Prix du Jockey Club and Arc. Stud record: First crop were two-year-olds in 2007. Sire of 2 classic winners from his first crop in Conduit (St Leger, Breeders Cup Turf (twice), King George VI & Queen Elizabeth Stakes) and Moonstone (Irish Oaks) and also worthy of note are the Group 2 winners Centennial, Chinese White, Armure and Democratie. With just four crops racing he's had an excellent start. Standing at Gilltown Stud, Ireland. 2011 fee: €35,000.

DANEHILL DANCER 1993 *Danehill – Mira Adonde (Sharpen Up)* Racing Record: Winner of 4 races, including Heinz 57 Phoenix Stakes and National Stakes at 2 yrs and Greenham at 3. Stud record: First runners in 2001. Sire of high-class performer Choisir (Golden Jubilee Stakes), multiple Group 1 winner Mastercraftsman, Irish 1,000 Guineas and Moyglare Stud Stakes winner Again, the US Grade 1 Garden City Stakes winner Alexander Tango, Queen Elizabeth II Stakes winner Where Or When, 1,000 Guineas winner Speciosa, dual Group 3 winner Indesatchel & numerous smart performers including Alexander Tango, Anna Pavlova, Blue Sky Thinking, Express Wish, Fast Company, Ice Queen, Jeremy, Lady Dominatrix, Lizard Island, Medicine Path, Miss Beatrix, Monsieur Bond, Pride Of Nation, Snaefell, Memory, Kissable and Samuel Morse. Standing at Coolmore Stud, Ireland. 2011 fee: Private.

DANSILI 1996 *Danehill – Hasili (Kahyasi)* Racing record: Won 5 races in France, and placed in six Group/Grade 1 events including Sussex Stakes and Breeders' Cup Mile. Stud record: First runners in 2004. Sire of top-class Rail Link (Arc, Grand Prix de Paris), Zambezi Sun (Group 1 Grand Prix de Paris), Zacinto (Group 2 Celebration Mile) and numerous very smart performers including Dansant, Delegator, Famous Name, Grecian Dancer, Home Affairs, Illustrious Blue, Passage Of Time, Price Tag (US Grade 1 winner and first past post in Poule d'Essai des Pouliches), Proviso, Sense Of Joy, Shaweel (Gimcrack Stakes), Silver Touch, Strategic Prince and Zoffany. Standing at Banstead Manor Stud, Newmarket. 2011 fee: £65,000.

DARK ANGEL 2005 *Acclamation – Midnight Angel (Machiavellian)* Racing record: Won 4 races at 2 yrs including Group 1 Middle Park Stakes and Group 2 Mill Reef Stakes. Standing at Morristown Lattin Stud, Ire 2011 fee €7,000. First runners 2011.

DIAMOND GREEN 2001 *Green Desert – Diamonaka (Akarad)* Racing Record: Won 3 races including the Group 3 Prix la Rochette 7f. First runners 2010, sire of 14 individual winners up to April 2011. Standing at Ballyhane Stud, Carlow, Ireland. 2011 fee €5,000.

DISTORTED HUMOR 1993 *Forty Niner – Danzig's Beauty (Danzig)* Racing record: Won 11 races in the USA including the Champagne Stakes, Futurity Stakes, Haskell Invitational and Travers Stakes (all Grade 1). Champion 2-y-o. Stud record: Sire of a host of Grade 1 winners including Any Given Saturday, Commentator, Coronado's Quest, Ecton Park, Editor's Note, Flower Alley, Funny Cide, Gold Fever, Marley Vale, Nine Keys Pathfork and Redharcnafarrige. Standing at Win Star Farm, Kentucky. 2011 fee $100,000.

DIXIE UNION 1997 *Dixieland Band – She's Tops (Capote)* Racing record: Won 7 races including the Haskell Invitational and the Malibu Stakes (both Grade 1 events in the USA). Stud record: Sire of the US Grade 1 winners Dixie Chatter and Hot Dixie Chick, Stud record: Group 2 Cherry Hinton Stakes winner Sander Camillo and the US Grade 2 winners Justwhistledixie, Most Distinguished and Nothing But Fun. Standing at Standing at Lane's End Farm, Kentucky. Died 2010.

DR FONG 1995 *Kris S – Spring Flight (Miswaki)* Racing record: Won 5 races, including St James's Palace Stakes. Stud record: First runners in 2003. Sire of the US Grade 1 winner Shamdinan, Italian Group winner Aoife Alainn and the Group 1 Prix Saint-Alary winner Ask For The Moon, the smart performers Andronikos, Celimene, Doctor Brown, Dubai's Touch, Fong's Thong, Forward Move, Group Captain, Metropolitan Man and Spotlight, and of numerous very useful performers. Standing at Haras Du Thenney, France. 2011 fee: €5,000.

DUBAI DESTINATION 1999 *Kingmambo – Mysterial (Alleged)* Racing record: Won 4 times, including Champagne Stakes and Queen Anne Stakes. Stud record: First crop were two-year-olds in 2007 and included the Group 1 winner Ibn Khaldun and the smart gelding Charm School. Subsequently, his best has been the smart colt Firebet, & Measuring Time. Standing at Glenview Stud, Ireland. 2011 fee: £3,500.

DUBAWI 2002 *Dubai Millennium – Zomaradah (Deploy)* Race record: Won the National Stakes at 2 and the Irish 2,000 Guineas and Prix Jacques le Marois at 3. Third in the Derby. Stud record: His first runners appeared in 2009 and he was the leading first-crop sire by number of winners. Best winners include the dual Group 1 winner Makfi, South African Group 1 winner Happy Archer, Australian Group 1 winner Secret Admirer and the Group 2 winners Irish Field, Monterosso, Prince Bishop, Worthadd, Poet's Voice and Sand Vixen. He also had the New Zealand Group 2 winner Cellarmaster and the smart Astrophysical Jet, Majestic Dubawi, Dubawi Heights, Titus Mills, Big Issue. Standing at Dalham Hall Stud, Newmarket. 2011 fee: €55,000.

DUTCH ART 2004 *Medicean – Hallana Park Lass (Spectrum)* Race record: Won 4 races at 2 Yrs including the Middle Park Stakes and the Prix Morny. Standing at Cheveley Park Stud. 2011 fee £5000.

DYLAN THOMAS 2003 *Danehill – Lagrion (Diesis)* Race record: Won 10 races including Prix de L'Arc de Triomphe and Irish Champion Stakes. Standing at Coolmore Stud. 2011 fee 17, 500€. First runners 2011.

DYNAFORMER 1985 *Roberto – Andover Way (His Majesty)* Racing record: 7 wins in USA including Grade 2 Florida Derby and Grade 2 Discovery Handicap. Stud record: Best winners include the Group 1 St Leger winner Lucarno, the Group 1 Fillies' Mile and Group 1 Matron Stakes winner Rainbow View, Melbourne Cup winner Americain and in the USA Grade 1 winners Barbaro, Dynaforce, Film Maker, Perfect Drift and Starrer, Dynever, Ocean Silk. Sharp Susan, Spanish John and White Moonstone. Standing at Three Chimneys Farm, Kentucky. 2011 fee: $150,000.

ECHO OF LIGHT 2002 *Dubai Millennium – Spirit of Tara (Sadler's Wells)* Race record: Won 7 races including Strensall Stakes, Prix Gontaut Biron, Prix Daniel Wildenstein. Standing at Kildangan Stud, Ire 2011 fee €3,000. First runners 2011.

ELNADIM 1994 *Danzig – E'le Seule (Exclusive Native)* Racing record: Won 5 races, notably Diadem Stakes and July Cup. Stud record: First runners in 2004, first European runners in 2005. Sire of smart performers Al Qasi (Group 3 Phoenix Stakes), Caldra (Group 3 Autumn Stakes), Culminate (New Zealand Group 1), Elletelle (Group 2 Queen Mary Stakes), Elnawin (Group 3 Sirenia Stakes) and Wi Dud (Group 2 Gimcrack Stakes) Soraya Standing at Derrinstown Stud, Ireland. 2011 fee: €6,000.

ELUSIVE CITY 2000 *Elusive Quality – Star of Paris (Dayjur)* Racing record: Won Group 1 Prix Morny and Group 2 Richmond Stakes. Also placed in Middle Park. Stud record: First crop were two-year-olds in 2008. His best winners include Elusive Wave (French 2,000 Guineas), Soul City (Group 3 Prix La Rochette and Goffs Million) and multiple listed winner Nashmiah. Standing at Haras D'Etreham. 2011 fee: €15,000.

ELUSIVE QUALITY 1993 *Gone West – Touch of Greatness (Hero's Honor)* Racing record: Won 9 races in USA, including Grade 3 events at 7f/1m. Stud record: Sire of top-class Kentucky Derby/Preakness Stakes winner Smarty Jones, Breeders Cup Classic and Queen Elizabeth II Stakes winner Raven's Pass, multiple Grade 1 winner Quality Road, Prix Morny winner Elusive City and numerous US graded stakes winners including Chimichurri, Elusive Diva, Girl Warrior, Maryfield, Omega Code, Quality Road, Royal Michele and True Quality, the smart dual listed winner Baharah and the Group 3 winning two-year-olds Elusive Pimpernel and Evasive. Standing at Darley Stud Farm Kentucky. 2011 fee: $50,000.

EMPIRE MAKER 2000 *Unbridled – Toussaud (El Gran Senor)* Racing record: Belmont Stakes. Florida Derby, Wood Memorial Stakes, Jim Dandy Stakes. Stud record: US Grade 1 winners Battle Plan, Mushka, Icon Project, Country Star and Pioneerofthe Nile. Standing in Japan. Fee Private.

EXCEED AND EXCEL 2000 *Danehill – Patrona (Lomond)* Racing record: Champion sprinter in Australia, won 7 races including the Grade 1 Newmarket H'cap, the Grade 1 Dubai Racing Club Cup and the Grade 2 Todman Stakes. Stud record: First northern hemisphere runners in 2008. His best winners include Infamous Angel (Lowther Stakes) and the Royal Ascot winner Flashmans Papers. His Australasian winners include the Group 1 winner Reward For Effort, Group 2 winner Wilander and the Group 3 winners Exceedingly Good, Sugar Babe and Believe 'n' Succeed. 51 two-year-old winner in England and Ireland in 2009 and 2010. Standing at Dalham Hall Stud, Newmarket. 2011 fee: £12,000.

EXCELLENT ART 2004 *Pivotal – Obsessive (Seeking The Gold)* Race record: Won 4 races including the St James's Palace Stakes. Stud record: Standing at Coolmore Stud. 2011 fee €10,000. First runners 2011.

EXCHANGE RATE 1997 *Danzig – Sterling Pound (Seeking The Gold)* Racing record: Won Risen Stakes, Tom Fool Handicap. Stud Record: Sire of US Grade 1 winners Ermine and Swap Fliparoo. Standing at Three Chimneys Farm, Ky. 2011 fee $25,000.

FOOTSTEPSINTHESAND 2002 *Giant's Causeway – Glatisant (Rainbow Quest)* Racing record: Won all 3 of his starts, notably the 2,000 Guineas. Stud record: Best performers to date include the Group winners Steinbeck, Sent From Heaven, Barefoot Lady and Formosina. Standing at Coolmore Stud, Ireland. 2011 fee: €10,000.

GALILEO 1998 *Sadler's Wells – Urban Sea (Miswaki)* Racing record: Won 6 races, including Derby, Irish Derby and King George And Queen Elizabeth Stakes. Stud record: First runners in 2005. Sire of champion 2-y-o's Frankel, Teofilo and New Approach (subsequent Derby, Champion Stakes and Irish Champion Stakes winner) and of the top-class double Group 1 winners Cape Blanco and Rip Van Winkle, Sixties Icon (St Leger), Red Rocks (Breeders' Cup Turf), Allegretto (Prix Royal-Oak), Lush Lashes (Coronation Stakes and Sun Chariot Stakes), Soldier Of Fortune (Irish Derby), Nightime (Irish 1000 Guineas), champion 2-y-o Frankel (Dewhurst Stakes), Roderick O'Connor (Group1 Criterium International) and Misty For Me (dual Group 1). Standing at Coolmore Stud, Ireland. 2011 fee: Private (was €150,000).

GIANT'S CAUSEWAY 1997 *Storm Cat – Mariah's Storm (Rahy)* Racing record: Won 9 races, 6 of them Group 1 events, including Prix de la Salamandre, Juddmonte International and Sussex Stakes. Stud record: First runners in 2004. Sire of high-class Shamardal (Dewhurst Stakes, St James's Palace Stakes and Prix du Jockey Club), very smart Footstepsinthesand (2000 Guineas) and a number of very smart performers including Ghanaati (1,000 Guineas and Coronation Stakes), Aragorn (dual US Grade winner), Heatseeker (Santa Anita Handicap), Maids Causeway (Coronation Stakes), My Typhoon, Swift Temper (US Grade 1 winners), Oonagh Maccool and First Samurai (US 2-y-o Grade 1 winner). Standing at Ashford Stud, Kentucky. 2011 fee: $85,000.

GREEN DESERT 1983 *Danzig – Foreign Courier (Sir Ivor)* Racing record: 5 wins including July Cup, Vernons Sprint Cup and Flying Childers Stakes. Stud record: Best winners (all very smart or better) include Alkaadhem, Cape Cross (Lockinge Stakes), Desert Lord (Prix de l'Abbaye), Desert Prince (Irish 2000 Guineas, Prix du Moulin, Queen Elizabeth Stakes), Desert Style, Desert Sun, Gabr, Invincible Spirit (Haydock Sprint Cup), Oasis Dream (Middle Park, July Cup, Nunthorpe Stakes), Owington (July Cup), Sheikh Albadou (Nunthorpe Stakes/ Haydock Sprint Cup), Tamarisk (Haydock Sprint Cup) and Tropical. Standing at Nunnery Stud, Norfolk. 2011 fee: Private.

HAAFHD 2001 *Alhaarth – Al Bahathri (Blushing Groom)* Racing record: Won 5 races, notably 2,000 Guineas and Champion Stakes. Stud record: First crop were two-year-olds in 2008. His best performer so far is the 2009 2-y-o Group 2 Superlative Stakes winner Silver Grecian. Also Emirates Champion who has won three valuable races at Meydan. Standing at Nunnery Stud, Norfolk. 2011 fee: £5,000.

HALLING 1991 *Diesis – Dance Machine (Green Dancer)* Racing record: Won 12 races including Coral-Eclipse Stakes (twice), Juddmonte International (twice) and Prix d'Ispahan. Stud record: First runners in 2000. Sire of the Group 1 Grand Prix de Paris winner Cavalryman, the high-class Norse Dancer, very smart Hala Bek and The Geezer, Group 2 King Edward VII Stakes winner Boscobel, and numerous smart performers including Bauer, Chancellor, Coastal Path, Cutlass Bay, Dandoun, Fisich, Foodbroker Fancy, Franklins Gardens, Giovani Imperatore, Harland, Hattan, Hero's Journey, Mkuzi, Nordhal, Parasol, Pinson and Vanderlin, Standing at Dalham Hall Stud, Newmarket. 2011 fee: £10,000.

HARD SPUN 2004 *Danzig – Turkish Tryst (Turkoman)* Racing record Ran 10, won 4 races including the Grade 1 King's Bishop St and second in Kentucky Derby. Standing at Darley, Ky. 2011 fee $30,000.

HERNANDO 1990 *Niniski – Whakilyric (Miswaki)* Racing record: Won 7 races including Prix Lupin and Prix du Jockey Club.

Stud record: First runners in 1999. His Group/Grade 1 winners are Look Here (Oaks), Holding Court (Prix du Jockey Club), Sulamani (Prix du Jockey Club, Arlington Million, Turf Classic Invitational, Juddmonte International), Casual Conquest (Tattersalls Gold Cup), Rainbow Peak (Gran Premio del Jockey Club) and Gitano Hernando. Also responsible for the US Grade 2 winners Arvada, Atlando and Herboriste, the very smart performers Asian Heights, Foreign Affairs, Mr Combustible, Samando, Songerie and Tau Ceti and numerous smart performers. Standing at Lanwades Stud, Newmarket. 2011 fee: Private.

HIGH CHAPARRAL 2000 *Sadler's Wells – Kasora (Darshaan)* Racing record: Won 10 races, including Derby, Irish Champion Stakes and Breeders' Cup Turf (last event twice). Stud record: First crop were two-year-olds in 2007. Best performers to date include the US Grade 1 winner Redwood, Australian Grade 1 winners So You Think, Monaco Consul and Shoot Out, St Leger runner-up Unsung Heroine, Group 2 Park Hill Stakes winner The Miniver Rose and the Group 3 winners Above Average, Golden Sword, High Heeled, Joanna, Magadan and Senlis. Standing at Coolmore Stud, Ireland. 2011 fee: €15,000.

HOLY ROMAN EMPEROR (2004) *Danehill – L'On Vite (Secretariat)* Racing Record: Won 4 races at 2 yrs including the Group 1 7f Prix Jean-Luc Lagardere, the Group 1 6f Waterford Phoenix Stakes and Group 2 6f Railway Stakes. Stud record: First runners 2010. Best winner to date Banimpire (Group 3 Ballysax Stakes). Standing at Coolmore Stud, Ireland. 2011 fee: €10,000.

HURRICANE RUN 2002 *Montjeu – Hold On (Surumu)* Racing Record: Won 8 races including the Group 1 12f King George VI & Queen Elizabeth Diamond Stakes, Group 1 10.5f Tattersalls Gold Cup and Group 1 12f Prix de l'Arc de Triomphe. Stud record: First runners 2010. Sire of 18 individual first crop 2-y-o winners including Group 2 placed Cochabamba. Standing at Coolmore Stud, Ireland. 2011 fee €15,000.

ICEMAN 2002 *Polar Falcon – Virtuous (Exit To Nowhere)* Racing record: Won the Group 2 6f Coventry Stakes at 2 yrs at Royal Ascot. Stud record: First two-year-olds in 2010. Dead.

IFFRAAJ 2001 *Zafonic – Pastorale (Nureyev)* Racing Record: Won 7 races including the Group 2 7f Park Stakes (twice), Group 2 7f Betfair Cup (Lennox St) and the 6f Wokingham Stakes. Stud record: First runners 2010. Among his winners are Wootton Bassett & Espirita. Sire of the winners of 68 races to April 2011. He sired more 2-y-o winners in 2011 than any first crop sire ever. Standing at Kildangan Stud, Ireland. 2011 fee €15,000.

IMPERIAL DANCER 1998 *Primo Dominie – Gorgeous Dancer (Nordico)* Race record: Won 11 races from 65 races including Festival Stakes, Scottish Classic, Meld Stakes, St Simon Stakes. Premio Roma. Stud record: Sire of one listed winner - Imperial Guest. Standing in Egypt.

INDESATCHEL 2002 *Danehill Dancer – Floria (Petorius)* Racing Record: Won 4 races including the Group 3 7f Tetrarch Stakes and the Group 3 7f Greenham Stakes. Stud record: First runners 2010 included the smart Galtymore Lad. Standing at Bearstone Stud, Shropshire. 2011 fee: POA (£3,000 in 2010).

INDIAN HAVEN 2000 *Indian Ridge – Madame Dubois (Legend Of France)* Racing record: Won 3 races including the Group 1 Irish 2,000 Guineas. Stud record: His first crop were 2-y-o's of 2008. His best winners have been the smart Group 3 winners Ashram and Aspen Darlin and the Irish Group 2 placed In Some Respect. Standing at the Irish National Stud. 2011 fee: €3,000.

INTIKHAB 1994 *Red Ransom – Crafty Example (Crafty Prospector)* Racing record: 8 wins including Diomed and Queen Anne Stakes. Stud record: First runners in 2003. Sire of Snow Fairy (multiple Group 1 winner), Red Evie (Lockinge Stakes & Matron Stakes), Paita (Group 1 Criterium de Saint-Cloud) and the smart Bonnie Charlie, Hoh Mike, Khabfair, Moon Unit, Motashaar and Without A Prayer. Standing at Derrinstown Stud, Ireland. 2011 fee: £5,500.

INVINCIBLE SPIRIT 1997 *Green Desert – Rafha (Kris)* Racing record: 7 wins, notably Sprint Cup at 5 yrs. Stud record: First runners in 2006. Sire of dual Group 1 winner Lawman (French Derby & Prix Jean Prat), Fleeting Spirit (July Cup, Temple Stakes, Flying Childers Stakes and Molecomb Stakes), Grade 1 Breeders Cup Juvenile winner Vale Of York, Cheveley Park Stakes winner Hooray, Gimcrack Stakes and Stewards Cup winner Conquest, Group 2 Criterium de Maisons-Lafitte winner Our Jonathan, Group 2 Flying Childers winner Madame Trop Vite, the smart performers Allied Powers, Campfire Glow, Captain Marvelous and Staying On, and the useful performers Bahama Mama, Hurricane Spirit, Invincible Force and Kingship Spirit. Standing at Irish National Stud. 2011 fee: €60,000.

ISHIGURU 1998 *Danzig – Strategic Maneuver (Cryptoclearance)* Race record: Won 3 races including the Group 3 Flying Five at Leopardstown and the listed Belgrave Stakes at the Curragh. Stud record: His best winners are Ferneley (5 wins including the Grade 2 1m Del Mar Handicap), Hellvelyn (5 wins including the Group 2 6f Coventry Stakes) and She's Our Mark (6 wins including the Group 3 10f Meld Stakes, the Group 3 1m Desmond Stakes and two listed events). Died 2009.

JAZIL 2003 *Seeking The Gold – Better Than Honour (Deputy Minister)* Race record: Won the Grade 1 Belmont Stakes. Stud record: Standing at Shadwell Farm Inc, Kentucky. 2011 $7,500. First runners 2011.

JEREMY 2003 *Danehill Dancer – Glint in Her Eye (Arazi)* Race record: Won four races including the Group 2 Betfred Mile and Group 3 Jersey Stakes. Stud record: Standing at the Irish National Stud. 2011 fee €6,000. First runners 2011.

JOHANNESBURG 1999 *Hennessy – Myth (Ogygian)* Racing record: Unbeaten at 2 yrs, when 7 wins included Phoenix Stakes, Prix Morny, Middle Park and Breeders' Cup Juvenile. Below form at 3 yrs. Stud record: First runners in 2006. Sire of the Group 1 Prix d'Ispahan winner Sageburg, Group 2 Norfolk Stakes winner Radiohead, US Grade 1 winner Scat Daddy, US Grade 2 winners Eaton's Gift and Teuflesburg, Australian dual Group 1 winner Turffontein and the smart performers Diamond Tycoon, Hammody, Jupiter Pluvius, Rabatash and Tombi. Standing in Japan for 2011.

KHELEYF 2001 *Green Desert – Society Lady (Mr Prospector)* Racing record: Won 3 races including the Group 3 Jersey Stakes. Stud record: From just two crops racing he is the sire of an exceptional 51 two-year-old winners. The best so far are Sayif (Group 2 Diadem Stakes), Percolator (Group 3 Prix du Bois) and the listed winners Captain Ramius and Playfellow and the Group 3 placed Deposer. Standing at Dalham Hall Stud, Newmarket. 2010 fee: £8,000.

KINGMAMBO 1990 *Mr Prospector – Miesque (Nureyev)* Racing record: Won the French 2,000 Guineas, the Prix du Moulin and the St James's Palace Stakes. Stud record: His European Group 1 winners include the multiple Group 1 winner Henrythenavigator, King's Best (both 2,000 Guineas), Russian Rhythm, Virginia Waters (both 1,000 Guineas), Rule Of Law (St Leger), Divine Proportions, Bluemamba (both French 1,000 Guineas), Light Shift (Oaks), Malhub (Golden Jubilee Stakes), Dubai Destination, (Queen Anne Stakes) and Okawango (Grand Criterium). Also the Japan Cup and French Group 1 winner Alkaased, Belmont Stakes winner Lemon Drop Kid, the Japanese champions El Condor Pasa and Kingkamehameha and the Hong Kong Q E II Stakes winner Archipenko. Retired from stud duties.

KING'S BEST 1997 *Kingmambo – Allegretta (Lombard)* Racing record: Won 3 races, including 2000 Guineas. Stud record: First runners in 2004. Sire of the Derby and Prix l'Arc de Triomphe winner Workforce, the Japanese Group 1 winner Eishin Flash, Proclamation (Sussex Stakes), Dubai Surprise (Premio Lydia Tesio) and Creachadoir (Lockinge Stakes), the very smart Allybar, Ancient Regime, Army Of Angels, Best Alibi, Best Name, King's Apostle (Group 1 Prix Maurice de Gheest) and Spice Route and the smart performers Elliots World, Notability, Not Just Swing, Oiseau Rare and Runaway. Sire of 21 stakes winners to April 2011. Standing at Haras Du Logis, France. 2011 fee: €15,000.

SIRES REFERENCE 349

KODIAC 2001 *Danehill – Rafha (Kris)* Racing Record: Won 4 races here and in the UAE over 6f and 7f including the Datel Trophy and Group 3 placed. Stud record: First runners 2010, sire of 3 listed winners. Standing at Tally Ho Stud, County Westmeath, Ireland. 2011 fee: Private.

KYLLACHY 1998 *Pivotal – Pretty Poppy (Song)* Racing record: Winner of 6 races, including Nunthorpe Stakes at 4 yrs. Stud record: First runners in 2006. Sire of the Group 1 Nunthorpe Stakes winner Sole Power, the Group 2 winners Arabian Gleam and Tariq, Hong Kong Group 1 winner Dim Sum, the very smart sprinter Corrybrough, and numerous smart performers including Awinnersgame, Befortyfour, Mabait and Mood Music. Standing at Cheveley Park Stud, Newmarket. 2011 fee: £12,000.

LAWMAN 2004 *Invincible Spirit – Laramie (Gulch)* Race record: Won 4 races, all in France including Prix du Jockey Club and Prix Jean Prat,. Stud record: First runners 2011. Standing at Ballylinch Stud, Ire 2011 fee €15,000.

LEMON DROP KID (1996) *Kingmambo – Charming Lassie (Seattle Slew)* Racing record: Won Belmont Stakes, Whitney Hcp and Woodward Stakes. Stud record: Bronze Cannon (Hardwicke Stakes), Jockey Club Stakes) and US Grade 1 winners Richard's Kid, Santa Teresita, Christmas Kid, Cittronade and Lemon's Forever. Standing at Lane's End, USA. 2011 fee $35,000.

LE VIE DEI COLORI 2000 *Efisio – Mystic Tempo (El Gran Senor)* Racing record: Won 12 races in Italy (notably the Premio Parioli and the Premio Vittorio di Capua) and 2 races here including the Challenge Stakes. Stud record: His first runners appeared in 2009 and included some smart two-year-olds including Carnaby Street, Classic Colori, Perfect Symmetry and Za Za Zoom. Died.

LIBRETTIST 2002 *Danzig – Mysterial (Alleged)* Racing Record: Won 7 races including the Group 1 Prix du Moulin and the Group 1 Prix Jacques Le Marois (both 1m). Stud record: First runners 2010 included the dual Group 2 winner Libranno. Standing at Haras du Logis, France. 2011 fee: €6,000.

LUCKY STORY 2001 *Kris S – Spring Flight (Miswaki)* Racing record: Won 4 races including the Group 2 Champagne Stakes and Group 2 Vintage Stakes. Stud record: First crop (bred in Japan) were two-year-olds in 2007. His first two European crops include the high-class Group 1 Golden Jubilee and Group 2 Coventry Stakes winner Art Connoisseur, the listed Redcar Two-Year-Old Trophy winner Lucky Like, the Group-placed Lucky Rave and several listed-placed horses. Standing at Tweenhills Stud. 2011 fee: £3,000.

MAJESTIC MISSILE 2003 *Royal Applause – Tshusick (Dancing Brave)* Racing Record: Won 6 including the Molecomb Stakes, Cornwallis Stakes and Prix du Petit Couvert (all 5f events). Stud record: First runners 2010. Standing at Ballyhane Stud, County Carlow, Ireland. 2011 fee €4,000.

MANDURO 2002 *Monsun – Mandellicht (Be My Guest)* Race record: Won 10 races including the Prix Jacques Le Marois, the Prince of Wales's Stakes and the Prix de Ispahan. Stud record: First runners in 2011. Kildangan Stud, Ire 2011 fee €15,000.

MARJU 1988 *Last Tycoon – Flame of Tara (Artaius)* Racing record: 3 wins including St James's Palace Stakes and runner-up in Derby. Stud record: First runners in 1993. Sire of the high-class Soviet Song (5 Group 1 events, including Sussex Stakes), the multiple Hong Kong Group 1 winner Viva Pataca and numerous smart performers including Asset, Brunel, Marju Snip (Group 1 Australasian Oaks), My Emma (Prix Vermeille), Sil Sila (Prix de Diane). Standing at Derrinstown Stud, Ireland. 2011 fee: €15,000.

MEDAGLIA D'ORO 1999 *El Prado – Cappucino Bay (Bailjumper)* Racing record, Won the Travers Stakes, Jim Dandy, San Felipe Stakes. Stud record: Best winners include champion Rachel Alexandra and the US Grade 1 winner Gabby's Golden Gal and Passion For Gold. Stud record: Standing at Darley, Ky, USA 2011 fee $100,000.

MEDICEAN 1997 *Machiavellian – Mystic Goddess (Storm Bird)* Racing record: 6 wins included Lockinge Stakes and Eclipse. Stud record: First runners in 2005. Sire of very smart Dutch Art (Prix Morny, Middle Park), Al Shemali (Group 1 Dubai Duty Free), the smart performer Nannina (Fillies' Mile, Coronation Stakes), the very smart miler Bankable (Dubai Group 2 1m winner), Almerita (Group 1 German Oaks), Chevron (Group 1 Raffles International Cup), German Group 3 winner Love Academy and the very smart Abigail Pett, Al Shemali, Cartimandua, Mr Medici and Medici Code. Stud record: Standing at Cheveley Park Stud. 2011 fee: £30,000.

MIZZEN MAST 1998 *Cozzene – Kinema (Graustark)* Racing record: Won the Grade 1 Malibu Stakes and the Grade 2 Strub Stakes. Stud record: Best winners include Midships (Charles Whittingham Stakes), Mast Track (Hollywood Gold Cup), Jibboom (Buena Vista Hcp), Madeo (Del Mar Derby(. Standing at Juddmonte Farms Ky. 2011 fee $12,500.

MONSUN 1990 *Konigsstuhl – Mosella (Sururm)* Racing record: Won three Grade 1 races in Germany. Stud record: Among notable winners Manduro (3 Grade 1 wins) and Shirocco (4 Grade 1 wins). Standing at Gestut Schlenderhan. 2011 stud fee: Private.

MONTJEU 1996 *Sadler's Wells – Floripedes (Top Ville)* Racing record: Won 11 races, including Prix de l'Arc de Triomphe and King George VI and Queen Elizabeth Diamond Stakes. Stud record: First runners in 2004. A top-class stallion son of Sadler's Wells. Sire of top-class Hurricane Run (Irish Derby, Prix de l'Arc de Triomphe, Tattersalls Gold Cup and King George), Authorized (Racing Post Trophy, Derby & Juddmonte International), Motivator (Racing Post Trophy and Derby) and Fame And Glory (Irish Derby and Racing Post Trophy), the 2009 Group 1 winning two-year-olds Jan Vermeer and St Nicholas Abbey and the high-class Alessandro Volta, Frozen Fire, Honolulu, Corre Caminos, Jukebox Jury, Macarthur, Montmartre, Papal Bull, Scorpion and Recital. Standing at Coolmore Stud, Ireland. 2011 fee: €75,000.

MOSS VALE (2001) *Shinko Forest – Wolf Cleugh (Last Tycoon)* Ran 42, won 8 including 6f Phoenix Sprint Stakes; G2 Prix Gros Chene, 5f. Weatherby Greenland Stakes G3 6f. Rathbarry Stud, 2011 fee €4,000. First runners 2011.

MOTIVATOR 2002 *Montjeu – Out West (Gone West)* Racing record: Won the Derby, the Racing Post Trophy and the Dante Stakes. Stud record: His first runners came in 2009 and they included the Group 2 May Hill Stakes winner Pollenator, the Italian listed winner Super Motiva and the Group 3 Autumn Stakes second Prompter. Standing at The Royal Studs. 2011: £8,000.

MR GREELEY 1992 *Gone West – Long Legend (Reviewer)* Racing record: Triple Grade 3 winner in USA and runner-up in Breeders' Cup Sprint. Stud record: First runners in 1999. Sire of Finsceal Beo (English & Irish 1,000 Guineas), Saoirse Abu (Phoenix Stakes, Moyglare Stud Stakes), Reel Buddy (Sussex Stakes), US Grade 1 winners El Corredor, Celtic Melody, Nonsuch Bay and Whywhywhy, the Australian Group 1 winner Miss Kournikova and numerous other Group/Graded stakes winners including Laughing Lashes winner of Debutante St. Died 2010.

MUJADIL 1988 *Storm Bird – Vallee Secrete (Secretariat)* Racing record: 3 wins (at 2 yrs) including Group 3 Cornwallis Stakes. Stud record: Best winners include Kingsgate Native (Group 1 Nunthorpe Stakes & Group 1 Golden Jubilee Stakes), Bouncing Bowdler (Group 2 Mill Reef Stakes), Galeota (Group 2 Mill Reef Stakes), the Group 3 winners Dancal (in Australia), Daunting Lady, Leggy Lou, Lesson In Humility, Master Plasta, Satri and Show Me The Money. Standing at Rathasker Stud, Ireland. 2011 fee: €7,500.

MULTIPLEX 2003 *Danehill – Shirley Valentine (Shirley Heights)* Won 4 races from 2 to 4 yrs including the 7f Prix la Rochette. Stud record: First runners 2011. Standing at Mickley Stud, 2011 fee £3,000.

NAMID 1996 *Indian Ridge – Dawnsio (Tate Gallery)* Racing record: Won 5 races, including Prix de l'Abbaye. Stud record: First runners in 2004. Sire of Total Gallery (Group 1 Prix de l'Abbaye), Pout (Group 2 Ridgewood Pearl Stakes), Redstone Dancer (Group 3 Brownstown Stakes), Blue Dakota (Group 3 Norfolk Stakes), Belle Artiste (Group 2 Leopardstown 1,000 Guineas Trial) and the smart performers Hogmaneigh and Resplendent Glory and several useful performers including Buachaill Dona, Burning Incense, Damika, Pike Bishop and That's Hot. Standing at Haras Du Hoguenet, France. 2011 fee: €5,000.

NAYEF 1999 *Gulch – Height of Fashion (Bustino)* Racing record: Won 9 races, including Champion Stakes and Juddmonte International Stakes. Stud record: First crop were two-year-olds in 2007. His best winners are Tamayiz (dual Group 1 winner in France), Lady Marian (Prix de l'Opera), Spacious (dual Group 2 winner and 1,000 Guineas second), the 2009 2-y-o Group 3 7f Oh So Sharp Stakes winner Tabassum, the very smart Confront (Group 3 1m Joel Stakes) and the smart Group 1 placed Top Lock. Standing at Nunnery Stud, Norfolk. 2011 fee: £12,000.

NORSE DANCER 2000 *Halling – River Patrol (Rousillon)* Racing record: Won 4 races including the Earl of Sefton Stakes and placed in numerous Group 1 events. Stud record: This is Norse Dancer's second crop of two-year-old runners. Sired four individual winners in 2010. Standing at Wood Farm Stud. 2011 fee Private.

NOTNOWCATO 2002 *Inchinor – Rambling Rose (Cadeaux Genereux)* Race record: Won seven races including the Group 1 Eclipse Stakes, Group 1 Tattersalls Gold Cup and Group 1 Juddmonte International. Stud record: First runners 2011. Standing at Stanley House Stud, Newmarket, 2011 fee £5,000.

OASIS DREAM 2001 *Green Desert – Hop (Dancing Brave)* Racing record: Won 4 races, including Middle Park Stakes, July Cup and Nunthorpe Stakes (all Group 1 events) Stud record: His first crop were two-year-olds in 2007 and he's built himself an outstanding reputation already with the Group 1 winners Aqlaam (Prix du Moulin), Arcano (Prix Morny), Midday (Nassau Stakes, Breeders Cup Filly & Mare Turf) and Naaqoos (Prix Jean-Luc Lagardere), along with over 10 other Group/

Graded stakes winners including Approve, Captain Gerrard, Main Aim, Misheer, Monitor Closely, Querari, Showcasing (Gimcrack Stakes), Sri Putra, Starlit Sands, Tuscan Evening, Visit, Young Pretender. Standing at Banstead Manor Stud, Newmarket. 2011 fee: £85,000.

ONE COOL CAT 2001 *Storm Cat – Tacha (Mr Prospector)* Racing record: At two in Ireland won the Group 1 6f Phoenix Stakes and the Group 1 7f National Stakes. Stud record: First crop were two-year-olds in 2008. Best performers include the Group 3 placed Hallie's Comet, Irish Cat and One Clever Cat and the listed winners Cool Contest, Icesolator, Layla's Hero, Lungwa and Magic Cat, Sarabia and Smokey Storm. Standing at Coolmore Stud, Ireland. 2011 fee: €9,000.

ORATORIO 2002 *Danehill – Mahrah (Vaguely Noble)* Racing record: Won the Prix Jean-Luc Lagardere (at 2 yrs). the Eclipse Stakes and Irish Champion Stakes. Stud record: His first crop were two-year-olds in 2009 and they included the first two home in the Group 1 Dewhurst Stakes, Beethoven and Fencing Master. He's also had the triple Group 3 winner Lolly For Dolly, the dual listed winner Big Audio, the Group 1 winning 2-y-o in New Zealand Banchee and King Torus (Vintage Stakes). Standing at Coolmore Stud, Ireland. 2011 fee: €9,000.

PASTORAL PURSUITS 2001 *Bahamian Bounty – Star (Most Welcome)* Racing record: Won 6 races including the July Cup, Sirenia Stakes and Park Stakes. Stud record: His first crop were runners in 2009. His best winners to date have been the Group 3 winner Rose Blossom, the 2-y-o listed winner Marine Commando and the Group 2 Mill Reef Stakes second Angel's Pursuit. Standing at the National Stud. 2011 fee: £7,000.

PEINTRE CELEBRE 1994 *Nureyev – Peinture Bleue (Alydar)* Racing record: Won 5 races including Prix du Jockey Club, Grand Prix de Paris, Prix de L'Arc de Triomphe. Stud record: His best winners include Pride (3 Group 1 wins), Byword (Group 1 Prince Of Wales's Stakes), Dai Jin (German Derby) and Valle Enchantee (Hong Kong Vase). Standing at Coolmore Stud, 2011 fee €15,000.

PICCOLO 1991 *Warning – Woodwind (Whistling Wind)* Racing record: 4 wins including Nunthorpe Stakes and Kings Stand Stakes. Stud record: Sire of the Group 1 Nunthorpe Stakes winner La Cucaracha, the Australian Group 1 winner Picaday, the Group 2 winners Ajigolo, Express Air, St Trinians and Winker Watson and numerous other smart performers including Aegean Dancer, Bond Boy (Steward's Cup winner), Hoh Hoh Hoh, Hunting Lion, Lipocco, Pan Jammer and Pickle. Standing at Throckmorton Court Stud. 2011 fee: £3,000.

PIVOTAL 1993 *Polar Falcon – Fearless Revival (Cozzene)* Racing record: 4 wins including the Nunthorpe Stakes and King's Stand Stakes. Stud record: First runners in 2000. An outstanding sire whose best winners include the high-class Excellent Art (St James's Palace Stakes), Falco (French 2,000 Guineas), Halfway To Heaven (Irish 1,00 Guineas, Nassau Stakes and Sun Chariot Stakes, Kyllachy (Nunthorpe Stakes), Sariska (Oaks and Irish Oaks), and Somnus (Sprint Cup, Prix de la Foret, Prix Maurice de Gheest), the very smart Beauty Is Truth (Group 2 Prix du Gros-Chene), Captain Rio (Group 2 Criterium des Maisons-Laffitte), Chorist (Pretty Polly Stakes), Golden Apples (triple US Grade 1 winner), Leo (Group 2 Royal Lodge Stakes), Peeress (Lockinge Stakes, Sun Chariot Stakes), Pivotal Point (Group 2 Diadem Stakes) and Virtual (Lockinge Stakes) and numerous smart performers including Falco (French 2,000 Guineas), Megahertz (2 US Grade 1 events), Regal Parade (Haydock Sprint Cup), Silvester Lady (German Oaks), Siyouni (2009 2-y-o Group 1 Prix Jean-Luc Lagardere) and Saoire (Irish 1000 Guineas). Salto. Standing at Cheveley Park Stud, Newmarket. 2011 fee: £55,000.

PROUD CITIZEN 1999 *Gone West –Drums Of Freedom (Green Forest)* Racing record: Won 3 races including the Grade 3 Lexington Stakes and second the Kentucky Derby. Stud record: Retired to stud in 2004. First crop were 2-y-o's in 2007. Sire of the US dual Grade 1 winner Proud Spell, the Group 3 Somerville Tattersall Stakes winner River Proud, the US Grade 3 winner Motovato and a number of other US stakes winners. Standing at Airdrie Stud, Kentucky. 2011 fee: $10,000.

RAIL LINK 2003 *Dansili – Docklands (Theatrical)* Race record: Won the Prix de L'Arc de Triomphe, Prix Niel, Grand Prix de Paris, Prix du Lys. Stud record: First runners 2011. Standing at Banstead Manor Stud, 2011 fee £7,000.

RED CLUBS 2003 *Red Ransom – Two Clubs (First Trump)* Race record: Won 6 races including the Group 1 Betfred Sprint Cup ,Group 2 Diadem Stakes and Group 3 Greenham Stakes. Stud record: Stands at Tally Ho Stud, Ireland €6,500. First runners 2011.

RED RANSOM 1987 *Roberto – Arabia (Damascus)* Racing record: 2 wins in US, at 5f and 6f, from three outings. Stud record: Best performers include outstanding miler Intikhab, high-class Ekraar (Group 1 Italian Derby) and Electrocutionist (Dubai World Cup, Juddmonte International), very smart performers Casual Look (Oaks), China Visit (Group 2 Prix du Rond-Point), Bail Out Becky (Del Mar Oaks), Perfect Sting (Queen Elizabeth II Challenge Cup and BC Filly and Mare Turf), Red Clubs (Haydock Park Sprint Cup), Australian Grade 1 winners Red Dazzler, Charge Forward & Typhoon Tracy (four Group 1 wins), the German Group 1 winner Ransom O'War and the dual Group 2 winning 2-y-o Sri Pekan. Died 2009.

REFUSE TO BEND 2000 *Sadler's Wells – Market Slide (Gulch)* Racing record: Won 7 races including National Stakes, 2,000 Guineas, Eclipse Stakes & Queen Anne Stakes. Stud record: His first crop were two-year-olds in 2008 and his best to date include the French dual Group 1 winner Sarafina, the smart dual winner Liberation, the Group 3 winners Grace O'Malley and Neon Light and the listed winners Alaiyma, Croisultan and Mibar. Standing at Whitsbury Manor Stud. 2011 fee: £4,500.

ROCK OF GIBRALTAR 1999 *Danehill – Offshore Boom (Be My Guest)* Racing record: Won 7 G1 races including Dewhurst Stakes, Sussex Stakes. Stud record: Sire of Eagle Mountain, Mount Nelson. South African Grade 1 winner Seventh Rock, US Grade 1 winner Diamondrella, Varenar (Prix de la Foret) and also Yellowstone, General Elliott and Kitty Macham. Standing at Coolmore Stud, Ire. 2011 fee €17,500.

ROYAL APPLAUSE 1993 *Waajib – Flying Melody (Auction Ring)* Racing record: Winner of 9 races, including Middle Park at 2 yrs and Haydock Park Sprint Cup at 4. Stud record First runners in 2001. Sire of the US dual Grade 1 winner Ticker Tape, Group/Grade 2 winners Acclamation, Battle Of Hastings, Finjaan, Lovelace, Mister Cosmi, Nevisian Lad, Please Sing and Whatsthescript and numerous very smart performers including Crime Scene, Majestic Missile, Peak To Creek and Prince Siegfried. Standing at The Royal Studs, Norfolk. 2011 fee: £9,000.

SAKHEE 1997 *Bahri – Thawakib (Sadler's Wells)* Racing record: Won 8 races, including Juddmonte International and Prix de l'Arc de Triomphe, and runner-up in Derby. Stud record: First runners in 2006. Sire of the Group 1 July Cup winner Sakhee's Secret, the Hong Kong and Dubai Group 1 winner Presvis and the very smart Regal Flush, Royal Rock and Samuel, Tin Horse. Standing at Nunnery Stud, Norfolk. 2011 fee: £5,000.

SELKIRK 1988 *Sharpen Up – Annie Edge (Nebbiolo)* Racing record: 6 wins including Queen Elizabeth II Stakes, Lockinge Stakes, Beefeater Gin Celebration Mile and Challenge Stakes. Stud record: A leading British-based stallion, he has sired 11 Group 1 winners. His best include Leadership (Gran Premio d'Italia), the Premio Presidente Repubblica winners Altieri and Selmis, Cityscape, Border Arrow, Etlaala, Favourable Terms (Nassau Stakes), Field of Hope (Prix de la Foret), Highest, Kastoria (Irish St Leger), Pipedreamer, Prince Kirk (Prix d'Ispahan), Red Bloom (Fillies' Mile), Scott's View, Squeak (Beverly Hills Handicap), Sulk (Prix Marcel Boussac), Tam Lin, The Trader, Tranquil Tiger, Trans Island, Wince (1000 Guineas) and Wordly. Rainbow Springs. Standing at Lanwades Stud in Newmarket. 2011 fee: £20,000.

SHAMARDAL 2002 *Giant's Causeway – Helsinki (Machiavellian)* Racing record: Won Dewhurst Stakes, French 2,000 Guineas, French Derby and St James's Palace Stakes. Stud record: His first European runners appeared in 2009. His best performers to date have been dual French Group 1 winner Lope de Vega, Group 1 Racing Post Trophy winner Casamento, Arctic (Group 3 Round Tower Stakes), Shakespearian (Group 2 Hungeford Stakes), Zazou (third in the Group 1 Criterium de Saint-Cloud) and the listed UAE 1,000 Guineas winner Siyaadah. In Australia he's had the Group 1 winner Faint Perfume. Standing at Kildangan Stud, Ireland. 2011 fee: €50,000.

SHIROCCO 2001 *Monsun – So Sedulous (The Minstrel)* Racing Record: Won 7 races including the German Derby, French Derby, Breeders Cup Turf and Coronation Cup (all Group 1, 12f events). Stud record: First runners 2010. Standing at Dalham Hall Stud. 2011 fee: £10,000.

SINGSPIEL 1992 *In The Wings – Glorious Song (Halo)* Racing record: Winner of 9 races, notably Canadian International and Japan Cup at 4 yrs and Dubai World Cup, Coronation Cup and Juddmonte International at 5. Stud record: First runners in 2001. Sire of triple Group 1 winner Dar Ri Me, Dubai World Cup winner Moon Ballad, US dual Grade 1 winner Lahudood, high-class Lohengrin (in Japan), very smart Asakusa Den'en (Japanese Group 1 winner), Confidential Lady (Prix de Diane), Eastern Anthem (Dubai Sheema Classic), Folk Opera (E P Taylor Stakes), Lateral (Gran Criterium), Papineau (Gold Cup), Silkwood (Ribblesdale Stakes), Singhalese (Del Mar Oaks) and of numerous smart performers. Died 2010.

SINNDAR 1997 *Grand Lodge – Sinntara (Lashkari)* Racing record: Won 7 races, including Derby and Prix de l'Arc de Triomphe. Stud record: First runners in 2004. Sire of the top-class colt and multiple Group 1 winner Youmzain, the 2009 2-y-o Group 1 Prix Marcel Boussac winner Rosanara, the very smart performer Shawanda (Irish Oaks and Prix Vermeille), the smart Albahja, Aqaleem, Four Sins (Blandford Stakes), Pictavia and Visindar (Prix Greffulhe) and the very useful Gale Force, Kerashan and Red Gala. Standing at Haras du Bonneval, France. 2011 fee: €9,500

SIR PERCY 2003 *Mark of Esteem – Percy's Lass (Blakeney)* Race record: Won 5 races including the Derby and the Dewhurst Stakes. Stud record: Standing at Lanwades Stud. Newmarkey, 2011 fee £6,000. First runners 2011.

SLEEPING INDIAN 2001 *Indian Ridge – Las Flores (Sadler's Wells)* Racing Record: Won 6 races including the Group 2, 7f Challenge Stakes the Group 3 7f Hungerford Stakes and three listed events. Stud record: First runners 2010. Standing at Tweenhills Stud. 2011 fee: £3,000.

SMART STRIKE 1992 *Mr Prospector – Classy 'n Smart (Smarten)* Racing record: Won 8 races in the USA including the Grade 2 8.5f Philip H Iselin Handicap and the Grade 3 Salvator Mile. Stud record: Best winners include the top-class colt Curlin (Preakness Stakes, Dubai World Cup, Breeders Cup Classic), the US Grade 1 winners English Channel, Fabulous Strike, Furthest Land, Lookin At Lucky, Shadow Cast, Soaring Free and Square Eddie, and the Japan Cup winner Fleetstreet Dancer. Standing at Lane's End Farm. 2011 fee: €75,000.

SOVIET STAR 1984 *Nureyev – Veruschka (Venture)* Racing record: Trusthouse Forte Mile, July Cup, Prix Moulin de Longchamp. Stud record: Best winners include Starcraft (Queen Elizabeth 11 Stakes, Prix du Moulin), Freedom Cry, Ashkalani, Starborough, Pressing, Soviet Line and Russian Pearl. Standing at Ballylinch Stud Ireland. 2011 fee €8,000.

SPEIGHTSTOWN 1998 *Gone West – Silken Cat (Storm Cat)* Racing record: Won Breeders Cup Sprint, Churchill Downs Hcp, True North Breeders Cup Hcp, Alfred Vanderbilt Handicap. Stud record: Best winners include Haynesfield (US Grade 1 Jockey Club Gold Cup), Jersey Town (US Grade 1 Cigar Mile), Munnings & Lord Shanakill. Standing at Winstar Farm, Ky 2011 fee: $50,000.

STORMY ATLANTIC 1994 *Storm Cat – Hail Atlantis (Seattle Slew)* Stud Record: Has sired 8 crops, winners include Stormello (Hollywood Futurity St, Norfolk Breeders Cup Stakes). Standing at Hill N'Dale Farms, Ky. 2011 fee $30,000.

STRATEGIC PRINCE 2004 *Dansili – Ausherra (Diesis)* Race record: Won 3 races including the July Stakes and the Vintage Stakes. Stud record: Standing at Coolmore, Ire, 2011 fee €4,000. First runners 2011.

STREET CRY 1998 *Machiavellian – Helen Street (Troy)* Racing record: 5 wins including Dubai World Cup. Stud record: First runners in 2006. Sire of the outstanding multiple Grade 1 winning race mare Zenyatta and the Group/ Grade 1 winners Street Sense (Breeders' Cup Juvenile, Kentucky Derby, Travers Stakes), Majestic Roi (Sun Chariot Stakes), Street Boss (Triple Bend Invitational, Bing Crosby H'cap), Seventh Street (dual US Grade 1), Street Hero (Norfolk Stakes), the Australian Group 1 winners Shocking (Melbourne Cup) and Whobegotyou, and Saamidd (Champagne Stakes). Standing at Darley Stud, Kentucky. 2011 fee: $150,000.

STREET SENSE 2004 *Street Cry – Bedazzle (Dixieland Band)* Race record: Won the Breeders Cup Juvenile and the Kentucky Derby. Stud record: Standing at Jonabell Farm, Kentucky, 2011, fee $40,000. First runners 2011.

TAGULA 1993 *Taufan – Twin Island (Standaan)* Racing record: Won 4 races including the Group 1 6f Prix Morny (at 2 yrs) and the Group 3 7f Supreme Stakes. Stud record: Sires plenty of winners, amongst the best being Canford Cliffs (triple Group 1 winner), the Group 2 Prix du Gros-Chene winner Tax Free, the Group 2 Royal Lodge Stakes winner Atlantis Prince, the German Group 2 winner Tagshira, the smart Group 2 placed Beaver Patrol and the listed winners Bakewell Tart, Double Vie, Drawnfromthepast, King Orchisios, Macaroon, Pure Poetry and Red Millennium. Standing at the Rathbarry Stud. 2011 fee: €4,000.

TEOFILO 2004 *Galileo – Speirbhhean (Danehill)* Race record: Won 5 races at 2 yrs including the Group 1 Dewhurst Stakes and the Group 1 National Stakes. Champion 2-y-o. Stud record: Standing at Kildangan Stud, Ire, 2011 fee €15,000. First runners 2011.

THREE VALLEYS 2001 *Diesis – Skiable (Niniski)* Race record: Won 5 races including the Group 2 Coventry Stakes at 2 yrs and subsequently two Graded stakes in the USA. Stud Record: Standing at Banstead Manor Stud, Newmarket, 2011 fee £5,000. First runners 2011.

TIGER HILL 1995 *Danehill – The Filly (Appiani II)* Racing record: Won 17 races including three Group 1 events in Germany. Stud record: Compiled an excellent record in Germany (including the Group 1 winners Iota and Konigstiger and a multitude of other stakes winners). Also sire of thr Group 1 Dubai Sheema Classic winner Rewilding. Standing at Gestut Fahrhof. 2011 fee: €9,500.

TRADE FAIR 2000 *Zafonic – Danefair (Danehill)* Racing record: Won the Group 3 Criterion Stakes, the Group 3 Minstrel Stakes and two listed events. Stud record: His first runners appeared in 2009. Sire of numerous minor winners. Standing at Tweenhills Stud. 2011 fee: £3,000.

VAN NISTLEROOY (2000) *Storm Cat – Halory (Halo)* Race record: Won the Group 2 7f Futurity Stakes in Ireland at 2 yrs. Stud record: Sire of winners Set Play (Grade 1 Del Mar Debutante), More Bountiful (Chairman's Trophy Sha Tin), Strike The Deal (Group 3 Dubai Duty Free Trophy). Standing at Ashford Stud, Ky. 2011 fee $5,000.

VERGLAS 1994 *Highest Honor – Rahaam (Secreto)* Racing record: Won 3 races including the Group 3 6f Coventry Stakes. Stud record: Sire of the Group 1 French 2,000 Guineas winner Silver Frost, the Group 1 Prix Jean Prat winner Stormy River, the US dual Grade 2 winner Blackdoun, the Group 3 winners Love Lockdown, Ozone Bere, Spirited One, Glass Harmonium and Wilside, and numerous listed winners. Standing at the Irish National Stud. 2010 fee: €10,000.

VITAL EQUINE 2004 *Danetime – Bayaka (Selkirk)* Racing Record: Won the Group 2 7f Champagne Stakes at 2 yrs and second n the 2,000 Guineas. Stud Record: Standing at Bearstone Stud. £3,500. First two-year-olds 2011.

WAR CHANT 1997 *Danzig – Hollywood Wildcat (Kris S)* Racing record: Won 5 races including the Grade 1 Breeders Cup Mile. Stud record: Sire of the 2-y-o Group 1 National Stakes winner Kingsfort, the US Grade 2 winners Brilliant and War Kill, Group 3 Nell Gwyn Stakes winner Karen's Caper, US Grade 2 winner Chamberlaine Bridge, the US Grade 3 winners Ballymore Lady, Chattahoochee War and En Roblar & Sea Chanter, Irish Group 3 winner Norman Invader and the French Group 3 winner Asperity. Standing at Three Chimneys Farm, Kentucky. 2011 fee: $12,500.

WHIPPER 2001 *Miesque's Son – Myth To Reality (Sadler's Wells)* Racing record: Won the Prix Morny and the Prix Maurice de Gheest. Stud record: Had his first runners in 2009. Best winners to date include French Group 2 winner Royal Bench, listed winner Yaa Wayl, Group 3 winner Dolled Up and the Group 2 Rockfel Stakes second Atasari. Standing at Haras du Mezeray. 2011 fee: €7,500.

WINDSOR KNOT 2002 *Pivotal – Triple Tie (The Minstrel)* Racing record: Won 4 races including the Solario Stakes at 2yrs and the Darley Stakes (both Group 3). Stud record: Standing at Rossenarra Stud Ireland. 2011 fee €3,000. First runners 2011.

ZAFEEN 2000 *Zafonic – Shy Lady (Kaldoun)* Racing record: Won the Group 1 St James's Palace Stakes and the Group 2 Mill Reef Stakes and second in the 2,000 Guineas. Stud record: His first runners appeared in 2009, he has had a number of winners but none at stakes level. Standing at Haras Du Petit Tellier. 2011 fee: €4000.

ZAMINDAR 1994 *Gone West – Zaizafon (The Minstrel)* Racing record: Won the Group 3 Prix de Cabourg at 2 yrs and was placed in the Prix Morny and the Prix de la Salamandre. Stud record: Has sired a number of very good fillies, notably the outstanding Zarkava (five Group 1 wins including the Prix de l'Arc de Triomphe), Darjina (three Group 1 wins), the Group 1 Prix Saint-Alary winner Coquerelle and the Group 1 French 1,000 Guineas winner Zenda. He also has the Group 2 winners Crossharbour and Modern Look. Standing at Banstead Manor Stud, Newmarket. 2011 fee: £15,000.

Sires index

Sires appear under the reference number of their offspring.

A P Indy 922
Acclamation 45, 92, 152, 174, 206, 287, 433, 450, 467, 675, 712, 713, 744, 755, 766, 782, 814, 823, 828, 832, 884, 929, 970, 1061, 1086, 1140, 1191, 1222, 1223, 1380, 1408, 1573, 1589, 1639, 1652, 1656
Act One 1519, 1522
Afraz 1293
Aldebaran 986
Alhaarth 34, 977
Amadeus Wolf 64, 106, 110, 372, 395, 414, 496, 745, 779, 1120, 1134, 1188, 1288, 1366, 1421, 1424, 1641, 1654
Anabaa 58, 378, 385
Antonius Pius 974
Any Given Saturday 1014
Aptitude 867, 1342
Araafa 1170, 1382
Arakan 804
Arch 440, 1322, 1619
Atraf 1117
Auction House 163, 495
Aussie Rules 270, 407, 890, 949, 966, 1058, 1351, 1352, 1397
Authorized 127, 147, 149, 156, 205, 234, 282, 283, 305, 376, 508, 555, 573, 608, 657, 720, 907, 962, 1549, 1629
Avonbridge 15, 159, 169, 816, 1138, 1369, 1645, 1648
Awesome Again 191, 1386
Azamour 202, 351, 514, 533, 586, 707, 1224, 1307, 1311, 1312, 1359

Bachelor Duke 1193, 1590
Bahamian Bounty 271, 272, 306, 399, 507, 544, 661, 714, 751, 797, 971, 1088, 1420, 1516, 1589
Baltic King 229, 824, 899, 1156
Barathea 1385
Beat Hollow 50, 310
Bernardini 562, 570, 1109, 1453, 1620
Bertolini 125, 136, 139, 241, 387, 526, 650, 826, 972
Big Bad Bob 457
Byron 160, 170, 278, 786, 1124, 1146

Cadeaux Genereux 55, 150, 172, 732, 734, 736, 969, 1101, 1172, 1650
Camacho 410, 523
Cape Cross 21, 43, 94, 126, 175, 181, 246, 282, 334, 444, 561, 605, 640, 667, 803, 833, 834, 941, 992, 1082, 1136, 1177, 1179, 1230, 1399, 1433, 1492, 1532, 1545, 1617
Captain Rio 161
Catcher In The Rye 1461
Celtic Swing 490
Cherokee Run 117
Chevalier 411, 530
Chineur 1030, 1115
Choisir 138, 141, 142, 417, 419, 528, 725, 759, 806, 877, 1005, 1053, 1145, 1338, 1653
Clodovil 113, 237, 245, 266, 379, 491, 517, 541, 596, 709, 730, 926, 979, 1114, 1149, 1169, 1280, 1285, 1326, 1436, 1600
Cockney Rebel 274, 416, 471, 538, 796, 838, 1039, 1077, 1144, 1435
Compton Place 8, 41, 103, 133, 227, 546, 976

Dalakhani 20, 33, 93, 221, 599, 636, 651, 809, 1073, 1302, 1320, 1459, 1643
Danehill Dancer 23, 85, 204, 254, 360, 681, 689, 739, 750, 798, 811, 819, 893, 934, 1071, 1196, 1229, 1248, 1335, 1392, 1403, 1465, 1509, 1513
Dansili 65, 184, 187, 194, 195, 196, 209, 216, 217, 219, 323, 326, 336, 337, 356, 441, 459, 556, 588, 618, 625, 662, 686, 830, 861, 1080, 1099, 1132, 1265, 1304, 1323, 1344, 1391, 1407, 1479, 1490, 1494, 1498, 1565, 1611, 1634
Dark Angel 75, 91, 137, 332, 438, 486, 501, 512, 658, 829, 840, 871, 888, 955, 965, 1015, 1043, 1049, 1060, 1121, 1206, 1282, 1348, 1410, 1416, 1528, 1608, 1632, 1637
Desert Style 793, 864
Diamond Green 280, 357, 391, 421, 503, 901, 1155
Discreet Cat 639, 1330, 1527
Distorted Humor 185, 462, 784, 1021, 1111, 1569
Dixie Union 48, 1064, 1105, 1538
Doyen 1350
Dr Fong 39, 1439
Dubai Destination 498, 563, 571, 695, 701, 923, 930, 994, 1178, 1556, 1566
Dubawi 148, 154, 294, 344, 350, 353, 366, 400, 439, 539, 540, 568, 656, 996, 1094, 1153, 1294, 1306, 1441, 1499, 1547, 1551, 1575
Dutch Art 27, 70, 281, 426, 487, 488, 489, 500, 509, 516, 589, 761, 911, 953, 982, 1010, 1055, 1062, 1069, 1137, 1164, 1197, 1210, 1401, 1415, 1448, 1449, 1558
Dylan Thomas 32, 121, 224, 300, 333, 364, 478, 548, 582, 630, 631, 678, 789, 900, 946, 1167, 1239, 1262, 1268, 1275, 1325

STALLIONS INDEX

Dynaformer 307, 352, 430, 612, 842
Echo Of Light 143, 164, 275, 585, 1646
Elnadim 279, 434, 951, 968, 1143
Elusive City 380, 469, 493, 719, 726, 738, 769, 781, 783, 787, 1052, 1083, 1205, 1464
Elusive Quality 3, 54, 247, 362, 464, 545, 622, 1198
Empire Maker 188, 220, 818
Exceed And Excel 61, 96, 134, 176, 251, 288, 313, 320, 358, 377, 386, 425, 427, 428, 466, 524, 557, 576, 587, 645, 792, 807, 860, 870, 902, 905, 927, 931, 936, 943, 944, 1036, 1040, 1160, 1443, 1548, 1570, 1578, 1612, 1618, 1630, 1649
Excellent Art 62, 297, 418, 492, 513, 694, 753, 757, 758, 846, 863, 886, 894, 960, 1037, 1050, 1068, 1131, 1240, 1244, 1246, 1327, 1504, 1605, 1644
Exchange Rate 455, 591

Flower Alley 1642
Footstepsinthesand 71, 223, 232, 365, 402, 717, 1074, 1096, 1627
Forest Wildcat 1333

Galileo 100, 119, 178, 179, 186, 200, 203, 208, 215, 218, 339, 343, 579, 580, 592, 594, 595, 601, 602, 610, 616, 624, 690, 696, 889, 897, 998, 1135, 1233, 1241, 1247, 1249, 1251, 1253, 1254, 1255, 1256, 1257, 1258, 1259, 1263, 1264, 1269, 1270, 1273, 1300, 1313, 1314, 1357, 1365, 1383, 1387, 1393, 1404, 1442, 1469, 1477, 1483, 1485, 1506, 1510, 1579, 1601, 1624, 1636
Giant's Causeway 817, 920, 1209, 1228, 1236, 1272, 1303, 1319, 1472, 1635

Gold Away 752
Gone West 1324
Green Desert 42, 151, 201, 302, 361, 460, 647, 673, 908, 1412, 1455

Haafhd 277, 293, 408, 497, 688, 692, 849, 912, 967, 1152, 1234, 1332, 1356, 1372, 1374, 1562, 1596, 1598
Halling 25, 167, 480, 484, 494, 655, 919, 1315, 1523, 1525
Hard Spun 554, 574, 649, 862, 935, 1546
Hawk Wing 1106
Henny Hughes 446, 879
Hernando 57, 84, 1396
High Chaparral 843, 1126, 1297, 1489
Holy Roman Emperor 16, 22, 63, 82, 265, 268, 285, 286, 289, 296, 329, 338, 398, 401, 448, 465, 506, 644, 762, 773, 774, 881, 885, 896, 904, 915, 928, 956, 961, 1004, 1009, 1085, 1173, 1218, 1237, 1242, 1243, 1245, 1278, 1281, 1286, 1423, 1460, 1461, 1470, 1493, 1609
Hurricane Run 2, 13, 711, 1019, 1305, 1606

Iceman 31, 162, 521
Iffraaj 111, 371, 468, 510, 511, 619, 702, 735, 749, 844, 942, 1045, 1046, 1227, 1276, 1279, 1451, 1561, 1583, 1584
Imperial Dancer 239, 240, 264
Include 1318
Indesatchel 422, 1422, 1425
Indian Haven 633, 1041
Intikhab 29, 66, 98, 412, 424, 799, 981, 1376, 1544
Invasor 238, 1090
Invincible Spirit 116, 210, 354, 367, 409, 437, 451, 481, 559, 565, 569, 627, 679, 684, 710, 1024, 1066, 1076, 1217, 1220, 1221,
1298, 1309, 1360, 1362, 1378, 1398, 1444, 1452, 1474, 1476, 1495, 1554, 1614, 1628
Ishiguru 1016, 1029, 1116, 1291
Istan 165
Ivan Denisovich 1032

Jazil 461, 671, 852, 1616
Jeremy 83, 276, 327, 632, 698, 820, 1020, 1368, 1559, 1638
Johannesburg 56, 839, 1195, 1232

Key Of Luck 420
Kheleyf 46, 101, 236, 743, 997, 1047, 1070, 1154, 1174, 1185, 1552, 1587
King's Best 131, 1023, 1129, 1180, 1299, 1434, 1480, 1501
Kingmambo 553, 1250, 1261, 1266, 1530
Kitten's Joy 1607
Kodiac 105, 397, 534, 583, 1001, 1054, 1345, 1426, 1457, 1458
Kyllachy 230, 322, 394, 499, 505, 522, 603, 643, 754, 763, 765, 767, 771, 973, 1056, 1075, 1084, 1119, 1161, 1183, 1231, 1440

Lando 77
Latent Heat 312, 854
Lawman 95, 115, 436, 621, 660, 748, 776, 831, 847, 948, 988, 1012, 1087, 1331, 1373
Le Vie Dei Colori 502, 1414
Lemon Drop Kid 81, 895, 1316
Librettist 235, 535, 665, 909
Lion Heart 1166
Lucky Story 406, 1048, 1647

Majestic Missile 381, 825
Manduro 18, 135, 578, 634, 729, 768, 989, 1007, 1377, 1379, 1602
Marju 199, 740, 869, 1025, 1287, 1301

Medaglia D'Oro 1437
Medicean 26, 86, 314, 355, 638, 708, 724, 872, 914, 925, 1000, 1002, 1011, 1063, 1171, 1204, 1216, 1388, 1400, 1409
Medicis 415
Mizzen Mast 214, 315, 328, 600, 856, 868, 1003, 1336, 1343, 1496
Monsieur Bond 1511
Monsun 207, 346, 423, 614, 1571
Montjeu 49, 72, 197, 309, 311, 432, 617, 822, 940, 1194, 1267, 1271, 1390, 1402
Moss Vale 102, 104, 109, 259, 715, 742, 845, 878, 950, 1013, 1018, 1027, 1190
Motivator 90, 347, 374, 693, 827, 947, 1118, 1514, 1518, 1563
Mr Greeley 80, 129, 231, 609, 668, 683, 685, 898, 1081, 1133, 1201, 1211, 1482, 1557
Mujadil 263, 383, 1187
Multiplex 704, 760, 1503

Namid 67, 876, 1125, 1127
Nayef 24, 44, 52, 99, 140, 304, 331, 405, 447, 453, 477, 518, 520, 543, 558, 575, 653, 654, 659, 666, 780, 1157, 1165, 1317, 1341, 1491, 1540, 1553, 1555, 1585, 1595
Norse Dancer 473, 474, 475
Notnowcato 6, 295, 324, 664, 785, 836, 1139, 1159, 1176, 1328, 1354, 1364, 1487, 1610

Oasis Dream 14, 79, 128, 198, 212, 250, 303, 382, 393, 443, 527, 577, 581, 584, 606, 607, 646, 669, 697, 716, 723, 778, 795, 841, 875, 939, 984, 993, 1059, 1092, 1163, 1213, 1219, 1235, 1238, 1246, 1292, 1339, 1481, 1488, 1507, 1533, 1541, 1564, 1568, 1577, 1621, 1626, 1633

Observatory 1515
One Cool Cat 848, 952, 1192
Oratorio 73, 171, 370, 404, 529, 547, 728, 741, 775, 791, 794, 800, 851, 883, 910, 957, 987, 1147, 1208, 1277, 1296, 1310, 1347, 1456, 1466, 1588, 1657
Osorio 4

Passing Glance 19
Pastoral Pursuits 375, 687, 1158
Peintre Celebre 359, 637, 1371
Piccolo 51, 158, 252, 255, 262, 396, 620, 1429, 1526
Pivotal 35, 348, 369, 525, 567, 642, 682, 721, 747, 880, 1057, 1200, 1207, 1212, 1252, 1406, 1473, 1475, 1497, 1500, 1508, 1572, 1576, 1597, 1615
Pleasant Tap 850, 1329
Proclamation 1128
Proud Citizen 11, 273, 1089, 1104, 1260
Pursuit Of Love 1044

Rahy 560, 1102
Rail Link 770, 887, 891, 985, 1108, 1321, 1447, 1521, 1625
Rakti 269
Red Clubs 5, 108, 144, 260, 429, 449, 483, 733, 855, 865, 866, 954, 1017, 1026, 1033, 1079, 1093, 1095, 1103, 1225, 1375, 1417
Red Ransom 36, 290, 705, 815, 916, 1367, 1535, 1536
Redback 107, 222, 853, 958, 963, 1148, 1539
Refuse To Bend 17, 74, 132, 699, 983, 1308, 1381
Rock Hard Ten 549
Rock Of Gibraltar 9, 47, 60, 87, 88, 253, 256, 299, 363, 413, 537, 604, 615, 623, 635, 674, 790, 964, 999, 1130, 1337, 1413, 1427, 1512
Royal Applause 28, 173, 213, 318, 340, 341, 431, 515, 532, 652, 663, 737, 772, 802, 835, 1008, 1123, 1142, 1162, 1181, 1184, 1215, 1274, 1283, 1289, 1431, 1468, 1471, 1505, 1581, 1586

Sakhee 1, 458, 519, 959, 975, 1097, 1141, 1593
Selkirk 317, 319, 1384, 1389, 1395, 1486, 1567, 1604, 1640
Shamardal 12, 68, 146, 153, 157, 257, 281, 445, 463, 626, 628, 641, 672, 680, 873, 874, 990, 1042, 1199, 1349, 1363, 1446, 1450, 1531, 1542, 1613
Sharp Humor 1290
Shirocco 485, 550, 718, 746, 1182, 1574
Singspiel 89, 145, 166, 228, 243, 373, 472, 542, 597, 892, 1353, 1520, 1622
Sinndar 859
Sir Percy 233, 267, 330, 435, 479, 903, 906, 921, 1078, 1175, 1405, 1529, 1534, 1537
Sleeping Indian 1186, 1346, 1428
Smart Strike 124, 670, 1098, 1203, 1478
Soviet Star 40, 244, 335
Speightstown 261, 676, 882, 1599
Stevie Wonderboy 1067
Stormy Atlantic 938, 1394
Stormy River 403
Strategic Prince 10, 226, 284, 727, 764, 777, 788, 801, 808, 813, 1035, 1370, 1419
Street Cry 76, 78, 349, 368, 442, 454, 590, 593, 598, 706, 857, 924, 933, 945, 1295, 1484, 1580, 1582, 1623
Street Sense 1543

Tagula 37, 756, 837, 1100, 1651, 1658
Tapit 1031
Teofilo 97, 112, 114, 118, 120, 155, 180, 182, 189, 190, 192, 248, 301, 388, 536, 551, 564, 566, 572, 700, 731, 810, 821, 858,

932, 937, 980, 991, 995, 1168, 1226, 1358, 1411, 1430, 1438, 1550, 1592, 1603
Teuflesburg 703
Theatrical 1594
Three Valleys 225, 298, 308, 316, 321, 345, 384, 389, 504, 531, 552, 611, 805, 913, 917, 1006, 1038, 1418, 1524, 1560
Tiger Hill 211, 470, 476, 1022, 1517
Titus Livius 258, 1150
Tiznow 613
Trade Fair 38, 168, 1113, 1122
Trans Island 1655
Val Royal 452
Van Nistelrooy 1072, 1112, 1463, 1631

Verglas 53, 59, 342, 1051, 1091, 1107, 1110, 1151, 1202, 1361, 1454, 1502
Vital Equine 249, 390, 691, 1065

War Chant 130, 812
War Front 69, 677, 1445
Whipper 122, 123, 392, 629, 648, 1128, 1355
Windsor Knot 30, 1189, 1467

Yes It's True 1034, 1340

Zafeen 177, 242
Zamindar 7, 183, 193, 325, 456, 482, 722, 918, 978, 1214, 1334, 1432

Racing Trends

The following tables focus on those two-year-old races that seem to produce winners that improve the following year as three-year-olds. This type of analysis can enable us to select some of the best of this year's classic generation.

In the tables, the figure in the third column indicates the number of wins recorded as a three-year-old, with GW signifying a Group race winner at that age.

The horses listed below are the winners of the featured races in 2010. Anyone looking for horses to follow in the Group and Classic events of this season might well want to bear them in mind. I feel that those in bold text are particularly worthy of close scrutiny.

Cape Dollar	Moriarty
Casamento	**Pathfork**
Dubai Prince	Rerouted
Frankel	Sister Red
Hooray	Waiters Dream
Indigo Way	White Moonstone
Janood	**Wootton Bassett**
King Torus	

Lowther Stakes		
York, 6 furlongs, August.		
1991	Culture Vulture	2 GW
1992	Niche	2 GW
1993	Velvet Moon	1
1994	Harayir	4 GW
1995	Dance Sequence	0
1996	Bianca Nera	0
1997	Cape Verdi	1 GW
1998	Bint Allayl	NR
1999	Jemima	0
2000	Enthused	0
2001	Queen's Logic	1 GW
2002	Russian Rhythm	3 GW
2003	Carry On Katie	0
2004	Soar	0
2005	Flashy Wings	0
2006	Silk Blossom	0
2007	Nahoodh	1 GW
2008	Infamous Angel	0
2009	Lady of the Desert	1 GW
2010	Hooray	

Despite a few disappointing years, this race often has a big say in the following season's Group 1 events for fillies. For example Harayir, Cape Verdi and Russian Rhythm won the English 1,000 Guineas whilst Culture Vulture and Al Bahathri took the respective French and Irish versions. Add the top-class sprinters Habibti and Polonia (both winners prior to 1991) and the Falmouth Stakes win for Nahoodh and it's clear this race is an important pointer. If she doesn't stay a mile it could well be that she remains a high-class filly for sprint distances. She certainly ought to train on and I expect her to win more races.

Dewhurst Stakes		
Newmarket, 7 furlongs, October.		
1991	Dr Devious	2 GW
1992	Zafonic	1 GW
1993	Grand Lodge	1 GW
1994	Pennekamp	2 GW
1995	Alhaarth	1 GW
1996	In Command	0
1997	Xaar	1 GW
1998	Mujahid	0
1999	Distant Music	1 GW
2000	Tobougg	0
2001	Rock Of Gibraltar	5 GW
2002	Tout Seul	0
2003	Milk It Mick	0
2004	Shamardal	3 GW
2005	Sir Percy	1 GW
2006	Teofilo	NR
2007	New Approach	3 GW
2008	Intense Focus	0
2009	Beethoven	1 GW
2010	Frankel	

The Dewhurst Stakes remains our premier race for two-year-old colts. Rock of Gibraltar was a real star of course, but other outstanding colts in this line up include Shamardal, Zafonic, Dr Devious, Grand Lodge and Sir Percy. New Approach can now be added to that illustrious list, with 3 Group 1 wins to his name in 2008 (the Derby, Champion Stakes and Irish Champion). Frankel was a very impressive 2-y-o and it seems highly likely that he'll be equally talented this year. He'll win more races at the top level.

Zetland Stakes
Newmarket, 10 furlongs, October/November.

Year	Horse	
1991	Bonny Scot	2 GW
1992	Bob's Return	3 GW
1993	Double Trigger	1 GW
1994	Double Eclipse	1
1995	Gentilhomme	0
1996	Silver Patriarch	2 GW
1997	Trigger Happy	0
1998	Adnaan	1
1999	Monte Carlo	0
2000	Worthily	0
2001	Alexandra Three D	2 GW
2002	Forest Magic	NR
2003	Fun And Games	NR
2004	Ayam Zaman	0
2005	Under The Rainbow	0
2006	Empire Day	NR
2007	Twice Over	2 GW
2008	Heliodor	1
2009	Take It To The Max	0
2010	Indigo Way	

As one can see from the list, previous winners include the St Leger and Coronation Cup winner Silver Patriarch, the good four-year-olds Double Eclipse and Rock Hopper, Bob's Return (also a St Leger hero) and the Ascot Gold Cup winner Double Trigger – surely the most notable of them all. Despite being a very smart 3-y-o, Twice Over is another that improved again at four (and five) and took the Champion Stakes twice for Henry Cecil. Indigo Way has been sent to Hong Kong where he'll surely win more races.

Cheveley Park Stakes
Newmarket, 6 furlongs, October.

Year	Horse	
1991	Marling	3 GW
1992	Sayyedati	2 GW
1993	Prophecy	0
1994	Gay Gallanta	0
1995	Blue Duster	1
1996	Pas de Reponse	2 GW
1997	Embassy	NR
1998	Wannabe Grand	1
1999	Seazun	0
2000	Regal Rose	NR
2001	Queen's Logic	1 GW
2002	Airwave	1 GW
2003	Carry On Katie	0
2004	Magical Romance	0
2005	Donna Blini	1
2006	Indian Ink	1 GW
2007	Natagora	2 GW
2008	Serious Attitude	1 GW
2009	Special Duty	2 GW
2010	Hooray	

A number of these fillies have gone on to further Group race success. Indian Ink saved her best day for Royal Ascot having previously been fifth in the 1,000 Guineas. Natagora raised the profile of this race even further when winning the 1,000 Guineas and Serious Attitude returned to sprinting for another Group race success after a stab at a Guineas glory floundered through lack of stamina. By the time this book is printed we should know whether or not Hooray stays a mile. I expect she'll revert to sprinting and win more Group 1 events.

Washington Singer Stakes
Newbury, 7 furlongs, August.

Year	Horse	
1991	Rodrigo de Triano	4 GW
1992	Tenby	2 GW
1993	Colonel Collins	0
1994	Lammtarra	3 GW
1995	Mons	0
1996	State Fair	0
1997	Bahr	2 GW
1998	Valentine Girl	0
1999	Mana-Mou-Bay	0
2000	Prizeman	0
2001	Funfair Wane	1
2002	Muqbil	1 GW
2003	Haafhd	3 GW
2004	Kings Quay	0
2005	Innocent Air	1
2006	Dubai's Touch	2
2007	Sharp Nephew	1
2008	Cry of Freedom	0
2009	Azmeel	2 GW
2010	Janood	

As can be seen from the table, this race can often provide us with Group race or Classic pointers and in that regard Lammtarra, Rodrigo de Triano and Haafhd were outstanding. Azmeel trained on to win the Sandown Classic Trial and the Dee Stakes. The Godolphin owned Janood, whose dam is a half-sister to the Derby winner New Approach, disappointed in the National Stakes after winning this race, but hopefully he can return to form and win again.

Veuve Clicquot Vintage Stakes
Goodwood, 7 furlongs, July.

1991	Dr Devious	2 GW
1992	Maroof	1
1993	Mister Baileys	1 GW
1994	Eltish	0
1995	Alhaarth	1 GW
1996	Putra	0
1997	Central Park	2 GW
1998	Aljabr	1 GW
1999	Ekraar	3 GW
2000	No Excuse Needed	1 GW
2001	Naheef	1 GW
2002	Dublin	1
2003	Lucky Story	0
2004	Shamardal	3 GW
2005	Sir Percy	1 GW
2006	Strategic Prince	0
2007	Rio De La Plata	0
2008	Orizaba	0
2009	Xtension	0
2010	King Torus	

All in all, this race is very informative in terms of sorting out future stars, with the classic winners Sir Percy, Shamardal, Don't Forget Me, Dr Devious and Mister Baileys and the King George winner Petoski standing out. Aljabr, Central Park, Ekraar and No Excuse Needed were all high-class colts too. King Torus is a smart colt and he'll win more races at up to a mile.

National Stakes, Curragh, 7f, September.

1991	El Prado	0
1992	Fatherland	0
1993	Manntari	1
1994	Definite Article	1
1995	Danehill Dancer	1 GW
1996	Desert King	3 GW
1997	King Of Kings	1 GW
1998	Mus-If	0
1999	Sinndar	5 GW
2000	Beckett	1
2001	Hawk Wing	1 GW
2002	Refuse To Bend	3 GW
2003	One Cool Cat	1 GW
2004	Dubawi	2 GW
2005	George Washington	2 GW
2006	Teofilo	NR
2007	New Approach	3 GW
2008	Mastercraftsman	3 GW
2009	Kingsfort	1
2010	Pathfork	

As one can see by the list of recent winners, this race is as important as any for figuring out the following year's top performers. For instance New Approach was outstanding when winning the Derby, the Champion Stakes and the Irish Champion, and Mastercraftsman also managed a couple of Group One wins at 3 yrs. A high-class and promising colt, Pathfork will win more races at a mile or more. Whether he'll stay a mile and a half we'll have to wait and see.

Racing Post Trophy
Doncaster, 8 furlongs, October.

1991	Seattle Rhyme	0
1992	Armiger	1 GW
1993	King's Theatre	2 GW
1994	Celtic Swing	2 GW
1995	Beauchamp King	1 GW
1996	Medaaly	0
1997	Saratoga Springs	1 GW
1998	Commander Collins	0
1999	Aristotle	0
2000	Dilshaan	1 GW
2001	High Chapparal	5 GW
2002	Brian Boru	1 GW
2003	American Post	3 GW
2004	Motivator	2 GW
2005	Palace Episode	0
2006	Authorized	3 GW
2007	Ibn Khaldun	0
2008	Crowded House	0
2009	St Nicholas Abbey	0
2010	Casamento	

Some notable performers have won this race, including one of my own favourites the French Derby winner Celtic Swing, the outstanding colt High Chaparral and the Derby heroes Motivator and Authorized (both by Montjeu – also the sire of St Nicholas Abbey). A son of the admirable Shamardal, Casamento seems sure to train on and win more races this year.

Fillies Conditions Race Newbury, 7 furlongs, September.		
1991	Freewheel	1
1992	Sueboog	1 GW
1993	Balanchine	2 GW
1994	Musetta	1
1995	Wild Rumour	0
1996	Etoile	0
1997	Amabel	NR
1998	Fragrant Oasis	1
1999	Veil Of Avalon	1
2000	Palatial	1
2001	Fraulein	2 GW
2002	L'Ancresse	1
2003	Silk Fan	1
2004	Shanghai Lily	0
2005	Mostaqeleh	0
2006	Darrfonah	1
2007	Rosa Grace	1
2008	Lassarina	0
2009	Silver Rock	0
2010	Sister Red	

The brilliant fillies Balanchine and Mill gram stand out in this group and although the race has thrown up a few disappointments of late, both Fraulein and L'Ancresse came up with excellent performances over the Atlantic, with the former taking Canada's Grade 1 E P Taylor Stakes and Ballydoyle's L'Ancresse only just getting touched off in the Breeders Cup Filly & Mare Turf. Having said that it's been a while since any of the winners trained on to good effect and Sister Red may also have to settle for lesser honours if she's to win more races.

Haynes, Hanson and Clark Stakes Newbury, 8 furlongs, September.		
1991	Zinaad	1
1992	Pembroke	1
1993	King's Theatre	2 GW
1994	Munwar	2 GW
1995	Mick's Love	1
1996	King Sound	1
1997	Duck Row	0
1998	Boatman	0
1999	Ethmaar	0
2000	Nayef	4 GW
2001	Fight Your Corner	1 GW
2002	Saturn	0
2003	Elshadi	0
2004	Merchant	NR
2005	Winged Cupid	NR
2006	Teslin	2
2007	Centennial	2 GW
2008	Taameer	0
2009	Ameer	0
2010	Moriarty	

The high-class horses Rainbow Quest, Unfuwain, King's Theatre and Nayef have all won this race and indeed Shergar won it in 1980, but it's been a while since those glory days although Centennial managed two Group race wins in 2008. Moriarty looks the type to win more races this year at a mile or ten furlongs.

Meon Valley Stud Fillies' Mile Ascot, 8 furlongs, September.		
1991	Midnight Air	0
1992	Ivanka	0
1993	Fairy Heights	0
1994	Aqaarid	1 GW
1995	Bosra Sham	3 GW
1996	Reams of Verse	2 GW
1997	Glorosia	0
1998	Sunspangled	0
1999	Teggiano	0
2000	Crystal Music	0
2001	Gossamer	1 GW
2002	Soviet Song	0
2003	Red Bloom	1 GW
2004	Playful Act	1 GW
2005	Nannina	1 GW
2006	Simply Perfect	1 GW
2007	Listen	0
2008	Rainbow View	1 GW
2009	Hibaayeb	2 GW
2010	White Moonstone	

Diminuendo (in 1987), Bosra Sham, Reams of Verse, Gossamer and Soviet Song stand out amongst recent winners of this race, although the latter had to wait until after her 4-y-o career before reaching her full potential. Hibaayib won the Ribblesdale Stakes and then crossed the Atlantic to win the Grade 1 Yellow

Ribbon. The high-class Dynaformer filly White Moonstone will also be expected to win at the highest level this year.

Somerville Tattersall Stakes Newmarket, 7 furlongs, September/October.		
1991	Tertian	0
1992	Nominator	0
1993	Grand Lodge	1 GW
1994	Annus Mirabilis	1
1995	Even Top	1 GW
1996	Grapeshot	1
1997	Haami	1
1998	Enrique	1 GW
1999	Scarteen Fox	0
2000	King Charlemagne	3 GW
2001	Where Or When	2 GW
2002	Governor Brown	NR
2003	Milk It Mick	0
2004	Diktatorial	0
2005	Aussie Rules	2 GW
2006	Thousand Words	0
2007	River Proud	1
2008	Ashram	2
2009	Sir Parky	0
2010	Rerouted	

The bare figures in this table don't really tell the whole story, for there are some very good horses here. The Group winners speak for themselves but Milk It Mick, Opening Verse and Annus Mirabilis all went on to win good races abroad and Haami was certainly a smart colt too. Aussie Rules won the French 2,000 Guineas and a Grade 1 event in the USA and both River Proud and Ashram won listed races in their 3-y-o season. After winning this race Rerouted was fourth in a Group 1 in France over mile on soft ground, so he certainly stays that far. He should win again this year.

Killavullan Stakes. Leopardstown, 7 furlongs October.		
1991	Misako-Togo	3
1992	Asema	3 GW
1993	Broadmara	0
1994	Kill The Crab	2 GW
1995	Aylesbury	0
1996	Shell Ginger	0
1997	Kincara Palace	1
1998	Athlumney Lady	0
1999	Monashee Mountain	2 GW
2000	Perigee Moon	0
2001	Stonemason	0
2002	New South Wales	1
2003	Grey Swallow	2 GW
2004	Footstepsinthesand	1 GW
2005	Frost Giant	1 GW
2006	Confuchias	1 GW
2007	Jupiter Pluvius	0
2008	Rayeni	1
2009	Free Judgement	1 GW
2010	Dubai Prince	

During the period researched, eight of the winners subsequently went on to Group success as three-year-olds, most notably the Irish Derby winner Grey Swallow and the English 2,000 Guineas winner Footstepsinthesand. Dubai Prince was very impressive when winning this race and further Group race glory awaits. Whether that will be over a mile or further we'll have to see, as he's not certain to stay the Derby trip.

Rockfel Stakes, 7 furlongs, Newmarket.		
1991	Musicale	1 GW
1992	Yawl	0
1993	Relatively Special	0
1994	Germane	0
1995	Bint Salsabil	1
1996	Moonlight Paradise	0
1997	Name Of Love	NR
1998	Hula Angel	1 GW
1999	Lahan	1 GW
2000	Sayedah	0
2001	Distant Valley	0
2002	Luvah Girl	1 in USA
2003	Cairns	0
2004	Maids Causeway	1 GW
2005	Speciosa	1 GW
2006	Finsceal Beo	2 GW
2007	Kitty Matcham	0
2008	Lahaleeb	2 GW
2009	Music Show	2 GW
2010	Cape Dollar	

Three Newmarket 1,000 Guineas winners have hailed from the winners of this race in the last 10 years – Lahan, Speciosa and Finsceal Beo. For good measure Maids Causeway won the Coronation Stakes and Hula Angel won the Irish 1,000 Guineas (a race Finsceal Beo also added to her tally). The Mick Channon trained pair Lahaleeb and Music Show both went on to record Group 1 successes. The prospects for Cape Dollar are excellent and she'll be probably be suited by distances of a mile to ten furlongs this year.

Prix Jean-Luc Lagardere – formerly the Grand Criterium, Longchamp, 7 furlongs (1 mile before 2001).		
2001	Rock Of Gibraltar	5 GW
2002	Hold That Tiger	0
2003	American Post	3 GW
2004	Oratorio	2 GW
2005	Horatio Nelson	0
2006	Holy Roman Emperor	NR
2007	Rio de la Plata	0
2008	Naaqoos	0
2009	Siyouni	0
2010	Wootton Bassett	

The last four winners have all failed to win as three-year-olds, but sadly they include Horatio Nelson who had to be put down after an injury in the Derby. Wootton Bassett was an admirable 2-y-o last year and unbeaten. He has it to do if he's to improve the fortunes of this race as a pointer to better things, but his handler will surely find another nice race for him.

Beresford Stakes, Curragh, 1m.		
1991	El Prado	0
1992	Frenchpark	0
1993	Sheridan	0
1994	Burden Of Proof	1
1995	Ahkaam	0
1996	Johan Cruyff	1 GW
1997	Saratoga Springs	1 GW
1998	Festival Hall	0
1999	Lermontov	0
2000	Turnberry Isle	0
2001	Castle Gandolfo	1
2002	Alamshar	3 GW
2003	Azamour	2 GW
2004	Albert Hall	0
2005	Septimus	1 GW
2006	Eagle Mountain	1 GW
2007	Curtain Call	1
2008	Sea The Stars	6 GW
2009	St Nicholas Abbey	0
2010	Casamento	

John Oxx must be very fond of this race because he's trained Sea The Stars, Alamshar and Azamour to win it and they've all subsequently hit the headlines as three-year-olds. Among the others, Frenchpark was a Grade 1 winner in the USA at 4 yrs, Eagle Mountain also went on to win as a 4-y-o in a Group 1 event (in Hong Kong) and Curtain Call won a Group 3 event at that age. Casamento has good prospects of adding another Group 1 win to his record this year.

Acomb Stakes York, 7 furlongs, August.		
1991	Torrey Canyon	1
1992	Woodchat	0
1993	Concordial	0
1994	Options Open	0
1995	Bijou d'Inde	1 GW
1996	Revoque	1
1997	Saratoga Springs	1 GW
1998	Auction House	0
1999	King's Best	1 GW
2000	Hemingway	NR
2001	Comfy	NR
2002	Bourbonnais	0
2003	Rule Of Law	2 GW
2004	Elliots World	1
2005	Palace Episode	0
2006	Big Timer	0
2007	Fast Company	0
2008	ABANDONED	
2009	Elusive Pimpernel	1 GW
2010	Waiter's Dream	

There have been a few disappointing seasons since the victories of such as King's Best (2,000 Guineas) and Bijou d'Inde (St James's Palace Stakes), but Rule Of Law turned things around in 2004 with his St Leger victory and Elusive Pimpernel was successful in the Group 3 Craven Stakes last year. Waiter's Dream was fourth in Dewhurst Stakes in October. He's by the top-class sprinter and sire Oasis Dream and Brian Meehan will be trying to add another Group race win to his tally this year, probably in races at up to a mile.

Horse Index

A'Juba 553
Aaraas 1356
Aazif 453
Abarrat (IRE) 1545
Absolute Crackers (IRE) 817
Abstain 1382
Accustomed 947
Acorn Valley (USA) 1607
Across Arabia (IRE) 1066
Actor (IRE) 1194
Adverse (IRE) 74
Aegaeus 423
Aegean Sky (IRE) 1357
Afaal (USA) 649
Afnoon (USA) 454
Afraah (USA) 1546
Afraz (IRE) 1293
Ahimsa (IRE) 1237
Ailanthus 168
Aim Higher 576
Airborne Again (IRE) 712
Aird Snout (USA) 920
Akeed Mofeed 1294
Akeed Wafi (IRE) 1295
Al Jabreiah 650
Al Kahn 279
Al Mamzar (IRE) 1430
Al Saham 555
Alareef 577
Albamara 1383
Albanka (USA) 1472
Albaspina (IRE) 1384
Alejandro 486
Alfaateh (USA) 1067
Alfursaan 830
Alhira 1431
Ali Hope (IRE) 298
Aliante 921
Alice Rose (IRE) 634
Alice's Dancer (IRE) 1169
Alizari (IRE) 1296
Aljamaaheer (IRE) 1547
All That Rules 178
Almaas (USA) 554
Almond Branches 1137
Almost Gemini (IRE) 333
Almunder 424
Alnaahee (IRE) 1358
Alraased (USA) 455
Altaria 1321
Altona (IRE) 222
Alupka (IRE) 713
Alwaffaa (USA) 1527

Alzahra 1548
Amaraja (GER) 179
Amber Silk (IRE) 831
Ambivalent (IRE) 1549
American Bling (USA) 1195
Amhrasach (IRE) 112
Amis Reunis 714
Among Equals 1238
Amoure Medici 1409
Amphora 14
Andalieb 1432
Angel Bright (IRE) 1608
Angelic Note (IRE) 1068
Angels Will Fall (IRE) 832
Aniseed (IRE) 651
Anisha (IRE) 113
Apostle (IRE) 75
Apothecary 578
Appealing (IRE) 125
Applaudere 1274
Aquilla (IRE) 180
Arabian Falcon 1069
Arabian Flight 425
Arch Villain (IRE) 1322
Archers Prize (IRE) 1049
Ardmay (IRE) 1419
Armed Guard (IRE) 1000
Armiger 1170
Arnold Lane 223
Art Law (IRE) 1070
Art News (IRE) 1132
Art Of Stone 488
Art Show 426
Artful Lady (IRE) 1037
Artistic Dawn 1644
Artistic Jewel (IRE) 1050
Artistic Thread (IRE) 1385
Artists Corner 487
Ashbina 652
Ashdown Lad 903
Ashkan 653
Ashyane (IRE) 344
Astrogold 1514
Astronomy Domine 579
Athb (IRE) 1550
Athens (IRE) 1239
Attain 1323
Atticus Finch (IRE) 1001
Autarch (USA) 1324
Autonomous 698
Autumn Fire 15
Available (IRE) 715
Avalanche 345

Avon Pearl 169
Awesome Pearl (USA) 1386
Azamata 1359

B Fifty Two (IRE) 888
Baccarat 489
Backcourt (USA) 76
Backtrade (IRE) 16
Badged 1297
Bahama Spirit (IRE) 1360
Baheeja 1551
Balady 456
Balcary Bay 482
Balm 716
Balty Boys (IRE) 833
Barolo Top (IRE) 372
Basseterre (IRE) 834
Bayan (IRE) 1071
Bayleyf (IRE) 101
Be My Rock 635
Beach Candy (IRE) 717
Beat The Stars (IRE) 1361
Beechey's Beauty 410
Bella Ophelia (IRE) 1156
Bella Vento 718
Beloved Leader 1002
Bensoon (IRE) 699
Benzanno (IRE) 17
Beograd Sniper 126
Berlusca (IRE) 904
Berwin (IRE) 948
Better Be Mine (IRE) 457
Between Us 1387
Beyond Conceit (IRE) 1506
Biba Diva (IRE) 1196
Big Blue Spirit 1362
Big Time Charlie (IRE) 719
Billyrayvalentine (CAN) 3
Binabee 580
Bishop Roko 299
Black Mascara (IRE) 720
Black Minstrel (IRE) 1325
Blackdown Fair 1113
Blank Czech (IRE) 1326
Bling King 912
Blonde (IRE) 721
Blue Corner (IRE) 700
Blue Surf 1327
Bluebells Are Blue (IRE) 913
Bogart 1420
Bohemian Rhapsody (IRE) 889
Bonfire 18

HORSE INDEX

Boomerang Bob (IRE) 890
Border Revia 490
Boris Grigoriev (IRE) 1240
Born To Sea (IRE) 1298
Boudoir 491
Bounty Seeker (USA) 922
Bramshill Lass 1328
Breaking The Bank 1171
Bridgehampton 77
Brief Chat (USA) 1329
Brilliantine (FR) 722
Brimstone Hill (IRE) 835
Brockwell 373
Bronterre 723
Bronze Angel (IRE) 1528
Bryant Park (USA) 78
Bulbul (IRE) 1363
Bull Bay 272
Bulldog Beasley (USA) 1072
Bunaaji (IRE) 1552
Burano (IRE) 1073
Burnham 1157
Burnie Braes (IRE) 1013
Burwaaz 427
Buster Brown (IRE) 542
Buzkashi (IRE) 1553
Bypass 19
Byron Blue (IRE) 1275
Byton 170

Cades Reef (IRE) 20
Caitlin 224
Caledonian Lad 1158
Calendar King 225
Call To Battle (IRE) 1299
Cantal 1473
Cape Crossing 21
Cape Ferrat (IRE) 654
Cape Pride 181
Cape Savannah 1433
Caphene 458
Cappielow Park 905
Captain Cardington 226
Captain Cat (IRE) 300
Carabinieri 836
Cardinal Walter (IRE) 334
Caribbean Ace (IRE) 483
Cashmere Or Caviar 837
Castilo Del Diablo (IRE) 182
Catamount 1364
Cataract 1645
Caterina 724
Cavaleiro (IRE) 1529
Celestial Dawn 1646
Cellist 655
Chalet Girl 581

Chandlery (IRE) 725
Chankillo 1515
Chapter Seven 492
Charitable Act (FR) 1172
Charity Box 1596
Charles The Great (IRE) 22
Checkpoint 183
Chester Aristocrat 1
Chevanah (IRE) 411
Cheviot Quest (IRE) 906
Chil The Kite 1159
Choice Pearl 1014
Cholesky (IRE) 1300
Chonberg 1516
Choral Bee 171
Chunky Diamond 280
Church Music 1421
City Dazzler 726
City Of Canton 346
Clapped 1586
Clare Is and Boy (IRE) 727
Clareti-theblood 493
Classic Falcon 656
Classy Strike (IRE) 728
Clean Bowled (IRE) 1074
Clowance Estate (IRE) 301
Coach Montana (IRE) 273
Cockney Dancer 838
Cockney Rocker 274
Code Cracker 1388
Coffee King (IRE) 1434
Commissar 335
Commitment 347
Complacent (IRE) 1587
Confirmed 127
Confucious Elite 136
Conquerata 374
Continuum 184
Coplow 729
Corn Rigs 428
Correct 79
Corsetry (USA) 185
Cosmic Halo 494
Countess Ferrama 657
Coupe De Ville (IRE) 730
Courtland Avenue 1345
Cravat 923
Crazylittlething (IRE) 1456
Cresta Star 731
Crimson Sunrise (IRE) 1609
Cristal Gem 732
Cristal Groove (IRE) 1301
Crowring Star 1142
Cryptic Choice (IRE) 839
Custom Cut (IRE) 1610
Cutie Pie (IRE) 1276

Daffyd (IRE) 302
Damask (IRE) 733
Dana's Present 4
Dance Company 966
Dance With Me (IRE) 23
Dandy (GER) 24
Daneking 582
Dansable (IRE) 336
Dante Inferno (IRE) 1365
Dark Ages 1410
Dark Ambition (IRE) 658
Dark Don (IRE) 840
Dark Passion (IRE) 1015
Dark Ranger (IRE) 1366
Darling Grace 659
Dawn Glory 303
Dawn Lightning 1043
Debating Society (IRE) 1474
Defy The Odds 186
Delft 1197
Democretes 734
Denton Dancer 484
Desert Spree 1124
Despatch 52
Devlin 495
Diamond Finesse (IRE) 429
Diamondhead (IRE) 1075
Dick Bos 281
Dickens Rules 949
Dilizan (IRE) 701
Dimitar 1003
Disagree 1016
Discression 1422
Distant Love (IRE) 25
District Attorney 660
Divine Pamina (IRE) 137
Divine Success 496
Doctor Banner 227
Dogstar (IRE) 304
Dollar Bill 26
Don't Tempt Me 950
Dora's Sister 1416
Double Cee 497
Dovils Date 1114
Dr Yes (FR) 187
Dream Attraction 661
Dream Lioness 823
Drummoyne (USA) 924
Duke Of Destiny 1591
Duke Of Firenze 1475
Dulkashe (IRE) 348
Dutch Master 27
Dutch Supreme 982
Dynamic Duo (IRE) 735

Eanans Bay 1517

368 TWO-YEAR-OLDS OF 2011

Eastern Destiny 498
Eastern Sun (IRE) 583
Ebble 584
Eben Zaabeel (IRE) 1076
Ebony Clarets 499
Ebtisama 1530
Echo Of Dubai (IRE) 143
Edge Lane 500
Eesti Poiss (IRE) 1277
Eight Letters (USA) 80
Eightfold 736
Ekbaal 1367
Ekraam 1531
Ektihaam (IRE) 1554
El Diamante (FR) 737
Electric Qatar 375
Electrician 585
Elite 1476
Ellaal 841
Elmora 951
Elusive Flame 469
Elusive Light (FR) 738
Elyassaat 1555
Elysian 1477
Emirates Jack 5
Emirates Queen 349
Emperor Vespasian 28
Empressive 1173
Encrypted Message (IRE) 1611
Endangered Species 1647
Endowing (IRE) 739
English Night (IRE) 1302
Engrossing 470
Enjoying 740
Ensejaam (IRE) 842
Enthrall (IRE) 329
Entifaadha 662
Epoque (USA) 188
Equalizer 376
Eraada 925
Ernest Hemingway (IRE) 1241
Esentepe (IRE) 741
Eshaab (USA) 430
Essell 228
Essexvale (IRE) 742
Estabsaal (IRE) 459
Estemaala (IRE) 1532
Estrela 305
Eureka (IRE) 743
Eurystheus (IRE) 744
Everlong 282
Evervescent (IRE) 1143
Ewell Place 1125
Ex Oriente 586

Excavator 306
Expense Claim (IRE) 29
Extol 587

Fa'Iz (IRE) 556
Factor Three 1038
Factory Time 229
Fairest (IRE) 1198
Fairy Moss (IRE) 745
Falcon In Flight 1199
Falconinthedesert (IRE) 926
Fallen For You 588
Famous Poet (IRE) 557
Fanoos 589
Faraway 663
Fareedha 460
Farraaj (IRE) 1556
Fast Fox (IRE) 307
Fast On (IRE) 1051
Fast Or Free 664
Fastideous 1612
Fencing 590
Fiery Ambition 1613
Fillionaire 230
Finbar 543
Finley Connolly (IRE) 1077
Firdaws (USA) 1557
Firestarter 471
Fistful Of Dollars (IRE) 1278
Flaming Ferrari (IRE) 283
Flashy Star 231
Flaxen Flare (IRE) 30
Flexible Flyer 1160
Fluctuate 591
Flugelhorn (IRE) 1052
Fly Haaf (IRE) 967
Fly In Style 330
Flying Pickets (IRE) 158
Foolscap (IRE) 138
Force Three (FR) 746
Forevertheoptimist (IRE) 1502
Forget Me Not Lane (IRE) 1423
Forgive 747
Forgotten Hero (IRE) 843
Fort Bastion (IRE) 748
Fortieth And Fifth (IRE) 81
Fortrose Academy 31
Foxtrot India (IRE) 1651
Fragonard 189
Framed 968
Freddy Q (IRE) 749
Free House 1078
Free Spin (IRE) 702
Free Verse 750

Freedom Reigns (IRE) 1368
French Emperor (IRE) 1004
Fresa 1389
Frosty Secret 275
Fulbright 927
Furbelow 1200
Furzanah 350

Gabrial (IRE) 501
Gabriel's Lad (IRE) 332
Galletto 351
Gallipot 592
Garrarufa 1115
Gassin Golf 1390
Gatepost (IRE) 232
Gathering 593
Geniality 1391
Ghost Protocol (IRE) 1435
Ghost Train (IRE) 928
Gifted Dancer 172
Gin Rummy 1017
Ginger Monkey (IRE) 1144
Gingernut 594
Giorgio's Dragon 502
Glasgow Boy (IRE) 844
Glaze 1161
Glee 751
Glen Moss (IRE) 845
Glitterball (IRE) 1478
Go Dutch (IRE) 1558
Goal Hanger 377
Going Grey 503
Gold Coin 891
Gold Edition 1201
Gold Sceptre (FR) 752
Gold Show 233
Golden Song 472
Goldoni (IRE) 32
Gondolier (FR) 378
Gone By Sunrise 504
Good Clodora (IRE) 1079
Good Of Luck 234
Goodfellows Quest (IRE) 412
Gooseberry Fool 1392
Grand Gold 235
Grande Illusion 892
Grandeur (IRE) 1202
Graphic (IRE) 753
Gray Pearl 846
Great Heavens 595
Great Namoos 1080
Greatest Dancer (IRE) 1279
Greek Canyon (IRE) 1018
Green Legacy (USA) 1330
Gregorian 596
Grey Falcon (FR) 1436

Elbe 216

Grey Mirage 128
Gripper 159
Guava 754
Gucci D'Oro 1437
Guiletta (IRE) 636
Gulf Port 308
Gung Ho Jack 102
Gush (USA) 818

Habita 309
Hadrian's Rule (IRE) 465
Hajras (IRE) 930
Hamble 665
Hamis Al Bin (IRE) 929
Hamza (IRE) 1424
Handsome Man (IRE) 558
Harbour Sands 544
Harbour Watch (IRE) 755
Harmonie 1411
Harvard N Yale (USA) 1203
Haseen (IRE) 1614
Hattaak 431
Havin' A Good Time (IRE) 1559
Headline News (IRE) 637
Hearts And Minds 1280
Heavy Weight (IRE) 114
Hefner (IRE) 756
Hello Dubai 1438
Henry Allingham 1560
Hepworth 597
Herbaceous 1204
Hestian (IRE) 1457
Hey Fiddle Fiddle (IRE) 848
Heyaaraat (IRE) 847
Hidden Justice (IRE) 1331
High Endeavour 1126
Hill Street 598
Hillcroft 505
Hint Of Promise 310
Hit The Jackpot (IRE) 1615
Hollywood All Star 1174
Hologram 190
Holy Empress (IRE) 82
Holy Roman Warrior 506
Homecoming Queen (IRE) 1242
Homeric 432
Honour 1479
Hoonose 969
Hugenot (IRE) 1005
Hummingbird 666
Hurricane Hugo (IRE) 1019
Hyacinth 1332

I'm Harry 849

Iberian Rock 413
Ibtaha 559
Ice (IRE) 1205
Ice Missile 952
Idler (IRE) 931
Idyllic Star 1145
Ihsas (USA) 560
Illustrious Lad (IRE) 139
Imelda Mayhem 1146
Impassive 1053
Impel (IRE) 757
Imperial Legend (IRE) 1187
Imperial Order (IRE) 758
Inchina 311
Indepub 1425
Indigo Iris (IRE) 759
Infinite Hope (USA) 352
Infinite Jest 893
Infinitum 599
Inniscastle Boy 1175
Integrity (IRE) 1206
Intense Pink 1597
Intent (IRE) 83
Interlocking (USA) 191
Intimacy (IRE) 192
Intuition 760
Inundate (USA) 850
Iron Butterfly 485
Ironically 983
Isatis 193
Ishi 1116
Ishvara (IRE) 1243
Island Melody (IRE) 1147
Isobel a 1162
Isola Bella 1346
Isolde's Return 1138
Istan Star (USA) 165
It's A Privilege 53
Italian Riviera 1393
Ivor's Princess 1117

J J Leary (IRE) 1188
Jacob Cats 761
Jafocl 667
Jambobo 970
Jamming 1020
Janey Muddles (IRE) 115
Jasie Lac 1127
Jemima's Pearl (USA) 1021
Jennifer J 1518
Jimtown 1369
Joe The Coat 1519
John Lightbody 932
Johnno 894
Jorum 194
Joy For Life 1207

Jubilance (IRE) 1208
Judge Jeremy 276
Junior Diary (USA) 1081
Jupiter Storm 1135
Just Dixie 1648
Just Facts (IRE) 116
Just When 33
Juvenal (IRE) 762

Kaaseb (USA) 1616
Kahruman 668
Kalily 353
Karuga 763
Kashgar 84
Kashmir Peak (IRE) 1022
Kastovia (USA) 1303
Keep It Dark 354
Keep Swinging (IRE) 1507
Kelner's Cross 1082
Key Appointment 1508
Key To Dance (IRE) 1304
Keyaadi 1561
Khajool (IRE) 1562
Khazeena 669
Khyber Pass 1006
Kinetica 1394
King Laertis (IRE) 824
King Of Dudes 195
King Of Paradise (IRE) 2
King's Guest (IRE) 1480
King's Warrant (IRE) 1023
Kiwayu 355
Knight Express 507
Know (IRE) 1244
Knoydart 1333
Kodiac Island 1054
Kodiac King (IRE) 1426
Kogershin (USA) 1209
Kung Hei Fat Choy (USA) 545
Kylin 765

L'Arlesienne 953
La Baracca (IRE) 1305
La Bocca (USA) 312
La Collina (IRE) 1370
La Passionata 1128
Ladram Bay (IRE) 1347
Lady Author 508
Lady Bellatrix 1520
Lady Rochford (IRE) 1024
Lady Victory 236
Lady's First 509
Ladyship 1481
Lambeau Field 34
Lancaster Gate 1334

Lanett Lady (IRE) 703
Lashyn (USA) 1482
Last Fighter (USA) 561
Last Shadow 1176
Latte 1503
Laugh Out Loud 237
Laurel Lad (IRE) 851
Lawn Jamil (USA) 852
Le Cagnard 85
Lean On Pete (IRE) 984
Leatherwood (IRE) 1371
Lelaps (USA) 129
Lemon Rock 1412
Leqqaa (USA) 933
Let Your Love Flow 510
Letsgoroundagain (IRE) 853
Lexi's Darling (IRE) 1189
Lexi's Prince (IRE) 379
Lexington Pearl (USA) 54
Lexington Spirit (IRE) 511
Liebesziel 1044
Light Zabeel 238
Lightening Pearl (IRE) 1025
Lightning Jet 1055
Like Clockwork 1521
Lilbourne Lad (IRE) 766
Lily's Angel 512
Lilygloves 239
Limoncello 895
Lisiere 513
Litmus (USA) 854
Little Mr Sunshine 514
Livia's Dream (IRE) 1592
Llanarmon Lad (IRE) 855
Lonan (IRE) 1306
London Welsh 1177
Lone Foot Laddie (IRE) 954
Look Here's Lady 1056
Looks Like Rain 86
Lord Ali McJones 380
Lord Ofthe Shadows (IRE) 767
Lost Highway (IRE) 934
Lothian Sky (IRE) 907
Lotus Roots 629
Lovage 313
Loved By All (IRE) 1083
Lucifers Shadow (IRE) 955
Lucky Money 1395
Lulla 1533
Lunar Deity 914
Lyrical Gangster (IRE) 1148

Mabroor (USA) 935
Maccabees 1118
Macchiara 638
Macdonald Mor (IRE) 337
Macy Anne 1129
Madeira Pack (IRE) 1372
Madgenta (IRE) 768
Magic City (IRE) 769
Maglev 770
Mahaazen (IRE) 1617
Mahkama (USA) 562
Maid To Master (IRE) 819
Main Focus 600
Main Line 985
Main Sequence (USA) 986
Majestic Rose 240
Majestic South 241
Majestic Zafeen 242
Makalali 1458
Make Up 771
Malekov (IRE) 196
Malindi 546
Mama Quilla (USA) 670
Manbaa (USA) 461
Mankini 356
Manmanmanman (IRE) 772
Maqaraat 433
Marching On (IRE) 1427
Marcus Augustus (IRE) 773
Marford Missile (IRE) 381
Margate 856
Maria Anna (IRE) 414
Maria Letizia 601
Maria Medecis (IRE) 415
Maroosh 1084
Martin Chuzzlewit (IRE) 1483
Mashaer (USA) 857
Master Of Ages (IRE) 936
Mawasem 1484
Mayo Lad (IRE) 774
Mazeydd 1563
Mean It (IRE) 1509
Mehidi (IRE) 1085
Melodrama (IRE) 987
Meloneras 1119
Menelik (IRE) 382
Mention (IRE) 1086
Merkel (IRE) 1007
Merv 173
Mexican Wave 87
Mezmaar 858
Mezzotint (IRE) 357
Mfiftythreeford (IRE) 515
Michelangelo 602
Midnight Tryst 416
Mikdaar (IRE) 434
Min Banat Alreeh (IRE) 1564
Mince 314
Minoan Dancer (IRE) 1485

Miss Astragal (IRE) 775
Miss Blakeney 1534
Miss Work Of Art 516
Mississippi 1618
Missus Mills (IRE) 6
Misteireach 117
Mister Musicmaster 1120
Misty Conquest (IRE) 383
Mizbah 563
Model Pupil 859
Modern Tutor 1486
Mokbil (IRE) 1565
Moldowney 1459
Moment In The Sun 1178
Money Never Sleeps 603
Monnoyer 1210
Monopoli 55
Monymusk 473
Moody Dancer 1179
Moon Pearl (USA) 56
Moonshed (USA) 1619
Moonville 517
Morant Bay (IRE) 197
Moratab (IRE) 1566
More Than Words (IRE) 776
Morocco 604
Morphius 198
Mossbrae 1567
Most Improved (IRE) 1087
Mount McLeod 1281
Mount Meru 1026
Mount St Mistress 7
Mr Fong 1439
Mr Knightley (IRE) 764, 777
Mr Majeika (IRE) 778
Mr Maynard 1487
Mrs Cash (IRE) 956
Mrs Huffey 174
Mrs Mop (IRE) 779
Muckle Bahoochie (IRE) 1027
Mujannad (IRE) 1535
Mujannada 671
Mukhadram 672
Mulheb (USA) 1620
Multitasking 704
Munro Bagger 1028
Munther (IRE) 1373
Muraafiqah 1374
Murmur (IRE) 199
Musical Valley 384
Musically 243
Mutaaleq (IRE) 1568
Mutanawwer 1536
Mutasadder (USA) 1569
Mutual Regard (IRE) 1396

HORSE INDEX

Muzdaan (IRE) 1570
My Body Is A Cage (IRE) 284
My Colleen (USA) 639
My Pearl (IRE) 1428
My Propeller (IRE) 285
My Queenie 780

Najm Kabir 564
Nant Saeson (IRE) 781
Naseem Alyasmeen 245
Nassau Storm 971
Nastrovia (IRE) 244
Natural Bloom (IRE) 200
Nawwaar (USA) 462
Nayarra 246
Nayef Flyer 518
Neige D'Antan 1397
Nemushka 519
Nero Emperor (IRE) 1460
Net Whizz (USA) 1211
Never Perfect (IRE) 1510
New Romantic 166
Nice Rose 937
Niceofyoutotellme 57
Nifty Shiftin 474
Niger (IRE) 1212
Night Angel (IRE) 1121
Night Flash (GER) 547
Nile Venture 1621
Nimble Thimble 315
Nimiety 938
Nine Realms 673
Nip And Tuck 908
No Dominion (IRE) 548
Noble Thought 674
Nocturn 1213
Noor Zabeel 247
Norfolk Sky 1598
Norse Gold 475
North Star Boy (IRE) 782
Northern Jewel 520
Not Bad For A Boy (IRE) 783
Nude (IRE) 958

Oasis Love 939
Oblitereight (IRE) 972
Ocean Myth 675
Oh So Blue (IRE) 825
Omar Khayyam 35
One Kool Dude 521
Oneniteinheaven (IRE) 417
Oojooba 1571
Opera Buff 957
Opera Cloak 605
Operation Tracer 88
Opinion 1488

Opus (IRE) 1335
Orders From Rome (IRE) 915
Orrell Fost 522
Orwellian 1088
Our Boy Jack 523
Out Do 358
Outlaw Torn (IRE) 1045

Pale Mimosa (IRE) 1622
Palmette 606
Palmetto (FR) 385
Palome's Prince (IRE) 140
Palus San Marco (IRE) 286
Papal Power (IRE) 896
Paramythi (IRE) 359
Parc De Launay 1511
Party Line 940
Pashan Garh 58
Pategonia 607
Patto D'Acciaio 130
PC Henry 1029
Pea Shooter 1429
Pearl Charm (USA) 784
Pearl City (IRE) 1214
Pearl Diva (IRE) 287
Pearl Frost 59
Pearl Magic 1599
Pearl Nation 676
Pearl Spirit (IRE) 1398
Pearl War 677
Pen Bal Crag 524
Peninsula 60
Penniston Line (IRE) 1461
Percythepinto (IRE) 476
Perfect Day 338
Personal Touch 525
Petaluma 248
Peters Pursuit 526
Petrol 360
Phantom Ranch 1522
Philipstown 785
Pick Three 316
Pickled Pelican 678
Picura 1180
Piece Of Cake 860
Pink Damsel (IRE) 339
Pink Delight (IRE) 1512
Pinkisthecolour (IRE) 1375
Pistol 1489
Pitlochry (IRE) 1030
Pitt Rivers 249
Pivota Bay 1057
Place In My Heart 8
Plum Bay 477
Plus Fours (USA) 1336
Plutonius (IRE) 1245

Poetic Lord 786
Poetic Power (IRE) 478
Point Made (IRE) 1058
Poisson D'Or 640
Poker Hospital 9
Polar Venture 679
Poly Pomona 201
Polydamos 447
Poncho 1399
Pond Life (IRE) 1603
Poole Harbour (IRE) 787
Port Charlotte 1163
Portraitofmylove (IRE) 202
Position 1400
Possibly 288
Power 1246
Premier Choice 466
Price List 36
Priceless Jewel 317
Pride And Joy (IRE) 1282
Prime Run 1490
Prince Gabrial (IRE) 1190
Princess Banu 250
Princess Highway (USA) 1623
Princess Kaiulani (IRE) 1181
Princess Sinead (IRE) 820
Private Means 861
Professor Tim (IRE) 1151
Profit Again (IRE) 37
Proofreader 608
Protanto 988
Proud Pearl (USA) 1089
Proximity 1491
Purple 'N Gold 10
Purple Affair (IRE) 1149
Purple Angel 1348
Pussycat Dream 1059
Pyman's Theory (IRE) 386

Qanaas (USA) 862
Qanan 361
Qasser (IRE) 1376
Qatar's Pearl (USA) 1031
Quality Pearl (USA) 362
Quick Glimpse 1624
Quiet Appeal (IRE) 941
Quite A Thing 1401
Quizzed 1588

Radio Call 1625
Rafaella 448
Rafeej 942
Raffinn 959
Raheeba 565
Rainbow Chorus 340

Ralphy Boy (IRE) 1191
Ransomed Rose 1626
Raphael Santi (IRE) 1246
Raspberry Fizz 916
Rawaafed (IRE) 1090
Rayadour (IRE) 1307
Rayon Rouge (IRE) 1377
Rayvin Black 1523
Red Aggressor (IRE) 144
Red Art (IRE) 863
Red Bay 277
Red Danzig (IRE) 864
Red Hand (USA) 609
Red Mischief 449
Red Senor (IRE) 865
Red Trump (IRE) 866
Red Tyke (IRE) 1417
Redact (IRE) 788
Redoubtable (IRE) 1378
Refreshestheparts (USA) 11
Regal Acclaim (IRE) 467
Regal Entrance 1215
Regal Power 1008
Regal Realm 1216
Regency (GER) 203
Reigns Of Gold (IRE) 789
Remember Alexander 821
Renegotiate 38
Repeater 1402
Represent (IRE) 251
Responsive 1164
Reve Du Jour (IRE) 1046
Reveal The Star (USA) 867
Revelette (USA) 868
Rex Imperator 318
Rhagori 61
Right Divine (IRE) 1091
Right Expectation (IRE) 289
Right Reason 1379
Right Regal (IRE) 131
Right To Dream (IRE) 1092
Rigoletta (IRE) 118
Ring For Baileys 973
Rio Grande 1217
Riot Of Colour 62
Riviera Poet (IRE) 1627
Rivington 527
Roccotaki (IRE) 1182
Rock Band 790
Rock Canyon 1130
Rock Of Monet 1440
Rock On Candy 960
Rock Song 1337
Rockalong (IRE) 363
Roedean (IRE) 791
Roman Around 974

Roman General (IRE) 1009
Roman Myst (IRE) 961
Roman Soldier (IRE) 1218
Rooknrasbryripple 252
Rose Madder 89
Rosslyn Castle 319
Roughlyn 1152
Roxelana (IRE) 1219
Royal Academician 1133
Royal Blush 341
Royal Dutch 331
Royal Empire (IRE) 566
Royal Red 63
Royal Sea (IRE) 1308
Rubina (IRE) 1309
Ruby Glass (IRE) 1093
Rugged Cross 175
Run Of The Day 917
Running The Show 435
Russian Ballet 1283

Sabusa 1047
Safari Storm (USA) 1094
Safarjal (IRE) 869
Saitaia 680
Sajwah (IRE) 870
Salford Dancer (IRE) 479
Salford Dream 480
Sally Pepper (USA) 549
Samaah (IRE) 1492
Samba Night (IRE) 1060
Samitar 253
Samminder 290
Samuel Pickwick (IRE) 1493
Sanad (IRE) 1095
Sandbetweenourtoes (IRE) 1096
Savanna Days 254
Scarabocio 291
Scarlet Belle 1537
Scripturist 910
Scrupul 364
Sea Fever 365
Sea Fret 1165
Sea Odyssey (IRE) 871
Season Spirit 550
Secretary Of State (IRE) 1248
Secrets Away (IRE) 132
See Emily Play 610
Seema (USA) 366
Seemples (IRE) 792
Selective Spirit 1649
Self Centred 872
Selinda 255
Sentaril 681
Sequoia 873

Serious Spender (IRE) 64
Seven Veils (IRE) 1403
Seventeen Seventy 278
Seventh Sign 682
Shajja 567
Shalaman (IRE) 1310
Shaleek 1572
Shamakat 641
Shame On You (IRE) 874
Shamooda (IRE) 1311
Shamrocked (IRE) 256
Shanghai Blaze (IRE) 1652
Shareni (IRE) 1312
Shark In The Sea 1097
Shatter (IRE) 683
Shawka 875
She's Flawless (USA) 1098
Shelford (IRE) 1313
Shestheman 989
Shevington 528
Shihab 568
Sholaan 684
Shot In The Dark (IRE) 39
Show Flower 257
Shukhov (IRE) 1032
Shy Rosa (USA) 1538
Sign Manual 90
Signifer (IRE) 258
Signor Sassi 1573
Silent Laughter 1349
Silent Place 133
Silke Top 909
Silver Lace (IRE) 1600
Silverheels (IRE) 342
Sinetta (IRE) 705
Singspiel Spirit 145
Sir Bedivere (IRE) 1099
Sir Fredlot (IRE) 1653
Sir Glanton (IRE) 1338
Sir Lexington (IRE) 793
Sir Palomides 685
Size (IRE) 794
Slade Power (IRE) 1010
Sleigh Bells 1524
Small Steps (IRE) 1061
Snooky 176
Solar Deity (IRE) 134
Solar View (IRE) 1404
Something Graceful 119
Songbird (IRE) 204
Soon (IRE) 1247
Sottenment (FR) 135
Sovereign Debt 91
Sparks Might Fly 1593
Speaking Of Which (IRE) 1628

HORSE INDEX

Special Boy (IRE) 569
Spinnacle 642
Spinning Silk (IRE) 1539
Spirit Of Concorde 1629
Spiritoftomintoul 205
Spiritual Star (IRE) 40
Split Second 259
Sporting Gold (IRE) 1574
Spring Daisy (IRE) 387
Spunky 367
Sputnik Sweetheart 795
St Barths 1101
Stagecoach 1011
Star Bonita (IRE) 1220
Star Rating (IRE) 1494
Starfly (IRE) 1221
Statementofintent (IRE) 1100
Stateos (IRE) 206
Stencive 686
Stepper Point 1183
Stepturn 1495
Still I'm A Star (IRE) 436
Stirring Ballad 41
Storm Lightning 1630
Stormbound (IRE) 343, 1249
Story Writer 975
Strada Facendo (USA) 368
Stradater (IRE) 1462
Strictly Private 1102
Stringer Bell 796
Subtle Embrace 450
Subtraction (IRE) 369
Sugarpine 529
Summer Lane 530
Sundrenched Coast (USA) 1631
Supaheart 1166
Superciliary 65
Supreme Quest 320
Surrey Spirit 451
Swan Song 42
Sweet Liberta (IRE) 43
Sweet Mystery (IRE) 1632
Sweet Ophelia 12
Sweetscot (IRE) 1604
Swerve 1633
Swing It 797
Swiss Spirit 481
Symfony (IRE) 207
Symposia 208
Syncopate 370

Ta Ajaab 687
Tadmir (USA) 570
Tahlia Ree (IRE) 92
Tajamal (IRE) 571

Tajriba (IRE) 572
Takeitfromalady (IRE) 66
Talwar (IRE) 1222
Tamarrud (IRE) 573
Tango Sky (IRE) 67
Tarkoor 292
Tarquin (IRE) 1504
Tasrih (USA) 574
Tawaasul 688
Tazweed (IRE) 1575
Tea Cup 798
Teacher 689
Tell Dad 799
Telwaar 293
Tendern 1634
Tenderly Place 976
Teofolina (IRE) 120
Thane Of Cawdor (IRE) 1513
That's Dangerous 321
Thawabel (IRE) 1540
The Baronet 1405
The Blue Banana (IRE) 1103
The Firm (IRE) 1380
The Kernigal (IRE) 1033
The New Black (IRE) 800
The Nile 611
Thomas Chippendale (IRE) 209
Thomas Dylan (IRE) 121
Thought Worthy 612
Throne 802
Tickled Pink (IRE) 210
Tidal Way 260
Tidentime 261
Tiger Cliff (IRE) 211
Tightlaced (USA) 613
Tioman Legend 322
Titus Star 1150
Tones (IRE) 801
Top Billing 614
Top Cop 45
Top Hana (IRE) 1576
Top Offer 323
Toparga Canyon 44
Topccat (IRE) 943
Toptempo 1525
Touch Gold (IRE) 212
Transfix 1406
Traveller's Tales 803
Treasured Dream 1339
Triggerlo 262
Trove (IRE) 615
True Pearl (USA) 1034
True Prince (USA) 1340
Trumpet Major (IRE) 804
Tuibama (IRE) 826

Tundridge 962
Turn Of The Sun 616
Turn The Page 1048
Twelve Strings (IRE) 371
Two Paths (USA) 1635

Ultrasonic (USA) 1496
Umayyad (IRE) 617
Uprise 1497
Urban Ball (IRE) 1314
Ustura (USA) 575
Utterance 618

Valbchek (IRE) 1223
Valiant 690
Valley Ace 1418
Valley Of Destiny 805
Valley Of Hope 531
Van Rooney (IRE) 1463
Variety Show (IRE) 213
Varnish 806
Vastly (USA) 214
Vegas Rocks (IRE) 1464
Venegazzu (IRE) 294
Venetian View (IRE) 1134
Ventura Spirit 532
Verbeeck 1062
Verge 1589
Very French 619
Very Social (IRE) 1465
Vespasia 1063
Vexillum (IRE) 263
Viewpoint (IRE) 807
Villa Royale 452
Vinnie Jones 620
Viola D'Amour (IRE) 388
Viola Da Gamba (IRE) 977
Virginia Gallica (IRE) 897
Viscount Vert (IRE) 46
Vital Gold 691
Vivid Blue 692
Vocational (USA) 944
Vociferous (USA) 945
Voodoo Rhythm (USA) 1104
Vow 693
Vulcan Mission (IRE) 418

Waafid 1541
Warcrown 533
Waterclock (IRE) 324
Waveguide (IRE) 1441
Weaam (IRE) 1542
Well Painted 694
Welsh Nayber 1341
Welsh Royale 1184
West Leake Diman (IRE) 876

West Leake Hare (IRE) 877
Westward Hope (USA) 898
While You Wait (IRE) 122
Whimsical (IRE) 808
Whinging Willie (IRE) 1136
Whip Rule (IRE) 123
Whisky Bravo 160
White Flight 1350
White Nile (IRE) 1636
Widyaan (IRE) 621
Wild Silk 1498
Willie Wagtail (USA) 1594
Willies Wonder (IRE) 878
Willow Island (IRE) 1637
Windsor County 622
Windy Lane 695
Winter Hill 389
World Class 1601
Worthington 534
Wot A Shot (IRE) 1381
Wreaths Of Empire (IRE) 809

Xinbama (IRE) 899
Xyzzy 1505

Yazdi (IRE) 1442
Yellow Rosebud (IRE) 1638
Yeomanoftheguard 535
Yours Ever 1407

Zaahya (IRE) 463
Zaffy (IRE) 468
Zaidaan (IRE) 1639
Zalanga (IRE) 707
Zamarelle 325
Zambelot (IRE) 706
Zamurai 978
Ze King 1602
Zenaad (USA) 879
Zermatt (IRE) 1035
Zeyran (IRE) 215
Zimira (IRE) 437
Zingana 918
Zip Top (IRE) 124
Zumbi (IRE) 1499
Zuzu Angel (IRE) 979

Unnamed 13, 47-51, 68-73, 93-100, 103-111, 141-142, 146-157, 161-164, 167, 177, 216-221, 264-271, 295-297, 326-328, 390-409, 419-422, 438-446, 464, 536-541, 551-552, 623-628, 630-633, 643-648, 696-697, 708-711, 810-816, 822, 827-829, 880-887, 900-902, 911, 919, 946, 963-965, 980-981, 990-999, 1012, 1036, 1039-1042, 1064-1065, 1105-1112, 1122-1123, 1131, 1139-1141, 1153-1155, 1167-1168, 1185-1186, 1192-1193, 1224-1236, 1250-1273, 1285-1292, 1315-1320, 1342-1344, 1351-1355, 1408, 1413-1415, 1443-1455, 1466-1471, 1500-1501, 1526, 1543-1544, 1577-1585, 1590, 1595, 1605-1606, 1640-1643, 1650, 1654-1658

Dams index

Dams appear under the reference number of their offspring.

A Footstep Away 343, 1249
Aberavon 145
Aberdovey 1341
Absolute Pleasure 438
Abunai 518
Acatama 1172
Achieve 1323
Adaala 1356
Addaya 977
Adelfia 1293
Adeptation 1185
Adraaj 424
Adrastea 928
Adultress 491
Ae Kae Ae 655
Agnus 1332
Agrippina 1063
Aguilas Perla 810
Ahdaab 1403
Aileen's Gift 253
Akariyda 1149
Akoya 1351
Akuna Bay 1248
Al Saqiya 432
Al Theraab 1102
Alabaq 455
Alabastrine 1384
Alambic 1357
Alattrah 649
Alaya 1296
Alba Stella 178
Albahja 1575
Albanova 1383
Alexander Ballet 390
Alexander Duchess 298
Alexander Phantom 954
Alexandrine 921
Alexandrova 1250
Alidiva 1472
Alikhlas 533
Alinea 1489
Alkaffeyah 226
All Began 863
All Elegance 1005
All For Laura 1630
All My Loving 209
All Time Great 1019
Almaaseh 1245
Almurooj 830

Alovera 716
Alphilca 844
Alsharq 772
Alta Anna 1483
Alta Meda 1133
Alvarinho Lady 161
Always Friendly 583
Am I 1654
Amazed 1401
Ameerat 1571
American Jewel 1195
Aminata 436
Amira 747
Amorous Pursuits 391
Amoureux 1224
Anbella 1550
Andramad 1590
Angel Rays 1593
Angry Bark 953
Ann Veronica 435
Anna Amalia 1382
Anna Karenina 651
Anna Oleanda 729
Annabelle Ja 718
Annalina 597
Annmarie's Magic 769
Anse Victorin 451
Anthos 642
Antibes 903
Anyaas 654
Aoife 394
Apache Dream 674
Applaud 341
Appointed One 1508
Apsara 179
Aptina 1352
Aquatirt 357
Arabescato 1561
Arabesque 606
Arameen 708
Arasorg 242
Arboresque 1031
Arculirge 170
Areyaam 1443
Arlette 553
Array Of Stars 713
Arsad 439
Artistic Blue 666
Aryaarm 571
Ascutney 622
Asfurah 557
Ashdali 1381
Ashforc Cross 804

Ashraakat 238
Ask Annie 1023
Ask For The Moon 1251
Aspen Falls 1380
Aspiring Diva 1625
Atamana 1552
Athlumney Dancer 1655
Atnab 873
Attraction 369
Aunt Ruby 264
Aunty Mary 1548
Auspicious 31
Australian Dreams 880
Autumn Pearl 230
Autumn Wealth 1395
Ava's Crown 69
Avila 1430
Avoidance 1633
Await 1035
Aweigh 415
Ayla 265
Ayun 453
Azra 122

B. W. Chargit 677
Babaraja 1124
Badminton 76
Bahamamia 392
Bahr 1566
Baileys Cream 1190
Baileys First 37
Baize 1444
Bakhoor 292
Balance The Books 280
Baldemosa 257
Ball Chairman 1314
Ball Gown 1445
Ballet 761
Balnaha 41
Banco Solo 1156
Banutan 950
Baraka 1506
Barakat 905
Baralinka 543
Barathiki 393
Barnabas 749
Barnacla 982
Barzah 1322
Bay Tree 858
Baya 568
Bayswater 1334
Be My Charm 1008
Bea's Ruby 419

Beacon Silver 103
Bedara 536
Bee One 473
Before The Storm 778
Behra 1315
Belle Genius 1570
Belsay 865
Bent Al Fala 379
Bermuxa 420
Bianca Cappello 1083
Bianca Nera 93
Bible Box 1596
Bidding Time 836
Bijan 102
Biloxi 308
Bint Al Hammour 840
Bionic 326
Birdsong 1372
Birthday Present 429
Black Belt Shopper 643
Black Tribal 1047
Bling Bling 912
Blixen 608
Blue Bamboo 913
Blue Cloud 1237
Blue Crystal 855
Blue Echo 431
Blue Iris 1460
Blue Mistral 959
Blue Parade 146
Blue Sail 1362
Blue Symphony 1555
Bluebell Wood 1466
Bluebelle Dancer 1179
Boast 548
Bold Assumption 634
Bolshaya 763
Bonne Mere 738
Bordighera 696
Bounce 630
Bourbonella 673
Braari 16
Brand 15
Brave Madam 1359
Brave The Storm 247
Brazilia 1060
Brazilian Samba 739
Braziliz 1360
Brecon 1184
Brennie 719
Briery 881
Brigadiers Bird 266
Brilliantly 722
Brindisi 1592
Broadways Millie 502
Bronwen 1446
Bronze Star 806

Broughtons Revival 507
Buffy Boo 272
Bumble 1353
Bunditten 712
Bunood 459
Bunting 147
Burn 158
Bush Cat 1438

Cache Creek 615
Cajun Two Step 1543
Cala 78
Calando 575
Callanish 1096
Camassina 1174
Camlet 706
Canda 1473
Candice 563
Cant Hurry Love 83
Cap Serena 752
Capannina 7
Cape Grace 33
Cape Merino 1252
Cape Trafalgar 500
Capistrano Day 841
Cappella 1421
Capriole 223
Cara Fantasy 457
Carafe 14
Carallia 486
Carenage 267
Caribbean Escape 483
Carisolo 556
Carry On Katie 944
Cassandra Go 210
Cassydora 1241
Castaway Queen 638
Castilian Queen 1069
Casting Call 261
Catch The Ring 842
Catherine Wheel 332
Catspraddle 1645
Caumshinaun 572
Cavernista 136
Cayman Sound 1598
Cedar Sea 506
Celestial Princess 975
Celestial Welcome 1646
Celtic Guest 104
Certain Charm 467
Chalice Wells 478
Champenoise 1425
Champoluc 276
Change Partners 918
Chantress 482
Charita 94
Charlotti Carlotti 387

Charmed Gift 784
Chartres 1306
Chasenthebluesaway 1333
Chatham Islands 833
Chatifa 1565
Che Chic 1122
Cheerleader 990
Chehalis Sunset 1464
Cherokee Stream 47
Chervil 215
Chetwynd 827
Chica Roca 382
Chief Bee 171
Chingford 1345
Chorus 1116
Christmas Tart 771
Cidaris 1637
Cinnamon Bay 856
Clancassie 1016
Clare Hills 68
Classic Park 1247
Classic Style 756
Classical Dancer 44
Claxon 458
Clear Vision 989
Clepsydra 184
Cliché 448
Clincher Club 1597
Clinet 900
Clochette 1285
Cocabana 1348
Coconut Squeak 832
Coffee To Go 1503
Coh Sho No 485
Collada 735
College Fund Girl 1085
Colonel's Daughter 162
Combloux 380
Coming Home 1078
Common Cause 263
Compete 1203
Conference 25
Confidante 1387
Confidential Lady 1388
Contiguous 1491
Cooden Beach 985
Cool Chron 1151
Copy-Cat 1159
Corndavon 428
Corps De Ballet 966
Corryvreckan 414
Cosmic Case 494
Cosmic Countess 281
Costa Rica 1321
Counting Blessings 963
Courting 347
Cover Girl 1608

DAMS INDEX

Coveted 908
Cozy Maria 607
Cozzene's Pride 890
Craigmill 251
Cresta Gold 61
Crimson Year 89
Crinolette 923
Croeso Cariad 1177
Crooked Wood 282
Cross Channel 1081
Crossanza 17
Crystal 95
Crystal Cavern 1487
Crystal Music 1478
Crystal Power 652
Crystal Valkyrie 848
Ctesiphon 1338
Cushat Law 906
Cut Short 591
Cutspurse Moll 1656
Czarna Roza 394

Dakota Sioux 537
Dame Blanche 522
Dame De Noche 519
Dame Hester 21
Dame's Violet 388
Danccalli 742
Dance Clear 1627
Dance Of Light 587
Dance The Classics 1299
Dance Troupe 180
Danceabout 558
Dancing Loma 495
Danehill's Dream 1459
Danemarque 123
Dangle 1121
Danish Gem 1050
Danzante 312
Danzelline 1366
Dapprima 1510
Darby Shaw 395
Daring Diva 1640
Darrery 1549
Date Mate 658
Dawn Raid 134
Dazzling Dancer 1361
Dazzling View 105
Decision Maid 790
Dedicated Lady 200
Delicia 1375
Delicieuse Lady 189
Delphie Queen 709
Delta 611
Descriptive 765
Desert Cristal 732
Desert Daisy 1038

Dessert Storm 1569
Deveron 991
Diacada 24
Diamond Line 205
Dibiya 701
Diese 1342
Dietrich 1253
Digger Girl 306
Dilly Dally 931
Dime Bag 1152
Dimelight 469
Disco Ball 1328
Disco Lights 295
Discove Roma 828
Diva 1098
Divert 715
Divine Grace 846
Divine Pursuit 496
Dixie Belle 1413
Dixie Eyes Blazing 1072
Dixie Favor 167
Dock Leaf 188
Doctrine 972
Dodo 1173
Dolls House 1524
Dolma 304
Dominante 254
Dominica 1533
Don't Tell Mum 799
Donnelly's Hollow 637
Dora Carrington 92
Dorrati 1572
Dossier 1142
Drama Class 1474
Dream State 1051
Dream Vision 823
Dreams Come True 644
Drei 746
Dress Design 160
Dubai Spirit 916
Dubai Sunrise 627
Dubai Surprise 96
Duena 27
Dust Dancer 980
Dust Flicker 744
Dusty Answer 79
Dutch Auction 983
Duty Paid 947
Dynah Mo Hum 1127

Easter Parade 1276
Easy Lover 1076
Easy Mover 159
Ebaza 1316
Echeon 1477
Ego 872
El Laoob 817

Elaflaak 1527
Elegant Hawk 262
Elegant Times 322
Elfaslah 925
Elhareer 1022
Elhida 1029
Elidore 318
Ellebanna 1210
Ellen 1404
Ellens Princess 1033
Eloquent Rose 70
Elrehaan 464
Elshamms 1614
Elutrah 1532
Emirates First 425
Emma's Surprise 764, 777
Emplane 208
Empress Anna 9
En Garde 934
Enchanted Kiss 1104
Endure 717
Enemy Action 576
Engaging 191
Enlightened Way 1153
Enthused 818
Esclarmonde 1002
Esterlina 1225
Estivau 1657
Eswarah 1557
Eternelle 59
Etica 1013
Euro Empire 4
Evanesce 255
Evangeline 1068
Eve 992
Evita 623
Ewenny 664
Exciting Times 1135
Exclusive Approval 1139
Exorcet 952
Exotic Mix 791
Exponent 1467
Express Way 560
Extravagance 258
Extreme Beauty 97
Eyrecourt 809
Ezilla 569

Fabine 1468
Fabuco 1641
Face The Storm 1115
Fairest Of All 1000
Fairy Contessa 1573
Fairy Glade 854
Fairy Godmother 303
Fairy Queen 1176
Fallen Star 588

Fancy Theory 743
Fanny's Fancy 225
Fantastic Account 730
Faraday Light 831
Farbenspiel 465
Fashion Statement 356
Fatat Alarab 915
Favoritely 371
Fawaayid 148
Faydah 456
Fear And Greed 1037
Feather Bride 1456
Feathers Flying 1364
Feet Of Flame 1148
Felicita 71
Felicitous 1612
Fen Guest 620
Fermion 1218
Festivite 511
Fey Rouge 1282
Ffestiniog 302
Fictitious 750
Film Script 36
Final Opinion 762
First 1238
First Ace 1418
First Approval 849
First Bloom 72
First Eclipse 687
Fizzy Treat 396
Flanders 1559
Flashing Green 202
Flashy Wings 1080
Flavian 28
Flawless 222
Fleet Hill 731
Flor Y Nata 1389
Florida Heart 19
Flower Bowl 958
Fly In Style 330
Fly South 1648
Follow My Lead 753
Foodbroker Fancy 594
For Evva Silca 1244
For Example 1447
For Freedom 1368
Forever Times 296
Four Roses 1254
Franglais 1511
Frappe 1246
Free Lance 787
French Fern 748
Frigid 1053
Frog 693
Frond 745
Frosty Welcome 1567
Fully Invested 186

Funny Girl 237
Funsie 1300
Fur Will Fly 274
Fuschia 1123

Galapagar 1175
Galileo's Star 231
Galleta 351
Gallivant 1207
Gandini 1283
Garah 1476
Gay Gallanta 1495
Gaze 77
Gazebo 386
Geht Schnell 1079
General Jeanne 1105
Gentle Night 1131
Gentle Wind 633
Gerobies Girl 397
Ghazal 667
Gibraltar Bay 538
Gilah 1129
Gilded 776
Gilded Vanity 398
Gimasha 290
Girl Power 1010
Give A Whistle 1106
Glatisant 685
Glint 1055
Gold Bar 1093
Gold Dodger 542
Gold Hush 1517
Gold Pattern 920
Golden Angel 30
Golden Dew 10
Golden Nun 691
Golden Shadow 767
Goldster 728
Goldthroat 733
Golly Gosh 907
Good Girl 471
Gorband 755
Gorgeous Dancer 1369
Got To Go 971
Gottcha Last 1386
Graceful Air 327
Grail 194
Granny Kelly 1092
Grecian Dancer 1485
Greek Symphony 137
Green Tambourine 1126
Grenade 378
Greta d'Argent 530
Gretna 1082
Grey Way 128
Guajira 501
Guerre Et Paix 933

Guilia 636
Gwyneth 1162
Gwynn 1255

Haiyfoona 797
Half Glance 1624
Halland Park Girl 1146
Hallowed Park 256
Hammrah 1075
Handaza 1317
Hankering 1502
Happy Nation 676
Haretha 1448
Harmonist 1411
Hartstown House 1632
Harve De Grace 1631
Hasty Words 1551
Haute Volta 13
Hawattef 1458
Hayley's Affair 1001
Hazimah 1541
Heart's Desire 1280
Heckle 796
Helena Molony 609
Helsinki 822
Hemaca 864
Hendrina 43
Here To Me 252
Heres The Plan 1414
Hi Katriona 101
Hidden Charm 1396
High Society 1275
High Spot 363
High Walden 882
Highbrook 1522
Higher Love 834
Highland Shot 39
Hippogator 86
Hiraeth 521
Historian 936
Hoh Dancer 1560
Hoity Toity 1305
Holly's Kid 1090
Holy Nola 1513
Honour Bright 1220
Horns Gray 1014
Hotelgenie Dot Com 1391
Hovering 970
Hufflepuff 1140
Humility 1520
Hundred Year Flood 182
Hureya 1535
Hydro Calido 1577
Hymn Of Love 1635
Hypnotize 1406

I'm Right 1064

DAMS INDEX 379

Ice Box 1205
Icing 227
Idle Fancy 534
Idolize 1145
Ikat 986
Ile Deserte 1101
Imperial Beauty 337
Impetious 1077
Imroz 216
In My Life 1469
In Safe Hands 811
Incendio 503
Incheni 311
Incise 285
Incoming Call 988
Indian Belle 700
Indian Mystery 978
Indication 217
Indolente 29
Innclassic 1617
Insan Mala 440
Insinuate 624
Intellibet One 399
Interpose 710
Intrigued 602
Intriguing 329
Intrum Morshaan 1578
Inveraray 1054
Irish Question 112
Irresistible Jewel 1623
Isis 193
Isla Azul 782
Islandagore 1169
Islington 1494
Itnab 461
Its Another Gift 1065

Jacaranda Ridge 981
Jackie's Opera 1337
Jaish 430
Jakarta 149
Jaleela 668
Jalissa 532
Jamrah 1246
Janaat 943
Janayen 1308
Janoubi 617
Jardin 26
Jasmick 1158
Jathaabeh 1563
Jazan 98
Jazz Up 684
Jazzy Jan 740
Jeed 434
Jellett 1385
Jemima 1021
Jewel In The Sand 1057

Jina 523
Jinskys Gift 631
Jioconda 1025
Joan Joan Joan 1198
Jojeema 22
Jude 1256
Judhoor 857
Jules 150
Jumairah Sun 786
Jump Ship 55
Just One Smile 1032
Just Special 20
Justbetweenfriends 487

Kahira 82
Kalima 183
Kalimanta 1073
Kalinova 166
Kardelle 325
Karliyna 577
Karsiyaka 413
Kasora 1257
Kassiopeia 224
Kastoria 1303
Katch Me Katie 1622
Katina 641
Kayah 60
Kelly Nicole 1547
Kelsey Rose 91
Kelucia 508
Key Change 1304
Key Girl 1100
Khawafi 381
Khazeyin 852
Khibraat 1529
Khulcod 1562
Kibara 355
Kiltubber 1488
Kimola 113
Kind 218
Kindling 1071
Kiralik 527
Kirk 299
Kiswahili 1394
Kitharga 35
Knapton Hill 1030
Knockatotaun 1095
Kobalt Sea 106
Kokacrie 1209
Koniya 974
Kootenay 1226
Kozmna 1354
Krasivaya 141
Kylemore 286

L'Extra Honor 38
La Belga 87

La Caprice 1107
La Chunga 1258
La Gandilie 614
La Sila 549
La Spezia 1011
Lac Dessert 689
Lacework 516
Ladood 1544
Lady Causeway 400
Lady Cruella 879
Lady Elgar 441
Lady Grace 659
Lady High Havens 1433
Lady Lahar 1259
Lady Links 1412
Lady Livius 621
Lady Lucia 107
Lady Natilda 177
Lady Power 781
Lady Shanghai 1424
Lady Succeed 545
Lady Windley 5
Lady Zonda 132
Lady's View 807
Lagrion 1242
Laheen 1652
Lambroza 910
Landmark 1579
Lanzana 847
Larousse 892
Lassie's Gold 287
Lasso 32
Last Second 1392
Last Tango 1061
Latent Lover 350
Latice 590
Launch Time 561
Laurel Delight 851
Lauren Louise 1420
Law Review 1206
Lazaretta 1018
Legend Maker 1260
Let Alone 1274
Lethal Temper 1538
Leto 195
Level Pegging 1440
Lexington Girl 54
Lifetime Romance 1409
Light Ballet 1634
Light Of Morn 625
Light Shift 187
Like A Dame 509
Lila 987
Lilissa 1509
Lille Hammer 640
Limit 1227
Lindfield Belle 927

Lingerie 185
Liscanna 1261
Liscune 1554
Lisfannon 949
Literacy 1208
Litewska 1017
Little Whisper 586
Livius Lady 656
Lizzy Cool 1228
Local Spirit 555
Lochsong 42
Lolita's Gold 789
Londolozi 1094
Londonnetdotcom 228
Lonely Heart 8
Look Here's Carol 1056
Look Who's Dancing 779
Lost In Wonder 803
Loulwa 697
Louve Sereine 883
Love And Laughter 365
Love Divine 190
Love Everlasting 1407
Lucky 1132
Lucky Date 1114
Lucky Dip 1647
Lucky Spin 1442
Lucky Token 1629
Ludynosa 358
Lulua 773
Lumiere Rouge 737
Luminda 914
Lunathea 939
Lunda 175
Lyrical 1313

Ma Paloma 140
Macadamia 1219
Mackenzie's Friend 401
Madame Dubois 657
Madamoiselle Jones 1084
Madeira Mist 686
Maganda 201
Magic Number 316
Magic Tree 672
Magical Cliché 539
Magical Romance 1486
Magnificent Style 595
Maid For Romance 515
Maid For Running 1048
Maid To Measure 1339
Mail Express 353
Malyana 1545
Mambo With G 1607
Mambodorga 1587
Mana Pools 546
Mandama 232

Mandavilla 268
Mango Groove 1301
Mango Mischief 626
Mansiya 775
Mantesera 135
Maraami 490
Marasem 108
March Hare 877
Marching West 310
Margarula 319
Margay 780
Marghelan 1591
Maria Luisa 529
Maria Theresa 1163
Marianka 362
Marianne's Dancer 955
Marienbad 1580
Marine City 1199
Marisa 1039
Mark One 229
Market Day 273
Market Forces 861
Marlene-D 946
Marliana 1589
Maroussies Wings 559
Mary Arnold 206
Masai Queen 725
Masandra 911
Maskaya 1167
Massarra 246
Maugusta 81
May Kiersey 1229
Mayfair 1651
Mayfield 935
Mazarine Blue 1581
Meanya 64
Mega 1514
Megdale 99
Mehtaaf 1582
Melaaya 1046
Melisendra 402
Merayaat 1542
Meshhed 1297
Messelina 126
Midnight Mist 1644
Midsummer 198
Migygian 165
Millay 479
Millennium Tale 1398
Million Spirits 40
Million Waves 1441
Millistar 370
Millyant 645
Milly-M 884
Mimisel 58
Min Alhawa 1553
Mina 646

Mine Excavation 204
Minnie Habit 309
Mira Costa 1330
Misaaayef 632
Mise 926
Misplace 1534
Miss Anabaa 647
Miss Corniche 1393
Miss Delila 1427
Miss Dixie 528
Miss Gibraltar 1125
Miss Hawai 1214
Miss Hepburn 573
Miss Interpret 1144
Miss Intimate 711
Miss Ivanhoe 1099
Miss Katmandu 84
Miss Kilroy 812
Miss Lacey 1230
Miss Madame 1128
Miss Odlum 510
Miss Otis 589
Miss Provence 85
Miss Respect 1449
Miss Riviera Golf 1390
Miss Satamixa 1595
Misskinta 1202
Misterah 1530
Misty Eyed 1120
Mix It Up 410
Mixed Blessing 1335
Miznapp 1074
Model Queen 662
Modesta 859
Molaaf 901
Molasses 307
Monevassia 1262
Monkshill 1108
Monsoon Wedding 699
Monsusu 1192
Mooching Along 1658
Mood Indigo 660
Moon Unit 120
Moonavvara 56
Moone Cross 517
Moonlight Wish 284
Moonshadow 1286
Moore's Melody 1222
Morning Cry 898
Mostaqeleh 462
Mother Of Pearl 300
Mowaadah 1196
Mrs Arkada 1423
Mrs Gray 377
Mrs Marsh 774
Muffled 942
Mujadilly 449

Multiple 1027
Murani 813
Murrieta 1231
Musical Horizon 384
Musicanna 207
Muwakleh 688
My Amalie 151
My Branch 317
My First Romance 492
My Golly 1006
My Sara 291
My-Lorraine 1428
Mystery Ocean 675
Mystiara 961
Myth To Reality 670
Mythical Echo 1232
Mythie 741
Mythologie 1221

Nadeszhda 938
Naissance Royale 442
Najah 463
Name Of Love 313
Nan Jan 163
Nannina 1475
Napoleon's Sister 601
Nasheed 1536
Native Force 1492
Native Justice 219
Nature's Magic 1599
Nausicaa 821
Nautical Design 1188
Navasha 639
Nebraas 1638
Necklace 1263
Needles And Pins 152
Neila 680
Nell Gwyn 1264
Neshla 153
New Assembly 90
New Light 1
Nicola Bella 1537
Nidhaal 427
Night Frolic 18
Night Gypsy 1422
Night Haven 498
Night Risk 1594
Night Symphonie 235
Night Woman 547
Nihal 650
Ninette 1437
Ninotchka 1397
Nirvana 736
No Frills 48
No Rehearsal 53
Noble Plum 373
Noelani 893

Nofa's Magic 1066
Non Dimenticar Me 1470
Northern Gulch 1281
Notepad 138
Nouvelle Lune 805
Noyelles 512
Nufoos 930

Octalura 376
Oh So Rosie 825
Omanan 411
On The Nile 885
One Of The Family 288
Oomph 552
Oops Pettie 234
Opera Comique 605
Opera Glass 957
Opopmil 1471
Optimistic 1523
Oriental Fashion 1363
Original 1194
Otaki 1182
Ouija Board 423
Our Queen Of Kings 1500
Our Sheila 1649
Out Like Magic 1505
Out West 1601
Overcome 1119
Overlook 1325
Owsley 570
Oystermouth 1450

Pachanga 499
Pacific Grove 1136
Pacific Spell 1089
Paimpolaise 929
Paix Royale 1558
Palacoona 289
Pan Galactic 470
Papabile 143
Papering 897
Paradise Isle 250
Park Acclaim 374
Party 940
Pascarina 403
Passarelle 1434
Passe Passe 367
Passing Hour 174
Pastorale 1556
Patacake Patacake 932
Peace And Love 1003
Pearl Bright 233
Pearl Quest 364
Peeress 1481
Pelagia 243
Pelican Key 477
Penelewey 404

Perfect Sound 1020
Perpetual Time 23
Persian Empress 899
Pescia 49
Petite Arvine 1193
Petite Epaulette 734
Petite Maxine 888
Pharma West 1217
Phillippa 245
Photo Flash 968
Picolette 1180
Pillars Of Society 1465
Pina Colada 720
Pinheiros 66
Pink Sovietstaia 1355
Pink Stone 1574
Pivotal Role 421
Pivotalia 1277
Pixie Ring 1399
Pizzicato 1213
Platonic 579
Plenty Of Light 922
Plucky 1197
Poise 1400
Poised 567
Polaire 613
Polar Jem 1040
Polish Belle 383
Polished Gem 1610
Pongee 360
Popolo 279
Poppo's Song 248
Poppys Footprint 412
Porretta 385
Porthcawl 902
Pout 1147
Prashock 1028
Premier Prize 472
Prepare For War 1052
Pretty Majestic 1451
Pretty Miss 1044
Pretty Poppy 802
Primissima 794
Primrose Lane 585
Prince's Passion 1015
Princess Atoosa 820
Princess Caraboo 698
Princess Clara 1058
Princess Ellen 181
Princess Luna 405
Princess Mood 372
Princess Skippie 130
Princess Speedfit 1041
Private Status 1620
Prodigal Daughter 1426
Promenade Girl 1109
Prosaic Star 1410

Prospectress 993
Puck's Castle 418
Purepleasureseeker 1143
Purple Tiger 994
Puteri Sas 172
Putout 6

Qilin 1516
Quad's Melody 197
Quadrophenia 504
Que Puntual 119
Queen Of Fibres 269
Queen Of Narnia 239
Queen Of Palms 1007
Queens Jubilee 1137
Quenched 580
Quick To Please 1336
Quickfire 1496
Quiet Mouse 889
Quiet Storm 798
Quintrell 176
Quite Elusive 88

Race For The Stars 1265
Radiant Energy 125
Rafina 1239
Raghida 433
Rahayeb 682
Rahy Rose 562
Rainbow End 475
Rainbow Java 788
Raindrop 1161
Rapid Ransom 1626
Rapid Revalation 484
Rare Gift 574
Rawabi 1036
Rayyana 1307
Raze 275
Razzle 497
Reams Of Verse 220
Reason To Dance 1350
Rebecca Parisi 129
Rebelline 1378
Reboot 1211
Reciprocal 474
Red Blooded Woman 535
Red Blossom 1204
Red Dot 328
Red Evie 100
Red Letter 878
Red Shareef 919
Red Slipper 829
Red Tiara 1200
Red Zinnia 277
Redstone Dancer 1358
Reem Dubai 203
Reform Act 1452

Regal Riband 1216
Regalline 1377
Regina 426
Reign Of Fire 783
Reprise 886
Requested Pleasure 1373
Ribot's Guest 540
Right After Moyne 1419
Right As Rain 835
Right Key 1379
Rihana 1528
Ring Of Fire 956
Ring Of Love 973
Ringarooma 951
Ringmoor Down 1347
Rinneen 1103
Riotous Applause 62
Rise And Fall 941
Riskaverse 339
River Abouali 493
River Belle 443
River Crossing 1043
Riyafa 1309
Rock Candy 960
Rockahoolababy 1600
Rolexa 278
Romea 702
Roo 838
Roodeye 969
Rosa De Mi Corazon 891
Rosamixa 73
Rose Indien 967
Rose Of Zollern 1619
Roselyn 876
Rosina May 1117
Rosse 524
Rosy Dudley 75
Rouwaki 867
Royal Esteem 131
Royal Fupeg 839
Royal Lady 1154
Royal Shyness 1463
Royal Tigress 1453
Royals Special 1287
Roystonea 1110
Ruby Affair 768
Ruby Rocket 1618
Russian Dance 1171
Russian Revolution 116
Ryan's Quest 704

Saabiq 995
Sabah 50
Sachet 795
Sacre Coeur 1183
Sadie Thompson 582
Sadima 1501

Sahara Lady 1454
Sahara Silk 544
Sahara Sky 513
Saik 348
Sail With The Wind 845
Sakhya 1432
Salanka 962
Salim Toto 1157
Sambac 1329
Sander Camillo 945
Sandtime 297
Sandystones 837
Sao Gabriel 758
Sarayir 1546
Saree 1484
Sari 335
Sassenach 1302
Sauterne 581
Savage 648
Save The Table 1493
Scottish Exile 1181
Scylla Cadeaux 270
Se La Vie 1004
Search Mission 1642
Seasonal Blossom 1515
Seasonal Style 1279
Secret History 792
See You Later 564
Seebe 593
Seek Easy 212
Selkirk Sky 1439
Sensasse 213
Senta's Dream 724
Sequoyah 1266
Seraphine 1371
Seren Devious 340
Shadow Dancing 550
Shadow Roll 74
Shadow Song 1267
Shady Nook 726
Shahaamah 460
Shaken And Stirred 416
Shalama 1310
Shall We Run 917
Shallow Ground 760
Shamaiel 669
Shambodia 1326
Shangazi 1026
Shanghai Lily 604
Shared Dreams 352
Sharesha 1312
Sharplaw Venture 679
Shauna's Honey 173
Shawahid 1531
Sheepscot 336
Sheer Bliss 1268
Sheer Spirit 334

Sheezalady 1024
Shemaka 1311
Shemanikha 904
Shersha 331
Shielaligh 1113
Shifting Mist 1165
Shine Like A Star 603
Shohrah 1540
Showery 12
Shulammite Woman 793
Shy Lady 1295
Siena Gold 1605
Silca Boo 249
Silca-Cisa 1490
Silcasue 1191
Silent Miracle 133
Silent Waters 345
Silk Point 1539
Silken Dalliance 51
Silkie Smooth 468
Silly Game 2
Silver Arrow 1049
Silverskaya 1269
Simply Perfect 1233
Simply Times 466
Sindirana 1318
Single Market 1343
Siniyya 705
Siphon Melody 199
Sirindiya 1155
Siringas 1568
Sirocco Dream 1034
Sister Angelina 114
Sister Bluebird 1650
Sister Golden Hair 721
Sister Maria 578
Skiable 315
Skimble 868
Skiphall 192
Sky Galaxy 67
Skyelady 505
Sleepytime 1482
Slieve 1288
Slip Dance 115
Smile Awhile 244
Smoken Rosa 703
Snap Crackle Pop 144
Snippets 1070
Snow Crystal 346
So Silk 1498
So Sweet 1604
Soar 1497
Social Honour 801
Social Storm 271
Soft Touch 406
Sogno Verde 766
Solmorin 240

Somagcia 1086
Somersault 663
Something Mon 616
Song of The Sea 1243
Sosumi 1526
South Club Hill 653
Souvenance 937
Soviet Terms 1455
Spanish Quest 320
Sparkling Eyes 1429
Special Moment 1178
Spectacular Show 1223
Speed Cop 45
Spinning Queen 592
Spirit Of Pearl 283
Spiritual Air 1583
Spitting Image 480
Spotlight 447
Spring Clean 714
Spunger 754
Squeak 139
St Edith 321
St Francis Wood 11
Star Express 996
Star Of Akkar 629
Star Studded 1499
Starfish 1370
Starlight Dreams 819
Starlit Sky 444
Starring 353
Starring Role 1462
Starry Messenger 964
Starship 678
Starstone 488
Statuette 422
Sticky Green 407
Strategy 1240
Streetcar 333
Strike Hard 924
Strike Lightly 1621
Strings 361
Stroke Of Six 1435
Strut 314
Subtle Affair 450
Sugar 1436
Suitably Discreet 1628
Sulk 584
Summer Dream Girl 554
Summerhill Parkes 896
Sundae Girl 860
Sundown 843
Sunrise 1189
Sunsetter 445
Suntory 1168
Supa Sal 635
Super Gift 1636
Supereva 65

Superfonic 984
Supermova 1166
Superstar Leo 681
Supportive 826
Surrender To Me 1376
Susun Kelapa 1586
Swain's Gold 57
Sweet And Careless 3
Sweet Namibia 808
Sweet Pickle 142
Sweet Surrender 759
Swiss Lake 481
Sydney Star 164
Syrian Queen 751

Taatof 260
Taghreed 1431
Tagula Sunrise 514
Tahara 785
Tahrir 870
Tahtheeb 541
Takarna 1118
Taking Liberties 1278
Tamazug 1367
Tanda Tula 965
Tarabaya 344
Tarandot 1042
Tarascon 1270
Tarbela 997
Tarfah 1271
Tarfshi 1576
Tariysha 1564
Tarreem 354
Tasha's Dream 1639
Tashawak 454
Tawoos 1009
Tea Chest 727
Tease 1349
Tekindia 520
Temple Street 1480
Tenable 770
Tencarola 757
Tender 976
Tenpence 1521
Teodora 1416
Tesary 1062
Tetravella 1346
Teutonic 1417
Thara 80
Thawakib 1616
The Abbess 168
The Cat's Whiskers 1059
The Oldladysays No 1150
The Sound Of Music 366
The Spirit Of Pace 359
Theben 1012
Three Days In May 596

Three Gifts 1289
Tidal 1415
Tidal Chorus 241
Tides 1457
Tilbury 998
Timarwa 1319
Time For Tea 665
Time Honoured 599
Time Over 1402
Time Saved 52
Time To Dream 871
Tinaca 895
Tinge 850
Tintern 1186
Tip The Scale 1290
Tipsy Me 1141
Tis Me 999
Tithcar 1212
Titian Saga 1187
To The Woods 1291
Token Gesture 1615
Tonnara 1087
Top Crystal 221
Top Flight Queen 1602
Top Row 814
Topatoo 1525
Topiary 948
Torcross 1519
Touch And Love 1045
Treble Heights 408
Treble Seven 154
Tree Peony 1588
Tree Tops 610
Trew Class 1518
Trinny 1088
Triple Edition 1201
Triton Dance 155
Truly Mine 1643
Tsar's Pride 600
Tuesday Morning 1130
Tullawadgeen 476
Tuning 1344
Turkana Girl 1512
Twenty Questions 259
Twilight Tango 1134

Ugo Fire 1365
Ulfah 1374
Umlani 1504
Umniya 1215
Uncharted Haven 1331
Up And About 1138
Urban Sea 1298
Utrecht 598

Vade Retro 109
Valandraud 375

Valentine Band 214
Valentine Waltz 618
Validate 525
Valjarv 1234
Vallee Des Reves 1272
Varenka 1235
Vargas Girl 1324
Vas Y Carla 127
Vasilia 342
Vax Star 661
Venturi 1292
Verbania 211
Vermilliann 63
Vert Val 894
Very Nice 619
Victoria Lodge 236
Vignette 612
Villa Carlotta 452
Vintage Tipple 294
Violette 1606
Virginia Rose 121
Virtuous 1479
Viscountess Brave 46
Vital Laser 110
Vivianna 692
Vltava 824

Waafiah 293
Walker's Gal 1236
Wannabe Grand 305
Warden Rose 169
Wasnah 671
Wassendale 1097
Water Feature 1603
Waterfall One 324
Watership Crystal 683
Wavy Up 1327
Well Warned 887
Welsh Valley 1170
Wendylina 695
Weqaar 34
Westlife 417
What A Treasure 368
Whazzis 690
Whenthedoveflies 1340
Where We Left Off 1611
Whirly Bird 301
Whisper To Dream 1507
White Turf 389
Whoopsie 815
Why Now 1584
Wijdan 869
Wild Gardenia 565
Wild Heaven 117
Wile Cat 1111
Willowbridge 1461
Wimple 156

Windermere Island 1160
Winding 409
Windmill 1405
Winds Of Time 1273
Windsong 862
Winner Takes All 1067
Wissal 875
Wolf Cleugh 866
Wonder Why 1294
Wondrous Story 723
Woodbeck 628
Woodlass 874
Wunders Dream 551
Wurfklinge 1653
Wychwood Wanderer 111

Xaluna Bay 1613
Xarzee 526
Xtrasensory 1164

Yaqeen 1585
Yellow Trumpet 1091
Yesterday 338
Young And Daring 196
Yousefia 1112

Zalaiyma 1320
Zamhrear 157
Zanara 707
Zanida 1609
Zanoubia 446
Zante 323
Zaragossa 531
Zarawa 800
Zavaleta 118
Zaza Top 909
Zeiting 566
Zephrina 816
Zibilene 437
Ziria 1408
Zither 979
Zofzig 124
Zomaradah 349
Zut Alors 489